PYTHON

HOW TO PROGRAM

Deitel™ Books, Cyber Classrooms, Complete Training Courses and Web-Based Training Courses published by Prentice Hall

How to Program Series

Advanced Java™ 2 Platform How to Program
C How to Program, 3/E
C++ How to Program, 3/E
C# How to Program
e-Business and e-Commerce How to Program
*Internet and World Wide Web How
    to Program, 2/E*
Java™ How to Program, 4/E
Perl How to Program
Python How to Program
Visual Basic® 6 How to Program
Visual Basic® .NET How to Program, 2/E
Visual C++® .NET How to Program (2002)
*Wireless Internet & Mobile Business How
    to Program*
XML How to Program

Multimedia Cyber Classroom and *Web-Based Training* Series

(for information regarding Deitel™ Web-based
training visit **www.ptgtraining.com**)
*Advanced Java™ 2 Platform Multimedia
    Cyber Classroom*
C++ Multimedia Cyber Classroom, 3/E
C# Multimedia Cyber Classroom
*e-Business and e-Commerce Multimedia
    Cyber Classroom*
*Internet and World Wide Web Multimedia
    Cyber Classroom, 2/E*
Java™ 2 Multimedia Cyber Classroom, 4/E
Perl Multimedia Cyber Classroom
Python Multimedia Cyber Classroom
Visual Basic® 6 Multimedia Cyber Classroom
*Visual Basic® .NET Multimedia Cyber
    Classroom, 2/E*
Visual C++® .NET M/M Cyber Classroom (2002)
*Wireless Internet & Mobile Business
    Programming Multimedia Cyber Classroom*
XML Multimedia Cyber Classroom

The Complete Training Course Series

*The Complete Advanced Java™ 2 Platform
    Training Course*
The Complete C++ Training Course, 3/E
The Complete C# Training Course
*The Complete e-Business and e-Commerce
    Programming Training Course*
*The Complete Internet and World Wide Web
    Programming Training Course, 2/E*
The Complete Java™ 2 Training Course, 4/E
The Complete Perl Training Course
The Complete Python Training Course
The Complete Visual Basic® 6 Training Course
*The Complete Visual Basic® .NET
    Training Course, 2/E*
*The Complete Visual C++® .NET
    Training Course (2002)*
*The Complete Wireless Internet & Mobile
    Business Programming Training Course*
The Complete XML Training Course

.NET Series

C# How to Program
Visual Basic® .NET How to Program, 2/E
Visual C++® .NET How to Program (2002)

Visual Studio® Series

*Getting Started with Microsoft® Visual C++™ 6
    with an Introduction to MFC*
Visual Basic® 6 How to Program
C# How to Program
Visual Basic® .NET How to Program, 2/E
Visual C++® .NET How to Program (2002)

For Managers Series

e-Business and e-Commerce for Managers

Coming Soon

e-books and e-whitepapers
*Course Compass, WebCT and Blackboard
    Multimedia Cyber Classrooms versions*

To communicate with the authors, send e-mail to:

deitel@deitel.com

For information on corporate on-site seminars and public seminars offered by Deitel & Associates, Inc. worldwide and to register for the *Deitel Buzz* e-mail newsletter, visit:

www.deitel.com

For continuing updates on Prentice Hall and Deitel & Associates, Inc. publications visit the Prentice Hall Deitel Web site or the InformIT Deitel kiosk:

www.prenhall.com/deitel   or   **www.InformIT.com/deitel**

PYTHON
HOW TO PROGRAM

H. M. Deitel
Deitel & Associates, Inc.

P. J. Deitel
Deitel & Associates, Inc.

J. P. Liperi
Deitel & Associates, Inc.

B. A. Wiedermann
Deitel & Associates, Inc.

Prentice Hall

PRENTICE HALL, Upper Saddle River, New Jersey 07458

Library of Congress Cataloging-in-Publication Data

On file

Vice President and Editorial Director: *Marcia Horton*
Acquisitions Editor: *Petra J. Recter*
Associate Editor: *Jennifer Cappello*
Assistant Editor: *Sarah Burrows*
Project Manager: *Crissy Statuto*
Vice President and Director of Production and Manufacturing, ESM: *David W. Riccardi*
Executive Managing Editor: *Vince O'Brien*
Assistant Managing Editor: *Camille Trentacoste*
Formatter: *Chirag Thakkar*
Software Production Editor: *Bob Engelhardt*
Software Formatter: *Edward Cadillo*
Director of Creative Services: *Paul Belfanti*
Senior Manager, Artworks: *Patricia Burns*
Managing Editor, Audio-Visual Assets: *Grace Hazeldine*
Audio-Visual Editor: *Xiaohong Zhu*
Creative Director: *Carole Anson*
Design Technical Support: *John Christiana*
Chapter Opener and Cover Designer: *Tamara L. Newnam*
Cover Illustration: *Tamara L. Newnam, Steve Lefkowitz*
Manufacturing Manager: *Trudy Pisciotti*
Manufacturing Buyer: *Lisa McDowell*
Marketing Assistant: *Barrie Rheinhold*

© 2002, by Prentice-Hall, Inc.
Upper Saddle River, New Jersey 07458

10 9 8 7 6 5 4 3 2 1

ISBN 0-13-092361-3

Prentice-Hall International (UK) Limited, *London*
Prentice-Hall of Australia Pty. Limited, *Sydney*
Prentice-Hall Canada Inc., *Toronto*
Prentice-Hall Hispanoamericana, S.A., *Mexico*
Prentice-Hall of India Private Limited, *New Delhi*
Prentice-Hall of Japan, Inc., *Tokyo*
Pearson Education Asia Pte. Ltd., *Singapore*
Editora Prentice-Hall do Brasil, Ltda., *Rio de Janeiro*

To Guido van Rossum:

For creating Python,
for your steadfast commitment to its evolution,
for your commitment to excellence in Python education,
for sharing with us your vision and your insights, and
for your encouragement.

Harvey Deitel
Paul Deitel
Jonathan Liperi
Ben Wiedermann

To Mom and Dad, for your love, support, encouragement and understanding.

Jonathan Liperi

To my brother Michael, who keeps me on a strict diet of inspiration and candy.

Ben Wiedermann

Trademarks

Contents

Illustrations

9 Object-Oriented Programming: Inheritance   296

10 Graphical User Interface Components: Part 1   342

17 Database Application Programming Interface (DB-API) 569

18   Process Management   613

19   Multithreading   645

24 Multimedia   867

25 Python Server Pages (PSP)   917

A   Operator Precedence Chart   971

B   ASCII Character Set   973

C   Number Systems   974

D   Python Development Environments   988

E   Career Opportunities   998

Preface

Live in fragments no longer. Only connect.
Edward Morgan Forster

Welcome to the world of Python programming! Python is a powerful general-purpose programming language that is extremely effective for developing Internet and Web-based, database intensive, multi-tier, client/server systems. This book presents a great variety of leading edge computing technologies, and is our second book on open-source programming languages.[1]

As we write these words, Python 2.2 has just been released, almost to the minute! We have worked hard to incorporate the 2.2 functionality throughout the book. Appendix O presents a few additional 2.2 features.

We hope you will find *Python How to Program* educational, entertaining and challenging. It was a joy to work on this project. The team at Deitel & Associates develops programming language textbooks and e-Learning materials. We work in almost every major programming language. We noticed something special while working on this book. Our developers and writers commented on how much they like Python. They appreciate its power, its readability and its conciseness. They like its pizzazz. They like the world of open-source software development that is generating an ever-growing base of modules.

Whether you are an instructor, a student, an experienced professional programmer or a novice, this book has much to offer you. Python is an excellent first programming language and is an equally excellent language for developing industrial-strength, commercial applications. For the student and the novice programmer, the early chapters of the book establish a solid foundation in the basics of programming. We discuss many programming models including structured programming, object-based programming, object-oriented programming and event-driven programming. For the professional developer, we have employed the "heavy-duty" Python functionality to create substantial, fully implemented

---

1. *Perl How to Program* was published in January, 2001.

systems. The capstone is the case study on building an online bookstore in Chapter 23—this occupies approximately 70 pages of the text.

The standard basic topics are all here—data types, operators, control structures, arithmetic, strings, decision making, algorithm development, functions, and random numbers and simulation.

The book features a solid treatment of data structures with an early introduction to Python's built-in structures—lists, tuples and dictionaries—and a later rigorous treatment of traditional data structures including queues, stacks, linked lists and binary trees.

The book emphasizes Internet and Web development—we feature an early introduction to CGI then use it in several chapters to build Web-based applications. We include a full-chapter treatment of PSP (Python Server Pages) where we re-engineer the message forum case study presented in Chapter 16.

The book features a detailed, three-chapter treatment of object-oriented programming covering classes, encapsulation, objects, attributes, methods, constructors, destructors, customization, operator overloading, inheritance, base classes, derived classes and polymorphism.

We include a thorough treatment of graphical user interface (GUI) programming, with **Tkinter**, using event-driven programming, labels, buttons, check buttons, radio buttons, mouse-event handling, keyboard-event handling, layout managers, and a whole range of advanced GUI capabilities for creating and manipulating menus and scrolling components.

We discuss exception handling for making programs more robust. We present a substantial treatment of Python's powerful string-manipulation capabilities and we tackle head-on the difficult—yet enormously powerful—topic of regular expressions.

We discuss file processing, sequential access files, random-access files (and the **shelve** module). We develop a transaction-processing program and consider object serialization. The discussions of file processing provide a nice lead-in to our treatment of database programming with Python's Database Application Programming Interface (DB-API). We discuss the relational database model and present an introduction to SQL (Structured Query Language).

Many people are familiar with HTML; yet few know that the World Wide Web Consortium—creator of HTML technology—has declared HTML to be a legacy technology that will undergo no further development. Nevertheless, HTML is still important, so we have provided two appendices on it. The world is evolving towards XML (eXtensible Markup Language). In the interim, contemporary Web development is using a transition technology called XHTML. We present two appendices on this important subject and use XHTML in various applications throughout the book. We present a chapter-length general introduction to XML, an absolute must subject for today's Web applications developers. We then include a full-chapter treatment of Python-specific XML processing and include a detailed case study in which we use CGI and XML to build message forums.

Computer applications have generally been good at doing one thing at a time; today's more sophisticated applications need to be able to do many things in parallel, or as we prefer to say in the computer field—concurrently. We provide full chapters on process management and multithreading. These technologies give the Python applications programmer capabilities that used to be available only to systems programmers working down at the operating systems level.

We discuss networking, including the HTTP protocol of the Web, client/server networking with stream sockets, connectionless client/server interaction using datagrams, and we implement a client/server tic-tac-toe game using a multithreaded server.

We present a thorough general discussion of computer security, then deal with some Python-specific security issues. We discuss executing potentially harmful code in a restricted environment using module **Bastion**. We demonstrate encrypting text with module **rotor**.

As a capstone exercise for the book, in Chapter 23 we present a detailed case study that implements online bookstore e-business using a great many technologies discussed in the earlier chapters and the appendices. We introduce HTTP sessions and session tracking and build our bookstore as a multi-tier, client/server system able to handle a variety of clients, including a standard Web browser (using XHTML) and wireless clients (using WML and XHTML Basic).

We present a full chapter on multimedia, including an introduction to **PyOpenGL** with 3-D graphics examples and an introduction to Alice, a 3-D environment that provides objects which can be animated with Python scripts. We demonstrate **pygame** by designing a CD player, a movie player and a space-cruiser game.

Recognizing the importance of server-side development, we introduce PSP (Python Server Pages) as an alternative to CGI, and we convert the message forum case study from CGI technology to PSP.

The book is loaded with valuable appendices, including the Operator Precedence Chart, ASCII Character Set, Number Systems (binary, octal, decimal, hexadecimal), Python Development Environments, HTML, XHTML, CSS (Cascading Style Sheets), Career Opportunities (with lots of Web resources) and Unicode. We include an appendix on Accessibility (which overviews issues affecting, and resources for, people with disabilities). We close with an appendix on Additional Python 2.2 Features, including discussions on iterators, generators and nested scopes.

As you read this book, if you have an questions, just send an e-mail to **deitel@deitel.com**. We will respond promptly. Please visit with us from time to time at **www.deitel.com** and be sure to sign up there for *The DEITEL™ BUZZ* e-mail newsletter. We use the Web site and the newsletter to keep our readers up to the minute on Python and our products and services.

Features in Python How to Program

This text contains many additional features, including:

- *"Code Washing."* This is our term for the process we use to format the programs in the book so that they have a carefully commented, open layout. *Python How to Program* code appears in two colors with easy-to-read, syntax highlighting, including Python keywords, strings and comments. Program code is grouped into small, well-documented pieces. This greatly improves code readability—an especially important goal for us, considering that this book contains 14,930 lines of code.

- *Object-Oriented Programming.* Object-oriented programming is the most widely employed technique for developing robust, reusable software. Python was designed to be an object-oriented language, and this text offers a rigorous discussion of Python's various object-oriented features. Data integrity is of particular concern in Python. All Python class data is public by default, but several techniques exist for ensuring data integrity. We discuss these and other object-oriented topics over three detailed chapters. Chapter 7, Object-Based Programming, introduces how to create classes and discusses public, "private" and *get/set* methods. Chapter 8, Customizing Classes, discusses how to create classes with customized behavior, such as operator overloading, string representation, list and dictionary behavior and methods for customizing attribute access. These concepts are extended in Chapter 9, Object-Oriented Programming: Inheritance, in which we discuss how programmers can create new classes that "absorb" the capabilities of existing classes. This chapter familiarizes the reader with the crucial concepts of polymorphism, abstract classes and concrete classes, which facilitate powerful manipulations of objects belonging to an inheritance hierarchy. The chapter concludes with a discussion of additional object-oriented capabilities available in Python 2.2, including properties.

• ***Database Application Programming Interface***. Databases store vast amounts of information that individuals and organizations must access to conduct business. Database management systems (DBMS) are used by organizations and individuals to manipulate databases—Python offers the database application programming interface (DB-API) to access database management systems. Chapter 17, Database Applications Programming Interface (DB-API), details these capabilities and the Structured Query Language (SQL) to query MySQL databases.

• ***XML.*** Use of Extensible Markup Language (XML) is exploding in the software-development industry, and in the e-business and e-commerce communities. Because XML is a platform-independent technology for describing data and for creating markup languages, XML's data portability integrates well with Python's portable applications and services. Chapter 15, Extensible Markup Language (XML), introduces XML. In this chapter, we discuss basic XML markup and technologies such as DTDs and Schema, which are used to validate XML document contents. In Chapter 16, Python XML Processing, we explain how to manipulate XML documents using the Document Object Model (DOM™) and how to transform XML documents into other types of documents via Extensible Stylesheet Language Transformations (XSLT). This chapter also presents an alternative to DOM, called Simple API for XML (SAX), which acts as an event-based API for XML.

• ***Common Gateway Interface (CGI) and Python Server Pages (PSP).*** The Internet and World Wide Web are pervasive in today's world, and interactive Web sites are crucial for businesses. Chapter 6, Introduction to the Common Gateway Interface (CGI), and Chapter 25, Python Server Pages (PSP), provide server-side Web technologies with which developers create interactive Web-based applications. A detailed case study in Chapter 23, Case Study: Online Bookstore, employs MySQL, XML, XHTML, XHTML Basic, Cascading Stylesheets, XSLT, CGI and the Wireless Markup Language (WML) to construct a dynamic e-commerce application. The book demonstrates two implementations of an XML message forum in which users post messages to an online message board. The version in Chapter 16 uses CGI, and the version in Chapter 25 uses PSP.

- *Graphical User Interface (GUI)*. Python does not have built-in graphical user interface capabilities, but many modules are available that provide access to existing GUI software. Chapter 10, Graphical User Interface Components: Part 1, and Chapter 11, Graphical User Interface Components: Part 2, discuss the **Tkinter** module (included in the Python standard library) that provides a Python programmer access to the Tool Command Language/Tool Kit (Tcl/Tk), a popular GUI toolkit. Using these programming tools, a developer can create graphical programs quickly and easily. These chapters provide the reader with the ability to program the GUI portions of the programs in the rest of the text. Chapter 11 also discusses module **Pmw**, which uses **Tkinter** to provide more complex GUI components.

- *Multimedia.* Multimedia capabilities produce powerful applications using sound and color, thereby enhancing users' experiences. Several Python modules are available for creating impressive multimedia applications. Chapter 24, Multimedia, explores the capabilities of **PyOpenGL** and Alice for creating and animating 3D graphics. The chapter also discusses **pygame**, which contains modules that enable a developer to access powerful multimedia libraries. Chapter 24 uses **pygame** to create a compact-disc player, a computer game and a video-player application.

- *Multithreading and Process Management.* Computers can perform many tasks concurrently (i.e., in parallel), such as printing documents, downloading files from a network and surfing the Web. Multithreading is a technology through which programmers can develop applications that perform concurrent tasks. Python's multithreading and process management capabilities are appropriate for today's sophisticated multimedia-intensive, database-intensive, network-based, multiprocessor-based, distributed applications. Chapter 18, Process Management, discusses concurrency and interprocess communication, and Chapter 19, Multithreading, provides a detailed discussion of multithreading, including an explanation of Python's Global Interpreter Lock, which controls and manages thread execution. The chapter also introduces common thread synchronization mechanisms in the context of several examples.

- *File Processing and Serialization*. Most industrial applications read and write data to a disk. Python provides several high-level capabilities for data storage and retrieval. In Chapter 14, File Processing and Serialization, we discuss basic file objects for the storage of sequential data; **shelve** objects for the storage of random-access data and module **cPickle** for serializing entire objects to a disk.

- *XHTML.* The *World Wide Web Consortium (W3C)* has declared HTML to be a legacy technology that will undergo no further development. HTML is being replaced by the Extensible Hypertext Markup Language (XHTML)—an XML-based technology that is rapidly becoming the standard for describing Web content. We use XHTML in Chapter 6, Introduction to the Common Gateway Interface (CGI); Chapter 16, Python XML Processing; Chapter 17, Database Application Programming Interface (DB-API); Chapter 23, Case Study: Online

Bookstore and Chapter 25, Python Server Pages (PSP). We introduce the technology in Appendix I, Introduction to XHTML: Part 1, and Appendix J, Introduction to XHTML: Part 2. These appendices overview headers, images, lists, image maps and other features of this emerging markup language. (We also present a treatment of HTML in Appendices G and H, because the message forums in Chapter 16 and Chapter 25 use scripts that generate HTML).

- *Career Opportunities.* Appendix E, Career Resources, introduces career services available on the Internet. We explore online career services from both the employer's and employee's perspectives. We list many Web sites at which you can submit applications, search for jobs and review applicants (if you are interested in hiring someone). We also review services that build recruiting pages directly into e-businesses. One of our reviewers told us that he had used the Internet as a primary tool in a recent job search, and that this appendix would have helped him expand his search dramatically.

- *Unicode.* As computer systems evolved worldwide, computer vendors developed numeric representations of character sets and special symbols for the local languages spoken in different countries. In some cases, different representations were developed for the same languages. Such disparate character sets hindered communication among computer systems. Python supports the *Unicode Standard*, which is developed and maintained by a non-profit organization called the *Unicode Consortium*). This standard contains a single character set that specifies unique numeric values for characters and special symbols in most of the world's languages. Appendix F, Unicode, discusses the standard, overviews the Unicode Consortium Web site (**www.unicode.org**) and presents a Python application that displays "Welcome to Unicode!" in many languages.

- *Accessibility.* Using the Web presents many challenges to people with disabilities. Individuals with hearing and visual impairments, in particular, have difficulty accessing multimedia-rich Web sites. In an attempt to improve this situation, the World Wide Web Consortium (W3C) launched the Web Accessibility Initiative (WAI), which provides guidelines for making Web sites accessible to people with disabilities. Appendix L, Accessibility, describes these guidelines and highlights various products and services designed to improve the Web-browsing experiences of individuals with disabilities. For example, the chapter introduces VoiceXML and CallXML—two XML-based technologies for increasing the accessibility of Web-based content for people with visual impairments.

This text provides many other topics in addition to the features previously listed. For a complete list of each chapter's features, visit page 15 of Chapter 1, Tour of the Book.

Python Version 2.2 Features

This text went to publication at the same time that the final version of Python 2.2 was released. However, all the code examples in this book were tested in Python 2.2b2 (Python Version 2.2 Beta 2) and with Release Candidate 1, on both the Windows and Linux operating systems, and the text demonstrates 2.2 features and functionality in every applicable chapter.[2] This section overviews the 2.2 capabilities presented in *Python How to Program*.

Floor Division and True Division. Python 2.2 introduces a new operator (**//**) for "floor" (integer) division. In the current and previous versions of Python, the default behavior of the **/** division operator is floor division; in future versions, the default behavior will be "true" (floating-point) division. By defining two division operators, the new versions of Python eliminates the type ambiguity that results in programs that use both integer and floating-point values for division. Section 2.6 discusses the difference between floor division and true division and explains how a program can change the default behavior of the **/** operator to perform true division.

Nested Scopes. Python 2.2 introduces nested scopes, which means that nested classes, methods and functions now have access to variables defined in their enclosing scope. This behavior is particularly helpful for writing **lambda** expressions. Chapter 4 discusses Python's basic scoping rules and provides a footnote that contains a Web resource for further information on nested scopes. The nested scoping behavior is most important to programmers who use Python in a functional-programming idiom. We also discuss nested scopes in Appendix O, Additional Python features. As this book focuses mainly on the object-oriented style of programming, we provide only a high-level motivation for nested scopes and suggest further resources where the reader can learn more about nested scopes and functional programming in Python.

More Object-Oriented Functionality. Most of the new features in Python 2.2 add more object-oriented functionality to the language. Chapters 8 and 9 introduce several of these new features. In Chapter 8, we discuss the methods that a programmer-defined class can overload to define behavior for operators, including the new **//** operator. We also introduce a dictionary method, new to 2.2, that enables programs to use **if/in** statements to test whether a dictionary contains a particular key. In Chapter 9, we discuss the most anticipated new feature—the ability for programmer-defined classes to inherit from built-in types. We present a substantial example that inherits from built-in type **list** to implement a programmer-defined list that contains only unique elements. We also discuss other new object-oriented features, including static methods, **__slots__** (for defining the attributes an object of a class may contain), method **__getattribute__** (that executes each time a client accesses an object's attribute) and properties (that allow classes to define *get/set* methods that execute when a client accesses an attribute).

Iterators. Appendix O contains additional 2.2 features that are not covered in the main text. We begin with a thorough treatment of iterators—special objects for progressing through the values of a sequence. Section O.2 contains two examples that present programmer-defined iterator classes and demonstrate a client of the class using an iterator to obtain values from a sequence. The first example illustrates how to define a class whose objects support iterators; the second example presents a computer guessing game that shows how iterators can be used to process sequences of indeterminate size. The new iterator mechanism in Python 2.2 enables the language to provide a significant performance enhancement over previous versions and improves software design by allowing programmers to separate iteration behavior from random-access behavior.

---

2. Before reading this book, download the most recent release of Python from the **python.org** Web site. As new versions are released, we will test our code and update the **www.deitel.com** Web site. Before you read each chapter, please go to our Web site for these updates.

Generators. Generators also provide new performance and design benefits. A generator is a "resumable function" that remembers its state between invocations. Often, a program writes a generator to define how to produce elements of a sequence in a simple, straightforward manner. Generators also are useful for performing recursive tasks or tasks that would require complex logic and state information to implement with "traditional" functions. Section O.2 discusses generators in the context of these issues and defines two versions of a generator that computes the Fibonacci sequence. The first version produces the next value in the sequence indefinitely; the second produces all the sequence values up through and including a user-defined nth value.

Some Notes to Instructors

Students Enjoy Learning a Leading-Edge Language
Students are highly motivated by the fact that they are learning a leading-edge language, Python, and a leading-edge programming paradigm (object-oriented programming) that will be immediately useful to them as they enter the business world. This increases their enthusiasm for the material—which is essential when you consider that there is much more to learn in a Python course now that students must master both the base language and substantial modules as well.

A World of Object Orientation
In the late 1990s, universities were still emphasizing procedural programming. The leading-edge courses were using object-oriented C++, but these courses generally mixed a substantial amount of procedural programming with object-oriented programming—something that C++ lets programmers do. Many instructors now are emphasizing a pure object-oriented programming approach. This book takes a predominantly object-oriented approach because of the object orientation provided in Python.

Focus of the Book
Our goal was clear: Produce a Python textbook for introductory-level university courses in computer programming aimed at students with little or no programming experience, yet offer the depth and the rigorous treatment of theory and practice demanded by both professionals and students in traditional, upper-level programming courses. To meet these objectives, we produced a comprehensive book that patiently teaches the principles of computer programming and of the Python language, including control structures, object-oriented programming, Python modules, graphical-user-interface concepts, event-driven programming and more. After mastering the material in this book, students will be well-prepared to program "industrial-strength" applications in Python.

Multimedia-Intensive Communications
People want to communicate. Sure, they have been communicating since the dawn of civilization, but the potential for information exchange has increased dramatically with the evolution of various technologies. Until recently, even computer communications were limited mostly to digits, alphabetic characters and special characters. The current wave of communication technology involves the distribution of multimedia—people enjoy using applications that transmit color pictures, animations, voices, audio clips and even

full-motion color video over the Internet. At some point, we will insist on three-dimensional, moving-image transmission.

There have been predictions that the Internet will eventually replace radio and television as we know them today. Similarly, it is not hard to imagine newspapers, magazines and books delivered to "the palm of your hand" (or even to special eyeglasses) via wireless communications. Many newspapers and magazines already offer Web-based versions, and some of these services have spread to the wireless world. When cell phones were first introduced, they were large and cumbersome. Today, they are small devices that fit in our pockets, and many are Internet-enabled. Wireless technology already enables streaming-video and graphics-intensive services, such as video conference calls and multi-player video games. Chapter 23, Case Study: Online Bookstore and Chapter 24, Multimedia demonstrate the possibilities of wireless Internet and multimedia applications.

Teaching Approach

Python How to Program contains a rich collection of examples, exercises and projects drawn from many fields and designed to provide students with a chance to solve interesting, real-world problems. The code examples in this text have been tested on Windows 2000 and Linux. The book concentrates on the principles of good software engineering, and stresses program clarity. We are educators who teach edge-of-the-practice topics in industry classrooms worldwide. We avoid arcane terminology and syntax specifications in favor of teaching by example. The text emphasizes good pedagogy.[3]

LIVE-CODE™ Teaching Approach

Python How to Program is loaded with numerous examples. This style exemplifies the way we teach and write about programming and is the focus of our multimedia *Cyber Classrooms* and Web-based training courses. Each new concept is presented in the context of a complete, working example that is immediately followed by one or more windows showing the program's input/output dialog or graphical display. We call this method of teaching and writing the *LIVE-CODE™ Approach*. *We use programming languages to teach programming languages.* Reading the examples in the text is much like entering and running them on a computer.

World Wide Web Access

All of the examples for *Python How to Program* (and our other publications) are available on the Internet free for download from the following Web sites:

```
www.deitel.com
www.prenhall.com/deitel
```

Registration is quick and easy. We suggest downloading all the examples, then running each program as you read the corresponding text. Make changes to the examples and immediately see the effects of those changes—this is a great way to learn programming. We also provide instructions for installing various software used in this book (e.g., Apache

---

3. We use a different font from the text font when referring to the elements in a graphical user interface (GUI) or when referring to a location on a computer disk. Our convention is to emphasize GUI features in a sans-serif bold Helvetica font (e.g., **Edit** menu) and to emphasize programming elements in a serif bold Courier font (e.g., **def**).

Software Foundation's Apache Web Server). Additional setup instructions for other Web servers and software can be found at our Web sites with the examples. [*Note*: This is copyrighted material. Feel free to use it as you study, but you may not republish any portion of it in any form without explicit permission from Prentice Hall and the authors.]

Objectives

Each chapter begins with objectives that inform students of what to expect and give them an opportunity, after reading the chapter, to determine whether they have met the intended goals. The objectives serve as confidence builders and as a source of positive reinforcement.

Quotations

The chapter objectives are followed by sets of quotations. Some are humorous, some are philosophical and some offer interesting insights. We have found that students enjoy relating the quotations to the chapter material. Many of the quotations are worth a "second look" *after* you read each chapter.

Outline

The chapter outline enables students to approach the material in top-down fashion. Along with the chapter objectives, the outline helps students anticipate future topics and set a comfortable and effective learning pace.

Approximately 14,930 Lines of Code in 281 Example Programs (with Program Outputs)

We present Python features in the context of complete, working Python programs. The programs range in size from just a few lines of code to substantial examples containing several hundred lines of code. All examples are available on the book's CD or free for download at `www.deitel.com`.

589 Illustrations/Figures

An abundance of charts, line drawings and program outputs is included. The discussion of control structures, for example, features carefully drawn flowcharts. [*Note*: We do not teach flowcharting as a program-development tool, but we do use a brief, flowchart-oriented presentation to explain the precise operation of each Python control structure.]

412 Programming Tips

We have included programming tips to help students focus on important aspects of program development. We highlight hundreds of these tips in the form of *Good Programming Practices*, *Common Programming Errors*, *Testing and Debugging Tips*, *Performance Tips*, *Portability Tips*, *Software Engineering Observations* and *Look-and-Feel Observations*. These tips and practices represent the best the authors have gleaned from a combined seven decades of programming and teaching experience. One of our students—a mathematics major—told us that she feels this approach is like the highlighting of axioms, theorems and corollaries in mathematics books; it provides a foundation on which to build good software.

73 Good Programming Practices

Good Programming Practices *are tips that call attention to techniques that will help students produce better programs. When we teach introductory courses to nonprogrammers, we state that the "buzzword" for each course is "clarity," and we tell the students that we will highlight (in these Good Programming Practices) techniques for writing programs that are clearer, more understandable and more maintainable.*

125 Common Programming Errors

Students learning a language—especially in their first programming course—tend to make certain kinds of errors frequently. Pointing out these Common Programming Errors *reduces the likelihood that students will make the same mistakes. It also shortens long lines outside instructors' offices during office hours!*

31 Testing and Debugging Tips

When we first designed this "tip type," we thought the tips would contain suggestions strictly for exposing bugs and removing them from programs. In fact, many of the tips describe aspects of Python that prevent "bugs" from getting into programs in the first place, thus simplifying the testing and debugging process.

35 Performance Tips

In our experience, teaching students to write clear and understandable programs is by far the most important goal for a first programming course. But students also want to write programs that run the fastest, use the least memory, require the smallest number of keystrokes or dazzle in other ways. Students really care about performance and they want to know what they can do to produce the most efficient programs. We have included 35 Performance Tips *that highlight opportunities for improving program performance—making programs run faster or minimizing the amount of memory that they occupy.*

23 Portability Tips

We include Portability Tips *to help students write portable code and to provide insights on how Python achieves its high degree of portability.*

92 Software Engineering Observations

The object-oriented-programming paradigm necessitates a complete rethinking of the way we build software systems. Python is an effective language for achieving good software engineering. The Software Engineering Observations *highlight architectural and design issues that affect the construction of software systems, especially large-scale systems. Much of what the student learns here will be useful in upper-level courses and in industry as the student begins to work with large, complex real-world systems.*

21 Look-and-Feel Observations

We provide Look-and-Feel Observations *to highlight graphical-user-interface conventions. These observations help students design attractive, user-friendly graphical user interfaces that conform to industry norms.*

Summary (1462 Summary bullets)

Each chapter ends with additional pedagogical devices. We present a thorough, bullet-list-style summary of the chapter. On average, there are 43 summary bullets per chapter. This helps the students review and reinforce key concepts.

Terminology (2485 Terms)

We include an alphabetized list of the important terms defined in the chapter in a *Terminology* section. Again, this serves as further reinforcement. On average, there are 73 terms per chapter. Each term also appears in the index, so the student can locate terms and definitions quickly.

615 Self-Review Exercises and Answers (Count Includes Separate Parts)

Extensive self-review exercises and answers are included for self-study. These questions and answers give the student a chance to build confidence with the material and prepare for the regular exercises. Students should be encouraged to attempt all the self-review exercises and check their answers.

370 Exercises (Solutions in Instructor's Manual; Count Includes Separate Parts)

Each chapter concludes with a substantial set of exercises that involve simple recall of important terminology and concepts; writing individual Python statements; writing small portions of Python methods and classes; writing complete Python methods, classes and applications; and writing major projects. These exercises cover a wide variety of topics, enabling instructors to tailor their courses to the unique needs of their audiences and to vary course assignments each semester. Instructors can use the exercises to form homework assignments, short quizzes and major examinations. The solutions for the exercises are included in the *Instructor's Manual* and on the disks *available only to instructors* through their Prentice-Hall representatives. [*NOTE:* **Please do not write to us requesting the instructor's manual. Distribution of this publication is strictly limited to college professors teaching from the book. Instructors may obtain the solutions manual from their regular Prentice Hall representatives. We regret that we cannot provide the solutions to professionals.**] Solutions to approximately half the exercises are included on the *Python Multimedia Cyber Classroom* CD-ROM (available in April 2002 at `www.InformIT.com/cyberclassrooms`; also see the last few pages of this book or visit `www.deitel.com` for ordering instructions). Also available in April 2002 is the boxed product, *The Complete Python Training Course*, which includes both our textbook, *Python How to Program* and the *Python Multimedia Cyber Classroom*. All of our *Complete Training Course* products are available at bookstores and online booksellers, including `www.InformIT.com`.

Approximately 4212 Index Entries (with approximately 5733 Page References)

We have included an extensive Index at the back of the book. Using this resource, students can search for any term or concept by keyword. The Index is especially useful to practicing programmers who use the book as a reference. Each of the 2485 terms in the Terminology sections appears in the Index (along with many more index items from each chapter). Students can use the Index in conjunction with the Terminology sections to ensure that they have covered the key material in each chapter.

"Double Indexing" of All Python Live-Code™ Examples

Python How to Program has 281 Live-Code™ examples, which we have "double in-dexed." For every Python source-code program in the book, we took the file name with the **.py** extension, such as **Book.py**, and indexed it both alphabetically (in this case, under "B") and as a subindex item under "Examples." This makes it easier to find examples that are demonstrating particular features.

Software Included with Python How to Program

There are a number of Python products available for download from the Internet. We wrote *Python How to Program* using the Python Core Language 2.2 final release, and other soft-ware we have included on the CD-ROM that accompanies this text. This software includes the Apache Web Server 1.3.22, from the Apache Software Foundation and Alice99, a mul-timedia application for creating 2D and 3D graphics. The CD-ROM includes the wireless browser, Pixo 2.1, the IBM WebSphere Voice Server 1.5, a text-to-speech engine and Web-ware 0.6 for Python, which contains PSP software components for developing Web-based server-side applications. As we mentioned earlier, Python 2.2 was released almost to the minute that we released *Python How to Program* to Prentice Hall for publication. Some of the Python software packages you many want to use may not yet work with Python 2.2. If that is the case, please try running those software packages on Python 2.1, which you can download from **www.python.org**. If you still experience problems, please check the Python FAQs at **www.deitel.com**. The CD-ROM contains Windows and Linux ver-sions of the software, where possible.

Ancillary Package for Python How to Program

Python How to Program has extensive ancillary materials for instructors teaching from the book. The *Instructor's CD* contains the *Instructor's Manual* with solutions to the vast ma-jority of the end-of-chapter exercises and a *Test Item File* of multiple-choice questions (ap-proximately two per book section). In addition, we provide PowerPoint® slides containing all the code and figures in the text. You are free to customize these slides to meet your own classroom needs. Prentice Hall provides a *Companion Web Site* (**www.prenhall.com/deitel**) that includes resources for instructors and students. For instructors, the Web site has a *Syllabus Manager* for course planning, links to the PowerPoint slides and reference materials from the appendices of the book (such as operator precedence chart, character set and Web resources). For students, the Web site provides chapter objectives, additional self-review exercises and answers, chapter highlights and reference materials.

Python Multimedia Cyber Classroom and The Complete Python Training Course

We have prepared an interactive, multimedia, CD-ROM-based, software version of *Python How to Program,* called the *Python Multimedia Cyber Classroom.* This resource is loaded with e-learning features that are ideal for both education and reference. The *Cyber Class-room* is packaged with the textbook at a discount in *The Complete Python Training Course.* If you already have the book and would like to purchase the *Python Multimedia Cyber Classroom* separately, please visit **www.InformIT.com/cyberclassrooms**. The

ISBN number for the CD-ROM format of the *Python Multimedia Cyber Classroom* is 0-13-067376-5 and the Web-based training format is ISBN number 0-13-067381-1. Many Deitel™ *Cyber Classrooms* are available in CD-ROM and Web-based formats.

The CD provides an introduction in which the authors overview the *Cyber Classroom*'s features. The textbook's 281 LIVE-CODE™ example Python programs truly "come alive" in the *Cyber Classroom*. If you are viewing a program and want to execute it, you simply click the lightning-bolt icon, and the program will run. You immediately will see—and hear, when working with audio-based multimedia programs—the program's outputs. If you want to modify a program and see the effects of your changes, simply click the floppy-disk icon that causes the source code to be "lifted off" the CD and "dropped into" one of your own directories so you can edit the text, recompile the program and try out your new version. Click the audio icon, and one of the authors will discuss the program and "walk you through" the code.

The *Cyber Classroom* also provides navigational aids, including extensive hyper-linking. The *Cyber Classroom* is browser based, so it remembers sections that you have visited recently and allows you to move forward or backward among these sections. The thousands of index entries are hyperlinked to their text occurrences. Furthermore, when you enter a term using the "find" feature, the *Cyber Classroom* will locate occurrences of that term throughout the text. The Table of Contents entries are "hot," so clicking a chapter name takes you immediately to that chapter.

Students like the fact that solutions to approximately half the exercises in the book are included with the *Cyber Classroom*. Studying and running these extra programs is a great way for students to enhance their learning experience.

Students and professional users of our *Cyber Classrooms* tell us that they like the inter-activity and that the *Cyber Classroom* is an effective reference due to its extensive hyper-linking and other navigational features. We received an e-mail from a person who said that he lives "in the boonies" and cannot take a live course at a university, so the *Cyber Classroom* provided an ideal solution to his educational needs.

Professors tell us that their students enjoy using the *Cyber Classroom* and spend more time on the courses and master more of the material than in textbook-only courses. For a complete list of the available and forthcoming *Cyber Classrooms* and *Complete Training Courses*, see the *Deitel™ Series* page at the beginning of this book, the product listing and ordering information at the end of this book or visit **www.deitel.com**, **www.pren-hall.com/deitel** and **www.InformIT.com/deitel**.

Deitel e-Learning Initiatives

e-Books and Support for Wireless Devices

Wireless devices will play an enormous role in the future of the Internet. Given recent band-width enhancements and the emergence of 2.5 and 3G technologies, it is projected that, within two years, more people will access the Internet through wireless devices than through desktop computers. Deitel & Associates, Inc., is committed to wireless accessibility and has recently published *Wireless Internet & Mobile Business How to Program*. To fulfill the needs of a wide range of customers, we are developing our content both in traditional print formats and in newly developed electronic formats, such as e-books so that students and professors can access content virtually anytime, anywhere. Visit **www.deitel.com** for periodic updates on these initiatives.

e-Matter

Deitel & Associates, Inc., is partnering with Prentice Hall's parent company, Pearson PLC, and its information technology Web site, **InformIT.com**, to launch the Deitel e-Matter series at **www.InformIT.com/deitel**. This series will provide professors, students and professionals with an additional source of information on specific programming topics. e-Matter consists of stand-alone sections taken from published texts, forthcoming texts or pieces written during the Deitel research-and-development process. Developing e-Matter based on pre-publication books allows us to offer significant amounts of the material to early adopters for use in courses. Some possible Python e-Matter titles we are considering include *Object-Oriented Programming in Python*; *Graphical User Interface Programming in Python* and *Multithreading in Python*.

Course Management Systems: WebCT, Blackboard, and CourseCompass

We are working with Prentice Hall to integrate our *How to Program Series* courseware into three Course Management Systems: WebCT, Blackboard™ and CourseCompass. These Course Management Systems enable instructors to create, manage and use sophisticated Web-based educational programs. Course Management System features include course customization (such as posting contact information, policies, syllabi, announcements, assignments, grades, performance evaluations and progress tracking), class and student management tools, a gradebook, reporting tools, communication tools (such as chat rooms), a whiteboard, document sharing, bulletin boards and more. Instructors can use these products to communicate with their students, create online quizzes and tests from questions directly linked to the text and automatically grade and track test results. For more information about these upcoming products, visit **www.deitel.com/whatsnew.html**. For demonstrations of existing WebCT, Blackboard and CourseCompass courses, visit **cms.pren_hall.com/WebCT**, **cms.prenhall.com/Blackboard** and **cms.prenhall.com/CourseCompass**, respectively.

Deitel and InformIT Newsletters

Deitel Column in the InformIT Newsletters

Deitel & Associates, Inc., contributes a weekly column to the popular *InformIT* newsletter, currently subscribed to by more than 800,000 IT professionals worldwide. For opt-in registration, visit **www.InformIT.com**.

Deitel Newsletter

Our own free, opt-in newsletter includes commentary on industry trends and developments, links to articles and resources from our published books and upcoming publications, information on future publications, product-release schedules, programming tips, errata, additional insights and more. For opt-in registration, visit **www.deitel.com**.

Acknowledgments

One of the great pleasures of writing a textbook is acknowledging the efforts of many people whose names may not appear on the cover, but whose hard work, cooperation, friendship and understanding were crucial to the production of the book.

Many other people at Deitel & Associates, Inc., devoted long hours to this project.

- Rashmi Jayaprakash, a graduate of Boston University with a degree in Computer Science, co-authored Appendices D, F and L and served as the project manager. She edited and reviewed Chapters 1–25 and the appendices and managed the review process for the book.

- Su Zhang, a graduate of McGill University with a Master's in Computer Science, co-authored Chapters 24 and 25 and contributed to Chapters 3, 5, 6, 17, 18 and 21.

- Tem R. Nieto, a graduate of the Massachusetts Institute of Technology, is Director of Product Development at Deitel & Associates, Inc. He is co-author of *Internet & World Wide Web How to Program, Second Edition*; *XML How to Program*; *Perl How to Program*; *Visual Basic .NET How to Program, Second Edition*; *C# How to Program* and *Wireless Internet and Mobile Business How to Program*. Tem co-authored Chapters 15–16 and edited Chapters 23–25 and Appendices D and F–L.

- Sean E. Santry, a graduate of Boston College with degrees in Computer Science and Philosophy, is Director of Software Development at Deitel & Associates, Inc., and co-author of *Advanced Java 2 Platform How to Program*. Sean contributed to Chapters 7, 12, 16–21, 23 and 25 and tested examples on Linux. Sean was instrumental in the finishing stages of the project.

- Kyle Lomelí, a graduate of Oberlin College with a degree in Computer Science and a minor in East Asian Studies, contributed to Chapters 7, 10–13, 17–19 and 24–25 and tested all the examples on Windows.

- Matthew R. Kowalewski, a graduate of Bentley College with a degree in Accounting Informations Systems, is the Director of Wireless Development at Deitel & Associates, Inc. He contributed to Chapter 16, 23 and 25 and Appendices G–N. He also reviewed Appendices A–F and edited the Index.

- Jonathan Gadzik, a graduate of the Columbia University School of Engineering and Applied Science with a major in Computer Science, contributed to Chapters 15 and 16 and reviewed Chapters 7, 12–14, 18–20 and 25.

- Betsy DuWaldt, a graduate of Metropolitan State College of Denver with a major in Technical Communications (Writing and Editing emphasis) and a minor in Computer Information Systems, is Editorial Director at Deitel & Associates, Inc. She co-authored the Preface and Chapter 1, edited the manuscript and managed the permissions process for the book.

- Laura Treibick, a graduate of the University of Colorado at Boulder with a degree in Photography and Multimedia, is Director of Multimedia at Deitel & Associates, Inc. She contributed to Chapters 18 and 24 and enhanced many of the graphics throughout the text.

- Barbara Deitel applied the copy edits to the manuscript. She did this in parallel with handling her extensive financial and administrative responsibilities at Deitel & Associates, Inc., which include serving as Chief Financial Officer. [Everyone at the company works on book content.]

- Abbey Deitel, a graduate of Carnegie Mellon University's Industrial Management Program and President of Deitel & Associates, Inc., co-authored Chapter 21, and edited the Preface and several of the book's chapters. She recruited 40 additional full-time employees and interns during 2001 and leased, equipped and furnished our second building to create the work environment from which *Python How to Program* and our other year 2001 publications were produced. She also suggested the title for the *How to Program* series.

We would also like to thank the participants in the Deitel & Associates, Inc., College Internship Program.[4]

- Christina J. Courtemarche, a senior at Boston University in Computer Science, was instrumental in the development of this manuscript. She co-authored Appendix D and contributed to Chapters 1–17, 19–22, 24, and Appendix F. She coded and tested the examples and solved the exercises for Chapters 1–14, 16, 20 and 22.

- Alex Rasin, a graduate of Brandeis University with a degree in Computer Science and a graduate student at Brown University, coded examples in Chapters 5, 9, 10, 11, 13, 21 and 24.

- Jeffrey Hamm, a sophomore at Northeastern University in Computer Science, reviewed Chapter 24.

- Christina Carney, a senior in Psychology and Business at Framingham State College, helped with the Preface and the Bibliography.

- Brian Foster, a sophomore at Northeastern University in Computer Science, contributed to ancillaries for book and helped with the Preface and Bibliography.

- Mike Preshman, a sophomore at Northeastern University with a major in Computer Science and minors in Electrical Engineering and Math, contributed to Appendices G–L, tested the code examples and helped with the Bibliography and ancillary materials.

- Matthew Rubino, a sophomore at Northeastern University in Computer Science, contributed to the ancillary materials.

- Adam Sparrow, a senior at Bentley College with a major in Computer Information Systems, contributed to the ancillary materials.

---

4. The *Deitel & Associates, Inc. College Internship Program* offers a limited number of salaried positions to Boston-area college students majoring in Computer Science, Information Technology, Marketing, Management and English. Students work at our corporate headquarters in Sudbury, Massachusetts full-time in the summers and (for those attending college in the Boston area) part-time during the academic year. We also offer full-time internship positions for students interested in taking a semester off from school to gain industry experience. Regular full-time positions are available to college graduates. For more information about this competitive program, please contact Abbey Deitel at **deitel@deitel.com** and visit our Web site, **www.deitel.com**.

We are fortunate to have been able to work on this project with the talented and dedicated team of publishing professionals at Prentice Hall. We especially appreciate the extraordinary efforts of our Computer Science editor, Petra Recter and her boss—our mentor in publishing—Marcia Horton, Editorial Director of Prentice-Hall's Engineering and Computer Science Division. Camille Trentacoste and her boss Vince O'Brien did a marvelous job managing the production of the book. Sarah Burrows handled editorial responsibilities on the book's extensive ancillary package.

The *Python Multimedia Cyber Classroom* was developed in parallel with *Python How to Program*. We sincerely appreciate the "new media" insight, savvy and technical expertise of our electronic-media editors, Mark Taub and Karen McLean. They and project manager Mike Ruel did a wonderful job bringing the *Python Multimedia Cyber Classroom* and *The Complete Python Training Course* to publication.

We owe special thanks to the creativity of Tamara Newnam (`smart_art@earthlink.net`), who produced the art work for our programming-tip icons and for the cover. She created the delightful creature who shares with you the book's programming tips. Barbara Deitel and Harvey Deitel contributed the bugs' names for the front cover.

We wish to acknowledge the efforts of our first- and second-round reviewers and to thank Crissy Statuto of Prentice Hall, who recruited the reviewers and managed the review process. Adhering to a tight time schedule, these reviewers scrutinized the text and the programs, providing countless suggestions for improving the accuracy and completeness of the presentation.

Python How to Program reviewers:

Guido Van Rossum (Creator of Python)
Mike Fletcher (PyOpenGL Project)
Jeremy Hylton (Pythonlabs at Digital Creations)
Andreas Jung (Zope Corporation)
Alex Martelli (Senior Software Consultant, think3, Inc.)
Russell Nelson (Vice President, Open Source Initiative)
Uche Ogbuji (CEO, Fourthought, Inc.)
Pete Shinners (Pygame Maintainer)
Aahz (Writer & Trainer)
Rob Andrews (Webmaster, Useless Python)
Ian Bicking (Colorstudy Web Design)
Carl Burnham (Southpoint)
Nathan Clegg (Geerbox)
Luis Cortes (Consultant)
David Currie (Netdecisions)
Kevin Dorff (Honeywell)
Cam Farnell (Consultant)
Doug Fort (Downright Software LLC)
Charles Fry (thesundancekid.org)
Robert Fulkerson (University of Nebraska at Omaha)
Gnanavel Gnana Arun Ganesh (Arun Microsystems)
Alan Gauld (Author of *Learn to Program Using Python*)
Dean Goodmanson (Renaissance Learning, Inc.)

Chris Gonnerman (Owner, New Century Computers)
David den Harring (Consultant)
Michael Hudson (University of Bristol)
Wayne Izatt (Independent Software Developer)
Curtis Jensen (University of California, San Diego)
Nicolas Kauer (University of Wisconsin)
Tim Keating (QA Engineer, Origin Systems)
Andredi Kulakov (Python Programmer)
Cameron Laird (Phasit, Inc.)
Tripp Lilley (Webware)
Andrew Markebo (Telelogic AB)
Rick McGowen (Unicode Consortium)
Sean McGrath (Propylon)
Zan Ouyang (Core Technology)
Todd Pitts (Consultant)
Brandon Rogers (Washington State University student)
Richard H.C. Seabrook (Anne Arundel Community College)
Christine Shannon (Centre College)
John W. Shipman (New Mexico Tech Computer Center)
David R. Sopha (Sopha Consulting, Inc.)
Ken Stone (Tellium)
Terry Sullivan (pantos.org)
Geoff Talvola (Webware)
Vladimir Toncar (Tiny Software)
Howard Whitston (Lawrence Technological University)
Collin Williams (Consultant)
Jesse Wilkins (Metalinear Media)
Jody Winston (xprt Computer Consulting Inc.)
Joerg Volelke (FeLis)
Kirby Urner (Curriculum Writer, 4D Solutions)

We would like to thank the Python Software Foundation for permission to use their software (Python, IDLE and **Tkinter**) in our illustrations to demonstrate many Python concepts. Copyright © 2001 Python Software Foundation; Copyright © 2000 BeOpen.com; Copyright © 1995–2001 Corporation for National Research Initiatives; Copyright © 1991-1995 Stichting Mathematisch Centrum, Amsterdam.

Modules and their Copyrights

The nature of Python is that members of the Python community create additions to the language called modules. Like Python, many of these modules are created as open source and are available for anyone to use in their Python programs. Here, we present a list of the modules used in this book and their creators.

- **Pmw (`pmw.sourceforge.net`)**. Copyright © 1997, 1998, 1999, 2000, 2001 Telstra Corporation Limited, Australia (ACN 051 775 556).
  PyXML (`pyxml.sourceforge.net`). Author: PyXML Special Interest Group.

- **4Suite** (`4suite.org/4SuiteIndex.html`). Copyright © 2000–2001 Fourthought, Inc.

- **MySQLdb** (`sourceforge.net/projects/mysql-python`). Author: Andy Dustman.

- **PyOpenGL** (`pyopengl.sourceforge.net`). Copyright © 1997–1998 by James Hugunin, Cambridge MA, USA, Thomas Schwaller, Munich, Germany and David Ascher, San Francisco CA, USA. PyOpenGL 1.5.6 Copyright © 1997–1998, 2000–2001.

- **Pygame** (`www.pygame.org`). Author: Pete Shinners. Copyright © Pygame, 2001 Python Game Development.

- **Webware** (`webware.sourceforge.net`). Copyright © 1999–2001 by Chuck Esterbrook.

We would sincerely appreciate your comments, criticisms, corrections and suggestions for improving the text. Please address all correspondence to:

deitel@deitel.com

We will respond promptly.

Well, that's it for now. Welcome to the exciting world of Python programming. We hope you enjoy this look at leading-edge computer applications development. Good luck!

Dr. Harvey M. Deitel
Paul J. Deitel
Jonathan Liperi
Ben Wiedermann

About the Authors

Dr. Harvey M. Deitel, CEO and Chairman of Deitel & Associates, Inc., has 41 years experience in the computing field, including extensive industry and academic experience. Dr. Deitel earned B.S. and M.S. degrees from the Massachusetts Institute of Technology and a Ph.D. from Boston University. He worked on the pioneering virtual-memory operating-systems projects at IBM and MIT that developed techniques now widely implemented in systems such as UNIX, Linux and Windows NT. He has 20 years of college teaching experience, including earning tenure and serving as the Chairman of the Computer Science Department at Boston College before founding Deitel & Associates, Inc., with his son, Paul J. Deitel. He is the author or co-author with Paul Deitel of several dozen books and multimedia packages and is writing many more. With translations published in Japanese, Russian, Spanish, Traditional Chinese, Simplified Chinese, Korean, French, Polish, Italian and Portuguese, Dr. Deitel's texts have earned international recognition. Dr. Deitel has delivered hundreds of professional seminars to major corporations, government organizations and various branches of the military.

Paul J. Deitel, Executive Vice President and Chief Technical Officer of Deitel & Associates, Inc., is a graduate of the Massachusetts Institute of Technology's Sloan School of Management, where he studied Information Technology. Through Deitel & Associates, Inc., he has delivered Java, C, C++ and Internet and World Wide Web courses to industry clients including Compaq, Sun Microsystems, White Sands Missile Range, Rogue Wave Software, Boeing, Dell, Stratus, Fidelity, Cambridge Technology Partners, Open Environment Corporation, One Wave, Hyperion Software, Lucent Technologies, Adra Systems, Entergy, CableData Systems, NASA at the Kennedy Space Center, the National Severe Storm Laboratory, IBM and many other organizations. He has lectured on C++ and Java for the Boston Chapter of the Association for Computing Machinery and has taught satellite-based Java courses through a cooperative venture of Deitel & Associates, Inc., Prentice Hall and the Technology Education Network. He and his father, Dr. Harvey M. Deitel, are the world's best-selling Computer Science textbook authors.

Jonathan Liperi is a senior at Boston University where he has been accepted into the Computer Science department's BA/MA program. He will earn his Master's degree in Computer Science in May 2003. His coursework has included advanced algorithms, queueing theory, computer architecture, computer networks, artificial intelligence, computer graphics, database systems, software engineering and various programming courses (C, C++, Python and Java).

Ben Wiedermann graduated from Boston University *magna cum laude* with a degree in Computer Science and a minor in Theater Arts. Ben plans to pursue post-graduate work in programming-language theory. Other Deitel publications to which he has contributed include *Java How to Program, Fourth Edition*; *C++ How to Program, Third Edition*; *Perl How to Program*; *Internet and World Wide Web How to Program, Second Edition*; *XML How to Program*; *e-Business & e-Commerce How to Program* and *C How to Program, Third Edition*.

About Deitel & Associates, Inc.

Deitel & Associates, Inc., is an internationally recognized corporate training and content-creation organization specializing in Internet/World Wide Web software technology, e-business/e-commerce software technology, object technology and computer programming languages education. The company provides courses on Internet and World Wide Web programming, wireless Internet programming, object technology and major programming platforms and languages, such as Visual Basic .NET, C#, Java, advanced Java, C, C++, XML, Perl, Python and more. The founders of Deitel & Associates, Inc., are Dr. Harvey M. Deitel and Paul J. Deitel. The company's clients include many of the world's largest computer companies, government agencies, branches of the military and business organizations. Through its 25-year publishing partnership with Prentice Hall, Deitel & Associates, Inc., publishes leading-edge programming textbooks, professional books, interactive CD-ROM-based multimedia *Cyber Classrooms, Complete Training Courses*, e-books, e-matter, Web-based training courses and course management systems e-content. Deitel & Associates, Inc., and the authors can be reached via e-mail at:

`deitel@deitel.com`

To register for *THE DEITEL™ BUZZ* e-mail newsletter and to learn more about Deitel & Associates, Inc., its publications and its worldwide corporate on-site curriculum, see the last few pages of this book or visit:

```
www.deitel.com
```

Individuals wishing to purchase Deitel books, *Cyber Classrooms*, *Complete Training Courses* and Web-based training courses can do so through bookstores, online booksellers and:

```
www.deitel.com
www.prenhall.com/deitel
www.InformIT.com/deitel
www.InformIT.com/cyberclassrooms
```

Bulk orders by corporations and academic institutions should be placed directly with Prentice Hall. See the last few pages of this book for worldwide ordering details. To register for the InformIT e-mail newsletter which contains a weekly column by the Deitels, visit `www.InformIT.com`.

The World Wide Web Consortium (W3C)

Deitel & Associates, Inc., is a member of the *World Wide Web Consortium (W3C)*. The W3C was founded in 1994 "to develop common protocols for the evolution of the World Wide Web." As a W3C member, Deitel & Associates, Inc., holds a seat on the W3C Advisory Committee (the company's representative is our Chief Technology Officer, Paul Deitel). Advisory Committee members help provide "strategic direction" to the W3C through meetings held around the world. Member organizations also help develop standards recommendations for Web technologies (such as XHTML, XML and many others) through participation in W3C activities and groups. Membership in the W3C is intended for companies and large organizations. To obtain information on becoming a member of the W3C visit `www.w3.org/Consortium/Prospectus/Joining`.

Introduction to Computers, Internet and World Wide Web

Objectives

- To understand basic computer concepts.
- To become familiar with different types of programming languages.
- To become familiar with the history of the Python programming language.
- To preview the remaining chapters of the book.

Things are always at their best in their beginning.
Blaise Pascal

High thoughts must have high language.
Aristophanes

Our life is frittered away by detail...Simplify, simplify.
Henry David Thoreau

Outline

1.1   Introduction
1.2   What Is a Computer?
1.3   Computer Organization
1.4   Evolution of Operating Systems
1.5   Personal Computing, Distributed Computing and Client/Server Computing
1.6   Machine Languages, Assembly Languages and High-Level Languages
1.7   Structured Programming
1.8   Object-Oriented Programming
1.9   Hardware Trends
1.10   History of the Internet and World Wide Web
1.11   World Wide Web Consortium (W3C)
1.12   Extensible Markup Language (XML)
1.13   Open-Source Software Revolution
1.14   History of Python
1.15   Python Modules
1.16   General Notes about Python and This Book
1.17   Tour of the Book
1.18   Internet and World Wide Web Resources

Summary • Terminology • Self-Review Exercises • Answers to Self-Review Exercises • Exercises

1.1 Introduction

Welcome to Python! We have worked hard to create what we hope will be an informative and entertaining learning experience for you. The manner in which we approached this topic created a book that is unique among Python textbooks for many reasons. For instance, we introduce early in the text the use of Python with the *Common Gateway Interface (CGI)* for programming Web-based applications. We do this so that we can demonstrate a variety of dynamic, Web-based applications in the remainder of the book. This text also introduces a range of topics, including *object-oriented programming (OOP)*, the Python *database application programming interface (DB-API)*, graphics, the *Extensible Markup Language (XML)*, security and an appendix on Web accessibility that addresses programming and technologies relevant to people with impairments. Whether you are a novice or an experienced programmer, there is much here to inform, entertain and challenge you.

Python How to Program is designed to be appropriate for readers at all levels, from practicing programmers to individuals with little or no programming experience. How can one book appeal to both novices and skilled programmers? The core of this book emphasizes achieving program clarity through proven techniques of *structured programming* and *object-based programming*. Nonprogrammers learn basic skills that underlie good programming; experienced programmers receive a rigorous explanation of the language and may improve their programming styles. To aid beginning programmers, we have written this text in a clear and straightforward manner, with abundant illustrations. Perhaps most importantly, the book presents hundreds of complete working Python programs and shows the outputs produced when those programs are run on a computer. We call this our *Live-Code™ approach*. All of the book's examples are available on the CD-ROM that accompanies this book and on our Web site, **www.deitel.com**.

Most people are at least somewhat familiar with the exciting capabilities of computers. Using this textbook, you will learn how to command computers to exercise those capabilities. It is *software* (i.e., the instructions you write to command the computer to perform *actions* and make *decisions*) that controls computers (often referred to as *hardware*).

Computer use is increasing in almost every field. In an era of steadily rising costs, the expense of owning a computer has been decreasing dramatically due to rapid developments in both hardware and software technology. Computers that filled large rooms and cost millions of dollars 25 to 30 years ago now are inscribed on the surfaces of silicon chips smaller than a fingernail and that cost perhaps a few dollars each. Silicon is one of the most abundant materials on the earth—it is an ingredient in common sand. Silicon-chip technology has made computing so economical that hundreds of millions of general-purpose computers are in use worldwide, helping people in business, industry, government and their personal lives. Given the current rate of technological development, this number could easily double over the next few years.

In beginning to study this text, you are starting on a challenging and rewarding educational path. As you proceed, if you would like to communicate with us, please send us e-mail at **deitel@deitel.com** or browse our World Wide Web sites at **www.deitel.com**, **www.prenhall.com/deitel** and **www.InformIT.com/deitel**. We hope you enjoy learning Python with *Python How to Program*.

1.2 What Is a Computer?

A *computer* is a device capable of performing computations and making logical decisions at speeds millions and even billions of times faster than those of human beings. For example, many of today's personal computers can perform hundreds of millions—even billions—of additions per second. A person operating a desk calculator might require decades to complete the same number of calculations that a powerful personal computer can perform in one second. (*Points to ponder*: How would you know whether the person added the numbers correctly? How would you know whether the computer added the numbers correctly?) Today's fastest *supercomputers* can perform hundreds of billions of additions per second—about as many calculations as hundreds of thousands of people could perform in one year! Trillion-instruction-per-second computers are already functioning in research laboratories!

Computers process *data* under the control of sets of instructions called *computer programs*. These programs guide computers through orderly sets of actions that are specified by individuals known as *computer programmers*.

A computer is composed of various devices (such as the keyboard, screen, mouse, disks, memory, CD-ROM and processing units) known as *hardware*. The programs that run on a computer are referred to as *software*. Hardware costs have been declining dramatically in recent years, to the point that personal computers have become a commodity. Software-development costs, however, have been rising steadily, as programmers develop ever more powerful and complex applications without being able to improve significantly the technology of software development. In this book, you will learn proven software-development methods that can reduce software-development costs—top-down, stepwise refinement, functionalization and object-oriented programming. Object-oriented programming is widely believed to be the significant breakthrough that can greatly enhance programmer productivity.

1.3 Computer Organization

Virtually every computer, regardless of differences in physical appearance, can be envisioned as being divided into six *logical units*, or sections:

1. *Input unit.* This "receiving" section of the computer obtains information (data and computer programs) from various *input devices*. The input unit then places this information at the disposal of the other units to facilitate the processing of the information. Today, most users enter information into computers via keyboards and mouse devices. Other input devices include microphones (for speaking to the computer), scanners (for scanning images) and digital cameras and video cameras (for taking photographs and making videos).

2. *Output unit.* This "shipping" section of the computer takes information that the computer has processed and places it on various *output devices,* making the information available for use outside the computer. Computers can output information in various ways, including displaying the output on screens, playing it on audio/video devices, printing it on paper or using the output to control other devices.

3. *Memory unit.* This is the rapid-access, relatively low-capacity "warehouse" section of the computer, which facilitates the temporary storage of data. The memory unit retains information that has been entered through the input unit, enabling that information to be immediately available for processing. In addition, the unit retains processed information until that information can be transmitted to output devices. Often, the memory unit is called either *memory* or *primary memory— random access memory* (*RAM*) is an example of primary memory. Primary memory is usually volatile, which means that it is erased when the machine is powered off.

4. *Arithmetic and logic unit* (*ALU*). The ALU is the "manufacturing" section of the computer. It is responsible for the performance of calculations such as addition, subtraction, multiplication and division. It also contains decision mechanisms, allowing the computer to perform such tasks as determining whether two items stored in memory are equal.

5. *Central processing unit* (*CPU*). The CPU serves as the "administrative" section of the computer. This is the computer's coordinator, responsible for supervising the operation of the other sections. The CPU alerts the input unit when information should be read into the memory unit, instructs the ALU about when to use information from the memory unit in calculations and tells the output unit when to send information from the memory unit to certain output devices.

6. *Secondary storage unit.* This unit is the long-term, high-capacity "warehousing" section of the computer. Secondary storage devices, such as hard drives and disks,

normally hold programs or data that other units are not actively using; the computer then can retrieve this information when it is needed—hours, days, months or even years later. Information in secondary storage takes much longer to access than does information in primary memory. However, the price per unit of secondary storage is much less than the price per unit of primary memory. Secondary storage is usually *nonvolatile*—it retains information even when the computer is off.

1.4 Evolution of Operating Systems

Early computers were capable of performing only one *job* or *task* at a time. In this mode of computer operation, often called single-user *batch processing,* the computer runs one program at a time and processes data in groups called *batches.* Users of these early systems typically submitted their jobs to a computer center on decks of punched cards. Often, hours or even days elapsed before results were returned to the users' desks.

To make computer use more convenient, software systems called *operating systems* were developed. Early operating systems oversaw and managed computers' transitions between jobs. By minimizing the time it took for a computer operator to switch from one job to another, the operating system increased the total amount of work, or *throughput*, computers could process in a given time period.

As computers became more powerful, single-user batch processing became inefficient, because computers spent a great deal of time waiting for slow input/output devices to complete their tasks. Developers then looked to multiprogramming techniques, which enabled many tasks to *share* the resources of the computer to achieve better utilization. *Multiprogramming* involves the "simultaneous" operation of many jobs on a computer that splits its resources among those jobs. However, users of early multiprogramming operating systems still submitted jobs on decks of punched cards and waited hours or days for results.

In the 1960s, several industry and university groups pioneered *timesharing* operating systems. Timesharing is a special type of multiprogramming that allows users to access a computer through *terminals* (devices with keyboards and screens). Dozens or even hundreds of people can use a timesharing computer system at once. It is important to note that the computer does not actually run all the users' requests simultaneously. Rather, it performs a small portion of one user's job and moves on to service the next user. However, because the computer does this so quickly, it can provide service to each user several times per second. This gives users' programs the appearance of running simultaneously. Timesharing offers major advantages over previous computing systems in that users receive prompt responses to requests, instead of waiting long periods to obtain results.

The UNIX operating system, which is now widely used for advanced computing, originated as an experimental timesharing operating system. Dennis Ritchie and Ken Thompson developed UNIX at Bell Laboratories beginning in the late 1960s and developed C as the programming language in which they wrote it. They freely distributed the source code to other programmers who wanted to use, modify and extend it. A large community of UNIX users quickly developed. The operating system and the world of the C language grew as UNIX users contributed their own programs and tools. Through a collaborative effort among numerous researchers and developers, UNIX became a powerful and flexible operating system able to handle almost any type of task that a user required. Many versions of UNIX have evolved, including today's phenomenally popular, *open-source*, Linux operating system.

1.5 Personal Computing, Distributed Computing and Client/Server Computing

In 1977, Apple Computer popularized the phenomenon of *personal computing*. Initially, it was a hobbyist's dream. However, the price of computers soon dropped so far that large numbers of people could buy them for personal or business use. In 1981, IBM, the world's largest computer vendor, introduced the IBM Personal Computer. Personal computing rapidly became legitimate in business, industry and government organizations.

The computers first pioneered by Apple and IBM were "stand-alone" units—people did their work on their own machines and transported disks back and forth to share information. (This process was often called "sneakernet.") Although early personal computers were not powerful enough to timeshare several users, the machines could be linked together into computer networks, either over telephone lines or via *local area networks* (*LANs*) within an organization. These networks led to the *distributed computing* phenomenon, in which an organization's computing is distributed over networks to the sites at which the work of the organization is performed, instead of being performed only at a central computer installation. Personal computers were powerful enough to handle both the computing requirements of individual users and the basic tasks involved in the electronic transfer of information between computers. *N-tier applications* split up an application over numerous distributed computers. For example, a *three-tier application* might have a user interface on one computer, business-logic processing on a second and a database on a third; all interact as the application runs.

Today's most advanced personal computers are as powerful as the million-dollar machines of just two decades ago. High-powered desktop machines—called *workstations*—provide individual users with enormous capabilities. Information is easily shared across computer networks, in which computers called *servers* store programs and data that can be used by *client* computers distributed throughout the network. This type of configuration gave rise to the term *client/server computing*. Today's popular operating systems, such as UNIX, Solaris, MacOS, Windows 2000, Windows XP and Linux, provide the kinds of capabilities discussed in this section.

1.6 Machine Languages, Assembly Languages and High-Level Languages

Programmers write instructions in various programming languages, some directly understandable by computers and others that require intermediate *translation* steps. Although hundreds of computer languages are in use today, the diverse offerings can be divided into three general types:

1. Machine languages

2. Assembly languages

3. High-level languages

Any computer can understand only its own *machine language* directly. As the "natural language" of a particular computer, machine language is defined by the computer's hardware design. Machine languages generally consist of streams of numbers (ultimately reduced to 1s and 0s) that instruct computers how to perform their most elementary operations. Machine languages are *machine-dependent*, which means that a particular machine language can be used on only one type of computer. The following section of a machine-language program, which adds *overtime* pay to *base pay* and stores the result in *gross pay*, demonstrates the incomprehensibility of machine language to the human reader.

```
+1300042774
+1400593419
+1200274027
```

As the popularity of computers increased, machine-language programming proved to be excessively slow, tedious and error prone. Instead of using the strings of numbers that computers could directly understand, programmers began using English-like abbreviations to represent the elementary operations of the computer. These abbreviations formed the basis of *assembly languages. Translator programs* called *assemblers* convert assembly language programs to machine language at computer speeds. The following section of an assembly-language program also adds *overtime pay* to *base pay* and stores the result in *gross pay*, but presents the steps more clearly to human readers than does its machine-language equivalent:

```
LOAD    BASEPAY
ADD     OVERPAY
STORE   GROSSPAY
```

Such code is clearer to humans but incomprehensible to computers until translated into machine language.

Although computer use increased rapidly with the advent of assembly languages, these languages still required many instructions to accomplish even the simplest tasks. To speed up the programming process, *high-level languages*, in which single statements accomplish substantial tasks, were developed. Translation programs called *compilers* convert high-level-language programs into machine language. High-level languages enable programmers to write instructions that look almost like everyday English and contain common mathematical notations. A payroll program written in a high-level language might contain a statement such as

```
grossPay = basePay + overTimePay
```

Obviously, programmers prefer high-level languages to either machine languages or assembly languages. C, C++, C# (pronounced "C sharp"), Java, Visual Basic, Perl and Python are among the most popular high-level languages.

Compiling a high-level language program into machine language can require a considerable amount of time. This problem was solved by the development of *interpreter* programs that can execute high-level language programs directly, bypassing the compilation step, and interpreters can start running a program immediately without "suffering" a compilation delay. Although programs that are already compiled execute faster than interpreted programs, interpreters are popular in program-development environments. In these environments, developers change programs frequently as they add new features and correct errors. Once a program is fully developed, a compiled version can be produced so that the program runs at maximum efficiency. As we will see throughout this book, interpreted languages—like Python—are particularly popular for implementing World Wide Web applications.

1.7 Structured Programming

During the 1960s, many large software-development efforts encountered severe difficulties. Development typically ran behind schedule, costs often greatly exceeded budgets and the finished products were unreliable. People began to realize that software development was a far more complex activity than they had imagined. Research activity, intended to address these issues, resulted in the evolution of *structured programming*—a disciplined approach to the creation of programs that are clear, demonstrably correct and easy to modify.

One of the more tangible results of this research was the development of the *Pascal* programming language in 1971. Pascal, named after the seventeenth-century mathematician and philosopher Blaise Pascal, was designed for teaching structured programming in academic environments and rapidly became the preferred introductory programming language in most universities. Unfortunately, because the language lacked many features needed to make it useful in commercial, industrial and government applications, it was not widely accepted in these environments. By contrast, C, which also arose from research on structured programming, did not have the limitations of Pascal, and became extremely popular.

The *Ada* programming language was developed under the sponsorship of the United States Department of Defense (DOD) during the 1970s and early 1980s. Hundreds of programming languages were being used to produce DOD's massive command-and-control software systems. DOD wanted a single language that would meet its needs. Pascal was chosen as a base, but the final Ada language is quite different from Pascal. The language was named after Lady Ada Lovelace, daughter of the poet Lord Byron. Lady Lovelace is generally credited with writing the world's first computer program, in the early 1800s (for the Analytical Engine mechanical computing device designed by Charles Babbage). One important capability of Ada is *multitasking*, which allows programmers to specify that many activities are to occur in parallel. As we will see in Chapters 18–19, Python offers process management and *multithreading*—two capabilities that enable programs to specify that various activities are to proceed in parallel.

1.8 Object-Oriented Programming

One of the authors, HMD, remembers the great frustration felt in the 1960s by software-development organizations, especially those developing large-scale projects. During the summers of his undergraduate years, HMD had the privilege of working at a leading computer vendor on the teams developing time-sharing, virtual-memory operating systems. It was a great experience for a college student, but, in the summer of 1967, reality set in. The company "decommitted" from producing as a commercial product the particular system that hundreds of people had been working on for several years. It was difficult to get this software right. Software is "complex stuff."

As the benefits of structured programming (and the related disciplines of *structured systems analysis and design*) were realized in the 1970s, improved software technology did begin to appear. However, it was not until the technology of object-oriented programming became widely used in the 1980s and 1990s that software developers finally felt they had the necessary tools to improve the software-development process dramatically.

Actually, object technology dates back to at least the mid-1960s, but no broad-based programming language incorporated the technology until C++. Although not strictly an object-oriented language, C++ absorbed the capabilities of C and incorporated Simula's ability to create and manipulate objects. C++ was never intended for widespread use beyond the research laboratories at AT&T, but grass-roots support rapidly developed for the hybrid language.

What are objects, and why are they special? Object technology is a packaging scheme that facilitates the creation of meaningful software units. These units are large and focused on particular applications areas. There are date objects, time objects, paycheck objects, invoice objects, audio objects, video objects, file objects, record objects and so on. In fact, almost any noun can be reasonably represented as a software object. Objects have *properties* (i.e., *attributes*, such as color, size and weight) and perform *actions* (i.e., *behaviors*, such as moving, sleeping or drawing). Classes represent groups of related objects. For example, all cars belong to the "car" class, even though individual cars vary in make, model, color and options packages. A class specifies the general format of its objects; the properties and actions available to an object depend on its class.

We live in a world of objects. Just look around you—there are cars, planes, people, animals, buildings, traffic lights, elevators and so on. Before object-oriented languages appeared, *procedural programming languages* (such as Fortran, Pascal, BASIC and C) focused on actions (verbs) rather than things or objects (nouns). We live in a world of objects, but earlier programming languages forced individuals to program primarily with verbs. This paradigm shift made program writing a bit awkward. However, with the advent of popular object-oriented languages, such as C++, Java, C# and Python, programmers can program in an object-oriented manner that reflects the way in which they perceive the world. This process, which seems more natural than procedural programming, has resulted in significant productivity gains.

One of the key problems with procedural programming is that the program units created do not mirror real-world entities effectively and therefore are not particularly reusable. Programmers often write and rewrite similar software for various projects. This wastes precious time and money as people repeatedly "reinvent the wheel." With object technology, properly designed software entities (called objects) can be reused on future projects. Using libraries of reusable componentry can greatly reduce the amount of effort required to implement certain kinds of systems (as compared to the effort that would be required to reinvent these capabilities in new projects).

Some organizations report that software reusability is not, in fact, the key benefit of object-oriented programming. Rather, they indicate that object-oriented programming tends to produce software that is more understandable because it is better organized and has fewer maintenance requirements. As much as 80 percent of software costs are not associated with the original efforts to develop the software, but instead are related to the continued evolution and maintenance of that software throughout its lifetime. Object orientation allows programmers to abstract the details of software and focus on the "big picture." Rather than worrying about minute details, the programmer can focus on the behaviors and interactions of objects. A roadmap that showed every tree, house and driveway would be difficult, if not impossible, to read. When such details are removed and only the essential information (roads) remains, the map becomes easier to understand. In the same way, a program that is divided into objects is easy to understand, modify and update because it hides much of the detail. It is clear that object-oriented programming will be the key programming methodology for at least the next decade.

1.9 Hardware Trends

Every year, people generally expect to pay at least a little more for most products and services. The opposite has been the case in the computer and communications fields, especially with regard to the costs of hardware supporting these technologies. For many decades, and continuing into the foreseeable future, hardware costs have fallen rapidly, if not precipitously. Every year or two, the capacities of computers approximately double.[1] This is especially true in relation to the amount of memory that computers have for programs, the amount of secondary storage (such as disk storage) computers have to hold programs and data over longer periods of time and their processor speeds—the speeds at which computers execute their programs (i.e., do their work). Similar improvements have occurred in the communications field, in which costs have plummeted as enormous demand for *bandwidth* (i.e., information-carrying capacity of communication lines) has attracted tremendous competition. We know of no other fields in which technology moves so quickly and costs fall so rapidly. Such phenomenal improvement in the computing and communications fields is truly fostering the so-called *Information Revolution*.

When computer use exploded in the 1960s and 1970s, many people discussed the dramatic improvements in human productivity that computing and communications would cause. However, these improvements did not materialize. Organizations were spending vast sums of capital on computers and employing them effectively, but without fully realizing the expected productivity gains. The invention of microprocessor chip technology and its wide deployment in the late 1970s and 1980s laid the groundwork for the productivity improvements that individuals and businesses have achieved in recent years.

1.10 History of the Internet and World Wide Web

In the late 1960s, one of the authors (HMD) was a graduate student at MIT. His research at MIT's Project Mac (now the Laboratory for Computer Science—the home of the World Wide Web Consortium) was funded by ARPA—the Advanced Research Projects Agency of the Department of Defense. ARPA sponsored a conference at which several dozen ARPA-funded graduate students were brought together at the University of Illinois at Urbana-Champaign to meet and share ideas. During this conference, ARPA rolled out the blueprints for networking the main computer systems of approximately a dozen ARPA-funded universities and research institutions. The computers were to be connected with communications lines operating at a then-stunning 56 Kbps (1 Kbps is equal to 1,024 bits per second), at a time when most people (of the few who had access to networking technologies) were connecting over telephone lines to computers at a rate of 110 bits per second. HMD vividly recalls the excitement at that conference. Researchers at Harvard talked about communicating with the Univac 1108 "supercomputer," which was located across the country at the University of Utah, to handle calculations related to their computer graphics research. Many other intriguing possibilities were discussed. Academic research was about to take a giant leap forward. Shortly after this conference, ARPA proceeded to implement what quickly became called the *ARPAnet*, the grandparent of today's *Internet*.

Things worked out differently from the original plan. Although the ARPAnet did enable researchers to network their computers, its chief benefit proved to be the capability for quick and easy communication via what came to be known as *electronic mail* (*e-mail*). This is true even on today's Internet, with e-mail, instant messaging and file transfer facilitating communications among hundreds of millions of people worldwide.

---

1. This often is called *Moore's Law*.

The network was designed to operate without centralized control. This meant that, if a portion of the network should fail, the remaining working portions would still be able to route data packets from senders to receivers over alternative paths.

The protocol (i.e., set of rules) for communicating over the ARPAnet became known as the *Transmission Control Protocol (TCP)*. TCP ensured that messages were properly routed from sender to receiver and that those messages arrived intact.

In parallel with the early evolution of the Internet, organizations worldwide were implementing their own networks to facilitate both intra-organization (i.e., within the organization) and inter-organization (i.e., between organizations) communication. A huge variety of networking hardware and software appeared. One challenge was to enable these diverse products to communicate with each other. ARPA accomplished this by developing the *Internet Protocol (IP)*, which created a true "network of networks," the current architecture of the Internet. The combined set of protocols is now commonly called *TCP/IP*.

Initially, use of the Internet was limited to universities and research institutions; later, the military adopted the technology. Eventually, the government decided to allow access to the Internet for commercial purposes. When this decision was made, there was resentment among the research and military communities—it was felt that response times would become poor as "the Net" became saturated with so many users.

In fact, the opposite has occurred. Businesses rapidly realized that, by making effective use of the Internet, they could refine their operations and offer new and better services to their clients. Companies started spending vast amounts of money to develop and enhance their Internet presence. This generated fierce competition among communications carriers and hardware and software suppliers to meet the increased infrastructure demand. The result is that bandwidth on the Internet has increased tremendously, while hardware costs have plummeted. It is widely believed that the Internet played a significant role in the economic growth that many industrialized nations experienced over the last decade.

The *World Wide Web (WWW)* allows computer users to locate and view multimedia-based documents (i.e., documents with text, graphics, animations, audios and/or videos) on almost any subject. Even though the Internet was developed more than three decades ago, the introduction of the World Wide Web was a relatively recent event. In 1989, Tim Berners-Lee of CERN (the European Organization for Nuclear Research) began to develop a technology for sharing information via hyperlinked text documents. Basing the new language on the well-established *Standard Generalized Markup Language (SGML)*—a standard for business data interchange—Berners-Lee called his invention the *HyperText Markup Language (HTML)*. He also wrote communication protocols to form the backbone of his new hypertext information system, which he referred to as the World Wide Web.

Historians will surely list the Internet and the World Wide Web among the most important and profound creations of humankind. In the past, most computer applications ran on "stand-alone" computers (computers that were not connected to one another). Today's applications can be written to communicate among the world's hundreds of millions of computers. The Internet and World Wide Web merge computing and communications technologies, expediting and simplifying our work. They make information instantly and conveniently accessible to large numbers of people. They enable individuals and small businesses to achieve worldwide exposure. They are profoundly changing the way we do business and conduct our personal lives. People can search for the best prices on virtually any product or service. Special-interest communities can stay in touch with one another. Researchers can be made instantly aware of the latest breakthroughs worldwide.

We have written two books for academic courses that convey fundamental principles of computing in the context of Internet and World Wide Web programming—*Internet and World Wide Web How to Program: Second Edition* and *e-Business and e-Commerce How to Program.*

1.11 World Wide Web Consortium (W3C)

In October 1994, Tim Berners-Lee founded an organization, called the *World Wide Web Consortium (W3C)*, that is devoted to developing nonproprietary, interoperable technologies for the World Wide Web. One of the W3C's primary goals is to make the Web universally accessible—regardless of disabilities, language or culture.

The W3C is also a standardization organization and is comprised of three *hosts*—the Massachusetts Institute of Technology (MIT), France's INRIA (Institut National de Recherche en Informatique et Automatique) and Keio University of Japan—and over 400 members, including Deitel & Associates, Inc. Members provide the primary financing for the W3C and help provide the strategic direction of the Consortium. To learn more about the W3C, visit **www.w3.org**.

Web technologies standardized by the W3C are called *Recommendations*. Current W3C Recommendations include *Extensible HyperText Markup Language (XHTML™)*, *Cascading Style Sheets (CSS™)* and the *Extensible Markup Language (XML)*. Recommendations are not actual software products, but documents that specify the role, syntax and rules of a technology. Before becoming a W3C Recommendation, a document passes through three major phases: *Working Draft*—which, as its name implies, specifies an evolving draft; *Candidate Recommendation*—a stable version of the document that industry can begin to implement; and *Proposed Recommendation*—a Candidate Recommendation that is considered mature (i.e., has been implemented and tested over a period of time) and is ready to be considered for W3C Recommendation status. For detailed information about the W3C Recommendation track, see "6.2 The W3C Recommendation track" at

```
www.w3.org/Consortium/Process/Process-19991111/
process.html#RecsCR
```

1.12 Extensible Markup Language (XML)

As the popularity of the Web exploded, HTML's limitations became apparent. HTML's lack of *extensibility* (the ability to change or add features) frustrated developers, and its ambiguous definition allowed erroneous HTML to proliferate. In response to these problems, the W3C added limited extensibility to HTML. This was, however, only a temporary solution—the need for a standardized, fully extensible and structurally strict language was apparent. As a result, XML was developed by the W3C. XML combines the power and extensibility of its parent language, Standard Generalized Markup Language (SGML), with the simplicity that the Web community demands. At the same time, the W3C began developing XML-based standards for style sheets and advanced hyperlinking. *Extensible Stylesheet Language (XSL)* incorporates elements of both Cascading Style Sheets (CSS), which is used to format HTML documents and *Document Style and Semantics Specification Language (DSSSL)*, which is used to format SGML documents. Similarly, the *Exten-*

sible Linking Language (*XLink*) combines ideas from *HyTime* and the *Text Encoding Initiative* (*TEI*), to provide extensible linking of resources.

Data independence, the separation of content from its presentation, is the essential characteristic of XML. Because an XML document describes data, any application conceivably can process an XML document. Recognizing this, software developers are integrating XML into their applications to improve Web functionality and interoperability. XML's flexibility and power make it perfect for the middle tier of client/server systems, which must interact with a wide variety of clients. Much of the processing that was once limited to server computers now can be performed by client computers, because XML's semantic and structural information enables it to be manipulated by any application that can process text. This reduces server loads and network traffic, resulting in a faster, more efficient Web.

XML is not limited to Web applications. Increasingly, XML is being employed in databases—the structure of an XML document enables it to be integrated easily with database applications. As applications become more Web enabled, it seems likely that XML will become the universal technology for data representation. All applications employing XML would be able to communicate, provided that they could understand each other's XML markup, or *vocabulary*.

Simple Object Access Protocol (SOAP) is a technology for the distribution of objects (marked up as XML) over the Internet. Developed primarily by Microsoft and Develop-Mentor, SOAP provides a framework for expressing application semantics, encoding that data and packaging it in modules. SOAP has three parts: The *envelope*, which describes the content and intended recipient of a SOAP message; the SOAP *encoding rules*, which are XML-based; and the SOAP *Remote Procedure Call (RPC) representation* for commanding other computers to perform a task. SOAP is supported by many platforms, because of its foundations in XML and HTTP. We discuss XML in Chapter 15, Extensible Markup Language (XML) and in Chapter 16, XML Processing.

1.13 Open-Source Software Revolution

When the source code of a program is freely available to any developer to modify, to redistribute and to use as a basis for other software, it is called *open-source software*.[2] In contrast, *closed-source software* restricts other developers from creating software programs whose source code is based on closed-source programs.

The concept of open-source technologies is not new. The development of open-source technologies was an important factor in the growth of modern computing in 1960s. Specifically, the United States government funded what became today's Internet and encouraged computer scientists to develop technologies that could facilitate distributed computing on various computer platforms.[3] Out of these efforts came technologies such as the protocols used to communicate over today's Internet. After the Internet was established, closed-source technologies and software became the norm in the software industry, and open-source fell from popular use in the 1980s and early 1990s. In response to the "closed"

---

2. The Open Source Initiative's definition includes nine requirements to which software must comply before it is considered "open source." To view the entire definition, visit **<www.open-source.org/docs/definition.html>**.

3. **<www.opensource.org>**.

nature of most commercial software and programmers' frustrations with the lack of responsiveness from closed-source vendors, open-source software, regained popularity. Today, Python is part of a growing open-source software community, which includes the Linux operating system, the Perl scripting language, the Apache Web server and hundreds of other software projects.

Some people in the computer industry equate open-source with "free" software. In most cases, this is true. However, "free" in the context of open-source software is thought of most appropriately as "freedom"—the freedom for any developer to modify source code, to exchanges ideas, to participate in the software-development process and to develop new software programs based on existing open-source software. Most open-source software is copyrighted and licenses are associated with the use of the software. Open-source licenses vary in their terms; some impose few restrictions (e.g., the Artistic license[4]), whereas others require many restrictions on the manner in which the software may be modified and used. Usually, either an individual developer or an organization maintains the software copyrights. To view an example of a license, visit **www.python.org/2.2/license.html** to read the Python agreement.

Typically, the source code for open-source products is available for download over the Internet. This enables developers to learn from, validate and modify the source code to meet their own needs. With a community of developers, more people review the code so issues such as performance and security problems are detected and resolved faster than they would be in closed-source software development. Additionally, a larger community of developers can contribute more features. Often, code fixes are available within hours, and new versions of open-source software are available more frequently than are versions of closed-source software. Open-source licenses often require that developers publish any enhancements they make so that the open-source community can continue to evolve those products. For example, Python developers participate in the **comp.lang.python** newsgroup to exchange ideas regarding the development of Python. Python developers also can document and submit their modifications to the Python Software Foundation through Python Enhancement Proposals (PEPS), which enables the Python group to evaluate the proposed changes and incorporate the ones they choose in future releases.[5]

Many companies, (e.g., IBM, Red Hat and Sun) support open-source developers and projects. Sometimes companies take open-source applications and sell them commercially (this depends on software licensing). For-profit companies also provide services such as support, custom-made software and training. Developers can offer their services as consultants or trainers to businesses implementing the software.[6] For more information about open-source software, visit the Open Source Initiative's Web site at **www.opensource.org**.

1.14 History of Python

Python began in late 1989. At that time, Guido van Rossum, a researcher at the *National Research Institute for Mathematics and Computer Science in Amsterdam (CWI)*, needed a high-level scripting language to accomplish administrative tasks for his research group's

---

4. <www.opensource.org/licenses/artistic-license.html>.
5. <www.python.org>.
6. <www-106.ibm.com/developerworks/opensource/library/license.html?dwzone=opensource>.

Amoeba distributed operating system. To create this new language, he drew heavily from *All Basic Code (ABC)*—a high-level teaching language—for syntax, and from *Modula-3*, a systems programming language, for error-handling techniques. However, one major shortcoming of ABC was its lack of extensibility; the language was not open to improvements or extensions. So, van Rossum decided to create a language that combined many of the elements he liked from existing languages, but one that could be extended through classes and programming interfaces. He named this language Python, after the popular comic troupe Monty Python.

Since its public release in early 1991, a growing community of Python developers and users have improved it to create a mature and well-supported programming language. Python has been used to develop a variety of applications, from creating online e-mail programs to controlling underwater vehicles, configuring operating systems and creating animated films. In 2001, the core Python development team moved to Digital Creations, the creators of *Zope*—a Web application server written in Python. It is expected that Python will continue to grow and expand into new programming realms.

1.15 Python Modules

Python is a modularly extensible language; it can incorporate new *modules* (reusable pieces of software). These new modules, which can be written by any Python developer, extend Python's capabilities. The primary distribution center for Python source code, modules and documentation is the Python Web site—**www.python.org**—with plans to develop a site dedicated solely to maintaining Python modules.

1.16 General Notes about Python and This Book

Python was designed so that novice and experienced programmers could learn and understand the language quickly and use it with ease. Unlike its predecessors, Python was designed to be portable and extensible. Python's syntax and design promote good programming practices and tend to produce surprisingly rapid development times without sacrificing program scalability and maintenance.

Python is simple enough to be used by beginning programmers, but powerful enough to attract professionals. *Python How to Program* introduces programming concepts through abundant, complete, working examples and discussions. As we progress, we begin to explore more complex topics by creating practical applications. Throughout the book, we emphasize good programming practices and portability tips and explain how to avoid common programming errors.

Python is one of the most highly portable programming languages in existence. Originally, it was implemented on UNIX, but has since spread to many other platforms, including Microsoft Windows and Apple Mac OS X. Python programs often can be ported from one operating system to another without any change and still execute properly.

1.17 Tour of the Book

In this section, we take a tour of the subjects introduced in *Python How to Program*. Some chapters end with an Internet and World Wide Web Resources section, which lists resources that provide additional information on Python programming.

Chapter 1—Introduction to Computers, Internet and World Wide Web

In this chapter, we discuss what computers are, how they work and how they are programmed. The chapter introduces structured programming and explains why this set of techniques has fostered a revolution in the way programs are written. A brief history of the development of programming languages—from machine languages, to assembly languages to high-level languages—is included. We present some historical information about computers and computer programming and introductory information about the Internet and the World Wide Web. We discuss the origins of the Python programming language and overview the concepts introduced in the remaining chapters of the book.

Chapter 2—Introduction to Python Programming

Chapter 2 introduces a typical Python programming environment and the basic syntax for writing Python programs. We discuss how to run Python from the command line. In addition to the interpreter, Python can execute statements in an interactive mode in which Python statements can be typed and executed. Throughout the chapter and the book, we include several interactive sessions to highlight and illustrate various subtle programming points. In this chapter, we discuss variables and introduce arithmetic, assignment, equality, relational and string operators. We introduce decision-making and arithmetic operations. Strings are a basic and powerful built-in data type. We introduce some standard output-formatting techniques. We discuss the concept of *objects* and *variables*. Objects are containers for values and variables are names that reference objects. Our Python programs use syntax coloring to highlight keywords, comments and regular program text. After studying this chapter, readers will understand how to write simple but complete Python programs.

Chapter 3—Control Structures

This chapter introduces *algorithms* (procedures) for solving problems. It explains the importance of using control structures effectively in producing programs that are understandable, debuggable, maintainable and more likely to work properly on the first try. The chapter introduces selection structures (**if**, **if/else** and **if/elif/else**) and repetition structures (**while** and **for**). It examines repetition in detail and compares counter-controlled and sentinel-controlled loops. We explain the technique of top-down, stepwise refinement which is critical to the production of properly structured programs and the creation of the popular program design aid, *pseudocode*. The chapter examples and case studies demonstrate how quickly and easily pseudocode algorithms can be converted to working Python code. The chapter contains an explanation of **break** and **continue**—statements that alter the flow of control. We show how to use the logical operators **and**, **or** and **not** to enable programs to make sophisticated decisions. The chapter includes several interactive sessions that demonstrate how to create a **for** structure and how to avoid several common programming errors that arise in structured programming. The chapter concludes with a summary of structured programming. The techniques presented in Chapter 3 are applicable for effective use of control structures in any programming language, not just Python. This chapter helps the student develop good programming habits in preparation for dealing with the more substantial programming tasks in the remainder of the text.

Chapter 4—Functions

Chapter 4 discusses the design and construction of *functions*. Python's function-related capabilities include built-in functions, programmer-defined functions and recursion. The techniques presented in Chapter 4 are essential for creating properly structured programs—especially the larger programs and software that system programmers and application programmers are likely to develop in real-world applications. The "divide and conquer" strategy is presented as an effective means for solving complex problems by dividing them into simpler interacting components. We begin by introducing modules as containers for groups of useful functions. We introduce module **math** and discuss the many mathematics-related functions the module contains. Students enjoy the treatment of random numbers and simulation, and they are entertained by a study of the dice game, craps, which makes elegant use of control structures. The chapter illustrates how to solve a Fibonacci and factorial problem using a programming technique called *recursion* in which a function calls itself. Scope rules are discussed in the context of an example that examines local and global variables. The chapter also discusses the various ways a program can import a module and its elements and how the **import** statement affects the program's *namespace*. Python functions can specify default arguments and keyword arguments. We discuss both ways of passing information to functions and illustrate some common programming errors in an interactive session. The exercises present traditional mathematics and computer-science problems, including how to solve the famous Towers of Hanoi problem using recursion. Another exercise asks the reader to display the prime numbers from 2–100.

Chapter 5—Lists, Tuples and Dictionaries

This chapter presents a detailed introduction to three high-level Python data types: *lists*, *tuples* and *dictionaries*. These data types enable Python programmers to accomplish complex tasks through minimal lines of code. Strings, lists and tuples are all *sequences*—a data type that can be manipulated through indexing and "slicing." We discuss how to create, access and manipulate sequences and present an example that creates a histogram from a sequence of values. We consider the different ways lists and tuples are used in Python programs. Dictionaries are "mappable" types—keys are stored with (or mapped to) their associated values. We discuss how to create, initialize and manipulate dictionaries in an example that stores student grades. We introduce *methods*—functions that perform the operations of objects, such as lists and dictionaries—and how to use methods to access, sort and search data. These methods easily perform algorithmic tasks that normally require abundant lines of code in other languages. We consider immutable sequences—which cannot be altered—and mutable sequences—which can be altered. An important and perhaps unexpected "side effect" occurs when passing mutable sequences to functions—we present an example to show the ramifications of this side effect. The exercises at the end of the chapter address elementary sorting and searching algorithms and other programming techniques.

Chapter 6—Introduction to the Common Gateway Interface (CGI)

Chapter 6 illustrates a protocol for interactions between applications (CGI programs or scripts) and Web servers. The chapter introduces the *HyperText Transfer Protocol (HTTP)*, which is a fundamental component in the communication of data between a Web server and a Web browser. We explain how a client computer connects to a server computer to request information over the Internet and how a Web server runs a CGI program then sends a response to the client. The most common data sent from a Web server to a Web browser is a Web page—a document that is formatted with the *Extensible HyperText Markup Language (XHTML)*. In this chapter, we learn how to create simple CGI scripts. We also show how to send user input from a browser to a CGI script with an example that displays a person's name in a Web browser. We then focus on how to send user input to a CGI script by using an XHTML form to pass data between the client and the CGI program on the server. We demonstrate how to use module `cgi` to process form data. The chapter contains descriptions of various HTTP headers used with CGI. We conclude by integrating the CGI material into a Web portal case study that allows the user to log in to a fictional travel Web site and to view information about special offers.

Chapter 7—Object-Based Programming

In this chapter, we begin our discussion of object-based programming. The chapter represents a wonderful opportunity for teaching *data abstraction* the "right way"—through the Python language that was designed from the ground up to be object-oriented. In recent years, data abstraction has become an important topic in introductory computing courses. We discuss how to implement a time abstract data type with a class and how to initialize and access data members of the class. Unlike other languages, Python does not permit programmers to prohibit attribute access. In this and the next two chapters, we discuss several access-control techniques. We introduce "private" attributes as well as *get* and *set* methods that control access to data. All objects and classes have attributes in common, and we discuss their names and values. We discuss default constructors and expand our example further. We also introduce the **raise** statement for indicating errors. Classes can contain class attributes—data that are created once and used by all instances of the class. We also discuss an example of composition, in which instances contain references to other instances as data members. The chapter concludes with a discussion of software reusability. The more mathematically inclined reader will enjoy the exercise on creating class **Rational** (for rational numbers).

Chapter 8—Customizing Classes

This chapter discusses the several methods Python provides for customizing the behavior of a class. These methods extend the access-control mechanism introduced in the previous chapter. Perhaps the most powerful of the customization techniques is operator overloading, which enables the programmer to tell the Python interpreter how to use existing operators with objects of new types. Python already knows how to use these operators with objects of built-in types such as integers, lists and strings. But suppose we create a new **Rational** class—what would the plus sign (**+**) denote when used between **Rational** objects? In this chapter, the programmer will learn how to "overload" the plus sign so that, when it is written between two **Rational** objects in an expression, the interpreter will generate a method call to an "operator method" that "adds" the two **Rational** objects. The chapter discusses the fundamentals of operator overloading, restrictions in operator overloading, overloading unary and binary operators and converting between types. The chapter also discusses how to customize a class so it contains list- or dictionary-like behaviors. The more mathematically inclined student will enjoy creating class **Polynomial**.

Chapter 9—Object-Oriented Programming: Inheritance

This chapter introduces one of the most fundamental capabilities of object-oriented programming languages: *inheritance*. Inheritance is a form of software reusability in which new classes are developed quickly and easily by absorbing the capabilities of existing classes and adding appropriate new capabilities. The chapter discusses the notions of base classes and derived classes, direct-base classes, indirect-base classes, constructors and destructors in base classes and derived classes, and software engineering with inheritance. This chapter compares various object-oriented relationships, such as inheritance and composition. Inheritance leads to programming techniques that highlight one of Python's most powerful built-in features—*polymorphism*. When many classes are related through inheritance to a common base class, each derived-class object may be treated as a base-class instance. This enables programs to be written in a general manner independent of the specific types of the derived-class objects. New kinds of objects can be handled by the same program, thus making systems more extensible. This style of programming is commonly used to implement today's popular *graphical user interfaces (GUIs)*. The chapter concludes with a discussion of the new object-oriented programming techniques available in Python version 2.2.

Chapter 10—Graphical User Interface Components: Part 1

Chapter 10 introduces **Tkinter**, a module that provides a Python interface to the popular *Tool Command Language/Tool Kit (Tcl/Tk)* graphical-user-interface (GUI) toolkit. The chapter begins with a detailed overview of the **Tkinter** module. Using **Tkinter**, the programmer can create graphical programs quickly and easily. We illustrate several basic **Tkinter** *components*—**Label**, **Button**, **Entry**, **Checkbutton** and **Radiobutton**. We discuss the concept of event-handling that is central to GUI programming and present examples that show how to handle mouse and keyboard events in GUI applications. We conclude the chapter with a more in-depth examination of the **pack**, **grid** and **place** Tk layout managers. The exercises ask the reader to use the concepts presented in the chapter to create practical applications, such as a program that allows the user to convert temperature values between scales. Another exercise asks the reader to create a GUI calculator. After completing this chapter, the reader should be able to understand most **Tkinter** applications.

Chapter 11—Graphical User Interface Components: Part 2

Chapter 11 discusses additional GUI-programming topics. We introduce module **Pmw**, which extends the basic Tk GUI widget set. We show how to create menus, popup menus, scrolled text boxes and windows. The examples demonstrate copying text from one window to another, allowing the user to select and display images, changing the text font and changing the background color of a window. Of particular interest is the 35-line program that allows the user to draw pictures on a **Canvas** component with a mouse. The chapter concludes with a discussion of alternative GUI toolkits available to the Python programmer, including **pyGTK**, **pyOpenGL** and **wxWindows**. One of the chapter exercises asks the reader to enhance the temperature-conversion example from the previous chapter. A second exercise asks the reader to create a simple program that draws a shape on the screen. In another exercise, the reader fills the shape with a color selected from menu. Many examples throughout the remainder of the book use the GUI techniques shown in Chapters 10 and 11. After completing Chapters 10 and 11, the reader will be prepared to write the GUI portions of programs that perform database operations, networking tasks and simple games.

Chapter 12—Exception Handling

This chapter enables the programmer to write programs that are more robust, more fault tolerant and more appropriate for business-critical and mission-critical environments. We begin the chapter with an explanation of exception-handling techniques. We then discuss when exception handling is appropriate and introduce the basics of exception handling with **try/except/else** statements in an example that gracefully handles the fatal logic error of dividing by zero. The programmer can raise exceptions specifically using the **raise** statement; we discuss the syntax of this statement and demonstrate its use. The chapter explains how to extract information from exceptions and how and when to raise exceptions. We explain the **finally** statement and provide a detailed explanation of when and where exceptions are caught in programs. In Python, exceptions are classes. We discuss how exceptions relate to classes by examining the exception hierarchy and how to create custom exceptions. The chapter concludes with an example that takes advantage of the capabilities of module **traceback** to examine the nature and contents of Python exceptions.

Chapter 13—String Manipulation and Regular Expressions

This chapter explores how to manipulate string appearance, order and contents. Strings form the basis of most Python output. The chapter discussion includes methods **count**, **find** and **index**, which search strings for substrings. Method **split** breaks a string into a list of strings. Method **replace** replaces a substring of a string with another substring. These methods provide basic text manipulation capabilities, but programmers often require more powerful pattern-based text manipulation. The **re** regular-expression module provides pattern-based text manipulation in Python. Regular-expression processing can be a complex subject, with many pitfalls. We present several sections that range from basic regular expressions to more substantial topics. We point out the most common programming mistakes and include examples that highlight how these mistakes occur and how to avoid them. The sections discuss the common functions and classes of module **re** and the common regular-expression metacharacters and sequences. We demonstrate grouping, which enables programmers to retrieve information from regular-expression processing results. Python regular expressions can be compiled to improve regular-expression processing performance, so we discuss when it is appropriate to do this. The exercises ask the reader to explore common applications of regular expressions.

Chapter 14—File Processing and Serialization

In this chapter, we discuss the techniques for processing sequential-access and random-access text files. The chapter overviews the data hierarchy among bits, bytes, fields, records and files. Next, Python's simple view of files and filehandles is presented. Sequential-access files are discussed using programs that show how to open and close files, how to store data sequentially in a file and how to read data sequentially from a file. The examples use the string-formatting techniques from the previous chapter to output data read from a file. We include a more substantial program that simulates a credit-inquiry program that retrieves data from a sequential-access file and formats the output based on data obtained from the file. One feature of the chapter is the discussion of how the **print** statement can redirect text to an arbitrary file, including the *standard error file* to which programs display error messages. Our discussion of random-access files uses module **shelve**, which provides a dictionary-like interface to random-access files. We use **shelve** to create a file for random access and to read and write data to a **shelve** file. We include a larger transaction-processing programming example that employs the techniques discussed in the chapter. One benefit of Python's high-level data types and modules is that programs can serialize (save to disk) arbitrary Python objects. We present an example that uses module **cPickle** to store a Python dictionary to disk for later use.

Chapter 15—Extensible Markup Language (XML)

XML is a language for creating markup languages. Unlike HTML, which formats information for display, XML structures information. It does not have a fixed set of tags as HTML does, but instead enables the document author to create new ones. This chapter provides a brief overview of *parsers*, which are programs that process XML documents and their data, and the requirements for a *well-formed document* (i.e., a document that is syntactically correct). We also introduce *namespaces*, which differentiate elements with the same name, and *Document Type Definition (DTD)* files and *schema* files, which provide a structural definition for an XML document by specifying the type, order, number and attributes of the elements in an XML document. By defining an XML document's structure, a DTD or Schema reduces the validation and error-checking work of the application using the document. This chapter provides an introduction to an extremely popular XML-related technology—called the *Extensible Stylesheet Language (XSL)*—for transforming XML documents into other document formats such as XHTML. This chapter provides an overview of XML; Chapter 16 discusses XML processing in Python.

Chapter 16—XML Processing

In this chapter, we discuss how Python XML processing and manipulation can be accomplished simply and powerfully using standard and third-party modules. This chapter overviews several ways to process XML documents. The W3C *Document Object Model (DOM)*—an *Application Programming Interface (API)* for XML that is platform and language neutral—is discussed. The DOM API provides a standard set of interfaces (i.e., methods, objects, etc.) for manipulating an XML document's contents. XML documents are hierarchically structured, thus, the DOM represents XML documents as tree structures. Using DOM, programs can modify the content, structure and formatting of documents dynamically. We also present an alternative to DOM called the *Simple API for XML (SAX)*. Unlike DOM, which builds a tree structure in memory, SAX calls specific methods when start tags, end tags, attributes, etc., are encountered in a document. For this reason, SAX is often referred to as an *event-based API*. Python XML support is available through modules **xml.dom.ext** (DOM) and **xml.sax** (SAX). In the chapter, we use *4Suite* (developed by FourThought, Inc.) and PyXML—two collections of Python XML modules. The major feature of this chapter is a case study that uses XML to implement a Web-based message forum.

Chapter 17—Database Application Programming Interface (DB-API)

This chapter enables programs to query and manipulate databases. Most substantial business and Web applications are based on *database management systems (DBMS)*. To support DBMS applications, Python offers the *database application programming interface (DB-API)*. This chapter uses *Structured Query Language (SQL)* to query and manipulate *Relational Database Management Systems (RDBMS)*, specifically a MySQL database. To interface with a MySQL database, Python uses module **MySQLdb**. This chapter contains three examples. The first is a CGI program that displays information about authors, based on criteria provided by the user. The second creates a GUI program that allows the user to enter an SQL query, then displays the results of the query. The third example is a more substantial GUI program that enables the user to maintain a list of contacts. The user can add, remove, update and find contacts in the database. The exercises ask the reader to modify these programs to provide more functionality, such as verifying that the database does not contain identical entries.

Chapter 18—Process Management

In this chapter, we discuss *concurrency*. Most programming languages provide a simple set of control structures that enable programmers to perform one action at a time and proceed to the next action after the previous one is finished. Such control structures do not allow most programming languages to perform concurrent actions. The kind of concurrency that computers perform today normally is implemented as operating-system *primitives* available only to highly experienced *systems programmers*. Python makes concurrency primitives available to application programmers. We show how to use the **fork** command, which creates a new process, and the **exec** and **system** commands, which execute separate programs. Techniques for controlling input and output with the **popen** command are demonstrated and explained. Some of these commands are available on the Unix platform only, so we point this out when appropriate. We also explore Python's cross-platform capabilities through examples that perform specific tasks based on the operating system on which the program is executing. We discuss methods for communicating between processes, including pipes and signals. The signal-handling examples demonstrate how to discover when a user tries to interrupt a program and how to specify an action that the program takes when such an event occurs.

Chapter 19—Multithreading

This chapter introduces *threads*, which are "light-weight processes." They often are more efficient than full-fledged processes created as a result of commands like **fork** presented in the previous chapter. We examine basic threading concepts, including the various states in which a thread can exist throughout its life. We discuss how to include threads in a program by subclassing **threading.Thread** and overriding method **run**. The latter half of the chapter contains examples that address the classic producer/consumer relationship. We develop several solutions to this problem and introduce the concept of thread synchronization and resource allocation. We introduce threading control primitives, such as locks, condition variables, semaphores and events. The final solution uses module **Queue** to protect access to shared data stored in a queue. The examples demonstrate the hazards of threaded programs and show how to avoid these hazards. Our solution also demonstrates the value of writing classes for reuse. We reuse our producer and consumer classes to access various synchronized and unsynchronized data types. After completing this chapter, the reader will have many of the tools necessary to write substantial, extensible and professional programs in Python.

Chapter 20—Networking

In this chapter, we explore applications that can communicate over computer networks. A major benefit of a high-level language like Python is that potentially complex topics can be presented and discussed easily through small, working examples. We discuss basic networking concepts and present two examples—a CGI program that displays a chosen Web page in a browser and a GUI example that displays page content (e.g., XHTML) in a text area. We also discuss client-server communication over sockets. The programs in this section demonstrate how to send and receive messages over the network, using connectionless and connection-based protocols. A key feature of the chapter is the live-code implementation of a collaborative client/server Tic-Tac-Toe game in which two clients play Tic-Tac-Toe by interacting with a multithreaded server that maintains the state of the game. As part of the exercises, readers will write programs that send and receive messages and files. We ask the reader to modify the Tic-Tac-Toe game to determine when a player wins the game.

Chapter 21—Security

This chapter discusses Web programming security issues. Web programming allows the rapid creation of powerful applications, but it also exposes computers to outside attack. We focus on defensive programming techniques that help the programmer prevent security problems by using certain techniques and tools. One of those tools is encryption. We provide an example of encryption and decryption with module **rotor**, which acts as a substitution cipher. Another tool is module **sha**, which is used to hash values. A third tool is Python's restricted-access (**rexec**) module, which creates a restricted environment in which untrusted code can execute without damaging the local computer. This chapter examines technologies, such as *Public Key Cryptography*, *Secure Socket Layer (SSL)*, *digital signatures*, *digital certificates*, *digital steganography* and *biometrics*, which provide network security. Other types of network security, such as firewalls and antivirus programs, are also covered, and common security threats including cryptanalytic attacks, viruses, worms and Trojan horses are discussed.

Chapter 22—Data Structures

Chapter 22 explores the techniques used to create and manipulate standard data structures in Python. Although high-level data types are built into Python, we believe the reader will benefit from this conceptual and programmatic examination of common data structures. The chapter begins with a discussion of self-referential structures and proceeds with a discussion of how to create and maintain various data structures, including *linked lists*, *queues* (or *waiting lines*), *stacks* and *binary trees*. We reuse the linked-list class to implement queues and stacks, so that the code for the inherited class is minimized and emphasis is placed on code reuse. The binary tree class contains methods for pre-, in- and post-order traversals. For each type of data structure, we present complete, working programs and show sample outputs.

Chapter 23—Case Study: Multi-Tier Online Bookstore

This chapter implements an online bookstore that uses MySQL, XML and XSLT to send Web pages to different clients. We begin the chapter with an introduction to an HTTP-session framework that maintains client information over several pages. The client information is "pickled" (serialized) on the server's computer, to be used by the server at a later time. We then discuss WML, a markup language used by wireless clients to pass documents over the Web. Although we demonstrate the application with XHTML, XHTML Basic and WML clients, we designed the bookstore to be extensible, so new client types can be added easily. The Python CGI programs do not change, but the programmer can modify the bookstore to service new clients by simply creating new XML and XSLT documents for those clients. The bookstore program determines the client type and sends the appropriate data to the client. This chapter encompasses many topics from the previous chapters in the book and illustrates a major strength of Python—its ability to integrate several technologies quickly and easily. The topics covered include file processing, serialization (module **cPickle**), CGI form processing (module **cgi**), database access (module **MySQLdb**), XML DOM manipulation and XSLT processing (the 4Suite set of modules.)

Chapter 24—Multimedia

This chapter presents Python's capabilities for making computer applications come alive. It is remarkable that students in entry-level programming courses will be writing Python applications with all these capabilities. Some exciting multimedia applications include *PyOpenGL*, a module that binds Python to OpenGL API to create colorful, interactive graphics; *Alice*, an environment for creating and manipulating 3D graphical worlds in an object-oriented manner; and **Pygame**, a large collection of Python modules for creating cross-platform, multimedia applications, such as interactive games. In our PyOpenGL examples, we create rotating objects and three-dimensional shapes. In the Alice example, we create a graphical game version of a popular riddle. The world we create contains a fox, a chicken and a plant. The goal is to move all three objects across a river, without leaving a predator-prey pair alone at any one time. Our first **Pygame** example combines **Tkinter** and **Pygame** to create a GUI compact disc player. The second example illustrates how to play an MPEG movie. The final **Pygame** example creates a video game where the user steers a spaceship through an asteroid field to gather energy cells. We discuss many graphics program pitfalls and techniques in the context of this example. With many other programming languages, these projects would be too complex or detailed to present in a book such as this. However, Python's high-level nature, simple syntax and ample modules enable us to present these exciting examples all in the same chapter!

Chapter 25—Python Server Pages (PSP)

In this chapter, we create dynamic Web content using familiar *Extensible HyperText Markup Language (XHTML)* syntax and Python scripts. We discuss both sides of a client-server relationship. The tools used in this chapter include Apache and *Webware for Python*—a suite of software for writing dynamic Web content. An explanation of Python servlets is presented at the beginning of this chapter. In addition to illustrating how PSP handles Python's unique indentation style, our examples illustrate *scriptlets*, *actions* and *directives*. The exercises ask the reader to modify these examples by adding database connections to PSP.

Appendix A—Operator Precedence Chart

This appendix contains the Python operator precedence chart.

Appendix B—ASCII Character Set

Appendix B contains a table of the 128 ASCII alphanumeric symbols.

Appendix C—Number Systems

Appendix C explains the binary, octal, decimal and hexadecimal number systems. We also cover how to convert between bases and perform arithmetic operations in each base.

Appendix D—Python Development Environments

This appendix presents a brief overview of several Python Development environments, including *IDLE*.

Appendix E—Career Resources

This appendix provides resources related to careers in Python and related technologies. The Internet presents valuable resources and services for job seekers and employers. Automatic search features allow employees to scan the Web for open positions. Employers also can find job candidates using the Internet. This reduces the amount of time spent preparing and reviewing resumes, and can minimize travel expenses for distance recruiting and interviewing. In this chapter, we explore career services on the Web from the perspectives of job seekers and employers. We introduce comprehensive job sites, industry-specific sites (including sites geared specifically for Python programmers) and contracting opportunities, as well as additional resources and career services designed to meet the needs of a variety of individuals.

Appendix F—Unicode®

This appendix introduces the *Unicode Standard*, an encoding scheme that assigns unique numeric values to the characters of most of the world's languages. It includes a Python program that uses Unicode encoding to print a welcome message in 10 different languages.

Appendices G and H—Introduction to HyperText Markup Language 4: 1 & 2 (on CD)

These appendices provide an introduction to HTML—the HyperText Markup Language. HTML is a markup language for describing the elements of an HTML document (Web page) so that a browser, such as Microsoft's Internet Explorer, can render (i.e., display) that page. These appendices are included for our readers who do not know HTML. Some key topics covered in Appendix G include incorporating text and images in an HTML document, linking to other HTML documents on the Web, incorporating special characters (such as copyright and trademark symbols) into an HTML document and separating parts of an HTML document with horizontal rules. In Appendix H, we discuss more substantial HTML elements and features. We demonstrate how to present information in lists and tables. We discuss how to collect information from people browsing a site. We explain how to use internal linking and image maps to make Web pages easier to navigate. We also discuss how to use frames to display multiple documents in the browser window.

Appendices I and J—Introduction to XHTML: Part 1 & 2

In these appendices, we introduce the *Extensible HyperText Markup Language (XHTML)*. XHTML is a W3C technology designed to replace HTML as the primary means of describing Web content. As an XML-based language, XHTML is more robust and extensible than HTML. XHTML incorporates most of HTML 4's elements and attributes—the focus of these appendices. Appendix I introduces the X*HTML* and write many simple Web pages. We introduce basic XHTML *tags* and *attributes*. A key issue when using XHTML is the separation of the *presentation of a document* (i.e., how the document is rendered on the screen by a browser) from the *structure of that document*. Appendix J continues our XHTML discussion with more substantial XHTML elements and features. We demonstrate how to present information in *lists* and *tables* and discuss how to collect information from people browsing a site. We explain *internal linking* and *image maps*—techniques that make Web pages easier to navigate. We show how to use *frames* to make attractive Web sites.

Appendix K—Cascading Style Sheets™ (CSS)

Appendix K discusses how document authors can control how the browser renders a Web page. In earlier versions of XHTML, Web browsers controlled the appearance (i.e., the rendering) of every Web page. For example, if a document author placed an **h1** (i.e., a large heading) element in a document, the browser rendered the element in its own manner, which was often different than the way other Web browsers would render the same document. *Cascading Style Sheets (CSS)* technology allows document authors to specify the styles of their page elements (spacing, margins, etc.) separately from the structure of their documents (section headers, body text, links, etc.). This separation of structure from content allows greater manageability and makes changing the style of the document easier and faster.

Appendix L—Accessibility

This appendix discusses how to design accessible Web sites. Currently, the World Wide Web presents challenges to people with various disabilities. Multimedia-rich Web sites hinder text readers and other programs designed to help people with visual impairments, and the increasing amount of audio on the Web is inaccessible to people with hearing impairments. To rectify this situation, the federal government has issued several key legislation that address Web accessibility. For example, the *Americans with Disabilities Act (ADA)* prohibits discrimination on the basis of a disability. The W3C started the *Web Accessibility Initiative (WAI)*, which provides guidelines describing how to make Web sites accessible to people with various impairments. This chapter provides a description of these methods, such as use of the `<headers>` tag to make tables more accessible to page readers, use of the `alt` attribute of the `<img>` tag to describe images, and the proper use of XHTML and related technologies to ensure that a page can be viewed on any type of display or reader. *VoiceXML* also can increase accessibility with speech synthesis and recognition.

Appendix M—HTML/XHTML Special Characters (on CD)

This appendix provides many commonly used HTML/XHTML special characters, called *character entity references*.

Appendix N—HTML/XHTML Colors (on CD)

This appendix lists commonly used HTML/XHTML color names and their corresponding hexadecimal values.

Appendix O—Additional Python 2.2 Features

This book was published as the release of Python 2.2 was impending. We integrated many Python 2.2 features throughout the book. However, there were a few features that we were unable to insert in the text. We assembled these additional features into Appendix O. As you read each chapter, peak ahead to Appendix O for additional discussions and live-code examples.

Resources on Our Web Site

Our Web site, `www.deitel.com`, provides a number of Python-related resources to help you install and configure Python on your Windows or UNIX/Linux systems. The resources include *Installing Python, Installing the Apache Web Server, Installing MySQL, Installing Database Application Programming Interface (DB-API) modules, Installing Webware for Python* and *Installing Third-Party Modules*.

Well, there you have it! We have worked hard to create this book and its optional interactive multimedia *Cyber Classroom*. The book is loaded with hundreds of working, Live-Code™ examples, programming tips, self-review exercises and answers, challenging exercises and projects and numerous study aids to help you master the material. The technologies we introduce will help you write Web-based applications quickly and effectively. As you read the book, if something is not clear, or if you find an error, please write to us at `deitel@deitel.com`. We will respond promptly, and we will post corrections and clarifications at `www.deitel.com`.

Prentice Hall maintains **www.prenhall.com/deitel**—a Web site dedicated to our Prentice Hall textbooks, multimedia packages and Web-based training products. The site contains "Companion Web Sites" for each of our books that include frequently asked questions (FAQs), downloads, errata, updates, self-test questions and other resources.

Deitel & Associates, Inc., contributes a weekly column to the popular *InformIT* newsletter, currently subscribed to by more than 800,000 IT professionals worldwide. For opt-in registration, visit **www.InformIT.com**.

Deitel & Associates, Inc. also offers a free, opt-in newsletter that includes commentary on industry trends and developments, links to articles and resources from published books and upcoming publications, information on future publications, product-release schedules and more. For opt-in registration, visit **www.deitel.com**.

You are about to start on a challenging and rewarding path. We hope you enjoy learning with *Python How to Program* as much as we enjoyed writing it!

1.18 Internet and World Wide Web Resources

www.python.org
This site is the first place to look for information about Python. The Python home page provides up-to-date news, a FAQ, and a collection of links to Python resources on the Internet including Python software, tutorials, user groups and demos.

www.zope.com
www.zope.org
Zope is an extensible, open-source Web application server written in Python. It was created by Digital Creations—the company where the Python development team resides.

www.activestate.com
ActiveState creates open-source tools for programmers. The company provides a Python distribution called ActivePython and Komodo, an open-source *Integrated Development Environment (IDE)* for many languages, including Python, XML, Tcl and PHP. ActiveState supplies Python tools for Windows and a collection of Python programs called the *Python Cookbook*.

homepage.ntlworld.com/tibsnjoan/python.html
This page contains many links to people and groups that develop and use Python.

www.ddj.com/topics/pythonurl/
Dr. Dobb's Journal, a programming publication, maintains a list of Python links at this site.

SUMMARY

[Note: Because Section 1.17 is primarily a summary of the rest of the book, we do not provide summary bullets for that section.]

- Software controls computers (often referred to as hardware).
- A computer is a device capable of performing computations and making logical decisions at speeds millions, even billions, of times faster than human beings can.
- Computers process data under the control of sets of instructions called computer programs. These computer programs guide the computer through orderly sets of actions specified by people called computer programmers.
- The various devices that comprise a computer system (such as the keyboard, screen, disks, memory and processing units) are referred to as hardware.
- The computer programs that run on a computer are referred to as software.

- The input unit is the "receiving" section of the computer. It obtains information (data and computer programs) from various input devices and places this information at the disposal of the other units so that the information may be processed.

- The output unit is the "shipping" section of the computer. It takes information processed by the computer and places it on output devices to make it available for use outside the computer.

- The memory unit is the rapid access, relatively low-capacity "warehouse" section of the computer. It retains information that has been entered through the input unit so that the information may be made immediately available for processing when it is needed and retains information that has already been processed until that information can be placed on output devices by the output unit.

- The arithmetic and logic unit (ALU) is the "manufacturing" section of the computer. It is responsible for performing calculations such as addition, subtraction, multiplication and division and for making decisions.

- The central processing unit (CPU) is the "administrative" section of the computer. It is the computer's coordinator and is responsible for supervising the operation of the other sections.

- The secondary storage unit is the long-term, high-capacity "warehousing" section of the computer. Programs or data not being used by the other units are normally placed on secondary storage devices (such as disks) until they are needed, possibly hours, days, months or even years later.

- Early computers were capable of performing only one job or task at a time. This form of computer operation often is called single-user batch processing.

- Software systems called operating systems were developed to help make it more convenient to use computers. Early operating systems managed the smooth transition between jobs and minimized the time it took for computer operators to switch between jobs.

- Multiprogramming involves the "simultaneous" operation of many jobs on the computer—the computer shares its resources among the jobs competing for its attention.

- Timesharing is a special case of multiprogramming in which dozens or even hundreds of users share a computer through terminals. The computer runs a small portion of one user's job, then moves on to service the next user. The computer does this so quickly that it might provide service to each user several times per second, so programs appear to run simultaneously.

- An advantage of timesharing is that the user receives almost immediate responses to requests rather than having to wait long periods for results, as with previous modes of computing.

- In 1977, Apple Computer popularized the phenomenon of personal computing.

- In 1981, IBM introduced the IBM Personal Computer, legitimizing personal computing in business, industry and government organizations.

- Although early personal computers were not powerful enough to timeshare several users, these machines could be linked together in computer networks, sometimes over telephone lines and sometimes in local area networks (LANs) within an organization. This led to the phenomenon of distributed computing, in which an organization's computing is distributed over networks to the sites at which the real work of the organization is performed.

- Today, information is shared easily across computer networks, where some computers called file servers offer a common store of programs and data that may be used by client computers distributed throughout the network—hence the term client/server computing.

- Computer languages may be divided into three general types: machine languages, assembly languages and high-level languages.

- Any computer can directly understand only its own machine language. Machine languages generally consist of strings of numbers (ultimately reduced to 1s and 0s) that instruct computers to perform their most elementary operations one at a time. Machine languages are machine dependent.

- English-like abbreviations formed the basis of assembly languages. Translator programs called assemblers convert assembly-language programs to machine language at computer speeds.

- Compilers translate high-level language programs into machine-language programs. High-level languages (like Python) contain English words and conventional mathematical notations.

- Interpreter programs directly execute high-level language programs without the need for first compiling those programs into machine language.

- Although compiled programs execute much faster than interpreted programs, interpreters are popular in program-development environments in which programs are recompiled frequently as new features are added and errors are corrected. Interpreters are also popular for developing Web-based applications.

- Objects are essentially reusable software components that model items in the real world. Modular, object-oriented design and implementation approaches make software-development groups more productive than is possible with previous popular programming techniques. Object-oriented programs are often easier to understand, correct and modify than programs developed with earlier methodologies.

- FORTRAN (FORmula TRANslator) was developed by IBM Corporation between 1954 and 1957 for scientific and engineering applications that require complex mathematical computations.

- COBOL (COmmon Business Oriented Language) was developed in 1959 by a group of computer manufacturers and government and industrial computer users. COBOL is used primarily for commercial applications that require precise and efficient manipulation of large amounts of data.

- C evolved from two previous languages, BCPL and B, as a language for writing operating-systems software and compilers.

- Both BCPL and B were "typeless" languages—every data item occupied one "word" in memory and the burden of typing variables fell on the shoulders of the programmer. The C language was evolved from B by Dennis Ritchie at Bell Laboratories.

- Pascal was designed at about the same time as C. It was created by Professor Nicklaus Wirth and was intended for academic use.

- Structured programming is a disciplined approach to writing programs that are clearer than unstructured programs, easier to test and debug and easier to modify.

- The Ada language was developed under the sponsorship of the United States Department of Defense (DOD) during the 1970s and early 1980s. One important capability of Ada is called multitasking; this allows programmers to specify that many activities are to occur in parallel.

- Most high-level languages generally allow the programmer to write programs that perform only one activity at a time. Python, through techniques called process management and multithreading, enables programmers to write programs with parallel activities.

- Objects are essentially reusable software components that model items in the real world.

- Object technology dates back at least to the mid-1960s. The C++ programming language, developed at AT&T by Bjarne Stroustrup in the early 1980s, is based C and Simula 67.

- In the early 1990s, researchers at Sun Microsystems® developed a purely object-oriented language called Java.

- In the late 1960's, the Advanced Research Projects Agency of the Department of Defense (ARPA) rolled out the blueprints for networking the main computer systems of about a dozen ARPA-funded universities and research institutions. ARPA proceeded to implement what quickly became called the ARPAnet, the grandparent of today's Internet.

- Originally designed to connect the main computer systems of about a dozen universities and research organizations, the Internet today is accessible by hundreds of millions of computers worldwide.

- One of ARPA's primary goals for the network was to allow multiple users to send and receive information at the same time over the same communications paths (such as phone lines). The network operated with a technique called packet switching (still in wide use today), in which digital data are sent in small packages called packets. The packets contain data, address information, error-control information and sequencing information. The address information routes the packets of data to their destination. The sequencing information helps reassemble the packets (which—because of complex routing mechanisms—can actually arrive out of order) into their original order for presentation to the recipients.

- The protocol for communicating over the ARPAnet became known as TCP—Transmission Control Protocol. TCP ensured that messages were routed properly from sender to receiver and that those messages arrived intact.

- Bandwidth is the information-carrying capacity of communications lines.

- In 1990, Tim Berners-Lee of CERN (the European Laboratory for Particle Physics) developed the World Wide Web and several communication protocols that form its backbone.

- The Web allows computer users to locate and view multimedia-intensive documents over the Internet.

- Browsers view HTML (Hypertext Markup Language) documents on the World Wide Web.

- Python is a modular extensible language; Python can incorporate new modules (reusable pieces of software).

- The primary distribution center for Python source code, modules and documentation is the Python Web site—**www.python.org**—with plans to develop a site dedicated solely to maintaining Python modules.

- Python is portable, practical and extensible.

TERMINOLOGY

Ada	hardware platform
ALU	high-level language
arithmetic and logic unit (ALU)	input unit
assembler	input/output (I/O)
assembly language	interpreter
batch processing	Java
C	machine dependent
C++	machine independent
central processing unit (CPU)	machine language
clarity	memory
client	memory unit
client/server computing	multiprocessor
COBOL	multiprogramming
computer	multitasking
computer program	object-oriented programming
computer programmer	output unit
data	Pascal
distributed computing	Python
file server	personal computer
FORTRAN	portability
function	primary memory
functionalization	programming language
hardware	run a program

screen	terminal
software	timesharing
software reusability	top-down, stepwise refinement
stored program	translator program
structured programming	UNIX
supercomputer	workstation
task	

SELF-REVIEW EXERCISES

1.1   Fill in the blanks in each of the following statements:

a) The company that popularized the phenomenon of personal computing was _____.

b) The computer that made personal computing legitimate in business and industry was the _____.

c) Computers process data under the control of sets of instructions called computer _____.

d) The six key logical units of the computer are the _____, _____, _____, _____, _____ and the _____.

e) Python can incorporate new _____ (reusable pieces of software), which can be written by any Python developer.

f) The three classes of languages discussed in the chapter are _____, _____ and _____.

g) The programs that translate high-level language programs into machine language are called _____.

h) C is widely known as the development language of the _____ operating system.

i) In 2001, the core Python development team moved to Digital Creations, the creators of _____—a Web application server written in Python.

j) The Department of Defense developed the Ada language with a capability called _____, which allows programmers to specify activities that can proceed in parallel.

1.2   State whether each of the following is *true* or *false*. If *false*, explain why.

a) Hardware refers to the instructions that command computers to perform actions and make decisions.

b) The **re** regular-expression module provides pattern-based text manipulation in Python.

c) The ALU provides temporary storage for data that has been entered through the input unit.

d) Software systems called batches manage the transition between jobs.

e) Assemblers convert high-level language programs to assembly language at computer speeds.

f) Interpreter programs compile high-level language programs into machine language faster than compilers.

g) Structured programming is a disciplined approach to writing programs that are clear and easy to modify.

h) Unlike other programming languages, Python is non-extensible.

i) Objects are reusable software components that model items in the real world.

j) Several **Canvas** components include **Label**, **Button**, **Entry**, **Checkbutton** and **Radiobutton**.

ANSWERS TO SELF-REVIEW EXERCISES

1.1   a) Apple. b) IBM Personal Computer. c) programs. d) input unit, output unit, memory unit, arithmetic and logic unit (ALU), central processing unit (CPU), secondary storage unit. e) modules.

f) machine languages, assembly languages, high-level languages. g) compilers. h) UNIX. i) Zope. j) multitasking.

1.2   a) False. Software refers to the instructions that control computers, also referred to as hardware. Hardware refers to the computer's devices. b) True. c) False. The memory unit provides temporary storage for data that have been entered through the input unit. The arithmetic and logic unit (ALU) performs the calculations and contains the decision mechanisms of the computer. d) False. Software systems called operating systems manage the transition between jobs; in single-user batch processing, the computer runs a single program at a time while processing data in batches. e) False. Assemblers convert assembly-language programs to machine language at computer speeds. f) False. Interpreter programs can directly execute high-level language programs without compiling them into machine language. g) True. h) False. Unlike other programming languages, Python is extensible. i) True. j) False. Several **Tkinter** components include **Label**, **Button**, **Entry**, **Checkbutton** and **Radiobutton**.

EXERCISES

1.3   Categorize each of the following items as either hardware or software:
   a) CPU.
   b) ALU.
   c) Input unit.
   d) A word-processor program.
   e) Python modules.

1.4   Translator programs, such as assemblers and compilers, convert programs from one language (referred to as the *source* language) to another language (referred to as the *object* language). Determine which of the following statements are *true* and which are *false*:
   a) A compiler translates high-level language programs into object language.
   b) An assembler translates source-language programs into machine-language programs.
   c) A compiler converts source-language programs into object-language programs.
   d) High-level languages are generally machine dependent.
   e) A machine-language program requires translation before it can be run on a computer.

1.5   Fill in the blanks in each of the following statements:
   a) Python can provide information about itself, a technique called _____.
   b) A computer program that converts assembly-language programs to machine language programs is called _____.
   c) The logical unit of the computer that receives information from outside the computer for use by the computer is called _____.
   d) The process of instructing the computer to solve specific problems is called _____.
   e) Three high-level Python data types are: _____, _____ and _____.
   f) _____ is the logical unit of the computer that sends information that has already been processed by the computer to various devices so that the information may be used outside the computer.
   g) The general name for a program that converts programs written in a certain computer language into machine language is _____.

1.6   Fill in the blanks in each of the following statements:
   a) _____ is the logical unit of the computer that retains information.
   b) _____ is the logical unit of the computer that makes logical decisions.
   c) The commonly used abbreviation for the computer's control unit is _____.
   d) The level of computer language most convenient to the programmer for writing programs quickly and easily is _____.
   e) _____ are "mappable" types—keys are stored with their associated values.

f) The only language that a computer can understand directly is called that computer's _____.

g) The _____ is the logical unit of the computer that coordinates the activities of all the other logical units.

1.7   What do each of the following acronyms stand for:
a) W3C.
b) XML.
c) DB-API.
d) CGI.
e) XHTML.
f) TCP/IP.
g) PSP.
h) Tcl/Tk.
i) SSL.
j) HMD.

1.8   State whether each of the following is *true* or *false*. If *false*, explain your answer.
a) Inheritance is a form of software reusability in which new classes are developed quickly and easily by absorbing the capabilities of existing classes and adding appropriate new capabilities.
b) **Pmw** is a module that provides an interface to the popular Tcl/Tk graphical-user-interface toolkit.
c) Like other high-level languages, Python is generally considered to be machine-independent.

Introduction to Python Programming

Objectives

- To understand a typical Python program-development environment.
- To write simple computer programs in Python.
- To use simple input and output statements.
- To become familiar with fundamental data types.
- To use arithmetic operators.
- To understand the precedence of arithmetic operators.
- To write simple decision-making statements.

High thoughts must have high language.
Aristophanes

Our life is frittered away by detail…Simplify, simplify.
Henry Thoreau

My object all sublime
I shall achieve in time.
W.S. Gilbert

Outline

2.1 Introduction

Python facilitates a disciplined approach to computer-program design. In this first programming chapter, we introduce Python programming and present several examples that illustrate important features of the language. To understand each example, we analyze the code one statement at a time. After presenting basic concepts in this chapter, we examine the *structured programming* approach in Chapters 3–5. At the same time that we explore introductory Python topics, we also begin our discussion of object-oriented programming—the key programming methodology presented throughout this text. For this reason, we conclude this chapter with Section 2.10, Thinking About Objects.

2.2 First Program in Python: Printing a Line of Text[1]

We begin by considering a simple program that prints a line of text. Figure 2.1 illustrates the program and its screen output.

```
1   # Fig. 2.1: fig02_01.py
2   # Printing a line of text in Python.
3
4   print "Welcome to Python!"
```

```
Welcome to Python!
```

Fig. 2.1   Text-printing program.

---

1. The resources for this book, including step-by-step instructions for installing Python on Windows and Unix/Linux platforms, are posted at **www.deitel.com**.

This program illustrates several important features of the Python language. Let us consider each line of the program. Each program we present in this book has line numbers included for the reader's convenience; line numbers are not part of actual Python programs. Line 4 does the "real work" of the program, namely displaying the phrase **Welcome to Python!** on the screen. However, let us consider each line in order.

Lines 1–2 begin with the pound symbol (**#**), which indicates that the remainder of each line is a *comment*. Programmers insert comments to *document* programs and to improve program readability. Comments also help other programmers read and understand your program. Comments do not cause the computer to perform any action when the program is run—Python ignores comments. We begin every program with a comment indicating the figure number and the file name in which that program is stored (line 1). We can place any text we choose in comments. All of the Python programs for this book are included on the enclosed CD and also are available free for download at **www.deitel.com**.

A comment that begins with **#** is called a *single-line comment*, because the comment terminates at the end of the current line. A **#** comment also can begin in the middle of a line and continue until the end of that line. Such a comment typically documents the Python code that appears at the beginning of that line. Unlike other programming languages, Python does not have a separate symbol for a multiple-line comment, so each line of multiple-line comment must start with the **#** symbol. The comment text "**Printing a line of text in Python.**" describes the purpose of the program (line 2).

Good Programming Practice 2.1

Place abundant comments throughout a program. Comments help other programmers understand the program, assist in debugging a program (i.e., discovering and removing errors in a program) and list useful information. Comments also help you understand your programs when you revisit the code for modifications or updates.

Good Programming Practice 2.2

Every program should begin with a comment describing the purpose of the program.

Line 3 is simply a blank line. Programmers use blank lines and space characters to make programs easier to read. Together, blank lines, space characters and tab characters are known as *white space*. (Space characters and tabs are known specifically as *white-space characters*.) Blank lines are ignored by Python.

Good Programming Practice 2.3

Use blank lines to enhance program readability.

The Python **print** command (line 4) instructs the computer to display the *string* of characters contained between the quotation marks. A string is a sequence of characters contained inside double quotes. The entire line is called a *statement*. In some programming languages, like C++ and Java, statements must end with a semicolon. In Python, most statements simply end when the lines on which they are written end. When the statement on line 4 executes, it displays the message **Welcome to Python!** on the screen. Note that the double quotes that delineate the string do not appear in the output.

Output (i.e., displaying information) and input (i.e., receiving information) in Python are accomplished with *streams* of characters. When the preceding statement executes, it sends the stream of characters **Welcome to Python!** to the *standard output stream*. The standard output stream is the channel through which an application presents information to the user—this information typically is displayed on the screen, but may be printed on a printer, written to a file, etc. It may even be spoken or issued to braille devices, so users with visual impairments can receive the outputs.

Python statements can be executed two ways. The first is by typing statements into an editor to create a program and saving the file with a **.py** extension (as in Fig. 2.1). Python files typically end with **.py**, although other extensions (e.g., **.pyw** on Windows) can be used. To use the Python interpreter to *execute* (run) the program in the file, type

> **python** *file*.**py**

at the DOS or Unix *shell command line*, in which *file*.**py** is the name of the Python file. The shell command line is a text "terminal" in which the user can type commands that cause the computer system to respond. [*Note:* To invoke Python, the system path variable must be set properly to include the **python** *executable*—a file containing the Python interpreter program that can be run. The resources for this book—posted at our Web site **www.deitel.com**—include instructions on how to set the appropriate system path variable.]

When the Python interpreter runs a program stored in the file, the interpreter starts at the first line of the file and executes statements until the end of the file. The output box in Fig. 2.1 contains the results of the Python interpreter running **fig02_01.py**.

The second way to execute Python statements is *interactively*. Typing

> **python**

at the shell command line runs the Python interpreter in *interactive mode*. With this mode, the programmer types statements directly to the interpreter, which executes these statements one at a time.

Testing and Debugging Tip 2.1

In interactive mode, Python statements are entered and interpreted one at a time. This mode often is useful when debugging a program.

Testing and Debugging Tip 2.2

*When the Python interpreter is invoked on a file, the interpreter exits after the last statement in the file executes. However, invoking the interpreter on a file using the **-i** flag (for example, **python -i file.py**) causes the interpreter to enter interactive mode after executing the statements in the file. This is useful when debugging a program.*

Figure 2.2 shows Python 2.2 running in interactive mode on Windows. The first three lines display information about the version of Python being used (2.2b2 means "version 2.2 beta 2"). The fourth line contains the *Python prompt* (**>>>**). When a programmer types a statement at the Python prompt and presses the *Enter* key (sometimes labeled the *Return* key), the interpreter executes the statement.

The **print** statement on the fifth line of Fig. 2.2 displays the text **Welcome to Python!** to the screen (note, again, that the double quotes delineating the screen do not print). After printing the text to the screen, the interpreter waits for the user to enter the next statement. We exit interactive mode by typing the *Ctrl-Z* end-of-file character (on Microsoft Windows systems) and pressing the *Enter* key. Figure 2.3 lists the keyboard combinations for the end-of-file character for various computer systems.

```
Python 2.2b2 (#26, Nov 16 2001, 11:44:11) [MSC 32 bit (Intel)] on
win32
Type "help", "copyright", "credits" or "license" for more
information.
>>> print "Welcome to Python!"
Welcome to Python!
>>> ^Z
```

Fig. 2.2   Interactive mode. (Python interpreter software Copyright © 2001 Python Software Foundation.)

2.3 Modifying our First Python Program

This section continues our introduction to Python programming with two examples that modify Fig. 2.1 to display text on one line using multiple statements and to display text on several lines using a single statement.

2.3.1 Displaying a Single Line of Text with Multiple Statements

Welcome to Python! can be printed in several ways. For example, Fig. 2.4 uses two **print** statements (lines 4–5), yet produces the same output as the program in Fig. 2.1. Most of the program is identical to that of Fig. 2.1, so we discuss only the changes here.

Line 4 displays the string **"Welcome"**. Normally, after the **print** statement displays its string, Python begins a new line—subsequent outputs are displayed on the line or lines that follow the **print** statement's string. However, the comma (**,**) at the end of line 4 tells Python not to begin a new line but instead to add a space after the string; thus, the next string the program displays (line 5) appears on the same line as the string **"Welcome"**.

Computer system	Keyboard combination
UNIX/Linux systems	*Ctrl-D* (on a line by itself)
DOS/Windows	*Ctrl-Z* (sometimes followed by pressing *Enter*)
Macintosh	*Ctrl-D*

Fig. 2.3   End-of-file key combinations for various popular computer systems.

```
1   # Fig. 2.4: fig02_04.py
2   # Printing a line with multiple statements.
3
4   print "Welcome",
5   print "to Python!"
```

```
Welcome to Python!
```

Fig. 2.4   Printing one line using several **print** statements.

2.3.2 Displaying Multiple Lines of Text with a Single Statement

A single statement can display multiple lines using *newline characters*. Newline characters are "special characters" that position the screen cursor to the beginning of the next line. Figure 2.5 outputs four lines of text, using newline characters to determine when to begin each new line.

Most of the program is identical to those of Fig. 2.1 and Fig. 2.4, so we discuss only the changes here. Line 4 displays four separate lines of text to the screen. Normally, the characters in a string display exactly as they appear in the double quotes. Notice, however, that the two characters \ and **n** (which appear three times in line 4) do not appear in the output. Python offers *special characters* that perform certain tasks, such as backspace and carriage return. A special character is formed by combining the backslash (\) character, also called the *escape character*, with a letter. When a backslash exists in a string of characters, the backslash and the character immediately following the backslash form an *escape sequence*. An example of an escape sequence is \n, which represents the newline character. Each occurrence of the \n escape sequence causes the screen cursor that controls where the next character will appear to move to the beginning of the next line. To print a blank line, simply place two newline characters back-to-back. Figure 2.6 lists other common escape sequences.

```
1   # Fig. 2.5: fig02_05.py
2   # Printing multiple lines with a single statement.
3
4   print "Welcome\nto\n\nPython!"
```

```
Welcome
to

Python!
```

Fig. 2.5   Printing multiple lines using a single **print** statement.

Escape Sequence	Description
\n	Newline. Move the screen cursor to the beginning of the next line.
\t	Horizontal tab. Move the screen cursor to the next tab stop.
\r	Carriage return. Move the screen cursor to the beginning of the current line; do not advance to the next line.
\b	Backspace. Move the screen cursor back one space.
\a	Alert. Sound the system bell.
\\	Backslash. Print a backslash character.
\"	Double quote. Print a double quote character.
\'	Single quote. Print a single quote character.

Fig. 2.6   Escape sequences.

2.4 Another Python Program: Adding Integers

Our next program inputs two integers (whole numbers, like –22, 7 and 1024) typed by a user at the keyboard, computes the sum of the values and displays the result. This program invokes Python functions ***raw_input*** and ***int*** to obtain the two integers. Again, the program uses the **print** statement to display the sum of the integers. Figure 2.7 contains the program and its output.

Lines 1–2 contain comments that state the figure number, file name and the purpose of the program. Line 5 calls Python's *built-in function* **raw_input** to request user input. A built-in function is a piece of code provided by Python that performs a task. The task is performed by *calling the function*—writing the function name, followed by parentheses (**()**). After performing its task, a function may return a value that represents the result of the task. We study functions in depth in Chapter 4, where we mention many other built-in functions and show how programmers can create their own *programmer-defined functions*.

Python function **raw_input** takes the *argument*, **"Enter first integer:\n"** that requests user input. An argument is a value that a function accepts and uses to perform its task. In this case, function **raw_input** accepts the "prompt" argument (that requests user input) and displays that prompt to the screen. In response to viewing this prompt, the user enters a number and presses the *Enter* key—this sends the number to function **raw_input** in the form of a string.

The result of **raw_input** (a string containing the characters typed by the user) is assigned to *variable* **integer1** using the *assignment symbol*, **=**. In Python, variables are more specifically referred to as *objects*. An object resides in the computer's memory and contains information used by the program. The term object normally implies that *attributes* (data) and *behaviors* (methods) are associated with the object. The object's methods use the attributes to perform tasks. A variable name (e.g., **integer1**) consists of letters, digits and underscores (_) and does not begin with a digit. Python is *case sensitive*—uppercase and lowercase letters are different, so **a1** and **A1** are different variables. An object can have multiple names, called *identifiers*. Each identifier (or variable name) *references* (points to) the object (or variable) in memory. The statement in line 5 is normally read as "Variable **integer1** is assigned the value returned by **raw_input("Enter first integer:\n")**." The actual meaning of such a line, however, is "**integer1** references the value returned by **raw_input("Enter first integer:\n")**."

```
1   # Fig. 2.7: fig02_07.py
2   # Simple addition program.
3
4   # prompt user for input
5   integer1 = raw_input( "Enter first integer:\n" )   # read string
6   integer1 = int( integer1 )      # convert string to integer
7
8   integer2 = raw_input( "Enter second integer:\n" ) # read string
9   integer2 = int( integer2 )      # convert string to integer
10
11  sum = integer1 + integer2       # compute and assign sum
12
13  print "Sum is", sum             # print sum
```

Fig. 2.7   Addition program. (Part 1 of 2.)

```
Enter first integer:
45
Enter second integer:
72
Sum is 117
```

Fig. 2.7   Addition program. (Part 2 of 2.)

Good Programming Practice 2.4

Choosing meaningful variable names helps a program to be "self-documenting," i.e., it is easier to understand the program simply by reading it, rather than having to read manuals or use excessive comments.

Good Programming Practice 2.5

Avoid identifiers that begin with underscores and double underscores, because the Python interpreter or other Python code may reserve those characters for internal use. This prevents names you choose from being confused with names the interpreter chooses.

In addition to a name and value, each object has a *type*. An object's type identifies the kind of information (e.g., integer, string, etc.) stored in the object. Integers are whole numbers that encompass negative numbers (–14), zero (0) and positive numbers (6). In languages like C++ and Java, the programmer must *declare* (state) the object type before using the object in the program. However, Python uses *dynamic typing*, which means that Python determines an object's type during program execution. For example, if object **a** is initialized to **2**, then the object is of type "integer" (because the number 2 is an integer). Similarly, if object **b** is initialized to **"Python"**, then the object is of type "string." Function **raw_input** returns values of type "string," so the object referenced by **integer1** (line 5) is of type "string."

To perform integer addition on the value referenced by **integer1**, the program must convert the string value to an integer value. Python function **int** (line 6) converts a string or a number to an integer value and returns the new value. If we do not obtain an integer value for variable **integer1**, we will not achieve the desired results—the program would combine the two strings instead of adding two integers. Figure 2.8 demonstrates this with an interactive session.

```
Python 2.2b2 (#26, Nov 16 2001, 11:44:11) [MSC 32 bit (Intel)] on
win32
Type "help", "copyright", "credits" or "license" for more informa-
tion.
>>> value1 = raw_input( "Enter an integer: " )
Enter an integer: 2
>>> value2 = raw_input( "Enter an integer: " )
Enter an integer: 4
>>> print value1 + value2
24
```

Fig. 2.8   Adding values from **raw_input** (incorrectly) without converting to integers (the result should be 6).

The *assignment statement* (line 11 of Fig. 2.7) calculates the sum of the variables **integer1** and **integer2** and assigns the result to variable **sum**, using the assignment symbol **=**. The statement is read as, "**sum** references the value of **integer1 + integer2**." Most calculations are performed through assignment statements.

The **+** symbol is an *operator*—a special symbol that performs a specific operation. In this case, the **+** operator performs addition. The **+** operator is called a *binary operator*, because it has two *operands* (values) on which it performs its operation. In this example, the operands are **integer1** and **integer2**. [*Note*: In Python, the **=** symbol is not an operator. Rather, it is referred to as the assignment symbol.]

Common Programming Error 2.1

Trying to access a variable that has not been given a value is a run-time error.

Good Programming Practice 2.6

Place spaces on either side of a binary operator or symbol. This helps the operator or symbol stand out, making the program more readable.

Line 13 displays the string **"Sum is"** followed by the numerical value of variable **sum**. Items we want to output are separated by commas (**,**). Note that this **print** statement outputs values of different types, namely a string and an integer.

Calculations also can be performed in output statements. We could have combined the statements in lines 11 and 13 into the statement

```
print "Sum is", integer1 + integer2
```

thus eliminating the need for variable **sum**. You should make such combinations only if you feel it makes your programs clearer.

2.5 Memory Concepts

Variable names such as **integer1**, **integer2** and **sum** actually correspond to Python objects. Every object has a *type,* a *size*, a *value* and a *location* in the computer's memory. A program cannot change an object's type or location. Some object types permit programmers to change the object's value. We discuss these types beginning in Chapter 5, Tuples, Lists and Dictionaries.

When the addition program in Fig. 2.7, executes the statement

```
integer1 = raw_input( "Enter first integer:\n" )
```

Python first creates an object to hold the user-entered string and places the object into a memory location. The **=** assignment symbol then binds (associates) the name **integer1** with the newly created object. Suppose the user enters **45** at the **raw_input** prompt. Python places the string **"45"** into memory at a starting location to which the name **integer1** is bound, as shown in Fig. 2.9. When the statement

```
integer1 = int( integer1 )
```

executes, function **int** creates a new object to store the integer value **45**. This integer object begins at a new memory location and Python binds the name **integer1** to this new memory location (Fig. 2.10). Variable **integer1** no longer refers to the memory location that contains the string value **"45"**.

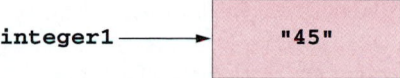

integer1 ⟶ **"45"**

Fig. 2.9 Memory location showing value of a variable and the name bound to the value.

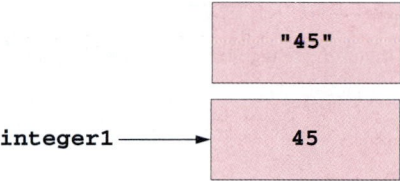

"45"

integer1 ⟶ 45

Fig. 2.10 Memory location showing the name and value of a variable.

Returning to our addition program, when the statements

```
integer2 = raw_input( "Enter second integer:\n" )
integer2 = int( integer2 )
```

execute, suppose the user enters the string **"72"**. After the program converts this value to the integer value **72** and places the value into a memory location to which **integer2** is bound, memory appears as in Fig. 2.11. Note that the locations of these objects are not necessarily adjacent in memory.

Once the program has obtained values for **integer1** and **integer2**, the program adds these values and assigns the sum to variable **sum**. After the statement

```
sum = integer1 + integer2
```

performs the addition, memory appears as in Fig. 2.12. Note that the values of **integer1** and **integer2** appear exactly as they did before they were used in the calculation of **sum**. These values were used, but not modified, as the computer performed the calculation. Thus, when a value is read out of a memory location, the value is not changed.

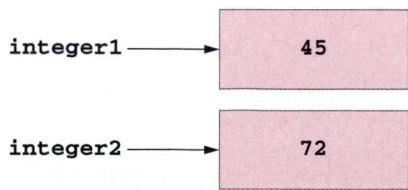

integer1 ⟶ 45

integer2 ⟶ 72

Fig. 2.11 Memory locations after values for two variables have been input.

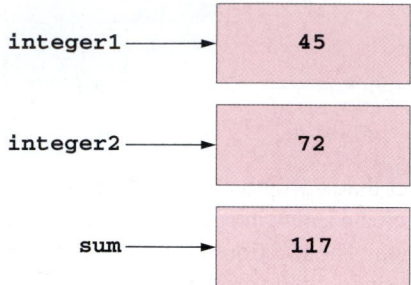

Fig. 2.12   Memory locations after a calculation.

Figure 2.13 demonstrates that each Python object has a location, a type and a value and that these object *properties* are accessed through an object's name. This program is identical to the program in Fig. 2.7, except that we have added statements that display the memory location, type and value for each object at various points in the program.

```
1   # Fig. 2.13: fig02_13.py
2   # Displaying an object's location, type and value.
3
4   # prompt the user for input
5   integer1 = raw_input( "Enter first integer:\n" )   # read a string
6   print "integer1: ", id( integer1 ), type( integer1 ), integer1
7   integer1 = int( integer1 )    # convert the string to an integer
8   print "integer1: ", id( integer1 ), type( integer1 ), integer1
9
10  integer2 = raw_input( "Enter second integer:\n" ) # read a string
11  print "integer2: ", id( integer2 ), type( integer2 ), integer2
12  integer2 = int( integer2 )    # convert the string to an integer
13  print "integer2: ", id( integer2 ), type( integer2 ), integer2
14
15  sum = integer1 + integer2    # assignment of sum
16  print "sum: ", id( sum ), type( sum ), sum
```

```
Enter first integer:
5
integer1:   7956744 <type 'str'> 5
integer1:   7637688 <type 'int'> 5
Enter second integer:
27
integer2:   7776368 <type 'str'> 27
integer2:   7637352 <type 'int'> 27
sum:   7637436 <type 'int'> 32
```

Fig. 2.13   Object's location, type and value.

Line 6 prints **integer1**'s location, type and value after the call to **raw_input**. Python function *id* returns the interpreter's representation of the variable's location. Function *type* returns the type of the variable. We print these values again (line 8), after converting the string value in **integer1** to an integer value. Notice that both the type and the location of variable **integer1** change as a result of the statement

```
integer1 = int( integer1 )
```

The change underscores the fact that a program cannot change a variable's type. Instead, the statement causes Python to create a new integer value in a new location and assigns the name **integer1** to this location. The location to which **integer1** previously referred is no longer accessible. The remainder of the program prints the location type and value for variables **integer2** and **sum** in a similar manner.

2.6 Arithmetic

Many programs perform arithmetic calculations. Figure 2.14 summarizes the *arithmetic operators*. Note the use of various special symbols not used in algebra. The *asterisk (*)* indicates multiplication and the *percent sign (%)* is the *modulus operator* that we discuss shortly. The arithmetic operators in Fig. 2.14 are binary operators, (i.e., operators that take two operands). For example, the expression **integer1 + integer2** contains the binary operator **+** and the two operands **integer1** and **integer2**.

Python is an evolving language, and as such, some of its features change over time. Starting with Python 2.2, the behavior of the **/** division operator will begin to change from "floor division" to "true division." *Floor division* (sometimes called *integer division*), divides the numerator by the denominator and returns the highest integer value that is not greater than the result. For example, dividing 7 by 4 with floor division yields 1 and dividing 17 by 5 with floor division yields 3. Note that any fractional part in floor division is simply discarded (i.e., *truncated*)—no rounding occurs. *True division* yields the precise *floating-point* (i.e., numbers with a decimal point such as 7.0, 0.0975 and 100.12345) result of dividing the numerator by the denominator. For example, dividing 7 by 4 with true division yields 1.75.

Python operation	Arithmetic operator	Algebraic expression	Python expression
Addition	+	$f + 7$	f + 7
Subtraction	−	$p - c$	p - c
Multiplication	*	bm	b * m
Exponentiation	**	x^y	x ** y
Division	/ // (new in Python 2.2)	x/y or $\frac{x}{y}$ or $x \div y$	x / y x // y
Modulus	%	$r \bmod s$	r % s

Fig. 2.14 Arithmetic operators.

In prior versions, Python contained only one operator for division—the **/** operator. The behavior (i.e., floor or true division) of the operator is determined by the type of the operands. If the operands are both integers, the operator performs floor division. If one or both of the operands are floating-point numbers, the operator performs true division.

The language designers and many programmers disliked the ambiguity of the **/** operator and decided to create two operators for version 2.2—one for each type of division. The **/** operator performs true division and the **//** operator performs floor division. However, this decision could introduce errors into programs that use older versions of Python. Therefore, the designers came up with a compromise: Starting with Python 2.2 all future 2.x versions will include two operators, but if a program author wants to use the new behavior, the programmer must state their intention explicitly with the statement

```
from __future__ import division
```

After Python sees this statement, the **/** operator performs true division and the **//** operator performs floor division. The interactive session in Fig. 2.15 demonstrates floor division and true division.

We first evaluate the expression **3 / 4**. This expression evaluates to the value **0**, because the default behavior of the **/** operator with integer operands is floor division. The expression **3.0 / 4.0** evaluates to **0.75**. In this case, we use floating-point operands, so the **/** operator performs true division. The expressions **3 // 4** and **3.0 // 4.0** evaluate to **0** and **0.0**, respectively, because the **//** operator always performs floor division, regardless of the types of the operands. Then, in line 13 of the interactive session, we change the behavior of the **/** operator with the special **import** statement. In effect, this statement turns on the true division behavior for operator **/**. Now the expression **3 / 4** evaluates to **0.75**. [*Note:* In this text, we use only the default 2.2 behavior for the **/** operator, namely floor division for integers (lines 5–6 of Fig. 2.15) and true division for floating-point numbers (lines 7–8 of Fig. 2.15).]

```
Python 2.2b2 (#26, Nov 16 2001, 11:44:11) [MSC 32 bit (Intel)] on
win32
Type "help", "copyright", "credits" or "license" for more informa-
tion.
>>> 3 / 4          # floor division (default behavior)
0
>>> 3.0 / 4.0    # true division (floating-point operands)
0.75
>>> 3 // 4         # floor division (only behavior)
0
>>> 3.0 // 4.0   # floating-point floor division
0.0
>>> from __future__ import division
>>> 3 / 4          # true division (new behavior)
0.75
>>> 3.0 / 4.0    # true division (same as before)
0.75
```

Fig. 2.15   Difference in behavior of the **/** operator.

Portability Tip 2.1

In Python version 3.0 (due to be released no sooner than 2003), the / operator can perform only true division. After the release of version 3.0, programmers need to update applications to compensate for the new behavior. For more information on this future change, see `python.sourceforge.net/peps/pep-0238.html`

Python provides the modulus operator (%), which yields the remainder after integer division. The expression **x % y** yields the remainder after **x** is divided by **y**. Thus, **7 % 4** yields **3** and **17 % 5** yields **2**. This operator is most commonly used with integer operands, but also can be used with other arithmetic types. In later chapters, we discuss many interesting applications of the modulus operator, such as determining whether one number is a multiple of another. (A special case of this is determining whether a number is odd or even.) [*Note*: The modulus operator can be used with both integer and floating-point numbers.]

Arithmetic expressions in Python must be entered into the computer in *straight-line form*. Thus, expressions such as "**a** divided by **b**" must be written as **a / b**, so that all constants, variables and operators appear in a straight line. The algebraic notation

$$\frac{a}{b}$$

is generally not acceptable to compilers or interpreters, although some special-purpose software packages do exist that support more natural notation for complex mathematical expressions.

Parentheses are used in Python expressions in much the same manner as in algebraic expressions. For example, to multiply **a** times the quantity **b + c**, we write

```
a * (b + c)
```

Python applies the operators in arithmetic expressions in a precise sequence determined by the following *rules of operator precedence,* which are generally the same as those followed in algebra:

1. Expressions contained within pairs of parentheses are evaluated first. Thus, parentheses may force the order of evaluation to occur in any sequence desired by the programmer. Parentheses are said to be at the "highest level of precedence." In cases of *nested,* or *embedded,* parentheses, the operators in the innermost pair of parentheses are applied first.

2. Exponentiation operations are applied next. If an expression contains several exponentiation operations, operators are applied from right to left.

3. Multiplication, division and modulus operations are applied next. If an expression contains several multiplication, division and modulus operations, operators are applied from left to right. Multiplication, division and modulus are said to be on the same level of precedence.

4. Addition and subtraction operations are applied last. If an expression contains several addition and subtraction operations, operators are applied from left to right. Addition and subtraction also have the same level of precedence.

Not all expressions with several pairs of parentheses contain nested parentheses. For example, the expression

```
a * (b + c) + c * (d + e)
```

does not contain nested parentheses. Rather, the parentheses in this expression are said to be "on the same level."

When we say that certain operators are applied from left to right, we are referring to the *associativity* of the operators. For example, in the expression

```
a + b + c
```

the addition operators (**+**) associate from left to right. We will see that some operators associate from right to left.

Figure 2.16 summarizes these rules of operator precedence. This table will be expanded as additional Python operators are introduced. A complete precedence chart is included in the appendices.

Now let us consider several expressions in light of the rules of operator precedence. Each example lists an algebraic expression and its Python equivalent. The following is an example of an arithmetic mean (average) of five terms:

Algebra: $\quad m = \dfrac{a + b + c + d + e}{5}$

Python: `m = ( a + b + c + d + e ) / 5`

The parentheses are required because division has higher precedence than addition and, hence, the division will be applied first. The entire quantity **(a + b + c + d + e)** is to be divided by **5**. If the parentheses are erroneously omitted, we obtain **a + b + c + d + e / 5**, which evaluates incorrectly as

$$a + b + c + d + \dfrac{e}{5}$$

The following is an example of the equation of a straight line:

Algebra: $\quad y = mx + b$

Python: `y = m * x + b`

No parentheses are required. The multiplication is applied first, because multiplication has a higher precedence than addition.

The following example contains modulus (**%**), multiplication, division, addition and subtraction operations:

Algebra: $\quad z = pr\%q + w/x - y$

Python: `z = p * r % q + w / x - y`
                               ①   ②   ④   ③   ⑤

Operator(s)	Operation(s)	Order of Evaluation (Precedence)
( )	Parentheses	Evaluated first. If the parentheses are nested, the expression in the innermost pair is evaluated first. If there are several pairs of parentheses "on the same level" (i.e., not nested), they are evaluated left to right.
**	Exponentiation	Evaluated second. If there are several, they are evaluated right to left.
* / // %	Multiplication Division Modulus	Evaluated third. If there are several, they are evaluated left to right. [*Note:* The // operator is new in version 2.2]
+ -	Addition Subtraction	Evaluated last. If there are several, they are evaluated left to right.

Fig. 2.16 Precedence of arithmetic operators.

The circled numbers under the statement indicate the order in which Python applies the operators. The multiplication, modulus and division are evaluated first, in left-to-right order (i.e., they associate from left to right) because they have higher precedence than addition and subtraction. The addition and subtraction are applied next. These are also applied left to right. Once the expression has been evaluated, Python assigns the result to variable **z**.

To develop a better understanding of the rules of operator precedence, consider how a second-degree polynomial is evaluated:

$$y = a * x ** 2 + b * x + c$$
$$\quad\quad\,\, 2 \quad\,\, 1 \quad 4 \quad\,\, 3 \quad\,\, 5$$

The circled numbers under the statement indicate the order in which Python applies the operators.

Suppose variables **a**, **b**, **c** and **x** are initialized as follows: **a = 2**, **b = 3**, **c = 7** and **x = 5**. Figure 2.17 illustrates the order in which the operators are applied in the preceding second-degree polynomial.

The preceding assignment statement can be parenthesized with unnecessary parentheses, for clarity, as

$$y = (a * (x ** 2)) + (b * x) + c$$

Good Programming Practice 2.7

As in algebra, it is acceptable to place unnecessary parentheses in an expression to make the expression clearer. These parentheses are called redundant parentheses. Redundant parentheses are commonly used to group subexpressions in a large expression to make that expression clearer. Breaking a large statement into a sequence of shorter, simpler statements also promotes clarity.

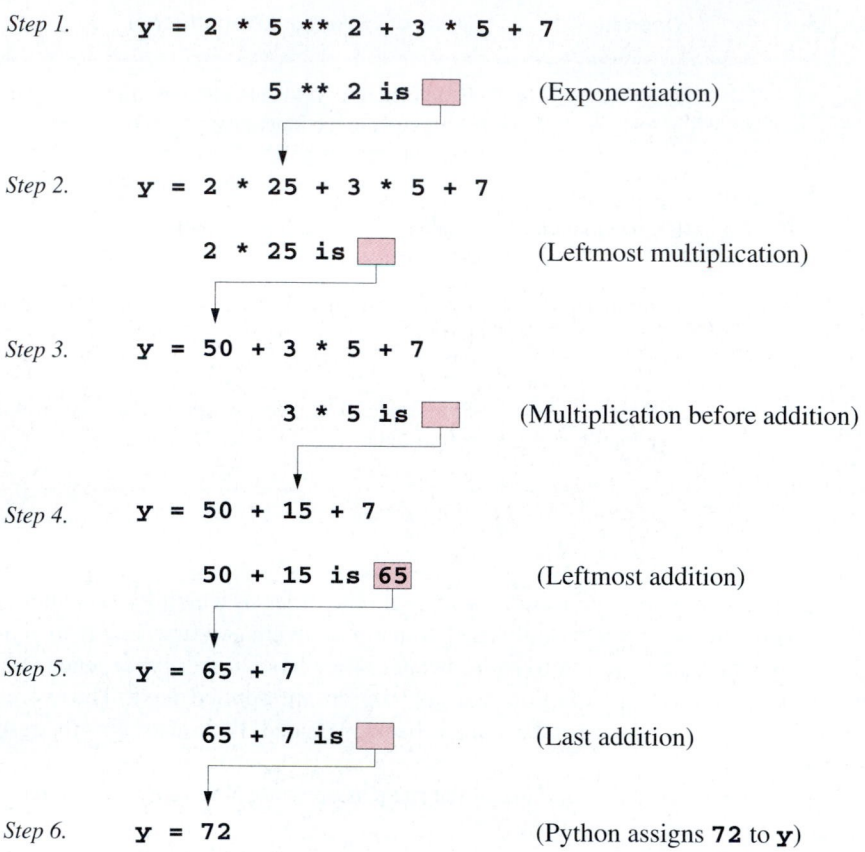

Step 1.   y = 2 * 5 ** 2 + 3 * 5 + 7

5 ** 2 is ☐   (Exponentiation)

Step 2.   y = 2 * 25 + 3 * 5 + 7

2 * 25 is ☐   (Leftmost multiplication)

Step 3.   y = 50 + 3 * 5 + 7

3 * 5 is ☐   (Multiplication before addition)

Step 4.   y = 50 + 15 + 7

50 + 15 is 65   (Leftmost addition)

Step 5.   y = 65 + 7

65 + 7 is ☐   (Last addition)

Step 6.   y = 72   (Python assigns **72** to **y**)

Fig. 2.17 Order in which a second-degree polynomial is evaluated.

2.7 String Formatting

Now that we have investigated numeric values, let us turn our attention to strings. Unlike some other popular programming languages, Python provides strings as a built-in data type, thereby enabling Python programs to perform powerful text-based operations easily. We have already learned how to create a string by placing text inside double quotes (**"**). Python strings can be created in a variety of other ways, as Fig. 2.18 demonstrates.

Line 4 creates a string with the familiar double-quote character (**"**). If we want such a string to print double quotes to the screen, we must use the escape sequence for the double-quote character (**\"**), rather than the double-quote character itself.

Strings also can be created using the single-quote character (**'**) as shown in line 5. If we want to use the double-quote character inside a string created with single quotes, we do not need to use the escape character. Similarly, if we want to use a single-quote character inside a string created with double quotes, we do not need to use the escape sequence (line 7). However, if we want to use the single-quote character inside a string created with single quotes (line 6), we must use the escape sequence (**\'**).

```
1   # Fig. 2.18: fig02_18.py
2   # Creating strings and using quote characters in strings.
3
4   print "This is a string with \"double quotes.\""
5   print 'This is another string with "double quotes."'
6   print 'This is a string with \'single quotes.\''
7   print "This is another string with 'single quotes.'"
8   print """This string has "double quotes" and 'single quotes'.
9      You can even do multiple lines."""
10  print '''This string also has "double" and 'single' quotes.'''
```

```
This is a string with "double quotes."
This is another string with "double quotes."
This is a string with 'single quotes.'
This is another string with 'single quotes.'
This string has "double quotes" and 'single quotes'.
   You can even do multiple lines.
This string also has "double" and 'single' quotes.
```

Fig. 2.18　Creating Python strings.

Python also supports *triple-quoted strings* (lines 8–10). Triple-quoted strings are useful for programs that output strings with special characters, such as quote characters. Single- or double-quote characters inside a triple-quoted string do not need to use the escape sequence. Triple-quoted strings also are used for large blocks of text, because triple-quoted strings can span multiple lines. We use triple-quoted strings in this book when we write programs that output large blocks of text for the Web.

Python strings support simple, but powerful, output formatting. We can create strings that format output in several ways:

1. Rounding floating-point values to an indicated number of decimal places.

2. Representing floating-point numbers in *exponential notation*.

3. Aligning a column of numbers with decimal points appearing one above the other.

4. *Right-justifying* and *left-justifying* outputs.

5. Inserting characters or strings at precise locations in a line of output.

6. Displaying all types of data with fixed-size *field widths* and *precision*.

The program in Fig. 2.19 demonstrates basic string-formatting capabilities.

```
1   # Fig. 2.19: fig02_19.py
2   # String formatting.
3
4   integerValue = 4237
5   print "Integer ", integerValue
6   print "Decimal integer %d" % integerValue
7   print "Hexadecimal integer %x\n" % integerValue
8
```

Fig. 2.19　String-formatting operator **%**. (Part 1 of 2.)

```
 9    floatValue = 123456.789
10    print "Float", floatValue
11    print "Default float %f" % floatValue
12    print "Default exponential %e\n" % floatValue
13
14    print "Right justify integer (%8d)" % integerValue
15    print "Left justify integer  (%-8d)\n" % integerValue
16
17    stringValue = "String formatting"
18    print "Force eight digits in integer %.8d" % integerValue
19    print "Five digits after decimal in float %.5f" % floatValue
20    print "Fifteen and five characters allowed in string:"
21    print "(%.15s) (%.5s)" % ( stringValue, stringValue )
```

```
Integer  4237
Decimal integer 4237
Hexadecimal integer 108d

Float 123456.789
Default float 123456.789000
Default exponential 1.234568e+005

Right justify integer (    4237)
Left justify \integer  (4237    )

Force eight digits in integer 00004237
Five digits after decimal in float 123456.78900
Fifteen and five characters allowed in string:
(String formatti) (Strin)
```

Fig. 2.19   String-formatting operator %. (Part 2 of 2.)

Lines 4–7 demonstrate how to represent integers in a string. Line 5 displays the value of variable **integerValue** without string formatting. The % *formatting operator* inserts the value of a variable in a string (line 6). The value to the left of the operator is a string that contains one or more *conversion specifiers*—place holders for values in the string. Each conversion specifier begins with a percent sign (**%**)—not to be confused with the **%** formatting operator—and ends with a *conversion-specifier symbol*. Conversion-specifier symbol *d* indicates that we want to place an integer within the current string at the specified point. Figure 2.20 lists several conversion-specifier symbols for use in string formatting. [*Note:* See Appendix C, Number Systems, for a discussion of numeric terminology in Fig. 2.20.]

Conversion Specifier Symbol	Meaning
c	Single character (i.e., a string of length one) or the integer representation of an ASCII character.
s	String or a value to be converted to a string.

Fig. 2.20   String-formatting characters. (Part 1 of 2.)

Conversion Specifier Symbol	Meaning
d	Signed decimal integer.
u	Unsigned decimal integer.
o	Unsigned octal integer.
x	Unsigned hexadecimal integer (with hexadecimal digits **a** through **f** in lowercase letters).
X	Unsigned hexadecimal integer (with hexadecimal digits **A** through **F** in uppercase letters).
f	Floating-point number.
e, E	Floating-point number (using scientific notation).
g, G	Floating-point number (using least-significant digits).

Fig. 2.20 String-formatting characters. (Part 2 of 2.)

The value to the right of the **%** formatting operator specifies what replaces the place-holders in the strings. In line 6, we specify the value **integerValue** to replace the **%d** placeholder in the string. Line 7 inserts the hexadecimal representation of the value assigned to variable **integerValue** into the string.

Lines 9–12 demonstrate how to insert floating-point values in a string. The **f** conversion specifier acts as a place holder for a floating-point value (line 11). To the right of the **%** formatting operator, we use variable **floatValue** as the value to be displayed. The **e** conversion specifier acts as a place holder for a floating-point value in exponential notation. *Exponential notation* is the computer equivalent of scientific notation used in mathematics. For example, the value 150.4582 is represented in *scientific notation* as **1.504582 X 10^2** and is represented in exponential notation as **1.504582E+002** by the computer. This notation indicates that **1.504582** is multiplied by **10** raised to the second power (**E+002**). The **E** stands for "exponent."

Lines 14–15 demonstrate string formatting with *field widths*. A field width is the minimum size of a field in which a value is printed. If the field width is larger than the value being printed, the data is normally *right-justified* within the field. To use field widths, place an integer representing the field width between the percent sign and the conversion-specifier symbol. Line 14 right-justifies the value of variable **integerValue** in a field width of size eight. To *left-justify* a value, specify a negative integer as the field width (line 15).

Lines 17–21 demonstrate string formatting with precision. *Precision* has different meaning for different data types. When used with integer conversion specifiers, precision indicates the minimum number of digits to be printed. If the printed value contains fewer digits than the specified precision, zeros are prefixed to the printed value until the total number of digits is equivalent to the precision. To use precision, place a decimal point (**.**) followed by an integer representing the precision between the percent sign and the conversion specifier. Line 18 prints the value of variable **integerValue** with eight digits of precision.

When precision is used with a floating-point conversion specifier, the precision is the number of digits to appear after the decimal point. Line 19 prints the value of variable **floatValue** with five digits of precision.

When used with a string-conversion specifier, the precision is the maximum number of characters to be written from the string. Line 21 prints the value of variable **stringValue** twice—once with a precision of fifteen and once with a precision of five. Notice that the conversion specifications are contained within parentheses. When the string to the left of the **%** formatting operator contains more than one conversion specifier, the value to the right of the operator must be a comma-separated sequence of values. This sequence is contained within parentheses and must have the same number of values as the string has conversion specifiers. Python constructs the string from left to right by matching a placeholder with the next value specified between parentheses and replacing the formatting character with that value.

Python strings support even more powerful string-formatting capabilities through *string methods*, which we discuss in detail in Chapter 13, Strings Manipulation and Regular Expressions.

2.8 Decision Making: Equality and Relational Operators

This section introduces a simple version of Python's *if structure* that allows a program to make a decision based on the truth or falsity of some *condition*. If the condition is met, (i.e., the condition is *true)*, the statement in the body of the **if** structure is executed. If the condition is not met (i.e., the condition is *false*), the body statement does not execute. We will see an example shortly.

Conditions in **if** structures can be formed with the *equality operators* and *relational operators* summarized in Fig. 2.21. The relational operators all have the same level of precedence and associate from left to right. All equality operators have the same level of precedence, which is lower than the precedence of the relational operators. The equality operators also associate from left to right.

Standard algebraic equality operator or relational operator	Python equality or relational operator	Example of Python condition	Meaning of Python condition
Relational operators			
>	>	x > y	x is greater than y
<	<	x < y	x is less than y
≥	>=	x >= y	x is greater than or equal to y
≤	<=	x <= y	x is less than or equal to y
Equality operators			
=	==	x == y	x is equal to y
≠	!=, <>	x != y,	x is not equal to y
		x <> y	

Fig. 2.21   Equality and relational operators.

Common Programming Error 2.2

A syntax error occurs if any of the operators **==**, **!=**, **>=** *and* **<=** *appears with spaces between its pair of symbols.*

Common Programming Error 2.3

Reversing the order of the pair of operators in any of the operators **!=**, **<>**, **>=** *and* **<=** *(by writing them as* **=!**, **><**, **=>** *and* **=<**, *respectively) is a syntax error.*

Common Programming Error 2.4

Confusing the equality operator **==** *with the assignment symbol* **=** *is an error. The equality operator should be read "is equal to" and the assignment symbol should be read "gets," "gets the value of" or "is assigned the value of." Some people prefer to read the equality operator as "double equals." In Python, the assignment symbol causes a syntax error when used in a conditional statement.*

The following example uses six **if** structures to compare two user-entered numbers. If the condition in any of these **if** structures is true, the assignment statement associated with that **if** structure executes. The user inputs two values, and the program converts the input values to integers and assigns them to variables **number1** and **number2**. Then, the program compares the numbers and displays the results of the comparisons. Figure 2.22 shows the program and sample executions.

```
1   # Fig. 2.22: fig02_22.py
2   # Compare integers using if structures, relational operators
3   # and equality operators.
4
5   print "Enter two integers, and I will tell you"
6   print "the relationships they satisfy."
7
8   # read first string and convert to integer
9   number1 = raw_input( "Please enter first integer: " )
10  number1 = int( number1 )
11
12  # read second string and convert to integer
13  number2 = raw_input( "Please enter second integer: " )
14  number2 = int( number2 )
15
16  if number1 == number2:
17     print "%d is equal to %d" % ( number1, number2 )
18
19  if number1 != number2:
20     print "%d is not equal to %d" % ( number1, number2 )
21
22  if number1 < number2:
23     print "%d is less than %d" % ( number1, number2 )
24
25  if number1 > number2:
26     print "%d is greater than %d" % ( number1, number2 )
27
```

Fig. 2.22   Equality and relational operators used to determine logical relationships. (Part 1 of 2.)

```
28   if number1 <= number2:
29       print "%d is less than or equal to %d" % ( number1, number2 )
30
31   if number1 >= number2:
32       print "%d is greater than or equal to %d" % ( number1, number2 )
```

```
Enter two integers, and I will tell you
the relationships they satisfy.
Please enter first integer: 37
Please enter second integer: 42
37 is not equal to 42
37 is less than 42
37 is less than or equal to 42
```

```
Enter two integers, and I will tell you
the relationships they satisfy.
Please enter first integer: 7
Please enter second integer: 7
7 is equal to 7
7 is less than or equal to 7
7 is greater than or equal to 7
```

```
Enter two integers, and I will tell you
the relationships they satisfy.
Please enter first integer: 54
Please enter second integer: 17
54 is not equal to 17
54 is greater than 17
54 is greater than or equal to 17
```

Fig. 2.22 Equality and relational operators used to determine logical relationships. (Part 2 of 2.)

The program uses Python functions **raw_input** and **int** to input two integers (lines 8–14). First a value is obtained for variable **number1**, then a value is obtained for variable **number2**.

The **if** structure in lines 16–17 compares the values of variables **number1** and **number2** to test for equality. If the values are equal, the statement displays a line of text indicating that the numbers are equal (line 17). If the conditions are met in one or more of the **if** structures starting at lines 19, 22, 25, 28 and 31, the corresponding **print** statement displays a line of text.

Each **if** structure consists of the word **if**, the condition to be tested and a colon (**:**). An **if** structure also contains a body (called a *suite*). Notice that each **if** structure in Fig. 2.22 has a single statement in its body and that each body is indented. Some languages, like C++, Java and C# use braces, **{ }**, to denote the body of **if** structures; Python requires indentation for this purpose. We discuss indentation in the next section.

Common Programming Error 2.5

*Failure to insert a colon (:) in an **if** structure is a syntax error.*

Common Programming Error 2.6

*Failure to indent the body of an **if** structure is a syntax error.*

Good Programming Practice 2.8

Set a convention for the size of indent you prefer, then apply that convention uniformly. The tab key may create indents, but tab stops may vary. We recommend using three spaces to form a level of indent.

In Python, syntax evaluation is dependent on white space; thus, the inconsistent use of white space can cause syntax errors. For instance, splitting a statement over multiple lines can result in a syntax error. If a statement is long, the statement can be spread over multiple lines using the \ line-continuation character. Some Python interpreters use **"..."** to denote a continuing line. The interactive session in Fig. 2.23 demonstrates the line-continuation character.

Good Programming Practice 2.9

*A lengthy statement may be spread over several lines with the \ continuation character. If a single statement must be split across lines, choose breaking points that make sense, such as after a comma in a **print** statement or after an operator in a lengthy expression.*

Figure 2.24 shows the precedence of the operators introduced in this chapter. The operators are shown from top to bottom in decreasing order of precedence. Notice that all these operators, except exponentiation, associate from left to right.

Testing and Debugging Tip 2.3

Refer to the operator-precedence chart when writing expressions containing many operators. Confirm that the operators in the expression are performed in the order you expect. If you are uncertain about the order of evaluation in a complex expression, break the expression into smaller statements or use parentheses to force the order, exactly as you would do in an algebraic expression. Be sure to observe that some operators, such as exponentiation (******), associate from right to left rather than from left to right.

```
Python 2.2b2 (#26, Nov 16 2001, 11:44:11) [MSC 32 bit (Intel)] on
win32
Type "help", "copyright", "credits" or "license" for more informa-
tion.
>>> print 1 +
  File "<string>", line 1
    print 1 +
            ^
SyntaxError: invalid syntax
>>> print 1 + \
... 2
3
>>>
```

Fig. 2.23   Line-continuation (\) character.

Operators				Associativity	Type
()				left to right	parentheses
**				right to left	exponential
*	/	//	%	left to right	multiplicative
+	-			left to right	additive
<	<=	>	>=	left to right	relational
==	!=	<>		left to right	equality

Fig. 2.24   Precedence and associativity of operators discussed so far.

2.9 Indentation

Python uses indentation to delimit (distinguish) sections of code. Other programming languages often use braces to delimit sections of code. A *suite* is a section of code that corresponds to the body of a control structure. We study *blocks* in the next chapter. The Python programmer chooses the number of spaces to indent a suite or block, and the number of spaces must remain consistent for each statement in the suite or block. Python recognizes new suites or blocks when there is a change in the number of indented spaces.

 Common Programming Error 2.7

If a single section of code contains lines of code that are not uniformly indented, the Python interpreter reads those lines as belonging to other sections, causing syntax or logic errors.

Figure 2.25 contains a modified version of the code in Fig. 2.22 to illustrate improper indentation. Lines 21–22 show the improper indentation of an **if** statement. Even though the program does not produce an error, it skips an equality operator. The

```
if number1 != number2:
```

statement (line 21) executes only if the **if number1 == number2:** statement (line 16) executes. In this case, the **if** statement in line 21 never executes, because two equal numbers will never be unequal (i.e., 2 will never unequal 2). Thus, the output of Fig. 2.25 does not state that **1 is not equal to 2** as it should.

```
1   # Fig. 2.25: fig02_25.py
2   # Using if statements, relational operators and equality
3   # operators to show improper indentation.
4
5   print "Enter two integers, and I will tell you"
6   print "the relationships they satisfy."
7
8   # read first string and convert to integer
9   number1 = raw_input( "Please enter first integer: " )
10  number1 = int( number1 )
11
```

Fig. 2.25   **if** statements used to show improper indentation. (Part 1 of 2.)

```
12    # read second string and convert to integer
13    number2 = raw_input( "Please enter second integer: " )
14    number2 = int( number2 )
15
16    if number1 == number2:
17        print "%d is equal to %d" % ( number1, number2 )
18
19        # improper indentation causes this if statement to execute only
20        # when the above if statement executes
21        if number1 != number2:
22            print "%d is not equal to %d" % ( number1, number2 )
23
24    if number1 < number2:
25        print "%d is less than %d" % ( number1, number2 )
26
27    if number1 > number2:
28        print "%d is greater than %d" % ( number1, number2 )
29
30    if number1 <= number2:
31        print "%d is less than or equal to %d" % ( number1, number2 )
32
33    if number1 >= number2:
34        print "%d is greater than or equal to %d" % ( number1, number2 )
```

```
Enter two integers, and I will tell you
the relationships they satisfy.
Please enter first integer: 1
Please enter second integer: 2
1 is less than 2
1 is less than or equal to 2
```

Fig. 2.25 `if` statements used to show improper indentation. (Part 2 of 2.)

Testing and Debugging Tip 2.4

To avoid subtle errors, ensure consistent and proper indentation within a Python program.

2.10 Thinking About Objects: Introduction to Object Technology

In each of the first six chapters, we concentrate on the "conventional" methodology of structured programming, because the objects we will build will be composed in part of structured-program pieces. Now we begin our early introduction to object orientation. In this section, we will see that object orientation is a natural way of thinking about the world and of writing computer programs.

We begin our introduction to object orientation with some key concepts and terminology. First, look around you in the real world. Everywhere you look you see them—*objects*!—people, animals, plants, cars, planes, buildings, computers, etc. Humans think in terms of objects. We have the marvelous ability of *abstraction* that enables us to view images on a computer screen as objects such as people, planes, trees and mountains, rather than as individual dots of color. We can, if we wish, think in terms of beaches rather than grains of sand, forests rather than trees and buildings rather than bricks.

We might be inclined to divide objects into two categories—animate objects and inanimate objects. Animate objects are "alive" in some sense. They move around and do things. Inanimate objects, like towels, seem not to do much at all. They just "sit around." All these objects, however, do have some things in common. They all have *attributes*, like size, shape, color and weight, and they all exhibit *behaviors* (e.g., a ball rolls, bounces, inflates and deflates; a baby cries, sleeps, crawls, walks and blinks; a car accelerates, brakes and turns; a towel absorbs water).

Humans learn about objects by studying their attributes and observing their behaviors. Different objects can have similar attributes and can exhibit similar behaviors. Comparisons can be made, for example, between babies and adults and between humans and chimpanzees. Cars, trucks, little red wagons and roller skates have much in common.

Object-oriented programming (OOP) models real-world objects using software counterparts. It takes advantage of *class* relationships, where objects of a certain class—such as a class of vehicles—have the same characteristics. It takes advantage of *inheritance* relationships, and even *multiple inheritance* relationships, where newly created classes of objects are derived by absorbing characteristics of existing classes and adding unique characteristics of their own. An object of class "convertible" certainly has the characteristics of the more general class "automobile," but a convertible's roof goes up and down.

Object-oriented programming gives us a more natural and intuitive way to view the programming process, by *modeling* real-world objects, their attributes and their behaviors. OOP also models communications between objects. Just as people send *messages* to one another (e.g., a sergeant commanding a soldier to stand at attention), objects communicate via messages.

OOP *encapsulates* data (attributes) and functions (behavior) into packages called *objects;* the data and functions of an object are intimately tied together. Objects have the property of *information hiding*. This means that, although objects may know how to communicate with one another, objects normally are not allowed to know how other objects are implemented—implementation details are hidden within the objects themselves. Surely it is possible to drive a car effectively without knowing the details of how engines, transmissions and exhaust systems work internally. We will see why information hiding is so crucial to good software engineering.

In C and other *procedural programming languages,* programming tends to be *action-oriented;* in Python, programming is *object-oriented* (ideally). The function is the unit of programming in procedural programming. In object-oriented programming, the unit of programming is the *class* from which objects are eventually *instantiated* (a fancy term for "created"). Python classes contain functions (that implement class behaviors) and data (that implements class attributes).

Procedural programmers concentrate on writing functions. Groups of actions that perform some task are formed into functions, and functions are grouped to form programs. Data is certainly important in procedural programming, but the view is that data exists primarily in support of the actions that functions perform. The verbs in a system specification help the procedural programmer determine the set of functions that will work together to implement the system.

Object-oriented programmers concentrate on creating their own *user-defined types* called *classes*. Each class contains both data and the set of functions that manipulate the data. The data components of a class are called *data members* or *attributes*. The functional components of a class are called *methods* (or *member functions* in other object-oriented languages). The focus of attention in object-oriented programming is on classes rather than functions. The *nouns* in a system specification help the object-oriented programmer determine the set of classes that will be used to create the instances that will work together to implement the system.

Classes are to objects as blueprints are to houses. We can build many houses from one blueprint, and we can create many objects from one class. Classes can also have relationships with other classes. For example, in an object-oriented design of a bank, the **Bank-Teller** class needs to relate to the **Customer** class. These relationships are called *associations*.

We will see that, when software is packaged as classes, these classes can be *reused* in future software systems. Groups of related classes are often packaged as reusable *components* or *modules*. Just as real-estate brokers tell their clients that the three most important factors affecting the price of real estate are "location, location and location," we believe the three most important factors affecting the future of software development are "reuse, reuse and reuse."

Indeed, with object technology, we will build most future software by combining "standardized, interchangeable parts" called components. This book will teach you how to "craft valuable classes" for reuse, reuse and reuse. Each new class you create will have the potential to become a valuable software asset that you and other programmers can use to speed and enhance the quality of future software-development efforts. This is an exciting possibility.

In this chapter, we have introduced many important features of Python, including printing data on the screen, inputting data from the keyboard, performing calculations and making decisions. In Chapter 3, Control Structures, we build on these techniques as we introduce *structured programming*. We will study how to specify and vary the order in which statements are executed—this order is called *flow of control*. Also, we introduced the basic concepts and terminology of object orientation. In Chapters 7–9, we expand our discussion on object-oriented programming.

SUMMARY

- Programmers insert comments to document programs and to improve program readability. Comments also help other programmers read and understand your program. In Python, comments are denoted by the pound symbol (**#**).
- A comment that begins with **#** is called a single-line comment, because the comment terminates at the end of the current line.
- Comments do not cause the computer to perform any action when the program is run. Python ignores comments.
- Programmers use blank lines and space characters to make programs easier to read. Together, blank lines, space characters and tab characters are known as white space. (Space characters and tabs are known specifically as white-space characters.)
- Blank lines are ignored by Python.
- The standard output stream is the channel by which information presented to the user by an application—this information typically is displayed on the screen, but may be printed on a printer, writ-

ten to a file, etc. It may even be spoken or issued to braille devices, so users with visual impairments can receive the outputs.

- The **print** statement instructs the computer to display the string of characters contained between the quotation marks. A string is a Python data type that contains a sequence of characters.

- A **print** statement normally sends a newline character to the screen. After a newline character is sent, the next string displayed on the screen appears on the line below the previous string. However, a comma (**,**) tells Python not to send the newline character to the screen. Instead, Python adds a space after the string, and the next string printed to the screen appears on the same line.

- Output (i.e., displaying information) and input (i.e., receiving information) in Python are accomplished with streams of characters.

- Python files typically end with **.py**, although other extensions (e.g., **.pyw** on Windows) can be used.

- When the Python interpreter executes a program, the interpreter starts at the first line of the file and executes statements until the end of the file.

- The backslash (****) is an escape character. It indicates that a "special" character is to be output. When a backslash is encountered in a string of characters, the next character is combined with the backslash to form an escape sequence.

- The escape sequence **\n** means newline. Each occurrence of a **\n** (newline) escape sequence causes the screen cursor to position to the beginning of the next line.

- A built-in function is a piece of code provided by Python that performs a task. The task is performed when the function is invoked or called. After performing its task, a function may return a value that represents the end result of the task.

- In Python, variables are more specifically referred to as objects. An object resides in the computer's memory and contains information used by the program. The term object normally implies that attributes (data) and behaviors (methods) are associated with the object. The object's methods use the attributes to perform tasks.

- A variable name consists of letters, digits and underscores (_) and does not begin with a digit.

- Python is case sensitive—uppercase and lowercase letters are different, so **a1** and **A1** are different variables.

- An object can have multiple names, called identifiers. Each identifier (or variable name) references (points to) the object (or variable) in memory.

- Each object has a type. An object's type identifies the kind of information (e.g., integer, string, etc.) stored in the object.

- In Python, every object has a type, a size, a value and a location.

- Function **type** returns the type of an object. Function **id** returns a number that represents the object's location.

- In languages like C++ and Java, the programmer must declare the object type before using the object in the program. In Python, the type of an object is determined automatically, as the program executes. This approach is called dynamic typing.

- Binary operators take two operands. Examples of binary operators are **+** and **-**.

- Starting with Python version 2.2, the behavior of the **/** division operator will change from "floor division" to "true division."

- Floor division (sometimes called integer division), divides the numerator by the denominator and returns the highest integer value that is not greater than the result. Any fractional part in floor division is simply discarded (i.e., truncated)—no rounding occurs.

- True division yields the precise floating-point result of dividing the numerator by the denominator.
- The behavior (i.e., floor or true division) of the **/** operator is determined by the type of the operands. If the operands are both integers, the operator performs floor division. If one or both of the operands are floating-point numbers, the operator perform true division.
- The **//** operator performs floor division.
- Programmers can change the behavior of the **/** operator to perform true division with the statement **from __future__ import division**.
- In Python version 3.0, the only behavior of the **/** operator will be true division. After the release of version 3.0, all programs are expected to have been updated to compensate for the new behavior.
- Python provides the modulus operator (**%**), which yields the remainder after integer division. The expression **x % y** yields the remainder after **x** is divided by **y**. Thus, **7 % 4** yields **3** and **17 % 5** yields **2**. This operator is most commonly used with integer operands, but also can be used with other arithmetic types.
- The modulus operator can be used with both integer and floating-point numbers.
- Arithmetic expressions in Python must be entered into the computer in straight-line form. Thus, expressions such as "**a** divided by **b**" must be written as **a / b**, so that all constants, variables and operators appear in a straight line.
- Parentheses are used in Python expressions in much the same manner as in algebraic expressions. For example, to multiply **a** times the quantity **b + c**, we write **a * (b + c)**.
- Python applies operators in arithmetic expressions in a precise sequence determined by the rules of operator precedence, which are generally the same as those followed in algebra.
- When we say that certain operators are applied from left to right, we are referring to the associativity of the operators.
- Python provides strings as a built-in data type and can perform powerful text-based operations.
- Strings can be created using the single-quote (**'**) and double-quote characters (**"**). Python also supports triple-quoted strings. Triple-quoted strings are useful for programs that output strings with quote characters or large blocks of text. Single- or double-quote characters inside a triple-quoted string do not need to use the escape sequence, and triple-quoted strings can span multiple lines.
- A field width is the minimum size of a field in which a value is printed. If the field width is larger than that needed by the value being printed, the data normally is right-justified within the field. To use field widths, place an integer representing the field width between the percent sign and the conversion-specifier symbol.
- Precision has different meaning for different data types. When used with integer conversion specifiers, precision indicates the minimum number of digits to be printed. If the printed value contains fewer digits than the specified precision, zeros are prefixed to the printed value until the total number of digits is equivalent to the precision.
- When used with a floating-point conversion specifier, the precision is the number of digits to appear to the right of the decimal point.
- When used with a string-conversion specifier, the precision is the maximum number of characters to be written from the string.
- Exponential notation is the computer equivalent of scientific notation used in mathematics. For example, the value 150.4582 is represented in scientific notation as 1.504582×10^2 and is represented in exponential notation as **1.504582E+002** by the computer. This notation indicates that **1.504582** is multiplied by **10** raised to the second power (**E+002**). The **E** stands for "exponent."

- An **if** structure allows a program to make a decision based on the truth or falsity of a condition. If the condition is true, (i.e., the condition is met), the statement in the body of the **if** structure is executed. If the condition is not met, the body statement is not executed.

- Conditions in **if** structures can be formed with equality relational operators. The relational operators all have the same level of precedence and associate from left to right. The equality operators both have the same level of precedence, which is lower than the precedence of the relational operators. The equality operators also associate from left to right.

- Each **if** structure consists of the word **if**, the condition to be tested and a colon (**:**). An **if** structure also contains a body (called a suite).

- Python uses indentation to delimit (distinguish) sections of code. Other programming languages often use braces to delimit sections of code. A suite is a section of code that corresponds to the body of a control structure. We study blocks in the next chapter.

- The Python programmer chooses the number of spaces to indent a suite or block, and the number of spaces must remain consistent for each statement in the suite or block.

- Splitting a statement over two lines can also cause a syntax error. If a statement is long, the statement can be spread over multiple lines using the **** line-continuation character.

- Object-oriented programming (OOP) models real-world objects with software counterparts. It takes advantage of class relationships where objects of a certain class—such as a class of vehicles—have the same characteristics.

- OOP takes advantage of inheritance relationships, and even multiple-inheritance relationships, where newly created classes of objects are derived by absorbing characteristics of existing classes and adding unique characteristics of their own.

- Object-oriented programming gives us a more natural and intuitive way to view the programming process, namely, by modeling real-world objects, their attributes and their behaviors. OOP also models communication between objects.

- OOP encapsulates data (attributes) and functions (behavior) into packages called objects; the data and functions of an object are intimately tied together.

- Objects have the property of information hiding. Although objects may know how to communicate with one another across well-defined interfaces, objects normally are not allowed to know how other objects are implemented—implementation details are hidden within the objects themselves.

- In Python, programming can be object-oriented. In object-oriented programming, the unit of programming is the class from which instances are eventually created. Python classes contain methods (that implement class behaviors) and data (that implements class attributes).

- Object-oriented programmers create their own user-defined types called classes and components. Each class contains both data and the set of functions that manipulate the data. The data components of a class are called data members or attributes.

- The functional components of a class are called methods (or member functions, in some other object-oriented languages).

- The focus of attention in object-oriented programming is on classes rather than on functions. The nouns in a system specification help the object-oriented programmer determine the set of classes that will be used to create the instances that will work together to implement the system.

TERMINOLOGY

abstraction

alert escape sequence (**\a**)

argument

arithmetic operator

assignment statement

assignment symbol (**=**)

association
associativity
associativity of operators
asterisk (**)
attribute
backslash (****) escape sequence
backspace (**\b**)
behavior
binary operator
block
built-in function
calculation
calling a function
carriage return (**\r**)
case sensitive
class
comma-separated list
comment
component
condition
conversion specifier
data member
debugging
design
dynamic typing
embedded parentheses
encapsulation
equality operators
escape character
escape sequence
execute
exponential notation
exponentiation
field width
floating-point division
floor division
flow of control
function
id function
identifier
indentation
information hiding
inheritance
instance
int function
integer division
left justify
left-to-right evaluation
member function
memory

memory location
method
modeling
modulus
modulus operator (**%**)
multiple inheritance
newline character (**\n**)
object
object orientation
OOP (object-oriented programming)
operand
operator overloading
operator precedence
overloading
percent sign (**%**)
polynomial
precedence
precision
procedural programming language
pseudocode
.py extension
.pyw extension
raw_input function
readability
redundant parentheses
relational operator
reused class
right justify
scientific notation
screen output
second-degree polynomial
self-documentation
single-line comment
single quote
software asset
standard output stream
statement
stream of characters
string of characters
string type
structured programming
suite
system path variable
triple-quoted string
true division
truncate
type
type function
user-defined type
variable

SELF-REVIEW EXERCISES

2.1   Fill in the blanks in each of the following:
   a) The _____ statement instructs the computer to display information on the screen.
   b) A _____ is a Python data type that contains a sequence of characters.
   c) _____ are simply names that reference objects.
   d) The _____ is the modulus operator.
   e) _____ are used to document a program and improve its readability.
   f) Each **if** structure consists of the word _____, the _____ to be tested, a _____ and a _____.
   g) The _____ function converts non-integer values to integer values.
   h) A Python statement can be spread over multiple lines using the _____.
   i) Arithmetic expressions enclosed in _____ are evaluated first.
   j) An object's _____ describes the information stored in the object.

2.2   State whether each of the following is *true* or *false*. If *false*, explain why.
   a) The Python function **get_input** requests input from the user.
   b) A valid Python arithmetic expression with no parentheses is evaluated left to right.
   c) The following are invalid variable names: **3g**, **87** and **2h**.
   d) The operator **!=** is an example of a relational operator.
   e) A variable name identifies the kind of information stored in the object.
   f) In Python, the programmer must declare the object type before using the object in the program.
   g) If parentheses are nested, the expression in the innermost pair is evaluated first.
   h) Python treats the variable names, **a1** and **A1**, as the same variable.
   i) The backslash character is called an escape sequence.
   j) The relational operators all have the same level of precedence and evaluate left to right.

ANSWERS TO SELF-REVIEW EXERCISES

2.1   a) **print**. b) string. c) Identifiers. d) percent sign (**%**). e) Comments. f) **if**, condition, colon (**:**), body/suite. g) **int**. h) line-continuation character (****). i) parentheses. j) type.

2.2   a) False. The Python function **raw_input** gets input from the user. b) False. Python arithmetic expressions are evaluated according to the rules of operator precedence and associativity—not left to right. c) True. d) False. The operator **!=** is an example of an equality operator. e) False. An object type identifies the kind of information stored in the object. f) False. In Python, the object type is determined as the program executes. g) True. h) False. Python is case sensitive, so **a1** and **A1** are different variables. i) False. The backslash is called an escape character. j) True.

EXERCISES

2.3   State the order of evaluation of the operators in each of the following Python statements and show the value of **x** after each statement is performed.

```
a) x = 7 + 3 * 6 / 2 - 1
b) x = 2 % 2 + 2 * 2 - 2 / 2
c) x = ( 3 * 9 * ( 3 + ( 9 * 3 / ( 3 ) ) ) )
```

2.4   Write a program that requests the user to enter two numbers and prints the sum, product, difference and quotient of the two numbers.

2.5   Write a program that reads in the radius of a circle and prints the circle's diameter, circumference and area. Use the constant value 3.14159 for π. Do these calculations in output statements.

2.6   Write a program that prints a box, an oval, an arrow and a diamond, as shown:

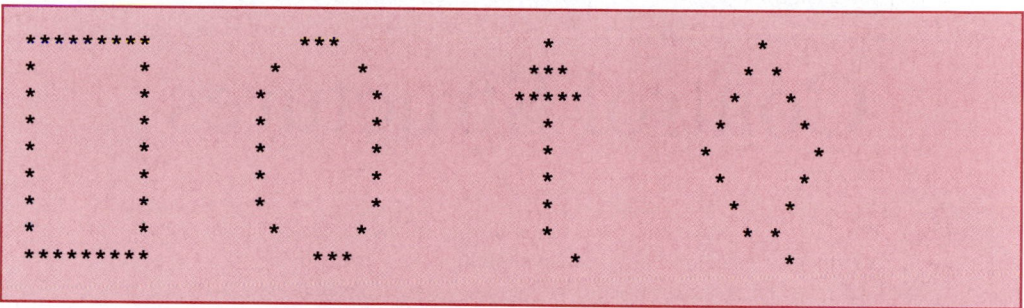

2.7   Write a program that reads in two integers and determines and prints whether the first is a multiple of the second. (Hint: Use the modulus operator.)

2.8   Give a brief answer to each of the following "object think" questions:
   a) Why does this text choose to discuss structured programming in detail before proceeding with an in-depth treatment of object-oriented programming?
   b) What aspects of an object need to be determined before an object-oriented program can be built?
   c) How is inheritance exhibited by human beings?
   d) What kinds of messages do people send to one another?
   e) Objects send messages to one another across well-defined interfaces. What interfaces does a car radio (object) present to its user (a person object)?

Control Structures

Objectives

- To understand basic problem-solving techniques.
- To develop algorithms through the process of top-down, stepwise refinement.
- To use the **if**, **if/else** and **if/elif/else** structures to select appropriate actions.
- To use the **while** and **for** repetition structures to execute statements in a program repeatedly.
- To understand counter-controlled and sentinel-controlled repetition.
- To use augmented assignment symbols and logical operators.
- To use the **break** and **continue** program control statements.

Let's all move one place on.
Lewis Carroll

The wheel is come full circle.
William Shakespeare

Who can control his fate?
William Shakespeare

The used key is always bright.
Benjamin Franklin

3.1 Introduction

Before writing a program to solve a particular problem, it is essential to have a thorough understanding of the problem and a carefully planned approach to solving the problem. When writing a program, it is equally essential to understand the types of building blocks that are available and to use proven program-construction principles. In this chapter, we discuss these issues in our presentation of the theory and principles of structured programming. The techniques that you learn are applicable to most high-level languages, including Python. When we begin our treatment of object-oriented programming in Chapter 7, we use the control structures presented in this chapter to build and manipulate objects.

3.2 Algorithms

Any computing problem can be solved by executing a series of actions in a specified order. An *algorithm* is a *procedure* for solving a problem in terms of

1.   *actions* to be executed and

2.   the *order* in which these actions are to be executed.

The following example demonstrates that specifying the order in which the actions are to be executed is important.

Consider the "rise-and-shine" algorithm followed by one junior executive for getting out of bed and going to work: (1) Get out of bed, (2) take off pajamas, (3) take a shower, (4) get dressed, (5) eat breakfast, (6) carpool to work. This routine gets the executive to work to make critical decisions.

Suppose that the same steps are performed in a slightly different order: (1) Get out of bed, (2) take off pajamas, (3) get dressed, (4) take a shower, (5) eat breakfast, (6) carpool to work. In this case, our junior executive shows up for work soaking wet.

Specifying the order in which statements are to be executed in a computer program is called *program control*. In this chapter, we investigate Python's program-control capabilities.

3.3 Pseudocode

Pseudocode is an artificial and informal language that helps programmers develop algorithms. Pseudocode consists of descriptions of *executable statements*—those that are executed when the program has been converted from pseudocode to Python. The pseudocode we present here is useful for developing algorithms that will be converted to Python programs. Pseudocode is similar to everyday English; it is convenient and user-friendly, although it is not an actual computer programming language.

Pseudocode programs are not executed on computers. Rather, pseudocode helps the programmer "plan" a program before attempting to write it in a programming language, such as Python. In this chapter, we provide several examples of how pseudocode can be used effectively in developing Python programs.

Software Engineering Observation 3.1

Pseudocode often is used to "think out" a program during the program design process. Then the pseudocode program is converted to Python.

The style of pseudocode we present consists purely of characters, so programmers can conveniently type pseudocode programs using a text-editor program. This way, a computer can display a fresh copy of a pseudocode program on demand. A carefully prepared pseudocode program can be converted easily to a corresponding Python program. In many cases, this is done simply by replacing pseudocode statements with their Python equivalents.

3.4 Control Structures

Normally, statements in a program are executed in the order in which they are written. This is called *sequential execution*. Various Python statements enable the programmer to specify that the next statement to be executed may be other than the next one in sequence. This is called *transfer of control*. Transfer of control is achieved with Python *control structures*. This section discusses the background of control structure development and the specific tools Python uses to transfer control in a program.

During the 1960s, it became clear that the indiscriminate use of control transfers caused the difficulty experienced by software-development groups. The finger of blame was pointed at the **goto** *statement* (used in several programming languages, including C and Basic), which allows a programmer to specify a transfer of control to one of a wide range of possible destinations in a program. The notion of so-called *structured programming* became almost synonymous with "goto elimination."

The research of Bohm and Jacopini[1] demonstrated that programs could be written without any **goto** statements. The challenge, then became for programmers to alter their programming styles to "**goto**-less programming." When programmers began to take structured programming seriously beginning in the 1970s, the notion of structured programming became almost synonymous with goto elimination. Since then, the results have been impressive, as software development groups have reported reduced development times, more frequent on-time delivery of systems and more frequent within-budget completion of software projects. Structured programming has enabled these improvements because structured programs are clearer, easier to debug and modify and more likely to be bug-free in the first place.

Bohm and Jacopini's work demonstrated that all programs could be written in terms of three *control structures*—namely, the *sequence structure*, the *selection structure* and the *repetition structure*. The sequence structure is built into Python. Unless directed otherwise, the computer executes Python statements sequentially. The *flowchart* segment of Fig. 3.1 illustrates a typical sequence structure in which two calculations are performed sequentially. A flowchart is a tool that provides graphical representation of an algorithm or a portion of an algorithm.

Flowcharts are drawn using certain special-purpose symbols, such as rectangles, diamonds, ovals and small circles; these symbols are connected by arrows called *flowlines*, which indicate the order in which the actions of the algorithm execute. Like pseudocode, flowcharts aid in the development and representation of algorithms. Although most programmers prefer pseudocode, flowcharts illustrate clearly how control structures operate. The reader should carefully compare the pseudocode and flowchart representations of each control structure.

The flowchart segment for the sequence structure in Fig. 3.1 uses the *rectangle* symbol, called the *action* symbol, to indicate an action, (e.g., calculation or an input/output operation). The flowlines in the figure indicate the order in which the actions are to be performed—first, **grade** is added to **total**, then **1** is added to **counter**. Python allows us to have as many actions as we want in a sequence structure—anywhere a single action may be placed, we can place several actions in sequence.

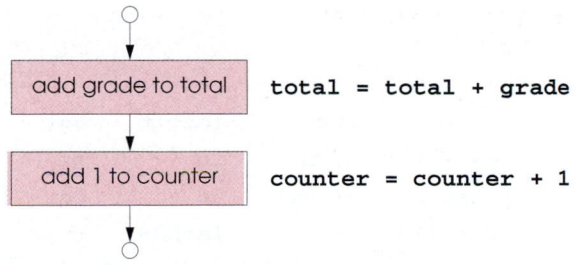

Fig. 3.1   Sequence structure flowchart.

1. Bohm, C., and G. Jacopini, "Flow Diagrams, Turing Machines, and Languages with Only Two Formation Rules," *Communications of the ACM*, Vol. 9, No. 5, May 1966, pp. 336–371.

In a flowchart that represents a *complete* algorithm, an *oval* symbol containing the word "Begin" represents the start of the flowchart; an oval symbol containing the word "End" represents the end of the flowchart. When drawing a portion of an algorithm, as in Fig. 3.1, the oval symbols are omitted in favor of *small circle* symbols, also called *connector* symbols.

Perhaps the most important flowchart symbol is the *diamond* symbol, also called the *decision* symbol, which indicates a decision is to be made. We discuss the diamond symbol in the next section. The pseudocode we present here is useful for developing algorithms that will be converted to structured Python programs.

Python provides three types of selection structures: **if**, **if/else** and **if/elif/else**. We discuss each of these in this chapter. The **if** selection structure either performs (selects) an action if a condition (predicate) is true or skips the action if the condition is false. The **if/else** selection structure performs an action if a condition is true or performs a different action if the condition is false. The **if/elif/else** selection structure performs one of many different actions, depending on the truth or falsity of several conditions.

The **if** selection structure is a *single-selection* structure because it selects or ignores a single action. The **if/else** selection structure is a *double-selection* structure because it selects between two different actions. The **if/elif/else** selection structure is a *multiple-selection* structure because it selects the action to perform from many different actions.

Python provides two types of repetition structures: **while** and **for**. The **if**, **elif**, **else**, **while** and **for** structures are Python *keywords*. These keywords are reserved by the language to implement various Python features, such as control structures. Keywords cannot be used as identifiers (i.e., variable names). Figure 3.2 lists all Python keywords.[2]

 Common Programming Error 3.1

Using a keyword as an identifier is a syntax error.

In all, Python has only the six control structures: the sequence structure, three types of selection structures and two types of repetition structures. Each Python program is formed by combining as many control structures as is appropriate for the algorithm the program implements. As with the sequence structure shown in Fig. 3.1, we will see that each control structure is flowcharted with two small circle symbols, one at the entry point to the control structure and one at the exit point.

Python keywords						
and	continue	else	for	import	not	raise
assert	def	except	from	in	or	return
break	del	exec	global	is	pass	try
class	elif	finally	if	lambda	print	while

Fig. 3.2   Python keywords.

2. Python 2.3 will introduce the keyword **yield** among others. Visit the Python Web site (**www.python.org**) to view a tentative list of such keywords, and avoid using them as identifiers.

These *single-entry/single-exit control structures* make it easy to build programs. The control structures are attached to one another by connecting the exit point of one control structure to the entry point of the next. This is similar to the way a child stacks building blocks; hence, the term *control-structure stacking*. *Control-structure nesting* also connects control structures; we discuss this technique later in the chapter.

Software Engineering Observation 3.2

Any Python program can be constructed from six different types of control structures (se-quence, **if**, **if/else**, **if/elif/else**, **while** *and* **for**) *combined in two ways (control-structure stacking and control-structure nesting).*

3.5 `if` Selection Structure

Selection structures choose among alternative courses of action. For example, suppose that the passing grade on an examination is 60. Then the pseudocode statement

> *If student's grade is greater than or equal to 60*
> *Print "Passed"*

determines whether the condition "student's grade is greater than or equal to 60" is true or false. If the condition is true, then "Passed" is printed, and the next pseudocode statement in order is "performed." (Remember that pseudocode is not a real programming language.) If the condition is false, the print statement is ignored, and the next pseudocode statement is performed. Note that the second line of this selection structure is indented. Such indentation is optional (for pseudocode), but it is highly recommended because indentation emphasizes the inherent hierarchy of structured programs. When we convert pseudocode into Python code, indentation is required.

The preceding pseudocode *if* statement may be written in Python as

```
if grade >= 60:
    print "Passed"
```

Notice that the Python code corresponds closely to the pseudocode. This similarity is the reason that pseudocode is a useful program development tool. The statement in the body of the **if** structure outputs the character string **"Passed"**.

The flowchart of Fig. 3.3 illustrates the single-selection **if** structure and the diamond symbol. The decision symbol contains an expression, such as a condition, that can be either true or false. The diamond has two flowlines emerging from it: One indicates the direction to follow when the expression in the symbol is true; the other indicates the direction to follow when the expression is false. We learned, in Chapter 2, Introduction to Python Programming, that decisions can be based on conditions containing relational or equality operators. Actually, a decision can be based on any expression. For instance, if an expression evaluates to zero, it is treated as false, and if an expression evaluates to nonzero, it is treated as true.

Note that the **if** structure is a single-entry/single-exit structure. We will soon learn that the flowcharts for the remaining control structures also contain (besides small circle symbols and flowlines) rectangle symbols that indicate the actions to be performed and diamond symbols that indicate decisions to be made. This type of flowchart emphasizes the *action/decision model of programming*.

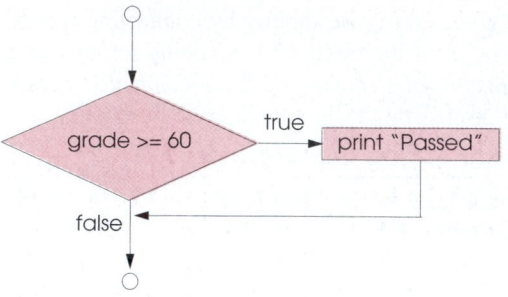

Fig. 3.3   **if** single-selection structure flowchart.

We can envision six bins, each containing control structures of one of the six types. These control structures are empty—nothing is written in the rectangles or in the diamonds. The programmer's task, then, is assembling a program from as many of each type of control structure as the algorithm demands, combining those control structures in only two possible ways (stacking or nesting), then filling in the actions and decisions in a manner appropriate for the algorithm. We will discuss the variety of ways in which actions and decisions may be written.

3.6 if/else and if/elif/else Selection Structures

The **if** selection structure performs a specified action only when the condition is true; otherwise, the action is skipped. The **if/else** selection structure allows the programmer to specify that a different action is to be performed when a condition is true from an action when a condition is false. For example, the pseudocode statement

>*If student's grade is greater than or equal to 60*
>>*Print "Passed"*
>*else*
>>*Print "Failed"*

prints *Passed* if the student's grade is greater than or equal to 60 and prints *Failed* if the student's grade is less than 60. In either case, after printing occurs, the next pseudocode statement in sequence is "performed." Note that the body of the *else* is indented. The indented body of a control structure is called a *suite*. Remember that indentation conventions you choose should be applied uniformly throughout programs. It is imperative for Python when it is executing code, and programs that do not obey uniform spacing conventions also are difficult to read.

Good Programming Practice 3.1

If there are several levels of indentation, each suite must be indented. Different suites at the same level do not have to be indented by the same amount, but doing so is good programming practice.

The preceding pseudocode *if/else* structure can be written in Python as

```
if grade >= 60:
    print "Passed"
else:
    print "Failed"
```

Common Programming Error 3.2

*Failure to indent all statements that belong to an **if** suite or an **else** suite results in a syntax error.*

The flowchart of Fig. 3.4 illustrates the flow of control in the **if/else** structure. Once again, note that (besides small circles and arrows) the symbols in the flowchart are rectangles (for actions) and diamonds (for decisions). We continue to emphasize this action/decision model of computing. Imagine again a bin containing empty double-selection structures. The programmer's job is to assemble these selection structures (by stacking and nesting) with other control structures required by the algorithm and to fill in the rectangles and diamonds with actions and decisions appropriate to the algorithm being implemented.

*Nested **if/else** structures* test for multiple cases by placing **if/else** selection structures inside other **if/else** selection structures. For example, the following pseudocode statement prints **A** for exam grades greater than or equal to 90, **B** for grades 80–89, **C** for grades 70–79, **D** for grades 60–69 and **F** for all other grades.

> *If student's grade is greater than or equal to 90*
>   *Print "A"*
> *else*
>   *If student's grade is greater than or equal to 80*
>   *Print "B"*
>   *else*
>   *If student's grade is greater than or equal to 70*
>   *Print "C"*
>   *else*
>   *If student's grade is greater than or equal to 60*
>   *Print "D"*
>   *else*
>   *Print "F"*

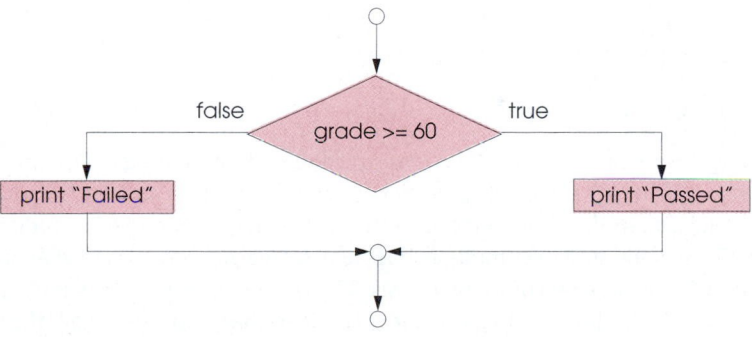

Fig. 3.4   if/else double-selection structure flowchart.

This pseudocode can be written in Python as

```
if grade >= 90:
    print "A"
else:
    if grade >= 80:
        print "B"
    else:
        if grade >= 70:
            print "C"
        else:
            if grade >= 60:
                print "D"
            else:
                print "F"
```

If **grade** is greater than or equal to 90, the first four conditions are met, but only the **print** statement after the first test executes. After that **print** executes, the **else** part of the "outer" **if/else** statement skips.

Performance Tip 3.1

*A nested **if/else** structure is faster than a series of single-selection **if** structures because the testing of conditions terminates after one of the conditions is satisfied.*

Performance Tip 3.2

*In a nested **if/else** structure, place the conditions that are more likely to be true at the beginning of the nested **if/else** structure. This enables the nested **if/else** structure to run faster and exit earlier than an equivalent **if/else** structure in which infrequent cases appear first.*

Many Python programmers prefer to write the preceding **if** structure as

```
if grade >= 90:
    print "A"
elif grade >= 80:
    print "B"
elif grade >= 70:
    print "C"
elif grade >= 60:
    print "D"
else:
    print "F"
```

thus replacing the double-selection **if/else** structure with the *multiple-selection* **if/elif/else** *structure*. The two forms are equivalent. The latter form is popular because it avoids the deep indentation of the code to the right. Such indentation often leaves little room on a line, forcing lines to be split over multiple lines and decreasing program readability.

Each **elif** can have one or more actions. The flowchart in Fig. 3.5 shows the general **if/elif/else** multiple-selection structure. The flowchart indicates that, after an **if** or **elif** statement executes, control immediately exits the **if/elif/else** structure. Again, note that (besides small circles and arrows) the flowchart contains rectangle symbols and diamond symbols. Imagine that the programmer has access to a deep bin of empty **if/elif/else** structures—as many as the programmer might need to stack and nest with

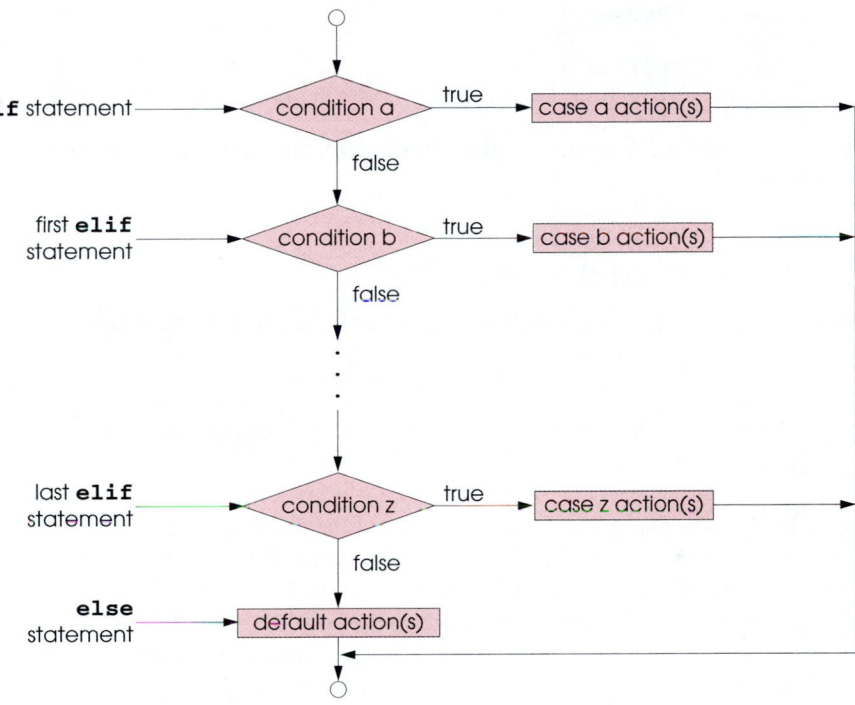

Fig. 3.5   **if/elif/else** multiple-selection structure.

other control structures to form a structured implementation of an algorithm's flow of control. The rectangles and diamonds are then filled with actions and decisions appropriate to the algorithm.

The **else** statement of the *if/elif/else* structure is optional. However, most programmers include an **else** statement at the end of a series of **elif** statements to handle any condition that does not match the conditions specified in the **elif** statements. We call the condition handled by the **else** statement the *default* condition. If an **if/elif** structure specifies an **else** statement, it must be the last statement in the structure.

Good Programming Practice 3.2

*Provide a default condition in **if/elif** structures. Conditions not explicitly tested in an **if/elif** structure without a default condition are ignored. Including a default condition focuses the programmer on the need to process exceptional conditions.*

Software Engineering Observation 3.3

A suite can be placed anywhere in a program that a single statement can be placed.

The **if** selection structure can contain several statements in its body (suite), and all these statements must be indented. The following example includes a suite in the **else** part of an **if/else** structure that contains two statements. A suite that contains more than one statement is sometimes called a *compound statement*.

```
if grade >= 60:
    print "Passed."
else:
    print "Failed."
    print "You must take this course again."
```

In this case, if **grade** is less than 60, the program executes both statements in the body of the **else** and prints

```
Failed.
You must take this course again.
```

Notice that both statements of the **else** suite are indented. If the statement

```
print "You must take this course again."
```

was not indented, the statement executes regardless of whether the grade is less than 60 or not. This is an example of a *logic error*.

A programmer can introduce two major types of errors into a program: *syntax errors* and logic errors. A syntax error violates the rules of the programming language. Examples of syntax errors include using a keyword as an identifier or forgetting the colon (**:**) after an **if** statement. The interpreter catches a syntax error and displays an error message.

A logic error causes the program to produce unexpected results and may not be caught by the interpreter. A *fatal logic error* causes a program to fail and terminate prematurely. For fatal errors, Python prints an error message called a *traceback* and exits. A *nonfatal logic error* allows a program to continue executing, but produces incorrect results.

Common Programming Error 3.3

Forgetting to indent all the statements in a suite can lead to syntax or logic errors in a program.

The interactive session in Fig. 3.6 attempts to divide two user-entered values and demonstrates one syntax error and two logic errors. The syntax error is contained in the line

```
print value1 +
```

The **+** operator needs a right-hand operand, so the interpreter indicates a syntax error.
The first logic error is contained in the line

```
print value1 + value2
```

The intention of this line is to **print** the sum of the two user-entered integer values. However, the strings were not converted to integers, thus the statement does not produce the desired result. Instead, the statement produces the concatenation of the two strings—formed by linking the two strings together. Notice that the interpreter does not display any messages because the statement is legal.
The second logic error occurs in the line

```
print int( value1 ) / int( value2 )
```

The program does not check whether the second user-entered value is **0**, so the program attempts to divide by zero. Dividing by zero is a fatal logic error.

```
Python 2.2b2 (#26, Nov 16 2001, 11:44:11) [MSC 32 bit (Intel)] on
win32
Type "help", "copyright", "credits" or "license" for more informa-
tion.
>>> value1 = raw_input( "Enter a number: " )
Enter a number: 3
>>> value2 = raw_input( "Enter a number: " )
Enter a number: 0
>>> print value1 +
  File "<stdin>", line 1
    print value1 +
                  ^
SyntaxError: invalid syntax
>>> print value1 + value2
30
>>> print int( value1 ) / int( value2 )
Traceback (most recent call last):
  File "<stdin>", line 1, in ?
ZeroDivisionError: integer division or modulo by zero
```

Fig. 3.6   Syntax and logic errors.

Common Programming Error 3.4

An attempt to divide by zero causes a fatal logic error.

Just as multiple statements can be placed anywhere a single statement can be placed, it is possible to have no statements at all, (i.e., *empty statements*). The empty statement is represented by placing keyword **pass** where a statement normally resides (Fig. 3.7).

Common Programming Error 3.5

All control structures must contain at least one statement. A control structure that contains no statements causes a syntax error.

3.7 `while` Repetition Structure

A *repetition structure* allows the programmer to specify that a program should repeat an action while some condition remains true. The pseudocode statement

While there are more items on my shopping list
Purchase next item and cross it off my list

```
Python 2.2b2 (#26, Nov 16 2001, 11:44:11) [MSC 32 bit (Intel)] on
win32
Type "help", "copyright", "credits" or "license" for more informa-
tion.
>>> if 1 < 2:
...     pass
...
```

Fig. 3.7   Keyword **pass**.

describes the repetition that occurs during a shopping trip. The condition, "there are more items on my shopping list" is either true or false. If it is true, the program performs the action "Purchase next item and cross it off my list." This action is performed repeatedly while the condition remains true.

The statement(s) contained in the *while* repetition structure constitute the body (suite) of the *while*. The *while* structure body can consist of a single statement or multiple statements. Eventually, the condition should evaluate to false (in the above example, when the last item on the shopping list has been purchased and crossed off the list). At this point, the repetition terminates, and the program executes the first statement after the repetition structure.

Common Programming Error 3.6

A logic error, called an infinite loop *(the repetition structure never terminates), occurs when an action that causes the condition in the* **while** *structure to become false is missing from the body of a* **while** *structure.*

Common Programming Error 3.7

Spelling the keyword **while** *with an uppercase* **W**, *as in* **While** *(remember that Python is a case-sensitive language), is a syntax error. All of Python's reserved keywords, such as* **while**, **if**, **elif** *and* **else**, *contain only lowercase letters.*

As an example of a **while** structure, consider a program segment designed to find the first power of 2 larger than 1000. Suppose variable **product** has been created and initialized to 2. When the following **while** repetition structure finishes executing, product will contain the desired answer:

```
product = 2

while product <= 1000:
    product = 2 * product
```

At the start of the **while** structure, **product** is 2. The variable **product** is multiplied by 2, successively taking on the values 4, 8, 16, 32, 64, 128, 256, 512 and 1024. When the value of **product** equals 1024, the **while** structure condition, **product <= 1000**, evaluates to false. This terminates the repetition—the final value of **product** is 1024. Program execution continues with the next statement after the **while** structure.

The flowchart of Fig. 3.8 illustrates the flow of control in the **while** structure that corresponds to the preceding **while** structure. Once again, note that (besides small circles and arrows) the flowchart contains a rectangle symbol and a diamond symbol.

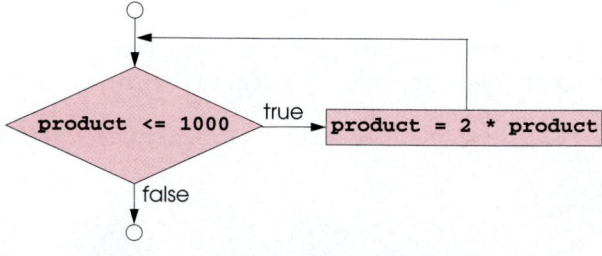

Fig. 3.8   **while** repetition structure flowchart.

Imagine a bin of empty **while** structures that can be stacked and nested with other control structures to implement an algorithm's flow of control. The empty rectangles and diamonds are then filled in with appropriate actions and decisions. The flowchart shows the repetition. The flowline emerging from the rectangle wraps back to the decision that is tested each time through the loop until the decision becomes false. Then, the **while** structure exits and control passes to the next statement in the program.

3.8 Formulating Algorithms: Case Study 1 (Counter-Controlled Repetition)

To illustrate how algorithms are developed, we solve several variations of a class-averaging problem. Consider the following problem statement:

> *A class of ten students took a quiz. The grades (integers in the range 0 –100) for this quiz are available. Determine the class average on the quiz.*

The class average is equal to the sum of the grades divided by the number of students. The algorithm for solving this problem requests each of the grades, performs the averaging calculation and prints the result.

Using pseudocode, we list the actions to be executed and specify the order in which these actions should be executed. We use *counter-controlled repetition* to input the grades one at a time. This technique uses a variable called a *counter* to control the number of times a set of statements executes. Repetition terminates when the counter exceeds 10. In this section, we present a pseudocode algorithm (Fig. 3.9) and the corresponding program (Fig. 3.10). In the next section, we show how to develop pseudocode algorithms. Counter-controlled repetition often is called *definite repetition* because the number of repetitions is known before the loop begins executing.

Note the references in the algorithm to the variables *total* and *counter*. In the program of Fig. 3.10, the variable **total** (line 5) accumulates the sum of a series of values, while the variable **counter** counts—in this case, it counts the number of user-entered grades. Variables that store totals normally are initialized to zero.

Set total to zero
Set grade counter to one

While grade counter is less than or equal to ten
    Input the next grade
    Add the grade into the total
    Add one to the grade counter

Set the class average to the total divided by ten
Print the class average

Fig. 3.9   Pseudocode algorithm that uses counter-controlled repetition to solve the class-average problem.

```
1   # Fig. 3.10: fig03_10.py
2   # Class average program with counter-controlled repetition.
3
4   # initialization phase
5   total = 0            # sum of grades
6   gradeCounter = 1     # number of grades entered
7
8   # processing phase
9   while gradeCounter <= 10:                # loop 10 times
10      grade = raw_input( "Enter grade: " ) # get one grade
11      grade = int( grade )     # convert string to an integer
12      total = total + grade
13      gradeCounter = gradeCounter + 1
14
15  # termination phase
16  average = total / 10             # integer division
17  print "Class average is", average
```

```
Enter grade: 98
Enter grade: 76
Enter grade: 71
Enter grade: 87
Enter grade: 83
Enter grade: 90
Enter grade: 57
Enter grade: 79
Enter grade: 82
Enter grade: 94
Class average is 81
```

Fig. 3.10   Counter-controlled repetition used to solve class-average problem.

Good Programming Practice 3.3

Initialize counters and totals.

Lines 5–6 are assignment statements that initialize **total** to 0 and **gradeCounter** to 1. Line 9 indicates that the **while** structure should continue as long as **grade-Counter**'s value is less than or equal to 10.

Lines 10–11 correspond to the pseudocode statement *Input the next grade*. Function **raw_input** displays the prompt "**Enter grade:**" on the screen and accepts user input. Line 11 converts the user-entered string to an integer.

Next, the program updates **total** with the new **grade** entered by the user—line 12 adds **grade** to the previous value of **total** and assigns the result to **total**.

Then, the program increments the variable **gradeCounter** to indicate that a grade has been processed. Line 13 increments **gradeCounter** by one, allowing the condition in the **while** structure to evaluate to false and terminate the loop.

Line 16 executes after the **while** structure terminates and assigns the results of the average calculation to variable **average**. Line 17 displays the string "**Class average is**", followed by a space (inserted by **print**), followed by the value of variable **average**.

Note that the averaging calculation in the program produces an integer result. Actually, the sum of the grades in this example is 817, which, when divided by 10, yields 81.7—a number with a decimal point. We discuss how to deal with floating-point numbers in the next section.

In Fig. 3.10, if line 16 used **gradeCounter** rather than 10 for the calculation, the output for this program would display an incorrect value, **74**, because **gradeCounter** contains the values **11**, after the termination of the **while** loop. Fig. 3.11 uses an interactive session to demonstrate the value of **gradeCounter** after the **while** loop iterates ten times.

3.9 Formulating Algorithms with Top-Down, Stepwise Refinement: Case Study 2 (Sentinel-Controlled Repetition)

Let us generalize the class-average problem. Consider the following problem:

> *Develop a class-averaging program that processes an arbitrary number of grades each time the program is executed.*

In the first class-average example, the program knows the number of grades (10) to be entered by the user. In this example, no indication is given of how many grades will be entered. The program processes an arbitrary number of grades. How can the program determine when to stop the input of grades? How will it know when to calculate and print the class average?

One way to solve this problem is to use a special value called a *sentinel value* (also called a *signal value*, a *dummy value* or a *flag value*) to indicate "end of data entry." The user inputs grades until all legitimate grades have been entered. The user then inputs the sentinel value to indicate that the last grade has been entered. Sentinel-controlled repetition often is called *indefinite repetition* because the number of repetitions is not known before the start of the loop.

Clearly, the sentinel value must be chosen so that it cannot be confused with an acceptable input value. As grades on a quiz normally are nonnegative integers, –1 is an acceptable sentinel value for this problem. Thus, executing the class-average program might process a stream of inputs such as 95, 96, 75, 74, 89 and –1. The program then computes and prints the class average for the grades 95, 96, 75, 74 and 89.

 Common Programming Error 3.8

Choosing a sentinel value that is a legitimate data value results in a logic error.

```
Python 2.2b2 (#26, Nov 16 2001, 11:44:11) [MSC 32 bit (Intel)] on
win32
Type "help", "copyright", "credits" or "license" for more informa-
tion.
>>> gradeCounter = 1
>>> while gradeCounter <= 10:
...     gradeCounter = gradeCounter + 1
...
>>> print gradeCounter
11
```

Fig. 3.11   Counter value used after termination of counter-controlled loop.

We approach the class-average program with a technique called *top-down, stepwise refinement*, which is essential to the development of well-structured programs. We begin with a pseudocode representation of the *top:*

Determine the class average for the quiz

The top is a single statement that conveys the overall function of the program. As such, the top is, in effect, a complete representation of a program. Unfortunately, the top (as in this case) rarely conveys a sufficient amount of detail from which to write the Python program. So we now begin the refinement process. We divide the top into a series of smaller tasks and list these in the order in which they need to be performed. This results in the following *first refinement*:

Initialize variables
Input, sum and count the quiz grades
Calculate and print the class average

In this case, the sequence control structure is used—the steps listed are executed successively.

Software Engineering Observation 3.4

Each refinement, as well as the top itself, is a complete specification of the algorithm; only the level of detail varies.

Software Engineering Observation 3.5

Many programs can be divided logically into three phases: An initialization phase *which initializes the program variables; a* processing phase *which inputs data values and adjusts program variables accordingly; and a* termination phase *which calculates and prints the final results.*

The preceding *Software Engineering Observation* often is all you need for the first refinement in the top-down process. To proceed to the next level of refinement (i.e., the *second refinement*), we commit to specific variables. The program needs to maintain a running total of the numbers, a count of how many numbers have been processed, a variable that contains the value of each grade and a variable that contains the calculated average. The pseudocode statement

Initialize variables

can be refined as follows:

Initialize total to zero
Initialize counter to zero

The pseudocode statement

Input, sum and count the quiz grades

requires a repetition structure (i.e., a loop) that successively inputs each grade. We do not know how many grades will be entered, so we use sentinel-controlled repetition. The user inputs legitimate grades successively. After the last legitimate grade has been entered, the user inputs the sentinel value. The program tests for the sentinel value after each grade is input and terminates the loop when it has been entered. The second refinement of the preceding pseudocode statement is

> *Input the first grade (possibly the sentinel)*
> *While the user has not as yet entered the sentinel*
>   *Add this grade into the running total*
>   *Add one to the grade counter*
>   *Input the next grade (possibly the sentinel)*

The pseudocode statement

> *Calculate and print the class average*

can be refined as follows:

> *If the counter is not equal to zero*
>   *Set the average to the total divided by the counter*
>   *Print the average*
> *else*
>   *Print "No grades were entered"*

Notice that we are testing for the possibility of division by zero—a fatal logic error which, if undetected, causes the program to fail (often called *bombing* or *crashing*). The complete second refinement of the pseudocode for the class average problem is shown in Fig. 3.12.

Good Programming Practice 3.4

When performing division by an expression whose value could be zero, explicitly test for this case and handle it appropriately in your program (such as by printing an error message) rather than allowing the fatal error to occur. In chapter 12, we discuss how to write programs that recognize such errors and take appropriate action. This is known as exception handling.

In Fig. 3.9 and Fig. 3.12, we included some blank lines in the pseudocode to improve the readability of the pseudocode. The blank lines separate these statements into their various phases.

Initialize total to zero
Initialize counter to zero

Input the first grade (possibly the sentinel)
While the user has not as yet entered the sentinel
    Add this grade into the running total
    Add one to the grade counter
    Input the next grade (possibly the sentinel)

If the counter is not equal to zero
    Set the average to the total divided by the counter
    Print the average
else
    Print "No grades were entered"

Fig. 3.12   Pseudocode algorithm that uses sentinel-controlled repetition to solve the class-average problem.

The pseudocode algorithm in Fig. 3.12 solves the more general class-averaging problem. This algorithm was developed after two refinements; sometimes more refinements are necessary.

Software Engineering Observation 3.6

The programmer terminates the top-down, stepwise refinement process when the pseudocode algorithm is specified in sufficient detail for the programmer to convert the pseudocode to Python. After this step, implementing the Python program normally is straightforward.

Figure 3.13 shows the Python program and a sample execution. Although each grade is an integer, the averaging calculation is likely to produce a number with a decimal point, (i.e., a real number). The integer data type cannot represent real numbers. The program uses the floating-point data type to handle numbers with decimal points and introduces function **float**, which forces the averaging calculation to produce a floating-point numeric result.

```
1   # Fig. 3.13: fig03_13.py
2   # Class average program with sentinel-controlled repetition.
3
4   # initialization phase
5   total = 0            # sum of grades
6   gradeCounter = 0     # number of grades entered
7
8   # processing phase
9   grade = raw_input( "Enter grade, -1 to end: " )    # get one grade
10  grade = int( grade )    # convert string to an integer
11
12  while grade != -1:
13      total = total + grade
14      gradeCounter = gradeCounter + 1
15      grade = raw_input( "Enter grade, -1 to end: " )
16      grade = int( grade )
17
18  # termination phase
19  if gradeCounter != 0:
20      average = float( total ) / gradeCounter
21      print "Class average is", average
22  else:
23      print "No grades were entered"
```

```
Enter grade, -1 to end: 75
Enter grade, -1 to end: 94
Enter grade, -1 to end: 97
Enter grade, -1 to end: 88
Enter grade, -1 to end: 70
Enter grade, -1 to end: 64
Enter grade, -1 to end: 83
Enter grade, -1 to end: 89
Enter grade, -1 to end: -1
Class average is 82.5
```

Fig. 3.13   Sentinel-controlled repetition used to solve class-average problem.

In this example, we see that control structures can be stacked on top of one another (in sequence) just as a child stacks building blocks. The **while** structure (lines 12–16) is immediately followed by an **if/else** structure (lines 19–23) in sequence. Much of the code in this program is identical to the code in Fig. 3.10, so in this section, we will concentrate on the new features and issues.

Line 6 initializes the variable **gradeCounter** to 0, because no grades have been entered. To keep an accurate record of the number of grades entered, variable **grade-Counter** is incremented only when a grade value is entered.

Good Programming Practice 3.5

In a sentinel-controlled loop, the prompts requesting data entry should explicitly remind the user of the sentinel value.

Study the difference between the program logic for sentinel-controlled repetition in Fig. 3.13 and counter-controlled repetition in Fig. 3.10. In counter-controlled repetition, the program reads a value from the user during each pass of the **while** structure, for a specified number of passes. In sentinel-controlled repetition, the program reads one value (lines 9–10) before the program reaches the **while** structure. This value determines whether the program's flow of control should enter the body of the **while** structure. If the **while** structure condition is false (i.e., the user has already typed the sentinel), the program does not execute the **while** loop (no grades were entered). On the other hand, if the condition is true, the program executes the **while** loop and processes the value entered by the user (i.e., adds the **grade** to **total**). After processing the **grade**, the program requests the user to enter another **grade**. After executing the last (indented) line of the **while** loop (line 16), execution continues with the next test of the **while** structure condition, using the new value just entered by the user to determine whether the **while** structure's body should execute again. Notice that the program requests the next value before evaluating the **while** structure. This allows for determining whether the value just entered by the user is the sentinel value *before* processing the value (i.e., adding it to **total**). If the value entered is the sentinel value, the **while** structure terminates, and the value is not added to **total**.

Lines 9–10 and 15–16 contain identical lines of code. In Section 3.15, we introduce programming constructs that help the programmer avoid repeating code.

Averages do not always evaluate to integer values. Often, an average is a value that contains a fractional part, such as 7.2 or –93.5. These values are referred to as *floating-point numbers*.

The calculation **total / gradeCounter** results in an integer, because **total** and **counter** contain integer values. Dividing two integers results in integer division, in which any fractional part of the calculation is discarded (i.e., truncated). The calculation is performed first, the fractional part is discarded before assigning the result to **average**. To produce a floating-point calculation with integer values, convert one (or both) of the values to a floating-point value with function **float**. Recall that functions are pieces of code that accomplish a task; in line 20, function **float** converts the integer value of variable sum to a floating-point value. The calculation now consists of a floating-point value divided by the integer **gradeCounter**.

The Python interpreter knows how to evaluate expressions in which the data types of the operands are identical. To ensure that the operands are of the same type, the interpreter performs an operation called *promotion* (also called *implicit conversion*) on selected oper-ands. For example, in an expression containing integer and floating-point data, integer operands are *promoted* to floating point. In our example, the value of **gradeCounter** is promoted to a floating-point number. Then, the calculation is performed, and the result of the floating-point division is assigned to variable **average**.

Common Programming Error 3.9

Assuming that all floating-point numbers are precise can lead to incorrect results. Most com-puters approximate floating-point numbers.

Despite the fact that floating-point numbers are not precise, they have numerous appli-cations. For example, when we speak of a "normal" body temperature of 98.6, we do not need to be precise to a large number of digits. When we view the temperature on a ther-mometer and read it as 98.6, it may actually be 98.5999473210643. The point here is that calling this number simply 98.6 is adequate for most applications.

Another way floating-point numbers develop is through division. When we divide 10 by 3, the result is 3.3333333…, with the sequence of 3s repeating infinitely. The computer allocates a fixed amount of space to hold such a value, so the stored floating-point value only can be an approximation.

3.10 Formulating Algorithms with Top-Down, Stepwise Refinement: Case Study 3 (Nested Control Structures)

Let us work another complete problem. We once again formulate the algorithm using pseudocode and top-down, stepwise refinement and we develop a corresponding Python program. Consider the following problem statement:

A college offers a course that prepares students for the state licensing exam for real estate brokers. Last year, several of the students who completed this course took the licensing examination. Naturally, the college wants to know how well its students did on the exam. You have been asked to write a program to summarize the results. You have been given a list of these 10 students. Next to each name is written a 1 if the student passed the exam and a 2 if the student failed.

Your program should analyze the results of the exam as follows:

1. *Input each test result (i.e., a 1 or a 2). Display the message "Enter result" on the screen each time the program requests another test result.*

2. *Count the number of test results of each type.*

3. *Display a summary of the test results indicating the number of students who passed and the number of students who failed.*

4. *If more than 8 students passed the exam, print the message "Raise tuition."*

After reading the problem statement carefully, we make the following observations about the problem:

1. The program must process 10 test results. A counter-controlled loop will be used.

2. Each test result is a number—either a 1 or a 2. Each time the program reads a test result, the program must determine if the number is a 1 or a 2. We test for a 1 in our algorithm. If the number is not a 1, we assume that it is a 2. (An exercise at the end of the chapter considers the consequences of this assumption.)

3. Two counters are used—one to count the number of students who passed the exam and one to count the number of students who failed the exam.

4. After the program has processed all the results, it must decide if more than eight students passed the exam.

Let us proceed with top-down, stepwise refinement. We begin with a pseudocode representation of the top:

Analyze exam results and decide if tuition should be raised

Once again, it is important to emphasize that the top is a complete representation of the program, but several refinements are likely to be needed before the pseudocode can evolve naturally into a Python program. Our first refinement is

Initialize variables
Input the ten exam grades and count passes and failures
Print a summary of the exam results and decide if tuition should be raised

Here, too, even though we have a complete representation of the entire program, further refinement is necessary. We now commit to specific variables. We need counters to record the passes and failures, a counter to control the looping process and a variable to store the user input. The pseudocode statement

Initialize variables

can be refined as follows:

Initialize passes to zero
Initialize failures to zero
Initialize student counter to one

Notice that only the counters for the number of passes, number of failures and number of students are initialized. The pseudocode statement

Input the ten exam grades and count passes and failures

requires a loop that successively inputs the result of each exam. Here it is known in advance that there are precisely ten exam results, so counter-controlled looping is appropriate. Inside the loop (i.e., *nested* within the loop), a double-selection structure determines whether each exam result is a pass or a failure and increments the appropriate counter accordingly. The refinement of the preceding pseudocode statement is

While student counter is less than or equal to ten
  Input the next exam result

  If the student passed
      Add one to passes
  else
      Add one to failures

  Add one to student counter

Notice the use of blank lines to set off the *If/else* control structure to improve program readability. The pseudocode statement

Print a summary of the exam results and decide if tuition should be raised

may be refined as follows:

> *Print the number of passes*
> *Print the number of failures*
>
> *If more than eight students passed*
> *   Print "Raise tuition"*

The complete second refinement appears in Fig. 3.14. Notice that the pseudocode also uses blank lines to set off the while structure for program readability.

This pseudocode is now sufficiently refined for conversion to Python. Figure 3.15 shows the Python program and two sample executions.

Initialize passes to zero
Initialize failures to zero
Initialize student counter to one

While student counter is less than or equal to ten
*   Input the next exam result*

*   If the student passed*
*   Add one to passes*
*   else*
*   Add one to failures*

*   Add one to student counter*

Print the number of passes
Print the number of failures

If more than eight students passed
*   Print "Raise tuition"*

Fig. 3.14   Pseudocode for examination-results problem.

```
1   # Fig. 3.15: fig03_15.py
2   # Analysis of examination results.
3
4   # initialize variables
5   passes = 0                          # number of passes
6   failures = 0                        # number of failures
7   studentCounter = 1                  # student counter
8
9   # process 10 students; counter-controlled loop
10  while studentCounter <= 10:
11      result = raw_input( "Enter result (1=pass,2=fail): " )
12      result = int( result )    # one exam result
```

Fig. 3.15   Examination-results problem. (Part 1 of 2.)

```
13
14      if result == 1:
15          passes = passes + 1
16      else:
17          failures = failures + 1
18
19      studentCounter = studentCounter + 1
20
21  # termination phase
22  print "Passed", passes
23  print "Failed", failures
24
25  if passes > 8:
26      print "Raise tuition"
```

```
Enter result (1=pass,2=fail): 1
Enter result (1=pass,2=fail): 1
Enter result (1=pass,2=fail): 1
Enter result (1=pass,2=fail): 1
Enter result (1=pass,2=fail): 2
Enter result (1=pass,2=fail): 1
Enter result (1=pass,2=fail): 1
Enter result (1=pass,2=fail): 1
Enter result (1=pass,2=fail): 1
Enter result (1=pass,2=fail): 1
Passed 9
Failed 1
Raise tuition
```

```
Enter result (1=pass,2=fail): 1
Enter result (1=pass,2=fail): 2
Enter result (1=pass,2=fail): 2
Enter result (1=pass,2=fail): 1
Enter result (1=pass,2=fail): 1
Enter result (1=pass,2=fail): 1
Enter result (1=pass,2=fail): 2
Enter result (1=pass,2=fail): 1
Enter result (1=pass,2=fail): 1
Enter result (1=pass,2=fail): 2
Passed 6
Failed 4
```

Fig. 3.15   *Examination-results problem. (Part 2 of 2.)*

Note that line 14 uses the equality operator (**==**) to test whether the value of variable **result** equals 1. Be careful not to confuse the equality operator with the assignment symbol (**=**). Such confusion can cause syntax or logic errors in Python.

 Common Programming Error 3.10

*Using the **=** symbol for equality in a conditional statement is a syntax error.*

Common Programming Error 3.11

Using operator == for assignment is a logic error.

Software Engineering Observation 3.7

Experience has shown that the most difficult part of solving a problem on a computer is developing an algorithm for the solution. Once a correct algorithm has been specified, the process of producing a working Python program from the algorithm normally is straightforward.

Software Engineering Observation 3.8

Many experienced programmers write programs without ever using program-development tools like pseudocode. These programmers feel that their ultimate goal is to solve the problem on a computer and that writing pseudocode merely delays the production of final outputs. Although this may work for simple and familiar problems, it can lead to serious errors and delays on large, complex projects.

3.11 Augmented Assignment Symbols

Python provides several *augmented assignment symbols* for abbreviating assignment expressions. For example, the statement

```
c = c + 3
```

can be abbreviated with the *augmented addition assignment symbol* **+=** as

```
c += 3
```

The **+=** symbol adds the value of the expression on the right of the **+=** sign to the value of the variable on the left of the sign and stores the result in the variable on the left of the sign. Any statement of the form

variable **=** *variable operator expression*

where *operator* is a binary operator, such as **+, −, **, *, /**, or **%**, can be written in the form

*variable operator***=** *expression*

A statement that uses an augmented assignment symbol is called an *augmented assignment statement*. Figure 3.16 shows the augmented arithmetic assignment symbols.

Assignment symbol	Sample expression	Explanation	Assigns
Assume: c = 3, d = 5, e = 4, f = 2, g = 6, h = 12			
+=	c += 7	c = c + 7	10 to c
-=	d -= 4	d = d - 4	1 to d

Fig. 3.16 Augmented arithmetic assignment symbols. (Part 1 of 2.)

Assignment symbol	Sample expression	Explanation	Assigns
*=	e *= 5	e = e * 5	20 to e
**=	f **= 3	f = f ** 3	8 to f
/=	g /= 3	g = g / 3	2 to g
%=	h %= 9	h = h % 9	3 to h

Fig. 3.16 Augmented arithmetic assignment symbols. (Part 2 of 2.)

Portability Tip 3.1

Augmented assignment symbols were introduced in Python version 2.0. Attempting to use an augmented assignment symbol with an earlier version of Python is a syntax error.

Common Programming Error 3.12

Attempting to use an augmented assignment before the variable to the left of the assignment symbol has been initialized is an error.

3.12 Essentials of Counter-Controlled Repetition

Counter-controlled repetition requires the following:

1. the *name* of a control variable (or loop counter),

2. the *initial value* of the control variable,

3. the amount of *increment* (or *decrement*) by which the control variable is modified each time through the loop (also known as each iteration of the loop), and

4. the condition that tests for the *final value* of the control variable (i.e., whether looping should continue).

Consider the simple program in Fig. 3.17, which prints the numbers from 0 to 9. Line 4 names the control variable (**counter**) and sets it to an *initial value* of **0**. Line 8 in the **while** structure *increments* the loop counter by 1 for each iteration of the loop. The loop-continuation condition in the **while** structure tests for whether the value of the control variable is less than **10**. The loop terminates when the control variable is greater than or equal to **10** (i.e., **counter** becomes **10**).

```
1   # Fig. 3.17: fig03_17.py
2   # Counter-controlled repetition.
3
4   counter = 0
5
6   while counter < 10:
7       print counter
8       counter += 1
```

Fig. 3.17 Counter-controlled repetition. (Part 1 of 2.)

Fig. 3.17   Counter-controlled repetition. (Part 2 of 2.)

Common Programming Error 3.13

Because floating-point values may be approximate, controlling the counting of loops with floating-point variables may result in imprecise counter values and inaccurate tests for termination. Programs should control counting loops with integer values.

Good Programming Practice 3.6

Put a blank line before and after each control structure to make it stand out in the program.

Good Programming Practice 3.7

Too many levels of nesting can make a program difficult to understand. As a general rule, try to avoid using more than three levels of indentation.

Good Programming Practice 3.8

Inserting a blank line above and below each control structure, and indenting the body of each control structure, give programs a two-dimensional appearance that enhances readability.

3.13 `for` Repetition Structure

The **for** repetition structure handles all the details of counter-controlled repetition. To illustrate the power of **for**, let us rewrite the program of Fig. 3.17. Figure 3.18 shows the result.

The program operates as follows. When the **for** structure begins executing, function **range** creates a *sequence* of values in the range 0–9 (Fig. 3.19). The first value in this sequence is assigned to variable **counter**, and the body of the **for** structure (line 6) executes. For each subsequent value in the sequence, the value is assigned to variable **counter**, and the body of the **for** structure executes. This process continues until all values in the sequence have been processed.

Fig. 3.19 shows the sequence returned by function **range**. This sequence is a Python *list* containing integers in the range 0–9. Note that values in a list are enclosed in square brackets (e.g., **[ ]**) and separated by commas. Lists are covered in detail in Chapter 5, Lists, Tuples and Dictionaries.

Notice that the last value of the sequence returned by function **range** is one less than the argument passed to the function. If the programmer incorrectly wrote

```
for counter in range( 9 ):
    print counter
```

then the loop executes nine times. This is a common logic error called an *off-by-one* error.

```
1   # Fig. 3.18: fig03_18.py
2   # Counter-controlled repetition with the
3   # for structure and range function.
4
5   for counter in range( 10 ):
6       print counter
```

```
0
1
2
3
4
5
6
7
8
9
```

Fig. 3.18   Counter-controlled repetition with the **for** structure.

Function **range** can take one, two or three arguments. If we pass one argument to the function (as in Fig. 3.19), that argument, called **end**, is one greater than the *upper bound* (highest value) of the sequence. In this case, **range** returns a sequence in the range:

> `0-( end-1 )`

If we pass two arguments, the first argument, called **start**, is the *lower bound*—the lowest value in the returned sequence—and the second argument is **end**. In this case, **range** returns a sequence in the range:

> `( start )-( end-1 )`

If we pass three arguments, the first two arguments are **start** and **end**, respectively, and the third argument, called **increment**, is the *increment value*. The sequence produced by a call to **range** with an increment value progresses from **start** to **end** in multiples of the increment value. If **increment** is positive, the last value in the sequence is the largest multiple less than **end**. The following three calls to **range** produce the same sequence as in Fig. 3.19.

```
range( 10 )
range( 0, 10 )
range( 0, 10, 1 )
```

```
Python 2.2b2 (#26, Nov 16 2001, 11:44:11) [MSC 32 bit (Intel)] on
win32
Type "help", "copyright", "credits" or "license" for more informa-
tion.
>>> range( 10 )
[0, 1, 2, 3, 4, 5, 6, 7, 8, 9]
```

Fig. 3.19   Function **range**.

Common Programming Error 3.14

*Forgetting that the first value of the sequence returned by function **range**, if no lower bound is provided, is zero can lead to an off-by-one logic error.*

Common Programming Error 3.15

*Forgetting that the last value of the sequence returned by function **range** is one less than the value of the function's **end** argument can lead to an off-by-one logic error.*

The increment value of **range** also can be negative. In this case, it is a decrement and the sequence produced progresses downwards from **start** to **end** in multiples of the increment value. The last value in the sequence is the smallest multiple greater than **end** (Fig. 3.20).

The sequence used in a **for** structure does not have to be generated using the **range** function. The general format of the **for** structure is

```
for element in sequence:
    statement(s)
```

where *sequence* is a set of items (sequences are explained in detail in Chapter 5). At the first iteration of the loop, variable *element* is assigned the first item in the sequence and *statement* is executed. At each subsequent iteration of the loop, variable *element* is assigned the next item in the sequence before the execution of *statement*. Once the loop has been executed once for each item in the *sequence*, the loop terminates. In most cases, the **for** structure can be represented by an equivalent **while** structure, as in

```
initialization

while loopContinuationTest:
    statement(s)
    increment
```

where the *initialization* expression initializes the loop's control variable, *loopContinuationTest* is the loop-continuation condition and *increment* increments the control variable.

Common Programming Error 3.16

*Creating a **for** structure that contains no body statements is a syntax error.*

If the *sequence* part of the **for** structure is empty (i.e., the sequence contains no values), the program does not perform the body of the **for** structure. Instead, execution proceeds with the statement following the **for** structure.

```
Python 2.2b2 (#26, Nov 16 2001, 11:44:11) [MSC 32 bit (Intel)] on
win32
Type "help", "copyright", "credits" or "license" for more informa-
tion.
>>> range( 10, 0, -1 )
[10, 9, 8, 7, 6, 5, 4, 3, 2, 1]
```

Fig. 3.20 Function **range** with a third value.

Programs frequently display the control variable (*element*) or use it in calculations in the loop body. However, this use is not required. It is common to use the control variable for controlling repetition while never mentioning it in the body of the **for** structure.

 Good Programming Practice 3.9

*Avoid changing the value of the control variable in the body of a **for** loop, because this practice can cause subtle logic errors.*

The flowchart of the **for** structure is similar to that of the **while** structure. Figure 3.21 illustrates the flowchart of the following **for** statement

```
for x in y:
    print x
```

The flowchart shows the initialization and the update processes. Note that update occurs each time *after* the program performs the body statement. Besides small circles and arrows, the flowchart contains only rectangle symbols and a diamond symbol. The programmer fills the rectangles and diamonds with actions and decisions appropriate to the algorithm.

3.14 Using the **for** Repetition Structure

The following examples show techniques for varying the control variable (loop counter) in a **for** structure. In each case, we write the appropriate **for** header. Note the change in the third argument to **range** for loops that decrement the control variable.

a)   Vary the control variable from **1** to **100** in increments of **1**.

```
for counter in range( 1, 101 ):
```

b)   Vary the control variable from **100** to **1** in increments of **−1** (decrements of **1**).

```
for counter in range( 100, 0, -1 ):
```

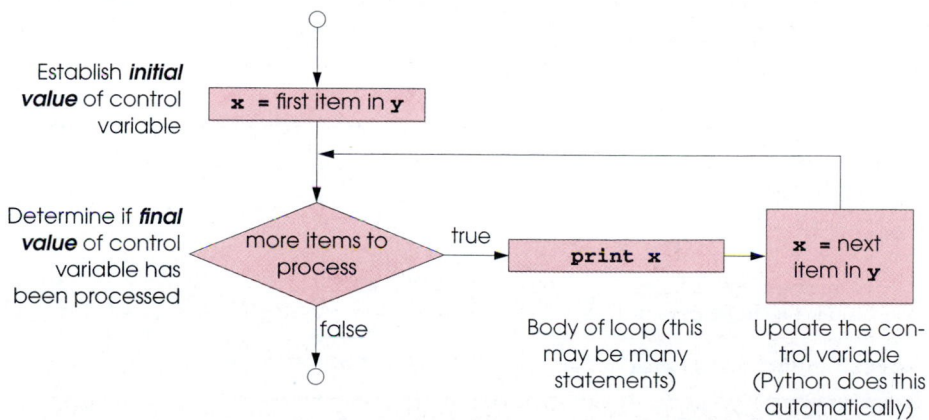

Fig. 3.21   **for** repetition structure flowchart.

c)   Vary the control variable from **7** to **77** in steps of **7**.

```
for counter in range( 7, 78, 7 ):
```

d)   Vary the control variable from **20** to **2** in steps of **-2**.

```
for counter in range( 20, 1, -2 ):
```

e)   Vary the control variable over the following sequence of values: **2, 5, 8, 11, 14, 17, 20**.

```
for counter in range( 2, 21, 3 ):
```

f)   Vary the control variable over the following sequence of values: **99, 88, 77, 66, 55, 44, 33, 22, 11, 0**.

```
for counter in range( 99, -1, -11 ):
```

The next two examples provide simple applications of the **for** structure. The program in Fig. 3.22 uses the **for** structure to sum all the even integers from **2** to **100**.

The next example computes compound interest using the **for** structure. Consider the following problem statement:

> *A person invests $1000 in a savings account yielding 5 percent interest. Assuming that all interest is left on deposit in the account, calculate and print the amount of money in the account at the end of each year for 10 years. Use the following formula for determining these amounts:*
>
> $$a = p (1 + r)^n$$
>
> *where*
>
> p is the original amount invested (i.e., the principal),
> r is the annual interest rate,
> n is the number of years and
> a is the amount on deposit at the end of the nth year.

This problem involves a loop that performs the indicated calculation for each of the 10 years the money remains on deposit. Figure 3.23 shows the solution. The **for** structure executes the body of the loop 10 times, incrementing a control variable (**year**) from 1 to 10. In this example, the algebraic expression $(1 + r)^n$ is written as **(1 + rate) ** year**, where variable **rate** represents r and variable **year** represents n.

```
1   # Fig. 3.22: fig03_22.py
2   # Summation with for.
3
4   sum = 0
5
6   for number in range( 2, 101, 2 ):
7       sum += number
8
9   print "Sum is", sum
```

```
Sum is 2550
```

Fig. 3.22 Summation with **for**.

```
1   # Fig. 3.23: fig03_23.py
2   # Calculating compound interest.
3
4   principal = 1000.0    # starting principal
5   rate = .05            # interest rate
6
7   print "Year %21s" % "Amount on deposit"
8
9   for year in range( 1, 11 ):
10      amount = principal * ( 1.0 + rate ) ** year
11      print "%4d%21.2f" % ( year, amount )
```

```
Year          Amount on deposit
   1                     1050.00
   2                     1102.50
   3                     1157.63
   4                     1215.51
   5                     1276.28
   6                     1340.10
   7                     1407.10
   8                     1477.46
   9                     1551.33
  10                     1628.89
```

Fig. 3.23   **for** structure used to calculate compound interest.

The output statement before the **for** loop (line 7) and the output statement in the **for** loop (line 11) combine to print the values of the variables **year** and **amount** with the formatting specified by the **%** formatting operator specifications. The characters **%4d** specify that the **year** column is printed with a field width of four (i.e., the value is printed with at least four character positions). If the value to be output is fewer than four character positions wide, the value is right justified in the field by default. If the value to be output is more than four character positions wide, the field width is extended to accommodate the entire value.

The characters **%21.2f** indicate that variable **amount** is printed as a float-point value (specified with the character **f**) with a decimal point. The column has a total field width of 21 character positions and two digits of precision to the right of the decimal point; the total field width includes the decimal point and the two digits to its right, hence 18 of the 21 positions appear to the left of the decimal point.

Notice that the variables **amount**, **principal** and **rate** are floating point values. We did this for simplicity, because we are dealing with fractional parts of dollars and thus need a type that allows decimal points in its values. Unfortunately, this can cause trouble. Here is an example of what can go wrong when using floating point values to represent dollar amounts (assuming that dollar amounts are displayed with two digits to the right of the decimal point): Two dollar amounts stored in the machine could be 14.234 (which would normally be rounded to 14.23 for display purposes) and 18.673 (which would normally be rounded to 18.67 for display purposes). When these amounts are added, they produce the internal sum 32.907, which would normally be rounded to 32.91 for display purposes. Thus, your printout could appear as

```
    14.23
  + 18.67
  -------
    32.91
```

but a person adding the individual numbers as printed would expect the sum to be 32.90. You have been warned!

Good Programming Practice 3.10

Be careful when using floating-point values to perform monetary calculations. Rounding errors may lead to undesired results.

Note that the body of the **for** structure contains the calculation **1.0 + rate** (line 10). In fact, this calculation produces the same result each time through the loop, so repeating the calculation is wasteful. A better solution would be to define a variable (e.g., **final-Rate** that references the value of **1.0 + rate** before the start of the **for** structure. Then, replace the calculation **1.0 + rate** (line 10) with variable **finalRate**.

Performance Tip 3.3

Avoid placing expressions whose values do not change inside loops.

3.15 break and continue Statements

Python offers the ***break*** and ***continue*** statements, which alter the flow of control. The **break** statement, when executed in a **while** or **for** structure, causes immediate exit from that structure. Program execution continues with the first statement after the structure. Figure 3.24 demonstrates the **break** statement in a **for** repetition structure. When the **if** structure detects that **x** equals **5**, it executes the **break** statement. This terminates the **for** statement and the program continues with the **print** statement (line 11). The loop outputs four numbers.

Figure 3.25 is a modified version of Fig. 3.13, the class-average program illustrating sentinel-controlled repetition. This version eliminates the repeated code found in the original program. Line 9 introduces an infinite **while** loop. The condition of the **while** loop never evaluates to false because 1 is always true. Lines 10–11 prompt the user for a grade and convert the input to an integer. If the grade is the sentinel value, –1, the program exits the loop (line 16).

```
1   # Fig. 3.24: fig03_24.py
2   # Using the break statement in a for structure.
3
4   for x in range( 1, 11 ):
5
6       if x == 5:
7           break
8
9       print x,
10
11  print "\nBroke out of loop at x =", x
```

Fig. 3.24 **break** statement used in a **for** structure. (Part 1 of 2.)

```
1 2 3 4
Broke out of loop at x = 5
```

Fig. 3.24 **break** statement used in a **for** structure. (Part 2 of 2.)

```
1    # Fig. 3.25: fig03_25.py
2    # Using the break statement to avoid repeating code
3    # in the class-average program.
4
5    # initialization phase
6    total = 0            # sum of grades
7    gradeCounter = 0     # number of grades entered
8
9    while 1:
10       grade = raw_input( "Enter grade, -1 to end: " )
11       grade = int( grade )
12
13       # exit loop if user inputs -1
14       if grade == -1:
15          break
16
17       total += grade
18       gradeCounter += 1
19
20   # termination phase
21   if gradeCounter != 0:
22       average = float( total ) / gradeCounter
23       print "Class average is", average
24   else:
25       print "No grades were entered"
```

```
Enter grade, -1 to end: 75
Enter grade, -1 to end: 94
Enter grade, -1 to end: 97
Enter grade, -1 to end: 88
Enter grade, -1 to end: 70
Enter grade, -1 to end: 64
Enter grade, -1 to end: 83
Enter grade, -1 to end: 89
Enter grade, -1 to end: -1
Class average is 82.5
```

Fig. 3.25 **break** statement used to eliminate code repetition.

The **continue** statement, when executed in a **while** or a **for** structure, skips the remaining statements in the body of that structure and proceeds with the next iteration of the loop. In **while** structures, the loop-continuation test is evaluated immediately after the execution of the **continue** statement. In the **for** structure, the control variable is assigned the next value in the sequence (if the sequence contains more values). Earlier, we stated that the **while** structure usually can represent the **for** structure. The one exception occurs when the increment expression in the **while** structure follows the **continue** statement. In this case, the increment is not executed before the repetition-continuation condition is tested, and the **while** does not execute in the same manner as the **for**. Figure 3.26 uses the **continue** statement in a **for** structure to skip the output statement in the structure and begin the next iteration of the loop.

Good Programming Practice 3.11

*Some programmers feel that **break** and **continue** violate structured programming. Because the effects of these statements can be achieved by structured programming techniques we discuss, these programmers do not use **break** and **continue**.*

3.16 Logical Operators

So far, we have studied *simple conditions*, such as **counter <= 10**, **total > 1000** and **number != sentinelValue**. We have expressed these conditions in terms of the relational operators **>**, **<**, **>=** and **<=** and the equality operators **==** and **!=**. Each decision tested precisely one condition. To test multiple conditions while making a decision, we performed these tests in separate statements or in nested **if** or **if/else** structures.

Python provides *logical operators* that are used to form more complex conditions by combining simple conditions. The logical operators are **and** *(logical AND)*, **or** *(logical OR)* and **not** *(logical NOT, also called logical negation)*. We now consider examples of each of these operators.

Suppose we wish to ensure that two conditions are *both* true before we choose a certain path of execution. In this case, we can use the logical **and** operator as follows:

```
if gender == "Female" and age >= 65:
    seniorFemales += 1
```

This **if** statement contains two simple conditions. The condition **gender == "Female"** is evaluated here to determine whether a person is a female. The condition **age >= 65** is evaluated to determine whether a person is a senior citizen. The simple condition to the left of the **and** operator is evaluated first, because the precedence of **==** is higher than the precedence of **and**. If necessary, the simple condition to the right of the **and** operator is evaluated next, because the precedence of **>=** is higher than the precedence of **and** (as we will discuss shortly, the right side of a logical AND expression is evaluated only if the left side is true). The **if** statement then considers the combined condition:

```
1   # Fig. 3.26: fig03_26.py
2   # Using the continue statement in a for/in structure.
3
4   for x in range( 1, 11 ):
5
6      if x == 5:
7         continue
8
9      print x,
10
11  print "\nUsed continue to skip printing the value 5"
```

Fig. 3.26 **continue** statement used in a **for** structure. (Part 1 of 2.)

```
1 2 3 4 6 7 8 9 10
Used continue to skip printing the value 5
```

Fig. 3.26 **continue** statement used in a **for** structure. (Part 2 of 2.)

```
gender == "Female" and age >= 65
```

This condition is true only if both of the simple conditions are true. Finally, if this combined condition is indeed true, then the count of **seniorFemales** is incremented by 1. If either or both of the simple conditions are false, then the program skips the incrementing and proceeds to the statement following the **if**. The preceding combined condition can be made more readable by adding redundant parentheses

```
( gender == "Female" ) and ( age >= 65 )
```

The table of Fig. 3.27 summarizes the **and** operator. The table shows all four possible combinations of false and true values for **expression1** and **expression2**. Such tables are often called *truth tables.*

Python evaluates to false or true all expressions that include relational operators and equality operators. A simple condition (e.g., **age >= 65**) that is false evaluates to the integer value 0; a simple condition that is true evaluates to the integer value 1. A Python expression that evaluates to the value 0 is false; a Python expression that evaluates to a non-zero integer value is true. The interactive session of Fig. 3.28 demonstrates these concepts.

Lines 5–10 of the interactive session demonstrate that the value 0 is false. Lines 11–18 show that any non-zero integer value is true. The simple condition in line 19 evaluates to true (line 20). The combined conditions in lines 21 and 23 demonstrate the return values of the **and** operator. If a combined condition evaluates to false (line 21), the **and** operator returns the first value which evaluated to false (line 22). Conversely, if the combined condition evaluates to true (line 23), the **and** operator returns the last value in the condition (line 24).

Now let us consider the **or** (logical OR) operator. Suppose we wish to ensure at some point in a program that either one *or* both of two conditions are true before we choose a certain path of execution. In this case, we use the **or** operator, as in the following program segment:

```
if semesterAverage >= 90 or finalExam >= 90:
    print "Student grade is A"
```

expression1	expression2	expression1 **and** expression2
false	false	false
false	true	false
true	false	false
true	true	true

Fig. 3.27 Truth table for the **and** (logical AND) operator.

```
Python 2.2b2 (#26, Nov 16 2001, 11:44:11) [MSC 32 bit (Intel)] on
win32
Type "help", "copyright", "credits" or "license" for more informa-
tion.
>>> if 0:
...     print "0 is true"
... else:
...     print "0 is false"
...
0 is false
>>> if 1:
...     print "non-zero is true"
...
non-zero is true
>>> if -1:
...     print "non-zero is true"
...
non-zero is true
>>> print 2 < 3
1
>>> print 0 and 1
0
>>> print 1 and 3
3
```

Fig. 3.28   Truth values.

This preceding condition also contains two simple conditions. The simple condition **semesterAverage >= 90** is evaluated to determine whether the student deserves an "A" in the course because of a solid performance throughout the semester. The simple condition **finalExam >= 90** is evaluated to determine whether the student deserves an "A" in the course because of an outstanding performance on the final exam. The **if** statement then considers the combined condition

> **semesterAverage >= 90 or finalExam >= 90**

and awards the student an "A" if either one or both of the simple conditions are true. Note that the message **Student grade is A** is not printed when both of the simple conditions are false. Fig. 3.29 is a truth table for the logical OR operator (**or**).

expression1	expression2	expression1 or expression2
false	false	false
false	true	true
true	false	true
true	true	true

Fig. 3.29   Truth table for the **or** (logical OR) operator.

If a combined condition evaluates to true, the **or** operator returns the first value which evaluated to true. Conversely, if the combined condition evaluates to false, the **or** operator returns the last value in the condition.

The **and** operator has a higher precedence than the **or** operator. Both operators associate from left to right. An expression containing **and** or **or** operators is evaluated until its truth or falsity is known. This is called *short circuit evaluation*. Thus, evaluation of the expression

```
gender == "Female" and age >= 65
```

will stop immediately if **gender** is not equal to **"Female"** (i.e., the entire expression is false), but continue if **gender** is equal to **"Female"** (i.e., the entire expression could still be true, if the condition **age >= 65** is true).

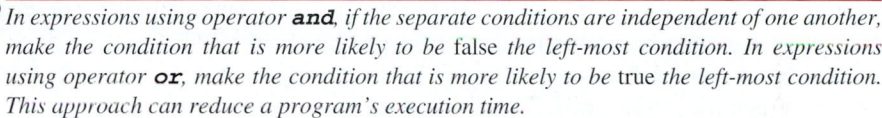

Performance Tip 3.4

*In expressions using operator **and**, if the separate conditions are independent of one another, make the condition that is more likely to be false the left-most condition. In expressions using operator **or**, make the condition that is more likely to be true the left-most condition. This approach can reduce a program's execution time.*

Python provides the **not** (logical negation) operator to enable a programmer to "reverse" the meaning of a condition. Unlike the **and** and **or** operators, which combine two conditions (binary operators), the logical negation operator has a single condition as an operand (i.e., **not** is a *unary* operator). The logical negation operator is placed before a condition when we are interested in choosing a path of execution if the original condition (without the logical negation operator) is false, such as in the following program segment:

```
if not grade == sentinelValue:
    print "The next grade is", grade
```

Figure 3.30 is a truth table for the logical negation operator. In many cases, the programmer can avoid using logical negation by expressing the condition differently with an appropriate relational or equality operator. For example, the preceding statement can also be written as follows:

```
if grade != sentinelValue:
    print "The next grade is", grade
```

This flexibility can often help a programmer express a condition in a more "natural" or convenient manner.

expression	not expression
false	true
true	false

Fig. 3.30   Truth table for operator **not** (logical negation).

Figure 3.31 shows the precedence and associativity of the Python operators introduced to this point. The operators are shown from top to bottom, in decreasing order of precedence.

3.17 Structured-Programming Summary

Just as architects design buildings by employing the collective wisdom of their profession, so should programmers design their programs. The field of computer programming is younger than architecture, and our collective wisdom is considerably sparser. We have learned that structured programming produces programs that are easier than unstructured programs to understand and hence are easier to test, debug, modify, and even prove correct in a mathematical sense.

Figure 3.32 summarizes Python's control structures. Small circles are used in the figure to indicate the single entry point and the single exit point of each structure. Connecting individual flowchart symbols arbitrarily can lead to unstructured programs. Therefore, the programming profession has chosen to combine flowchart symbols to form a limited set of control structures and to build structured programs by properly combining control structures in only two simple ways.

For simplicity, single-entry/single-exit control structures are used—there is one way to enter and one way to exit each control structure. Connecting control structures in sequence to form structured programs is simple—the exit point of one control structure is connected to the entry point of the next control structure, so that control structures are simply placed one after another in a program; we have called this "control-structure stacking." The rules for forming structured programs also allow for control structures to be nested.

Figure 3.33 shows the rules for forming properly structured programs. The rules assume that the rectangle flowchart symbol may be used to indicate any action, including input and output. The rules also assume that we begin with the simplest flowchart (Fig. 3.34).

Operators	Associativity	Type
( )	left to right	parentheses
**	right to left	exponentiation
* / %	left to right	multiplicative
+	left to right	additive
< <= > >=	left to right	relational
== != <>	left to right	equality
and	left to right	logical AND
or	left to right	logical OR
not	right to left	logical NOT

Fig. 3.31 Operator precedence and associativity.

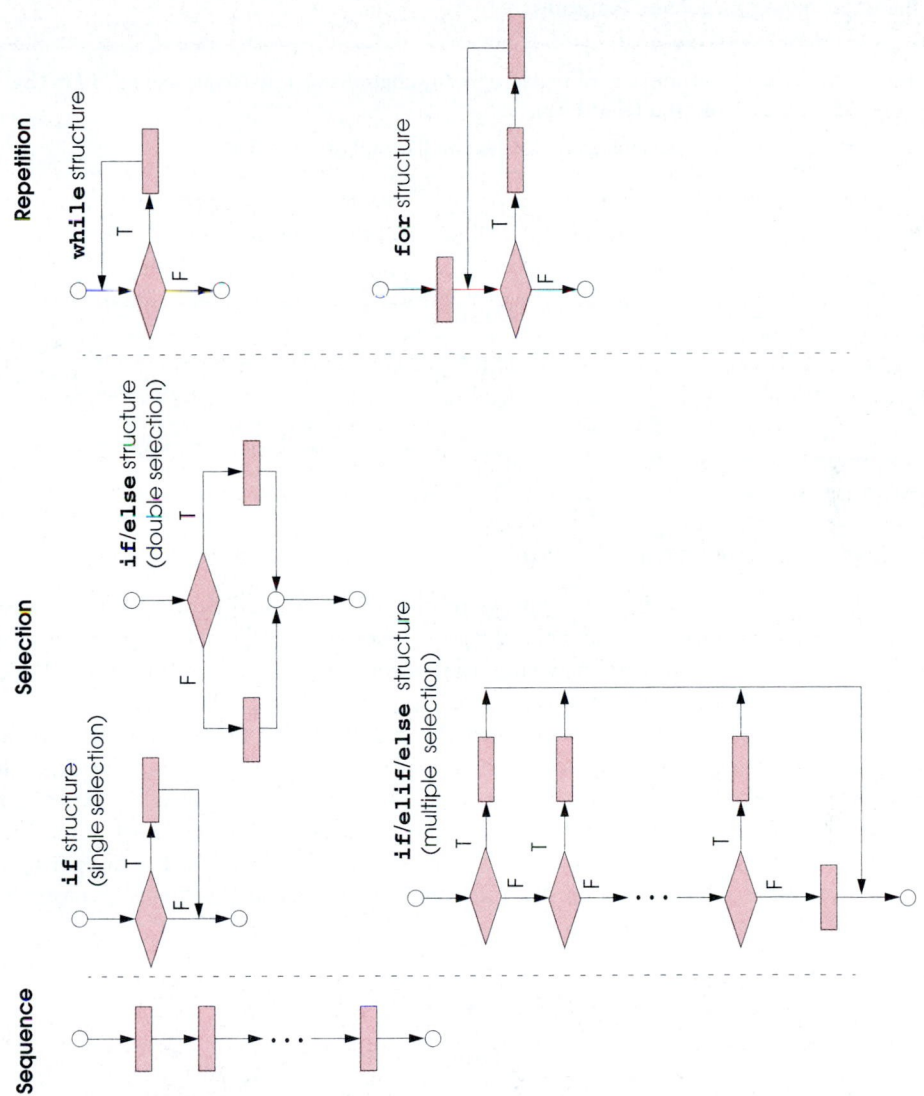

Fig. 3.32 Single-entry/single-exit sequence, selection and repetition structures.

Rules for Forming Structured Programs

1) Begin with the so called simplest flowchart (Fig. 3.34).

2) Any rectangle (action) can be replaced by two rectangles (actions) in sequence.

Fig. 3.33 Rules for forming structured programs. (Part 1 of 2.)

Rules for Forming Structured Programs

3)   Any rectangle (action) can be replaced by any control structure (sequence, **if**, **if/else**, **if/elif/else**, **while** or **for**).

4)   Rules 2 and 3 can be applied as often as you like and in any order.

Fig. 3.33   Rules for forming structured programs. (Part 2 of 2.)

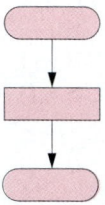

Fig. 3.34   Simplest flowchart.

Applying the rules of Fig. 3.33 always results in a structured flowchart with a neat, building-block appearance. For example, repeatedly applying rule 2 to the simplest flowchart results in a structured flowchart containing many rectangles in sequence (Fig. 3.35). Notice that rule 2 generates a stack of control structures, so let us call rule 2 the *stacking rule*.

Rule 3 is called the *nesting rule*. Repeatedly applying rule 3 to the simplest flowchart results in a flowchart with neatly nested control structures. For example, in Fig. 3.36, the rectangle in the simplest flowchart is first replaced with a double-selection (**if/else**) structure. Then rule 3 is applied again to both of the rectangles in the double-selection structure, replacing each of these rectangles with double-selection structures. The dashed boxes around each of the double-selection structures represent the rectangles that were replaced.

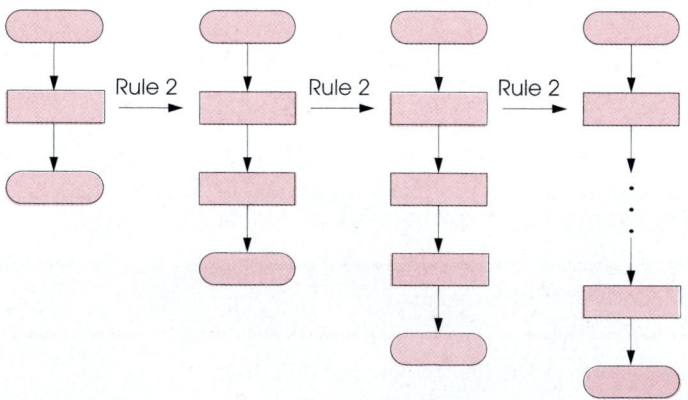

Fig. 3.35   Applying (repeatedly) rule 2 of Fig. 3.33 to the simplest flowchart.

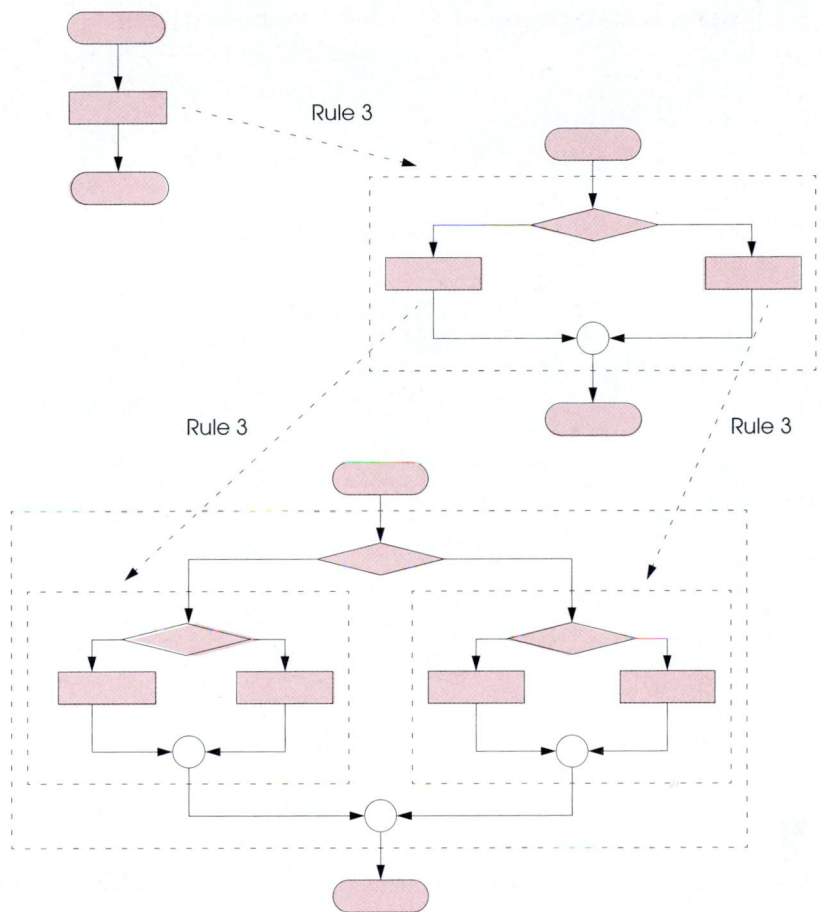

Fig. 3.36 Applying rule 3 of Fig. 3.35 to the simplest flowchart.

Rule 4 generates larger, more involved and more deeply nested structures. The flowcharts that emerge from applying the rules in Fig. 3.33 constitute the set of all possible structured flowcharts and hence the set of all possible structured programs.

The beauty of the structured approach is that we use only six simple single-entry/single-exit pieces, and we assemble them in only two simple ways. Figure 3.37 shows the kinds of stacked building blocks that emerge from applying rule 2 and the kinds of nested building blocks that emerge from applying rule 3. The figure also shows the kind of overlapped building blocks that cannot appear in structured flowcharts (because of the elimination of the **goto** statement).

If the rules in Fig. 3.33 are followed, an unstructured flowchart (such as that in Fig. 3.38) cannot be created. If you are uncertain of whether a particular flowchart is structured, apply the rules of Fig. 3.33 in reverse to try to reduce the flowchart to the simplest flowchart. If the flowchart is reducible to the simplest flowchart, the original flowchart is structured; otherwise, it is not.

Nested building blocks   Nested building blocks

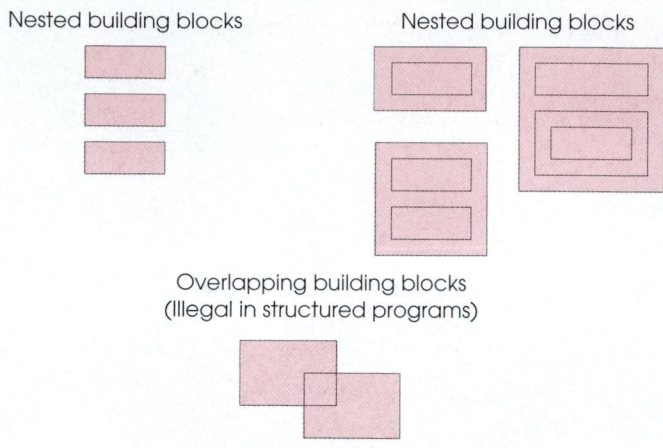

Overlapping building blocks
(Illegal in structured programs)

Fig. 3.37   Stacked, nested and overlapped building blocks.

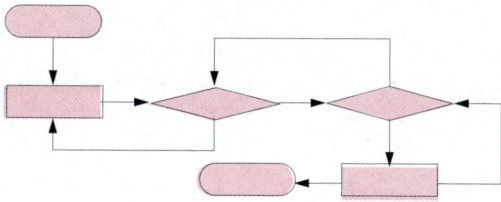

Fig. 3.38   Unstructured flowchart.

Structured programming promotes simplicity. Bohm and Jacopini have given us the result that only three forms of control are needed:

- Sequence
- Selection
- Repetition

Sequence is trivial. Selection is implemented in one of three ways:

- **if** structure (single selection)
- **if/else** structure (double selection)
- **if/elif/else** structure (multiple selection)

In fact, it is straightforward to prove that the simple **if** structure is sufficient to provide any form of selection—everything that can be done with the **if/else** structure and the **if/elif/else** structure can be implemented by combining **if** structures (although perhaps not as clearly and efficiently).

Repetition is implemented in one of two ways:

- **while** structure
- **for** structure

It is straightforward to prove that the **while** structure is sufficient to provide any form of repetition. Everything that can be done with the **for** structure can be done with the **while** structure (although perhaps not as smoothly).

Combining these results illustrates that any form of control ever needed in a Python program can be expressed in terms of the following:

- sequence
- **if** structure (selection)
- **while** structure (repetition)

Also, these control structures can be combined in only two ways—stacking and nesting. Indeed, structured programming promotes simplicity.

In this chapter, we discussed how to compose programs from control structures containing actions and decisions. In Chapter 4, Functions, we introduce another program-structuring unit, called the *function*. We learn to compose large programs by combining functions that, in turn, are composed of control structures. We also discuss how functions promote software reusability. In Chapter 7, Object-Oriented Programming, we introduce Python's other program-structuring unit, called the *class*. We then create objects from classes and proceed with our treatment of *object-oriented programming (OOP)*.

SUMMARY

- Any computing problem can be solved by executing a series of actions in a specified order. An algorithm solves problems in terms of the actions to be executed and the order in which these actions are executed.
- Specifying the order in which statements execute in a computer program is called program control.
- Pseudocode is an artificial and informal language that helps programmers develop algorithms. Pseudocode is similar to everyday English; it is convenient and user-friendly, although it is not an actual computer programming language.
- A carefully prepared pseudocode program can be converted easily to a corresponding Python program. In many cases, this is done simply by replacing pseudocode statements with their Python equivalents.
- Normally, statements in a program execute successively in the order in which they appear. This is called sequential execution. Various Python statements enable the programmer to specify that the next statement to be executed may be other than the next one in sequence. This is called transfer of control.
- The **goto** statement allows a programmer to specify a transfer of control to one of a wide range of possible destinations in a program.
- The research of Bohm and Jacopini demonstrated that programs could be written without any **goto** statements. The challenge of the era became for programmers to shift their styles to "**goto**-less programming."
- Bohm and Jacopini demonstrated that all programs could be written in terms of only three control structures—the sequence, selection and repetition structures.
- The sequence structure is built into Python. Unless directed otherwise, the computer executes Python statements sequentially.
- A flowchart is a graphical representation of an algorithm or of a portion of an algorithm. Flowcharts are drawn using certain special-purpose symbols, such as rectangles, diamonds, ovals and small circles; these symbols are connected by arrows called flowlines.

- Like pseudocode, flowcharts aid in the development and representation of algorithms. Although most programmers prefer pseudocode, flowcharts nicely illustrate how control structures operate.

- The rectangle symbol, also called the action symbol, indicates an action, including a calculation or an input/output operation. Python allows for as many actions as necessary in a sequence structure.

- Perhaps the most important flowchart symbol is the diamond symbol, also called the decision symbol, which indicates a decision is to be performed.

- Python provides three types of selection structures: **if**, **if/else** and **if/elif/else**.

- The **if** selection structure either performs (selects) an action if a condition (predicate) is true or skips the action if the condition is false.

- The **if/else** selection structure performs an action if a condition is true or performs a different action if the condition is false.

- The **if/elif/else** selection structure performs one of many different actions, depending on the validity of several conditions.

- The **if** selection structure is a single-selection structure—it selects or ignores a single action. The **if/else** selection structure is a double-selection structure—it selects between two different actions. The **if/elif/else** selection structure is a multiple-selection structure—it selects from many possible actions.

- Python provides two types of repetition structures: **while** and **for**.

- The words **if**, **elif**, **else**, **while** and **for** are Python keywords. These keywords are reserved by the language to implement various Python features, such as control structures. Keywords cannot be used as identifiers (e.g., variable names).

- Python has six control structures: sequence, three types of selection and two types of repetition. Each Python program is formed by combining as many control structures of each type as is appropriate for the algorithm the program implements.

- Single-entry/single-exit control structures make it easy to build programs—the control structures are attached to one another by connecting the exit point of one control structure to the entry point of the next. This is similar to the way a child stacks building blocks; hence, the term control-structure stacking.

- Indentation emphasizes the inherent structure of structured programs and, unlike in most other programming languages, is actually required in Python.

- Nested **if/else** structures test for multiple cases by placing **if/else** selection structures inside other **if/else** selection structures.

- Nested **if/else** structures and the multiple-selection **if/elif/else** structure are equivalent. The latter form is popular because it avoids deep indentation of the code. Such indentation often leaves little room on a line, forcing lines to be split over multiple lines and decreasing program readability.

- The **else** block of the **if/elif/else** structure is optional. However, most programmers include an **else** block at the end of a series of **elif** blocks to handle any condition that does not match the conditions specified in the **elif** statements. If an **if/elif** statement specifies an **else** block, the **else** block must be the last block in the statement.

- The **if** selection structure can contain several statements in the body of an **if** statement, and all these statements must be indented. A set of statements contained within an indented code block is called a suite.

- A fatal logic error causes a program to fail and terminate prematurely. For fatal errors, Python prints an error message called a traceback and exits. A nonfatal logic error allows a program to continue executing, but might produce incorrect results.

- Just as multiple statements can be placed anywhere a single statement can be placed, it is possible to have no statements at all, (i.e., empty statements). The empty statement is represented by placing keyword **pass** where a statement normally resides.

- A repetition structure allows the programmer to specify that a program should repeat an action while some condition remains true.

- Counter-controlled repetition uses a variable called a counter to control the number of times a set of statements executes. Counter-controlled repetition often is called definite repetition because the number of repetitions must be known before the loop begins executing.

- A sentinel value (also called a signal value, a dummy value or a flag value) indicates "end of data entry." Sentinel-controlled repetition often is called indefinite repetition because the number of repetitions is not known before the start of the loop.

- In top-down, stepwise refinement, which is essential to the development of well-structured programs, the top is a single statement that conveys the overall function of the program. As such, the top is, in effect, a complete representation of a program. Thus, it is necessary to divide (refine) the top into a series of smaller tasks and list these in the order in which they need to be performed.

- Floating-point numbers contain a decimal point, as in 7.2 or –93.5.

- Dividing two integers results in integer division, in which any fractional part of the calculation is discarded (i.e., truncated).

- To produce a floating-point calculation with integer values, convert one (or both) of the values to a floating-point value with function **float**.

- The Python interpreter evaluates expressions in which the data types of the operands are identical. To ensure that the operands are of the same type, the interpreter performs an operation called promotion (also called implicit conversion) on selected operands.

- Python provides several augmented assignment symbols for abbreviating assignment expressions run together.

- Any statement of the form *variable = variable operator expression* where operator is a binary operator, such as **+**, **-**, ******, *****, **/**, and **%**, can be written in the form *variable operator= expression*.

- Function **range** can take one, two or three arguments. If we pass one argument to the function, that argument, called **end**, is one greater than the upper bound (highest value) of the sequence.

- If we pass two arguments, the first argument, called **start**, is the lower bound—the lowest value in the returned sequence—and the second argument is **end**.

- If we pass three arguments, the first two arguments are **start** and **end**, respectively, and the third argument, called **increment**, is the increment value. The sequence produced by a call to **range** with an increment value progresses from **start** to **end** in multiples of the increment value. If **increment** is positive, the last value in the sequence is the largest multiple less than **end**.

- The increment value of **range** also can be negative. In this case, it is a decrement and the sequence produced progresses downwards from **start** to **end** in multiples of the increment value. The last value in the sequence is the smallest multiple greater than **end**.

- The **break** statement, when executed in a **while** or **for** structure, causes immediate exit from that structure. Program execution continues with the first statement after the structure.

- The **continue** statement, when executed in a **while** or a **for** structure, skips the remaining statements in the body of that structure and proceeds with the next iteration of the loop.

- Python provides logical operators that form more complex conditions by combining simple conditions. The logical operators are **and** (logical AND), **or** (logical OR) and **not** (logical NOT, also called logical negation).

- Python evaluates to false or true all expressions that include relational operators and equality operators. A simple condition (e.g., **age >= 65**) that is false evaluates to the integer value 0; a simple condition that is true evaluates to the integer value 1. A Python expression that evaluates to the value 0 is false; a Python expression that evaluates to a non-zero integer value is true.

- If a combined condition evaluates to false, the **and** operator returns the first value which evaluated to false. Conversely, if the combined condition evaluates to true, the **and** operator returns the last value in the condition.

- If a combined condition evaluates to true, the **or** operator returns the first value which evaluated to true. Conversely, if the combined condition evaluates to false, the **or** operator returns the last value in the condition.

- The **and** operator has a higher precedence than the **or** operator. Both operators associate from left to right. An expression containing **and** or **or** operators is evaluated until its truth or falsity is known. This is called short circuit evaluation.

- The **not** (logical negation) operator enables a programmer to "reverse" the meaning of a condition. Unlike the **and** and **or** operators, which combine two conditions (binary operators), the logical negation operator has a single condition as an operand (i.e., **not** is a unary operator).

TERMINOLOGY

action/decision model of programming
action symbol
algorithm
and (logical AND) operator
augmented addition assignment symbol
augmented assignment statement
augmented assignment symbol
break statement
compound statement
connector symbols
continue statement
control structure
control-structure nesting
control-structure stacking
counter
counter-controlled repetition
decision symbol
default condition
definite repetition
double-selection structure
diamond symbol
dummy value
empty statement
end argument of **range** function
exception handling
fatal logic error
first refinement
flag value
float function
flowchart
for repetition structure

function
goto elimination
goto statement
if selection structure
if/elif/else selection structure
if/else selection structure
implicit conversion
increment argument of **range** function
increment value
indefinite repetition
initialization phase
int function
keyword
list
logic error
logical negation
logical operator
loop-continuation test
lower bound
multiple-selection structure
nested **if/else** structure
nesting
nesting rule
nonfatal logic error
not (logical NOT) operator
off-by-one error
or (logical OR) operator
oval symbol
pass keyword
procedure
processing phase

program control
promotion
pseudocode
range function
rectangle symbol
repetition structure
second refinement
selection structure
sentinel value
sequence
sequence structure
sequential execution
short-circuit evaluation
signal value
simple condition
single-entry/single-exit control structure

single-selection structure
small circle symbol
stacking rule
start argument of **range** function
structured programming
suite
termination phase
top-down, stepwise refinement
total
traceback
transfer of control
truth table
unary operator
upper bound
while repetition structure

SELF-REVIEW EXERCISES

3.1   Fill in the blanks in each of the following statements:
   a) The **if/elif/else** structure is a _____ structure.
   b) The words **if** and **else** are examples of reserved words called Python _____.
   c) Sentinel-controlled repetition is called _____ because the number of repetitions is not known before the loop begins executing.
   d) The augmented assignment symbol ***=** performs _____.
   e) Function _____ creates a sequence of integers.
   f) A procedure for solving a problem is called a(n) _____.
   g) The keyword _____ represents an empty statement.
   h) A set of statements within an indented code block in Python is called a _____.
   i) All programs can be written in terms of three control structures, namely, _____, _____ and _____.
   j) A _____ is a graphical representation of an algorithm.

3.2   State whether each of the following is *true* or *false*. If *false*, explain why.
   a) Pseudocode is a simple programming language.
   b) The **if** selection structure performs an indicated action when the condition is true.
   c) The **if/else** selection structure is a single-selection structure.
   d) A fatal logic error causes a program to execute and produce incorrect results.
   e) A repetition structure performs the statements in its body while some condition remains true.
   f) Function **float** converts its argument to a floating-point value.
   g) The exponentiation operator ****** associates left to right.
   h) Function call **range(1, 10)** returns the sequence 1 to 10, inclusive.
   i) Sentinel-controlled repetition uses a counter variable to control the number of times a set of instructions executes.
   j) The symbol **=** tests for equality.

ANSWERS TO SELF-REVIEW EXERCISES

3.1   a) multiple-selection. b) keywords. c) indefinite repetition. d) multiplication. e) **range**. f) algorithm. g) **pass**. h) suite. i) the sequence structure, the selection structure, the repetition structure. j) flowchart.

3.2   a) False. Pseudocode is an artificial and informal language that helps programmers develop algorithms. b) True. c) False. The **if/else** selection structure is a double-selection structure—it selects between two different actions. d) False. A fatal logic error causes a program to terminate. e) True. f) True. g) False. The exponentiation operator associates from right to left. h) False. Function call **range(1, 10)** returns the sequence 1–9, inclusive. i) False. Counter-controlled repetition uses a counter variable to control the number of repetitions; sentinel-control repetition waits for a sentinel value to stop repetition. j) False. The operator **==** tests for equality; the symbol **=** is **for** assignment.

EXERCISES

3.3   Drivers are concerned with the mileage obtained by their automobiles. One driver has kept track of several tankfuls of gasoline by recording miles driven and gallons used for each tankful. Develop a Python program that prompts the user to input the miles driven and gallons used for each tankful. The program should calculate and display the miles per gallon obtained for each tankful. After processing all input information, the program should calculate and print the combined miles per gallon obtained for all tankful (= total miles driven divide by total gallons used).

```
Enter the gallons used (-1 to end): 12.8
Enter the miles driven: 287
The miles / gallon for this tank was 22.421875
Enter the gallons used (-1 to end): 10.3
Enter the miles driven: 200
The miles / gallon for this tank was 19.417475
Enter the gallons used (-1 to end): 5
Enter the miles driven: 120
The miles / gallon for this tank was 24.000000
Enter the gallons used (-1 to end): -1
The overall average miles/gallon was 21.601423
```

3.4   A palindrome is a number or a text phrase that reads the same backwards or forwards. For example, each of the following five-digit integers is a palindrome: 12321, 55555, 45554 and 11611. Write a program that reads in a five-digit integer and determines whether it is a palindrome. (*Hint*: Use the division and modulus operators to separate the number into its individual digits.)

3.5   Input an integer containing 0s and 1s (i.e., a "binary" integer) and print its decimal equivalent. Appendix C, Number Systems, discusses the binary number system. (*Hint*: Use the modulus and division operators to pick off the "binary" number's digits one at a time from right to left. Just as in the decimal number system, where the rightmost digit has the positional value 1 and the next digit leftward has the positional value 10, then 100, then 1000, etc., in the binary number system, the rightmost digit has a positional value 1, the next digit leftward has the positional value 2, then 4, then 8, etc. Thus, the decimal number 234 can be interpreted as 2 * 100 + 3 * 10 + 4 * 1. The decimal equivalent of binary 1101 is 1 * 8 + 1 * 4 + 0 * 2 + 1 * 1.)

3.6   The factorial of a nonnegative integer n is written $n!$ (pronounced "n factorial") and is defined as follows:

$n! = n \cdot (n - 1) \cdot (n - 2) \cdot \ldots \cdot 1$ (for values of n greater than or equal to 1)

and

$n! = 1$ (for $n = 0$).

For example, $5! = 5 \cdot 4 \cdot 3 \cdot 2 \cdot 1$, which is 120. Factorials increase in size very rapidly. What is the largest factorial that your program can calculate before leading to an overflow error?

a) Write a program that reads a nonnegative integer and computes and prints its factorial.

b) Write a program that estimates the value of the mathematical constant e by using the formula [*Note*: Your program can stop after summing 10 terms.]

$$e = 1 + \frac{1}{1!} + \frac{1}{2!} + \frac{1}{3!} + \dots$$

c) Write a program that computes the value of e^x by using the formula [*Note*: Your program can stop after summing 10 terms.]

$$e^x = 1 + \frac{x}{1!} + \frac{x^2}{2!} + \frac{x^3}{3!} + \dots$$

3.7 Write a program that prints the following patterns separately, one below the other each pattern separated from the next by one blank line. Use **for** loops to generate the patterns. All asterisks (*****) should be printed by a single statement of the form

        print '*',

(which causes the asterisks to print side by side separated by a space). (*Hint*: The last two patterns require that each line begin with an appropriate number of blanks.) Extra credit: Combine your code from the four separate problems into a single program that prints all four patterns side by side by making clever use of nested **for** loops. For all parts of this program—minimize the numbers of asterisks and spaces and the number of statements that print these characters.

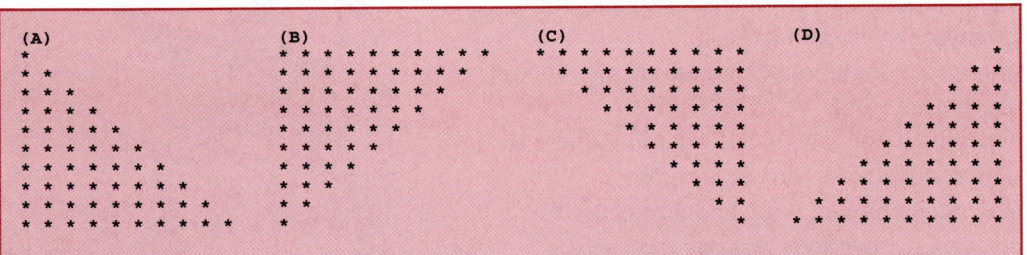

3.8 (*Pythagorean Triples*) A right triangle can have sides that are all integers. The set of three integer values for the sides of a right triangle is called a Pythagorean triple. These three sides must satisfy the relationship that the sum of the squares of two of the sides is equal to the square of the hypotenuse. Find all Pythagorean triples for **side1**, **side2** and **hypotenuse** all no larger than 20. Use a triple-nested **for**-loop that tries all possibilities. This is an example of "brute force" computing. You will learn in more advanced computer science courses that there are many interesting problems for which there is no known algorithmic approach other than sheer brute force.

Functions

Objectives

- To understand how to construct programs modularly from small pieces called functions.
- To create new functions.
- To understand the mechanisms of exchanging information between functions.
- To introduce simulation techniques using random number generation.
- To understand how the visibility of identifiers is limited to specific regions of programs.
- To understand how to write and use recursive functions, i.e., functions that call themselves.
- To introduce default and keyword arguments.

Form ever follows function.
Louis Henri Sullivan

E pluribus unum.
(One composed of many.)
Virgil

O! call back yesterday, bid time return.
William Shakespeare
Richard II

When you call me that, smile.
Owen Wister

Outline

4.1 Introduction

Most computer programs that solve real-world problems are larger than the programs presented in the previous chapters. Experience has shown that the best way to develop and maintain a large program is to construct it from smaller pieces or *components*, each of which is more manageable than the original program. This technique is called *divide and conquer*. This chapter describes many features of the Python language that facilitate the design, implementation, operation and maintenance of large programs.

4.2 Program Components in Python

Program components in Python are called functions, classes, modules and packages. Typically, Python programs are written by combining *programmer-defined* (programmer-created) functions and classes with functions or classes already available in existing Python modules. A *module* is a file that contains definitions of functions and classes. Many modules can be grouped together into a collection, called a package. In this chapter, we concentrate on functions and we introduce modules and packages; we discuss classes in detail in Chapter 7, Object-Based Programing.

    Programmers can define functions to perform specific tasks that execute at various points in a program. These functions are referred to as *programmer-defined* functions. The actual statements defining the function are written only once, but may be called upon "to do their job" from many points throughout a program. Thus functions are a fundamental unit of *software reuse* in Python because functions allow us to reuse program code.

Python *modules* provide functions that perform such common tasks as mathematical calculations, string manipulations, character manipulations, Web programming, graphics programming and many other operations. These functions simplify the programmer's work, because the programmer does not have to write new functions to perform common tasks. A collection of modules, the *standard library*, is provided as part of the core Python language. These modules are located in the library directory of the Python installation (e.g., **/usr/lib/python2.2** or **/usr/local/lib/python2.2** on Unix/Linux; **\Python\Lib** or **\Python22\Lib** on Windows).

Just as a module groups related definitions, a *package* groups related modules. The package as a whole provides tools to help the programmer accomplish a general task (e.g., graphics or audio programming). Each module in the package defines classes, functions or data that perform specific, related tasks (e.g., creating colors, processing **.wav** files and the like). This text introduces many available Python packages, but creating a robust package is a software engineering exercise beyond the scope of the text.

Good Programming Practice 4.1

Familiarize yourself with the collection of functions and classes in the core Python modules.

Software Engineering Observation 4.1

Avoid "reinventing the wheel." When possible, use standard library module functions in-stead of writing new functions. This reduces program development time and increases reliability, because you are using well-designed, well-tested code.

Portability Tip 4.1

Using the functions in the core Python modules usually makes programs more portable.

Performance Tip 4.1

Do not try to rewrite existing module functions to make them more efficient. These functions are written to perform well.

A function is *invoked* (i.e., made to perform its designated task) by a *function call*. The function call specifies the function name and provides information (as *arguments*) that the called function needs to perform its job. A common analogy for this is the hierarchical form of management. A boss (the *calling function* or *caller*) requests a worker (the *called function*) to perform a task and *return* (i.e., report back) the results after performing the task. The boss function is unaware of *how* the worker function performs its designated tasks. The worker might call other worker functions, yet the boss is unaware of this decision. We will discuss how "hiding" implementation details promotes good software engineering. Figure 4.1 shows the **boss** function communicating with worker functions **worker1**, **worker2** and **worker3** in a hierarchical manner. Note that **worker1** acts as a boss function to **worker4** and **worker5**. The **boss** function when calling **worker1** need not know about **worker1**'s relationship with **worker4** and **worker5**. Relationships among functions might not always be a hierarchical structure like the one in this figure.

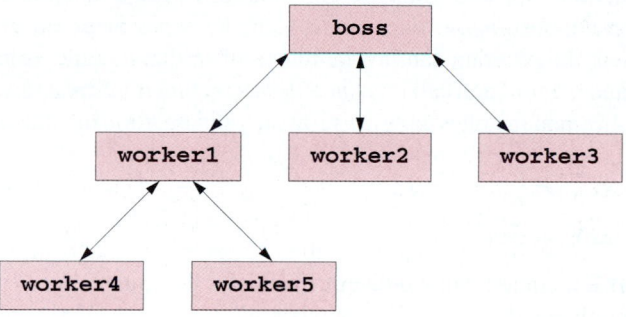

Fig. 4.1   Hierarchical boss-function/worker-function relationship.

4.3 Functions

Functions allow the programmer to modularize a program. All variables created in function definitions are *local variables*—they are known only to the function in which they are declared. Most functions have a list of *parameters* (which are also local variables) that provide the means for communicating information between functions.

There are several motivations for "functionalizing" a program. The divide-and-conquer approach makes program development more manageable. Another motivation is *software reusability*—using existing functions as building blocks for creating new programs. Software reusability is a major benefit of object-oriented programming as we will see in Chapter 7, Object-Based Programming, Chapter 8, Customizing Classes, and Chapter 9, Object-Based Programming: Inheritance. With good function naming and definition, programs can be created from standardized functions that accomplish specific tasks, rather than having to write customized code for every task. A third motivation is to avoid repeating code in a program. Packaging code as a function allows the code to be executed in several locations just by calling the function rather than rewriting it in every instance it is used.

Software Engineering Observation 4.2

Each function should be limited to performing a single, well-defined task, and the function name should effectively express that task. This promotes software reusability.

Software Engineering Observation 4.3

If you cannot choose a concise name that expresses a function's task, it is possible that the function is performing too many diverse tasks. Usually, it is best to divide such a function into smaller functions.

4.4 Module `math` Functions

A *module* contains function definitions and other elements (e.g., class definitions) that perform related tasks. The **math** module contains functions that allow programmers to perform certain mathematical calculations. We use various **math** module functions to introduce the concept of functions and modules. Throughout this text, we discuss many other functions in the core Python modules.

Generally, functions are invoked by writing the name of the function, followed by a left parenthesis, followed by the *argument* (or a comma-separated list of arguments) being passed to the function, followed by a right parenthesis. To use a function that is defined in a module, a program must *import the module*, using keyword **import**. After the module has been imported, the program can invoke functions in that module, using the module's name, a dot (**.**) and the function call (i.e., *moduleName* **.** *functionName* **( )**). The interactive session in Fig. 4.2 demonstrates how to print the square root of 900 using the **math** module.

When the line

    print math.sqrt(900)

executes, the **math** module's function **sqrt** calculates the square root of the number contained in the parentheses (e.g., 900). The number 900 is the *argument* of the **math.sqrt** function. The function *returns* (i.e., gives back as a result) the floating-point value 30.0, which is displayed on the screen.

When the line

    print math.sqrt(-900)

executes, the function call generates an error, also called an exception, because function **sqrt** cannot handle a negative argument. The interpreter displays information about this error to the screen. Exceptions and exception handling are discussed in Chapter 12, Exception Handling.

Common Programming Error 4.1

*Failure to import the **math** module when using **math** module functions is a runtime error. A program must import each module before using its functions and variables.*

Common Programming Error 4.2

*When a module is imported via an **import** statement, forgetting to prefix one of its functions with the module name is a runtime error.*

Function arguments can be values, variables or expressions. If **c1 = 13.0**, **d = 3.0** and **f = 4.0**, then the statement

    print math.sqrt(c1 + d * f)

calculates and prints the square root of **13.0 + 3.0 * 4.0 = 25.0**, (namely, **5.0**). Some other **math** module functions are summarized in Fig. 4.3. (*Note*: Some results are rounded.)

```
Python 2.2b2 (#26, Nov 16 2001, 11:44:11) [MSC 32 bit (Intel)] on
win32
Type "help", "copyright", "credits" or "license" for more informa-
tion.
>>> import math
>>> print math.sqrt( 900 )
30.0
>>> print math.sqrt( -900 )
Traceback (most recent call last):
  File "<stdin>", line 1, in ?
ValueError: math domain error
```

Fig. 4.2   Function **sqrt** of module **math**.

Method	Description	Example
`acos( x )`	Trigonometric arc cosine of x (result in radians)	`acos( 1.0 )` is `0.0`
`asin( x )`	Trigonometric arc sine of x (result in radians)	`asin( 0.0 )` is `0.0`
`atan( x )`	Trigonometric arc tangent of x (result in radians)	`atan( 0.0 )` is `0.0`
`ceil( x )`	Rounds x to the smallest integer not less than x	`ceil( 9.2 )` is `10.0` `ceil( -9.8 )` is `-9.0`
`cos( x )`	Trigonometric cosine of x (x in radians)	`cos( 0.0 )` is `1.0`
`exp( x )`	Exponential function e^x	`exp( 1.0 )` is `2.71828` `exp( 2.0 )` is `7.38906`
`fabs( x )`	Absolute value of x	`fabs( 5.1 )` is `5.1` `fabs( -5.1 )` is `5.1`
`floor( x )`	Rounds x to the largest integer not greater than x	`floor( 9.2 )` is `9.0` `floor( -9.8 )` is `-10.0`
`fmod( x, y )`	Remainder of x/y as a floating point number	`fmod( 9.8, 4.0 )` is `1.8`
`hypot( x, y )`	hypotenuse of a triangle with sides of length x and y: sqrt($x^2 + y^2$)	`hypot( 3.0, 4.0 )` is `5.0`
`log( x )`	Natural logarithm of x (base e)	`log( 2.718282 )` is `1.0` `log( 7.389056 )` is `2.0`
`log10( x )`	Logarithm of x (base 10)	`log10( 10.0 )` is `1.0` `log10( 100.0 )` is `2.0`
`pow( x, y )`	x raised to power y (x^y)	`pow( 2.0, 7.0 )` is `128.0` `pow( 9.0, .5 )` is `3.0`
`sin( x )`	trigonometric sine of x (x in radians)	`sin( 0.0 )` is `0.0`
`sqrt( x )`	square root of x	`sqrt( 900.0 )` is `30.0` `sqrt( 9.0 )` is `3.0`
`tan( x )`	trigonometric tangent of x (x in radians)	`tan( 0.0 )` is `0.0`

Fig. 4.3   `math` module functions.

4.5 Function Definitions

Each program we have presented thus far has consisted of a series of statements that sometimes called predefined Python functions to accomplish the program's tasks. We refer to these statements as the *main portion of the program* for the duration of the book, to differentiate it from the part of the program that contains function definitions. We now discuss how programmers write customized functions.

Software Engineering Observation 4.4

In programs containing many functions, the main portion of the program should be imple-mented as a group of calls to functions that perform the bulk of the program's work.

Consider a program, with a user-defined function **square**, that calculates the squares of the integers from 1 to 10 (Fig. 4.4). Functions must be defined before they are used.

Good Programming Practice 4.2

Place a blank line between function definitions to separate the functions and enhance pro-gram readability.

Line 9 of the main program invokes function **square** (defined at lines 5–6) with the statement

```
print square( x ),
```

Function **square** receives a copy of **x** in the parameter **y**.[1] Then **square** calculates **y * y** (line 6). The result is returned to the statement that invoked **square**. The function call (line 9) evaluates to the value returned by the function. This value is displayed by the **print** statement. The value of **x** is not changed by the function call. This process is re-peated 10 times using the **for** repetition structure.

The format of a function definition is

def *function-name* **(** *parameter-list* **) :**
   statements

where *function-name* is any valid identifier, and *parameter-list* is a comma-separated list of parameter names received by *function-name*. If a function does not receive any values, the parameter list is empty, but the parentheses are still required. The indented statements that fol-low a **def** statement form the *function body*. The function body is referred to as a *block*.

```
1   # Fig. 4.4: fig04_04.py
2   # Creating and using a programmer-defined function.
3
4   # function definition
5   def square( y ):
6      return y * y
7
8   for x in range( 1, 11 ):
9      print square( x ),
10
11  print
```

```
1 4 9 16 25 36 49 64 81 100
```

Fig. 4.4   Programmer-defined function.

---

1. Actually, **y** receives a reference to **x**, but **y** behaves as if it were a copy of **x**'s value. This is the concept of pass-by-object-reference, which we introduce in Chapter 5, Lists, Tuples and Dictio-naries.

Common Programming Error 4.3

Failure to place a colon (:) after a function's parameter list is a syntax error.

Common Programming Error 4.4

*The pair of parentheses ( ) in a function call is a Python operator. It causes the function to be called. The function is not invoked if the parentheses are missing from a function call. Normally, control passes through the statement. If a **print** statement includes a function call without parentheses, it displays the memory location of the function. If the user intends to assign the result of a function call to a variable, a function call without parentheses binds the function itself to the variable.*

Common Programming Error 4.5

Failure to indent the body of a function is a syntax error.

Good Programming Practice 4.3

It is not advisable to use identical names for the arguments passed to a function and the corresponding parameters in the function definition.

Good Programming Practice 4.4

Choosing meaningful function names and meaningful parameter names ensures program readability and reduces the amount of comments. Writing programs this way creates "self-commenting code."

Software Engineering Observation 4.5

If possible, a function should fit in an editor window. Regardless of the length of a function, it should perform one task well. Small functions promote software reusability.

Testing and Debugging Tip 4.1

Updating a function is easier than updating repeated code throughout a program.

Software Engineering Observation 4.6

Programs should be written as collections of small functions. This makes programs easier to write, debug, maintain and modify.

Software Engineering Observation 4.7

*A function requiring a large number of parameters might be performing too many tasks. Consider dividing the function into smaller functions that perform separate tasks. The function's **def** statement should fit on one line, if possible.*

When a function completes its task, the function returns control to the caller. There are three ways to return control to the point from which a function was invoked. If the function does not return a result explicitly, control is returned either when the last indented line is reached or upon execution of the statement

```
return
```

In either case, the function returns **None**, a Python value that represents null—indicating that no value has been declared—and evaluates to false in conditional expressions.

If the function does return a result, the statement

> **return** *expression*

returns the value of *expression* to the caller.

Our second example (Fig. 4.5) uses a programmer-defined function, **maximum-Value**. This function is independent of the type of its arguments. We use function **maximumValue** to determine and return the largest of three integers, the largest of three floats and the largest of three strings.

Line 15 combines two function calls—**raw_input** and **int**—into one statement. In this case, function **raw_input** reads a value from the user, then the result is passed to function **int** as an argument. The call to function **maximumValue** (line 20) passes the three integers to the programmer-defined function (lines 4–13). The **return** statement in **maximumValue** (line 13) returns the largest integer value to the main program. The **print** statement (line 20) displays the returned value. The same function also returns the maximum float (line 26) and the maximum string (line 32).

```
1   # Fig. 4.5: fig04_05.py
2   # Finding the maximum of three integers.
3
4   def maximumValue( x, y, z ):
5      maximum = x
6
7      if y > maximum:
8         maximum = y
9
10     if z > maximum:
11        maximum = z
12
13     return maximum
14
15  a = int( raw_input( "Enter first integer: " ) )
16  b = int( raw_input( "Enter second integer: " ) )
17  c = int( raw_input( "Enter third integer: " ) )
18
19  # function call
20  print "Maximum integer is:", maximumValue( a, b, c )
21  print    # print new line
22
23  d = float( raw_input( "Enter first float: " ) )
24  e = float( raw_input( "Enter second float: " ) )
25  f = float( raw_input( "Enter third float: " ) )
26  print "Maximum float is: ", maximumValue( d, e, f )
27  print
28
29  g = raw_input( "Enter first string: " )
30  h = raw_input( "Enter second string: " )
31  i = raw_input( "Enter third string: " )
32  print "Maximum string is: ", maximumValue( g, h, i )
```

Fig. 4.5   Programmer-defined **maximum** function. (Part 1 of 2.)

```
Enter first integer: 27
Enter second integer: 12
Enter third integer: 36
Maximum integer is: 36

Enter first float: 12.3
Enter second float: 45.6
Enter third float: 9.03
Maximum float is:  45.6

Enter first string: hello
Enter second string: programming
Enter third string: goodbye
Maximum string is:  programming
```

Fig. 4.5   Programmer-defined **maximum** function. (Part 2 of 2.)

4.6 Random-Number Generation

We now take a brief diversion into a popular programming application—simulation and game playing—to illustrate most of the control structures we have studied. In this and the next section, we develop a game-playing program that incorporates multiple functions.

There is something in the air of a gambling casino that invigorates every type of person from the high-rollers at the plush mahogany-and-felt craps tables to the quarter-poppers at the one-armed bandits. It is the *element of chance,* the possibility that luck will convert a pocketful of money into a mountain of wealth, that drives scores of people to gambling casinos. The element of chance can be introduced into computer applications through module **random**.

Function **random.randrange** generates an integer in the range of its first argument upto, but not including, its second argument. If **randrange** truly produces integers at random, every number in that range has an equal *chance* (or *probability*) of being chosen each time the function is called.

Figure 4.6 displays the results of 20 rolls of a six-sided die to demonstrate module **random**. Function call **random.randrange(1, 7)** produces integers in the range 1–6.

```
1   # Fig. 4.6: fig04_06.py
2   # Random integers produced by randrange.
3
4   import random
5
6   for i in range( 1, 21 ):    # simulates 20 die rolls
7       print "%10d" % ( random.randrange( 1, 7 ) ),
8
9       if i % 5 == 0:  # print newline every 5 rolls
10          print
```

Fig. 4.6   Random integers produced by **random.randrange(1, 7)**. (Part 1 of 2.)

5	3	3	3	2
3	2	3	3	4
2	3	6	5	4
6	2	4	1	2

Fig. 4.6   Random integers produced by **random.randrange(1, 7)**. (Part 2 of 2.)

To show that these numbers occur with approximately equal likelihood, let us simulate 6000 rolls of a die (Fig. 4.7). Each integer from 1 to 6 should appear approximately 1000 times.

```
1   # Fig. 4.7: fig04_07.py
2   # Roll a six-sided die 6000 times.
3
4   import random
5
6   frequency1 = 0
7   frequency2 = 0
8   frequency3 = 0
9   frequency4 = 0
10  frequency5 = 0
11  frequency6 = 0
12
13  for roll in range( 1, 6001 ):           # 6000 die rolls
14      face = random.randrange( 1, 7 )
15
16      if face == 1:                       # frequency counted
17          frequency1 += 1
18      elif face == 2:
19          frequency2 += 1
20      elif face == 3:
21          frequency3 += 1
22      elif face == 4:
23          frequency4 += 1
24      elif face == 5:
25          frequency5 += 1
26      elif face == 6:
27          frequency6 += 1
28      else:                               # simple error handling
29          print "should never get here!"
30
31  print "Face %13s" % "Frequency"
32  print "   1 %13d" % frequency1
33  print "   2 %13d" % frequency2
34  print "   3 %13d" % frequency3
35  print "   4 %13d" % frequency4
36  print "   5 %13d" % frequency5
37  print "   6 %13d" % frequency6
```

Fig. 4.7   Rolling a six-sided die 6000 times. (Part 1 of 2.)

Face	Frequency
1	946
2	1003
3	1035
4	1012
5	987
6	1017

Fig. 4.7   Rolling a six-sided die 6000 times. (Part 2 of 2.)

As the program output shows, function **random.randrange** simulates the rolling of a six-sided die. Note that program execution should not reach the **else** condition (lines 28–29) provided in the **if/elif/else** structure, but we provide the condition for good practice.

 Testing and Debugging Tip 4.2

*Provide a default **else** case in an **if/elif/else** to catch errors even if you absolutely are certain that the program contains no bugs!*

4.7 Example: A Game of Chance

One of the most popular games of chance is a dice game known as "craps," which is played in casinos and back alleys throughout the world. The rules of the game are straightforward:

> *A player rolls two dice. Each die has six faces. These faces contain 1, 2, 3, 4, 5 and 6 spots. After the dice have come to rest, the sum of the spots on the two upward faces is calculated. If the sum is 7 or 11 on the first throw, the player wins. If the sum is 2, 3 or 12 on the first throw (called "craps"), the player loses (i.e., the "house" wins). If the sum is 4, 5, 6, 8, 9 or 10 on the first throw, then that sum becomes the player's "point." To win, you must continue rolling the dice until you "make your point." The player loses by rolling a 7 before making the point.*

The program in Fig. 4.8 simulates the game of craps and shows several sample executions.

```
1   # Fig. 4.8: fig04_08.py
2   # Craps.
3
4   import random
5
6   def rollDice():
7       die1 = random.randrange( 1, 7 )
8       die2 = random.randrange( 1, 7 )
9       workSum = die1 + die2
10      print "Player rolled %d + %d = %d" % ( die1, die2, workSum )
11
12      return workSum
13
14  sum = rollDice()                                # first dice roll
15
```

Fig. 4.8   Game of craps. (Part 1 of 2.)

```
16   if sum == 7 or sum == 11:               # win on first roll
17      gameStatus = "WON"
18   elif sum == 2 or sum == 3 or sum == 12:  # lose on first roll
19      gameStatus = "LOST"
20   else:                                    # remember point
21      gameStatus = "CONTINUE"
22      myPoint = sum
23      print "Point is", myPoint
24
25   while gameStatus == "CONTINUE":     # keep rolling
26      sum = rollDice()
27
28      if sum == myPoint:               # win by making point
29         gameStatus = "WON"
30      elif sum == 7:                   # lose by rolling 7:
31         gameStatus = "LOST"
32
33   if gameStatus == "WON":
34      print "Player wins"
35   else:
36      print "Player loses"
```

```
Player rolled 2 + 5 = 7
Player wins
```

```
Player rolled 1 + 2 = 3
Player loses
```

```
Player rolled 1 + 5 = 6
Point is 6
Player rolled 1 + 6 = 7
Player loses
```

```
Player rolled 5 + 4 = 9
Point is 9
Player rolled 4 + 4 = 8
Player rolled 2 + 3 = 5
Player rolled 5 + 4 = 9
Player wins
```

Fig. 4.8   Game of craps. (Part 2 of 2.)

Notice that the player must roll two dice on each roll. Function **rollDice** simulates rolling the dice (lines 6–12). Function **rollDice** is defined once, but it is called from two places in the program (lines 14 and 26). The function takes no arguments, so the parameter list is empty. Function **rollDice** prints and returns the sum of the two dice (lines 10–12).

The game is reasonably involved. The player could win or lose on the first roll or on any subsequent roll. The variable **gameStatus** keeps track of the win/loss status. Variable **gameStatus** is one of the strings **"WON"**, **"LOST"** or **"CONTINUE"**. When the player wins the game, **gameStatus** is set to **"WON"** (lines 17 and 29). When the player loses the game, **gameStatus** is set to **"LOST"** (lines 19 and 31). Otherwise, **gameStatus** is set to **"CONTINUE"**, allowing the dice to be rolled again (line 21).

If the game is won or lost after the first roll, the body of the **while** structure (lines 25–31) is skipped, because **gameStatus** is not equal to **"CONTINUE"** (line 25). Instead, the program proceeds to the **if/else** structure (lines 33–36), which prints **"Player wins"** if **gameStatus** equals **"WON"**, but **"Player loses"** if **gameStatus** equals **"LOST"**.

If the game is not won or lost after the first roll, the value of **sum** is assigned to variable **myPoint** (line 22). Execution proceeds with the **while** structure, because **gameStatus** equals **"CONTINUE"**. During each iteration of the **while** loop, **rollDice** is invoked to produce a new **sum** (line 26). If **sum** matches **myPoint**, **gameStatus** is set to **"WON"** (lines 28–29), the **while** test fails (line 25), the **if/else** structure prints **"Player wins"** (lines 33–34) and execution terminates. If **sum** is equal to **7**, **gameStatus** is set to **"LOST"** (lines 30–31), the **while** test fails (line 25), the **if/else** statement prints **"Player loses"** (lines 35–36) and execution terminates. Otherwise, the **while** loop continues executing.

Note the use of the various program-control mechanisms discussed earlier. The craps program uses one programmer-defined function—**rollDice**—and the **while**, **if/else** and **if/elif/else** structures. The program uses both stacked control structures (the **if/elif/else** in lines 16–23 and the **while** in lines 25–31) and nested control structures (the **if/elif** in lines 28–31 is nested inside the **while** in lines 25–31).

4.8 Scope Rules[2]

Until now, we have not discussed how a Python program stores and retrieves a variable's value. It appears that the value is simply "there" when the program needs it. In fact, Python has strict rules that describe how and when a variable's value can be accessed. These rules are described in terms of *namespaces* and *scopes*. In this section, we discuss how namespaces and scopes affect a program's execution.

We use an example to explain these concepts. Assume that a function contains the following line of code:

```
print x
```

Before a value can be printed to the screen, Python must first find the identifier named **x** and determine the value associated with that identifier. Namespaces store information about an identifier and the value to which it is bound. Python defines three namespaces—local, global and built-in. When a program attempts to access an identifier's value, Python searches the namespaces in a certain order—local, global and built-in namespaces—to see whether and where the identifier exists.

---

2. Nested scopes are not discussed in this text. Nested scopes are a complex topic and were optional in Python 2.1 but are mandatory in Python 2.2. Information about nested scopes can be found in PEP 227 at **www.python.org/peps/pep-0227.html**.

The first namespace that Python searches is the *local namespace*, which stores bindings created in a block. Function bodies are blocks, so all function parameters and any identifiers the function creates are stored in the function's local namespace. Each function has a unique local namespace—one function cannot access the local namespace of another function. In the example above, Python first searches the function's local namespace for an identifier named **x**. If the function's local namespace contains such an identifier, the function prints the value of **x** to the screen. If the function's local namespace does not contain an identifier named **x** (e.g., the function does not define any parameters or create any identifiers named **x**), Python searches the next outer namespace—the *global namespace* (sometimes called the *module namespace*).

The global namespace contains the bindings for all identifiers, function names and class names defined within a module or file. Each module or file's global namespace contains an identifier called **__name__** that states the module's name (e.g., **"math"** or **"random"**). When a Python interpreter session starts or when the Python interpreter begins executing a program stored in a file, the value of **__name__** is **"__main__"**. In the example above, Python searches for an identifier named **x** in the global namespace. If the global namespace contains the identifier (i.e., the identifier was bound to the global namespace before the function was called), Python stops searching for the identifier and the function prints the value of **x** to the screen. If the global namespace does not contain an identifier named **x**, Python searches the next outer namespace—the *built-in namespace*.

The built-in namespace contains identifiers that correspond to many Python functions and error messages. For example, functions **raw_input**, **int** and **range** belong to the built-in namespace. Python creates the built-in namespace when the interpreter starts, and programs normally do not modify the namespace (e.g., by adding an identifier to the namespace). In the example above, the built-in namespace does not contain an identifier named **x**, so Python stops searching and prints an error message stating that the identifier could not be found.

An identifier's *scope* describes the region of a program that can access the identifier's value. If an identifier is defined in the local namespace (e.g., in a function), all statements in the block may access that identifier. Statements that reside outside the block (e.g., in the main portion of a program or in another function) cannot access the identifier. Once the code block terminates (e.g., after a **return** statement), all identifiers in that block's local namespace "go out of scope" and are inaccessible.

If an identifier is defined in the global namespace, the identifier has *global scope*. A global identifier is known to all code that executes, from the point at which the identifier is created until the end of the file. Furthermore, if certain criteria are met, functions may access global identifiers. We discuss this issue momentarily. Identifiers contained in built-in namespaces may be accessed by code in programs, modules or functions.

One pitfall that can arise in a program that uses functions is called *shadowing*. When a function creates a local identifier with the same name as an identifier in the module or built-in namespaces, the local identifier shadows the global or built-in identifier. A logic error can occur if the programmer references the local variable when meaning to reference the global or built-in identifier.

Common Programming Error 4.6

Shadowing an identifier in the module or built-in namespace with an identifier in the local namespace may result in a logic error.

Good Programming Practice 4.5

Avoid variable names that shadow names in outer scopes. This can be accomplished by avoiding the use of an identifier with the same name as an identifier in the built-in namespace and by avoiding the use of duplicate identifiers in a program.

Python provides a way for programmers to determine what identifiers are available from the current namespace. Built-in function **dir** returns a list of these identifiers. Figure 4.9 shows the namespace that Python creates when starting an interactive session. Calling function **dir** tells us that the current namespace contains three identifiers: **__builtins__**, **__doc__** and **__name__**. The next command in the session prints the value for identifier **__name__**, to demonstrate that this value is **__main__** for an interactive session. The subsequent command prints the value for identifier **__builtins__**. Notice that we get back a value indicating that this identifier is bound to a module. This indicates that the identifier **__builtins__** can be used to refer to the module **__builtin__**. We explore this further in Section 4.9. The next command in the interactive session creates a new identifier **x** and binds it to the value **3**. Calling function **dir** again reveals that identifier **x** has been added to the session's namespace.

The interactive session in Fig. 4.9 only hints at a Python program's powerful ability to provide information about the identifiers in a program (or interactive session). This is called *introspection*. Python provides many other introspective capabilities, including functions **globals** and **locals** that return additional information about the global and local namespaces, respectively.

Although functions help make a program easier to debug, scoping issues can introduce subtle errors into a program if the developer is not careful. The program in Fig. 4.10 demonstrates these issues, using global and local variables. Line 4 creates variable **x** with the value 1. This variable resides in the global namespace for the program and has global scope. In other words, variable **x** can be accessed and changed by any code that appears after line 4. This global variable is shadowed in any function that creates a local variable named **x**. In the main program, line 22 prints the value of variable **x** (i.e., 1). Lines 24–25 assign the value 7 to variable **x** and print its new value.

```
Python 2.2b2 (#26, Nov 16 2001, 11:44:11) [MSC 32 bit (Intel)] on
win32
Type "help", "copyright", "credits" or "license" for more informa-
tion.
>>> dir()
['__builtins__', '__doc__', '__name__']
>>> print __name__
__main__
>>> print __builtins__
<module '__builtin__' (built-in)>
>>> x = 3    # bind new identifier to global namespace
>>> dir()
['__builtins__', '__doc__', '__name__', 'x']
```

Fig. 4.9   Function **dir**.

```
1   # Fig. 4.10: fig04_10.py
2   # Scoping example.
3
4   x = 1 # global variable
5
6   # alters the local variable x, shadows the global variable
7   def a():
8      x = 25
9
10     print "\nlocal x in a is", x, "after entering a"
11     x += 1
12     print "local x in a is", x, "before exiting a"
13
14  # alters the global variable x
15  def b():
16     global x
17
18     print "\nglobal x is", x, "on entering b"
19     x *= 10
20     print "global x is", x, "on exiting b"
21
22  print "global x is", x
23
24  x = 7
25  print "global x is", x
26
27  a()
28  b()
29  a()
30  b()
31
32  print "\nglobal x is", x
```

```
global x is 1
global x is 7

local x in a is 25 after entering a
local x in a is 26 before exiting a

global x is 7 on entering b
global x is 70 on exiting b

local x in a is 25 after entering a
local x in a is 26 before exiting a

global x is 70 on entering b
global x is 700 on exiting b

global x is 700
```

Fig. 4.10 Scopes and keyword `global`.

The program defines two functions that neither receive nor return any arguments. Function **a** (lines 7–12) declares a local variable **x** and initializes it to 25. Then, function **a** prints local variable **x**, increments it and prints it again (lines 10–12). Each time the program invokes the function, function **a** recreates local variable **x** and initializes the variable to 25, then increments it to 26.

Function **b** (lines 15–20) does not declare any variables. Instead, line 16 designates **x** as having global scope with keyword **global**. Therefore, when function **b** refers to variable **x**, Python searches the global namespace for identifier **x**. When the program first invokes function **b** (line 28), the program prints the value of the global variable (7), multiplies the value by 10 and prints the value of the global variable (70) again before exiting the function. The second time the program invokes function **b** (line 30), the global variable contains the modified value, 70. Finally, line 32 prints the global variable **x** in the main program again (700) to show that function **b** has modified the value of this variable.

4.9 Keyword **import** and Namespaces

We have discussed how to import a module and use the functions defined in that module. In this section, we explore how importing a module affects a program's namespace and discuss various ways to import modules into a program.

4.9.1 Importing One or More Modules

Consider a program that needs to perform one of the specialized mathematical operations defined in module **math**. The program must first import the module with the line

```
import math
```

The code that imports the module now has a reference to the **math** module in its namespace. After the **import** statement, the program may access any identifiers defined in the **math** module.

The interactive session in Fig. 4.11 demonstrates how an **import** statement affects the session's namespace and how a program can access identifiers defined in a module's namespace. The first line imports the **math** module. The next line then calls function **dir**, to demonstrate that the identifier **math** has been inserted in the session's namespace. As the subsequent **print** statement shows, the identifier is bound to an object that represents the **math** module. If we pass identifier **math** to function **dir**, the function returns a list of all the identifiers in the **math** module's namespace.[3] [*Note*: Earlier versions of Python may output different results for **dir()**.]

The next command in the session invokes function **sqrt**. To access an identifier in the **math** module's namespace, we must use the dot (**.**) access operator. The line

```
math.sqrt( 9.0 )
```

first accesses (with the dot access operator) function **sqrt** defined in the **math** module's namespace. The line then invokes (with the parentheses operator) the **sqrt** function, passing an argument of **9.0**.

If a program needs to import several modules, the program can include a separate **import** statement for each module. A program can also import multiple modules in one statement, by separating the module names with commas. Each imported module is added to the program's namespace as demonstrated in the interactive session of Fig. 4.12.

---

3. Actually, function **dir** returns a list of attributes for the object passed as an argument. In the case of a module, this information amounts to a list of all identifiers (e.g., functions and data) defined in the module.

```
Python 2.2b2 (#26, Nov 16 2001, 11:44:11) [MSC 32 bit (Intel)] on
win32
Type "help", "copyright", "credits" or "license" for more informa-
tion.
>>> import math
>>> dir()
['__builtins__', '__doc__', '__name__', 'math']
>>> print math
<module 'math' (built-in)>
>>> dir( math )
['__doc__', '__name__', 'acos', 'asin', 'atan', 'atan2', 'ceil',
'cos', 'cosh','e', 'exp', 'fabs', 'floor', 'fmod', 'frexp', 'hy-
pot', 'ldexp', 'log', 'log10','modf', 'pi', 'pow', 'sin', 'sinh',
'sqrt', 'tan', 'tanh']
>>> math.sqrt( 9.0 )
3.0
```

Fig. 4.11   Importing a module.

```
Python 2.2b2 (#26, Nov 16 2001, 11:44:11) [MSC 32 bit (Intel)] on
win32
Type "help", "copyright", "credits" or "license" for more informa-
tion.
>>> import math, random
>>> dir()
['__builtins__', '__doc__', '__name__', 'math', 'random']
```

Fig. 4.12   Importing more than one module.

4.9.2 Importing Identifiers from a Module

In the previous example, we discussed how to access an identifier defined in another module's namespace. To access that identifier, the programmer must use the dot (**.**) access operator. Sometimes, a program uses only one or a few identifiers from a module. In this case,
it may be useful to import only those identifiers the program needs. Python provides the
from/import statement to import one or more identifiers from a module directly into the
program's namespace.

The interactive session in Fig. 4.13 imports the **sqrt** function directly into the session's namespace. When the interpreter executes the line

> **from** math **import** sqrt

the interpreter creates a reference to function **math.sqrt** and places the reference directly into the session's namespace. Now, we can call the function directly without using the
dot operator. Just as a program can import multiple modules in one statement, a program
can import multiple identifiers from a module in one statement. The line

> **from** math **import** sin, cos, tan

imports **math** functions **sin**, **cos** and **tan** directly into the session's namespace. After
the **import** statement, a call to function **dir** reveals references to each of these functions.

```
Python 2.2b2 (#26, Nov 16 2001, 11:44:11) [MSC 32 bit (Intel)] on
win32
Type "help", "copyright", "credits" or "license" for more informa-
tion.
>>> from math import sqrt
>>> dir()
['__builtins__', '__doc__', '__name__', 'sqrt']
>>> sqrt( 9.0 )
3.0
>>> from math import sin, cos, tan
>>> dir()
['__builtins__', '__doc__', '__name__', 'cos', 'sin', 'sqrt',
'tan']
```

Fig. 4.13   Importing an identifier from a module.

The interactive session in Fig. 4.14 demonstrates that a program also may import *all* identifiers defined in a module. The statement

```
from math import *
```

imports all identifiers that do not start with an underscore from the **math** module into the interactive session's namespace. Now the programmer can invoke any of the functions from the **math** module, without accessing the function through the dot access operator. However, importing a module's identifiers in this way can lead to serious errors and is considered a dangerous programming practice. Consider a situation in which a program had defined an identifier named **e** and assigned it the string value **"e"**. After executing the preceding **import** statement, identifier **e** is bound to the mathematical floating-point constant *e*, and the previous value for **e** is no longer accessible. In general, a program should never import all identifiers from a module in this way.

Testing and Debugging Tip 4.3

In general, avoid importing all identifiers from a module into the namespace of another module. This method of importing a module should be used only for modules provided by trusted sources, whose documentation explicitly states that such a statement may be used to import the module.

```
Python 2.2b2 (#26, Nov 16 2001, 11:44:11) [MSC 32 bit (Intel)] on
win32
Type "help", "copyright", "credits" or "license" for more informa-
tion.
>>> from math import *
>>> dir()
['__builtins__', '__doc__', '__name__', 'acos', 'asin', 'atan',
'atan2', 'ceil', 'cos', 'cosh', 'e', 'exp', 'fabs', 'floor',
'fmod', 'frexp', 'hypot', 'ldexp','log', 'log10', 'modf', 'pi',
'pow', 'sin', 'sinh', 'sqrt', 'tan', 'tanh']
```

Fig. 4.14   Importing all identifiers from a module.

4.9.3 Binding Names for Modules and Module Identifiers

We have already seen how a program can import a module or specific identifiers from a module. Python's syntax gives the programmer considerable control over how the **import** statement affects a program's namespace. In this section, we discuss this control in more detail and explain further how the programmer can customize the references to imported elements.

The statement

```
import random
```

imports the **random** module and places a reference to the module named **random** in the namespace. In the interactive session in Fig. 4.15, the statement

```
import random as randomModule
```

also imports the **random** module, but the *as* clause of the statement allows the programmer to specify the name of the reference to the module. In this case, we create a reference named **randomModule**. Now, if we want to access the **random** module, we use reference **randomModule**.

A program can also use an **import/as** statement to specify a name for an identifier that the program imports from a module. The line

```
from math import sqrt as squareRoot
```

imports the **sqrt** function from module **math** and creates a reference to the function named **squareRoot**. The programmer may now invoke the function with this reference.

Typically, module authors use **import/as** statements, because the imported element may define names that conflict with identifiers already defined by the author's module. With the **import/as** statement, the module author can specify a new name for the imported elements and thereby avoid the naming conflict. Programmers also use the **import/as** statement for convenience. A programmer may use the statement to rename a particularly long identifier that the program uses extensively. The programmer specifies a shorter name for the identifier, thus increasing readability and decreasing the amount of typing.

```
Python 2.2b2 (#26, Nov 16 2001, 11:44:11) [MSC 32 bit (Intel)] on
win32
Type "help", "copyright", "credits" or "license" for more informa-
tion.
>>> import random as randomModule
>>> dir()
['__builtins__', '__doc__', '__name__', 'randomModule']
>>> randomModule.randrange( 1, 7 )
1
>>> from math import sqrt as squareRoot
>>> dir()
['__builtins__', '__doc__', '__name__', 'randomModule', 'square-
Root']
>>> squareRoot( 9.0 )
3.0
```

Fig. 4.15 Specifying names for imported elements.

Python's capabilities for importing elements into a program supports component-based programming. The programmer should choose syntax Python appropriate for each situation, keeping in mind that the goal of component-based programming is to create programs that are easier to construct and maintain.

4.10 Recursion

The programs we have discussed thus far generally are structured as functions that call one another in a disciplined, hierarchical manner. For some problems, however, it is useful to have functions call themselves. A *recursive function* is a function that calls itself, either directly or indirectly (through another function). Recursion is an important topic discussed at length in upper-level computer-science courses. In this section and the next, we present simple examples of recursion.

We first consider recursion conceptually and then illustrate several recursive functions. Recursive problem-solving approaches have a number of elements in common. A recursive function is called to solve a problem. The function actually knows how to solve only the simplest case(s), or so-called *base case(s)*. If the function is not called with a base case, the function divides the problem into two conceptual pieces—a piece that the function knows how to solve (a base case) and a piece that the function does not know how to solve. To make recursion feasible, the latter piece must resemble the original problem, but be a slightly simpler or slightly smaller version of the original problem. Because this new problem looks like the original problem, the function invokes (calls) a fresh copy of itself to go to work on the smaller problem; this is referred to as a *recursive call* and is also called the *recursion step*. The recursion step normally includes the keyword **return**, because this result will be combined with the portion of the problem the function knew how to solve to form a result that will be passed back to the original caller.

The recursion step executes while the original call to the function is still open (i.e., while it has not finished executing). The recursion step can result in many more such recursive calls, as the function divides each new subproblem into two conceptual pieces. For the recursion eventually to terminate, the sequence of smaller and smaller problems must converge on a base case. At that point, the function recognizes the base case and returns a result to the previous copy of the function, and a sequence of returns ensues up the line until the original function call eventually returns the final result to the caller. This process sounds exotic when compared with the conventional problem solving techniques we have used to this point. As an example of these concepts at work, let us write a recursive program to perform a popular mathematical calculation.

The factorial of a nonnegative integer n, written $n!$ (and pronounced "n factorial"), is the product

$$n \cdot (n-1) \cdot (n-2) \cdot \ldots \cdot 1$$

with 1! equal to 1, and 0! equal to 1. For example, 5! is the product $5 \cdot 4 \cdot 3 \cdot 2 \cdot 1$, which is equal to 120.

The factorial of an integer, **number**, greater than or equal to 0 can be calculated iteratively (nonrecursively) using **for**, as follows:

```
factorial = 1

for counter in range( 1, number + 1 ):
    factorial *= counter
```

A recursive definition of the factorial function is obtained by observing the following relationship:

$$n! = n \cdot (n - 1)!$$

For example, 5! is clearly equal to 5 * 4!, as is shown by the following equations:

$$5! = 5 \cdot 4 \cdot 3 \cdot 2 \cdot 1$$
$$5! = 5 \cdot (4 \cdot 3 \cdot 2 \cdot 1)$$
$$5! = 5 \cdot (4!)$$

The evaluation of 5! would proceed as shown in Fig. 4.16. Figure 4.16 (a) shows how the succession of recursive calls proceeds until 1! evaluates to 1, which terminates the recursion. Figure 4.16 (b) shows the values returned from each recursive call to its caller until the final value is calculated and returned.

Figure 4.17 uses recursion to calculate and print the factorials of the integers from 0 to 10. The recursive function **factorial** (lines 5–10) first tests to determine whether a terminating condition is true (line 7)—if **number** is less than or equal to **1** (the base case), **factorial** returns 1, no further recursion is necessary and the function terminates. Otherwise, if **number** is greater than **1**, line 10 expresses the problem as the product of **number** and a recursive call to **factorial** evaluating the factorial of **number - 1**. Note that **factorial(number - 1)** is a simpler version of the original calculation, **factorial(number)**.

Common Programming Error 4.7

Either omitting the base case or writing the recursion step incorrectly so that it does not converge on the base case will cause infinite recursion, eventually exhausting memory. This is analogous to the problem of an infinite loop in an iterative (nonrecursive) solution.

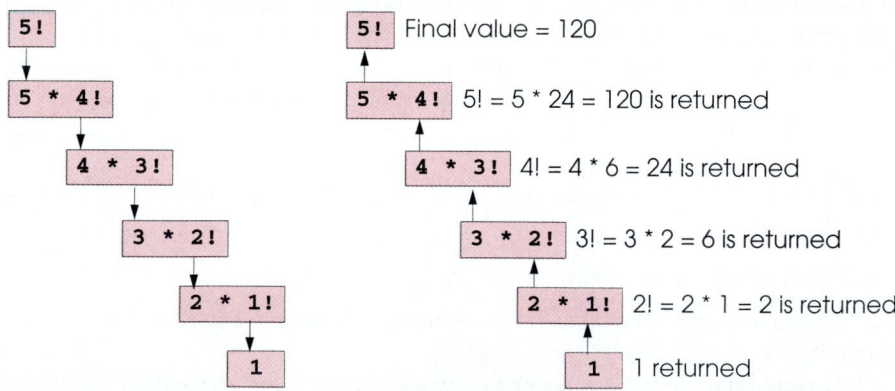

(a) Procession of recursive calls   (b) Values returned from each recursive call

Fig. 4.16   Recursive evaluation of 5!.

```
1   # Fig. 4.17: fig04_17.py
2   # Recursive factorial function.
3
4   # Recursive definition of function factorial
5   def factorial( number ):
6
7       if number <= 1:    # base case
8           return 1
9       else:
10          return number * factorial( number - 1 )   # recursive call
11
12  for i in range( 11 ):
13      print "%2d! = %d" % ( i, factorial( i ) )
```

```
 0! = 1
 1! = 1
 2! = 2
 3! = 6
 4! = 24
 5! = 120
 6! = 720
 7! = 5040
 8! = 40320
 9! = 362880
10! = 3628800
```

Fig. 4.17 Recursive function used to calculate factorials.

4.11 Example Using Recursion: The Fibonacci Series

The Fibonacci series

0, 1, 1, 2, 3, 5, 8, 13, 21, …

begins with 0 and 1 and has the property that each subsequent Fibonacci number is the sum of the previous two Fibonacci numbers.

The series occurs in nature, in particular, describing a spiral. The ratio of successive Fibonacci numbers converges on a constant value of 1.618…. This number, too, repeatedly occurs in nature and has been called the *golden ratio*, or the *golden mean.* Humans tend to find the golden mean aesthetically pleasing. Architects often design windows, rooms, and buildings whose length and width are in the ratio of the golden mean. Postcards often are designed with a golden-mean length/width ratio.

The Fibonacci series can be defined recursively as follows:

fibonacci(0) = 0
fibonacci(1) = 1
fibonacci(n) = fibonacci($n - 1$) + fibonacci($n - 2$)

Note that there are two base cases for the Fibonacci calculation—fibonacci(0) is defined to be 0 and fibonacci(1) is defined to be 1. The program of Fig. 4.18 calculates the ith Fibonacci number recursively, using function **fibonacci** (lines 4–14). Notice that Fibonacci numbers increase rapidly. Each output box shows a separate execution of the program.

```
1   # Fig. 4.18: fig04_18.py
2   # Recursive fibonacci function.
3
4   def fibonacci( n ):
5
6      if n < 0:
7        print "Cannot find the fibonacci of a negative number."
8
9      if n == 0 or n == 1:    # base case
10        return n
11     else:
12
13        # two recursive calls
14        return fibonacci( n - 1 ) + fibonacci( n - 2 )
15
16  number = int( raw_input( "Enter an integer: " ) )
17  result = fibonacci( number )
18  print "Fibonacci(%d) = %d" % ( number, result )
```

```
Enter an integer: 0
Fibonacci(0) = 0
```

```
Enter an integer: 1
Fibonacci(1) = 1
```

```
Enter an integer: 2
Fibonacci(2) = 1
```

```
Enter an integer: 3
Fibonacci(3) = 2
```

```
Enter an integer: 4
Fibonacci(4) = 3
```

```
Enter an integer: 6
Fibonacci(6) = 8
```

```
Enter an integer: 10
Fibonacci(10) = 55
```

Fig. 4.18 Recursively generating Fibonacci numbers. (Part 1 of 2.)

```
Enter an integer: 20
Fibonacci(20) = 6765
```

Fig. 4.18 Recursively generating Fibonacci numbers. (Part 2 of 2.)

The initial call to **fibonacci** (line 17) is not a recursive call, but all subsequent calls to **fibonacci** performed from the body of **fibonacci** are recursive. Each time **fibonacci** is invoked, it tests for the base case—**n** equal to 0 or 1. If this condition is true, **fibonacci** returns **n** (line 10). Interestingly, if **n** is greater than 1, the recursion step generates *two* recursive calls (line 14), each of which is a simpler problem than the original call to **fibonacci**. Figure 4.19 illustrates **fibonacci** evaluating **fibonacci(3)**.

A word of caution is in order about recursive programs like the one we use here to generate Fibonacci numbers. Each invocation of the **fibonacci** function that does not match one of the base cases (i.e., 0 or 1) results in two more recursive calls to **fibonacci**. This set of recursive calls rapidly gets out of hand. Calculating the Fibonacci value of 20 using the program in Fig. 4.18 requires 21,891 calls to the **fibonacci** function; calculating the Fibonacci value of 30 requires 2,692,537 calls to the **fibonacci** function.

As you try to calculate larger Fibonacci values, you will notice that each consecutive Fibonacci number results in a substantial increase in calculation time and number of calls to the **fibonacci** function. For example, the Fibonacci value of 31 requires 4,356,617 calls, and the Fibonacci value of 32 requires 7,049,155 calls. As you can see, the number of calls to fibonacci is increasing quickly—2,692,538 additional calls between Fibonacci values of 31 and 32. This difference in number of calls made between Fibonacci values of 31 and 32 is more than 1.5 times the number of calls for Fibonacci values between 30 and 31. Computer scientists refer to this as *exponential complexity*. Problems of this nature humble even the world's most powerful computers! In the field of complexity theory, computer scientists study how hard algorithms work to complete their tasks. Complexity issues are discussed in detail in the upper-level computer-science course generally called "Algorithms" or "Complexity."

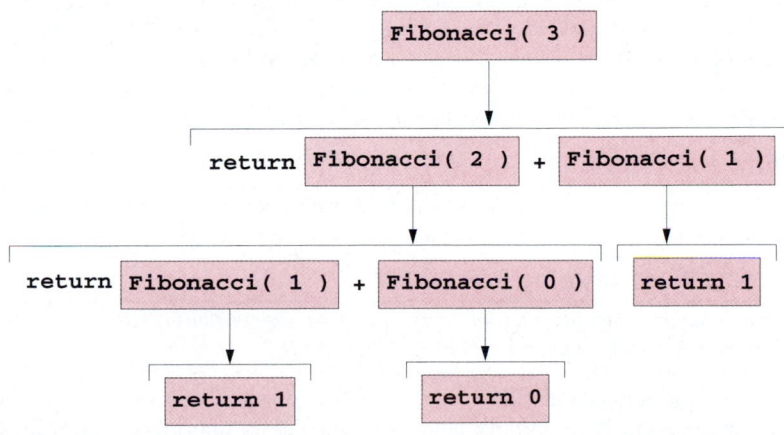

Fig. 4.19 Recursive call to function **fibonacci**.

Performance Tip 4.2

Avoid Fibonacci-style recursive programs that result in an exponential "explosion" of calls.

4.12 Recursion vs. Iteration

In the previous sections, we studied two functions that can be implemented either recursively or iteratively. In this section, we compare the two approaches and discuss why the programmer might choose one approach over the other in a particular situation.

Both iteration and recursion are based on a control structure: Iteration uses a repetition structure (such as **for** and **while**); recursion uses a selection structure (such as **if** and **if/else**). Both iteration and recursion involve repetition: Iteration explicitly uses a repetition structure; recursion achieves repetition through repeated function calls. Iteration and recursion both involve a termination test: Iteration terminates when the loop-continuation condition fails; recursion terminates when a base case is recognized. Iteration with counter-controlled repetition and recursion each gradually approach termination: Iteration keeps modifying a counter until the counter assumes a value that makes the loop-continuation condition fail; recursion keeps producing simpler versions of the original problem until the base case is reached. Both iteration and recursion can occur infinitely: An infinite loop occurs with iteration if the loop-continuation test never becomes false; infinite recursion occurs if the recursion step does not reduce the problem each time in a manner that converges on the base case.

Recursion has many negatives. It repeatedly invokes the mechanism and, consequently, the overhead of function calls. This repetition can be expensive in both processor time and memory space. Each recursive call causes another copy of the function (actually only the function's variables) to be created; this set of copies can consume considerable memory. Iteration normally occurs within a function, so the overhead of repeated function calls and extra memory assignment is omitted. So why choose recursion?

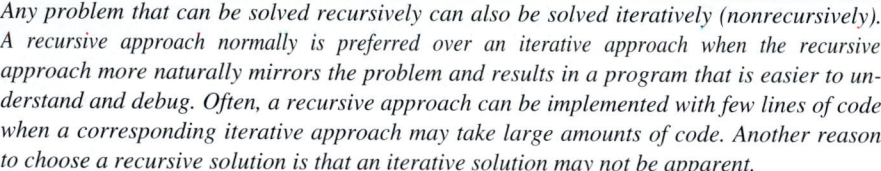

Software Engineering Observation 4.8

Any problem that can be solved recursively can also be solved iteratively (nonrecursively). A recursive approach normally is preferred over an iterative approach when the recursive approach more naturally mirrors the problem and results in a program that is easier to understand and debug. Often, a recursive approach can be implemented with few lines of code when a corresponding iterative approach may take large amounts of code. Another reason to choose a recursive solution is that an iterative solution may not be apparent.

Performance Tip 4.3

Avoid using recursion in performance situations. Recursive calls take time and consume additional memory.

Common Programming Error 4.8

Accidentally having a function that solves a non-recursive algorithm call itself, either directly or indirectly (through another function), is a logic error.

Let us reconsider some observations that we make repeatedly throughout the book. Good software engineering is important. High performance is important. Unfortunately, these goals are often at odds with one another. Good software engineering is key to making more manageable the task of developing the larger and more complex software systems. High performance in these systems is key to realizing the systems of the future, which will place ever-greater computing demands on hardware. Where do functions fit in here?

Software Engineering Observation 4.9

Functionalizing programs in a neat, hierarchical manner promotes good software engineering, but it has a price.

Performance Tip 4.4

A heavily functionalized program—as compared with a monolithic (i.e., one-piece) program without functions—makes potentially large numbers of function calls, and these consume execution time and memory space on a computer's processor(s). But monolithic programs are difficult to program, test, debug and maintain.

So functionalize programs judiciously, always keeping in mind the delicate balance between performance and good software engineering.

4.13 Default Arguments

Function calls may commonly pass a particular value of an argument. When defining a function, the programmer can specify an argument as a *default argument,* and the programmer can provide a default value for that argument. Default arguments are a convenience; they allow the programmer to specify fewer arguments when calling a function. When a default argument is omitted in a function call, the interpreter inserts the default value of that argument and passes the argument in the call.

Default arguments must appear to the right of any non-default arguments in a function's parameter list. When calling a function with two or more default arguments, if an omitted argument is not the rightmost argument in the argument list, all arguments to the right of that argument also must be omitted.

Figure 4.20 demonstrates using default arguments in calculating the volume of a box. The function definition for **boxVolume** in line 5 specifies that all three arguments have been given default values of 1. Note that default values should be defined only in the function's **def** statement.

```
1   # Fig. 4.20: fig04_20.py
2   # Using default arguments.
3
4   # function definition with default arguments
5   def boxVolume( length = 1, width = 1, height = 1 ):
6      return length * width * height
7
8   print "The default box volume is:", boxVolume()
9   print "\nThe volume of a box with length 10,"
10  print "width 1 and height 1 is:", boxVolume( 10 )
11  print "\nThe volume of a box with length 10,"
12  print "width 5 and height 1 is:", boxVolume( 10, 5 )
13  print "\nThe volume of a box with length 10,"
14  print "width 5 and height 2 is:", boxVolume( 10, 5, 2 )
```

Fig. 4.20   Default arguments. (Part 1 of 2.)

```
The default box volume is: 1

The volume of a box with length 10,
width 1 and height 1 is: 10

The volume of a box with length 10,
width 5 and height 1 is: 50

The volume of a box with length 10,
width 5 and height 2 is: 100
```

Fig. 4.20   Default arguments. (Part 2 of 2.)

The first call to **boxVolume** (line 8) specifies no arguments and thus uses all three default values. The second call (line 10) passes a **length** argument and thus uses default values for the **width** and **height** arguments. The third call (line 12) passes arguments for **length** and **width** and thus uses a default value for the **height** argument. The last call (line 14) passes arguments for **length**, **width** and **height**, thus using no default values.

Good Programming Practice 4.6

Using default arguments can simplify writing function calls. However, some programmers feel that explicitly specifying all arguments makes programs easier to read.

Common Programming Error 4.9

Default arguments must be the rightmost (trailing) arguments. Omitting an argument other than a rightmost argument is a syntax error.

4.14 Keyword Arguments

The programmer can specify that a function receives one or more *keyword arguments*. The function definition assigns a default value to each keyword. A function may use a default value for a keyword or a function call may assign a new value to the keyword using the format **keyword = value**. When using keyword arguments, the position of arguments in the function call is not required to match the position of the corresponding parameters in the function definition. Figure 4.21 demonstrates using keyword arguments in a Python program that displays information about a requested Web site.

```
1   # Fig. 4.21: fig04_21.py
2   # Keyword arguments example.
3
4   def generateWebsite( name, url = "www.deitel.com",
5      Flash = "no", CGI = "yes" ):
6      print "Generating site requested by", name, "using url", url
7
8      if Flash == "yes":
9         print "Flash is enabled"
10
```

Fig. 4.21   Keyword parameters. (Part 1 of 2.)

```
11       if CGI == "yes":
12           print "CGI scripts are enabled"
13       print  # prints a new line
14
15   generateWebsite( "Deitel" )
16
17   generateWebsite( "Deitel", Flash = "yes",
18       url = "www.deitel.com/new" )
19
20   generateWebsite( CGI = "no", name = "Prentice Hall" )
```

```
Generating site requested by Deitel using url www.deitel.com
CGI scripts are enabled

Generating site requested by Deitel using url www.deitel.com/new
Flash is enabled
CGI scripts are enabled

Generating site requested by Prentice Hall using url www.deitel.com
```

Fig. 4.21   Keyword parameters. (Part 2 of 2.)

Function **generateWebsite** takes four arguments. The keyword argument names **url**, **Flash** and **CGI** are assigned the default values **"www.deitel.com"**, **"no"** and **"yes"**, respectively (lines 4–5). The function identifies who is requesting the Web site and displays a message if the Web site is Flash- or CGI-enabled (lines 6–13).

The function call in line 15 passes one argument, a value for **name**, to function **generateWebsite**. The function uses the default values given in the definition for the other parameters.

The function call in lines 17–18 passes three arguments to **generateWebsite**. Variable **name** again has the value **"Deitel"**. The call also assigns the value **"yes"** to keyword argument **Flash** and **"www.deitel.com/new"** to keyword argument **url**. This function call illustrates that the order of keyword arguments is more flexible than that of regular arguments in an ordinary function call. The Python interpreter matches the value **"Deitel"** with variable **name** by its position in the function call. The Python interpreter matches the values passed to **url** and **Flash** by their keyword argument names rather than by their positions in the function call. The value of **name** must come first in any call to **generateWebsite** if it is not referenced by specifying a value for **name** in the argument list. Line 20 demonstrates that any function argument can be referenced as a keyword even if it has no default value.

The interactive session of Fig. 4.22 demonstrates common errors when mixing non-keyword and keyword arguments. Function call **test(number1 = "two", "Name")** causes an error, because the non-keyword argument is placed after the keyword argument. Function call **test(number1 = "three")** is incorrect, because function test expects one non-keyword argument.

Common Programming Error 4.10

Misplacing or omitting the value for a non-keyword argument in a function call is an error.

```
Python 2.2b2 (#26, Nov 16 2001, 11:44:11) [MSC 32 bit (Intel)] on
win32
Type "help", "copyright", "credits" or "license" for more informa-
tion.
>>> def test( name, number1 = "one", number2 = "two" ):
...     pass
...
>>> test( number1 = "two", "Name" )
SyntaxError: non-keyword arg after keyword arg
>>> test( number1 = "three" )
Traceback (most recent call last):
  File "<stdin>", line 1, in ?
TypeError: test() takes at least 1 non-keyword argument (0 given)
```

Fig. 4.22 Errors with keyword arguments.

SUMMARY

- Constructing a large program from smaller components, each of which is more manageable than the original program, is a technique called divide and conquer.

- Components in Python are called functions, classes, modules and packages.

- Python programs typically are written by combining new functions and classes the programmer writes with "pre-packaged" functions or classes available in numerous Python modules.

- The programmer can write programmer-defined functions to define specific tasks that could be used at many points in a program.

- A module defines related classes, functions and data. A package groups related modules. The package as a whole provides tools to help the programmer accomplish a general task.

- A function is invoked (i.e., made to perform its designated task) by a function call.

- The function call specifies the function name and provides information (as a comma-separated list of arguments) that the called function needs to do its job.

- All variables created in function definitions are local variables—they are known only in the function in which they are created.

- Most functions have a list of parameters that provide the means for communicating information between functions. A function's parameters are also local variables.

- The divide-and-conquer approach makes program development more manageable.

- Another motivation for using the divide-and-conquer approach is software reusability—using existing functions as building blocks to create new programs.

- A third motivation for using the divide-and-conquer approach is to avoid repeating code in a program. Packaging code as a function allows the code to be executed from several locations in a program simply by calling the function.

- The **math** module functions allow the programmer to perform certain common mathematical calculations.

- Functions normally are called by writing the name of the function, followed by a left parenthesis, followed by the argument (or a comma-separated list of arguments) of the function, followed by a right parenthesis.

- To use a function that is defined in a module, a program has to import the module, using keyword **import**. After the module has been imported, the program can access a function or a variable in the module, using the module name, a dot (**.**) and the function or variable name.

- Functions are defined with keyword **def**.
- The indented statements that follow a **def** statement form the function body. The function body also is referred to as a block.
- There are three ways to return control to the point at which a function was invoked. If the function does not return a result, control is returned simply when the last indented line is reached, or upon executing **return**. If the function does return a result, the statement **return expression** returns the value of **expression** to the caller.
- **None** is a Python value that represents null— indicating that no value has been declared—and that evaluates to false in conditional expressions.
- The element of chance can be introduced into computer applications using module **random**.
- Function **randrange** generates an integer in the range of its first argument to, but not including, its second argument. If **randrange** truly produces integers at random, every number between the first argument and the second argument has an equal chance (or probability) of being chosen each time the function is called.
- Python has strict rules that describe how and when a variable's value can be accessed. These rules are described in terms of namespaces and scopes.
- Namespaces store information about an identifier and the value to which it is bound.
- Python defines three namespaces; when a program attempts to access an identifier's value, Python searches the namespaces in a specific order to see whether and where the identifier exists.
- The local namespace stores bindings created in a block. All function parameters and any identifiers the function creates are stored in the function's local namespace.
- The global (or module) namespace contains the bindings for all identifiers, function names and class names defined in a file or module.
- Each module's global namespace contains an identifier called **__name__** that provides the name for that module. When a Python interpreter session is started or when the Python interpreter is invoked on a program stored in a file, the value of **__name__** is **"__main__"**.
- The built-in namespace contains identifiers that correspond to many Python functions and errors. Python creates the built-in namespace when the interpreter starts, and programs normally do not modify the namespace (e.g., by adding an identifier to the namespace).
- An identifier's scope describes the region of a program that can access the identifier's value.
- If an identifier is defined in the local namespace (e.g., of a function), that identifier has local scope. Once the code block terminates (e.g., when a function returns), all identifiers in that block's local namespace "go out of scope" and no longer can be accessed.
- If an identifier is defined in the global namespace, the identifier has global scope. A global identifier is known to all code that executes within that module, from the point at which the identifier is created until the end of the file.
- When a function creates a local identifier with the same name as an identifier in the module or built-in namespaces, the local identifier is said to shadow the global or built-in identifier. The programmer can introduce a logic error into the program if the programmer refers to the local variable, but intends to refer to the global or built-in identifier.
- A recursive function is a function that calls itself, either directly or indirectly.
- A recursive function actually knows how to solve only the simplest case(s) or so-called base case(s) of a problem.
- If a recursive function is not called with a base case, the function divides the problem into two conceptual pieces: A piece that the function knows how to do (base case), and a piece that the function does not know how to do.

- A recursive function invokes a fresh copy of itself to go to work on a smaller version of the problem; this procedure is referred to as a recursive call and is also called the recursion step.

- Both iteration and recursion are based on a control structure: Iteration uses a repetition structure; recursion uses a selection structure.

- Both iteration and recursion also involve repetition: Iteration explicitly uses a repetition structure; recursion achieves repetition through repeated function calls.

- Iteration and recursion both involve a termination test: Iteration terminates when the loop-continuation condition fails; recursion terminates when a base case is recognized.

- Iteration with counter-controlled repetition and recursion both gradually approach termination: Iteration keeps modifying a counter until the counter assumes a value that makes the loop-continuation condition fail; recursion keeps producing simpler versions of the original problem until the base case is reached.

- Iteration and recursion can both occur infinitely: An infinite loop occurs with iteration if the loop-continuation test never becomes false; infinite recursion occurs if the recursion step does not reduce the problem each time in a manner that converges on the base case.

- Recursion repeatedly invokes the mechanism and, consequently, the overhead of function calls. This can be expensive in both processor time and memory space. Iteration normally occurs within a function, so the overhead of repeated function calls and extra memory assignment is omitted.

- Some function calls commonly pass a particular value of an argument. The programmer can specify that such an argument is a default argument, and the programmer can provide a default value for that argument. When a default argument is omitted in a function call, the interpreter automatically inserts the default value of that argument and passes the argument in the call.

- Default arguments must be the rightmost (trailing) arguments in a function's parameter list. When calling a function with two or more default arguments, if an omitted argument is not the rightmost argument in the argument list, all arguments to the right of that argument also must be omitted.

- The programmer can specify that a function receives one or more keyword arguments. The function definition can assign a value to a keyword argument. Either a function may a default value for a keyword argument or a function call may assign a new value to the keyword argument, using the format **keyword = value**.

TERMINOLOGY

acos function
asin function
atan function
base case
built-in namespace
__builtins__
calling function
ceil function
comma-separated list of arguments
cos function
def statement
default argument
dir function
divide and conquer
dot (**.**) operator
exp function
expression

fabs function
factorial
Fibonacci series
floor function
fmod function
function
function argument
function body
function call
function definition
function name
function parameter
global keyword
global namespace
global variable
globals function
hypot function

identifier
import keyword
iterative function
keyword argument
local namespace
local variable
locals function
log function
log10 function
"__main__"
main program
math module
module
module namespace

__name__
package
parameter list
probability
random module
randrange function
recursion
recursive function
return keyword
scope
sin function
sqrt function
tan function

SELF-REVIEW EXERCISES

4.1 Fill in the blanks in each of the following statements.
a) Constructing a large program from smaller components is called _____.
b) Components in Python are called _____, _____, _____ and _____.
c) "Pre-packaged" functions or classes are available in Python _____.
d) The _____ module functions allow programmers to perform common mathematical calculations.
e) The indented statements that follow a _____ statement form a function body.
f) The _____ in a function call is the operator that causes the function to be called.
g) The _____ module introduces the element of chance into Python programs.
h) A program can obtain the name of its module through identifier _____.
i) During code execution, three namespaces can be accessed: _____, _____ and _____.
j) A recursive function converges on the _____.

4.2 State whether each of the following is *true* or *false*. If *false*, explain why.
a) All variables declared in a function are global to the program containing the function.
b) An **import** statement must be included for every module function used in a program.
c) Function **fmod** returns the floating-point remainder of its two arguments.
d) The keyword **return** displays the result of a function.
e) A function's parameter list is a comma-separated list containing the names of the parameters received by the function when it is called.
f) Function call **random.randrange (1, 7)** produces a random integer in the range 1 to 7, inclusive.
g) An identifier's scope is the portion of the program in which the identifier has meaning.
h) Every call to a recursive function is a recursive call.
i) Omitting the base case in a recursive function can lead to "infinite" recursion.
j) A recursive function may call itself indirectly.

ANSWERS TO SELF-REVIEW EXERCISES

4.1 a) divide and conquer. b) functions, classes, modules, packages. c) modules. d) **math**. e) **def**. f) pair of parentheses. g) **random**. h) __name__. i) the local namespace, the global namespace, the built-in namespace. j) base case.

4.2   a) False. All variables declared in a function are local—known only in the function in which they are defined. b) False. Functions included in the __**builtin**__ module do not need to be imported. c) True. d) False. Keyword **return** passes control and optionally, the value of an expression, back to the point from which the function was called. e) True. f) False. Function call **random.randrange (1, 7)** produces a random integer in the range from 1 to 6, inclusive. g) True. h) False. The initial call to the recursive function is not recursive. i) True. j) True.

EXERCISES

4.3   Implement the following function **fahrenheit** to return the Fahrenheit equivalent of a Celsius temperature.

$$F = \frac{9}{5}C + 32$$

Use this function to write a program that prints a chart showing the Fahrenheit equivalents of all Celsius temperatures 0–100 degrees. Use one position of precision to the right of the decimal point for the results. Print the outputs in a neat tabular format that minimizes the number of lines of output while remaining readable.

4.4   An integer greater than 1 is said to be prime if it is divisible by only 1 and itself. For example, 2, 3, 5 and 7 are prime numbers, but 4, 6, 8 and 9 are not.
   a)   Write a function that determines whether a number is prime.
   b)   Use this function in a program that determines and prints all the prime numbers between 2 and 1,000.
   c)   Initially, you might think that $n/2$ is the upper limit for which you must test to see whether a number is prime, but you need go only as high as the square root of n. Rewrite the program and run it both ways to show that you get the same result.

4.5   An integer number is said to be a perfect number if the sum of its factors, including 1 (but not the number itself), is equal to the number. For example, 6 is a perfect number, because $6 = 1 + 2 + 3$. Write a function **perfect** that determines whether parameter **number** is a perfect number. Use this function in a program that determines and prints all the perfect numbers between 1 and 1000. Print the factors of each perfect number to confirm that the number is indeed perfect. Challenge the power of your computer by testing numbers much larger than 1000.

4.6   Computers are playing an increasing role in education. The use of computers in education is referred to as *computer-assisted instruction (CAI)*. Write a program that will help an elementary school student learn multiplication. Use the random module to produce two positive one-digit integers. The program should then display a question, such as

```
How much is 6 times 7?
```

The student then types the answer. Next, the program checks the student's answer. If it is correct, print the string **"Very good!"** on the screen and ask another multiplication question. If the answer is wrong, display **"No. Please try again."** and let the student try the same question again repeatedly until the student finally gets it right. A separate function should be used to generate each new question. This method should be called once when the program begins execution and each time the user answers the question correctly. (*Hint*: To convert the numbers for the problem into strings for the question, use function **str**. For example, **str(7)** returns **"7"**.)

4.7   Write a program that plays the game of "guess the number" as follows: Your program chooses the number to be guessed by selecting an integer at random in the range 1 to 1000. The program then displays

```
I have a number between 1 and 1000.
Can you guess my number?
Please type your first guess.
```

The player then types a first guess. The program responds with one of the following:

```
1. Excellent! You guessed the number!
   Would you like to play again (y or n)?
2. Too low. Try again.
3. Too high. Try again.
```

If the player's guess is incorrect, your program should loop until the player finally gets the number right. Your program should keep telling the player **Too high** or **Too low** to help the player "zero in" on the correct answer. After a game ends, the program should prompt the user to enter **"y"** to play again or **"n"** to exit the game.

4.8   *(Towers of Hanoi)* Every budding computer scientist must grapple with certain classic problems. The Towers of Hanoi (see Fig. 4.23) is one of the most famous of these. Legend has it that, in a temple in the Far East, priests are attempting to move a stack of disks from one peg to another. The initial stack had 64 disks threaded onto one peg and arranged from bottom to top by decreasing size. The priests are attempting to move the stack from this peg to a second peg, under the constraints that exactly one disk is moved at a time and that at no time may a larger disk be placed above a smaller disk. A third peg is available for holding disks temporarily. Supposedly, the world will end when the priests complete their task, so there is little incentive for us to facilitate their efforts.

Let us assume that the priests are attempting to move the disks from peg 1 to peg 3. We wish to develop an algorithm that will print the precise sequence of peg-to-peg disk transfers.

If we were to approach this problem with conventional methods, we would rapidly find ourselves hopelessly knotted up in managing the disks. Instead, if we attack the problem with recursion in mind, it immediately becomes tractable. Moving n disks can be viewed in terms of moving only $n - 1$ disks (hence, the recursion), as follows:

a)   Move $n - 1$ disks from peg 1 to peg 2, using peg 3 as a temporary holding area.
b)   Move the last disk (the largest) from peg 1 to peg 3.
c)   Move the $n - 1$ disks from peg 2 to peg 3, using peg 1 as a temporary holding area.

The process ends when the last task involves moving n = 1 disk, i.e., the base case. This is accomplished trivially by moving the disk without the need for a temporary holding area.

Write a program to solve the Towers of Hanoi problem. Use a recursive function with four parameters:

a)   The number of disks to be moved
b)   The peg on which these disks are initially threaded
c)   The peg to which this stack of disks is to be moved
d)   The peg to be used as a temporary holding area

Your program should print the precise instructions it will take to move the disks from the starting peg to the destination peg. For example, to move a stack of three disks from peg 1 to peg 3, your program should print the following series of moves:

$1 \rightarrow 3$ (This means move one disk from peg 1 to peg 3.)
$1 \rightarrow 2$
$3 \rightarrow 2$
$1 \rightarrow 3$
$2 \rightarrow 1$
$2 \rightarrow 3$
$1 \rightarrow 3$

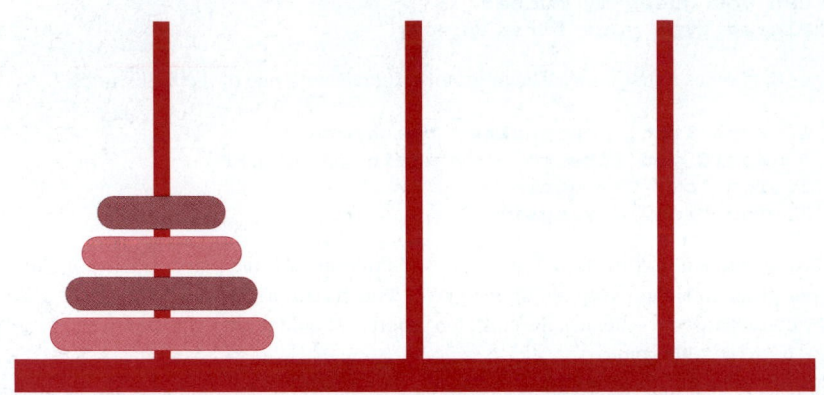

Fig. 4.23   The Towers of Hanoi for the case with 4 disks.

Lists, Tuples and Dictionaries

Objectives

- To understand Python sequences.
- To introduce the list, tuple and dictionary data types.
- To understand how to create, initialize and refer to individual elements of lists, tuples and dictionaries.
- To understand the use of lists to sort and search sequences of values.
- To be able to pass lists to functions.
- To introduce list and dictionary methods.
- To create and manipulate multiple-subscript lists and tuples.

With sobs and tears he sorted out
Those of the largest size …
Lewis Carroll

Attempt the end, and never stand to doubt;
Nothing's so hard, but search will find it out.
Robert Herrick

Now go, write it before them in a table,
and note it in a book.
Isaiah 30:8

'Tis in my memory lock'd,
And you yourself shall keep the key of it.
William Shakespeare

Outline

5.1 Introduction

This chapter introduces Python's data-handling capabilities that use *data structures*. Data structures hold and organize information (data). Many types of data structures exist, and each type has features appropriate for certain tasks. *Sequences*, often called *arrays* in other languages, are data structures that store (usually) related data items. Python supports three basic sequence data types: the string, the *list* and the *tuple*. *Mappings*, often called associative arrays or *hashes* in other languages, are data structures that store data in *key-value* pairs. Python supports one mapping data type: the *dictionary*. This chapter discusses Python's sequence and mapping types in the context of several examples. Chapter 22, Data Structures, introduces some high-level data structures (*linked lists*, *queues*, *stacks* and *trees*) that extend Python's basic data types.

5.2 Sequences

A sequence is a series of contiguous values that often are related. We already have encountered sequences in several programs: Python strings are sequences, as is the value returned by function **range**—a Python built-in function that returns a list of integers. In this section, we discuss sequences in detail and explain how to refer to a particular *element*, or location, in the sequence.

Figure 5.1 illustrates sequence **c**, which contains 12 integer elements. Any element may be referenced by writing the sequence name followed by the element's *position number* in square brackets (**[]**). The first element in every sequence is the *zeroth element*. Thus, in sequence **c**, the first element is **c[0]**, the second element is **c[1]**, the sixth element of sequence **c** is **c[5]**. In general, the *i*th element of sequence **c** is **c[i - 1]**.

Name of sequence (c)

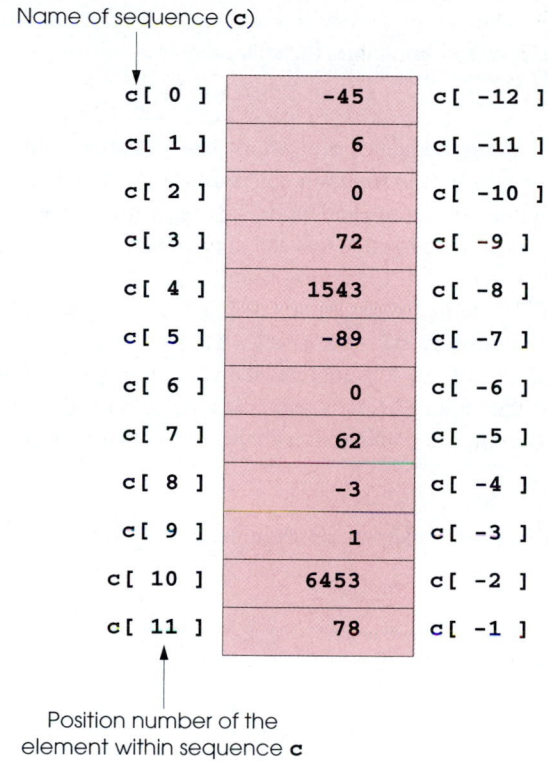

c[0]	-45	c[-12]
c[1]	6	c[-11]
c[2]	0	c[-10]
c[3]	72	c[-9]
c[4]	1543	c[-8]
c[5]	-89	c[-7]
c[6]	0	c[-6]
c[7]	62	c[-5]
c[8]	-3	c[-4]
c[9]	1	c[-3]
c[10]	6453	c[-2]
c[11]	78	c[-1]

Position number of the
element within sequence **c**

Fig. 5.1   Sequence with elements and indices.

Sequences also can be accessed from the end. The last element is c[-1], the second to last element is c[-2] and the *i*th-from-the-end is c[-i]. Sequences follow the same naming conventions as variables.

The position number more formally is called a *subscript* (or an *index*), which must be an integer or an integer expression. If a program uses an integer expression as a subscript, Python evaluates the expression to determine the index. For example, if variable **a** equals **5** and variable **b** equals **6**, then the statement

```
print c[ a + b ]
```

prints the value of c[11]. Integer expressions used as subscripts can be useful for iterating over a sequence in a loop.

Python lists and dictionaries are *mutable*—they can be altered. For example, if sequence **c** in Fig. 5.1 were mutable, the statement

```
c[ 11 ] = 0
```

modifies the value of element **11** by assinging it a new value of **0** to replace the original value of **78**.

On the other hand, some types of sequences are *immutable*—they cannot be altered (e.g., by changing element values). Python strings and tuples are immutable sequences. For example, if the sequence **c** were immutable, the statement

```
c[ 11 ] = 0
```

would be illegal. Let us examine sequence **c** in detail. The sequence *name* is **c**. The *length* of the sequence is determined by the function call **len(c)**. It is useful to know a sequence's length, because referring to an element outside the sequence results in an "out-of-range" error. Most of the errors discussed in this chapter can be caught as exceptions. [*Note:* We discuss exceptions in Chapter 12, Exception Handling.]

Sequence **c** contains 12 elements, namely **c[0]**, **c[1]**, ..., **c[11]**. The range of elements also can be referenced by **c[-12]**, **c[-11]**, ..., **c[-1]**. In this example, **c[0]** contains the *value* **-45**, **c[1]** contains the value **6**, **c[-9]** contains the value **72** and **c[-2]** contains the value **6453**. To calculate the sum of the values contained in the first three elements of sequence **c** and assign the result to variable **sum**, we would write

```
sum = c[ 0 ] + c[ 1 ] + c[ 2 ]
```

To divide the value of the seventh element of sequence **c** by 2 and assign the result to the variable **x**, we would write

```
x = c[ 6 ] / 2
```

Common Programming Error 5.1

*It is important to note the difference between the "seventh element of the sequence" and "sequence element seven." Sequence subscripts begin at 0, thus the "seventh element of the sequence" has a subscript of 6. On the other hand, "sequence element seven" references subscript 7 (i.e., **c[7]**), which is the eighth element of the sequence. This confusion often leads to "off-by-one" errors.*

Testing and Debugging Tip 5.1

In other programming languages that do not allow negative subscripts, if a negative subscript is accidentally calculated, a run-time error occurs. In Python, such an accidental negative subscript could cause a non-fatal logic error, with the program running to completion and producing invalid results.

The pair of square brackets enclosing the subscript of a sequence is a Python operator. Figure 5.2 shows the precedence and associativity of the operators introduced to this point in the text. They are shown from top to bottom in decreasing order of precedence, with their associativity and types.

5.3 Creating Sequences

Different Python sequences (strings, lists and tuples) require different syntax. We illustrated how Python strings are created by placing the text of the string within quotes. To create an empty string, use a statement like

```
aString = ""
```

Note that we could have used single quotes (**'**) or triple quotes (**"""** or **'''**) to create the string.

Operators	Associativity	Type
`()`	left to right	parentheses
`[]`	left to right	subscript
`.`	left to right	member access
`**`	right to left	exponentiation
`*   /  //  %`	left to right	multiplicative
`+   -`	left to right	additive
`<    <=   >   >=`	left to right	relational
`==  !=   <>`	left to right	equality

Fig. 5.2   Precedence and associativity of the operators discussed so far.

To create an empty list, use a statement like

```
aList = []
```

To create a list that contains a sequence of values, separate the values by commas inside square brackets (`[]`)

```
aList = [ 1, 2, 3 ]
```

To create an empty tuple, use the statement

```
aTuple = ()
```

To create a tuple that contains a sequence of values, simply separate the values with commas.

```
aTuple = 1, 2, 3
```

Creating a tuple is sometimes referred to as *packing a tuple*. Tuples also can be created by surrounding the comma-separated list of tuple values with optional parentheses. It is the commas that create tuples, not the parentheses.

```
aTuple = ( 1, 2, 3 )
```

When creating a one-element tuple—called a *singleton*—use a statement like

```
aSingleton = 1,
```

Notice that a comma (`,`) follows the value. The comma identifies the variable—**aSingleton**—as a tuple. If the comma were omitted, **aSingleton** would simply contain the integer value 1.

5.4 Using Lists and Tuples

Lists and tuples both contain sequences of values. For example, a list or a tuple may contain the sequence of integers from 1 to 5

```
aList = [ 1, 2, 3, 4, 5 ]
aTuple = ( 1, 2, 3, 4, 5 )
```

In practice, however, Python programmers distinguish between the two data types to represent different kinds of sequences, based on the context of the program. In the next subsections, we discuss the situations for which lists and tuples are best suited.

5.4.1 Using Lists

Although lists are not restricted to homogeneous data types (i.e., values of the same data type), Python programmers typically use lists to store sequences of homogeneous values. For example, either a list may store a sequence of integers that represent test scores or a sequence of strings representing employee names. In general, a program uses a list to store homogeneous values for the purpose of looping over these values and performing the same operation on each value. Usually, the length of the list is not predetermined and may vary over the course of the program. The program in Fig. 5.3 demonstrates how to create, augment and retrieve values from a list.

```
 1   # Fig. 5.3: fig05_03.py
 2   # Creating, accessing and changing a list.
 3
 4   aList = []     # create empty list
 5
 6   # add values to list
 7   for number in range( 1, 11 ):
 8      aList += [ number ]
 9
10   print "The value of aList is:", aList
11
12   # access list values by iteration
13   print "\nAccessing values by iteration:"
14
15   for item in aList:
16      print item,
17
18   print
19
20   # access list values by index
21   print "\nAccessing values by index:"
22   print "Subscript    Value"
23
24   for i in range( len( aList ) ):
25      print "%9d %7d" % ( i, aList[ i ] )
26
27   # modify list
28   print "\nModifying a list value..."
29   print "Value of aList before modification:", aList
30   aList[ 0 ] = -100
31   aList[ -3 ] = 19
32   print "Value of aList after modification:", aList
```

Fig. 5.3   List of homogeneous values. (Part 1 of 2.)

```
The value of aList is:  [1, 2, 3, 4, 5, 6, 7, 8, 9, 10]

Accessing values by iteration:
1 2 3 4 5 6 7 8 9 10

Accessing values by index:
Subscript      Value
       0           1
       1           2
       2           3
       3           4
       4           5
       5           6
       6           7
       7           8
       8           9
       9          10

Modifying a list value...
Value of aList before modification:  [1, 2, 3, 4, 5, 6, 7, 8, 9, 10]
Value of aList after modification:  [-100, 2, 3, 4, 5, 6, 7, 19, 9, 10]
```

Fig. 5.3   List of homogeneous values. (Part 2 of 2.)

Line 4 creates an empty list, **aList**. Lines 7–8 use a **for** loop to insert the values 1–10 into **aList**, using the **+=** augmented assignment statement. When the value to the left of the **+=** statement is a sequence, the value to the right of the statement also must be a sequence. Thus, line 8 places square brackets around the value to be added to the list. Line 10 prints variable **aList**. Python displays the list as a comma-separated sequence of values inside square brackets. Variable **aList** represents a typical Python list—a sequence containing homogeneous data.

Lines 13–18 demonstrate the most common way of accessing a list's elements. The **for** structure actually iterates over a sequence

```
for item in aList:
```

The **for** structure (lines 15–16) starts with the first element in the sequence, assigns the value of the first element to the control variable (**item**) and executes the body of the **for** loop (i.e., prints the value of the control variable). The loop then proceeds to the next element in the sequence and performs the same operations. Thus, lines 15–16 print each element of **aList**.

List elements also can be accessed through their corresponding indices. Lines 21–25 access each element in **aList** in this manner. The function call in line 24

```
range( len( aList ) )
```

returns a sequence that contains the values **0, ...**, **len(aList) - 1**. This sequence contains all possible element positions for **aList**. The **for** loop iterates through this sequence and, for each element position, prints the position and the value stored at that position.

Lines 30–31 modify some of the list's elements. To modify the value of a particular element, we assign a new value to that element. Line 30 changes the value of the list's first element from 0 to -100; line 31 changes the value of the list's third-from-the-end element from 8 to 19.

If the program attempts to access a nonexistent index (e.g., index 13) in **aList**, the program exits and Python displays an out-of-range error message. The interactive session in Fig. 5.4 demonstrates the results of accessing an out-of-range list element.

Common Programming Error 5.2

Referring to an element outside the sequence is an error.

Testing and Debugging Tip 5.2

When looping through a sequence, the positive sequence subscript should be less than the total number of elements in the sequence (i.e., the subscript should not be larger than the length of the sequence); whereas, the negative sequence subscript should be equal to or greater than the negation of the total number of elements in the sequence. Make sure the loop-terminating condition prevents accessing elements outside this range.

Generally, a program does not concern itself with the length of a list, but simply iterates over the list and performs an operation for each element in the list. Figure 5.5 demonstrates one practical application of using lists in such a manner—creating a *histogram* (a bar graph of frequencies) from a collection of data.

```
Python 2.2b2 (#26, Nov 16 2001, 11:44:11) [MSC 32 bit (Intel)] on
win32
Type "help", "copyright", "credits" or "license" for more informa-
tion.
>>> aList = [ 1 ]
>>> print aList[ 13 ]
Traceback (most recent call last):
  File "<stdin>", line 1, in ?
IndexError: list index out of range
```

Fig. 5.4   Out-of-range error.

```
1   # Fig. 5.5: fig05_05.py
2   # Creating a histogram from a list of values.
3
4   values = []    # a list of values
5
6   # input 10 values from user
7   print "Enter 10 integers:"
8
9   for i in range( 10 ):
10     newValue = int( raw_input( "Enter integer %d: " % ( i + 1 ) ) )
11     values += [ newValue ]
12
```

Fig. 5.5   Histogram created from a list of values. (Part 1 of 2.)

```
13    # create histogram
14    print "\nCreating a histogram from values:"
15    print "%s %10s %10s" % ( "Element", "Value", "Histogram" )
16
17    for i in range( len( values ) ):
18        print "%7d %10d  %s" % ( i, values[ i ], "*" * values[ i ] )
```

```
Enter 10 integers:
Enter integer 1: 19
Enter integer 2: 3
Enter integer 3: 15
Enter integer 4: 7
Enter integer 5: 11
Enter integer 6: 9
Enter integer 7: 13
Enter integer 8: 5
Enter integer 9: 17
Enter integer 10: 1

Creating a histogram from values:
Element        Value  Histogram
      0           19  *******************
      1            3  ***
      2           15  ***************
      3            7  *******
      4           11  ***********
      5            9  *********
      6           13  *************
      7            5  *****
      8           17  *****************
      9            1  *
```

Fig. 5.5   Histogram created from a list of values. (Part 2 of 2.)

The program creates an empty list called **values** (line 4). Lines 7–11 input 10 integers from the user and insert those integers into the list. Lines 14–18 create the histogram. For each element in the list, the program prints the element's index and value and a string that contains the same number of asterisks (*****) as the value. The expression

```
"*" * values[ i ]
```

uses the multiplication operator (*****) to create a string with the number of asterisks specified by **values[i]**.

5.4.2 Using Tuples

Whereas lists typically store sequences of homogeneous data, tuples typically store sequences of heterogeneous data—this is a convention, not a rule, that Python programmers follow. Each data item in a tuple provides a part of the total information represented by the tuple. For example, a tuple can represent a student in a class. The tuple could contain the student's name (represented as a string) and age (represented as an integer). Or, a tuple can represent the time of day, using three parts—the hour, minute and second. Although all these values might be represented as integers, each integer has its own meaning, and the full representation of the time is obtained only by taking all three values together. The length of the tuple (i.e., its number of data items) is predetermined and cannot change during a program's execution.

By convention, each data item in the tuple represents a unique portion of the overall data. Therefore, a program usually does not iterate over a tuple, but accesses the parts of the tuple the program needs to perform its task. Figure 5.6 demonstrates how to create and access a tuple using this idiom.

Lines 5–7 ask the user to enter three integers that represent the hour, minutes and seconds, respectively. Line 9 creates a tuple called **currentTime** to store the user-entered values. Lines 14–16 print the number of seconds that have passed since midnight. We perform a different operation (i.e., multiply each value by a different factor) for each value in the tuple; therefore, the program accesses each value by its index.

As tuples are immutable, Python provides error handling that notifies users when they attempt to modify tuples. For example, if the program attempts to change the first element in **currentTime** to contain the value 0,

```
currentTime[ 0 ] = 0
```

the program exits and Python displays a runtime error

```
Traceback (most recent call last):
  File "fig05_06.py", line 18, in ?
    currentTime[ 0 ] = 0
TypeError: object doesn't support item assignment
```

to indicate that the program illegally attempted to change the value of the immutable tuple.

```
1   # Fig. 5.6: fig05_06.py
2   # Creating and accessing tuples.
3
4   # retrieve hour, minute and second from user
5   hour = int( raw_input( "Enter hour: " ) )
6   minute = int( raw_input( "Enter minute: " ) )
7   second = int( raw_input( "Enter second: " ) )
8
9   currentTime = hour, minute, second   # create tuple
10
11  print "The value of currentTime is:", currentTime
12
13  # access tuple
14  print "The number of seconds since midnight is", \
15      ( currentTime[ 0 ] * 3600 + currentTime[ 1 ] * 60 +
16        currentTime[ 2 ] )
```

```
Enter hour: 9
Enter minute: 16
Enter second: 1
The value of currentTime is: (9, 16, 1)
The number of seconds since midnight is 33361
```

Fig. 5.6   Tuples created and accessed.

Note that the use of lists and tuples introduced in Section 5.4.1 and Section 5.4.2 is not a rule, but rather a convention that Python programmers follow. Python does not limit the data type stored in lists and tuples (i.e., they can contain homogeneous or heterogeneous data). The primary difference between lists and tuples is that lists are mutable whereas tuples are immutable.

5.4.3 Sequence Unpacking

Recall that creating a tuple with

```
aTuple = 1, 2, 3
```

or

```
aTuple = ( 1, 2, 3 )
```

is called packing a tuple, because the values are "packed into" the tuple. Tuples and other sequences also can be *unpacked*—the values stored in the sequence are assigned to various identifiers. Unpacking is a useful programming shortcut for assigning values to multiple variables in a single statement. The program in Fig. 5.7 demonstrates the results of unpacking strings, lists and tuples.

Lines 5–7 create a string, a list and a tuple, each containing three elements. Sequences are unpacked with an assignment statement. The assignment statement in line 11 unpacks the elements in variable **aString** and assigns each element to a variable. The first element is assigned to variable **first**, the second to variable **second** and the third to variable **third**. Line 12 prints the variables to confirm that the string unpacked properly. Lines 14–20 perform similar operations for the elements in variables **aList** and **aTuple**. When unpacking a sequence, the number of variable names to the left of the = symbol should equal the number of elements in the sequence to the right of the symbol; otherwise, a runtime error occurs. Notice that when unpacking a sequence, parentheses or brackets are optional to the left of the = symbol because there usually are no precedence issues.

```
1   # Fig. 5.7: fig05_07.py
2   # Unpacking sequences.
3
4   # create sequences
5   aString = "abc"
6   aList = [ 1, 2, 3 ]
7   aTuple = "a", "A", 1
8
9   # unpack sequences to variables
10  print "Unpacking string..."
11  first, second, third = aString
12  print "String values:", first, second, third
13
14  print "\nUnpacking list..."
15  first, second, third = aList
16  print "List values:", first, second, third
17
```

Fig. 5.7   Unpacking strings, lists and tuples. (Part 1 of 2.)

```
18    print "\nUnpacking tuple..."
19    first, second, third = aTuple
20    print "Tuple values:", first, second, third
21
22    # swapping two values
23    x = 3
24    y = 4
25
26    print "\nBefore swapping: x = %d, y = %d" % ( x, y )
27    x, y = y, x       # swap variables
28    print "After swapping: x = %d, y = %d" % ( x, y )
```

```
Unpacking string...
String values: a b c

Unpacking list...
List values: 1 2 3

Unpacking tuple...
Tuple values: a A 1

Before swapping: x = 3, y = 4
After swapping: x = 4, y = 3
```

Fig. 5.7   *Unpacking strings, lists and tuples. (Part 2 of 2.)*

Lines 22–28 demonstrate one benefit of sequence packing and unpacking—swapping the value of two variables. Lines 23–24 create two variables **x** and **y**, with the values 3 and 4, respectively. Line 27

```
    x, y = y, x
```

swaps the values assigned to each variable. Python swaps the value by first packing the right-hand side of the statement into a tuple (e.g., **(4, 3)**), then unpacking that tuple to variables **x** and **y**, respectively. Thus, the value assigned to variable **x** is now assigned to variable **y**, and the value assigned to variable **y** is now assigned to variable **x**.

5.4.4 Sequence Slicing

We have discussed how to create sequences and access them through the **[ ]** operator (to access one element) or a **for** statement (to access all the elements iteratively). Sometimes, a program may need to access a series of sequential values (e.g., the characters of a person's last name in a string that stores the person's full name). For these cases, Python allows programs to *slice* a sequence.

Figure 5.8 demonstrates Python sequence-slicing capabilities. The program creates three sequences—a string, a tuple and a list. The program prompts the user to enter a starting and ending index, creates the specified slice for each sequence and prints the slice to the screen.

```
1    # Fig. 5.8: fig05_08.py
2    # Slicing sequences.
3
```

Fig. 5.8   Sequence slices. (Part 1 of 3.)

```
 4   # create sequences
 5   sliceString = "abcdefghij"
 6   sliceTuple = ( 1, 2, 3, 4, 5, 6, 7, 8, 9, 10 )
 7   sliceList = [ "I", "II", "III", "IV", "V",
 8                 "VI", "VII", "VIII", "IX", "X" ]
 9
10   # print strings
11   print "sliceString: ", sliceString
12   print "sliceTuple: ", sliceTuple
13   print "sliceList: ", sliceList
14   print
15
16   # get slices
17   start = int( raw_input( "Enter start: " ) )
18   end = int( raw_input( "Enter end: " ) )
19
20   # print slices
21   print "\nsliceString[", start, ":", end, "] = ", \
22       sliceString[ start:end ]
23
24   print "sliceTuple[", start, ":", end, "] = ", \
25       sliceTuple[ start:end ]
26
27   print "sliceList[", start, ":", end, "] = ", \
28       sliceList[ start:end ]
```

```
sliceString:  abcdefghij
sliceTuple:  (1, 2, 3, 4, 5, 6, 7, 8, 9, 10)
sliceList:  ['I', 'II', 'III', 'IV', 'V', 'VI', 'VII', 'VIII',
'IX', 'X']

Enter start: 3
Enter end: 3

sliceString[ 3 : 3 ] =
sliceTuple[ 3 : 3 ] =  ()
sliceList[ 3 : 3 ] =  []
```

```
sliceString:  abcdefghij
sliceTuple:  (1, 2, 3, 4, 5, 6, 7, 8, 9, 10)
sliceList:  ['I', 'II', 'III', 'IV', 'V', 'VI', 'VII', 'VIII',
'IX', 'X']

Enter start: -4
Enter end: -1

sliceString[ -4 : -1 ] =  ghi
sliceTuple[ -4 : -1 ] =  (7, 8, 9)
sliceList[ -4 : -1 ] =  ['VII', 'VIII', 'IX']
```

Fig. 5.8   Sequence slices. (Part 2 of 3.)

```
sliceString:  abcdefghij
sliceTuple:  (1, 2, 3, 4, 5, 6, 7, 8, 9, 10)
sliceList:  ['I', 'II', 'III', 'IV', 'V', 'VI', 'VII', 'VIII',
'IX', 'X']

Enter start: 0
Enter end: 10

sliceString[ 0 : 10 ] =  abcdefghij
sliceTuple[ 0 : 10 ] =  (1, 2, 3, 4, 5, 6, 7, 8, 9, 10)
sliceList[ 0 : 10 ] =  ['I', 'II', 'III', 'IV', 'V', 'VI', 'VII',
'VIII', 'IX', 'X']
```

Fig. 5.8   Sequence slices. (Part 3 of 3.)

Lines 5–18 create the three sequences and request the user to specify a beginning and ending index for the slice. Lines 21–28 print the specified slice for each sequence. A slice is simply a new sequence, created from an existing sequence. The expression in line 22

sliceString[start:end]

creates (slices) a new sequence from variable **sliceString**. This new sequence contains the values stored at indices **sliceString[start]**, ..., **sliceString[end - 1]**. In general, to obtain from *sequence* a slice of the *i*th element through the *j*th element, inclusive, use the expression

sequence[*i:j + 1*]

Figure 5.8 includes three sample outputs from the program. The first sample creates a slice from indices 0 to 10 (e.g., the entire sequence). Recall that the first element in every sequence is the zeroth element. The sequence created from this slice is equivalent to the sequence created with the expression

sequence[:]

This expression creates a new sequence that is a copy of the original sequence. The above expression is equivalent to the following expressions:

sequence[0 : **len(** *sequence* **)**]
sequence[: **len(** *sequence* **)**]
sequence[0 :]

The syntax for sequence slicing provides a useful shortcut for selecting a portion of an existing sequence. A program can use sequence slicing to create a copy of a list when passing the list to a function. We discuss this issue in Section 5.7 and 5.8.

Note that negative slices cannot access the last element of a list directly (i.e.,**sliceString[-4 : -1] = ghi**) because slices apply to points between elements. With negative slices, the last point between elements is the point between elements with indices -2 and -1.

5.5 Dictionaries

In addition to lists and tuples, Python supports another powerful data type, called the *dictionary*. Dictionaries (called *hashes* or *associative arrays* in other languages) are *mapping* constructs consisting of *key-value pairs*. Dictionaries can be thought of as unordered collections of values where each value is referenced through its corresponding key. For example, a dictionary might store phone numbers that can be referenced by a person's name.

The statement

```
emptyDictionary = {}
```

creates an empty dictionary. Notice that curly braces (**{}**) denote dictionaries. To initialize key-value pairs for a dictionary, use the statement

```
dictionary = { 1 : "one", 2 : "two" }
```

Each key-value pair is of the form

key **:** *value*

A comma separates each key-value pair. Dictionary keys must be immutable values, such as strings, numbers or tuples. Dictionary values can be of any Python data type.

Common Programming Error 5.3

Using a list or a dictionary for a dictionary key is an syntax error.

Figure 5.9 demonstrates how to create, initialize, access and manipulate simple dictionaries. Lines 5–6 create and print an empty dictionary. Line 9 creates a dictionary **grades** and initializes the dictionary to contain four key-value pairs. The keys are strings that contain student names, and the integer values represent the students' grades. Line 10 prints the value assigned to variable **grades**. Observe that the application displays **grades** in a different order than the declaration; this is because a dictionary is an unordered collection of key-value pairs. Also, notice in the output that the dictionary keys appear in single quotes, because Python displays strings in single quotes.

```
1   # Fig. 5.09: fig05_09.py
2   # Creating, accessing and modifying a dictionary.
3
4   # create and print an empty dictionary
5   emptyDictionary = {}
6   print "The value of emptyDictionary is:", emptyDictionary
7
8   # create and print a dictionary with initial values
9   grades = { "John": 87, "Steve": 76, "Laura": 92, "Edwin": 89 }
10  print "\nAll grades:", grades
11
12  # access and modify an existing dictionary
13  print "\nSteve's current grade:", grades[ "Steve" ]
14  grades[ "Steve" ] = 90
15  print "Steve's new grade:", grades[ "Steve" ]
```

Fig. 5.9   Dictionaries created, accessed and modified. (Part 1 of 2.)

```
16
17    # add to an existing dictionary
18    grades[ "Michael" ] = 93
19    print "\nDictionary grades after modification:"
20    print grades
21
22    # delete entry from dictionary
23    del grades[ "John" ]
24    print "\nDictionary grades after deletion:"
25    print grades
```

```
The value of emptyDictionary is: {}

All grades: {'Edwin': 89, 'John': 87, 'Steve': 76, 'Laura': 92}

Steve's current grade: 76
Steve's new grade: 90

Dictionary grades after modification:
{'Edwin': 89, 'Michael': 93, 'John': 87, 'Steve': 90, 'Laura': 92}

Dictionary grades after deletion:
{'Edwin': 89, 'Michael': 93, 'Steve': 90, 'Laura': 92}
```

Fig. 5.9   Dictionaries created, accessed and modified. (Part 2 of 2.)

Line 13 accesses a particular dictionary value, using the **[]** operator. Dictionary values are accessed with the expression

   dictionaryName **[** *key* **]**

In line 13, the *dictionaryName* is **grades** and the *key* is the string **"Steve"**. This expression evaluates to the value stored in the dictionary at key **"Steve"**, namely, **76**. Line 14 assigns a new value, **90**, to the key **"Steve"**. Dictionary values are modified using syntax similar to that of modifying lists. Line 15 prints the result of changing the dictionary value.

Line 18 inserts a new key-value pair into the dictionary. Although this statement resembles the syntax for modifying an existing dictionary value, it inserts a new key-value pair because **Michael** is a new key. The statement

   dictionaryName **[** *key* **]** **=** *value*

modifies the *value* associated with *key*, if the dictionary already contains that key. Otherwise, the statement inserts the key-value pair into the dictionary.

 ### Software Engineering Observation 5.1

When adding a key-value pair to a dictionary, mis-typing the key could be a source of inadvertent errors.

Lines 19–20 print the results of adding a new key-value pair to the dictionary. The order in which the key-value pairs are printed is entirely arbitrary (remember that a dictionary is an unordered collection of key-value pairs).

The expression *dictionaryName* [*key*] can lead to subtle programming errors. If this expression appears on the left-hand side of an assignment statement and the dictionary does not contain the key, the assignment statement inserts the key-value pair into the dictionary. However, if the expression appears to the right of an assignment statement (or any statement that simply attempts to access the value stored at the specified key), then the statement causes the program to exit and to display an error message, because the program is trying to access a nonexistent key.

Common Programming Error 5.4

Attempting to access a nonexistent dictionary key is a "key error," a runtime error.

Line 23 deletes an entry from the dictionary. The statement

del *dictionaryName* [*key*]

removes the specified key and its value from the dictionary. If the specified key does not exist in the dictionary, then the above statement causes the program to exit and to display an error message. Again, this is because the program is accessing a nonexistent key. This runtime error can be caught through exception handling, which we discuss in Chapter 12.

Dictionaries are powerful data types that help programmers accomplish sophisticated tasks. Many Python modules provide data types similar to dictionaries that facilitate access and manipulation of more complex data. In the next section, we explore the dictionary's capabilities further.

5.6 List and Dictionary Methods

We have seen how sequences and dictionaries enable programmers to accomplish high-level data manipulation, such as storing and retrieving data. We now introduce a new programming concept, the *method*, to extend data-manipulation capabilities.

As discussed in Chapter 2, Introduction to Python Programming, all Python data types contain at least three properties: a value, a type and a location. Some Python data types (e.g., strings, lists and dictionaries) also contain methods. A method is a function that performs the behaviors (tasks) of an object. In this section, we discuss list and dictionary methods; we discuss string methods in Chapter 13, Strings Manipulation and Regular Expressions.

List methods implement several behaviors, such as appending a value to the end of a list or determining the index of a particular element in the list. The program of Fig. 5.10 appends items to the end of a list, using a list method. The program asks the user to enter the names of Shakespearean plays and appends the names to a list. Line 4 creates an empty list, **playList**, to store the names of the plays entered by the user. The **for** structure (lines 8–10) uses list method **append** to append items to the end of variable **playList**. Method **append** takes as an argument the new element to insert at the end of the list. To invoke the list method, specify the name of the list, followed by the dot (**.**) access operator, followed by the method call (i.e., method name and necessary arguments). Lines 14–15 define another **for** loop that prints the names of the user-entered Shakespearean plays. Notice that line 15 uses the – formatting character to left align the names.

Figure 5.10 demonstrates how a data type's methods provide a way for programmers to create applications that perform useful data-manipulation tasks. Figure 5.11 uses another list method to perform a more typical data-manipulation task—counting the number of times a

```
1   # Fig. 5.10: fig05_10.py
2   # Appending items to a list.
3
4   playList = []      # list of favorite plays
5
6   print "Enter your 5 favorite Shakespearean plays.\n"
7
8   for i in range( 5 ):
9      playName = raw_input( "Play %d: " % ( i + 1 ) )
10     playList.append( playName )
11
12  print "\nSubscript      Value"
13
14  for i in range( len( playList ) ):
15     print "%9d      %-25s" % ( i + 1, playList[ i ] )
```

```
Enter your 5 favorite Shakespearean plays.

Play 1: Richard III
Play 2: Henry V
Play 3: Twelfth Night
Play 4: Hamlet
Play 5: King Lear

Subscript      Value
        1      Richard III
        2      Henry V
        3      Twelfth Night
        4      Hamlet
        5      King Lear
```

Fig. 5.10   Appending items to a list.

particular value occurs in a list. Lines 4–7 create a list (**responses**) that contains several values between 1–10. Lines 11–12 contain a **for** loop that calls list method **count** to return the amount of times an element appears in a list. Method **count** takes as an argument a value of any data type. If the list contains no elements with the specified value, method **count** returns 0. Lines 11–12 print the frequency of each value in the list.

```
1   # Fig. 5.11: fig05_11.py
2   # Student poll program.
3
4   responses = [ 1, 2, 6, 4, 8, 5, 9, 7, 8, 10,
5                 1, 6, 3, 8, 6, 10, 3, 8, 2, 7,
6                 6, 5, 7, 6, 8, 6, 7, 5, 6, 6,
7                 5, 6, 7, 5, 6, 4, 8, 6, 8, 10 ]
8
9   print "Rating      Frequency"
10
11  for i in range( 1, 11 ):
12     print "%6d %13d" % ( i, responses.count( i ) )
```

Fig. 5.11   List method **count**. (Part 1 of 2.)

```
Rating      Frequency
  1             2
  2             2
  3             2
  4             2
  5             5
  6            11
  7             5
  8             7
  9             1
 10             3
```

Fig. 5.11   List method **count**. (Part 2 of 2.)

Lists provide several other useful methods. Figure 5.12 summarizes these methods. Throughout the text, we create programs that invoke list methods to accomplish tasks.

Method	Purpose
append (*item* **)**	Inserts *item* at the end of the list.
count (*element* **)**	Returns the number of occurrences of *element* in the list.
extend (*newList* **)**	Inserts the elements of *newList* at the end of the list.
index (*element* **)**	Returns the index of the first occurrence of *element* in the list. If element is not in the list, a **ValueError** exception occurs. [*Note*: We discuss exceptions in Chapter 12, Exception Handling.]
insert (*index*, *item* **)**	Inserts *item* at position *index*.
pop (*[index]* **)**	Parameter index is optional. If this method is called without arguments, it removes and returns the last element in the list. If parameter *index* is specified, this method removes and returns the element at position *index*.
remove (*element* **)**	Removes the first occurrence of *element* from the list. If *element* is not in the list, a **ValueError** exception occurs.
reverse ()	Reverses the contents of the list in place (rather than creating a reversed copy).
sort (*[compare-function]* **)**	Sorts the content of the list in place. The optional parameter *compare-function* is a function that specifies the compare criteria. The *compare-function* takes any two elements of the list (x and y) and returns -1 if x should appear before y, 0 if the orders of x and y do not matter and 1 if x should appear after y. [*Note*: We discuss sorting in Section 5.9.]

Fig. 5.12   List methods.

The dictionary data type also provides many methods that enable the programmer to manipulate the stored data. Figure 5.13 demonstrates three dictionary methods. Lines 4–7 create the dictionary **monthsDictionary** that represents the months of the year. Line 10 uses dictionary method *items* to print the dictionary's key-value pairs to the screen. The method returns a list of tuples, where each tuple contains a key-value pair.

```
1   # Fig. 5.13: fig05_13.py
2   # Dictionary methods.
3
4   monthsDictionary = { 1 : "January", 2 : "February", 3 : "March",
5                        4 : "April", 5 : "May", 6 : "June", 7 : "July",
6                        8 : "August", 9 : "September", 10 : "October",
7                        11 : "November", 12 : "December" }
8
9   print "The dictionary items are:"
10  print monthsDictionary.items()
11
12  print "\nThe dictionary keys are:"
13  print monthsDictionary.keys()
14
15  print "\nThe dictionary values are:"
16  print monthsDictionary.values()
17
18  print "\nUsing a for loop to get dictionary items:"
19
20  for key in monthsDictionary.keys():
21      print "monthsDictionary[", key, "] =", monthsDictionary[ key ]
```

```
The dictionary items are:
[(1, 'January'), (2, 'February'), (3, 'March'), (4, 'April'), (5,
'May'), (6, 'June'), (7, 'July'), (8, 'August'), (9, 'September'), (10,
'October'), (11, 'November'), (12, 'December')]

The dictionary keys are:
[1, 2, 3, 4, 5, 6, 7, 8, 9, 10, 11, 12]

The dictionary values are:
['January', 'February', 'March', 'April', 'May', 'June', 'July', 'Au-
gust', 'September', 'October', 'November', 'December']

Using a for loop to get dictionary items:
monthsDictionary[ 1 ] = January
monthsDictionary[ 2 ] = February
monthsDictionary[ 3 ] = March
monthsDictionary[ 4 ] = April
monthsDictionary[ 5 ] = May
monthsDictionary[ 6 ] = June
monthsDictionary[ 7 ] = July
monthsDictionary[ 8 ] = August
monthsDictionary[ 9 ] = September
monthsDictionary[ 10 ] = October
monthsDictionary[ 11 ] = November
monthsDictionary[ 12 ] = December
```

Fig. 5.13 Dictionary methods **items**, **keys** and **values**.

Dictionary method **keys** (line 13) returns an unordered list of the dictionary's keys. Similarly, dictionary method **values** (line 16) returns an unordered list of the dictionary's values. Lines 20–21 demonstrate a common use of dictionary method **keys**. The **for** loop iterates over the dictionary keys. Each key is assigned to control variable **key**. Line 21 prints both the key and the value associated with that key. Figure 5.14 summarizes the dictionary methods.

Method	Description
clear()	Deletes all items from the dictionary.
copy()	Creates and returns a shallow copy of the dictionary (the elements in the new dictionary are references to the elements in the original dictionary).
get(*key [, returnValue]* **)**	Returns the value associated with *key*. If *key* is not in the dictionary and if *returnValue* is specified, returns the specified value. If *returnValue* is not specified, returns **None**.
has_key(*key* **)**	Returns **1** if *key* is in the dictionary; returns **0** if *key* is not in the dictionary.
items()	Returns a list of tuples that are key-value pairs.
keys()	Returns a list of keys in the dictionary.
popitem()	Removes and returns an arbitrary key-value pair as a tuple of two elements. If dictionary is empty, a **Key-Error** exception occurs. [*Note*: We discuss exceptions in Chapter 12, Exception Handling.] This method is useful for accessing an element (i.e., print the key-value pair) before removing it from the dictionary.
setdefault(*key* [, *dummyValue*] **)**	Behaves similarly to method **get**. If key is not in the dictionary and *dummyValue* is specified, inserts the key and the specified value into dictionary. If *dummyValue* is not specified, value is **None**.
update(*newDictionary* **)**	Adds all key-value pairs from *newDictionary* to the current dictionary and overrides the values for keys that already exist.
values()	Returns a list of values in the dictionary.
iterkeys()	Returns an iterator of dictionary keys. [*Note*: We discuss iterators in Appendix O, Additional Python 2.2 Features.]
iteritems()	Returns an iterator of key-value pairs. [*Note*: We discuss iterators in Appendix O, Additional Python 2.2 Features.]
itervalues()	Returns an iterator of dictionary values. [*Note*: We discuss iterators in Appendix O, Additional Python 2.2 Features.]

Fig. 5.14 Dictionary methods.

Dictionary method **copy** returns a new dictionary that is a *shallow* copy of the original dictionary. In a shallow copy, the elements in the new dictionary are references to the elements in the original dictionary.

The interactive session in Fig. 5.15 demonstrates the difference between shallow and *deep* copies. We first create **dictionary**, which contains one value—a list of numbers. We then invoke dictionary method **copy** to create a shallow copy of **dictionary**, and we assign the copy to variable **shallowCopy**. The values stored for key **"listKey"** in both dictionaries reference the same object. To underscore this fact, we insert the value 4 at the end of the list stored in **dictionary**. We then print the value of variables **dictionary** and **shallowCopy**. Notice that the list has been changed in both copies of the dictionary. This is a consequence of doing a shallow copy, which does not create a fully independent copy of the original dictionary.

Sometimes, a shallow copy is sufficient for a program, especially if the dictionaries contain no references to other Python objects (i.e., they contain only literal numeric values or immutable values). However, sometimes it is necessary to create a copy—called a *deep copy*—that is independent of the original dictionary. To create a deep copy, Python provides module *copy*. The remainder of the interactive session in Fig. 5.15 creates a deep copy of variable **dictionary**. We first import function *deepcopy* from module **copy**. We then call **deepcopy** and pass **dictionary** as an argument. The function call returns a deep copy of **dictionary**, and we assign the copy to variable **deepCopy**. The value associated with **deepCopy["listKey"]** is now independent of the value associated with that key in variables **dictionary** and **shallowCopy**. To demonstrate this fact, we append a new value to **dictionary**'s list and print the values for **dictionary**, **shallowCopy** and **deepCopy**.

```
Python 2.2b2 (#26, Nov 16 2001, 11:44:11) [MSC 32 bit (Intel)] on
win32
Type "help", "copyright", "credits" or "license" for more informa-
tion.
>>> dictionary = { "listKey" : [ 1, 2, 3 ] }
>>> shallowCopy = dictionary.copy()          # make a shallow copy
>>> dictionary[ "listKey" ].append( 4 )
>>> print dictionary
{'listKey': [1, 2, 3, 4]}
>>> print shallowCopy
{'listKey': [1, 2, 3, 4]}

>>> from copy import deepcopy
>>> deepCopy = deepcopy( dictionary )        # make a deep copy
>>> dictionary[ "listKey" ].append( 5 )
>>> print dictionary
{'listKey': [1, 2, 3, 4, 5]}
>>> print shallowCopy
{'listKey': [1, 2, 3, 4, 5]}
>>> print deepCopy
{'listKey': [1, 2, 3, 4]}
```

Fig. 5.15   Difference between a shallow copy and a deep copy.

Shallow and deep copies reflect how Python handles references (i.e., names of objects). The programmer should exercise caution when dealing with references to objects like lists and dictionaries, because changing an object affects the value of all the names that refer to that object. In the next two sections, we discuss how passing a reference to a function affects an object's value.

Software Engineering Observation 5.2

`deepCopyList = originalList[:]` does a deep copy which means that the **`deepCopyList`** *is a deep copy of the* **`originalList`**.

5.7 References and Reference Parameters

To perform tasks, functions require certain input values, which the main program or functions have (or know). The main program (e.g., a program that simulates a calculator) may ask users for input, and those input values are sent, in turn, to functions (e.g., **add**, **subtract**). The values, or arguments, have to be passed to the functions through a certain protocol. In many programming languages, the two ways to pass arguments to functions are *pass-by-value* and *pass-by-reference*. When an argument is passed by value, a copy of the argument's value is made and passed to the called function.

Testing and Debugging Tip 5.3

With pass-by-value, changes to the called function's copy do not affect the original variable's value in the calling code. This prevents accidental side effects that can hinder the development of correct and reliable software systems.

With pass-by-reference, the caller allows the called function to access the caller's data directly and to modify that data. Pass-by-reference can improve performance by eliminating the overhead of copying large amounts of data. However, pass-by-reference can weaken security, because the called function can access the caller's data.

Unlike many other languages, Python does not allow programmers to choose between pass-by-value and pass-by-reference when passing arguments. Python arguments are always *passed by object reference*—the function receives references to the values passed as arguments. In practice, pass-by-object-reference can be thought of as a combination of pass-by-value and pass-by-reference. If a function receives a reference to a mutable object (e.g., a dictionary or a list), the function can modify the original value of the object. It is as if the object had been passed by reference. If a function receives a reference to an immutable object (e.g., a number, a string or a tuple, whose elements are immutable values), the function cannot modify the original object directly. It is as if the object had been passed by value.

As always, it is important for the programmer to be aware of when an object may be modified by the function to which it is passed. Remembering the preceding rules and understanding how Python treats references to objects is essential to creating large and sophisticated Python systems.

5.8 Passing Lists to Functions

In this section, we discuss references further by examining what happens when a program passes a list to a function. The results we discover hold true for other mutable Python objects, such as dictionaries. To pass a list argument to a function, specify the name of the list without square brackets. For example, if list **hourlyTemperatures** has been created as

```
        hourlyTemperatures = [ 39, 43, 45 ]
```

the function call

```
        modifyList( hourlyTemperatures )
```

passes list **hourlyTemperatures** to function **modifyList**.

Although entire lists can be changed by a function, individual list elements that are numeric or immutable sequence data types cannot be changed. To pass a list element to a function, use the subscripted name of the list element as an argument in the function call.

The program of Fig. 5.16 demonstrates the difference between passing an entire list and passing a list element. Line 12 creates variable **aList**. The **for** loop at lines 17–18 prints the items of the list. Line 20 invokes function **modifyList** and passes the function variable **aList**. Function **modifyList** (lines 4–7) multiplies each element by 2. To illustrate that **aList**'s elements are modified, the **for** loop at lines 24–25 displays the list elements again. As the output shows, the elements of **aList** were modified by **modifyList**.

```
1   # Fig. 5.16: fig05_16.py
2   # Passing lists and individual list elements to functions.
3
4   def modifyList( aList ):
5
6       for i in range( len( aList ) ):
7           aList[ i ] *= 2
8
9   def modifyElement( element ):
10      element *= 2
11
12  aList = [ 1, 2, 3, 4, 5 ]
13
14  print "Effects of passing entire list:"
15  print "The values of the original list are:"
16
17  for item in aList:
18      print item,
19
20  modifyList( aList )
21
22  print "\n\nThe values of the modified list are:"
23
24  for item in aList:
25      print item,
26
27  print "\n\nEffects of passing list element:"
28  print "aList[ 3 ] before modifyElement:", aList[ 3 ]
29  modifyElement( aList[ 3 ] )
30  print "aList[ 3 ] after modifyElement:", aList[ 3 ]
31
32  print "\nEffects of passing slices of list:"
33  print "aList[ 2:4 ] before modifyList:", aList[ 2:4 ]
34  modifyList( aList[ 2:4 ] )
35  print "aList[ 2:4 ] after modifyList:", aList[ 2:4 ]
```

Fig. 5.16   Passing lists and individual list elements to methods. (Part 1 of 2.)

```
Effects of passing entire list:
The values of the original list are:
1 2 3 4 5

The values of the modified list are:
2 4 6 8 10

Effects of passing list element:
aList[ 3 ] before modifyElement: 8
aList[ 3 ] after modifyElement: 8

Effects of passing slices of list:
aList[ 2:4 ] before modifyList: [6, 8]
aList[ 2:4 ] after modifyList: [6, 8]
```

Fig. 5.16   Passing lists and individual list elements to methods. (Part 2 of 2.)

Lines 27–30 demonstrate passing a list element (**aList[3]**, which contains a number, recall that numbers are immutable) to a function. The program first prints the value of **aList[3]**, which is 8. Then, the program calls function **modifyElement** (lines 9–10) passing to parameter **element** the value 8. Function **modifyElement** multiplies **element** by 2. When the function terminates, the local variable **element** is destroyed. The value of the original element, **aList[3]**, in the list is not modified because the value of **aList[3]** is immutable. Thus, when control is returned to the main portion of the program, the unmodified value of **aList[3]** is printed.

Slicing creates a new sequence; therefore, when a program passes a slice to a function, the original sequence is not affected. Line 33 prints the slice **aList[2:4]** to the screen. Line 34 calls function **modifyList** and passes **aList[2:4]**. Line 35 prints the result of calling function **modifyList**—demonstrating that the original list was not modified.

Notice that function **modifyList** iterates through its list by accessing the elements using the square bracket operator. If the function contained the code

```
for item in aList:
    item *= 2
```

the list would remain unchanged, because the function would modify the value of local variable **item** and not the value stored at a particular index in the list.

5.9 Sorting and Searching Lists

Sorting data (i.e., placing the data into a particular order, such as ascending or descending) is a common computing application. For instance, a bank sorts checks by account number to prepare individual monthly bank statements. Telephone companies sort accounts by last names and, within that, by first names, to simplify the search for phone numbers. Almost all organizations sort data—in many cases, massive amounts of data. Sorting data is an intriguing problem that has attracted some of the most intense research efforts in the field of computer science. In this section, we discuss how to sort a list using list method *sort*.

Figure 5.17 sorts the values of the 10-element list **aList** (line 4) into ascending order. Lines 8–9 print the list items. Line 11 calls list method *sort*—this method sorts the elements of **aList** in ascending order. The remainder of the program prints the results of sorting the list.

Much research has been performed in the area of list-sorting algorithms, resulting in the design of many algorithms. Some of these algorithms are simple to express and program, but are inefficient. Other algorithms are complex and sophisticated, but provide increased performance. The exercises at the end of this chapter investigate a well-known sorting algorithm.

Performance Tip 5.1

Sometimes, the simplest algorithms perform poorly. Their virtue is that they are easy to write, test and debug. Sometimes complex algorithms are needed to realize maximum performance.

Often, programmers work with large amounts of data stored in lists. It might be necessary to determine whether a list contains a value that matches a certain *key value.* The process of locating a particular element value in a list is called *searching.*

The program in Fig. 5.18 searches a list for a value. Line 5 creates list **aList**, which contains the even numbers between 0 and 198, inclusive. Line 7 then retrieves the *search key* from the user and assigns the value to variable **searchKey**. Keyword **in** tests whether list **aList** contains the user-entered search key (line 9). If the list contains the value stored in variable **searchKey**, the expression (line 9) evaluates to true; otherwise, the expression evaluates to false.

```
1   # Fig. 5.17: fig05_17.py
2   # Sorting a list.
3
4   aList = [ 2, 6, 4, 8, 10, 12, 89, 68, 45, 37 ]
5
6   print "Data items in original order"
7
8   for item in aList:
9      print item,
10
11  aList.sort()
12
13  print "\n\nData items after sorting"
14
15  for item in aList:
16     print item,
17
18  print
```

```
Data items in original order
2 6 4 8 10 12 89 68 45 37

Data items after sorting
2 4 6 8 10 12 37 45 68 89
```

Fig. 5.17   Sorting a list.

```
1    # Fig. 5.18: fig05_18.py
2    # Searching a list for an integer.
3
4    # Create a list of even integers 0 to 198
5    aList = range( 0, 199, 2 )
6
7    searchKey = int( raw_input( "Enter integer search key: " ) )
8
9    if searchKey in aList:
10       print "Found at index:", aList.index( searchKey )
11   else:
12       print "Value not found"
```

```
Enter integer search key: 36
Found at index: 18
```

```
Enter integer search key: 37
Value not found
```

Fig. 5.18 Searching a list for an integer.

If the list contains the search key, line 10 invokes list method **index** to obtain the index of the search key. List method **index** takes a search key as a parameter, searches through the list and returns the index of the first list value that matches the search key. If the list does not contain any value that matches the search key, the program displays an error message. [*Note*: Figure 5.18 searches **aList** twice (lines 9–10), which, for large sequences, can result in poor performance. To improve performance, the program can use list method **index** and trap the exception that occurs if the argument is not in the list. We discuss exception-handling techniques in Chapter 12.]

As with sorting, a great deal of research has been devoted to the task of searching. In the exercises at the end of this chapter, we explore some of the more sophisticated ways of searching a list.

5.10 Multiple-Subscripted Sequences

Sequences can contain elements that are also sequences (i.e., lists and tuples). Such sequences have multiple subscripts. A common use of multiple-subscripted sequences is to represent *tables* of values consisting of information arranged in *rows* and *columns*. To identify a particular table element, we must specify two subscripts—by convention, the first identifies the element's row, the second the element's column.

Sequences that require two subscripts to identify a particular element are called *double-subscripted sequences* or *two-dimensional sequences*. Note that multiple-subscripted sequences can have more than two subscripts. Python does not support multiple-subscripted sequences directly, but allows programmers to specify single-subscripted tuples and lists whose elements are also single-subscripted tuples and lists, thus achieving the same effect. Figure 5.19 illustrates a double-subscripted sequence, **a**, containing three rows and four columns (i.e., a 3-by-4 sequence). In general, a sequence with *m* rows and *n* columns is called an *m-by-n sequence*.

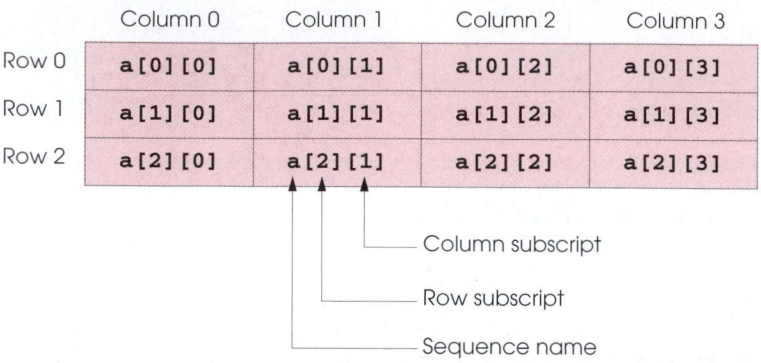

Fig. 5.19   Double-subscripted sequence with three rows and four columns.

Every element in sequence **a** is identified in Fig. 5.19 by an element name of the form
a[i][j]; **a** is the name of the sequence, and **i** and **j** are the subscripts that uniquely
identify the row and column of each element in **a**. Notice that the names of the elements in
the first row all have 0 as the first subscript; the names of the elements in the fourth column
all have 3 as the second subscript.

Multiple-subscripted sequences can be initialized during creation in much the same
way as a single-subscripted sequence. A double-subscripted list with two rows and columns
could be created with

```
b = [ [ 1, 2 ], [ 3, 4 ] ]
```

The values are grouped by row—the first row is the first element in the list, and the second
row is the second element in the list. So, **1** and **2** initialize **b[0][0]** and **b[0][1]**,
and **3** and **4** initialize **b[1][0]** and **b[1][1]**. Multiple-subscripted sequences are
maintained as sequences of sequences. The statement

```
c = ( ( 1, 2 ), ( 3, 4, 5 ) )
```

creates a tuple **c** with row 0 containing two elements (**1** and **2**) and row 1 containing three
elements (**3**, **4** and **5**). Python allows multiple-subscripted sequences to have rows of different lengths.

Figure 5.20 demonstrates creating and initializing double-subscripted sequences and
using nested **for** structures to traverse the sequences (i.e., manipulate every element of the
sequence).

```
1   # Fig. 5.20: fig05_20.py
2   # Making tables using lists of lists and tuples of tuples.
3
4   table1 = [ [ 1, 2, 3 ], [ 4, 5, 6 ] ]
5   table2 = ( ( 1, 2 ), ( 3, ), ( 4, 5, 6 ) )
6
```

Fig. 5.20   Tables created using lists of lists and tuples of tuples. (Part 1 of 2.)

```
7   print "Values in table1 by row are"
8
9   for row in table1:
10
11      for item in row:
12          print item,
13
14      print
15
16  print "\nValues in table2 by row are"
17
18  for row in table2:
19
20      for item in row:
21          print item,
22
23      print
```

```
Values in table1 by row are
1 2 3
4 5 6

Values in table2 by row are
1 2
3
4 5 6
```

Fig. 5.20   Tables created using lists of lists and tuples of tuples. (Part 2 of 2.)

The program declares two sequences. Line 4 creates the multiple-subscript list **table1** and provides six values in two sublists (i.e., two lists-within-lists). The first sublist (row) of the sequence contains the values 1, 2 and 3; the second sublist contains the values 4, 5 and 6.

Line 5 creates multiple-subscript tuple **table2** and provides six values in three subtuples (i.e., tuples-within-tuples). The first subtuple (row) contains two elements with values 1 and 2, respectively. The second subtuple contains one element with value 3. The third subtuple contains three elements with values 4, 5 and 6. Lines 9–14 use a nested **for** structure to output the rows of list **table1**. The outer **for** structure iterates over the rows in the list. The inner **for** structure iterates over each column in the row. The remainder of the program prints the values for variable **table2** in a similar manner.

The program in Fig. 5.20 demonstrates one case in a which a **for** structure is useful for manipulating a multiple-subscripted sequence. Many other common sequence manipulations use **for** repetition structures. For example, the following **for** structure sets all the elements in the third row of sequence **a** in Fig. 5.19 to 0:

```
for column in range( len( a[ 2 ] ) ):
    a[ 2 ][ column ] = 0
```

We specified the *third* row; thus, the first subscript is always 2 (0 is the first row and 1 is the second row). The **for** structure varies only the second subscript (i.e., the column subscript). The preceding **for** structure is equivalent to the assignment statements

```
a[ 2 ][ 0 ] = 0
a[ 2 ][ 1 ] = 0
a[ 2 ][ 2 ] = 0
a[ 2 ][ 3 ] = 0
```

The following nested **for** structure determines the total of all the elements in sequence **a**:

```
total = 0

for row in a:
    for column in row:
        total += column
```

The **for** structure totals the elements of the sequence one row at a time. The outer **for** structure iterates over the rows in the table so that the elements of each row may be totaled by the inner **for** structure. The **total** is displayed when the nested **for** structure terminates.

The program in Fig. 5.21 performs several other common sequence manipulations on the 3-by-4 list **grades**. Each row of the list represents a student, and each column represents a grade on one of the four exams the students took during the semester. The list manipulations are performed by four functions. Function **printGrades** (lines 5–25) prints the data stored in list **grades** in a tabular format. Function **minimum** (lines 28–38) determines the lowest grade of any student for the semester. Function **maximum** (lines 41–51) determines the highest grade of any student for the semester. Function **average** (lines 54–60) determines a particular student's semester average. Notice that line 55 initializes **total** to **0.0**, so the function returns a floating-point value.

```
1   # Fig. 5.21: fig05_21.py
2   # Double-subscripted list example.
3
4
5   def printGrades( grades ):
6       students = len( grades )        # number of students
7       exams = len( grades[ 0 ] )      # number of exams
8
9       # print table headers
10      print "The list is:"
11      print "             ",
12
13      for i in range( exams ):
14          print "[%d]" % i,
15
16      print
17
18      # print scores, by row
19      for i in range( students ):
20          print "grades[%d]   " % i,
21
22          for j in range( exams ):
23              print grades[ i ][ j ], "",
24
25          print
```

Fig. 5.21   Double-scripted tuples. (Part 1 of 3.)

```
26
27
28  def minimum( grades ):
29      lowScore = 100
30
31      for studentExams in grades:       # loop over students
32
33          for score in studentExams:    # loop over scores
34
35              if score < lowScore:
36                  lowScore = score
37
38      return lowScore
39
40
41  def maximum( grades ):
42      highScore = 0
43
44      for studentExams in grades:       # loop over students
45
46          for score in studentExams:    # loop over scores
47
48              if score > highScore:
49                  highScore = score
50
51      return highScore
52
53
54  def average( setOfGrades ):
55      total = 0.0
56
57      for grade in setOfGrades:         # loop over student's scores
58          total += grade
59
60      return total / len( setOfGrades )
61
62
63  # main program
64  grades = [ [ 77, 68, 86, 73 ],
65             [ 96, 87, 89, 81 ],
66             [ 70, 90, 86, 81 ] ]
67
68  printGrades( grades )
69  print "\n\nLowest grade:", minimum( grades )
70  print "Highest grade:", maximum( grades )
71  print "\n"
72
73  # print average for each student
74  for i in range( len( grades ) ):
75      print "Average for student", i, "is", average( grades[ i ] )
```

Fig. 5.21   Double-scripted tuples. (Part 2 of 3.)

```
The list is:
          [0] [1] [2] [3]
grades[0]  77  68  86  73
grades[1]  96  87  89  81
grades[2]  70  90  86  81


Lowest grade: 68
Highest grade: 96


Average for student 0 is 76.0
Average for student 1 is 88.25
Average for student 2 is 81.75
```

Fig. 5.21   Double-scripted tuples. (Part 3 of 3.)

Function **printGrades** uses the list **grades** and variables **students** (number of rows in the list) and **exams** (number of columns in the list). The function loops through list **grades**, using nested **for** structures to print out the grades in tabular format. The outer **for** structure (lines 19–25) iterates over **i** (i.e., the row subscript), the inner **for** structure (lines 22–23) over **j** (i.e., the column subscript).

Functions **minimum** and **maximum** loop through list **grades**, using nested **for** structures. Function **minimum** compares each grade to variable **lowScore**. If a grade is less than **lowScore**, **lowScore** is set to that grade (line 36). When execution of the nested structure is complete, **lowScore** contains the smallest grade in the double-subscripted list. Function **maximum** works similarly to function **minimum**.

Function **average** takes one argument—a single-subscripted list of test results for a particular student. When line 75 invokes **average**, the argument is **grades[i]**, which specifies that a particular row of the double-subscripted list **grades** is to be passed to **average**. For example, the argument **grades[1]** represents the four values (a single-subscripted list of grades) stored in the second row of the double-subscripted list **grades**. Remember that, in Python, a double-subscripted list is a list with elements that are single-subscripted lists. Function **average** calculates the sum of the list elements, divides the total by the number of test results and returns the floating-point result.

In the above example, we demonstrated how to use double-subscripted lists. However, when we need to compute pure numerical problems (i.e., multi-dimensional arrays), the basic Python language cannot handle them efficiently. In this case, a package called **NumPy** should be used. The **NumPy** (numerical python) package contains modules that handle arrays, and it provides multi-dimensional array objects for efficient computation. For more information on **NumPy**, visit **sourceforge.net/projects/numpy**.

Chapters 2–5 introduced the basic-programming techniques of Python. In Chapter 6, Introduction to the Common Gateway Interface (CGI), we will use these techniques to design Web-based applications. In Chapters 7–9, we will introduce object-oriented programming techniques that will allow us to build complex applications in the latter half of the book.

SUMMARY

- Data structures hold and organize information (data).

- Sequences, often called arrays in other languages, are data structures that store related data items. Python supports three basic sequence data types: a string, a list and a tuple.

- A sequence element may be referenced by writing the sequence name followed by the element's position number in square brackets (**[ ]**). The first element in a sequence is the zeroth element.

- Sequences can be accessed from the end of the sequence by using negative subscripts.

- The position number more formally is called a subscript (or an index), which must be an integer or an integer expression. If a program uses an integer expression as a subscript, Python evaluates the expression to determine the location of the subscript.

- Some types of sequences are immutable—the sequence cannot be altered (e.g., by changing the value of one of its elements). Python strings and tuples are immutable sequences.

- Some sequences are mutable—the sequence can be altered. Python lists are mutable sequences.

- The length of the sequence is determined by the function call **len(** *sequence* **)**.

- To create an empty string, use the empty quotes (i.e., **" "**, **' '**,**""" """** or **''' '''**)

- To create an empty list, use empty square brackets (i.e., **[ ]**). To create a list that contains a sequence of values, separate the values with commas, and place the values inside square brackets.

- To create an empty tuple, use the empty parentheses (i.e., **( )**). To create a tuple that contains a sequence of values, simply separate the values with commas. Tuples also can be created by surrounding the tuple values with parentheses; however, the parentheses are optional.

- Creating a tuple is sometimes referred to as packing a tuple.

- When creating a one-element tuple—called a singleton—write the value, followed by a comma (**,**).

- In practice, Python programmers distinguish between tuples and lists to represent different kinds of sequences, based on the context of the program.

- Although lists are not restricted to homogeneous data types, Python programmers typically use lists to store sequences of homogeneous values—values of the same data type. In general, a program uses a list to store homogeneous values for the purpose of looping over these values and performing the same operation on each value. Usually, the length of the list is not predetermined and may vary over the course of the program.

- The **+=** augmented assignment statement can insert a value in a list. When the value to the left of the **+=** symbol is a sequence, the value to the right of the symbol must be a sequence also.

- The **for/in** structure iterates over a sequence. The **for** structure starts with the first element in the sequence, assigns the value of the first element to the control variable and executes the body of the **for** structure. Then, the **for** structure proceeds to the next element in the sequence and performs the same operations.

- If a program attempts to access a nonexistent index, the program exits and displays an "out-of-range" error message. This error can be caught as an exception.

- Tuples store sequences of heterogeneous data. Each data piece in a tuple represents a part of the total information represented by the tuple. Usually, the length of the tuple is predetermined and does not change over the course of a program's execution. A program usually does not iterate over a sequence, but accesses the parts of the tuple the program needs to perform its task.

- If a program attempts to modify a tuple, the program exits and displays an error message.

- Sequences can be unpacked—the values stored in the sequence are assigned to various identifiers. Unpacking is a useful programming shortcut for assigning values to multiple variables in a single statement.

- When unpacking a sequence, the number of variable names to the left of the = symbol must equal the number of elements in the sequence to the right of the symbol.
- Python provides the slicing capability to obtain contiguous regions of a sequence.
- To obtain a slice of the *i*th element through the *j*th element, inclusive, use the expression *sequence*[**i:j + 1**].
- The dictionary is a mapping construct that consists of key-value pairs. Dictionaries (called hashes or associative arrays in other languages), can be thought of as unordered collections of values where each value is accessed through its corresponding key.
- To create an empty dictionary, use empty curly braces (i.e., **{}**).
- To create a dictionary with values, use a comma-separated sequence of key-value pairs, inside curly braces. Each key-value pair is of the form *key* : *value*.
- Python dictionary keys must be immutable values, like strings, numbers or tuples, whose elements are immutable. Dictionary values can be of any Python data type.
- Dictionary values are accessed with the expression *dictionaryName*[*key*].
- To insert a new key-value pair in a dictionary, use the statement *dictionaryName*[*key*] = *value*.
- The statement *dictionaryName*[*key*] = *value* modifies the value associated with key, if the dictionary already contains that key. Otherwise, the statement inserts the key-value pair into the dictionary.
- Accessing a non-existent dictionary key causes the program to exit and to display a "key error" message.
- A method performs the behaviors (tasks) of an object.
- To invoke an object's method, specify the name of the object, followed by the dot (**.**) access operator, followed by the method invocation.
- List method **append** adds an items to the end of a list.
- List method **count** takes a value as an argument and returns the number of elements in the list that have that value. If the list contains no elements with the specified value, method **count** returns 0.
- Dictionary method **items** returns a list of tuples, where each tuple contains a key-value pair. Dictionary method **keys** returns an unordered list of the dictionary's keys. Dictionary method **values** returns an unordered list of the dictionary's values.
- Dictionary method **copy** returns a new dictionary that is a shallow copy of the original dictionary. In a shallow copy, the elements in the new dictionary are references to the elements in the original dictionary.
- If the programmer wants to create a copy—called a deep copy—that is independent of the original dictionary, Python provides module **copy**. Function **copy.deepcopy** returns a deep copy of it argument.
- In many programming languages, the two ways to pass arguments to functions are pass-by-value and pass-by-reference (also called pass-by-value and pass-by-reference).
- When an argument is passed by value, a copy of the argument's value is made and passed to the called function.
- With by reference, the caller allows the called function to access the caller's data directly and to modify that data.
- Unlike many other languages, Python does not allow programmers to choose between pass-by-value and pass-by-reference to pass arguments. Python arguments are always passed by object reference—the function receives references to the values passed as arguments. In practice, pass-by-object-reference can be thought of as a combination of pass-by-value and pass-by-reference.

- If a function receives a reference to a mutable object (e.g., a dictionary or a list), the function can modify the original value of the object. It is as if the object had been passed by reference.
- If a function receives a reference to an immutable object (e.g., a number, a string or a tuple whose elements are immutable values), the function cannot modify the original object directly. It is as if the object had been passed by value.
- To pass a list argument to a function, specify the name of the list without square brackets.
- Although entire lists can be changed by a function, individual list elements that are numeric and immutable sequence data types cannot be changed. To pass a list element to a function, use the subscripted name of the list element as an argument in the function call.
- Slicing creates a new sequence; therefore, when a program passes a slice to a function, the original sequence is not affected.
- Sorting data is the process of placing data into a particular order.
- By default, list method **sort** sorts the elements of a list in ascending order.
- Some sorting algorithms are simple to express and program, but are inefficient. Other algorithms are complex and sophisticated, but provide increased performance.
- Often, programmers work with large amounts of data stored in lists. It might be necessary to determine whether a list contains a value that matches a certain key value. The process of locating a particular element value in a list is called searching.
- Keyword **in** tests whether a sequence contains a particular value.
- List method **index** takes a search key as a parameter, searches through the list and returns the index of the first list value that matches the search key. If the list does not contain any value that matches the search key, the program displays an error message.
- Sequences can contain elements that are also sequences. Such sequences have multiple subscripts. A common use of multiple-subscripted sequences is to represent tables of values consisting of information arranged in rows and columns.
- To identify a particular table element, we must specify two subscripts—by convention, the first identifies the element's row, the second identifies the element's column.
- Sequences that require two subscripts to identify a particular element are called double-subscripted sequences or two-dimensional sequences.
- Python does not support multiple-subscripted sequences directly, but allows programmers to specify single-subscripted tuples and lists whose elements are also single-subscripted tuples and lists, thus achieving the same effect.
- A sequence with m rows and n columns is called an m-by-n sequence. It is more commonly know as two-dimensional sequence.
- The name of every element in a multiple-subscripted sequence is of the form **a[i][j]**, where **a** is the name of the sequence, and i and j are the subscripts that uniquely identify the row and column of each element in the sequence.
- To compute pure numerical problems (i.e., multi-dimensional arrays), use package **NumPy** (numerical Python). This package contains modules that handle arrays and provides multi-dimensional array objects for efficient computation.

TERMINOLOGY

append method of list	bracket operator (**[]**)
array	**clear** method of dictionary
associative array	column

comma (**,**)
copy method of dictionary
count list method
data structure
deep copy of a dictionary
dictionary
dictionary method
dot access operator (**.**)
double-subscripted sequence
element
empty curly braces **{}**
empty dictionary
empty list
empty parentheses **()**
empty quotes
empty square brackets **[]**
empty string
empty tuple
for structure
get method of dictionary
hash
has_key method of dictionary
heterogeneous data (in tuples)
histogram
homogeneous data (in lists)
immutable sequence
in keyword
index
index method of list
in-place sorting
items method of dictionary
iteritems method of dictionary
iterkeys method of dictionary
itervalues method of dictionary
keys method of dictionary
key value
key-value pair
length (sequence)
list
list method

m-by-*n* sequence
mapping construct
method
method invocation
multiple-subscripted sequence
mutable sequence
name (sequence)
NumPy package (numerical Python)
one-element tuple (singleton)
out-of-range error message
packed
packing a tuple
pass-by-object-reference
pass-by-reference
pass-by-value
popitem method of dictionary
position number
row
search
search key
sequence
sequence slicing
sequence unpacking
setdefault method of dictionary
shallow copy of a dictionary
singleton
slice a sequence
slicing operator (**[:]**)
sort
sort list method
subscript
table
tuple
two-dimensional sequence
update method of dictionary
unpacked sequence
value (sequence)
values dictionary method
zeroth element

SELF-REVIEW EXERCISES

5.1   Fill in the blanks in each of the following statements:
a) _____ are "associative arrays" that consist of _____ pairs.
b) The last element in a sequence can always be accessed with subscript _____.
c) Statement _____ creates a singleton **aTuple**.
d) Function _____ returns the length of a sequence.
e) Selecting a portion of a sequence with the operator **[:]** is called _____.
f) Dictionary method _____ returns a list of key-value pairs.

g) When an argument is passed _____, a copy of the argument's value is made and passed to the called method.

h) Use the expression _____ to obtain the *i*th element through the *j*th element of list **sequence**, inclusive.

i) A sequence with *m* rows and *n* columns is called an _____.

j) List method _____ returns the number of times a specified element occurs in a list.

5.2 State whether each of the following is *true* or *false*. If *false*, explain why.

a) A sequence begins at subscript 1.

b) Strings and tuples are mutable sequences.

c) Each key-value pair in a dictionary has the form *key* **:** *value*.

d) Using a tuple as a dictionary key is an error.

e) Dictionary values are accessed with the dot operator.

f) Method **insert** adds one element to the end of a list.

g) The **+=** statement appends items into lists.

h) List method **sort** sorts the elements of a list in place.

i) If list method **search** finds a list value that matches the search key, it returns the subscript of the list value.

j) Unlike other languages, Python does not allow the programmer to choose whether to pass each argument pass-by-value or pass-by-reference.

ANSWERS TO SELF-REVIEW EXERCISES

5.1   a) Dictionaries, key-value. b) -1. c) **aTuple = 1,**. d) **len**. e) slicing. f) **items**. g) pass-by-value. h) **sequence[i:j + 1]**. i) m-by-n sequence. j) **count**.

5.2   a) False. The first element in every sequence has subscript 0. b) False. Strings and tuples are immutable sequences—their values cannot be altered. c) True. d) False. Dictionary keys must be immutable data types, such as tuples. e) False. Dictionary values are accessed with the expression *dictionaryName*[*key*]. f) False. Method **append** adds one element to the end of a list. g) True. h) True. i) False. If list method **index** finds a list value that matches the search key, it returns the subscript of the list value. j) True.

EXERCISES

5.3   Use a list to solve the following problem: Read in 20 numbers. As each number is read, print it only if it is not a duplicate of a number already read.

5.4   Use a list of lists to solve the following problem. A company has four salespeople (1 to 4) who sell five different products (1 to 5). Once a day, each salesperson passes in a slip for each different type of product sold. Each slip contains:

a) The salesperson number.

b) The product number.

c) The number of that product sold that day.

Thus, each salesperson passes in between 0 and 5 sales slips per day. Assume that the information from all of the slips for last month is available. Write a program that will read all this information for last month's sales and summarize the total sales by salesperson by product. All totals should be stored in list **sales**. After processing all the information for last month, display the results in tabular format, with each of the columns representing a particular salesperson and each of the rows representing a particular product. Cross-total each row to get the total sales of each product for last month; cross-total each column to get the total sales by salesperson for last month. Your tabular printout should include these cross-totals to the right of the totaled rows and at the bottom of the totaled columns.

5.5   (*The Sieve of Eratosthenes*) A prime integer is any integer greater than 1 that is evenly divisible only by itself and 1. The Sieve of Eratosthenes is a method of finding prime numbers. It operates as follows:

    a) Create a list with all elements initialized to 1 (true). List elements with prime subscripts will remain 1. All other list elements will eventually be set to zero.

    b) Starting with list element 2, every time a list element is found whose value is 1, loop through the remainder of the list and set to zero every element whose subscript is a multiple of the subscript for the element with value 1. For list subscript 2, all elements beyond 2 in the list that are multiples of 2 will be set to zero (subscripts 4, 6, 8, 10, etc.); for list subscript 3, all elements beyond 3 in the list that are multiples of 3 will be set to zero (subscripts 6, 9, 12, 15, etc.); and so on.

When this process is complete, the list elements that are still set to 1 indicate that the subscript is a prime number. These subscripts can then be printed. Write a program that uses a list of 1000 elements to determine and print the prime numbers between 2 and 999. Ignore element 0 of the list.

5.6   (*Bubble Sort*) Sorting data (i.e. placing data into some particular order, such as ascending or descending) is one of the most important computing applications. Python lists provide a **sort** method. In this exercise, readers implement their own sorting function, using the bubble-sort method. In the bubble sort (or *sinking* sort), the smaller values gradually "bubble" their way upward to the top of the list like air bubbles rising in water, while the larger values sink to the bottom of the list. The process that compares each adjacent pair of elements in a list in turn and swaps the elements if the second element is less than the first element is called a pass. The technique makes several passes through the list. On each pass, successive pairs of elements are compared. If a pair is in increasing order, bubble sort leaves the values as they are. If a pair is in decreasing order, their values are swapped in the list. After the first pass, the largest value is guaranteed to sink to the highest index of a list. After the second pass, the second largest value is guaranteed to sink to the second highest index of a list, and so on. Write a program that uses function **bubbleSort** to sort the items in a list.

5.7   (*Binary Search*) When a list is sorted, a high-speed binary search technique can find items in the list quickly. The binary search algorithm eliminates from consideration one-half of the elements in the list being searched after each comparison. The algorithm locates the middle element of the list and compares it with the search key. If they are equal, the search key is found, and the subscript of that element is returned. Otherwise, the problem is reduced to searching one half of the list. If the search key is less than the middle element of the list, the first half of the list is searched. If the search key is not the middle element in the specified piece of the original list, the algorithm is repeated on one-quarter of the original list. The search continues until the search key is equal to the middle element of the smaller list or until the smaller list consists of one element that is not equal to the search key (i.e. the search key is not found.)

    Even in a worst-case scenario, searching a list of 1024 elements will take only 10 comparisons during a binary search. Repeatedly dividing 1024 by 2 (because after each comparison we are able to eliminate from the consideration half the list) yields the values 512, 256, 128, 64, 32, 16, 8, 4, 2 and 1. The number 1024 (210) is divided by 2 only ten times to get the value 1. Dividing by 2 is equivalent to one comparison in the binary-search algorithm. A list of 1,048,576 (2^{20}) elements takes a maximum of 20 comparisons to find the key. A list of one billion elements takes a maximum of 30 comparisons to find the key. The maximum number of comparisons needed for the binary search of any sorted list can be determined by finding the first power of 2 greater than or equal to the number of elements in the list.

    Write a program that implements function **binarySearch**, which takes a sorted list and a search key as arguments. The function should return the index of the list value that matches the search key (or -1, if the search key is not found).

5.8   Create a dictionary of 20 random values in the range 1–99. Determine whether there are any duplicate values in the dictionary. (*Hint*: you many want to sort the list first.)

Introduction to the Common Gateway Interface (CGI)

Objectives

- To understand the Common Gateway Interface (CGI) protocol.
- To understand the Hypertext Transfer Protocol (HTTP).
- To implement CGI scripts.
- To use XHTML forms to send information to CGI scripts.
- To understand and parse query strings.
- To use module **cgi** to process information from XHTML forms.

This is the common air that bathes the globe.
Walt Whitman

The longest part of the journey is said to be the passing of the gate.
Marcus Terentius Varro

Railway termini...are our gates to the glorious and unknown. Through them we pass out into adventure and sunshine, to them, alas! we return.
E. M. Forster

There comes a time in a man's life when to get where he has to go—if there are no doors or windows—he walks through a wall.
Bernard Malamud

6.1 Introduction

The *Common Gateway Interface (CGI)* describes a set of protocols through which applications (commonly called *CGI programs* or *CGI scripts*) interact with Web servers and indirectly with Web browsers (e.g., client applications). A Web server is a specialized software application that responds to client application requests by providing resources (e.g. Web pages). CGI protocols often generate Web content dynamically. A Web page is dynamic if a program on the Web server generates that page's content each time a user requests the page. For example, a form in a Web page could request that a user enter a zip code. When the user types and submits the zip code, the Web server can use a CGI program to create a page that displays information about the weather in that client's region. In contrast, *static* Web page content never changes unless the Web developers edit the document.

CGI is "common" because it is not specific to any operating system (e.g., Linux or Windows), to any programming language or to any Web server software. CGI can be used with virtually any programming or scripting language, such as C, Perl and Python. In this chapter, we explain how Web clients and servers interact. We introduce the basics of CGI and use Python to write CGI scripts.

The CGI protocol was developed in 1993 by the *National Center for Supercomputing Applications* (*NCSA*—**www.ncsa.uiuc.edu**), for use with its *HTTPd Web server*. NCSA developed CGI to be a simple tool to produce dynamic Web content. The simplicity of CGI resulted in its widespread use and in its adoption as an unofficial worldwide protocol. CGI was quickly incorporated into additional Web servers, such as Microsoft *Internet Information Services (IIS)* and Apache (**www.apache.org**).

6.2 Client and Web Server Interaction

In this section, we discuss the interactions between a Web server and a client application. A Web page, in its simplest form, is either a *Hypertext Markup Language* (*HTML*) document or an *Extensible Hypertext Markup Language (XHTML)* document. (In this chapter, we use XHTML.) An XHTML document is a plain-text file that contains markup, or *tags*, which describe how the document should be displayed by a Web browser. For example, the XHTML markup

```
<title>My Web Page</title>
```

indicates that the text between the opening *<title>* tag and the closing *</title>* tag is the Web page's title. The browser renders the text between these tags in a specific manner.

XHTML requires *syntactically* correct documents—markup must follow specific rules. For example, XHTML tags must be in all lowercase letters and all opening tags must have corresponding closing tags. We discuss XHTML in detail in Appendix I and Appendix J.

Each Web page has a unique *Uniform Resource Locator* (*URL*) associated with it—an address of sorts. The URL contains information that directs a browser to the resource (most often a Web page) the user wishes to access. For example, consider the URL

```
http://www.deitel.com/books/downloads.html
```

The first part of the address, **http://**, indicates that the resource is to be obtained using the *Hypertext Transfer Protocol (HTTP)*. During this interaction, the Web server and the client communicate using the platform-independent HTTP, a protocol for transferring requests and files over the Internet (e.g., between Web servers and Web browsers). Section 6.2.3 discusses HTTP.

The next section of the URL—**www.deitel.com**—is the *hostname* of the server, which is the name of the server computer, the *host*, on which the resource resides. A *domain name system (DNS)* server translates the hostname (**www.deitel.com**) into an *Internet Protocol* (*IP*) *address* (e.g., **207.60.134.230**) that identifies the server computer (just as a telephone number uniquely identifies a particular phone line). This translation operation is a *DNS lookup*. A DNS server maintains a database of hostnames and their corresponding IP addresses.

The remainder of the URL specifies the requested resource—**/books/downloads.html**. This portion of the URL specifies both the name of the resource (**downloads.html**—an HTML/XHTML document) and its path (**/books**). The Web server maps the URL to a file (or other resource, such as a CGI program) on the server, or to another resource on the server's network. The Web server then returns the requested document to the client. The path represents a directory in the Web server's file system. It also is possible that the resource is created dynamically and does not reside anywhere on the server computer. In this case, the URL uses the hostname to locate the correct server, and the server uses the path and resource information to locate (or create) the resource to respond to the client's request. As we will see, URLs also can provide input to a CGI program residing on a server.

6.2.1 System Architecture

A Web server often is part of a *multi-tier application*, sometimes referred to as an *n-tier application*. Multi-tier applications divide functionality into separate *tiers* (i.e., logical groupings of functionality). Tiers can be located on a single computer or on multiple computers. Figure 6.1 presents the basic structure of a three-tier application.

The *information tier* (also called the *data tier* or the *bottom tier*) maintains data for the application. This tier typically stores data in a *relational database management system (RDBMS)*. We discuss relational database management systems in further detail in Chapter 17, Database Application Programming Interface (DB-API). For example, a retail store may have a database for product information, such as descriptions, prices and quantities in stock. The same database also may contain customer information, such as user names, billing addresses and credit-card numbers.

The *middle tier* implements *business logic* and *presentation logic* to control interactions between application clients and application data. The middle tier acts as an intermediary between data in the information tier and the application clients. The middle-tier *controller logic* processes client requests from the client tier (e.g., a request to view a product catalog) and retrieves data from the database. The middle-tier presentation logic then processes data from the information tier and presents the content to the client.

Business logic in the middle tier enforces *business rules* and ensures that data are reliable before updating the database or presenting data to a client. Business rules dictate how clients can and cannot access application data and how applications process data.

The middle tier also implements the application's presentation logic. Web applications typically present information to clients as XHTML documents (older applications present information as HTML). Many Web applications present information to wireless clients as Wireless Markup Language (WML) documents. We discuss WML in detail in Chapter 23, Case Study: Online Bookstore.

The *client tier*, or *top tier*, is the application's user interface. Users interact with the application through the user interface. This causes the client to interact with the middle tier to make requests and to retrieve data from the information tier. The client then displays to the user the data retrieved from the middle tier.

6.2.2 Accessing Web Servers

To request documents from Web servers, users must know the machine names (called hostnames) on which Web server software resides. Users can request documents from *local Web servers* (i.e, those that reside on users' machines) or *remote Web servers* (i.e., those that reside on different machines).

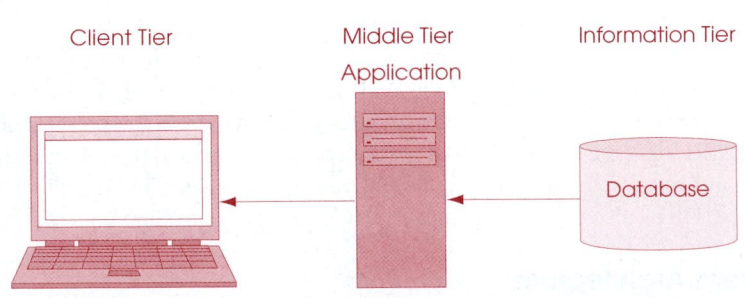

Fig. 6.1   Three-tier application model.

We can request document from local Web servers through the machine name or through `localhost`—a hostname that references the local machine. We use `localhost` in this book. To determine the machine name in Windows 98, right-click **Network Neighborhood**, and select **Properties** from the context menu to display the **Network** dialog. In the **Network** dialog, click the **Identification** tab. The computer name displays in the **Computer name:** field. Click **Cancel** to close the **Network** dialog. In Windows 2000, right click **My Network Places** and select **Properties** from the context menu to display the **Network and Dialup Connections** explorer. In the explorer, click **Network Identification**. The **Full Computer Name:** field in the **System Properties** window displays the computer name. To determine the machine name on most Linux machines, simply type the command **hostname** at a shell prompt.

A client also can access a server by specifying the server's domain name or IP address (e.g., in a Web browser's **Address** field). A domain name represents a group of hosts on the Internet; it combines with a hostname (such as **www**—a common hostname for Web servers) and a *top-level domain (TLD)* to form a *fully qualified hostname*, which provides a user-friendly way to identify a site on the Internet. In a fully qualified hostname, the TLD often describes the type of organization that owns the domain name. For example, the **com** TLD usually refers to a commercial business, whereas the **org** TLD usually refers to a non-profit organization. In addition, each country has its own TLD, such as **cn** for China, **et** for Ethiopia, **om** for Oman and **us** for the United States.

6.2.3 HTTP Transactions

Before exploring how CGI operates, it is necessary to have a basic understanding of networking and the World Wide Web. In this section, we discuss the technical aspects of how a browser interacts with a Web server to display a Web page and we examine the Hypertext Transfer Protocol (HTTP). We also explore HTTP's components that enable clients and servers to interact and exchange information uniformly and predictably.

An HTTP request often posts data to a *server-side form handler* that processes the data. For example, when a user participates in a Web-based survey, the Web server receives the information specified in the XHTML form as part of the request.

When a user enters a URL, the client has to request that resource. The two most common *HTTP request types* (also known as *request methods*) are *get* and *post*. These request types retrieve resources from a Web server and send client form data to a Web server. A *get* request sends form content as part of the URL. For example, in the URL

www._somesite_**.com/search?query=**_value_

the information following the **?** (**query=**_value_) indicates the user-specified input. For example, if the user performs a search on "Massachusetts," the last part of the URL would be **?query=Massachusetts**. Most Web servers limit *get* request query strings to 1024 characters. If the query string exceeds this limit, the *post* request must be used. The data sent in a *post* request is not part of the URL and cannot be seen by the user. Forms that contain many fields are submitted most often by *post* requests. Sensitive form fields, such as passwords, usually are sent using this request type.

To make the request, the browser sends an HTTP request message to the server (step 1, Fig. 6.2). HTTP has two request types, *get* and *post*. The *get* request (in its simplest form) follows the format: **GET /books/downloads.html HTTP/1.1**. The word *GET* is an

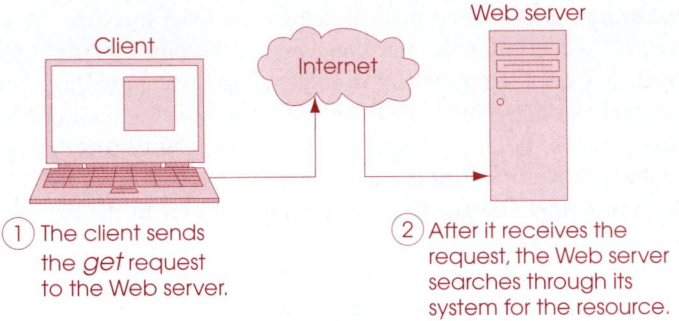

① The client sends the *get* request to the Web server.

② After it receives the request, the Web server searches through its system for the resource.

Fig. 6.2   Client interacting with server and Web server. Step 1: The request, **GET /books/downloads.html HTTP/1.1**.

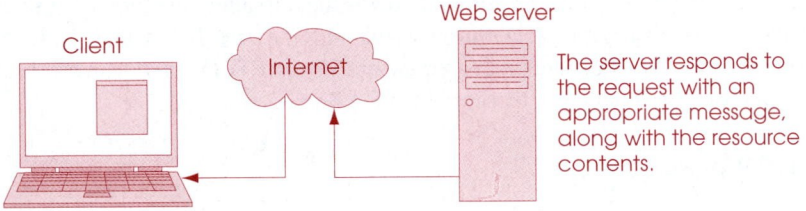

The server responds to the request with an appropriate message, along with the resource contents.

Fig. 6.2   Client interacting with server and Web server. Step 2: The HTTP response, **HTTP/1.1 200 OK**.

HTTP method indicating that the client is requesting a resource. The next part of the request provides the name (**downloads.html**) and path (**/books/**) of the resource (an HTML/XHTML document). The final part of the request provides the protocol's name and version number (**HTTP/1.1**).

Servers that understand HTTP version 1.1 translate this request and respond (step 2, Fig. 6.2). The server responds with a line indicating the HTTP version, followed by a status code that consists of a numeric code and phrase describing the status of the transaction. For example,

    HTTP/1.1 200 OK

indicates success, while

    HTTP/1.1 404 Not found

informs the client that the requested resource was not found on the server in the location specified by the URL.

Browsers often *cache* (save on a local disk) Web pages for quick reloading, to reduce the amount of data that the browser needs to download. However, browsers typically do not cache server responses to *post* requests, because subsequent *post* requests may not contain the same information. For example, several users who participate in a Web-based survey may request the same Web page. Each user's response changes the overall results of the survey, thus the data on the Web server is changed.

On the other hand, Web browsers cache server responses to *get* requests. With a Web-based search engine, a *get* request normally supplies the search engine with search criteria specified in an XHTML form. The search engine then performs the search and returns the results as a Web page. These pages are cached in the event that the user performs the same search again.

The server normally sends one or more *HTTP headers,* which provide additional information about the data sent in response to the request. In this case, the server is sending an HTML/XHTML text document, so the HTTP header reads

```
Content-type: text/html
```

This information is known as the *MIME (Multipurpose Internet Mail Extensions) type* of the content. MIME is an Internet standard that specifies how messages should be formatted and clients use the content type to determine how to represent the content to the user. Each type of data sent has a MIME type associated with it that helps the browser determine how to process the data it receives. For example, the MIME type **text/plain** indicates that the data is text that should be displayed without attempting to interpret any of the content as HTML or XHTML markup. Similarly, the MIME type **image/gif** indicates that the content is a *GIF (Graphics Interchange Format)* image. When this MIME type is received by the browser, it attempts to display the image. For more information on MIME, visit

```
www.nacs.uci.edu/indiv/ehood/MIME/MIME.html
```

The header (or set of headers) is followed by a blank line (a carriage return, line feed or combination of both) which indicates to the client that the server is finished sending HTTP headers. The server then sends the text in the requested HTML/XHTML document (**downloads.html**). The connection terminates when the transfer of the resource completes. The client-side browser interprets the text it receives and displays (or renders) the results.

This section examined how a simple HTTP transaction is performed between a Web-browser application on the client side (e.g., Microsoft Internet Explorer or Netscape Communicator) and a Web-server application on the server side (e.g., Apache or IIS). Next, we introduce CGI programming.

6.3 Simple CGI Script

Two types of scripting are used in Web-based applications: *server-side* and *client-side*. CGI scripts are an example of server-side scripts because they run on the server. Programmers have greater control over Web page content when using server-side scripts, because server-side scripts can manipulate databases and other server resources. An example of client-side scripting is JavaScript. Client-side scripts can access the browser's features, manipulate browser documents, validate user input and much more.

Scripts executed on the server usually generate custom responses for clients. For example, a client might connect to an airline's Web server and request a list of all flights from Boston to San Antonio between September 19th and November 5th. The server queries the database, dynamically generates XHTML content containing the flight list and sends the XHTML to the client. This technology allows clients to obtain the most current flight information from the database by connecting to an airline's Web server.

Server-side scripting languages have a wider range of programmatic capabilities than their client-side equivalents. For example, server-side scripts can access the server's file directory structure, whereas client-side scripts cannot access the client's file directory structure.

Server-side scripts also have access to server-side software that extends server functionality. These pieces of software are called *COM components* for Microsoft Web servers and *modules* for Apache Web servers. Components and modules range from programming language support to counting the number of times a Web page has been visited (known as the number of *hits*).

Software Engineering Observation 6.1

Server-side scripts are not visible to the client; only the content the server delivers is visible to the client.

As long as a file on the server remains unchanged, its associated URL will display the same content in clients' browsers each time the file is accessed. For the content in the file to change (e.g., to include new links or the latest company news), someone must alter the file manually (probably with a text editor or Web-page design software) then load the changed file back onto the server.

Manually changing Web pages is not feasible for those who want to create interesting and dynamic Web pages. For example, if you want your Web page always to display the current date or weather, the page would require continuous updating.

The examples in this chapter rely heavily upon XHTML and *Cascading Style Sheets (CSS)*. CSS allows document authors to specify the presentation of elements on a Web page (spacing, margins, etc.) separately from the structure of the document (section headers, body text, links, etc.). Readers not familiar with these technologies will want to read Appendix I and Appendix J, which describe XHTML in detail and Appendix K, Cascading Style Sheets, which introduces CSS.

Figure 6.3 illustrates the full program listing for our first CGI script. Line 1

```
#!c:\Python\python.exe
```

is a *directive* (sometimes called the *pound-bang* or *sh-bang*) that specifies the location of the Python interpreter on the server. This directive must be the first line in a CGI script. The examples in this chapter are for Window users. For UNIX or Linux-based machines, the directive typically is one of the following:

```
#!/usr/bin/python
#!/usr/local/bin/python
#!/usr/bin/env python
```

depending on the location of the Python interpreter. [*Note*: If you do not know where the Python interpreter resides, contact the server administrator.]

Common Programming Error 6.1

*Forgetting to put the directive (**#!**) in the first line of a CGI script is an error if the Web server running the script does not understand the **.py** filename extension.*

Line 5 **import**s module *time*. This module obtains the current time on the Web server and displays it in the user's browser. Lines 7–17 define function **printHeader**. This function takes argument **title**, which corresponds to the title of the Web page. Line

```
1    #!c:\Python\python.exe
2    # Fig. 6.3: fig06_03.py
3    # Displays current date and time in Web browser.
4
5    import time
6
7    def printHeader( title ):
8       print """Content-type: text/html
9
10   <?xml version = "1.0" encoding = "UTF-8"?>
11   <!DOCTYPE html PUBLIC
12      "-//W3C//DTD XHTML 1.0 Strict//EN"
13      "DTD/xhtml1-strict.dtd">
14   <html xmlns = "http://www.w3.org/1999/xhtml">
15   <head><title>%s</title></head>
16
17   <body>""" % title
18
19   printHeader( "Current date and time" )
20   print time.ctime( time.time() )
21   print "</body></html>"
```

Fig. 6.3   CGI script displaying the date and time.

8 prints the HTTP header. Notice that line 9 is blank, which denotes the end of the HTTP headers. The line that follows the last HTTP header must be a blank line, otherwise Web browsers cannot render the content properly. Lines 10–14 print the XML declaration, document type declaration and opening **<html>** tag. For more information on XML, see Chapter 15. Lines 15–17 contain the XHTML document header and title and begin the XHTML document body.

 Common Programming Error 6.2

Failure to place a blank line after an HTTP header is an error.

Line 19 begins the main portion of the program by calling function **printHeader** and passing an argument that represents the title of the Web page. Line 20 calls two functions in module **time** to print the current time. Function **_time.time_** returns a floating-point value that represents the number of seconds since midnight, January 1, 1970 (called the *epoch*). Function `time.ctime` takes as an argument the number of seconds since the epoch and returns a human-readable string that represents the current time. We conclude the program by printing the XHTML body and document closing tags. For a complete list of functions in module `time`, visit

`www.python.org/doc/current/lib/module-time.html`

Note that the program consists almost entirely of **print** statements. Until now, the output of **print** has always displayed on the screen. However, technically speaking, the default target for **print** is *standard output*—an information stream presented to the user by an application. Typically, standard output is displayed on the screen, but it may be sent to a printer, written to a file, etc. When a Python program executes as a CGI script, the server redirects the standard output to the client Web browser. The browser interprets the headers and tags as if they were part of a normal server response to an XHTML document request.

Executing the program requires a properly configured server. [*Note*: In this book, we use the Apache Web server. For information on obtaining and configuring Apache, refer to our Python Web resources at **www.deitel.com**.] Once a server is available, the Web server site administrator specifies where CGI scripts can reside and what names are allowed for them. In our example, we place the Python file in the Web server's **cgi-bin** directory. For UNIX and Linux users, it also is necessary to set the permissions before executing the program. For example, UNIX and Linux command

`chmod 755 fig06_02.py`

gives the client the permission to read and execute **fig06_02.py**.

Assuming that the server is on the local computer, execute the program by typing

`http://localhost/cgi-bin/fig06_02.py`

in the browser's **Address** or **Location** field. If the server resides on a different computer, replace **localhost** with the server's hostname or IP address. [*Note*: The IP address of **localhost** is always **127.0.0.1**.] Requesting the document causes the server to execute the program and return the results.

Figure 6.4 illustrates the process of calling a CGI script. First, the client requests the resource named **fig06_02.py** from the server, just as the client requested **downloads.html** in the previous example (Step 1). If the server has not been configured to handle CGI scripts, it might return the Python code as text to the client.

A properly configured Web server, however, recognizes that certain resources need to be processed differently. For example, when the resource is a CGI script, the script must be executed by the Web server. A resource usually is designated as a CGI script in one of two ways—either it has a special filename extension (such as **.cgi** or **.py**), or it is located in a specific directory (often **cgi-bin**). In addition, the server administrator must grant explicit permission for remote access and CGI-script execution.

The server recognizes that the resource is a Python script and invokes Python to execute the script (Step 2). The program executes, and the text sent to standard output is returned to the Web server (Step 3). Finally, the Web server prints an additional line to the output that indicates the status of the HTTP transaction (such as **HTTP/1.1 200 OK**, for success) and sends the whole body of text to the client (Step 4).

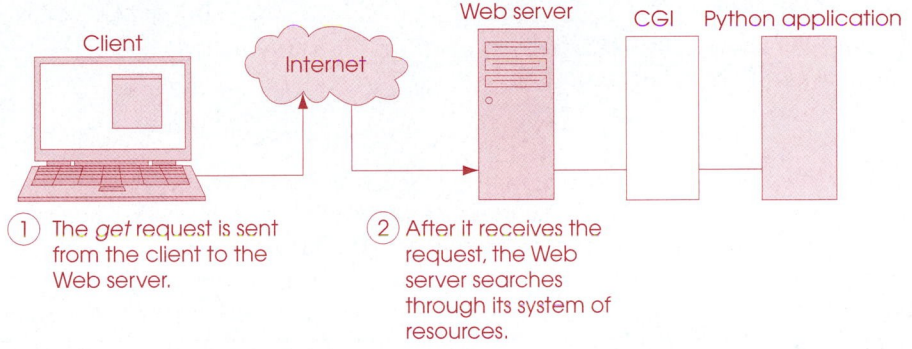

① The *get* request is sent from the client to the Web server.

② After it receives the request, the Web server searches through its system of resources.

Fig. 6.4   Step 1: The **GET** request, **GET /cgi-bin/fig06_02.py HTTP/ 1.1**. (Part 1 of 4.)

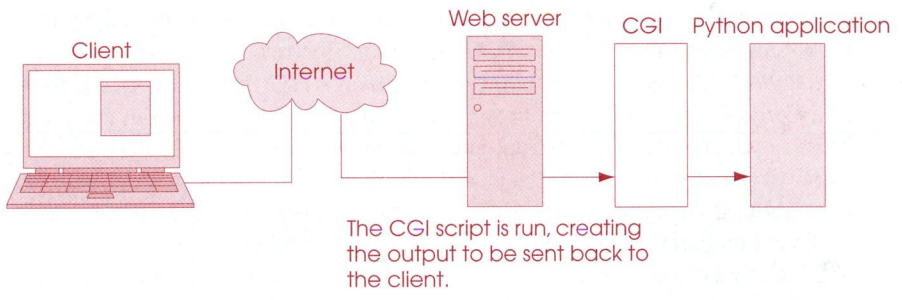

The CGI script is run, creating the output to be sent back to the client.

Fig. 6.4   Step 2: The Web server starts the CGI script. (Part 2 of 4.)

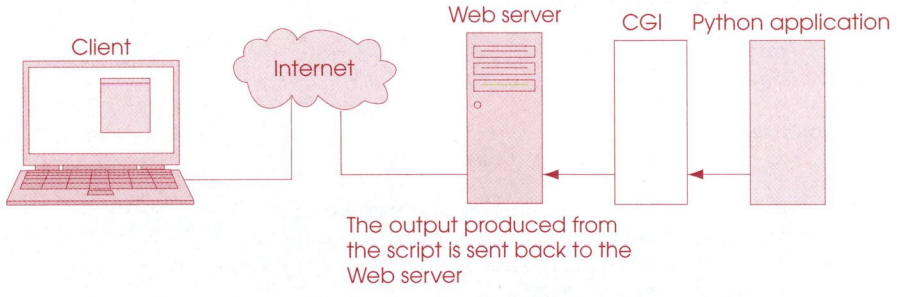

The output produced from the script is sent back to the Web server

Fig. 6.4   Step 3: The output of the script is sent to the Web server. (Part 3 of 4.)

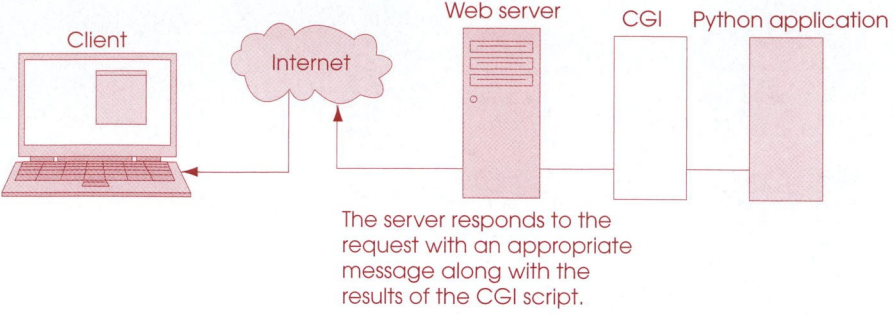

The server responds to the
request with an appropriate
message along with the
results of the CGI script.

Fig. 6.4   Step 4: The HTTP response, **HTTP/1.1 200 OK**. (Part 4 of 4.)

The browser on the client side then processes the XHTML output and displays the results. It is important to note that the browser does not know about the work the server has done to execute the CGI script and return XHTML output. As far as the browser is concerned, it is requesting a resource like any other and receiving a response like any other. The client computer is not required to have a Python interpreter installed, because the script executes on the server. The client simply receives and processes the script's output.

We now consider a more involved CGI program. Figure 6.5 organizes all *CGI environment variables* and their corresponding values in an XHTML table, which is then displayed in a Web browser. Environment variables contain information about the execution environment in which script is being run. Such information includes the current user name and the name of the operating system. A CGI program uses environment variables to obtain information about the client (e.g., the client's IP address, operating system type, browser type, etc.) or to obtain information passed from the client to the CGI program.

Line 6 **import**s module *cgi*. This module provides several CGI-related capabilities, including text-formatting, form-processing and URL parsing. In this example, we use module **cgi** to format XHTML text; in later examples, we use module **cgi** to process XHTML forms.

```
1   #!c:\Python\python.exe
2   # Fig. 6.5: fig06_05.py
3   # Program displaying CGI environment variables.
4
5   import os
6   import cgi
7
8   def printHeader( title ):
9      print """Content-type: text/html
10
11  <?xml version = "1.0" encoding = "UTF-8"?>
12  <!DOCTYPE html PUBLIC
13     "-//W3C//DTD XHTML 1.0 Strict//EN"
14     "DTD/xhtml1-strict.dtd">
15  <html xmlns = "http://www.w3.org/1999/xhtml">
16  <head><title>%s</title></head>
```

Fig. 6.5   CGI program to display environment variables. (Part 1 of 2.)

```
17
18   <body>""" % title
19
20   rowNumber = 0
21   backgroundColor = "white"
22
23   printHeader( "Environment Variables" )
24   print """<table style = "border: 0">"""
25
26   # print table of cgi variables and values
27   for item in os.environ.keys():
28      rowNumber += 1
29
30      if rowNumber % 2 == 0:            # even row numbers are white
31         backgroundColor = "white"
32      else:                            # odd row numbers are grey
33         backgroundColor = "lightgrey"
34
35      print """<tr style = "background-color: %s">
36      <td>%s</td><td>%s</td></tr>""" % ( backgroundColor,
37         cgi.escape( item ), cgi.escape( os.environ[ item ] ) )
38
39   print """</table></body></html>"""
```

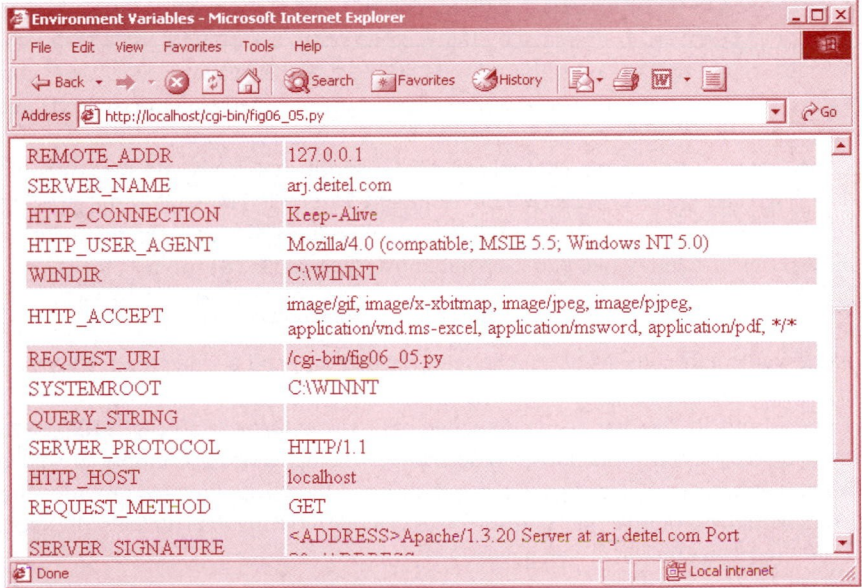

Fig. 6.5   CGI program to display environment variables. (Part 2 of 2.)

Lines 8–18 define function **printHeader**, which is identical to the function we defined in the previous example. The main program prints an XHTML table that contains the environment variables (lines 24–39). The ***os.environ*** data member holds all the environment variables (line 27). This data member acts like a dictionary; therefore, we can access its keys via the **keys** method and its values via the **[]** operator. Lines 30–33 set the background color for each row. For each environment variable, lines 35–37 create a new row in the table containing that key and the corresponding value.

Note that line 37 calls function ***cgi.escape*** and passes as values each environment variable name and value. This function takes a string and returns a properly formatted XHTML string. Proper formatting means that special XHTML characters, such as the less-than and greater-than signs (**<** and **>**), are "escaped." For example, function **escape** returns a string where "**<**" is replaced by "**<**", "**>**" is replaced by "**>**" and "**&**" is replaced by "**&**". The replacement signifies that the browser should display a character instead of treating the character as markup. After we have printed all the environment variables, we close the **table**, **body** and **html** tags (line 39).

6.4 Sending Input to a CGI Script

You have seen one example of a CGI script processing preset environment variables. We now use an environment variable to supply data (e.g., client's name, search-engine query, etc.) to a CGI script. This section presents the environment variable **QUERY_STRING** that provides such a mechanism. The **QUERY_STRING** variable contains extra information that is appended to a URL in a **GET** request, following a question mark (**?**). For example, the URL

www._somesite_**.com/cgi-bin/script.py?state=California**

causes the Web browser to request a resource from **www.**_somesite_**.com**. The resource uses a CGI script (**cgi-bin/script.py**) to execute. The information following the **?** (**state=California**) is assigned by the Web server to the **QUERY_STRING** environment variable. Note that the question mark is not part of the resource requested, nor is it part of the query string; it serves as a *delimiter* (or separator) between the resource and the query string.

Figure 6.6 shows a simple example of a CGI script that reads and responds to data passed through the **QUERY_STRING** environment variable. The CGI script reading the string needs to know how to interpret the formatted data. In the example, the query string contains a series of name-value pairs separated by ampersands (**&**), as in

country=USA&state=California&city=Sacramento

Each name-value pair consists of a name (e.g., **country**) and a value (e.g., **USA**), delimited by an equal sign.

In line 24 of Fig. 6.6, we assign the value of environment-variable **QUERY_STRING** to variable **query**. Line 26 then tests to determine whether **query** is empty. If so, a message prints instructing the user to add a query string to the URL. We also provide a link to a URL that includes a sample query string. Note that query-string data may also be specified as part of a hypertext link in a Web page.

```
1   #!c:\Python\python.exe
2   # Fig. 6.6: fig06_06.py
3   # Example using QUERY_STRING.
4
5   import os
6   import cgi
```

Fig. 6.6   Reading input from **QUERY_STRING**. (Part 1 of 3.)

```
7
8   def printHeader( title ):
9       print """Content-type: text/html
10
11  <?xml version = "1.0" encoding = "UTF-8"?>
12  <!DOCTYPE html PUBLIC
13      "-//W3C//DTD XHTML 1.0 Strict//EN"
14      "DTD/xhtml1-strict.dtd">
15  <html xmlns = "http://www.w3.org/1999/xhtml">
16  <head><title>%s</title></head>
17
18  <body>""" % title
19
20  printHeader( "QUERY_STRING example" )
21  print "<h1>Name/Value Pairs</h1>"
22
23  query = os.environ[ "QUERY_STRING" ]
24
25  if len( query ) == 0:
26      print """<p><br />
27          Please add some name-value pairs to the URL above.
28          Or try
29          <a href = "fig06_06.py?name=Veronica&amp;age=23">this</a>.
30          </p>"""
31  else:
32      print """<p style = "font-style: italic">
33          The query string is '%s'.</p>""" % cgi.escape( query )
34      pairs = cgi.parse_qs( query )
35
36      for key, value in pairs.items():
37          print "<p>You set '%s' to value %s</p>""" % \
38              ( key, value )
39
40  print "</body></html>"
```

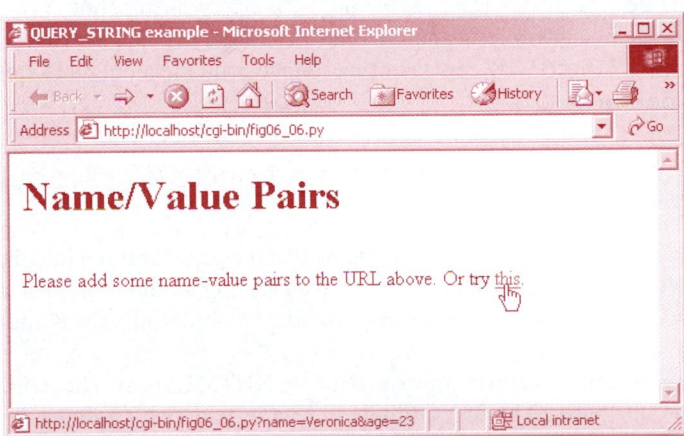

Fig. 6.6   Reading input from **QUERY_STRING**. (Part 2 of 3.)

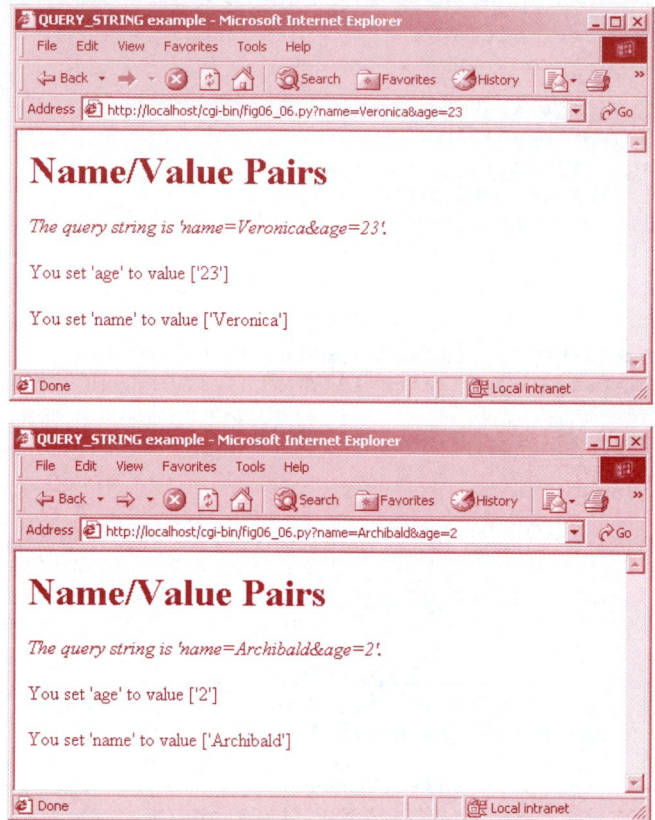

Fig. 6.6   Reading input from **QUERY_STRING**. (Part 3 of 3.)

If the query string is not empty, the value of the query string (lines 31–32) prints. Function **cgi.parse_qs** parses (i.e., "splits-up") the query string (line 33). This function takes as an argument a query string and returns a dictionary of name-value pairs contained in the query string. Lines 35–37 contain a **for** loop to print the names and values contained in dictionary **pairs**.

6.5 Using XHTML Forms to Send Input and Using Module `cgi` to Retrieve Form Data

If Web page users had to type all the information that the page required into the page's URL every time the user wanted to access the page, Web surfing would be quite a laborious task. XHTML provides *forms* on Web pages that provide a more intuitive way for users to input information to CGI scripts.

The **<form>** and **</form>** *tags* surround an XHTML form. The **<form>** tag typically takes two attributes. The first attribute is **action**, which specifies the operation to perform when the user submits the form. For our purposes, the operation usually will be to call a CGI script to process the form data. The second attribute is **method**, which is either *get* or *post*. In this section, we show examples using both methods. An XHTML form may contain any number of elements. Figure 6.7 gives a brief description of several possible elements to include.

Figure 6.8 demonstrates a basic XHTML form that uses the HTTP *get* method. Lines 21–26 output the form. Notice that the **method** attribute is *get* and the **action** attribute is **fig06_08.py** (i.e., the script calls itself to handle the form data once they are submitted—this is called a *postback*).

The form contains two input fields. The first is a single-line text field (**type = "text"**) with the name **word** (line 23). The second displays a button, labeled **Submit word**, to submit the form data (line 24).

The first time the script executes, **QUERY_STRING** should contain no value (unless the user has specifically appended a query string to the URL). However, once the user enters a word into the **word** text field and clicks the **Submit word** button, the script is called again. This time, the **QUERY_STRING** environment variable contains the name of the text-input field (**word**) and the user-entered value. For example, if the user enters the word **python** and clicks the **Submit word** button, **QUERY_STRING** would contain the value **"word=python"**.

Tag name	type attribute (for `<input>` tags)	Description
`<input>`	`button`	A standard push button.
	`checkbox`	Displays a checkbox that can be checked (true) or unchecked (false).
	`file`	Displays a text field and button so the user can specify a file to upload to a Web server. The button displays a file dialog that allows the user to select a file.
	`hidden`	Hides data information from clients so that hidden form data can be used only by the form handler on the server.
	`image`	The same as **submit**, but displays an image rather than a button.
	`password`	Like **text**, but each character typed appears as an asterisk (*****) to hide the input (for security).
	`radio`	Radio buttons are similar to checkboxes, except that only one radio button in a group of radio buttons can be selected at a time.
	`reset`	A button that resets form fields to their default values.
	`submit`	A push button that submits form data according to the form's **action**.
	`text`	Provides single-line text field for text input. This attribute is the default input type.
`<select>`		Drop-down menu or selection box. When used with the `<option>` tag, `<select>` specifies items to select.
`<textarea>`		Multiline area in which text can be input or displayed.

Fig. 6.7   XHTML form elements.

```
1   #!c:\Python\python.exe
2   # Fig. 6.8: fig06_08.py
3   # Demonstrates get method with an XHTML form.
4
5   import cgi
6
7   def printHeader( title ):
8      print """Content-type: text/html
9
10  <?xml version = "1.0" encoding = "UTF-8"?>
11  <!DOCTYPE html PUBLIC
12     "-//W3C//DTD XHTML 1.0 Strict//EN"
13     "DTD/xhtml1-strict.dtd">
14  <html xmlns = "http://www.w3.org/1999/xhtml">
15  <head><title>%s</title></head>
16
17  <body>""" % title
18
19  printHeader( "Using 'get' with forms" )
20  print """<p>Enter one of your favorite words here:<br /></p>
21     <form method = "get" action = "fig06_08.py">
22        <p>
23        <input type = "text" name = "word" />
24        <input type = "submit" value = "Submit word" />
25        </p>
26     </form>"""
27
28  pairs = cgi.parse()
29
30  if pairs.has_key( "word" ):
31     print """<p>Your word is:
32        <span style = "font-weight: bold">%s</span></p>""" \
33        % cgi.escape( pairs[ "word" ][ 0 ] )
34
35  print "</body></html>"
```

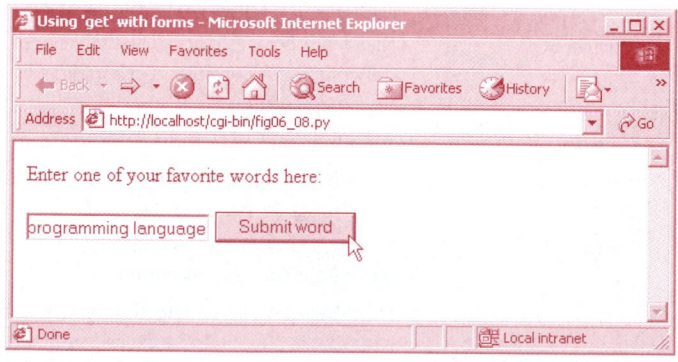

Fig. 6.8   *get* used with an XHTML form. (Part 1 of 2.)

Fig. 6.8   *get* used with an XHTML form. (Part 2 of 2.)

Line 28 uses function **cgi.parse** to parse the form data. This function is similar to function **cgi.parse_qs**, except that **cgi.parse** parses the data from standard input (as opposed to the query string) and returns the name-value pairs in a dictionary.

Thus, during the second execution of the script, when the query string is parsed, line 28 assigns the returned dictionary to variable **pairs**. If dictionary **pairs** contains the key **"word"**, the user has submitted at least one word and the program prints the word(s) to the browser. The words are passed to function **cgi.escape** in case the input includes some special characters (such as **<, >** or a space). Lines 31–33 use CSS to display the result. CSS is discussed in Appendix K, Cascading Style Sheets (CSS). In Fig. 6.8, we see that the spaces in the address bar are replace by plus signs because Web browsers URL-encode XHTML-form data they send, which means that spaces are turned into plus signs and that certain other symbols (such as the apostrophe) are translated into their ASCII value in hexadecimal and preceded with a percent sign.

Using *get* with an XHTML form passes data to the CGI script in the same way that we saw in Fig. 6.6—through environment variables. Another way that CGI scripts interact with servers is via standard input and the *post* method. For comparison purposes, let us now reimplement the application of Fig. 6.8 using *post*. Notice that the code in the two figures is virtually identical. The XHTML form indicates that we are now using the *post* method to submit the form data (line 21).

```
1   #!c:\Python\python.exe
2   # Fig. 6.9: fig06_09.py
3   # Demonstrates post method with an XHTML form.
4
5   import cgi
6
7   def printHeader( title ):
8       print """Content-type: text/html
9
10  <?xml version = "1.0" encoding = "UTF-8"?>
11  <!DOCTYPE html PUBLIC
12      "-//W3C//DTD XHTML 1.0 Strict//EN"
13      "DTD/xhtml1-strict.dtd">
```

Fig. 6.9   *post* used with an XHTML form. (Part 1 of 2.)

```
14    <html xmlns = "http://www.w3.org/1999/xhtml">
15    <head><title>%s</title></head>
16
17    <body>""" % title
18
19    printHeader( "Using 'post' with forms" )
20    print """<p>Enter one of your favorite words here:<br /></p>
21       <form method = "post" action = "fig06_09.py">
22          <p>
23          <input type = "text" name = "word" />
24          <input type = "submit" value = "Submit word" />
25          </p>
26       </form>"""
27
28    pairs = cgi.parse()
29
30    if pairs.has_key( "word" ):
31       print """<p>Your word is:
32          <span style = "font-weight: bold">%s</span></p>""" \
33          % cgi.escape( pairs[ "word" ][ 0 ] )
34
35    print "</body></html>"
```

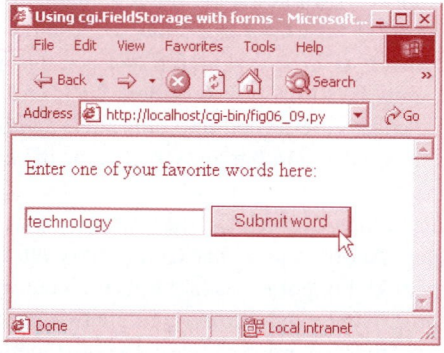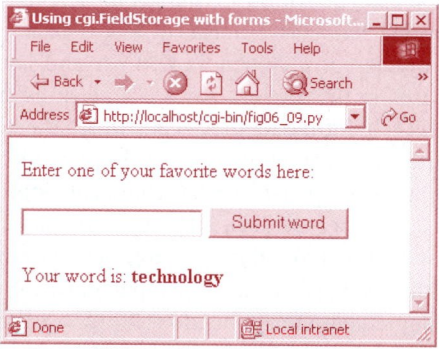

Fig. 6.9   *post* used with an XHTML form. (Part 2 of 2.)

The *post* method sends data to a CGI script via standard input. The data are encoded just as in **QUERY_STRING** (that is, with name-value pairs connected by equals signs and ampersands), but the **QUERY_STRING** environment variable is not set. Instead, the *post* method sets the environment variable **CONTENT_LENGTH**, to indicate the number of characters of data that were sent (or posted). A benefit of the *post* method is that the number of characters of data can vary in size.

Although methods *get* and *post* are similar, some important differences exist. A *get* request sends form content as part of the URL. A *post* request posts form content to the end of an HTTP request. Another difference is the manner in which browsers process responses. Browsers often *cache* (save on disk) Web pages, so that when the Web page is requested a second time, the browser need not download the page again, but can load the page from the cache. This process speeds up the user's browsing experience by reducing the amount of data downloaded to view a Web page. Browsers do not cache the server responses to *post* requests, however, because subsequent *post* requests might not contain the same information.

This method of handling responses is different from that of handling *get* requests. When a Web-based search engine is used, a *get* request normally supplies the search engine with the information specified in the XHTML form. The search engine then performs the search and returns the results as a Web page.

Software Engineering Observation 6.2

Most Web servers limit get request query strings to 1024 characters. If a query string exceeds this limit, use the post request.

Software Engineering Observation 6.3

Forms that contain many fields are submitted most often using a post *request. Sensitive form fields, such as passwords, usually are sent using* post *request.*

6.6 Using `cgi.FieldStorage` to Read Input

Figure 6.10 reimplements the example from Fig. 6.9 to take advantage of a high-level data abstraction provided by module **cgi**. Line 28 creates an object of class **cgi.FieldStorage**. [*Note*: Classes are discussed in Chapter 7, Object-Based Programming.] In our example, the high-level data type (or class) is called **cgi.FieldStorage** and resembles the dictionary returned by the parsing function.

```
1   #!c:\Python\python.exe
2   # Fig. 6.10: fig06_10.py
3   # Demonstrates use of cgi.FieldStorage an with XHTML form.
4
5   import cgi
6
7   def printHeader( title ):
8       print """Content-type: text/html
9
10  <?xml version = "1.0" encoding = "UTF-8"?>
11  <!DOCTYPE html PUBLIC
12      "-//W3C//DTD XHTML 1.0 Strict//EN"
13      "DTD/xhtml1-strict.dtd">
14  <html xmlns = "http://www.w3.org/1999/xhtml">
15  <head><title>%s</title></head>
16
17  <body>""" % title
18
19  printHeader( "Using cgi.FieldStorage with forms" )
20  print """<p>Enter one of your favorite words here:<br /></p>
21      <form method = "post" action = "fig06_10.py">
22          <p>
23          <input type = "text" name = "word" />
24          <input type = "submit" value = "Submit word" />
25          </p>
26      </form>"""
27
```

Fig. 6.10   `cgi.FieldStorage` used with an XHTML form. (Part 1 of 2.)

```
28   form = cgi.FieldStorage()
29
30   if form.has_key( "word" ):
31      print """<p>Your word is:
32         <span style = "font-weight: bold">%s</span></p>""" \
33         % cgi.escape( form[ "word" ].value )
34
35   print "</body></html>"
```

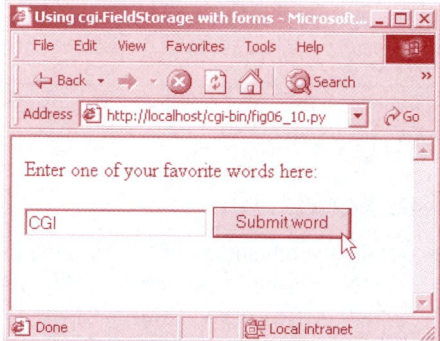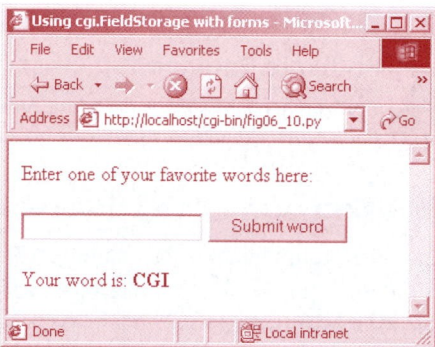

Fig. 6.10   cgi.FieldStorage used with an XHTML form. (Part 2 of 2.)

Line 30 calls dictionary method **has_key** and passes **form**, to determine whether the dictionary contains the key **"word"**. If so, the user has entered a word, and the program prints the word to the browser (lines 31–33). Note that, to access the value of any key in a **cgi.FieldStorage** object, we must access the value attribute of the key's corresponding value.

6.7 Other HTTP Headers

We mentioned at the close of Section 6.2.3 that there are alternatives to the standard HTTP header

```
Content-type: text/html
```

For example,

```
print "Content-type: text/plain"
```

prints the **Content-type** header with the **text/plain** content type. If the **content-type** of a page is specified as **text/plain**, the page is processed as plain text instead of as an HTML or XHTML document.

In addition to HTTP header **Content-type**, a CGI script can supply other HTTP headers. In most cases, the server passes these extra headers to the client untouched. For example, the following *Refresh* header redirects the client to a new location after a specified amount of time:

```
Refresh: "5; URL = http://www.deitel.com/newpage.html"
```

Five seconds after the Web browser receives this header, the browser requests the resource at the specified URL. Alternatively, the **Refresh** header can omit the URL, in which case it refreshes the current page at the given time interval.

The CGI protocol indicates that certain types of headers output by a CGI script are to be handled by the server, rather than be passed directly to the client. The first of these is the **Location** header. Like the **Refresh** header, **Location** redirects the client to a new location:

```
Location: http://www.deitel.com/newpage.html
```

If used with a *relative URL* (e.g., **Location: /newpage.html**), the **Location** header indicates to the server that the redirection is to be performed on the server side, without sending the **Location** header back to the client. In this case, it appears to the user as if the browser originally requested that resource. When a Python script uses the **Location** header, the **Content-type** header is not necessary because the new resource has its own content type.

The CGI specification also includes a **Status** header, which tells the server to output a status-header line (e.g., **HTTP/1.1 200 OK**). Normally, the server sends the appropriate status line to the client (adding, for example, the **200 OK** status code in most cases). However, CGI allows you to change the response status if you so desire. For example, sending a

```
Status: 204 No Response
```

header indicates that, although the request was successful, the browser should continue to display the same page. This header might be useful if you want to allow users to submit forms without moving to a new page.

We now have covered the fundamentals of the CGI protocol. To review, the CGI protocol allows scripts to interact with servers in three basic ways:

1. through the output of headers and content to the client via standard output;

2. by the server's setting of environment variables (including the URL-encoded **QUERY_STRING**) whose values are available within the script (via **os.environ**); and

3. through posted, URL-encoded data that the server sends to the script's standard input.

6.8 Example: Interactive Portal

Figure 6.11 and Fig. 6.12 show the implementation of a simple interactive portal (login page) for the fictional Bug2Bug Travel Web site. The example queries the client for a name and password, then displays information based on data entered. For simplicity, the example does not encrypt the data sent to the server.

Figure 6.11 displays the opening page. It is a static XHTML document containing a form that posts data to the **fig06_12.py** CGI script (line 14). The form contains one field to collect the client's name (line 17) and one to collect the member password (line 20). To make this XHTML file available from an Apache server, place **fig06_11.html** in the root directory of the Apache server (e.g., **Apache Group\Apache\htdocs**). For more information on Apache servers, visit **www.apache.org**.

```
1   <?xml version = "1.0" encoding = "UTF-8"?>
2   <!DOCTYPE html PUBLIC
3      "-//W3C//DTD XHTML 1.0 Strict//EN"
4      "DTD/xhtml1-strict.dtd">
5   <!-- Fig. 6.11: fig06_11.html     -->
6   <!-- Bug2Bug Travel log-in page. -->
7
8   <html xmlns = "http://www.w3.org/1999/xhtml">
9      <head><title>Enter here</title></head>
10
11     <body>
12        <h1>Welcome to Bug2Bug Travel</h1>
13
14        <form method = "post" action = "/cgi-bin/fig06_12.py">
15
16           <p>Please enter your name:<br />
17           <input type = "text" name = "name" /><br />
18
19           Members, please enter the password:<br />
20           <input type = "password" name = "password" /><br />
21           </p>
22
23           <p style = "font-size: em - 1; font-style: italic" >
24           Note that password is not encrypted.<br /><br />
25           <input type = "submit" />
26           </p>
27
28        </form>
29     </body>
30  </html>
```

Fig. 6.11   Interactive portal to create a password-protected Web page.

Figure 6.12 is the CGI script that processes the data received from the client. Line 20 retrieves the form data in a **cgi.FieldStorage** instance and assigns the result to local

variable **form**. The **if** structure that begins in line 22 tests whether **form** contains the key
"name". If **form** does not contain that key, the user has not entered a name, and we
print a **Location** HTTP header (line 23) to redirect the user to the XHTML file where
the user can enter a name (**fig06_11.html**). The document **fig06_11.html** is contained in the Web server's main document root (as indicated by the **/** that precedes the page
name). The effect of line 23 is that clients who try to access **fig06_12.py** directly,
without going through the login procedure, must enter through the portal.

```
1   #!c:\Python\python.exe
2   # Fig. 6.12: fig06_12.py
3   # Handles entry to Bug2Bug Travel.
4
5   import cgi
6
7   def printHeader( title ):
8      print """Content-type: text/html
9
10  <?xml version = "1.0" encoding = "UTF-8"?>
11  <!DOCTYPE html PUBLIC
12     "-//W3C//DTD XHTML 1.0 Strict//EN"
13     "DTD/xhtml1-strict.dtd">
14  <html xmlns = "http://www.w3.org/1999/xhtml">
15  <head><title>%s</title></head>
16
17  <body>""" % title
18
19  form = cgi.FieldStorage()
20
21  if not form.has_key( "name" ):
22     print "Location: /fig06_11.html\n"
23  else:
24     printHeader( "Bug2Bug Travel" )
25     print "<h1>Welcome, %s!</h1>" % form[ "name" ].value
26     print """<p>Here are our weekly specials:<br /></p>
27        <ul><li>Boston to Taiwan for $300</li></ul>"""
28
29     if not form.has_key( "password" ):
30        print """<p style = "font-style: italic">
31           Become a member today for more great deals!</p>"""
32     elif form[ "password" ].value == "Coast2Coast":
33        print """<hr />
34           <p>Current specials just for members:<br /></p>
35           <ul><li>San Diego to Hong Kong for $250</li></ul>"""
36     else:
37        print """<p style = "font-style: italic">
38           Sorry, you have entered the wrong password.
39           If you have the correct password, enter
40           it to see more specials.</p>"""
41
42     print "<hr /></body></html>"
```

Fig. 6.12 Interactive portal handler. (Part 1 of 2.)

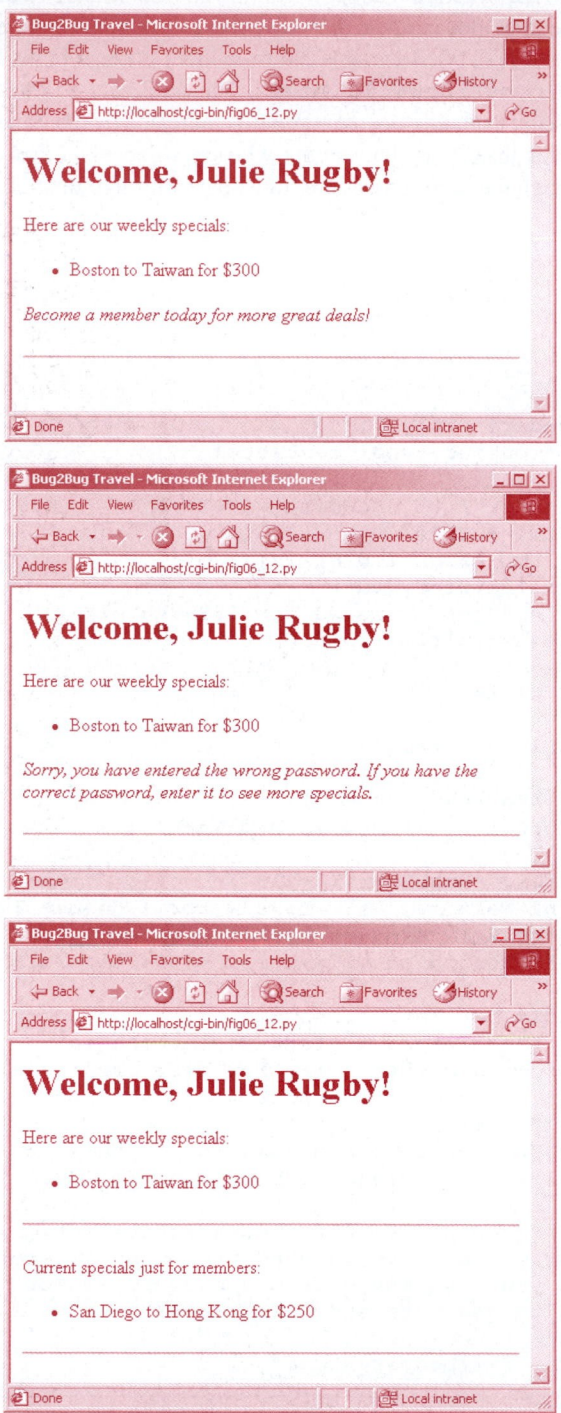

Fig. 6.12   Interactive portal handler. (Part 2 of 2.)

If a user has entered a name, we print a greeting that includes the user's name and the weekly specials (lines 26–28). Line 30 tests whether the user entered a password. If the user has not entered a password, we invite the user to become a member (line 31). If the user has entered a password, line 32 determines whether the password is equal to the string **"Coast2Coast"**. If true, we print the member specials to the browser. Note that the password, weekly specials and member specials are hard-coded (i.e., their values are supplied in the code). If the user-entered password does not equal **"Coast2Coast"**, the application requests the user to enter a valid password (lines 36–38).

Performance Tip 6.1

In response to each CGI request, a Web server executes a CGI program to create the response to the client. This process often takes more time than returning a static document. When implementing a Web site, define content that does not change frequently as static content. This practice allows the Web server to respond to clients more quickly than if only CGI scripting were used.

6.9 Internet and World Wide Web Resources

www.w3.org/CGI
The World Wide Web Consortium page on CGI is concerned with security issues involving the Common Gateway Interface. This page provides links to CGI specifications, as indicated by the National Center for Supercomputing Applications (NCSA).

www.nacs.uci.edu/indiv/ehood/MIME/MIME.html
This document provides links to MIME RFCs (Request for Comments), MIME related RFCs and other MIME-related information.

www.speakeasy.org/~cgires
This is a collection of tutorials and scripts related to CGI.

www.fastcgi.com
This is the home page of fast CGI—an extension to CGI that for high performance Internet applications

bel-epa.com/pyapache
This site is the resource center for **PyApache**. **PyApache** is a module that embeds the Python interpreter into the Apache server.

www.modpython.org
This is the home page of **mod_python**. Module **mod_python** is another module that embeds the Python interpreter within the Apache server. This module lets scripts run much faster than traditional CGI scripts.

SUMMARY

- The Common Gateway Interface (CGI) describes a set of protocols through which applications (commonly called CGI programs or CGI scripts) can interact with Web servers and (indirectly) with clients.

- The content of dynamic Web pages does not require modification by programmers, however the content of static Web pages requires modification by programmers.

- The Common Gateway Interface is "common" in the sense that it is not specific to any particular operating system (such as Linux or Windows) or to any one programming language.

- HTTP describes a set of methods and headers that allow clients and servers to interact and exchange information in a uniform and predictable way.

- A Web page in its simplest form is nothing more than an XHTML (Extensible Hypertext Markup Language) document. An XHTML document is just a plain-text file containing markings (markup, or tags) that describe to a Web browser how to display and format the information in the document.

- Hypertext information creates links to different pages or to other portions of the same page.

- Any XHTML file available for viewing over the Internet has a URL (Universal Resource Locator) associated with it. The URL contains information that directs a browser to the resource that the user wishes to access.

- The hostname is the name of the computer where a resource (such as an XHTML document) resides. The hostname is translated into an IP address, which identifies the server on the Internet.

- To request a resource, the browser first sends an HTTP request message to the server. The server responds with a line indicating the HTTP version, followed by a numeric code and a phrase describing the status of the transaction.

- The server normally sends one or more HTTP headers, which provide additional information about the data being sent. The header or set of headers is followed by a blank line, which indicates that the server has finished sending HTTP headers.

- Once the server sends the contents of the requested resource, the connection is terminated. The client-side browser processes the XHTML it receives and displays the results.

- *get* is an HTTP method that indicates that the client wishes to obtain a resource.

- The function **time.ctime**, when called with **time.time()**, returns a string value such as **Wed Jul 18 10:54:57 2001**.

- Redirecting output means sending output to somewhere other than the standard output, which is normally the screen.

- Just as standard input refers to the standard method of input into a program (usually the keyboard), standard output refers to the standard method of output from a program (usually the screen).

- If a server is not configured to handle CGI scripts, the server may return the Python program as text to display in a Web browser.

- A properly configured Web server will recognize a CGI script and execute it. A resource is usually designated as a CGI script in one of two ways: Either it has a specific filename extension or it is located in a specific directory. The server administrator must explicitly give permission for remote clients to access and execute CGI scripts.

- When the server recognizes that the resource requested is a Python script, the server invokes Python to execute the script. The Python program executes and the Web server sends the output to the client as the response to the request.

- With a CGI script, we must explicitly include the **Content-type** header, whereas, with an XHTML document, the header would be added by the Web server.

- The CGI protocol for output to be sent to a Web browser consists of printing to standard output the **Content-type** header, a blank line and the data (XHTML, plain text, etc.) to be output.

- Module **cgi** provides functions that simplify the creation of CGI scripts. Among other things, **cgi** includes a set of functions to aid in dynamic XHTML generation.

- The **os.environ** dictionary contains the names and values of all the environment variables.

- CGI-enabled Web servers set environment variables that provide information about both the server's and the client's script-execution environment.

- The environment variable **QUERY_STRING** provides a mechanism that enables programmers to supply any type of data to CGI scripts. The **QUERY_STRING** variable contains extra information that is appended to a URL, following a question mark (**?**). The question mark is not part of the resource requested or of the query string. It simply serves as a delimiter.

- Data put into a query string can be structured in a variety of ways, provided that the CGI script that reads the string knows how to interpret the formatted data.
- Forms provide another way for users to input information that is sent to a CGI script.
- The **<form>** and **</form>** tags surround an XHTML form.
- The **<form>** tag generally takes two attributes. The first attribute is **action**, which specifies the action to take when the user submits the form. The second attribute is **method**, which is either *get* or *post*.
- Using *get* with an XHTML form causes data to be passed to the CGI script through environment variable **QUERY_STRING**, which is set by the server.
- Web browsers URL-encode XHTML-form data that they send. This means that spaces are turned into plus signs and that certain other symbols (such as the apostrophe) are translated into their ASCII value in hexadecimal and preceded with a percent sign.
- A CGI script can supply HTTP headers in addition to **Content-type**. In most cases, the server passes these extra headers to the client untouched.
- The **Location** header redirects the client to a new location. If used with a relative URL, the **Location** header indicates to the server that the redirection is to be performed without sending the **Location** header back to the client.
- The CGI specification also includes a **Status** header, which informs the server to output a corresponding status header line. Normally, the server adds the appropriate status line to the output sent to the client. However, CGI allows users to change the response status.

TERMINOLOGY

#! directive
? in query string
127.0.0.1 IP address
action attribute
button attribute
protocol
CSS (Cascading Style Sheet)
CGI (Common Gateway Interface)
CGI environment variable
.cgi file extension
cgi module
CGI Script
cgi module
cgi.escape function
cgi.FieldStorage object
cgi.parse function
cgi.parse_qs function
cgi-bin directory
checkbox attribute value (**type**)
CONTENT_LENGTH
Content-type HTTP header
domain name system (DNS)
dynamic Web content
environment variable
file attribute value (**type**)
form XHTML element (**<form>...</form>**)

get method
HTTP header
hidden attribute value (**type**)
HTML (Hypertext Markup Language)
HTTP (Hypertext Transfer Protocol)
HTTP method
HTTP transaction
image attribute value (**type**)
image/gif MIME type
input HTML element
IP (Internet Protocol) address
localhost
Location HTTP header
method of XHTML form
MIME (Multipurpose Internet Mail Extensions)
os.environ data member
password attribute value (**type**)
.py file extension
post method
portal
pound-bang directive
QUERY_STRING environment variable
radio attribute value (**type**)
redirect
Refresh HTTP header
relative URL

reset attribute value (**type**)
select XHTML element (**form**)
sh-bang directive (**#!**)
static Web content
Status HTTP header
submit attribute value (**type**)
text attribute value (**type**)
text/html MIME type
text/txt MIME type
textarea XHTML element
time module
time.ctime function

time.time function
title XHTML element
   (**<title>...</title>**)
URL (Universal Resource Locator)
value attribute of
   cgi.FieldStorage object
virtual URL
document root
XHTML (Extensible Hypertext
   Markup Language)
XHTML form
XHTML tag

SELF-REVIEW EXERCISES

6.1   Fill in the blanks in each of the following statements:
   a) CGI is an acronym for _____.
   b) HTTP describes a set of _____ and _____ that allow clients and servers to interact.
   c) The translation of a hostname into an IP address normally is performed by a _____.
   d) The _____, which is part of the HTTP header sent with every type of data, helps the browser determine how to process the data it receives.
   e) _____ are reserved memory locations that an operating systems maintains to keep track of system information.
   f) Function _____ takes a string and returns a properly formatted XHTML string.
   g) Variable _____ contains extra information that is appended to a URL in a *get* request, following a question mark.
   h) The default target for **print** is _____.
   i) The _____ data member contains all the environment variables.
   j) XHTML _____ allow users to input information to a CGI script.

6.2   State whether each of the following is *true* or *false*. If *false*, explain why.
   a) The CGI protocol is not specific to any particular operating system or programming language.
   b) Function **time.ctime** returns a floating-point value that represents the number of seconds since the epoch.
   c) The first directive of a CGI script provides the location of the Python interpreter.
   d) The forward slash character acts as a delimiter between the resource and the query string in a URL.
   e) CGI scripts are executed on the client's machine.
   f) The **Status: 204 No Response** header indicates that a request to the server failed.
   g) Redirection sends output to somewhere other than the screen.
   h) The **action** attribute of the **form** element specifies the action to take when the user submits the form.
   i) A *post* request posts form contents to the end of an HTTP request.
   j) Form data can be stored in an object of class **cgi.FormStorage**.

ANSWERS TO SELF REVIEW EXERCISES

6.1 a) Common Gateway Interface. b) methods, headers. c) domain name server (DNS). d) MIME type. e) Environment variables. f) **cgi.escape**. g) **QUERY_STRING**. h) standard output. i) **os.environ**. j) forms.

6.2   a) True. b) False. Function **ctime.time** takes a floating-point value that represents the number of seconds since the epoch as an argument and returns a human-readable string representing the current time. c) True. d) False. A question mark acts as a delimiter between the resource and the query string in a URL. e) False. The server executes CGI scripts. f) False. The **Status: 204 No Response** header indicates that, although the request was successful, the browser should continue to display the same page. g) True. h) True. i) True. j) False. Form data can be stored in an object of class **cgi.FieldStorage**.

EXERCISES

6.3   Write a CGI script that prints the squares of the integers from 1 to 10 on separate lines.

6.4   Modify your solution to Exercise 6.3 to display its output in an XHTML table. The left column should be the number, and the right column should be the square of that number.

6.5   Write a CGI script that receives as input three numbers from the client and returns a statement indicating whether the three numbers could represent an equilateral triangle (all three sides are the same length), an isosceles triangle (two sides are the same length) or a right triangle (the square of one side is equal to the sum of the squares of the other two sides).

6.6   Write a soothsayer CGI program that allows the user to submit a question. When the question is submitted, the server should display a random response from a list of vague answers.

6.7   You are provided with a portal page (see the code and output below) where people can buy products. Write the CGI script to enable this interactive portal. The user should specify how many of each item to buy. The total cost of the items purchased should be displayed to the user.

```
1   <!DOCTYPE html PUBLIC "-//W3C//DTD HTML 4.0 Transitional//EN">
2   <!-- Exercise 6.7: ex06_07.html                              -->
3   <!-- Interactive portal that compiles shopping list based -->
4   <!-- on user input.                                          -->
5
6   <html>
7      <head>
8         <title>Buy Something</title>
9      </head>
10
11     <body>
12        <h1>Clearance!</h1>
13        <p>Please enter how many of each product you would like to
14           order into the box in the right-hand column.</p>
15
16        <form method = "post" action =
17              "http://localhost/cgi-bin/ex06_07.py">
18
19           <table width = "100%" border = "3">
20              <tr>
21                 <th>Product Name</th>
22                 <th>Description</th>
23                 <th>Price</th>
24                 <th>Order</th>
25              </tr>
26
```

```
27                <tr>
28                    <td>CD</td>
29                    <td>Buy this really cool CD</td>
30                    <td>$12.00</td>
31                    <td><input type = "text" name = "CD" /></td>
32                </tr>
33
34                <tr>
35                    <td>Book</td>
36                    <td>Buy this really cool book</td>
37                    <td>$19.99</td>
38                    <td><input type = "text" name = "book" /></td>
39                </tr>
40
41                <tr>
42                    <td>Airplane</td>
43                    <td>Buy this really cool airplane</td>
44                    <td>$1,000,000</td>
45                    <td><input type = "text" name = "airplane" /></td>
46                </tr>
47            </table>
48
49        <input type = "submit" value = "submit">
50      </form>
51    </body>
52  </html>
```

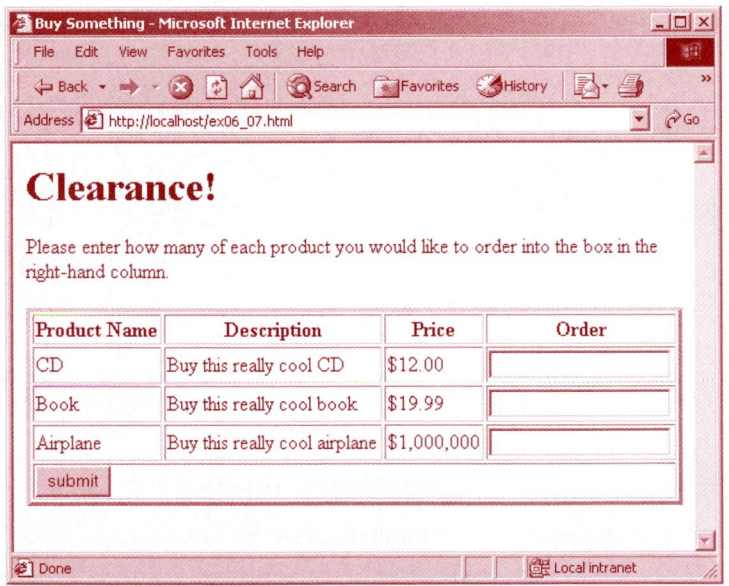

6.8   Write a CGI script for a TV show survey. List five TV shows, let the survey participant rank the TV shows with numbers from 1 (least favorite) to 5 (most favorite). Display the participant's most favorite TV show.

7

Object-Based Programming

Objectives

- To understand the software-engineering concepts of "encapsulation" and "data hiding."
- To understand the notions of data abstraction and abstract data types (ADTs).
- To create Python ADTs, namely classes.
- To understand how to create, use and destroy objects of a class.
- To control access to object attributes and methods.
- To begin to appreciate the value of object orientation.

My object all sublime
I shall achieve in time.
W. S. Gilbert

Is it a world to hide virtues in?
William Shakespeare

Your public servants serve you right.
Adlai Stevenson

Classes struggle, some classes triumph, others are eliminated.
Mao Zedong

This above all: to thine own self be true.
William Shakespeare

7.1 Introduction

Now we begin our deeper study of object orientation. Through our discussion of Python programs in Chapters 2–6, we have already encountered many basic concepts (i.e., "object think") and terminology (i.e., "object speak"). Let us briefly overview some key concepts and terminology of object orientation. *Object-oriented programming (OOP) encapsulates* (i.e., wraps) data (*attributes*) and functions (*behaviors*) into components called *classes*. The data and functions of a class are intimately tied together. A class is like a blueprint. Using a blueprint, a builder can build a house. Using a class, a programmer can create an *object* (also called an *instance*). One blueprint can be reused many times to make many houses. One class can be reused many times to make many objects of the same class. Classes have a property called *information hiding*. This means that, although objects may know how to communicate with one another across well-defined *interfaces,* one object normally should not be allowed to know how another object is implemented—implementation details are hidden within the objects themselves. Surely it is possible to drive a car effectively without knowing the details of how engines, transmissions and exhaust systems work internally. We will see why information hiding is crucial to good software engineering.

In C and other *procedural programming languages,* programming tends to be *action-oriented*; in Python, programming can be *object-oriented*. In procedural programming, the unit of programming is the *function*. In object-oriented programming, the unit of programming is the *class* from which objects eventually are *instantiated* (i.e., created).

Procedural programmers concentrate on writing functions. Groups of actions that perform some task are formed into functions, and functions are grouped to form programs. Data certainly is important in procedural programming, but the view is that data exists primarily in support of the actions that functions perform. The *verbs* in a system specification—a document that describes the services an application should provide—help the procedural programmer determine the set of functions that will work together to implement the system.

Object-oriented programmers concentrate on creating their own *user-defined types*, called *classes*. Classes are also referred to as *programmer-defined types*. Each class contains data and the set of functions that manipulate the data. The data components of a class are called *attributes* (or *data members*). The functional components of a class are called *methods* (or *member functions*, in other object-oriented languages). The focus of attention in object-oriented programming is on classes rather than on functions. The *nouns* in a system specification help the object-oriented programmer determine the set of classes that will be used to create the objects that will work together to implement the system.

Software Engineering Observation 7.1

A central theme of this book is "reuse, reuse, reuse." We will carefully discuss a number of techniques for "polishing" classes to encourage reuse. We focus on "crafting valuable classes" and creating valuable "software assets."

7.2 Implementing a Time Abstract Data Type with a Class

Classes enable programmers to model objects that have data (represented as attributes) and behaviors—or *operations*—(represented as methods). Methods are invoked in response to *messages* sent to objects. A message corresponds to a method call sent from one object to another.

Classes simplify programming because the *clients* (or users of the class) need to be concerned only with the operations encapsulated or embedded in the object—the object interface. Such operations usually are designed to be client-oriented rather than implementation-oriented. Clients do not need to be concerned with a class's implementation (although clients, of course, want correct and efficient implementations). When an implementation changes, implementation-dependent code must change accordingly. Hiding the implementation eliminates the possibility of other program parts becoming dependent on the details of the class implementation.

Often, classes do not have to be created "from scratch." Rather, they may be *derived* from other classes that provide attributes and behaviors the new classes can use—or classes can include objects of other classes as members. Such *software reuse* can greatly enhance programmer productivity. Deriving new classes from existing classes is called *inheritance* and is discussed in detail in Chapter 9, Object-Oriented Programming: Inheritance.

Figure 7.1 contains a simple definition for class **Time**. The class contains information that describes the time of day and contains methods for printing the time in two formats. The class maintains the time internally in a 24-hour format (i.e., military time), but allows the client to display the time in either 24-hour format or in "standard" (AM, PM) format. Later in this section, we present a program (Fig. 7.2) that demonstrates how to create an object of class **Time**.

Keyword **class** (line 4) begins a class definition. The keyword is followed by the name of the class (**Time**), which is followed by a colon (**:**). The line that contains keyword **class** and the class name is called the class's *header*. The *body* of the class is an indented code block (lines 5–37) that contains methods and attributes that belong to the class. Class names usually follow the same naming conventions as variable names, except that the first word of the class name is capitalized.

```
1    # Fig. 7.1: Time1.py
2    # Simple definition of class Time.
3
4    class Time:
5        """Time abstract data type (ADT) definition"""
6
7        def __init__( self ):
8            """Initializes hour, minute and second to zero"""
9
10           self.hour = 0       # 0-23
11           self.minute = 0     # 0-59
12           self.second = 0     # 0-59
13
14       def printMilitary( self ):
15           """Prints object of class Time in military format"""
16
17           print "%.2d:%.2d:%.2d" % \
18               ( self.hour, self.minute, self.second ),
19
20       def printStandard( self ):
21           """Prints object of class Time in standard format"""
22
23           standardTime = ""
24
25           if self.hour == 0 or self.hour == 12:
26               standardTime += "12:"
27           else:
28               standardTime += "%d:" % ( self.hour % 12 )
29
30           standardTime += "%.2d:%.2d" % ( self.minute, self.second )
31
32           if self.hour < 12:
33               standardTime += " AM"
34           else:
35               standardTime += " PM"
36
37           print standardTime,
```

Fig. 7.1   **Time** class—contains attributes and methods for storing and displaying time of day.

Common Programming Error 7.1

Failure to include a colon at the end of a class definition header is a syntax error.

Common Programming Error 7.2

Failure to indent the body of a class is a syntax error.

Line 5 contains the class's optional *documentation string*—a string that describes the class. If a class contains a documentation string, the string must appear in the line or lines following the class header. A user can view a class's documentation string by executing the following statement

```
print ClassName.__doc__
```

Modules, methods and functions also may specify a documentation string.

Good Programming Practice 7.1

Include documentation strings, where appropriate, to enhance program clarity.

Good Programming Practice 7.2

By convention, docstrings are triple-quoted strings. This convention allows the class author to expand a program's documentation (e.g., by adding several more lines) without having to change the quote style.

Line 7 begins the definition for special method **__init__**, the *constructor* method of the class. A constructor is a special method that executes each time an object of a class is created. The constructor (method **__init__**) initializes the attributes of the object and returns **None**. Python classes may define several other special methods, identified by leading and trailing double-underscores (**__**) in the name. We discuss many of these special methods in Chapter 8, Customizing Classes.

Common Programming Error 7.3

*Returning a value other than **None** from a constructor is a fatal, runtime error.*

Software Engineering Observation 7.2

Ensure that objects are initialized before client code invokes those objects' methods. Do not rely on client code to initialize objects properly.

Good Programming Practice 7.3

When appropriate (almost always), provide a constructor to ensure that every object is initialized with meaningful values.

All methods, including constructors, must specify at least one parameter. This parameter represents the object of the class for which the method is called. This parameter often is referred to as the *class instance object*. This term can be confusing, so we refer to the first argument of any method as the *object reference argument*, or simply the *object reference*. Methods must use the object reference to access attributes and other methods that belong to the class. By convention, the object reference argument is called **self**.

Common Programming Error 7.4

*Failure to specify an object reference (usually called **self**) as the first parameter in a method definition causes fatal logic errors when the method is invoked at runtime.*

Good Programming Practice 7.4

*Name the first parameter of all methods **self**. This naming convention helps ensure conformity across Python programs written by different programmers.*

Each object has its own namespace that contains the object's methods and attributes. The class's constructor starts with an empty object (**self**) and adds attributes to the object's namespace. For example, the constructor for class **Time** (lines 7–12) adds three attributes (**hour**, **minute** and **second**) to the new object's namespace. Line 10 binds attribute **hour** to the object's namespace and initializes the attribute's value to 0. Once an attribute has been added to an object's namespace, a client that uses the object may access the attribute's value.

Class **Time** also defines methods **printMilitary** and **printStandard**. Notice that methods can specify a docstring, in the line or lines following the method header. In this example, each method specifies one parameter (**self**) that refers to the object of the class for which the method is invoked. Each method accesses the object's attributes through parameter **self**. Method **printMilitary** (lines 14–18) prints the time in military (24-hour) format. Method **printStandard** (lines 20–37) prints the time in standard (12-hour) format.

Once a class has been defined, programs can create objects of that class. Many objects of a class can exist and programmers can create objects as necessary. This is one reason why Python is said to be an *extensible language*. The program in Fig. 7.2 creates an object of class **Time**, defined in Fig. 7.1. We first import the class definition from file **Time1.py**—the file that contains the class definition. Line 4 imports the definition in the same way a program would import any element from a module.

```
1   # Fig. 7.2: fig07_02.py
2   # Creating and manipulating objects of class Time.
3
4   from Time1 import Time  # import class definition from file
5
6   time1 = Time()  # create object of class Time
7
8   # access object's attributes
9   print "The attributes of time1 are: "
10  print "time1.hour:", time1.hour
11  print "time1.minute:", time1.minute
12  print "time1.second:", time1.second
13
14  # access object's methods
15  print "\nCalling method printMilitary:",
16  time1.printMilitary()
17
18  print "\nCalling method printStandard:",
19  time1.printStandard()
20
21  # change value of object's attributes
22  print "\n\nChanging time1's hour attribute..."
23  time1.hour = 25
24  print "Calling method printMilitary after alteration:",
25  time1.printMilitary()
```

```
The attributes of time1 are:
time1.hour: 0
time1.minute: 0
time1.second: 0

Calling method printMilitary: 00:00:00
Calling method printStandard: 12:00:00 AM

Changing time1's hour attribute...
Calling method printMilitary after alteration: 25:00:00
```

Fig. 7.2   Creating an object.

One of the fundamental principles of good software engineering is that a client should not need to know how a class is implemented to use that class. Python's use of modules facilitates this data abstraction—the program in Fig. 7.2 simply imports the **Time** definition and uses class **Time** without knowing how the class is implemented.

Software Engineering Observation 7.3

Clients of a class do nost need access to the class's source code to use the class.

To create an object of class **Time**, simply "call" the class name as if it were a function (line 6). This call invokes the constructor for class **Time**. Even though the class definition stipulates that the constructor (**__init__**) takes one argument, line 6 does not pass any arguments to the constructor. Python inserts the first (object reference) argument into every method call, including a class's constructor call. The constructor initializes the object's attributes. Once the constructor exits, Python assigns the newly created object to **time1**.

Client code must access an object's attributes through a reference to that object. Lines 10–12 demonstrate how a program can access an object's attributes through the dot (**.**) access operator. The name of the object appears to the left of the dot, and the attribute appears to the right of the dot. The output demonstrates the initial values that the constructor assigned to attributes **hour**, **minute** and **second**.

Client code can access an object's methods in a similar manner. Line 16 calls **time1**'s **printMilitary** method. Notice again that the method call passes no arguments, even though the method definition specifies one parameter called **self**. Python passes a reference to **time1** in the **printMilitary** call, so the method may access the object's attributes.

Line 23 modifies the value assigned to attribute **time1.hour**. The output from lines 24–25 shows a problem that often arises when a client indiscriminately accesses an object's data. The meaning of attribute **hour** is unclear, because that data member now has a value of 25. We say that the data member is in an *inconsistent state* (it contains an invalid value). Some other programming languages provide ways to prevent a client from accessing an object's data. Python, on the other hand, does not provide such strict programming constructs. Later in this chapter, we discuss the various ways Python programmers ensure that an object's data remains in a consistent state.

Common Programming Error 7.5

Directly accessing an object's attributes may cause the data to enter an inconsistent state.

7.3 Special Attributes

Classes and objects of classes both have special attributes that can be manipulated. These attributes, which Python creates when a class is defined or when an object of a class is created, provide information about the class or object of a class to which they belong. Figure 7.3 lists the special attributes that all classes contain. The interactive session in Fig. 7.4 prints the value of each of these attributes for class **Time**.

Additionally, all objects of classes have attributes in common. Figure 7.5 lists these attributes, and the interactive session in Fig. 7.6 prints the attributes' values for an object of class **Time**. Notice that objects can access the **__doc__** and **__module__** attributes that belong to the object's class.

Attribute	Description
__bases__	A tuple that contains base classes from which the class directly inherits. If the class does not inherit from other classes, the tuple is empty. [*Note:* We discuss base classes and inheritance in Chapter 9, Object-Oriented Programming: Inheritance.]
__dict__	A dictionary that corresponds to the class's namespace. Each key-value pair represents an identifier and its value in the namespace.
__doc__	A class's docstring. If the class does not specify a docstring, the value is **None**.
__module__	A string that contains the module (file) name in which the class is defined.
__name__	A string that contains the class's name.

Fig. 7.3   Special attributes of a class.

```
Python 2.2b2 (#26, Nov 16 2001, 11:44:11) [MSC 32 bit (Intel)] on
win32
Type "help", "copyright", "credits" or "license" for more informa-
tion.
>>>
>>> from Time1 import Time
>>> print Time.__bases__
()
>>> print Time.__dict__
{'printMilitary': <function printMilitary at 0x0079BF80>,
'__module__': 'Time1', '__doc__': 'Time abstract data type (ADT)
definition', '__init__': <function __init__ at 0x0077AB00>,
'printStandard': <function printStandard at 0x00769990>}
>>>
>>> print Time.__doc__
Time abstract data type (ADT) definition
>>> print Time.__module__
Time1
>>> print Time.__name__
Time
```

Fig. 7.4   Special attributes of a class.

Attribute	Description
__class__	A reference to the class from which the object was instantiated.
__dict__	A dictionary that corresponds to the object's namespace. Each key-value pair represents an identifier and its value in the namespace.

Fig. 7.5   Special attributes of an object of a class.

```
Python 2.2b2 (#26, Nov 16 2001, 11:44:11) [MSC 32 bit (Intel)] on
win32
Type "help", "copyright", "credits" or "license" for more informa-
tion.
>>>
>>> from Time1 import Time
>>> time1 = Time()
>>> print time1.__class__
Time1.Time
>>> print time1.__dict__
{'second': 0, 'minute': 0, 'hour': 0}
>>> print time1.__doc__
Time abstract data type (ADT) definition
>>> print time1.__module__
Time1
```

Fig. 7.6   Special attributes of an object.

These attributes contribute to Python's strong *introspection* capabilities (i.e., Python's ability to provide information about itself). Many programmers use these capabilities to create advanced, dynamic and flexible applications. In this text, we use these capabilities mostly to explore how Python works and to further our understanding of programming concepts.

7.4 Controlling Access to Attributes

In this chapter we already have discussed how clients can access an object's attributes directly and how this practice can place an object's data in an inconsistent state. Most object-oriented programming languages allow an object to prevent its clients from accessing the object's data directly. However, in Python, the programmer uses attribute naming conventions to hide data from clients. In this section, we discuss the advantages and disadvantages of this practice.

7.4.1 Get and Set Methods

Although a client can access an object's data directly (and perhaps cause the data to enter an inconsistent state), a programmer can design classes to encourage correct use. One technique is for the class to provide *access methods* through which the data of the class can be read and written in a carefully controlled manner.

Predicate methods are read-only access methods that test the validity of a condition. An example of a predicate method is an **isEmpty** method for a *container* class—a class capable of holding many objects. A program calls **isEmpty** before reading another item from the container object. An **isFull** predicate method tests a container object to determine whether it has additional space in which a program can place an item. Some appropriate predicate methods for our **Time** class might be **isAM** and **isPM**.

When a class defines access methods, a client should access an object's attributes only through those access methods. A typical manipulation might be the adjustment of a customer's bank-account balance (e.g., an attribute of an object of class **BankAccount**) by a method **computeInterest**.

Classes often provide methods that allow clients to *set* (write) or *get* (read) the values of attributes. Although these methods need not be called *set* and *get*, they often are, by conven-

tion. More specifically, a method that *sets* data member **interestRate** typically would be named **setInterestRate**, and a method that *gets* the **interestRate** typically would be named **getInterestRate**. *Get* methods also are called "query" methods.

It may seem that providing both *set* and *get* capabilities provides no benefit over accessing the attributes directly, but there is a subtle difference. A *get* method seems to allow clients to read the data at will, but the *get* method can control the formatting of the data. A *set* method can—and most likely should—scrutinize attempts to modify the value of the attribute. This ensures that the new value is appropriate for that data item. For example, a set method can reject the following values: the value 37 as the date, a negative value as a person's body weight and the value 185 on an exam (when the grade range is 0–100).

Software Engineering Observation 7.4

Controlling access, especially write access, to attributes through access methods helps ensure data integrity.

Testing and Debugging Tip 7.1

Data integrity is not automatic, even if the programmer provides access methods—the programmer must provide for validity checking.

A class's *set* methods sometimes return values that indicate attempts were made to assign invalid data to an object of the class. Clients of the class then test the return values of *set* methods to determine whether the object it is manipulating is a valid object and to take appropriate actions if the object is not valid. Alternatively, a *set* method may specify that an error message—called an *exception*—be sent ("raised") to the client when the client attempts to assign an invalid value to an attribute. *Raising exceptions* is a topic we explore in detail in Chapter 12, Exception Handling. Exceptions are the preferred technique for handling invalid attribute values in Python.

Good Programming Practice 7.5

Methods that set *the values of data should verify that the intended new values are proper. If they are not, the* set *methods should indicate that an error has occurred.*

Software Engineering Observation 7.5

Accessing data through set *and* get *methods not only protects the data from assuming invalid values, but also insulates clients of the class from the representation of the data. Thus, if the representation of the data changes (typically to reduce the amount of storage required or to improve performance), only the method bodies need to change—the clients need not change as long as the interface provided by the methods remains the same.*

Figure 7.7—**Time2.py**—defines a modified **Time** class that uses access methods to protect access to the data stored in the class.

```
1   # Fig: 7.7: Time2.py
2   # Class Time with accessor methods.
3
4   class Time:
5       """Class Time with accessor methods"""
6
```

Fig. 7.7   Access methods defined for class **Time**. (Part 1 of 3.)

```
7       def __init__( self ):
8           """Time constructor initializes each data member to zero"""
9
10          self._hour = 0      # 0-23
11          self._minute = 0    # 0-59
12          self._second = 0    # 0-59
13
14      def setTime( self, hour, minute, second ):
15          """Set values of hour, minute, and second"""
16
17          self.setHour( hour )
18          self.setMinute( minute )
19          self.setSecond( second )
20
21      def setHour( self, hour ):
22          """Set hour value"""
23
24          if 0 <= hour < 24:
25              self._hour = hour
26          else:
27              raise ValueError, "Invalid hour value: %d" % hour
28
29      def setMinute( self, minute ):
30          """Set minute value"""
31
32          if 0 <= minute < 60:
33              self._minute = minute
34          else:
35              raise ValueError, "Invalid minute value: %d" % minute
36
37      def setSecond( self, second ):
38          """Set second value"""
39
40          if 0 <= second < 60:
41              self._second = second
42          else:
43              raise ValueError, "Invalid second value: %d" % second
44
45      def getHour( self ):
46          """Get hour value"""
47
48          return self._hour
49
50      def getMinute( self ):
51          """Get minute value"""
52
53          return self._minute
54
55      def getSecond( self ):
56          """Get second value"""
57
58          return self._second
59
```

Fig. 7.7   Access methods defined for class **Time**. (Part 2 of 3.)

```
60      def printMilitary( self ):
61          """Prints Time object in military format"""
62
63          print "%.2d:%.2d:%.2d" % \
64              ( self._hour, self._minute, self._second ),
65
66      def printStandard( self ):
67          """Prints Time object in standard format"""
68
69          standardTime = ""
70
71          if self._hour == 0 or self._hour == 12:
72              standardTime += "12:"
73          else:
74              standardTime += "%d:" % ( self._hour % 12 )
75
76          standardTime += "%.2d:%.2d" % ( self._minute, self._second )
77
78          if self._hour < 12:
79              standardTime += " AM"
80          else:
81              standardTime += " PM"
82
83          print standardTime,
```

Fig. 7.7   Access methods defined for class **Time**. (Part 3 of 3.)

Notice that the constructor creates attributes with single leading underscores (_) in lines 10–12. Attribute names that begin with a single underscore have no special meaning in the syntax of the Python language itself. However, the single leading underscore is a convention among Python programmers who use the class. When a class author creates an attribute with a single leading underscore, the author does not want users of the class to access the attribute directly. If a program requires access to the attributes, the class author provides some other means for doing so. In this case, we provide access methods through which clients should manipulate the data.

Good Programming Practice 7.6

An attribute with a single leading underscore conveys information about a class's interface. Clients of a class that defines such attributes should access and modify the attributes' values only through the access methods that the class provides. Failing to do so often causes unexpected errors to occur during program execution.

Software Engineering Observation 7.6

Python's classes and modularity encourage programs to be implementation independent. When the implementation of a class used by implementation-independent code changes, that code need not be modified.

Method **setTime** (lines 14–19) is the *set* method that clients should use to set all values in an object's time. This method receives as arguments values for attributes **_hour**, **_minute** and **_second**. Methods **setHour** (lines 21–27), **setMinute** (lines 29–35) and **setSecond** (lines 37–43) are *set* methods for the individual attributes. These methods provide more flexibility to clients that modify the time.

Software Engineering Observation 7.7

Not all methods need to serve as part of a class's interface. Some methods serve as utility methods to other methods of the class and are not intended to be used by clients of the class.

Common Programming Error 7.6

*When inside a method, forgetting to use the object reference (often called **self**) to access another method defined by the object's class is either a fatal runtime error or a logic error. The logic error occurs when the global namespace contains a function with the same name as one of the class's methods. In this case, forgetting to access the method name through the object reference actually calls the global function.*

The comparison expressions in lines 24, 32 and 40 demonstrate Python's comparison "chaining" syntax that enables programmers to write comparison expressions in familiar, arithmetic terms. Chained comparison expressions can be re-written with syntax familiar from other languages, using an appropriate **and** or **or** operation. For example, the statement in line 24 also could be written as

```
hour >= 0 and hour < 24
```

Performance Tip 7.1

Chained comparison expressions can be more efficient than their non-chained equivalents, because each term in the chained comparison expression is evaluated only once.

Method **setHour** (lines 21–27) changes an object's **_hour** attribute. The method checks whether the value passed as a parameter is in the range 0–23, inclusive. If the hour is valid, the method updates attribute **_hour** with the new value. Otherwise, the method *raises an exception*, to indicate that the client has attempted to place the object's data in an inconsistent state. An *exception* is a Python object that indicates a special event (most often an error) has occurred. For example, when a program attempts to access a nonexistent dictionary key, Python raises an exception.

When an exception is raised a program either can *catch* the exception and *handle* it; or the exception can go uncaught, in which case the program prints an error message and terminates immediately. Catching and handling an exception enables a program to recognize and potentially fix errors that might otherwise cause a program to terminate. For example, a client that uses class **Time** can catch an exception and detect that the program has attempted to place data in an inconsistent state (i.e., set an invalid time). Catching and handling exceptions is a broad topic that we discuss in detail in Chapter 12, Exception Handling. For now, we discuss only how to raise an exception to indicate invalid data assignments and prevent data corruption.

The statement in line 27 uses keyword ***raise*** to raise an exception. The keyword **raise** is followed by the name of the exception, a comma and a value that the exception object stores as an attribute. When Python executes a **raise** statement, an exception is raised; if the exception is not caught, Python prints an error message that contains the name of the exception and the exception's attribute value, as shown in Fig. 7.8.

The remaining methods—**setMinute** (lines 29–35) and **setSecond** (lines 37–43) change attributes **_minute** and **_second**, respectively. Each method ensures that the values remain in the range 0–59, inclusive. If the values are invalid, the methods raise exceptions and specify appropriate error-message arguments.

```
Python 2.2b2 (#26, Nov. 16 2001, 11:44:11) [MSC 32 bit (Intel)] on
win32
Type "help", "copyright", "credits" or "license" for more informa-
tion.
>>>
>>> raise ValueError, "This is an error message"
Traceback (most recent call last):
  File "<stdin>", line 1, in ?
ValueError: This is an error message
```

Fig. 7.8   Raising an exception.

Lines 45–58 contain the *get* methods for class **Time**. Clients use these methods (**getHour**, **getMinute** and **getSecond**) to retrieve the values of an attributes **_hour**, **_minute** and **_second**, respectively. The remainder of the class definition does not differ from the previous definition we presented.

Software Engineering Observation 7.8

If a class provides access methods for its data, clients should use only access methods to retrieve/modify data. This "agreement" between class and client helps maintain data in a consistent state.

Software Engineering Observation 7.9

The class designer need not provide set *or* get *methods for each data item; these capabilities should be provided only when appropriate. If the service is appropriate for clients, that service should be provided in the class's interface.*

Software Engineering Observation 7.10

Every method that modifies the data of an object should ensure that the data remains in a consistent state.

Figure 7.9 contains a *driver* for modified class **Time**. A driver is a program that tests a class's interface. Lines 4–6 **import** class **Time** from module **Time2** and create an object of the class. Lines 9–12 call methods **printMilitary** and **printStandard** to display the initial time values of the object.

```
1   # Fig. 7.9: fig07_09.py
2   # Driver to test class TimeControl.
3
4   from Time2 import Time
5
6   time1 = Time()
7
8   # print initial time
9   print "The initial military time is",
10  time1.printMilitary()
11  print "\nThe initial standard time is",
12  time1.printStandard()
```

Fig. 7.9   Access methods called to change data. (Part 1 of 2.)

```
13
14   # change time
15   time1.setTime( 13, 27, 6 )
16   print "\n\nMilitary time after setTime is",
17   time1.printMilitary()
18   print "\nStandard time after setTime is",
19   time1.printStandard()
20
21   time1.setHour( 4 )
22   time1.setMinute( 3 )
23   time1.setSecond( 34 )
24   print "\n\nMilitary time after setHour, setMinute, setSecond is",
25   time1.printMilitary()
26   print "\nStandard time after setHour, setMinute, setSecond is",
27   time1.printStandard()
```

```
The initial military time is 00:00:00
The initial standard time is 12:00:00 AM

Military time after setTime is 13:27:06
Standard time after setTime is 1:27:06 PM

Military time after setHour, setMinute, setSecond is 04:03:34
Standard time after setHour, setMinute, setSecond is 4:03:34 AM
```

Fig. 7.9   Access methods called to change data. (Part 2 of 2.)

Line 15 calls **time1**'s method **setTime**, passing values that correspond to 1:27:06 PM, to change the object's time values. Lines 16–19 call the appropriate methods to display the formatted times. The interactive session in Fig. 7.10 creates an object of class **Time** and calls method **setTime** to attempt to place the object's data in an inconsistent state. Each call to method **setTime** contains an invalid value, and each call results in an error message.

```
Python 2.2b2 (#26, Nov 16 2001, 11:44:11) [MSC 32 bit (Intel)] on
win32
Type "help", "copyright", "credits" or "license" for more informa-
tion.
>>>
>>> from Time2 import Time
>>> time1 = Time()
>>>
>>> time1.setHour( 30 )
Traceback (most recent call last):
  File "<stdin>", line 1, in ?
  File "Time2.py", line 27, in setHour
    raise ValueError, "Invalid hour value: %d" % hour
ValueError: Invalid hour value: 30
```

(continued top of next page)

Fig. 7.10   *set* method called with invalid values. (Part 1 of 2.)

```
                                                    (continued from previous page)

>>>
>>> time1.setMinute( 99 )
Traceback (most recent call last):
  File "<stdin>", line 1, in ?
  File "Time2.py", line 35, in setMinute
    raise ValueError, "Invalid minute value: %d" % minute
ValueError: Invalid minute value: 99
>>>
>>> time1.setSecond( -99 )
Traceback (most recent call last):
  File "<stdin>", line 1, in ?
  File "Time2.py", line 43, in setSecond
    raise ValueError, "Invalid second value: %d" % second
ValueError: Invalid second value: -99
```

Fig. 7.10   *set* method called with invalid values. (Part 2 of 2.)

7.4.2 Private Attributes

In programming languages such as C++ and Java, a class may state explicitly which attributes or methods may be accessed by clients of the class. These attributes or methods are said to be *public*. Attributes and methods that may not be accessed by clients of the class are said to be *private*.

In Python, an object's attributes may always be accessed—there is no way to prevent other code from accessing the data. However, Python does provide a way to prevent indiscriminate access to data. Suppose we want to create an object of class **Time** and to prevent the following assignment statement

```
time1.hour = 25
```

To prevent such access, we prefix the name of the attribute with two underscore characters (__). When Python encounters an attribute name that begins with two underscores, the interpreter performs *name mangling* on the attribute, to prevent indiscriminate access to the data. Name mangling changes the name of an attribute by including information about the class to which the attribute belongs. For example, if the **Time** constructor contained the line

```
self.__hour = 0
```

Python creates an attribute called **_Time__hour**, instead of an attribute called **__hour**. Figure 7.11 contains an example in which we define a class **PrivateClass** that contains one public attribute **publicData** (line 10) and one private attribute **__privateData** (line 11). The interactive session that follows (Fig. 7.12) demonstrates how to access an object's data.

First, in Fig. 7.12, we import the class from module **Private** and create an object called **private**. The statement

```
print private.publicData
```

```
1   # Fig. 7.11: Private.py
2   # Class with private data members.
3
4   class PrivateClass:
5      """Class that contains public and private data"""
6
7      def __init__( self ):
8         """Private class, contains public and private data members"""
9
10        self.publicData = "public"      # public data member
11        self.__privateData = "private"  # private data member
```

Fig. 7.11   Class **PrivateClass** with private data.

```
Python 2.2b2 (#26, Nov 16 2001, 11:44:11) [MSC 32 bit (Intel)] on
win32
Type "help", "copyright", "credits" or "license" for more informa-
tion.
>>>
>>> from Private import PrivateClass
>>> private = PrivateClass()
>>> print private.publicData
public
>>> print private.__privateData
Traceback (most recent call last):
  File "<stdin>", line 1, in ?
AttributeError: PrivateClass instance has no attribute
'__privateData'
>>>
>>> print private._PrivateClass__privateData
private
>>> private._PrivateClass__privateData = "modified"
>>> print private._PrivateClass__privateData
modified
```

Fig. 7.12   Private data accessed.

behaves as expected—Python prints the value of the public attribute. When we write the statement

```
        print private.__privateData
```

Python prints an error message which explains that class **PrivateClass** does not contain an attribute called **__privateData**. We prefixed our attribute name with double underscores, so Python changed the name of the attribute in the class definition.

However, we can still access the data, because we know that Python renames attribute **__privateData** to attribute **_PrivateClass__privateData**. Therefore, the line

```
        print private._PrivateClass__privateData
```

successfully prints the value assigned to the private attribute. The final two statements in the session demonstrate that private data may be modified in the same way as public data.

However, accessing and modifying private attributes in this manner violates the data encapsulation the class author intended. A client should never perform such a manipulation, but instead should use any access methods the class provides.

Software Engineering Observation 7.11

Make private any data that the client should not access.

Python programmers use private attributes for different reasons. Some programmers use private attributes to avoid common scoping problems that may arise in inheritance hierarchies. [*Note*: We discuss inheritance in Chapter 9, Object-Oriented Programming: Inheritance.] Other programmers use private attributes for data or methods the client should never access. These attributes or methods are essential to the inner workings of the class, but are not part of the class's interface. For example, a class author might designate a utility method by prepending the method name with two underscores. In this chapter, we use private attributes to demonstrate access methods and to introduce a basic data integrity technique. In the next chapter, we discuss other ways to ensure data integrity. The techniques we discuss in the next chapter allow programmers to use public access syntax but also to take advantage of the data integrity provided by access methods. This practice enables programmers to add data integrity to a project as the project grows and matures, without having to change the interface on which the project's clients have come to rely.

7.5 Using Default Arguments With Constructors

Thus far, the client has supplied all the values that the constructor for class **Time** needed to initialize a new object. However, constructors can define default arguments that specify initial values for an object's attributes, if the client does not specify an argument at construction time. Constructors also can define keyword arguments that enable the client to specify values for only certain, named arguments. Figure 7.13—**Time3.py**—defines a modified version of class **Time** that redefines the **Time** constructor to include the default value 0 for each argument. Providing a default constructor guarantees that objects will be initialized to consistent states, even if no values are provided in constructor calls. Programmer-supplied constructors that default all their arguments (or explicitly require no arguments) are also called *default constructors* (i.e., constructors that can be invoked with no arguments.)

```
1   # Fig: 7.13: Time3.py
2   # Class Time with default constructor.
3
4   class Time:
5      """Class Time with default constructor"""
6
7      def __init__( self, hour = 0, minute = 0, second = 0 ):
8         """Time constructor initializes each data member to zero"""
9
10        self.setTime( hour, minute, second )
11
```

Fig. 7.13 Default constructor defined for class **Time**. (Part 1 of 3.)

```
12      def setTime( self, hour, minute, second ):
13          """Set values of hour, minute, and second"""
14
15          self.setHour( hour )
16          self.setMinute( minute )
17          self.setSecond( second )
18
19      def setHour( self, hour ):
20          """Set hour value"""
21
22          if 0 <= hour < 24:
23              self.__hour = hour
24          else:
25              raise ValueError, "Invalid hour value: %d" % hour
26
27      def setMinute( self, minute ):
28          """Set minute value"""
29
30          if 0 <= minute < 60:
31              self.__minute = minute
32          else:
33              raise ValueError, "Invalid minute value: %d" % minute
34
35      def setSecond( self, second ):
36          """Set second value"""
37
38          if 0 <= second < 60:
39              self.__second = second
40          else:
41              raise ValueError, "Invalid second value: %d" % second
42
43      def getHour( self ):
44          """Get hour value"""
45
46          return self.__hour
47
48      def getMinute( self ):
49          """Get minute value"""
50
51          return self.__minute
52
53      def getSecond( self ):
54          """Get second value"""
55
56          return self.__second
57
58      def printMilitary( self ):
59          """Prints Time object in military format"""
60
61          print "%.2d:%.2d:%.2d" % \
62              ( self.__hour, self.__minute, self.__second ),
63
```

Fig. 7.13 Default constructor defined for class **Time**. (Part 2 of 3.)

```
64       def printStandard( self ):
65          """Prints Time object in standard format"""
66
67          standardTime = ""
68
69          if self.__hour == 0 or self.__hour == 12:
70             standardTime += "12:"
71          else:
72             standardTime += "%d:" % ( self.__hour % 12 )
73
74          standardTime += "%.2d:%.2d" % ( self.__minute, self.__second )
75
76          if self.__hour < 12:
77             standardTime += " AM"
78          else:
79             standardTime += " PM"
80
81          print standardTime,
```

Fig. 7.13   Default constructor defined for class **Time**. (Part 3 of 3.)

In this example, the constructor invokes method **setTime** with the values passed to the constructor (or the default values). The class uses private attributes to store data. As with the previous definition of **Time**, **setTime** uses the class's other methods, which ensure that the value supplied for **__hour** is in the range 0–23 and that the values for **__minute** and **__second** are each in the range 0–59. If a value is out of range, the appropriate method raises an exception (this is an example of ensuring that a data member remains in a consistent state).

The **Time** constructor could have included the same statements as method **setTime**. This may be slightly more efficient because the extra call to **setTime** is eliminated. Coding the **Time** constructor and method **setTime** identically, however, makes maintaining this class more difficult. If the implementation of method **setTime** changes, the implementation of the **Time** constructor should change accordingly. Instead, any changes to the implementation of **setTime** need to be made only once, because the **Time** constructor calls **setTime** directly. This reduces the likelihood of a programming error when altering the implementation.

Software Engineering Observation 7.12

If a method of a class already provides all or part of the functionality required by a constructor (or other method) of the class, call that method from the constructor (or other method). This simplifies the maintenance of the code and reduces the likelihood of an error if the implementation of the code is modified. As a general rule: Avoid repeating code.

Figure 7.14 initializes four objects of class **Time** (defined in Fig. 7.13)—one with all three arguments defaulted in the constructor call, one with one argument specified, one with two arguments specified and one with three arguments specified. The values of each object's attributes after initialization are displayed by calling **printTimeValues** (lines 6–10).

If no constructor is defined for a class, the interpreter creates a default constructor (i.e., one that can be called with no arguments). However, the constructor that Python provides does not perform any initialization, so, when an object is created, the object is not guaranteed to be in a consistent state.

```
1   # Fig. 7.14: fig07_14.py
2   # Demonstrating default constructor method for class Time.
3
4   from Time3 import Time
5
6   def printTimeValues( timeToPrint ):
7       timeToPrint.printMilitary()
8       print
9       timeToPrint.printStandard()
10      print
11
12  time1 = Time()              # all default
13  time2 = Time( 2 )           # minute, second default
14  time3 = Time( 21, 34 )      # second default
15  time4 = Time( 12, 25, 42 ) # all specified
16
17  print "Constructed with:"
18
19  print "\nall arguments defaulted:"
20  printTimeValues( time1 )
21
22  print "\nhour specified; minute and second defaulted:"
23  printTimeValues( time2 )
24
25  print "\nhour and minute specified; second defaulted:"
26  printTimeValues( time3 )
27
28  print "\nhour, minute and second specified:"
29  printTimeValues( time4 )
```

```
Constructed with:

all arguments defaulted:
00:00:00
12:00:00 AM

hour specified; minute and second defaulted:
02:00:00
2:00:00 AM

hour and minute specified; second defaulted:
21:34:00
9:34:00 PM

hour, minute and second specified:
12:25:42
12:25:42 PM
```

Fig. 7.14 Objects created with default constructor.

7.6 Destructors

A constructor is a method that initializes a newly created object. Conversely, a *destructor* executes when an object is destroyed (e.g., after no more references to the object exist). A class can define a special method called **___del___** that executes when the last reference to an object is deleted or goes out of scope[1]. The method itself does not actually destroy the object—it performs *termination housekeeping* before the interpreter reclaims the object's memory, so that memory may be reused. A destructor normally specifies no parameters other than **self** and returns **None**.

We have not defined method **___del___** for the classes presented to this point. In programming languages such as C++, destructors often allocate and recycle memory. Python handles most of these issues for the programmer, so **___del___** normally is not included in the class definition. Occasionally, a class defines **___del___** to close a network or a database connection before destroying an object. We discuss these issues throughout the text, as appropriate. In the next section, we define method **___del___** for a class, to maintain a count of all objects of the class that have been created.

7.7 Class Attributes

Each object of a class has copies of all the attributes created in the constructor. In certain cases, only one copy of an attribute should be shared by all objects of a class. A *class attribute* is used for this reason. A class attribute represents "class-wide" information (i.e., a property of the class, not of a specific object of the class).

We now consider a video-game example to justify the need for class-wide data. Suppose that we have a video game with **Martian**s and other space creatures. Each **Martian** tends to be brave and willing to attack other space creatures when the **Martian** is aware that there are at least four other **Martian**s present. If there are fewer than five **Martian**s present, each **Martian** becomes cowardly. For this reason, each **Martian** must know the **martianCount**. We could endow each object of class **Martian** with **martianCount** as an attribute. However, if we do this, then every **Martian** would have a separate copy of the attribute, and, each time we create a **Martian**, we would have to update attribute **martianCount** in every **Martian**. The redundant copies waste space, and updating those copies is time-consuming. Instead, we create **martianCount** as a class attribute so that **martianCount** is class-wide data. Each **Martian** can see the **martianCount** as if it were an attribute of that **Martian**, but Python maintains only one copy of the **martianCount** attribute to save space. This technique also saves time; because there is only one copy, we do not have to increment separate copies of **martianCount** for each object of class **Martian**.

Performance Tip 7.2

When a single copy of the data will suffice, use class attributes to save storage.

---

1. Actually, there are some cases in which **___del___** does not execute immediately after the last reference to an object is deleted. However, in most cases, it is safe to assume that the method executes when expected. See **www.python.org/doc/current/ref/customization.html** for more information.

Although class attributes may seem like global variables, each class attribute resides in the namespace of the class in which it is created. Class attributes should be initialized once (and only once) in the class definition. A class's class attributes can be accessed through any object of that class. A class's class attributes also exist even when no object of that class exists. To access a class attribute when no object of the class exists, prefix the class name, followed by a period, to the name of the attribute.

Software Engineering Observation 7.13

A class's class attributes can be used even if no objects of that class have been instantiated.

Class **Employee** (Fig. 7.15) demonstrates how to define a class attribute that maintains a count of the number of objects of the class that have been instantiated. The class attribute **count** is initialized to 0 in the class definition (line 7). Notice that the creation of class attribute **count** appears in the body of the class definition, not inside a method. The statement has the effect of defining a new variable named **count**, with value 0, and adding that variable to class **Employee**'s namespace.

```
1   # Fig. 7.15: EmployeeWithClassAttribute.py
2   # Class Employee with class attribute count.
3
4   class Employee:
5       """Represents an employee"""
6
7       count = 0        # class attribute
8
9       def __init__( self, first, last ):
10          """Initializes firstName, lastName and increments count"""
11
12          self.firstName = first
13          self.lastName = last
14
15          Employee.count += 1    # increment class attribute
16
17          print "Employee constructor for %s, %s" \
18              % ( self.lastName, self.firstName )
19
20      def __del__( self ):
21          """Decrements count and prints message"""
22
23          Employee.count -= 1    # decrement class attribute
24
25          print "Employee destructor for %s, %s" \
26              % ( self.lastName, self.firstName )
```

Fig. 7.15 Class attributes—class **Employee**.

```
1   # Fig. 7.16: fig07_16.py
2   # Demonstrating class attribute access.
3
```

Fig. 7.16 Class attributes—**fig07_16.py**. (Part 1 of 2.)

```
 4    from EmployeeWithClassAttribute import Employee
 5
 6    print "Number of employees before instantiation is", \
 7        Employee.count
 8
 9    # create two Employee objects
10    employee1 = Employee( "Susan", "Baker" )
11    employee2 = Employee( "Robert", "Jones" )
12    employee3 = employee1
13
14    print "Number of employees after instantiation is", \
15        employee1.count
16
17    # explicitly delete employee objects by removing references
18    del employee1
19    del employee2
20    del employee3
21
22    print "Number of employees after deletion is", \
23        Employee.count
```

```
Number of employees before instantiation is 0
Employee constructor for Baker, Susan
Employee constructor for Jones, Robert
Number of employees after instantiation is 2
Employee destructor for Jones, Robert
Employee destructor for Baker, Susan
Number of employees after deletion is 0
```

Fig. 7.16   Class attributes—`fig07_16.py`. (Part 2 of 2.)

Figure 7.16 access **Employee**'s class attribute. Class attribute **count** maintains a count of the number of existing objects of class **Employee** and can be accessed whether or not objects of class **Employee** exist. If no objects of the class exist, a program can reference **count** through the class name (line 7). Lines 10–11 create two **Employee** objects. When each **Employee** object is created, its constructor is called. In the output, notice that creating identifier **employee3** (line 12) does not create a new object of class **Employee** and therefore does not call **Employee**'s constructor. The statement simply binds a new name to the object created in line 18, so that **employee3** and **employee1** refer to the same object. Lines 18–20 use keyword **del** to delete all references to the two **Employee** objects. Method **__del__** for the object created in line 10 does not execute until the last reference to that object is deleted in line 20.

7.8 Composition: Object References as Members of Classes

Until now, we have defined classes whose objects have attributes of basic types. Sometimes, a programmer needs objects whose attributes are themselves references to objects of other classes. For example, an object of class **AlarmClock** needs to know when it is supposed to sound its alarm, so why not include an object of class **Time** as a member of the object of class **AlarmClock**? Such a capability is called *composition*.

Software Engineering Observation 7.14

One form of software reusability is composition, in which a class has references to objects of other classes as members.

Software Engineering Observation 7.15

If a class has as a member a reference to an object of another class, making that member object publicly accessible does not violate the encapsulation and hiding of that member object's private members.

Figure 7.17 uses a class **Date** (Fig. 7.17) a modified class **Employee** (Fig. 7.18) and to demonstrate references to objects as members of other objects. Class **Employee** contains attributes **firstName**, **lastName**, **birthDate** and **hireDate**. Attributes **birthDate** and **hireDate** are objects of class **Date**, which contains attributes **month**, **day** and **year**. The program (Fig. 7.19) instantiates an object of class **Employee** and initializes and displays its attributes.

```python
1   # Fig. 7.17: Date.py
2   # Definition of class Date.
3
4   class Date:
5       """Class that represents dates"""
6
7       # class attribute lists number of days in each month
8       daysPerMonth = [
9           0, 31, 28, 31, 30, 31, 30, 31, 31, 30, 31, 30, 31 ]
10
11      def __init__( self, month, day, year ):
12          """Constructor for class Date"""
13
14          if 0 < month <= 12:    # validate month
15              self.month = month
16          else:
17              raise ValueError, "Invalid value for month: %d" % month
18
19          if year >= 0:          # validate year
20              self.year = year
21          else:
22              raise ValueError, "Invalid value for year: %y" % year
23
24          self.day = self.checkDay( day )   # validate day
25
26          print "Date constructor:",
27          self.display()
28
29      def __del__( self ):
30          """Prints message when called"""
31
32          print "Date object about to be destroyed:",
33          self.display()
34
```

Fig. 7.17   Member objects—**Date.py**. (Part 1 of 2.)

```
35    def display( self ):
36        """Prints Date information"""
37
38        print "%d/%d/%d" % ( self.month, self.day, self.year )
39
40    def checkDay( self, testDay ):
41        """Validates day of the month"""
42
43        # validate day, test for leap year
44        if 0 < testDay <= Date.daysPerMonth[ self.month ]:
45            return testDay
46        elif self.month == 2 and testDay == 29 and \
47            ( self.year % 400 == 0 or
48              self.year % 100 != 0 and self.year % 4 == 0 ):
49            return testDay
50        else:
51            raise ValueError, "Invalid day: %d for month: %d" % \
52                ( testDay, self.month )
```

Fig. 7.17   Member objects—**Date.py**. (Part 2 of 2.)

In Fig. 7.18, the **Employee** constructor (lines 9–20) takes nine arguments—**self**, **firstName**, **lastName**, **birthMonth**, **birthDay**, **birthYear**, **hireMonth**, **hireDay** and **hireYear**—and creates objects of class **Date** from the last six arguments. Arguments **birthMonth**, **birthDay** and **birthYear** are passed to object **birthDate**'s constructor, and arguments **hireMonth**, **hireDay** and **hireYear** are passed to object **hireDate**'s constructor. Class **Date** and class **Employee** each define method **__del__** to print a message when an object of class **Date** or an object of class **Employee** is destroyed, respectively.

```
1    # Fig. 7.18: EmployeeComposition.py
2    # Definition of Employee class with composite members.
3
4    from Date import Date
5
6    class Employee:
7        """Employee class with Date attributes"""
8
9        def __init__( self, firstName, lastName, birthMonth,
10            birthDay, birthYear, hireMonth, hireDay, hireYear ):
11            """Constructor for class Employee"""
12
13            self.birthDate = Date( birthMonth, birthDay, birthYear )
14            self.hireDate = Date( hireMonth, hireDay, hireYear )
15
16            self.lastName = lastName
17            self.firstName = firstName
18
19            print "Employee constructor: %s, %s" \
20                % ( self.lastName, self.firstName )
```

Fig. 7.18   Member objects—**EmployeeComposition.py**. (Part 1 of 2.)

```
21
22      def __del__( self ):
23          """Called before Employee destruction"""
24
25          print "Employee object about to be destroyed: %s, %s" \
26              % ( self.lastName, self.firstName )
27
28      def display( self ):
29          """Prints employee information"""
30
31          print "%s, %s" % ( self.lastName, self.firstName )
32          print "Hired:",
33          self.hireDate.display()
34          print "Birth date:",
35          self.birthDate.display()
```

Fig. 7.18   Member objects—**EmployeeComposition.py**. (Part 2 of 2.)

```
1    # Fig. 7.19: fig07_19.py
2    # Demonstrating composition: an object with member objects.
3
4    from Date import Date
5    from EmployeeComposition import Employee
6
7    employee = Employee( "Bob", "Jones", 7, 24, 1949, 3, 12, 1988 )
8    print
9
10   employee.display()
11   print
```

```
Date constructor: 7/24/1949
Date constructor: 3/12/1988
Employee constructor: Jones, Bob

Jones, Bob
Hired: 3/12/1988
Birth date: 7/24/1949

Employee object about to be destroyed: Jones, Bob
Date object about to be destroyed: 3/12/1988
Date object about to be destroyed: 7/24/1949
```

Fig. 7.19   Member objects—**fig07_19.py**.

7.9 Data Abstraction and Information Hiding

As we pointed out at the beginning of this chapter, classes normally hide the details of their implementation from their clients. This is called *information hiding*. As an example of information hiding, let us consider a data structure called a *stack*.

Students can think of a stack as analogous to a pile of dishes. When a dish is placed on the pile, it is always placed at the top (referred to as *pushing* the dish onto the stack). Similarly, when a dish is removed from the pile, it is always removed from the top (referred to as *pop-*

ping the dish off the stack). Stacks are known as *last-in, first-out (LIFO) data structures*—the last item pushed (inserted) on the stack is the first item popped (removed) from the stack.

Stacks can easily be implemented with lists, and in fact, Python lists contain methods that programers can use to make lists "act" like stacks. (We also implement our own class **Stack** in Chapter 22, Data Structures.) A client of a stack class need not be concerned with the stack's implementation. The client knows only that when data items are placed in the stack, these items will be recalled in last-in, first-out order. The client cares about *what* functionality a stack offers, but not about *how* that functionality is implemented. This concept is referred to as *data abstraction*. Although programmers might know the details of a class's implementation, they should not write code that depends on these details. This enables a particular class (such as one that implements a stack and its operations, *push* and *pop*) to be replaced with another version without affecting the rest of the system. As long as the services of the class do not change (i.e., every method still has the same name, returns the same type of value and defines the same parameter list in the new class definition), the rest of the system is not affected.

The job of a high-level language is to create a view convenient for programmers to use. There is no single accepted standard view—that is one reason why there are so many programming languages. Object-oriented programming in Python presents yet another view.

Most programming languages emphasize actions. In these languages, data exists to support the actions that programs must take. Data is "less interesting" than actions. Data is "crude." Only a few built-in data types exist, and it is difficult for programmers to create their own data types. The object-oriented style of programming in Python elevates the importance of data. The primary activities of object-oriented programming in Python is the creation of data types (i.e., classes) and the expression of the interactions among objects of those data types. To create languages that emphasize data, the programming-languages community needed to formalize some notions about data. The formalization we consider here is the notion of *abstract data types (ADTs)*. ADTs receive as much attention today as structured programming did decades earlier. ADTs, however, do not replace structured programming. Rather, they provide an additional formalization to improve the program-development process.

Consider the built-in integer type, which most people would associate with an integer in mathematics. Rather, the integer type is an abstract representation of an integer. Unlike mathematical integers, computer integers are fixed in size. For example, the integer type on some computers is limited approximately to the range –2 billion to +2 billion. If the result of a calculation falls outside this range, an error occurs, and the computer responds in some machine-dependent manner. It might, for example, "quietly" produce an incorrect result. Mathematical integers do not have this problem. Therefore, the notion of a computer integer is only an approximation of the notion of a real-world integer. The same is true of the floating-point type and other built-in types.

We have taken the notion of the integer type for granted until this point, but we now consider it from a new perspective. Types like integer, floating-points, strings and others are all examples of abstract data types. These types are representations of real-world notions to some satisfactory level of precision within a computer system.

An ADT actually captures two notions: A *data representation* and the *operations* that can be performed on that data. For example, in Python, an integer contains an integer value (data) and provides addition, subtraction, multiplication, division and modulus operations;

however, division by zero is undefined. Python programmers use classes to implement abstract data types.

Software Engineering Observation 7.16

Programmers can create types through the use of the class mechanism. These new types can be designed so that they are as convenient to use as the built-in types. This marks Python as an extensible language. Although the language is easy to extend via new types, the programmer cannot alter the base language itself.

Another abstract data type we discuss is a *queue*, which is similar to a "waiting line." Computer systems use many queues internally. A queue offers well-understood behavior to its clients: Clients place items in a queue one at a time via an *enqueue* operation, then get those items back one at a time via a *dequeue* operation. A queue returns items in *first-in, first-out (FIFO)* order, which means that the first item inserted in a queue is the first item removed. Conceptually, a queue can become infinitely long, but real queues are finite.

The queue hides an internal data representation that keeps track of the items currently waiting in line, and it offers a set of operations to its clients (*enqueue* and *dequeue*). The clients are not concerned about the implementation of the queue—clients simply depend upon the queue to operate "as advertised." When a client enqueues an item, the queue should accept that item and place it in some kind of internal FIFO data structure. Similarly, when the client wants the next item from the front of the queue, the queue should remove the item from its internal representation and deliver the item in FIFO order (i.e., the item that has been in the queue the longest should be the next one returned by the next dequeue operation).

The queue ADT guarantees the integrity of its internal data structure. Clients cannot manipulate this data structure directly—only the queue ADT has access to its internal data. Clients are able to perform only allowable operations on the data representation; the ADT rejects operations that its interface does not provide. This could mean issuing an error message, terminating execution, raising an exception (as discussed in Chapter 12, Exception Handling) or simply ignoring the operation request.

7.10 Software Reusability

Python programmers concentrate both on crafting new classes and on reusing classes from the standard library, which contains hundreds of predefined classes. Developers construct software by combining programmer-defined classes with well-defined, carefully tested, well-documented, portable and widely available standard library classes. This kind of software reusability speeds the development of powerful, high-quality software. *Rapid applications development (RAD)* is of great interest today.

The standard library enables Python developers to build applications faster by reusing preexisting, extensively tested classes. In addition to reducing development time, standard library classes also improve programmers' abilities to debug and maintain applications, because proven software components are being used. For programmers to take advantage of the standard library's classes, they must familiarize themselves with the standard library's rich set of capabilities.

In this chapter, we discussed how to define a class and to create objects of the class. When a new object is created, the class constructor initializes the new object's attributes. We discussed several ways to initialize and modify attributes—default constructors, *set* methods and raising exceptions for invalid attribute values. We also discussed data integrity, how all object attributes may be accessed directly by the client, how the single leading underscore (_) indicates that clients should not access attributes and how the double leading underscore (__) mangles an attribute's name to prevent casual attribute access. Python's direct attribute access encourages rapid application development and facilitates dynamic introspection; however, direct access is often insufficient for large-scale software projects. In the next chapter, we discuss how class authors can ensure data integrity, while still taking advantage of direct access syntax. This data integrity functionality can be added to the class without changing the interface the client uses to access an object's data. This promotes both the safe, modular programming techniques and rapid development practices that Python programmers desire.

SUMMARY

- Object-oriented programming (OOP) encapsulates (i.e., wraps) data (attributes) and functions (behaviors) into components called classes. The data and functions of a class are intimately tied together.

- A class is like a blueprint. Using a blueprint, a builder can build a house. Using a class, a programmer can create an object (also called an instance).

- Classes have a property called *information hiding*. Although objects may know how to communicate with one another across well-defined interfaces, one object normally should not be allowed to know how another object is implemented—implementation details are hidden within the objects themselves.

- In procedural programming, the unit of programming is the function. In object-oriented programming, the unit of programming is the class from which objects eventually are instantiated.

- Procedural programmers concentrate on writing functions. The verbs in a system specification help the procedural programmer determine the set of functions that will work together to implement the system.

- Object-oriented programmers concentrate on creating their own user-defined types, called classes. The nouns in a system specification help the object-oriented programmer determine the set of classes that will be used to create the objects that will work together to implement the system.

- Classes simplify programming because the clients need to be concerned only with the operations encapsulated or embedded in the object—the object interface.

- Keyword **class** begins a class definition. The keyword is followed by the name of the class, which is followed by a colon (**:**). The line that contains keyword **class** and the class name is called the class's header.

- The body of the class is an indented code block that contains methods and attributes that belong to the class.

- A class's optional documentation string describes the class. If a class contains a documentation string, the string must appear in the line or lines following the class header.

- Method **__init__** is the constructor method of a class. A constructor is a special method that executes each time an object of a class is created. The constructor initializes the attributes of the object and returns **None**.

- All methods, including constructors, must specify at least one parameter—the object reference. This parameter represents the object of the class for which the method is called. Methods must use the object reference to access attributes and other methods that belong to the class.

- By convention, the object reference argument is called **self**.

- Each object has its own namespace that contains the object's methods and attributes. The class's constructor starts with an empty object (**self**) and adds attributes to the object's namespace.

- Once a class has been defined, programs can create objects of that class. Programmers can create objects as necessary. This is one reason why Python is said to be an *extensible language*.

- One of the fundamental principles of good software engineering is that a client should not need to know how a class is implemented to use that class. Python's use of modules facilitates this data abstraction—a program can import a class definition and use the class without knowing how the class is implemented.

- To create an object of a class, simply "call" the class name as if it were a function. This call invokes the constructor for the class.

- Classes and objects of classes both have special attributes that can be manipulated. These attributes, which Python creates when a class is defined or when an object of a class is created, provide information about the class or object of a class to which they belong.

- Directly accessing an object's data can leave the data in an inconsistent state.

- Most object-oriented programming languages allow an object to prevent its clients from accessing the object's data directly. However, in Python, the programmer uses attribute naming conventions to hide data from clients.

- Although a client can access an object's data directly (and perhaps cause the data to enter an inconsistent state), a programmer can design classes to encourage correct use. One technique is for the class to provide access methods through which the data of the class can be read and written in a carefully controlled manner.

- Predicate methods are read-only access methods that test the validity of a condition.

- When a class defines access methods, a client should access an object's attributes only through those access methods.

- Classes often provide methods that allow clients to *set* or *get* the values of attributes. Although these methods need not be called *set* and *get*, they often are. *Get* methods also are called "query" methods.

- A *get* method can control the formatting of the data. A *set* method can—and most likely should—scrutinize attempts to modify the value of the attribute. This ensures that the new value is appropriate for that data item.

- A *set* method may specify that an error message—called an exception—be raised to the client when the client attempts to assign an invalid value to an attribute.

- When a class author creates an attribute with a single leading underscore, the author does not want users of the class to access the attribute directly. If a program requires access to the attributes, the class author provides some other means for doing so.

- Python comparisons may be chained. The chaining syntax that enables programmers to write comparison expressions in familiar, arithmetic terms.

- When an exception is raised a program either can catch the exception and handle it; or the exception can go uncaught, in which case the program prints an error message and terminates immediately.

- The keyword **raise** is followed by the name of the exception, a comma and a value that the exception object stores as an attribute. When Python executes a **raise** statement, an exception is raised. If the exception is not caught, Python prints an error message that contains the name of the exception and the exception's attribute value.

- In programming languages such as C++ and Java, a class may state explicitly which attributes or methods may be accessed by clients of the class. These attributes or methods are said to be public. Attributes and methods that may not be accessed by clients of the class are said to be private.

- To prevent indiscriminate attribute access, prefix the name of the attribute with two underscore characters (__).

- When Python encounters an attribute name that begins with two underscores, the interpreter performs name mangling on the attribute, to prevent indiscriminate access to the data. Name mangling changes the name of an attribute by including information about the class to which the attribute belongs.

- Constructors can define default arguments that specify initial values for an object's attributes, if the client does not specify an argument at construction time.

- Constructors can define keyword arguments that enable the client to specify values for only certain, named arguments.

- Programmer-supplied constructors that default all their arguments (or explicitly require no arguments) are also called default constructors

- If no constructor is defined for a class, the interpreter creates a default constructor. However, the constructor that Python provides does not perform any initialization, so, when an object is created, the object is not guaranteed to be in a consistent state.

- A destructor executes when an object is destroyed (e.g., after no more references to the object exist).

- A class can define a special method called **__del__** that executes when the last reference to an object is deleted or goes out of scope. A destructor normally specifies no parameters other than **self** and returns **None**.

- A class attribute represents "class-wide" information (i.e., a property of the class, not of a specific object of the class).

- Although class attributes may seem like global variables, each class attribute resides in the namespace of the class in which it is created. Class attributes should be initialized once (and only once) in the class definition.

- A class's class attributes can be accessed through any object of that class. A class's class attributes also exist even when no object of that class exists. To access a class attribute when no object of the class exists, prefix the class name, followed by a period, to the name of the attribute.

- Sometimes, a programmer needs objects whose attributes are themselves references to objects of other classes. Such a capability is called composition.

- Stacks are known as last-in, first-out (LIFO) data structures—the last item pushed (inserted) on the stack is the first item popped (removed) from the stack.

- Types like integer, floating-points, strings and others are all examples of abstract data types. These types are representations of real-world notions to some satisfactory level of precision within a computer system.

- An ADT actually captures two notions: A data representation and the operations that can be performed on that data. Python programmers use classes to implement abstract data types.

- A queue, is a "waiting line." A queue offers well-understood behavior to its clients: Clients place items in a queue one at a time via an enqueue operation, then get those items back one at a time via a dequeue operation.

- A queue returns items in first-in, first-out (FIFO) order, which means that the first item inserted in a queue is the first item removed.

- Python programmers concentrate both on crafting new classes and on reusing classes from the standard library. This kind of software reusability speeds the development of powerful, high-quality software.

- The standard library enables Python developers to build applications faster by reusing preexisting, extensively tested classes. In addition to reducing development time, standard library classes also improve programmers' abilities to debug and maintain applications.

TERMINOLOGY

abstract data type (ADT)
access method
attribute
__bases__ attribute of a class
behavior
built-in data type
__class__ attribute of an object
class body
class instance object
class keyword
class library
class scope
composition
consistent state
constructor
container class
data abstraction
data member
data type
data validation
del keyword
__del__ method
dequeue
destructor
__dict__ attribute of a class
__dict__ attribute of an object
__doc__ attribute of a class
double underscore (__)
encapsulation
enqueue
extensible language
first in, first out (FIFO)

get access method
inconsistent state
information hiding
__init__ method
instantiate
interface
last in, first out (LIFO)
member function
method
module
__module__ attribute of a class
__name__ attribute of a class
name mangling
object
object-oriented programming (OOP)
popping off a stack
predicate method
private
public
pushing onto a stack
queue
rapid application development (RAD)
reference
self
set access method
single underscore (_)
software reuse
stack
structured programming
termination housekeeping
user-defined type
utility method

SELF-REVIEW EXERCISES

7.1   Fill in the blanks in each of the following statements:
   a) Object-oriented programming _____ data and functions into _____.
   b) Method _____ is called the constructor.
   c) Classes enable programmers to model objects that have _____ (represented as data members) and behaviors (represented as _____).
   d) A class's methods are often referred to as _____ in other object-oriented programming languages.
   e) A _____ method tests the truth or falsity of a condition.
   f) A _____ is a variable shared by all objects of a class.
   g) _____ are known as last-in, first-out data structures.
   h) A user of an object is referred to as a _____.
   i) Python performs name mangling on attributes that begin with _____ underscore(s).
   j) Describing the functionality of a class independent of its implementation is called _____.

7.2   State whether each of the following is *true* or *false*. If *false*, explain why.
   a)   Object-oriented programming languages do not use functions to perform actions.
   b)   The parameter **self** must be the first item in a method's argument list.
   c)   The class constructor returns an object of the class.
   d)   Programmer-defined and built-in modules are imported in the same way.
   e)   Constructors may specify keyword arguments and default arguments.
   f)   An attribute that begins with a single underscore is a private attribute.
   g)   The destructor is called when the keyword **del** is used on an object.
   h)   A shared class attribute should be initialized in the constructor.
   i)   When invoking an object's method, a program does not need to pass a value that corresponds to the object reference parameter.
   j)   Every class should have a ___**del**___ method to reclaim an object's memory.

ANSWERS TO SELF-REVIEW EXERCISES

7.1   a) encapsulates, classes. b) ___**init**___. c) attributes, methods. d) member functions.
e) predicate. f) class attribute. g) Stacks. h) client. i) two. j) data abstraction.

7.2   a) False. Object-oriented programmers use methods, or functions, as components of classes.
b) False. The first parameter in a method's argument must be an object of the class, which is called
self by convention. c) False. The class constructor initializes an object of the class and implicitly
returns **None**. d) True. e) True. f) False. An attribute that begins with a single underscore conveys the
convention that a client of a class should not access the attribute directly. g) False. A destructor executes when the last reference to an object is destroyed. h) False. A shared class attribute should be
initialized exactly once, at class scope, outside the class's methods. i) True. j) False. The programmer
is not required to write a ___**del**___ method for a class.

EXERCISES

7.3   Create a class called **Complex** for performing arithmetic with complex numbers. Write a
driver program to test your class.
      Complex numbers have the form

            realPart + imaginaryPart * i

where *i* is

$$\sqrt{-1}$$

Use floating-point numbers to represent the data of the class. Provide a constructor that enables an
object of this class to be initialized when it is created. The constructor should contain default values
in case no initializers are provided. Provide methods for each of the following:
   a)   Adding two **ComplexNumber**s: The real parts are added to form the real part of the result, and the imaginary parts are added to form the imaginary part of the result.
   b)   Subtracting two **ComplexNumber**s: The real part of the right operand is subtracted from the real part of the left operand to form the real part of the result, and the imaginary part of the right operand is subtracted from the imaginary part of the left operand to form the imaginary part of the result.
   c)   Printing **ComplexNumber**s in the form **(a, b)**, where **a** is the real part and **b** is the imaginary part.

7.4   Create a class called **RationalNumber** for performing arithmetic with fractions. Write a
driver program to test your class.

Use integer variables to represent the data of the class—the numerator and the denominator. Provide a constructor that enables an object of this class to be initialized when it is declared. The constructor should contain default values, in case no initializers are provided, and should store the fraction in reduced form (i.e., the fraction

$$\frac{2}{4}$$

would be stored in the object as 1 in the numerator and 2 in the denominator). Provide methods for each of the following:

    a) Adding two **RationalNumber**s. The result should be stored in reduced form.
    b) Subtracting two **RationalNumber**s. The result should be stored in reduced form.
    c) Multiplying two **RationalNumber**s. The result should be stored in reduced form.
    d) Dividing two **RationalNumber**s. The result should be stored in reduced form.
    e) Printing **RationalNumber**s in the form **a/b**, where **a** is the numerator and **b** is the denominator.
    f) Printing **RationalNumber**s in floating-point format.

7.5   Modify the **Time** class of Fig. 7.13 to include a **tick** method that increments the time stored in a **Time** object by one second. The **Time** object should always remain in a consistent state. Write a driver program that tests the **tick** method. Be sure to test the following cases:

    a) Incrementing into the next minute.
    b) Incrementing into the next hour.
    c) Incrementing into the next day (i.e., 23:59:59 to 0:00:00).

7.6   Create a class **Rectangle**. The class has attributes __length and __width, each of which defaults to 1. It has methods that calculate the **perimeter** and the **area** of the rectangle. It has *set* and *get* methods for both __length and __width. The *set* methods should verify that __length and __width are each floating-point numbers larger than 0.0 and less than 20.0. Write a driver program to test the class.

7.7   Create a more sophisticated **Rectangle** class than the one you created in Exercise 7.6. This class stores only the *x-y* coordinates of the upper left-hand and lower right-hand corners of the rectangle. The constructor calls a *set* function that accepts two tuples of coordinates and verifies that each of these is in the first quadrant, with no single *x* or *y* coordinate larger than 20.0. Methods calculate the **length**, **width**, **perimeter** and **area**. The length is the larger of the two dimensions. Include a predicate method **isSquare** that determines whether the rectangle is a square. Write a driver program to test the class.

7.8   Create a class **TicTacToe** that will enable you to write a complete program to play the game of tic-tac-toe. The class contains a 3-by-3 double-subscripted list of letters. The constructor should initialize the empty board to all zeros. Allow two human players. Wherever the first player moves, place an **"X"** in the specified square; place an **"O"** wherever the second player moves. Each move must be to an empty square. After each move, determine whether the game has been won and whether the game is a draw. [*Note:* If you feel ambitious, modify your program so that the computer makes the moves for one of the players automatically. Also, allow the player to choose whether to go first or second.]

Customizing Classes

Objectives

- To understand how to write special methods that customize a class.
- To be able to represent an object as a string.
- To use special methods to customize attribute access.
- To understand how to redefine (overload) operators to work with new classes.
- To learn when to, and when not to, overload operators.
- To learn how to overload sequence operations.
- To learn how to overload mapping operations.
- To study interesting, customized classes.

The whole difference between construction and creation is exactly this: that a thing constructed can only be loved after it is constructed; but a thing created is loved before it exists.
Gilbert Keith Chesterton

The die is cast.
Julius Caesar

Our doctor would never really operate unless it was necessary. He was just that way. If he didn't need the money, he wouldn't lay a hand on you.
Herb Shriner

8.1 Introduction

In Chapter 7, we introduced the basics of Python classes and the notion of abstract data types (ADTs). We discussed how methods **___init___** and **___del___** execute when an object is created and destroyed, respectively. These methods are two examples of the many *special methods* that a class may define. A special method is a method that has a special meaning in Python; the Python interpreter calls one of an object's special methods when the client performs a certain operation on the object. For example, when a client creates an object of a class, Python invokes the **___init___** special method of that class.

A class author implements special methods to *customize* the behavior of the class. The purpose of customization is to provide the clients of a class with a simple notation for manipulating objects of the class. For example, in Chapter 7, manipulations on objects were accomplished by sending messages (in the form of method calls) to the objects. This method-call notation is cumbersome for certain kinds of classes, especially mathematical classes. For such classes, it would be nice to use Python's rich set of built-in operators and statements to manipulate objects. In this chapter, we show how to define special methods that enable Python's operators to work with objects—a process called *operator overloading*. It is straightforward and natural to extend Python with these new capabilities. Operator overloading also requires great care, because, when overloading is misused, it can make a program difficult to understand.

Operator **+** has multiple purposes in Python, for example, integer addition and string concatenation. This is an example of operator overloading. The Python language itself overloads operators **+** and *****, among others. These operators perform differently to suit the context in integer arithmetic, floating-point arithmetic, string manipulation and other operations.

Python enables the programmer to overload most operators to be sensitive to the context in which they are used. The interpreter takes the appropriate action based on the manner in which the operator is used. Some operators are overloaded frequently, especially operators like **+** and **-**. The job performed by overloaded operators also can be performed by explicit method calls, but operator notation is often clearer.

In this chapter, we discuss when to use operator overloading and when not to use it. We show how to overload operators, and we present complete programs using overloaded operators.

Customization provides other benefits, as well. A class may define special methods that cause an object of the class to behave like a list or like a dictionary. A class also may define special methods to control how a client accesses object attributes through the dot access operator. In this chapter, we introduce the appropriate special methods and create classes that implement them.

8.2 Customizing String Representation: Method __str__

Python is able to output the built-in data types with the **print** statement. What if a programmer wants to define a class whose objects also can be output with the **print** statement? A Python class can define special method **__str__**, to provide an informal (i.e., human-readable) string representation of an object of the class. If a client program of the class contains the statement

```
print objectOfClass
```

Python calls the object's **__str__** method and outputs the string returned by that method. Figure 8.1 demonstrates how to define special method **__str__** to handle data of a user-defined telephone number class called **PhoneNumber**. This program assumes telephone numbers are input correctly.

```
1  # Fig. 8.1: PhoneNumber.py
2  # Representation of phone number in USA format: (xxx) xxx-xxxx.
3
4  class PhoneNumber:
5     """Simple class to represent phone number in USA format"""
6
7     def __init__( self, number ):
8        """Accepts string in form (xxx) xxx-xxxx"""
9
10       self.areaCode = number[ 1:4 ]   # 3-digit area code
11       self.exchange = number[ 6:9 ]   # 3-digit exchange
12       self.line = number[ 10:14 ]   # 4-digit line
13
14    def __str__( self ):
15       """Informal string representation"""
16
17       return "(%s) %s-%s" % \
18          ( self.areaCode, self.exchange, self.line )
19
```

Fig. 8.1   String representation—special method **__str__**. (Part 1 of 2.)

```
20   def test():
21
22      # obtain phone number from user
23      newNumber = raw_input(
24         "Enter phone number in the form (123) 456-7890:\n" )
25
26      phone = PhoneNumber( newNumber )   # create PhoneNumber object
27      print "The phone number is:",
28      print phone   # invokes phone.__str__()
29
30   if __name__ == "__main__":
31      test()
```

```
Enter phone number in the form (123) 456-7890:
(800) 555-1234
The phone number is: (800) 555-1234
```

Fig. 8.1   String representation—special method **__str__**. (Part 2 of 2.)

Method **__init__** (lines 7–12) accepts a string in the form **"(xxx) xxx-xxxx"**, where each **x** in the string is a digit in the phone number. The method slices the string and stores the pieces of the phone number as attributes.

Method **__str__** (lines 14–18) is a special method that constructs and returns a string representation of an object of class **PhoneNumber**. When the interpreter encounters the statement

```
print phone
```

in line 28, the interpreter executes the statement

```
print phone.__str__()
```

When a program passes a **PhoneNumber** object to built-in function **str** or when a program uses a **PhoneNumber** object with the **%** string-formatting operator (e.g., **"%s" % phone**), Python also calls method **__str__**.

Common Programming Error 8.1

*Returning a non-string value from method **__str__** is a fatal, runtime error.*

Function **test**, (lines 20–28) requests a phone number from the user, creates a new **PhoneNumber** object, and prints the string representation of the object. Recall that when a module runs as a stand-alone program (i.e., the user invokes the Python interpreter on the module), Python assigns the value **"__main__"** to the namespace's name (stored in built-in variable **__name__**). Line 31 calls function **test**, if **PhoneNumber.py** is executed as a stand-alone program. This practice of defining a driver function and testing a module's namespace to execute the function is employed by many Python modules. The benefit of this practice is that a module author can define different behaviors for the module, based on the context in which the module is used. If another program imports the module, the value of **__name__** will be the module name (e.g., **"PhoneNumber"**), and the test function does not execute. If the module is executed as a stand-alone program, the value of **__name__** is **"__main__"**, and the test function executes. In Chapters 10 and 11, we create graphical programs that use test functions to display the graphical components we define.

 Good Programming Practice 8.1

Provide test functions for modules you create, when necessary. These functions help ensure that the module works correctly, and they provide additional information to clients of the class by demonstrating the ways in which a module's operations may be performed.

8.3 Customizing Attribute Access

In the previous chapter, we discussed two techniques for a client to access an object's attributes. The client can access the attributes directly (through the dot access operator), or the class author can give the attributes special names to signify that a client should access the attributes through access methods. In this section, we discuss another technique—defining special methods that customize the behavior of direct attribute access.

Python provides three special methods (Fig. 8.2) that a class can define to control how the dot access operator behaves on objects of the class. This technique of redefining an operator's behavior is called "operator overloading," a topic we discuss in detail in the next several sections. Overloading the dot access operator combines the two attribute access techniques we discussed in the previous chapter—a client may access the attributes directly (i.e., through the dot access operator), but doing so actually executes code that performs the operations of access methods.

Figure 8.3 contains a modified definition of class **Time**, the class we used to explore attribute access in the previous chapter. The new definition uses special methods **__getattr__** and **__setattr__** to control how a client accesses and modifies an object's attributes.

Lines 7–13 contain a default constructor for class **Time**. The constructor simply assigns the argument values to the new object's attributes. If a class defines special method **__setattr__**, Python calls this method every time a program makes an assignment to an object's attribute through the dot operator. Therefore, the statement in line 11 actually results in the call

```
self.__setattr__( "hour", hour )
```

Method	Description
__delattr__	Executes when a client deletes an attribute (e.g., **del anObject.attribute**)
__getattr__	Executes when a client accesses an attribute name that cannot be located in the object's **__dict__** attribute (e.g., **anObject.unfoundName**)
__setattr__	Executes when a client assigns a value to an object's attribute (e.g., **anObject.attribute = value**)

Fig. 8.2   Attribute access customization methods.

```
1   # Fig: 8.3: TimeAccess.py
2   # Class Time with customized attribute access.
3
4   class Time:
5      """Class Time with customized attribute access"""
6
7      def __init__( self, hour = 0, minute = 0, second = 0 ):
8         """Time constructor initializes each data member to zero"""
9
10        # each statement invokes __setattr__
11        self.hour = hour
12        self.minute = minute
13        self.second = second
14
15     def __setattr__( self, name, value ):
16        """Assigns a value to an attribute"""
17
18        if name == "hour":
19
20           if 0 <= value < 24:
21              self.__dict__[ "_hour" ] = value
22           else:
23              raise ValueError, "Invalid hour value: %d" % value
24
25        elif name == "minute" or name == "second":
26
27           if 0 <= value < 60:
28              self.__dict__[ "_" + name ] = value
29           else:
30              raise ValueError, "Invalid %s value: %d" % \
31                 ( name, value )
32
33        else:
34           self.__dict__[ name ] = value
35
36     def __getattr__( self, name ):
37        """Performs lookup for unrecognized attribute name"""
38
39        if name == "hour":
40           return self._hour
41        elif name == "minute":
42           return self._minute
43        elif name == "second":
44           return self._second
45        else:
46           raise AttributeError, name
47
48     def __str__( self ):
49        """Returns Time object string in military format"""
50
51        # attribute access does not call __getattr__
52        return "%.2d:%.2d:%.2d" % \
53           ( self._hour, self._minute, self._second )
```

Fig. 8.3   Customized attribute access—class **Time**. (Part 1 of 2.)

```
Python 2.2b2 (#26, Nov 16 2001, 11:44:11) [MSC 32 bit (Intel)] on win32
Type "help", "copyright", "credits" or "license" for more information.
>>>
>>> from TimeAccess import Time
>>> time1 = Time( 4, 27, 19 )
>>> print time1
04:27:19
>>> print time1.hour, time1.minute, time1.second
4 27 19
>>> time1.hour = 16
>>> print time1
16:27:19
>>> time1.second = 90
Traceback (most recent call last):
  File "<stdin>", line 1, in ?
  File "TimeAccess.py", line 30, in __setattr__
    raise ValueError, "Invalid %s value: %d" % \
ValueError: Invalid second value: 90
```

Fig. 8.3   Customized attribute access—class **Time**. (Part 2 of 2.)

Method **__setattr__** (lines 15–34) contains the error-checking code needed to maintain the object's data in a consistent state. The method accepts three arguments—the object reference (**self**), the name of the attribute to set and the value to be assigned to the attribute. Line 18 tests whether the attribute to be set is named **"hour"**. If so, lines 20–23 determine whether the specified value falls within the appropriate range. If the value is in the appropriate range, line 21 assigns the value to attribute **_hour** by accessing the appropriate key-value pair in the object's **__dict__** attribute; otherwise, lines 22–23 raise an exception to indicate an invalid value.

It is important that method **__setattr__** uses an object's **__dict__** attribute to set an object's attributes. If line 21 contained the statement

```
self._hour = value
```

method **__setattr__** would execute again, with the arguments **"_hour"** and **value**, resulting in infinite recursion. Assigning a value through the object's **__dict__** attribute, however, does not invoke method **__setattr__**, but simply inserts the appropriate key–value pair in the object's **__dict__**.

Common Programming Error 8.2

*In method **__setattr__**, assigning a value to an object's attribute through the dot access operator results in infinite recursion. Use the object's **__dict__** instead.*

Lines 25–31 of method **__setattr__** perform similar tests for when the client attempts to assign a value to attributes **minute** or **second**. If the specified value falls within the appropriate range, the method assigns the value to the object's attribute (either **_minute** or **_second**). If the client attempts to assign a value to an attribute other than **hour**, **minute** or **second**, line 33 assigns the value to the specified attribute name, to preserve Python's default behavior for adding attributes to an object.

Common Programming Error 8.3

Assigning a value to an object's attribute, but mistakenly typing the wrong name for that attribute is a logic error. Python adds a new attribute to the object's namespace with the incorrect name.

Lines 36–46 contain the definition for method **__getattr__**. When a client program contains the expression

    time1.*attribute*

as an *rvalue* (i.e., the right-hand value in an operator expression), Python first looks in **time1**'s **__dict__** attribute for the attribute name. If the attribute name is in **__dict__**, Python simply returns the attribute's value. If the attribute name is not in the object's **__dict__**, Python generates the call

    time1.__getattr__(*attribute*)

where **_attribute_** is the name of the attribute that the client is attempting to access. The method tests for whether the client is attempting to access **hour**, **minute** or **second** and, if so, returns the value of the appropriate attribute. Otherwise the method raises an exception (line 46).

Software Engineering Observation 8.1

*The **__getattr__** definition for every class should raise the **AttributeError** exception if the attribute name cannot be found, to preserve Python's default behavior for locating nonexistent attributes.*

The interactive session that follows the class definition in Fig. 8.3 demonstrates the benefit of defining special methods **__getattr__** and **__setattr__**. The client program can access the attributes of an object of class **Time** in a transparent manner, through the dot access operator. The interface to class **Time** appears identical to the interface we presented in the first definition of the class in Chapter 7, but it has the advantage of maintaining data in a consistent state. In Chapter 9, Inheritance, we discuss a similar technique—called *properties*—that enables class authors to specify a method that executes when a client attempts to access or modify a particular attribute.

Software Engineering Observation 8.2

*Designers of large systems that require strict access to data should use **__getattr__** and **__setattr__** to ensure data integrity. Developers of large systems that use Python 2.2 can use properties, a more efficient technique to take advantage of the syntax allowed by **__getattr__** and **__setattr__**.*

8.4 Operator Overloading

Operators provide programmers with a concise notation for expressing manipulations of objects of built-in types. Programmers can also use operators with objects of a class. Although Python does not allow new operators to be created, it does allow most existing operators to be overloaded such that, when these operators are used with objects of a programmer-defined type, the operators have meaning appropriate to the new types.

Software Engineering Observation 8.3

Operator overloading contributes to Python's extensibility, one of the language's most appealing qualities.

Good Programming Practice 8.2

Use operator overloading when it makes a program clearer than accomplishing the same operations with explicit method calls.

Good Programming Practice 8.3

Avoid excessive or inconsistent use of operator overloading; overloaded operators can make a program cryptic and difficult to read.

Although operator overloading may sound like an exotic capability, most programmers implicitly use overloaded operators regularly. For example, the addition operator (+) operates quite differently on integers, floating-point numbers and strings. But addition nevertheless works fine with variables of these types and other built-in types, because the addition operator (+) has been overloaded in the Python language itself.

Operators are overloaded by writing a method definition as you normally would, except that the method name corresponds to the Python special method for that operator. For example, the method name **__add__** overloads the addition operator (+). To use an operator on an object of a class, the class *must* overload (i.e., define a special method for) that operator.

Overloading is most appropriate for mathematical classes. These often require that a substantial set of operators be overloaded to ensure consistency with the way these mathematical classes are handled in the real world. For example, it would be unusual to overload, for rational numbers, only addition, because other arithmetic operators also are used commonly with rational numbers.

Python is an operator-rich language. Python programmers who understand the meaning and context of each operator are likely to make reasonable choices when it comes to overloading operators for new classes.

Operator overloading provides the same concise expressions for user-defined classes that Python provides with its rich collection of operators for built-in types. However, operator overloading is not automatic; the programmer must write operator overloading methods to perform the desired operations.

Extreme misuses of overloading are possible, such as overloading operator + to perform subtraction-like operations or overloading operator – to perform multiplication-like operations. Such non-intuitive uses of overloading make a program extremely difficult to comprehend and should be avoided.

Good Programming Practice 8.4

Overload operators to perform the same function or similar functions on objects as the operators perform on objects of built-in types. Avoid nonintuitive uses of operators.

8.5 Restrictions on Operator Overloading

Most Python operators and augmented assignment symbols can be overloaded.[1] These are shown in Fig. 8.4.

---

1. Two operators cannot be overloaded: **{}** and **lambda**. [*Note:* **lambda** is a keyword that supports functional programming—a technique that is beyond the scope of this book.]

Common operators and augmented assignment statements that can be overloaded							
+	-	*	**	/	//	%	<<
>>	&	|	^	~	<	>	<=
>=	==	!=	+=	-=	*=	**=	/=
//=	%=	<<=	>>=	&=	^=	|=	[]
()	.	` `	in				

Fig. 8.4   Operators and augmented assignment statements that can be overloaded.

The precedence of an operator cannot be changed by overloading. However, parentheses can be used to force the order of evaluation of overloaded operators in an expression. The associativity of an operator cannot be changed by overloading.

It is not possible to change the "arity" of an operator (i.e., the number of operands an operator takes)—overloaded unary operators remain unary operators, and overloaded binary operators remain binary operators. Operators + and – each have both unary and binary versions; these unary and binary versions can be overloaded separately, using different method names. It is not possible to create new operators; only existing operators can be overloaded.

Common Programming Error 8.4

Attempting to change the "arity" of an operator via operator overloading causes a fatal runtime error when the overloaded operator's method executes.

The meaning of how an operator works on objects of built-in types cannot be changed by operator overloading. The programmer cannot, for example, change the meaning of how + adds two integers. Operator overloading works only with objects of user-defined classes or with a mixture of an object of a user-defined class and an object of a built-in type.

Overloading a binary mathematical operator (e.g., +, –, *) automatically overloads the operator's corresponding augmented assignment statement. For example, overloading an addition operator to allow statements like

```
object2 = object2 + object1
```

implies that the += augmented assignment statement also is overloaded to allow statements such as

```
object2 += object1
```

Although (in this case) the programmer does not have to define a method to overload the += assignment statement, such behavior also can be achieved by defining the method explicitly for that class.

Performance Tip 8.1

Sometimes it is preferable to overload an augmented assignment version of an operator to perform the operation "in place" (i.e., without using extra memory by creating a new object).

8.6 Overloading Unary Operators

A unary operator for a class is overloaded as a method that takes only the object reference argument (**self**). When overloading a unary operator (such as ~) as a method, if **object1** is an object of class **Class**, when the interpreter encounters the expression

    ~object1

the interpreter generates the call

    object1.__invert__()

The operand **object1** is the object for which the **Class** method __invert__ is invoked. Figure 8.5 lists the unary operators and their corresponding special methods.

8.7 Overloading Binary Operators

A binary operator or statement for a class is overloaded as a method with two arguments: **self** and **other**. Later in this chapter, we will overload the + operator to indicate addition of two objects of class **Rational**. When overloading binary operator +, if **y** and **z** are objects of class **Rational**, then **y + z** is treated as if **y.__add__(z)** had been written, invoking the __add__ method. If **y** is not an object of class **Rational**, but **z** is an object of class **Rational**, then **y + z** is treated as if **z.__radd__(y)** had been written. The method is named __radd__, because the object for which the method executes appears to the right of the operator. Usually, overloaded binary operator methods create and return new objects of their corresponding class.

When overloading assignment statement += as a **Rational** method that accepts two arguments, if **y** and **z** are objects of class **Rational**, then **y += z** is treated as if **y.__iadd__(z)** had been written, invoking the __iadd__ method. The method is named __iadd__, because the method performs its operations "in-place" (i.e., the method uses no extra memory to perform its behavior). Usually, this means that the method performs any necessary calculations on the object reference argument (**self**), then returns the updated reference. Figure 8.6 lists the binary operators and assignment statements and their corresponding special methods.

What happens if we evaluate the expression **y + z** or the statement **y += z**, and only **y** is an object of class **Rational**? In both cases, **z** must be *coerced* (i.e., converted) to an object of class **Rational**, before the appropriate operator overloading method executes. We cover coercion and the special methods that provide coercion behavior in Section 8.9.

Unary operator	Special method
-	__neg__
+	__pos__
~	__invert__

Fig. 8.5   Unary operators and their corresponding special methods.

Binary operator/ statement	Special method
+	__add__, __radd__
-	__sub__, __rsub__
*	__mul__, __rmul__
/	__div__, __rdiv__, __truediv__ (for Python 2.2), __rtruediv__ (for Python 2.2)
//	__floordiv__, __rfloordiv__ (for Python version 2.2)
%	__mod__, __rmod__
**	__pow__, __rpow__
<<	__lshift__, __rlshift__
>>	__rshift__, __rrshift__
&	__and__, __rand__
^	__xor__, __rxor__
|	__or__, __ror__
+=	__iadd__
-=	__isub__
*=	__imul__
/=	__idiv__, __itruediv__ (for Python version 2.2)
//=	__ifloordiv__ (for Python version 2.2)
%=	__imod__
**=	__ipow__
<<=	__ilshift__
>>=	__irshift__
&=	__iand__
^=	__ixor__
|=	__ior__
==	__eq__
!+, <>	__ne__
>	__gt__
<	__lt__
>=	__ge__
<=	__le__

Fig. 8.6   Binary operators and their corresponding special methods.

8.8 Overloading Built-in Functions

A class also may define special methods that execute when certain built-in functions are called on an object of the class. For example, we may define special method __*abs*__ for class **Rational**, to execute when a program calls **abs(rationalObject)** to compute the absolute value of an object of that class. The table in Fig. 8.7 contains a list of common built-in functions and the corresponding special methods that the class may define.

8.9 Converting Between Types

Most programs process information of a variety of types. Sometimes all the operations "stay within a type." For example, adding (concatenating) a string to a string produces a string. But, it is often necessary to convert or *coerce* data of one type to data of another type. This can happen in assignments and in calculations. The interpreter knows how to perform certain conversions among built-in types. Programmers can force conversions among built-in types by calling the appropriate Python function, such as **int** or **float**.

But what about user-defined classes? The interpreter cannot know how to convert among user-defined classes and built-in types. The programmer must specify how such conversions are to occur with special methods that override the appropriate Python functions. For example, a class can define special method **___int___** that overloads the behavior of the call **int(anObject)** to return an integer representation of the object. The table in Fig. 8.8 lists the special methods that a class may define to implement type coercion. Each special method has a corresponding built-in function.

Built-in Function	Description	Special method
abs(x)	Returns the absolute value of *x*.	**___abs___**
divmod(x, y)	Returns a tuple that contains the integer and remainder components of *x* **%** *y*.	**___divmod___**
len(x)	Returns the length of *x* (*x* should be a sequence).	**___len___**
pow(x, y[, z])	Returns the result of x^y. With three arguments, returns (x^y) **%** *z*.	**___pow___**
repr(x)	Returns a formal string representation of x (i.e., a string from which object *x* can be replicated).	**___repr___**

Fig. 8.7   Common built-in functions and their corresponding special methods.

Method	Description
___coerce___	Converts two values to the same type.
___complex___	Converts object to complex number type.
___float___	Converts object to floating-point number type.
___hex___	Converts object to hexidecimal string type.

Fig. 8.8   Coercion methods. (Part 1 of 2.)

Method	Description
__int__	Converts object to integer number type.
__long__	Converts object to long integer number type.
__oct__	Converts object to octal string type.
__str__	Converts object to string type. Also used to obtain informal string representation of object (i.e., a string that simply describes object).

Fig. 8.8   Coercion methods. (Part 2 of 2.)

8.10 Case Study: A **Rational** Class

Figure 8.9 illustrates a **Rational** class. The class uses overloaded numerical operators, built-in functions and statements to manipulate rational numbers. A rational number is a fraction represented as a numerator (top) and a denominator (bottom). A rational number can be positive, negative or zero. Class **Rational**'s interface includes a default constructor, string representation method, overloaded **abs** function, equality operators and several mathematical operators. The class also defines one method **simplify** that reduces the rational number. Reducing a rational number is the process of dividing the numerator and denominator by their greatest common divisor, to express the rational number in "simplest terms." The file defines a **gcd** function, used by class **Rational** to compute the greatest common divisor of two values.

In the class definition (Fig. 8.9), lines 4–12 define function **gcd**, which computes the greatest common divisor of two values. Class **Rational** uses this function to simplify the rational number.

The **Rational** constructor (lines 17–30) takes two arguments—**top** and **bottom**—that default to 1. If the client attempts to create an object of class **Rational** with denominator 0, the constructor raises an exception (**ZeroDivisionError**) to indicate an error (lines 21–22). **ZeroDivisionError** is the name of an exception object that Python places in the built-in namespace when the interpreter begins. We discuss this exception and others (e.g., **IndexErrror**, **KeyError**, etc.) in Chapter 12, Exception Handling. Lines 25–26 assign the object's numerator and denominator as the absolute value of the arguments passed to the constructor. Lines 27–28 compute and assign the object's sign to attribute **sign**. Line 30 calls method **simplify**, to reduce the rational number to its simplest form.

```
1   # Fig. 8.9: RationalNumber.py
2   # Definition of class Rational.
3
4   def gcd( x, y ):
5       """Computes greatest common divisor of two values"""
6
7       while y:
8           z = x
9           x = y
10          y = z % y
```

Fig. 8.9   Operator overloading—**Rational.py**. (Part 1 of 4.)

```
11
12      return x
13
14   class Rational:
15      """Representation of rational number"""
16
17      def __init__( self, top = 1, bottom = 1 ):
18         """Initializes Rational instance"""
19
20         # do not allow 0 denominator
21         if bottom == 0:
22            raise ZeroDivisionError, "Cannot have 0 denominator"
23
24         # assign attribute values
25         self.numerator = abs( top )
26         self.denominator = abs( bottom )
27         self.sign = ( top * bottom ) / ( self.numerator *
28            self.denominator )
29
30         self.simplify()   # Rational represented in reduced form
31
32      # class interface method
33      def simplify( self ):
34         """Simplifies a Rational number"""
35
36         common = gcd( self.numerator, self.denominator )
37         self.numerator /= common
38         self.denominator /= common
39
40      # overloaded unary operator
41      def __neg__( self ):
42         """Overloaded negation operator"""
43
44         return Rational( -self.sign * self.numerator,
45                          self.denominator )
46
47      # overloaded binary arithmetic operators
48      def __add__( self, other ):
49         """Overloaded addition operator"""
50
51         return Rational(
52            self.sign * self.numerator * other.denominator +
53            other.sign * other.numerator * self.denominator,
54            self.denominator * other.denominator )
55
56      def __sub__( self, other ):
57         """Overloaded subtraction operator"""
58
59         return self + ( -other )
60
61      def __mul__( self, other ):
62         """Overloaded multiplication operator"""
63
```

Fig. 8.9   Operator overloading—**Rational.py**. (Part 2 of 4.)

```
64          return Rational( self.numerator * other.numerator,
65                          self.sign * self.denominator *
66                          other.sign * other.denominator )
67
68      def __div__( self, other ):
69          """Overloaded / division operator."""
70
71          return Rational( self.numerator * other.denominator,
72                          self.sign * self.denominator *
73                          other.sign * other.numerator )
74
75      def __truediv__( self, other ):
76          """Overloaded / division operator. (For use with Python
77          versions (>= 2.2) that contain the // operator)"""
78
79          return self.__div__( other )
80
81      # overloaded binary comparison operators
82      def __eq__( self, other ):
83          """Overloaded equality operator"""
84
85          return ( self - other ).numerator == 0
86
87      def __lt__( self, other ):
88          """Overloaded less-than operator"""
89
90          return ( self - other ).sign < 0
91
92      def __gt__( self, other ):
93          """Overloaded greater-than operator"""
94
95          return ( self - other ).sign > 0
96
97      def __le__( self, other ):
98          """Overloaded less-than or equal-to operator"""
99
100         return ( self < other ) or ( self == other )
101
102     def __ge__( self, other ):
103         """Overloaded greater-than or equal-to operator"""
104
105         return ( self > other ) or ( self == other )
106
107     def __ne__( self, other ):
108         """Overloaded inequality operator"""
109
110         return not ( self == other )
111
112     # overloaded built-in functions
113     def __abs__( self ):
114         """Overloaded built-in function abs"""
115
116         return Rational( self.numerator, self.denominator )
```

Fig. 8.9   Operator overloading—**Rational.py**. (Part 3 of 4.)

```
117
118    def __str__( self ):
119       """String representation"""
120
121       # determine sign display
122       if self.sign == -1:
123          signString = "-"
124       else:
125          signString = ""
126
127       if self.numerator == 0:
128          return "0"
129       elif self.denominator == 1:
130          return "%s%d" % ( signString, self.numerator )
131       else:
132          return "%s%d/%d" % \
133             ( signString, self.numerator, self.denominator )
134
135    # overloaded coercion capability
136    def __int__( self ):
137       """Overloaded integer representation"""
138
139       return self.sign * divmod( self.numerator,
140          self.denominator )[ 0 ]
141
142    def __float__( self ):
143       """Overloaded floating-point representation"""
144
145       return self.sign * float( self.numerator ) / self.denominator
146
147    def __coerce__( self, other ):
148       """Overloaded coercion. Can only coerce int to Rational"""
149
150       if type( other ) == type( 1 ):
151          return ( self, Rational( other ) )
152       else:
153          return None
```

Fig. 8.9   Operator overloading—**Rational.py**. (Part 4 of 4.)

```
1    # Fig. 8.10: fig08_10.py
2    # Driver for class Rational.
3
4    from RationalNumber import Rational
5
6    # create objects of class Rational
7    rational1 = Rational()   # 1/1
8    rational2 = Rational( 10, 30 )   # 10/30 (reduces to 1/3)
9    rational3 = Rational( -7, 14 )   # -7/14 (reduces to -1/2)
10
11   # print objects of class Rational
12   print "rational1:", rational1
```

Fig. 8.10   Operator overloading—**fig08_10.py**. (Part 1 of 2.)

```
13    print "rational2:", rational2
14    print "rational3:", rational3
15    print
16
17    # test mathematical operators
18    print rational1, "/", rational2, "=", rational1 / rational2
19    print rational3, "-", rational2, "=", rational3 - rational2
20    print rational2, "*", rational3, "-", rational1, "=", \
21       rational2 * rational3 - rational1
22
23    # overloading + implicitly overloads +=
24    rational1 += rational2 * rational3
25    print "\nrational1 after adding rational2 * rational3:", rational1
26    print
27
28    # test comparison operators
29    print rational1, "<=", rational2, ":", rational1 <= rational2
30    print rational1, ">", rational3, ":", rational1 > rational3
31    print
32
33    # test built-in function abs
34    print "The absolute value of", rational3, "is:", abs( rational3 )
35    print
36
37    # test coercion
38    print rational2, "as an integer is:", int( rational2 )
39    print rational2, "as a float is:", float( rational2 )
40    print rational2, "+ 1 =", rational2 + 1
```

```
rational1: 1
rational2: 1/3
rational3: -1/2

1 / 1/3 = 3
-1/2 - 1/3 = -5/6
1/3 * -1/2 - 1 = -7/6

rational1 after adding rational2 * rational3: 5/6

5/6 <= 1/3 : 0
5/6 > -1/2 : 1

The absolute value of -1/2 is: 1/2

1/3 as an integer is: 0
1/3 as a float is: 0.333333333333
1/3 + 1 = 4/3
```

Fig. 8.10   Operator overloading—`fig08_10.py`. (Part 2 of 2.)

Method **simplify** (lines 33–38) reduces an object of class **Rational**. The method first calls function **gcd** to determine the greatest common divisor of the object's numerator and denominator (line 36). The method then uses the greatest common divisor to simplify the rational object (lines 37–38).

Method **__neg__** (lines 41–45) overloads the unary negation operator. If **rational** is an object of class **Rational**, when the interpreter encounters the expression

```
-rational
```

the interpreter generates method call

```
rational.__neg__()
```

which simply creates a new object of class **Rational** with the negated sign of the original object.

Method **__add__** (lines 48–54) overloads the addition operator. This method takes two arguments—the object reference (**self**), and a reference to another object of class **Rational**. If **rational1** and **rational2** are two objects of class **Rational**, when the interpreter encounters the expression

```
rational1 + rational2
```

the interpreter generates method call

```
rational1.__add__( rational2 )
```

This method creates and returns a new object of class **Rational** that represents the results of adding **self** to **other**. The numerator of this new value is computed with the expression

```
self.sign * self.numerator * other.denominator +
other.sign * other.numerator * self.denominator
```

and the denominator is computed with the expression

```
self.denominator * other.denominator
```

Method **__sub__** (lines 56–59) overloads the binary subtraction operator. This method uses the overloaded **+** and **–** operators to create and return the results of subtracting the method's second argument from the method's first argument.

Method **__mul__** (lines 61–66) overloads the binary multiplication operator. This method creates and returns a new object of class **Rational** that represents the product of the method's two arguments.

Method **__div__** (lines 68–73) overloads the binary division operator **/** and creates and returns a new object of class **Rational** that represents the results of dividing the method's two arguments. Method **__truediv__** (lines 75–79) overloads the binary division operator **/** for Python versions 2.2 and greater that use floating-point division. This method simply calls method **__div__**, because the **/** operator should perform the same operation, regardless of the Python version. [*Note:* See Chapter 2, Introduction to Python Programming, for more information on the difference in the **/** operator between Python versions.]

Method **__eq__** (lines 82–85) overloads the binary equality operator (**==**). If **rational1** and **rational2** are two objects of class **Rational**, when the interpreter encounters the expression

```
rational1 == rational2
```

the interpreter generates method call

```
rational1.__eq__( rational2 )
```

This method subtracts the two objects and determines whether the numerator of the result is 0. **Rational** objects are reduced to their simplest form when created; therefore, we do not need to reduce the method's argument values before testing whether they are equal.

Method **__lt__** (lines 87–90) overloads the binary less-than operator (**<**). This method subtracts its second argument from its first argument and tests whether the sign of the result is less than 0. Method **__gt__** (lines 92–95) overloads the binary greater-than operator (**>**). This method subtracts its second argument from its first and tests whether the sign of the result is greater than 0.

Methods **__le__** (lines 97–100), **__ge__** (lines 102–105) and **__ne__** (lines 107–110) overload the **<=**, **>=** and inequality operators (**!=** and **<>**) for objects of class **Rational**. These methods use the overloaded equality (**==**), greater-than (**>**) and less-than (**<**) operators to performs their operations.

Lines 113–116 define special method **__abs__** to overload the functionality of the built-in **abs** function. If **rational** is an object of class **Rational**, when the interpreter encounters the expression

```
abs( rational )
```

the interpreter generates the method call

```
rational.__abs__()
```

This method creates a new object of class **Rational** using the values of the numerator and denominator of the object reference argument (recall that the constructor stores these values as positive integers).

Lines 118–133 define method **__str__** so that clients may use the **print** statement or built-in function **str** to display information about an object of class **Rational**. If the object's numerator is 0, **__str__** returns the string representation of integer value 0; if the object's denominator is 1, **__str__** returns the string representation of the object's sign and numerator. Otherwise, the method returns the string representation of the object's sign, followed by the string representation of the object's numerator, followed by **"/"**, followed by the string representation of the object's denominator.

Lines 136–153 define special methods for coercion behavior. Method **__int__** (lines 136–140) executes when a client invokes built-in function **int** on an object of class **Rational**. The method calls built-in function **divmod** to compute the integer division and remainder components of dividing the numerator by the denominator. The method returns the first element in the tuple returned from **divmod**, which represents the integer division component. Method **__float__** (lines 142–145) executes when a client invokes built-in function **float** on an object of class **Rational**. The method multiplies the object's sign (-1 or 1) by the result of dividing the numerator by the denominator and ensures a floating-point return value by call function **float** on the numerator.

Method **__coerce__** (lines 147–153) executes when a client calls built-in function **coerce** on an object of class **Rational** and another object or when the client performs so-called "mixed-mode" arithmetic. An example of mixed-mode arithmetic is the statement

```
rational + 1
```

which attempts to add an integer to an object of class **Rational**. This statement results in the method call

```
rational.__add__( rational.__coerce__( 1 ) )
```

Special method **__coerce__** should contain code that converts the object and the other type to the same type and should return a tuple that contains the two converted values. Method **__coerce__** for class **Rational** converts only integer values. Line 150 determines whether the type of the method's second argument is an integer. If so, the method returns a tuple that contains the object reference argument and a new object of class **Rational**, created by passing the integer argument to **Rational**'s constructor. Python expects special method **__coerce__** to return **None** if a coercion of the two types is not possible; therefore, line 153 returns **None** if the method's argument is not an integer.

The driver program (Fig. 8.10) creates objects of class **Rational**—**rational1** is initialized by default to 1/1, **rational2** is initialized to 10/30 and **rational3**, which is initialized to -7/14. The **Rational** constructor calls method **simplify** to reduce the specified numerator and denominator. Thus, **rational2** represents the value 1/3, and **rational3** represents the value -1/2.

The driver program outputs each of the constructed objects of class **Rational**, using the **print** statement. Lines 17–21 demonstrate the results of using overloaded arithmetic operators **/**, **-** and *****. Lines 24–26 demonstrate that overloading the **+** addition operator implicitly overloads the **+=** assignment statement. The program uses the **+=** augmented assignment statement to add to **rational1** the product of **rational2 * rational3**, then prints the results. The driver then prints the results of comparing the objects of class **Rational** through the overloaded comparison operators (lines 29–31). Line 34 prints the absolute value of object **rational3**. Lines 38-40 tests **Rational**'s coercion capability by printing the integer representation (invoking method **__int__**) and the floating-point representation (invoking method **__float__**) and by adding an object of class **Rational** and an integer (invoking method **__coerce__**).

8.11 Overloading Sequence Operations

We have seen how to use special methods to define a class that behaves like a numeric type. A class also can define several special methods to implement sequence operations, providing a list-based interface to its clients. An object of the class can provide access to its elements through subscripts and slices, can be passed to function **len** to determine its length and can support the operators and provide the methods that lists support. The table in Fig. 8.11 contains some methods that a sequence class should provide. In the next section, we define several of these methods for a list-based class that contains only unique values.

Method	Description
__add__, **__radd__**, **__iadd__**	Overloads addition operator for concatenating sequences (e.g., **sequence1 + sequence2**)

Fig. 8.11   Sequence methods. (Part 1 of 2.)

Method	Description
append	Called to append an element to a mutable sequence (e.g., **sequence.append(element)**)
__contains__	Called to test for membership (e.g., **element in sequence**)
count	Called to determine number of occurrences of element in a mutable sequence (e.g., **sequence.count(element)**)
__delitem__	Called to delete an item from a mutable sequence (e.g., **del sequence[index]**)
__getitem__	Called for subscript access (e.g., **sequence[index]**)
index	Called to obtain index of first occurrence of an element in a mutable sequence (e.g., **sequence.index(element)**)
insert	Called to insert an element at a given index in a mutable sequence (e.g., **sequence.insert(index, element)**)
__len__	Called for length of sequence (e.g., **len(sequence)**)
__mul__, **__rmul__**, **__imul__**	Overloads multiplication operator for repeating sequences (e.g., **sequence * 3**)
pop	Called to remove an element from a mutable sequence (e.g., **sequence.pop()**)
remove	Called to remove first occurrence of a value from a mutable sequence (e.g., **sequence.remove()**)
reverse	Called to reverse a mutable sequence in place (e.g., **sequence.reverse()**)
__setitem__	Called for assignment to a mutable sequence (e.g., **sequence[index] = value**)
sort	Called to sort a mutable sequence in place (e.g., **sequence.sort()**)

Fig. 8.11   Sequence methods. (Part 2 of 2.)

8.12 Case Study: A **SingleList** Class

We now present an example of a class that "wraps" (contains) a list to illustrate how to define several special methods to create a class that behaves like a sequence. The list allows clients to insert only new (unique) values in the list and allows the list to be displayed in tabular form. This example will sharpen your appreciation of data abstraction. You will probably want to suggest enhancements to this example. Class development is an interesting, creative and intellectually challenging activity—always with the goal of "crafting valuable classes."

The program of Fig. 8.12 demonstrates class **SingleList** and its overloaded operators, statements and other special methods. First we walk through the driver program (Fig. 8.13). Then we consider the class definition and each of the class's methods.

```
 1   # Fig. 8.12: NewList.py
 2   # Simple class SingleList.
 3
 4   class SingleList:
 5
 6      def __init__( self, initialList = None ):
 7         """Initializes SingleList instance"""
 8
 9         self.__list = []  # internal list, contains no duplicates
10
11         # process list passed to __init__, if necessary
12         if initialList:
13
14            for value in initialList:
15
16               if value not in self.__list:
17                  self.__list.append( value )  # add original value
18
19      # string representation method
20      def __str__( self ):
21         """Overloaded string representation"""
22
23         tempString = ""
24         i = 0
25
26         # build output string
27         for i in range( len( self ) ):
28            tempString += "%12d" % self.__list[ i ]
29
30            if ( i + 1 ) % 4  == 0:  # 4 numbers per row of output
31               tempString += "\n"
32
33         if i % 4 != 0:  # add newline, if necessary
34            tempString += "\n"
35
36         return tempString
37
38      # overloaded sequence methods
39      def __len__( self ):
40         """Overloaded length of the list"""
41
42         return len( self.__list )
43
44      def __getitem__( self, index ):
45         """Overloaded sequence element access"""
46
47         return self.__list[ index ]
48
49      def __setitem__( self, index, value ):
50         """Overloaded sequence element assignment"""
51
```

Fig. 8.12 **SingleList** class with operator overloading—**SingleList.py**. (Part 1 of 2.)

```
52          if value in self.__list:
53              raise ValueError, \
54                  "List already contains value %s" % str( value )
55
56          self.__list[ index ] = value
57
58      # overloaded equality operators
59      def __eq__( self, other ):
60          """Overloaded == operator"""
61
62          if len( self ) != len( other ):
63              return 0  # lists of different sizes
64
65          for i in range( 0, len( self ) ):
66
67              if self.__list[ i ] != other.__list[ i ]:
68                  return 0  # lists are not equal
69
70          return 1  # lists are equal
71
72      def __ne__( self, other ):
73          """Overloaded != and <> operators"""
74
75          return not ( self == other )
```

Fig. 8.12 **SingleList** class with operator overloading—**SingleList.py**. (Part 2 of 2.)

```
1   # Fig. 8.13: fig08_13.py
2   # Driver for simple class SingleList.
3
4   from NewList import SingleList
5
6   def getIntegers():
7       size = int( raw_input( "List size: " ) )
8
9       returnList = []  # the list to return
10
11      for i in range( size ):
12          returnList.append(
13              int( raw_input( "Integer %d: " % ( i + 1 ) ) ) )
14
15      return returnList
16
17  # input and create integers1 and integers2
18  print "Creating integers1..."
19  integers1 = SingleList( getIntegers() )
20
21  print "Creating integers2..."
22  integers2 = SingleList( getIntegers() )
23
```

Fig. 8.13 **SingleList** class with operator overloading—**fig08_13.py**. (Part 1 of 3.)

```
24   # print integers1 size and contents
25   print "\nSize of list integers1 is", len( integers1 )
26   print "List:\n", integers1
27
28   # print integers2 size and contents
29   print "\nSize of list integers2 is", len( integers2 )
30   print "List:\n", integers2
31
32   # use overloaded comparison operator
33   print "Evaluating: integers1 != integers2"
34
35   if integers1 != integers2:
36      print "They are not equal"
37
38   print "\nEvaluating: integers1 == integers2"
39
40   if integers1 == integers2:
41      print "They are equal"
42
43   print "integers1[ 0 ] is", integers1[ 0 ]
44   print "Assigning 0 to integers1[ 0 ]"
45   integers1[ 0 ] = 0
46   print "integers1:\n", integers1
```

```
Creating integers1...
List size: 8
Integer 1: 1
Integer 2: 2
Integer 3: 3
Integer 4: 4
Integer 5: 5
Integer 6: 6
Integer 7: 7
Integer 8: 8
Creating integers2...
List size: 10
Integer 1: 9
Integer 2: 10
Integer 3: 11
Integer 4: 12
Integer 5: 13
Integer 6: 14
Integer 7: 15
Integer 8: 16
Integer 9: 17
Integer 10: 18

Size of list integers1 is 8
List:
          1              2              3              4
          5              6              7              8
```

Fig. 8.13 **SingleList** class with operator overloading—**fig08_13.py**. (Part 2 of 3.)

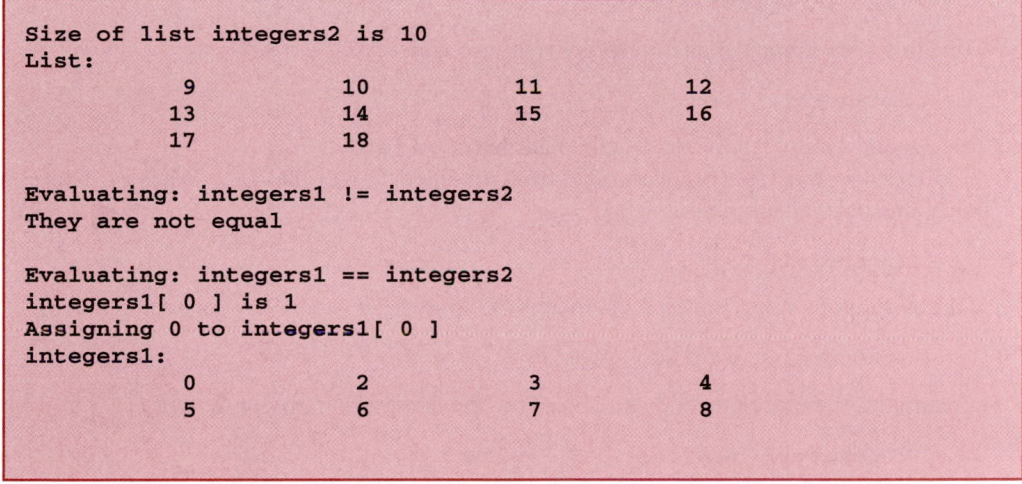

```
Size of list integers2 is 10
List:
            9           10           11           12
           13           14           15           16
           17           18

Evaluating: integers1 != integers2
They are not equal

Evaluating: integers1 == integers2
integers1[ 0 ] is 1
Assigning 0 to integers1[ 0 ]
integers1:
            0            2            3            4
            5            6            7            8
```

Fig. 8.13 **SingleList** class with operator overloading—**fig08_13.py**. (Part 3 of 3.)

The program (Fig. 8.13) begins by creating two objects of class **SingleList** (lines 18–22). This class's constructor takes a list as an argument. To create this list, we call function **getIntegers** (lines 6–15). This function prompts the user to enter integers and returns a list of these integers. Lines 25–26 use overloaded Python function **len** to determine the size of **integers1** and use the **print** statement (which implicitly calls method **__str__**) to confirm that the list elements were initialized correctly by the constructor. Next, lines 29–30 output the size and contents of **integers2**.

Lines 35–41 test the overloaded equality operator (**==**) and inequality operator (**!=**) by first evaluating the condition

        integers1 != integers2

The program prints a message if the two objects are not equal (line 36). Similarly, line 41 prints a message if the two objects are identical.

Line 43 uses the overloaded subscript operator to refer to **integers1[0]**. This subscripted name is used as an *rvalue* to print the value in **integers1[0]**. Line 45 uses **integers1[0]** as an *lvalue* on the left side of an assignment statement to assign a new value, **0**, to element 0 of **integers1**.

Now that we have seen how this program operates, let us walk through the class's method definitions (Fig. 8.12). Lines 6–17 define the constructor for the class. The constructor initializes attribute **_list** to be the empty list. If the user specified a value for parameter **initialList**, the constructor inserts all unique elements from **initial-List** into **_list**.

Lines 20–36 define method **__str__** for representing objects of class **Integer-List** as a string. This method builds a string (**tempString**) by iterating over the elements in the list and formatting the elements in tabular format, with four elements in each row. Line 36 returns the formatted string.

Lines 39–42 define method **__len__**, which overrides the Python **len** function. When the interpreter encounters the expression

```
len( integers1 )
```

in the driver program, the interpreter generates the call

```
integers1.__len__()
```

This method simply returns the length of attribute __list.

Lines 44–56 define two overloaded subscript operators for the class. When the interpreter encounters the expression

```
integers1[ 0 ]
```

in the driver program, the interpreter invokes the appropriate method by generating the call

```
integers1.__getitem__( 0 )
```

to return the value of element 0 (e.g., line 43 in the driver program), or the call

```
integers1.__setitem__( 0, value )
```

to set the value of a list element (e.g., line 45 in the driver program). When the **[]** operator is used in an *rvalue* expression, method **__getitem__** is called; when the **[]** operator is used in an *lvalue* expression, method **__setitem__** is called.

Method **__getitem__** (lines 44–47) simply returns the value of the appropriate element. Method **__setitem__** (lines 49–56) first ascertains whether the list already contains the new element. If the list contains the new element, the method raises an exception; otherwise, the method sets the new value. Because **SingleList** methods manipulate a basic list, any out-of-range errors that apply to regular list data types apply to our **SingleList** type.

Lines 59–70 define the overloaded equality operator (**==**) for the class. When the interpreter encounters the expression

```
integers1 == integers2
```

the interpreter invokes the **__eq__** method by generating the call

```
integers1.__eq__( integers2 )
```

The **__eq__** method immediately returns 0 if the length of the lists are different (lines 62–63). Otherwise, the method compares each pair of elements (lines 65–68). If they are all the same, the method returns 1 (line 70). The first pair of elements to differ causes the method to return 0 immediately (line 68). Line 72–75 define method **__ne__** for testing whether two **NewLists** are unequal. The method simply uses the overloaded **==** operator to determine whether the two objects are unequal.

Class **SingleList** defines only some of the methods suggested for sequences in Fig. 8.11. The exercises contain instructions for implementing some of the remaining methods.

8.13 Overloading Mapping Operations

Python defines several special methods to provide a mapping-based interface to its clients. An object of a class that implements these methods can provide access to its elements through subscripts, can be passed to function **len** to determine the object's length (i.e., the number of key–value pairs) and can support the methods that dictionaries support. The table in Fig. 8.14 contains some methods that a mapping class should provide. In the next section, we show an example of a class that defines many of these methods, to provide a dictionary interface to a basic object.

8.14 Case Study: A **SimpleDictionary** Class

Recall that an object of a class has a namespace that contains identifiers and their values. Attribute __**dict**__ contains this information for each object. We can take advantage of this fact to provide a dictionary interface to every object of a class. Figure 8.15 demonstrates class **SimpleDictionary**, which defines special methods to implement mapping behaviors of the class.

Method	Description
clear	Called to remove all items from mapping (e.g., **mapping.clear()**)
__**contains**__	Called to test for membership; should return same value as method **has_key** (e.g., **key in mapping**) [*Note:* This is new for Python 2.2 dictionaries.]
copy	Called to return a shallow copy of mapping (e.g., **mapping.copy()**)
__**delitem**__	Called to delete an item from mapping (e.g., **del mapping[key]**)
get	Called to obtain the value of a key in mapping (e.g., **mapping.get(key)**)
__**getitem**__	Called for subscript access through key (e.g., **mapping[key]**)
has_key	Called to determine if mapping contains a key (e.g., **mapping.has_key(key)**)
items	Called to obtain a list of key-value pairs in mapping (e.g., **mapping.items()**)
keys	Called to obtain a list of keys in mapping (e.g., **mapping.keys()**)
__**len**__	Called for length of mapping (e.g., **len(mapping)**)
__**setitem**__	Called for insertion or assignment through key (e.g., **mapping[key] = value**)
values	Called to return a list of values in mapping (e.g., mapping.values())
update	Called to insert items from another mapping (e.g., **mapping.update(otherMapping)**)

Fig. 8.14   Mapping methods.

```python
1   # Fig. 8.15: NewDictionary.py
2   # Definition of class SimpleDictionary.
3
4   class SimpleDictionary:
5      """Class to make an instance behave like a dictionary"""
6
7      # mapping special methods
8      def __getitem__( self, key ):
9         """Overloaded key-value access"""
10
11         return self.__dict__[ key ]
12
13      def __setitem__( self, key, value ):
14         """Overloaded key-value assignment/creation"""
15
16         self.__dict__[ key ] = value
17
18      def __delitem__( self, key ):
19         """Overloaded key-value deletion"""
20
21         del self.__dict__[ key ]
22
23      def __str__( self ):
24         """Overloaded string representation"""
25
26         return str( self.__dict__ )
27
28      # common mapping methods
29      def keys( self ):
30         """Returns list of keys in dictionary"""
31
32         return self.__dict__.keys()
33
34      def values( self ):
35         """Returns list of values in dictionary"""
36
37         return self.__dict__.values()
38
39      def items( self ):
40         """Returns list of items in dictionary"""
41
42         return self.__dict__.items()
```

Fig. 8.15 Mapping interface—class **SimpleDictionary**.

```python
1   # Fig. 8.16: fig08_16.py
2   # Driver for class SimpleDictionary.
3
4   from NewDictionary import SimpleDictionary
5
6   # create and print SimpleDictionary object
7   simple = SimpleDictionary()
```

Fig. 8.16 Mapping interface—**fig08_16.py**. (Part 1 of 2.)

```
 8   print "The empty dictionary:", simple
 9
10   # add values to simple (invokes simple.__setitem__)
11   simple[ 1 ] = "one"
12   simple[ 2 ] = "two"
13   simple[ 3 ] = "three"
14   print "The dictionary after adding values:", simple
15
16   del simple[ 1 ]   # remove a value
17   print "The dictionary after removing a value:", simple
18
19   # use mapping methods
20   print "Dictionary keys:", simple.keys()
21   print "Dictionary values:", simple.values()
22   print "Dictionary items:", simple.items()
```

```
The empty dictionary: {}
The dictionary after adding values: {1: 'one', 2: 'two', 3: 'three'}
The dictionary after removing a value: {2: 'two', 3: 'three'}
Dictionary keys: [2, 3]
Dictionary values: ['two', 'three']
Dictionary items: [(2, 'two'), (3, 'three')]
```

Fig. 8.16 Mapping interface—`fig08_16.py`. (Part 2 of 2.)

Each method in the class (Fig. 8.15) simply calls the appropriate method for the object's __dict__ attribute. Method __getitem__ (lines 8–11) accepts a key argument that contains the key value to retrieve from the dictionary. Line 11 simply uses the [] operator to retrieve the specified key from the object's __dict__. Method __setitem__ (lines 13–16) accepts as arguments a key and a value. The method simply inserts or updates the key-value pair in the object's __dict__. Method __delitem__ (lines 18–21) executes when the client uses keyword **del** to remove a key-value pair from the dictionary. The method simply removes the key-value pair from the object's __dict__. Method __str__ (lines 23–26) returns a string representation of an object of class **SimpleDictionary** by passing the object's __dict__ to built-in function **str**. Methods **keys** (lines 29–32), **values** (lines 34–37) and **items** (lines 39—42) each return their appropriate value by calling the corresponding method on the object's __dict__.

The driver program (Fig. 8.16) creates one object of class **SimpleDictionary** and uses the **print** statement to output the object's value (lines 7–8). Lines 11–13 add new values to the object with the [] operator, invoking method **simple.__setitem__**. Line 16 uses keyword **del** to delete an element from the object, invoking method **object.__delitem__**. Lines 20–22 call methods **keys**, **values** and **items**, to print the key-value pairs that the object stores.

In this chapter, we introduced the concept of class customization, wherein a class defines certain special methods to provide a syntax-based interface. These special methods perform a wide variety of tasks in Python, including string representation, attribute access, operator overloading and subscript access. We discussed the methods that provide each of these behaviors, and implemented three case studies that demonstrated how these methods can be used. In the next chapter, we discuss inheritance, a feature that allows programmers to define new classes that take advantage of the attributes and behaviors of existing classes. This ability is a key advantage of object-oriented programming, because it lets programmers focus only on the new behaviors a class should exhibit. For example, the technique we employed in this chapter of implementing a dictionary interface by calling the methods of an object's underlying **__dict__** attribute leads to some amount of redundant code. With inheritance, we can define a class that "re-uses" the behaviors of the standard dictionary type, without having to define every mapping method explicitly.

SUMMARY

- A special method is a method that has a special meaning in Python; the Python interpreter calls one of an object's special methods when the client performs a certain operation on the object.

- A class author implements special methods to customize the behavior of the class. The purpose of customization is to provide the clients of a class with a simple notation for manipulating objects of the class.

- Operator overloading consists of defining special methods to describe how operators behave with objects of programmer-defined types.

- Python enables programmers to overload most operators to be sensitive to the context in which they are used. The interpreter takes the action appropriate for the manner in which the operator is used.

- A Python class can define special method **__str__**, to provide an informal (i.e., human-readable) string representation of an object of the class. This method executes when a client uses an object with the **print** statement, the **%** string formatting operator or built-in function **str**.

- Python provides three special methods—**__getattr__**, **__setattr__** and **__delattr__**—that a class can define to control how the dot access operator behaves on objects of the class.

- If a class defines special method **__setattr__**, Python calls this method every time a program makes an assignment to an object's attribute through the dot operator.

- Assigning a value through the object's **__dict__** attribute does not invoke method **__setattr__**, but simply inserts the appropriate key–value pair in the object's **__dict__**.

- When a client program accesses an object attribute as an *rvalue*, Python first looks in the object's **__dict__** attribute for the attribute name. If the attribute name is not in **__dict__**, Python invokes the object's **__getattr__** method.

- The **__getattr__** definition for every class should raise the **AttributeError** exception if the attribute name cannot be found, to preserve Python's default behavior for looking up nonexistent attributes.

- Although Python does not allow new operators to be created, it does allow most existing operators to be overloaded so that, when these operators are used with objects of a programmer-defined type, the operators have meaning appropriate to the new types.

- Operators are overloaded by writing a method definition as you normally would, except that the method name corresponds to the Python special method for that operator. To use an operator on an object of a class, the class *must* overload (i.e., define a special method for) that operator.

- Operator overloading is not automatic; the programmer must write operator-overloading methods to perform the desired operations.

- The precedence of an operator cannot be changed by overloading.

- It is not possible to change the "arity" of an operator (i.e., the number of operands an operator takes): Overloaded unary operators remain unary operators; overloaded binary operators remain binary operators.

- The meaning of how an operator works on objects of built-in types cannot be changed by operator overloading. Operator overloading works only with objects of user-defined classes or with a mixture of an object of a user-defined class and an object of a built-in type.

- Overloading a binary mathematical operator automatically overloads the operator's corresponding augmented assignment statement, although the programmer can overload the augmented assignment statement explicitly.

- A unary operator for a class is overloaded as a method that takes only the object reference argument (**self**).

- A binary operator or statement for a class is overloaded as a method with two arguments: **self**, and **other**.

- A class also may define special methods that execute when certain built-in functions are called on an object of the class.

- The interpreter knows how to perform certain conversions among built-in types. Programmers can force conversions among built-in types by calling the appropriate function, such as **int** or **float**.

- The programmer must specify how conversions among user-defined classes and built-in types are to occur. Such conversions can be performed with special methods that override the appropriate Python functions.

- Method **__truediv__** overloads the binary division operator **/** for Python versions 2.2 and greater that use floating-point division.

- Method **__coerce__** executes when a client calls built-in function **coerce** on an object of class **Rational** and another object or when the client performs so-called "mixed-mode" arithmetic.

- Special method **__coerce__** should contain code that converts the reference object and the other type to the same type and should return a tuple that contains the two converted values. Python expects special method **__coerce__** to return **None** if a coercion of the two types is not possible.

- A class also can define several special methods to implement sequence operations, providing a list-based interface to its clients.

- When a program accesses an element of a sequence- or dictionary-like object as an *rvalue*, the object's **__getitem__** method executes. When a program assigns a value to an element of a sequence- or dictionary-like object, the object's **__setitem__** method executes.

- Python defines several special methods to provide a mapping-based interface to its clients.

TERMINOLOGY

__abs__ method (overloads built-in function **abs**)

__add__ method (overloads operator **+**)

__and__ method (overloads operator **&**)

append

"arity"

binary operator

clear

__coerce__ method (overloads coercion behavior)

__complex__ method (overloads built-in function **complex**)

__contains__ method (overloads operator **in**)

copy

count

__delattr__ method (overloads attribute deletion)

__delitem__ method (overloads sequence/mapping element deletion)

__div__ method (overloads operator **/**)

__divmod__ method (overloads built-in function **divmod**)

__float__ method (overloads built-in function **float**)

__floordiv__ method (overloads operator **//**)

get

__getattr__ method (overloads attribute retrieval)

__getitem__ method (overloads
   sequence/mapping element retrieval)
has_key
__hex__ method (overloads built-in
   function hex)
__iadd__ method (overloads symbol +=)
__iand__ method (overloads symbol &=)
__idiv__ method (overloads symbol /=)
__ifloordiv__ method (overloads
   symbol //=)
__ilshift__ method (overloads
   symbol <<=)
__imod__ method (overloads symbol %=)
__imul__ method (overloads symbol *=)
index
insert
__int__ method (overloads built-in
   function int)
__invert__ method (overloads operator ~)
__ior__ method (overloads symbol |=)
__ipow__ method (overloads symbol **=)
__irshift__ method (overloads
   symbol >>=)
__isub__ method (overloads symbol -=)
items
__ixor__ method (overloads symbol ^=)
keys
__len__ method (overloads built-in
   function len)
__long__ method (overloads built-in
   function long)
__lshift__ method (overloads operator <<)
__mod__ method (overloads operator %)
__mul__ method (overloads operator *)
__neg__ method (overloads operator -)
__oct__ method (overloads built-in
   function oct)
operator overloading
__or__ method (overloads operator |)
pop
__pos__ method (overloads operator +)
__pow__ method (overloads operator **)

__radd__ method (overloads
   right-hand addition)
__rand__ method (overloads
   right-hand bitwise AND)
__rdiv__ method (overloads
   right-hand division)
remove
__repr__ method (formal
   string representation)
reverse
__rfloordiv__ method (overloads
   right-hand floor division)
__rlshift__ method (overloads
   right-hand left-shift)
__rmod__ method (overloads
   right-hand modulus)
__rmul__ method (overloads
   right-hand multiplication)
__ror__ method (overloads right-hand
   bitwise OR)
__rpow__ method (overloads
   right-hand exponentiation)
__rrshift__ method (overloads
   right-hand right-shift)
__rshift__ method (overloads operator >>)
__rsub__ method (overloads
   right-hand subtraction)
__rxor__ method (overloads
   right-hand bitwise exclusive OR)
__setattr__ method (overloads
   attribute assignment)
__setitem__ method (overloads
   sequence/mapping element assignment)
sort
special method
__str__ method (informal string
   string representation)
__sub__ method (overloads operator -)
unary operator
update
values
__xor__ method (overloads operator ^)

SELF-REVIEW EXERCISES

8.1   Fill in the blanks in each of the following statements:
   a) Special methods _____, _____ and _____ customize attribute access
      through the dot access operator.
   b) Suppose **a** and **b** are integer variables and a program calculates the sum **a + b**. Now sup-
      pose **c** and **d** are string variables and a program performs the concatenation **c + d**. The

two **+** operators here are clearly being used for different purposes. This is an example of
_____.

c) The method name _____ overloads the **+** operator.
d) The _____, _____ and _____ of an operator cannot be changed by over-
    loading.
e) The **print** statement implicitly invokes special method _____.
f) Special method **__coerce__** should return _____ if no coercion can be made.
g) Special method **__ne__** overloads the _____.
h) Special method _____ customizes the behavior of built-in function **abs**.
i) Special method _____ overloads the exponentiation operator _____.
j) Special methods _____, _____ and _____ control attribute access
    through the **[]** subscript operators for list- and dictionary-like types.

8.2 State whether each of the following is *true* or *false*. If *false*, explain why.
a) Customization is accomplished by implementing special methods.
b) Python allows the programmer to create new operators to overload.
c) Overloading a mathematical operator implicitly overloads its augmented assignment
    counterpart.
d) User-defined objects can use Python's implicit operator overloading to get the expected
    results.
e) A class may overload the operation of the **=** assignment symbol.
f) Unary operators can be overloaded to accept two operands.
g) Operator overloading cannot change how an operator works with built-in types.
h) Comparison operators can be overloaded.
i) Subtraction can be overloaded with either special method **__neg__** or **__sub__**.
j) A class must define special methods to provide a dictionary-like interface.

ANSWERS TO SELF-REVIEW EXERCISES

8.1 a) **__getattr__**, **__setattr__**, **__delattr__**. b) operator overloading.
c) **__add__**. d) precedence, associativity, "arity." e) **__str__**. f) **None**. g) **!=** and **<>** inequality
operators. h) **__abs__**. i) **__pow__**, ******. j) **__getitem__**, **__setitem__**, **__delitem__**.

8.2 a) True. b) False. Python prohibits the programmer from creating new operators. c) True.
d) False. To use an operator or a statement on objects, that operator or statement must be overloaded.
e) False. The assignment symbol cannot be overloaded. f) False. Unary operators can be overloaded,
but the number of operands an operator takes cannot be changed. g) True. h) True. i) False. Subtraction can be overloaded only with **__sub__**; the unary operator **-** can be overloaded with method
__neg__. j) False. A class may define special methods to provide a dictionary-like interface, but
may also use inheritance.

EXERCISES

8.3 The definition for class **SimpleDictionary** in Fig. 8.15 does not include all the methods
suggested for providing a dictionary interface. Review the list of mapping methods in Fig. 8.14, and
modify the definition for class **SimpleDictionary** to include definitions for methods **clear**,
copy, **get**, **has_key** and **update**. Each method of class **SimpleDictionary** should call attribute **__dict__**'s corresponding method, passing any necessary arguments. Review the description of dictionary methods in Section 5.6—the corresponding methods of class
SimpleDictionary should specify the same arguments and should return the same value.

8.4 Implement methods **append**, **count**, **index**, **insert**, **pop**, **remove**, **reverse** and
sort for class **SingleList**. Review the description of list methods in Section 5.6—the corre-

sponding **SingleList** methods should specify the same arguments and should return the same value. Any new method that modifies the list should ensure that only unique values are inserted. The method should raise an exception if the client attempts to insert an existing value. Also, implement methods **__delitem__** and **__contains__** to enable clients to delete list elements with keyword **del** or perform membership tests with keyword **in**.

8.5   Review the **Rational** class definition (Fig. 8.9) and driver (Fig. 8.10). What happens when Python executes the following statement?

```
x = 1 + Rational( 3, 4 )
```

Special methods **__radd__**, **__rsub__** and so on overload the mathematical operators for a user-defined class when an object of that class is used as the right-hand value of an operator. For each operator overloaded in Fig. 8.9 (i.e., operators **+**, **-**, *****, **/** and **//**), add a corresponding method for overloading the operator when a **Rational** appears to the right of that operator.

8.6   As class **Rational** is currently implemented, the client may modify the attributes (i.e., **sign**, **numerator** and **denominator**) and place the data in an inconsistent state. Modify the definition for class **Rational** from Exercise 8.5 to include method **__setitem__**. If a client attempts to change the numerator or denominator of an object of class **Rational**, **__setitem__** determines whether the change affects the sign of the object. If so, the method changes the object's sign and sets the numerator or denominator as the absolute value of the client-specified value. The method also should call method **simplify** to reduce the object. Beware: If **__setitem__** assigns a value to an attribute through the dot access operator, Python invokes **__setitem__** again, resulting in infinite recursion. Make sure the method makes assignments through the object's **__dict__** attribute instead. [*Note:* Methods **__init__** and **simplify** also must be updated to use the object's **__dict__**, to avoid infinite recursion].

8.7   Consider a class **Complex** that simulates the built-in complex data type. The class enables operations on so-called *complex numbers*. These are numbers of the form **realPart + imaginaryPart *** *i*, where *i* has the value

$$\sqrt{-1}$$

a) Modify the class to enable output of complex numbers in the form (*realPart*, *imaginaryParti*), through the overloaded **__str__** method.

b) Overload the multiplication operator to enable multiplication of two complex numbers as in algebra, using the equation
   (a, b*i***) * (c, d***i***) = (a*c - b*d, (a*d + b*c)***i***)**

c) Overload the **==** operator to allow comparisons of complex numbers. [*Note:* **(a, b***i***)** is equal to **(c, d***i***)** if **a** is equal to **c** and **b** is equal to **d**.]

```
1   # Exercise 8.7: Complex.py
2   # Complex number class.
3
4   class Complex:
5       """Complex numbers of the form realPart + imaginaryPart * i"""
6
7       def __init__( self, real = 0, imaginary = 0 ):
8           """Assigns values to realPart and imaginaryPart"""
9
10          self.realPart = real
11          self.imaginaryPart = imaginary
```

```
12
13        def __add__( self, other ):
14            """Returns the sum of two Complex instances"""
15
16            real = self.realPart + other.realPart
17            imaginary = self.imaginaryPart + other.imaginaryPart
18
19            # create and return new complexNumber
20            return Complex( real, imaginary )
21
22        def __sub__( self, other ):
23            """Returns the difference of two Complex instance"""
24
25            real = self.realPart - other.realPart
26            imaginary = self.imaginaryPart - other.imaginaryPart
27
28            # create and return new complexNumber
29            return Complex( real, imaginary )
```

8.8   Develop class **Polynomial**. The internal representation of a **Polynomial** is a dictionary of terms. Each term is a key–value pair that contains an exponent and a coefficient. The term

$$2x^4$$

has the coefficient 2 and the exponent 4. For simplicity, assume the polynomial contains only non-negative exponents. Develop the class with a dictionary-based interface for accessing terms that includes the following elements:

a) The class's constructor accepts a dictionary of *exponent* : *coefficient* pairs.

b) Coefficient values in a **Polynomial** are accessed by exponent keys (e.g., **polynomial[exponent] = coefficient**). If a polynomial does not have a coefficient for a specified exponent, the expression **polynomial[exponent]** evaluates to 0.

c) The length of a **Polynomial** is the value of its highest exponent.

d) Define method **__str__** for representing a Polynomial as a string with terms of the form cx^y.

e) Include an overloaded addition operator (**+**) to add two **Polynomial**s.

f) Include an overloaded subtraction operator (**-**) to subtract two **Polynomial**s.

Object-Oriented Programming: Inheritance

Objectives

- To create new classes by inheriting from existing classes.
- To understand how inheritance promotes software reusability.
- To understand the notions of base class and derived class.
- To understand the concept of polymorphism.
- To learn about classes that inherit from base-class **object**.

Say not you know another entirely, till you have divided an inheritance with him.
Johann Kasper Lavater

This method is to define as the number of a class the class of all classes similar to the given class.
Bertrand Russell

A deck of cards was built like the purest of hierarchies, with every card a master to those below it, a lackey to those above it.
Ely Culbertson

Good as it is to inherit a library, it is better to collect one.
Augustine Birrell

Save base authority from others' books.
William Shakespeare

Outline

9.1 Introduction

In this chapter we discuss *inheritance*—one of the most important capabilities of object-oriented programming. Inheritance is a form of software reusability in which new classes are created from existing classes by absorbing their attributes and behaviors, and overriding or embellishing these with capabilities the new classes require. Software reusability saves time in program development. It encourages programmers to reuse proven and debugged high-quality software, thus reducing problems after a system becomes functional. These are exciting possibilities.

When creating a new class, instead of writing completely new attributes and methods, the programmer can designate that the new class is to *inherit* the attributes and methods of a previously defined *base class*. The new class is referred to as a *derived class*. Each derived class itself can be a base class for some future derived class. With *single inheritance,* a class is derived from one base class. With *multiple inheritance,* a derived class inherits from several base classes. Single inheritance is straightforward—we show several examples that should enable the reader to become proficient quickly. Multiple inheritance is beyond the scope this edition—we do not show a live-code example and issue a strong caution urging the reader to pursue further study before using this powerful capability. For more information on Python 2.2's multiple inheritance capabilities, visit:

```
www.python.org/2.2/descrintro.html
python.sourceforge.net/peps/pep-0253.html
```

A derived class can add attributes and methods of its own, so an object of a derived class can be larger than object of that derived-class's base class. A derived class is more specific than its base class and represents a smaller set of objects. With single inheritance, the derived class starts out essentially the same as the base class. The real strength of inheritance comes from the ability to define in the derived class additions, replacements or refinements for the features inherited from the base class.

With inheritance, every object of a derived class also may be treated as an object of that derived class's base class. We can take advantage of this "derived-class-object-is-a-base-class-object" relationship to perform some interesting manipulations. For example, we can thread a wide variety of different objects related through inheritance into a list where each element of the list is treated as a base-class object. This allows a variety of objects to be processed in a general way. As we will see, this capability—called *polymorphism*—is a key thrust of object-oriented programming (OOP).

With polymorphism, it is possible to design and implement systems that are more easily *extensible*. Programs can be written to process generically—as base-class objects—objects of all existing classes in a hierarchy. Classes that do not exist during program development can be added with little or no modification to the generic part of the program—as long as those classes are part of the hierarchy that is being processed generically. The only parts of a program that need modification are those parts that require direct knowledge of the particular class that is added to the hierarchy. Polymorphism enables us to write programs in a general fashion to handle many existing and yet-to-be-specified related classes. Inheritance and polymorphism are effective techniques for managing software complexity.

Experience in building software systems indicates that significant portions of the code deal with closely related special cases. It becomes difficult in such systems to see the "big picture" because the designer and the programmer become preoccupied with the special cases. Object-oriented programming provides several ways of "seeing the forest through the trees"—a process called *abstraction*.

We distinguish between *"is-a" relationships* and *"has-a" relationships*. "Is a" is inheritance. In an "is a" relationship, an object of a derived-class type may also be treated as an object of the base-class type. "Has a" is composition (see Fig. 7.18). In a "has a" relationship, an object *has* references to one or more objects of other classes as members.

A derived class can access the attributes and methods of its base class. One problem with inheritance is that a derived class can inherit method implementations that it does not need to have or should expressly not have. When a base-class method implementation is inappropriate for a derived class, that method can be *overridden* (i.e., redefined) in the derived class with an appropriate implementation.

Perhaps most exciting is the notion that new classes can inherit from classes in existing *class libraries*. Organizations develop their own class libraries and use other libraries available worldwide. Eventually, software will be constructed predominantly from *standardized reusable components* just as hardware is often constructed today. This will help to meet the challenges of developing the ever more powerful software we will need in the future.

9.2 Inheritance: Base Classes and Derived Classes

Often an object of one class really "is an" object of another class as well. A rectangle certainly *is a* quadrilateral (as are a square, a parallelogram and a trapezoid). Thus, class **Rectangle** can be said to inherit from class **Quadrilateral**. In this context, class

Quadrilateral is a base class and class **Rectangle** is a derived class. A rectangle *is a* specific type of quadrilateral, but it is incorrect to claim that a quadrilateral *is a* rectangle (the quadrilateral could, for example, be a parallelogram). Figure 9.1 shows several simple inheritance examples.

Other object-oriented programming languages such as Smalltalk and Java use different terminology: In inheritance, the base class is called the *superclass* and the derived class is called the *subclass.* Because inheritance normally produces derived classes with *more* features than their base classes, the terms superclass and subclass can be confusing; we avoid these terms.

Inheritance forms tree-like hierarchical structures. A base class exists in a hierarchical relationship with its derived classes. A class can certainly exist by itself, but it is when a class is used with the mechanism of inheritance that the class becomes either a base class that supplies attributes and behaviors to other classes or a derived class that inherits attributes and behaviors.

Let us develop a simple inheritance hierarchy (Fig. 9.2). A typical university community has thousands of people who are community members. These people consist of employees, students and alumni. Employees are either faculty members or staff members. Faculty members are either administrators (such as deans and department chairpersons) or teaching faculty. This yields the inheritance hierarchy shown in Fig. 9.2. Note that some administrators also teach classes, so we have used multiple inheritance to form class **AdministratorTeacher**. Because students often work for their universities, and because employees often take courses, it would also be reasonable to use multiple inheritance to create a class called **EmployeeStudent**.

Another inheritance hierarchy is the **Shape** hierarchy of Fig. 9.3. A common observation among students learning object-oriented programming is that there are abundant examples of hierarchies in the real world. It is just that these students are not accustomed to categorizing the real world in this manner, so it takes some adjustment in their thinking.

Base class	Derived classes
Student	GraduateStudent
	UndergraduateStudent
Shape	Circle
	Triangle
	Rectangle
Loan	CarLoan
	HomeImprovementLoan
	MortgageLoan
Employee	FacultyMember
	StaffMember
Account	CheckingAccount
	SavingsAccount

Fig. 9.1　Inheritance examples.

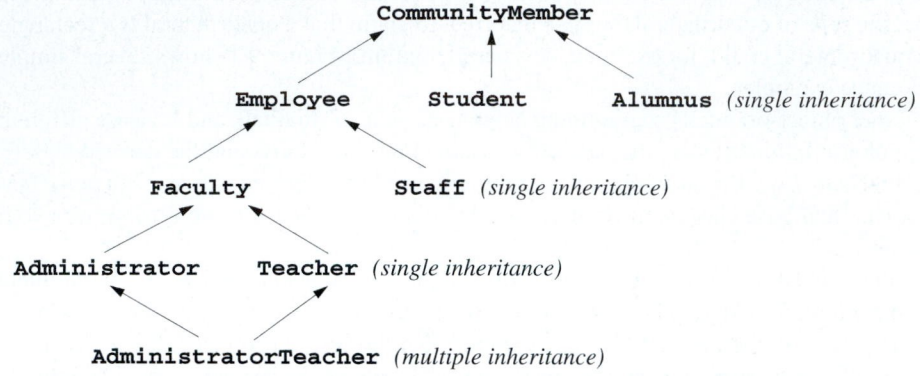

Fig. 9.2   Inheritance hierarchy for university community members.

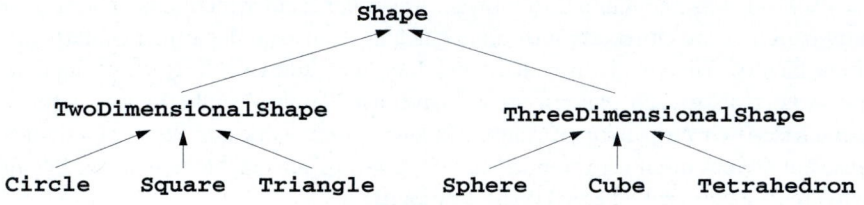

Fig. 9.3   **Shape** class hierarchy.

Let us consider the syntax for indicating inheritance. To specify that class **Two-DimensionalShape** is derived from class **Shape**, class **TwoDimensionalShape** typically would be defined as follows:

```
class TwoDimensionalShape( Shape ):
    ...
```

With inheritance, all attributes and methods of the base class are inherited as attributes and methods of the derived class.

A base class may be either a *direct base class* of a derived class or an *indirect base class* of a derived class. A direct base class of a derived class is explicitly listed inside parentheses (**()**) when the derived class is defined. An indirect base class is not explicitly listed when the derived class is defined; rather, the indirect base class is inherited from two or more levels up the class hierarchy. In Fig. 9.3, class **Circle** has a direct base class **TwoDimensionalShape** and an indirect base class **Shape**. Although the class definition for class **Circle** would list only class **TwoDimensionalShape** as a base class, class **Circle** would inherit all the attributes and methods of class **TwoDimensional-Shape** and of class **Shape**.

It is possible to treat base-class objects and derived-class objects similarly; that commonality is expressed in the attributes and behaviors of the base class. Objects of any class derived with inheritance from a common base class can all be treated as objects of that base class. In Section 9.10, we consider an example in which we can take advantage of this relationship.

9.3 Creating Base Classes and Derived Classes

This section creates an inheritance hierarchy and instantiates objects from the classes in that hierarchy. Python provides two built-in functions—*issubclass* and *isinstance*—that enable us to determine whether one class is derived from another class and whether a value is an object of a particular class or of a subclass of that class. We discuss these functions in Fig. 9.4 that demonstrates how to derive one class from another class and that underscores the fact that a derived-class object "is a" base-class object. In Fig. 9.4, lines 6–13 show a **Point** class and constructor definition. Lines 15–28 show a **Circle** class and method definitions. Lines 30–52 contain a driver program. We offer this hierarchy as an example of so-called *structural inheritance*. Although it may not appear to be a natural series of "is-a" relationships (i.e., many readers will be uncomfortable with any claim that a circle is a point), the fact that we derive **Circle** from **Point** makes a **Circle** a **Point** in a mechanical sense. We find that this example helps the student understand the mechanics of inheritance. Later in the chapter, we present a natural example of inheritance.

```python
1   # Fig 9.4: fig09_04.py
2   # Derived class inheriting from a base class.
3
4   import math
5
6   class Point:
7       """Class that represents geometric point"""
8
9       def __init__( self, xValue = 0, yValue = 0 ):
10          """Point constructor takes x and y coordinates"""
11
12          self.x = xValue
13          self.y = yValue
14
15  class Circle( Point ):
16      """Class that represents a circle"""
17
18      def __init__( self, x = 0, y = 0, radiusValue = 0.0 ):
19          """Circle constructor takes x and y coordinates of center
20          point and radius"""
21
22          Point.__init__( self, x, y )   # call base-class constructor
23          self.radius = float( radiusValue )
24
25      def area( self ):
26          """Computes area of a Circle"""
27
28          return math.pi * self.radius ** 2
29
30  # main program
31
32  # examine classes Point and Circle
33  print "Point bases:", Point.__bases__
34  print "Circle bases:", Circle.__bases__
```

Fig. 9.4   Derived class inheriting from a base class. (Part 1 of 2.)

```
35
36    # demonstrate class relationships with built-in function issubclass
37    print "\nCircle is a subclass of Point:", \
38       issubclass( Circle, Point )
39    print "Point is a subclass of Circle:", issubclass( Point, Circle )
40
41    point = Point( 30, 50 )  # create Point object
42    circle = Circle( 120, 89, 2.7 )    # create Circle object
43
44    # demonstrate object relationship with built-in function isinstance
45    print "\ncircle is a Point object:", isinstance( circle, Point )
46    print "point is a Circle object:", isinstance( point, Circle )
47
48    # print Point and Circle objects
49    print "\npoint members:\n\t", point.__dict__
50    print "circle members:\n\t", circle.__dict__
51
52    print "\nArea of circle:", circle.area()
```

```
Point bases: ()
Circle bases: (<class __main__.Point at 0x00767250>,)

Circle is a subclass of Point: 1
Point is a subclass of Circle: 0

circle is a Point object: 1
point is a Circle object: 0

point members:
        {'y': 50, 'x': 30}
circle members:
        {'y': 89, 'x': 120, 'radius': 2.7000000000000002}

Area of circle: 22.9022104447
```

Fig. 9.4   Derived class inheriting from a base class. (Part 2 of 2.)

The constructor for class **Point** (lines 9–13) takes two arguments that correspond to the point's *x*- and *y*-coordinates. Class **Circle** (lines 15–28) inherits from class **Point**. The parentheses (**()**) in the first line of the class definition indicate inheritance. The name of the base class (**Point**) is placed inside the parentheses. Class **Circle** inherits all attributes of class **Point**. This means that class **Circle** contains the **Point** members (i.e., **x** and **y**) as well as the **Circle** members.

A derived class inherits the methods defined in its base class, including the base-class constructor. Often, the derived class *overrides* the base-class constructor by defining a derived-class __**init**__ method. A derived class overrides a base-class method when the derived class defines a method with the same name as a base-class method. The overridden derived-class constructor usually calls the base-class constructor, to initialize base-class attributes before initializing derived-class attributes. Line 22 in the **Circle** constructor calls the base-class constructor through an *unbound method call*. Until now, we have invoked only *bound method calls*. A bound method call is invoked by accessing the method name through an object (e.g., **anObject.method()**). We have seen that Python inserts the object-reference argument for bound method calls. An unbound method call is invoked by accessing the method through its class name and specifically passing an object reference. For example, line 22 calls method **Point.__init__** and passes **self** (an object of class **Circle**) as the object reference. The unbound method call also passes the values for **x** and **y** so the **Point** constructor can initialize the **Point** attributes for the object of class **Circle**. We explore method overriding and bound and unbound method calls further in the next section. After the base-class constructor terminates, control returns to the **Circle** constructor so it can perform any **Circle**-specific initialization. Line 23 adds a new attribute—**radius**—to **Circle**'s namespace.

Software Engineering Observation 9.1

A derived class (like any class) is not required to define a constructor. If a derived class does not define a constructor, the class's base-class constructor executes when the client creates a new object of the class.

Common Programming Error 9.1

If a derived class's overridden constructor needs to invoke the base-class constructor to initialize base-class members, the derived-class constructor must invoke the base-class constructor explicitly. Failure to call the base-class constructor from a derived class often is a logic error.

Common Programming Error 9.2

Failure to specify an object reference as the first argument to an unbound method call is a logic error.

Lines 25–28 define method **area** for class **Circle**. This method demonstrates how the derived class can define new methods to extend the functionality of the base class. In this example, derived class **Circle** provides extra functionality that computes the area of an object of class **Circle**.

The driver program in Fig. 9.4 first prints the value of each class's **__bases__** attribute (lines 33–34). Recall from Chapter 7 that each class contains special attributes, including **__bases__**, which is a tuple that contains references to each of the class's base classes. Notice from the output that **Point.__bases__** is an empty tuple, because **Point** does not inherit from any other class. However, **Circle.__bases__** is a tuple that contains one value—a reference to base-class **Point**. Lines 37–39 call built-in function **issubclass** to demonstrate that **Circle** is a subclass of **Point**, but that **Point** is not a subclass of **Circle**. Function **issubclass** takes two arguments that are classes and returns true if the first argument is a class that inherits from the second argument (or if the first argument is the same class as the second argument).

Lines 41–42 create **point** as a reference to an object of class **Point** and **circle** as a reference to an object of class **Circle**. Lines 45–46 demonstrate built-in function **isinstance**. This function takes two arguments—an object and a class. If the object argument is an object of the type specified by the class argument, or if the object argument is an object of a derived class of the type specified by the class argument, function **isinstance** returns 1. Otherwise, the function returns 0. The two calls to function **isinstance** demonstrate that a derived class is an object of its base class (e.g., **circle** is a **Point**), but the reverse is not true (e.g., **point** is not a **Circle**).

Common Programming Error 9.3

Treating a base-class object as a derived-class object can cause runtime errors. A program terminates if the program attempts to call a derived-class method from a base-class object and the base class does not define that method.

Lines 49–50 print the **__dict__** attribute **point** and **circle**, respectively. Notice from the output that **circle**'s **__dict__** contains attributes **x** and **y**, initialized in the base-class constructor. Line 52 calls **circle** method **area**, to demonstrate class **Circle**'s extended functionality.

In this section, we demonstrated the mechanics of defining base and derived classes and discussed bound and unbound methods. This material establishes the foundation we need for our deeper treatment of object-oriented programming with inheritance in the remainder of this chapter.

9.4 Overriding Base-Class Methods in a Derived Class

A derived class can override a base-class method by supplying a new version of that method with the same name. When that method is mentioned by name in the derived class, the derived-class version is selected. The name of the base class may be used to access the base-class version from the derived class by passing the derived-class object in an unbound call to the base-class's method.

Common Programming Error 9.4

When a base-class method is overridden in a derived class, it is common to have the derived-class version call the base-class version and perform some additional work. Not using the base-class name to reference (i.e., prepending the base-class name and a dot to) the base-class method causes infinite recursion, because the derived-class method actually calls itself. This eventually will cause the system to exhaust memory—a fatal error.

Consider a simplified class **Employee**. It stores the employee's **firstName** and **lastName**. This information is common to all employees, including classes derived from class **Employee**. From class **Employee**, now derive classes **HourlyWorker**, **Piece-Worker**, **Boss** and **CommissionWorker**. The **HourlyWorker** gets paid by the hour, with "time-and-a-half" for overtime hours in excess of 40 hours per week. The **Piece-Worker** gets paid a fixed rate per item produced—for simplicity, assume this person makes only one type of item, so the data members are number of items produced and rate per item. The **Boss** gets a fixed wage per week. The **CommissionWorker** gets a small fixed weekly base salary plus a fixed percentage of that person's gross sales for the week. For simplicity, this and the next section present only class **Employee** and derived class **HourlyWorker**. In Section 9.10, we present a case study that addresses the entire hierarchy.

Our next example appears in Fig. 9.5. Lines 4–16 show the **Employee** class definition and **Employee** methods. Lines 18–40 show the **HourlyWorker** class definition and **HourlyWorker** method definitions. Lines 42–49 show a driver program for the **Employee/HourlyWorker** inheritance hierarchy that creates an object of class **HourlyWorker** and invokes its **__str__** method implicitly, then explicitly with a bound method call, then explicitly with an unbound method call.

The **Employee** class definition consists of two attributes (**firstName** and **last-Name**) and two methods (**__init__** and **__str__**). The constructor receives two arguments and assigns their values to **firstName** and **lastName**. Class **HourlyWorker** inherits from class **Employee**. The members of **HourlyWorker** include attributes **hours** and **wage** and methods **__init__**, **getPay** and **__str__**.

```
1   # Fig. 9.5: fig09_05.py
2   # Overriding base-class methods.
3
4   class Employee:
5      """Class to represent an employee"""
6
7      def __init__( self, first, last ):
8         """Employee constructor takes first and last name"""
9
10        self.firstName = first
11        self.lastName = last
12
13     def __str__( self ):
14        """String representation of an Employee"""
15
16        return "%s %s" % ( self.firstName, self.lastName )
17
18  class HourlyWorker( Employee ):
19     """Class to represent an employee paid by hour"""
20
21     def __init__( self, first, last, initHours, initWage ):
22        """Constructor for HourlyWorker, takes first and last name,
23        initial number of hours and initial wage"""
24
25        Employee.__init__( self, first, last )
26        self.hours = float( initHours )
27        self.wage = float( initWage )
28
29     def getPay( self ):
30        """Calculates HourlyWorker's weekly pay"""
31
32        return self.hours * self.wage
33
34     def __str__( self ):
35        """String representation of HourlyWorker"""
36
37        print "HourlyWorker.__str__ is executing"""
38
39        return "%s is an hourly worker with pay of $%.2f" % \
40           ( Employee.__str__( self ), self.getPay() )
41
42  # main program
43  hourly = HourlyWorker( "Bob", "Smith", 40.0, 10.00 )
44
45  # invoke __str__ method several ways
46  print "Calling __str__ several ways..."
47  print hourly  # invoke __str__ implicitly
48  print hourly.__str__()  # invoke __str__ explicitly
49  print HourlyWorker.__str__( hourly )  # explicit, unbound call
```

Fig. 9.5   Overriding base-class methods in a derived class. (Part 1 of 2.)

```
Calling __str__ several ways...
 HourlyWorker.__str__ is executing
Bob Smith is an hourly worker with pay of $400.00
HourlyWorker.__str__ is executing
Bob Smith is an hourly worker with pay of $400.00
HourlyWorker.__str__ is executing
Bob Smith is an hourly worker with pay of $400.00
```

Fig. 9.5   Overriding base-class methods in a derived class. (Part 2 of 2.)

The **HourlyWorker** constructor uses an unbound method call to pass the strings **first** and **last** to the **Employee** constructor so the base-class attributes can be initialized, then initializes attributes **hours** and **wage**. Method **getPay** uses attributes **hours** and **wage** to calculate the salary of the **HourlyWorker**.

HourlyWorker method **__str__** overrides the **Employee __str__** method. Often, base-class methods are overridden in a derived class to provide more functionality. The overridden method sometimes calls the base-class version of the method to perform part of the new task. In this example, the derived-class **__str__** method calls the base-class **__str__** method (with an unbound method call on line 40) to output the employee's name. The derived-class **__str__** method also outputs the employee's pay.

The driver program invokes an hourly object's **__str__** method in three different ways. Line 47 simply uses the object in a **print** statement, which implicitly invokes the object's **__str__** method. Line 48 makes an explicit, bound call to the object's **__str__** method. Line 49 makes an unbound call to class **HourlyWorker**'s **__str__** method and passes **hourly** as the object reference argument.

9.5 Software Engineering with Inheritance

We can use inheritance to customize existing software. We inherit the attributes and behaviors of an existing class, then add attributes and behaviors (or override base-class behaviors) to customize the class to meet our needs. It can be difficult for students to appreciate the problems faced by designers and implementors on large-scale software projects. People experienced on such projects will invariably state that a key to improving the software development process is software reuse. Object-oriented programming in general, and Python in particular, certainly do this.

The availability of substantial and useful modules delivers the maximum benefits of software reuse through inheritance. As interest in Python grows, interest in creating useful modules also grows. Just as shrink-wrapped software produced by independent software vendors became an explosive growth industry with the arrival of the personal computer, so, too, is the creation and distribution of class libraries. Application designers build their applications with these libraries, and library designers are being rewarded by having their libraries wrapped with the applications.

Software Engineering Observation 9.2

Creating a derived class does not affect its base class's source code; the integrity of a base class is preserved by inheritance.

A base class specifies commonality—all classes derived from a base class inherit the capabilities of that base class. In the object-oriented design process, the designer looks for commonality and "factors it out" to form desirable base classes. Derived classes are then customized beyond the capabilities inherited from the base class.

Software Engineering Observation 9.3

In an object-oriented system, classes often are closely related. "Factor out" common attributes and behaviors and place these in a base class. Then use inheritance to form derived classes.

Just as the designer of non-object-oriented systems seeks to avoid unnecessary proliferation of functions, the designer of object-oriented systems should avoid unnecessary proliferation of classes. Such a proliferation of classes creates management problems and can hinder software reusability, simply because it is more difficult for a potential reuser of a class to locate that class in a large collection. The trade-off is to create fewer classes, each providing substantial additional functionality, but such classes might be too rich for certain users.

Performance Tip 9.1

If classes produced through inheritance are larger than they need to be, memory and processing resources may be wasted. Inherit from the class "closest" to what you need.

Note that reading a set of derived-class definitions can be confusing because inherited members are not shown, but they are nevertheless present in the derived classes. A similar problem can exist in the documentation of derived classes.

Software Engineering Observation 9.4

A derived class contains the attributes and behaviors of its base class. A derived class can also contain additional attributes and behaviors.

Software Engineering Observation 9.5

Modifications to a base class do not require derived classes to change as long as the interfaces to the base class remain unchanged.

9.6 Composition vs. Inheritance

We have discussed *is-a* relationships, which are supported by inheritance. We have also discussed *has-a* relationships (and seen an example in Chapter 7, Object-Based Programming) in which a class may have references to other classes as members. "hassuch relationships create new classes by *composition* of existing classes. For example, given the classes **Employee**, **BirthDate** and **TelephoneNumber**, it is improper to say that an **Employee** *is a* **BirthDate** or that an **Employee** *is a* **TelephoneNumber**. But it is certainly appropriate to say that an **Employee** *has a* **BirthDate** and that an **Employee** *has a* **TelephoneNumber**.

Software Engineering Observation 9.6

Program modifications to a class that is a member of another class do not require the enclosing class to change as long as the interface to the member class remains unchanged.

9.7 "Uses A" and "Knows A" Relationships

Inheritance and composition each encourage software reuse by creating new classes that have much in common with existing classes. There are other ways to use the services of classes. Although a person object is not a car and a person object does not contain a car, a person object certainly *uses a* car. A program uses an object simply by calling a method of that object through a reference.

An object can be *aware of* another object. Knowledge networks frequently have such relationships. One object can contain a reference to another object to be aware of that object. In this case, one object is said to have a *knows a* relationship with the other object; this is sometimes called an *association*.

9.8 Case Study: Point, Circle, Cylinder

Consider a more substantial example using a point, circle, cylinder structural-inheritance hierarchy. First we develop and use class **Point** (Fig. 9.6). Then we present an example in which we derive class **Circle** from class **Point** (Fig. 9.7). Finally, we present an example in which we derive class **Cylinder** from class **Circle** (Fig. 9.8).

Figure 9.6 shows class **Point**. The constructor (lines 7–11) takes two arguments that correspond to the *x*- and *y*-coordinates of the point. Method **__str__** (lines 13–16) creates a string representation of an object of class **Point**. The driver program in function **main** (lines 19–30) creates an object of class **point**, prints its **x** and **y** attributes, changes the value of its attributes and prints the changed **point** object.

```
1   # Fig 9.6: PointModule.py
2   # Definition and test function for class Point.
3
4   class Point:
5      """Class that represents a geometric point"""
6
7      def __init__( self, xValue = 0, yValue = 0 ):
8         """Point constructor takes x and y coordinates"""
9
10        self.x = xValue
11        self.y = yValue
12
13     def __str__( self ):
14        """String representation of a Point"""
15
16        return "( %d, %d )" % ( self.x, self.y )
17
18  # main program
19  def main():
20     point = Point( 72, 115 )   # create object of class Point
21
22     # print point attributes
23     print "X coordinate is:", point.x
24     print "Y coordinate is:", point.y
25
26     # change point attributes and output new location
27     point.x = 10
28     point.y = 10
29
30     print "The new location of point is:", point
```

Fig. 9.6   Class **Point—PointModule.py**. (Part 1 of 2.)

```
31
32  if __name__ == "__main__":
33      main()
```

```
X coordinate is: 72
Y coordinate is: 115
The new location of point is: ( 10, 10 )
```

Fig. 9.6   Class **Point—PointModule.py**. (Part 2 of 2.)

Figure 9.7 demonstrates class **Circle**, which inherits from class **Point** (Fig. 9.6). Lines 7–26 show the **Circle** class definition, and lines 29–45 contain the driver program for class **Circle**. Note that, because class **Circle** inherits from class **Point**, the interface to **Circle** includes the **Point** methods as well as the **Circle** method **area**.

```
1   # Fig. 9.7: CircleModule.py
2   # Definition and test function for class Circle.
3
4   import math
5   from PointModule import Point
6
7   class Circle( Point ):
8      """Class that represents a circle"""
9
10     def __init__( self, x = 0, y = 0, radiusValue = 0.0 ):
11        """Circle constructor takes center point and radius"""
12
13        Point.__init__( self, x, y )  # call base-class constructor
14        self.radius = float( radiusValue )
15
16     def area( self ):
17        """Computes area of a Circle"""
18
19        return math.pi * self.radius ** 2
20
21     def __str__( self ):
22        """String representation of a Circle"""
23
24        # call base-class __str__ method
25        return "Center = %s Radius = %f" % \
26           ( Point.__str__( self ), self.radius )
27
28  # main program
29  def main():
30     circle = Circle( 37, 43, 2.5 )  # create Circle object
31
32     # print circle attributes
33     print "X coordinate is:", circle.x
34     print "Y coordinate is:", circle.y
35     print "Radius is:", circle.radius
```

Fig. 9.7   Class **Circle—CircleModule.py**. (Part 1 of 2.)

```
36
37          # change circle attributes and print new values
38          circle.radius = 4.25
39          circle.x = 2
40          circle.y = 2
41
42          print "\nThe new location and radius of circle are:", circle
43          print "The area of circle is: %.2f" % circle.area()
44
45          print "\ncircle printed as a Point is:", Point.__str__( circle )
46
47   if __name__ == "__main__":
48       main()
```

```
X coordinate is: 37
Y coordinate is: 43
Radius is: 2.5

The new location and radius of circle are: Center = ( 2, 2 ) Radius =
4.250000
The area of circle is: 56.75

circle printed as a Point is: ( 2, 2 )
```

Fig. 9.7   Class `Circle—CircleModule.py`. (Part 2 of 2.)

The driver program creates an object of class **Circle**, then prints the attributes of the object. The driver program then changes the values of the object's attributes and prints the changed object. Line 43 calls **circle** method **area** to display the object's area. Finally, line 45 calls **Point** method **__str__** as an unbound method and passes **circle** as the object reference. This call prints the object of class **Circle** as an object of class **Point**, demonstrating how a derived-class object can be used as a base-class object.

Our last example reuses the **Point** and **Circle** class definitions from Fig. 9.6 and Fig. 9.7. Lines 8–32 show the **Cylinder** class definition, and lines 35–61 are the driver program for class **Cylinder**. Note that class **Cylinder** inherits from class **Circle**, so the interface to **Cylinder** includes the **Circle** methods and **Point** methods as well as the **Cylinder** methods **area** (overridden from **Circle**) and **volume**. Note that the **Cylinder** constructor invokes the constructor for its direct base class **Circle**, but not its indirect base class **Point**. Each derived-class constructor is responsible only for calling the constructors of that class's immediate base class.

The driver program creates an object of class **Cylinder** (line 38), then prints the values of the object's attributes (lines 41–44). The driver program then changes the values of the height, radius and coordinates of the cylinder (lines 47–49) and outputs the results of the changes (lines 50–51). Finally, the program makes unbound method calls to the **Point** and **Circle __str__** methods (lines 57 and 61) to print the object of class **Cylinder** as an object of classes **Point** and **Circle**, respectively.

This example nicely demonstrates inheritance. The reader should now be confident with the basics of inheritance. In the remainder of the chapter, we show how to program with inheritance hierarchies in a general manner.

```
1   # Fig. 9.8: CylinderModule.py
2   # Definition and test function for class Cylinder.
3
4   import math
5   from PointModule import Point
6   from CircleModule import Circle
7
8   class Cylinder( Circle ):
9      """Class that represents a cylinder"""
10
11     def __init__( self, x, y, radius, height ):
12        """Constructor for Cylinder takes x, y, height and radius"""
13
14        Circle.__init__( self, x, y, radius )
15        self.height = float( height )
16
17     def area( self ):
18        """Calculates (surface) area of a Cylinder"""
19
20        return 2 * Circle.area( self ) + \
21           2 * math.pi * self.radius * self.height
22
23     def volume( self ):
24        """Calculates volume of a Cylinder"""
25
26        return Circle.area( self ) * height
27
28     def __str__( self ):
29        """String representation of a Cylinder"""
30
31        return "%s; Height = %f" % \
32           ( Circle.__str__( self ), self.height )
33
34  # main program
35  def main():
36
37     # create object of class Cylinder
38     cylinder = Cylinder( 12, 23, 2.5, 5.7 )
39
40     # print Cylinder attributes
41     print "X coordinate is:", cylinder.x
42     print "Y coordinate is:", cylinder.y
43     print "Radius is:", cylinder.radius
44     print "Height is:", cylinder.height
45
46     # change Cylinder attributes
47     cylinder.height = 10
48     cylinder.radius = 4.25
49     cylinder.x, cylinder.y = 2, 2
50     print "\nThe new points, radius and height of cylinder are:", \
51        cylinder
52
53     print "\nThe area of cylinder is: %.2f" % cylinder.area()
```

Fig. 9.8   Class **Cylinder—CylinderModule.py**. (Part 1 of 2.)

```
54
55      # display the Cylinder as a Point
56      print "\ncylinder printed as a Point is:", \
57          Point.__str__( cylinder )
58
59      # display the Cylinder as a Circle
60      print "\ncylinder printed as a Circle is:", \
61          Circle.__str__( cylinder )
62
63   if __name__ == "__main__":
64       main()
```

```
X coordinate is: 12
Y coordinate is: 23
Radius is: 2.5
Height is: 5.7

The new points, radius and height of cylinder are: Center = ( 2, 2 )
Radius = 4.250000; Height = 10.000000

The area of cylinder is: 380.53

cylinder printed as a Point is: ( 2, 2 )

cylinder printed as a Circle is: Center = ( 2, 2 ) Radius = 4.250000
```

Fig. 9.8   Class **Cylinder—CylinderModule.py**. (Part 2 of 2.)

9.9 Abstract Base Classes and Concrete Classes

When we think of a class as a type, we assume that objects of that type will be created. However, there are cases in which it is useful to define classes for which the programmer never intends to create any objects. Such classes are called *abstract classes*. Because these are used as base classes in inheritance situations, we normally refer to them as *abstract base classes*.

We do not create objects of abstract classes. The sole purpose of an abstract class is to provide an appropriate base class from which classes may inherit interface and possibly implementation. Classes from which objects can be created are called *concrete classes*.

We could have an abstract base class **TwoDimensionalShape** and derive concrete classes, such as **Square**, **Circle** and **Triangle**. We could also have an abstract base class **ThreeDimensionalShape** and derive concrete classes such as **Cube**, **Sphere** and **Cylinder**. Abstract base classes are too generic to define real objects; we need to be more specific before we can think of creating objects. That is what concrete classes do; they provide the specifics that make it reasonable to create objects.

A hierarchy need not contain any abstract classes; but, as we will see, many good object-oriented systems have class hierarchies headed by an abstract base class. In some cases, abstract classes constitute the top few levels of the hierarchy. A good example of this is a shape hierarchy. The hierarchy could be headed by abstract base class **Shape**. On the next level down, we can have two more abstract base classes, namely **TwoDimensionalShape** and **ThreeDimensionalShape**. The next level down would start defining concrete classes for two-dimensional shapes such as circles and squares and concrete classes for three-dimensional shapes such as spheres and cubes.

9.10 Case Study: Inheriting Interface and Implementation

Our next example reexamines the **Employee** hierarchy introduced in Section 9.4. This time, we implement the entire class hierarchy, heading it with abstract base class **Employee**. The derived classes of **Employee** are **Boss**, who gets paid a fixed weekly salary regardless of the number of hours worked; **CommissionWorker**, who gets a flat base salary plus a percentage of sales; **PieceWorker**, who gets paid by the number of items produced; and **HourlyWorker**, who gets paid by the hour and receives "time-and-a-half" overtime pay for hours worked in excess of 40 hours.

Each concrete **Employee** class defines method **earnings**. An **earnings** method call certainly applies generically to all employees. However, the earnings calculation for each employee differs based on the class of the employee. These classes are all derived from the base class **Employee**, so each derived class provides appropriate implementations of **earnings**. To calculate any employee's earnings, the program simply invokes the **earnings** method on that employee's object.

Let us now consider the example (Fig. 9.9). We begin with class **Employee** (lines 4–35). The methods include a constructor that takes the first name and last name as arguments; an **__str__** method; a utility method **_checkPositive** that ensures an attribute is initialized with a positive value and an abstract method **earnings**. Method **earnings** simply raises a **NotImplementedError** exception when called. [*Note*: We discuss exceptions in Chapter 12, Exception Handling.] Why does **earnings** raise an exception? The answer is that it does not make sense to provide an implementation of this method in the **Employee** class. We cannot calculate the earnings for a generic employee—we first must know the type of employee to perform a proper earnings calculation. By raising an exception in the body of the method, we ensure that each class that inherits from **Employee** must override method **earnings** with a more specific definition. The programmer never intends to call this method on an object of abstract base class **Employee**. If a derived class neglects to override **earnings** with an appropriate definition, the abstract method in the base class raises an exception when the program attempts to call **earnings** from the derived class. Similar to **earnings**, the **Employee** constructor raises an exception if a program attempts to create an object of the abstract base class. Lines 11–13 determine whether **self** is an object of class **Employee** and, if so, raise an appropriate exception.

Class **Boss** (lines 37–54) derives from class **Employee**. The **Boss**'s methods include a constructor (lines 40–44), the overridden **earnings** method (lines 46–49) and an **__str__** method (lines 51–54). The constructor (method **__init__**) takes a first name, a last name and a weekly salary as arguments and passes the first and last names to the **Employee** constructor to initialize the **firstName** and **lastName** members of the base-class part of the derived-class object. Method **earnings** performs the **Boss**-specific earnings calculations. Method **__str__** creates a string with the type and name of the employee.

Class **CommissionWorker** (lines 56–77) derives from class **Employee**. The methods include a constructor (lines 59–66), the overridden **earnings** method (lines 68–71) and an **__str__** method (lines 73–77). The constructor takes a first name, a last name, a salary, a commission and a quantity of items sold as arguments and passes the first and last names to the **Employee** constructor. Method **earnings** performs the

CommissionWorker-specific earnings calculations. Method **__str__** creates a string with the type and name of the employee.

```
1   # Fig 9.9: fig09_09.py
2   # Creating a class hierarchy with an abstract base class.
3
4   class Employee:
5      """Abstract base class Employee"""
6
7      def __init__( self, first, last ):
8         """Employee constructor, takes first name and last name.
9         NOTE: Cannot create object of class Employee."""
10
11        if self.__class__ == Employee:
12           raise NotImplementedError, \
13              "Cannot create object of class Employee"
14
15        self.firstName = first
16        self.lastName = last
17
18     def __str__( self ):
19        """String representation of Employee"""
20
21        return "%s %s" % ( self.firstName, self.lastName )
22
23     def _checkPositive( self, value ):
24        """Utility method to ensure a value is positive"""
25
26        if value < 0:
27           raise ValueError, \
28              "Attribute value (%s) must be positive" % value
29        else:
30           return value
31
32     def earnings( self ):
33        """Abstract method; derived classes must override"""
34
35        raise NotImplementedError, "Cannot call abstract method"
36   class Boss( Employee ):
37      """Boss class, inherits from Employee"""
38
39
40      def __init__( self, first, last, salary ):
41         """Boss constructor, takes first and last names and salary"""
42
43         Employee.__init__( self, first, last )
44         self.weeklySalary = self._checkPositive( float( salary ) )
45
46      def earnings( self ):
47         """Compute the Boss's pay"""
48
49         return self.weeklySalary
```

Fig. 9.9   Abstract class-based hierarchy. (Part 1 of 3.)

```
50
51      def __str__( self ):
52          """String representation of Boss"""
53
54          return "%17s: %s" % ( "Boss", Employee.__str__( self ) )
55
56  class CommissionWorker( Employee ):
57      """CommissionWorker class, inherits from Employee"""
58
59      def __init__( self, first, last, salary, commission, quantity ):
60          """CommissionWorker constructor, takes first and last names,
61          salary, commission and quantity"""
62
63          Employee.__init__( self, first, last )
64          self.salary = self._checkPositive( float( salary ) )
65          self.commission = self._checkPositive( float( commission ) )
66          self.quantity = self._checkPositive( quantity )
67
68      def earnings( self ):
69          """Compute the CommissionWorker's pay"""
70
71          return self.salary + self.commission * self.quantity
72
73      def __str__( self ):
74          """String representation of CommissionWorker"""
75
76          return "%17s: %s" % ( "Commission Worker",
77              Employee.__str__( self ) )
78
79  class PieceWorker( Employee ):
80      """PieceWorker class, inherits from Employee"""
81
82      def __init__( self, first, last, wage, quantity ):
83          """PieceWorker constructor, takes first and last names, wage
84          per piece and quantity"""
85
86          Employee.__init__( self, first, last )
87          self.wagePerPiece = self._checkPositive( float( wage ) )
88          self.quantity = self._checkPositive( quantity )
89
90      def earnings( self ):
91          """Compute PieceWorker's pay"""
92
93          return self.quantity * self.wagePerPiece
94
95      def __str__( self ):
96          """String representation of PieceWorker"""
97
98          return "%17s: %s" % ( "Piece Worker",
99              Employee.__str__( self) )
100
101 class HourlyWorker( Employee ):
102     """HourlyWorker class, inherits from Employee"""
```

Fig. 9.9   Abstract class-based hierarchy. (Part 2 of 3.)

```
103
104    def __init__( self, first, last, wage, hours ):
105        """HourlyWorker constructor, takes first and last names,
106        wage per hour and hours worked"""
107
108        Employee.__init__( self, first, last )
109        self.wage = self._checkPositive( float( wage ) )
110        self.hours = self._checkPositive( float( hours ) )
111
112    def earnings( self ):
113        """Compute HourlyWorker's pay"""
114
115        if self.hours <= 40:
116            return self.wage * self.hours
117        else:
118            return 40 * self.wage + ( self.hours - 40 ) *\
119                self.wage * 1.5
120
121    def __str__( self ):
122        """String representation of HourlyWorker"""
123
124        return "%17s: %s" % ( "Hourly Worker",
125            Employee.__str__( self ) )
126
127 # main program
128
129 # create list of Employees
130 employees = [ Boss( "John", "Smith", 800.00 ),
131               CommissionWorker( "Sue", "Jones", 200.0, 3.0, 150 ),
132               PieceWorker( "Bob", "Lewis", 2.5, 200 ),
133               HourlyWorker( "Karen", "Price", 13.75, 40 ) ]
134
135 # print Employee and compute earnings
136 for employee in employees:
137    print "%s earned $%.2f" % ( employee, employee.earnings() )
```

```
            Boss: John Smith earned $800.00
Commission Worker: Sue Jones earned $650.00
    Piece Worker: Bob Lewis earned $500.00
  Hourly Worker: Karen Price earned $550.00
```

Fig. 9.9   Abstract class-based hierarchy. (Part 3 of 3.)

Class **PieceWorker** (lines 79–99) derives from class **Employee**. The methods include a constructor (lines 82–88), the overridden **earnings** method (lines 90–93), and an **__str__** method (lines 95–99). The constructor takes a first name, a last name, a wage per piece and a quantity of items produced as arguments and passes the first and last names to the **Employee** constructor. Method **earnings** performs the **PieceWorker**-specific earnings calculations. Method **__str__** method creates a string with the type and name of the employee.

Class **HourlyWorker** (lines 101–125) derives from class **Employee**. The methods include a constructor (lines 104–110), the overridden **earnings** method (lines 112–119), and an **__str__** method (lines 121–125). The constructor takes a first name, a last name, a wage and the number of hours worked as arguments and passes the first and last names to the **Employee** constructor. Method **earnings** performs the **HourlyWorker**-specific earnings calculations.

The driver program is shown in lines 127–137. We create a list of four concrete objects of class **Employee**—an object of class **Boss**, an object of class **CommissionWorker**, an object of class **PieceWorker** and an object of class **HourlyWorker**. Lines 136–137 iterate over the list of objects of class **Employee** and call method **earnings** for each object in the list. This technique—generically processing a list of objects of various classes—is possible because of Python's inherent *polymorphic* behavior, a topic we discuss in the next section.

9.11 Polymorphism

Python enables *polymorphism*—the ability for objects of different classes related by inheritance to respond differently to the same message (i.e., method call). The same message sent to many different types of objects takes on "many forms"—hence the term polymorphism. If, for example, class **Rectangle** is derived from class **Quadrilateral**, then a **Rectangle** *is a* more specific version of a **Quadrilateral**. An operation (such as calculating the perimeter or the area) that can be performed on an object of class **Quadrilateral** also can be performed on an object of class **Rectangle**. Python is inherently polymorphic because the language is "dynamically typed." This means that Python determines at runtime whether an object defines a method or contains an attribute. If so, Python calls the appropriate method or accesses the appropriate attribute. Also, Python's dynamic typing enables programs to perform generic processing on objects of classes that are not related by inheritance. If the objects in a list all provide the same operations (e.g., all the objects define a certain method), then a program can process a list of those objects generically. The term polymorphism normally refers to the behavior of objects of classes related by inheritance, so we discuss polymorphic behavior in the context of class hierarchies in which all the classes in the hierarchy provide a common interface.

Consider the following example using the **Employee** base class and **HourlyWorker** derived class of Fig. 9.9. Our **Employee** base class and **HourlyWorker** derived class each define their own **__str__** methods. Calling the **__str__** method through an **Employee** reference invokes **Employee.__str__**, and calling the **__str__** method through an **HourlyWorker** reference invokes **HourlyWorker.__str__**. The base-class **__str__** method also is available to the derived class. To call the base-class **__str__** method for a derived-class object, the method must be called explicitly as follows

```
Employee.__str__( hourlyReference )
```

This specifies that the base-class **__str__** should be called explicitly, using **hourlyReference** as the object reference argument.

Through polymorphism, one method call can cause different actions to occur depending on the class of the object receiving the call. This gives the programmer tremendous expressive capability.

Software Engineering Observation 9.7

With polymorphism, the programmer can deal in generalities and let the execution-time environment concern itself with the specifics. The programmer can command a wide variety of objects to behave in manners appropriate to those objects without even knowing the types of those objects.

Software Engineering Observation 9.8

Polymorphism promotes extensibility: Software written to invoke polymorphic behavior is written independently of the types of the objects to which messages are sent. Thus, new types of objects that can respond to existing messages can be added into such a system without modifying the base system.

Software Engineering Observation 9.9

An abstract class defines an interface for the various members of a class hierarchy. The abstract class contains methods that will be defined in the derived classes. All methods in the hierarchy can use this same interface through polymorphism.

Let us consider applications of polymorphism. A screen manager needs to display many objects of different classes, including new types that will be added to the system even after the screen manager is written. The system may need to display various shapes (i.e., base class is **Shape**) such as squares, circles, triangles, rectangles, points, lines and the like (each shape class is derived from the base class **Shape**). The screen manager uses base-class references (to **Shape**) to manage all the objects to be displayed. To draw any object (regardless of the level at which that object appears in the inheritance hierarchy), the screen manager simply sends a **draw** message to the object. Method **draw** has been overridden in each of the derived classes. Each object of class **Shape** knows how to draw itself. The screen manager does not have to worry about what type each object is or whether the object is of a type the screen manager has seen before—the screen manager simply tells each object to **draw** itself.

Polymorphism is particularly effective for implementing layered software systems. In operating systems, for example, each type of physical device may operate differently from the others. Regardless of this, commands to *read* or *write* data from and to devices can have a certain uniformity. The *write* message sent to a device-driver object needs to be interpreted specifically in the context of that device driver and how that device driver manipulates devices of a specific type. However, the *write* call itself is really no different from the *write* to any other device in the system—it simply places some number of bytes from memory onto that device. An object-oriented operating system might use an abstract base class to provide an interface appropriate for all device drivers. Then, through inheritance from that abstract base class, derived classes are formed that all operate similarly. The capabilities (i.e., the interface) offered by the device drivers are provided as methods in the abstract base class. Implementations of these methods are provided in the derived classes that correspond to the specific types of device drivers.

With polymorphic programming, a program might walk through a container, such as a list of objects from various levels of a class hierarchy. For example, a list of objects of class **TwoDimensionalShape** could contain objects from the derived classes **Square**, **Circle**, **Triangle**, **Rectangle**, **Line**, etc. Sending a message to draw each object in the list would, using polymorphism, draw the correct picture on the screen. This example of polymorphic programming highlights the benefits of a naturally polymorphic language like Python, for building large, layered systems.

9.12 Classes and Python 2.2

In versions of Python before 2.2, classes and types were two distinct programming elements. The differences between types and classes contradicts the notion that classes *are* programmer-defined types. Many Python programmers, as well as the developers of the language also disliked the limitations of this needless difference between classes and types. For example, because types are not classes, programmers cannot inherit from built-in types to take advantage of Python's high-level data manipulation capabilities provided by lists, dictionaries and other objects.

Beginning with Python 2.2, the nature and behavior of classes will change, to remove the difference between types and classes. In all future 2.x releases, a programmer can distinguish between two kinds of classes—so-called "classic" classes that behave in the same manner as the classes presented earlier in this chapter and the two preceding chapters, and "new" classes that exhibit new behavior. Python 2.2 provides type **object** to define new classes. Any class that directly or indirectly inherits from **object** exhibits all the behaviors defined for a new class, which include many advanced object-oriented features. The remainder of this section overviews some of these features in the context of live-code examples.

9.12.1 Static Methods

In Python 2.2 all classes (not only classes that inherit from **object**) can define *static methods*. A static method can be called by a client of the class, even if no objects of the class exist. Typically, a static method is a utility method of a class that does not require an object of the class to execute. Figure 9.10 contains an example in which we redefine class **Employee** to provide information about the employee's working conditions. In this example, employees work in a small office—only 10 employees can work in the office comfortably. If more than 10 employees are working in the office, it becomes too crowded and the employees are uncomfortable. Class **Employee** maintains a class attribute **numberOfEmployees** that stores the number of objects of class **Employee** that have been instantiated. The class also defines static method **isCrowded**, which determines whether the employees are working in overcrowded conditions.

Lines 4–58 contain the class **Employee** definition. The class defines two class attributes—**numberOfEmployees**, which is the number of objects of class **Employee** that have been created; and **maxEmployees**, the maximum number of employees that can work in the office comfortably.

Method **isCrowded** (lines 10–13) returns true if the number of existing objects of class **Employee** is greater than the maximum number of employees that can work in the office comfortably. The method accesses class attributes **numberOfEmployees** and **maxEmployees** through the class name (**Employee**). Line 16 specifies that method **isCrowded** is a static method for class **Employee**. A class designates a method as static by passing the method's name to built-in function ***staticmethod*** and binding a name to the value returned from the function call. Static methods differ from regular methods because, when a program calls a static method, Python does not pass the object-reference argument to the method. Therefore, a static method does not specify **self** as the first argument. This allows a static method to be called even if no objects of the class exist.

```
1   # Fig. 9.10: EmployeeStatic.py
2   # Class Employee with a static method.
3
4   class Employee:
5      """Employee class with static method isCrowded"""
6
7      numberOfEmployees = 0   # number of Employees created
8      maxEmployees = 10   # maximum number of comfortable employees
9
10     def isCrowded():
11        """Static method returns true if the employees are crowded"""
12
13        return Employee.numberOfEmployees > Employee.maxEmployees
14
15     # create static method
16     isCrowded = staticmethod( isCrowded )
17
18     def __init__( self, firstName, lastName ):
19        """Employee constructor, takes first name and last name"""
20
21        self.first = firstName
22        self.last = lastName
23        Employee.numberOfEmployees += 1
24
25     def __del__( self ):
26        """Employee destructor"""
27
28        Employee.numberOfEmployees -= 1
29
30     def __str__( self ):
31        """String representation of Employee"""
32
33        return "%s %s" % ( self.first, self.last )
34
35   # main program
36   def main():
37      answers = [ "No", "Yes" ]   # responses to isCrowded
38
39      employeeList = []   # list of objects of class Employee
40
41      # call static method using class
42      print "Employees are crowded?",
43      print answers[ Employee.isCrowded() ]
44
45      print "\nCreating 11 objects of class Employee..."
46
47      # create 11 objects of class Employee
48      for i in range( 11 ):
49         employeeList.append( Employee( "John", "Doe" + str( i ) ) )
50
51         # call static method using object
52         print "Employees are crowded?",
53         print answers[ employeeList[ i ].isCrowded() ]
```

Fig. 9.10 Static methods—class **Employee**. (Part 1 of 2.)

```
54
55      print "\nRemoving one employee..."
56      del employeeList[ 0 ]
57
58      print "Employees are crowded?", answers[ Employee.isCrowded() ]
59
60  if __name__ == "__main__":
61      main()
```

```
Employees are crowded? No

Creating 11 objects of class Employee...
Employees are crowded? No
Employees are crowded? No
Employees are crowded? No
Employees are crowded? No
Employees are crowded? No
Employees are crowded? No
Employees are crowded? No
Employees are crowded? No
Employees are crowded? No
Employees are crowded? No
Employees are crowded? Yes

Removing one employee...
Employees are crowded? No
```

Fig. 9.10 Static methods—class **Employee**. (Part 2 of 2.)

Method __init__ (lines 18–23) takes two arguments that correspond to the employee's first and last name. The method also increments the value of **Employee** class attribute **numberOfEmployees**. Method __del__ (lines 25–28) decrements the value of **Employee** class attribute **numberOfEmployees**. Method __str__ (lines 30–33) simply returns a string that contains the employee's first and last name.

Static methods can be called either by using the class name in which the method is defined or by using the name of an object of that class. Function **main** (lines 36–58) demonstrates the ways in which a client program can call a static method. Variable **answers** (line 37) is a list that contains the possible answers (**"Yes"** or **"No"**) to the question, "Are the employees crowded?" Line 43 calls static method **isCrowded** using the class name (**Employee**). The method returns 0, because no objects of the class have been created. Lines 48–53 contain a **for** loop that creates 11 objects of class **Employee** and adds each object to list **employeeList**. For each object, the program calls static method **isCrowded** using the newest object of that class. The program prints **"Yes"** in response to the eleventh call to **isCrowded**, because the number of existing **Employees** (class attribute **numberOfEmployees**) is greater than the maximum number that can work in the office comfortably (class attribute **maxEmployees**). Line 56 deletes one of the objects from **employeeList**, which invokes that object's destructor. Line 58 calls static method **isCrowded** once more to demonstrate that the number of employees has dropped to an acceptable level.

Static methods are crucial in languages like Java which require the programmer to place all program code in a class definition. In these languages, programmers often define classes that contain only static utility methods. Clients of the class can then call the static utility methods, much in the same way the Python programs invoke functions defined in a module. In Python, static methods enable programmers to define a class interface more precisely. When a method of a class does not require an object of the class to perform its task, the programmer designates that method as static.

9.12.2 Inheriting from Built-in Types

The goal of the new class behavior is to remove the separation that existed between Python types and classes before version 2.2. The type-class unification enables programmers to define a derived class that inherits from one of Python's built-in types (e.g., integer, string and list) in the same manner that a derived class inherits from any base class. In Python 2.2, the interpreter places a reference to each type in the **__builtin__** namespace. Figure 9.11 lists common built-in type names from which a programmer-defined class can inherit. A programmer-defined class inherits from a built-in type by placing the type's name in the class's base-class list.

Figure 9.12 redefines class **SingleList**—from Section 8.12—a list that contains only unique values. The previous definition of **SingleList** (Chapter 8) defined every method for class **SingleList** that should be exposed to the client. In this example, **SingleList** inherits from base-class **list** and overrides only those methods that should provide customized behaviors in class **SingleList**. The class inherits the other methods of base-class **list**, so the programmer does not need to define the remaining **list** methods to include them as part of the new class's interface.

Class **SingleList** (Fig. 9.12) inherits from base-class **list** by placing the name **list** in the parentheses that follow the class name. Every built-in type (except **object**) inherits from **object**, so classes that inherit from built-in types (including **SingleList**)

Type name	Python data type
complex	complex number
dict	dictionary
file	file
float	floating point
int	integer
list	list
long	long integer
object	base object (*Note:* Inherit from **object** to create a "new" class.)
str	string
tuple	tuple
unicode	unicode string (*Note:* see Appendix F for information on Unicode.)

Fig. 9.11   Built-in type names in Python 2.2.

display the behaviors of "new" classes. This definition for class **SingleList** differs from our previous definition, because this definition does not maintain as an attribute an internal list of values. **SingleList** is a **list**, so all methods of the class can treat the object reference as a **list** object—an extra attribute is not necessary. Class **SingleList**'s constructor (lines 7–14) first calls the base-class constructor, to initialize the list. If the client passes an initial list value to the class's constructor, line 14 calls **SingleList** method **merge** (discussed shortly) to add unique values from the list argument to the empty list initialized by the base-class constructor.

```python
1   # Fig 9.12: NewList.py
2   # Definition for class SingleList,
3
4   class SingleList( list ):
5
6       # constructor
7       def __init__( self, initialList = None ):
8           """SingleList constructor, takes initial list value.
9           New SingleList object contains only unique values"""
10
11          list.__init__( self )
12
13          if initialList:
14              self.merge( initialList )
15
16      # utility method
17      def _raiseIfNotUnique( self, value ):
18          """Utility method to raise an exception if value
19          is in list"""
20
21          if value in self:
22              raise ValueError, \
23                  "List already contains value %s" % value
24
25      # overloaded sequence operation
26      def __setitem__( self, subscript, value ):
27          """Sets value of particular index. Raises exception if list
28          already contains value"""
29
30          # terminate method on non-unique value
31          self._raiseIfNotUnique( value )
32
33          return list.__setitem__( self, subscript, value )
34
35      # overloaded mathematical operators
36      def __add__( self, other ):
37          """Overloaded addition operator, returns new SingleList"""
38
39          return SingleList( list.__add__( self, other ) )
40
```

Fig. 9.12 Inheriting from built-in type **list**—class **SingleList**. (Part 1 of 3.)

```
41      def __radd__( self, otherList ):
42          """Overloaded right addition"""
43
44          return SingleList( list.__add__( other, self ) )
45
46      def __iadd__( self, other ):
47          """Overloaded augmented assignment. Raises exception if list
48          already contains any of the values in otherList"""
49
50          for value in other:
51              self.append( value )
52
53          return self
54
55      def __mul__( self, value ):
56          """Overloaded multiplication operator. Cannot use
57          multiplication on SingleLists"""
58
59          raise ValueError, "Cannot repeat values in SingleList"
60
61      # __rmul__ and __imul__ have same behavior as __mul__
62      __rmul__ = __imul__ = __mul__
63
64      # overridden list methods
65      def insert( self, subscript, value ):
66          """Inserts value at specified subscript. Raises exception if
67          list already contains value"""
68
69          # terminate method on non-unique value
70          self._raiseIfNotUnique( value )
71
72          return list.insert( self, subscript, value )
73
74      def append( self, value ):
75          """Appends value to end of list. Raises exception if list
76          already contains value"""
77
78          # terminate method on non-unique value
79          self._raiseIfNotUnique( value )
80
81          return list.append( self, value )
82
83      def extend( self, other ):
84          """Adds to list the values from another list. Raises
85          exception if list already contains value"""
86
87          for value in other:
88              self.append( value )
89
90      # new SingleList method
91      def merge( self, other ):
92          """Merges list with unique values from other list"""
93
```

Fig. 9.12 Inheriting from built-in type **list**—class **SingleList**. (Part 2 of 3.)

```
94          # add unique values from other
95          for value in other:
96
97              if value not in self:
98                  list.append( self, value )
```

Fig. 9.12 Inheriting from built-in type **list**—class **SingleList**. (Part 3 of 3.)

Lines 17–23 define utility method **_raiseIfNotUnique**. This method takes as an argument a potential value to add to the list and raises an exception if the list already contains the value. All **SingleList** methods that add new elements to a list first call method **_raiseIfNotUnique**, to ensure that the client inserts only unique values in the list. Typically, a client program contains code that detects the exception, to determine whether the value was inserted successfully. [*Note*: We discuss how to detect exceptions in Chapter 12, Exception Handling.]

Method **__setitem__** (lines 26–33) executes when a client assigns a value to a particular index. The method first calls utility method **_raiseIfNotUnique** with the value to insert. If the value already is in the list, the utility method raises an exception, method **__setitem__** terminates and the value is not added to the list. If the utility method does not raise an exception, line 33 calls **__setitem__** in the base class, which either assigns the value at the specified index or, if the index is out-of-bounds, raises an exception.

```
1   # Fig. 9.13: fig09_13.py
2   # Program that uses SingleList
3
4   from NewList import SingleList
5
6   duplicates = [ 1, 2, 2, 3, 4, 3, 6, 9 ]
7   print "List with duplicates is:", duplicates
8
9   single = SingleList( duplicates )  # create SingleList object
10  print "SingleList, created from duplicates, is:", single
11  print "The length of the list is:", len( single )
12
13  # search for values in list
14  print "\nThe value 2 appears %d times in list" % single.count( 2 )
15  print "The value 5 appears %d times in list" % single.count( 5 )
16  print "The index of 9 in the list is:", single.index( 9 )
17
18  if 4 in single:
19      print "The value 4 was found in list"
20
21  # add values to list
22  single.append( 10 )
23  single += [ 20 ]
24  single.insert( 3, "hello" )
25  single.extend( [ -1, -2, -3 ] )
26  single.merge( [ "hello", 2, 100 ] )
27  print "\nThe list, after adding elements is:", single
```

Fig. 9.13 Inheriting from built-in type **list**—**fig09_13.py**. (Part 1 of 2.)

```
28
29   # remove values from list
30   popValue = single.pop()
31   print "\nRemoved", popValue, "from list:", single
32   single.append( popValue )
33   print "Added", popValue, "back to end of list:", single
34
35   # slice list
36   print "\nThe value of single[ 1:4 ] is:", single[ 1:4 ]
```

```
List with duplicates is: [1, 2, 2, 3, 4, 3, 6, 9]
SingleList, created from duplicates, is: [1, 2, 3, 4, 6, 9]
The length of the list is: 6

The value 2 appears 1 times in list
The value 5 appears 0 times in list
The index of 9 in the list is: 5
The value 4 was found in list

The list, after adding elements is: [1, 2, 3, 'hello', 4, 6, 9, 10, 20,
-1, -2, -3, 100]

Removed 100 from list: [1, 2, 3, 'hello', 4, 6, 9, 10, 20, -1, -2, -3]
Added 100 back to end of list: [1, 2, 3, 'hello', 4, 6, 9, 10, 20, -1,
-2, -3, 100]

The value of single[ 1:4 ] is: [2, 3, 'hello']
```

Fig. 9.13   Inheriting from built-in type `list`—`fig09_13.py`. (Part 2 of 2.)

Lines 36–44 overload the **+** operator for addition when a **SingleList** appears to the left or right of the operator. Methods **__add__** and **__radd__** each return a new object of class **SingleList** that is initialized with the elements of the two arguments passed to either method. This operation has the same effect as merging two lists into one list of unique values. Lines 46–53 overload the augmented assignment **+=** symbol. The method performs its operation in-place (i.e., on the object reference itself). For each value in the right-hand operand, method **__iadd__** calls **SingleList** method **append**, which either inserts a new value at the end of the list or if the list already contains that value, raises an exception. Python expects an overloaded, augmented-assignment method to return an object of the class for which the method is defined, so line 53 returns the augmented object reference. Lines 55–62 overload the multiplication operation (i.e., list repetition) for objects of class **SingleList**. By definition, a **SingleList** cannot contain more than one occurrence of any value, so method **__mul__** raises an exception if the client attempts such an operation. Line 62 binds the names for methods **__rmul__** (right multiplication) and **__imul__** (augmented assignment multiplication) to the method defined for **__mul__**; when clients invoke these operations, the corresponding methods also raise exceptions.

Lines 65–88 define methods **insert**, **append** and **extend** for adding values to a list. Methods **insert** and **append** first invoke utility method **_raiseIfNotUnique**— to prevent the client from adding duplicate values to the list—before invoking the base-class version of the corresponding method. Method **extend** uses method **append** to add elements from another list to the reference object.

Method **merge** (lines 91–98) provides clients the ability to merge a **SingleList** with another list that possibly contains duplicate values. Method **merge** provides the same behavior that base-class **list** provides with method **extend**. However, method **extend** in the derived class raises an exception if the client attempts to extend the **SingleList** with a list that would insert duplicate values in the **SingleList**. By providing method **merge**, we give clients a way to extend a **SingleList** without raising an exception. The method adds only unique values to the **SingleList**, by calling **list.append** for every unique value in the client-supplied list.

The driver program of Fig. 9.13 uses both **SingleList**-specific functionality and functionality inherited from base-class **list**. Lines 6–7 create and print list **duplicates**, which contains duplicate values. Line 9 creates an object of class **SingleList**, which passes **duplicates** to the constructor. The new object—**single**—of class **SingleList** contains one of each of the values from list **duplicates**. The remainder of the driver program demonstrates **SingleList**'s capabilities. Line 10 prints **single**, which implicitly invokes the object's base-class **__str__** method. Line 11 passes **single** to function **len**, which calls the object's base-class **__len__** method to determine the number of elements in the list.

Lines 14–16 call **single**'s methods **count** and **index** to determine whether certain elements exist in the list and to locate an element in the list, respectively. Line 18 uses keyword **in**, which implicitly invokes the base-class **__contains__** method, to determine whether the list contains the integer element 4. Lines 22–25 call overridden **SingleList** methods to add elements to the list. Line 22 calls method **append** to add an element to the list. Line 23 appends an element with symbol **+=**, which implicitly invokes the object's **__iadd__** method. Line 24 calls method **insert** to insert the element **"hello"** at index 3. Line 25 calls method **extend** to add elements from another list to **single**. All these methods add unique elements to the list; if one of the method calls attempted to add a duplicate value to the list, the method would raise an exception (as shown in Fig. 9.14). The call to method **merge** in line 26 merges the values in **single** with values from another list. Notice, from the output, that the effect of call in line 26 is to add only the integer element 100, because this element is the only value that **single** did not yet contain.

Lines 30–33 of Fig. 9.13 remove an element from the list, add the element back in to the list and print the results. These statements demonstrate that the client can remove a value from the list, using base-class method **pop**, and that reinserting the removed value does not raise an exception. Line 36 demonstrates that class **SingleList** inherits slicing capabilities from base-class **list**. This underscores the benefit of inheritance-based software reuse. In the previous definition of class **SingleList**, we would have had to program this capability explicitly. In this version, we simply inherit the capability from the base class.

9.12.3 __getattribute__ Method

In Chapter 8, Customizing Classes, we discussed method **__getattr__**, which executes when a client attempts to access an object attribute and that attribute name is not in the object's **__dict__**, the **__dict__** of the object's class or the **__dict__** of the class's di-

```
Python 2.2b2 (#26, Nov 16 2001, 11:44:11) [MSC 32 bit (Intel)] on win32
Type "help", "copyright", "credits" or "license" for more information.
>>>
>>> from NewList import SingleList
>>> single = SingleList( [ 1, 2, 3 ] )
>>>
>>> single.append( 1 )
Traceback (most recent call last):
  File "<stdin>", line 1, in ?
  File "NewList.py", line 79, in append
    self._raiseIfNotUnique( value )
  File "NewList.py", line 22, in _raiseIfNotUnique
    raise ValueError, \
ValueError: List already contains value 1
>>>
>>> single += [ 2 ]
Traceback (most recent call last):
  File "<stdin>", line 1, in ?
  File "NewList.py", line 51, in __iadd__
    self.append( value )
  File "NewList.py", line 79, in append
    self._raiseIfNotUnique( value )
  File "NewList.py", line 22, in _raiseIfNotUnique
    raise ValueError, \
ValueError: List already contains value 2
>>>
>>> single.insert( 0, 1 )
Traceback (most recent call last):
  File "<stdin>", line 1, in ?
  File "NewList.py", line 70, in insert
    self._raiseIfNotUnique( value )
  File "NewList.py", line 22, in _raiseIfNotUnique
    raise ValueError, \
ValueError: List already contains value 1
>>>
>>> single.extend( [ 3, 4 ] )
Traceback (most recent call last):
  File "<stdin>", line 1, in ?
  File "NewList.py", line 88, in extend
    self.append( value )
  File "NewList.py", line 79, in append
    self._raiseIfNotUnique( value )
  File "NewList.py", line 22, in _raiseIfNotUnique
    raise ValueError, \
ValueError: List already contains value 3
```

Fig. 9.14   Class **SingleList**—inserting non-unique values.

rect and indirect base classes. Classes that inherit from base-class **object** also can define
method __*getattribute*__, which executes for every attribute access. Figure 9.15 contains a simple example. We define class **DemostrateAccess** (lines 4–29), which inherits
from base-class **object** and provides both __**getattr**__ and __**getattribute**__
methods. The constructor creates one attribute—**value**—and initializes it to 1.

Method **__getattribute__** (lines 13–19) executes every time the client attempts to access an object's attribute through the dot (**.**) access operator. The method prints a line indicating that the method is executing and a line that displays the name of the attribute that the client is attempting to access. Line 19 returns the result of calling base-class method **__getattribute__**, passing the specified attribute name. Method **__getattribute__** in a derived class must call the base-class version of the method to retrieve an attribute's value, because attempting to access the attribute's value through the object's **__dict__** would result in another call to **__getattribute__**.

Common Programming Error 9.5

To ensure proper attribute access, a derived-class version of method **__getattribute__** *should call the base-class version of the method. Attempting to return the attribute's value by accessing the object's* **__dict__** *causes infinite recursion.*

Lines 21–29 define method **__getattr__**, which performs the same behavior as in "classic" classes; namely, the method executes when the client attempts to access an attribute that the object's **__dict__** does not contain. The method displays output that indicates the method is executing and provides the name of the attribute that the client attempted to access (lines 24–26). Lines 28–29 raise an exception to preserve Python's default behavior of raising an exception when a client accesses a nonexistent attribute.

```
1   # Fig. 9.15: fig09_15.py
2   # Class that defines method __getattribute__
3
4   class DemonstrateAccess( object ):
5      """Class to demonstrate when method __getattribute__ executes"""
6
7      def __init__( self ):
8         """DemonstrateAccess constructor, initializes attribute
9         value"""
10
11        self.value = 1
12
13     def __getattribute__( self, name ):
14        """Executes for every attribute access"""
15
16        print "__getattribute__ executing..."
17        print "\tClient attempt to access attribute:", name
18
19        return object.__getattribute__( self, name )
20
21     def __getattr__( self, name ):
22        """Executes when client access attribute not in __dict__"""
23
24        print "__getattr__ executing..."
25        print "\tClient attempt to access non-existent attribute:",\
26           name
27
28        raise AttributeError, "Object has no attribute %s" \
29           % name
```

Fig. 9.15 **__getattribute__** method and attribute access. (Part 1 of 2.)

```
Python 2.2b2 (#26, Nov 16 2001, 11:44:11) [MSC 32 bit (Intel)] on win32
Type "help", "copyright", "credits" or "license" for more information.
>>>
>>> from fig09_15 import DemonstrateAccess
>>> access = DemonstrateAccess()
>>>
>>> access.value
__getattribute__ executing...
        Client attempt to access attribute: value
1
>>>
>>> access.novalue
__getattribute__ executing...
        Client attempt to access attribute: novalue
__getattr__ executing...
        Client attempt to access non-existent attribute: novalue
Traceback (most recent call last):
  File "<stdin>", line 1, in ?
  File "fig09_15.py", line 28, in __getattr__
    raise AttributeError, "Object has no attribute %s" \
AttributeError: Object has no attribute novalue
```

Fig. 9.15   **__getattribute__** method and attribute access. (Part 2 of 2.)

The interactive session in the output box for Fig. 9.15 demonstrates when methods **__getattribute__** and **__getattr__** execute. We first create an object of class **DemonstrateAccess**, then access attribute **value**, using the dot access operator. The output indicates that method **__getattribute__** executes in response to the attribute access; Python displays the return value (**1**) in the interactive session. Next, the program accesses attribute **novalue**, a nonexistent attribute. Method **__getattribute__** executes first, because the method executes every time the client attempts to access an attribute. When the base-class version of the method determines that the object does not contain a **novalue** attribute, method **__getattr__** executes. The method raises an exception to indicate that the client has accessed a nonexistent attribute.

9.12.4 __slots__ Class Attribute

Python's dynamism enables programmers to write applications that can change as they execute. Often, this is useful for software development purposes. For example, during the development cycle, a graphical-application programmer might create software that enables the programmer to change the application's appearance (i.e., some of the application's code) without terminating the application. This technique also is valuable for applications like Web servers that must continue executing for long periods of time, but that may need to change periodically to incorporate new features. Dynamism also has drawbacks—usually dynamic applications or applications programmed in a dynamic language exhibit poorer performance than do their non-dynamic counterparts.

One side-effect of Python's dynamic nature is that a program can add attributes to an object's namespace after the object has been created. This practice sometimes can lead to unexpected results. For example, the programmer could incorrectly type an attribute name in an assignment statement. Rather than printing an error, such an assignment statement simply binds a new attribute name and value to the object, and the program continues executing. Python 2.2 allows new classes to define a __*slots*__ attribute listing the only attributes that objects of the class are allowed to have. Figure 9.16 presents two simplified definitions of a point—classes **PointWithoutSlots** and **PointWithSlots**. A program can add attributes to objects of class **PointWithoutSlots**, but cannot add attributes to objects of class **PointWithSlots**.

```
1   # Fig. 9.16: Slots.py
2   # Simple class with slots
3
4   class PointWithoutSlots:
5      """Programs can add attributes to objects of this class"""
6
7      def __init__( self, xValue = 0.0, yValue = 0.0 ):
8         """Constructor for PointWithoutSlots, initializes x- and
9         y-coordinates"""
10
11        self.x = float( xValue )
12        self.y = float( yValue )
13
14  class PointWithSlots( object ):
15     """Programs cannot add attributes to objects of this class"""
16
17     # PointWithSlots objects can contain only attributes x and y
18     __slots__ = [ "x", "y" ]
19
20     def __init__( self, xValue = 0.0, yValue = 0.0 ):
21        """Constructor for PointWithoutSlots, initializes x- and
22        y-coordinates"""
23
24        self.x = float( xValue )
25        self.y = float( yValue )
26
27  # main program
28  def main():
29     noSlots = PointWithoutSlots()
30     slots = PointWithSlots()
31
32     for point in [ noSlots, slots ]:
33        print "\nProcessing an object of class", point.__class__
34
35        print "The current value of point.x is:", point.x
36        newValue = float( raw_input( "Enter new x coordinate: " ) )
37        print "Attempting to set new x-coordinate value..."
38
39        # Logic error: create new attribute called X, instead of
40        # changing the value of attribute X
41        point.X = newValue
42
43        # output unchanged attribute x
44        print "The new value of point.x is:", point.x
```

Fig. 9.16 __**slots**__ attribute—specifying object attributes. (Part 1 of 2.)

```
45
46   if __name__ == "__main__":
47       main()
```

```
Processing an object of class __main__.PointWithoutSlots
The current value of point.x is: 0.0
Enter new x coordinate: 1.0
Attempting to set new x-coordinate value...
The new value of point.x is: 0.0

Processing an object of class <class '__main__.PointWithSlots'>
The current value of point.x is: 0.0
Enter new x coordinate: 1.0
Attempting to set new x-coordinate value...
Traceback (most recent call last):
  File "Slots.py", line 47, in ?
    main()
  File "Slots.py", line 41, in main
    point.X = newValue
AttributeError: 'PointWithSlots' object has no attribute 'X'
```

Fig. 9.16   **__slots__** attribute—specifying object attributes. (Part 2 of 2.)

The **PointWithoutSlots** definition (lines 4–12) simply defines a constructor (lines 7–12) that initializes the point's *x*- and *y*-coordinates. Class **PointWithSlots** (lines 14–25) inherits from base-class **object**, and defines an attribute **__slots__**—a list of attribute names that objects of the class may contain. When a new class defines the **__slots__** attribute, objects of the class can assign values only to attributes whose names appear in the **__slots__** list. If a client attempts to assign a value to an attribute whose name does not appear in **__slots__**, Python raises an exception.

Software Engineering Observation 9.10

If a new class defines attribute **__slots__***, but the class's constructor does not initialize the attributes' values, Python assigns **None** to each attribute in* **__slots__** *when an object of the class is created.*

Software Engineering Observation 9.11

A derived class inherits its base-class **__slots__** *attribute. However, if programs should not be allowed to add attributes to objects of the derived class, the derived class must define its own* **__slots__** *attribute. The derived-class* **__slots__** *contains only the allowed derived-class attribute names, but clients still can set values for attributes specified by the derived class's direct and indirect bases classes.*

The driver program (lines 28–44) demonstrates the difference between an object of a class that defines **__slots__** and an object of a class that does not define **__slots__**. Lines 29–30 create objects of classes **PointWithoutSlots** and **PointsWithSlots**, respectively. The **for** loop in lines 32–44 iterates over each object and attempts to replace the value of the object's **x** attribute with a user-supplied value, obtained in line 36. Line 41 contains a logic error—the program intends to modify the value of the object's **x** attribute, but mistakenly creates an attribute called **X** and assigns the user-entered value to the new attribute. For objects of class **PointWithoutSlots** (e.g., object **noSlots**), line 41 executes without raising an exception, and line 44 prints the unchanged value of attribute **x**. For objects of class **PointWithSlots** (e.g., **slots**), line 41 raises an exception, because the object's **__slots__** attribute does not contain the name **"X"**.

The example in Fig. 9.16 demonstrates one benefit of defining the **__slots__** attribute for new classes, namely preventing accidental attribute creation. Programs that use new classes also gain performance benefits, because Python knows in advance that programs cannot add new attributes to an object; therefore, Python can store and manipulate the objects in a more efficient manner. A disadvantage of **__slots__** is that experienced Python programmers sometimes expect the ability to add object attributes dynamically. Defining **__slots__** can inhibit programmers' abilities to create dynamic applications quickly.

9.12.5 Properties

Python's new classes can contain *properties* that describe object attributes. A program accesses an object's properties using object-attribute syntax. However, a class definition creates a property by specifying up to four components—a *get* method that executes when a program accesses the property's value, a *set* method that executes when a program sets the property's value, a *delete* method that executes when a program deletes the value (e.g., with keyword **del**) and a docstring that describes the property. The *get*, *set* and *delete* methods can perform the tasks that maintain an object's data in a consistent state. Thus, properties provide an additional way for programmers to control access to an object's data.

Figure 9.17 redefines class **Time**—the class previously used to demonstrate attribute access—to contain attributes **hour**, **minute** and **second** as properties. The constructor (lines 7–12) creates private attributes **__hour**, **__minute** and **__second**. Typically, classes that use properties define their attributes to be private, to hide the data from clients of the class. The clients of the class then access the public properties of that class, which *get* and *set* the values of the private attributes.

Method **deleteValue** (lines 20–23) raises an exception to prevent a client from deleting an attribute. We use this method to create properties that the client cannot delete. Each property (**hour**, **minute** and **second**) defines corresponding *get* and *set* methods. Each *get* method takes only the object reference as an argument and returns the property's value. Each *set* method takes two arguments—the object-reference argument and the new value for the property. Lines 25–32 define the *set* method (**setHour**) for the **hour** property. If the new value is within the appropriate range, the method assigns the new value to the property; otherwise, the method raises an exception. Method **getHour** (lines 34–37) is the **hour** property's *get* method, which simply returns the value of the corresponding private attribute (**__hour**).

```
1   # Fig. 9.17: TimeProperty.py
2   # Class Time with properties
3
4   class Time( object ):
5      """Class Time with hour, minute and second properties"""
6
```

Fig. 9.17   Properties—class **Time**. (Part 1 of 3.)

```
 7      def __init__( self, hourValue, minuteValue, secondValue ):
 8          """Time constructor, takes hour, minute and second"""
 9
10          self.__hour = hourValue
11          self.__minute = minuteValue
12          self.__second = secondValue
13
14      def __str__( self ):
15          """String representation of an object of class Time"""
16
17          return "%.2d:%.2d:%.2d" % \
18              ( self.__hour, self.__minute, self.__second )
19
20      def deleteValue( self ):
21          """Delete method for Time properties"""
22
23          raise TypeError, "Cannot delete attribute"
24
25      def setHour( self, value ):
26          """Set method for hour attribute"""
27
28          if 0 <= value < 24:
29              self.__hour = value
30          else:
31              raise ValueError, \
32                  "hour (%d) must be in range 0-23, inclusive" % value
33
34      def getHour( self ):
35          """Get method for hour attribute"""
36
37          return self.__hour
38
39      # create hour property
40      hour = property( getHour, setHour, deleteValue, "hour" )
41
42      def setMinute( self, value ):
43          """Set method for minute attribute"""
44
45          if 0 <= value < 60:
46              self.__minute = value
47          else:
48              raise ValueError, \
49                  "minute (%d) must be in range 0-59, inclusive" % value
50
51      def getMinute( self ):
52          """Get method for minute attribute"""
53
54          return self.__minute
55
56      # create minute property
57      minute = property( getMinute, setMinute, deleteValue, "minute" )
58
```

Fig. 9.17 Properties—class **Time**. (Part 2 of 3.)

```
59          def setSecond( self, value ):
60              """Set method for second attribute"""
61
62              if 0 <= value < 60:
63                  self.__second = value
64              else:
65                  raise ValueError, \
66                      "second (%d) must be in range 0-59, inclusive" % value
67
68          def getSecond( self ):
69              """Get method for second attribute"""
70
71              return self.__second
72
73      # create second property
74      second = property( getSecond, setSecond, deleteValue, "second" )
```

```
Python 2.2b2 (#26, Nov 16 2001, 11:44:11) [MSC 32 bit (Intel)] on win32
Type "help", "copyright", "credits" or "license" for more information.
>>>
>>> from TimeProperty import Time
>>>
>>> time1 = Time( 5, 27, 19 )
>>> print time1
05:27:19
>>> print time1.hour, time1.minute, time1.second
5 27 19
>>>
>>> time1.hour, time1.minute, time1.second  = 16, 1, 59
>>> print time1
16:01:59
>>>
>>> time1.hour = 25
Traceback (most recent call last):
  File "<stdin>", line 1, in ?
  File "TimeProperty.py", line 31, in setHour
    raise ValueError, \
ValueError: hour (25) must be in range 0-23, inclusive
>>>
>>> time1.minute = -3
Traceback (most recent call last):
  File "<stdin>", line 1, in ?
  File "TimeProperty.py", line 48, in setMinute
    raise ValueError, \
ValueError: minute (-3) must be in range 0-59, inclusive
>>>
>>> time1.second = 99
Traceback (most recent call last):
  File "<stdin>", line 1, in ?
  File "TimeProperty.py", line 65, in setSecond
    raise ValueError, \
ValueError: second (99) must be in range 0-59, inclusive
```

Fig. 9.17 Properties—class **Time**. (Part 3 of 3.)

Built-in function ***property*** (line 40) takes as arguments a *get* method, a *set* method, a *delete* method and a docstring and returns a property for the class. Line 40 creates the **hour** property by passing to function **property** methods **getHour**, **setHour** and **deleteValue** and the string **"hour"**. Clients access properties, using the dot (**.**) access operator. When the client uses a property as an *rvalue*, the property's *get* method executes. When the client uses the property as an *lvalue*, the property's *set* method executes. When the client deletes the property with keyword **del**, the property's *delete* method executes. The remainder of the class definition (lines 42–74) defines *get* and *set* methods for properties **minute** (created in line 57) and **second** (created in line 74).

Software Engineering Observation 9.12

*Function **property** does not require that the caller pass all four arguments. Instead, the caller can pass values for keyword arguments **fget**, **fset**, **fdel** and **doc** to specify the property's* get, set *and* delete *methods and the docstring, repsectively.*

The interactive session in Fig. 9.17 highlights the benefits of properties. A client of the class can access an object's attributes, using the dot access operator, but the class author also can ensure data integrity. Properties have added advantages over implementing methods **__setattr__**, **__getattr__** and **__delattr__**. For example, class authors can state explicitly the attributes for which the client may use the dot access notation. Additionally, the class author can write separate *get*, *set* and *delete* methods for each attribute, rather than using **if/else** logic to determine which attribute to access.

In this chapter, we discussed the mechanics of inheritance and how inheritance promotes software reuse and data abstraction. We discussed two examples of inheritance—one example of structural inheritance and one example of a class hierarchy headed by an abstract base class. We also introduced new object-oriented-programming features available in Python 2.2. We continued our discussion of data integrity by presenting properties—a feature that allows clients of the class to access data with the dot access operator and allows classes to maintain private data in a consistent state. Data hiding and data integrity are fundamental object-oriented software design principles. The topics discussed in this and the previous two chapters provide a solid foundation for programmers who want to build large, industrial-strength software systems in Python.

SUMMARY

- Inheritance is a form of software reusability in which new classes are created from existing classes by absorbing their attributes and behaviors and then overriding or embellishing these with capabilities the new classes require.

- When creating a new class, instead of writing completely new attributes and methods, the programmer can designate that the new class is to inherit the attributes and methods of a previously defined base class.

- The class that inherits from a base class is referred to as a derived class. Each derived class itself becomes a candidate to be a base class for some future derived class.

- With single inheritance, a class is derived from one base class.

- With multiple inheritance, a derived class inherits from multiple (possibly unrelated) base classes. Multiple inheritance can be complex and error prone.

- The real strength of inheritance comes from the ability to define in the derived class additions, replacements or refinements for the features inherited from the base class.

- With inheritance, every object of a derived class also may be treated as an object of that derived class's base class. However, the converse is not true—base-class objects are not objects of that base class's derived classes.

- With polymorphism, it is possible to design and implement systems that are more easily extensible. Programs can be written to process generically—as base-class objects—objects of all existing classes in a hierarchy.

- Polymorphism enables us to write programs in a general fashion to handle a wide variety of existing and yet-to-be-specified related classes.

- Object-oriented programming provides several ways of "seeing the forest through the trees"—a process called abstraction.

- "Is a" is inheritance. In an "is-a" relationship, an object of a derived-class type may also be treated as an object of the base-class type.

- "Has a" is composition. In a "has-a" relationship, an object *has* references to one or more objects of other classes as members.

- A derived class can access the attributes and methods of its base class. When a base-class member implementation is inappropriate for a derived class, that member can be overridden (i.e., replaced) in the derived class with an appropriate implementation.

- Inheritance forms tree-like hierarchical structures. A base class exists in a hierarchical relationship with its derived classes.

- Function **issubclass** takes two arguments that are classes and returns true if the first argument is a class that inherits from the second argument (or if the first argument is the same class as the second argument)

- Python provides a built-in function—**isinstance**—that determines whether an object is an object of a given class or of a subclass of that class.

- Parentheses, **()**, in the first line of the class definition indicates inheritance. The name of the base class (or base classes) is placed inside the parentheses.

- A direct base class of a derived class is explicitly listed inside parentheses when the derived class is defined.

- An indirect base class is not explicitly listed when the derived class is defined; rather the indirect base class is inherited from two or more levels up the class hierarchy.

- To initialize an object of a derived class, the derived-class constructor must call the base-class constructor.

- A bound method call is invoked by accessing the method name through an object. Python automatically inserts the object reference argument for bound method calls.

- An unbound method call is invoked by accessing the method through its class name then specifically passing an object.

- A class's __**bases**__ attribute is a tuple that contains references to each of the class's base classes.

- A derived class can override a base-class method by supplying a new version of that method with the same name. When that method is mentioned by name in the derived class, the derived-class version is automatically selected.

- A base class specifies commonality. In the object-oriented design process, the designer looks for commonality and "factors it out" to form base classes. Derived classes are then customized beyond the capabilities inherited from the base class.

- A program *uses* an object if the program simply calls a method of that object through a reference.

- An object is said to have a *knows a* relationship with a second object if the first object is aware of (i.e., has a reference to) the second object. This is sometimes called an association.

- There are cases in which it is useful to define classes for which the programmer never intends to create any objects. Such classes are called abstract classes.

- The sole purpose of an abstract class is to provide an appropriate base class from which classes may inherit interface and possibly implementation. Classes from which objects can be created are called concrete classes.

- Python does not provide a way to designate an abstract class. However, the programmer can implement an abstract class by raising an exception in the class's **__init__** method.

- Python is inherently polymorphic because the language is dynamically typed. This means that Python determines at runtime whether an object defines a method or contains an attribute and, if so, calls the appropriate method or accesses the appropriate attribute.

- Using polymorphism, one method call can cause different actions to occur depending on the class of the object receiving the call. This gives the programmer tremendous expressive capability.

- Beginning with Python 2.2, the nature and behavior of classes will change. In all future 2.x releases, a programmer can distinguish between two kinds of classes: "classic" classes and "new" classes. In Python 3.0, all classes will behave like "new" classes.

- Python 2.2 provides type **object** for defining "new" classes. Any class that inherits from **object** exhibits the new-class behaviors.

- "New" classes can define static methods. A static method can be called by a client of the class, even if no objects of the class exist.

- A class designates a method as static by passing the method's name to built-in function **staticmethod** and binding a name to the value returned from the function call.

- Static methods differ from regular methods in that when a program calls a static method, Python does not pass the object reference argument to the method. Therefore, a static method does not specify **self** as the first argument.

- The goal of the new class behavior is to remove the dichotomy that existed between Python types and classes before version 2.2. The most practical use of this type-class unification is that programmers now can inherit from Python's built-in types.

- Classes that inherit from base-class **object** also can define method **__getattribute__**, which executes for every attribute access.

- Method **__getattribute__** in a derived class must call the base-class version of the method to retrieve an object's attribute; otherwise, infinite recursion occurs.

- Python 2.2 allows "new" classes to define a **__slots__** attribute listing the attributes that objects of the class are allowed to have.

- When a "new" class defines the **__slots__** attribute, objects of the class can assign values only to attributes whose names appear in the **__slots__** list. If a client attempts to assign a value to an attribute whose name does not appear in **__slots__**, Python raises an exception.

- ""New" classes can contain properties that describe object attributes. A program accesses an object's properties in the same manner as accessing the object's attributes.

- A class definition creates a property by specifying four components—a *get* method, a *set* method, a *delete* method and a docstring that describes the property. The *get*, *set* and *delete* methods can perform any tasks necessary for maintaining data in a consistent state.

- Classes that use properties most often define their attributes to be private, to hide the data from clients of the class. The clients of the class then access the public properties of that class, which *get* and *set* the values of the private attributes.

- Built-in function **property** takes as arguments a *get* method, a *set* method, a *delete* method and a docstring and returns a property for the class.

TERMINOLOGY

abstract class
abstract method
abstraction
association
base class
__bases__ attribute of a class
bound method call
class library
complex type
composition
concrete class
derived class
dict type
direct base class
extensible
file type
float type
__getattribute__ method
"has-a" relationship
indirect base class
inherit
inheritance
int type
"is-a" relationship
isinstance function
issubclass function

"knows-a" relationship
list type
long type
multiple inheritance
NotImplementedError exception
object base class
object type
overriding a method
polymorphism
property
property function
reusability
single inheritance
__slots__ attribute of a class
standardized reusable components
static method
staticmethod function
str type
structural inheritance
subclass
superclass
tuple type
unbound method call
unicode type
"uses-a" relationship

SELF-REVIEW EXERCISES

9.1   Fill in the blanks in each of the following:
  a) With _____, a class is derived from several base classes.
  b) In other object-oriented programming languages, like Java, the base class is called the _____ and the derived class is the _____.
  c) A *has-a* relationship creates new classes by _____ of existing classes.
  d) When an object has a *knows a* relationship with another object, this is an _____.
  e) A base class exists in a _____ relationship with its derived classes.
  f) _____ in the first line of a class definition are used to indicate inheritance.
  g) An _____ is inherited from two or more levels up the class hierarchy.
  h) A base class specifies _____—all classes derived from a base class inherit the capabilities of that base class.
  i) _____ are classes for which the programmer never intends to create objects.
  j) A _____ method does not require an object of the class to perform its operation.

9.2   State whether each of the following is *true* or *false*. If *false*, explain why.
  a) The derived class inherits all the attributes and methods of its base class.
  b) A derived class must define a constructor that calls the base class's constructor.
  c) All base classes of a derived class are explicitly listed inside parentheses when the derived class is defined.
  d) To use an object of another class, a class must inherit from that class.

e) A derived class uses only the base-class methods that it overrides.

f) A derived class's constructor can invoke the base class's constructor through an unbound method call.

g) The name of the base class can be used to access the base class version of an overridden method from the derived class.

h) Placing a comma-separated list of base classes inside parentheses in a class definition indicates multiple inheritance.

i) Polymorphism enables multiple inheritance.

j) Python does not implement polymorphism.

ANSWERS TO SELF-REVIEW EXERCISES

9.1   a) multiple inheritance.   b) superclass, subclass.   c) composition.   d) association. e) hierarchical. f) Parentheses. g) indirect base class. h) commonality. i) Abstract classes. j) static.

9.2   a) True. b) False. If a derived class does not define a constructor, Python calls the base class's constructor. c) False. Only the direct base classes of a derived class are explicitly listed. d) False. A program uses an object of another class by importing the class and creating the object or using composition to define a class that contains a reference to an object of that class. e) False. A derived class has access to all of its base class's methods. f) True. g) True. h) True. i) False. Polymorphism is the ability for objects of different classes related by inheritance to respond differently to the same message. j) False. Python is inherently polymorphic because it is dynamically typed.

EXERCISES

9.3   Study the inheritance hierarchy of Fig. 9.2. For each class, indicate some common attributes and behaviors consistent with the hierarchy. Add some other classes (e.g., **UndergraduateStudent**, **GraduateStudent**, **Freshman**, **Sophomore**, **Junior**, **Senior**, etc.) to enrich the hierarchy.

9.4   Consider the class **Bicycle**. Given your knowledge of some common components of bicycles, show a class hierarchy in which the class **Bicycle** inherits from other classes, which, in turn, inherit from yet other classes. Discuss the creation of various objects of class **Bicycle**. Discuss inheritance from class **Bicycle** for other closely related derived classes.

9.5   Many programs written with inheritance could be solved with composition instead, and vice versa. Discuss the relative merits of these approaches in the context of the **Point**, **Circle**, **Cylinder** class hierarchy in this chapter. Rewrite the classes in Figs. 8.6–8.8 (and the supporting programs) to use composition rather than inheritance. After you do this, reassess the relative merits of the two approaches both for the **Point**, **Circle**, **Cylinder** problem and for object-oriented programs in general.

9.6   Write an inheritance hierarchy for class **Quadrilateral**, **Trapezoid**, **Parallelogram**, **Rectangle** and **Square**. Use **Quadrilateral** as the base class of the hierarchy. Make the hierarchy as deep (i.e., as many levels) as possible. The data of **Quadrilateral** should be the (x, y) coordinate pairs for the four endpoints of the **Quadrilateral**. Write a driver program that creates and displays objects of each of these classes.

9.7   Write a function that prints a class hierarchy. The function should take one argument that is an object of a class. The function should determine the class of that object and all direct and indirect base classes of the object. [*Note:* For simplicity, assume each class in the hierarchy uses only single inheritance.] The function prints each class name on a separate line. The first line contains the topmost class in the hierarchy, and each level in the hierarchy is indented by three spaces. For example, the output for the function, when passed an object of class **Cylinder** from Fig. 9.8, should be:

```
Point
   Circle
      Cylinder
```

9.8   Create a class **Date** that has data members for the day, the month and the year. Modify the payroll system of Fig. 9.9 to add data members **birthDate** (an object of class **Date**) and **departmentCode** (a number) to class **Employee**. Assume this payroll is processed once per month. Then, as your program calculates the payroll for each **Employee**, add a $100.00 bonus to the person's payroll amount if this is the month in which the **Employee**'s birthday occurs.

10

Graphical User Interface Components: Part 1

Objectives

- To understand the design principles of graphical user interfaces.
- To use the **Tkinter** module to build graphical user interfaces.
- To create and manipulate labels, text fields, buttons, check boxes and radio buttons.
- To learn to use mouse events and keyboard events.
- To understand and use layout managers.

… the wisest prophets make sure of the event first.
Horace Walpole

Do you think I can listen all day to such stuff?
Lewis Carroll

Speak the affirmative; emphasize your choice by utter ignoring of all that you reject.
Ralph Waldo Emerson

You pays your money and you takes your choice.
Joseph Keppler

Guess if you can, choose if you dare.
Pierre Corneille

All hope abandon, ye who enter here!
Dante Alighieri

Exit, pursued by a bear.
William Shakespeare

10.1 Introduction

A *graphical user interface (GUI)* allows a user to interact with a program. A GUI (pronounced "GOO-ee") gives a program a distinctive "look" and "feel." Providing different programs with a consistent set of intuitive interface components provides users with a basic level of familiarity with GUI programs before they ever use them. In turn, this reduces the time users require to learn programs and increases their ability to use the programs in a productive manner.

 Look-and-Feel Observation 10.1

Consistent user interfaces enable users to learn new applications faster.

GUIs are built from *GUI components* (called *widgets*—shorthand for *window gadgets*). A GUI component is an object with which a user interacts via a mouse or a keyboard. Figure 10.1 contains an example of a GUI, an Internet Explorer window with some of its GUI components labeled. There is a *menu bar* containing such *menus* as **File**, **Edit** and **View**. Below the menu bar is a set of *buttons* (e.g., **Back**, **Search**, and **History**), each of which has a defined task in Internet Explorer. Below the buttons is a *text field* in which a user can type a Web site address. To the left of the text field is a *label* (i.e., **Address**) that indicates the purpose of the text field. The menus, buttons, text fields and labels are part of the Internet Explorer GUI. These components enable a user to interact with the Internet Explorer program by just pointing with a mouse and clicking an element.

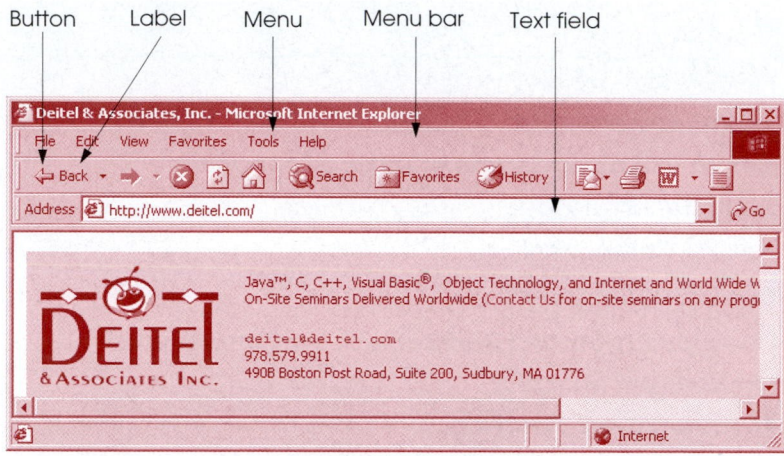

Fig. 10.1   GUI components in an Internet Explorer window.

Python programmers can construct GUIs by using the *Tool Command Language (TCL)* program and its graphic interface development tool, *Tool Kit (Tk)*. (Information about this scripting language and its components can be found at **www.scriptics.com**.) Figure 10.2 lists several common GUI components found in Tk. This chapter and the next discuss these and other GUI components in detail.

Component	Description
Frame	Serves as a container for other components.
Label	Displays uneditable text or icons.
Entry	Accepts user input from the keyboard, or displays information. A single-line input area.
Text	Accepts user input from the keyboard, or displays information. A multiple-line input area.
Button	Triggers an event when clicked.
Checkbutton	Selection component that is either chosen or not chosen.
Radiobutton	Selection component that allows the user to choose only one option.
Menu	Displays a list of items from which the user can select.
Canvas	Displays text, images, lines or shapes.
Scale	Allows the user to select from a range of integers using a slider.
Listbox	Displays a list of text options.
Menubutton	Displays popup or pull-down menu.
Scrollbar	Displays a scrollbar for canvases, text fields and lists.

Fig. 10.2   GUI components.

10.2 **Tkinter** Overview

The ***Tkinter*** module often is used to program GUIs in Python because it is Python's standard GUI package—it comes packaged with the Python program.[1] (Other GUI packages also are available for use with Python, but for this text, we use **Tkinter**). The **Tkinter** library provides an objected-oriented interface to the Tk GUI toolkit. As an object-oriented layer on top of Tk/TCL, each Tk GUI component in the **Tkinter** module is a class that inherits from class **Widget** (Fig. 10.3). All **Widget**-derived classes have common attributes and behaviors.

A GUI consists of a *top-level* (or, *parent*) *component* that can contain other GUI components. The components that are contained in the parent are *children* of the top-level component, and each child may contain other children. The concept of parent-child components

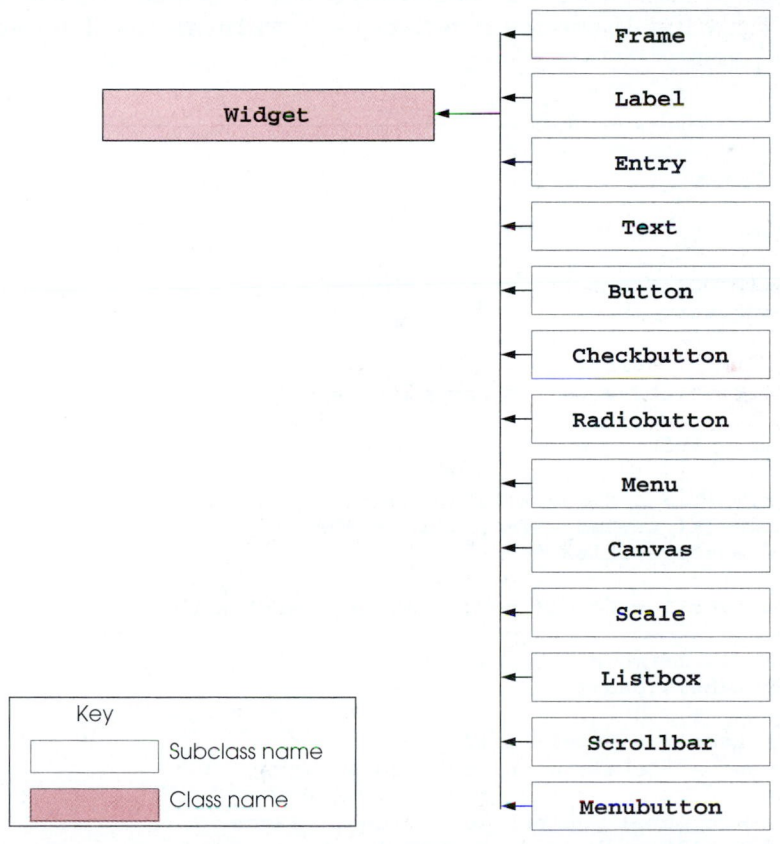

Fig. 10.3 **Widget** subclasses.

---

1. The **Tkinter** module is portable across many platforms. Some platforms, however, need to have Tcl/Tk and **Tkinter** installed. The Deitel & Associates, Inc. Web site, **www.deitel.com**, contains installation instructions for various platforms.

should not be confused with the relationship between a base class and a derived class. A program builds a GUI from the top-level component by creating new components and placing each new component in the parent component.

Each program in this chapter implements a GUI by inheriting from **Widget**'s subclass **Frame**. In our programs, **Frame** will serve as the top-level component to which children are added to extend the GUI's functionality. This inheritance enables the reuse of components in other GUI programs and promotes object-orientation.

 Portability Tip 10.1

The **Tkinter** *module can design graphical user interfaces for Unix, Macintosh and Windows platforms.*

10.3 Simple **Tkinter** Example: **Label** Component

Labels display text or images that provide instructions or other information in graphical user interfaces. Figure 10.4 demonstrates class **Label**—the **Tkinter** class that represents a label component.

```
1   # Fig. 10.4: fig10_04.py
2   # Label demonstration.
3
4   from Tkinter import *
5
6   class LabelDemo( Frame ):
7      """Demonstrate Labels"""
8
9      def __init__( self ):
10         """Create three Labels and pack them"""
11
12         Frame.__init__( self )  # initializes Frame object
13
14         # frame fills all available space
15         self.pack( expand = YES, fill = BOTH )
16         self.master.title( "Labels" )
17
18         self.Label1 = Label( self, text = "Label with text" )
19
20         # resize frame to accommodate Label
21         self.Label1.pack()
22
23         self.Label2 = Label( self,
24            text = "Labels with text and a bitmap" )
25
26         # insert Label against left side of frame
27         self.Label2.pack( side = LEFT )
28
29         # using default bitmap image as label
30         self.Label3 = Label( self, bitmap = "warning" )
31         self.Label3.pack( side = LEFT )
32
```

Fig. 10.4 **Label**s demonstration. (Part 1 of 2.)

```
33   def main():
34       LabelDemo().mainloop()   # starts event loop
35
36   if __name__ == "__main__":
37       main()
```

Fig. 10.4   Labels demonstration. (Part 2 of 2.)

Line 4 imports **Tkinter** class definitions and predefined values, or *constants*. In Chapter 4, Functions, we discussed how to import all elements from a module

```
from module import *
```

This statement allows us to write less code because specific definitions do not need to be accessed through the module's name. However, importing all definitions can cause errors. For example, if we **import *** from a module that defines a function **len**, this new definition overrides the definition for Python function **len**. If this is the case, a program cannot determine the length of a sequence. As a safeguard, only use **import *** from modules (e.g., **Tkinter**) that explicitly state that an **import *** statement may be used.

Class **LabelDemo** (lines 6–31) defines the GUI for our program. This class inherits from class **Frame** and serves as the parent container for three **Label** components. The entire GUI is constructed when a client creates a **LabelDemo** object and the class's **__init__** method (lines 9–31) executes. Line 12 calls the base class **Frame** constructor, which creates a top-level component for the entire application and initializes the **Frame**.

Once a component has been created and initialized, the component must be placed into its parent container (e.g., the top-level component created by the call to the base class constructor). Method **pack** (line 15) and its keyword arguments specify how and where the component should be placed in its parent. Each parent component has a certain amount of space into which child components can be placed, and each child has an original default size. When method **pack** executes, a *layout manager* determines the size and location of the child component, based on the available space in the parent container. We discuss layout managers in detail in Section 10.10.1.

The keyword argument values for method **pack** influence the size of the component. Keyword argument **fill** specifies how much space the component occupies, beyond its default size. Possible values for **fill** are **X** (all available horizontal space), **Y** (all available vertical space), **BOTH** (both vertical and horizontal available space) and **NONE** (the default value—occupies no additional space). Once all child components have been placed in their parent, the parent may still have available space. Keyword argument **expand** specifies whether a child component should occupy any extra space in its parent component (i.e., any space not yet occupied by other components). The keyword takes a value of either **YES** (expand to occupy extra space) or **NO** (do not expand to occupy extra space). The **Label-Demo** object occupies all available space provided by its parent (top-level) component because options **expand** and **fill** are set to **YES** and **BOTH**, respectively (line 15).

Look-and-Feel Observation 10.2

If no options are set, method **pack** *uses is default settings to places components in a GUI. If a programmer desires to alter the position of a component, the programmer changes the keyword arguments.*

Good Programming Practice 10.1

Before using a GUI class, read the Python online documentation to learn the methods and options of the class to understand its capabilities.

Every child component has an attribute called **master** that references the child's parent component. Line 16 accesses the **LabelDemo**'s parent (top-level) component and calls method **title** to change the title of the GUI to **Labels**, which then appears in the GUI title bar.

Line 18 creates a **Label** object. Each GUI component's class constructor takes a first argument that corresponds to the new object's parent. In this case, **self** is the first argument, indicating that the **Label** is a child of the **LabelDemo** component. The value of keyword argument **text** indicates the contents of the **Label** component. Method **pack** (line 21) inserts **Label1** into the GUI, using the default settings. By default, **Label1** occupies the top of the window.

Lines 23–24 create a second **Label** component. Line 27 calls method **pack** and passes a value for keyword argument **side**, which describes where the new component is placed. Value **LEFT** indicates that **Label2** appears against the left side of the window. Other possible values for the **side** option are **BOTTOM**, **RIGHT** and **TOP** (the default setting). These options also determine the placing and sizing of child components when the parent container resizes. Figure 10.4 displays the resulting arrangement after the window size increases. As specified by the side option, **label1** remains at the top of the container, while **label2** and **label3** stay at the left side of the container. Section 10.10.1 discusses different settings for method pack and the effects of resizing parent containers.

A **Label**s can display an image when a programmer specifies values for the keyword argument **bitmap**. For example, a value of **"warning"** (line 30) displays a warning *bitmap* image on **label3**. Figure 10.5 lists other values for **bitmap** that are available

Bitmap image name	Image	Bitmap image name	Image
error	⊘	hourglass	⧖
gray75	▓	info	𝒊
gray50	▒	questhead	☹

Fig. 10.5 Bitmap images available. (Part 1 of 2.)

Bitmap image name	Image	Bitmap image name	Image
gray25		question	
gray12		warning	

Fig. 10.5   Bitmap images available. (Part 2 of 2.)

In addition to using existing bitmap images, programmers can create images to insert in a GUI by using keyword argument *image*. Note that a hierarchy exists between **image**, **bitmap** and **text** keyword arguments (in that order). For example, if an image option is specified, any **bitmap** or **text** options are ignored. Similarly, if **bitmap** and **text** options both are specified, the **text** option is ignored. Label options follow a precedence hierarchy—the value of the option with the highest precedence appears on the GUI, and other labels are ignored. Labels with the highest precedence are **image**, next is **bitmap**, and the lowest precedence is **text**.

The third label component, **Label3**, has the **side** option set to **LEFT** (line 31). This setting left-justifies the label against **Label2**, not against the edge of the GUI. Section 10.10.1 offers for more information about how the **pack** method arranges components in a GUI.

Lines 33–37 introduce a convention common to many GUI programs. Lines 36–37 test whether the namespace is **"__main__"** and calls function **main** if the condition is true (i.e., the interpreter has been invoked on the file) and false if the file has been imported as a module. Function **main** executes if the program is run by itself, rather than imported as a module for use in another program.

Function **main** creates a **LabelDemo** object and calls its **mainloop** method (line 34). Method **mainloop** starts the **labelDemo** GUI. The method redraws the GUI when necessary (e.g., when the user changes the size of the GUI) and sends events to the appropriate components. [Note: We discuss events in Section 10.4.] Method **mainloop** terminates when the user destroys (closes) the GUI.

10.4 Event Handling Model

GUIs are *event driven*—GUI components generate *events* (actions) when users of the programs interact with the GUIs. Some common interactions include moving a mouse, clicking a mouse button, typing in a text field, selecting an item from a menu and closing a window. When a user interaction occurs, an event is sent to the program. GUI event information is stored in an object of a class **Event**. An event-driven program is *asynchronous*—the program does not know when events will occur.

To process a GUI event, a program must *bind* an event to a graphical component and implement an *event handler* (or *callback*). A program binds, or associates, an event with a graphical component and specifies an action to perform. An event handler is a method that is invoked in response to an associated event.

When an event occurs, the GUI component with which the user interacted determines whether an event handler has been specified for the event. If an event handler has been specified, the event handler associated with the event executes. For example, a "rollover" event occurs when the user moves the mouse over a component. A program might require that the appearance of a label changes (e.g., by changing the background color of the label) when a rollover event occurs. In this case, the programmer defines a method that changes the label's appearance and binds the rollover event to the method. When the user moves the mouse over the label, the method executes.

10.5 Entry Component

Entry components are areas in which users can enter text or programmers can display a line of text. This section demonstrates entry components in a program. When the user types text into an **Entry** component and presses the *Enter* key, a **<Return>** event occurs. If an event handler is bound to that event for the **Entry** component, the event is processed. In our example, the **<Return>** event signals that the user has finished entering text in the **Entry**. Figure 10.6 defines class **EntryDemo**, which creates and manipulates four **Entry** text fields. When a user presses the *Enter* key in the active field, the program displays the field's text. The program contains two **Frame** objects, each of which contains two **Entry** components.

```
1   # Fig. 10.6: fig10_06.py
2   # Entry components and event binding demonstration.
3
4   from Tkinter import *
5   from tkMessageBox import *
6
7   class EntryDemo( Frame ):
8      """Demonstrate Entrys and Event binding"""
9
10     def __init__( self ):
11        """Create, pack and bind events to four Entrys"""
12
13        Frame.__init__( self )
14        self.pack( expand = YES, fill = BOTH )
15        self.master.title( "Testing Entry Components" )
16        self.master.geometry( "325x100" )   # width x length
17
18        self.frame1 = Frame( self )
19        self.frame1.pack( pady = 5 )
20
21        self.text1 = Entry( self.frame1, name = "text1" )
22
23        # bind the Entry component to event
24        self.text1.bind( "<Return>", self.showContents )
25        self.text1.pack( side = LEFT, padx = 5 )
26
27        self.text2 = Entry( self.frame1, name = "text2" )
28
```

Fig. 10.6 **Entry** components and event binding demonstration. (Part 1 of 3.)

```
29              # insert text into Entry component text2
30              self.text2.insert( INSERT, "Enter text here" )
31              self.text2.bind( "<Return>", self.showContents )
32              self.text2.pack( side = LEFT, padx = 5 )
33
34              self.frame2 = Frame( self )
35              self.frame2.pack( pady = 5 )
36
37              self.text3 = Entry( self.frame2, name = "text3" )
38              self.text3.insert( INSERT, "Uneditable text field" )
39
40              # prohibit user from altering text in Entry component text3
41              self.text3.config( state = DISABLED )
42              self.text3.bind( "<Return>", self.showContents )
43              self.text3.pack( side = LEFT, padx = 5 )
44
45              # text in Entry component text4 appears as *
46              self.text4 = Entry( self.frame2, name = "text4",
47                  show = "*" )
48              self.text4.insert( INSERT, "Hidden text" )
49              self.text4.bind( "<Return>", self.showContents )
50              self.text4.pack( side = LEFT, padx = 5 )
51
52      def showContents( self, event ):
53          """Display the contents of the Entry"""
54
55              # acquire name of Entry component that generated event
56              theName = event.widget.winfo_name()
57
58              # acquire contents of Entry component that generated event
59              theContents = event.widget.get()
60              showinfo( "Message", theName + ": " + theContents )
61
62  def main():
63      EntryDemo().mainloop()
64
65  if __name__ == "__main__":
66      main()
```

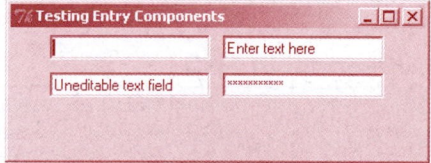

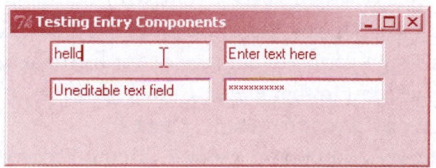

Fig. 10.6 Entry components and event binding demonstration. (Part 2 of 3.)

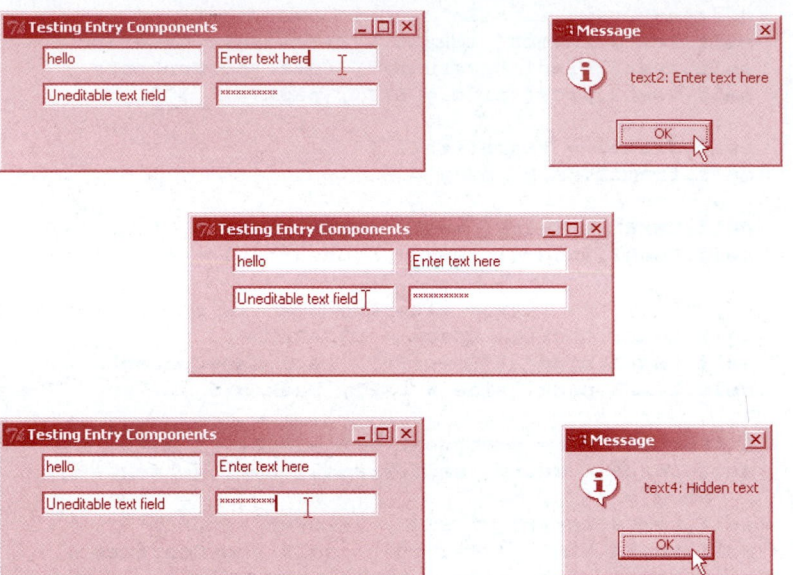

Fig. 10.6   Entry components and event binding demonstration. (Part 3 of 3.)

Line 5 imports the class definitions and constants from module **tkMessageBox**. Module **tkMessageBox** contains functions that display *dialogs*, which present messages to users.

Class **EntryDemo**'s **__init__** method calls the base class constructor, packs the **EntryDemo** and titles the program (lines 13–15). Method **geometry** configures the length and width of the top-level component in pixels (line 16). Line 18 creates the first **Frame** component, **frame1**. The **pack** method call (line 19) introduces another option, **pady**, which specifies the amount of empty vertical space between **frame1** and other GUI components in the parent container. Similarly, option **padx**, used later in the program, specifies the amount of empty horizontal space between components.

Lines 21 create **Entry** component **text1**. Option **name** assigns a name to **Entry**. We assign a name so the event handler can use that name to identify the component in which an event has occurred.

Look-and-Feel Observation 10.3

*If a name is not specified by the programmer, **Tkinter** assigns each component a unique name. To obtain the full name of a component, pass the component object to function **str**.*

Method **bind** (line 24) associates a **<Return>** event with component **text1**. A **<Return>** event occurs when the user presses the *Enter* key. Method **bind** takes two arguments. The first argument is the type of the event (the event format), and the second argument is the name of the method to bind to that event. In this example, method **show-Contents** executes when a **<Return>** event occurs in **text1**.

Lines 30–32 create and pack **Entry** component **text2**. Method *insert* writes text in the **Entry** component (line 30). Method *insert* takes two arguments—a position at which text is to be inserted and a string that contains the text to insert. Passing a value of

INSERT as the first argument causes the text to be inserted at the cursor's current position. Text also can be inserted at the end of an **Entry** component. For example, the call

```
insert( END, text )
```

appends **text** to the end of text already displayed in the component.

A program also can delete text from an **Entry** component with method *delete*. The call

```
delete( start, finish )
```

removes all text in an **Entry** component in the range *start* to *finish*. If **END** is the second argument, the method removes text up to the end of the text area. The first position in an **Entry** component is position 0; therefore, **delete(0, END)** removes all text in an **Entry** component.

Lines 34–35 creates and packs the second **Frame** component, **frame2**. The program packs the **Frame**s one below the other to create two rows into which the **Entry**s are inserted. The program inserts **Entry** components **text1** and **text2** in **frame1**, while **text3** and **text4** are packed into **frame2**.

Lines 41–43 create and pack **text3** in the same way as the first two **Entry**s. In this case, the component is bound to the **<Return>** event (line 42). In this example, we demonstrate disabling **text3** with method *config*. Method **config** allows the user to configure a component by specifying keyword-value pairs (line 41). Specifying the value **DISABLED** for option *state* disables the **Entry** component, preventing the user from editing its text. As a result, **text3** cannot generate a **<Return>** event. Disabling an **Entry** can be useful to a program that wants to display text but does not want the user to edit that text.

Lines 46–50 create and pack **Entry** component **text4** in the same way as the first three **Entry**s. This component enables the user to enter confidential information. Option *show* specifies a character that will be displayed in the text box instead of the user-entered text (line 47). In this example, asterisks (*****) appear in place of the default text, **"Hidden text"**. Asterisks also appear in place of any text that the user types into the **Entry** component.

Method *showContents* (lines 52–60) is the event handler for each **<Return>** event generated in the **Entry** components. In Python, most event handlers take as a reference to an **Event** object as an argument; an **Event** object can have various attributes. The component that generated the event is obtained from the object's **widget** attribute (i.e., **event.widget**). In our program, **event.widget** refers to one of the four **Entry** components whose **<Return>** event is bound to method **showContents**.

Common Programming Error 10.1

Failure to bind an event handler to an event type for a particular GUI component results in no events being handled for that component for that event type.

Widget method *winfo_name* (line 56) returns the name of the component. **Entry** method *get* (line 59) returns the contents of the **Entry**. The event handler uses both return values to construct a message to display to the user. The **tkMessageBox** function *showinfo* (line 60) displays a dialog box labeled **"Message"** that contains the name and contents of the **Entry** that generated the event. The screenshots that appear at the end of Fig. 10.6 demonstrate what happens when each **Entry** component receives the **<Enter>** event.

10.6 Button Component

A button is a GUI component that generates an event when it is selected. Buttons facilitate and simplify the selection of events by allowing users to select the appropriate button to execute an action, instead of manually typing commands. Buttons are created with class **Button**, which inherits from class **Widget**. The text or image appearing on a **Button** component is a *button label*. A GUI can display many **Button**s, but, typically, each button should have a unique button label.

Look-and-Feel Observation 10.4

*Having more than one **Button** with the same label results in ambiguity. Provide a unique label for each button.*

Figure 10.7 creates two **Button**s and demonstrates that **Button**s, like **Label**s, can display both images and text.

```python
1   # Fig. 10.7: fig10_07.py
2   # Button demonstration.
3
4   from Tkinter import *
5   from tkMessageBox import *
6
7   class PlainAndFancy( Frame ):
8      """Create one plain and one fancy button"""
9
10     def __init__( self ):
11        """Create two buttons, pack them and bind events"""
12
13        Frame.__init__( self )
14        self.pack( expand = YES, fill = BOTH )
15        self.master.title( "Buttons" )
16
17        # create button with text
18        self.plainButton = Button( self, text = "Plain Button",
19           command = self.pressedPlain )
20        self.plainButton.bind( "<Enter>", self.rolloverEnter )
21        self.plainButton.bind( "<Leave>", self.rolloverLeave )
22        self.plainButton.pack( side = LEFT, padx = 5, pady = 5 )
23
24        # create button with image
25        self.myImage = PhotoImage( file = "logotiny.gif" )
26        self.fancyButton = Button( self, image = self.myImage,
27           command = self.pressedFancy )
28        self.fancyButton.bind( "<Enter>", self.rolloverEnter )
29        self.fancyButton.bind( "<Leave>", self.rolloverLeave )
30        self.fancyButton.pack( side = LEFT, padx = 5, pady = 5 )
31
```

Fig. 10.7 **Button**s demonstration. (Part 1 of 2.)

```
32      def pressedPlain( self ):
33          showinfo( "Message", "You pressed: Plain Button" )
34
35      def pressedFancy( self ):
36          showinfo( "Message", "You pressed: Fancy Button" )
37
38      def rolloverEnter( self, event ):
39          event.widget.config( relief = GROOVE )
40
41      def rolloverLeave( self, event ):
42          event.widget.config( relief = RAISED )
43
44  def main():
45      PlainAndFancy().mainloop()
46
47  if __name__ == "__main__":
48      main()
```

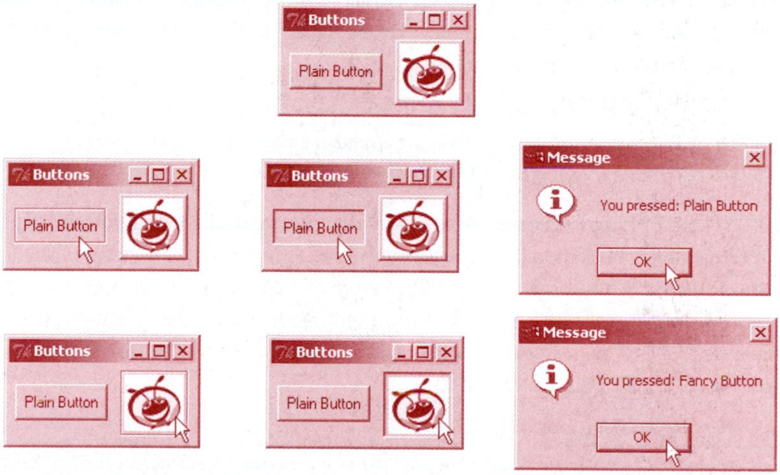

Fig. 10.7   **Button**s demonstration. (Part 2 of 2.)

Lines 18–19 create a **Button** called **plainButton**. Option **text** sets the button's label. Keyword argument **command** specifies the event handler that executes when a user selects the button. In our example, **plainButton**'s label is **"PlainButton"**, and its event handler is method **pressedPlain**.

Lines 20–21 bind methods *rolloverEnter* and *rolloverLeave* to **plain-Button** events **<Enter>** and **<Leave>** events, respectively. The **<Enter>** event occurs when the user places the mouse cursor over the button; the **<Leave>** event occurs when the user removes the mouse cursor from the button. Section 10.8 discusses mouse events in detail.

Many **Tkinter** components, including **Button**s, can display images by specifying *image* arguments to their constructors or their **config** methods. The image to display must be an object of a **Tkinter** class that loads an image file. One such class is *Photo-Image*, which supports three image formats—*Graphics Interchange Format (GIF)*, *Joint*

Photographic Experts Group (JPEG) and *Portable Greymap Format (PGM)*. File names for each of these types typically end with **.gif**, **.jpg** (or **.jpeg**) or **.pgm** (or **.ppm**), respectively. An additional image class is class ***BitmapImage***, which supports the *Bitmap (BMP) image* format (**.bmp**). Line 25 creates a **PhotoImage** object. File **logotiny.gif** contains the image to load and store in the **PhotoImage** object. (This file resides in the same directory as the program.) The program assigns the newly created **PhotoImage** object to reference **myImage**.

Lines 26–27 create **fancyButton** with **image** attribute **myImage**. As with **Labels**, the **image** attribute takes precedence over **text** and **bitmap** attributes, and if text or bitmap are specified, they are ignored.

The event handler for **fancyButton** is **pressedFancy**. Note that methods **pressedPlain** (lines 32–33) and **pressedFancy** (lines 35–36) do not take an **Event** object as an argument. This is because **Button** callbacks do not take **Event** objects as arguments. Without an **Event** object, a callback cannot determine for which component the event occurred; therefore, it is important to specify a separate callback method for each **Button**, to ensure that the calling component can be identified. Methods **pressed-Plain** and **pressedFancy** create the **"Message"** dialog boxes, which notify users of the buttons that generated the events.

Good Programming Practice 10.2

*Defining a separate callback method for each **Button** avoids confusion, ensures desired behavior and makes debugging a GUI easier.*

Methods **rolloverEnter** (lines 38–39) and **rolloverLeave** (lines 41–42) create a *rollover effect* for their respective events. A rollover effect changes the appearance of a component. Both methods change the *relief* of the component—how the component appears in relation to its surrounding components—for which the event occurred. Method **rolloverEnter** sets the component's ***relief*** option to **GROOVE**; method **roll-overLeave** sets **relief** to **RAISED**

Look-and-Feel Observation 10.5

*Using rollovers for **Button**s provides users with visual feedbacks alerting them of actions that occur if the **Button**s are selected.*

10.7 Checkbutton and Radiobutton Components

Tkinter defines two GUI components—**Checkbutton** and **Radiobutton**—that have on/off or true/false values. Classes **Checkbutton** and **Radiobutton** are subclasses of **Widget**. Although they take the same values, class **Checkbutton** and class **Radiobutton** are used for different situations. We first discuss class **Checkbutton**.

A checkbox is a small white square that either is blank or contains a checkmark. When a checkbox is selected, a black checkmark appears in the box. There are no restrictions on how checkboxes are used—any number of boxes can be selected at a time. The text that appears alongside a checkbox is referred to as the *checkbox label*.

Figure 10.8 uses two **Checkbutton** objects to modify the font style of the text displayed in an **Entry** component. When selected, one **Checkbutton** applies a bold style, and the other applies an italic style. If both are selected, the style of the font is bold and italic. Initially, the **Checkbutton**s are not selected.

```
1    # Fig. 10.8: fig10_08.py
2    # Checkbuttons demonstration.
3
4    from Tkinter import *
5
6    class CheckFont( Frame ):
7       """An area of text with Checkbutton controlled font"""
8
9       def __init__( self ):
10          """Create an Entry and two Checkbuttons"""
11
12          Frame.__init__( self )
13          self.pack( expand = YES, fill = BOTH )
14          self.master.title( "Checkbutton Demo" )
15
16          self.frame1 = Frame( self )
17          self.frame1.pack()
18
19          self.text = Entry( self.frame1, width = 40,
20             font = "Arial 10" )
21          self.text.insert( INSERT, "Watch the font style change" )
22          self.text.pack( padx = 5, pady = 5 )
23
24          self.frame2 = Frame( self )
25          self.frame2.pack()
26
27          # create boolean variable
28          self.boldOn = BooleanVar()
29
30          # create "Bold" checkbutton
31          self.checkBold = Checkbutton( self.frame2, text = "Bold",
32             variable = self.boldOn, command = self.changeFont )
33          self.checkBold.pack( side = LEFT, padx = 5, pady = 5 )
34
35          # create boolean variable
36          self.italicOn = BooleanVar()
37
38          # create "Italic" checkbutton
39          self.checkItalic = Checkbutton( self.frame2,
40             text = "Italic", variable = self.italicOn,
41             command = self.changeFont )
42          self.checkItalic.pack( side = LEFT, padx = 5, pady = 5 )
43
44       def changeFont( self ):
45          """Change the font based on selected Checkbuttons"""
46
47          desiredFont = "Arial 10"
48
49          if self.boldOn.get():
50             desiredFont += " bold"
51
52          if self.italicOn.get():
53             desiredFont += " italic"
```

Fig. 10.8 **Checkbutton**s font style selection. (Part 1 of 2.)

```
54
55          self.text.config( font = desiredFont )
56
57  def main():
58      CheckFont().mainloop()
59
60  if __name__ == "__main__":
61      main()
```

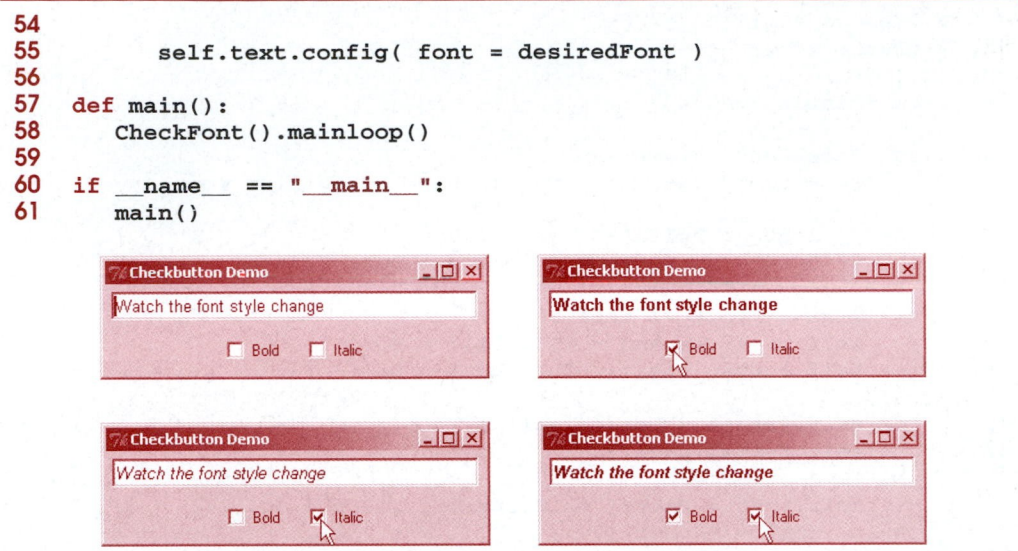

Fig. 10.8   Checkbuttons font style selection. (Part 2 of 2.)

Lines 19–20 create an **Entry** component named **text**. The inserted text, **"Watch the font style change"** (line 21), has font style **"Arial 10"**. The *font* attribute indicates the font of the **Entry** component. One way of representing a font is by using a string containing the font name, size and style. It is possible to specify no font style, in addition to specifying multiple font styles. The online *Introduction to Tkinter*

```
www.pythonware.com/library/tkinter/introduction/x444-
fonts.htm
```

includes a discussion of available fonts and font styles.

BooleanVar objects, *boldOn* (line 28) and *italicOn* (line 36), are **Tkinter** integer variables that have values of either 0 or 1. The option **variable** requires an object of the **Tkinter Variable** class. **Tkinter** provides the *Variable* class from which **BooleanVar** inherits. The **Variable** class acts as a container for Python variables. Various **Tkinter** classes use **Variable** objects to maintain information about a particular component. For example, the **CheckButton** class uses a **BooleanVar** object to store the *state*—checked or unchecked—of the button. Our program creates and passes **BooleanVar** references to the **CheckButton** constructors, so the event handlers can determine whether the user has selected one or both of the buttons.

Lines 31–32 create a **Checkbutton** called **checkBold**. The **text** option indicates that the text, **"Bold"**, appears next to the checkbox to provide information about the purpose of the checkbox. The **command** attribute of a **Checkbutton** component is the event handler that executes when a user selects or de-selects the button. In this case, we specify method **changeFont** as the event handler. The component's *variable* option passes the **BooleanVar** object that the component uses to maintain its state information. When a user clicks the **CheckButton**, two things happen—its **BooleanVar** value changes from **0** to **1**, or **1** to **0**, and the event handler **changeFont** executes. Lines 38–40 create **checkItalic**, a **CheckButton** object that behaves similarly to object **checkBold**.

Method **changeFont** (lines 44–55) initializes string **desiredFont** to the original **"Arial 10"** font. Method **get** (of class **BooleanVar**) returns the variable's value. If a user selects **checkBold**, the program appends **" bold"** to **desiredFont** (line 50). The process repeats for **checkItalic**, using **italicOn**. Likewise, if a user selects **checkItalic**, the program appends the string **" italic"** to **desiredFont** (line 53). Each string begins with a space so that when the style is appended to the font, a space is included (e.g., **"Arial 10 italic"**). The method then calls **config** to change **text**'s font to **desiredFont**.

Radio buttons, created with class **Radiobutton**, resemble checkboxes because they have two states—*selected* and *not selected* (also called *deselected*). Unlike checkboxes, radio buttons represent a set of *mutually exclusive* options—only one radio button in a group can be selected at a time. Selecting a different radio button in the group forces all other radio buttons in the group to be deselected.

Look-and-Feel Observation 10.6

*Use **RadioButton**s when the user should choose only one option in a group.*

Look-and-Feel Observation 10.7

*Use **CheckBox**es when the user should be able to choose multiple options in a group.*

Figure 10.9 is similar to the program in Fig. 10.8 in that the user can alter the font style of an **Entry**'s text. However, this example permits only a single font style in the group to be selected at a time, using radio buttons.

```
1   # Fig. 10.9: fig10_09.py
2   # Radiobuttons demonstration.
3
4   from Tkinter import *
5
6   class RadioFont( Frame ):
7      """An area of text with Radiobutton controlled font"""
8
9      def __init__( self ):
10        """Create an Entry and four Radiobuttons"""
11
12        Frame.__init__( self )
13        self.pack( expand = YES, fill = BOTH )
14        self.master.title( "Radiobutton Demo" )
15
16        self.frame1 = Frame( self )
17        self.frame1.pack()
18
19        self.text = Entry( self.frame1, width = 40,
20           font = "Arial 10" )
21        self.text.insert( INSERT, "Watch the font style change" )
22        self.text.pack( padx = 5, pady = 5 )
23
```

Fig. 10.9   **Radiobutton**s selecting font styles. (Part 1 of 2.)

```
24          self.frame2 = Frame( self )
25          self.frame2.pack()
26
27          fontSelections = [ "Plain", "Bold", "Italic",
28                             "Bold/Italic" ]
29          self.chosenFont = StringVar()
30
31          # initial selection
32          self.chosenFont.set( fontSelections[ 0 ] )
33
34          # create group of Radiobutton components with same variable
35          for style in fontSelections:
36             aButton = Radiobutton( self.frame2, text = style,
37                variable = self.chosenFont, value = style,
38                command = self.changeFont )
39             aButton.pack( side = LEFT, padx = 5, pady = 5 )
40
41      def changeFont( self ):
42          """Change the font based on selected Radiobutton"""
43
44          desiredFont = "Arial 10"
45
46          if self.chosenFont.get() == "Bold":
47             desiredFont += " bold"
48          elif self.chosenFont.get() == "Italic":
49             desiredFont += " italic"
50          elif self.chosenFont.get() == "Bold/Italic":
51             desiredFont += " bold italic"
52
53          self.text.config( font = desiredFont )
54
55  def main():
56      RadioFont().mainloop()
57
58  if __name__ == "__main__":
59      main()
```

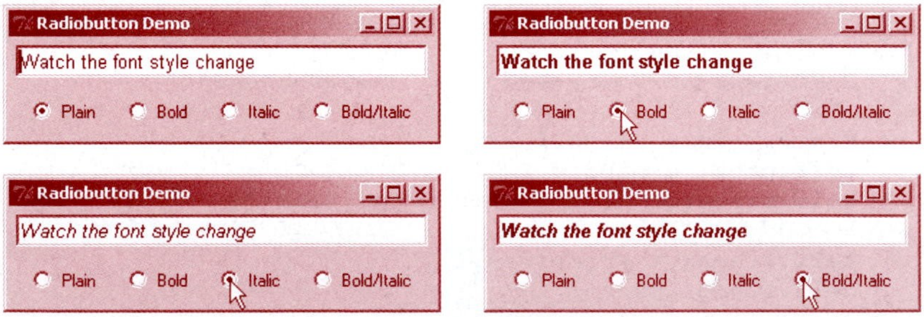

Fig. 10.9 **Radiobutton**s selecting font styles. (Part 2 of 2.)

Sequence ***fontSelections*** (lines 27–28) lists several font styles. Lines 29–32 define a ***StringVar*** object, ***chosenFont***, and **set**s the initial value to the default style, **"Plain"**. Like **BooleanVar**, **StringVar** is a subclass of **Tkinter** class **Variable**, and it acts as a container for a string variable. Unlike our **CheckButton**s example, which uses a **BooleanVar** to track a button's state, a grouping of **RadioButton**s in Fig. 10.9 use a **StringVar** to store the value (i.e., name) of the selected button. Groups of RadioButtons modify the same Variable object. To define mutually exclusive groups of RadioButtons, programmers must assign one Variable object to each group. When a user selects a given radio button, the selected radio button modifies the assigned Variable object and class the appropriate event handler. Our event handler (**changeFont**) retrieves the value of the group's **StringVar** object to determine the selected button.

Lines 35–39 create and pack a **Radiobutton** component for each **style** in the **fontSelection**s list—**"Plain"**, **"Bold"**, **"Italic"** and **"Bold/Italic"**. The **for** loop assigns a **style** to each button's **text** and **value** options—the option that determines the button's name. Option **text** indicates the text to be displayed next to the **Radiobutton** component. Attribute **variable** associates **StringVar** object **chosenFont** with each **Radiobutton** component, and option **command** registers method **changeFont** as the event handler for each button. When the user clicks a **Radiobutton**, the string contained in the **StringVar** object is changed to contain the button's value, and method **changeFont** executes.

Method **changeFont** (lines 41–53) initializes string **desiredFont** to **"Arial 10"**. If a **Radiobutton** is selected, **changeFont** appends the desired style to **desiredFont**. Method **get** obtains the current value of **chosenFont**. In this example, **changeFont** uses an **if/elif** structure to emphasize that, unlike **Checkbutton**s, only one **Radiobutton** (using the same variable) may be selected at a time.

10.8 Mouse Event Handling

This section demonstrates how programs handle *mouse events*—events that occur as a result of user interaction with a mouse. Figure 10.10 summarizes several common mouse event formats and Fig. 10.11 demonstrates how a GUI program can handle them. All **Tkinter** events are described by strings following the pattern *<modifier-type-detail>*. The *type* (for instance, **Button** and **Return**) specifies the kind of event. The prefix **Double** is an example of a modifier while the specific mouse button is a detail.

Event format	Description
<ButtonPress-*n***>**	Mouse button *n* has been selected while the mouse pointer is over the component. *n* may be 1 (left button), 2 (middle button) or 3 (right button). (e.g., **<ButtonPress-1>**).
<Button-*n***>**, **<***n***>**	Shorthand notations for **<ButtonPress-***n***>**.
<ButtonRelease-*n***>**	Mouse button *n* has been released.
<B*n***-Motion>**	Mouse is moved with button *n* held down.
*<Prefix-***Button-***n***>**	Mouse button *n* has been *Prefix* clicked over the component. *Prefix* may be **Double** or **Triple**.
<Enter>	Mouse pointer has entered the component.
<Leave>	Mouse pointer has exited the component.

Fig. 10.10 Mouse event formats.

```
1   # Fig. 10.11: fig10_11.py
2   # Mouse events example.
3
4   from Tkinter import *
5
6   class MouseLocation( Frame ):
7      """Demonstrate binding mouse events"""
8
9      def __init__( self ):
10        """Create a Label, pack it and bind mouse events"""
11
12        Frame.__init__( self )
13        self.pack( expand = YES, fill = BOTH )
14        self.master.title( "Demonstrating Mouse Events" )
15        self.master.geometry( "275x100" )
16
17        self.mousePosition = StringVar() # displays mouse position
18        self.mousePosition.set( "Mouse outside window" )
19        self.positionLabel = Label( self,
20           textvariable = self.mousePosition )
21        self.positionLabel.pack( side = BOTTOM )
22
23        # bind mouse events to window
24        self.bind( "<Button-1>", self.buttonPressed )
25        self.bind( "<ButtonRelease-1>", self.buttonReleased )
26        self.bind( "<Enter>", self.enteredWindow )
27        self.bind( "<Leave>", self.exitedWindow )
28        self.bind( "<B1-Motion>", self.mouseDragged )
29
30     def buttonPressed( self, event ):
31        """Display coordinates of button press"""
32
33        self.mousePosition.set( "Pressed at [ " + str( event.x ) +
34           ", " + str( event.y ) + " ]" )
35
36     def buttonReleased( self, event ):
37        """Display coordinates of button release"""
38
39        self.mousePosition.set( "Released at [ " + str( event.x ) +
40           ", " + str( event.y ) + " ]" )
41
42     def enteredWindow( self, event ):
43        """Display message that mouse has entered window"""
44
45        self.mousePosition.set( "Mouse in window" )
46
47     def exitedWindow( self, event ):
48        """Display message that mouse has left window"""
49
50        self.mousePosition.set( "Mouse outside window" )
51
```

Fig. 10.11 Mouse events demonstration. (Part 1 of 2.)

```
52      def mouseDragged( self, event ):
53          """Display coordinates of mouse being moved"""
54
55          self.mousePosition.set( "Dragged at [ " + str( event.x ) +
56              ", " + str( event.y ) + " ]" )
57
58  def main():
59      MouseLocation().mainloop()
60
61  if __name__ == "__main__":
62      main()
```

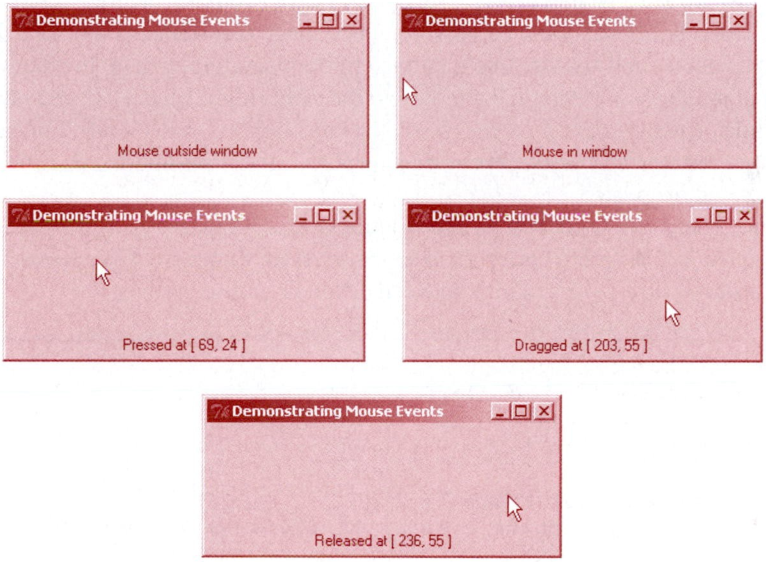

Fig. 10.11 Mouse events demonstration. (Part 2 of 2.)

Lines 17–18 create a **StringVar** object **mousePosition** and initializes its value to **"Mouse outside window"**. Lines 19–21 create and pack **Label** *position-Label* with *textvariable* option **mousePosition**. Option **textvariable** associates the text displayed by a **Label** component with a **StringVar** object. Option **textvariable** must be associated with a **Tkinter Variable** object. (Note that in Fig. 10.4 we demonstrated the Label component's text option which is associated with a Python variable.) When the string value of the object—in this case **mousePosition**—changes, the text of the label, **positionLabel**, is updated.

Lines 24–28 bind a few common mouse events to the window. An event is generated when the left mouse button is selected or released while the mouse pointer is in the window, when the mouse pointer enters or leaves the window or when the mouse is moved with the left button pressed.

When a **<Button-1>** event or a **<ButtonRelease-1>** event is generated, method **buttonPressed** (lines 30–34) or method **buttonReleased** (lines 36–40), respectively, calls method **set** to change the value of variable **mousePosition** to inform the user of the event. A mouse event's **Event** object contains the *x*- and *y*-coordinates, stored in the **x** and **y** attributes of the **Event** object, that describe where the event occurred.

When a mouse pointer enters the application area, method **enteredWindow** (lines 42–45) executes. When a mouse pointer exits the application area, method **exited-Window** (lines 47–50) executes. As the screen captures demonstrate, each method prints an appropriate message indicating whether the mouse is over or not over the **MouseLocation** object. The methods modify the value in **StringVar** object **mousePosition** to update the **Label**'s text.

Event handler **mouseDragged** (lines 52–56) is triggered under different circumstances than event handlers **buttonPressed** and **buttonReleased**. There are two conditions which must be met before a **<B1-Motion>** event is triggered: button **B1** must be pressed and the mouse must be moving. Once these requirements are met, the **<B1-Motion>** event is fired at a rate that is defined by the operating system. In other words, on on one operating system, dragging a mouse to the right might trigger 50 **<B1-Motion>** events, while on a different operating system the rate might be much lower. For each **<B1-Motion>** event, method **mouseDragged** displays the events and the coordinates from which the event originated.

A mouse may have one, two, or three buttons. A program may need to take different actions, depending on which button the user has pressed. Figure 10.12 contains a program that demonstrates how to distinguish between different mouse buttons.

```
1   # Fig. 10.12: fig10_12.py
2   # Mouse button differentiation.
3
4   from Tkinter import *
5
6   class MouseDetails( Frame ):
7      """Demonstrate mouse events for different buttons"""
8
9      def __init__( self ):
10         """Create a Label, pack it and bind mouse events"""
11
12         Frame.__init__( self )
13         self.pack( expand = YES, fill = BOTH )
14         self.master.title( "Mouse clicks and buttons" )
15         self.master.geometry( "350x150" )
16
17         # create mousePosition variable
18         self.mousePosition = StringVar()
19         positionLabel = Label( self,
20            textvariable = self.mousePosition )
21         self.mousePosition.set( "Mouse not clicked" )
22         positionLabel.pack( side = BOTTOM )
23
24         # bind event handler to events for each mouse button
25         self.bind( "<Button-1>", self.leftClick )
26         self.bind( "<Button-2>", self.centerClick )
27         self.bind( "<Button-3>", self.rightClick )
28
```

Fig. 10.12 Mouse button differentiation. (Part 1 of 2.)

```
29      def leftClick( self, event ):
30          """Display coordinates and indicate left button clicked"""
31
32          self.showPosition( event.x, event.y )
33          self.master.title( "Clicked with left mouse button" )
34
35      def centerClick( self, event ):
36          """Display coordinates and indicate center button used"""
37
38          self.showPosition( event.x, event.y )
39          self.master.title( "Clicked with center mouse button" )
40
41      def rightClick( self, event ):
42          """Display coordinates and indicate right button clicked"""
43
44          self.showPosition( event.x, event.y )
45          self.master.title( "Clicked with right mouse button" )
46
47      def showPosition( self, x, y ):
48          """Display coordinates of button press"""
49
50          self.mousePosition.set( "Pressed at [ " + str( x ) + ", " +
51              str( y ) + " ]" )
52
53  def main():
54      MouseDetails().mainloop()
55
56  if __name__ == "__main__":
57      main()
```

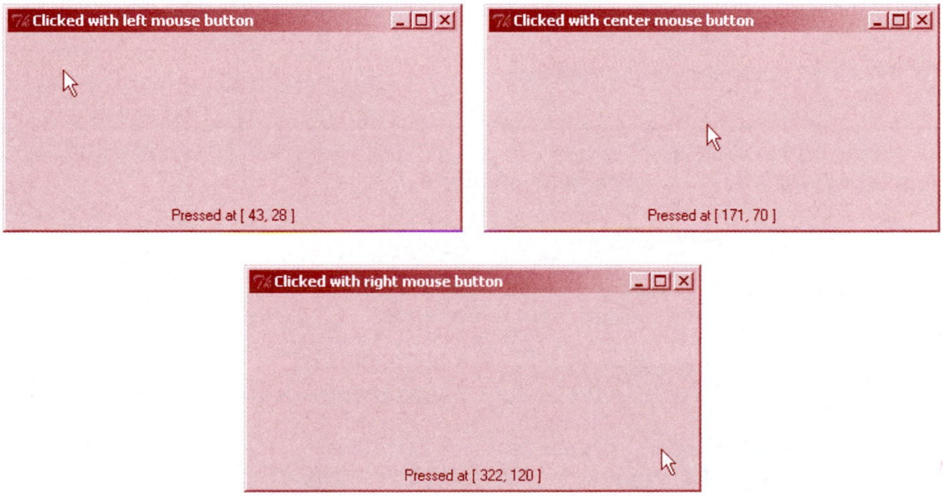

Fig. 10.12 Mouse button differentiation. (Part 2 of 2.)

Figure 10.12 is similar to Fig. 10.11 except that lines 25–27 bind methods to events for different mouse buttons by changing the number in the event format (**<Button-*n*>**). When the user presses a button while the mouse pointer is inside the window, the window's title changes to indicate which button was pressed. Each event handler calls method **showPosition** (lines 47–51), which displays the coordinates of the mouse event.

10.9 Keyboard Event Handling

This section presents binding event handlers to *keyboard events*. These events are generated when keyboard keys are pressed and released. Figure 10.13 presents all available formats for keyboard events.

Figure 10.14 demonstrates binding methods to keyboard events. For clarity, we do not use the shorthand notations of **<KeyPress>** and **<KeyPress-***key***>** events.

Event format	Description of event
<KeyPress>	Any key has been selected.
<KeyRelease>	Any key has been released.
<KeyPress-*key***>** **<KeyRelease-***key***>**	*key* has been selected or released.
<Key>, **<Key-***key***>**	Shorthand notation for **<KeyPress>** and **<KeyPress-***key***>**.
<key>	Shorthand notation for **<KeyPress-***key***>**. This format works only for printable characters (excluding space and less-than sign).
<Prefix-key>	*key* has been selected while *Prefix* is held down. Possible prefixes are **Alt**, **Shift** and **Control**. Note that multiple prefixes are also possible (e.g., **<Control-Alt-***key***>**).

Fig. 10.13 Keyboard event formats.

```
1   # Fig. 10.14: fig10_14.py
2   # Binding keys to keyboard events.
3
4   from Tkinter import *
5
6   class KeyDemo( Frame ):
7      """Demonstrate keystroke events"""
8
9      def __init__( self ):
10        """Create two Labels and bind keystroke events"""
11
12        Frame.__init__( self )
13        self.pack( expand = YES, fill = BOTH )
14        self.master.title( "Demonstrating Keystroke Events" )
15        self.master.geometry( "350x100" )
16
17        self.message1 = StringVar()
18        self.line1 = Label( self, textvariable = self.message1 )
```

Fig. 10.14 Keyboard events demonstrated. (Part 1 of 3.)

```
19            self.message1.set( "Type any key or shift" )
20            self.line1.pack()
21
22            self.message2 = StringVar()
23            self.line2 = Label( self, textvariable = self.message2 )
24            self.message2.set( "" )
25            self.line2.pack()
26
27            # binding any key
28            self.master.bind( "<KeyPress>", self.keyPressed )
29            self.master.bind( "<KeyRelease>", self.keyReleased )
30
31            # binding specific key
32            self.master.bind( "<KeyPress-Shift_L>", self.shiftPressed )
33            self.master.bind( "<KeyRelease-Shift_L>",
34                self.shiftReleased )
35
36        def keyPressed( self, event ):
37            """Display the name of the pressed key"""
38
39            self.message1.set( "Key pressed: " + event.char )
40            self.message2.set( "This key is not left shift" )
41
42        def keyReleased( self, event ):
43            """Display the name of the released key"""
44
45            self.message1.set( "Key released: " + event.char )
46            self.message2.set( "This key is not left shift" )
47
48        def shiftPressed( self, event ):
49            """Display a message that left shift was pressed"""
50
51            self.message1.set( "Shift pressed" )
52            self.message2.set( "This key is left shift" )
53
54        def shiftReleased( self, event ):
55            """Display a message that left shift was released"""
56
57            self.message1.set( "Shift released" )
58            self.message2.set( "This key is left shift" )
59
60    def main():
61        KeyDemo().mainloop()
62
63    if __name__ == "__main__":
64        main()
```

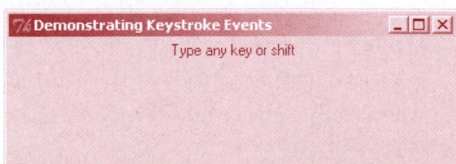

Fig. 10.14 Keyboard events demonstrated. (Part 2 of 3.)

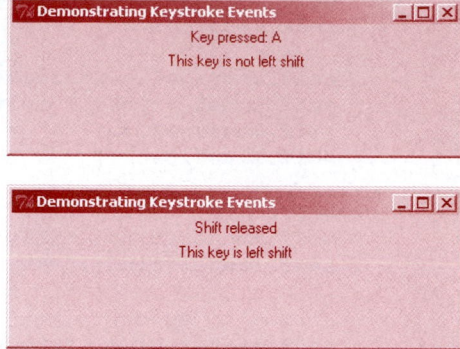

Fig. 10.14 Keyboard events demonstrated. (Part 3 of 3.)

Lines 17–25 create and pack two **Labels**—**line1** and **line2**—that display information about the key events. Lines 28–29 bind methods **keyPressed** and **keyReleased** to **<KeyPress>** and **<KeyRelease>** events, respectively. Method **bind** (lines 32–34) associates the **<KeyPress-***n***>** and **<KeyRelease-***n***>** events for the left **Shift** key (*Shift_L*) to methods **shiftPressed** and **shiftReleased**, respectively.

Methods **shiftPressed** (lines 50–54) and **shiftReleased** (lines 56–60) display messages in the **Label** components when the user presses and releases the left **Shift** key, respectively. If the user selects a key other than the **Shift** key, methods **keyPressed** and **keyReleased** display messages in **line1** and **line2** indicating which key generated the event. Methods **keyPressed** and **keyReleased** obtain the name of the key with the *char* attribute of the **Event** object.

Portability Tip 10.2

Not all systems can distinguish between the left and right Shift keys.

10.10 Layout Managers

Layout managers arrange the placement of GUI components. Most layout managers provide basic layout capabilities that a programmer can use, rather than having to determine the exact position and size of every GUI component. Allowing layout managers to process most of the design details enables the programmer to concentrate on the basic "look and feel" of the GUI. Figure 10.15 summarizes the available layout managers.

Layout manager	Description
Pack	Places components in the order in which they were added.
Grid	Arranges components into rows and columns.
Place	Allows the programmer to specify the size and location of components and windows.

Fig. 10.15 GUI layout managers.

Good Programming Practice 10.3

Choosing the best layout manager can make programming a GUI much easier. Before programming, draw your design and select the manager that best suits it.

Common Programming Error 10.2

*Using more than one type of layout manager in the same container causes the application to freeze while **Tkinter** attempts to reconcile the different demands of each manager.*

10.10.1 Pack

All the previous GUI examples used the most basic layout manager, **Pack**. Unless a programmer specifies a different order, **Pack** places GUI components in a *container* from top to bottom in the order in which they listed in the program. A container is a GUI component into which other components may be placed. Containers are useful for managing the layout of GUI components. When the edge of the container is reached, the container expands, if possible. If the container cannot expand, the remaining components are not visible.

A programmer has several options when packing components in a container. Option **side** indicates the side of the container against which the component is placed. Setting **side** to **TOP** (the default value) packs components vertically. Other possible values are **BOTTOM**, **LEFT** (for horizontal placement) and **RIGHT**. The **fill** option, which can be set to **NONE** (default), **X**, **Y** or **BOTH**, allots the amount of space the component should occupy in the container. Setting **fill** to **X**, **Y** or **BOTH** ensures that a component occupies all the space the container has allocated to it in the specified direction. The **expand** option can be set to **YES** or **NO** (**1** or **0**). The default value is **NO**. If **expand** is set to **YES**, the component expands to fill any extra space in the container. The **padx** and **pady** options insert padding, or empty space, around a component. The method **pack_forget** removes a packed component from a container.

Good Programming Practice 10.4

Review the list of options and methods for layout managers found in the Python on-line documentation before using layout managers.

Common Programming Error 10.3

*Method **pack** places components in a container in the order in which they were packed; therefore, an incorrect packing order can cause undesired results. Packing components with specified values for options **side**, **expand**, **fill**, **padx** and **pady** can create the desired results regardless of packing order.*

Figure 10.16 creates four **Button**s and adds them to the application using the **Pack** layout manager. The example manipulates the button locations and sizes.

The **Frame** constructor (line 12) allows the base class to perform any initialization that it requires before we add components. Method **title** (line 13) displays the title in the GUI. Method **geometry** (line 14) sets the width and height to 300 and 150 pixels, respectively. The **expand** and **fill** options (line 15) are set to **YES** and **BOTH**, respectively, ensuring that the **packDemo** GUI fills the entire window. The second screen capture illustrates the GUI's appearance after it has been resized by dragging the borders with the mouse.

```
1   # Fig. 10.16: fig10_16.py
2   # Pack layout manager demonstration.
3
4   from Tkinter import *
5
6   class PackDemo( Frame ):
7      """Demonstrate some options of Pack"""
8
9      def __init__( self ):
10        """Create four Buttons with different pack options"""
11
12        Frame.__init__( self )
13        self.master.title( "Packing Demo" )
14        self.master.geometry( "400x150" )
15        self.pack( expand = YES, fill = BOTH )
16
17        self.button1 = Button( self, text = "Add Button",
18           command = self.addButton )
19
20        # Button component placed against top of window
21        self.button1.pack( side = TOP )
22
23        self.button2 = Button( self,
24           text = "expand = NO, fill = BOTH" )
25
26        # Button component placed against bottom of window
27        # fills all available vertical and horizontal space
28        self.button2.pack( side = BOTTOM, fill = BOTH )
29
30        self.button3 = Button( self,
31           text = "expand = YES, fill = X" )
32
33        # Button component placed against left side of window
34        # fills all available horizontal space
35        self.button3.pack( side = LEFT, expand = YES, fill = X )
36
37        self.button4 = Button( self,
38           text = "expand = YES, fill = Y" )
39
40        # Button component placed against right side of window
41        # fills all available vertical space
42        self.button4.pack( side = RIGHT, expand = YES, fill = Y )
43
44     def addButton( self ):
45        """Create and pack a new Button"""
46
47        Button( self, text = "New Button" ).pack( pady = 5 )
48
49   def main():
50      PackDemo().mainloop()
51
52   if __name__ == "__main__":
53      main()
```

Fig. 10.16 Pack layout manager demonstration. (Part 1 of 2.)

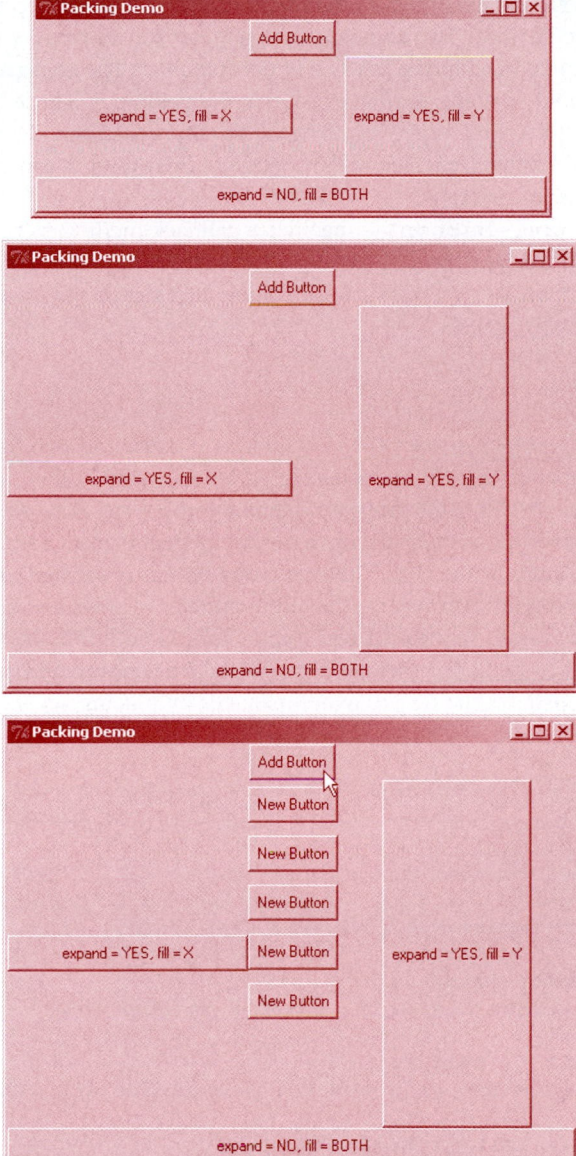

Fig. 10.16 Pack layout manager demonstration. (Part 2 of 2.)

Lines 17–42 create and pack four **Button**s, specifying different packing options for each **Button**. The **Pack** layout manager places each item on the top-level component in the order that they appear in the program. The specified values for options **side**, **expand** and **fill** ensure that the buttons appear as they do in the screenshots. Method **pack** (line 21) places **button1** at the top of the container as specified by option **side**. Since **fill** and **expand** are false by default, the **Button** component maintains its default size. The next component, **button2**, (line 28) is placed at the bottom of the container. The **fill** option's value, **BOTH**, indicates that the **Button** component should occupy all space allocated to it by the container. The **expand** option is set for **button3** (line 35). Method **pack** places this component on the left side of the container. The **expand** option specifies that the button should take any available space in the container. The **X** fill option sets the button to fill all horizontal space given to it by the container. The last component, **button4**, is placed on the right side of the container. Fill option **Y** causes the button to fill all its allocated vertical space.

Only one **Button**—**button1**—specifies a callback method. When the user presses **button1**, method **addButton** (lines 44–47) creates and packs a new **Button**. The newly created **Button**s are packed vertically below **button1** and are each padded in the vertical direction by five pixels.

10.10.2 **Grid**

The *Grid* layout manager divides the container into a grid, so that components can be placed in rows and columns. Components are added to a grid at their specified **row** and **column** indices; every cell in the grid can contain a component. Row and column numbers begin at 0. If the **row** option is not specified, the component is placed in the first empty row and the default **column** value is 0. If the **column** option is omitted, the **column** value defaults to 0. The programmer may set the initial number of rows and columns in the grid by specifying both options in a **grid** constructor call. In addition, the rows and columns can be set with calls to methods **rowconfigure** and **columnconfigure**, respectively. Figure 10.17 demonstrates the **Grid** layout manager by placing several types of components in the GUI.

```
1   # Fig. 10.17: fig10_17.py
2   # Grid layout manager demonstration.
3
4   from Tkinter import *
5
6   class GridDemo( Frame ):
7      """Demonstrate the Grid geometry manager"""
8
9      def __init__( self ):
10         """Create and grid several components into the frame"""
11
12         Frame.__init__( self )
13         self.master.title( "Grid Demo" )
14
15         # main frame fills entire container, expands if necessary
16         self.master.rowconfigure( 0, weight = 1 )
17         self.master.columnconfigure( 0, weight = 1 )
18         self.grid( sticky = W+E+N+S )
19
20         self.text1 = Text( self, width = 15, height = 5 )
21
```

Fig. 10.17 **Grid** layout manager demonstration. (Part 1 of 3.)

```
22              # text component spans three rows and all available space
23              self.text1.grid( rowspan = 3, sticky = W+E+N+S )
24              self.text1.insert( INSERT, "Text1" )
25
26              # place button component in first row, second column
27              self.button1 = Button( self, text = "Button 1",
28                 width = 25 )
29              self.button1.grid( row = 0, column = 1, columnspan = 2,
30                 sticky = W+E+N+S )
31
32              # place button component in second row, second column
33              self.button2 = Button( self, text = "Button 2" )
34              self.button2.grid( row = 1, column = 1, sticky = W+E+N+S )
35
36              # configure button component to fill all it allocated space
37              self.button3 = Button( self, text = "Button 3" )
38              self.button3.grid( row = 1, column = 2, sticky = W+E+N+S )
39
40              # span two columns starting in second column of first row
41              self.button4 = Button( self, text = "Button 4" )
42              self.button4.grid( row = 2, column = 1, columnspan = 2,
43                 sticky = W+E+N+S )
44
45              # place text field in fourth row to span two columns
46              self.entry = Entry( self )
47              self.entry.grid( row = 3, columnspan = 2,
48                 sticky = W+E+N+S )
49              self.entry.insert( INSERT, "Entry" )
50
51              # fill all available space in fourth row, third column
52              self.text2 = Text( self, width = 2, height = 2 )
53              self.text2.grid( row = 3, column = 2, sticky = W+E+N+S )
54              self.text2.insert( INSERT, "Text2" )
55
56              # make second row/column expand
57              self.rowconfigure( 1, weight = 1 )
58              self.columnconfigure( 1, weight = 1 )
59
60  def main():
61      GridDemo().mainloop()
62
63  if __name__ == "__main__":
64      main()
```

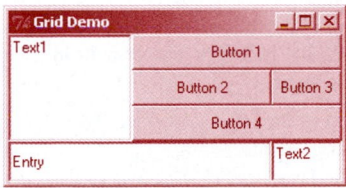
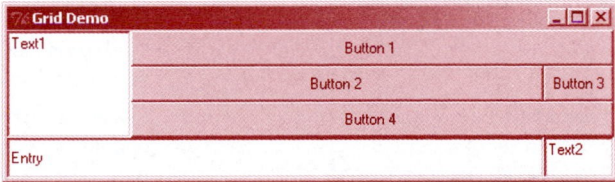

Fig. 10.17 Grid layout manager demonstration. (Part 2 of 3.)

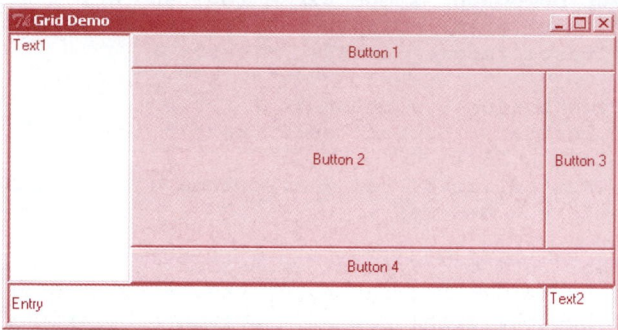

Fig. 10.17 Grid layout manager demonstration. (Part 3 of 3.)

Method **grid** (line 18) places the top-level component in row 0 and column 0, by default. The *sticky* option for the **gridDemo** object is **W+E+N+S**; this causes the main frame to expand to fill the entire cell. The **sticky** option specifies the component's alignment and whether the component stretches to fill the cell. Possible values for **sticky** are any combination of **W**, **E**, **N**, **S**, **NW**, **NE**, **SW** and **SE**. A **sticky** value of **W+E**, for example, is similar to setting **fill** to **X** when packing a component—the component stretches from the left (**W**) to the right (**E**) to fill the cell. Setting **sticky** to **W+E+N+S** produces results similar to those produced by the **Pack** layout manager's **fill** value of **BOTH**. Specifying only one value for **sticky** is analogous to the **side** option of **Pack**—the component aligns with the indicated cell border without being stretched. The second screenshot shows the GUI after being resized with the mouse.

The **Grid** manager supports several methods that control the placement of components in the container. Methods *rowconfigure* and *columnconfigure* change row and column options, respectively. For example, to ensure that row 0 stretches when the window is resized, method *rowconfigure* (line 16) sets the *weight* option to 1. The **weight** option indicates the relative weight of growth for a row or column. Weight describes the rate at which the row or column grows as the window is resized. For object, a row with a weight of three increases at three times the rate of a row whose weight is one. The default is 0—cells will not change size if a user resizes the window. Figure 10.18 describes the most common **Grid** methods.

Grid Methods	Description
columnconfigure(*column, options* **)**	Sets *column* options, such as **minsize** (minimum size), **pad** (add padding to largest component in the column) and **weight**.
grid()	Places a component in **Grid** as described by optional keyword arguments.
grid_forget()	Removes, but does not destroy, a component.

Fig. 10.18 Grid methods. (Part 1 of 2.)

Grid Methods	Description
grid_remove()	Removes a component, storing its associated options in case the component is re-inserted.
grid_info()	Returns current options as a dictionary.
grid_location(x, y)	Returns the grid position closest to the given pixel coordinates as a tuple (*column*, *row*).
grid_size()	Returns the grid size as a tuple (*column*, *row*).
rowconfigure(*row*, *options*)	Sets *row*'s options, such as **minsize** (minimum size), **pad** (add padding to largest component in the row) and **weight**.

Fig. 10.18 Grid methods. (Part 2 of 2.)

Line 20 introduces the ***Text*** component, which creates a multiple-line text area **text1**. Method **grid** (line 23) inserts component **text1** into the grid and introduces keyword argument ***rowspan***. The **rowspan** option sets the number of rows that a component occupies in the GUI.

Component **button1** (line 27) spans two columns, as indicated by keyword argument ***columnspan***. Option **columnspan** causes a component to stretch across a specified number of columns. Lines 27–43 create four buttons and explicitly insert each button at a certain **row** and **column**.

The **Entry** component inserted at row 3 (lines 46–49) spans two columns and fills all available space in the cell. In line 47, **columnspan** is assigned 2 and **sticky** is set to **W+E+N+S**—creating an **Entry** component that fills the first two columns of row 3. Methods **rowconfigure** and **columnconfigure** ensure that the second row and column expand when a user resizes the window (lines 57–58).

As in the **Pack** layout manager, **Grid** options **padx** and **pady** set the size of vertical and horizontal padding around a component in a cell. To place padding inside the component, use options **ipadx** and **ipady**. When a component is smaller than its cell, it is centered in the cell by default.

 It is possible to specify overlapping components. The components that are packed earliest in the code are obscured by the most recently added component.

10.10.3 Place

The ***Place*** layout manager allows the user to set the position and size of a GUI component absolutely or relatively to the position and size of another component. The component being referenced is specified with the **in_** option and may be only the parent of the component being placed (default) or a descendant of its parent.

Layout manager **Place** is more complicated than the other managers. For this reason, we do not discuss the **Place** layout manager in detail, although Fig. 10.19 lists the most common **Place** methods. Figure 10.20 lists the common **place** and **place_configure** method options. For more information on layout manager **Place**, visit **www.python.org**.

Place Method	Description
place()	Inserts a component as specified by keyword arguments.
place_forget()	Removes, but does not destroy, a component.
place_info()	Returns current options in a dictionary.
place_configure()	Positions a component as specified by keyword arguments.

Fig. 10.19 Place methods.

Place Option	Description
x	Designates the absolute horizontal position of the component.
y	Designates the absolute vertical position of the component.
relx	Indicates the horizontal position of the component, relative to that of another component.
rely	Specifies the vertical position of the component, relative to that of another component.
width	Specifies the absolute width of the component.
height	Indicates the absolute height of the component.
relwidth	Specifies the width of the component, relative to that of another component.
relheight	Specifies the height of the component, relative to that of another component.
in_	Specifies a reference component. The newly inserted component, which must be a sibling or a child of the reference component, is placed relative to it.
anchor	Indicates which part of the component to "fix" at the given position. Possible values are **NW** (default), **N**, **NE**, **E**, **SE**, **S**, **SW**, **W** and **CENTER**.

Fig. 10.20 Place options.

10.11 Card Shuffling and Dealing Simulation

In this section. we use random number generation to develop a card shuffling and dealing simulation program. This program then can be used to implement programs that play specific card games.

We develop GUI class **Deck** (Fig. 10.21), which creates a deck of 52 playing cards using **Card** objects, then enables the user to deal each card by clicking on a **"Deal card"** button. Each card dealt is displayed in a **Label**. The user can shuffle the deck at any time by clicking on a **"Shuffle cards"** button.

Class **Card** (lines 7–26) contains two lists—**faces** and **suits**—that store every possible card face and suit. The constructor for the class (lines 17–21) receives a string from list **faces** and a string from list **suits**. Method **__str__** (lines 23–26) returns a string consisting of the **face** of the card, the string **" of "** and the **suit** of the card.

Class **Deck** (lines 32–95) consists of a list deck of 52 **Card** objects, an integer **currentCard** representing the most recently dealt card in the deck list and the GUI components used to manipulate the deck of cards. The constructor uses the **for** structure (lines 41–43) to fill the deck list with **Card** objects. Each **Card** is instantiated and initialized with two strings—one from the **faces** list (Strings **"Ace"** through **"King"**) and one from the **suits** list (**"Hearts"**, **"Diamonds"**, **"Clubs"** and **"Spades"**). Note that the lists are referenced as **Card.faces** and **Card.suits**, respectively, because they are class attributes of class **Card**. The calculation **i % 13** always results in a value from 0 to 12 (the thirteen subscripts of the **faces** list), and the calculation **i / 13** always results in a value from 0 to 3 (the four subscripts in the **suits** list).

```
1   # Fig. 11.21: fig11_21.py
2   # Card shuffling and dealing program
3
4   import random
5   from Tkinter import *
6
7   class Card:
8       """Class that represents one playing card"""
9
10      # class attributes faces and suits contain strings
11      # that correspond to card face and suit values
12      faces = [ "Ace", "Deuce", "Three", "Four", "Five",
13                "Six", "Seven", "Eight", "Nine", "Ten",
14                "Jack", "Queen", "King" ]
15      suits = [ "Hearts", "Diamonds", "Clubs", "Spades" ]
16
17      def __init__( self, face, suit ):
18          """Card constructor, takes face and suit as strings"""
19
20          self.face = face
21          self.suit = suit
22
23      def __str__( self ):
24          """String representation of a card"""
25
26          return "%s of %s" % ( self.face, self.suit )
27
28  class Deck( Frame ):
29      """Class to represent a GUI card deck shuffler"""
30
31      def __init__( self ):
32          """Deck constructor"""
33
34          Frame.__init__( self )
35          self.master.title( "Card Dealing Program" )
36
37          self.deck = []   # list of card objects
38          self.currentCard = 0   # index of current card
39
```

Fig. 10.21 Card-dealing program. (Part 1 of 3.)

```
40          # create deck
41          for i in range( 52 ):
42             self.deck.append( Card( Card.faces[ i % 13 ],
43                Card.suits[ i / 13 ] ) )
44
45          # create buttons
46          self.dealButton = Button( self, text = "Deal Card",
47             width = 10, command = self.dealCard )
48          self.dealButton.grid( row = 0, column = 0 )
49
50          self.shuffleButton = Button( self, text = "Shuffle cards",
51             width = 10, command = self.shuffle )
52          self.shuffleButton.grid( row = 0, column = 1 )
53
54          # create labels
55          self.message1 = Label( self, height = 2,
56             text = "Welcome to Card Dealer!" )
57          self.message1.grid( row = 1, columnspan = 2 )
58
59          self.message2 = Label( self, height = 2,
60             text = "Deal card or shuffle deck" )
61          self.message2.grid( row = 2, columnspan = 2 )
62
63          self.shuffle()
64          self.grid()
65
66      def shuffle( self ):
67          """Shuffle the deck"""
68
69          self.currentCard = 0
70
71          for i in range( len( self.deck ) ):
72             j = random.randint( 0, 51 )
73
74             # swap the cards
75             self.deck[ i ], self.deck[ j ] = \
76                self.deck[ j ], self.deck[ i ]
77
78          self.message1.config( text = "DECK IS SHUFFLED" )
79          self.message2.config( text = "" )
80          self.dealButton.config( state = NORMAL )
81
82      def dealCard( self ):
83          """Deal one card from the deck"""
84
85          # display the card, if it exists
86          if self.currentCard < len( self.deck ):
87             self.message1.config(
88                text = self.deck[ self.currentCard ] )
89             self.message2.config(
90                text = "Card #: %d" % self.currentCard )
```

Fig. 10.21 Card-dealing program. (Part 2 of 3.)

```
91            else:
92                self.message1.config( text = "NO MORE CARDS TO DEAL" )
93                self.message2.config( text =
94                   "Shuffle cards to continue" )
95                self.dealButton.config( state = DISABLED )
96
97            self.currentCard += 1   # increment card for next turn
98
99   def main():
100      Deck().mainloop()
101
102   if __name__ == "__main__":
103      main()
```

Fig. 10.21 Card-dealing program. (Part 3 of 3.)

When the user clicks the **Deal card** button, method **dealCard** (lines 82–95) gets the next card in the list. If **currentCard** is less than 52 (the length of deck), lines 87–88 display the face and suit of the card in **Label message1**. **Label message2** (lines 89–90) displays the number of the card (**currentCard**). If there are no more cards to deal (i.e., **currentCard** is greater than or equal to 52), the string **"NO MORE CARDS TO DEAL"** is displayed in **message1** and string **"Shuffle cards to continue"** is displayed in **message2**.

When the user clicks the **Shuffle cards** button, method **shuffle** (lines 66–80) shuffles the cards. The method loops through all 52 cards (list subscripts 0 to 51). For each card, a number between 0 and 51 is picked randomly. Next, the current **Card** object and the randomly selected **Card** object are swapped in the list. A total of only 52 swaps are made in a single pass of the entire list, and the list of **Card** objects is shuffled! When the shuffling is complete, **"DECK IS SHUFFLED"** is displayed in a **Label**.

10.12 Internet and World Wide Web Resources

This section presents several Internet and World Wide Web resources related to using module **Tkinter** with Python.

faqts.com/knowledge_base/index.phtml/fid/264
This **python.faqts** page contains questions and answers concerning **Tkinter** and Python interaction.

faqts.com/knowledge_base/index.phtml/fid/265
This page lists questions and answers concerning handling events.

www.pythonware.com/library/tkinter/introduction
Fredrik Lundh's *An Introduction to Tkinter* offers information about **Widget** classes and event handling.

www.python.org/topics/tkinter
This Web page provides links to documentation about **Tkinter**, additional **Widget** classes and troubleshooting tips.

www.csis.hku.hk/~kkto/doc-tkinter/tkinter/tkinter.html
Isaac K. K. To's *Building GUI Programs Using Tkinter: A Tkinter Manual* provides information about layout managers, events, the **Widget** class and subclasses.

SUMMARY

- A graphical user interface (GUI) presents a pictorial interface to a program.

- A GUI (pronounced "GOO-eE") gives a program a distinctive "look" and "feel."

- By providing different applications with a consistent set of intuitive user-interface components, GUIs allow the user to spend less time trying to remember which keystroke sequences do what and spend more time using the program in a productive manner.

- GUIs are built from GUI components (sometimes called controls or widgets—shorthand for window gadgets).

- A GUI component is an object with which a user interacts via a mouse or a keyboard.

- The **Tkinter** module is the most frequently used module for programming graphical user interfaces in Python.

- The **Tkinter** library provides an interface to the Tk (Tool Kit) GUI toolkit–the graphical interface development tool for the Tool Command Language (TCL).

- **Tkinter** implements each Tk GUI component as a class that inherits from class **Widget**.

- All **Widget**s have common attributes and behaviors.

- A GUI consists of a top-level component that may contain more GUI components. The top-level component is the parent component. The remaining components are children of the top-level component and each child of the top-level component may itself contain children (descendants of the parent component). A program builds a GUI from the top-level component by creating new components and placing each new component in its parent.

- Inheriting from class **Frame** extends the GUI's functionality. This inheritance enables the reuse of components in other GUI programs and promotes object-orientation in GUI programs.

- The **Tkinter** module, like the rest of Python, is portable across many platforms.

- Labels display text or images and usually provide instructions or other information on a graphical user interface.

- The **Frame** constructor initializes the **Frame** and creates a top-level component into which the **Frame** is placed.

- The creation of a GUI object initially does not display it on the screen. The program must specify where and how to draw the object.

- Method **pack** places components in the GUI.

- Keyword argument **fill** specifies how much available space the component occupies, beyond the component's default size. Possible values for fill are **X** (all available horizontal space), **Y** (all available vertical space), **BOTH** (both vertical and horizontal available space) and **NONE** (the default value—do not take up available space).

- Keyword argument **expand** specifies whether a child component should take up any extra space in its parent component (i.e., any space not yet occupied once all other components have been placed).

- Each GUI component's class constructor takes a first argument that corresponds to the new object's parent.

- The value of keyword argument **text** specifies the contents of the **Label** component.

- The keyword argument **side** describes where the new component is drawn. Value **LEFT** specifies that a component is placed against the left side of the window. Other possible values for the **side** option are **BOTTOM**, **RIGHT** and **TOP**, the default setting.

- Many components display images by specifying a value for the keyword argument **bitmap**.

- Keyword argument **image** inserts a programmer-defined image. Label options have the following precedence, from highest to lowest: **image**, **bitmap** and **text**. Each **Label** component displays only one bitmap, image or text message. The value of the option with the highest precedence appears on the GUI. Any other values are ignored.

- If the interpreter is running the program, method **mainloop** method starts the GUI, redraws the GUI as needed and sends events to the appropriate components. It terminates when the user destroys (closes) the GUI.

- GUIs are event driven (i.e., they generate events when the user of the program interacts with the GUI). Some common interactions are moving the mouse, clicking a mouse button, typing in a text field, selecting an item from a menu and closing a window. When a user interaction occurs, an event is sent to the program.

- GUI event information is stored in an object of a class **Event**.

- An event-driven program is asynchronous—the program does not know when events will happen.

- To process a GUI event, the programmer must perform two key tasks—bind an event to a graphical component and implement an event handler. A program explicitly binds, or associates, an event with a graphical component and specifies an action to perform when that event occurs. Typically, the action is performed by an event handler—a method that is called in response to its associated event.

- When an event occurs, the GUI component with which the user interacted determines whether an event handler has been specified for the event. If an event handler has been specified, that event handler executes. The program can specify an event handler that executes when this event occurs.

- **Entry** components are areas in which users can enter or programmers can display a single line of text.

- When the user types data into an **Entry** component and presses the *Enter* key, a **<Return>** event occurs. If an event handler is bound to that event for the **Entry** component, the event is processed and the data in the **Entry** can be used by the program.

- Module **tkMessageBox** contains functions that display dialogs. Dialogs present messages to the user.

- Method **geometry** specifies the length and width of the top-level component in pixels.

- Option **pady** of method **pack** specifies the amount of empty vertical space between GUI components. Similarly, option **padx** specifies the amount of empty horizontal space between components.

- The **Entry** constructor's **width** argument specifies that 20 columns of text can appear in the text area on the GUI, although the **Entry** component accommodates larger inputs. The width of the text field will be the width, in pixels, of the average character in the text field's current font multiplied by 20.

- Option **name** assigns a name to the **Entry**. A program can use the name to identify the component in which an event has occurred.

- Method **bind** associates an event with a component. Method **bind** takes two arguments. The first argument is the type of the event, and the second argument is the name of the method to bind to that event.

- Method **insert** writes text in the **Entry** component. Method **insert** takes two arguments— a position at which text is to be inserted and a string that contains the text to insert.

- Passing a value of **INSERT** as the first argument to method **insert** causes the text to be inserted at the cursor's current position.

- Method call **insert(END, text)** appends **text** to the end of any text already displayed in the component.

- Method call **delete(start, finish)** removes all text in an **Entry** component in the range **start** to **finish**. Using **END** as the second argument removes text up to the end of the text area. The first position in an **Entry** component is position 0; **delete(0, END)** removes all text in an **Entry** component.

- Method **config** configures a component's options.

- Specifying the value **DISABLED** for option **state** disables the **Entry** component, preventing the user from editing its text.

- Option **show** sets the character that appears in place of the actual text.

- Most event handlers take as an argument an **Event** object, which has various attributes. The component that generated the event is obtained from the **widget** attribute of the **Event** object (i.e., **event.widget**).

- **Widget** method **winfo_name** and **Entry** method **get** acquire the name and contents of an **Entry**, respectively.

- The **tkMessageBox** function **showinfo** displays a dialog box.

- A button is a component the user clicks to trigger a specific action. A button generates an event when the user clicks the button with the mouse.

- Buttons are created with class **Button**, which inherits from class **Widget**.

- The text or image on the face of a **Button** component is called a button label.

- **Button**s (like **Label**s) can display both images and text.

- Option **text** sets the button's label.

- Keyword argument **command** specifies the event handler (or callback) that is invoked when the button is selected.

- Many **Tkinter** components, including **Button**s, can display images by specifying an **image** argument to their constructor or their **config** method.

- A specified image must be an object of a **Tkinter** class that loads an image file. One such class is **PhotoImage**, which supports three image formats—Graphics Interchange Format (GIF), Joint Photographic Experts Group (JPEG) and Portable Greymap Format (PGM). File names for each of these types typically end with **.gif**, **.jpg** (or **.jpeg**) or **.pgm** (or **.ppm**), respectively.

- Class is **BitmapImage** supports the Bitmap (BMP) image format (**.bmp**).

- As with **Label**s, the **image** attribute of a **Button** component takes precedence over **text** and **bitmap** attributes.

- The **relief** option of the **Button**s is changed to **GROOVE** or **RAISED** to create rollover effects.

- **Tkinter** contains two GUI components—**Checkbutton** and **Radiobutton**—that have on/off or true/false values.

- Classes **Checkbutton** and **Radiobutton** are subclasses of **Widget**.

- A **Radiobutton** is different than a **Checkbutton** in that there are normally several **Radiobutton**s that are grouped together, and only one of the **Radiobutton**s in the group can be selected (true) at any time. Radio buttons are used to represent a set of mutually exclusive options (i.e., multiple options in the group cannot be selected at the same time).

- **Entry** fonts are specified using the **font** attribute. One way of representing a font is a string containing the name, size and style of the font. It is possible to specify no font style, as well as more than one font style.

- **BooleanVar** objects are **Tkinter** integer variables that have value 0 or 1.

- **Tkinter** provides a **Variable** class from which **BooleanVar** inherits. The **Variable** class acts as a container for Python variables.

- The **CheckButton** class uses a **BooleanVar** object to store the state—checked or unchecked—of the button.

- **StringVar**, like **BooleanVar**, is a subclass of **Tkinter** class **Variable**. A **StringVar** object acts as the interface to a string variable.

- Attribute **variable** associates **chosenFont** with each **Radiobutton** component.

- Keyword argument **value** specifies the value to assign to the associated variable when a radio button is selected.

- All **Tkinter** events described by strings follow the pattern *<modifier–type–detail>*. The type specifies the kind of event.

- An **Event** object for a mouse event contains information about the mouse event that occurred, including the *x*- and *y*-coordinates of the location where the event occurred. The *x*- and *y*-coordinates of the location of the mouse pointer when the event occurred are stored in the **x** and **y** attributes of the **Event** object.

- The name of a selected key can be obtained with the **char** attribute of the **Event** object.

- Layout managers arrange GUI components on a container for presentation purposes. Most layout managers provide basic layout capabilities that are easier to use than determining the exact position and size of every GUI component.

- Letting layout managers process most of the layout details enables the programmer to concentrate on the basic "look and feel" of the GUI.

- **Pack** is the most basic layout manager. GUI components are placed on a container from top to bottom in the order in which they are added to the container (unless otherwise specified). When the edge of the container is reached, the container is expanded (if possible), or the remaining components are not visible.

- A programmer can specify several options when packing components in a container.

- The **padx** and **pady** options place padding around the component.

- To remove a packed component from a container, use the component's **pack_forget** method.

- Method **title** displays the title in the GUI.

- Method **geometry** sets the width and height of a GUI.

- The **Grid** layout manager divides the container into a grid, so that components can be placed in rows and columns, where the numbering of the rows and columns starts at 0.

- Every cell in the grid can contain a component.

- Components are added to a grid at their specified **row** and **column** indices. If the **row** option is not specified, the component is placed in the first empty row. The default **column** value is 0.

- The **sticky** option specifies the component's alignment or stretches the component to fill the cell. Possible values for **sticky** are any combination of **W, E, N, S, NW, NE, SW** and **SE**.

- A **sticky** value of **W+E** is similar to setting **fill** to **X** when packing a component—the component stretches from the left (**W**) to the right (**E**). The component stretches horizontally to fill the cell.

- Setting **sticky** to **W+E+N+S** produces results similar to those produced by a **fill** value of **BOTH**.

- Specifying only one value for **sticky** is analogous to the **side** option of **Pack**. The component aligns to the specified cell border without being stretched.

- The **Grid** manager, the component into which other components have been placed, supports several methods that control the grid.

- Methods **rowconfigure** and **columnconfigure** change options of rows and columns, respectively.

- The **weight** option specifies the relative weight of growth for a row or column. The default is 0, therefore, cells will not change size if the window is resized unless the **weight** option has been changed.

- The **Text** component creates a multiple-line text area.

- The **rowspan** option sets the number of rows that a component occupies in the GUI.

- Option **columnspan** causes a component to span the specified number of columns.

- As in the **Pack** layout manager, **Grid** options **padx** and **pady** specify the size of vertical and horizontal padding around a component in a cell.

- To place padding inside the component, use options **ipadx** and **ipady**. If a component is smaller than its cell, it is centered in the cell by default.

- The **Place** layout manager allows the user to set the position and size of a GUI component in relation to the position and size of another component relatively or absolutely. The component being referenced is specified with the **in_** option and may be only the parent of the component being placed (default) or a descendant of its parent.

- The **Place** layout manager is more complicated than the other managers, so most programmers prefer to use the other, more simpler managers.

TERMINOLOGY

anchor option of layout manger **Place**
bitmap image
bitmap option of **Button** component
bitmap option of **Entry** component
BitmapImage class
<B*n***-motion>** event
BooleanVar class
BOTTOM value of option **side** of method **pack**
Button component
button label
<Button-*n***>** event
<ButtonPress-*n***>** event
<ButtonRelease-*n***>** event
callback
CENTER value of option **anchor** of
    layout manger **Place**
char attribute of the **Event** object
check box

Checkbutton component
children
columnconfigure method of
    layout manager **Grid**
column option of method **grid**
columnspan option of method **grid**
config method of class **Widget**
E value of option **anchor** of
    layout manger **Place**
E value of option **sticky** of method **grid**
<Enter> event
Entry component
Event class
event handler
expand option of method **pack**
fill option of method **pack**
font attribute of component **Entry**
Frame component

Tk (Tool Kit)
Tkinter module
tkMessageBox module
Tool Command Language (TCL)
TOP value of option **side** of method **pack**
top-level component
value option of component **Checkbutton**
value option of component **Radiobutton**
variable option of component
   Checkbutton
variable option of component
   Radiobutton

W value of option anchor of
   layout manager **Place**
W value of option sticky of method **grid**
weight option of layout manager **Grid**
Widget class
width option of layout manager **Place**
winfo_name method of class **Widget**
X option of layout manager **Place**
x value of option **fill** of method **pack**
Y option of layout manager **Place**
y value of option **fill** of method **pack**
YES value of option **expand** of method **pack**

SELF-REVIEW EXERCISES

10.1   Fill in the blanks in each of the following:
a) A _____ presents a pictorial user interface to a program.
b) Labels are defined with class _____— a subclass of _____.
c) _____ are single-line areas in which text can be displayed.
d) Method _____ displays text in an **Entry**.
e) Method _____ displays a message dialog.
f) A _____ is a container for other components.
g) Use method _____ of class _____ to acquire the name of an **Entry**.
h) _____ arrange GUI components on a container for presentation purposes.
i) A _____ is a component that the user clicks to trigger an action.
j) The _____ places components in the specified row and column.

10.2   State whether each of the following is *true* or *false*. If *false*, explain why.
a) All Tkinter classes inherit from **Frame**.
b) A **Label** displays only text.
c) The **Entry** component creates multiple-line text areas.
d) When the user types data into an **Entry** and presses the Enter key, an **<Enter>** event occurs.
e) **Tkinter Button** components display images using method **img**.
f) Class **PhotoImage** supports GIF, JPEG and PGM images.
g) Only one **Radiobutton** can be selected at a time.
h) **Boolean** objects are **Tkinter** integer variables that can have a value of 0 or 1.
i) Event format **<Left>** handles the event in which a mouse pointer has exited the component.
j) Layout managers arrange the placement of GUI components.

ANSWERS TO SELF-REVIEW EXERCISES

10.1   a) graphical user interface (GUI). b) **Label**, **Widget**. c) **Entry**s. d) **insert**. e) **show-info**. f) **Frame**. g) **winfo_name**, **Widget**. h) Layout managers. i) button. j) **Grid** layout manager.

10.2   a) False. All Tkinter classes inherit from **Widget**. b) False. A **Label** can display text or an image. c) False. The **Entry** component creates single-line text areas. A **Text** widget creates multiple-line text areas. d) False. When the user types data into an **Entry** and presses the Enter key, a **<Return>** event occurs. e) False. **Tkinter Button** components display images using method **image**. f) True. g) True. h) False. **BooleanVar** objects are **Tkinter** integer variables that can have a value of 0 or 1. i) False. Event format **<Leave>** handles the event in which a mouse pointer has left the component. j) True.

EXERCISES

10.3   Create the following GUI using the **Grid** layout manager. You do not have to provide any functionality.

10.4   Write a temperature conversion program that converts Fahrenheit to Celsius. Use the **Pack** layout manager. The Fahrenheit temperature should be entered from the keyboard via an **Entry** component. A **tkMessageBox** should display the converted temperature. Use the following formula for the conversion:

```
Celsius = 5 /9 * (Fahrenheit - 32)
```

10.5   Enhance the temperature conversion program of Exercise 10.4 by adding the Kelvin temperature scale. The program should also allow the user to make conversions between any two scales. Use the following formula for the conversion between Kelvin and Celsius (in addition to the formula in Exercise 10.4):

```
Kelvin = Celsius + 273
```

10.6   Add functionality—addition, subtraction, multiplication and division—to the calculator created in Exercise 10.3. Use the built-in Python function **eval** to evaluates strings. For instance, **eval("34+24")** returns the integer 58.

10.7   Write a program that allows the user to practice typing. When the user clicks a button, the program generates and displays a random sequence of letters in an **Entry** component. The user repeats the sequence in another **Entry** component. When the user enters an incorrect letter, the program displays an error message until the user types the correct letter. Use keyboard events.

10.8   Create a GUI for a matching game. Initially, buttons should cover pairs of images. When the user clicks a button, the image displays. If the user finds a matching pair, disable the buttons and display their images. If the user's choices do not match, hide the images.

11

Graphical User Interface Components: Part 2

Objectives

- To create a scrolled list of items from which a user can make a selection.
- To create scrolled text areas.
- To create menus and popup menus.
- To create and manipulate canvases and scales.

I claim not to have controlled events, but confess plainly that events have controlled me.
Abraham Lincoln

A good symbol is the best argument, and is a missionary to persuade thousands.
Ralph Waldo Emerson

Capture its reality in paint!
Paul Cézanne

Outline

11.1 Introduction

In this chapter, we continue our study of GUIs. We discuss more advanced components and lay the groundwork for building complex GUIs.

We discuss *Python megawidgets (**Pmw**)*—a toolkit that provides high-level GUI components developed from smaller components provided by the **Tkinter** module. For example, a **Pmw** *ScrolledListBox* component allows the user to select an item from a drop-down list. We continue our discussion with a look at the *ScrolledText* component that allows a user to manipulate multiple lines of text. We also discuss menus; **Pmw** class **MenuBar** creates a component that helps a user organize a menu.

We also introduce more **Tkinter** classes. We use **Tkinter** class *Menu* to create popup menus—context-sensitive menus that typically appear when the user right clicks on components that have popup menus. Finally, we discuss the **Tkinter** *Canvas* component for displaying and manipulating text, images, lines and shapes. There are many GUI components and toolkits available to Python programmers, so we end this chapter with a description of several other toolkits.

11.2 Overview of **Pmw**

Python Megawidgets (**Pmw**) is a collection of useful GUI components built using module **Tkinter**. Each **Pmw** component combines one or more **Tkinter** components to create a useful, more complex component. Each **Tkinter** component can be referred to as a *subcomponent* of the **Pmw** component. For example, the **Pmw** *ComboBox* component combines an **Entry** component and a **Listbox** component to create a more complex component that enables users to select an item from a **Listbox** and edit the selection in an **Entry**.

Each subcomponent of a **Pmw** component can be configured independently—the appearance and functionality of the subcomponent can be modified. **Pmw** options have names of the form *subcomponent_option*, and the programmer configures a **Pmw** component by setting values for these options. Each component can be configured by passing option values in the constructor call either when the component is created or at a later time by passing option values in a call to method *configure*. For example, the following statement creates a **ScrolledListBox Pmw** component and configures the **Listbox** subcomponent with a height of 3:

```
Pmw.ScrolledListBox( self, listbox_height = 3 )
```

The following line configures the height of the **text** component in an existing **Pmw** *TextDialog* component

```
textdialog.configure( text_height = 10 )
```

Although **Pmw** extends the functionality of the **Tkinter** module by providing additional components, **Pmw** is not packaged with Python. To download the product, visit **pmw.sourceforge.net**. For installation instructions, visit the Deitel & Associates Web site at **www.deitel.com**.

11.3 ScrolledListbox Component

A *list box* (sometimes called a *drop-down list*) provides a list of items from which the user can select. **Tkinter** class *Listbox* (a derived class of **Widget**) implements list boxes.

In some cases, the number of items in a list prevents the list from being displayed entirely on the screen. In such cases, it is desirable to allow the user to scroll through the list. Scrolling can be implemented by configuring a **Scrollbar** and a **Listbox** to work together. However, **Pmw** offers a simpler option, the *ScrolledListBox megawidget*.

Figure 11.1 uses the **ScrolledListBox** component to provide a list of four image filenames. When the user selects an image filename, the program displays the corresponding image in a **Label**. The screen captures show the **ScrolledListBox** list after a selection.

```
1   # Fig. 11.1: fig11_01.py
2   # ScrolledListBox used to select image.
3
4   from Tkinter import *
5   import Pmw
6
7   class ImageSelection( Frame ):
8      """List of available images and an area to display them"""
9
10     def __init__( self, images ):
11        """Create list of PhotoImages and Label to display them"""
12
13        Frame.__init__( self )
14        Pmw.initialise()
15        self.pack( expand = YES, fill = BOTH )
16        self.master.title( "Select an image" )
17
18        self.photos = []
19
20        # add PhotoImage objects to list photos
21        for item in images:
22           self.photos.append( PhotoImage( file = item ) )
```

Fig. 11.1 ScrolledListBox used to select an image. (Part 1 of 2.)

```
23
24        # create scrolled list box with vertical scrollbar
25        self.listBox = Pmw.ScrolledListBox( self, items = images,
26           listbox_height = 3, vscrollmode = "static",
27           selectioncommand = self.switchImage )
28        self.listBox.pack( side = LEFT, expand = YES, fill = BOTH,
29           padx = 5, pady = 5 )
30
31        self.display = Label( self, image = self.photos[ 0 ] )
32        self.display.pack( padx = 5, pady = 5 )
33
34     def switchImage( self ):
35        """Change image in Label to current selection"""
36
37        # get tuple containing index of selected list item
38        chosenPicture = self.listBox.curselection()
39
40        # configure label to display selected image
41        if chosenPicture:
42           choice = int( chosenPicture[ 0 ] )
43           self.display.config( image = self.photos[ choice ] )
44
45  def main():
46     images = [ "bug1.gif", "bug2.gif",
47                "travelbug.gif", "buganim.gif" ]
48     ImageSelection( images ).mainloop()
49
50  if __name__ == "__main__":
51     main()
```

Fig. 11.1   ScrolledListBox used to select an image. (Part 2 of 2.)

Line 5 imports module **Pmw**. In line 14, function **Pmw.initialise** initializes **Pmw**. The call to function **initialise** enables the program to access the full functionality of the **Pmw** module.

Testing and Debugging Tip 11.1

*A program that uses module **Pmw** but does not invoke **Pmw.initialise** is not able to access the full functionality of module **Pmw**.*

Method **main** (lines 45–48) creates a list of image filenames, **images**, that the program passes to the constructor method of class **ImageSelection** (lines 7–43). Lines 21–22 create a list of **PhotoImage** instances from the filenames in **images**. Lines 25–

27 create a new **ScrolledListBox** component called **listBox**. The *items* option contains the list of items to be displayed in **listBox**. When the user selectes an entry in **listBox** with the left-mouse button, the method assigned to *selectioncommand* (**switchImage**) executes.

Note that the *vscrollmode* option for **listBox** is set to **"static"** (line 26). This setting ensures that the **vertscrollbar** subcomponent of the **ScrolledListBox** (a **Tkinter Scrollbar**) is always present. Other possible values are **"dynamic"** (which displays the **vertscrollbar** only if necessary) and **"none"** (which never displays the **vertscrollbar**). The default value is **"dynamic"**.

Line 31 creates a **Label** to display the selected image. By default, the label contains the image of the first item in the list. When the user selects an item in **listBox**, method **switchImage** (lines 34–43) changes the image. The call to **ScrolledListBox** method **curselection** (line 38) returns a tuple that contains one string. This string corresponds to the index of the user-selected listbox item. For example, if the user selects the **bug1.gif** image (the first image in the list), method **curselection** returns (**"0"**). If the tuple is not empty, **Tkinter** method **config** changes the **Label** component's **image** attribute to the user-selected image. The **ScrolledListBox** component also provides method *getcurselection* that returns a tuple of the currently selected values, rather than indices of those values.

By default, the user can select only one option in a **ScrolledListbox** component. A *multiple-selection list* enables the user to select several items from a **Scrolled-Listbox**. A **ScrolledListbox**'s *listbox_selectmode* option determines how many items a user may select. Possible values are **SINGLE**, **BROWSE** (default), **MUL-TIPLE** and **EXTENDED**. Value **SINGLE** allows the user to select one item at a time. Value **BROWSE** is the same as **SINGLE**, except that the user also may move the selection by dragging the mouse, rather than simply clicking an item. Value **MULTIPLE** allows the user to select multiple options, by clicking on multiple values. Value **EXTENDED** is similar to **BROWSE**, except that dragging the mouse selects multiple values. To select a contiguous range of items in a multiple-selection list, select the first item then press the *Shift* key while selecting the last item in the range. To select multiple, nonconsecutive items, press the *Ctrl* key while selecting each item. To deselect an item, hold the *Ctrl* key while clicking the item a second time.

A multiple-selection list does not have a specific event associated with making multiple selections. Normally, an *external event* generated by another GUI component (e.g., a **Button**) specifies when the multiple selections in a **ScrolleListbox** should be processed. We illustrate an example of an external event in the next section.

Look-and-Feel Observation 11.1

*Often an external event determines when a program should process the selected items in a multiple-selection **ScrolledListBox***

11.4 ScrolledText Component

Tkinter *Text* components provide areas for manipulating multiple lines of text. **Pmw** defines a *ScrolledText* component, which is a scrolled **Tkinter Text** component. Figure 11.2 contains two **ScrolledText** components—one displays text that the user can select and the other displays the text the user selected in the first **ScrolledText** component. Sometimes, no event types are bound for a **ScrolledText**. Instead, an external event, (i.e., an event generated by a different GUI component) indicates when to process the text in a **ScrolledText** component. For example, many graphical e-mail programs provide a **Send** button to send the text of the message to the recipient. In this program, a button generates the external event that determines when the program copies the selected text in the left **ScrolledText** component into in the right **ScrolledText** component.

```python
1   # Fig. 11.2: fig11_02.py
2   # Copying selected text from one text area to another.
3
4   from Tkinter import *
5   import Pmw
6
7   class CopyTextWindow( Frame ):
8       """Demonstrate ScrolledTexts"""
9
10      def __init__( self ):
11          """Create two ScrolledTexts and a Button"""
12
13          Frame.__init__( self )
14          Pmw.initialise()
15          self.pack( expand = YES, fill = BOTH )
16          self.master.title( "ScrolledText Demo" )
17
18          # create scrolled text box with word wrap enabled
19          self.text1 = Pmw.ScrolledText( self,
20              text_width = 25, text_height = 12, text_wrap = WORD,
21              hscrollmode = "static", vscrollmode = "static" )
22          self.text1.pack( side = LEFT, expand = YES, fill = BOTH,
23              padx = 5, pady = 5 )
24
25          self.copyButton = Button( self, text = "Copy >>>",
26              command = self.copyText )
27          self.copyButton.pack( side = LEFT, padx = 5, pady = 5 )
28
29          # create uneditable scrolled text box
30          self.text2 = Pmw.ScrolledText( self, text_state = DISABLED,
31              text_width = 25, text_height = 12, text_wrap = WORD,
32              hscrollmode = "static", vscrollmode = "static" )
33          self.text2.pack( side = LEFT, expand = YES, fill = BOTH,
34              padx = 5, pady = 5 )
35
36      def copyText( self ):
37          """Set the text in the second ScrolledText"""
38
39          self.text2.settext( self.text1.get( SEL_FIRST, SEL_LAST ) )
40
41  def main():
42      CopyTextWindow().mainloop()
43
44  if __name__ == "__main__":
45      main()
```

Fig. 11.2 Text copied from one component to another. (Part 1 of 2.)

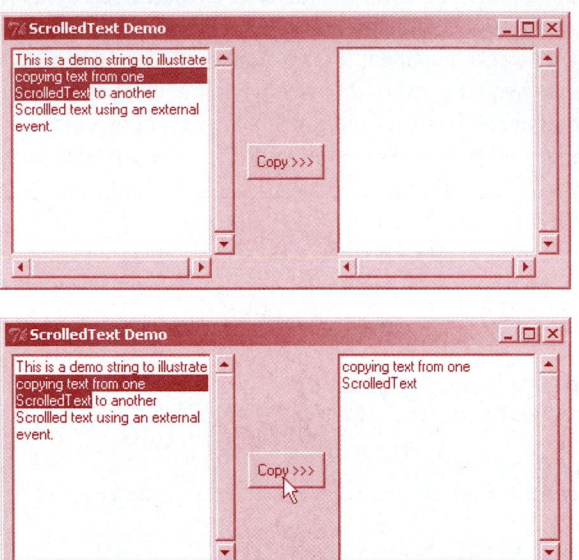

Fig. 11.2 Text copied from one component to another. (Part 2 of 2.)

Lines 19–23 create and pack the first **ScrolledText** component—**text1**—with a 25-column and 12-row **Text** subcomponent. The **ScrolledText** component's **text_wrap** option determines whether text lines that are too long to display in the component wrap. Value **NONE** (default) does not continue text on the next line and displays only the text that fits in the component's width. Value **CHAR** splits the text across multiple lines at the character location where the text becomes too long for the component. Value **WORD** is similar to value **CHAR**, except that the component splits the text on word boundaries (i.e., whitespace characters such as tabs and spaces). This last value enables word-wrapping, a common feature in many text editors.

Look-and-Feel Observation 11.2

*To provide automatic word-wrap functionality for a **Text** component, specify the **text_wrap** option as **WORD** rather than **NONE**.*

Lines 25–27 create and pack **copyButton** and bind callback method **copyText**. Lines 30–34 create and pack the second **ScrolledText** component, **text2**. Line 30 sets **text2**'s **text_state** option to **DISABLED**, rendering the text area uneditable by disabling calls to **insert** and **delete** for the component.

When the user clicks **copyButton**, method **copyText** (lines 36–39) executes. This method retrieves the user-entered text from **text1** by invoking the component's method **get**. Method **get** takes two arguments that specify the range of text to retrieve from the component. Line 39 retrieves the **text1**'s selected text by specifying a range that starts at the beginning of the selection (**SEL_FIRST**) and stops at the end of the selection (**SEL_LAST**). Method **settext** deletes the current text in the component and inserts the text the method receives as an argument. In this case, method **settext** inserts text returned by method **get** into **text2**. If the user has not selected any text, the program raises a **TclError** exception and displays the error in an error dialog. We discussed exceptions briefly in Chapter 7, Object-Based Programming. In Chapter 12, Exception Handling, we discuss in detail how to handle exceptions (e.g., to prevent the program from displaying the error dialog).

11.5 MenuBar Component

Menus are an integral part of GUIs because they contain a list of actions, which, when selected by users, are performed by the applications. Menus simplify the appearances of graphical user interfaces by not "cluttering" the GUI with extra components (buttons, links, etc.). Simple **Tkinter** GUIs create menus with **Menu** components. Module **Pmw** includes class **MenuBar**, which contains the methods necessary to manage a *menu bar*, a container for menus.

Look-and-Feel Observation 11.3

Menus simplify GUIs by reducing the number of components the user views at one time.

A *menu item* is a GUI component inside a menu that performs an action when selected by a user. Menu items can be of different forms. The **command** menu item initiates an action. When a user selects a **command** menu item, the application invokes the item's call-back method. The **checkbutton** menu item can be toggled on or off. When a user selects a **checkbutton** menu item, a checkmark appears to the left of the menu item. A user can select multiple **checkbutton**s (i.e, they are not mutually exclusive). Selecting a checked **checkbutton** removes the checkmark.

The **radiobutton** menu item is another menu item that can be toggled on or off. When multiple **radiobutton** menu items are grouped together, a user can select only one item from each **radiobutton**-menu-item group. After selecting a **radiobutton** menu item, a checkmark appears to the left of the menu item. When a user selects another **radiobutton** menu item from the same group, the application removes the checkmark from the previously selected menu item. Like **radioButton**s (discussed in Chapter 10, Graphical User Interface Components: Part 1), **radiobutton** menu items are grouped logically by a shared variable.

The **separator** menu item is a horizontal line in a menu. The **cascade** menu item is a *submenu* (or *cascade menu*) that provides more menu items from which the user can select.

Look-and-Feel Observation 11.4

*The **separator** menu item can be used to group related menu items.*

A menu bar contains menu items and submenus. When a menu is clicked, the menu expands to show its list of menu items and submenus. Clicking a menu item generates an event. Figure 11.3 provides menus and menu items that enable a user to change the properties of a line of text. The program also introduces *balloons* (also called a *tool-tips*) that display decriptions of menus and menu items. When the user moves the mouse cursor over a menu or menu item with a balloon, the program displays a specified help message.

Line 20 creates **myBalloon**—a **Pmw Balloon** component. Lines 21–23 create and pack a **MenuBar** component **choices**. Option **balloon** specifies a **Balloon** component that is attached to the menubar. Lines 26–34 build the program's menu bar. Method **addmenu** (line 26) adds a new menu to **choices**. The method's first argument (**"File"**) is the menu name. The second argument (**"Exit"**) contains the text that appears in the menu's balloon. When the user places the mouse cursor over the **File** menu, the program displays this text in a floating label next to the cursor.

```
1   # Fig. 11.3: fig11_03.py
2   # MenuBars with Balloons demonstration.
3
4   from Tkinter import *
5   import Pmw
6   import sys
7
8   class MenuBarDemo( Frame ):
9      """Create window with a MenuBar"""
10
11     def __init__( self ):
12        """Create a MenuBar with items and a Canvas with text"""
13
14        Frame.__init__( self )
15        Pmw.initialise()
16        self.pack( expand = YES, fill = BOTH )
17        self.master.title( "MenuBar Demo" )
18        self.master.geometry( "500x200" )
19
20        self.myBalloon = Pmw.Balloon( self )
21        self.choices = Pmw.MenuBar( self,
22           balloon = self.myBalloon )
23        self.choices.pack( fill = X )
24
25        # create File menu and items
26        self.choices.addmenu( "File", "Exit" )
27        self.choices.addmenuitem( "File", "command",
28           command = self.closeDemo, label = "Exit" )
29
30        # create Format menu and items
31        self.choices.addmenu( "Format", "Change font/color" )
32        self.choices.addcascademenu( "Format", "Color" )
33        self.choices.addmenuitem( "Format", "separator" )
34        self.choices.addcascademenu( "Format", "Font" )
35
36        # add items to Format/Color menu
37        colors = [ "Black", "Blue", "Red", "Green" ]
38        self.selectedColor = StringVar()
39        self.selectedColor.set( colors[ 0 ] )
40
41        for item in colors:
42           self.choices.addmenuitem( "Color", "radiobutton",
43              label = item, command = self.changeColor,
44              variable = self.selectedColor )
45
```

Fig. 11.3 **MenuBar**s created with **Balloon**s. (Part 1 of 3.)

```
46          # add items to Format/Font menu
47          fonts = [ "Times", "Courier", "Helvetica" ]
48          self.selectedFont = StringVar()
49          self.selectedFont.set( fonts [ 0 ] )
50
51          for item in fonts:
52             self.choices.addmenuitem( "Font", "radiobutton",
53                label = item, command = self.changeFont,
54                variable = self.selectedFont )
55
56          # add a horizontal separator in Font menu
57          self.choices.addmenuitem( "Font", "separator" )
58
59          # associate checkbutton menu item with BooleanVar object
60          self.boldOn = BooleanVar()
61          self.choices.addmenuitem( "Font", "checkbutton",
62             label = "Bold", command = self.changeFont,
63             variable = self.boldOn )
64
65          # associate checkbutton menu item with BooleanVar object
66          self.italicOn = BooleanVar()
67          self.choices.addmenuitem( "Font", "checkbutton",
68             label = "Italic", command = self.changeFont,
69             variable = self.italicOn )
70
71          # create Canvas with text
72          self.display = Canvas( self, bg = "white" )
73          self.display.pack( expand = YES, fill = BOTH )
74
75          self.sampleText = self.display.create_text( 250, 100,
76             text = "Sample Text", font = "Times 48" )
77
78       def changeColor( self ):
79          """Change the color of the text on the Canvas"""
80
81          self.display.itemconfig( self.sampleText,
82             fill = self.selectedColor.get() )
83
84       def changeFont( self ):
85          """Change the font of the text on the Canvas"""
86
87          # get selected font and attach size
88          newFont = self.selectedFont.get() + " 48"
89
90          # determine which checkbutton menu items selected
91          if self.boldOn.get():
92             newFont += " bold"
93
94          if self.italicOn.get():
95             newFont += " italic"
96
97          # configure sample text to be displayed in selected style
98          self.display.itemconfig( self.sampleText, font = newFont )
```

Fig. 11.3 **MenuBar**s created with **Balloon**s. (Part 2 of 3.)

```
99
100    def closeDemo( self ):
101        """Exit the program"""
102
103        sys.exit()
104
105  def main():
106      MenuBarDemo().mainloop()
107
108  if __name__ == "__main__":
109      main()
```

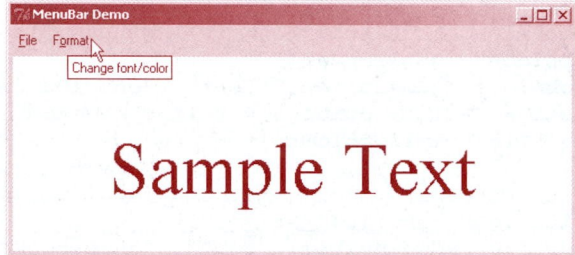

Fig. 11.3   MenuBars created with **Balloon**s. (Part 3 of 3.)

Lines 27–28 invoke method **addmenuitem** to insert a **command** menu item in the **File** menu. This method requires two arguments—the name of the menu to which the item belongs and the menu item's type. This example adds the **Exit** menu item to the **File** menu. The method's keyword argument **label** specifies the menu item's text. The keyword argument **command** specifies the menu item's callback. When the user selects menu item **Exit** from the **File** menu, callback method **closeDemo** (lines 100–103) exits the program.

Line 31 adds menu **Format** to the **choices** menubar. Method **addcascademenu** (line 34) adds a submenu to an existing menu. The method requires two arguments—the name of the menu to which the submenu belongs and the submenu's text. When the user opens the **Format** menu and selects **Color**, the program displays the **Color** submenu. Lines 33–34 add a **separator** menu item and a **Font** submenu to menu **Format**. The **separator** menu item is a line dividing the **Color** and **Font** submenus.

Look-and-Feel Observation 11.5

Menu items appear in the order in which they are added. Be sure to add them in the correct order.

Look-and-Feel Observation 11.6

Menus normally appear from left to right in the order that they are added.

Line 37 defines the list of color choices for the sample text. Lines 38–39 create **StringVar selectedColor** and initialize it to the first element of the list of color choices. Lines 41–44 add a **radiobutton** menu item to the **Color** submenu for each item in a list of colors. Note that each **radiobutton** menu item shares the same callback method (**changeColor**) and the same variable (**selectedColor**). When the user selects an item, **selectedColor**'s value changes to the item's text value and method **changeColor** is invoked. Variable **selectedColor** is shared by the radiobutton menu items in the group.

Lines 51–54 add a **radiobutton** menu item for each item in a list of fonts to the **Format** menu's **Font** submenu. Each **radiobutton** menu item shares the same callback method (**changeFont**) and the same variable (**selectedFont**).

Line 57 adds a **separator** menu item to the **"Font"** submenu. Lines 60–69 then add **"Bold"** and **"Italic"** **checkbutton** menu items to the **Font** submenu. Lines 60 and 66 create two **BooleanVar** variables to represent whether these menue items are checked or unchecked). These values are passed to method **addmenuitem** through its **variable** keyword parameter. Although both **checkbutton** menu items share the same callback method (**changeFont**), they each have a different **BooleanVar** variable. The menu items' **BooleanVar** variables serve the same purpose as in **Tkinter Checkbutton** components. When the user selects the menu item, the **BooleanVar**'s value changes to 1. When the user deselects the menu item, the **BooleanVar**'s value changes to 0.

Lines 72–73 create and pack **display**—a **Tkinter** *Canvas* with a white background on which a program can display text, lines and shapes. A **Canvas** displays a *canvas item*—an object, like a string or a shape, that is drawn on the **Canvas** component. Each **Canvas** has a method that corresponds to a canvas item. Each of these methods creates a canvas item and adds it to the **Canvas**. For example, method **create_text** (lines 75–76) creates a canvas text item. This method draws the text **"Sample Text"** onto **display** in the font (**"Times 48"**) specified by keyword parameter **font**. We discuss **Canvas** components in more detail in Section 11.7.

When the user selects a **Color** menu item, method **changeColor** (lines 78–82) configures **sampleText** to be filled (colored) with the value of **selectedColor**. Method *itemconfig* configures items on **Canvas**. Lines 77–78 set the color of **sampleText** to the selected color by specifying option *fill*.

When the user selects a **radiobutton** menu item in the **Font** submenu of the **Format** menu, method **changeFont** (lines 84–98) changes the font of **sampleText**. Line 98 retrieves the desired font name from **selectedFont**. Lines 91–95 determine whether any **checkbutton** menu items of the **Font** submenu are selected. If so, the program appends the specified style to the font name. Line 92 then updates the text with the specified font.

11.6 Popup Menus

Many of today's computer applications provide *context-sensitive popup menus*. Such menus can be created easily with **Tkinter** class **Menu**. These menus provide options that are specific to the component for which the *popup trigger event* was generated. On most systems, the popup trigger event occurs when the user presses and releases the right mouse button. However, with **Tkinter**, a popup trigger event must be specified by binding a callback to the desired trigger for a component.

Figure 11.4 creates a **Menu** that allows the user to select one of three colors as the background color of the **Frame**. When the user clicks the right mouse button on the **Frame**, the program displays a popup menu containing a list of colors. If the user selects one of the **radiobutton** menu items that represents a color, the program changes the background color of the **Frame**.

```python
1   # Fig. 11.4: fig11_04.py
2   # Popup menu demonstration.
3
4   from Tkinter import *
5
6   class PopupMenuDemo( Frame ):
7      """Demonstrate popup menus"""
8
9      def __init__( self ):
10         """Create a Menu but do not add it to the Frame"""
11
12         Frame.__init__( self )
13         self.pack( expand = YES, fill = BOTH )
14         self.master.title( "Popup Menu Demo" )
15         self.master.geometry( "300x200" )
16
17         # create and pack frame with initial white background
18         self.frame1 = Frame( self, bg = "white" )
19         self.frame1.pack( expand = YES, fill = BOTH )
20
21         # create menu without packing it
22         self.menu = Menu( self.frame1, tearoff = 0 )
23
24         colors = [ "White", "Blue", "Yellow", "Red" ]
25         self.selectedColor = StringVar()
26         self.selectedColor.set( colors[ 0 ] )
27
28         for item in colors:
29            self.menu.add_radiobutton( label = item,
30               variable = self.selectedColor,
31               command = self.changeBackgroundColor )
32
33         # popup menu on right-mouse click
34         self.frame1.bind( "<Button-3>", self.popUpMenu )
35
36      def popUpMenu( self, event ):
37         """Add the Menu to the Frame"""
38
39         self.menu.post( event.x_root, event.y_root )
40
```

Fig. 11.4   Popup menu implementation. (Part 1 of 2.)

```
41        def changeBackgroundColor( self ):
42            """Change the Frame background color"""
43
44            self.frame1.config( bg = self.selectedColor.get() )
45
46    def main():
47        PopupMenuDemo().mainloop()
48
49    if __name__ == "__main__":
50        main()
```

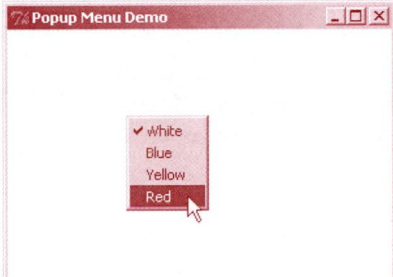
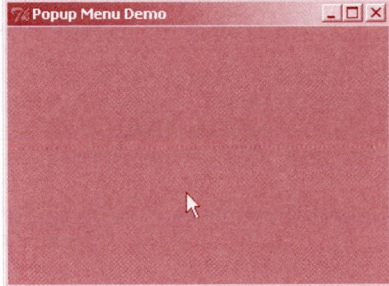

Fig. 11.4   Popup menu implementation. (Part 2 of 2.)

The **Frame** constructor's **bg** option is a string that specifies the **Frame**'s background color. Lines 18–19 create and pack **frame1** with a white background. Line 22 creates a **Tkinter Menu** component called **menu**. Note that **Menu**'s **tearoff** option is set to 0. This setting removes the dashed separator line that is, by default, the first entry in a **Menu**. Lines 28–31 add a **radiobutton** menu item to **menu** for each item in a list of colors. Each **radiobutton** menu item has the same callback method (**changeBackground-Color**) and the same variable (**selectedColor**).

Line 34 binds method **popUpMenu** to a right-mouse click (**<Button-3>**) for **frame1**. When the user right-clicks in **frame1**, the **popUpMenu** callback (lines 36–39) executes. Line 39 calls **Menu** method **post**, which displays a **Menu** at a given position. This method accepts two arguments that correspond to the position on the top-level component at which the menu is displayed. Event attributes **x_root** and **y_root** contain the coordinates of the mouse cursor when the event was triggered.

When a user selects one of the **radiobutton** menu items, method **changeBack-groundColor** executes. This method (lines 41–44) calls the **config** method of **frame1**, specifying the new **bg** to be the value of **selectedColor** (line 44). This method call changes **frame1**'s background color.

11.7 Canvas Component

Figure 11.3 used a *Canvas* to display formatted text. **Canvas** is a **Tkinter** component that displays text, images, lines and shapes. **Canvas** inherits from **Widget**. By default, a **Canvas** is blank. To display items on a **Canvas**, a program creates *canvas items*. New items are drawn on top of existing items unless otherwise specified.

Figure 11.5 uses the **<B1-Motion>** event and a **Canvas** to create a simple drawing program. The user draws pictures by dragging the mouse cursor over a **Canvas**.

```
1   # Fig. 11.5: fig11_05.py
2   # Canvas paint program.
3
4   from Tkinter import *
5
6   class PaintBox( Frame ):
7      """Demonstrate drawing on a Canvas"""
8
9      def __init__( self ):
10        """Create Canvas and bind paint method to mouse dragging"""
11
12        Frame.__init__( self )
13        self.pack( expand = YES, fill = BOTH )
14        self.master.title( "A simple paint program" )
15        self.master.geometry( "300x150" )
16
17        self.message = Label( self,
18           text = "Drag the mouse to draw" )
19        self.message.pack( side = BOTTOM )
20
21        # create Canvas component
22        self.myCanvas = Canvas( self )
23        self.myCanvas.pack( expand = YES, fill = BOTH )
24
25        # bind mouse dragging event to Canvas
26        self.myCanvas.bind( "<B1-Motion>", self.paint )
27
28     def paint( self, event ):
29        """Create an oval of radius 4 around the mouse position"""
30
31        x1, y1 = ( event.x - 4 ), ( event.y - 4 )
32        x2, y2 = ( event.x + 4 ), ( event.y + 4 )
33        self.myCanvas.create_oval( x1, y1, x2, y2, fill = "black" )
34
35  def main():
36     PaintBox().mainloop()
37
38  if __name__ == "__main__":
39     main()
```

Fig. 11.5 Canvas paint program.

Lines 17–19 create and pack a **Label** with user instructions. Lines 22–23 create and pack **Canvas** instance **myCanvas**. Line 26 binds the mouse-drag event (**<B1-Motion>**) for the canvas to method **paint** (lines 28–33). When the user moves the mouse while holding down the left button, method **paint** executes. This method draws an oval on the **Canvas myCanvas**. **Canvas** method *create_oval* creates an *oval Canvas* item with a radius of 4 and a fill color of **"black"** centered at the current mouse cursor position (line 33).

11.8 Scale Component

The *Scale* component enables the user to select from a range of integer values. Class **Scale** inherits from **Widget**. Figure 11.6 shows a horizontal **Scale** with *numeric values* and a *slider* that allows the user to select a value.

Scales have either a *horizontal orientation* or a *vertical orientation*. On a horizontal **Scale**, the minimum value is at the extreme left and the maximum value is at the extreme right of the **Scale**. On a vertical **Scale**, the minimum value is at the extreme top and the maximum value is at the extreme bottom of the **Scale**.

Figure 11.7 enables the user to specify the size of a circle drawn on a **Canvas** by using a **Scale** component. The diameter of the circle is controlled with a horizontal **Scale**. The radius changes when the user interacts with the **Scale**.

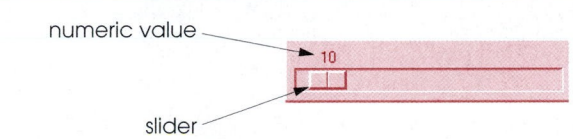

numeric value

slider

Fig. 11.6   Horizontal **Scale**.

```
1   # Fig. 11.7: fig11_07.py
2   # Scale used to control the size of a circle.
3
4   from Tkinter import *
5
6   class ScaleDemo( Frame ):
7      """Demonstrate Canvas and Scale"""
8
9      def __init__( self ):
10        """Create Canvas with a circle controlled by a Scale"""
11
12        Frame.__init__( self )
13        self.pack( expand = YES, fill = BOTH )
14        self.master.title( "Scale Demo" )
15        self.master.geometry( "220x270" )
16
17        # create Scale
18        self.control = Scale( self, from_ = 0, to = 200,
19           orient = HORIZONTAL, command = self.updateCircle )
```

Fig. 11.7   **Scale** used to control the size of a circle on a **Canvas**. (Part 1 of 2.)

```
20          self.control.pack( side = BOTTOM, fill = X )
21          self.control.set( 10 )
22
23          # create Canvas and draw circle
24          self.display = Canvas( self, bg = "white" )
25          self.display.pack( expand = YES, fill = BOTH )
26
27      def updateCircle( self, scaleValue ):
28          """Delete the circle, determine new size, draw again"""
29
30          end = int( scaleValue ) + 10
31          self.display.delete( "circle" )
32          self.display.create_oval( 10, 10, end, end,
33              fill = "red", tags = "circle" )
34
35  def main():
36      ScaleDemo().mainloop()
37
38  if __name__ == "__main__":
39      main()
```

Fig. 11.7   **Scale** used to control the size of a circle on a **Canvas**. (Part 2 of 2.)

Lines 18–20 create and pack **control**, the **Scale** used to change the size of the circle. The constructor's **orient** option (**HORIZONTAL** or **VERTICAL**) determines whether the new **Scale** instance has a horizontal or vertical orientation. Options **from_** and **to** specify the **Scale** component's minimum and maximum values, respectively. The option values in lines 18–19 create a horizontal **Scale** with a minimum value of 0 and a maximum value of 200. The **Scale**'s callback is method **updateCircle**, which executes when the user moves the slider to change the numerical value. Note that although nothing is drawn on **display** in **__init__**, the circle appears on **display** when the program starts. This is because when the **Scale** is created, its callback method (**updateCircle**) is invoked. Line 21 sets **control**'s value to 10, so that when the program starts, a circle of diameter 10 appears on the screen. Lines 24–25 create and pack **display**, a **Canvas** with a white background.

When the user drags the slider, method **updateCircle** (lines 27–33) executes. The callback accepts as an argument the current value of the scale, represented as a string. Line 30 converts this value to an integer, adds 10 to it and stores the value in variable **end**.

Canvas method *delete* (line 31) deletes the old circle before drawing a new one. Method **delete** accepts one argument—either an *item handle* or a *tag*. Item handles are integer values that identify a newly drawn item. A tag is a name that can be attached to a canvas item at creation. To attach a tag to a canvas item, pass a string value to the *tags* option of the item's **create** method.

Method *create_oval* (lines 32–33) draws an oval with coordinates (**10**, **10**, **end**, **end**), specifying option **fill** to be **"red"** and option **tags** to be **"circle"**. The coordinates specify points on the oval's bounding rectangle. **Canvas** method *create_item* allows the user to create the following items by substituting their names for *item*—arc, line, oval, rectangle, polygon, image, bitmap, text and window.

11.9 Other GUI Toolkits

Many different GUI Toolkits for Python exist. **PyGTK** (**www.daa.com.au/~james/ pygtk**) provides an object-oriented interface for the *Gimp ToolKit (GTK)* component set (**www.gtk.org**). GTK is an advanced component set used primarily under the X Windows system (a graphics system providing a common interface for displaying windowed graphics). PyGTK is a part of GTK+, a Python toolkit for creating graphical user interfaces.

Another popular GUI toolkit is **wxPython** (**www.wxpython.org**)—a Python extension module that enables access to **wxWindows**, a GUI library written in C++. This toolkit currently supports Microsoft Windows and most of the Unix-like systems. Python module **wxPython** wraps around wxWindows, providing the interface to manipulate wxWindows classes and methods.

PyOpenGL (**pyopengl.sourceforge.net**) provides a Python interface to the OpenGL (**www.opengl.org**) library. OpenGL is one of the most widely used libraries designed for developing interactive two-dimensional and three-dimensional graphical applications. It is available under Microsoft Windows, MacOS and most Unix-like systems. **PyOpenGL** can be used with **Tkinter**, **wxPython** and other windowing libraries. Chapter 24, Multimedia, discusses module **PyOpenGL**.

SUMMARY

- The **Pmw** (Python Mega Widgets) toolkit provides high-level GUI components composed of **Tkinter** components.

- Megawidgets can also be configured for a particular use. The appearance and functionality of the components and their subcomponents can be modified.

- The components can be configured either during or after creation with method **configure**.

- In general, subcomponent options are named *subcomponent_option*.

- A list box provides a list of items from which the user can make a selection. List boxes are implemented with **Tkinter** class **Listbox**, which inherits from class **Widget**.

- Often, it is desirable to allow the user to scroll up and down a list. Scrolling can be achieved by creating a **Tkinter Scrollbar** and a **Listbox** separately and configuring them properly. Conveniently, **Pmw** provides a megawidget called **ScrolledListBox** that serves this purpose.

- Function **Pmw.initialise** initializes **Pmw**. This function call allows a list of top-level components to be maintained. This call also ensures that **Pmw** is notified after the destruction of a component.

- The **items** option contains the list of items that will be displayed in a **ScrolledListBox**.

- The method specified as a value for option **selectioncommand** executes each time an entry in a **ScrolledListBox** is selected.

- Setting the **vscrollmode** option for a **ScrolledListBox** to **"static"** ensures that the **vertscrollbar** subcomponent of the **ScrolledListBox** (a **Tkinter Scrollbar**) will always be present. Other possible values are **"dynamic"** (display the **vertscrollbar** only if necessary) and **"none"** (the **vertscrollbar** will never be displayed). The default value is **"dynamic"**.

- Method **curselection** returns a tuple of the indices of the currently selected items in a **ScrolledListBox**.

- The **ScrolledListBox** component also supports a **getcurselection** method that returns a tuple of the currently selected values, rather than the values' indices.

- By default, the user can select only one option in a **ScrolledListbox** component.

- A multiple-selection list enables the user to select many items from a **ScrolledListbox**.

- A **ScrolledListbox**'s **listbox_selectmode** option controls how many items a user may select. Possible values are **SINGLE**, **BROWSE** (default), **MULTIPLE** and **EXTENDED**. Value **SINGLE** allows the user to select only one item in the **ScrolledListbox** at a time. Value **BROWSE** is the same as **SINGLE**, except that the user also may move the selection by dragging the mouse, rather than simply clicking an item. Value **MULTIPLE** allows the user to select multiple options, by clicking on multiple values. Value **EXTENDED** acts like **BROWSE**, except that when the user drags the mouse, the user selects multiple values.

- A multiple-selection list does not have a specific event associated with making multiple selections. Normally, an external event generated by another GUI component specifies when the multiple selections in a **ScrolledListbox** should be processed.

- **Tkinter Text** components provide an area for manipulating multiple lines of text. **Pmw** defines a **ScrolledText** component, which is a scrolled **Tkinter Text**.

- Sometimes, no event types are bound for a **ScrolledText**. Instead, an external event indicates when the text in a **ScrolledText** should be processed.

- The **ScrolledText** component's **wrap** option controls the appearance of text lines that are too long to display in the component. Value **NONE** (default) for **wrap** means that the component truncates the line and displays only the text that fits in the component. Value **CHAR** for **wrap** means that the text is broken up when it becomes too long; the remainder of the text is displayed on the next line. Value **WORD** for **wrap** is similar to value **CHAR**, except that the component breaks the text on word boundaries. This last value enables word-wrapping, a common feature in many popular text editors.

- Setting a text subcomponent's state as **DISABLED** renders the text area uneditable by disabling calls to **insert** and **delete** for the component.

- The **ScrolledText** component's method **get** retrieves the user-entered text. Method **get** takes two arguments that specify the range of text to retrieve from the component. Constant **SEL_FIRST** specifies the beginning of the selection. Constant **SEL_LAST** specifies the end of the selection.

- Method **settext** deletes the current text in the component and inserts the specified text.

- Menus are an integral part of GUIs. Menus allow the user to perform actions without unnecessarily "cluttering" a graphical user interface with extra GUI components.

- Simple **Tkinter** GUIs create menus with **Menu** components. However, **Pmw** supplies class **MenuBar**, which contains the methods necessary to manage a menu bar, a container for menus.

- A menu item is a GUI component inside a menu that causes an action to be performed when selected. Menu items can be of different forms.

- A **command** menu item initiates an action. When the user selects a **command** menu item, the item's callback method is invoked.
- A **checkbutton** menu item can be toggled on or off. When a **checkbutton** menu item is selected, a check appears to the left of the menu item. When the **checkbutton** menu item is selected again, the check to the left of the menu item is removed.
- When multiple **radiobutton** menu items are assigned to the same variable, only one item in the group can be selected at a given time. When a **radiobutton** menu item is selected, a check appears to the left of the menu item. When another **radiobutton** menu item is selected, the check to the left of the previously selected menu item is removed.
- A **separator** menu item is a horizontal line in a menu that groups menu items logically.
- A **cascade** menu item is a submenu. A submenu (or cascade menu) provides more menu items from which the user can select.
- When a menu is clicked, the menu expands to show its list of menu items and submenus.
- Clicking a menu item generates an event.
- A balloon (also called a tool-tip) displays helpful text for menus and menu items. When the user moves the mouse cursor over a menu or menu item with a balloon, the program displays a specified help message.
- Option **balloon** specifies a **Balloon** component that is attached to the menu.
- Method **addmenu** of **Pmw** class **MenuBar** adds a new menu. The method's first argument contains the name of the menu; the second argument contains the text that appears in the menu's balloon. When the user places the mouse cursor over the menu, the program displays this text.
- Method **addmenuitem** of **Pmw** class **MenuBar** adds a menu item to a menu. This method requires two arguments: the name of the menu to which the item belongs and the menu item's type.
- **MenuBar** method **addmenuitem**'s keyword argument **label** specifies the menu item's text. Keyword argument **command** specifies the item's callback.
- Method **addcascademenu** of **Pmw** class **MenuBar** adds a submenu to an existing menu. The method requires two arguments: the name of the menu to which the submenu belongs and the submenu's text.
- Many of today's computer applications provide context-sensitive popup menus. These menus provide options that are specific to the component for which the popup trigger event was generated.
- Context menus be created easily with **Tkinter** class **Menu** (a subclass of **Widget**). A popup trigger event must be specified by binding a callback to the desired trigger for a component.
- The **Frame** constructor's **bg** option takes a string specifying the **Frame**'s background color.
- Setting a **Menu**'s **tearoff** option to 0 removes the dashed separator line that is, by default, the first entry in a **Menu**.
- **Menu** method **post** displays a **Menu** at a given position. This method accepts two arguments that correspond to the position on the top-level component at which the menu is displayed.
- The current mouse position is specified by the **x_root** and **y_root** attributes of the **Event** instance passed to an event handler.
- **Canvas** is a **Tkinter** component that displays text, images, lines and shapes. **Canvas** inherits from **Widget**.
- By default, a **Canvas** is blank. To display items on a **Canvas**, a program creates canvas items. New items are drawn on top of existing items unless otherwise specified.
- Adding canvas items to a **Canvas** displays something on the **Canvas**. Each canvas item has a corresponding **Canvas** method that creates the item and adds it to the canvas.

- Method **create_text** of class **Canvas** creates a canvas text item. **Canvas** method **create_oval** creates an **oval Canvas** item.

- Method **itemconfig** of class **Canvas** configures items on **Canvas**.

- Specifying a value for option **fill** sets the color of a canvas item.

- The **Scale** component enables the user to select from a range of integer values. Class **Scale** inherits from **Widget**. **Scale**s have either a horizontal orientation or a vertical orientation. For a horizontal **Scale**, the minimum value is at the extreme left and the maximum value is at the extreme right of the **Scale**. For a vertical **Scale**, the minimum value is at the extreme top and the maximum value is at the extreme bottom of the **Scale**.

- The **Scale** constructor's **orient** option (**HORIZONTAL** or **VERTICAL**) determines whether the new **Scale** instance has a horizontal or vertical orientation. Options **from_** and **to** specify the **Scale** component's minimum and maximum values. When the **Scale** is created, its callback method is invoked.

- Item handles are integer values that identify a newly drawn item.

- A tag is a name that can be attached to a canvas item when the item is created.

- **Canvas** method **delete** deletes a canvas item. Method **delete** accepts one argument—either an item handle or a tag.

- To attach a tag to a canvas item, pass a string value to the **tags** option of the item's **create** method.

- **Canvas** methods **create_item** allow the user to create the following items by substituting their names for **item**: arc, line, oval, rectangle, polygon, image, bitmap, text and window.

- **PyGTK** provides an object-oriented interface for the GTK component set (**www.gtk.org**). GTK is an advanced component set used primarily under the X Windows system (a graphics system providing a common interface for displaying windowed graphics).

- **wxPython** is a Python extension module that enables access of wxWindows. wxWindows is a GUI library written in C++. It currently supports Microsoft Windows and most of the Unix-like systems.

- **PyOpenGL** provides a Python interface to the OpenGL (**www.opengl.org**) library—one of the most widely used libraries designed for developing interactive two-dimensional and three-dimensional graphical applications. It is available under Microsoft Windows, MacOS and most Unix-like systems. **PyOpenGL** can be used with **Tkinter**, **wxPython** and other windowing libraries.

TERMINOLOGY

addcascademenu method of **MenuBar**
addmenu method of **MenuBar** component
addmenuitem method of **MenuBar**
balloon
balloon option of **MenuBar**
bg option of **Frame** component
BROWSE value of **listbox_selectmode** option of **ScrolledListbox**
Canvas component
cascade menu
cascade menu item
CHAR option of **wrap** option of **ScrolledText**
checkbutton menu item
command menu item
command option of **MenuBar**

configure method of **Pmw**
create_oval method of **Canvas**
curselection method of **ScrolledListBox**
"dynamic" value of **vscrollmode** option of **ScrolledListBox**
EXTENDED value of **listbox_selectmode** option of **ScrolledListbox**
external event
fill option of **Canvas**
font option of **Canvas**
from_ option of **Scale**
get method of **ScrolledText**
getcurselection method of **ScrolledListBox**
horizontal **Scale** component

HORIZONTAL value of **orient** option
    of **Scale**
item handle
itemconfig method of **Canvas**
items option of **ScrolledListBox**
Listbox component
menu
menu bar
Menu component
menu item
mnemonics
multiple-selection list
"none" option of **vscrollmode** option of
    ScrolledListBox
NONE value of **wrap** option of **ScrolledText**
orient option of **Scale**
Pmw.initialise function
popup trigger event
post method of **Menu** component
radiobutton menu item
Scale component
Scrollbar component
ScrolledListBox component
ScrolledText component
SEL_FIRST argument to method **get**
    of **ScrolledText**

SEL_LAST argument to method **get**
    of **ScrolledText**
listbox_selectmode option
    of **ScrolledListbox**
separator menu item
settext method of **ScrolledText**
SINGLE value of **listbox_selectmode**
    option of **ScrolledListbox**
"static" option of **vscrollmode** option of
    ScrolledListBox
tag
tags option of **create** method of **Canvas**
tearoff option of **Menu**
Text component
to option of **Scale**
tool-tip
traverseSpec option of **MenuBar**
variable keyword argument for
    method **addmenuitem**
vertical **Scale** component
VERTICAL value of **orient** option of **Scale**
vscrollmode option of **ScrolledListBox**
WORD option of **wrap** option
    of **ScrolledText**
word wrapping
wrap option of **ScrolledText** component

SELF-REVIEW EXERCISES

11.1 Fill in the blanks in each of the following:
   a) **Tkinter** class _____, which inherits from class _____, implement list boxes.
   b) If the **vscrollmode** of a vertical **ScrolledListBox** is set to _____, the scroll bar component will never be displayed.
   c) A _____ enables the user to select many items from a list box.
   d) Set **text_wrap** to _____ in a **ScrolledText** widget to enable word wrap.
   e) When the user selects a _____ menu item, its callback function is invoked.
   f) A _____ displays help text for menu items.
   g) **Tkinter** component _____ displays text, images, lines and shapes.
   h) The _____ component enables a user to select from a range of integer values.
   i) _____ are integer values identifying an item drawn on a **Canvas**.
   j) An _____ allows selection of a contiguous range of items in the list.

11.2 State whether each of the following is *true* or *false*. If *false*, explain why.
   a) **Tkinter** cannot provide a scrollbar with a list.
   b) By default, the scrollbar component of a **ScrolledListBox** is always displayed.
   c) The **Pmw** component **ScrolledText** is a scrolled **Tkinter Text**.
   d) **Tkinter Menu** components contain the methods necessary to manage a menu bar.
   e) A **cascade** menu is a submenu that provides more items from which the user can select.
   f) Method **addmenuitem** adds menus to a menu bar, which can contain menu items.
   g) **Tkinter** class **Menu** can create context-sensitive popup menus.
   h) The minimum and maximum value positions on a **Scale** can be specified by setting the **from_** and **to** options.

i)   A **Scale** must be horizontal with the maximum value at the extreme right and the minimum value at the extreme left.

j)   A **radiobutton** menu item can be toggled on and off.

ANSWERS TO SELF-REVIEW EXERCISES

11.1   a) **Listbox**, **Widget**. b) **"none"**. c) multiple-selection list. d) **WORD**. e) **command**. f) balloon. g) **Canvas**. h) **Scale**. i) Item handles. j) **EXTENDED Listbox**.

11.2   a) False. A **Tkinter Scrollbar** can be attached to a **Listbox** to create a scrollable list. b) False. By default, the scrollbar component of a **ScrolledListBox** is displayed only if it is necessary to navigate the list. c) True. d) False. Pmw class **MenuBar** contains the methods necessary to manage a menu bar. e) True. f) False. Method **addmenu** adds menus to a menu bar, which can contain menu items. g) True. h) True. i) False. A **Scale** may have either a horizontal or a vertical orientation. j) True.

EXERCISES

11.3   Modify Exercise 10.4. Allow the user to select a Fahrenheit temperature to be converted with a horizontal **Scale**. When the user interacts with the **Scale**, update the temperature conversion.

11.4   Rewrite the program of Fig. 11.2. Create a multiple-selection list of colors. Allow the user to select one or more colors and copy them to a **ScrolledText** component.

11.5   Write a program that allows the user to draw a rectangle by dragging the mouse on a **Canvas**. The drawing should begin when the user holds the left-mouse button down. With this button held down, the user should be able to resize the rectangle. The drawing ends when the user releases the left button. When the user next clicks on the **Canvas**, the rectangle should be deleted.

11.6   Modify Exercise 11.5. Allow the user to fill the rectangle with a color. Create a popup menu of possible colors. The popup menu should appear when the user presses the right-mouse button.

11.7   Write a menu designer program. The program allows the user to enter menu information and generates code to create that menu based on the user input. The GUI allows the user to enter the necessary input and displays the menu names in a **Pmw ScrolledListBox** as they are added. The program displays the generated code when the user has finished adding information. The program can be written with two distinct parts.

a)   Class **Menus** creates a GUI that allows the user to enter a menu name or a menu name, menu item and callback function. The program should issue a warning with a dialog box if the user does not enter the specified information. The GUI provides two **Entry** components for the menu name and the menu item and a **Pmw ScrolledText** component for the callback function. The program generates code based on the user input that the user could execute to create the menu. The GUI should have an **Add** button whose callback adds the user input to the generated menu code, a **Clear** button whose callback resets the GUI and a **Finish** button that ends the program, displaying the generated menu code.

b)   Class **MenusList** creates a single-selection list of the added menus. As the user adds menus, the **Pmw ScrolledListBox** should be updated with the new information. When the user selects a menu in the list, the menu items in that list are displayed in a **Pmw ScrolledText** component.

You may add extra error checking and special features. For instance, when the user selects a menu name in the **Pmw ScrolledListBox** display the menu name in the **Entry** component for menu names.

11.8   Modify Exercise 11.7 so that, as the user adds menus and menu items a sample menu displays and is updated with any new information.

12

Exception Handling

Objectives

- To understand exceptions and error handling.
- To use the **try** statement to delimit code in which exceptions may occur.
- To be able to **raise** exceptions.
- To use **except** clauses to specify exception handlers.
- To use the **finally** clause to release resources.
- To understand the Python exception class hierarchy.
- To understand Python's traceback mechanism.
- To create programmer-defined exceptions.

*It is common sense to take a method and try it. If it fails,
admit it frankly and try another. But above all, try something.*
Franklin Delano Roosevelt

*O! throw away the worser part of it,
And live the purer with the other half.*
William Shakespeare

*If they're running and they don't look where they're going
I have to come out from somewhere and catch them.*
Jerome David Salinger

*And oftentimes excusing of a fault
Doth make the fault the worse by the excuse.*
William Shakespeare

Outline

12.1 Introduction

In this chapter, we introduce *exception handling*. An *exception* is an indication of a "special event" that occurs during a program's execution. The name "exception" indicates that, although the event can occur, the event occurs infrequently. Often, the special event is an error (e.g., dividing by zero or adding two incompatible types); sometimes, the special event is something else (e.g., the termination of a **for** loop). Exception handling enables programmers to create applications that can *handle* (or *resolve*) exceptions. In many cases, handling an exception allows a program to continue executing as if no problems were encountered. More severe problems may prevent a program from continuing normal execution. In such cases, the program can notify the user of the problem, then terminate in a controlled manner. The features presented in this chapter enable programmers to write programs that are clear, robust and more *fault tolerant*.

The style and details of exception handling in Python are based on the work of the creators of the Modula-3 programming language. The exception-handling mechanism is similar to that used in C# and Java.

We begin with an overview of exception-handling concepts, then demonstrate basic exception-handling techniques. The chapter then overviews the exception-handling class hierarchy.

Programs typically request and release resources (such as files on disk) during program execution. Often, these resources are in limited supply or can be used only by one program at a time. We demonstrate a part of the exception-handling mechanism that enables a program to use a resource, then guarantee that the program releases the resource for use by other programs.

The chapter continues with an explanation and example of **traceback** objects—the objects that Python creates when it encounters an exception. The chapter concludes with an example that shows programmers how to create and use their own exception classes.

12.2 Raising an Exception

Chapter 7, Classes and Data Abstraction, introduced the **raise** statement, to signal that a client had attempted to assign an invalid value to an object's attribute. The **raise** statement indicates that an exception occurred (e.g., a function could not complete successful-ly). This is called *raising* (or sometimes *throwing*) *an exception*.

The simplest form of raising an exception consists of the keyword **raise**, followed by the name of the exception to raise. Exception names identify classes; Python exceptions are objects of those classes. When a **raise** statement executes, Python creates an object of the specified exception class. The **raise** statement also may specify arguments that initialize the exception object. To do so, follow the exception class name with a comma (**,**) and the argument (or a tuple of arguments). Programs can use an exception object's attributes to dis-cover more information about the exception that occurred. The **raise** statement has many forms. Section 12.7 discusses another form of **raise** that specifies no exception name.

Testing and Debugging Tip 12.1

The arguments used to initialize an exception object can be referenced in an exception han-dler to perform an appropriate task.

Testing and Debugging Tip 12.2

An exception can be raised without passing arguments to initialize the exception object. In this case, knowledge that an exception of this type occurred normally provides sufficient in-formation for the handler to perform its task.

Until now, we have seen only how a **raise** statement causes a program to terminate and print an error message. This chapter demonstrates how a program detects that an excep-tion occurred (called *catching* an exception), then, based on that exception, takes appro-priate action (called *handling* the exception). Catching and handling exceptions enables a program to know when an error has occurred, then to take actions to minimize the conse-quences of that error.

12.3 Exception-Handling Overview

The logic of a program frequently tests conditions that determine how program execution proceeds. Consider the following pseudocode:

> *Perform a task*
>
> *If the preceding task did not execute correctly*
>   *Perform error processing*
>
> *Perform next task*
>
> *If the preceding task did not execute correctly*
>   *Perform error processing*
>
>   *...*

This pseudocode begins by performing a task, then tests a condition to determine whether that task executed correctly. If not, error processing occurs. Otherwise, the pseudocode continues with the next task. Although this form of error handling may work, intermixing the logic of the program with the error-handling logic can make the program difficult to read, modify, maintain and debug—especially in large applications. In fact, if many of the potential problems occur infrequently, intermixing program logic and error handling can degrade the performance of the program, because the program must test extra conditions to determine whether the next task can be performed.

Exception handling enables programmers to remove error-handling code from the "main line" of the program's execution. This improves program clarity and enhances modifiability. Programmers can decide to handle whatever exceptions they choose—all types of exceptions, all exceptions of a certain type or all exceptions of a related type. Such flexibility reduces the likelihood that errors will be overlooked, thereby increasing a program's robustness.

Testing and Debugging Tip 12.3

Exception handling helps improve a program's fault tolerance. When it is easy to write error-processing code, programmers are more likely to use it.

With programming languages that do not support exception handling, programmers often delay writing error-processing code and sometimes simply forget to include it. This results in less robust software products. Python enables the programmer to deal with exception handling easily from the inception of a project. Still, the programmer must put considerable effort into incorporating an exception-handling strategy into software projects.

Software Engineering Observation 12.1

Incorporate your exception-handling strategy into a system from the inception of the design process. Adding effective exception handling after a system has been implemented is difficult.

Software Engineering Observation 12.2

In the past, programmers used many techniques to implement error-processing code. Exception handling provides a single, uniform technique for processing errors. This enables programmers working on large projects to understand each other's error-processing code.

The exception-handling mechanism also is useful for processing problems that occur when a program interacts with reusable software elements, such as functions, classes and modules. Rather than internally handling problems that occur, such software elements use exceptions to notify client code when problems occur. This enables programmers to implement error handling that is appropriate to each application.

Common Programming Error 12.1

Aborting a program component could leave a resource—such as a file or a network connection—in a state in which other programs are not able to acquire the resource. This is known as a "resource leak."

Performance Tip 12.1

When no exceptions occur, exception-handling code incurs little or no performance penalties. Thus, programs that implement exception handling operate more efficiently than programs that perform error handling throughout the program logic.

Software Engineering Observation 12.3

Complex applications normally consist of predefined software components (such as those defined in the Python standard library) and components specific to the application that use the predefined components. When a predefined component encounters a problem, that component needs a mechanism to communicate the problem to the application-specific component—the predefined component cannot know in advance how each application will process a problem that occurs. Exception handling simplifies combining software components and having them work together effectively by enabling predefined components to communicate problems that occur to application-specific components, which can then process the problems in an application-specific manner.

Software Engineering Observation 12.4

Although it is possible to do so, exceptions often are not used explicitly for conventional flow of control. It is more difficult to keep track the of consequently larger number of exception cases, which makes programs difficult to read and maintain.

Exception handling is geared to situations in which the code that detects an error is unable to handle it. Such code *raises* or *throws an exception*. There is no guarantee that there will be an *exception handler*—code that executes when the program detects an exception—to process that kind of exception. If there is, the exception will be *caught* (detected) and *handled*. The result of an *uncaught exception* depends on whether the program is a GUI program or a *console* (non-GUI) program and on whether the program is running in interactive mode. In a non-GUI program, an uncaught exception simply causes the program to print an error message and terminate. When a GUI program detects an uncaught exception, the program displays the error message (either in the console or in a dialog box, depending on the GUI package) and the program continues execution. Although a GUI program continues execution after an uncaught exception, the program may fail to behave as expected, because of the error that caused the exception. When a program running in interactive mode detects an uncaught exception, the program displays an error message, terminates execution and displays the interactive Python prompt.

Python uses **try** statements to enable exception handling. The **try** statement encloses other statements that potentially cause exceptions. A **try** statement begins with keyword **try**, followed by a colon (**:**), followed by a suite of code in which exceptions may occur. The **try** statement may specify one or more **except** *clauses* that immediately follow the **try** suite. Each **except** clause specifies zero or more exception class names that represent the type(s) of exceptions that the **except** clause can handle. An **except** clause (also called an **except** *handler*) also may specify an identifier that the program can use to reference the exception object that was caught. The handler can use the identifier to obtain information about the exception from the exception object. An **except** clause that specifies no exception type is called an *empty* **except** *clause*. Such a clause catches all exception types. After the last **except** clause, an optional **else** clause contains code that executes if the code in the **try** suite raised no exceptions. If a **try** statement specifies no **except** clauses, the statement must contain a **finally** clause, which always executes, regardless of whether an exception occurs. We discuss each possible combination of clauses over the next several sections.

Common Programming Error 12.2

It is a syntax error to write a **try** *statement that contains* **except** *and* **finally** *clauses. The only acceptable forms are* **try/except**, **try/except/else** *and* **try/finally**.

When code in a program causes an exception, or when the Python interpreter detects a problem, the code or the interpreter *raises* (or *throws*) *an exception*. Some programmers refer to the point in the program at which an exception occurs as the *throw point*—an important location for debugging purposes (as we demonstrate in Section 12.7). Exceptions are objects of classes that inherit from class **Exception**.[1] If an exception occurs in a **try**

---

1. Python exceptions also may be strings, to support programs that require earlier versions of the Python interpreter. For newer Python versions (greater than 1.5.2), the class-based exception-handling technique is preferred.

suite, the **try** suite *expires* (i.e., terminates immediately), and program control transfers to the first **except** handler (if there is one) following the **try** suite. Next, the interpreter searches for the first **except** handler that can process the type of exception that occurred. The interpreter locates the matching **except** by comparing the raised exception's type to each **except**'s exception type(s) until the interpreter finds a match. A match occurs if the types are identical or if the raised exception's type is a derived class of the handler's exception type. If no exceptions occur in a **try** suite, the interpreter ignores the exception handlers for the **try** statement and executes the **try** statement's **else** clause (if the statement specifies an **else** clause). If no exceptions occur, or if one of the **except** clauses successfully handles the exception, program execution resumes with the next statement after the **try** statement. If an exception occurs in a statement that is not in a **try** suite and that statement is in a function, the function containing that statement terminates immediately and the interpreter attempts to locate an enclosing **try** statement in a calling code—a process called *stack unwinding* (discussed in Section 12.7).

Python is said to use the *termination model of exception handling*, because the **try** suite that raises an exception expires immediately when that exception occurs.[2]

12.4 Example: **DivideByZeroError**

Let us consider a simple exception-handling example. The program in Fig. 12.1 uses **try**, **except** and **else** to detect and handle exceptions. The program prompts the user to enter two numbers that represent the numerator and denominator of a division. After the user enters the two numbers, the program calls function **float** on each user-entered string, to convert the user inputs to floating-point values. The program then attempts to divide the first value by the second value. If the user types 0 in response to the request for a denominator, an exception occurs when the program attempts to divide by zero. Also, if the user types a value that is not a number in response to either prompt, the program displays a message requesting that the user enter two numbers.

Before we discuss the program details, consider the sample outputs Fig. 12.1. The first shows a successful calculation in which the user inputs the numerator **100** and the denominator **7**. The output shows the result of the division. In the second output, the user enters the string **"hello"** at the second prompt. When the user presses *Enter* after typing the string, the program displays a message, indicating that the user must enter numbers. This occurs because **float** cannot convert a string argument to a floating-point value, so the function raises a *ValueError* exception. The program catches the exception and displays an appropriate message. The last output shows the result after an attempt to divide by zero. The Python interpreter itself tests for division by zero and raises a *Zero-DivisionError* exception if the denominator is zero. The program catches the exception and displays a message, indicating an attempt to divide by zero.

Let us consider the user interactions and flow of control that yield the results shown in the sample input/output dialogs. The user inputs values that represent the numerator and

---

2. Some languages use the *resumption model of exception handling* in which, after handling the exception, control returns to the point at which the exception was raised and execution resumes from that point.

```
 1   # Fig. 12.1: fig12_01.py
 2   # Simple exception handling example.
 3
 4   number1 = raw_input( "Enter numerator: " )
 5   number2 = raw_input( "Enter denominator: " )
 6
 7   # attempt to convert and divide values
 8   try:
 9      number1 = float( number1 )
10      number2 = float( number2 )
11      result = number1 / number2
12
13   # float raises a ValueError exception
14   except ValueError:
15      print "You must enter two numbers"
16
17   # division by zero raises a ZeroDivisionError exception
18   except ZeroDivisionError:
19      print "Attempted to divide by zero"
20
21   # else clause's suite executes if try suite raises no exceptions
22   else:
23      print "%.3f / %.3f = %.3f" % ( number1, number2, result )
```

```
Enter numerator: 100
Enter denominator: 7
100.000 / 7.000 = 14.286
```

```
Enter numerator: 100
Enter denominator: hello
You must enter two numbers
```

```
Enter numerator: 100
Enter denominator: 0
Attempted to divide by zero
```

Fig. 12.1   Exception handling with **try**, **except** and **else**.

denominator. The program then attempts to convert the user-entered values to floating-point values and to divide the numerator by the denominator. Lines 8–11 begin a **try** statement enclosing the code that may raise exceptions. Notice that the code in the **try** suite does not itself contain any **raise** statements and therefore may not appear to raise exceptions. In general, the statements in a **try** suite may call other code that possibly raises exceptions; or the statements in a **try** suite may raise exceptions if, for example, the code accesses an invalid sequence subscript, dictionary key or object attribute. In Fig. 12.1, the **try** suite makes two calls to function **float** (that may raise a **ValueError** exception) and performs one division operation (that may raise a **ZeroDivisionError** exception).

Software Engineering Observation 12.5

*Place in a **try** suite a significant logical section of program in which several statements can raise exceptions, rather than using a separate **try** statements for every statement that raises an exception. However, for proper exception-handling granularity, each **try** statement should enclose a section of code small enough that, when an exception occurs, the specific context is known and the **except** handlers can process the exception properly. If many statements in a **try** suite raise the same exception types, multiple **try** statements may be required to determine each exception's context.*

Function **float** converts the user-entered values to floating-point values (lines 9–10). This function raises a **ValueError** exception if it cannot convert its string argument to a floating-point value. If lines 9–10 properly convert the values (i.e., no exceptions occur), then line 11 divides the numerator by the denominator and assigns the result to variable **result**. If the denominator is zero, line 11 causes the Python interpreter to raise a **ZeroDivisionError** exception. If line 11 does not cause an exception, then the **try** suite completes its execution. If no exceptions occur in the **try** suite, the program ignores the **except** handlers in lines 14–15 and 18–19 and continues program execution with the first statement of the **else** suite (lines 22-23). The **else** suite contains a single line that prints the result of division. After the **else** suite terminates, program execution continues with the first statement after the entire **try** statement (i.e., after line 23). In this example, the program contains no more statements, so program execution terminates.

Common Programming Error 12.3

*It is a syntax error to place statements between a **try** suite and its first **except** handler, between **except** handlers, between the last **except** handler and the **else** clause, or between the **try** suite and the **finally** clause.*

Testing and Debugging Tip 12.4

*Although a **try** suite can contain any type of statement, generally a **try** suite should contain only statements that may raise exceptions. Place in an **else** suite could that does not raise exceptions and should execute only if no exceptions occur in the corresponding **try** suite.*

Immediately following the **try** suite are two **except** clauses (also called **except** handlers or exception handlers)—lines 14–15 define the exception handler for a **ValueError** exception and lines 18–19 define the exception handler for the **ZeroDivisionError** exception. Each **except** clause begins with keyword **except** followed by an exception name that specifies the type of exception handled by the **except** clause, followed by a colon (**:**). The exception-handling code appears in the body of the **except** clause (i.e., in the indented code suite). In general, when an exception occurs in a **try** suite, an **except** clause catches the exception and handles it. In Fig. 12.1, the first **except** clause specifies that it catches **ValueError** exceptions (raised by function **float**). The second **except** clause specifies that it catches **ZeroDivisionError** exceptions (raised by the interpreter). Only the matching **except** handler executes if an exception occurs. Both the exception handlers in this example display an error message. When program control reaches the last statement of an **except** handler's suite, the interpreter considers the exception handled, and program control continues with the first statement after the entire **try** statement (the end of the program in this example).

Testing and Debugging Tip 12.5

*An **except** handler always should specify the class name(s) of the exception(s) to catch. An empty **except** handler should be used only for a default catch-all case.*

In the second input/output dialog, the user input the string **"hello"** as the denominator. When line 10 executes, **float** cannot convert this string value to a floating-point value, so **float** raises a **ValueError** exception to indicate that the function was unable to perform the conversion. When an exception occurs, the **try** suite expires (terminates) immediately. Next, the interpreter attempts to locate a matching **except** handler starting with the **except** at line 14. The interpreter compares the type of the raised exception (**ValueError**) with the type following keyword **except** (also **ValueError**). A match occurs, so that exception handler executes, and the interpreter ignores all other exception handlers following the corresponding **try** suite. If a match did not occur, the interpreter compares the type of the raised exception with the next **except** handler in sequence and repeats the process until a match is found.

Software Engineering Observation 12.6

*An **except** clause can specify more than one exception with a comma-separated sequence of exception names in parentheses, following keyword **except**. If an **except** clause specifies more than one exception, the exceptions should be related in some way (e.g., the exceptions all are caused by mathematical errors). Use a separate **except** clause for each group of related exceptions.*

In the third input/output dialog of Fig. 12.1, the user input **0** as the denominator. When line 11 executes, the interpreter raises a **ZeroDivisionError** exception to indicate an attempt to divide by zero. Once again, the **try** suite terminates immediately upon encountering the exception and the interpreter attempts to locate a matching **except** handler, starting from the **except** handler at line 14. The interpreter compares the type of the raised exception (**ZeroDivisionError**) with the type following keyword **except** (**ValueError**). In this case, there is no match, because **ZeroDivisionError** and **ValueError** are not the same exception types and **ValueError** is not a base class of **ZeroDivisionError**. So, the interpreter proceeds to line 18 and compares the type of the raised exception (**ZeroDivisionError**) with the type following keyword **except** (**ZeroDivisionError**). A match occurs, so exception handler executes. If there were additional **except** handlers, the interpreter would ignore them.

12.5 Python **Exception** Hierarchy

This section overviews several of Python's exception classes. All exceptions inherit from base class ***Exception*** and are defined in module ***exceptions***. Python automatically places all exception names in the built-in namespace, so programs do not need to import the **exceptions** module to use exceptions. Python defines four primary classes that inherit from **Exception**—***SystemExit***, ***StopIteration***, ***Warning*** and ***StandardError***. Exception **SystemExit**, when raised and left uncaught, terminates program execution. If an interactive session encounters an uncaught **SystemExit** exception, the interactive session terminates. Python uses exception **StopIteration** (new in version 2.2) to determine when a **for** loop reaches the end of its sequence. Python uses **Warning** exceptions to indicate that certain elements of Python may change in the future.

For example, if a Python 2.2 program uses a variable named **yield**, Python raises a **Warning** exception, because future versions of Python, will reserve **yield** for use as a keyword. **StandardError** is the base class for all Python error exceptions (e.g., **ValueError** and **ZeroDivisionError**).

Figure 12.2 contains the exception hierarchy for Python 2.2. For any version of Python, the programmer can obtain the exception hierarchy with the statements

```
import exceptions
print exceptions.__doc__
```

Many **StandardError** exceptions can be caught at runtime and handled, so the program can continue running. Such exceptions often can be avoided by coding properly. For example, if a program attempts to access an out-of-range sequence subscript, the interpreter raises an exception of type ***IndexError***. Similarly, an ***AttributeError*** exception occurs when a program attempts to access a non-existent object attribute.

One of the benefits of the exception class hierarchy is that an **except** handler can catch exceptions of a particular type or can use a base-class type to catch exceptions in a hierarchy of related exception types. For example, Section 12.3 discussed the empty **except** handler, which catches exceptions of all types. An **except** handler that specifies an exception of type **Exception** also can catch all exceptions (assuming the raised exceptions inherit from class **Exception**), because **Exception** is the base class of all exception classes.

Using inheritance with exceptions enables an exception handler to catch related exceptions with a concise notation. An exception handler certainly could catch each derived-class exception individually, but it is more concise to catch the base-class exception if the handling behavior is the same for all derived classes. Otherwise, catch each derived-class exception individually.

Common Programming Error 12.4

*It is a syntax error to place an empty **except** clause before the last **except** clause following a particular **try** suite.*

Common Programming Error 12.5

*It is a logic error if two or more **except** clauses following a particular **try** suite specify the exact same exception type. Python executes the first **except** handler that matches a raised exception and ignores any additional **except** handlers that catch the same exception type.*

Common Programming Error 12.6

*Placing an **except** handler that catches type **Exception** before other **except** handlers is a logic error, because all exceptions would be caught before other exception handlers could be reached. Thus, subsequent exception handlers are unreachable.*

Determining when Python and standard and third-party components raise exceptions can be difficult—there is no way for a program to determine whether, for example, a function may raise a particular exception. The language reference and standard library documentation[3] often specify cases in which exceptions are raised. For example, in Fig. 12.1,

---

3. The library reference can be found at **www.python.org/doc/current/lib/lib.html**, and the language reference can be found at **www.python.org/doc/current/ref/ref.html**.

Python exceptions

```
Exception
    SystemExit
    StopIteration
    StandardError
        KeyboardInterrupt
        ImportError
        EnvironmentError
            IOError
            OSError
                WindowsError  (Note: Defined on Windows platforms only)
        EOFError
        RuntimeError
            NotImplementedError
        NameError
            UnboundLocalError
        AttributeError
        SyntaxError
            IndentationError
                TabError
        TypeError
        AssertionError
        LookupError
            IndexError
            KeyError
        ArithmeticError
            OverflowError
            ZeroDivisionError
            FloatingPointError
        ValueError
            UnicodeError
        ReferenceError
        SystemError
        MemoryError
    Warning
        UserWarning
        DeprecationWarning
        SyntaxWarning
        OverflowWarning
        RuntimeWarning
```

Fig. 12.2 Python exception hierarchy.

we demonstrated that Python raises a **ZeroDivisionError** exception when a program attempts to divide by zero. In the language reference, Section 5.6 discusses the division operator and states that division by zero causes a **ZeroDivisionError** exception. A third-party component intended for distribution and use in software development also should include documentation that indicates the exceptions raised by the component and why such exceptions occur.

Software Engineering Observation 12.7

If a component raises exceptions, the component documentation should state that the component raises the exception. Statements that use the component should be placed in **try** *suites, and those exceptions should be caught and handled.*

12.6 **finally** Clause

Programs frequently request and release resources dynamically (i.e., at execution time). For example, a program that reads a file from disk first asks to open that file. If that request succeeds, the program reads the contents of the file. Operating systems typically can prevent more than one program from manipulating a file at once. Therefore, when a program finishes processing a file, the program normally closes the file (i.e., releases the resource). This enables other programs to use the file. Closing the file helps prevent a *resource leak*, in which the file resource is not available to other programs because a program using the file never closed it. Programs that obtain certain types of resources (such as files) typically should return those resources explicitly to the system to avoid resource leaks.

In programming languages (e.g., C and C++) in which programmers are responsible for dynamic memory management, the most common type of resource leak is a *memory leak*. This happens when a program allocates (obtains) memory, but does not deallocate (release) the memory when it is no longer needed. In Python, normally this is not an issue, because the interpreter performs *garbage collection* of memory no longer needed by an executing program. However, other kinds of resource leaks (such as the unclosed files mentioned previously) can occur in Python.

Testing and Debugging Tip 12.6

The interpreter does not eliminate memory leaks completely. The interpreter will not garbage-collect an object while references to that object exist. Thus, memory leaks can occur if programmers erroneously keep references to unwanted objects.

Most resources that require explicit release have potential exceptions associated with processing those resources. For example, a program that processes a file might receive **IOError** exceptions during the processing. For this reason, file processing code normally appears in a **try** suite. Regardless of whether a program successfully processes a file, the program should close the file when the file is no longer needed.

Suppose a program places all resource-request and resource-release code in a **try** suite. If no exceptions occur, the **try** suite executes normally and releases the resources. However, if an exception occurs, the **try** suite expires before the resource-release code can execute. We could duplicate all resource-release code in the **except** handlers, but this makes the code more difficult to modify and maintain.

Python's exception handling mechanism provides the ***finally*** clause, which is guaranteed to execute if program control enters the corresponding **try** suite, regardless of whether that **try** suite executes successfully or an exception occurs. This guarantee makes the **finally** suite an ideal location to place resource-deallocation code for resources acquired and manipulated in the corresponding **try** suite. If the **try** suite executes successfully, the **finally** suite executes immediately after the **try** suite terminates. If an exception occurs in the **try** suite, the **finally** suite executes immediately after the line that caused the exception. The exception is then processed by the next enclosing **try** statement (if there is one).

Testing and Debugging Tip 12.7

*A **finally** suite typically contains code to release resources acquired in the corresponding **try** suite, making the **finally** suite an effective way to eliminate resource leaks.*

Testing and Debugging Tip 12.8

*The only reason a **finally** suite will not execute if program control entered the corresponding **try** suite is if the application terminates before the **finally** can execute.*

Performance Tip 12.2

As a rule, resources should be released as soon as they are no longer needed in a program. This makes those resources available for reuse immediately and enables other programs to access those resources.

Software Engineering Observation 12.8

Before raising an exception, the code that raises the exception should release any resources acquired in the code before the exception occurred.

Figure 12.3 demonstrates that the **finally** clause always executes, regardless of whether an exception occurs in the corresponding **try** suite. The program consists of two functions to demonstrate **finally**—**doNotRaiseException** (lines 4–14) and **raiseExceptionDoNotCatch** (lines 16–27). The main program calls these functions to demonstrate when **finally** clauses execute.

```
1   # Fig. 12.3: fig12_03.py
2   # Using finally clauses.
3
4   def doNotRaiseException():
5
6       # try block does not raise any exceptions
7       try:
8           print "In doNotRaiseException"
9
10      # finally executes because corresponding try executed
11      finally:
12          print "Finally executed in doNotRaiseException"
13
14      print "End of doNotRaiseException"
15
16  def raiseExceptionDoNotCatch():
17
18      # raise exception, but do not catch it
19      try:
20          print "In raiseExceptionDoNotCatch"
21          raise Exception
22
```

Fig. 12.3 **finally** always executes. (Part 1 of 2.)

```
23        # finally executes because corresponding try executed
24        finally:
25            print "Finally executed in raiseExceptionDoNotCatch"
26
27        print "Will never reach this point"
28
29    # main program
30
31    # Case 1: No exceptions occur in called function.
32    print "Calling doNotRaiseException"
33    doNotRaiseException()
34
35    # Case 2: Exception occurs, but is not handled in called function,
36    # because no except clauses exist in raiseExceptionDoNotCatch
37    print "\nCalling raiseExceptionDoNotCatch"
38
39    # call raiseExceptionDoNotCatch
40    try:
41        raiseExceptionDoNotCatch()
42
43    # catch exception from raiseExceptionDoNotCatch
44    except Exception:
45        print "Caught exception from raiseExceptionDoNotCatch " + \
46            "in main program."
```

```
Calling doNotRaiseException
In doNotRaiseException
Finally executed in doNotRaiseException
End of doNotRaiseException

Calling raiseExceptionDoNotCatch
In raiseExceptionDoNotCatch
Finally executed in raiseExceptionDoNotCatch
Caught exception from raiseExceptionDoNotCatch in main program.
```

Fig. 12.3 **finally** always executes. (Part 2 of 2.)

Line 33 of the main program calls function **doNotRaiseException** (lines 4–14)—a function that contains a **try/finally** form. The **try** suite (line 8) outputs a message. The **try** suite does not raise any exceptions, so program control reaches the end of the suite. Next, the **finally** clause's suite (line 12) executes and outputs a message. At this point, program control continues with the first statement after the **finally** suite, because no exception was raised. This statement (line 14) outputs a message indicating that the end of the function has been reached. Then, program control returns to the main program.

Common Programming Error 12.7

*It is a syntax error to write a **try** statement that does not contain either a **finally** clause or one or more **except** clauses. If a **try** statement does not have any **except** clauses, it must have a **finally** clause. If a **try** statement does not have a **finally** clause, it must have one or more **except** clauses.*

Lines 40–41 of the main program begin a **try** statement that invokes function **raiseExceptionDoNotCatch** (lines 16–27). The **try** statement enables the main program to catch any exceptions raised by **raiseExceptionDoNotCatch**. In **raiseExceptionDoNotCatch**, the **try** suite (lines 20–21) begins by outputting a message. Next, the **try** suite raises an **Exception** (line 21) and the **try** suite expires immediately. This **try** statement does not specify any **except** clauses; therefore, the exception is not caught in function **raiseExceptionDoNotCatch**. Normal program control cannot continue until that exception is caught and processed. Thus, the interpreter will terminate **raiseExceptionDoNotCatch** and program control will return to the main program. Before control returns to the main program, however, the **finally** clause's suite (line 25) executes and outputs a message. At this point, program control returns to the main program—any statements appearing after the **finally** suite (e.g., line 27) do not execute. In the main program, the **except** handler in lines 44–46 catches the exception and displays a message indicating that the exception was caught in the main program.

Common Programming Error 12.8

*Raising an exception in a **finally** suite is a potentially dangerous operation. If an uncaught exception is awaiting processing when the **finally** suite executes and the **finally** suite raises a new exception that the suite does not catch, the first exception is lost, and the new exception is passed to the next enclosing **try** statement.*

Testing and Debugging Tip 12.9

*In a **finally** suite, always enclose in a **try** statement code that may raise an exception. This prevents losing uncaught exceptions that occur before the **finally** suite executes.*

Software Engineering Observation 12.9

*If a **try** statement specifies a **finally** clause, the **finally** clause's suite executes even if the **try** suite is terminated by a **return** statement. Then, the **return** to the calling code occurs.*

Note that the point at which program control continues after the **finally** clause executes depends on the exception-handling state. If the **try** suite successfully completes, the **finally** suite executes and control continues with the next statement after the **finally** suite. If the **try** suite raises an exception, the **finally** suite executes then program control continues in the next enclosing **try** statement. The enclosing **try** may be in the calling function or one of its callers. It also is possible to nest a **try/except** form in a **try** suite, in which case the outer **try** statement's exception handlers would process any exceptions the were not caught in the inner **try** statement.

12.7 **Exception Objects** and Tracebacks

As we discussed in Section 12.5, exception data types—which derive from class **Exception**—can be created with zero or more arguments. These arguments frequently are used to formulate error messages for a raised exception. When Python creates an exception object in response to a **raise** statement, Python places any arguments from the **raise** statement in the exception object's **args** attribute.

When an exception occurs, Python "remembers" the exception that has been raised and the current state of the program. Python also maintains **traceback** objects that contain information about the function call stack from the time the exception occurred. Recall that exceptions can be raised in a deeply nested series of function calls. As the program calls each function, Python inserts the function name at the beginning of the *function call stack*. When an exception is raised, Python begins searching for an exception handler. If no exception handler exists in the current function, the current function terminates execution, and Python searches the current function's calling function, and so on, until either an exception handler is found or Python reaches the main program. This process of searching for an appropriate exception handler is called *stack unwinding*. Just as the interpreter maintains information about functions that are placed on the stack, the interpreter maintains information about functions that have been unwound from the stack.

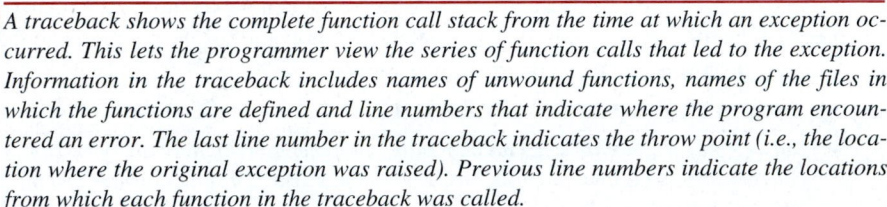

Testing and Debugging Tip 12.10

A traceback shows the complete function call stack from the time at which an exception occurred. This lets the programmer view the series of function calls that led to the exception. Information in the traceback includes names of unwound functions, names of the files in which the functions are defined and line numbers that indicate where the program encountered an error. The last line number in the traceback indicates the throw point (i.e., the location where the original exception was raised). Previous line numbers indicate the locations from which each function in the traceback was called.

Our next example (Fig. 12.4) demonstrates exception object's **args** attribute and exception object string representation. The example also demonstrates how to access **traceback** objects to print information about stack unwinding. As we discuss this example, we keep track of the functions on the call stack so we can discuss the **traceback** object and the stack-unwinding mechanism.

```
1   # Fig. 12.4: fig12_04.py
2   # Demonstrating exception arguments and stack unwinding.
3
4   import traceback
5
6   def function1():
7       function2()
8
9   def function2():
10      function3()
11
12  def function3():
13
14      # raise exception, catch exception, reraise exception
15      try:
16          raise Exception, "An exception has occurred"
17      except Exception:
18          print "Caught exception in function3. Reraising....\n"
19          raise   # reraises most recent exception
20
21  # call function1, any Exception it generates will be
22  # caught by the except clause that follows
23  try:
24      function1()
25
```

Fig. 12.4   Exception arguments and stack unwinding. (Part 1 of 2.)

```
26   # output exception arguments, string representation of exception,
27   # and the traceback
28   except Exception, exception:
29       print "Exception caught in main program."
30       print "\nException arguments:", exception.args
31       print "\nException message:", exception
32       print "\nTraceback:"
33       traceback.print_exc()
```

```
Caught exception in function3. Reraising....

Exception caught in main program.

Exception arguments: ('An exception has occurred',)

Exception message: An exception has occurred

Traceback:
Traceback (most recent call last):
  File "fig12_04.py", line 24, in ?
    function1()
  File "fig12_04.py", line 7, in function1
    function2()
  File "fig12_04.py", line 10, in function2
    function3()
  File "fig12_04.py", line 16, in function3
    raise Exception, "An exception has occurred"
Exception: An exception has occurred
```

Fig. 12.4 Exception arguments and stack unwinding. (Part 2 of 2.)

The interpreter begins executing the program with line 1. This is technically the first line in the main program. The main program is the first entry in the function call stack, because it is the entity that invokes all other functions. Line 24 of the **try** suite in the main program invokes **function1** (defined in lines 6–7), which becomes the second entry on the stack. If **function1** raises an exception, the **except** handler in lines 28–33 catch the exception and output information about the exception that occurred. Line 7 of **function1** invokes **function2** (defined in lines 9–10), which becomes the third entry on the stack. Then, line 10 of **function2** invokes **function3** (defined in lines 12–19) which becomes the fourth entry on the stack.

At this point, the call stack for the program is

> **function3** *(top)*
> **function2**
> **function1**
> *Main Program*

with the last function called (**function3**) at the top and the main program at the bottom. Line 16 in **function3** raises an **Exception** and passes the string **"An exception has occurred"** as an argument. In response to the **raise** statement, Python creates an **Exception** object, with the specified argument. The **except** clause in lines 17–19 catches the exception and first prints a message. Line 19 uses an empty **raise** statement to *reraise* the exception. Usually, reraising an exception indicates that the **except** handler performed partial processing of the exception and is now passing the exception back to the caller (in this case **function2**) for further processing. In this example, the **function3** demonstrates that keyword **raise**, with no specified exception name, reraises the most recently raised exception.

Software Engineering Observation 12.10

If a function is capable of handling a given type of exception, then let that function handle it, rather than passing the exception to another region of the program.

Next, **function3** terminates because the reraised exception is not caught in the function body. Thus, control will return to the statement that invoked **function3** in the prior function in the call stack (**function2**). This removes or *unwinds* **function3** from the function call stack (thus, terminating the function) and Python maintains information about the function call in a **traceback** object.

When control returns to line 10 in **function2**, the interpreter ascertains that line 10 is not in a **try** suite. Therefore, the exception cannot be caught in **function2**, and **function2** terminates. This unwinds **function2** from the function call stack, creates another **traceback** object (to represent the current level of unwinding) and returns control to line 7 in **function1**. Here again, line 7 is not in a **try** suite, so the exception cannot be caught in **function1**. The function terminates and unwinds from the call stack, creating another **traceback** object and returning control to line 24 in the main program, which is in a **try** suite. The **try** suite in the main program expires and the **except** handler in lines (28–33) catches the exception.

Notice that the **except** clause in line 28 differs from the **except** clauses presented thus far. When Python encounters an **except** clause in which **except** is followed by an exception type (or tuple of exception types), a comma, and an identifier, Python binds the identifier to the matching exception object. Now, the **except** handler can use the identifier to obtain information about the specific exception that occurred. The **except** suite in lines 29–33 prints the exception object's **args** attribute (line 30). Then, the handler prints the string representation of the exception. Python's string representation of an exception object depends on the value of its **args** attribute. If the **args** attribute is an empty tuple, Python represents the exception as the empty string. If an exception objects's **args** tuple contains only one value, Python's represents the exception as the string representation of that value. If an exception object's **args** tuple contains multiple items, Python represents the exception as the string representation of the **args** tuple. In this example, the exception object's **arg** attribute contains only one value, so Python represents the exception as that value (i.e., the string **"An exception has occurred"**).

Line 33 of the **except** handler calls function ***traceback.print_exc*** to print the traceback. Module **traceback** contains many functions for manipulating the **traceback** objects that Python creates during stack unwinding. Recall that stack unwinding continues until either an **except** handler catches the exception or the program terminates. Function **print_exc**, when called with no arguments, prints all the **traceback** objects accumulated thus far in the stack-unwinding process. This output is identical to the output Python produces when the interpreter encounters an uncaught exception. Let us examine the output from function **print_exc**. The first line

```
Traceback (most recent call last)
```

is the standard traceback line that Python prints when an error occurs. This line indicates that the most recent call (i.e., the call at the top of the call stack when the exception occurred) appears last in the traceback output. The next two lines in the traceback output contain information about the first call on the function call stack (i.e., the call to **function1** from the main program). The information includes the file in which the call occurred (**fig12_04.py**), the line number of the file that called the function (**24**) and the calling entity from which the function was invoked (**?**, which corresponds to the main program). The subsequent pairs of lines in the traceback output each correspond to a call on the function call stack. The second-to-last line contains the code that caused the exception (i.e., the code from line 16 in **function3** that contains the **raise** statement). This demonstrates the fact that the empty **raise** statement in line 19 simply reraises the exception from line 16. The final line of the output contains a string representation of the exception type and its argument. Note that traceback output contains information about the call stack from the point at which the exception occurred to the point at which the exception is caught (or the point at which the program terminates, if the exception is not caught).

Testing and Debugging Tip 12.11

When reading a traceback, start from the end of the traceback and read the error message first. Then, read up the remainder of the traceback, looking for the first line that indicates code that you wrote in your program. Normally, this is the location that caused the exception.

12.8 Programmer-Defined Exception Classes

In many cases, programmers can use existing exception classes from the Python hierarchy to indicate exceptions that occur in their programs. However, in some cases, programmers may wish to create new exception types that are more specific to the problems that occur in their programs. *Programmer-defined exception classes* should derive directly or indirectly from class **Exception**.

Good Programming Practice 12.1

Associating each type of malfunction with an appropriately named exception class improves program clarity.

Good Programming Practice 12.2

Before creating programmer-defined exception classes, investigate the existing exception classes in the Python hierarchy to discover whether an appropriate exception type already exists.

Good Programming Practice 12.3

Define new exception classes only if programmers need to catch and handle the new exceptions differently from other existing exception types.

Figure 12.5 demonstrates defining and using a programmer-defined exception class. Class **NegativeNumberError** (lines 6–8) is a programmer-defined exception class representing exceptions that occur when a program performs an illegal operation on a negative number, such as the square root of a negative number.

Lines 6–8 define a programmer-defined exception class. The Python exception class hierarchy defines many categories of exceptions, and programmer-defined exceptions should extend an appropriate exception from one of these categories. **NegativeNumberError**

```
 1   # Fig. 12.5: fig12_05.py
 2   # Demonstrating a programmer-defined exception class.
 3
 4   import math
 5
 6   class NegativeNumberError( ArithmeticError ):
 7      """Attempted improper operation on negative number."""
 8      pass
 9
10   def squareRoot( number ):
11      """Computes square root of number. Raises NegativeNumberError
12      if number is less than 0."""
13
14      if number < 0:
15         raise NegativeNumberError, \
16            "Square root of negative number not permitted"
17
18      return math.sqrt( number )
19
20   while 1:
21
22      # get user-entered number and compute square root
23      try:
24         userValue = float( raw_input( "\nPlease enter a number: " ) )
25         print squareRoot( userValue )
26
27      # float raises ValueError if input is not numerical
28      except ValueError:
29         print "The entered value is not a number"
30
31      # squareRoot raises NegativeNumberError if number is negative
32      except NegativeNumberError, exception:
33         print exception
34
35      # successful execution: terminate while loop
36      else:
37         break
```

```
Please enter a number: hello
The entered value is not a number

Please enter a number: -900
Square root of negative number not permitted

Please enter a number: 12.345
3.51354521815
```

Fig. 12.5   Programmer-defined exception class.

exceptions most likely occur during arithmetic, so it seems logical to derive class **Negativ-eNumberError** from class **ArithmeticError**. Creating simple, programmer-defined exceptions in Python is easy, because the new exception class inherits all its functionality from the base-class exception. Therefore, the body of the class contains only the keyword **pass**—the keyword that indicates a suite or block performs no work.

The remainder of the program (lines 10–37) demonstrates our programmer-defined exception class. The program enables the user to input a numeric value, then invokes function **squareRoot** (lines 10–18) to calculate the square root of that value. For this purpose, **squareRoot** invokes function **math.sqrt**, which wants a nonnegative value as its argument. If **math.sqrt** receives a negative value, the function raises a **ValueError** exception with the argument **"math domain error"**. In this program, we essentially write our own square root function that uses a programmer-defined exception to prevent the user from calculating the square root of a negative number. If the numeric value received from the user is negative, function **squareRoot** raises a **NegativeNumberError** (lines 14–16). Otherwise, **squareRoot** invokes function **math.sqrt** to compute the square root.

In the main program, a **while** loop (lines 20–37) continues executing until the user enters a nonnegative value. The **try** suite (lines 24–25) attempts to obtain a numerical value from the user and to pass that value to function **squareRoot**. When the user inputs a value and presses *Enter*, the program passes the user-entered value to function **float**. If the value is not a number, function **float** raises a **ValueError** exception, and the except handler in lines 28–29 prints an error message. Control then returns to the beginning of the **while** loop. If the user inputs a negative number, function **squareRoot** raises a **NegativeNumberError**. The except handler in lines 32–33 simply prints the exception object before control returns to the beginning of the **while** loop. If the user enters a valid, nonnegative number, line 25 prints the square root of the number before program control proceeds to the **else** clause in lines 36–37. The **else** suite contains only the keyword **break**, which terminates the **while** loop.

In this chapter, we demonstrated how the exception-handling mechanism works and discussed how to make applications more robust by writing exception handlers to process potential problems. When developing new applications, it is important to investigate potential exceptions raised by the functions your program invokes or by the interpreter, then implement appropriate exception-handling code to make those applications more robust. In Chapter 13, String Manipulation and Regular Expressions, we begin a discussing a series of techniques for developing substantial software. These techniques, when combined with disciplined exception handling, enable Python programmers to create viable, valuable software components.

SUMMARY

- An exception is an indication of a "special event" that occurs during a program's execution. Often the special event is an error (e.g., dividing by zero or adding two incompatible types). Sometimes the special event is something else (e.g., the termination of a **for** loop).

- Exception handling enables programmers to write clear, robust, more fault-tolerant programs that can resolve (or handle) exceptions.

- The style and details of exception handling in Python are based on the Modula-3 language. This exception-handling mechanism is similar to that used in C# and Java.

- The **raise** statement executes to indicate that an exception has occurred. This is called raising (or sometimes throwing) an exception.

- The simplest **raise** statement consists of the keyword **raise**, followed by the name of the exception to be raised.

- Exception names specify classes and Python exceptions are objects of those classes. When the **raise** statement executes, Python creates an object of the specified exception class.

- The **raise** statement may specify an argument or arguments that initialize the exception object. In this case, a comma follows the exception name, and the argument or a tuple of arguments follows the comma.

- Exception handling enables the programmer to remove error-handling code from the "main line" of the program's execution. This improves program clarity and enhances modifiability.

- Programmers can decide to handle whatever exceptions they choose—all types of exceptions, all exceptions of a certain type or all exceptions of related types.

- The exception-handling mechanism is useful for processing problems that occur when a program interacts with reusable software components. Rather than internally handling problems that occur, such components use exceptions to notify client code of problems. This enables programmers to implement error handling that is appropriate to each application.

- Exception handling is geared to situations in which the code that detects an error is unable to handle it. Such code raises or throws an exception.

- Python uses **try** statements to enable exception handling. The **try** statement encloses statements that potentially cause exceptions. A **try** statement consists of keyword **try**, followed by a colon (**:**), followed by a suite of code in which exceptions may occur, followed by one or more clauses.

- Immediately following the **try** suite may be one or more **except** clauses (also called **except** handlers). Each **except** clause specifies zero or more exception names that represent the type(s) of exceptions the **except** clause can handle.

- The **except** clause also may specify an identifier for the exception that was raised, and the handler can use the exception object to obtain information about that exception.

- An **except** clause that specifies no exception type is an empty **except** clause, which catches all exception types. It is a syntax error to place an empty **except** clause before any other **except** clauses in a particular **try** statement.

- After the last **except** clause, an optional **else** clause contains code that executes if the code in the **try** suite raised no exceptions.

- A **try** suite can be followed by zero **except** clauses; in that case, it must be followed by a **finally** clause. The code in the **finally** suite always executes, regardless of whether an exception occurs.

- Programmers sometimes refer to the point in the program at which an exception occurs as the throw point.

- Exceptions are objects of classes that inherit from class **Exception**.

- If an exception occurs in a **try** suite, the **try** suite expires and program control transfers to the first matching **except** handler (if there is one) following the **try** suite. A match occurs if the types are identical or if the raised exception's type is a derived class of the handler's exception type.

- If no exceptions occur in a **try** suite, the interpreter ignores the exception handlers for that **try** statement.

- If an exception occurs in a statement that is not in a **try** suite and that statement is in a function, the function containing that statement terminates immediately and the interpreter attempts to locate an enclosing **try** statement in a calling function—a process called stack unwinding.

- Python is said to use the termination model of exception handling, because the **try** statement enclosing a raised exception expires immediately when that exception occurs.

- Function **float** raises a **ValueError** exception if the function cannot convert its argument value to a floating-point value.

- The Python interpreter automatically tests for division by zero and raises a **ZeroDivision-Error** exception if the denominator is zero.

- As good programming practice, an **except** handler always should specify the name of the exception to catch. An empty **except** handler should be used only for a default catch-all case.

- The preferred exception-handling mechanism is to allow objects of class **Exception** and its derived classes to be raised and caught.

- An **except** handler can catch exceptions of a particular type or can use a base-class type to catch exceptions in a hierarchy of related exception types.

- A third-party component intended for distribution and use in software development also should include documentation that indicates which exceptions are raised by the component.

- Programs frequently request and release resources dynamically. Programs that obtain certain types of resources (such as files) sometimes must return those resources explicitly to the system to avoid resource leaks. Most resources that require explicit release have potential exceptions associated with processing those resources.

- The **finally** clause that guaranteed to execute if program control enters the corresponding **try** suite. The **finally** clause is an ideal location to place resource deallocation code for resources acquired and manipulated in the corresponding **try** suite.

- Objects of exception data types can be created with zero or more arguments. These arguments frequently are used to formulate error messages for a raised exception.

- When Python creates an exception object in a **raise** statement, Python places any arguments from the **raise** statement in the exception object's **args** attribute.

- When an exception occurs, Python remembers the exception that was raised and the current state of the program. Python also maintains **traceback** objects that contains information about the function call stack from the time the exception occurred.

- Python maintains information about functions that have been unwound from the stack with **traceback** objects.

- An empty **raise** statement reraises the most recently raised exception.

- When Python encounters an **except** clause in which **except** is followed by an exception type (or tuple of exception types), a comma and an identifier, Python binds the identifier to the exception object that the except handler catches.

- If an exception object's **args** attribute is an empty tuple, the exception's string representation is the empty string.

- If an exception objects's **args** tuple contains only one value, the exception's string representation is the string representation of that value.

- If an exception object's **args** tuple contains multiple items, the exception's string representation is the string representation of the **args** tuple.

- Module **traceback** contains many functions for manipulating the **traceback** objects that Python creates during stack unwinding.

- Function **traceback.print_exc**, when called with no arguments, prints all the **traceback** objects accumulated thus far in the stack-unwinding process.

- A Python **traceback** object stores information about a function call, including the file name, line numbers and the code that caused an error.

- Programmer-defined exception classes should derive directly or indirectly from class **Exception**.

- If a programmer-defined exception requires no extra functionality, the programmer can create the exception merely by inheriting from an existing exception class and placing keyword **pass** in the body of the class.

TERMINOLOGY

args attribute of exception object

automatic garbage collection

call stack

catch related errors

divide by zero

eliminate resource leaks

empty **except** clause

empty **raise** clause

error-processing code

except clause

except handler

except suite expires

exception

Exception class

exception handler

fault-tolerant program

finally clause

FormatException class

function call stack

garbage collection

IndexError exception

inheritance with exceptions

memory exhaustion

memory leak

Modula-3

out-of-range sequence subscript

print_exc function of module **traceback**

programmer-defined exception class

raise an exception

raise statement

release a resource

reraise an exception

resource leak

resumption model of exception handling

sqrt function of module **math**

stack unwinding

StandardError exception

StopIteration exception

SystemExit exception

termination model of exception handling

throw an exception

throw point

traceback module

traceback object

try statement

try/except form

try/except/else form of a **try** statement

try/finally form of a **try** statement

Warning exception

ZeroDivisionError exception

SELF-REVIEW EXERCISES

12.1 Fill in the blanks in each of the following statements:

a) Python uses exception handling to determine when a _____ loop terminates.

b) A function is said to _____ an exception when it detects that a problem occurred.

c) The _____ clause, if it appears after a **try** suite, always executes.

d) Most basic Python exceptions derive from class _____.

e) The statement that raises an exception is sometimes called the _____ of the exception.

f) A _____ statement encloses code that may raise an exception.

g) If the catch-all exception handler is specified before another exception handler, a _____ may occur.

h) An uncaught exception in a function causes that function to be _____ from the function call stack.

i) Function **float** can raise a(n) _____ exception if its argument cannot be converted to a floating-point value.

j) Python maintains information about the functions unwound from the stack in _____ objects.

12.2 State whether each of the following is *true* or *false*. If *false*, explain why.

a) Exceptions always are handled in the function that initially detects the exception.

b) Accessing a nonexistent object attribute causes an **AttributeError** exception.

c) Accessing an out-of-bounds sequence subscript causes the interpreter to raise an exception.

d) A **try** statement must contain one or more clauses.

e) If a **finally** clause appears in a function, that **finally** clause is guaranteed to execute.

f) In Python, it is possible to return to the throw point of an exception via keyword **return**.
g) Exceptions can be reraised.
h) Function **math.sqrt** raises a **NegativeNumberError** exception if called with a negative-integer argument.
i) Exception object attribute **args** contains a string that corresponds to the exception's error message.
j) Exceptions can be raised only by functions explicitly called in **try** statements.

ANSWERS TO SELF-REVIEW EXERCISES

12.1   a) **for**. b) raise (or throw). c) **finally**. d) **Exception**. e) throw point. f) **try**. g) syntax or logic error. h) unwound. i) **ValueError**. j) **traceback**.

12.2   a) False. Although it is possible to handle an exception in the function that originally detects the exception, often an exception is handled by a calling function on the function call stack. b) True. c) True. d) True. e) False. The **finally** clause will execute only if program control enters the corresponding **try** suite and if the **try** suite does not terminate the program. f) False. It is not possible to return control to the throw point of an exception in Python. g) True. h) False. Function **math.sqrt** raises a **ValueError** exception if called with a negative-integer argument. i) False. Exception object attribute **args** contains a tuple that corresponds to the arguments used to initialize the exception object. j) False. Exceptions can be raised by any code, regardless of whether it is called from a **try** statement. Also, the interpreter can raise exceptions.

EXERCISES

12.3   Use inheritance to create an exception base class and various exception-derived classes. Write a program to demonstrate that the **except** clause specifying the base class catches derived-class exceptions.

12.4   Write a Python program that demonstrates how various exceptions are caught with

    except Exception, *exception*

12.5   Write a Python program that shows the importance of the order of exception handlers. Write two programs, one with the correct order of **except** handlers and another with an order that causes a logic error. If you attempt to catch a base-class exception type before a derived-class type, the program may produce a logic error.

12.6   Exceptions can be used to indicate problems that occur when an object is being constructed. Write a Python program that shows a constructor passing information about constructor failure to an exception handler that occurs after a **try** statement. The exception raised also should contain the arguments sent to the constructor.

12.7   Write a Python program that illustrates reraising an exception.

12.8   Write a Python program that shows that a function with its own **try** statement does not have to catch every possible exception that occurs within the **try** suite. Some exceptions can slip through to, and be handled in, other scopes.

13

String Manipulation and Regular Expressions

Objectives

- To understand text processing in Python.
- To use Python's string data-type methods.
- To manipulate and search string contents.
- To understand and create regular expressions.
- To use regular expressions to match patterns in strings.
- To use metacharacters, special sequences and grouping to create complex regular expressions.

The chief defect of Henry King
Was chewing little bits of string.
Hilaire Belloc

Vigorous writing is concise. A sentence should contain no unnecessary words, a paragraph no unnecessary sentences.
William Strunk, Jr.

I have made this letter longer than usual, because I lack the time to make it short.
Blaise Pascal

The difference between the almost-right word and the right word is really a large matter—it's the difference between the lightning bug and the lightning.
Mark Twain

Mum's the word.
Miguel de Cervantes

13.1 Introduction

This chapter introduces Python's string and character processing capabilities and demonstrates using regular expressions to search for patterns in text. The techniques presented in this chapter can be employed to develop text editors, word processors, page-layout software, computerized typesetting systems and other text-processing software. Previous chapters presented several string-processing capabilities. In this chapter, we expand on this information by detailing the capabilities of various methods of the basic string data type and the powerful text-processing capabilities provided in the Python module **re**.

13.2 Fundamentals of Characters and Strings

Characters (digits, letters and symbols such as $, @, % and *) are the fundamental building blocks of Python programs. Every program is composed of characters that, when grouped meaningfully, represent a series of instructions that the interpreter uses to perform a task. Each character has a corresponding *character code* (sometimes called its *integer ordinal value*). For example, the integer value **122** corresponds to the character constant **"z"**. Python provides function **ord** that takes as an argument a character and returns its character code (as shown in the interactive session of Fig. 13.1). In most modern programming languages and systems, character values are established according to the *Unicode character set*—an international character set that contains many more symbols and letters than does the ASCII character set (see Appendix B, ASCII Character Set). To learn more about Unicode, see Appendix F.

Python supports strings as a basic data type. Recall that strings are immutable sequences—strings cannot be changed after they are created. We have seen how to obtain the length of a string with function **len**, how to concatenate strings with operator **+** and

```
Python 2.2b2 (#26, Nov 16 2001, 11:44:11) [MSC 32 bit (Intel)] on
win32
Type "help", "copyright", "credits" or "license" for more informa-
tion.
>>> ord( "z" )
122
>>> ord( "\n" )
10
```

Fig. 13.1   Integer ordinal value of a character.

how to format strings with format operator **%**. Strings also support methods that perform various other formatting and processing capabilities. The table in Fig. 13.2 lists the string methods. When a program invokes a string method that appears to modify the string, the method actually returns its results as a new string. In the table, the "original string" refers to the string on which a method is invoked. We discuss many of these methods in the following sections.

String Method	Description
capitalize()	Returns a version of the original string in which only the first letter is capitalized. Converts any other capital letters to lowercase.
center(*width* **)**	Returns a copy of the original string centered (using spaces) in a string of *width* characters.
count(*substring[, start[, end]]* **)**	Returns the number of times *substring* occurs in the original string. If argument *start* is specified, searching begins at that index. If argument *end* is indicated, searching begins at *start* and stops at *end*.
encode(*[encoding[, errors]* **)**	Returns an encoded string. Python's default encoding is normally ASCII. Argument *errors* defines the type of error handling used; by default, errors is ***"strict"***.
endswith(*substring[, start[, end]]* **)**	Returns 1 if the string ends with *substring*. Returns 0 otherwise. If argument *start* is specified, searching begins at that index. If argument *end* is specified, the method searches through the slice *start:end*.
expandtabs(*[tabsize]* **)**	Returns a new string in which all tabs are replaced by spaces. Optional argument *tabsize* specifies the number of space characters that replace a tab character. The default value is 8.

Fig. 13.2   String methods. (Part 1 of 3.)

String Method	Description
find(*substring[, start[, end]]*)	Returns the lowest index at which *substring* occurs in the string; returns −1 if the string does not contain *substring*. If argument *start* is specified, searching begins at that index. If argument *end* is specified, the method searches through the slice *start:end*.
index(*substring[, start[, end]]*)	Performs the same operation as **find**, but raises a **ValueError** exception if the string does not contain *substring*.
isalnum()	Returns 1 if the string contains only alphanumeric characters (i.e., numbers and letters); otherwise, returns 0.
isalpha()	Returns 1 if the string contains only alphabetic characters (i.e., letters); returns 0 otherwise.
isdigit()	Returns 1 if the string contains only numerical characters (e.g., **"0"**, **"1"**, **"2"**); otherwise, returns 0.
islower()	Returns 1 if all alphabetic characters in the string are lower-case characters (e.g., **"a"**, **"b"**, **"c"**); otherwise, returns 0.
isspace()	Returns 1 if the string contains only whitespace characters; otherwise, returns 0.
istitle()	Returns 1 if the first character of each word in the string is the only uppercase character in the word; otherwise, returns 0.
isupper()	Returns 1 if all alphabetic characters in the string are uppercase characters (e.g., **"A"**, **"B"**, **"C"**); otherwise, returns 0.
join(*sequence*)	Returns a string that concatenates the strings in *sequence* using the original string as the separator between concatenated strings.
ljust(*width*)	Returns a new string left-aligned in a whitespace string of *width* characters.
lower()	Returns a new string in which all characters in the original string are lowercase.
lstrip()	Returns a new string in which all leading whitespace is removed.
replace(*old, new[, maximum]*)	Returns a new string in which all occurrences of *old* in the original string are replaced with *new*. Optional argument *maximum* indicates the maximum number of replacements to perform.

Fig. 13.2   String methods. (Part 2 of 3.)

String Method	Description
rfind(*substring[, start[, end]]* **)**	Returns the highest index value in which *substring* occurs in the string or −1 if the string does not contain *substring*. If argument *start* is specified, searching begins at that index. If argument *end* is specified, the method searches the slice *start:end*.
rindex(*substring[, start[, end]]* **)**	Performs the same operation as **rfind**, but raises a **ValueError** exception if the string does not contain *substring*.
rjust(*width* **)**	Returns a new string right-aligned in a string of *width* characters.
rstrip()	Returns a new string in which all trailing whitespace is removed.
split(*[separator]* **)**	Returns a list of substrings created by splitting the original string at each *separator*. If optional argument *separator* is omitted or **None**, the string is separated by any sequence of whitespace, effectively returning a list of words.
splitlines(*[keepbreaks]* **)**	Returns a list of substrings created by splitting the original string at each newline character. If optional argument *keepbreaks* is 1, the substrings in the returned list retain the newline character.
startswith(*substring[, start[, end]]* **)**	Returns 1 if the string starts with *substring*; otherwise, returns 0. If argument *start* is specified, searching begins at that index. If argument *end* is specified, the method searches through the slice *start:end*.
strip()	Returns a new string in which all leading and trailing whitespace is removed.
swapcase()	Returns a new string in which uppercase characters are converted to lowercase characters and lower-case characters are converted to uppercase characters.
title()	Returns a new string in which the first character of each word in the string is the only uppercase character in the word.
translate(*table[, delete]* **)**	Translates the original string to a new string. The translation is performed by first deleting any characters in optional argument *delete*, then by replacing each character *c* in the original string with the value *table* **[ord(** *c* **)]**.
upper()	Returns a new string where all characters in the original string are uppercase.

Fig. 13.2   String methods. (Part 3 of 3.)

13.3 String Presentation

Strings require formatting for various reasons. For example, manipulating string presentations enables users to read and understand program instructions or output more easily. This section presents two simple examples that demonstrate string-formatting methods. Figure 13.3 uses three string methods—**center**, **ljust** and **rjust**—to align strings. These methods use white space characters to manipulate the string formatting.

String method **center** (line 6) takes one argument—an integer value—that corresponds to the total length of the output string. The method then creates a new string of this length and centers the original calling string (**string1**) in **50** spaces so that an equal number of spaces appears to the right and left of the calling string. String method **rjust** also aligns the **string1** by preceding the calling string with **50 – len(string1)** space characters to right-align the string (line 7). Line 8 uses method **ljust** to creates a new string that is left aligned by following the calling string with **50 – len(string1)** space characters. If the string is longer than the argument supplied to any of these methods, the method simply returns the original string.

Fig. 13.4 demonstrates methods that *strip* (remove) whitespace from strings. Line 4 creates a string, **string1**, that contains leading and trailing whitespace. String method **strip** removes leading and trailing whitespace from the original string (line 7). String method **lstrip** removes only leading whitespace (line 8) and method **rstrip** removes only trailing whitespace (line 9). As the output demonstrates, these methods remove all whitespace, including spaces, newlines and tabs.

```
1   # Fig. 13.3: fig13_03.py
2   # Simple output formatting example.
3
4   string1 = "Now I am here."
5
6   print string1.center( 50 )
7   print string1.rjust( 50 )
8   print string1.ljust( 50 )
```

```
                    Now I am here.
                                  Now I am here.
Now I am here.
```

Fig. 13.3   String justification.

```
1   # Fig. 13.4: fig13_04.py
2   # Stripping whitespace from a string.
3
4   string1 = "\t  \n   This is a test string. \t\t \n"
5
6   print 'Original string: "%s"\n' % string1
7   print 'Using strip: "%s"\n' % string1.strip()
8   print 'Using left strip: "%s"\n' % string1.lstrip()
9   print "Using right strip: \"%s\"\n" % string1.rstrip()
```

Fig. 13.4   Stripping whitespace from strings. (Part 1 of 2.)

```
Original string: "
  This is a test string.
"


Using strip: "This is a test string."

Using left strip: "This is a test string.
"


Using right strip: "
  This is a test string."
```

Fig. 13.4   Stripping whitespace from strings. (Part 2 of 2.)

13.4 Searching Strings

In many applications, it is necessary to search for a character or set of characters in a string. For example, a programmer creating a word processor would want to provide capabilities for searching through documents. To perform such tasks, Python provides methods such as **find** and **index**. When searching for a substring, we either can determine whether a string contains the substring, or we can retrieve the index at which a substring begins. Figure 13.5 searches for substrings at the beginning, middle and end of a string.

```python
1   # Fig. 13.5: fig13_05.py
2   # Searching strings for a substring.
3
4   # counting the occurrences of a substring
5   string1 = "Test1, test2, test3, test4, Test5, test6"
6
7   print '"test" occurs %d times in \n\t%s' % \
8       ( string1.count( "test" ), string1 )
9   print '"test" occurs %d times after 18th character in \n\t%s' % \
10      ( string1.count( "test", 18, len( string1 ) ), string1 )
11  print
12
13  # finding a substring in a string
14  string2 = "Odd or even"
15
16  print '"%s" contains "or" starting at index %d' % \
17      ( string2, string2.find( "or" ) )
18
19  # find index of "even"
20  try:
21      print '"even" index is', string2.index( "even" )
22  except ValueError:
23      print '"even" does not occur in "%s"' % string2
24
25  if string2.startswith( "Odd" ):
26      print '"%s" starts with "Odd"' % string2
27
```

Fig. 13.5   Strings searched for substrings. (Part 1 of 2.)

```
28    if string2.endswith( "even" ):
29        print '"%s" ends with "even"\n' % string2
30
31    # searching from end of string
32    print 'Index from end of "test" in "%s" is %d' \
33        % ( string1, string1.rfind( "test" ) )
34    print
35
36    # find rindex of "Test"
37    try:
38        print 'First occurrence of "Test" from end at index', \
39            string1.rindex( "Test" )
40    except ValueError:
41        print '"Test" does not occur in "%s"' % string1
42
43    print
44
45    # replacing a substring
46    string3 = "One, one, one, one, one, one"
47
48    print "Original:", string3
49    print 'Replaced "one" with "two":', \
50        string3.replace( "one", "two" )
51    print "Replaced 3 maximum:", string3.replace( "one", "two", 3 )
```

```
"test" occurs 4 times in
        Test1, test2, test3, test4, Test5, test6
"test" occurs 2 times after 18th character in
        Test1, test2, test3, test4, Test5, test6

"Odd or even" contains "or" starting at index 4
"even" index is 7
"Odd or even" starts with "Odd"
"Odd or even" ends with "even"

Index from end of "test" in "Test1, test2, test3, test4, Test5, test6"
is 35

First occurrence of "Test" from end at index 28

Original: One, one, one, one, one, one
Replaced "one" with "two": One, two, two, two, two, two
Replaced 3 maximum: One, two, two, two, one, one
```

Fig. 13.5   Strings searched for substrings. (Part 2 of 2.)

Lines 5–11 use string method **count** to return the number of occurrences of a substring in a string or a string slice. If the method does not find the specified substring, the method returns 0. Line 8 prints the number of times the substring **"test"** occurs in **string1**. Method **count** takes two optional arguments that specify a slice of the string to search. Line 10 passes arguments to **count** that cause the method to search **string1** starting at index 18 (i.e., character **"3"**) and terminating at the end of the string. This call produces the same result as the statement

```
string1[ 18:len( string1 ) ].count( "test" )
```

but the method call with optional arguments has the added benefit of better readability and better performance, because the program does not create a new slice.

Lines 14–29 demonstrate string that search for substrings. Line 17 uses method **find** to return the lowest index at which the substring occurs. If a string does not contain the substring, the method returns –1. Method **index** (line 21) resembles method **find**, except that if a string does not contain the substring, the method raises a **ValueError** exception. A program can catch this exception and handle it appropriately, in the case that the string does not contain the specified substring.

Lines 25–29 use methods that determine whether a string begins or ends with a specific substring. If the string begins with the substring, method **startswith** returns 1 (line 25). This call produces the same result as the expression

```
string2[ 0:len( "Odd" ) ] == "Odd"
```

If a string ends with the substring, method **endswith** returns 1 (line 28). Using this method produces the same result as the expression

```
string2[ -len( "even" ): ] == "even"
```

The program can search for a substring starting from the end of a string. Lines 32–43 use methods **rfind** and **rindex** to determine whether **string1** contains certain substrings. Method **rfind** returns the index of the first occurrence of the substring searching from the end of the string. If the method does not find the substring, it returns –1. Method **rindex** returns the highest index at which the substring begins and raises a **ValueError** if the method does not find the substring. Our program catches the exception to handle the case where the string does not contain the specified substring.

At times, a user may want to find substring to perform an action on that substring. For example, a user may perform a search for a current phrase in a document and replace that phrase with another phrase. Method **replace** takes two substrings and searches a document for the first substring then replaces that substring with the substring in the second argument. Line 50 replaces all occurrences of the substring **"one"** in **string3** with the substring **"two"**. Method **replace** takes an optional third argument that sets the maximum number of replacements. Line 51 replaces up to three occurrences of substring **"one"** with substring **"two"**.

13.5 Joining and Splitting Strings

A computer processes code in much the same way people process text when reading. When you read a sentence, your brain breaks the sentence into individual words, or *tokens,* each of which conveys a meaning. This process is known as tokenization. Interpreters perform tokenization because they break up statements into such individual components as keywords, identifiers, operators and other elements of a programming language. Tokens are separated by delimiters, typically whitespace characters such as blank, tab, newline and carriage return. Other characters also may be used as delimiters to separate tokens. In this section, we study string methods that perform delimiter-based string splitting and joining.

Figure 13.6 demonstrates string methods **split** and **join**. Line 5 creates **string1**, a comma-separated string of letters. Lines 7–11 demonstrate how to split a string into tokens using delimiters. Line 8 calls method **split** with no arguments, which splits the string at each occurrence of a whitespace character. The method returns a list of tokens and

```
1    # Fig. 13.6: fig13_06.py
2    # Token splitting and delimiter joining.
3
4    # splitting strings
5    string1 = "A, B, C, D, E, F"
6
7    print "String is:", string1
8    print "Split string by spaces:", string1.split()
9    print "Split string by commas:", string1.split( "," )
10   print "Split string by commas, max 2:", string1.split( ",", 2 )
11   print
12
13   # joining strings
14   list1 = [ "A", "B", "C", "D", "E", "F" ]
15   string2 = "___"
16
17   print "List is:", list1
18   print 'Joining with "%s": %s' \
19       % ( string2, string2.join ( list1 ) )
20   print 'Joining with "-.-":', "-.-".join( list1 )
```

```
String is: A, B, C, D, E, F
Split string by spaces: ['A,', 'B,', 'C,', 'D,', 'E,', 'F']
Split string by commas: ['A', ' B', ' C', ' D', ' E', ' F']
Split string by commas, max 2: ['A', ' B', ' C, D, E, F']

List is: ['A', 'B', 'C', 'D', 'E', 'F']
Joining with "___": A___B___C___D___E___F
Joining with "-.-": A-.-B-.-C-.-D-.-E-.-F
```

Fig. 13.6   Splitting and joining strings.

the program displays the tokens. In line 9, method **split** receives the argument **","**, which represents the delimiter (the string is split at each occurrence of a comma). In line 10, method **split** receives two arguments—the delimiter and an integer value that specifies the maximum number of splits to perform.

Given a list of tokens, method **join** combines the list with a pre-defined delimiter. Line 14 creates a list of letter tokens and line 15 creates a delimiter **string2** that contains three underscore (**"_"**) characters. Lines 18–19 show the results of calling **string2**'s **join** method. The method receives the list of tokens as an argument and returns a string where the tokens are joined by the underscore delimiter in **string2**. Line 20 demonstrates combining the **print** method with a call to a string's **join** method.

> ### Performance Tip 13.1
> *When building a complex string, it is more efficient to include the pieces in a list and then use method* **join** *to assemble the string, rather than using the concatenation (+) operator.*

13.6 Regular Expressions

String methods allow programs to search for a specific substring. For instance, to determine whether a string contains the substrings representing the days of the week (**"Monday"**,

"Tuesday", **"Wednesday"**, etc.), the program can invoke string method **find** for each substring (i.e., the program needs to invoke method **find** seven times to search for every day of the week). Depending on the search, a program may need to invoke method **find** numerous time, an inefficient way to solve a problem. *Regular expressions* provide a more efficient and powerful alternative. A regular expression is a *text pattern* that a program uses to find substrings that match patterns. In the remainder of this chapter, we discuss Python's various regular-expression capabilities.

Good Programming Practice 13.1

Use string methods where only simple processing is required. This prevents errors caused by the more complex regular expressions and increases program readability.

We begin our discussion with a simple example (Fig. 13.7) in which we search various welcoming phrases for **"hello"**, **"Hello"** and **"world!"**.

Line 4 imports the regular-expression module *re*, which provides regular-expression processing capabilities in Python. List **testStrings** (line 7) contains the strings that are searched with the regular expressions created in line 8. Note that the regular expressions closely resemble the strings.

```
1   # Fig. 13.7: fig13_07.py
2   # Simple regular-expression example.
3
4   import re
5
6   # list of strings to search and expressions used to search
7   testStrings = [ "Hello World", "Hello world!", "hello world" ]
8   expressions = [ "hello", "Hello", "world!" ]
9
10  # search every expression in every string
11  for string in testStrings:
12
13      for expression in expressions:
14
15          if re.search( expression, string ):
16              print expression, "found in string", string
17          else:
18              print expression, "not found in string", string
19
20      print
```

```
hello not found in string Hello World
Hello found in string Hello World
world! not found in string Hello World

hello not found in string Hello world!
Hello found in string Hello world!
world! found in string Hello world!

hello found in string hello world
Hello not found in string hello world
world! not found in string hello world
```

Fig. 13.7   Regular-expression example.

The remainder of the program consists of a nested **for** loop that tests each regular expression in list **expressions** against each string in list **testStrings**. Function *re.search* looks for the first occurrence of a regular expression in a string and returns an object that contains the substring matching the regular expression. If the string does not contain the pattern, **re.search** returns **None**. The program determines whether the function call returns a value, then prints an appropriate message. We discuss how to use the object returned by **re.search** in the next section.

Each regular expression in this example is a substring of one of the test strings. In fact, line 15 could be replaced with the expression

```
if string.find( expression ) >= 0:
```

and the program would produce the same result. In the remaining sections, we explore how to create more powerful regular-expression pattern strings.

13.7 Compiling Regular Expressions and Manipulating Regular Expression Objects

This section examines *compiled regular-expression objects* and introduces the object returned by function **re.search**, which contains the results of a search. The **re** module normally compiles a regular expression into a form that the module uses to process a string. If a program uses the same regular expression several times, compiling the regular expression in advance may make the program more efficient. Figure 13.8 demonstrates how to compile regular expressions in advance to create compiled regular-expression objects and shows how to use the object returned from **re.search** to view the search results.

Function *re.compile* (line 11) takes as an argument a regular expression and returns an *SRE_Pattern object* that represents a compiled regular expression. Compiled regular expression objects provide all the functionality available in module **re**. For example, compiled-expression object method **search** (line 22) corresponds to function **re.search** (line 20). As the output demonstrates, both approaches return an *SRE_Match object*. This object supports various methods for retrieving the results of regular-expression processing. Method *group* (lines 26–28) returns the substring that matches the pattern. We discuss this method further when we discuss grouping in Section 13.11.

```
1   # Fig. 13.08: fig13_08.py
2   # Compiled regular-expression and match objects.
3
4   import re
5
6   testString = "Hello world"
7   formatString = "%-35s: %s"    # string for formatting the output
8
9   # create regular expression and compiled expression
10  expression = "Hello"
11  compiledExpression = re.compile( expression )
12
13  # print expression and compiled expression
14  print formatString % ( "The expression", expression )
```

Fig. 13.8 Regular-expression compilation. (Part 1 of 2.)

```
15    print formatString % ( "The compiled expression",
16        compiledExpression )
17
18    # search using re.search and compiled expression's search method
19    print formatString % ( "Non-compiled search",
20        re.search( expression, testString ) )
21    print formatString % ( "Compiled search",
22        compiledExpression.search( testString ) )
23
24    # print results of searching
25    print formatString % ( "search SRE_Match contains",
26        re.search( expression, testString ).group() )
27    print formatString % ( "compiled search SRE_Match contains",
28        compiledExpression.search( testString ).group() )
```

```
The expression                       : Hello
The compiled expression              : <SRE_Pattern object at 0x00B60A20>
Non-compiled search                  : <SRE_Match object at 0x00D0F9B8>
Compiled search                      : <SRE_Match object at 0x00D0F9B8>
search SRE_Match contains            : Hello
compiled search SRE_Match contains : Hello
```

Fig. 13.8   Regular-expression compilation. (Part 2 of 2.)

13.8 Regular Expression Repetition and Placement Characters

We now begin our discussion on how to build more sophisticated pattern strings. Regular expressions are like a "language within a language." Much as Python has a strictly defined syntax for creating programs, regular expressions specify several characters for creating patterns. Most patterns are built using a combination of characters, *metacharacters* and *escape sequences*. A metacharacter is a regular-expression syntax element, just as keyword **if** is a Python syntax element. Characters match themselves. A metacharacter's task is to repeat, group, place or classify one or more characters. This section introduces metacharacters for repeating. We discuss escape sequences and other metacharacters in the following sections.

Figure 13.9 demonstrates the basic repetition metacharacters—**?**, **+** and *****. Line 7 creates a list of regular expressions that contain these symbols. Metacharacter **?** matches exactly zero or one occurrences of the *expression* it follows. An expression can be a single character, an escape sequence, a class of characters (discussed in Section 13.9) or a group (discussed in Section 13.11). In our simple example, we use only a single character for all the expressions that precede a repeating metacharacter. For example, the first regular expression in line 7, **"Hel?o"** matches the letter **H**, followed by the letter **e**, followed by zero or one occurrences of the letter **l**, followed by the letter **o**.

```
1    # Fig. 13.9: fig13_09.py
2    # Repetition patterns, matching vs searching.
3
4    import re
5
```

Fig. 13.9   Searching and matching strings with repetition metacharacters. (Part 1 of 2.)

```
6   testStrings = [ "Heo", "Helo", "Hellllo" ]
7   expressions = [ "Hel?o", "Hel+o", "Hel*o" ]
8
9   # match every expression with every string
10  for expression in expressions:
11
12     for string in testStrings:
13
14        if re.match( expression, string ):
15           print expression, "matches", string
16        else:
17           print expression, "does not match", string
18
19     print
20
21  # demonstrate the difference between matching and searching
22  expression1 = "elo"      # plain string
23  expression2 = "^elo"     # "elo" at beginning of string
24  expression3 = "elo$"     # "elo" at end of string
25
26  # match expression1 with testStrings[ 1 ]
27  if re.match( expression1, testStrings[ 1 ] ):
28     print expression1, "matches", testStrings[ 1 ]
29
30  # search for expression1 in testStrings[ 1 ]
31  if re.search( expression1, testStrings[ 1 ] ):
32     print expression1, "found in", testStrings[ 1 ]
33
34  # search for expression2 in testStrings[ 1 ]
35  if re.search( expression2, testStrings[ 1 ] ):
36     print expression2, "found in", testStrings[ 1 ]
37
38  # search for expression3 in testStrings[ 1 ]
39  if re.search( expression3, testStrings[ 1 ] ):
40     print expression3, "found in", testStrings[ 1 ]
```

```
Hel?o matches Heo
Hel?o matches Helo
Hel?o does not match Hellllo

Hel+o does not match Heo
Hel+o matches Helo
Hel+o matches Hellllo

Hel*o matches Heo
Hel*o matches Helo
Hel*o matches Hellllo


elo found in Helo
elo$ found in Helo
```

Fig. 13.9   Searching and matching strings with repetition metacharacters. (Part 2 of 2.)

Metacharacter **+** matches one or more occurrences of the expression it follows. For example, the second regular expression in line 7, **"Hel+o"**, matches the letter **H**, followed by the letter **e**, followed by one or more occurrences of the letter **l**, followed by the letter **o**. Metacharacter ***** matches zero or more occurrences of the expression it follows. For example, the third regular expression in line 7, **"Hel*o"**, matches the letter **H**, followed by the letter **e**, followed by zero or more occurrences of the letter **l**, followed by the letter **o**.

Lines 10–19 contain a nested **for** loop that applies each regular expression from line 7 to each string from line 6. Function **re.match** (line 14) matches an expression to a string. Unlike function **re.search** (which returns an **SRE_Match** object if any part of the string matches the expression), function **re.match** returns an **SRE_Match** object only if the beginning of the string matches the regular expression.

Regular expressions can contain two additional metacharacters to place a pattern within a string. Metacharacter **^** indicates placement at the beginning of the string; metacharacter **$** indicates placement at the end of the string. A search or a match returns a value only if a string contains the specified pattern at the beginning or end of the string, respectively. Lines 22–40 create regular expressions that contain these metacharacters and use functions **re.match** and **re.search** to process a string.

The regular expressions in lines 22–24 correspond to the sequence of characters **"elo"** anywhere in a string, at the beginning of a string and at the end of a string, respectively. Notice, from the output that function **re.match** returns **None** when passed arguments **expression1** and **testStrings[2]**, because the regular expression **"elo"** does not match the entire string **"Helo"**. Similarly, function **re.search** returns **None** when passed arguments **expression2** and **testStrings[1]**, because the string **"elo"** does not appear at the beginning of the string **"Helo"**.

13.9 Classes and Special Sequences

In this section, we explore two more basic regular-expression building blocks—*character classes* and *special sequences*. A character class specifies a group of characters to match in a string. A special sequence is a shortcut for a common class of characters.

The metacharacters **[** and **]** denote a *regular expression class*. A regular expression that contains a class matches one character in the class. For example, the regular expression class **"[abc]"** matches the letter **a**, the letter **b** or the letter **c**. Classes can use the **-** character to specify a range of consecutive characters. For example, the regular expression **"[a-d]"** is identical to the regular expression **"[abcd]"**.

When placed at the beginning of a class, the metacharacter **^** *negates* the class. This means that the regular expression matches all characters *except* those specified in the class. For example, the class **"[^a-c]"** matches any character but **a**, **b** and **c**. Special sequences (Fig. 13.10) describe commonly used classes of characters.

Figure 13.11 demonstrates regular expressions that contain classes and special sequences. We also demonstrate how to avoid common regular-expression errors. The regular expression in line 8 contains one new metacharacter and demonstrates an important point about using regular expressions. The metacharacter **|** matches either the regular expression to the left or to the right of the metacharacter. Another way to write the expression **"[abc]"** is **"a|b|c"**. Thus, the regular expression in line 8 matches either the string **"2x+5y"** or the string **"7y-3z"**.

Special Sequence	Describes
\d	The class of digits (**[0-9]**).
\D	The negation of the class of digits (**[^0-9]**).
\s	The whitespace characters class (**[\n\f\r\t\v]**).
\S	The negation of the whitespace characters class (**[^ \n\f\r\t\v]**).
\w	The alphanumeric characters class (**[a-zA-Z0-9_]**).
\W	The negation of the alphanumeric characters class (**[^a-zA-Z0-9_]**).
\\	The backslash (****).

Fig. 13.10 Regular-expression special sequences.

```python
# Fig. 13.11: fig13_11.py
# Program that demonstrates classes and special sequences.

import re

# specifying character classes with [ ]
testStrings = [ "2x+5y","7y-3z" ]
expressions = [ r"2x\+5y|7y-3z",
                r"[0-9][a-zA-Z0-9_].[0-9][yz]",
                r"\d\w-\d\w" ]

# match every expression with every string
for expression in expressions:

    for testString in testStrings:

        if re.match( expression, testString ):
            print expression, "matches", testString

# specifying character classes with special sequences
testString1 = "800-123-4567"
testString2 = "617-123-4567"
testString3 = "email: \t joe_doe@deitel.com"

expression1 = r"^\d{3}-\d{3}-\d{4}$"
expression2 = r"\w+:\s+\w+@\w+\.(com|org|net)"

# matching with character classes
if re.match( expression1, testString1 ):
    print expression1, "matches", testString1

if re.match( expression1, testString2 ):
    print expression1, "matches", testString2

if re.match( expression2, testString3 ):
    print expression2, "matches", testString3
```

Fig. 13.11 Regular expressions with classes and special sequences. (Part 1 of 2.)

```
2x\+5y|7y-3z matches 2x+5y
2x\+5y|7y-3z matches 7y-3z
[0-9][a-zA-Z0-9_].[0-9][yz] matches 2x+5y
[0-9][a-zA-Z0-9_].[0-9][yz] matches 7y-3z
\d\w-\d\w matches 7y-3z
^\d{3}-\d{3}-\d{4}$ matches 800-123-4567
^\d{3}-\d{3}-\d{4}$ matches 617-123-4567
\w+:\s+\w+@\w+\.(com|org|net) matches email:        joe_doe@deitel.com
```

Fig. 13.11 Regular expressions with classes and special sequences. (Part 2 of 2.)

Notice that \ the escape metacharacter, precedes the character **+** in the regular expression at line 8. This matches the character **+**, rather than using the repetition metacharacter **+**. If the **+** was not escaped, the regular expression would match one or more **x** characters, followed by the numeric character **5** (as shown in Fig. 13.12).

Note also that the regular expression in line 8 is a *raw string*—i.e., a string created by preceding the string with the character **r**. Usually, when a \ appears in a string, Python interprets this character as an escape character and attempts to replace the \ and the character that follows with the correct escape sequence. When a \ appears within a raw string, Python does not interpret the character as the escape character, but instead interprets the character as the literal backslash character. For example, Python interprets the string **"\n"** as one newline character, but it interprets the string **r"\n"** as two characters—a backslash and the character **n**.

Common Programming Error 13.1
Placing a backslash at the end of a raw string results in a syntax error.

Good Programming Practice 13.2
Regular expression pattern strings often contain backslash characters. Using raw strings to create pattern strings eliminates the need to escape each backslash in the pattern string, thus making the pattern string easier to read.

Lines 9–10 create two additional regular expressions. The metacharacter **.** matches any character in a string except for a newline. The regular expression in line 9 matches a digit, followed by an alphanumeric character, followed by any character except a newline,

```
Python 2.2b2 (#26, Nov 16 2001, 11:44:11) [MSC 32 bit (Intel)] on
win32
Type "copyright", "credits" or "license" for more information.
>>> import re
>>> print re.match( "2x+5y", "2x+5y" )
None
>>> print re.match( "2x+5y", "2x5y" )
<SRE_Match object at 0x00932268>
>>> print re.match( "2x+5y", "2xx5y" )
<SRE_Match object at 0x00949A88>
```

Fig. 13.12 \ metacharacter in regular expressions.

followed by a digit, followed by the letter **y** or the letter **z**. The regular expression in line 10 uses special sequences to create a similar regular expression. This expression matches a digit, followed by an alphanumeric character, followed by the character **-**, followed by a digit, followed by an alphanumeric character. Lines 13–18 contain a nested **for** loop that attempts to match each expression from lines 8–10 to each string in line 7.

The remainder of the program creates more complex regular expressions. The metacharacters **{** and **}** provide another way to repeat characters. The expression in line 25 matches three digits (as specified between curly brackets), followed by the character **-**, three digits, another **-** and four digits. By placing the regular expression between metacharacters **^** and **$**, we specify that we want the regular expression to match the entire string. We can also use the bracket metacharacters to specify a range of repetitions. For example, the expression **"\d{1,3}"** matches one, two or three digits.

Line 26 creates a regular expression that matches one or more alphanumeric characters, followed by a colon (**:**), followed by one or more whitespace characters, followed by one or more alphanumeric characters, followed by the **@** character, followed by one or more alphanumeric characters, followed by the **.** character (notice the backslash to escape this regular expression character), followed by the sequence of characters **com**, **org** or **net**. The remainder of the program attempts to match the regular expressions to the test strings.

13.10 Regular Expression String-Manipulation Functions

The first few sections of this chapter discussed basic string methods for string manipulation and promised a more powerful version of these methods that use regular expressions. Module **re** provides pattern-based, string-manipulation capabilities, such as substituting a substring in a string and splitting a string with a delimiter. Figure 13.13 demonstrates these capabilities.

```
1   # Fig. 13.13: fig13_13.py
2   # Regular-expression string manipulation.
3
4   import re
5
6   testString1 = "This sentence ends in 5 stars *****"
7   testString2 = "1,2,3,4,5,6,7"
8   testString3 = "1+2x*3-y"
9   formatString = "%-34s: %s"    # string to format output
10
11  print formatString % ( "Original string", testString1 )
12
13  # regular expression substitution
14  testString1 = re.sub( r"\*", r"^", testString1 )
15  print formatString % ( "^ substituted for *", testString1 )
16
17  testString1 = re.sub( r"stars", "carets", testString1 )
18  print formatString % ( '"carets" substituted for "stars"',
19      testString1 )
20
21  print formatString % ( 'Every word replaced by "word"',
22      re.sub( r"\w+", "word", testString1 ) )
```

Fig. 13.13 Regular-expression-based string manipulation. (Part 1 of 2.)

```
23
24  print formatString % ( 'Replace first 3 digits by "digit"',
25     re.sub( r"\d", "digit", testString2, 3 ) )
26
27  # regular expression splitting
28  print formatString % ( "Splitting " + testString2,
29     re.split( r",", testString2 ) )
30
31  print formatString % ( "Splitting " + testString3,
32     re.split( r"[+\-*/%]", testString3 ) )
```

```
Original string                      : This sentence ends in 5 stars *****
^ substituted for *                  : This sentence ends in 5 stars ^^^^^
"carets" substituted for "stars"     : This sentence ends in 5 carets ^^^^^
Every word replaced by "word"        : word word word word word word ^^^^^
Replace first 3 digits by "digit"    : digit,digit,digit,4,5,6,7
Splitting 1,2,3,4,5,6,7              : ['1', '2', '3', '4', '5', '6', '7']
Splitting 1+2x*3-y                   : ['1', '2x', '3', 'y']
```

Fig. 13.13 Regular-expression-based string manipulation. (Part 2 of 2.)

Function **re.sub** (line 14) takes three arguments. The second argument is a substring that is substituted for every substring in the third argument that matches the pattern described by the first argument. Line 14 substitutes the caret character (^) for the asterisk character (*) in string **testString1**. To replace the asterisk character, the method must use the regular expression **"*"**, because * is a metacharacter. Lines 21–22 replace every word (**"\w+"**) by the substring **"word"**. Lines 24–25 use the function's optional fourth argument to specify a maximum number of replacements to perform.

Function **re.split** takes two arguments. The first argument is a regular expression that describes a pattern delimiter. The function returns a list of tokens created by splitting the second argument at the delimiter. Lines 28–29 print the results of splitting variable **testString2** on commas (**,**). Line 32 calls **re.split**, passing a delimiter pattern that matches one of five mathematical operators. Notice that this regular expression defines a class and escapes the **–** character, but not the ***** character. This demonstrates a subtle regular expression feature. When any character—except **^** (for negation) or **–** (for a range)—appears inside a class that character is interpreted literally as the character. Therefore, metacharacters such as **$**, **+** or ***** do not need to be escaped when they appear inside a class.

13.11 Grouping

In Fig. 13.8, we saw how a program can use method **group** to extract matching substrings from an **SRE_Match** object. This method arises from a more sophisticated regular-expression technique—*grouping*. A regular expression may specify groups of substrings to match in a string. A program then searches or matches a string with the regular expression and extracts information from the matching groups. Figure 13.14 creates regular expressions with groups and prints the information extracted from these groups.

The regular expression in line 12 describes three groups. The metacharacters **(** and **)** denote a group. The first group matches a word (**\w+**), followed by a space, followed by another word. The second group matches three digits, followed by the character **–**, followed

```
1   # Fig. 13.14: fig13_14.py
2   # Program that demonstrates grouping and greedy operations.
3
4   import re
5
6   formatString1 = "%-22s: %s"   # string to format output
7
8   # string that contains fields and expression to extract fields
9   testString1 = \
10      "Albert Antstein, phone: 123-4567, e-mail: albert@bug2bug.com"
11  expression1 = \
12      r"(\w+ \w+), phone: (\d{3}-\d{4}), e-mail: (\w+@\w+\.\w{3})"
13
14  print formatString1 % ( "Extract all user data",
15      re.match( expression1, testString1 ).groups() )
16  print formatString1 % ( "Extract user e-mail",
17      re.match( expression1, testString1 ).group( 3 ) )
18  print
19
20  # greedy operations and grouping
21  formatString2 = "%-38s: %s"   # string to format output
22
23  # strings and patterns to find base directory in a path
24  pathString = "/books/2001/python"  # file path string
25
26  expression2 = "(/.+)/"  # greedy operator expression
27  print formatString1 % ( "Greedy error",
28      re.match( expression2, pathString ).group( 1 ) )
29
30  expression3 = "(/.+?)/"  # non-greedy operator expression
31  print formatString1 % ( "No error, base only",
32      re.match( expression3, pathString ).group( 1 ) )
```

```
Extract all user data : ('Albert Antstein', '123-4567', 'albert@
bug2bug.com')
Extract user e-mail    : albert@bug2bug.com

Greedy error           : /books/2001
No error, base only    : /books
```

Fig. 13.14 Regular-expression groups and greedy operators.

by four digits. The third group matches one or more alphanumeric characters, followed by the character **@**, followed by one or more alphanumeric characters, followed by the character **.**, followed by three alphanumeric characters. This regular expression matches the string in variable **testString1**. The three groups match the name, phone number and e-mail address of the person, respectively.

Lines 14–17 demonstrate the benefits of grouping. Line 15 calls function **re.match**, which returns an **SRE_Match** object. This object's *groups* method returns a list of substrings. Each substring in the list corresponds to the substring that matches a group in the regular expression. The first substring in the list matches the first group in the regular expression, and so on. The result of line 15 is that the program obtains the person's name, phone number and e-mail address. Line 17 calls the **SRE_Match**'s method **group**, passing integer value 3 as an argument. This call returns the substring that matches the third group in the regular expression, which retrieves the e-mail address substring from **testString1**.

Regular-expression grouping introduces another subtle regular-expression issue. The metacharacters **+** and ***** are called *greedy operators*. A greedy operator attempts to match as many characters as possible. Sometimes this is not the desired behavior. Lines 20–32 demonstrate the problem of greedy operators. Line 24 is a string that contains a sample path that might be part of a URL. Suppose we wish to write a regular expression that obtains the root directory name from the path (i.e., **/books** in this example). Lines 26–28 attempt this operation, but fail because of the greedy behavior of the **+** operator in **expression2**. When an operator is greedy the regular expression module tries to match as much of the expression that precedes the operator as possible. Initially, this causes **expression2** to match the entire string. However, the regular expression module must allow for the rest of the pattern to be matched. In this case, the group that contains the greedy operator must be immediately followed by a slash (**/**) as specified in **expression2**. Therefore, the regular expression module searches backwards in the string until the regular expression module can guarantee that there is a slash (**/**) that will follow the initial group in **expression2**. Thus, the group that contains the greedy operator matches **/books/2001**.

The regular expression in line 30 modifies the behavior of the greedy **+** operator to obtain the root directory name in the sample path correctly. Placing the **?** metacharacter after the greedy **+** operator changes the behavior of the **+** operator. Now, when the regular expression module searches the string using **expression3**, the module searches one character at a time until it finds the smallest string that matches the pattern in the group (i.e., **/books**).

This chapter presented basic string manipulation capabilities, as well as how to use the powerful regular-expression-processing capabilities of module **re**. Chapter 14 introduces file processing, which enables programs to read information from files on disk and write information to files on disk. Many programs that process files use regular expressions and other string-processing capabilities to search and manipulate the contents of those files.

13.12 Internet and World Wide Web Resources

The following resources offer more information about the complex topic of regular expressions.

etext.lib.virginia.edu/helpsheets/regex.html
This tutorial discusses common regular expression uses, writing complex regular expressions and other topics like escape characters and anchors.

www.zvon.org/other/reReference/Output
This reference describes common regular expression special sequences.

py-howto.sourceforge.net/regex/regex.html
This tutorial discusses using regular expressions and the **re** module. Topics covered include common problems, modifying strings and pattern matching.

www.devshed.com/Server_Side/Administration/RegExp
This article describes common uses of regular expressions.

py-howto.sourceforge.net/regex/regex.html
This document contains information about regular-expression processing with module **re**, and discusses greedy operators and how to use raw strings as regular-expression pattern strings.

SUMMARY

- Python represents strings as sequences of characters. Characters are the fundamental building blocks of Python source programs. Every program is composed of a sequence of characters that—when they are grouped together meaningfully—is interpreted by the computer as a series of instructions used to accomplish a task.

- Each character has a corresponding character code (sometimes called its integer ordinal value) the ASCII or Unicode character set.

- Python supports strings as a basic data type.

- Strings are immutable sequences—once a string is created, it cannot be changed.

- Methods **center**, **ljust** and **rjust** control how a string is output by "padding" the string with space characters. Method **center** takes one argument, which corresponds to the length of the output string. The method then creates a new string of this length and centers the calling string in the specified number of spaces. Method **rjust** right-justifies the calling string by preceding the string with the difference of the specified number of spaces and the length of the calling string. Method **ljust** creates a new string where the calling string is followed by the difference of the specified number of spaces and the length of the calling string.

- String method **strip** removes leading and trailing whitespace from the calling string. String method **lstrip** removes only leading whitespace. Method **rstrip** removes only trailing whitespace.

- String method **count** returns the number of times the substring occurs in the string. If the method does not find the specified substring, the method returns 0.

- Method **find** returns the lowest index in the string that begins the specified substring. If the string does not contain the specified substring, the method returns –1.

- Method **index** is similar to method **find**. However, if the method does not find the specified substring, the method raises a **ValueError** exception.

- Method **startswith** returns 1 if the string begins with the specified substring.

- Method **endswith** returns 1 if the string ends with the specified substring.

- Method **rfind** is similar to method **find**, except the former returns the highest index at which the specified substring begins. If the method does not find the specified substring, it returns –1.

- Method **rindex** is similar to method **index**, except that **rindex** returns the highest index at which the specified substring begins (and raises a **ValueError** if the method does not find the substring).

- Method **replace** receives two substrings as arguments. The method searches the calling string for the first substring and replaces that substring with the second argument. Method **replace** takes an optional third argument that specifies the maximum number of replacements.

- When you read a sentence, your mind breaks the sentence into words, or tokens, each of which conveys meaning to you. Interpreters also perform tokenization. They break up statements into individual pieces like keywords, identifiers, operators and other elements of a programming language.

- Tokens are separated from one another by delimiters, typically whitespace characters such as blank, tab, newline and carriage return. Other characters also may be used as delimiters to separate tokens.

- Method **split** returns a list of tokens. When a call to method **split** passes no arguments, the method splits the string by any whitespace. The method takes an optional second argument that specifies the maximum number of splits to perform.

- Given a list of tokens, method **join** joins that list with a delimiter. The method receives the list of tokens as an argument and returns a string where the tokens are joined by the delimiter specified in the calling string.

- A regular expression is a text pattern that a program uses to find substrings that match patterns.
- The **re** regular-expression module provides regular expression capability in Python.
- Function **re.search** looks for the first occurrence of a regular expression in a string and returns an object that contains the substring matching the regular expression. If the string does not contain the pattern, **re.search** returns **None**.
- Compiling regular expressions can make programs more efficient. To use a regular expression, the **re** module first compiles the expression into a form that the module uses to process a string.
- Function **re.compile** takes as an argument a regular expression and returns an **SRE_Pattern** object that represents a compiled regular expression. Compiled regular expression objects provide all the functionality available in module **re**.
- **SRE_Match** methods enable a program to retrieve the results of regular-expression processing.
- Most patterns are built using a combination of characters, metacharacters and escape sequences. A metacharacter is a regular-expression syntax element. A metacharacter's job is to repeat, group, place or classify.
- Metacharacter **?** matches exactly zero or one occurrences of the expression it follows. Metacharacter **+** matches one or more occurrences of the expression it follows. Metacharacter ***** matches zero or more occurrences of the expression it follows.
- Function **re.match** matches an expression to a string. Unlike function **re.search** (which returns an **SRE_Match** object if any part of the string matches the expression), function **re.match** returns an **SRE_Match** object only if the beginning of the string matches the regular expression.
- Metacharacter **^** indicates placement at the beginning of the string; metacharacter **$** indicates placement at the end of the string.
- A character class specifies a group of characters to match in a string.
- A special sequence is a shortcut for a common class of characters.
- The metacharacters **[** and **]** denote a regular expression class. A regular expression that contains a class matches one character in the class.
- Classes can use the **-** character to specify a range of consecutive characters.
- When placed within a class as the first character after the square bracket, metacharacter **^** negates the class—the regular expression matches all characters except those specified in the class.
- The metacharacter **|** matches either the regular expression to the left of the **|** or the regular expression to the right.
- A raw string is created by preceding the string with the character **r**.
- Usually, when a **** appears in a string, Python interprets this character as an escape character and attempts to replace the **** and the character that follows with the correct escape sequence.
- When a **** appears within a raw string, Python does not interpret the character as the escape character, but instead as the literal backslash character.
- The metacharacter **.** matches any character in a string except for a newline.
- The metacharacters **{** and **}** provide another way to repeat characters.
- By placing a regular expression between metacharacters **^** and **$**, we specify that we want the regular expression to match the entire string.
- Module **re** provides pattern-based, string-manipulation capabilities, such as substituting a substring in a string and splitting a string with a delimiter.
- Function **re.sub** takes three arguments. The second argument is a substring that is substituted for every substring in the third argument that matches the pattern described by the first argument. The function's optional fourth argument specifies a maximum number of replacements to perform.

- Function **re.split** takes two arguments. The first argument is a regular expression that describes a pattern delimiter. The function returns a list of tokens created by splitting the second argument at the delimiter.
- If metacharacters such as **$**, **+** or ***** appear inside a class, they do not need to be escaped.
- Method **group** extracts matching substrings from an **SRE_Match** object. A regular expression may specify groups of substrings to match in a string. The metacharacters **(** and **)** denote a group.
- Function **re.match** returns an **SRE_Match** object. This object's **groups** method returns a list of substrings. Each substring in the list corresponds to the substring that matches a group in the regular expression. The first substring in the list matches the first group in the regular expression, and so on.
- The metacharacters **+** and ***** are called greedy operators. A greedy operator attempts to match as many characters as possible.

TERMINOLOGY

$ metacharacter
% metacharacter
(metacharacter
) metacharacter
* metacharacter
+ metacharacter
. metacharacter
? metacharacter
**** metacharacter
[metacharacter
] metacharacter
^ metacharacter
{ metacharacter
} metacharacter
| metacharacter
capitalize method
character
character class
center method
count method
delimiter
encode method
endswith method
escape sequence
expandtabs method
find method
greedy operator
group method
groups method
index method
integer ordinal value
isalnum method
isalpha method
isdigit method
islower method
isspace method

istitle method
isupper method
join method
ljust method
lower method
lstrip method
metacharacter
ord function
raw string
re module
re.compile function
re.match function
re.search function
re.split function
re.sub function
regular expression
replace method
rfind method
rindex method
rjust method
rstrip method
search method
split method
splitlines method
SRE_MATCH object
SRE_Pattern object
startswith method
string
strip method
swapcase method
title method
token
tokenization
translate method
upper method
white space character

SELF REVIEW EXERCISES

13.1   Fill in the blanks in each of the following:
  a) Method _____ returns a new string where all leading and trailing whitespace has been removed.
  b) Python represents strings as sequences of _____.
  c) Method _____ returns the number of times a specified substring occurs in a string.
  d) Tokens are separated from one another by _____.
  e) A _____ is a text pattern that a program uses to process strings.
  f) Function _____ looks for the first occurrence of a regular expression in a string.
  g) The task of a _____ is to repeat, group, place or classify one or more characters.
  h) Method _____ takes a regular expression as an argument and returns an object that represents a compiled regular expression.
  i) Compiled regular expressions provide all the functionality available in module _____.
  j) The metacharacters _____ and _____ denote a regular expression class.

13.2   State whether each of the following is *true* or *false*. If *false*, explain why.
  a) String method **capitalize** returns a new string where the first character of each word in the string is the one and only uppercase character in the word.
  b) String method **find** searches a string for a substring and raises a **ValueError** exception if the string does not contain a substring.
  c) Method **rindex** returns the highest index at which the specified substring begins.
  d) Most string methods modify the string in-place.
  e) Any string can be treated as a regular expression.
  f) Metacharacter **?** matches exactly one occurrence of the expression it follows.
  g) Method **group** returns an **SRE_Match** object.
  h) Method **re.match** does not search through a string, but returns a match object only if the string matches the specified regular expression starting from the beginning.
  i) The class **[^0-9]** matches any digit but **0**.
  j) Preceding a string with the character **r** creates a raw string.

ANSWERS TO SELF REVIEW EXERCISES

13.1   a) **strip**. b) characters. c) **count**. d) delimiters. e) regular expression. f) **re.search**. g) metacharacter. h) **re.compile**. i) **re**. j) **[**, **]**.

13.2   a) False. String method **title** returns a new string where the first character of each word in the string is the one and only uppercase character in the word. b) False. String method **index** searches a string for a substring and raises a **ValueError** exception if the string does not contain a substring. c) True. d) False. Strings are immutable, so string methods that appear to modify a string actually return a new string. e) True. f) False. Metacharacter **?** matches exactly zero or one occurrences of the expression it follows. g) False. Method **group** returns the substring that matches a regular expression. h) True. i) False. The class **[^0-9]** excludes all digits. j) True.

EXERCISES

13.3   Use a regular expression to count the number of digits, non-digit characters, whitespace characters and words in a string.

13.4   Use a regular expression to search through an XHTML string and to locate all valid URLs. For the purpose of this exercise, assume that a valid URL is enclosed in quotes and begins with **http://**.

13.5   Write a regular expression that searches a string and matches a valid number. A number can have any number of digits, but it can have only digits and a decimal point. The decimal point is optional, but if it appears in the number, there must be only one, and it must have digits on its left and its right. There should be whitespace or a beginning or end-of-line character on either side of a valid number. Negative numbers are preceded by a minus sign.

13.6   Write a program that receives XHTML as input and outputs the number of XHTML tags in the string. The program should count the number of tags nested at each level. For example, the XHTML:

```
<p><strong>hi</strong></p>
```

has a **p** tag (nesting level 0—i.e., not nested in another tag) and a **strong** tag (nesting level 1).

13.7   Write a function that takes a list of dollar values separated by commas, converts each number from dollars to pounds (at an exchange rate 0.667 dollars per pound) and prints the results in a comma-separated list. Each converted value should have the £ symbol in front of it. This symbol can be obtained by passing the ASCII value of the symbol (**156**) to the **chr** function, which returns a string composed of that character. Ambitious programmers can attempt to do the conversion all in one statement.

13.8   Write a program that asks the user to enter a sentence and checks whether the sentence contains more than one space between words. If so, the program should remove the extra spaces. For example, **"Hello   World"** should be **"Hello World"**. (*Hint*: Use **split** and **join**.)

14

File Processing and Serialization

Objectives

- To create, read, write and update files.
- To become familiar with sequential-access file processing.
- To understand random-access file processing via module **shelve**.
- To specify high-performance, unformatted I/O operations.
- To understand the differences between formatted and raw data-file processing.
- To build a transaction-processing program with random-access file processing.
- To serialize complex objects for storage.

I read part of it all the way through.
Samuel Goldwyn

I can only assume that a "Do Not File" document is filed in a "Do Not File" file.
Senator Frank Church

Outline

14.1 Introduction

Variables and sequences offer only temporary storage of data—the data is lost when a local variable "goes out of scope" or when the program terminates. By contrast, *files* are used for long-term retention of large amounts of data, even after the program that created the data terminates. Data maintained in files often is called *persistent* data. Computers store files on *secondary storage devices*, such as magnetic disks, optical disks and tapes. In this chapter, we explain how Python programs create, update and process data files. We consider both *sequential-access files* and *random-access files*, indicating the types of applications for which each is best suited. We compare formatted data-file processing and raw data-file processing, and we also examine various file-based data storage mechanisms, such as the **shelve** and **cPickle** modules.

14.2 Data Hierarchy

Ultimately, all data items processed by computers are reduced to combinations of zeros and ones. This occurs because it is simple and economical to build electronic devices that can assume two stable states—**0** represents one state and **1** represents the other. It is remarkable that the impressive functions performed by computers involve only the most fundamental manipulations of **0**s and **1**s.

The smallest data item that computers support is called a *bit* (short for *"binary digit"*— a digit that can assume one of two values). Each data item, or bit, can assume either the value **0** or the value **1**. Computer circuitry performs various bit manipulations, such as examining the value of a bit, setting the value of a bit and reversing the value of a bit (from **1** to **0** or from **0** to **1**). For more information on binary numbers, refer to Appendix C, Number Systems.

Programming with data in the low-level form of bits is cumbersome. It is preferable to program with data in forms such as *decimal digits* (e.g., 0, 1, 2, 3, 4, 5, 6, 7, 8, and 9), *letters* (e.g., A through Z and a through z) and *special symbols* (e.g., \$, @, %, &, *, (,), -, +, ", :, ?, /, etc.). Digits, letters and special symbols are referred to as *characters*. The set of all characters used to write programs and represent data items on a particular computer is called that computer's *character set*. Because computers can process only **1**s and **0**s, every character in a computer's character set is represented as a pattern of **1**s and **0**s. *Bytes* are composed of eight bits. Programmers create programs and data items with characters; computers manipulate and process these characters as patterns of bits.

Just as characters are composed of bits, *fields* are composed of characters (or bytes). A field is a group of characters that convey a meaning. For example, a field consisting of only uppercase and lowercase letters can represent a person's name.

Data items processed by computers form a *data hierarchy* in which data items become larger and more complex in structure in the progression from bits, to characters (bytes), to fields and upto larger data structures.

Typically, a *record*, which we can represent as a tuple, dictionary or instance in Python, is composed of several fields. In a payroll system, for example, a record for a particular employee might consist of the following fields:

1. Employee identification number
2. Name
3. Address
4. Hourly salary rate
5. Number of exemptions claimed
6. Year-to-date earnings
7. Amount of federal taxes withheld

Thus, a record is a group of related fields. In the preceding example, each field is associated with a particular employee. A company has a payroll record for each employee. A *file* is a group of related records.[1] A company's payroll file normally contains one record for each employee. Thus, a payroll file for a small company might contain only 22 records, whereas a payroll file for a large company might contain 100,000 records. It is not unusual for a company to have many files, some containing millions of characters of information. Figure 14.1 illustrates the data hierarchy.

To facilitate the retrieval of specific records from a file, at least one field in each record is chosen as a *record key*. A record key identifies a record as belonging to a particular person or entity and distinguishes that record from all other records in the file. In the payroll record described previously, the employee-identification number would normally be chosen as the record key.

There are many ways to organize records in a file. The most common organization is called a *sequential file,* in which records typically are stored in order by the record-key field. In a payroll file, records usually are placed in order by employee-identification number. The first employee record in the file contains the lowest employee-identification number, and subsequent records contain increasingly higher employee-identification numbers.

---

1. Generally, a file can contain arbitrary data in arbitrary formats. In some operating systems, a file is viewed as nothing more than a collection of bytes. In such an operating system, any organization of bytes in a file (such as organizing the data into records) is a view created by the application's programmer.

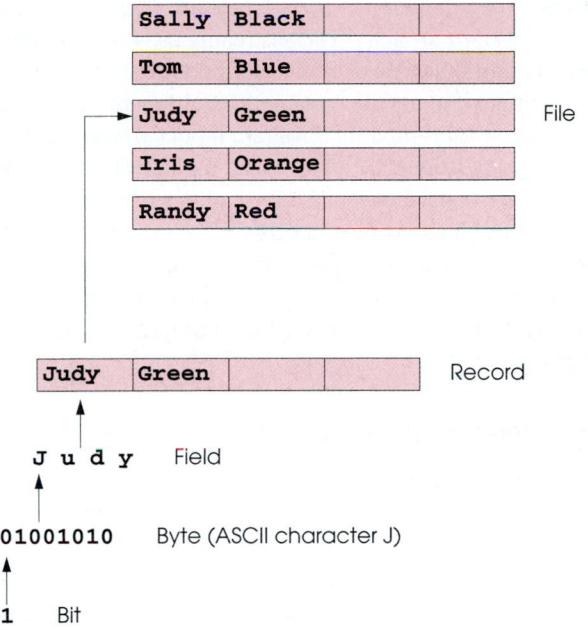

Fig. 14.1   Data hierarchy.

Most businesses use many different files to store data. For example, companies might have payroll files, accounts-receivable files (listing money due from clients), accounts-payable files (listing money due to suppliers), inventory files (listing facts about all the items handled by the business) and many other types of files. Sometimes, a group of related files is called a *database*. A collection of programs designed to create and manage databases is called a *database management system (DBMS)*. We discuss databases in detail in Chapter 17, Database Application Programming Interface (DB-API).

14.3 Files and Streams

Python views each file as a sequential stream of bytes (Fig. 14.2). Each file ends either with an *end-of-file marker* or at a specific byte number recorded in a system-maintained administrative data structure. When a program *opens* a file, Python creates an object and associates a *stream* with that object.

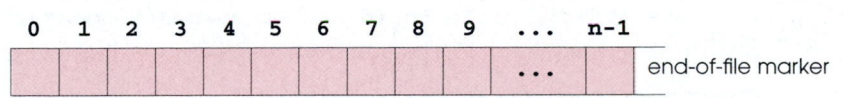

Fig. 14.2   Python's view of a file of **n** bytes.

When a Python program begins execution, Python creates three file streams—*sys.stdin* (*standard input stream*), *sys.stdout* (*standard output stream*) and *sys.stderr* (*standard error stream*). These streams provide communication channels between a program and a particular file or device. Python file streams are created regardless of whether a Python program imports the **sys** module, although a program must import the **sys** module to access the streams directly. Program input corresponds to **sys.stdin**. In fact, **raw_input** uses **sys.stdin** to retrieve user input. Program output corresponds to **sys.stdout**. The **print** statement sends information to the standard output stream, by default. Program errors are printed to **sys.stderr**.

The **sys.stdin** stream enables a program to receive input from the keyboard or other devices, the **sys.stdout** stream enables a program to output data to the screen or other devices and the **sys.stderr** stream enables a program to output error messages to the screen or other devices.

14.4 Creating a Sequential-Access File

Python imposes no structure on a file—notions like "records" do not exist in Python files. This means that the programmer must structure files to meet the requirements of applications. In the example in this section, we impose a record structure on a file.

Figure 14.3 creates a simple sequential-access file that might be used by an accounts-receivable system to track the money owed by a company's client. For each client, the program obtains an account number, the client's name and account balance (i.e., the amount the client owes the company). The data obtained for each client constitutes a record for that client. The account number represents the record key in this application; that is, the file will be created and maintained in account-number order. In our example, we assume a user enters the account information in account-number order. In a comprehensive accounts-receivable system, a sorting capability would be provided so the user could enter the records in any order—the records would then be sorted before being written to the file.

As stated previously, a programmer creates file-stream objects to open files. Function **open**, which receives one required argument and two optional arguments, creates a stream object (line 8). The required argument for the new stream object is the *file name*; the two optional arguments are the *file-open mode* and the *buffering mode*.

```
1   # Fig. 14.3: fig14_03.py
2   # Opening and writing to a file.
3
4   import sys
5
6   # open file
7   try:
8      file = open( "clients.dat", "w" )   # open file in write mode
9   except IOError, message:                # file open failed
10     print >> sys.stderr, "File could not be opened:", message
11     sys.exit( 1 )
12
13  print "Enter the account, name and balance."
14  print "Enter end-of-file to end input."
```

Fig. 14.3   File-stream objects for opening and writing data to a file. (Part 1 of 2.)

```
15
16   while 1:
17
18      try:
19         accountLine = raw_input( "? " )    # get account entry
20      except EOFError:
21         break                              # user entered EOF
22      else:
23         print >> file, accountLine         # write entry to file
24
25   file.close()
```

```
Enter the account, name and balance.
Enter end-of-file to end input.
? 100 Jones 24.98
? 200 Doe 345.67
? 300 White 0.00
? 400 Stone -42.16
? 500 Rich 224.62
? ^Z
```

Fig. 14.3   File-stream objects for opening and writing data to a file. (Part 2 of 2.)

The file-open mode indicates whether a user can open the file for reading, writing or both. File-open mode **"w"** opens a file to output data to the file. Existing files opened with mode **"w"** are *truncated*—all data in the file is deleted—and re-created with the new data. If the specified file does not yet exist, then a file is created. The newly created file is assigned the name provided in the *file name* argument (i.e., **clients.dat**). If the location of the file is not specified in the file name argument, Python attempts to create the file in the current directory. If the file open-mode argument is not specified, the default value is **"r"**, which opens a file for reading. Figure 14.4 lists various file-open modes. The third argument to function **open**—the buffering-mode argument—is for advanced control of file input and output and usually is not specified. We do not assign a value to the buffering-mode argument in this example.

Mode	Description
"a"	Writes all output to the end of the file. If the indicated file does not exist, it is created.
"r"	Opens a file for input. If the file does not exist, an **IOError** exception is raised.
"r+"	Opens a file for input and output. If the file does not exist, causes an **IOError** exception.
"w"	Opens a file for output. If the file exists, it is truncated. If the file does not exist, one is created.
"w+"	Opens a file for input and output. If the file exists, it is truncated. If the file does not exist, one is created.

Fig. 14.4   File-open modes. (Part 1 of 2.)

Mode	Description
`"ab"`, `"rb"`, `"r+b"`, `"wb"`, `"w+b"`	Opens a file for binary (i.e., non-text) input or output. [*Note*: These modes are supported only on the Windows and Macintosh platforms.]

Fig. 14.4   File-open modes. (Part 2 of 2.)

Common Programming Error 14.1

Opening an existing file for output (`"w"`) when the user wants to preserve the file is a logic error, because the contents of the file are discarded without warning.

When **open** encounters an error, the function raises an ***IOError*** exception. Some possible errors include attempting to open a file for reading that does not exist, opening a read-only file for writing and opening a file for writing when no disk space is available.

In Fig. 14.3, if **open** raises an **IOError** exception, line 10 prints the error message **"File could not be opened"** to **sys.stderr**. By default, the **print** statement sends output to the **sys.stdout** file object. Programs can *redirect* output from the **print** statement to print to a different file object. In our example, the statement

```
print >> sys.stderr, "File could not be opened:", message
```

redirects output to the **sys.stderr** (standard error) file object. When **>>** symbol follows the **print** keyword, the **print** statement redirects the output to the file object that appears to the right of **>>**. A comma follows the output file object, and the value to print follows the comma.

Common Programming Error 14.2

*When redirecting file output with **>>**, forgetting to put a comma (**,**) after the file object is a syntax error.*

Redirecting output with **>>** was added to Python in version 2.0. For earlier versions, or to support multiple versions, the effect of redirecting output with the **>>** symbol can be accomplished with file object method **write** as follows:

```
sys.stderr.write( output )
```

The table in Fig. 14.5 lists the file-object methods.

Method	Description
`close()`	Closes the file object.
`fileno()`	Returns an integer that is the file's *file descriptor* (i.e., the number the operating system uses to maintain information about the file).

Fig. 14.5   File-object methods. (Part 1 of 2.)

Method	Description
flush()	Flushes the file's *buffer*. A buffer contains the information to be written to or read from a file. Flushing the buffer performs the read or write operation.
isatty()	Returns **1** if the file object is a *tty* (terminal) device.
read(*[size]* **)**	Reads data from the file. If *size* is not specified, the method reads all data to the end of the file. If argument *size* is specified, the method reads at most *size* bytes from the file.
readline(*[size]* **)**	Reads one line from the file. If *size* is not specified, the method reads to the end of the line. If *size* is specified, the method reads at most *size* bytes from the line.
readlines(*[size]* **)**	Reads lines from the file and returns the lines in a list. If *size* is not specified, the method reads to the end of the file. If *size* is specified, the method reads at most *size* bytes.
seek(*offset[, location]* **)**	Moves the file position *offset* bytes. If *location* is not specified, the file position moves *offset* bytes from the beginning of the file. If *location* is specified, the file position moves *offset* bytes from *location*. Section 14.5 discusses **seek** in detail.
tell()	Returns the file's current position.
truncate(*[size]* **)**	Truncates data in the file. If *size* is not specified, all data is deleted. If *size* is specified, the file is truncated to contain at most *size* bytes.
write(*output* **)**	Writes the string *output* to the file.
writelines(*outputList* **)**	Writes each string in *outputList* to the file.
xreadlines()	Similar to **readlines**, except the method implements a more memory-efficient way to read a file. The method returns an **xreadlines** object that a program can iterate over to retrieve the information. See **www.python.org/doc/current/lib/ module-xreadlines.html** for information on **xreadlines** objects.

Fig. 14.5   File-object methods. (Part 2 of 2.)

If an error occurs when the program in Fig. 14.3 opens a file, function **sys.exit** (line 11) terminates the program. Function **sys.exit** returns its optional argument to the environment from which the program was invoked. Argument **0** (the default) indicates normal program termination; any other value indicates that the program terminated due to an error. The calling environment (most likely the operating system) uses the value returned by **sys.exit** to respond to the error appropriately.

If the file, **clients.dat**, opens successfully, the program processes data. Lines 13–14 prompt the user to enter the various fields for each record, or the end-of-file marker when data entry is completed.

Lines 16–23 extract each set of data from the standard input using a **try/except/ else** block in a repetition structure. Function **raw_input** retrieves a line of input from the user. If the user enters the end-of-file character, **raw_input** raises an *EOFError* exception. Lines 20–21 catch this error and use a **break** statement to exit the infinite **while** loop. If the user does not enter the end-of-file character, the **else** block (lines 22–23) executes and prints the user-entered line to the output file using the **>>** symbol.

The **close** method (line 25) closes the file object after the **while** loop terminates. Although Python closes open files when a program terminates, it is good practice to close a file with the **close** method as soon as the program no longer needs the file.

Performance Tip 14.1

Close each file explicitly as soon as it is known that the program will not reference the file again. This can reduce resource use in a program that continues executing after it no longer needs a particular file. This practice also improves program clarity.

In the sample execution for the program of Fig. 14.3, the user enters information for five accounts and signals that data entry is complete by entering end-of-file. This dialog does not show how the data records actually appear in the file. To verify that the file has been created successfully, the next section demonstrates a program that reads the file and displays its contents.

14.5 Reading Data from a Sequential-Access File

Data is stored in files so that the data can be retrieved for processing at a later time. The previous section demonstrated how to create a sequential-access file. In this section, we discuss how to read (or retrieve) data sequentially from a file.

Figure 14.6 reads records from the file **clients.dat** created by the program of Fig. 14.3 and displays the contents of each record. Files are opened for reading by passing an **"r"** as the second argument to function **open** (line 8). If the locatin of the file is not specified in the file name argument to **open**, Python attempts to locate the file in the current directory.

```
1   # Fig. 14.6: fig14_06.py
2   # Reading and printing a file.
3
4   import sys
5
6   # open file
7   try:
8       file = open( "clients.dat", "r" )
9   except IOError:
10      print >> sys.stderr, "File could not be opened"
11      sys.exit( 1 )
12
13  records = file.readlines()    # retrieve list of lines in file
14
15  print "Account".ljust( 10 ),
16  print "Name".ljust( 10 ),
17  print "Balance".rjust( 10 )
18
```

Fig. 14.6   Data read from a sequential-access file. (Part 1 of 2.)

```
19   for record in records:        # format each line
20       fields = record.split()
21       print fields[ 0 ].ljust( 10 ),
22       print fields[ 1 ].ljust( 10 ),
23       print fields[ 2 ].rjust( 10 )
24
25   file.close()
```

```
Account      Name         Balance
100          Jones          24.98
200          Doe           345.67
300          White           0.00
400          Stone         -42.16
500          Rich          224.62
```

Fig. 14.6   Data read from a sequential-access file. (Part 2 of 2.)

File objects are opened for reading by default, so the statement

```
file = open( "clients.dat" )
```

also opens **clients.dat** for reading.

Good Programming Practice 14.1

*A programmer should set a file to open for reading only (using **"r"**) if the contents of the file should not be modified. This prevents unintentional modifications of a file's contents. This is an example of the principle of least privilege.*

Method **readlines** (line 13) reads the entire file contents of Fig. 14.3 into the program. This method returns a list of the lines in the file, which the program stores in variable **records**. For each line (**record**) in the file, method **split** returns the words (**fields**) in the line as a list. Lines 19–23 output the fields. Methods **ljust** and **rjust** left- and right-justify the fields, respectively, to format the output. Method **close** (line 25) closes the file associated with the file object.

Python version 2.2 contains additional features that enable the programmer to use a file object in a **for** statement. For example, line 19 in the above example could be replaced by:

```
for record in file:
```

in a program that uses Python 2.2. This technique reads one line of **file** at a time and assigns the line to **record**. The program can process that line immediately. Iterating over the lines in a file in this manner can be more efficient than reading the contents of a large file with method **readlines**, which requires the program to wait for the entire file to be read into memory before any of the file's contents can be processed.

To retrieve data sequentially from a file, programs normally start from the beginning of the file and read all the data consecutively until the desired data is found. It sometimes is necessary to process a file sequentially several times (from the beginning of the file) during the execution of a program. File objects provide method **seek** for repositioning the *file-position pointer* (which contains the byte number of the next byte to be read from or written to the file). The statement

```
file.seek( 0, 0 )
```

repositions the file-position pointer at the beginning of the file. The first argument **seek** takes is the *offset*, which is an integer value that specifies the location in the file as a number of bytes from the *seek direction* of the file. The second (optional) argument is the seek direction, or *location*, from which the offset begins. The seek direction can be **0** (the default) for positioning relative to the beginning of a file, **1** for positioning relative to the current position in a file or **2** for positioning relative to the end of a file. Some examples of positioning the file position pointer are

```
# position to the nth byte of file
# assumes seek direction is 0
file.seek( n )

# position n bytes forward in file
file.seek( n, 1 )

# position n bytes backward from end of file
file.seek( -n, 2 )

# position at end of file
file.seek( 0, 2 )
```

File-object method **tell** returns the current location of the file-position pointer. The following statement assigns the current file-position pointer value to variable **location**

```
location = file.tell()
```

Figure 14.7 uses **seek** in a program that enables a credit manager to display the account information for customers with zero balances (i.e., customers who do not owe any money), credit balances (i.e., customers to whom the company owes money) and debit balances (i.e., customers who owe the company money for goods and services received in the past). The program displays a menu and allows the credit manager to enter one of three options to obtain credit information. Option 1 produces a list of accounts with zero balances (lines 56–57). Option 2 produces a list of accounts with credit balances (lines 58–59). Option 3 produces a list of accounts with debit balances (lines 60–61). Option 4 terminates the program execution (lines 62–63). Entering an invalid option causes the program to prompt the user to enter another choice (lines 64–65).

Lines 52–77 process the request for each request that is not option 4. Method **readline** (line 67) reads one line from the file and moves the file-position pointer to the next line in the file. When method **readline** has finished reading all lines from the file (i.e., the program has reached the end of the file), **readline** returns the empty string (**""**).

Method **split** (line 71) unpacks each record to three variables—**account, name** and **balance**. The program calls function **shouldDisplay** (lines 18–29), which returns **1** (true), if a record should be displayed. If applicable, function **outputLine** (lines 32–36) displays the record fields.

```
1   # Fig. 14.7: fig14_07.py
2   # Credit inquiry program.
3
```

Fig. 14.7   Credit-inquiry program. (Part 1 of 3.)

```python
4    import sys
5
6    # retrieve one user command
7    def getRequest():
8
9        while 1:
10           request = int( raw_input( "\n? " ) )
11
12           if 1 <= request <= 4:
13               break
14
15       return request
16
17   # determine if balance should be displayed, based on type
18   def shouldDisplay( accountType, balance ):
19
20       if accountType == 2 and balance < 0:     # credit balance
21           return 1
22
23       elif accountType == 3 and balance > 0:   # debit balance
24           return 1
25
26       elif accountType == 1 and balance == 0:  # zero balance
27           return 1
28
29       else: return 0
30
31   # print formatted balance data
32   def outputLine( account, name, balance ):
33
34       print account.ljust( 10 ),
35       print name.ljust( 10 ),
36       print balance.rjust( 10 )
37
38   # open file
39   try:
40       file = open( "clients.dat", "r" )
41   except IOError:
42       print >> sys.stderr, "File could not be opened"
43       sys.exit( 1 )
44
45   print "Enter request"
46   print "1 - List accounts with zero balances"
47   print "2 - List accounts with credit balances"
48   print "3 - List accounts with debit balances"
49   print "4 - End of run"
50
51   # process user request(s)
52   while 1:
53
54       request = getRequest()     # get user request
55
```

Fig. 14.7   Credit-inquiry program. (Part 2 of 3.)

```
56      if request == 1:          # zero balances
57          print "\nAccounts with zero balances:"
58      elif request == 2:        # credit balances
59          print "\nAccounts with credit balances:"
60      elif request == 3:        # debit balances
61          print "\nAccounts with debit balances:"
62      elif request == 4:        # exit loop
63          break
64      else:  # getRequest should never let program reach here
65          print "\nInvalid request."
66
67      currentRecord = file.readline()      # get first record
68
69      # process each line
70      while ( currentRecord != "" ):
71          account, name, balance = currentRecord.split()
72          balance = float( balance )
73
74          if shouldDisplay( request, balance ):
75              outputLine( account, name, str( balance ) )
76
77          currentRecord = file.readline() # get next record
78
79      file.seek( 0, 0 )                        # move to beginning of file
80
81  print "\nEnd of run."
82  file.close()                                 # close file
```

```
Enter request
1 - List accounts with zero balances
2 - List accounts with credit balances
3 - List accounts with debit balances
4 - End of run

? 1

Accounts with zero balances:
300       White                0.0

? 2

Accounts with credit balances:
400       Stone              -42.16

? 3

Accounts with debit balances:
100       Jones               24.98
200       Doe                345.67
500       Rich               224.62

? 4

End of run.
```

Fig. 14.7   Credit-inquiry program. (Part 3 of 3.)

14.6 Updating Sequential-Access Files

Data that is formatted and written to a sequential-access file (as shown in the previous sections) cannot be modified without the risk of destroying other data in the file. For example, if the name "**White**" needs to be changed to "**Williams**," the old name cannot simply be overwritten. In Fig. 14.7, the record for **White** was written to the file as

```
300 White 0.00
```

If a user overwrites this record with the name "**Williams**," the record appears as

```
300 Williams00
```

The new last name contains three more characters than the original last name, so the characters beyond the second "**i**" in "**Williams**" overwrite the other characters in the line. The problem here is that in the formatted input/output model, fields (records) can vary in size. For example, 7, 14, –117, 2074 and 27383 are all integers and are stored in the same number of "raw data" bytes internally, but when these integers are output as formatted text (character sequences) to the screen or to a file, they become different-sized fields. Therefore, the formatted input/output model usually is not used to update records in place.

Updating data in sequential-access files is possible, but it is awkward. For example, to make the preceding name change, the records before **300 White 0.00** in a sequential-access file could be copied to a separate file, the updated record could then be written to this file and the records after **300 White 0.00** could be copied to this file. However, this can be cumbersome, because it requires processing every record in the file to update one record. If many records are being updated in one pass of the file, then the effort this technique requires would be unacceptable.

14.7 Random-Access Files

We have explained how to create sequential-access files and how to search through such files to locate particular information. However, sequential-access files are inappropriate for so-called *"instant-access" applications*, in which a particular record of information must be located immediately. Popular instant-access applications include airline reservation systems, banking systems, point-of-sale systems, automated-teller machines (ATMs) and other kinds of *transaction-processing systems* that require rapid access to specific data. The bank at which an individual keeps an account may have hundreds of thousands or even millions of other customers; however, when that individual uses an ATM, the appropriate account is checked for sufficient funds in seconds. Instant access is possible with *random-access files* (sometimes called *direct-access files*). Individual records of a random-access file can be accessed directly (and quickly) without searching through other records.

As we discussed earlier in this chapter, Python does not impose structure on files, so applications that use random-access files must create the random-access capability. There are a variety of techniques for creating random-access files. Perhaps the simplest involves requiring that all records in a file be of uniform-fixed length. The use of fixed-length records enable a program to calculate (as a function of the record size and the record key) the exact location of any record in relation to the beginning of the file. We soon demonstrate how this facilitates immediate access to specific records, even in large files.

Figure 14.8 presents a view of a random-access file composed of fixed-length records. Each record is 100 bytes long. A random-access file is like a railroad train with many

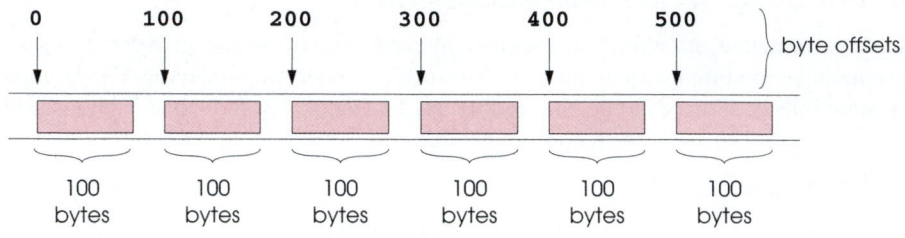

Fig. 14.8   Structure of a random-access file.

cars—some empty, some with contents. Data can be inserted into a random-access file without destroying other data in the file. In addition, previously stored data can be updated or deleted without rewriting the entire file. In the following sections, we explain how to create a random-access file, enter data to that file, read the data, update the data and delete data that is no longer needed.

14.8 Simulating a Random-Access File: The `shelve` Module

Random-access file-processing programs rarely write a single field to a file. Often, these programs write one record (or object) at a time. Random-access files can be created in other programming languages by defining a class that represents the record to be written to the file. In such programming languages, program that uses the class then reads and writes instances to a random-access file based on the size of the class (i.e., the number of bytes an instance of the class occupies). Python provides module **shelve** to simulate such behavior, so a programmer does not need to write a new class. We use this module in the following examples.

Consider the following problem statement for a credit-processing application:

> *Create a transaction-processing program capable of storing a maximum of 100 fixed-length records for a company that can have a maximum of 100 customers. Each record consists of an account number (that acts as a record key), a last name, a first name and a balance. The program can update an account, insert a new account, delete an account and list all the account records in a file.*

The next several sections introduce the techniques necessary to create this credit-processing program. We can use module **shelve** to read and write records in a file. To accomplish this, we create **shelve** objects to represent the records. These objects have a dictionary interface—the record key accesses a record's information. In our example, the record key is the account number, and the record value is a list that contains the customer's last name, first name and account balance.

14.9 Writing Data to a `shelve` File

Figure 14.9 retrieves account information from the user and writes the data to the **shelve** file **credit.dat**. Line 9 opens the **shelve** file **credit.dat** using function **shelve.open**. This function resembles the Python function **open** used for opening regular files. If the file does not exist, **shelve** function **open** creates the file. If an error occurs when opening the file, the function raises an **IOError** exception.

```
1   # Fig. 14.9: fig14_09.py
2   # Writing to shelve file.
3
4   import sys
5   import shelve
6
7   # open shelve file
8   try:
9       outCredit = shelve.open( "credit.dat" )
10  except IOError:
11      print >> sys.stderr, "File could not be opened"
12      sys.exit( 1 )
13
14  print "Enter account number (1 to 100, 0 to end input)"
15
16  # get account information
17  while 1:
18
19      # get account information
20      accountNumber = int( raw_input(
21          "\nEnter account number\n? " ) )
22
23      if 0 < accountNumber <= 100:
24
25          print "Enter lastname, firstname, balance"
26          currentData = raw_input( "? " )
27
28          outCredit[ str( accountNumber ) ] = currentData.split()
29
30      elif accountNumber == 0:
31          break
32
33  outCredit.close()    # close shelve file
```

```
Enter account number (1 to 100, 0 to end input)
? 37
Enter lastname, firstname, balance
? Barker Doug 0.00

Enter account number
? 29
Enter lastname, firstname, balance
? Brown Nancy -24.54

Enter account number
? 96
Enter lastname, firstname, balance
? Stone Sam 34.98

Enter account number
? 88
```

(continued on next page)

Fig. 14.9   Data written to a **shelve** file. (Part 1 of 2.)

```
                                                (continued from previous page)

Enter lastname, firstname, balance
? Smith Dave 258.34

Enter account number
? 33
Enter lastname, firstname, balance
? Dunn Stacey 314.33

Enter account number
? 0
```

Fig. 14.9   Data written to a **shelve** file. (Part 2 of 2.)

     Lines 20–21 prompt the user for the account numbers in the range 1–100, inclusive. Line 28 writes data to the **shelve** file. The program manipulates the data in a **shelve** file through a dictionary interface. Each key in a **shelve** file must be a string; therefore, function **str** converts the integer value **accountNumber** to a string (line 28). Method **split** converts the user-entered data into a list, which is stored as the record key's value (line 28). When the user enters **0** to indicate the end of data, the file object's **close** method closes the **shelve** file (line 33).

14.10 Retrieving Data from a `shelve` File

In the previous section, we created a **shelve** file and wrote data to that file. In this section, we present a program (Fig. 14.10) that iterates through the file and prints each record.

```
1   # Fig. 14.10: fig14_10.py
2   # Reading shelve file.
3
4   import sys
5   import shelve
6
7   # print formatted credit data
8   def outputLine( account, aList ):
9
10      print account.ljust( 10 ),
11      print aList[ 0 ].ljust( 10 ),
12      print aList[ 1 ].ljust( 10 ),
13      print aList[ 2 ].rjust( 10 )
14
15  # open shelve file
16  try:
17      creditFile = shelve.open( "credit.dat" )
18  except IOError:
19      print >> sys.stderr, "File could not be opened"
20      sys.exit( 1 )
21
22  print "Account".ljust( 10 ),
```

Fig. 14.10 Data read from a **shelve** file. (Part 1 of 2.)

```
23    print "Last Name".ljust( 10 ),
24    print "First Name".ljust( 10 ),
25    print "Balance".rjust( 10 )
26
27    # display each account
28    for accountNumber in creditFile.keys():
29        outputLine( accountNumber, creditFile[ accountNumber ] )
30
31    creditFile.close()    # close shelve file
```

Account	Last Name	First Name	Balance
37	Barker	Doug	0.00
88	Smith	Dave	258.34
33	Dunn	Stacey	314.33
29	Brown	Nancy	-24.54
96	Stone	Sam	34.98

Fig. 14.10 Data read from a **shelve** file. (Part 2 of 2.)

Method *keys* returns a list of the record keys in the **shelve** file (line 28). A **for** loop iterates over this list and passes each record key and its value to function **output-Line**. Function **outputLine** (lines 8–13) prints the record key and its associated values.

14.11 Example: A Transaction-Processing Program

We now develop a substantial transaction-processing program (Fig. 14.11) that uses a **shelve** file to achieve "instant-access" processing. The program maintains a bank's account information. Users of this program can update existing accounts, add new accounts, delete accounts and store formatted listings of all the current accounts in text files.

```
1     # Fig. 14.11: fig14_11.py
2     # Reads shelve file, updates data
3     # already written to file, creates data
4     # to be placed in file and deletes data
5     # already in file.
6
7     import sys
8     import shelve
9
10    # prompt for input menu choice
11    def enterChoice():
12
13        print "\nEnter your choice"
14        print "1 - store a formatted text file of accounts"
15        print "    called \"print.txt\" for printing"
16        print "2 - update an account"
17        print "3 - add a new account"
18        print "4 - delete an account"
19        print "5 - end program"
```

Fig. 14.11 Bank-account program. (Part 1 of 4.)

```
20
21       while 1:
22           menuChoice = int( raw_input( "? " ) )
23
24           if not 1 <= menuChoice <= 5:
25               print >> sys.stderr, "Incorrect choice"
26
27           else:
28               break
29
30       return menuChoice
31
32   # create formatted text file for printing
33   def textFile( readFromFile ):
34
35       # open text file
36       try:
37           outputFile = open( "print.txt", "w" )
38       except IOError:
39           print >> sys.stderr, "File could not be opened."
40           sys.exit( 1 )
41
42       print >> outputFile, "Account".ljust( 10 ),
43       print >> outputFile, "Last Name".ljust( 10 ),
44       print >> outputFile, "First Name".ljust( 10 ),
45       print >> outputFile, "Balance".rjust( 10 )
46
47       # print shelve values to text file
48       for key in readFromFile.keys():
49           print >> outputFile, key.ljust( 10 ),
50           print >> outputFile, readFromFile[ key ][ 0 ].ljust( 10 ),
51           print >> outputFile, readFromFile[ key ][ 1 ].ljust( 10 ),
52           print >> outputFile, readFromFile[ key ][ 2 ].rjust( 10 )
53
54       outputFile.close()
55
56   # update account balance
57   def updateRecord( updateFile ):
58
59       account = getAccount( "Enter account to update" )
60
61       if updateFile.has_key( account ):
62           outputLine( account, updateFile[ account ] ) # get record
63
64           transaction = raw_input(
65               "\nEnter charge (+) or payment (-): " )
66
67           # create temporary record to alter data
68           tempRecord = updateFile[ account ]
69           tempBalance = float( tempRecord[ 2 ] )
70           tempBalance += float( transaction )
71           tempBalance = "%.2f" % tempBalance
72           tempRecord[ 2 ] = tempBalance
```

Fig. 14.11 Bank-account program. (Part 2 of 4.)

```
73
74        # update record in shelve
75        del updateFile[ account ]   # remove old record first
76        updateFile[ account ] = tempRecord
77        outputLine( account, updateFile[ account ] )
78     else:
79        print >> sys.stderr, "Account #", account, \
80           "does not exist."
81
82  # create and insert new record
83  def newRecord( insertInFile ):
84
85     account = getAccount( "Enter new account number" )
86
87     if not insertInFile.has_key( account ):
88        print "Enter lastname, firstname, balance"
89        currentData = raw_input( "? " )
90        insertInFile[ account ] = currentData.split()
91     else:
92        print >> sys.stderr, "Account #", account, "exists."
93
94  # delete existing record
95  def deleteRecord( deleteFromFile ):
96
97     account = getAccount( "Enter account to delete" )
98
99     if deleteFromFile.has_key( account ):
100       del deleteFromFile[ account ]
101       print "Account #", account, "deleted."
102    else:
103       print >> sys.stderr, "Account #", account, \
104          "does not exist."
105
106
107 # output line of client information
108 def outputLine( account, record ):
109
110    print account.ljust( 10 ),
111    print record[ 0 ].ljust( 10 ),
112    print record[ 1 ].ljust( 10 ),
113    print record[ 2 ].rjust( 10 )
114
115 # get account number from keyboard
116 def getAccount( prompt ):
117
118    while 1:
119       account = raw_input( prompt + " (1 - 100): " )
120
121       if 1 <= int( account ) <= 100:
122          break
123
124    return account
125
```

Fig. 14.11 Bank-account program. (Part 3 of 4.)

```
126  # list of functions that correspond to user options
127  options = [ textFile, updateRecord, newRecord, deleteRecord ]
128
129  # open shelve file
130  try:
131      creditFile = shelve.open( "credit.dat" )
132  except IOError:
133      print >> sys.stderr, "File could not be opened."
134      sys.exit( 1 )
135
136  # process user commands
137  while 1:
138
139      choice = enterChoice()                    # get user menu choice
140
141      if choice == 5:
142          break
143
144      options[ choice - 1 ]( creditFile )   # invoke option function
145
146  creditFile.close()                            # close shelve file
```

Fig. 14.11 Bank-account program. (Part 4 of 4.)

Execute the program in Fig. 14.9 to insert data in the file that is used in this transaction-processing program (Fig. 14.11). The transaction-processing program offers a user five options (**1–5**) with which to work in the program. Option **1** calls function **textFile** (lines 33–54), which stores a formatted list of all the account information in a text file called **print.txt**. From this file, a user can print a list of account information. Function **text-File** takes a **shelve** file as an argument and uses the data in that **shelve** file to create the text file. Function **outputLine** (lines 108–113) outputs the data to file **stdout**. After a user chooses option **1**, the file **print.txt** contains the following text:

```
Account     Last Name   First Name    Balance
37          Barker      Doug             0.00
88          Smith       Dave           258.54
33          Dunn        Stacey         314.33
29          Brown       Nancy          -24.54
96          Stone       Sam             34.98
```

When a user selects option **2**, the program calls function **updateRecord** (lines 57–80) to update an account. First, the function determines whether the record that the user specifies exists, because the function can update only existing records. If the record exists, it is read into variable **tempRecord**. Lines 69–70 convert the string representation of the account balance to a floating-point value before manipulating its numerical value. Before updating a record in the **shelve** file, the program must delete the existing record for the specified account; keyword **del** (line 75) deletes the current record. Line 76 updates the record by assigning the new record values to the corresponding account number (record key). The program then outputs the updated values. The following is a typical output for this option:

```
Enter account to update (1 - 100): 37
37          Barker      Doug                    0.00

Enter charge (+) or payment (-): +87.99
37          Barker      Doug                   87.99
```

Portability Tip 14.1

*Not all Python platforms require the value of a record to be deleted from a **shelve** file before updating that record. However, using **del** to delete a record value before updating it, ensures that the update occurs properly across Python platforms.*

Option **3** calls function **newRecord** to enable a user to add a new account. This function adds an account in the same manner as that of the program of Fig. 14.9. If the user enters an account number for an existing account, **newRecord** displays a message that the account exists and the program allows the user to select the next operation to perform. A typical output for option **3** is as follows:

```
Enter new account number (1 - 100): 22
Enter lastname, firstname, balance
? Johnston Sarah 247.45
```

Option **4** calls function **deleteRecord** to remove a record that is no longer needed. The program prompts the user to enter an account number. If the account number exists, the program uses keyword **del** to delete that record from the **shelve** file, then displays a message to inform the user that the record has been deleted. However, if the account number does not exist, the program displays an error message. A typical output for option **4** is as follows:

```
Enter account to delete (1 - 100): 29
Account # 29 deleted.
```

Option **5** terminates the program. The main portion of the program (lines 127–146) creates a list of functions that correspond to the user-menu options (line 127). The program then opens the **shelve** file for the bank accounts and gets the user's menu choice.

Line 144 calls a function that corresponds with a user option. Recall that parentheses (**()**) are Python operators. When used in conjunction with the function name (e.g., **text-File**), the operator calls the function and passes any indicated arguments. Variable **options** holds a list of function names, so a statement such as

```
options[ 0 ]( creditFile )
```

invokes function **textFile** (the first function in the list) and passes **creditFile** as an argument. Statements like this avoid the need for long **if/else** statements that determine the user menu option and call the appropriate function.

14.12 Object Serialization

Serialization, or *pickling,* converts complex object types, such as user-defined classes, to sets of bytes for storage or for transmission over a network. Pickling also is referred to as *flattening* or *marshalling.* Python provides both modules **pickle** and **cPickle** to perform pickling. In this text we use **cPickle**, a module written in C, instead of the Python module **pickle**. We choose to use **cPickle**, because modules written in compiled languages, such as C, execute faster than do interpreted languages such as Python. Figure 14.12 demonstrates pickling and storing a list in a file.

Performance Tip 14.2

*Module **cPickle** executes more efficiently than does module **pickle**, because **cPickle** is implemented in C and compiled into native machine language on each platform.*

```python
1   # Fig. 14.12: fig14_12.py
2   # Opening and writing pickled object to file.
3
4   import sys, cPickle
5
6   # open file
7   try:
8       file = open( "users.dat", "w" )      # open file in write mode
9   except IOError, message:                 # file open failed
10      print >> sys.stderr, "File could not be opened:", message
11      sys.exit( 1 )
12
13  print "Enter the user name, name and date of birth."
14  print "Enter end-of-file to end input."
15
16  inputList = []
17
18  while 1:
19
20      try:
21          accountLine = raw_input( "? " )             # get user entry
22      except EOFError:
23          break                                       # user-entered EOF
24      else:
25          inputList.append( accountLine.split() ) # append entry
26
27  cPickle.dump( inputList, file )   # write pickled object to file
28
29  file.close()
```

```
Enter the user name, name and date of birth.
Enter end-of-file to end input.
? mike Michael 4/3/60
? joe Joseph 12/5/71
? amy Amelia 7/10/80
? jan Janice 8/18/74
? ^Z
```

Fig. 14.12 Pickled object written to a file.

Line 8 opens **user.dat**, the file in which the pickled object resides. Variable **inputList**, initialized in line 16, is a list that contains the user-entered information to pickle. Lines 18–25 prompt the user to enter information and append the user's entries to **inputList**. Function **cPickle.dump** (line 27) pickles **inputList** to the file. The first argument to **dump** is the object to pickle and the second argument is the file object that represents the file in which method **dump** will store the pickled object. The function converts **inputList** to a series of bytes and writes the stream to the file. Line 29 calls file object method **close** to close the file.

A program can convert pickled data back to the original format by *unpickling* the data. Figure 14.13 demonstrates unpickling. This example uses the pickled file created by the program in Fig. 14.12.

The program first opens file **users.dat** (lines 7–11). Function **cPickle.load** (line 13) unpickles the data in the file. The function takes as an argument a file object that contains a pickled object, converts the pickled object into a Python object and returns a reference to the unpickled object. We assign this reference to variable **records**. The program then closes the file, because the file is no longer needed (line 14). The remainder of the program (lines 16–23) displays the unpickled data by iterating over the list of lists.

```
1   # Fig. 14.13: fig14_13.py
2   # Reading and printing pickled object in a file.
3
4   import sys, cPickle
5
6   # open file
7   try:
8       file = open( "users.dat", "r" )
9   except IOError:
10      print >> sys.stderr, "File could not be opened"
11      sys.exit( 1 )
12
13  records = cPickle.load( file )   # retrieve list of lines in file
14  file.close()
15
16  print "Username".ljust( 15 ),
17  print "Name".ljust( 10 ),
18  print "Date of birth".rjust( 20 )
19
20  for record in records:              # format each line
21      print record[ 0 ].ljust( 15 ),
22      print record[ 1 ].ljust( 10 ),
23      print record[ 2 ].rjust( 20 )
```

```
Username        Name                   Date of birth
mike            Michael                     4/3/60
joe             Joseph                     12/5/71
amy             Amelia                     7/10/80
jan             Janice                     8/18/74
```

Fig. 14.13 Pickled object read from a file.

SUMMARY

- Files are used for long-term retention of large amounts of data.
- Computers store files on secondary storage devices, such as magnetic disks, optical disks and tapes.
- Ultimately, all data items processed by digital computers are reduced to combinations of zeros and ones. This occurs because it is simple and economical to build electronic devices that can assume two stable states—**0** represents one state, and **1** represents the other.
- The smallest data item that computers support is called a bit (short for "binary digit"—a digit that can assume one of two values). Each data item, or bit can assume either the value **0** or the value **1**.
- It is preferable to program with data forms such as decimal digits (e.g., 0, 1, 2, 3, 4, 5, 6, 7, 8 and 9), letters (e.g., A through Z and a through z) and special symbols (e.g., $, @, %, &, *, (,), -, +, ", :, ?, /, etc.).
- Digits, letters and special symbols are referred to as characters.
- The set of all characters used to write programs and represent data items on a particular computer is called that computer's character set.
- Because computers can process only **1**s and **0**s, every character in a computer's character set is represented as a sequence of **1**s and **0**s (called a byte). Bytes are composed of eight bits.
- Just as characters are composed of bits, fields are composed of characters (or bytes). A field is a group of characters that convey a meaning.
- Data items processed by computers form a data hierarchy in which data items become larger and more complex in structure in the progression from bits, to characters (bytes), to fields and up to larger data structures.
- A record, which we can implement as a tuple, a dictionary or instance in Python, is a group of related fields.
- To facilitate the retrieval of specific records from a file, at least one field in each record is chosen as a record key. A record key identifies a record as belonging to a particular person or entity and distinguishes that record from all other records in the file.
- There are many ways to organize records in a file. In the most common organization is a sequential file, in which records typically are stored in order by the record-key field.
- Sometimes, a group of related files is called a database.
- A collection of programs designed to create and manage databases is called a database management system (DBMS).
- Python views each file as a sequential stream of bytes.
- Python imposes no structure on a file—notions like "records" do not exist in Python files.
- Each file ends either with an end-of-file marker or at a specific byte number recorded in a system-maintained administrative data structure.
- When a file is opened, Python creates an object and associates a stream with that object.
- Python creates three file streams—**sys.stdin** (standard input stream), **sys.stdout** (standard output stream) and **sys.stderr** (standard error stream). These streams provide communication channels between a program and a particular file or device.
- A program must import the **sys** module to access the three file streams directly.
- Program input corresponds to **sys.stdin**. Function **raw_input** uses **sys.stdin** to get input from the user.
- Program output corresponds with **sys.stdout**. By default, the **print** statement sends information to the standard output stream.

- Program errors are printed to **sys.stderr**.

- Function **open**, which takes one required argument and two optional arguments, creates a new stream objects. The required argument, for the new stream object, is the file name; the two optional arguments are the file open mode and the buffering mode.

- The file open mode specifies whether the file should be opened for reading, writing or both.

- The file open mode **"w"** opens a file to output data to the file; the file open mode **"w+"** opens a file to append data to the end of the file (without modifying any data already in the file).

- Existing files opened with mode **"w"** are truncated—all data in the file is deleted. If the specified file does not yet exist, then a file is created. The newly created file is assigned the name provided in the file-name argument.

- The default file-open mode is **"r"**, which opens a file for reading.

- The third argument to function open—the buffering-mode argument—is for advanced control of file input and output and usually is not specified.

- When **open** encounters an error, the function raises an **IOError** exception.

- Programs can redirect output from the **print** statement to print to a different file object.

- When the **>>** symbol follows the **print**, **print** redirects output to the file object that appears to the right of **>>**. A comma follows the output file object; the value to be printed follows the comma.

- Function **sys.exit** terminates a program and returns its optional argument to the environment from which the program was invoked. Argument value **0** (the default) indicates normal program termination. Any other value indicates that the program terminated due to an error. The calling environment can use the value returned by **sys.exit** to respond appropriately to the error.

- Invoking methods **read**, **readline**, **readlines** and **xreadlines** on the end-of-file character raises an **EOFError** exception.

- Method **close** closes a file object. Although Python closes open files when a program terminates, it is good practice to close a file explicitly as soon as the program no longer needs the file.

- Data is stored in files so that they can be retrieved for processing.

- Method **readlines** reads an entire file into a program.

- Methods **ljust** and **rjust** left-and right-justify fields, respectively.

- To retrieve data sequentially from a file, programs normally start reading from the beginning of the file, and read all the data consecutively until the desired data is found.

- Method **seek** repositions the file position pointer. The first argument to **seek** is an offset, which is an integer value that specifies the location in the file as a number of bytes from the seek direction. The second (optional) argument is a seek direction, or location, from which the offset begins.

- File-object method **tell** returns the current location of the file-position pointer.

- Method **readline** reads one line from the file. This method returns one line from the file and moves the file-position pointer to the next line in the file. When the file contains no more lines (i.e., the program has reached the end of the file), **readline** returns the empty string (**""**).

- In the formatted input/output model, fields—and hence records—can vary in size. Therefore, the formatted input/output model usually is not used to update records.

- Sequential-access files are inappropriate for so-called "instant-access" applications in which a particular record of information must be located immediately.

- Individual records of a random-access file can be accessed directly (and quickly) without searching through other records. Random-access files sometimes are called direct-access files.

- Data can be inserted into a random-access file without destroying other data in the file. In addition, previously stored data can be updated or deleted without rewriting the entire file.

- Module **shelve** reads and writes objects to a random-access file.
- A program can create **shelve** file objects to represent records. These objects have a dictionary interface—the record key accesses a record's information.
- The **shelve.open** function resembles the Python function **open** that opens regular files.
- Method **keys** returns a list of the record keys in the **shelve** file.
- Serialization, or pickling, converts complex object types, such as programmer-defined classes, to sets of bytes for storage or for transmission over a network. Pickling also is referred to as flattening or marshalling.
- Python provides both modules **pickle** and **Pickle** to perform pickling.
- Module **cPickle**, which is implemented in C, executes much faster than does module **pickle**, which is implemented in Python. Modules written in compiled languages, such as C, execute faster than do interpreted languages such as Python.
- Function **cPickle.dump** pickles objects.
- Unpickling restores a pickled object to its original form.
- Function **cPickle.load** unpickles pickled objects in a file.

TERMINOLOGY

>> symbol	raw data processing
"a" file-open mode	**readline** method
"ab" file-open mode	**readlines** method
bit	record
buffering mode	record key
byte	redirection of output
character set	**"r"** file-open mode
close method	**"r+"** file-open mode
cPickle method	**"r+b"** file-open mode
data hierarchy	**"rb"** file-open mode
database	**seek** method
database management system (DBMS)	sequential-access file
end-of-file marker	serialization
EOFError exception	**shelve** file
field	**shelve** module
file	**split** method
file name	standard-error stream (**sys.stderr**)
file-open mode	standard-input stream (**sys.stdin**)
file-position pointer	standard-output stream (**sys.stdout**)
file-seek location	stream
instant-access processing	**sys.exit** function
IOError exception	**tell** method
keys method	transaction-processing systems
magnetic disk	truncate
offset	unpickling an object
open method	**"w"** file-open mode
persistent data	**"w+"** file-open mode
pickling an object	**"w+b"** file-open mode
random-access file	**"wb"** file-open mode

SELF-REVIEW EXERCISES

14.1 Fill in the blanks in each of the following statements:

a) Computers store files on _____, such as magnetic disks.

b) A record can be implemented as a _____, a _____ or a _____ in Python.

c) The set of all characters used to write programs on a computer is called its _____.

d) In a _____, records typically are stored in order by the record key.

e) Python creates three file streams—_____, _____ and _____.

f) A _____ is composed of several fields.

g) To facilitate the retrieval of specific records from a file, one field in each record is chosen as a _____.

h) At the lowest level, the functions performed by computers essentially involve the manipulation of _____ and _____.

i) Data items represented in computers form a _____, in which data items become larger and more complex as they progress from bits to fields.

j) A group of related files is called a _____.

14.2 State which of the following are *true* and which are *false*. If *false*, explain why.

a) The programmer must create the `sys.stderr` stream explicitly.

b) The smallest data item in a computer is a byte.

c) Python views each file as a dictionary.

d) File streams serve as communication channels.

e) It is not necessary to search through all the records in a random-access file to find a specific record.

f) Records in random-access files must be of uniform length.

g) Module `cPickle` performs more efficiently than does module `pickle` because `cPickle` is written in Python.

h) Serialization converts complex objects to a set of bytes.

i) Method `sys.exit` returns `1` by default to signify that no errors occurred.

j) Sequential-access files are inappropriate for instant-access applications in which records must be located quickly.

ANSWERS TO SELF-REVIEW EXERCISES

14.1 a) secondary storage devices. b) tuple, dictionary, instance. c) character set. d) random-access file. e) `sys.stdout`, `sys.stdin`, `sys.stderr`. f) record. g) record key. h) `0`'s, `1`'s. i) data hierarchy. j) database.

14.2 a) False. This stream is created for the programmer. b) False. The smallest data item in a computer is a bit. c) False. Python views each file as a stream. d) True. e) True. f) False. Records in random-access files normally are of uniform length, but are not required to be so. g) False. Module `cPickle` performs more efficiently because it is written in C and compiled into native machine language for each platform. h) True. i) False. Method `sys.exit` returns `0` by default to signify that no errors occurred. j) True.

EXERCISES

14.3 Fill in the blanks in each of the following statements:

a) A group of related characters that conveys meaning is called a _____.

b) Method _____ repositions the file-position pointer in a file.

c) Programs can _____ output from the print statement to print to a different file object.

d) If the user enters the end-of-file character, function raw_input raises an _____.

e) Method _____ returns a list of the lines in a file.

14.4   State which of the following are *true* and which are *false*. If *false*, explain why.
   a) People prefer to manipulate bits instead of characters and fields because bits are more compact.
   b) People specify programs and data items as characters; computers then manipulate and process these characters as groups of zeros and ones.
   c) Most organizations store all information in a single file to facilitate computer processing.
   d) Each statement that processes a file in a Python program explicitly refers to that file by name.
   e) Python imposes no structure on a file.

14.5   You are the owner of a hardware store and need to keep an inventory that can tell you what different tools you have, how many of each you have on hand and the cost of each one. Write a program that initializes the **shelve** file **"hardware.dat"**, lets you input the data concerning each tool and enables you to list all your tools. The tool identification number should be the record number. Use the following information to start your file:

14.6   Modify the inventory program of Exercise 14.5. The modified program allows you to delete a record for a tool that you no longer have and allows you to update *any* information in the file.

14.7   Create a simple text editor GUI that allows the user to open a file. The GUI should display the text of the file and then close the file. The user can modify the file's contents. When the user chooses to save the text, the modified contents should be written to the file, replacing any other contents. The user also should be able to clear the display.

14.8   Create four band members from the class **BandMember**. Pickle these objects and store them in a file. Unpickle, then output the objects.

Record Number	Tool name	Quantity	Cost
17	Hammer	76	11.99
37	Saw	88	12.00
68	Screwdriver	106	6.99
83	Wrench	34	7.50

Fig. 14.14 Data for Exercise 14.5.

```
1   class BandMember:
2      """Represent a band member"""
3
4      def __init__( self, name, instrument ):
5         """Initialize name and instrument"""
6
7         self.name = name
8         self.instrument = instrument
9
10     def __str__( self ):
11        """Overloaded string representation"""
12
13        return "%s plays the %s" % ( self.name, self.instrument )
```

Fig. 14.15 Class **BandMember**.

15

Extensible Markup Language (XML)

Objectives

- To understand XML.
- To mark up data using XML.
- To become familiar with the types of markup languages created with XML.
- To understand the relationships among DTDs, Schemas and XML.
- To understand the fundamentals of DOM-based and SAX-based parsing.
- To understand the concept of XML namespaces.
- To create simple XSLT documents.

Every country has its own language, yet the subjects of which the untutored soul speaks are the same everywhere.
Tertullian

The chief merit of language is clearness, and we know that nothing detracts so much from this as do unfamiliar terms.
Galen

Like everything metaphysical, the harmony between thought and reality is to be found in the grammar of the language.
Ludwig Wittgenstein

15.1 Introduction

The *Extensible Markup Language* (XML) was developed in 1996 by the *World Wide Web Consortium's (W3C's) XML Working Group*. XML is a portable, widely supported, *open technology* (i.e., non-proprietary technology) for describing data. XML quickly is becoming the standard for data that is exchanged between applications. Using XML, document authors can describe any type of data, including mathematical formulas, software configuration instructions, music, recipes and financial reports. An additional benefit of using XML is that documents are readable by both humans and machines.

This chapter explores XML and various XML-related technologies. The first three sections introduce XML and how it is used to mark up data. The next two sections describe two different programmatic libraries that can be used to manipulate XML documents. Later sections introduce several *XML vocabularies* (i.e., markup languages created with XML). This chapter also examines a technology called Extensible Stylesheet Language Transformations (XSLT), which transforms XML data into other text-based formats. Chapter 16, Python XML Processing, builds upon the concepts presented in this chapter by writing Python applications that use XML.

15.2 XML Documents

Our first XML document describes an article (Fig. 15.1). [*Note*: Every XML document we show has line numbers for the reader's convenience. These line numbers are not part of the XML documents.]

This document begins with an optional *XML declaration* (line 1), which identifies the document as an XML document. The **version** *information parameter* specifies the version

```
 1   <?xml version = "1.0"?>
 2
 3   <!-- Fig. 15.1: article.xml       -->
 4   <!-- Article structured with XML. -->
 5
 6   <article>
 7
 8      <title>Simple XML</title>
 9
10      <date>December 21, 2001</date>
11
12      <author>
13         <firstName>John</firstName>
14         <lastName>Doe</lastName>
15      </author>
16
17      <summary>XML is pretty easy.</summary>
18
19      <content>In this chapter, we present a wide variety of examples
20         that use XML.
21      </content>
22
23   </article>
```

Fig. 15.1 XML used to mark up an article.

of XML[1] that is used in the document. XML comments (lines 3–4) begin with **<!--** and end with **-->**, and can be placed almost anywhere in an XML document. As in a Python program, comments are used in XML for documentation purposes.

Common Programming Error 15.1

Placing any characters, including whitespace, before the XML declaration is an error.

Portability Tip 15.1

Although the XML declaration is optional, documents should include the declaration to identify the version of XML used. Otherwise, in the future, a document that lacks an XML declaration might be assumed to conform to the latest version of XML, and errors could result.

XML marks up data using *tags*, which are names enclosed in *angle brackets* (**<>**). Tags are used in pairs to delimit character data (e.g., **Simple XML**). A tag that begins *markup* (i.e., XML data) is called a *start tag*, whereas a tag that terminates markup is called an *end tag*. Examples of start tags are **<article>** and **<title>** (lines 6 and 8, respectively). End tags differ from start tags in that they contain a *forward slash* (**/**) character immediately after the **<** character. Examples of end tags are **</title>** and **</article>** (lines 8 and 23, respectively). XML documents can contain any number of tags.

Common Programming Error 15.2

Failure to provide a corresponding end tag for a start tag is an error.

---

1. Currently, there is only one version of XML, 1.0.

Individual units of markup (i.e., everything included between a start tag and its corresponding end tag) are called *elements*. An XML document includes one element (called a *root element*) that contains all other elements in the document. The root element must be the first element after the XML declaration. In Fig. 15.1, **article** (line 6) is the root element. Elements are *nested* to form hierarchies—with the root element at the top of the hierarchy. This allows document authors to create explicit relationships between data. For example, elements **title**, **date**, **author**, **summary** and **content** then are nested within **article**. Elements **firstName** and **lastName** are nested within **author**.

Common Programming Error 15.3

Attempting to create more than one root element in an XML document is an error.

Element **title** (line 8) contains the title of the article, **Simple XML**, as character data. Similarly, **date** (line 10), **summary** (line 17) and **content** (lines 19–21) contain character data that represent the article's publication date, summary and content, respectively. XML tag names can be of any length and may contain letters, digits, underscores, hyphens and periods—they must begin with a letter or an underscore.

Common Programming Error 15.4

XML is case sensitive. Using the wrong case for an XML tag name is an error.

By itself, this document is simply a text file named **article.xml**. Although it is not required, most XML-document file names end with the file extension **.xml**.[2] Processing an XML document requires a program called an *XML parser*. Parsers are responsible for checking an XML document's syntax and making the XML document's data available to applications. Often, XML parsers are built into applications or available for download over the Internet. Popular parsers include Microsoft's *msxml*, *4DOM* (a Python package that we use extensively in the Chapter 16), the Apache Software Foundation's *Xerces* and IBM's *XML4J*. In this chapter, we use msxml.

When the user loads **article.xml** into Internet Explorer (IE),[3] msxml parses the document and passes the parsed data to IE. IE then uses a built-in *style sheet* to format the data. Notice that the resulting format of the data (Fig. 15.2) is similar to the format of the XML document shown in Fig. 15.1. As we soon demonstrate, style sheets play an important and powerful role in the transformation of XML data into formats suitable for display.

Notice the minus (**–**) and plus (**+**) signs in Fig. 15.2. Although these are not part of the XML document, IE places them next to all *container elements* (i.e., elements that contain other elements). Container elements also are called *parent elements*. A minus sign indicates that the parent element's *child elements* (i.e., nested elements) currently are displayed. When clicked, a minus sign becomes a plus sign (which collapses the container element and hides all of its children). Conversely, clicking a plus sign expands the container element and changes the plus sign to a minus sign. This behavior is similar to the viewing of the directory structure on a Windows system using Windows Explorer. In fact, a directory structure often is modeled as a series of tree structures, in which each drive letter (e.g., **C:**, etc.) represents

---

2. Some applications that process XML documents may require this file extension.
3. IE 5 and higher.

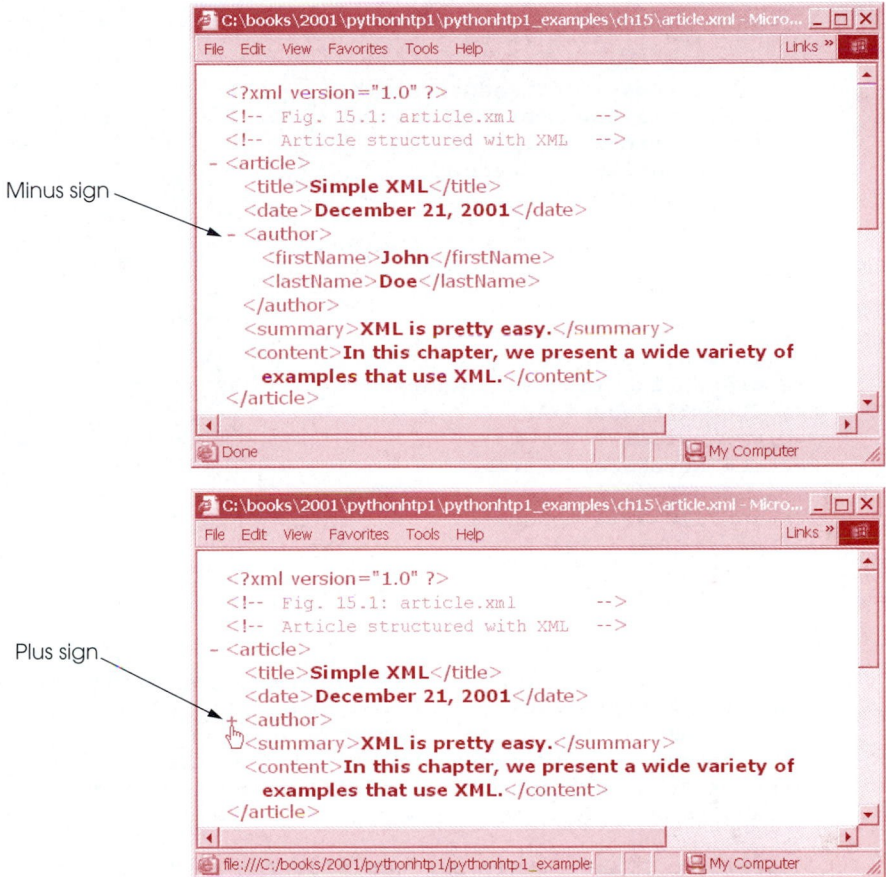

Minus sign

Plus sign

Fig. 15.2 `article.xml` displayed by Internet Explorer.

the *root* of a tree. Each folder is a *node* in the tree. Parsers often place XML data into trees to facilitate efficient manipulation, as discussed in Section 15.4.

 Common Programming Error 15.5

Nesting XML tags improperly is an error. For example, **<x><y>hello</x></y>** *is an error, because the* **</y>** *tag must precede the* **</x>** *tag.*

We now present a second XML document (Fig. 15.3), which marks up a business letter. This document contains significantly more data than did the previous XML document.

```
1   <?xml version = "1.0"?>
2
3   <!-- Fig. 15.3: letter.xml            -->
4   <!-- Business letter formatted with XML. -->
5
```

Fig. 15.3 Business letter marked up as XML. (Part 1 of 2.)

```
6   <letter>
7      <contact type = "from">
8         <name>Jane Doe</name>
9         <address1>Box 12345</address1>
10        <address2>15 Any Ave.</address2>
11        <city>Othertown</city>
12        <state>Otherstate</state>
13        <zip>67890</zip>
14        <phone>555-4321</phone>
15        <flag gender = "F" />
16     </contact>
17
18     <contact type = "to">
19        <name>John Doe</name>
20        <address1>123 Main St.</address1>
21        <address2></address2>
22        <city>Anytown</city>
23        <state>Anystate</state>
24        <zip>12345</zip>
25        <phone>555-1234</phone>
26        <flag gender = "M" />
27     </contact>
28
29     <salutation>Dear Sir:</salutation>
30
31        <paragraph>It is our privilege to inform you about our new
32        database managed with <technology>XML</technology>. This
33        new system allows you to reduce the load on
34        your inventory list server by having the client machine
35        perform the work of sorting and filtering the data.
36        </paragraph>
37
38        <paragraph>Please visit our Web site for availability
39        and pricing.
40        </paragraph>
41
42     <closing>Sincerely</closing>
43
44     <signature>Ms. Doe</signature>
45  </letter>
```

Fig. 15.3 Business letter marked up as XML. (Part 2 of 2.)

Root element **letter** (lines 6–45) contains the child elements **contact** (lines 7–16 and 18–27), **salutation**, **paragraph**, **closing** and **signature**. In addition to being placed between tags, data also can be placed in *attributes*, which are name-value pairs in start tags. Elements can have any number of attributes in their start tags. The first **contact** element (lines 7–16) has attribute **type** with attribute *value* **"from"**, which indicates that this **contact** element marks up information about the letter's sender. The second **contact** element (lines 18–27) has attribute **type** with value **"to"**, which indicates that this **contact** element marks up information about the letter's recipient. Like tag names, attribute names are case sensitive; can be any length; may contain letters, digits, underscores, hyphens and periods; and must begin with either a letter or underscore character. A **contact** element stores a contact's name, address and phone number. Element **salutation** (line 29) marks up the letter's salutation. Lines 31–40 mark up the letter's body with **paragraph** elements. Elements **closing** (line 42) and **signature** (line 44) mark up the closing sentence and the signature of the letter's author, respectively.

Common Programming Error 15.6

Failure to enclose attribute values in double (" ") or single (' ') quotes is an error.

In line 15, we introduce *empty element* **flag**, which indicates the gender of the contact. Empty elements do not contain character data (i.e., they do not contain text between the start and end tags). Such elements are closed either by placing a slash at the end of the element (as shown in line 15) or by explicitly writing a closing tag, as in

```
<flag gender = "F"></flag>
```

15.3 XML Namespaces

Languages such as Python provide massive class libraries that group their features into namespaces. These namespaces prevent *naming collisions* between programmer-defined identifiers and identifiers in class libraries. For example, we might use class **Book** to represent information on one of our publications; however, a stamp collector might use class **Book** to represent a book of stamps. Without using namespaces to differentiate the two **Book** classes, a naming collision would occur if we use these two classes in the same application.

Like Python, XML also provides *namespaces* for unique identification of XML elements. In addition, XML-based languages—called *vocabularies*, such as XML Schema (Section 15.6) and the Extensible Stylesheet Language (Section 15.8)—often use namespaces to identify their elements.

Namespace prefixes, which identify the namespace to which an element belongs, differentiate elements. For example,

```
<deitel:publication>
    Python How to Program
</deitel:publication>
```

qualifies element **publication** with namespace prefix **deitel**. This indicates that element **publication** is part of namespace **deitel**. Document authors can use any name for a namespace prefix except the reserved namespace prefix *xml*.

Common Programming Error 15.7

Attempting to create a namespace prefix named xml in any combination of uppercase and lowercase letters is an error.

The markup in Fig. 15.4 demonstrates the use of namespaces. This XML document contains two **file** elements that are differentiated using namespaces.

```
1   <?xml version = "1.0"?>
2
3   <!-- Fig. 15.4: namespace.xml  -->
4   <!-- Demonstrating namespaces. -->
```

Fig. 15.4 XML namespaces demonstration. (Part 1 of 2.)

```
5
6    <text:directory xmlns:text = "http://www.deitel.com/ns/python1e"
7       xmlns:image = "http://www.deitel.com/images/ns/120101">
8
9       <text:file filename = "book.xml">
10         <text:description>A book list</text:description>
11      </text:file>
12
13      <image:file filename = "funny.jpg">
14         <image:description>A funny picture</image:description>
15         <image:size width = "200" height = "100" />
16      </image:file>
17
18   </text:directory>
```

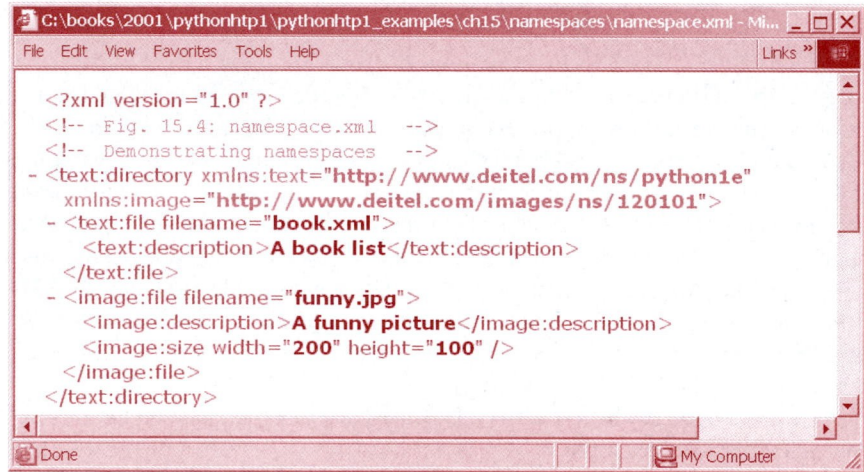

Fig. 15.4 XML namespaces demonstration. (Part 2 of 2.)

 Software Engineering Observation 15.1

Attributes need not be qualified with namespace prefixes, because they always are associated with elements.

Lines 6–7 use attribute **xmlns** to create two namespace prefixes: **text** and **image**. Each namespace prefix is bound to a series of characters called a *uniform resource identifier (URI)* that uniquely identifies the namespace. Document authors create their own namespace prefixes and URIs.

To ensure that namespaces are unique, document authors must provide unique URIs. Here, we use the text **http://www.deitel.com/ns/python1e** and **http://www.deitel.com/images/ns/120101** as URIs. A common practice is to use *Universal Resource Locators (URLs)* for URIs, because the domain names (such as, **www.deitel.com**) used in URLs are guaranteed to be unique. In this example, we use URLs related to the Deitel & Associates, Inc., domain name to identify namespaces. The parser never visits these URLs—they simply represent a series of characters used to differentiate names. The URLs need not refer to actual Web pages or be formed properly.

Lines 9–11 use the namespace prefix **text** to describe elements **file** and **description**. Notice that the namespace prefix **text** is applied to the end tag name as well. Lines 13–16 apply namespace prefix **image** to elements **file**, **description** and **size**.

To eliminate the need to precede each tag name with a namespace prefix, document authors can specify a *default namespace*. Figure 15.5 demonstrates the creation and use of default namespaces.

Line 6 defines a default namespace by binding a URI to attribute **xmlns**. Once this default namespace is defined, tag names in child elements belonging to the namespace need not be qualified by a namespace prefix. Element **file** (line 9–11) is in the namespace corresponding to the URI **http://www.deitel.com/ns/python1e**. Compare this to lines 9–11 of Fig. 15.4, where we prefixed elements **file** and **description** with **text**.

The default namespace applies to element **directory** and all elements that are not qualified with a namespace prefix. However, we can use a namespace prefix to specify a different namespace for particular elements. For example, line 13 prefixes tag name **file**

```
1    <?xml version = "1.0"?>
2
3    <!-- Fig. 15.5: defaultnamespace.xml -->
4    <!-- Using default namespaces.        -->
5
6    <directory xmlns = "http://www.deitel.com/ns/python1e"
7       xmlns:image = "http://www.deitel.com/images/ns/120101">
8
9       <file filename = "book.xml">
10          <description>A book list</description>
11      </file>
12
13      <image:file filename = "funny.jpg">
14          <image:description>A funny picture</image:description>
15          <image:size width = "200" height = "100" />
16      </image:file>
17
18   </directory>
```

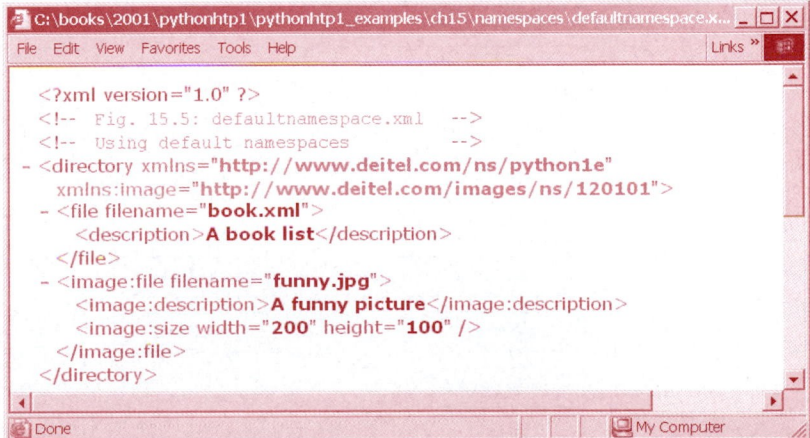

Fig. 15.5 Default namespace demonstration.

in with **image** to indicate that it is in the namespace corresponding to the URI **http://www.deitel.com/images/ns/120101**, rather than in the default namespace.

15.4 Document Object Model (DOM)

Although XML documents are text files, retrieving data from them via sequential-file access techniques is neither practical nor efficient, especially in situations where data must be added or deleted dynamically.

Upon successful parsing of documents, some XML parsers store document data as tree structures in memory. Figure 15.6 illustrates the tree structure for the document **article.xml** discussed in Fig. 15.1. This hierarchical tree structure is called a *Document Object Model (DOM)* tree, and an XML parser that creates this type of structure is known as a *DOM parser*. The DOM tree represents each component of the XML document (e.g., **article**, **date**, **firstName**, etc.) as a node in the tree. Nodes (such as, **author**) that contain other nodes (called *child nodes*) are called *parent nodes*. Nodes that have the same parent (such as, **firstName** and **lastName**) are called *sibling nodes*. A node's *descendant nodes* include that node's children, its children's children and so on. Similarly, a node's *ancestor nodes* include that node's parent, its parent's parent and so on.

The DOM has a single *root node*, called the *document root*, which contains all other nodes in a document. For example, the root node for **article.xml** (Fig. 15.1) contains a node for the XML declaration (line 1), two nodes for the comments (lines 3–4) and a node for the root element (line 6).

Each node is an object that has attributes and methods. Attributes associated with a node include tag names, values, child nodes, etc. Methods enable programs to create, delete and append nodes, load XML documents and so on. The XML parser exposes these methods as a programmatic library—called an *Application Programming Interface (API)*. We discuss how to use the DOM API in Chapter 16, Python XML Processing.

15.5 Simple API for XML (SAX)

Members of the *XML-DEV mailing list* developed the Simple API for XML (SAX), which they released in May, 1998. SAX is an alternate method for parsing XML documents that

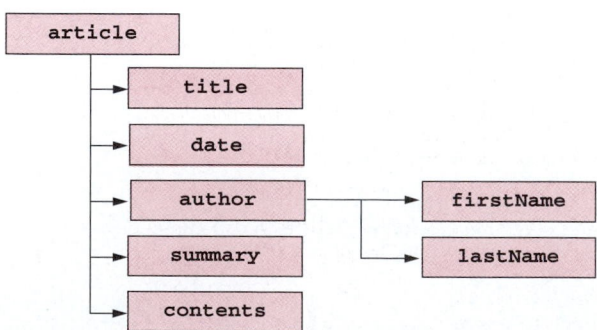

Fig. 15.6   Tree structure for **article.xml**.

uses an *event-based model—SAX-based parsers* generate notifications called *events* as the parser processes the document. Software programs can "listen" for these events to retrieve data from the document. For example, a program that builds mailing lists might read name and address information from an XML document that contains much more than just mailing address information (e.g., birthdays, phone numbers, email addresses, etc.). Such a program could use a SAX parser to parse the document, and might listen only for events that contain name and address information. SAX-based parsers are available for a variety of programming languages such as Python, Java and C++. We demonstrate SAX-based parsing in Chapter 16, Python XML Processing.

SAX and DOM provide dramatically different APIs for accessing XML document data. Each API has advantages and disadvantages. DOM is a tree-based model that stores the document's data in a hierarchy of nodes. Programs can access data quickly, because all the document's data is in memory. DOM also provides facilities for adding or removing nodes, which enables programs to modify XML documents easily.

SAX-based parsers invoke *listener methods* when the parser encounters markup. With this event-based model, the SAX-based parser does not create a tree structure to store the XML document's data—instead, the parser passes data to the application from the XML document as the parser finds that data. This results in greater performance and less memory overhead than with DOM-based parsers. In fact, many DOM parsers use SAX parsers "under the hood" to retrieve data from a document for building the DOM tree in memory. Many programmers find it easier to traverse and manipulate XML documents using the DOM tree structure. As a result, programs typically use SAX parsers for reading XML documents that the program will not modify.

Performance Tip 15.1

SAX-based parsing often is more efficient than DOM-based parsing for processing large XML documents—SAX-based parsers do not load entire XML documents into memory.

Performance Tip 15.2

SAX-based parsing is an efficient means of parsing documents that only need parsing once.

Performance Tip 15.3

DOM-based parsing often is more efficient than SAX-based parsing when a program must retrieve specific information from the document quickly.

Performance Tip 15.4

Programs that must conserve memory commonly use SAX-based parsers.

Software Engineering Observation 15.2

Members of the XML-DEV mailing list developed SAX independently of the W3C, although SAX has wide industry support. DOM is the official W3C recommendation.

15.6 Document Type Definitions (DTDs), Schemas and Validation

This section introduces *Document Type Definitions* (*DTDs*) and *Schemas*—documents that specify the structure of XML documents (i.e., what elements are permitted, what attributes an element can have and so on). When a DTD or Schema document is provided, some parsers (called *validating parsers*[4]) read the DTD or Schema and check the XML document's structure against it. If the XML document conforms to the DTD or Schema, then the XML document is *valid*. Parsers that cannot validate documents against DTDs or Schemas are called *non-validating parsers*. If an XML parser (validating or non-validating) is able to process an XML document (that does not reference a DTD or Schema), the XML document is considered to be *well formed* (i.e., it is syntactically correct). By definition, a valid XML document is a well-formed XML document. If a document is not well formed, the parser issues an error.

Software Engineering Observation 15.3

DTD and Schema documents are essential components for XML documents used in business-to-business (B2B) transactions and mission-critical systems.

Software Engineering Observation 15.4

Because XML document content can be structured in many different ways, an application cannot determine whether the document data it receives is complete, missing data or ordered properly. DTDs and Schemas solve this problem by providing an extensible means of describing a document's contents. An application can use a DTD or Schema document to perform a validity check on the document's contents.

15.6.1 Document Type Definition Documents

Document type definitions (DTDs) provide a means for type checking XML documents and thus verifying their *validity* (confirming that elements contain the proper attributes, elements are in the proper sequence, etc.). DTDs use *EBNF (Extended Backus-Naur Form) grammar* to describe an XML document's content. XML parsers need additional functionality to read EBNF grammar, because it is not XML syntax. Although DTDs are optional, they are recommended to ensure document conformity. The DTD in Fig. 15.7 defines the set of rules (i.e., the grammar) for structuring the business letter document contained in Fig. 15.8.

```
1    <!-- Fig. 15.7: letter.dtd         -->
2    <!-- DTD document for letter.xml. -->
3
4    <!ELEMENT letter ( contact+, salutation, paragraph+,
5       closing, signature )>
6
7    <!ELEMENT contact ( name, address1, address2, city, state,
8       zip, phone, flag )>
9    <!ATTLIST contact type CDATA #IMPLIED>
10
11   <!ELEMENT name ( #PCDATA )>
12   <!ELEMENT address1 ( #PCDATA )>
13   <!ELEMENT address2 ( #PCDATA )>
14   <!ELEMENT city ( #PCDATA )>
15   <!ELEMENT state ( #PCDATA )>
16   <!ELEMENT zip ( #PCDATA )>
17   <!ELEMENT phone ( #PCDATA )>
```

Fig. 15.7   Document Type Definition (DTD) for a business letter. (Part 1 of 2.)

---

4. Many DOM parsers and SAX parsers are validating parsers. Check you parser's documentation to
   determine whether it is a validating parser.

```
18    <!ELEMENT flag EMPTY>
19    <!ATTLIST flag gender (M | F) "M">
20
21    <!ELEMENT salutation ( #PCDATA )>
22    <!ELEMENT closing ( #PCDATA )>
23    <!ELEMENT paragraph ( #PCDATA )>
24    <!ELEMENT signature ( #PCDATA )>
```

Fig. 15.7   Document Type Definition (DTD) for a business letter. (Part 2 of 2.)

Portability Tip 15.2

DTDs can ensure consistency among XML documents generated by different programs.

Line 4 uses the ***ELEMENT*** *element type declaration* to define rules for element **letter**. In this case, **letter** contains one or more **contact** elements, one **salutation** element, one or more **paragraph** elements, one **closing** element and one **signature** element, in that sequence. The *plus sign* (**+**) *occurrence indicator* specifies that an element must occur one or more times. Other indicators include the *asterisk* (*****), which indicates an optional element that can occur any number of times, and the *question mark* (**?**), which indicates an optional element that can occur at most once. If an occurrence indicator is omitted, exactly one occurrence is expected.

The **contact** element definition (line 7) specifies that it contains the **name**, **address1**, **address2**, **city**, **state**, **zip**, **phone** and **flag** elements—in that order. Exactly one occurrence of each is expected.

Line 9 uses the ***ATTLIST*** *element type declaration* to define an attribute (i.e., **type**) for the **contact** element. Keyword ***#IMPLIED*** specifies that, if the parser finds a **contact** element without a **type** attribute, the application can provide a value or ignore the missing attribute. The absence of a **type** attribute cannot invalidate the document. Other types of default values include ***#REQUIRED*** and ***#FIXED***. Keyword ***#REQUIRED*** specifies that the attribute must be present in the document and the keyword ***#FIXED*** specifies that the attribute (if present) must always be assigned a specific value. For example,

```
<!ATTLIST address zip #FIXED "01757">
```

indicates that the value **01757** must be used for attribute **zip**; otherwise, the document is invalid. If the attribute is not present, then the parser, by default, uses the fixed value that is specified in the **ATTLIST** declaration. Flag ***CDATA*** specifies that attribute **type** contains text that is not processed by the parser, but instead is passed to the application as is.

Software Engineering Observation 15.5

DTD syntax cannot describe an element's (or attribute's) data type.

Flag ***#PCDATA*** (line 11) specifies that the element can store *parsed character data* (i.e., text). Parsed character data cannot contain markup. Because they are used in markup, the characters less than (**<**) and ampersand (**&**) must be replaced by their *entity references* (i.e., **<** and **&**). However, the ampersand character can be used with entity references. See Appendix M, HTML/XHTML Special Characters, for a list of pre-defined entities.

Line 18 defines an empty element named **flag**. Keyword ***EMPTY*** specifies that the element cannot contain character data. Empty elements commonly are used for their attributes.

Common Programming Error 15.8

Any element, attribute or relationship not explicitly defined by a DTD results in an invalid document.

XML documents must reference a DTD explicitly. Figure 15.8 is an XML document that conforms to **letter.dtd** (Fig. 15.7).

```
1   <?xml version = "1.0"?>
2
3   <!-- Fig. 15.8: letter2.xml            -->
4   <!-- Business letter formatted with XML. -->
5
6   <!DOCTYPE letter SYSTEM "letter.dtd">
7
8   <letter>
9      <contact type = "from">
10        <name>Jane Doe</name>
11        <address1>Box 12345</address1>
12        <address2>15 Any Ave.</address2>
13        <city>Othertown</city>
14        <state>Otherstate</state>
15        <zip>67890</zip>
16        <phone>555-4321</phone>
17        <flag gender = "F" />
18     </contact>
19
20     <contact type = "to">
21        <name>John Doe</name>
22        <address1>123 Main St.</address1>
23        <address2></address2>
24        <city>Anytown</city>
25        <state>Anystate</state>
26        <zip>12345</zip>
27        <phone>555-1234</phone>
28        <flag gender = "M" />
29     </contact>
30
31     <salutation>Dear Sir:</salutation>
32
33        <paragraph>It is our privilege to inform you about our new
34        database managed with XML. This new system
35        allows you to reduce the load on your inventory list
36        server by having the client machine perform the work of
37        sorting and filtering the data.
38        </paragraph>
39
40        <paragraph>Please visit our Web site for availability
41        and pricing.
42        </paragraph>
43     <closing>Sincerely</closing>
44     <signature>Ms. Doe</signature>
45   </letter>
```

Fig. 15.8   XML document referencing its associated DTD.

This XML document is similar to that in Fig. 15.3. Line 6 references a DTD file. This markup contains three pieces: The name of the root element (**letter** in line 8) to which the DTD is applied, the keyword ***SYSTEM*** (which in this case denotes an *external DTD*— a DTD defined in a separate file) and the DTD's name and location (i.e., **letter.dtd** in the current directory). Though almost any file extension can be used, DTD documents typically end with the *.dtd* extension.

Various tools (many of which are free) check document conformity against DTDs and Schemas (discussed momentarily). The output in Fig. 15.9 shows the results of validating **letter2.xml** against **letter.dtd** using Microsoft's *XML Validator*. Microsoft XML Validator is available free for download from **msdn.microsoft.com/downloads/ samples/Internet/xml/xml_validator/sample.asp**. For additional validation tools, visit **www.w3.org/XML/Schema.html**.

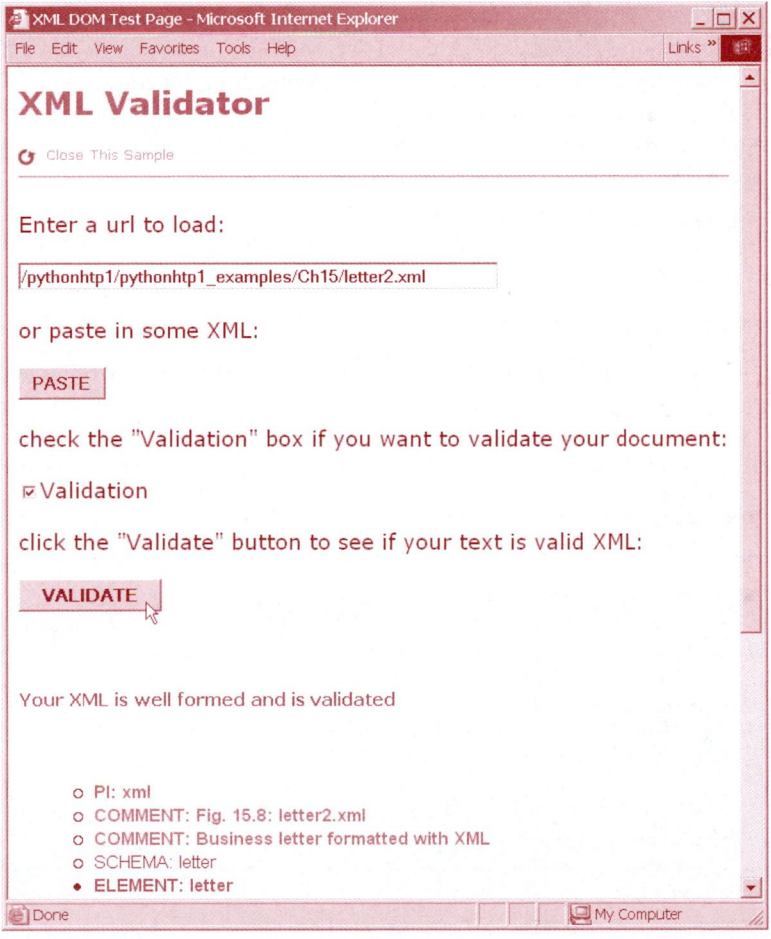

Fig. 15.9   XML Validator validating an XML document against a DTD.

The Microsoft XML Validator can validate XML documents against DTDs locally or by uploading the documents to the XML Validator Web site. Here, **letter2.xml** and **letter.dtd** are placed in folder **/pythonhtp1/pythonhtp1_examples/Ch15**. This XML document (**letter2.xml**) is valid because it conforms to **letter.dtd**.

XML documents that fail validation still may be well-formed documents. When a document fails to conform to a DTD or Schema, Microsoft XML Validator displays an error message. For example, the DTD in Fig. 15.8 indicates that the **contacts** element must contain child element **name**. If this element is omitted, the document is well formed, but not valid. In such a scenario, Microsoft XML Validator displays the error message shown in Fig. 15.10.

15.6.2 W3C XML Schema Documents

This section introduces *W3C XML Schema*[5]—a W3C *Recommendation* (i.e., a stable release suitable for use in industry). Many developers in the XML community believe DTDs are not flexible enough to meet today's programming needs. For example, programs cannot manipulate DTDs (e.g., search, transform into different representations such as XHTML, etc.) in the same manner as XML documents because DTDs are not themselves XML documents. These and other limitations led to the development of Schemas.

Unlike DTDs, Schemas do not use EBNF grammar. Instead, Schemas use XML syntax and are actually XML documents that can be manipulated programmatically. Like DTDs, Schemas require validating parsers. In the near future, Schemas likely will replace DTDs as the primary means of describing XML document structure.

A DTD describes an XML document's structure, not the content of that document's elements. For example,

> **<quantity>5</quantity>**

contains character data. If the document containing element **quantity** references a DTD, an XML parser can validate the document to confirm that this element indeed does contain **PCDATA** content, but the parser cannot validate whether the content is numeric; DTDs do not provide such capability. So, unfortunately, the parser also considers markup such as

> **<quantity>hello</quantity>**

Fig. 15.10 XML Validator displaying an error message.

---

5. For the latest information on W3C XML Schema, visit **www.w3.org/XML/Schema**.

to be valid. The application that uses the XML document containing this markup would need to test whether the data in element **quantity** is numeric and take appropriate action if the data is not numerics.

XML Schema enables Schema authors to specify that element **quantity**'s data must be numeric. When a parser validates the XML document against this Schema, the parser can determine that **5** conforms and that **hello** does not. An XML document that conforms to a schema document is *schema valid* and a document that does not conform is invalid.

In this section, we use *XSV* (*XML Schema Validator*) to validate XML documents against W3C XML Schema. To use XSV online, visit **www.w3.org/2000/09/webdata/xsv**, enter the name of the XML file to validate, then press the **Upload and Get Results** button. Visit **www.ltg.ed.ac.uk/~ht/xsv-status.html** to download XSV.

Software Engineering Observation 15.6

Many organizations and individuals are creating DTDs and schemas for a broad range of applications (e.g., financial transactions, medical prescriptions, etc.). These collections— called repositories—*often are available free for download from the Web (e.g., www.dtd.com).*

Figure 15.11 shows a Schema-valid XML document (**book.xml**) and Fig. 15.12 shows the W3C XML Schema document (**book.xsd**) that defines the structure for **book.xml**. W3C XML Schemas typically use the **.xsd** extension, although this is not required. Figure 15.11 shows the result of validating **book.xml** against Schema **book.xsd**. Note that the output is XML, and the **outcome='success'** and **schemaErrors='0'** attributes indicate that **book.xml** is valid.

W3C XML Schema use the namespace URI **http://www.w3.org/2001/XMLSchema** and often use *namespace prefix* **xsd** (line 6 in Fig. 15.12). Root element **schema** contains elements that define an XML document's structure. Line 7 binds the URI **http://www.deitel.com/booklist** to namespace prefix **deitel**. Line 8 specifies the **targetNamespace**, which is the namespace for elements and attributes that this Schema defines.

Good Programming Practice 15.1

By convention, W3C XML Schema authors use namespace prefix **xsd** *when referring to the URI* **http://www.w3.org/2001/XMLSchema**\

```
1   <?xml version = "1.0"?>
2
3   <!-- Fig. 15.11: book.xml                          -->
4   <!-- Document that conforms to a W3C XML Schema. -->
5
6   <deitel:books xmlns:deitel = "http://www.deitel.com/booklist">
7      <book>
8         <title>e-Business and e-Commerce How to Program</title>
9      </book>
10      <book>
11         <title>Python How to Program</title>
12      </book>
13   </deitel:books>
```

Fig. 15.11 XML document that conforms to a W3C XML Schema. (Part 1 of 2.)

```
C:\Program Files\XSV>xsv /pythonhtp1_examples/ch15/Schema/book.xml /
pythonhtp1_examples/ch15/Schema/book.xsd

<?xml version='1.0'?>
<xsv docElt='{http://www.deitel.com/booklist}books'
instanceAssessed='true' instanceErrors='0' rootType='{http://www.dei-
tel.com/booklist}:BooksType' schemaDocs='/pythonhtp1_examples/ch15/
Schema/book.xsd' schemaErrors='0' target='file:/pythonhtp1_examples/
ch15/Schema/book.xml' validation='strict' version='XSV 1.203.2.37/
1.106.2.19 of 2001/11/29 11:00:00'xmlns='http://www.w3.org/2000/05/
xsv'>
<schemaDocAttempt URI='file:/pythonhtp1_examples/ch15/Schema/book.xsd'
outcome='success' source='command line'/>
</xsv>
```

Fig. 15.11 XML document that conforms to a W3C XML Schema. (Part 2 of 2.)

```
1   <?xml version = "1.0"?>
2
3   <!-- Fig. 15.12: book.xsd           -->
4   <!-- Simple W3C XML Schema document. -->
5
6   <xsd:schema xmlns:xsd = "http://www.w3.org/2001/XMLSchema"
7      xmlns:deitel = "http://www.deitel.com/booklist"
8      targetNamespace = "http://www.deitel.com/booklist">
9
10     <xsd:element name = "books" type = "deitel:BooksType" />
11
12     <xsd:complexType name = "BooksType">
13        <xsd:sequence>
14           <xsd:element name = "book" type = "deitel:BookType"
15              minOccurs = "1" maxOccurs = "unbounded" />
16        </xsd:sequence>
17     </xsd:complexType>
18
19     <xsd:complexType name = "BookType">
20        <xsd:sequence>
21           <xsd:element name = "title" type = "xsd:string" />
22        </xsd:sequence>
23     </xsd:complexType>
24
25   </xsd:schema>
```

Fig. 15.12 XSD Schema document to which **book.xml** conforms.

In W3C XML Schema, element *element* (line 10) defines an element. Attributes *name* and *type* specify the **element**'s name and data type, respectively. In this case, the name of the element is **books** and the data type is **deitel:BooksType**. Any element (e.g., **books**) that contains attributes or child elements must define a *complex type*, which defines each attribute and child element. Type **deitel:BooksType** (lines 12–17) is an example of a complex type. We prefix **BooksType** with **deitel**, because this is a complex type that we have created, not an existing W3C XML Schema data type.

Lines 12–17 use element ***complexType*** to define an element type that has a child element named **book**. Because **book** contains a child element, its type must be a complex type (e.g., **BookType**). Attribute ***minOccurs*** specifies that **books** must contain a minimum of one **book** element. Attribute ***maxOccurs***, with value ***unbounded*** (line 14) specifies that **books** may have any number of **book** child elements. Element ***sequence*** specifies the order of elements in the complex type.

Lines 19–23 define the **complexType BookType**. Line 21 defines element **title** with **type *xsd:string***. When an element has a *simple type* such as **xsd:string**, it is prohibited from containing attributes and child elements. W3C XML Schema provides a large number of data types such as ***xsd:date*** for dates, ***xsd:int*** for integers, ***xsd:double*** for floating-point numbers and ***xsd:time*** for time.

The Schema in Fig. 15.12 indicates that every **book** element must contain child element **title**. If this element is omitted, the document is well formed, but not valid. If we remove line 8 from Fig. 15.11, XSV displays the error message shown in Fig. 15.13.

15.7 XML Vocabularies

XML allows document authors to create their own tags to describe data precisely. People and organizations in various fields of study have created many different XML vocabularies for structuring data. Some of these vocabularies are: *MathML* (*Mathematical Markup Language*), *Scalable Vector Graphics* (*SVG*), *Wireless Markup Language* (*WML*), *Extensible Business Reporting Language* (*XBRL*), *Extensible User Interface Language* (*XUL*) and *VoiceXML*™. Two other examples of XML vocabularies are W3C XML Schema and the

```
C:\PROGRA~1\XSV>xsv /pythonhtp1/pythonhtp1_examples/Ch15/Schema/
book.xml /pythonhtp1/pythonhtp1_examples/Ch15/Schema/book.xsd

<?xml version='1.0'?>
<xsv docElt='{http://www.deitel.com/booklist}books' instanceAs-
sessed='true' instanceErrors='1' rootType='{http://www.deitel.com/
booklist}:BooksType' schemaDocs='/pythonhtp1/pythonhtp1_examples/Ch15/
Schema/book.xsd' schemaErrors='0' target='file:/pythonhtp1/
pythonhtp1_examples/Ch15/Schema/book.xml' validation='strict' ver-
sion='XSV 1.203.2.37/1.106.2.19 of 2001/11/29 11:00:00' xmlns='http://
www.w3.org/2000/05/xsv'>
<schemaDocAttempt URI='file:/pythonhtp1/pythonhtp1_examples/Ch15/Sche-
ma/book.xsd' outcome='success' source='command line'/>
<invalid char='4' code='cvc-complex-type.1.2.4' line='8' re-
source='file:/pythonhtp1/pythonhtp1_examples/Ch15/Schema/
book.xml'>content of book is not allowed to end here (1), expecting
['{None}:title']:
<fsm>
<node id='1'>
<edge dest='2' label='{None}:title'/>
</node>
<node final='true' id='2'/>
</fsm></invalid>
</xsv>
```

Fig. 15.13 XML document that does not conform to a W3C XML Schema.

Extensible Stylesheet Language (XSL), which is introduced in Section 15.8. The following subsections describe MathML, Chemical Markup Language (CML) and other XML vocabularies.

15.7.1 MathML™

Until recently, computers typically required specialized software packages such as TeX and LaTeX to display complex mathematical expressions. This section introduces MathML, which the W3C developed for describing mathematical notations and expressions. One application that can parse and render MathML is the W3C's *Amaya*™ browser/editor, which can be downloaded at no charge from

www.w3.org/Amaya/User/BinDist.html

This Web page contains download links for the Windows 95/98/NT/2000, Linux® and Solaris™ platforms. Amaya documentation and installation notes also are available at the W3C Web site.

MathML markup describes mathematical expressions for display. Figure 15.14 uses MathML to mark up a simple expression. [*Note*: In this section, we provide sample outputs that illustrate how a MathML-enabled application might render the markup.]

```
1   <?xml version="1.0"?>
2
3   <!DOCTYPE html PUBLIC "-//W3C//DTD XHTML 1.0 Transitional//EN"
4       "http://www.w3.org/TR/xhtml1/DTD/xhtml1-transitional.dtd">
5
6   <!-- Fig. 15.14: mathml1.html -->
7   <!-- Simple MathML.           -->
8
9   <html xmlns = "http://www.w3.org/1999/xhtml">
10
11      <head><title>Simple MathML Example</title></head>
12
13      <body>
14
15         <math xmlns = "http://www.w3.org/1998/Math/MathML">
16
17            <mrow>
18               <mn>2</mn>
19               <mo>+</mo>
20               <mn>3</mn>
21               <mo>=</mo>
22               <mn>5</mn>
23            </mrow>
24
25         </math>
26
27      </body>
28   </html>
```

Fig. 15.14 Expression marked up with MathML. (Part 1 of 2.)

$$(2 + 3 = 5)$$

Fig. 15.14 Expression marked up with MathML. (Part 2 of 2.)

We embed the MathML content into an XHTML document by using a **math** element with the default namespace **http://www.w3.org/1998/Math/MathML** (line 15). The **mrow** *element* (line 17) is a container element for expressions that contain more than one element. In this case, the **mrow** element contains five children. The **mn** *element* (line 18) marks up a number. The **mo** *element* (line 19) marks up an operator (e.g., +). Using this markup, we define the expression $2 + 3 = 5$, which a software program that supports MathML could display.

Let us now consider using MathML to mark up an algebraic equation that uses exponents and arithmetic operators (Fig. 15.15).

```
1   <?xml version="1.0"?>
2
3   <!DOCTYPE html PUBLIC "-//W3C//DTD XHTML 1.0 Transitional//EN"
4       "http://www.w3.org/TR/xhtml1/DTD/xhtml1-transitional.dtd">
5
6   <!-- Fig. 15.15: mathml2.html -->
7   <!-- Simple MathML.            -->
8
9   <html xmlns = "http://www.w3.org/1999/xhtml">
10
11      <head><title>Algebraic MathML Example</title></head>
12
13      <body>
14
15         <math xmlns = "http://www.w3.org/1998/Math/MathML">
16            <mrow>
17
18               <mrow>
19                  <mn>3</mn>
20                  <mo>&InvisibleTimes;</mo>
21
22                  <msup>
23                     <mi>x</mi>
24                     <mn>2</mn>
25                  </msup>
26
27               </mrow>
28
29               <mo>+</mo>
30               <mi>x</mi>
31               <mo>-</mo>
32
33               <mfrac>
34                  <mn>2</mn>
35                  <mi>x</mi>
36               </mfrac>
```

Fig. 15.15 Algebraic equation marked up with MathML. (Part 1 of 2.)

```
37
38                    <mo>=</mo>
39                    <mn>0</mn>
40
41              </mrow>
42         </math>
43
44     </body>
45 </html>
```

$$3x^2 + x - \frac{2}{x} = 0$$

Fig. 15.15 Algebraic equation marked up with MathML. (Part 2 of 2.)

Element **mrow** behaves like parentheses, which allow the document author to group related elements properly. Line 20 uses entity reference **⁢** to indicate a multiplication operation without a *symbolic representation* (i.e., the multiplication symbol does not appear between the **3** and **x**). For exponentiation, line 22 uses the **msup** element, which represents a superscript. This **msup** element has two children—the expression to be superscripted (i.e., the base) and the superscript (i.e., the exponent). Similarly, the **msub** element represents a subscript. To display variables such as **x**, line 23 uses *identifier element **mi***.

To display a fraction, line 33 uses element **mfrac**. Lines 34–35 specify the numerator and the denominator for the fraction. If either the numerator or the denominator contains more than one element, it must be nested in an **mrow** element.

Figure 15.16 marks up a calculus expression that contains an integral symbol and a square-root symbol.

```
1  <?xml version="1.0"?>
2
3  <!DOCTYPE html PUBLIC "-//W3C//DTD XHTML 1.0 Transitional//EN"
4      "http://www.w3.org/TR/xhtml1/DTD/xhtml1-transitional.dtd">
5
6  <!-- Fig. 15.16: mathml3.html      -->
7  <!-- Calculus example using MathML. -->
8
9  <html xmlns = "http://www.w3.org/1999/xhtml">
10
11     <head><title>Calculus MathML Example</title></head>
12
13     <body>
14
15        <math xmlns = "http://www.w3.org/1998/Math/MathML">
16           <mrow>
17              <msubsup>
18
19                 <mo>&Integral;</mo>
20                 <mn>0</mn>
```

Fig. 15.16 Calculus expression marked up with MathML. (Part 1 of 2.)

```
21
22                    <mrow>
23                        <mn>1</mn>
24                        <mo>-</mo>
25                        <mi>y</mi>
26                    </mrow>
27
28                </msubsup>
29
30                <msqrt>
31                    <mrow>
32
33                        <mn>4</mn>
34                        <mo>&InvisibleTimes;</mo>
35
36                        <msup>
37                            <mi>x</mi>
38                            <mn>2</mn>
39                        </msup>
40
41                        <mo>+</mo>
42                        <mi>y</mi>
43
44                    </mrow>
45                </msqrt>
46
47                <mo>&delta;</mo>
48                <mi>x</mi>
49            </mrow>
50        </math>
51    </body>
52 </html>
```

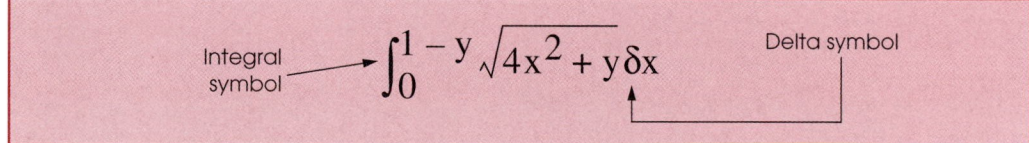

Fig. 15.16 Calculus expression marked up with MathML. (Part 2 of 2.)

The entity reference **∫** (line 19) represents the integral symbol, while the **msubsup** element (line 17) specifies the superscript and subscript. Element **mo** marks up the integral operator. Element **msubsup** requires three child elements—an operator (e.g., the integral entity reference), the subscript expression (line 20) and the superscript expression (lines 22–26). Element **mn** (line 20) marks up the number (i.e., **0**) that represents the subscript. Element **mrow** marks up the expression (i.e., **1-y**) that specifies the superscript expression

Element **msqrt** (lines 30–45) represents a square root expression. Line 31 uses element **mrow** to group the expression contained in the square root. Line 47 introduces entity reference **δ** for representing a delta symbol. Delta is an operator, so line 47 places this entity reference in element **mo**. To see other operations and symbols in MathML, visit **www.w3.org/Math**.

15.7.2 Chemical Markup Language (CML)

Chemical Markup Language (*CML*) is an XML vocabulary for representing molecular and chemical information. Although many of our readers will not know the chemistry required to understand the example in this section fully, we feel that CML so beautifully illustrates the purpose of XML that we chose to include the example for the readers who wish to see XML "at its best." Document authors can edit and view CML, using the *Jumbo browser*[6], which is available at **www.xml-cml.org**. Figure 15.17 shows an ammonia molecule marked up in CML.

Lines 1–2 contain a *processing instruction* (*PI*), which contains application-specific information embedded in an XML document. The characters **<?** and **?>** delimit a processing instruction. The processing instruction of lines 1–2 provides application-specific information to the Jumbo browser. Processing instructions consist of a *PI target* (e.g.,

```
1   <?jumbo:namespace ns = "http://www.xml-cml.org"
2      prefix = "C" java = "jumbo.cmlxml.*Node" ?>
3
4   <!-- Fig. 15.17: ammonia.xml -->
5   <!-- Structure of ammonia.    -->
6
7   <C:molecule id = "Ammonia">
8
9      <C:atomArray builtin = "elsym">
10        N H H H
11     </C:atomArray>
12
13     <C:atomArray builtin = "x2" type = "float">
14        1.5 0.0 1.5 3.0
15     </C:atomArray>
16
17     <C:atomArray builtin = "y2" type = "float">
18        1.5 1.5 0.0 1.5
19     </C:atomArray>
20
21     <C:bondArray builtin = "atid1">
22        1 1 1
23     </C:bondArray>
24
25     <C:bondArray builtin = "atid2">
26        2 3 4
27     </C:bondArray>
28
29     <C:bondArray builtin = "order" type = "integer">
30        1 1 1
31     </C:bondArray>
32
33   </C:molecule>
```

Fig. 15.17 CML markup for ammonia molecule. (Part 1 of 2.)

---

6. At the time of this writing, Jumbo did not allow users to load documents for rendering. For illustration purposes, we created the image shown in Fig. 15.17.

Ammonia

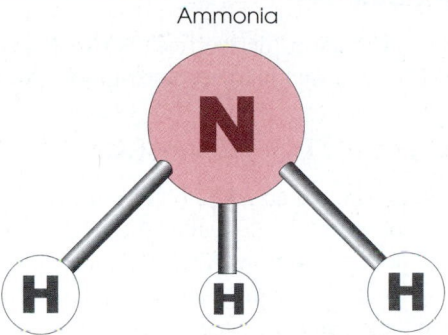

Fig. 15.17 CML markup for ammonia molecule. (Part 2 of 2.)

`jumbo:namespace`) and a *PI value* (e.g., `ns = "http://www.xml-cml.org"`
`prefix = "C" java = "jumbo.cmlxml.*Node"`).

Portability Tip 15.3

Processing instructions allow document authors to embed application-specific information in an XML document, without affecting that document's portability.

Line 7 defines an ammonia molecule using element *molecule*. Attribute *id* identifies this molecule as **Ammonia**. Lines 9–11 use element *atomArray* and attribute *builtin* to specify the molecule's atoms. Ammonia contains one nitrogen atom and three hydrogen atoms.

Lines 13–15 show element **atomArray** with attribute **builtin** assigned the value *x2* and *type float*. This specifies that the element contains a list of floating-point numbers, each of which indicates the *x*-coordinate of an atom. The first value (**1.5**) is the *x*-coordinate of the first atom (nitrogen), the second value (**0.0**) is the *x*-coordinate of the second atom (the first hydrogen atom) and so on.

Lines 17–19 show element **atomArray** with attribute **builtin** assigned the value *y2* and *type float*. This specifies that the element contains a list of *y*-coordinate values. The first value (**1.5**) is the *y*-coordinate of the first atom (nitrogen), the second value (**1.5**) is the *y*-coordinate of the second atom (the first hydrogen atom) and so on.

Lines 21–23 show element *bondArray* with attribute **builtin** assigned the value *atid1*. Element **bondArray** defines the bonds between atoms. This element has a **builtin** value of **atid1**, so the values this element specifies compose the first atom in a pair of atoms. We are defining three bonds, so we specify three values. For each value, we specify the first atom in the **atomArray**, the nitrogen atom.

Lines 25–27 show element **bondArray** with attribute **builtin** assigned the value *atid2*. The values of this element compose the second atom in a pair of atoms and denote the three hydrogen atoms.

Lines 29–31 show element **bondArray** with the attribute **builtin** assigned the value *order* and *type integer*. The values of this element are integers that represent the number of bonds between the pairs of atoms. Thus, the bond between the nitrogen atom and the first hydrogen is a single bond, the bond between the nitrogen atom and the second hydrogen atom is a single bond, and the bond between the nitrogen atom and the third hydrogen atom is a single bond.

15.7.3 Other XML Vocabularies

Literally hundreds of XML vocabularies derive from XML. Every day, developers find new uses for XML. In Fig. 15.18, we summarize some of these vocabularies.

15.8 Extensible Stylesheet Language (XSL)[7]

Extensible Stylesheet Language (XSL) is an XML vocabulary for formatting XML data. In this section, we discuss the portion of XSL—called *XSL Transformations* (*XSLT*)—that creates formatted text-based documents from XML documents. This process is called a *transformation* and involves two tree structures—the *source tree*, which is the XML document being transformed, and the *result tree*, which is the result (e.g., Extensible Hypertext Markup Language or XHTML[8]) of the transformation. The source tree is not modified when a transformation occurs.

Vocabulary	Description
VoiceXML™	The VoiceXML forum founded by AT&T, IBM, Lucent and Motorola developed VoiceXML. It provides interactive voice communication between humans and computers through a telephone, PDA (personal digital assistant) or desktop computer. IBM's VoiceXML SDK can process VoiceXML documents. Visit **www.voicexml.org** for more information on VoiceXML.
Synchronous Multimedia Integration Language (SMIL™)	SMIL is an XML vocabulary for multimedia presentations. The W3C was the primary developer of SMIL, with contributions from other companies. Visit **www.w3.org/AudioVideo** for more on SMIL.
Research Information Exchange Markup Language (RIXML)	RIXML, which a consortium of brokerage firms developed, marks up investment data. Visit **www.rixml.org** for more information on RIXML.
ComicsML	A language developed by Jason MacIntosh for marking up comics. Visit **www.jmac.org/projects/comics_ml** for more information on ComicsML.
Geography Markup Language (GML)	The OpenGIS developed the GML to describe geographic information. Visit **www.opengis.org** for more information on GML.
Extensible User Interface Language (XUL)	The Mozilla project created XUL for describing graphical user interfaces in a platform-independent way. For more information visit: **www.mozilla.org/xpfe/languageSpec.html**.

Fig. 15.18 XML Vocabularies.

---

7. The example in this section requires msxml 3.0 or higher to run. For more information on downloading and installing msxml 3.0, visit **www.deitel.com**.
8. XHTML is the W3C Recommendation that replaces HTML for marking up content for the Web. For more information on XHTML, see the XHTML Appendices I and J.

To perform transformations, an XSLT processor is required. Popular XSLT processors include Microsoft's msxml, the Apache Software Foundation's *Xalan 2* and the Python package *4XSLT* (which we use in Chapter 16, Python XML Processing). The XML document in Fig. 15.19 is transformed by msxml into an XHTML document using the XSLT document in Fig. 15.20.

Line 6 is a processing instruction specific to IE that specifies the location of the XSLT document to apply to this XML document. Figure 15.20 presents the XSLT document (**sorting.xsl**) that transforms **sorting.xml** (Fig. 15.19) to XHTML.

Performance Tip 15.5

Using Internet Explorer on the client to process XSLT documents conserves server resources by using the client's processing power (instead of having the server process XSLT documents for multiple clients).

```
1   <?xml version = "1.0"?>
2
3   <!-- Fig. 15.19: sorting.xml                      -->
4   <!-- XML document containing book information. -->
5
6   <?xml:stylesheet type = "text/xsl" href = "sorting.xsl"?>
7
8   <book isbn = "999-99999-9-X">
9      <title>Mary&apos;s XML Primer</title>
10
11     <author>
12        <firstName>Mary</firstName>
13        <lastName>White</lastName>
14     </author>
15
16     <chapters>
17        <frontMatter>
18           <preface pages = "2" />
19           <contents pages = "5" />
20           <illustrations pages = "4" />
21        </frontMatter>
22
23        <chapter number = "3" pages = "44">
24           Advanced XML</chapter>
25        <chapter number = "2" pages = "35">
26           Intermediate XML</chapter>
27        <appendix number = "B" pages = "26">
28           Parsers and Tools</appendix>
29        <appendix number = "A" pages = "7">
30           Entities</appendix>
31        <chapter number = "1" pages = "28">
32           XML Fundamentals</chapter>
33     </chapters>
34
35     <media type = "CD" />
36  </book>
```

Fig. 15.19 XML document containing book information.

Line 1 of Fig. 15.20 contains the XML declaration. This line is present because an XSLT document is an XML document. Line 6 is the *xsl:stylesheet* root element. Attribute *version* specifies the version of XSLT to which this document conforms. Namespace prefix **xsl** is defined and bound to the XSLT URI defined by the W3C. When processed, lines 11–13 write the document type declaration to the result tree. Attribute *method* is assigned *"xml"*, which indicates that XML is being output to the result tree. Attribute *omit-xml-declaration* is assigned **"no"**, which indicates that an XML declaration will be output to the result tree. Attribute *doctype-system* and *doctype-public* contain the **Doctype** DTD information that is output to the result tree.

```xml
1   <?xml version = "1.0"?>
2
3   <!-- Fig. 15.20: sorting.xsl                        -->
4   <!-- Transformation of book information into XHTML. -->
5
6   <xsl:stylesheet version = "1.0"
7       xmlns:xsl = "http://www.w3.org/1999/XSL/Transform">
8
9       <!-- write XML declaration and DOCTYPE DTD information -->
10      <xsl:output method = "xml" omit-xml-declaration = "no"
11          doctype-system =
12              "http://www.w3.org/TR/xhtml1/DTD/xhtml1-strict.dtd"
13          doctype-public = "-//W3C//DTD XHTML 1.0 Strict//EN"/>
14
15      <!-- match document root -->
16      <xsl:template match = "/">
17          <html xmlns = "http://www.w3.org/1999/xhtml">
18              <xsl:apply-templates />
19          </html>
20      </xsl:template>
21
22      <!-- match book -->
23      <xsl:template match = "book">
24          <head>
25              <title>ISBN <xsl:value-of select = "@isbn" /> -
26                  <xsl:value-of select = "title" /></title>
27          </head>
28
29          <body>
30              <h1 style = "color: blue">
31                  <xsl:value-of select = "title"/></h1>
32
33              <h2 style = "color: blue">by <xsl:value-of
34                  select = "author/lastName" />,
35                  <xsl:value-of select = "author/firstName" /></h2>
36
37              <table style =
38                  "border-style: groove; background-color: wheat">
```

Fig. 15.20 XSLT document that transforms **sorting.xml** into XHTML. (Part 1 of 3.)

```
39
40                     <xsl:for-each select = "chapters/frontMatter/*">
41                        <tr>
42                           <td style = "text-align: right">
43                              <xsl:value-of select = "name()" />
44                           </td>
45
46                           <td>
47                              ( <xsl:value-of select = "@pages" /> pages )
48                           </td>
49                        </tr>
50                     </xsl:for-each>
51
52                     <xsl:for-each select = "chapters/chapter">
53                        <xsl:sort select = "@number" data-type = "number"
54                           order = "ascending" />
55                        <tr>
56                           <td style = "text-align: right">
57                              Chapter <xsl:value-of select = "@number" />
58                           </td>
59
60                           <td>
61                              ( <xsl:value-of select = "@pages" /> pages )
62                           </td>
63                        </tr>
64                     </xsl:for-each>
65
66                     <xsl:for-each select = "chapters/appendix">
67                        <xsl:sort select = "@number" data-type = "text"
68                           order = "ascending" />
69                        <tr>
70                           <td style = "text-align: right">
71                              Appendix <xsl:value-of select = "@number" />
72                           </td>
73
74                           <td>
75                              ( <xsl:value-of select = "@pages" /> pages )
76                           </td>
77                        </tr>
78                     </xsl:for-each>
79                  </table>
80
81                  <p style = "color: blue">Pages:
82                     <xsl:variable name = "pagecount"
83                        select = "sum(chapters//*/@pages)" />
84                     <xsl:value-of select = "$pagecount" />
85                  <br />Media Type:
86                     <xsl:value-of select = "media/@type" /></p>
87            </body>
88      </xsl:template>
89
90   </xsl:stylesheet>
```

Fig. 15.20 XSLT document that transforms **sorting.xml** into XHTML. (Part 2 of 3.)

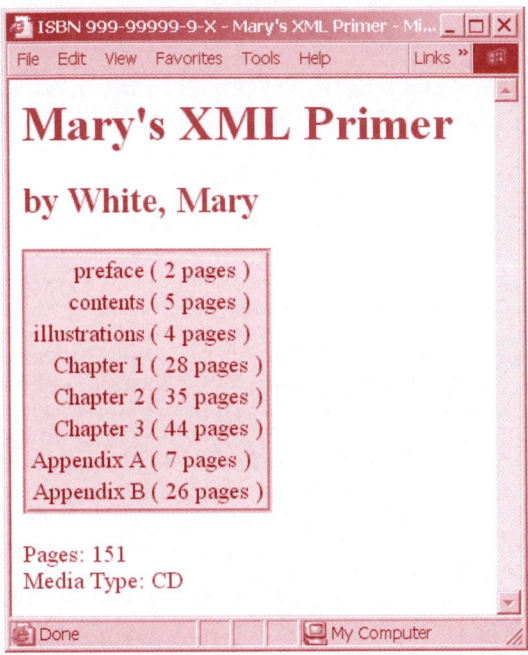

Fig. 15.20 XSLT document that transforms `sorting.xml` into XHTML. (Part 3 of 3.)

XSLT documents contain one or more **xsl:template** elements that specify which information the XSLT processor outputs to the result tree. The template on line 16 **match**es the source tree's document root. When the document root is encountered during the transformation, this **template** is applied, and any text marked up by this element that is not in the namespace referenced by **xsl** is outputted to the result tree. Line 18 calls for all the **template**s that **match** children of the document root to be applied. Line 23 specifies a **template** that **match**es element **book**.

Lines 25–26 create the title for the XHTML document. We use the ISBN of the book from attribute **isbn** and the contents of element **title** to create the title string **ISBN 999-99999-9-X - Mary's XML Primer**. Element **xsl:value-of** selects the **book** element's **isbn** attribute.

Lines 33–35 create a header element that contains the book's author. Because the *context node* (i.e., the current node being processed) is **book**, the expression **author/lastName** selects the author's last name, and the expression **author/firstName** selects the author's first name.

Line 40 selects each element (indicated by an asterisk) that is a child of element **frontMatter**. Line 43 calls *node-set function* **name** to retrieve the current node's element name (e.g., **preface**). The current node is the context node specified in the **xsl:for-each** (line 40).

Lines 53–54 sort **chapter**s by number in ascending order. Attribute **select** selects the value of context node **chapter**'s attribute **number**. Attribute *data-type* with value **"number"**, specifies a numeric sort and attribute *order* specifies **"ascending"** order. Attribute **data-type** also can be assigned the value ***"text"*** (line 67) and attribute **order** also may be assigned the value ***"descending"***.

Lines 82–83 use an *XSLT variable* to store the value of the book's page count and output it to the result tree. Attribute **name** specifies the variable's name, and attribute *select* assigns it a value. Function ***sum*** totals the values for all **page** attribute values. The two slashes between **chapters** and * indicate that all descendent nodes of **chapters** are searched for elements that contain an attribute named **pages**.

Figure 15.21 shows the XHTML that is generated when msxml applies **sorting.xsl** to **sorting.xml**. In Chapter 16, we use several of Python's XML-related packages to apply XSLT style sheets to XML documents.

Notice that the XHTML document contains an XML declaration that is different than what was shown previously. Value ***encoding*** indicates the type of *character encoding* (i.e., a set of numeric values associated with characters) the document uses. This document uses UTF-8, which is well suited for ASCII-based systems. UTF-8 is the default encoding for XML documents. More information on character encoding and UTF-8 may be found in Appendix F, Unicode.

```
 1  <?xml version="1.0" encoding="UTF-8"?>
 2  <!DOCTYPE html PUBLIC "-//W3C//DTD XHTML 1.0 Strict//EN"
 3     "http://www.w3.org/TR/xhtml1/DTD/xhtml1-strict.dtd">
 4
 5  <html xmlns="http://www.w3.org/1999/xhtml">
 6
 7     <head>
 8        <title>ISBN 999-99999-9-X - Mary's XML Primer</title>
 9     </head>
10
11     <body>
12        <h1 style="color: blue">Mary's XML Primer</h1>
13        <h2 style="color: blue">by White, Mary</h2>
14       <table style="border-style: groove; background-color: wheat">
15
16          <tr>
17             <td style="text-align: right">preface</td>
18             <td>( 2 pages )</td>
19          </tr>
20
21          <tr>
22             <td style="text-align: right">contents</td>
23             <td>( 5 pages )</td>
24          </tr>
25
26          <tr>
27             <td style="text-align: right">illustrations</td>
28             <td>( 4 pages )</td>
29          </tr>
30
31          <tr>
32             <td style="text-align: right">Chapter 1</td>
```

Fig. 15.21 XHTML generated when **sorting.xsl** is applied by msxml to **sorting.xml**. (Part 1 of 2.)

```
33              <td>( 28 pages )</td>
34          </tr>
35
36          <tr>
37              <td style="text-align: right">Chapter 2</td>
38              <td>( 35 pages )</td>
39          </tr>
40
41          <tr>
42              <td style="text-align: right">Chapter 3</td>
43              <td>( 44 pages )</td>
44          </tr>
45
46          <tr>
47              <td style="text-align: right">Appendix A</td>
48              <td>( 7 pages )</td>
49          </tr>
50
51          <tr>
52              <td style="text-align: right">Appendix B</td>
53              <td>( 26 pages )</td>
54          </tr>
55
56      </table>
57
58      <p style="color: blue">Pages: 11<br />Media Type: CD</p>
59
60  </body>
61 </html>
```

Fig. 15.21 XHTML generated when **sorting.xsl** is applied by msxml to **sorting.xml**. (Part 2 of 2.)

15.9 Internet and World Wide Web Resources

www.w3.org/xml
The W3C (World Wide Web Consortium) works to develop common protocols to ensure interoperability on the Web. Their XML page includes information about upcoming events, publications, software and discussion groups. Visit this site to read about the latest developments in XML.

www.xml.org
xml.org is a reference for XML, DTDs, Schemas and namespaces. This site also contains news on how XML relates to industry.

www.w3.org/style/XSL
This site provides information on XSL, including what is new in XSL, learning XSL, XSL-enabled tools, the XSL specification, FAQs and the history of XSL.

www.w3.org/TR
This W3C technical reports and publications page contains links to working drafts, proposed recommendations, recommendations and so on.

xml.apache.org
The Apache XML Web site provides many resources related to XML, which include tools and downloads.

www.xmlbooks.com
This site contains a list of XML books recommended by Charles Goldfarb—one of the original designers of GML (General Markup Language), from which XML's parent language SGML (Standard Generalized Markup Language) was derived.

wdvl.internet.com/Authoring/Languages/XML
The *Web Developer's Virtual Library XML* site includes tutorials, FAQ, the latest news and extensive links to XML sites and software downloads.

www.xml.com
Visit **xml.com** for the latest news and information about XML, conference listings, links to XML Web resources organized by topic, tools and more.

msdn.microsoft.com/xml/default.asp
The *MSDN Online XML Development Center* features articles on XML, Ask the Experts chat sessions, samples and demos, newsgroups and other helpful information.

www.oasis-open.org/cover/xml.html
The *SGML/XML Web Page* is an extensive resource that includes links to FAQs, online resources, industry initiatives, demos, conferences and tutorials.

www.gca.org/whats_xml/default.htm
The GCA site has an XML glossary, list of books, brief descriptions of the draft standards for XML and links to online drafts.

www.xmlinfo.com
XMLINFO is a resource site with tutorials, a list of recommended books, documentation, discussion forums and more.

developer.netscape.com/tech/xml/index.html
The *XML and Metadata Developer Central* site has demos, technical notes and news articles related to XML.

www.ucc.ie/xml
This site is a detailed XML FAQ. Submit your own questions through the site.

www.xml-cml.org
This site is a resource for the Chemical Markup Language (CML). It includes a FAQ list, documentation, software and XML links.

SUMMARY

- XML is a widely supported open technology (i.e., nonproprietary technology) for data exchange.

- XML permits document authors to create their own markup for virtually any type of information. This extensibility enables document authors to create entirely new markup languages (called vocabularies) to describe specific types of data, including mathematical formulas, chemical molecular structures, music and recipes.

- XML allows document authors to create their own tags, so naming collisions (i.e., different elements that have the same name) can occur. Namespaces enable document authors to prevent collisions among elements in an XML document.

- Namespace prefixes prepended to tag names specify the namespace in which the element can be found. Each namespace prefix has a corresponding uniform resource identifier (URI) that uniquely identifies the namespace. By definition, a URI is a series of characters that differentiates names. Document authors can create their own namespace prefixes. Document authors can use virtually any namespace prefix except the reserved namespace prefix **xml**.

- To eliminate the need to place a namespace prefix in each element, authors may specify a default namespace for an element and all of its child elements.

- XML documents are highly portable. Opening an XML document does not require special software—any text editor that supports ASCII/Unicode characters will suffice. One important characteristic of XML is that it is both human readable and machine readable.

- Processing an XML document—which typically ends in the **.xml** extension—requires a software program called an XML parser (or an XML processor). Parsers check an XML document's syntax and can support the Document Object Model (DOM) and/or the Simple API for XML (SAX) API.

- DOM-based parsers build a tree structure containing the XML document's data in memory. This allows programs to manipulate the document's data. SAX-based parsers process the document and generate events as the parser encounters tags, text, comments and so on. These events contain data from the XML document.

- An XML document can reference an optional document that defines the XML document's structure. This optional document can be either a Document Type Definition (DTD) or a Schema.

- A DOM tree has a single root node that contains all other nodes in the document. The XML parser exposes these methods and properties as a programmatic library, called an Application Programming Interface (API).

- A node that contains other nodes (called child nodes) is a parent node. Nodes that are peers are sibling nodes. A node's descendant nodes include that node's children, its children's children and so on. A node's ancestor nodes include that node's parent, its parent's parent and so on.

- If the XML document conforms to its DTD or Schema, then the XML document is valid. Parsers that cannot check for document conformity against DTDs or Schemas are called nonvalidating parsers. If an XML parser (validating or nonvalidating) can process an XML document that does not have a DTD or Schema successfully, the XML document is well formed (i.e., it is syntactically correct). By definition, a valid XML document also is a well-formed document.

- The **ATTLIST** element type declaration in a DTD defines an attribute. Keyword **#IMPLIED** specifies that, if the parser finds an element without the attribute, the application can provide a value or ignore the missing attribute. Keyword **#REQUIRED** specifies that the attribute must be in the document, and keyword **#FIXED** specifies that the attribute must have the given value. Flag **CDATA** specifies that an attribute contains data that the parser should not process as markup. Keyword **EMPTY** specifies that the element does not contain any text.

- Flag **#PCDATA** specifies that the element can store parsed character data (i.e., text). Document authors must replace the characters less than (**<**) and ampersand (**&**) with their corresponding entity references (i.e., **<** and **&**).

- Schemas use XML syntax.

- In XML Schema, element **element** defines an element. Attributes **name** and **type** specify the **element**'s name and data type, respectively. Any element that contains attributes or child elements must define a type—called a complex type—that defines each attribute and child element.

- Attribute **minOccurs** specifies the minimum number of occurrences for an element. Attribute **maxOccurs** specifies the maximum number of occurrences for an element.

- When an element is a simple type, such as **xsd:string**, that element cannot contain attributes and child elements.

- MathML markup describes mathematical expressions.

- Chemical Markup Language (CML) marks up molecular and chemical information.

- The characters **<?** and **?>** delimit processing instructions (PIs), which are application-specific information embedded in an XML document. A processing instruction consists of a PI target and a PI value.

- Extensible Stylesheet Language (XSL) documents specify how programs should render an XML document's data. A subset of XSL—XSL Transformations (XSLT)—provides elements that define rules for transforming data from one XML document into another text-based format such as XHTML.

- Transforming an XML document using XSLT involves two tree structures: The source tree (i.e., the XML document being transformed) and the result tree (i.e., the XML document to create).

TERMINOLOGY

ancestor node

asterisk (*****) occurrence indicator

atomArray element

ATTLIST element type declaration

CDATA flag

child node

complexType element

container element

context node

data-type attribute

default namespace

descendent node

doctype-public attribute

doctype-system attribute

document reuse

document root

Document Type Definition (DTD)

DOM (Document Object Model)

DOM API (Application Programming Interface)

DOM-based XML parser

EBNF (Extended Backus-Naur Form) grammar

ELEMENT element type declaration

empty element

EMPTY keyword

event

Extensible Stylesheet Language (XSL)

external DTD

forward slash

#IMPLIED flag

invalid document

match attribute

maxOccurs attribute

minOccurs attribute

mn element

molecule element

mrow element

msqrt element

msub element

msubsup element

msxml parser

name attribute

name node-set function

namespace prefix

node

nonvalidating XML parser

occurrence indicator

order attribute

parent node

parsed character data

parser

#PCDATA flag

PI (processing instruction)

PI target

PI value

plus sign (**+**) occurrence indicator

processing instruction

question mark (**?**) occurrence indicator

result tree

root element

root node

SAX (Simple API for XML)

SAX-based parser

schema element

Schema valid

select attribute

simple type

single-quote character (**'**)

source tree

stylesheet element

sum function

SYSTEM flag

targetNamespace attribute

tree-based model

type attribute

unbounded value

validating XML parser

well-formed document

XML (Extensible Markup Language)

XML declaration

.xml file extension

xml namespace prefix

XML parser

XML processor

XML Schema

XML **version**   **xsl:for-each** element
xmlns keyword   **xsl:output** element
.xsd extension   **xsl:sort** element
XSL (Extensible Stylesheet Language)   **xsl:value-of** element
.xsl extension   XSLT variable
XSL Transformations (XSLT)   XSV (XML Schema Validator)
xsl:apply-templates element

SELF-REVIEW EXERCISES

15.1   Which of the following tag names might be found in a well-formed XML document?
   a) **yearBorn**.
   b) **year.Born**.
   c) **year Born**.
   d) **year-Born1**.
   e) **2_year_born**.
   f) **--year/born**.
   g) **year*born**.
   h) **.year_born**.
   i) **_year_born_**.
   j) **y_e-a_r-b_o-r_n**.

15.2   State whether each of the following is *true* or *false*. If *false*, explain why.
   a) XML is a technology for creating markup languages.
   b) Forward and backward slashes (**/** and ****) delimit XML markup text.
   c) All XML start tags must have corresponding end tags.
   d) Parsers check an XML document's syntax.
   e) **XML**, in any mixture of case, is a reserved namespace prefix.
   f) When creating XML documents, document authors must use the set of XML tags that the W3C provides.
   g) In an XML document, the pound character (**#**), the dollar sign (**$**), ampersand (**&**), greater-than (**>**) and less-than (**<**) must be replaced with their corresponding entity references.

15.3   Fill in the blanks for each of the following statements:
   a) MathML element _____ defines a mathematical operator.
   b) _____ help avoid naming collisions.
   c) _____ embed application-specific information into an XML document.
   d) _____ is Microsoft's XML parser.
   e) XSL element _____ inserts a **DOCTYPE** in the result tree.
   f) XML Schema documents have root element _____.
   g) Element _____ marks up the **∫** MathML entity reference.
   h) _____ defines attributes in a DTD.
   i) XSL element _____ is the root element in an XSL document.
   j) XSL element _____ selects specific XML elements using repetition.

15.4   State whether each of the following is *true* or *false*. If *false*, explain why.
   a) XML is not case sensitive.
   b) An XML document may contain only one root element.
   c) XML is a formatting language.
   d) A DTD/Schema defines the style of an XML document.
   e) MathML is an XML vocabulary.
   f) XSL is an acronym for XML Stylesheet Language.

g) The `<!ELEMENT list (item*)>` defines element `list` as containing one or more `item` elements.

h) XML documents must have the `.xml` extension.

15.5 Find the error(s) in each of the following and explain how to correct it (them).

a) ```
<job>
    <title>Manager</title>
    <task number = "42">
</job>
```

b) ```
<mfrac>
    <mi>x</mi>
    <mo>+</mo>
    <mn>4</mn>
    <mi>y</mi>
</mfrac>
```

c) `<company name = "Deitel & Associates, Inc." />`

15.6 What is the `#PCDATA` flag used for?

15.7 Write a processing instruction for Internet Explorer that includes the style sheet `wap.xsl`.

ANSWERS TO SELF-REVIEW EXERCISES

15.1 a, b, d, i, j. [Choice c is incorrect because it contains a space; Choice e is incorrect because the first character is a number; Choice f is incorrect because it contains a division symbol (`/`) and does not begin with a letter or underscore; Choice g is incorrect because it contains an asterisk (`*`); Choice h is incorrect because the first character is a period (`.`) and does not begin with a letter or underscore.]

15.2 a) True. b) False. In an XML document, markup text is delimited by angle brackets (`<` and `>`) with a forward slash being used in the end tag. c) True. d) True. e) True. f) False. When creating tags, document authors may use any permissible name except the reserved word `xml` in any mixture of case. g) False. The ampersand (`&`) and the left-angle bracket (`<`) must be replaced with their entity references.

15.3 a) `mo`. b) namespaces. c) processing instructions. d) msxml. e) `xsl:output`. f) `Schema`. g) `mo`. h) `ATTLIST`. i) `xsl:stylesheet`. j) `xsl:for-each`.

15.4 a) False. XML is case sensitive. b) True. c) False. XML organizes data in a structured manner. d) False. A DTD/Schema defines an XML document's structure. e) True. f) False. XSL is an acronym for Extensible Stylesheet Language. g) False. Element `list` can contain any number of optional `item` elements. h) False. An XML document can have any extension.

15.5 a) The closing `/` in empty element `task` is missing:

`<task number = "42"/>`

b) `<mrow>` tag is needed to contain $x + 4$.

c) The ampersand must be replaced with `&amp;`:

`<company name = "Deitel &amp; Associates, Inc." />`

15.6 Flag `#PCDATA` denotes that parsed character data is contained in the element.

15.7 `<?xsl:stylesheet type = "text/xsl" href = "wap.xsl"?>`

EXERCISES

15.8 Create an XML document that marks up the nutrition facts for a package of Grandma Deitel's Cookies. A package of Grandma Deitel's Cookies has a serving size of 1 package and the following nutritional value per serving: 260 calories, 100 fat calories, 11 grams of fat, 2 grams of saturated fat,

5 milligrams of cholesterol, 210 milligrams of sodium, 36 grams of total carbohydrates, 2 grams of fiber, 15 grams of sugar and 5 grams of protein. Load the XML document in Internet Explorer. [*Hint*: Your markup should contain elements that describe the product name, serving size/amount, calories, sodium, cholesterol, protein, etc. Mark up each nutrition fact/ingredient listed above.]

15.9   Write an XSLT style sheet for your solution to Exercise 15.8 that displays the nutritional facts in an XHTML table.

15.10   Write an XML document that marks up the following information in Fig. 15.22.

15.11   Write a DTD for the XML document in Exercise 15.10.

15.12   Modify your solution to Exercise 15.10 to qualify each person with a namespace prefix corresponding to their job. Your solution should not contain any elements or attributes that identify a person's job.

15.13   Write an XSLT document that transforms the XML document of Exercise 15.10 into an XHTML sorted table.

15.14   Modify Fig. 15.20 (`sorting.xsl`) to sort each section (i.e., front matter, chapters and appendix) of the book by page number, rather than by section.

Name	Job	Department	Cubicle
Joe	Programmer	Engineering	5E
Erin	Designer	Marketing	9M
Melissa	Designer	Human Resources	8H
Craig	Administrator	Engineering	4E
Eileen	Project Coordinator	Marketing	3M
Danielle	Programmer	Engineering	12E
Frank	Salesperson	Marketing	17M
Corinne	Programmer	Technical Support	19T

Fig. 15.22 Information for Exercise 15.10.

16

Python XML Processing

Objectives

- To create XML markup programmatically.
- To use the Document Object Model (DOM™) to manipulate XML documents.
- To use the Simple API for XML (SAX) to retrieve data from XML documents.
- To create an XML-based message forum.

Knowing trees, I understand the meaning of patience.
Knowing grass, I can appreciate persistence.
Hal Borland

I think that I shall never see
A poem lovely as a tree.
Joyce Kilmer

I played with an idea, and grew willful; tossed it into the air;
transformed it; let it escape and recaptured it; made it
iridescent with fancy, and winged it with paradox.
Oscar Wilde

16.1 Introduction

In Chapter 15, we introduced XML and various XML-related technologies. In this chapter, we demonstrate how Python applications and scripts can process XML documents. Support for XML is provided through a large collection of freely available Python packages and modules. This chapter focuses on the two of these Python packages: **4DOM** and **xml.sax**.

In this chapter, we discuss how to generate XML content programatically. We introduce DOM- and SAX-based parsing for programmatically manipulating an XML document's data. The chapter concludes with a case study that uses XML to mark up an online message forum's data.

16.2 Generating XML Content Dynamically

The process by which Python applications can generate XML dynamically is similar to the process by which they generate XHTML. For example, to output XML from a Python script, we can use **print** statements or we can use XSLT.

In this section, we present a simple Python script that creates an XML document from data in a text file (Fig. 16.1). The XML markup is sent to the browser via **print** statements. In Section 16.4, we present more sophisticated techniques for creating and manipulating XML documents. Figure 16.2 is the Python script that marks up the text file's data as XML. [*Note*: Files **names.txt**, **fig16_02.py** and **contact_list.xsl** must be placed in the correct directories for this example to be served by Apache. Specifically, **names.txt** and **fig16_02.py** must be located in Apache's **cgi-bin** directory. **contact_list.xsl** must be located in a directory called **XML** under Apache's **htdocs** directory. The correct directory structure can also be seen in Fig. 16.19.]

```
1   O'Black, John
2   Green, Sue
```

Fig. 16.1   Text file **names.txt** used in Fig. 16.2. (Part 1 of 2.)

```
3    Red, Bob
4    Blue, Mary
5    White, Mike
6    Brown, Jane
7    Gray, Bill
```

Fig. 16.1   Text file **names.txt** used in Fig. 16.2. (Part 2 of 2.)

```
1    #!c:\Python\python.exe
2    # Fig. 16.2: fig16_02.py
3    # Marking up a text file's data as XML.
4
5    import sys
6
7    print "Content-type: text/xml\n"
8
9    # write XML declaration and processing instruction
10   print """<?xml version = "1.0"?>
11   <?xml:stylesheet type = "text/xsl"
12      href = "../XML/contact_list.xsl"?>"""
13
14   # open data file
15   try:
16      file = open( "names.txt", "r" )
17   except IOError:
18      sys.exit( "Error opening file" )
19
20   print "<contacts>" # write root element
21
22   # list of tuples: ( special character, entity reference )
23   replaceList = [ ( "&", "&amp;" ),
24                   ( "<", "&lt;" ),
25                   ( ">", "&gt;" ),
26                   ( '"', "&quot;" ),
27                   ( "'", "&apos;" ) ]
28
29   # replace special characters with entity references
30   for currentLine in file.readlines():
31
32      for oldValue, newValue in replaceList:
33         currentLine = currentLine.replace( oldValue, newValue )
34
35      # extract lastname and firstname
36      last, first = currentLine.split( ", " )
37      first = first.strip() # remove carriage return
38
39      # write contact element
40      print """   <contact>
41         <LastName>%s</LastName>
42         <FirstName>%s</FirstName>
43      </contact>""" % ( last, first )
44
```

Fig. 16.2   Marking up a text file's data as XML. (Part 1 of 2.)

```
45   file.close()
46
47   print "</contacts>"
```

Fig. 16.2   Marking up a text file's data as XML. (Part 2 of 2.)

Line 7 prints the HTTP header, which sets the MIME type to **text/xml**. Lines 10–12 print the XML declaration and a processing instruction for Internet Explorer. The processing instruction references the XSLT style sheet **contact_list.xsl** (Fig. 16.3).

After the script prints the headers, lines 15–18 open the file (or exit, if the file could not be opened). Line 20 prints the **<contacts>** start tag of the root element. A list of five tuples is created in lines 23–27. Each tuple contains two values: a character and an entity reference that corresponds to that character. The **for** loop in lines 30–43 generates XML elements for each name in the file. Lines 32–33 call method **replace** to substitute characters (e.g., **<, &,** etc.) with their corresponding entity references. The **split** method (line 36) extracts the last name and first name from the line read from the file. Line 37 removes any whitespace (e.g., a carriage return) from the first name. The XML element containing the person's name is printed in lines 40–43. Finally, line 47 prints the root element's end tag.

```
1    <?xml version = "1.0"?>
2    <!-- Fig. 16.3: contact_list.xsl -->
3    <!-- Formats a contact list      -->
4
5    <xsl:stylesheet version = "1.0"
6       xmlns:xsl = "http://www.w3.org/1999/XSL/Transform">
7
8       <!-- match document root -->
9       <xsl:template match = "/">
10
11          <html xmlns = "http://www.w3.org/1999/xhtml">
12
```

Fig. 16.3   XSLT used to format contact list. (Part 1 of 2.)

```
13                   <head>
14                       <title>Contact List</title>
15                   </head>
16
17                   <body>
18                       <table border = "1">
19
20                           <thead>
21                               <tr>
22                                   <th>First Name</th>
23                                   <th>Last Name</th>
24                               </tr>
25                           </thead>
26
27                           <!-- process each contact element -->
28                           <xsl:for-each select = "contacts/contact">
29                               <tr>
30                                   <td>
31                                       <xsl:value-of select = "FirstName" />
32                                   </td>
33                                   <td>
34                                       <xsl:value-of select = "LastName" />
35                                   </td>
36                               </tr>
37                           </xsl:for-each>
38
39                       </table>
40
41                   </body>
42
43               </html>
44
45       </xsl:template>
46
47   </xsl:stylesheet>
```

Fig. 16.3   XSLT used to format contact list. (Part 2 of 2.)

16.3 XML Processing Packages

In the remaining sections of this chapter, we provide several examples of XML processing using the Document Object Model (DOM) and Simple API for XML (SAX). At the time of this writing, the modules included with Python for DOM manipulation were **xml.minidom** and **xml.pulldom**. Neither of these DOM implementations is fully compliant with the W3C's DOM Recommendation. Therefore, we use a third-party package called **4DOM**, which fully complies with the W3C's DOM Recommendation. **4DOM** is included with the package **PyXML**[1] (**pyxml.sourceforge.net**). The classes and functions provided by **4DOM** are located in **xml.dom.ext**.

In Section 16.5, we use a package that is included with Python[2]—**xml.sax**—that contains classes and functions for SAX-based parsing.

---

1. Visit **www.deitel.com** for installation instructions.
2. Version 2.0 and higher.

Another package, *4XSLT*, contains an XSLT processor for transforming XML documents into other text-based formats. **4XSLT** is located in a package called *4Suite*[3] (**4suite.org**), from Fourthought, Inc. The classes and functions provided by **4XSLT** are located in **xml.xslt**.

16.4 Document Object Model (DOM)

In Chapter 15, we introduced the Document Object Model (DOM). In this section, we demonstrate how to use Python and the DOM API to manipulate XML documents programatically.

Figure 16.4 takes an XML document (Fig. 16.5) that marks up an article and uses the DOM implementation included in **4DOM** to display the document's element names and values.

```
1   # Fig. 16.4: fig16_04.py
2   # Using 4DOM to traverse an XML Document.
3
4   import sys
5   from xml.dom.ext import StripXml
6   from xml.dom.ext.reader import PyExpat
7   from xml.parsers.expat import ExpatError
8
9   # open XML file
10  try:
11      file = open( "article2.xml" )
12  except IOError:
13      sys.exit( "Error opening file" )
14
15  # parse contents of XML file
16  try:
17      reader = PyExpat.Reader()                # create Reader instance
18      document = reader.fromStream( file ) # parse XML document
19      file.close()
20  except ExpatError:
21      sys.exit( "Error processing XML file" )
22
23  # get root element
24  rootElement = StripXml( document.documentElement )
25  print "Here is the root element of the document: %s" % \
26      rootElement.nodeName
27
28  # traverse all child nodes of root element
29  print "The following are its child elements:"
30
31  for node in rootElement.childNodes:
32      print node.nodeName
33
```

Fig. 16.4   Traversing an XML document. (Part 1 of 2.)

3. **PyXML** must be installed prior to installing **4Suite**. Visit **www.deitel.com** for installation instructions.

```
34  # get first child node of root element
35  child = rootElement.firstChild
36  print "\nThe first child of root element is:", child.nodeName
37  print "whose next sibling is:",
38
39  # get next sibling of first child
40  sibling = child.nextSibling
41  print sibling.nodeName
42  print 'Value of "%s" is:' % sibling.nodeName,
43
44  value = sibling.firstChild
45
46  # print text value of sibling
47  print value.nodeValue
48  print "Parent node of %s is: %s" % \
49     ( sibling.nodeName, sibling.parentNode.nodeName )
50
51  reader.releaseNode( document ) # remove DOM tree from memory
```

```
Here is the root element of the document: article
The following are its child elements:
title
date
author
summary
content

The first child of root element is: title
whose next sibling is: date
Value of "date" is: December 19, 2001
Parent node of date is: article
```

Fig. 16.4   Traversing an XML document. (Part 2 of 2.)

Lines 10–11 attempt to open **article2.xml** for reading. If the file cannot be opened, the program exits with the message **"Error opening file"** (lines 12–13). Line 17 instantiates a *PyExpat Reader* object, which is an instance of a DOM-based parser. Module **PyExpat** is located in **4DOM**'s *reader* package. Line 18 passes the XML document referenced by **file** to **Reader** method *fromStream*, which parses the document and loads the XML document's data into memory. Variable **document** references the DOM tree (called a *Document*) returned by **fromStream**.

A **Document** object's *documentElement* attribute refers to the **Document**'s root element node. Line 24 passes the root element node to **4DOM**'s *StripXml* function, which removes insignificant whitespace (e.g., the carriage return line feeds and spaces used for indentation) from an XML DOM tree. If **StripXml** is not called, insignificant whitespace would be stored in the DOM tree. Recall from Chapter 15, that a DOM tree contains a set of nodes. Each node in a DOM tree is of a type derived from class *Node*. We say more about these derived classes momentarily.

Lines 25–26 print the name of **rootElement** via its *nodeName* attribute. A **Node** object's *childNodes* attribute is a list of that **Node**'s children. Lines 31–32 print the

nodeName of each child node of **rootElement**. Lines 35–49 then print the names of specific nodes. A **Node** object's *firstChild* attribute corresponds to the first child node in that **Node**'s list of children. Lines 35–36 assign the first child of **rootElement** to variable **child** and print the child's name.

Line 40 assigns the next sibling of **child** to variable **sibling**. Attribute *nextSibling* contains a node's next sibling (i.e., the next node that has the same parent node). For example, **title**, **date**, **author**, **summary** and **content** are sibling nodes. Line 41 prints **sibling**'s name.

Line 44 assigns the first child node of **sibling** to variable **value**. In this case, **value** is a *Text* node that represents the contents of **sibling**. **Text** nodes contain character data. Line 47 prints the text contained in **value** by accessing its *nodeValue* attribute. Lines 48–49 print **sibling**'s parent node. Parent nodes are obtained through the *parentNode* attribute. Finally, line 51 calls **Reader** method **releaseNode**, which removes the specified **Document** (i.e., DOM tree) from memory.

Good Programming Practice 16.1

*Although not required in Python version 2.0 and higher, calling method **releaseNode** ensures that a DOM tree is freed from memory.*

The classes that inherit from **Node** represent the various XML node types. The **Document** node represents the entire XML document (in memory) and provides methods for manipulating its data. **Element** nodes represent XML elements. **Text** nodes represent character data. **Attr** nodes represent XML attributes, and **Comment** nodes represent comments. **Document** nodes can contain **Element**, **Text** and **Comment** nodes. **Element** nodes can contain **Attr**, **Element**, **Text** and **Comment** nodes.

```
1   <?xml version = "1.0"?>
2
3   <!-- Fig. 16.5: article2.xml    -->
4   <!-- Article formatted with XML -->
5
6   <article>
7
8      <title>Simple XML</title>
9
10     <date>December 19, 2001</date>
11
12     <author>
13        <firstName>Jane</firstName>
14        <lastName>Doe</lastName>
15     </author>
16
17     <summary>XML is easy.</summary>
18
19     <content>Once you have mastered XHTML, XML is learned
20        easily. Remember that XML is not for displaying
21        information but for managing information.
22     </content>
23
24  </article>
```

Fig. 16.5 XML document used in Fig. 16.4.

The tables in Fig. 16.6–Fig. 16.12 summarize important DOM attributes and methods for navigating and updating DOM trees. Figure 16.6 describes some **Node** attributes and methods, Fig. 16.7 describes some *NodeList* (i.e., an ordered list of **Node**s) attributes and methods, Fig. 16.8 describes some *NamedNodeMap* (i.e., an unordered dictionary of **Node**s) attributes and methods, Fig. 16.9 describes some **Document** attributes and methods, Fig. 16.10 describes some **Element** attributes and methods, Fig. 16.11 describes some **Attr** attributes and Fig. 16.12 describes a **Text** and **Comment** attribute.

The program in Fig. 16.13 uses the DOM to add names to the contact list XML document, **contacts.xml** (Fig. 16.14). The XML document is loaded into memory, programmatically manipulated and saved to disk (overwriting the previous version).

Attribute/Method	Description
appendChild(*newChild* **)**	Appends *newChild* to the list of child nodes. Returns the appended child node.
attributes	**NamedNodeMap** that contains the attribute nodes for the current node.
childNodes	**NodeList** that contains the node's current children.
firstChild	First child node in the **NodeList** or **None**, if the node has no children.
insertBefore(*newChild,* *refChild* **)**	Inserts the *newChild* node before the *refChild* node. *refChild* must be a child node of the current node; otherwise, **insertBefore** raises a **ValueError** exception.
isSameNode(*other* **)**	Returns true if *other* is the current node.
lastChild	Last child node in the **NodeList** or **None**, if the current node has no children.
nextSibling	The next node in the **NodeList**, or **None**, if the node has no next sibling.
nodeName	Name of the node, or **None**, if the node does not have a name.
nodeType	Integer that represents the node type. Class **Node** defines several constants including: **ELEMENT_NODE** = 1 **ATTRIBUTE_NODE** = 2 **TEXT_NODE** = 3 **COMMENT_NODE** = 8 **DOCUMENT_NODE** = 9
nodeValue	The current node's value, or **None**, if the node has no value.
parentNode	Parent node or **None** if the node has no parent.

Fig. 16.6 **Node** attributes and methods. (Part 1 of 2.)

Attribute/Method	Description
previousSibling	The previous node in the **NodeList**, or **None**, if the node has no preceding sibling.
removeChild(*oldChild* **)**	Removes a child node. *oldChild* must be a child node of the current node; otherwise, a **ValueError** exception is raised.
replaceChild(*newChild,* *oldChild* **)**	Replaces *oldChild* with *newChild. oldChild* must be a child node of the current node; otherwise, **replaceChild** raises a **ValueError** exception.

Fig. 16.6   Node attributes and methods. (Part 2 of 2.)

Atrribute/Method	Description
item(*i* **)**	Returns the node at index *i*. Indices range from 0 to **length** – 1.
length	Number of nodes in the **NodeList**.

Fig. 16.7   NodeList attributes and methods.

Atrribute/Method	Description
item(*i* **)**	Returns the attribute node at index *i*. Indices range from 0 to **length** – 1.
length	Number of attribute nodes for the given element node.

Fig. 16.8   NamedNodeMap attributes and methods.

Atrribute/Method	Description
createAttribute(*name* **)**	Creates and returns an **Attr** node with the specified *name*.
createComment(*data* **)**	Creates and returns a **Comment** node that contains the specified *data*.
createElement(*tagName* **)**	Creates and returns an **Element** node with the specified *tagName*.
createTextNode(*data* **)**	Creates and returns a **Text** node that contains the specified *data*.
documentElement	Root element node of the document tree (DOM tree).

Fig. 16.9   Document attributes and methods. (Part 1 of 2.)

Atrribute/Method	Description
getElementsByTagName(*name*)	Returns a **NodeList** of all nodes in the subtree with the tag name *name*.

Fig. 16.9 **Document** attributes and methods. (Part 2 of 2.)

Attribute/Method	Description
getAttribute(*name*)	Returns XML attribute *name*'s value as a string.
getAttributeNode(*name*)	Returns the **Attr** node for XML attribute *name*.
getElementsByTagName(*name*)	Returns a **NodeList** of all nodes in the subtree with the tag name *name*.
removeAttribute(*name*)	Removes XML attribute *name* (specified as a string) from the XML attribute list for the given element node.
removeAttributeNode(*name*)	Removes **Attr** node *name* from the XML attribute list for the given **Element** node.
setAttribute(*name*, *value*)	Changes the value of XML attribute *name* to *value*. Both arguments are specified as strings.
setAttributeNode(*name*)	Adds new **Attr** node *name* to the attribute list for the given element node. If the attribute already exists, the new attribute replaces the current attribute.
tagName	Element's tag name.

Fig. 16.10 Element attributes and methods.

Attribute	Description
name	Name of the XML attribute.
prefix	Namespace prefix, if it exists, or **None**.

Fig. 16.11 Attr attributes.

Atrribute	Description
data	**Node**'s (**Text** or **Comment**) data.

Fig. 16.12 Text and **Comment** attribute.

```python
1   # Fig. 16.13: fig16_13.py
2   # Using 4DOM to manipulate an XML Document.
3
4   import sys
5   from xml.dom.ext.reader import PyExpat
6   from xml.dom.ext import PrettyPrint
7
8   def printInstructions():
9      print """\nEnter 'a' to add a contact.
10  Enter 'l' to list contacts.xml.
11  Enter 'i' for instructions.
12  Enter 'q' to quit."""
13
14  def printList( document ):
15     print "Your contact list is:"
16
17     # iterate over NodeList of contact elements
18     for contact in document.getElementsByTagName( "contact" ):
19        first = contact.getElementsByTagName( "FirstName" )[ 0 ]
20
21        # get first node's value
22        firstText = first.firstChild.nodeValue
23
24        # get NodeList for nodes that contain tag name "LastName"
25        last = contact.getElementsByTagName( "LastName" )[ 0 ]
26        lastText = last.firstChild.nodeValue
27
28        print firstText, lastText
29
30  def addContact( document ):
31     root = document.documentElement    # get root element node
32
33     name = raw_input(
34        "Enter the name of the person you wish to add: " )
35
36     first, last = name.split()
37
38     # create first name element node
39     firstNode = document.createElement( "FirstName" )
40     firstNodeText = document.createTextNode( first )
41     firstNode.appendChild( firstNodeText )
42
43     # create last name element node
44     lastNode = document.createElement( "LastName" )
45     lastNodeText = document.createTextNode( last )
46     lastNode.appendChild( lastNodeText )
47
48     # create contact node, append first name and last name nodes
49     contactNode = document.createElement( "contact" )
50     contactNode.appendChild( firstNode )
51     contactNode.appendChild( lastNode )
52
53     root.appendChild( contactNode ) # add contact node
```

Fig. 16.13 Manipulating an XML document. (Part 1 of 2.)

```
54
55   # open contacts file
56   try:
57       file = open( "contacts.xml", "r+" )
58   except IOError:
59       sys.exit( "Error opening file" )
60
61   # create DOM parser and parse XML document
62   reader = PyExpat.Reader()
63   document = reader.fromStream( file )
64
65   printList( document )
66   printInstructions()
67   character = "l"
68
69   while character != "q":
70       character = raw_input( "\n? " )
71
72       if character == "a":
73           addContact( document )
74       elif character == "l":
75           printList( document )
76       elif character == "i":
77           printInstructions()
78       elif character != "q":
79           print "Invalid command!"
80
81   file.seek( 0, 0 )                    # position to beginning of file
82   file.truncate()                      # remove data from file
83   PrettyPrint( document, file )        # print DOM contents to file
84   file.close()                         # close XML file
85   reader.releaseNode( document )       # free memory
```

```
Your contact list is:
John Black
Sue Green

Enter 'a' to add a contact.
Enter 'l' to list contacts.xml.
Enter 'i' for instructions.
Enter 'q' to quit.

? a
Enter the name of the person you wish to add: Michael Red

? l
Your contact list is:
John Black
Sue Green
Michael Red

? q
```

Fig. 16.13 Manipulating an XML document. (Part 2 of 2.)

Line 57 opens **contacts.xml** for reading and writing. A parser object is instantiated on line 62. Line 63 calls method **fromStream** to parse the XML document and build the DOM tree.

Line 65 calls function **printList** (lines 14–28) to print the contact list to the screen. Method **getElementsByTagName** (line 18) returns a **NodeList** that contains all **Element** nodes that have **contact** for a tag name. Line 19 calls **getElementsByTagName** to obtain a **NodeList** for all **Element** nodes that have **FirstName** for a tag name. Each node referenced by **contact** contains only one such node. This one node is accessed as the first element in the list (i.e., **[0]**). Line 22 assigns the value of **first**'s first child element (a **Text** node) to variable **firstText**. Lines 25–26 repeat the processes to obtain the last name. Line 28 prints the current contact's first name and last name to the screen.

Line 66 calls function **printInstructions** to print the program's instructions. Lines 69–79 get the user's choice and call the appropriate function.

The **addContact** function (lines 30–53) adds a contact to the list. The **Document**'s root element is obtained via its **documentElement** attribute (line 31). Lines 33–36 prompt the user for input and call string method **split** to separate the first name from the last name.

Line 39 calls the **Document**'s *createElement* method to create an **Element** node with the tag name **FirstName**. Lines 40–41 create and append a **Text** node to this **Element** node by calling the *createTextNode* and *appendChild* methods, respectively. Lines 44–46 create an **Element** node with the tag name **LastName** in a similar manner.

Line 49 creates an **Element** node with the tag name **contact**. Lines 50–51 call method **appendChild** to add the **Element** nodes referenced by **firstNode** and **lastNode** to the node referenced by **contactNode**. Line 53 calls method **appendChild** to add the node referenced by **contactNode** to the node referenced by **root**.

When the user has finished adding names to the contact list, the file is saved. The **seek** method (line 81) positions the file pointer to the beginning of the file and method **truncate** (line 82) deletes the contents of the file. Then, **4DOM**'s *PrettyPrint* function writes the updated XML to the file (line 83). Function **PrettyPrint** writes an XML DOM tree's data to a specified output stream (with indentation and carriage returns for readability). Lines 84–85 close the file and release the DOM tree from memory.

```
1   <?xml version="1.0" encoding="UTF-8"?>
2   <!DOCTYPE contacts>
3   <contacts>
4     <contact>
5       <LastName>Black</LastName>
6       <FirstName>John</FirstName>
7     </contact>
8     <contact>
9       <LastName>Green</LastName>
10      <FirstName>Sue</FirstName>
11    </contact>
12    <contact>
13      <FirstName>Michael</FirstName>
14      <LastName>Red</LastName>
15    </contact>
16  </contacts>
```

Fig. 16.14 Contact list output by Fig. 16.13.

16.5 Parsing XML with `xml.sax`

In this section, we discuss the **`xml.sax`** package, which provides a set of modules for SAX-based parsing. With SAX-based parsing, the parser reads the input to identify the XML markup. As the parser encounters markup, the parser calls *event handlers* (i.e., methods). For example, when the parser encounters a start tag, the **`startElement`** event handler is called; when the parser encounters character data, the **`characters`** event handler is called. Programmers override event handlers to provide specialized processing of the XML. Some common SAX event handlers are shown in Fig. 16.15.

Good Programming Practice 16.2

Review the Python on-line documentation for a complete listing of **`xml.sax`** *event handlers. This information can be found at:*
`www.python.org/doc/current/lib/content-handler-objects.html`

Figure 16.16 demonstrates SAX-based parsing. This program allows the user to specify a tag name to search for in an XML document. When the tag name is encountered, the program outputs the element's attribute-value pairs. Methods **`startElement`** and **`endElement`** are overriden to handle the events generated when start tags and end tags are encountered. Figure 16.17 contains the XML document used by this program.

Lines 42–43 obtain the name of the XML document to parse and the tag name to locate. Line 46 invokes **`xml.sax`** function **`parse`**, which creates a SAX parser object. Function **`parse`**'s first argument is either a Python file object or a filename. The second argument passed to **`parse`** must be an instance of class **`xml.sax.ContentHandler`** (or a derived class of **`ContentHandler`**, such as **`TagInfoHandler`**), which is the main callback handler in **`xml.sax`**. Class `ContentHandler` contains the methods (Fig. 16.15) for handling SAX events.

If an error occurs during the opening of the specified **`file`**, an **`IOError`** exception is raised, and line 50 displays an error message. If an error occurs while parsing the file (e.g., if the specified XML document is not well-formed), **`parse`** raises a **`SAXParseException`** exception, and line 54 displays an error message.

Event Handler	Description
`characters`(*content*)	Called when the parser encounters character data. The character data is passed as *content* to the event handler.
`endDocument`()	Called when the parser encounters the end of the document.
`endElement`(*name*)	Called when the parser encounters an end tag. The tag *name* is passed as an argument to the event handler.
`startDocument`()	Called when the parser encounters the beginning of the document.
`startElement`(*name*, *attrs*)	Called when the parser encounters a start tag. The tag *name* and its attributes (*attrs*) are passed as arguments to the event handler.

Fig. 16.15 `xml.sax` event-handler methods.

```
 1   # Fig. 16.16: fig16_16.py
 2   # Demonstrating SAX-based parsing.
 3
 4   from xml.sax import parse, SAXParseException, ContentHandler
 5
 6   class TagInfoHandler( ContentHandler ):
 7      """Custom xml.sax.ContentHandler"""
 8
 9      def __init__( self, tagName ):
10         """Initialize ContentHandler and set tag to search for"""
11
12         ContentHandler.__init__( self )
13         self.tagName = tagName
14         self.depth = 0 # spaces to indent to show structure
15
16      # override startElement handler
17      def startElement( self, name, attributes ):
18         """An Element has started"""
19
20         # check if this is tag name for which we are searching
21         if name == self.tagName:
22            print "\n%s<%s> started" % ( " " * self.depth, name )
23
24            self.depth += 3
25
26            print "%sAttributes:" % ( " " * self.depth )
27
28            # check if element has attributes
29            for attribute in attributes.getNames():
30               print "%s%s = %s" % ( " " * self.depth, attribute,
31                  attributes.getValue( attribute ) )
32
33      # override endElement handler
34      def endElement( self, name ):
35         """An Element has ended"""
36
37         if name == self.tagName:
38            self.depth -= 3
39            print "%s</%s> ended\n" % ( " " * self.depth, name )
40
41   def main():
42      file = raw_input( "Enter a file to parse: " )
43      tagName = raw_input( "Enter tag to search for: " )
44
45      try:
46         parse( file, TagInfoHandler( tagName ) )
47
48      # handle exception if unable to open file
49      except IOError, message:
50         print "Error reading file:", message
51
```

Fig. 16.16 SAX-based parsing example. (Part 1 of 2.)

```
52        # handle exception parsing file
53        except SAXParseException, message:
54            print "Error parsing file:", message
55
56    if __name__ == "__main__":
57        main()
```

```
Enter a file to parse: boxes.xml
Enter tag to search for: box

<box> started
   Attributes:
   size = big

   <box> started
      Attributes:
      size = medium
   </box> ended


   <box> started
      Attributes:
      type = small

      <box> started
         Attributes:
         type = tiny
      </box> ended

   </box> ended

</box> ended
```

Fig. 16.16 SAX-based parsing example. (Part 2 of 2.)

Our example overrides only two event handlers. Methods **startElement** and **endElement** are called when start tags and end tags are encountered. Method **start-Element** (lines 16–31) takes two arguments—the element's tag name as a string and the element's attributes. The attributes are passed as an instance of class **AttributesImpl**, defined in **xml.sax.reader**. This class provides a dictionary-like interface to the element's attributes.

Line 21 determines whether the element received from the event contains the tag name that the user specified. If so, line 22 prints the start tag, indented by **depth** spaces, and line 24 increments **depth** by **3** to ensure that the next tag printed indented further.

Lines 29–31 print the element's attributes. The **for** loop first obtains the attribute names by invoking the **getNames** method of **attributes**. The loop then prints each attribute name and its corresponding value—obtained by passing the current attribute name to the **getValue** method of **attributes**.

Method **endElement** (lines 34–39) executes when an end tag is encountered and receives the end tag's name as an argument. If **name** contains the tag name specified by the user, line 38 decreases the indent by decrementing **depth**. Line 39 prints that the specified end tag was found.

16.6 Case Study: Message Forums with Python and XML[4]

In this section, we use XML and several XML-related technologies to create one of the most popular types of Web sites: A *message forum*. Message forums are "virtual" bulletin boards where users discuss various topics. Common features of message forums include discussion groups, question-and-answer sections and general comments. Many Web sites host message forums. Some popular message forums are

```
groups.yahoo.com
web.eesite.com/forums
groups.google.com
```

Figure 16.18 summarizes the files that comprise the message forum. Figure 16.19 shows the directory structure for Apache running on Windows. Fig. 16.20 illustrates some of the key interactions between the files. The main XHTML page generated by **default.py** displays the list of available message forums, which are stored in the XML document **forums.xml**. Hyperlinks are provided to each XML message forum document and to script **addForum.py**, which adds a forum to **forums.xml** and creates an XML message forum, using the markup in **template.xml** as a starting point.

```
1   <?xml version = "1.0"?>
2
3   <!-- Fig. 16.17: boxes.xml              -->
4   <!-- XML document used in Fig. 16.16 -->
5
6   <boxlist>
7
8     <box size = "big">
9        This is the big box.
10
11       <box size = "medium">
12          Medium sized box
13          <item>Some stuff</item>
14          <thing>More stuff</thing>
15       </box>
16
17       <parcel />
18       <box type = "small">
19          smaller stuff
20          <box type = "tiny">tiny stuff</box>
21       </box>
22
23     </box>
24
25   </boxlist>
```

Fig. 16.17 XML document used in Fig. 16.16.

---

4. The implementation of this message forum requires Internet Explorer 5 or higher, and msxml 3.0 or higher. In Section 16.6.3, we discuss how other client browsers, such as Netscape, may be used.

Each XML document that contains a forum (e.g., **feedback.xml**) is transformed into an XHTML document by applying the XSLT document **formatting.xsl**. The XHTML generated is formatted by applying **site.css**. New messages are posted to a forum by **addPost.py**.

File Name	Description
forums.xml	XML document containing available forum titles and their filenames.
default.py	Main page that provides navigational links to the forums.
template.xml	Template for a message forum document.
addForum.py	Adds a new forum.
feedback.xml	Sample message forum.
formatting.xsl	XSLT document for transforming message forums into XHTML.
addPost.py	Adds a message to a forum.
error.html	Displays an error message.
site.css	Style sheet for formatting XHTML content.
forum.py	Transforms XML documents to HTML on the server for non-Internet Explorer clients.

Fig. 16.18 Message-forum documents.

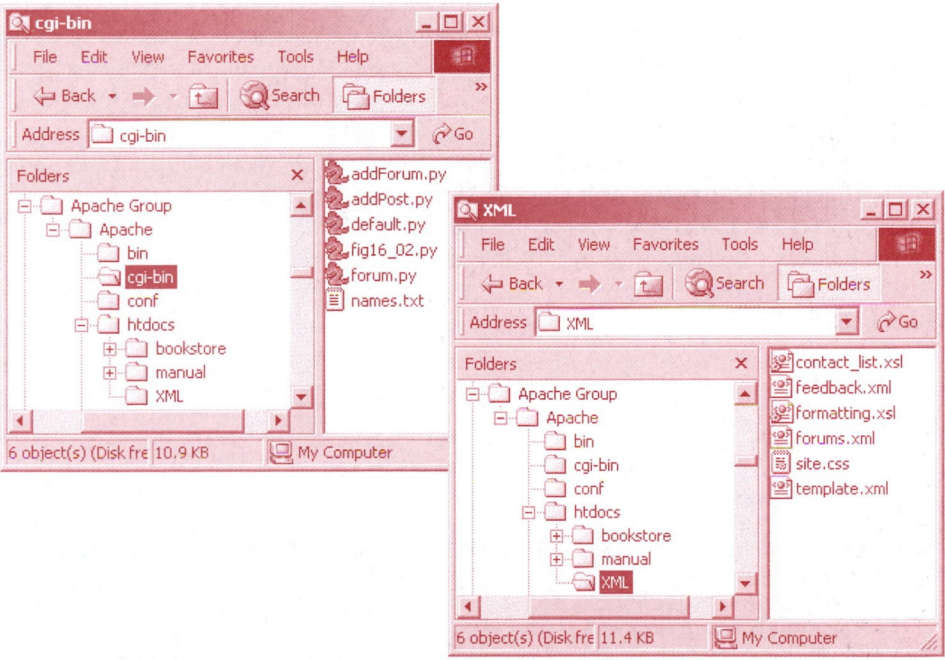

Fig. 16.19 Directory structure for the message forum.

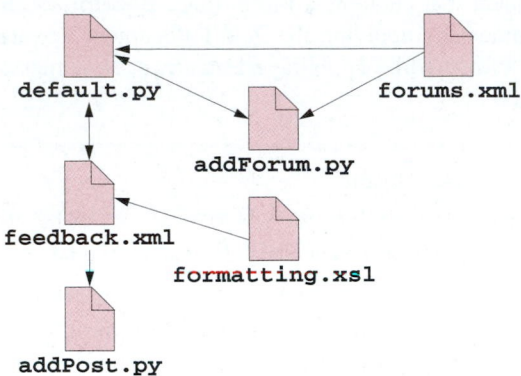

Fig. 16.20 Key interactions between message forum documents.

16.6.1 Displaying the Forums

This section discusses how XML is used to mark up message forum data and the Python script—**default.py**—that creates the message forum's main XHTML page. For this case study, we provide a sample forum named **feedback.xml** (Fig. 16.21) to show the structure of a forum document.

Notice the reference to the style sheet **formatting.xsl** (line 6). When applied by msxml, this XSLT document (which we discuss later in the chapter) transforms the XML into XHTML for display in Internet Explorer. Forum documents have root element **forum**, which contains attribute **file**. This attribute's value is the document's filename. Child elements include **name**, for specifying the title of the forum, and **message**, for marking up the message. Messages contain a user name, a title and the text, which are marked up by elements **user**, **title** and **text**, respectively. Messages also are given a **timestamp**.

The document **forums.xml** (Fig. 16.22) contains the filename and title for every message forum. As forums are created, this document is updated.

Root element **forums** (line 8) contains one or more **forum** child elements. Initially, one forum (i.e., **Feedback**) is present. Each **forum** element has attribute **filename** and child element **name**.

```
1   <?xml version = "1.0"?>
2
3   <!-- Fig. 16.21: feedback.xml          -->
4   <!-- XML document representing a forum -->
5
6   <?xml:stylesheet type = "text/xsl" href = "../XML/formatting.xsl"?>
7
8   <forum file = "feedback.xml">
9     <name>Feedback</name>
10
```

Fig. 16.21 XML document representing a forum containing one message. (Part 1 of 2.)

```
11        <message timestamp = "Wed Jun 27 12:53:22 2001">
12          <user>Jessica</user>
13          <title>Nice forums!</title>
14          <text>These forums are great! Well done, all.</text>
15        </message>
16
17      </forum>
```

Fig. 16.21 XML document representing a forum containing one message. (Part 2 of 2.)

```
1      <?xml version = "1.0"?>
2
3      <!-- Fig. 16.22: forums.xml                -->
4      <!-- XML document containing all forums -->
5
6      <?xml:stylesheet type = "text/xsl" href = "formatting.xsl"?>
7
8      <forums>
9
10        <forum filename = "feedback.xml">
11          <name>Feedback</name>
12        </forum>
13
14      </forums>
```

Fig. 16.22 XML document containing data for all available forums.

Visitors to the message forum are greeted initially by the Web page that **default.py** (Fig. 16.23) generates, which displays links to all forums and provides forum management options. Initially, only two links are active—one to view the **Feedback** forum (i.e., the sample forum) and one to create a forum. In the chapter exercises, we ask the reader to enhance the message forum by adding functionality for modifying and deleting forums.

```
1      #!c:\Python\python.exe
2      # Fig. 16.23: default.py
3      # Default page for message forums.
4
5      import os
6      import sys
7      from xml.dom.ext.reader import PyExpat
8
9      def printHeader( title, style ):
10         print """Content-type: text/html
11
12      <?xml version = "1.0" encoding = "UTF-8"?>
13      <!DOCTYPE html PUBLIC
14          "-//W3C//DTD XHTML 1.0 Strict//EN"
15          "DTD/xhtml1-strict.dtd">
16      <html xmlns = "http://www.w3.org/1999/xhtml">
17
```

Fig. 16.23 Default page for the message forum. (Part 1 of 3.)

```
18    <head>
19    <title>%s</title>
20    <link rel = "stylesheet" href = "%s" type = "text/css" />
21    </head>
22
23    <body>""" % ( title, style )
24
25    # open XML document that contains the forum names and locations
26    try:
27       XMLFile = open( "../htdocs/XML/forums.xml" )
28    except IOError:
29       print "Location: /error.html\n"
30       sys.exit()
31
32    # parse XML document containing forum information
33    reader = PyExpat.Reader()
34    document = reader.fromStream( XMLFile )
35    XMLFile.close()
36
37    # write XHTML to browser
38    printHeader( "Deitel Message Forums", "/XML/site.css" )
39    print """<h1>Deitel Message Forums</h1>
40    <p style="font-weight:bold">Available Forums</p>
41    <ul>"""
42
43    # determine client-browser type
44    if os.environ[ "HTTP_USER_AGENT" ].find( "MSIE" ) != -1:
45       prefix = "../XML/"    # Internet Explorer
46    else:
47       prefix = "forum.py?file="
48
49    # add links for each forum
50    for forum in document.getElementsByTagName( "forum" ):
51
52       # create link to forum
53       link = prefix + forum.attributes.item( 0 ).value
54
55       # get element nodes containing tag name "name"
56       name = forum.getElementsByTagName( "name" )[ 0 ]
57
58       # get Text node's value
59       nameText = name.childNodes[ 0 ].nodeValue
60       print '<li><a href = "%s">%s</a></li>' % ( link, nameText )
61
62    print """</ul>
63    <p style="font-weight:bold">Forum Management</p>
64    <ul>
65       <li><a href = "addForum.py">Add a Forum</a></li>
66       <li>Delete a Forum</li>
67       <li>Modify a Forum</li>
68    </ul>
69    </body>
70
```

Fig. 16.23 Default page for the message forum. (Part 2 of 3.)

```
71    </html>"""
72
73    reader.releaseNode( document )
```

Fig. 16.23 Default page for the message forum. (Part 3 of 3.)

This Python script uses modules in package **4DOM** to parse **forums.xml**. Lines 33–34 instantiate a parser object, then load and parse **forums.xml**. Lines 38–71 output XHTML to the browser. First, line 38 prints the XHTML header for the main page by calling function **printHeader** (lines 9–23). This function prints the XHTML header with a specified title and a link to a Cascading Style Sheet (CSS) that formats the page. In this case study, we would like to take advantage of msxml's XML parsing and XSLT processing capabilities to reduce the amount of processing the server must perform. Lines 44–45 determine whether the client is using Internet Explorer. If so, **prefix** is set to **"../ XML/"**. Otherwise, **prefix** is set to **"forum.py?file="**. Note that line 47 uses **prefix** to construct the hyperlinks to each forum. Clients who use Internet Explorer request the XML documents directly, while other clients request **forum.py**. We discuss this in greater detail in Section 16.6.3. The **for** loop (lines 50–60) retrieves all **Element** nodes that contain the tag name **forum**. Hyperlinks are created to each forum found in **forums.xml**. Lines 62–71 print the remaining XHTML, including a hyperlink to **addForum.py**. Finally, line 73 releases the **Document** object from memory.

16.6.2 Adding Forums and Messages

In this section, we discuss the Python scripts and documents that add forums and messages. The Python script that adds a new forum is shown in Fig. 16.24. This script uses modules in package **4DOM** to manipulate XML documents.

When the script is requested initially, it is not passed any parameters. The script begins by retrieving the form data (line 29). Because the form contains no values, execution begins with the **else** block at line 93. Lines 94–107 output a form that prompts the user for a forum name and a filename for the XML document to be created. When the form is submitted, the script is re-requested and passed the user-entered form values. When this occurs, the condition (line 32) is true, and lines 33–92 execute.

```
1   #!c:\Python\python.exe
2   # Fig. 16.24: addForum.py
3   # Adds a forum to the list
4
5   import re
6   import sys
7   import cgi
8
9   # 4DOM packages
10  from xml.dom.ext.reader import PyExpat
11  from xml.dom.ext import PrettyPrint
12
13  def printHeader( title, style ):
14      print """Content-type: text/html
15
16  <?xml version = "1.0" encoding = "UTF-8"?>
17  <!DOCTYPE html PUBLIC
18      "-//W3C//DTD XHTML 1.0 Strict//EN"
19      "DTD/xhtml1-strict.dtd">
20  <html xmlns = "http://www.w3.org/1999/xhtml">
21
22  <head>
23  <title>%s</title>
24  <link rel = "stylesheet" href = "%s" type = "text/css" />
25  </head>
26
27  <body>""" % ( title, style )
28
29  form = cgi.FieldStorage()
30
31  # if user enters data in form fields
32  if form.has_key( "name" ) and form.has_key( "filename" ):
33      newFile = form[ "filename" ].value
34
35      # determine whether file has xml extension
36      if not re.match( "\w+\.xml$", newFile ):
37          print "Location: /error.html\n"
38          sys.exit()
39      else:
40
41          # create forum files from xml files
42          try:
43              newForumFile = open( "../htdocs/XML/" + newFile, "w" )
44              forumsFile = open( "../htdocs/XML/forums.xml", "r+" )
45              templateFile = open( "../htdocs/XML/template.xml" )
46          except IOError:
47              print "Location: /error.html\n"
48              sys.exit()
49
```

Fig. 16.24 Script that adds a new forum to **forums.xml**. (Part 1 of 3.)

```
50          # parse forums document
51          reader = PyExpat.Reader()
52          document = reader.fromStream( forumsFile )
53
54          # add new forum element
55          forum = document.createElement( "forum" )
56          forum.setAttribute( "filename", newFile )
57
58          name = document.createElement( "name" )
59          nameText = document.createTextNode( form[ "name" ].value )
60          name.appendChild( nameText )
61          forum.appendChild( name )
62
63          # obtain root element of forum
64          documentNode = document.documentElement
65          firstForum = documentNode.getElementsByTagName(
66             "forum" )[ 0 ]
67          documentNode.insertBefore( forum, firstForum )
68
69          # write updated XML to disk
70          forumsFile.seek( 0, 0 )
71          forumsFile.truncate()
72          PrettyPrint( document, forumsFile )
73          forumsFile.close()
74
75          # create document for new forum from template file
76          document = reader.fromStream( templateFile )
77          forum = document.documentElement
78          forum.setAttribute( "file", newFile )
79
80          # create name element
81          name = document.createElement( "name" )
82          nameText = document.createTextNode( form[ "name" ].value )
83          name.appendChild( nameText )
84          forum.appendChild( name )
85
86          # write generated XML to new forum file
87          PrettyPrint( document, newForumFile )
88          newForumFile.close()
89          templateFile.close()
90          reader.releaseNode( document )
91
92          print "Location: default.py\n"
93   else:
94      printHeader( "Add a forum", "/XML/site.css" )
95      print """<form action = "addForum.py" method="post">
96   Forum Name<br />
97   <input type = "text" name = "name" size = "40" /><br />
98   Forum File Name<br />
99   <input type = "text" name = "filename" size = "40" /><br />
100  <input type = "submit" name = "submit" value = "Submit" />
101  <input type = "reset" value = "Reset" />
102  </form>
```

Fig. 16.24 Script that adds a new forum to **forums.xml**. (Part 2 of 3.)

```
103
104    <a href = "/cgi-bin/default.py">Return to Main Page</a>
105    </body>
106
107    </html>"""
```

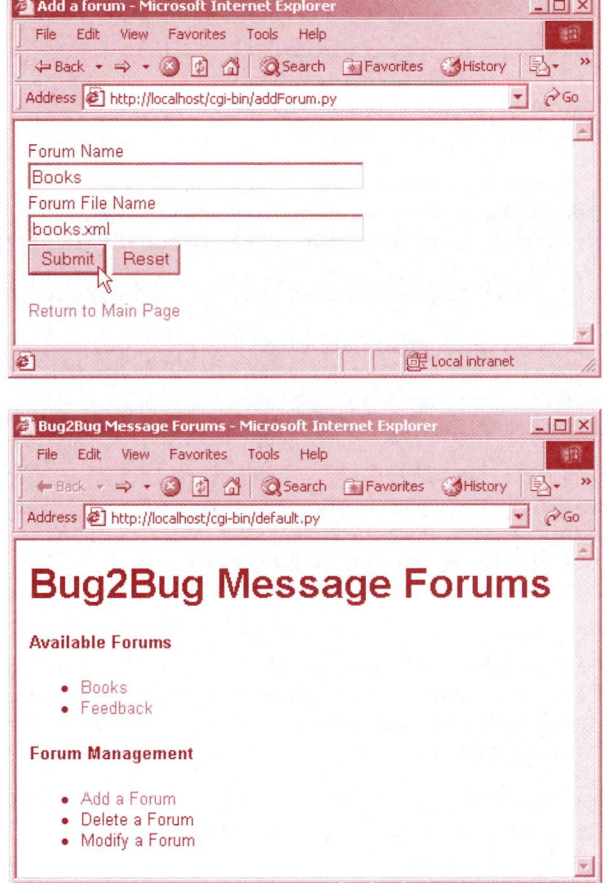

Fig. 16.24 Script that adds a new forum to **forums.xml**. (Part 3 of 3.)

Line 36 examines the filename posted to the script to make sure it contains only alpha-numeric characters and ends with **.xml**; if not, the script redirects the client to **error.html**. This prevents a malicious user from writing to a system file or otherwise gaining unrestricted access to the server. However, it is important to note that other solutions exist, such as generating filenames on the server. If the filename is permitted, line 43 attempts to create the file by calling function **open**.

Line 44 opens file **forums.xml** for reading and writing (**"r+"**). Line 40 opens the template XML document named **template.xml** (Fig. 16.25), which provides a forum's markup. The template contains an empty **forums** element, to which the forum name and filename are added programmatically. If an error occurs during an attempt to open any file, the client is redirected to **error.html**.

Line 51 instantiates a DOM parser and assigns it to variable **reader**. Line 52 loads and parses **forums.xml**; the **Document** object created is assigned to variable **document**. Because we wish to create a **forum** element within **forums**, line 55 calls the **Document** object's **createElement** method with the name of the new element (**"forum"**). The **filename** attribute of the new **Element** node is set by calling **setAttribute** and passing the attribute's name and value.

The **forum** element contains only one piece of information—the forum name—added by lines 58–61. Line 58 creates another **Element** node named **name**. To add character data to the new **Element** node, a child **Text** node must be created. We call method **createTextNode** (line 59) with the forum name from the form (i.e., **form["name"].value**). Line 60 appends the **Text** node to the **Element** node referenced by **name** by calling method **appendChild**. Line 61 adds the **Element** node referenced by **name** to the **Element** node referenced by **forum**.

Line 64 accesses the **documentElement** attribute of **document** to obtain the root element node (i.e., **forums**). Lines 65–66 obtain a **NodeList** of all **forum** elements by calling method **getElementsByTagName**, the first of which is assigned to variable **firstForum**. Line 67 inserts the new **Element** node referenced by **forum** before the first child node of **forums** by calling method **insertBefore**. With this technique, the most recently added forums appear first in the forum list.

To update **forums.xml**, line 70 **seek**s to the beginning and deletes any existing data (by truncating the file to size **0**). Line 72 then calls function **PrettyPrint** to write the updated XML to **forumsFile**.

Line 76 loads and parses file **template.xml** (Fig. 16.25) by calling method **fromStream** and assigns the **Document** object created to variable **document**. Line 77 uses **documentElement** to get the root element, and line 78 sets its **file** attribute's value to the specified filename. Lines 81–84 add the **name** node, and lines 87–88 output the updated XML to **newForumFile** and close the file. Lines 89–90 close **template.xml** and release the **Document** object from memory. The user is redirected to **default.py** in line 92.

Figure 16.26 contains the Python script that allows users to add messages to a forum. When **formatting.xsl** (Fig. 16.27) is applied to a forum document, a link to **addPost.py** is added to the page, which includes the current forum's filename. This filename is passed to **addPost.py** (e.g., **addPost.py?file=forum1.xml**).

```
1  <?xml version = "1.0"?>
2
3  <!-- Fig. 16.25: template.xml -->
4  <!-- Empty forum file         -->
5
6  <?xml:stylesheet type = "text/xsl" href = "../XML/formatting.xsl"?>
7  <forum>
8  </forum>
```

Fig. 16.25 XML template for generating new forums.

```
 1   #!c:\Python\python.exe
 2   # Fig. 16.26: addPost.py
 3   # Adds a message to a forum.
 4
 5   import re
 6   import os
 7   import sys
 8   import cgi
 9   import time
10
11   # 4DOM packages
12   from xml.dom.ext.reader import PyExpat
13   from xml.dom.ext import PrettyPrint
14
15   def printHeader( title, style ):
16      print """Content-type: text/html
17
18   <?xml version = "1.0" encoding = "UTF-8"?>
19   <!DOCTYPE html PUBLIC
20      "-//W3C//DTD XHTML 1.0 Strict//EN"
21      "DTD/xhtml1-strict.dtd">
22   <html xmlns = "http://www.w3.org/1999/xhtml">
23
24   <head>
25   <title>%s</title>
26   <link rel = "stylesheet" href = "%s" type = "text/css" />
27   </head>
28
29   <body>""" % ( title, style )
30
31   # identify client browser
32   if os.environ[ "HTTP_USER_AGENT" ].find( "MSIE" ) != -1:
33      prefix = "../XML/"    # Internet Explorer
34   else:
35      prefix = "forum.py?file="
36
37   form = cgi.FieldStorage()
38
39   # user has submitted message to post
40   if form.has_key( "submit" ):
41      filename = form[ "file" ].value
42
43      # add message to forum
44      if not re.match( "\w+\.xml$", filename  ):
45         print "Location: /error.html\n"
46         sys.exit()
47
48      try:
49         forumFile = open( "../htdocs/XML/" + filename, "r+" )
50      except IOError:
51         print "Location: /error.html\n"
52         sys.exit()
53
```

Fig. 16.26 Script that adds a message to a forum. (Part 1 of 3.)

```
54        # parse forum document
55        reader = PyExpat.Reader()
56        document = reader.fromStream( forumFile )
57        documentNode = document.documentElement
58
59        # create message element
60        message = document.createElement( "message" )
61        message.setAttribute( "timestamp", time.ctime( time.time() ) )
62
63        # add elements to message
64        messageElements = [ "user", "title", "text" ]
65
66        for item in messageElements:
67
68           if not form.has_key( item ):
69              text = "( Field left blank )"
70           else:
71              text = form[ item ].value
72
73           # create nodes
74           element = document.createElement( item )
75           elementText = document.createTextNode( text )
76           element.appendChild( elementText )
77           message.appendChild( element )
78
79        # append new message to forum and update document on disk
80        documentNode.appendChild( message )
81        forumFile.seek( 0, 0 )
82        forumFile.truncate()
83        PrettyPrint( document, forumFile )
84        forumFile.close()
85        reader.releaseNode( document )
86
87        print "Location: %s\n" % ( prefix + form[ "file" ].value )
88
89   # create form to obtain new message
90   elif form.has_key( "file" ):
91      printHeader( "Add a posting", "/XML/site.css" )
92      print """\n<form action = "addPost.py" method="post">
93   User<br />
94   <input type = "text" name = "user" size = "40" /><br />
95   Message Title<br />
96   <input type = "text" name = "title" size = "40" /><br />
97   Message Text<br />
98   <textarea name = "text" cols = "40" rows = "5"></textarea><br />
99   <input type = "hidden" name = "file" value = "%s" />
100  <input type = "submit" name = "submit" value = "Submit" />
101  <input type = "reset" value = "Reset" />
102  </form>
103
104  <a href = "%s">Return to Forum</a>
105  </body>
106
```

Fig. 16.26 Script that adds a message to a forum. (Part 2 of 3.)

```
107  </html>""" % ( form[ "file" ].value,
108     prefix + form[ "file" ].value )
109  else:
110     print "Location: /error.html\n"
```

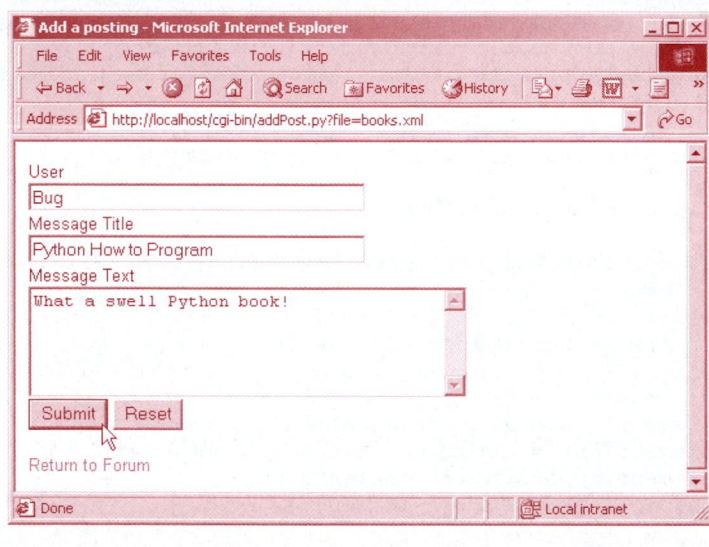

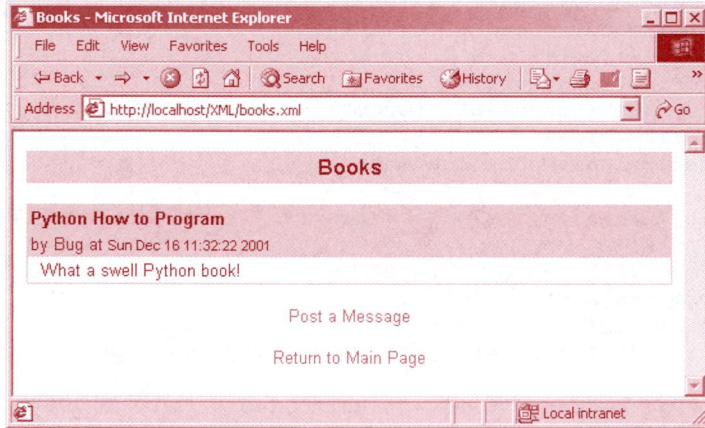

Fig. 16.26 Script that adds a message to a forum. (Part 3 of 3.)

Line 37 obtains the form values posted to the script. The user has not yet submitted a new message; therefore, the form does not contain the value **"submit"** (line 40), and execution proceeds to line 90. If the form contains a single value (i.e., the filename), lines 91–108 output a form, which includes fields for the user name, message title, message text and the forum filename as a hidden value (line 99). Note that, if no parameters are passed to the script, the script has been accessed in an inappropriate way, and the programs redirects the browser to **error.html** (line 110).

When the form data are submitted, the posted information is processed, starting at line 41. As in the previous figure, the filename is checked for an **.xml** extension, and the file is opened (lines 44–52). Lines 55–61 parse the forum file, create an **Element** node with tag name **message** and set the node's **timestamp** attribute by calling method **set-Attribute**.

Lines 64–77 create **Element** nodes that represent the **user**, **title** and **text** and add text that corresponds to the values entered in the form. Note that, if a field has been left blank, **"(Field left blank)"** is entered for that field. Each new **Element** node is appended to the node referenced by **message** (line 77).

Line 80 appends the node referenced by **message** to the node referenced by **documentNode**. Lines 81–82 then **seek** and **truncate** the XML file to eliminate the file's content and write the updated XML markup. Lines 84–85 close the file and free the **Document** object from memory. The user is redirected to the updated XML document in line 87.

16.6.3 Alterations for Browsers without XML and XSLT Support

This case study uses an XSLT style sheet (**formatting.xsl** in Fig. 16.27) to transform XML data into XHTML that is rendered in Internet Explorer. Recall that each XML document sent to Internet Explorer contains a processing instruction that references this style sheet.

Support for XSLT currently is available only for Internet Explorer 5 and higher. This means that our message forum application could send XML content to some browsers (e.g., Netscape Communicator 6) that do not have built-in XML parsers and XSLT processors. To create a more client-independent application, we can parse the XML on the server and apply the XSLT transformation on the server.

```
1   <?xml version = "1.0"?>
2
3   <!-- Fig. 16.27: formatting.xsl  -->
4   <!-- Style sheet for forum files -->
5
6   <xsl:stylesheet version = "1.0"
7      xmlns:xsl = "http://www.w3.org/1999/XSL/Transform">
8
9      <!-- match document root -->
10     <xsl:template match = "/">
11        <html xmlns = "http://www.w3.org/1999/xhtml">
12
13        <!-- apply templates for all elements -->
14        <xsl:apply-templates select = "*" />
15        </html>
16     </xsl:template>
17
18     <!-- match forum elements -->
19     <xsl:template match = "forum">
20        <head>
21           <title><xsl:value-of select = "name" /></title>
22           <link rel = "stylesheet" type = "text/css"
23              href = "../XML/site.css" />
24        </head>
25
```

Fig. 16.27 XSLT style sheet that transforms XML into XHTML. (Part 1 of 3.)

```
26          <body>
27              <table width = "100%" cellspacing = "0"
28                  cellpadding = "2">
29                  <tr>
30                      <td class = "forumTitle">
31                          <xsl:value-of select = "name" />
32                      </td>
33                  </tr>
34              </table>
35
36              <!-- apply templates for message elements -->
37              <br />
38                  <xsl:apply-templates select = "message" />
39              <br />
40
41              <div style = "text-align: center">
42                  <a>
43
44                      <!-- add href attribute to "a" element -->
45                      <xsl:attribute name = "href">../cgi-bin/
addPost.py?file=<xsl:value-of select = "@file" />
46                      </xsl:attribute>
47                      Post a Message
48                  </a>
49                  <br /><br />
50                  <a href = "../cgi-bin/default.py">Return to Main Page</a>
51              </div>
52
53          </body>
54      </xsl:template>
55
56      <!-- match message elements -->
57      <xsl:template match = "message">
58          <table width = "100%" cellspacing = "0"
59              cellpadding = "2">
60              <tr>
61                  <td class = "msgTitle">
62                      <xsl:value-of select = "title" />
63                  </td>
64              </tr>
65
66              <tr>
67                  <td class = "msgInfo">
68                      by
69                      <xsl:value-of select = "user" />
70                      at
71                      <span class = "date">
72                          <xsl:value-of select = "@timestamp" />
73                      </span>
74                  </td>
75              </tr>
76
```

Fig. 16.27 XSLT style sheet that transforms XML into XHTML. (Part 2 of 3.)

```
77              <tr>
78                  <td class = "msgText">
79                      <xsl:value-of select = "text" />
80                  </td>
81              </tr>
82
83          </table>
84      </xsl:template>
85
86  </xsl:stylesheet>
```

Fig. 16.27 XSLT style sheet that transforms XML into XHTML. (Part 3 of 3.)

4XSLT, which is a package included in **4Suite**, contains an XSLT processor for transforming XML into HTML. We can create an instance of this processor for applying style sheets to XML documents.

Recall how the **prefix** variable in **default.py** (Fig. 16.23) and **addPost.py** (Fig. 16.26) was used to define where links or redirection statements sent clients. By allowing Internet Explorer's XML parser and XSLT processor to parse the XML and apply a style sheet to the XML, we reduce the load on the server. For browsers without XML and XSLT support, however, we direct clients to a Python script that parses the XML document and sends HTML to the client.

We therefore insert a browser test at line 44 of **default.py** and at line 32 of **addPost.py**:

```
if os.environ[ "HTTP_USER_AGENT" ].find( "MSIE" ) != -1:
    prefix = "../XML/"
else:
    prefix = "forum.py?file="
```

Variable **prefix** is set according to whether **MSIE** (Microsoft Internet Explorer) appears in the **HTTP_USER_AGENT** environment variable. For simplicity, we assume Internet Explorer 5 or higher (with msxml 3.0 or higher) is the only version of MSIE being used and do not test for older versions.

Once **prefix** has been set, we may use its value to customize the URLs generated by the scripts. One example occurs in line 87 of **addPost.py**:

```
print "Location: %s\n" % ( prefix + form[ "file" ].value )
```

This line directs Internet Explorer users to the specified XML forum file located in **../ XML/**, but sends users of other browsers to **forum.py**, a Python script that receives a single parameter (i.e., the filename).

Figure 16.28 shows **forum.py**, which transforms XML documents to HTML on the server. The figure also includes the rendered HTML output displayed in Netscape Communicator.

If a filename is not passed to the script, the user is redirected to **error.html** (line 40). Otherwise, execution begins at line 16. Lines 16–18 determine whether the specified filename ends in **.xml**. If so, lines 21–22 open the XSLT style sheet (**formatting.xsl**) and the specified XML document, respectively. If an error occurs during an attempt to open one of these files, the user is redirected to **error.html** (line 24).

The XML then is transformed into HTML for display. Line 28 instantiates a **4XSLT Processor** object, which transforms XML into HTML, by applying an XSLT style sheet. Line 31 specifies the appropriate XSLT style sheet by invoking **processor**'s **appendStyleSheetStream** method. This method appends a style sheet to the list of style sheets a **Processor** can use. Note that more than one style sheet can be appended (i.e., **appendStyleSheetStream** can be called multiple times) so that the same **Processor** object can be used to transform an XML document to many different formats. The argument passed to **appendStyleSheetStream** must be a Python file object. Other methods for appending style sheets to a **4XSLT Processor** are **appendStyleSheet-String**, **appendStyleSheetNode** and **appendStyleSheetUri**, which accept as arguments a string containing an XSLT style sheet, a DOM tree containing a style sheet and a URI that references a style sheet, respectively. The specified URI may be a URL (in the form of a string) that represents the location of the style sheet on the Web.

```python
1   #!c:\Python\python.exe
2   # Fig. 16.28: forum.py
3   # Display forum postings for non-Internet Explorer browsers.
4
5   import re
6   import cgi
7   import sys
8   from xml.xslt import Processor
9
10  form = cgi.FieldStorage()
11
12  # form to display has been specified
13  if form.has_key( "file" ):
14
15      # determine whether file is xml
16      if not re.match( "\w+\.xml$", form[ "file" ].value ):
17          print "Location: /error.html\n"
18          sys.exit()
19
20      try:
21          style = open( "../htdocs/XML/formatting.xsl" )
22          XMLFile = open( "../htdocs/XML/" + form[ "file" ].value )
23      except IOError:
24          print "Location: /error.html\n"
25          sys.exit()
26
27      # create XSLT processor instance
28      processor = Processor.Processor()
29
30      # specify style sheet
31      processor.appendStylesheetStream( style )
32
```

Fig. 16.28 Script that transforms XML into HTML for browsers without XSLT support. (Part 1 of 2.)

```
33        # apply style sheet to XML document
34        results = processor.runStream( XMLFile )
35        style.close()
36        XMLFile.close()
37        print "Content-type: text/html\n"
38        print results
39    else:
40        print "Location: /error.html\n"
```

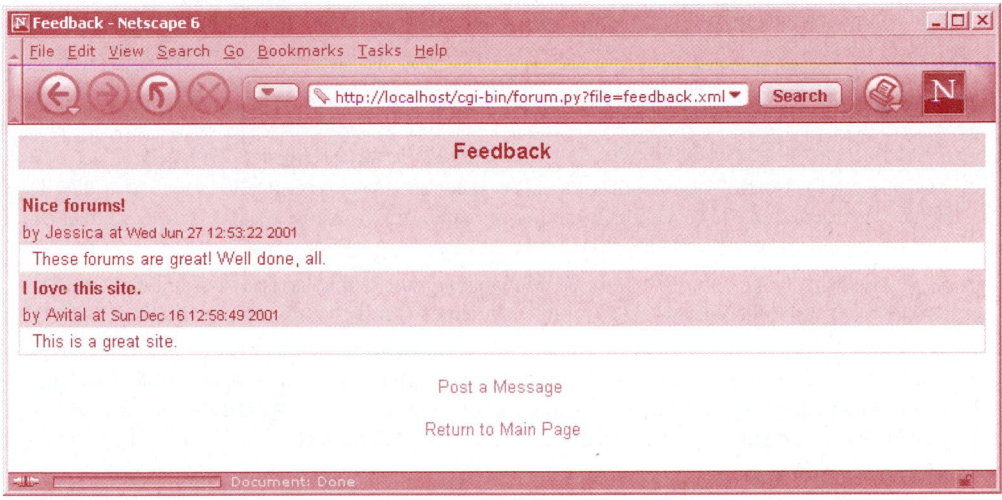

Fig. 16.28 Script that transforms XML into HTML for browsers without XSLT support. (Part 2 of 2.)

Line 34 invokes the **Processor**'s *runStream* method to apply the style sheet to the XML document. As with **appendStyleSheetStream**, the object passed to **runStream** must be a Python file object. Other methods used for applying style sheets are *runString*, *runNode* and *runUri*, which accept as arguments a string containing XML, a DOM tree containing XML and a URI that references an XML document, respectively.

Lines 35–36 close the XSLT and XML files used by the script. Line 37 prints the content type header for the Web browser. The transformed XML is then sent to the client as HTML (line 38).

In this chapter, we used the concepts presented in Chapter 15 to create XML-based applications. We used Python packages containing DOM implementations and SAX implementations to parse our XML documents, then used XSLT style sheets to display the XML document content in a browser. In Chapter 17, Database Application Programming Interface (DB-API), we discuss databases, the widely employed relational database model and the Structured Query Language (SQL), a language used to obtain database contents easily.

16.7 Internet and World Wide Web Resources

pyxml.sourceforge.net
The home page for **PyXML**, a Python XML processing package. **PyXML** contains several tools, such as a DOM-based and a SAX-based validating XML parsers.

4suite.org
The home page for **4Suite**, a Python XML processing package. **4Suite** contains several DOM implementations for DOM-based parsing and tools for other XML-related technologies.

www.python.org/doc/current/lib/content-handler-objects.html
This site contains documentation for **xml.sax.ContentHandler** event handlers.

SUMMARY

- Support for XML is provided through a large collection of freely available packages.

- The process by which Python applications can generate XML dynamically is similar to that by which they generate XHTML. For example, to output XML from a Python script, we can use **print** statements or we can use XSLT.

- The modules included with Python for DOM manipulation are **xml.minidom** and **xml.pulldom**. However, neither of these DOM implementations is fully compliant with the W3C's DOM Recommendation.

- A third-party package called **4DOM** is a fully compliant DOM implementation. **4DOM** is included with XML package **PyXML** (**pyxml.sourceforge.net**). Once **PyXML** is installed, the extended DOM components of **4DOM** are accessed via **xml.dom.ext**.

- **4XSLT**, used for applying a style sheet to an XML document, is located in another XML package called **4Suite** (**4suite.org**), from Fourthought, Inc.

- **4DOM**'s **reader** package includes module **PyExpat**.

- **PyExpat** contains class **Reader**, an XML parser. A **Reader** object takes an XML document and parses it, storing it in memory as a tree structure (called a DOM tree).

- The **Node** class, or a class derived from **Node**, represents an XML element, node, comment, etc. in an XML document. Other classes include **NodeList**, an ordered list of nodes, and **NamedNodeMap**, a dictionary of attribute nodes.

- A **Document** object represents the entire XML document (in memory) and provides methods for manipulating its data.

- **Element** nodes represent XML elements.

- **Text** nodes represent character data.

- **Attr** nodes represent attributes in start tags.

- **Comment** nodes represent comments.

- **Document** nodes can contain **Element**, **Text** and **Comment** nodes.

- **Element** nodes can contain **Attr**, **Element**, **Text** and **Comment** nodes.

- Method **fromStream** accepts as input a Python file object and returns a **Document** object.

- A **Document** object's **documentElement** attribute returns the **Document**'s root element node.

- Function **StripXml** removes insignificant whitespace from an XML DOM tree.

- A **Node** object's **childNodes** attribute contains a list of that **Node**'s children.

- A **Node** object's **firstChild** attribute corresponds to the first child in that **Node**'s list of children.

- Parent nodes are obtained through the **parentNode** attribute.

- Method **releaseNode** removes a specified **Document** (i.e., DOM tree) from memory.

- Method **getElementsByTagName** returns a **NodeList** whose **Element** nodes have a particular tag name.

- A **Document** object's **createElement** method creates an **Element** node.

- Function **PrettyPrint** writes an XML DOM tree to a specified output stream.

- For SAX-based parsing, programmers use a package that is included with Python (versions 2.0 and higher)—**xml.sax.** Package **xml.sax** contains SAX classes and functions. With SAX-based parsing, the parser reads the input to identify the XML markup. As the parser encounters markup, event handlers (i.e., methods) are called.

- Class **ContentHandler** contains methods for handling SAX events. These methods can be overridden to perform the desired parsing.

- The **xml.sax** function **parse** creates a SAX parser. The document passed to function **parse** may be specified as either a Python file object or a filename. The second argument passed to **parse** must be an instance of class **xml.sax.ContentHandler** (or a derived class of **ContentHandler**), the main callback handler in **xml.sax**.

- If an error occurs during parsing, **parse** raises a **SAXParseException** exception.

- Methods **startElement** and **endElement** are called when element start tags and end tags are encountered, respectively. Method **startElement** takes two arguments—the element's name as a string and the element's attributes. The attributes are passed as an instance of class **AttributesImpl**, defined in **xml.sax.reader**. Method **endElement** executes when an element's end tag is encountered and takes the end tag's name as an argument.

- A **4XSLT Processor** transforms XML to HTML by applying an XSLT style sheet.

- The **Processor**'s **appendStyleSheetStream** method specifies the XSLT style sheet to apply. This method appends a style sheet to the list of style sheets a **Processor** can use. The argument passed to **appendStyleSheetStream** must be a Python file object.

- The **Processor**'s **runStream** method applies the style sheet to the XML document. The object passed to **runStream** must be a Python file object.

TERMINOLOGY

4DOM package
4Suite package
4XSLT package
appendChild method of class **Node**
appendStyleSheetNode method of class **Processor**
appendStyleSheetStream method of class **Processor**
appendStyleSheetString method of class **Processor**
appendStyleSheetUri method of class **Processor**
Attr class
attributes attribute of class **Node**
characters method of class **ContentHandler**

childNodes attribute of class **Node**
Comment class
ContentHandler class
createAttribute method of class **Document**
createComment method of class **Document**
createElement method of class **Document**
createTextNode method of class **Document**
data attribute of class **Comment**
data attribute of class **Text**
Document class
Document Object Model (DOM)
DOM parser
DOM tree
documentElement attribute

Element class
endDocument method of class
    ContentHandler
endElement method of class
    ContentHandler
event handler
firstChild attribute of class **Node**
fromStream method of class **Reader**
getAttribute method of class **Element**
getAttributeNode method of class
    Element
getElementsByTagName method of class
    Document
getElementsByTagName method of class
    Element
insertBefore method of class **Node**
isSameNode method of class **Node**
item method of class **NamedNodeMap**
item method of class **NodeList**
lastChild attribute of class **Node**
length attribute of class **NamedNodeMap**
length attribute of class **NodeList**
name attribute of class **Attr**
NamedNodeMap class
nextSibling attribute of class **Node**
Node class
NodeList class
nodeName attribute of class **Node**
nodeType attribute of class **Node**
nodeValue attribute of class **Node**
parent node
parentNode attribute of class **Node**

parse function of package **xml.sax**
parser
prefix attribute of class **Attr**
PrettyPrint function of package **4DOM**
previousSibling attribute of class **Node**
Processor class
PyExpat module
PyXML package
Reader class
removeAttribute method of class
    Element
removeAttributeNode method of class
    Element
removeChild method of class **Node**
replaceChild method of class **Node**
runNode method
runStream method
runString method
runUri method
SAX-based parsing
SAX parser
setAttribute method of class **Element**
setAttributeNode method of class
    Element
sibling
startDocument method of class
    ContentHandler
startElement method of class
    ContentHandler
StripXml function of package **4DOM**
tagName attribute of class **Element**
Text class

SELF-REVIEW EXERCISES

16.1 Fill in the blanks for each of the following statements:
   a) A **PyExpat** _____ object takes an XML document and parses it, storing it in memory as a tree structure.
   b) A **Document** object's _____ attribute refers to the **Document**'s root element.
   c) **4DOM**'s _____ function prints an XML DOM tree to a specified output stream.
   d) **Node** method _____ appends a new child to the list of child nodes.
   e) Method _____ removes a specified DOM tree from memory, freeing resources.
   f) **xml.sax** class _____ contains methods for handling SAX events which can be overridden to perform desired parsing.
   g) A **4XSLT** _____ object transforms XML into HTML, by applying a specified XSLT style sheet.
   h) Method **fromStream** returns a _____ object.

16.2 State which of the following statements are *true* and which are *false*. If *false*, explain why.
   a) To create a Python script which outputs XML, programmers use module **xmlgen**.
   b) Method **insertBefore(_a_, _b_)** inserts node _a_ before node _b_.
   c) The different XML node types are represented in a DOM tree by class **XMLNode**.

d) **Node** attribute **childNodes** returns a **NodeList** object containing the node's children.

e) **4DOM**'s **StripXml** function parses an XML document.

f) With SAX-based parsing, the parser reads the input, storing it in memory as a tree structure.

g) The second argument passed to **parse** must be an instance of class **xml.sax.ContentHandler** (or a subclass of **ContentHandler**).

h) If an error occurs while parsing a file, **parse** raises a **SAXParseException** exception.

ANSWERS TO SELF-REVIEW EXERCISES

16.1   a) **Reader**.   b) **documentElement**.   c) **PrettyPrint**.   d) **appendChild**.
e) **releaseNode**. f) **ContentHandler**. g) **Processor**. h) **Document**.

16.2   a) False. Programmers can use **print** statements, XSLT or the DOM to generate XML markup. b) True. c) False. XML node types are represented by classes derived from **Node**. d) True. e) False. **StripXml** removes insignificant whitespace from an XML DOM tree. f) False. With SAX-based parsing, data is not stored in memory. As the parser encounters markup, event handlers are called. g) True. h) True.

EXERCISES

16.3   Modify the program in Fig. 16.13. Allow the user to add a new element to each **contact** element. For instance, if the user adds a **phoneNumber** element, the user should be prompted to provide a phone number for each contact. Each time a user adds a contact, the user should be prompted to provide information for any new elements in addition to the first and last names. Function **printList** should print any new information as well as the contact's first and last names.

16.4   Create a Python script that, given an XML document, creates an XHTML list of the document's elements in hierarchical order. Display the elements in Internet Explorer. For example, given the XML document in Fig. 16.29, create a Python script that lists the elements as shown in Fig. 16.29.

16.5   These lines of code are from lines 45–46 of **formatting.xsl** (Fig. 16.27). Explain why the **@** in front of **"@file"** is necessary in the **xsl:value-of** element.

```
<xsl:attribute name = "href">../cgi-bin/
addPost.py?file=<xsl:value-of select = "@file" />
</xsl:attribute>
```

16.6   Describe the purpose of Fig. 16.27 (**formatting.xsl**).

16.7   Implement the **Delete a Forum** option in **default.py**. Selecting this option should direct the user to a script named **deleteForum.py**. Here, the user can select a forum name from a list. Your script should remove the selected forum from **forums.xml** and delete the underlying XML document. After removing the forum, the script should redirect the browser to **default.py**.

```
1   <?xml version = "1.0"?>
2   <?xml:stylesheet type = "text/xsl" href = "games.xsl"?>
3
4   <!-- Fig. 16.29                        -->
5   <!-- Sports Database: sports.xml -->
```

Fig. 16.29 sports.xml for Exercise 16.4. (Part 1 of 2.)

```
6
7   <sports>
8      <game id = "783">
9         <name>Cricket</name>
10        <summary>
11           <paragraph>
12              More popular among commonwealth nations.
13           </paragraph>
14        </summary>
15     </game>
16
17     <game id = "239">
18        <name>Baseball</name>
19        <summary>
20           <paragraph>
21              More popular in America.
22           </paragraph>
23        </summary>
24     </game>
25  </sports>
```

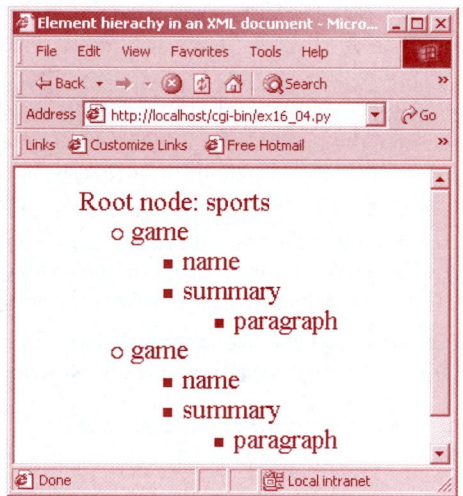

Fig. 16.29 `sports.xml` for Exercise 16.4. (Part 2 of 2.)

16.8   Implement the **Modify a Forum** option in `default.py` such that individual messages can be deleted. Selecting this option should direct the user to a script named **`modifyForum.py`**. Here, the user can select a forum name from a list. Script **`modifyForum.py`** should then display all the messages in the specified forum, allowing the user to select one for deletion. Once selected, **`modifyForum.py`** should remove the given message from the current forum and redirect the browser to `default.py`.

17

Database Application Programming Interface (DB-API)

Objectives

- To understand the relational database model.
- To understand basic database queries using Structured Query Language (SQL).
- To use the methods of the **MySQLdb** module to query a database, insert data into a database and update data in a database.

It is a capital mistake to theorize before one has data.
Arthur Conan Doyle

Now go, write it before them in a table, and note it in a book, that it may be for the time to come for ever and ever.
The Holy Bible: The Old Testament

Let's look at the record.
Alfred Emanuel Smith

True art selects and paraphrases, but seldom gives a verbatim translation.
Thomas Bailey Aldrich

Get your facts first, and then you can distort them as much as you please.
Mark Twain

I like two kinds of men: domestic and foreign.
Mae West

17.1 Introduction

In Chapter 14, File Processing and Serialization, we discussed sequential-access and random-access file processing. Sequential-file processing is appropriate for applications in which most or all of the file's information is to be processed. On the other hand, random-access file processing is appropriate for applications in which only a small portion of a file's data is to be processed. For instance, in transaction processing it is crucial to locate and, possibly, update an individual piece of data quickly. Python provides capabilities for both types of file processing.

A *database* is an integrated collection of data. Many companies maintain databases to organize employee information, such as names, addresses and phone numbers. There are many different strategies for organizing data to facilitate easy access and manipulation of the data. A *database management system (DBMS)* provides mechanisms for storing and organizing data in a manner consistent with the database's format. Database management systems allow for the access and storage of data without concern for the internal representation of databases.

Today's most popular database systems are *relational databases*, which store data in tables and define relationships between the tables. A language called *Structured Query*

Language (*SQL*—pronounced as its individual letters or as "sequel") is used almost universally with relational database systems to perform *queries* (i.e., to request information that satisfies given criteria) and to manipulate data. [*Note*: The writing in this chapter assumes that SQL is pronounced as its individual letters. For this reason, we often precede SQL with the article "an" as in "an SQL database" or "an SQL statement."]

Some popular relational database systems include Microsoft SQL Server, Oracle, Sybase, DB2, Informix and MySQL. In this chapter, we present examples using MySQL. All examples in this chapter use MySQL version 3.23.41. [*Note*: The Deitel & Associates, Inc. Web site (**www.deitel.com**) provides step-by-step instructions for installing MySQL and helpful MySQL commands for creating, populating and deleting tables.]

A programming language connects to, and interacts with, relational databases via an *interface*—software that facilitates communications between a database management system and a program. Python programmers communicate with databases using modules that conform to the Python *Database Application Programming Interface (DB-API)*. Section 17.5 discusses the DB-API specification.

17.2 Relational Database Model

The *relational database model* is a logical representation of data that allows relationships among data to be considered without concern for the physical structure of the data. A relational database is composed of *tables*. Figure 17.1 illustrates a table that might be used in a personnel system. The table name is **Employee**, and its primary purpose is to maintain the specific attributes of various employees. A particular row of the table is called a *record* (or *row*). This table consists of six records. The **number** *field* (or *column*) of each record in the table is the *primary key* for referencing data in the table. A primary key is a field (or combination of fields) in a table that contain(s) unique data—i.e, data that is not duplicated in other records of that table. This guarantees that each record can be identified by at least one distinct value. Examples of primary-key fields are columns that contain social security numbers, employee IDs and part numbers in an inventory system. The records of Fig. 17.1 are *ordered* by primary key. In this case, the records are listed in increasing order (they also could be listed in decreasing order).

Number	Name	Department	Salary	Location
23603	Jones	413	1100	New Jersey
24568	Kerwin	413	2000	New Jersey
34589	Larson	642	1800	Los Angeles
35761	Myers	611	1400	Orlando
47132	Neumann	413	9000	New Jersey
78321	Stephens	611	8500	Orlando

Record/Row {

Primary key   Field/Column

Fig. 17.1   Relational-database structure of an **Employee** table.

Each column of the table represents a different field. Records normally are unique (by primary key) within a table, but particular field values might be duplicated in multiple records. For example, three different records in the **Employee** table's **Department** field contain the number 413.

Often, different users of a database are interested in different data and different relationships among those data. Some users require only subsets of the table columns. To obtain table subsets, we use SQL statements to specify certain data we wish to *select* from a table. SQL provides a complete set of commands (including ***SELECT***) that enable programmers to define complex *queries* to select data from a table. The results of queries commonly are called *result sets* (or *record sets*). For example, we might select data from the table in Fig. 17.1 to create a new result set that contains only the location of each department. This result set appears in Fig. 17.2. SQL queries are discussed in detail in Section 17.4.

17.3 Relational Database Overview: Books Database

This section gives an overview of SQL in the context of a sample **Books** database we created for this chapter. Before we discuss SQL, we overview the tables of the **Books** database. [*Note*: The CD that accompanies this book contains a program called **DBSetup.py** that creates and populates a **Books** database with sample data.]

We use the **Books** database to introduce various database concepts, such as using SQL to obtain useful information from the database and to manipulate the database. We provide the database in the examples directory for this chapter on the CD that accompanies this book. Note that when using MySQL on Windows, the database name is case insensitive (i.e., the **Books** database and the **books** database refer to the same database). However, on Linux, the database name is case sensitive (i.e., the **Books** database and the **books** database refer to different databases).

The database consists of four tables: **Authors**, **Publishers**, **AuthorISBN** and **Titles**. The **Authors** table (described in Fig. 17.3) consists of three fields (or columns) that maintain each author's unique ID number, first name and last name. Figure 17.4 contains the sample data from the **Authors** table of the **Books** database.

The **Publishers** table (described in Fig. 17.5) consists of two fields, which represent each publisher's unique ID and name. Figure 17.6 contains the data from the **Publishers** table of the **Books** database.

Department	Location
413	New Jersey
611	Orlando
642	Los Angeles

Fig. 17.2 Result set formed by selecting **Department** and **Location** data from the **Employee** table.

Field	Description
AuthorID	Author's ID number in the database. In the **Books** database, this **int** field is defined as an *auto-incremented field*. For each new record inserted in this table, the database increments the **AuthorID** value, ensuring that each record has a unique **AuthorID**. This field is the table's primary key.
FirstName	Author's first name (a **string**).
LastName	Author's last name (a **string**).

Fig. 17.3 Authors table from **Books**.

AuthorID	FirstName	LastName
1	Harvey	Deitel
2	Paul	Deitel
3	Tem	Nieto
4	Kate	Steinbuhler
5	Sean	Santry
6	Ted	Lin
7	Praveen	Sadhu
8	David	McPhie
9	Cheryl	Yaeger
10	Marina	Zlatkina
11	Ben	Wiedermann
12	Jonathan	Liperi
13	Jeffrey	Listfield

Fig. 17.4   Data from the **Authors** table of **Books**.

Field	Description
PublisherID	The publisher's ID number in the database. This auto-incremented **int** field is the table's primary-key field.
PublisherName	The name of the publisher (a **string**).

Fig. 17.5 Publishers table from **Books**.

The **AuthorISBN** table (described in Fig. 17.7) consists of two fields that maintain the authors' ID numbers and the corresponding ISBN numbers of their books. This table helps associate the names of the authors with the titles of their books. Figure 17.8 contains a portion of the sample data from the **AuthorISBN** table of the **Books** database.

ISBN is an abbreviation for "International Standard Book Number"—a numbering scheme by which publishers worldwide assign every book a unique identification number. [*Note*: To save space, we split the contents of this figure into two columns, each containing the **AuthorID** and **ISBN** fields.]

PublisherID	PublisherName
1	Prentice Hall
2	Prentice Hall PTG

Fig. 17.6   Data from the **Publishers** table of **Books**.

Field	Description
AuthorID	The author's ID number, which allows the database to associate each book with a specific author. The integer ID number in this field must also appear in the **Authors** table.
ISBN	The ISBN number for a book (a **string**).

Fig. 17.7   **AuthorISBN** table from **Books**.

AuthorID	ISBN	AuthorID	ISBN
1	0130895725	1	0130284181
1	0132261197	1	0130895601
1	0130895717	2	0130895725
1	0135289106	2	0132261197
1	0139163050	2	0130895717
1	013028419x	2	0135289106
1	0130161438	2	0139163050
1	0130856118	2	013028419x
1	0130125075	2	0130161438
1	0138993947	2	0130856118
1	0130852473	2	0130125075
1	0130829277	2	0138993947
1	0134569555	2	0130852473
1	0130829293	2	0130829277
1	0130284173	2	0134569555

Fig. 17.8   Data from **AuthorISBN** table in **Books**. (Note: This table shows only a portion of the sample data.) (Part 1 of 2.)

AuthorID	ISBN	AuthorID	ISBN
2	0130829293	3	0130856118
2	0130284173	3	0134569555
2	0130284181	3	0130829293
2	0130895601	3	0130284173
3	013028419x	3	0130284181
3	0130161438	4	0130895601

Fig. 17.8 Data from **AuthorISBN** table in **Books**. (Note: This table shows only a portion of the sample data.) (Part 2 of 2.)

The **Titles** table (described in Fig. 17.9) consists of seven fields that maintain general information about the books in the database. This information includes each book's ISBN number, title, edition number, copyright year and publisher's ID number, as well as the name of a file that contains an image of the book cover and, finally, each book's price. Figure 17.10 contains the sample data from the **Titles** table.

Field	Description
ISBN	ISBN number of the book (a **string**).
Title	Title of the book (a **string**).
EditionNumber	Edition number of the book (a **string**).
Copyright	Copyright year of the book (an **int**).
PublisherID	Publisher's ID number (an **int**). This value must correspond to an ID number in the **Publishers** table.
ImageFile	Name of the file containing the book's cover image (a **string**).
Price	Suggested retail price of the book (a real number). [*Note*: The prices shown in this database are for example purposes only.]

Fig. 17.9 Titles table from **Books**.

ISBN	Title	Edition-Number	Publish-erID	Copy-right	ImageFile	Price
0130923613	Python How to Program	1	1	2002	**python.jpg**	$69.95
0130622214	C# How to Program	1	1	2002	**cshtp.jpg**	$69.95
0130341517	Java How to Program	4	1	2002	**jhtp4.jpg**	$69.95

Fig. 17.10 Data from the **Titles** table of **Books**. (Part 1 of 3.)

ISBN	Title	Edition-Number	Publish-erID	Copy-right	ImageFile	Price
0130649341	The Complete Java Training Course	4	2	2002	`javactc4.jpg`	$109.95
0130895601	Advanced Java 2 Platform How to Program	1	1	2002	`advjhtp1.jpg`	$69.95
0130308978	Internet and World Wide Web How to Program	2	1	2002	`iw3htp2.jpg`	$69.95
0130293636	Visual Basic .NET How to Program	2	1	2002	`vbnet.jpg`	$69.95
0130895636	The Complete C++ Training Course	3	2	2001	`cppctc3.jpg`	$109.95
0130895512	The Complete e-Business & e-Commerce Programming Training Course	1	2	2001	`ebecctc.jpg`	$109.95
013089561X	The Complete Internet & World Wide Web Programming Training Course	2	2	2001	`iw3ctc2.jpg`	$109.95
0130895547	The Complete Perl Training Course	1	2	2001	`perl.jpg`	$109.95
0130895563	The Complete XML Programming Training Course	1	2	2001	`xmlctc.jpg`	$109.95
0130895725	C How to Program	3	1	2001	`chtp3.jpg`	$69.95
0130895717	C++ How to Program	3	1	2001	`cpphtp3.jpg`	$69.95
013028419X	e-Business and e-Commerce How to Program	1	1	2001	`ebechtp1.jpg`	$69.95
0130622265	Wireless Internet and Mobile Business How to Program	1	1	2001	`wireless.jpg`	$69.95
0130284181	Perl How to Program	1	1	2001	`perlhtp1.jpg`	$69.95
0130284173	XML How to Program	1	1	2001	`xmlhtp1.jpg`	$69.95
0130856118	The Complete Internet and World Wide Web Programming Training Course	1	2	2000	`iw3ctc1.jpg`	$109.95

Fig. 17.10 Data from the **Titles** table of **Books**. (Part 2 of 3.)

ISBN	Title	Edition-Number	Publish-erID	Copy-right	ImageFile	Price
0130125075	Java How to Program (Java 2)	3	1	2000	`jhtp3.jpg`	$69.95
0130852481	The Complete Java 2 Training Course	3	2	2000	`javactc3.jpg`	$109.95
0130323640	e-Business and e-Commerce for Managers	1	1	2000	`ebecm.jpg`	$69.95
0130161438	Internet and World Wide Web How to Program	1	1	2000	`iw3htp1.jpg`	$69.95
0130132497	Getting Started with Visual C++ 6 with an Introduction to MFC	1	1	1999	`gsvc.jpg`	$49.95
0130829293	The Complete Visual Basic 6 Training Course	1	2	1999	`vbctc1.jpg`	$109.95
0134569555	Visual Basic 6 How to Program	1	1	1999	`vbhtp1.jpg`	$69.95
0132719746	Java Multimedia Cyber Classroom	1	2	1998	`javactc.jpg`	$109.95
0136325890	Java How to Program	1	1	1998	`jhtp1.jpg`	$69.95
0139163050	The Complete C++ Training Course	2	2	1998	`cppctc2.jpg`	$109.95
0135289106	C++ How to Program	2	1	1998	`cpphtp2.jpg`	$49.95
0137905696	The Complete Java Training Course	2	2	1998	`javactc2.jpg`	$109.95
0130829277	The Complete Java Training Course (Java 1.1)	2	2	1998	`javactc2.jpg`	$99.95
0138993947	Java How to Program (Java 1.1)	2	1	1998	`jhtp2.jpg`	$49.95
0131173340	C++ How to Program	1	1	1994	`cpphtp1.jpg`	$69.95
0132261197	C How to Program	2	1	1994	`chtp2.jpg`	$49.95
0131180436	C How to Program	1	1	1992	`chtp.jpg`	$69.95

Fig. 17.10 Data from the **Titles** table of **Books**. (Part 3 of 3.)

Figure 17.11 illustrates the relationships among the tables in the **Books** database. The first line in each table is the table's name. The field whose name appears in italics contains that table's primary key. A table's primary key uniquely identifies each record in the table. Every record must have a value in the primary-key field, and the value must be unique. This

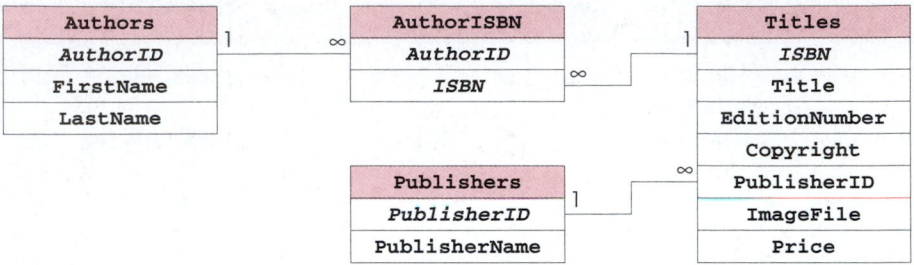

Fig. 17.11 Table relationships in **Books**.

is known as the *Rule of Entity Integrity*. Note that the **AuthorISBN** table contains two fields whose names are italicized. This indicates that these two fields form a *compound primary key*—each record in the table must have a unique **AuthorID–ISBN** combination. For example, several records might have an **AuthorID** of **2**, and several records might have an **ISBN** of **0130895601**, but only one record can have both an **AuthorID** of **2** and an **ISBN** of **0130895601**.

Common Programming Error 17.1

Failure to provide a value for a primary-key field in every record breaks the Rule of Entity Integrity and causes the DBMS to report an error.

Common Programming Error 17.2

Providing duplicate values for the primary-key field of multiple records causes the DBMS to report an error.

The lines connecting the tables in Fig. 17.11 represent the *relationships* among the tables. Consider the line between the **Publishers** and **Titles** tables. On the **Publishers** end of the line, there is a **1**, and, on the **Titles** end, there is an infinity (∞) symbol. This line indicates a *one-to-many relationship*, in which every publisher in the **Publishers** table can have an arbitrarily large number of books in the **Titles** table. Note that the relationship line links the **PublisherID** field in the **Publishers** table to the **PublisherID** field in **Titles** table. In the **Titles** table, the **PublisherID** field is a *foreign key*—a field for which every entry has a unique value in another table and where the field in the other table is the primary key for that table (e.g., **PublisherID** in the **Publishers** table). Programmers specify foreign keys when creating a table. The foreign key helps maintain the *Rule of Referential Integrity*: Every foreign-key field value must appear in another table's primary-key field. Foreign keys enable information from multiple tables to be *joined* together for analysis purposes. There is a one-to-many relationship between a primary key and its corresponding foreign key. This means that a foreign-key field value can appear many times in its own table, but must appear exactly once as the primary key of another table. The line between the tables represents the link between the foreign key in one table and the primary key in another table.

Common Programming Error 17.3

Providing a foreign-key value that does not appear as a primary-key value in another table breaks the Rule of Referential Integrity and causes the DBMS to report an error.

The line between the **AuthorISBN** and **Authors** tables indicates that, for each author in the **Authors** table, the **AuthorISBN** table can contain an arbitrary number of ISBNs for books written by that author. The **AuthorID** field in the **AuthorISBN** table is a foreign key of the **AuthorID** field (the primary key) of the **Authors** table. Note, again, that the line between the tables links the foreign key in table **AuthorISBN** to the corresponding primary key in table **Authors**. The **AuthorISBN** table links information in the **Titles** and **Authors** tables.

The line between the **Titles** and **AuthorISBN** tables illustrates another one-to-many relationship; a title can be written by any number of authors. In fact, the sole purpose of the **AuthorISBN** table is to represent a many-to-many relationship between the **Authors** and **Titles** tables; an author can write any number of books, and a book can have any number of authors.

17.4 Structured Query Language (SQL)

This section provides an overview of Structured Query Language (SQL) in the context of our **Books** sample database. The SQL queries discussed here form the foundation for the SQL used in the chapter examples.

Figure 17.12 lists SQL keywords and provides a description of each. In the next several subsections, we discuss these SQL keywords in the context of complete SQL queries. Other SQL keywords exist, but are beyond the scope of this text. [*Note*: To locate additional information on SQL, please refer to the bibliography at the end of this book.]

SQL keyword	Description
SELECT	Selects (retrieves) fields from one or more tables.
FROM	Specifies tables from which to get fields or delete records. Required in every **SELECT** and **DELETE** statement.
WHERE	Specifies criteria that determine the rows to be retrieved.
INNER JOIN	Joins records from multiple tables to produce a single set of records.
GROUP BY	Specifies criteria for grouping records.
ORDER BY	Specifies criteria for ordering records.
INSERT	Inserts data into a specified table.
UPDATE	Updates data in a specified table.
DELETE	Deletes data from a specified table.

Fig. 17.12 SQL query keywords.

17.4.1 Basic SELECT Query

Let us consider several SQL queries that extract information from database **Books**. A typical SQL query "selects" information from one or more tables in a database. Such selections are performed by *SELECT queries*. The basic format for a **SELECT** query is:

```
SELECT * FROM tableName
```

In this query, the asterisk (*****) indicates that all columns from the *tableName* table of the database should be selected. For example, to select the entire contents of the **Authors** table (i.e., all data depicted in Fig. 17.4), use the query:

```
SELECT * FROM Authors
```

To select specific fields from a table, replace the asterisk (*****) with a comma-separated list of the field names to select. For example, to select only the fields **AuthorID** and **LastName** for all rows in the **Authors** table, use the query:

```
SELECT AuthorID, LastName FROM Authors
```

This query returns only the data presented in Fig. 17.13. The result set contains the columns in the order that are specified by the query. [*Note*: If a field name contains spaces, the entire field name must be enclosed in square brackets (**[ ]**) in the query. For example, if the field name is **First Name**, it must appear in the query as **[First Name]**].

Common Programming Error 17.4

If a program assumes that an SQL statement using the asterisk (*) to select fields always returns those fields in the same order, the program could process the result set incorrectly. If the field order in the database table(s) changes, the order of the fields in the result set would change accordingly.

Performance Tip 17.1

If a program does not know the order of fields in a result set, the program must process the fields by name. This could require a linear search of the field names in the result set. If users specify the field names that they wish to select from a table (or several tables), the application receiving the result set knows the order of the fields in advance. When this occurs, the program can process the data more efficiently, because fields can be accessed directly by column number.

AuthorID	LastName	AuthorID	LastName
1	Deitel	8	McPhie
2	Deitel	9	Yaeger
3	Nieto	10	Zlatkina
4	Steinbuhler	12	Wiedermann
5	Santry	12	Liperi
6	Lin	13	Listfield
7	Sadhu		

Fig. 17.13 AuthorID and **LastName** from the **Authors** table.

17.4.2 WHERE Clause

In most cases, users search a database for records that satisfy certain *selection criteria*. Only records that match the selection criteria are selected. SQL uses the optional **WHERE** *clause* in a **SELECT** query to specify the selection criteria for the query. The simplest format for a **SELECT** query that includes selection criteria is:

> **SELECT** *fieldName1*, *fieldName2*, ... **FROM** *tableName* **WHERE** *criteria*

For example, to select the **Title**, **EditionNumber** and **Copyright** fields from those rows of table **Titles** in which the **Copyright** date is greater than **1999**, use the query:

```
SELECT Title, EditionNumber, Copyright
FROM Titles
WHERE Copyright > 1999
```

Figure 17.14 shows the result set of the preceding query. [*Note*: When we construct a query for use in Python, we create a string containing the entire query. However, when we display queries in the text, we often use multiple lines and indentation to enhance readability.]

Performance Tip 17.2

Using selection criteria improves performance, because queries that involve such criteria normally select a portion of the database that is smaller than the entire database. Working with a smaller portion of the data is more efficient than working with the entire set of data stored in the database.

Title	EditionNumber	Copyright
Internet and World Wide Web How to Program	2	2002
Java How to Program	4	2002
The Complete Java Training Course	4	2002
The Complete e-Business & e-Commerce Programming Training Course	1	2001
The Complete Internet & World Wide Web Programming Training Course	2	2001
The Complete Perl Training Course	1	2001
The Complete XML Programming Training Course	1	2001
C How to Program	3	2001
C++ How to Program	3	2001
The Complete C++ Training Course	3	2001
e-Business and e-Commerce How to Program	1	2001
Internet and World Wide Web How to Program	1	2000
The Complete Internet and World Wide Web Programming Training Course	1	2000
Java How to Program (Java 2)	3	2000

Fig. 17.14 Titles with copyrights after 1999 from table **Titles**. (Part 1 of 2.)

Title	EditionNumber	Copyright
The Complete Java 2 Training Course	3	2000
XML How to Program	1	2001
Perl How to Program	1	2001
Advanced Java 2 Platform How to Program	1	2002
e-Business and e-Commerce for Managers	1	2000
Wireless Internet and Mobile Business How to Program	1	2001
C# How To Program	1	2002
Python How to Program	1	2002
Visual Basic .NET How to Program	2	2002

Fig. 17.14 Titles with copyrights after 1999 from table **Titles**. (Part 2 of 2.)

The **WHERE** clause condition can contain operators **<**, **>**, **<=**, **>=**, **=**, **<>** and **LIKE**. Operator **LIKE** is used for *pattern matching* with wildcard characters *percent* (**%**) and *underscore mark* (**_**). Pattern matching allows SQL to search for strings that "match a pattern."

A pattern that contains a percent (**%**) searches for strings in which zero or more characters take the percent character's place in the pattern. For example, the following query locates the records of all authors whose last names start with the letter **D**:

```
SELECT AuthorID, FirstName, LastName
FROM Authors
WHERE LastName LIKE 'D%'
```

The preceding query selects the two records shown in Fig. 17.15, because two of the authors in our database have last names that begin with the letter **D** (followed by zero or more characters). The **%** in the **WHERE** clause's **LIKE** pattern indicates that any number of characters can appear after the letter **D** in the **LastName** field. Notice that the pattern string is surrounded by single-quote characters.

Portability Tip 17.1

*Not all database systems support the **LIKE** operator, so be sure to read the database system's documentation carefully before employing this operator.*

Portability Tip 17.2

*Some databases use the ***** character in place of the **%** character in **LIKE** expressions.*

AuthorID	FirstName	LastName
1	Harvey	Deitel
2	Paul	Deitel

Fig. 17.15 Authors from the **Authors** table whose last names start with **D**.

Portability Tip 17.3

In some databases, string data is case sensitive.

Portability Tip 17.4

In some databases, table names and field names are case sensitive.

Good Programming Practice 17.1

By convention, SQL keywords should be written entirely in uppercase letters on systems that are not case sensitive. This emphasizes the SQL keywords in an SQL statement.

A pattern string including an underscore (_) character searches for strings in which exactly one character takes the underscore's place in the pattern. For example, the following query locates the records of all authors whose last names start with any character (specified with _), followed by the letter **i**, followed by any number of additional characters (specified with **%**):

```
SELECT AuthorID, FirstName, LastName
FROM Authors
WHERE LastName LIKE '_i%'
```

The preceding query produces the records listed in Fig. 17.16; five authors in our database have last names in which the letter **i** is the second letter.

Portability Tip 17.5

*Some databases use the **?** character in place of the _ character in **LIKE** expressions.*

17.4.3 ORDER BY Clause

The results of a query can be arranged in ascending or descending order using the optional **ORDER BY** *clause*. The simplest forms for an **ORDER BY** clause are:

```
SELECT fieldName1, fieldName2, ... FROM tableName ORDER BY field ASC
SELECT fieldName1, fieldName2, ... FROM tableName ORDER BY field DESC
```

where **ASC** specifies ascending order (lowest to highest), **DESC** specifies descending order (highest to lowest) and *field* specifies the field whose values determine the sorting order.

AuthorID	FirstName	LastName
3	Tem	Nieto
6	Ted	Lin
11	Ben	Wiedermann
12	Jonathan	Liperi
13	Jeffrey	Listfield

Fig. 17.16 Authors from table **Authors** whose last names contain **i** as the second letter.

For example, to obtain a list of authors arranged in ascending order by last name (Fig. 17.17), use the query:

```
SELECT AuthorID, FirstName, LastName
FROM Authors
ORDER BY LastName ASC
```

Note that the default sorting order is ascending; therefore, **ASC** is optional.

To obtain the same list of authors arranged in descending order by last name (Fig. 17.18), use the query:

```
SELECT AuthorID, FirstName, LastName
FROM Authors
ORDER BY LastName DESC
```

AuthorID	FirstName	LastName
2	Paul	Deitel
1	Harvey	Deitel
6	Ted	Lin
12	Jonathan	Liperi
13	Jeffrey	Listfield
8	David	McPhie
3	Tem	Nieto
7	Praveen	Sadhu
5	Sean	Santry
4	Kate	Steinbuhler
11	Ben	Wiedermann
9	Cheryl	Yaeger
10	Marina	Zlatkina

Fig. 17.17 Authors from table **Authors** in ascending order by **LastName**.

AuthorID	FirstName	LastName
10	Marina	Zlatkina
9	Cheryl	Yaeger
11	Ben	Wiedermann
4	Kate	Steinbuhler
5	Sean	Santry

Fig. 17.18 Authors from table **Authors** in descending order by **LastName**. (Part 1 of 2.)

AuthorID	FirstName	LastName
7	Praveen	Sadhu
3	Tem	Nieto
8	David	McPhie
13	Jeffrey	Listfield
12	Jonathan	Liperi
6	Ted	Lin
2	Paul	Deitel
1	Harvey	Deitel

Fig. 17.18 Authors from table **Authors** in descending order by **LastName**. (Part 2 of 2.)

The **ORDER BY** clause also can be used to order records by multiple fields. Such queries are written in the form:

> **ORDER BY** *field1 sortingOrder*, *field2 sortingOrder*, ...

where *sortingOrder* is either **ASC** or **DESC**. Note that the *sortingOrder* does not have to be identical for each field. For example, the query:

```
SELECT AuthorID, FirstName, LastName
FROM Authors
ORDER BY LastName, FirstName
```

sorts all authors in ascending order by last name, then by first name. Thus, any authors have the same last name, their records are returned sorted by first name (Fig. 17.19).

AuthorID	FirstName	LastName
1	Harvey	Deitel
2	Paul	Deitel
6	Ted	Lin
12	Jonathan	Liperi
13	Jeffrey	Listfield
8	David	McPhie
3	Tem	Nieto
7	Praveen	Sadhu
5	Sean	Santry
4	Kate	Steinbuhler

Fig. 17.19 Authors from table **Authors** in ascending order by **LastName** and by **FirstName**. (Part 1 of 2.)

AuthorID	FirstName	LastName
11	Ben	Wiedermann
9	Cheryl	Yaeger
10	Marina	Zlatkina

Fig. 17.19 Authors from table **Authors** in ascending order by **LastName** and by **FirstName**. (Part 2 of 2.)

The **WHERE** and **ORDER BY** clauses can be combined in one query. For example, the query:

```
SELECT ISBN, Title, EditionNumber, Copyright, Price
FROM Titles
WHERE Title
LIKE '*How to Program' ORDER BY Title ASC
```

returns the ISBN, title, edition number, copyright and price of each book in the **Titles** table that has a **Title** ending with "**How to Program**;" it lists these records in ascending order by **Title**. The results of the query are depicted in Fig. 17.20.

ISBN	Title	Edition-Number	Copy-right	Price
0130895601	Advanced Java 2 Platform How to Program	1	2002	$69.95
0131180436	C How to Program	1	1992	$69.95
0130895725	C How to Program	3	2001	$69.95
0132261197	C How to Program	2	1994	$49.95
0130622214	C# How To Program	1	2002	$69.95
0135289106	C++ How to Program	2	1998	$49.95
0131173340	C++ How to Program	1	1994	$69.95
0130895717	C++ How to Program	3	2001	$69.95
013028419X	e-Business and e-Commerce How to Program	1	2001	$69.95
0130308978	Internet and World Wide Web How to Program	2	2002	$69.95
0130161438	Internet and World Wide Web How to Program	1	2000	$69.95
0130341517	Java How to Program	4	2002	$69.95
0136325890	Java How to Program	1	1998	$49.95

Fig. 17.20 Books from table **Titles** whose titles end with **How to Program** in ascending order by **Title**. (Part 1 of 2.)

ISBN	Title	Edition-Number	Copy-right	Price
0130284181	Perl How to Program	1	2001	$69.95
0130923613	Python How to Program	1	2002	$69.95
0130293636	Visual Basic .NET How to Program	2	2002	$69.95
0134569555	Visual Basic 6 How to Program	1	1999	$69.95
0130622265	Wireless Internet and Mobile Business How to Program	1	2001	$69.95
0130284173	XML How to Program	1	2001	$69.95

Fig. 17.20 Books from table **Titles** whose titles end with **How to Program** in ascending order by **Title**. (Part 2 of 2.)

17.4.4 Merging Data from Multiple Tables: INNER JOIN

Database designers often split related data into separate tables to ensure that a database does not store data redundantly. For example, the **Books** database has tables **Authors** and **Titles**. We use an **AuthorISBN** table to provide "links" between authors and their corresponding titles. If we did not separate this information into individual tables, we would need to include author information with each entry in the **Titles** table. This would result in the database storing duplicate author information for authors who wrote multiple books.

Often, it is necessary for analysis purposes to merge data from multiple tables into a single set of data—referred to as *joining* the tables. Joining is accomplished via an *INNER JOIN* operation in the **SELECT** query. An **INNER JOIN** merges records from two or more tables by testing for matching values in a field that is common to the tables. The simplest format for an **INNER JOIN** clause is:

```
SELECT fieldName1, fieldName2, …
FROM table1
INNER JOIN table2
   ON table1.fieldName = table2.fieldName
```

The **ON** part of the **INNER JOIN** clause specifies the fields from each table that are compared to determine which records are joined. For example, the following query produces a list of authors accompanied by the ISBN numbers for books written by each author:

```
SELECT FirstName, LastName, ISBN
FROM Authors
INNER JOIN AuthorISBN
   ON Authors.AuthorID = AuthorISBN.AuthorID
ORDER BY LastName, FirstName
```

The query merges the **FirstName** and **LastName** fields from table **Authors** with the **ISBN** field from table **AuthorISBN**, sorting the results in ascending order by **LastName** and **FirstName**. Notice the use of the syntax *tableName.fieldName* in the **ON** part of the **INNER JOIN**. This syntax (called a *fully qualified name*) specifies the fields from each table that should be compared to join the tables. The "*tableName*." syntax is required if the fields have the same name in both tables. The same syntax can be used in any query to distinguish among fields in different tables that have the same name. Fully qualified names that start with the database name can be used to perform cross-database queries.

Software Engineering Observation 17.1
If an SQL statement includes fields from multiple tables that have the same name, the statement must precede those field names with their table names and the dot operator (e.g., **Authors.AuthorID**).

Common Programming Error 17.5
In a query, failure to provide fully qualified names for fields that have the same name in two or more tables is an error.

As always, the query can contain an **ORDER BY** clause. Figure 17.21 depicts the results of the preceding query, ordered by **LastName** and **FirstName**. [*Note*: To save space, we split the results of the query into two columns, each containing the **FirstName**, **LastName** and **ISBN** fields.]

FirstName	LastName	ISBN	FirstName	LastName	ISBN
Harvey	Deitel	0130895601	Harvey	Deitel	0130829293
Harvey	Deitel	0130284181	Harvey	Deitel	0134569555
Harvey	Deitel	0130284173	Harvey	Deitel	0130829277
Harvey	Deitel	0130852473	Paul	Deitel	0130125075
Harvey	Deitel	0138993947	Paul	Deitel	0130856118
Harvey	Deitel	0130856118	Paul	Deitel	0130161438
Harvey	Deitel	0130161438	Paul	Deitel	013028419x
Harvey	Deitel	013028419x	Paul	Deitel	0139163050
Harvey	Deitel	0139163050	Paul	Deitel	0130895601
Harvey	Deitel	0135289106	Paul	Deitel	0135289106
Harvey	Deitel	0130895717	Paul	Deitel	0130895717
Harvey	Deitel	0132261197	Paul	Deitel	0132261197
Harvey	Deitel	0130895725	Paul	Deitel	0130895725
Harvey	Deitel	0130125075	Tem	Nieto	0130284181
Paul	Deitel	0130284181	Tem	Nieto	0130284173
Paul	Deitel	0130284173	Tem	Nieto	0130829293
Paul	Deitel	0130829293	Tem	Nieto	0134569555
Paul	Deitel	0134569555	Tem	Nieto	0130856118
Paul	Deitel	0130829277	Tem	Nieto	0130161438
Paul	Deitel	0130852473	Tem	Nieto	013028419x
Paul	Deitel	0138993947			

Fig. 17.21 Authors from table **Authors** and ISBN numbers of the authors' books, sorted in ascending order by **LastName** and **FirstName**.

17.4.5 Joining Data from Tables `Authors`, `AuthorISBN`, `Titles` and `Publishers`

The **Books** database contains one predefined query (**TitleAuthor**), which selects as its results the title, ISBN number, author's first name, author's last name, copyright year and publisher's name for each book in the database. For books that have multiple authors, the query produces a separate composite record for each author. The **TitleAuthor** query is depicted in Fig. 17.22. Figure 17.23 contains a portion of the query results.

```
1    SELECT Titles.Title, Titles.ISBN, Authors.FirstName,
2           Authors.LastName, Titles.Copyright,
3           Publishers.PublisherName
4    FROM
5       ( Publishers INNER JOIN Titles
6          ON Publishers.PublisherID = Titles.PublisherID )
7       INNER JOIN
8       ( Authors INNER JOIN AuthorISBN
9          ON Authors.AuthorID = AuthorISBN.AuthorID )
10      ON Titles.ISBN = AuthorISBN.ISBN
11   ORDER BY Titles.Title
```

Fig. 17.22 `TitleAuthor` query of **Books** database.

Title	ISBN	First-Name	Last-Name	Copy-right	Publisher-Name
Advanced Java 2 Platform How to Program	0130895601	Paul	Deitel	2002	Prentice Hall
Advanced Java 2 Platform How to Program	0130895601	Harvey	Deitel	2002	Prentice Hall
Advanced Java 2 Platform How to Program	0130895601	Sean	Santry	2002	Prentice Hall
C How to Program	0131180436	Harvey	Deitel	1992	Prentice Hall
C How to Program	0131180436	Paul	Deitel	1992	Prentice Hall
C How to Program	0132261197	Harvey	Deitel	1994	Prentice Hall
C How to Program	0132261197	Paul	Deitel	1994	Prentice Hall
C How to Program	0130895725	Harvey	Deitel	2001	Prentice Hall
C How to Program	0130895725	Paul	Deitel	2001	Prentice Hall
C# How To Program	0130622214	Tem	Nieto	2002	Prentice Hall
C# How To Program	0130622214	Paul	Deitel	2002	Prentice Hall
C# How To Program	0130622214	Jeffrey	Listfield	2002	Prentice Hall
C# How To Program	0130622214	Cheryl	Yaeger	2002	Prentice Hall
C# How To Program	0130622214	Marina	Zlatkina	2002	Prentice Hall

Fig. 17.23 Portion of the result set produced by the query in Fig. 17.22. (Part 1 of 2.)

Title	ISBN	First-Name	Last-Name	Copy-right	Publisher-Name
C# How To Program	0130622214	Harvey	Deitel	2002	Prentice Hall
C++ How to Program	0130895717	Paul	Deitel	2001	Prentice Hall
C++ How to Program	0130895717	Harvey	Deitel	2001	Prentice Hall
C++ How to Program	0131173340	Paul	Deitel	1994	Prentice Hall
C++ How to Program	0131173340	Harvey	Deitel	1994	Prentice Hall
C++ How to Program	0135289106	Harvey	Deitel	1998	Prentice Hall
C++ How to Program	0135289106	Paul	Deitel	1998	Prentice Hall
e-Business and e-Commerce for Managers	0130323640	Harvey	Deitel	2000	Prentice Hall
e-Business and e-Commerce for Managers	0130323640	Kate	Stein-buhler	2000	Prentice Hall
e-Business and e-Commerce for Managers	0130323640	Paul	Deitel	2000	Prentice Hall
e-Business and e-Commerce How to Program	013028419X	Harvey	Deitel	2001	Prentice Hall
e-Business and e-Commerce How to Program	013028419X	Paul	Deitel	2001	Prentice Hall
e-Business and e-Commerce How to Program	013028419X	Tem	Nieto	2001	Prentice Hall

Fig. 17.23 Portion of the result set produced by the query in Fig. 17.22. (Part 2 of 2.)

We added indentation to the query in Fig. 17.22 to make the query more readable. Let us now break down the query into its various parts. Lines 1–3 contain a comma-separated list of the fields that the query returns; the order of the fields from left to right specifies the fields' order in the returned table. This query selects fields **Title** and **ISBN** from table **Titles**, fields **FirstName** and **LastName** from table **Authors**, field **Copyright** from table **Titles** and field **PublisherName** from table **Publishers**. For purposes of clarity, we fully qualified each field name with its table name (e.g., **Titles.ISBN**).

Lines 5–10 specify the **INNER JOIN** operations used to combine information from the various tables. There are three **INNER JOIN** operations. It is important to note that, although an **INNER JOIN** is performed on two tables, either of those two tables can be the result of another query or another **INNER JOIN**. We use parentheses to nest the **INNER JOIN** operations; SQL evaluates the innermost set of parentheses first and then moves outward. We begin with the **INNER JOIN**:

```
( Publishers INNER JOIN Titles
    ON Publishers.PublisherID = Titles.PublisherID )
```

which joins the **Publishers** table and the **Titles** table **ON** the condition that the **PublisherID** numbers in each table match. The resulting temporary table contains information about each book and its publisher.

The other nested set of parentheses contains the **INNER JOIN**:

```
( Authors INNER JOIN AuthorISBN ON
    Authors.AuthorID = AuthorISBN.AuthorID )
```

which joins the **Authors** table and the **AuthorISBN** table **ON** the condition that the **AuthorID** fields in each table match. Remember that the **AuthorISBN** table has multiple entries for **ISBN** numbers of books that have more than one author. The third **INNER JOIN**:

```
( Publishers INNER JOIN Titles
    ON Publishers.PublisherID = Titles.PublisherID )
INNER JOIN
( Authors INNER JOIN AuthorISBN
    ON Authors.AuthorID = AuthorISBN.AuthorID )
ON Titles.ISBN = AuthorISBN.ISBN
```

joins the two temporary tables produced by the two prior inner joins **ON** the condition that the **Titles.ISBN** field for each record in the first temporary table matches the corresponding **AuthorISBN.ISBN** field for each record in the second temporary table. The result of all these **INNER JOIN** operations is a temporary table from which the appropriate fields are selected to produce the results of the query.

Finally, line 11 of the query:

```
ORDER BY Titles.Title
```

indicates that all the records should be sorted in ascending order (the default) by title.

17.4.6 INSERT Statement

The *INSERT* statement inserts a new record in a table. The simplest form for this statement is:

```
INSERT INTO tableName ( fieldName1, fieldName2, ..., fieldNameN )
    VALUES ( value1, value2, ..., valueN )
```

where *tableName* is the table in which to insert the record. The *tableName* is followed by a comma-separated list of field names in parentheses. The list of field names is followed by the SQL keyword **VALUES** and a comma-separated list of values in parentheses. The specified values in this list must match the field names listed after the table name in both order and type (for example, if *fieldName1* is specified as the **FirstName** field, then *value1* should be a string in single quotes representing the first name). The **INSERT** statement:

```
INSERT INTO Authors ( FirstName, LastName )
    VALUES ( 'Sue', 'Smith' )
```

inserts a record into the **Authors** table. The statement indicates that values will be inserted for the **FirstName** and **LastName** fields. The corresponding values to insert are **'Sue'** and **'Smith'**. [*Note*: The SQL statement does not specify an **AuthorID** in this example, because **AuthorID** is an *autoincrement field* in table **Authors**. For every new record added to this table, MySQL assigns a unique **AuthorID** value that is the next value in the autoincrement sequence (i.e., 1, 2, 3, etc.). In this case, MySQL assigns **AuthorID** number 8 to Sue Smith.] Figure 17.24 shows the **Authors** table after the **INSERT INTO** operation.

AuthorID	FirstName	LastName
1	Harvey	Deitel
2	Paul	Deitel
3	Tem	Nieto
4	Kate	Steinbuhler
5	Sean	Santry
6	Ted	Lin
7	Praveen	Sadhu
8	David	McPhie
9	Cheryl	Yaeger
10	Marina	Zlatkina
11	Ben	Wiedermann
12	Jonathan	Liperi
13	Jeffrey	Listfield
14	Sue	Smith

Fig. 17.24 Authors after an **INSERT** operation to add a record.

Common Programming Error 17.6

SQL statements use the single-quote (') character as a delimiter for strings. To specify a string containing a single quote (such as O'Malley) in an SQL statement, the string must include two single quotes in the position where the single-quote character should appear in the string (e.g., **'O''Malley'***). The first of the two single-quote characters acts as an escape character for the second. Failure to escape single-quote characters in a string that is part of an SQL statement is an SQL syntax error.*

17.4.7 UPDATE Statement

An **UPDATE** statement modifies data in a table. The simplest form for an **UPDATE** statement is:

```
UPDATE tableName
    SET fieldName1 = value1, fieldName2 = value2, ..., fieldNameN = valueN
    WHERE criteria
```

where *tableName* is the table in which to update a record (or records). The *tableName* is followed by keyword **SET** and a comma-separated list of field name/value pairs written in the format, *fieldName = value*. The **WHERE** clause specifies the criteria used to determine which record(s) to update. For example, the **UPDATE** statement:

```
UPDATE Authors
    SET LastName = 'Jones'
    WHERE LastName = 'Smith' AND FirstName = 'Sue'
```

updates a record in the **Authors** table. The statement indicates that **LastName** will be assigned the new value **Jones** for the record in which **LastName** currently is equal to

Smith and **FirstName** is equal to **Sue**. If we know the **AuthorID** in advance of the **UPDATE** operation (possibly because we searched for the record previously), the **WHERE** clause could be simplified as follows:

> **WHERE** AuthorID = 14

Figure 17.25 depicts the **Authors** table after we perform the **UPDATE** operation.

Common Programming Error 17.7

*Failure to use a **WHERE** clause with an **UPDATE** statement could lead to logic errors.*

17.4.8 DELETE Statement

An SQL **DELETE** statement removes data from a table. The simplest form for a **DELETE** statement is:

> **DELETE FROM** *tableName* **WHERE** *criteria*

where *tableName* is the table from which to delete a record (or records). The **WHERE** clause specifies the criteria used to determine which record(s) to delete. For example, the **DELETE** statement:

> **DELETE FROM** Authors
>   **WHERE** LastName = 'Jones' **AND** FirstName = 'Sue'

deletes the record for **Sue Jones** from the **Authors** table. Figure 17.26 depicts the **Authors** table after we perform the **DELETE** operation.

AuthorID	FirstName	LastName
1	Harvey	Deitel
2	Paul	Deitel
3	Tem	Nieto
4	Kate	Steinbuhler
5	Sean	Santry
6	Ted	Lin
7	Praveen	Sadhu
8	David	McPhie
9	Cheryl	Yaeger
10	Marina	Zlatkina
11	Ben	Wiedermann
12	Jonathan	Liperi
13	Jeffrey	Listfield
14	Sue	Jones

Fig. 17.25 Table **Authors** after an **UPDATE** operation to change a record.

AuthorID	FirstName	LastName
1	Harvey	Deitel
2	Paul	Deitel
3	Tem	Nieto
4	Kate	Steinbuhler
5	Sean	Santry
6	Ted	Lin
7	Praveen	Sadhu
8	David	McPhie
9	Cheryl	Yaeger
10	Marina	Zlatkina
11	Ben	Wiedermann
12	Jonathan	Liperi
13	Jeffrey	Listfield

Fig. 17.26 Table **Authors** after a **DELETE** operation to remove a record.

Common Programming Error 17.8

WHERE clauses can match multiple records. When deleting records from a database, be sure to define a WHERE clause that matches only the records to be deleted.

17.5 Python DB-API Specification

The code examples in this chapter use the MySQL database system; however, Python supports many databases in addition to MySQL. Modules have been written that can interface with most popular databases, thus hiding database details from the programmer. These modules follow the Python *Database Application Programming Interface (DB-API)*, a document that specifies common object and method names for manipulating any database.

Specifically, the DB-API describes a **Connection** object that accesses the database (connects to the database). A program then uses the **Connection** object to create the **Cursor** object, which manipulates and retrieves data. We discuss the methods and attributes of these objects in the context of live-code examples throughout the remainder of the chapter.

A **Cursor** enables a program to perform operations on a database (e.g., executing queries, inserting rows into a table, deleting rows from a table, etc.), as well as manipulate data returned from query execution. Three methods are available to fetch row(s) of a query result set—**fetchone**, **fetchmany** and **fetchall**. Method **fetchone** returns a tuple containing the next row in a result set stored in **Cursor**. Method **fetchmany** takes one argument—the number of rows to be fetched and returns the next set of rows of a result set as a tuple of tuples. Method **fetchall** returns all rows of a result set as a tuple of tuples. On a large database, a **fetchall** would be impractical.

A benefit of the DB-API is that a program does not need to know much about the database to which the program connects. Therefore, a program can use different databases with few modifications in the Python source code. For example, to switch from the MySQL database to another database, a programmer needs to change three or four lines of code. However, the switch between databases may require modifications to the SQL code (to compensate for case sensitivity, etc.).

17.6 Database Query Example

Figure 17.27 presents a CGI program that performs a simple query on the **Books** database. The query retrieves all information about the authors in the **Authors** table and displays the data in an XHTML table. The program demonstrates connecting to the database, querying the database and displaying the results. The discussion that follows presents the key DB-API aspects of the program. [Note: The CGI script in this example is defined for use with the Apache Web server running on Microsoft Windows. On the CD that accompanies this book, we provide a version of this example for use with Apache running on Linux.]

```python
1  #!c:\python\python.exe
2  # Fig. 17.27: fig17_27.py
3  # Displays contents of the Authors table,
4  # ordered by a specified field.
5
6  import MySQLdb
7  import cgi
8  import sys
9
10 def printHeader( title ):
11     print """Content-type: text/html
12
13 <?xml version = "1.0" encoding = "UTF-8"?>
14 <!DOCTYPE html PUBLIC
15     "-//W3C//DTD XHTML 1.0 Transitional//EN"
16     "DTD/xhtml1-transitional.dtd">
17 <html xmlns = "http://www.w3.org/1999/xhtml"
18     xml:lang = "en" lang = "en">
19 <head><title>%s</title></head>
20
21 <body>""" % title
22
23 # obtain user query specifications
24 form = cgi.FieldStorage()
25
26 # get "sortBy" value
27 if form.has_key( "sortBy" ):
28     sortBy = form[ "sortBy" ].value
29 else:
30     sortBy = "firstName"
31
32 # get "sortOrder" value
33 if form.has_key( "sortOrder" ):
34     sortOrder = form[ "sortOrder" ].value
35 else:
36     sortOrder = "ASC"
37
```

Fig. 17.27 Connecting to and querying a database. (Part 1 of 3.)

```
38   printHeader( "Authors table from Books" )
39
40   # connect to database and retrieve a cursor
41   try:
42      connection = MySQLdb.connect( db = "Books" )
43
44   # error connecting to database
45   except MySQLdb.OperationalError, error:
46      print "Error:", error
47      sys.exit( 1 )
48
49   # retrieve cursor
50   else:
51      cursor = connection.cursor()
52
53   # query all records from Authors table
54   cursor.execute( "SELECT * FROM Authors ORDER BY %s %s" %
55      ( sortBy, sortOrder ) )
56
57   allFields = cursor.description   # get field names
58   allRecords = cursor.fetchall()   # get records
59
60   # close cursor and connection
61   cursor.close()
62   connection.close()
63
64   # output results in a table
65   print """\n<table border = "1" cellpadding = "3" >
66         <tr bgcolor = "silver" >"""
67
68   # create table header
69   for field in allFields:
70      print "<td>%s</td>" % field[ 0 ]
71
72   print "</tr>"
73
74   # display each record as a row
75   for author in allRecords:
76      print "<tr>"
77
78      for item in author:
79         print "<td>%s</td>" % item
80
81      print "</tr>"
82
83   print "</table>"
84
85   # obtain sorting method from user
86   print """
87         \n<form method = "post" action = "/cgi-bin/fig17_27.py">
88         Sort By:<br />"""
89
```

Fig. 17.27 Connecting to and querying a database. (Part 2 of 3.)

```
90   # display sorting options
91   for field in allFields:
92       print """<input type = "radio" name = "sortBy"
93           value = "%s" />""" % field[ 0 ]
94       print field[ 0 ]
95       print "<br />"
96
97   print """<br />\nSort Order:<br />
98           <input type = "radio" name = "sortOrder"
99           value = "ASC" checked = "checked" />
100          Ascending
101          <input type = "radio" name = "sortOrder"
102          value = "DESC" />
103          Descending
104          <br /><br />\n<input type = "submit" value = "SORT" />
105          </form>\n\n</body>\n</html>"""
```

Fig. 17.27 Connecting to and querying a database. (Part 3 of 3.)

Line 6 imports module **MySQLdb**, which contains classes and functions for manipulating MySQL databases in Python (available from **sourceforge.net/projects/ mysql-python**). For installation instructions, please visit **www.deitel.com**.

Lines 86–105 create an XHTML form that enables the user to specify how to sort the records of the **Authors** table. Lines 24–36 retrieve and process this form. The records are sorted by the field assigned to variable **sortBy**. By default, the records are sorted by **AuthorID**. The user can select a radio button to sort the records by another field. Similarly, variable **sortOrder** has either the user-specified value or **"ASC"**.

Line 42 creates a **Connection** object called **connection** to manage the connection between the program and the database. Function **MySQLdb.connect** receives the name of the database as the value of keyword argument **db** and creates the connection. [*Note:* For operating systems other than Windows, MySQL may require a username and password to connect to the database. If so, pass the appropriate values as strings to keyword arguments **user** and **passwd** for function **MySQLdb.connect**.] If **MySQLdb.connect** fails, the function raises a **MySQLdb OperationalError** exception.

Line 51 calls **Connection** method *cursor* to create a **Cursor** object for the database. The **Cursor** method *execute* takes as an argument an SQL command to execute against the database. Lines 54–55 query and retrieve all records from the **Authors** table sorted by the field specified in **sortBy** and ordered by the value of **sortOrder**.

A **Cursor** object internally stores the results of a database query. The **Cursor** attribute *description* contains a tuple of tuples in which each tuple provides information about a field in the result set obtained by method **execute**. The first value of each field's tuple is the field name. Line 57 assigns the tuple of field name records to variable **allFields**. Cursor method *fetchall* returns a tuple of tuples that contains all the internally stored results obtained by invoking method execute. Each subtuple in the returned tuple represents one record from the database, and each element in the record represents a field's value for that record. Line 58 assigns the tuple of matching records to variable **allRecords**.

Cursor method *close* (line 61) closes the **Cursor** object; line 62 closes the **Connection** object with **Connection** method *close*. These methods explicitly close the **Cursor** and the **Connection** objects. Although the objects' **close** methods execute when the objects are destroyed at program termination, programmers should explicitly close the objects once they are no longer needed.

Good Programming Practice 17.2

*Explicitly close **Cursor** and **Connection** objects with their respective **close** methods as soon as the program no longer needs those objects.*

The remainder of the program displays the results of the database query in an XHTML table. Lines 65–83 display the **Authors** table's fields using a **for** loop. For each field, the program displays the first entry in that field's tuple (lines 69-70). Lines 75–83 display a table row for each record in the **Authors** table using nested **for** loops. The outer **for** loop (line 75) iterates through each record in the table to create a new row. The inner **for** loop (line 78) iterates over each field in the current record and displays each field in a new cell.

17.7 Querying the Books Database

Figure 17.28 enhances the example of Fig. 17.27 by allowing the user to enter any query into a GUI program. This example introduces database error handling and the **Pmw** components **ScrolledFrame** and **PanedWidget**. Module **Pmw** is introduced in Chapter 11, Graphical User Interface Components: Part 2. The GUI constructor (lines 13–39) creates four GUI elements.

The program display contains two sections. The top section provides a **Scrolled-Text** component (lines 24–25) for entering a query string. The attribute **text_height** sets the scrolled text area as eight lines high. A **Button** component (lines 28–30) calls the method that executes the query string on the database.

The bottom section contains a *ScrolledFrame* component (lines 33–35) for displaying the results of the query. A **ScrolledFrame** component is a scrollable area. The horizontal and vertical scroll bars are displayed because attributes **hscrollmode** and **vscrollmode** are assigned the value **"static"**. The **ScrolledFrame** contains a *PanedWidget* component (lines 37–39) for dividing the result records into fields. **Frame** method **interior** specifies that the **PanedWidget** is created within the **ScrolledFrame**. A **PanedWidget** is a subdivided frame that allows the user to change the size of the subdivisions. The **PanedWidget** constructor's *orient* argument takes the value *"horizontal"* or *"vertical"*. If the value is **"horizontal"**, the panes are placed left to right in the frame; if the value is **"vertical"**, the panes are placed top to bottom in the frame.

```
1   # Fig. 17.28: fig17_28.py
2   # Displays results returned by a
3   # query on Books database.
4
5   import MySQLdb
6   from Tkinter import *
7   from tkMessageBox import *
8   import Pmw
9
10  class QueryWindow( Frame ):
11     """GUI Database Query Frame"""
12
13     def __init__( self ):
14        """QueryWindow Constructor"""
15
16        Frame.__init__( self )
17        Pmw.initialise()
18        self.pack( expand = YES, fill = BOTH )
19        self.master.title( \
20           "Enter Query, Click Submit to See Results." )
21        self.master.geometry( "525x525" )
22
23        # scrolled text pane for query string
24        self.query = Pmw.ScrolledText( self, text_height = 8 )
25        self.query.pack( fill = X )
26
27        # button to submit query
28        self.submit = Button( self, text = "Submit query",
29           command = self.submitQuery )
30        self.submit.pack( fill = X )
```

Fig. 17.28 GUI application for submitting queries to a database. (Part 1 of 3.)

```
31
32          # frame to display query results
33          self.frame = Pmw.ScrolledFrame( self,
34             hscrollmode = "static", vscrollmode = "static" )
35          self.frame.pack( expand = YES, fill = BOTH )
36
37          self.panes = Pmw.PanedWidget( self.frame.interior(),
38             orient = "horizontal" )
39          self.panes.pack( expand = YES, fill = BOTH )
40
41      def submitQuery( self ):
42          """Execute user-entered query agains database"""
43
44          # open connection, retrieve cursor and execute query
45          try:
46             connection = MySQLdb.connect( db = "Books" )
47             cursor = connection.cursor()
48             cursor.execute( self.query.get() )
49          except MySQLdb.OperationalError, message:
50             errorMessage = "Error %d:\n%s" % \
51                ( message[ 0 ], message[ 1 ] )
52             showerror( "Error", errorMessage )
53             return
54          else:    # obtain user-requested information
55             data = cursor.fetchall()
56             fields = cursor.description   # metadata from query
57             cursor.close()
58             connection.close()
59
60          # clear results of last query
61          self.panes.destroy()
62          self.panes = Pmw.PanedWidget( self.frame.interior(),
63             orient = "horizontal" )
64          self.panes.pack( expand = YES, fill = BOTH )
65
66          # create pane and label for each field
67          for item in fields:
68             self.panes.add( item[ 0 ] )
69             label = Label( self.panes.pane( item[ 0 ] ),
70                text = item[ 0 ], relief = RAISED )
71             label.pack( fill = X )
72
73          # enter results into panes, using labels
74          for entry in data:
75
76             for i in range( len( entry ) ):
77                label = Label( self.panes.pane( fields[ i ][ 0 ] ),
78                   text = str( entry[ i ] ), anchor = W,
79                   relief = GROOVE, bg = "white" )
80                label.pack( fill = X )
81
82          self.panes.setnaturalsize()
83
```

Fig. 17.28 GUI application for submitting queries to a database. (Part 2 of 3.)

```
84   def main():
85       QueryWindow().mainloop()
86
87   if __name__ == "__main__":
88       main()
```

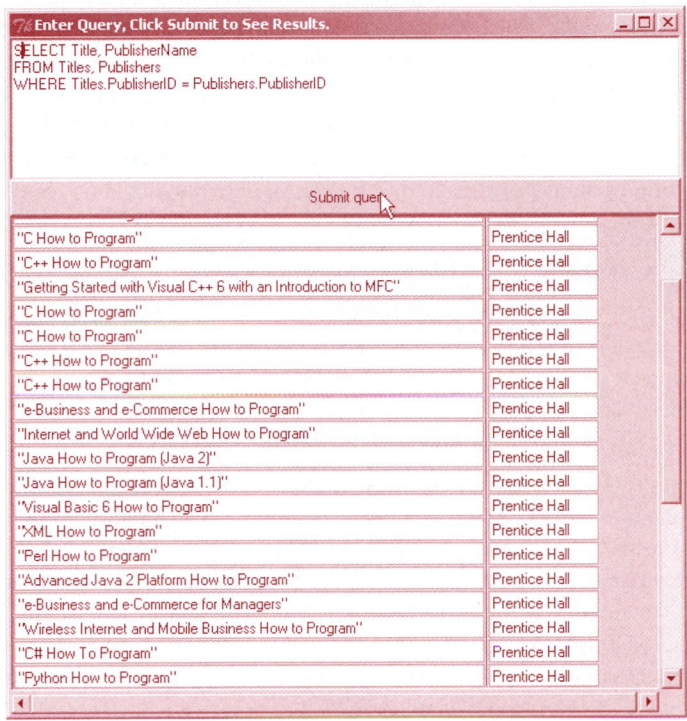

Fig. 17.28 GUI application for submitting queries to a database. (Part 3 of 3.)

When the user presses the **Submit query** button, method **submitQuery** (lines 41–82) performs the query and displays the results. Lines 45–58 contain a **try/except/else** statement that connects to and queries the database. The **try** statement creates a **Connection** and a **Cursor** object and uses **Cursor** method **execute** to perform the user-entered query. Function **MySQLdb.connect** (line 46) fails if the specified database does not exist. **Cursor** method **execute** (line 48) fails if the query string contains an SQL syntax error. Each method raises an **OperationalError** exception. Lines 49–53 handle this exception and call **tkMessageBox** function **showerror** with an appropriate error message.

If the user-entered query string successfully executes, the program retrieves the result of the query. The **else** clause (lines 54–58) assigns the queried records to variable **data** and assigns metadata to variable **fields**. *Metadata* is data that describes data. For example, the metadata for a result set may include the field names and field types. The metadata

```
fields = cursor.description
```

contains descriptive information about the result set of the user-entered query (line 56). **Cursor** attribute *description* contains a tuple of tuples that provides information about the fields obtained by method **execute**.

PanedWidget method *destroy* (line 61) removes the existing panes to display the query data in new panes (lines 62–64). Lines 67–71 iterate over the field information to display the names of the columns. For each field, method **add** adds a pane to the **PanedWidget**. This method takes a string that identifies the pane. The **Label** constructor adds a label to the pane that contains the name of the field with the **relief** attribute set to **RAISED**. **PanedWidget** method *pane* (line 69) identifies the parent of this new label. This method takes the name of a pane and returns a reference to that pane.

Lines 74–80 iterate over each record to create a label that contains the value of each field in the record. Method **pane** specifies the appropriate parent frame for each label. The expression

```
self.panes.pane( fields[ i ][ 0 ] )
```

evaluates to the pane whose name is the field name for the ith value in the record. Once the results have been added to the panes, the **PanedWidget** method *setnaturalsize* sets the size of each pane to be large enough to view the largest label in the pane.

17.8 Reading, Inserting and Updating a Database

The next example (Fig. 17.29) manipulates a simple MySQL **AddressBook** database that contains one table (**addresses**) with 11 columns—**ID** (a unique integer ID number for each person in the address book), **FirstName**, **LastName**, **Address**, **City**, **StateOrProvince**, **PostalCode**, **Country**, **EmailAddress**, **HomePhone** and **FaxNumber**. All fields, except **ID**, are strings. The program provides capabilities for inserting new records, updating existing records and searching for records in the database. [*Note*: The CD that accompanies this book contains a program called **DBSetup.py** that creates an empty **AddressBook** database.]

Class **AddressBook** uses **Button** and **Entry** components to retrieve and display address information. The constructor creates a list of fields for one address book entry (lines 32–34). Line 38 initializes dictionary data member **entries** to hold references to **Entry** components. A **for** loop (lines 44–60) then iterates over the length of this list to create an **Entry** component for each field (lines 47–48). The loop also adds a reference to the **Entry** component to data member **entries**. Lines 58–60 create a key name for each entry, based on that entry's field name.

```python
1   # Fig. 17.29: fig17_29.py
2   # Inserts into, updates and searches a database
3
4   import MySQLdb
5   from Tkinter import *
6   from tkMessageBox import *
7   import Pmw
8
9   class AddressBook( Frame ):
10      """GUI Database Address Book Frame"""
```

Fig. 17.29 Inserting, finding and updating records. (Part 1 of 5.)

```
11
12      def __init__( self ):
13          """Address Book constructor"""
14
15          Frame.__init__( self )
16          Pmw.initialise()
17          self.pack( expand = YES, fill = BOTH )
18          self.master.title( "Address Book Database Application" )
19
20          # buttons to execute commands
21          self.buttons = Pmw.ButtonBox( self, padx = 0 )
22          self.buttons.grid( columnspan = 2 )
23          self.buttons.add( "Find", command = self.findAddress )
24          self.buttons.add( "Add", command = self.addAddress )
25          self.buttons.add( "Update", command = self.updateAddress )
26          self.buttons.add( "Clear", command = self.clearContents )
27          self.buttons.add( "Help", command = self.help, width = 14 )
28          self.buttons.alignbuttons()
29
30
31          # list of fields in an address record
32          fields = [ "ID", "First name", "Last name",
33             "Address", "City", "State Province", "Postal Code",
34             "Country", "Email Address", "Home phone", "Fax Number" ]
35
36          # dictionary with Entry components for values, keyed by
37          # corresponding addresses table field names
38          self.entries = {}
39
40          self.IDEntry = StringVar()    # current address id text
41          self.IDEntry.set( "" )
42
43          # create entries for each field
44          for i in range( len( fields ) ):
45              label = Label( self, text = fields[ i ] + ":" )
46              label.grid( row = i + 1, column = 0 )
47              entry = Entry( self, name = fields[ i ].lower(),
48                  font = "Courier 12" )
49              entry.grid( row = i + 1 , column = 1,
50                  sticky = W+E+N+S, padx = 5 )
51
52              # user cannot type in ID field
53              if fields[ i ] == "ID":
54                  entry.config( state = DISABLED,
55                      textvariable = self.IDEntry, bg = "gray" )
56
57              # add entry field to dictionary
58              key = fields[ i ].replace( " ", "_" )
59              key = key.upper()
60              self.entries[ key ] = entry
61
62      def addAddress( self ):
63          """Add address record to database"""
```

Fig. 17.29 Inserting, finding and updating records. (Part 2 of 5.)

```
64
65          if self.entries[ "LAST_NAME" ].get() != "" and \
66             self.entries[ "FIRST_NAME"].get() != "":
67
68             # create INSERT query command
69             query = """INSERT INTO addresses (
70                     FIRST_NAME, LAST_NAME, ADDRESS, CITY,
71                     STATE_PROVINCE, POSTAL_CODE, COUNTRY,
72                     EMAIL_ADDRESS, HOME_PHONE, FAX_NUMBER
73                     ) VALUES (""" + \
74                     "'%s', " * 10 % \
75                     ( self.entries[ "FIRST_NAME" ].get(),
76                       self.entries[ "LAST_NAME" ].get(),
77                       self.entries[ "ADDRESS" ].get(),
78                       self.entries[ "CITY" ].get(),
79                       self.entries[ "STATE_PROVINCE" ].get(),
80                       self.entries[ "POSTAL_CODE" ].get(),
81                       self.entries[ "COUNTRY" ].get(),
82                       self.entries[ "EMAIL_ADDRESS" ].get(),
83                       self.entries[ "HOME_PHONE" ].get(),
84                       self.entries[ "FAX_NUMBER" ].get() )
85             query = query[ :-2 ] + ")"
86
87             # open connection, retrieve cursor and execute query
88             try:
89                 connection = MySQLdb.connect( db = "AddressBook" )
90                 cursor = connection.cursor()
91                 cursor.execute( query )
92             except MySQLdb.OperationalError, message:
93                 errorMessage = "Error %d:\n%s" % \
94                     ( message[ 0 ], message[ 1 ] )
95                 showerror( "Error", errorMessage )
96             else:
97                 cursor.close()
98                 connection.close()
99                 self.clearContents()
100
101        else:    # user has not filled out first/last name fields
102            showwarning( "Missing fields", "Please enter name" )
103
104    def findAddress( self ):
105        """Query database for address record and display results"""
106
107        if self.entries[ "LAST_NAME" ].get() != "":
108
109            # create SELECT query
110            query = "SELECT * FROM addresses " + \
111                    "WHERE LAST_NAME = '" + \
112                    self.entries[ "LAST_NAME" ].get() + "'"
113
114            # open connection, retrieve cursor and execute query
115            try:
116                connection = MySQLdb.connect( db = "AddressBook" )
```

Fig. 17.29 Inserting, finding and updating records. (Part 3 of 5.)

```
117                    cursor = connection.cursor()
118                    cursor.execute( query )
119               except MySQLdb.OperationalError, message:
120                    errorMessage = "Error %d:\n%s" % \
121                        ( message[ 0 ], message[ 1 ] )
122                    showerror( "Error", errorMessage )
123                    self.clearContents()
124               else:    # process results
125                  results = cursor.fetchall()
126                  fields = cursor.description
127
128                  if not results:    # no results for this person
129                      showinfo( "Not found", "Nonexistent record" )
130                  else:              # display information in GUI
131                      self.clearContents()
132
133                      # display results
134                      for i in range( len( fields ) ):
135
136                          if fields[ i ][ 0 ] == "ID":
137                              self.IDEntry.set( str( results[ 0 ][ i ] ) )
138                          else:
139                              self.entries[ fields[ i ][ 0 ] ].insert(
140                                  INSERT, str( results[ 0 ][ i ] ) )
141
142                  cursor.close()
143                  connection.close()
144
145          else:    # user did not enter last name
146              showwarning( "Missing fields", "Please enter last name" )
147
148      def updateAddress( self ):
149          """Update address record in database"""
150
151          if self.entries[ "ID" ].get():
152
153              # create UPDATE query command
154              entryItems= self.entries.items()
155              query = "UPDATE addresses SET"
156
157              for key, value in entryItems:
158
159                  if key != "ID":
160                      query += " %s='%s'," % ( key, value.get() )
161
162              query = query[ :-1 ] + " WHERE ID=" + self.IDEntry.get()
163
164              # open connection, retrieve cursor and execute query
165              try:
166                  connection = MySQLdb.connect( db = "AddressBook" )
167                  cursor = connection.cursor()
168                  cursor.execute( query )
```

Fig. 17.29 Inserting, finding and updating records. (Part 4 of 5.)

```
169              except MySQLdb.OperationalError, message:
170                  errorMessage = "Error %d:\n%s" % \
171                      ( message[ 0 ], message[ 1 ] )
172                  showerror( "Error", errorMessage )
173                  self.clearContents()
174              else:
175                  showinfo( "database updated", "Database Updated." )
176                  cursor.close()
177                  connection.close()
178
179          else:   # user has not specified ID
180              showwarning( "No ID specified", """
181                  You may only update an existing record.
182                  Use Find to locate the record,
183                  then modify the information and press Update.""" )
184
185      def clearContents( self ):
186          """Clear GUI panel"""
187
188          for entry in self.entries.values():
189              entry.delete( 0, END )
190
191          self.IDEntry.set( "" )
192
193      def help( self ):
194          "Display help message to user"
195
196          showinfo( "Help", """Click Find to locate a record.
197              Click Add to insert a new record.
198              Click Update to update the information in a record.
199              Click Clear to empty the Entry fields.\n""" )
200
201  def main():
202      AddressBook().mainloop()
203
204  if __name__ == "__main__":
205      main()
```

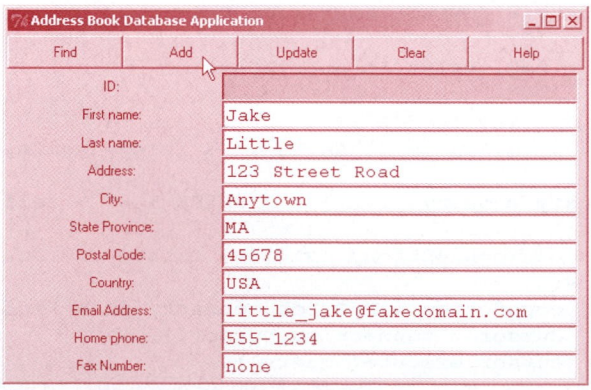

Fig. 17.29 Inserting, finding and updating records. (Part 5 of 5.)

Method **addRecord** (lines 62–102) adds a new record to the **AddressBook** database in response to the **Add** button in the GUI. The method first ensures that the user has entered values for the first and last name fields (lines 65–66). If the user enters values for these fields, the query string inserts a record into the database (lines 69–85). Otherwise, **tkMessageBox** function **showwarning** reminds the user to enter the information (lines 101–102). Line 74 includes ten string escape sequences whose values are replaced by the values contained in lines 75–84. Line 85 closes the values parentheses in the SQL statement.

Lines 88–99 contain a **try/except/else** statement that connects to and updates the database (i.e., inserts the new record in the database). Line 99 invokes method **clearContents** (lines 185–191) to clear the contents of the GUI. If an error occurs, **tkMessageBox** function **showerror** displays the error.

Method **findAddress** (lines 104–146) queries the **AddressBook** database for a specific record when the user clicks the **Find** button in the GUI. Line 107 tests whether the last name text field contains data. If the entry is empty, the program displays an error. If the user has entered data in the last name text field, a **SELECT** SQL statement searches the database for the user-specified last name. We used asterisk (*****) in the **SELECT** statement because line 126 uses metadata to get field names. Lines 115–143 contain a **try/except/else** statement that connects to and queries the database. If these operations succeed, the program retrieves the results from the database (lines 125–126). A message informs the user if the query does not yield results (lines 128–129). If the query does yield results, lines 134–140 display the results in the GUI. Each field value is inserted in the appropriate **Entry** component. The record's ID must be converted to a string before it can be displayed.

Method **updateAddress** (lines 148–183) updates an existing database record. The program displays a message if the user attempts to perform an update operation on a nonexistent record. Line 151 tests whether the **id** for the current record is valid. Lines 155–162 create the SQL **UPDATE** statement. Lines 165–177 connect to and update the database.

Method **clearContents** (lines 185–191) clears the text fields when the user clicks the **Clear** button in the GUI. Method **help** (lines 193–199) calls a **tkMessageBox** function to display instructions about how to use the program.

17.9 Internet and World Wide Web Resources

This section presents several Internet and World Wide Web resources related to database programming.

www.mysql.com
This site offers the free MySQL database for download, the most current documentation and information about open-source licensing.

ww3.one.net/~jhoffman/sqltut.html
The *Introduction to SQL* has a tutorial, links to sites with more information about the language and examples.

www.python.org/topics/databases
This **python.org** page has links to modules like **MySQLdb**, documentation, a list of useful books about database programming and the DB-API specification.

www.chordate.com/gadfly.html
Gadfly is a free relational database written completely in Python. From this home page, visitors can download the database and view its documentation.

SUMMARY

- A database is an integrated collection of data.

- A database management system (DBMS) provides mechanisms for storing and organizing data in a manner consistent with the database's format. Database management systems allow for the access and storage of data without worrying about the internal representation of databases.

- Today's most popular database systems are relational databases.

- A language called Structured Query Language (SQL—pronounced as its individual letters or as "sequel") is used almost universally with relational database systems to perform queries (i.e., to request information that satisfies given criteria) and to manipulate data.

- Python programmers communicate with databases using modules that conform to the Python Database Application Programming Interface (DB-API).

- The relational database model is a logical representation of data that allows the relationships between the data to be considered independent of the actual physical structure of the data.

- A relational database is composed of tables. Any particular row of the table is called a record (or row).

- A primary key is a field (or fields) in a table that contain(s) unique data, which cannot be duplicated in other records. This guarantees each record can be identified by a unique value.

- A foreign key is a field in a table for which every entry has a unique value in another table and where the field in the other table is the primary key for that table. The foreign key helps maintain the Rule of Referential Integrity—every value in a foreign-key field must appear in another table's primary-key field. Foreign keys enable information from multiple tables to be joined together and presented to the user.

- Each column of the table represents a different field (or column or attribute). Records normally are unique (by primary key) within a table, but particular field values may be duplicated between records.

- SQL enables programmers to define complex queries that select data from a table by providing a complete set of commands.

- The results of a query commonly are called result sets (or record sets).

- A typical SQL query selects information from one or more tables in a database. Such selections are performed by **SELECT** queries. The simplest format of a **SELECT** query is

        SELECT * **FROM** *tableName*

- An asterisk (*) indicates that all rows and columns from table *tableName* of the database should be selected.

- To select specific fields from a table, replace the asterisk (*) with a comma-separated list of field names.

- In most cases, it is necessary to locate records in a database that satisfy certain selection criteria. Only records that match the selection criteria are selected. SQL uses the optional **WHERE** clause in a **SELECT** query to specify the selection criteria for the query. The simplest format of a **SELECT** query with selection criteria is

        SELECT *fieldName1* **FROM** *tableName* **WHERE** *criteria*

- The **WHERE** clause condition can contain operators <, >, <=, >=, =, <> and **LIKE**.

- Operator **LIKE** is used for pattern matching with wildcard characters percent (**%**) and underscore (**_**). Pattern matching allows SQL to search for similar strings that "match a pattern."

- A pattern that contains a percent character (**%**) searches for strings that have zero or more characters at the percent character's position in the pattern.

- An underscore (**_**) in the pattern string indicates a single character at that position in the pattern.

- The results of a query can be arranged in ascending or descending order using the optional **ORDER BY** clause. The simplest form of an **ORDER BY** clause is

    SELECT * **FROM** *tableName* **ORDER BY** *field* **ASC**
    SELECT * **FROM** *tableName* **ORDER BY** *field* **DESC**

    where **ASC** specifies ascending order (lowest to highest), **DESC** specifies descending order (highest to lowest) and field specifies the field on which the sort is based.

- Multiple fields can be used for ordering purposes with an **ORDER BY** clause of the form

    ORDER BY *field1 sortingOrder,* *field2 sortingOrder,* ...

    where *sortingOrder* is either **ASC** or **DESC**. Note that the *sortingOrder* does not have to be identical for each field.

- The **WHERE** and **ORDER BY** clauses can be combined in one query.

- A join merges records from two or more tables by testing for matching values in a field that is common to both tables. The simplest format of a join is

    SELECT *fieldName1,* *fieldName2,* ...
    FROM *table1*
    INNER JOIN *table2*
        ON *table1.fieldName* **=** *table2.fieldName*

- A fully qualified name specifies the fields from each table that should be compared to join the tables. The "*tableName.*" syntax is required if the fields have the same name in both tables. The same syntax can be used in a query to distinguish fields in different tables that happen to have the same name. Fully qualified names that start with the database name can be used to perform cross-database queries.

- The **INSERT** statement inserts a new record in a table. The simplest form of this statement is

    INSERT INTO *tableName* **(** *fieldName1,* ..., *fieldNameN* **)**
    VALUES **(** *value1,...,* *valueN* **)**

    where *tableName* is the table in which to insert the record. The *tableName* is followed by a comma-separated list of field names in parentheses. (This list is not required if the **INSERT INTO** operation specifies a value for every column of the table in the correct order.) The list of field names is followed by the SQL keyword **VALUES** and a comma-separated list of values in parentheses. The values specified here should match the field names specified after the table name in order and type (i.e., if *fieldName1* is supposed to be the **FirstName** field, then *value1* should be a string in single quotes representing the first name).

- An **UPDATE** statement modifies data in a table. The simplest form for an **UPDATE** statement is

    UPDATE *tableName*
    SET *fieldName1* **=** *value1,* ..., *fieldNameN* **=** *valueN*
    WHERE *criteria*

    where *tableName* is the table in which to update a record (or records). The *tableName* is followed by keyword **SET** and a comma-separated list of field name/value pairs in the format *fieldName* **=** *value*. The **WHERE** clause specifies the criteria used to determine which record(s) to update.

- An SQL **DELETE** statement removes data from a table. The simplest form for a **DELETE** statement is

    DELETE FROM *tableName* **WHERE** *criteria*

    where *tableName* is the table from which to delete a record (or records). The **WHERE** clause specifies the criteria used to determine which record(s) to delete.

- Modules have been written that can interface with most popular databases, hiding database details from the programmer. These modules follow the Python Database Application Programming Interface (DB-API), a document that specifies common object and method names for manipulating any database.

- The DB-API describes a **Connection** object that programs create to connect to a database.

- A program can use a **Connection** object to create a **Cursor** object, which the program uses to execute queries against the database.

- The major benefit of the DB-API is that a program does not need to know much about the database to which the program connects. Therefore, the programmer can change the database a program uses without changing vast amounts of Python code. However, changing the DB often requires changes in the SQL code.

- Module **MySQLdb** contains classes and functions for manipulating MySQL databases in Python.

- Function **MySQLdb.connect** creates the connection. The function receives the name of the database as the value of keyword argument **db**. If **MySQLdb.connect** fails, the function raises an **OperationalError** exception.

- The **Cursor** method **execute** takes as an argument a query string to execute against the database.

- A **Cursor** object internally stores the results of a database query.

- The **Cursor** method **fetchall** returns a tuple of records that matched the query. Each record is represented as a tuple that contains the values of that records field.

- The **Cursor** method **close** closes the **Cursor** object.

- The **Connection** method **close** closes the **Connection** object.

- A **PanedWidget** is a subdivided frame that allows the user to change the size of the subdivisions. The **PanedWidget** constructor's **orient** argument takes the value **"horizontal"** or **"vertical"**. If the value is **"horizontal"**, the panes are placed left to right in the frame; if the value is **"vertical"**, the panes are placed top to bottom in the frame.

- Metadata are data that describe other data. The **Cursor** attribute **description** contains a tuple of tuples that provides information about the fields of the data obtained by function **execute**. The cursor and connection are closed.

- The **PanedWidget** method **pane** takes the name of a pane and returns a reference to that pane.

- The **PanedWidget** method **setnaturalsize** sets the size of each pane to be large enough to view the largest label in the pane.

TERMINOLOGY

AND keyword	**Connection** object
ASC keyword	**Cursor** object
asterisk (*****)	data attribute
close method	database
column	database management system (DBMS)

database table

DELETE statement

DESC keyword

escape character

execute method

fetchall method

field

foreign key

FROM keyword

fully qualified name

INSERT statement

INTO keyword

interior method

joining tables

LIKE keyword

MySQL

MySQLdb module

open source

ORDER BY keyword

PanedWidget

pattern matching

percent

percent (**%**) SQL wildcard character

primary key

Python Database Application Programming
        Interface (DB-API)

query

record

record set

relational database

result set

row

Rule of Referential Integrity

scalability

ScrolledFrame component

SELECT statement

selection criteria

SET keyword

shell

Structured Query Language (**SQL**)

table

underscore (_) wildcard character

UPDATE statement

VALUES keyword

WHERE clause

SELF-REVIEW EXERCISES

17.1   Fill in the blanks in each of the following statements:

  a) The most popular database query language is _____.
  b) A relational database is composed of _____.
  c) A table in a database consists of _____ and _____.
  d) The _____ uniquely identifies each record in a table.
  e) SQL provides a complete set of commands (including **SELECT**) that enable program-
      mers to define complex _____.
  f) SQL keyword _____ is followed by the selection criteria that specify the records to
      select in a query.
  g) SQL keyword _____ specifies the order in which records are sorted in a query.
  h) A _____ specifies the fields from multiple tables table that should be compared to
      join the tables.
  i) A _____ is an integrated collection of data which is centrally controlled.
  j) A _____ is a field in a table for which every entry has a unique value in another
      table and where the field in the other table is the primary key for that table.

17.2   State whether the following are *true* or *false*. If *false*, explain why.

  a) **DELETE** is not a valid SQL keyword.
  b) Tables in a database must have a primary key.
  c) Python programmers communicate with databases using modules that conform to the
      DB-API.
  d) **UPDATE** is a valid SQL keyword.
  e) The **WHERE** clause condition can not contain operator **<>**.
  f) Not all database systems support the **LIKE** operator.
  g) The **INSERT INTO** statement inserts a new record in a table.
  h) **MySQLdb.connect** is used to create a connection to database.

i) A **Cursor** object can execute queries in a database.

j) Once created, a connection with database can not be closed.

ANSWERS TO SELF-REVIEW EXERCISES

17.1   a) SQL. b) tables. c) rows, columns. d) primary key. e) queries. f) **WHERE**. g) **ORDER BY**. h) fully qualified name. i) database. j) foreign key.

17.2   a) False. **DELETE** is a valid SQL keyword—it is used to delete records. b) False. Tables in a database normally have primary keys. c) True. d) True. e) False. The **WHERE** clause can contain operator **<>** (not equals). f) True. g) True. h) True. i) True. j) False. **Connection.close** can close the connection.

EXERCISES

17.3   Write SQL queries for the **Books** database (discussed in Section 17.3) that perform each of the following tasks:
    a) Select all authors from the **Authors** table.
    b) Select all publishers from the **Publishers** table.
    c) Select a specific author and list all books for that author. Include the title, copyright year and ISBN number. Order the information alphabetically by title.
    d) Select a specific publisher and list all books published by that publisher. Include the title, copyright year and ISBN number. Order the information alphabetically by title.

17.4   Write SQL queries for the **Books** database (discussed in Section 17.3) that perform each of the following tasks:
    a) Add a new author to the **Authors** table.
    b) Add a new title for an author (remember that the book must have an entry in the **AuthorISBN** table). Be sure to specify the publisher of the title.
    c) Add a new publisher.

17.5   Modify Fig. 17.27 so that the user can read different tables in the books database.

17.6   Create a MySQL database that contains information about students in a university. Possible fields might include date of birth, major, current grade point average, credits earned, etc. Write a Python program to manage the database. Include the following functionality: sort all students according to GPA (descending), create a display of all students in one particular major and remove all records from the database where the student has the required amount of credits to graduate.

17.7   Modify the **FIND** capability in Fig. 17.29 to allow the user to scroll through the results of the query in case there is more than one person with the specified last name in the Address Book. Provide an appropriate GUI.

17.8   Modify the solution from Exercise 17.7 so that the program checks whether a record already exists in the database before adding it.

18

Process Management

Objectives

- To understand the notion of processes.
- To understand how to create and manage processes.
- To learn how to execute shell commands in Python.
- To understand how to control the input and output of processes.
- To learn to send and intercept signals.

A person with one watch knows what time it is; a person with two watches is never sure.
Proverb

Conversation is but carving!
Give no more to every guest,
Then he's able to digest.
Jonathan Swift

18.1 Introduction

The human body performs a great variety of operations *in parallel,* or, as we will say throughout this chapter, *concurrently.* Respiration, blood circulation and digestion, for example, can occur concurrently. Similarly, all the senses—sight, touch, smell, taste and hearing—can be stimulated at the same time. Computers, too, perform operations concurrently. It is common for a desktop personal computer to compile a program, send a file to a printer and receive electronic mail messages over a network concurrently.

There are two primary ways to implement concurrency. One is to have each *task,* or *process,* operate in a separate memory space, each with its own section of memory in which to execute. Although processes may have separate memory spaces in which to execute, processes do not actually run "at the same time" unless they are executed on separate processors. On single-processor systems, the operating system uses *time slicing* to divide processor time among the many processes. The operating system allocates a short span of execution time—called a *quantum*—to a process. The process executes for the quantum of time, then the operating system allocates a quantum of time to another process. The operating system performs *context switching* to move the first process and its dependent data into memory, and to move the new processes and its dependent data into the processor. On multi-processor systems, each process can run on a separate processor to achieve true concurrency.

Another way to implement concurrency is to program multiple executions, also known as *threads of execution*, that operate in the same memory space. This is known as *multi-threading*, a concept we discuss in Chapter 19, Multithreading. Creating a thread is more efficient than creating a process, because the operating system does not create a separate memory space for each thread.

Operating systems provide *shells*—programs that execute system commands on behalf of the user. UNIX users probably are familiar with shells such as the *Bourne shell* (**sh**) or the *C shell* (**csh**), which provide command-line interfaces for executing commands. Windows users probably are familiar with *Windows Explorer*, which is a graphical shell, and the *MS-DOS prompt*, which provides a command-line interface. Macintosh OS users probably are familiar with the *Finder*, which is another graphical shell. Through module **os**, Python enables developers to access the shell to run other programs and control those programs' input and output.

Some operating systems, (e.g., UNIX and Mac OS X) have built-in system commands that enable programmers to create and manage processes. The *Portable Operating System Interface for UNIX (POSIX)* standard defines these system commands for UNIX operating systems. Most UNIX operating systems implement the POSIX standard, and therefore provide the same set of functions for creating new processes programmatically. Python uses these underlying operating system commands to implement process management.

Portability Tip 18.1

Not all operating systems can create separate processes from within a running program. For this reason, process management is one of Python's least portable features.

18.2 os.fork Function

Creating new processes is useful in applications that can perform multiple tasks in parallel. For example, the Apache Web server (prior to version 2.0) used multiple processes to handle multiple client requests simultaneously. Each of these processes was an identical copy of the main Apache process. In this case, making identical copies of the main Apache process was useful, because each of these processes performed the same task (i.e., the serving of Web pages to clients).

One way to create a new process is to use function **os.fork**, which is available only on POSIX-compliant systems (e.g., most versions of UNIX and Linux). Module **os** on the Windows version of Python does not define function **os.fork**, because Windows does not support the creation of new processes by using **fork**. Instead, Windows applications programmers typically use multithreaded programming techniques to accomplish concurrency tasks.

Common Programming Error 18.1

Attempting to execute a Python program that invokes **os.fork** *on a Windows machine causes an* **AttributeError** *exception because the* **os** *module for Windows does not define function* **fork***.*

Figure 18.1 describes how function **os.fork** creates a new process. Each time a program executes, the operating system creates a new process to run the program's instructions (Step 1). A process also may cause the operating system to create a new process by calling **os.fork**. The *parent process* is the process that invokes **os.fork**. Any process that the parent process *forks* (creates) is a *child process*. Each process has a unique *process id* number, or *pid*, that identifies the process. When a process invokes function **fork**, the operating system creates a new child process that is essentially identical to the parent (original) process (Step 2). The child process inherits copies of many values, such as global variables and environment variables, from the parent process. The only difference between the two processes is the return value of **fork**: The **child** process receives a return value of 0, and the parent process receives the child's *pid* as the return value. After the call to function **fork**, the two processes execute the same program concurrently, starting with the line of code that follows the invocation of **fork**. The parent and child processes execute concurrently and independently of one another (i.e., they execute "asynchronously"). Figure 18.2 illustrates an example of function **os.fork**.

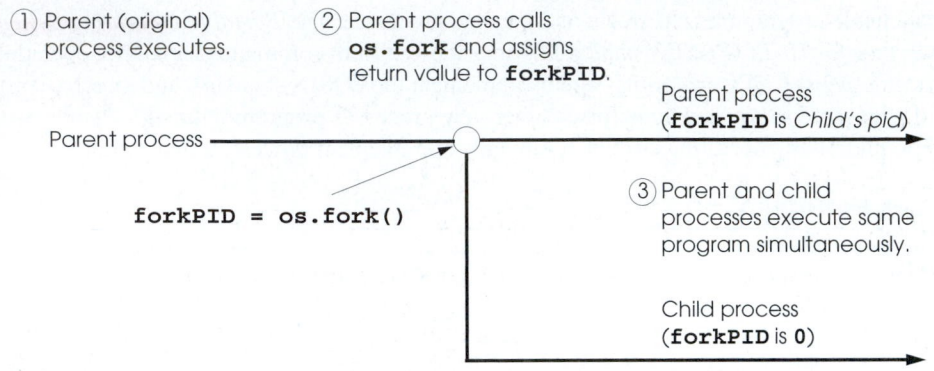

① Parent (original)
process executes.

② Parent process calls
os.fork and assigns
return value to **forkPID**.

Parent process
(**forkPID** is *Child's pid*)

Parent process ⎯⎯⎯⎯⎯⎯⎯⎯⎯⎯⎯⎯⎯⎯⎯⎯⎯⎯⎯⎯⎯➤

forkPID = os.fork()

③ Parent and child
processes execute same
program simultaneously.

Child process
(**forkPID** is **0**)

Fig. 18.1 os.fork creates a new process.

```
1   # Fig. 18.2: fig18_02.py
2   # Using fork to create child processes.
3
4   import os
5   import sys
6   import time
7
8   processName = "parent"  # only the parent is running now
9
10  print "Program executing\n\tpid: %d, processName: %s" \
11     % ( os.getpid(), processName )
12
13  # attempt to fork child process
14  try:
15     forkPID = os.fork()  # create child process
16  except OSError:
17     sys.exit( "Unable to create new process." )
18
19  if forkPID != 0:  # am I parent process?
20     print "Parent executing\n" + \
21        "\tpid: %d, forkPID: %d, processName: %s" \
22        % ( os.getpid(), forkPID, processName )
23
24  elif forkPID == 0:  # am I child process?
25     processName = "child"
26     print "Child executing\n" + \
27        "\tpid: %d, forkPID: %d, processName: %s" \
28        % ( os.getpid(), forkPID, processName )
29
30  print "Process finishing\n\tpid: %d, processName: %s" \
31     % ( os.getpid(), processName )
```

Fig. 18.2 os.fork used to create child processes. (Part 1 of 2.)

```
Program executing
        pid: 5428, processName: parent
Parent executing
        pid: 5428, forkPID: 5429, processName: parent
Process finishing
        pid: 5428, processName: parent
Child executing
        pid: 5429, forkPID: 0, processName: child
Process finishing
        pid: 5429, processName: child
```

```
Program executing
        pid: 5430, processName: parent
Child executing
        pid: 5431, forkPID: 0, processName: child
Process finishing
        pid: 5431, processName: child
Parent executing
        pid: 5430, forkPID: 5431, processName: parent
Process finishing
        pid: 5430, processName: parent
```

```
Program executing
        pid: 5888, processName: parent
Child executing
Parent executing
        pid: 5888, forkPID: 5889, processName: parent
Process finishing
        pid: 5888, processName: parent
        pid: 5889, forkPID: 0, processName: child
Process finishing
        pid: 5889, processName: child
```

Fig. 18.2 `os.fork` used to create child processes. (Part 2 of 2.)

Portability Tip 18.2

Function `os.fork` is unavailable for Windows versions of Python.

Line 8 initializes variable **processName** to **"parent"** to indicate that the current process is the parent process. Lines 10–11 print the *pid* and **processName** of the parent process. Line 15 then calls function **os.fork** to create a duplicate of the current process. If the operating system is unable to create a new process, function **os.fork** raises an **OSError** exception, and line 17 exits the program; otherwise, the operating system creates a new process. Both copies of the process—parent and child—continue execution from the point at which the child process was created (line 15), but in separate memory spaces.

If a program must perform different tasks in the parent and child processes, that program can use **if** statements to test the value that **fork** returns in each process. The processes then can perform the appropriate tasks based on the results of those **if** statements. Recall that **fork** returns 0 in the newly created child process; whereas in the parent process, **fork** returns the child's *pid*, which must be a positive integer. In the example of Fig. 18.2, the parent process performs different tasks than those that the child process performs. If the executing process is the parent, the return value from fork is the child's pid, and the condition on line 19 evaluates to true. The process then executes the parent-specific code on lines 20–22. If the executing process is the child, **forkPID** is 0 and the condition on line 19 evaluates to false. This prevents the child process from executing the parent-specific code. Instead, the condition on line 24 evaluates to true and the child-specific code on lines 25–28 executes.

The child process changes its copy of variable **processName** to the value **"child"** (line 25). If a program modifies the variable's value in one process, the value of the variable in the other process does not change, because each process contains a separate variable called **processName**. Function **os.getpid** (lines 22 and 28) returns the *pid* of the currently executing process. Notice in the sample outputs that the child's *pid* matches the value of **forkPID** in the parent process. The parent process can use the child's *pid* to manage the child process, as we demonstrate in Section 18.7.

Notice that the first two sample outputs of Fig. 18.2 differ. After the child process is created by calling **os.fork** (line 15), both processes—parent and child—proceed independently as *asynchronous* concurrent processes. Asynchronous means that they operate independently of one another without synchronization. Concurrent means that they can proceed in parallel (i.e., they execute at the same time). Thus, we cannot predict the relative speeds of the child process and parent process. For this reason, the output of Fig. 18.2 will differ on each execution. Sometimes, the parent process will execute line 20 before the child process executes line 26, and sometimes the child process will execute first. Notice in the last sample output, the parent process executes line 20 while the child process is executing line 26! This underscores the concurrency of the processes.

Another reason the output differs in the sample outputs is because each time a new process is run, the operating system assigns it a unique *pid*. Thus, the *pid* of each process— parent and child—changes with each execution of the program.

In some cases, the parent process must wait for a child process to finish before the parent can proceed. For example, a child process might perform a calculation whose result the parent requires before the parent can continue executing. Function **os.wait** (available only on UNIX-compatible systems) waits for anyone of the parent's child processes to complete before allowing the parent process to continue its execution. This function returns a two-element tuple that contains the *pid* of the finished child and the child's *exit status*— an integer that indicates the state in which the child process exited. An exit status of 0 indicates that the child process completed successfully; a positive integer indicates that the child process terminated with some error. Function **os.wait** raises an **OSError** exception if there are no children. Figure 18.3 demonstrates function **os.wait**.

The program creates two child processes, and the parent waits for both child processes to complete execution before the parent process terminates. Each child invokes function **time.sleep** to sleep for a random number of seconds (calculated on lines 10–11). The calls to function **sleep** make it seem that the child processes perform some work.

Line 15 creates the first child process, and line 23 creates the second child process. The outer **if** statement (line 19) evaluates **forkPID1**, the return value from the first call to

fork (line 14). If the parent process is executing, the code in lines 21–48 executes. The parent forks a new child (line 23), assigns the return value to **forkPID2** and checks the value of this variable to determine if this is still the parent running (line 27).

```python
1   # Fig. 18.3: fig18_03.py
2   # Demonstrates the wait function.
3
4   import os
5   import sys
6   import time
7   import random
8
9   # generate random sleep times for child processes
10  sleepTime1 = random.randrange( 1, 6 )
11  sleepTime2 = random.randrange( 1, 6 )
12
13  # parent ready to fork first child process
14  try:
15     forkPID1 = os.fork()  # create first child process
16  except OSError:
17     sys.exit( "Unable to create first child. " )
18
19  if forkPID1 != 0:  # am I parent process?
20
21     # parent ready to fork second child process
22     try:
23        forkPID2 = os.fork()  # create second child process
24     except OSError:
25        sys.exit( "Unable to create second child." )
26
27     if forkPID2 != 0:  # am I parent process?
28        print "Parent waiting for child processes...\n" + \
29           "\tpid: %d, forkPID1: %d, forkPID2: %d" \
30           % ( os.getpid(), forkPID1, forkPID2 )
31
32        # wait for any child process
33        try:
34           child1 = os.wait()[ 0 ]  # wait returns one child's pid
35        except OSError:
36           sys.exit( "No more child processes." )
37
38        print "Parent: Child %d finished first, one child left." \
39           % child1
40
41        # wait for another child process
42        try:
43           child2 = os.wait()[ 0 ]  # wait returns other child's pid
44        except OSError:
45           sys.exit( "No more child processes." )
46
47        print "Parent: Child %d finished second, no children left." \
48           % child2
```

Fig. 18.3 `os.wait` used to wait for a child process. (Part 1 of 2.)

```
49
50        elif forkPID2 == 0:  # am I second child process?
51           print """Child2 sleeping for %d seconds...
52           \tpid: %d, forkPID1: %d, forkPID2: %d""" \
53              % ( sleepTime2, os.getpid(), forkPID1, forkPID2 )
54           time.sleep( sleepTime2 )  # sleep to simulate some work
55
56     elif forkPID1 == 0:  # am I first child process?
57        print """Child1 sleeping for %d seconds...
58           \tpid: %d, forkPID1: %d""" \
59           % ( sleepTime1, os.getpid(), forkPID1 )
60        time.sleep( sleepTime1 )  # sleep to simulate some work
```

```
Child2 sleeping for 4 seconds...
        pid: 9578, forkPID1: 9577, forkPID2: 0
Child1 sleeping for 5 seconds...
        pid: 9577, forkPID1: 0
Parent waiting for child processes...
        pid: 9576, forkPID1: 9577, forkPID2: 9578
Parent: Child 9578 finished first, one child left.
Parent: Child 9577 finished second, no children left.
```

```
Parent waiting for child processes...
        pid: 9579, forkPID1: 9580, forkPID2: 9581
Child1 sleeping for 1 seconds...
        pid: 9580, forkPID1: 0
Child2 sleeping for 5 seconds...
        pid: 9581, forkPID1: 9580, forkPID2: 0
Parent: Child 9580 finished first, one child left.
Parent: Child 9581 finished second, no children left.
```

```
Parent waiting for child processes...
Child1 sleeping for 4 seconds...
        pid: 9583, forkPID1: 0
Child2 sleeping for 3 seconds...
        pid: 9584, forkPID1: 9583, forkPID2: 0
        pid: 9582, forkPID1: 9583, forkPID2: 9584
Parent: Child 9584 finished first, one child left.
Parent: Child 9583 finished second, no children left.
```

Fig. 18.3 `os.wait` used to wait for a child process. (Part 2 of 2.)

After creating the second child, the parent prints a message to indicate that the parent will wait for its children (lines 28–30). The parent then calls function **os.wait** (line 34). The parent process waits, or *blocks*, until either one of its child processes has finished. Note that this is not necessarily the first child that the parent created. Due to the nature of concurrent, asynchronous processes, the second child process may complete execution first. Function **os.wait** often is useful when a parent must use the results of the child process's task before the parent can continue its own task (e.g., a parent process that sends an e-mail that contains text output provided by a child process).

The first child process (lines 57–60) prints its *pid* and the value of **forkPID1**. It then calls function **time.sleep** (line 60), with an argument that specifies the length of time in seconds for which the process should remain asleep. We pass a random value (**sleepTime1**) to simulate performing some work. Although programmers cannot rely on function **time.sleep** to provide synchronization, when you run the program, notice that the parent does waits the correct number of seconds before terminating. After the first child process wakes up, it completes execution and terminates successfully. The second child process performs similar tasks (lines 51–54). This second process prints a message and sleeps for a random amount of time before terminating.

Function **os.wait** causes the parent to wait for any one of its child processes to complete execution. Function **os.wait** then returns the *pid* of the child process that completed, and the parent process resumes execution. When one child process terminates, the parent wakes up and prints a message to the screen that shows the *pid* of the child process that completed (lines 38–39). Recall that processes execute concurrently and asynchronously, so we cannot predict which child process will complete first. Line 43 calls function **os.wait** a second time, which causes the parent to block again until the remaining child process completes. When the remaining child terminates, the parent prints a message to the screen, which displays the *pid* of that child (lines 47–48).

Notice that the order in which the processes execute differs with each execution, as shown in the three sample outputs for Fig. 18.3. In the first output, the second child process (with pid 9578) completes execution first. This reminds us once again that all of the processes execute concurrently and asynchronously.

To cause the parent process to wait for a specific child process to terminate, the parent can use function *os.waitpid*. This function (available only on UNIX-compatible systems) waits for a process to finish then returns a two-element tuple that contains the process's *pid* and that process's exit status. If the *pid* does not exist or if the child terminated prior to the call to **waitpid**, function **waitpid** raises an **OSError** exception. The function call passes a process id as the first argument and an *option* as the second argument. If the first argument is greater than 0, **waitpid** waits for the process with the specified *pid*. If the first argument is −1, **waitpid** waits for any child of the current process, which is a identical behavior to **os.wait**. The *option* argument passed to **os.waitpid** should be 0 for normal operation. Passing the constant **os.WNOHANG** as argument *option* specifies that the call to **waitpid** should return immediately if no status information is available for the process with the given *pid*.

Figure 18.4 demonstrates **os.waitpid**. The program is similar to Fig. 18.3 except that line 29 passes the *pid* of the second child and an *option* value of 0 to **waitpid**. This means that the parent process always waits until the second child (i.e., the process with pid **forkPID2**) terminates before executing lines 33–34 (whether the first child has terminated or not). The three sample outputs again demonstrate the unpredictable nature of asynchronous concurrent processes.

```
1   # Fig. 18.4: fig18_04.py
2   # Demonstrates the waitpid function.
3
```

Fig. 18.4 os.waitpid used to wait for a specific child process. (Part 1 of 3.)

```
4   import os
5   import sys
6   import time
7
8   # parent about to fork first child process
9   try:
10      forkPID1 = os.fork()  # create first child process
11  except OSError:
12      sys.exit( "Unable to create first child. " )
13
14  if forkPID1 != 0:  # am I parent process?
15
16      # parent about to fork second child process
17      try:
18          forkPID2 = os.fork()  # create second child process
19      except OSError:
20          sys.exit( "Unable to create second child." )
21
22      if forkPID2 > 0:  # am I parent process?
23          print "Parent waiting for child processes...\n" + \
24              "\tpid: %d, forkPID1: %d, forkPID2: %d" \
25              % ( os.getpid(), forkPID1, forkPID2 )
26
27          # wait for second child process explicitly
28          try:
29              child2 = os.waitpid( forkPID2, 0 )[ 0 ]  # child's pid
30          except OSError:
31              sys.exit( "No child process with pid %d." % ( forkPID2 ) )
32
33          print "Parent: Child %d finished." \
34              % child2
35
36      elif forkPID2 == 0:  # am I second child process?
37          print "Child2 sleeping for 4 seconds...\n" + \
38              "\tpid: %d, forkPID1: %d, forkPID2: %d" \
39              % ( os.getpid(), forkPID1, forkPID2 )
40          time.sleep( 4 )
41
42  elif forkPID1 == 0:  # am I first child process?
43      print "Child1 sleeping for 2 seconds...\n" + \
44          "\tpid: %d, forkPID1: %d" % ( os.getpid(), forkPID1 )
45      time.sleep( 2 )
```

```
Parent waiting for child processes...
        pid: 6092, forkPID1: 6093, forkPID2: 6094
Child1 sleeping for 2 seconds...
        pid: 6093, forkPID1: 0
Child2 sleeping for 4 seconds...
        pid: 6094, forkPID1: 6093, forkPID2: 0
Parent: Child 6094 finished.
```

Fig. 18.4 **os.waitpid** used to wait for a specific child process. (Part 2 of 3.)

```
Child1 sleeping for 2 seconds...
        pid: 6089, forkPID: 0
Child2 sleeping for 4 seconds...
        pid: 6090, forkPID: 6089, forkPID2: 0
Parent waiting for child processes...
        pid: 6088, forkPID: 6089, forkPID2: 6090
Parent: Child 6090 finished.
```

```
Parent waiting for child processes...
Child1 sleeping for 2 seconds...
        pid: 6102, forkPID: 0
        pid: 6101, forkPID: 6102, forkPID2: 6103
Child2 sleeping for 4 seconds...
        pid: 6103, forkPID: 6102, forkPID2: 0
Parent: Child 6103 finished.
```

Fig. 18.4 `os.waitpid` used to wait for a specific child process. (Part 3 of 3.)

18.3 `os.system` Function and `os.exec` Family of Functions

Python provides several ways to execute system commands and other programs from Python code. One way is to call function *os.system*, which executes a system command using a shell, then returns control to the original process (after the command completes). Another way to execute a program is through the *os.exec* *family of functions*. Unlike **os.system**, each **os.exec** function does not return control to the calling process after executing the specified command. When a program invokes an **os.exec** function, the program that the **os.exec** function executes "takes over" the Python process. In fact, the Python process terminates as soon as it calls the **os.exec** function. The invoked program then executes with the same *pid* under which the Python process executed previously. Function **os.system** and the **os.exec** family of functions are available on both UNIX-compatible and Windows systems. In this section, we create programs that perform system-specific actions based on the user's operating system.

Figure 18.5 uses function **os.system** to create a simple text-processing application. This application requests that the user enter the name of a file to create. The user then enters the file's contents. The user can type **clear** to delete the contents of the file or **quit** to save the file and quit the program. Figure 18.6 displays the contents of a file created with this application. The first two sample outputs show the output on a Windows system and a UNIX-compatible system, respectively. The remaining outputs are identical for both system types.

```
1   # Fig. 18.5: fig18_05.py
2   # Uses the system function to clear the screen.
3
4   import os
5   import sys
```

Fig. 18.5 `os.system` used in a simple word-processor program. (Part 1 of 3.)

```
 6
 7   def printInstructions( clearCommand ):
 8       os.system( clearCommand )  # clear display
 9
10       print """Type the text that you wish to save in this file.
11   Type clear on a blank line to delete the contents of the file.
12   Type quit on a blank line when you are finished.\n"""
13
14   # determine operating system
15   if os.name == "nt" or os.name == "dos":  # Windows system
16       clearCommand = "cls"
17       print "You are using a Windows system."
18   elif os.name == "posix":  # UNIX-compatible system
19       clearCommand = "clear"
20       print "You are using a UNIX-compatible system."
21   else:
22       sys.exit( "Unsupported OS" )
23
24   filename = raw_input( "What file would you like to create? " )
25
26   # open file
27   try:
28       file = open( filename, "w+" )
29   except IOError, message:
30       sys.exit( "Error creating file: %s" % message )
31
32   printInstructions( clearCommand )
33   currentLine = ""
34
35   # write input to file
36   while currentLine != "quit\n":
37       file.write( currentLine )
38       currentLine = sys.stdin.readline()
39
40       if currentLine == "clear\n":
41
42           # seek to beginning and truncate file
43           file.seek( 0, 0 )
44           file.truncate()
45
46           currentLine = ""
47           printInstructions( clearCommand )
48
49   file.close()
```

```
You are using a Windows system.
What file would you like to create? welcome.txt
```

```
You are using a UNIX-compatible system.
What file would you like to create? welcome.txt
```

Fig. 18.5   os.system used in a simple word-processor program. (Part 2 of 3.)

```
Type the text that you wish to save in this file.
Type clear on a blank line to delete the contents of the file.
Type quit on a blank line when you are finished.

This will not be written to the file.
The following line will call clear.
clear
```

```
Type the text that you wish to save in this file.
Type clear on a blank line to delete the contents of the file.
Type quit on a blank line when you are finished.
```

```
Type the text that you wish to save in this file.
Type clear on a blank line to delete the contents of the file.
Type quit on a blank line when you are finished.

Wilkommen!
Bienvenue!
Welcome!
quit
```

Fig. 18.5 `os.system` used in a simple word-processor program. (Part 3 of 3.)

```
Wilkommen!
Bienvenue!
Welcome!
```

Fig. 18.6 `welcome.txt` file contents for a Windows or UNIX system.

Different operating systems have different commands for clearing text from a console. Lines 15–22 attempt to make the program portable by identifying the user's operating system and setting variable **clearCommand** appropriately. Variable *os.name* contains the name of the user's operating system. If the name is *"nt"* or *"dos"*, the user is using a Windows or MS-DOS machine, so variable **clearCommand** is set to **"cls"**, which clears a console on these operating systems (line 16). If the operating system name is *"posix"*, the program is running on an operating system that implements the POSIX standard (such as most versions of UNIX), so variable **clearCommand** is set to **"clear"** (line 19). If the name does not match either of these strings, the program exits and displays an error message (line 22).

Once the application determines the type of the operating system, the program prompts the user to enter a file name (line 24) and attempts to create the file (lines 27–30). Line 32 calls function **printInstructions** (lines 7–12) to clear the screen and print the program instructions. Line 8 calls **os.system** to execute the system-specific shell command to clear the console. The program passes the shell command to execute as a string argument to this function; the program then waits while the shell command executes. After the command has completed, control returns to the program, and lines 10–12 print the instructions.

Lines 36–47 write the user-entered lines to the file. Line 37 calls file-object method **write** to write the text to the file. The program then retrieves the next line from the user. If this line is the command **"clear"**, lines 43–44 move to the beginning of the file and truncate it to erase the contents of the file. The application also calls function **printInstructions** to clear the console and reprint the instructions (line 47). If the user types **"quit"**, the program terminates the **while** loop, closes the file (line 49) and exits.

Figure 18.7 shows a slightly more complicated text-editing example. The example uses function *urlretrieve* of module *urllib* to get a Web page and store it in a file. Then, it uses function *os.execvp* to start a native editing program to edit this page. Function **os.execvp** replaces the Python process with the program executed via **os.execvp**. This is useful if one process wishes to terminate after handing control over to another process. When you run the program, you will notice that the Python program does not wait, but terminates as soon as the editor is started. The first sample output shows the command that invokes the program. The last two sample outputs show the program running on a UNIX-compatible machine and a Windows machine, respectively.

On many systems—DOS and UNIX in particular—it is possible to pass information to programs from the command line as *command-line arguments*. Python stores command-line arguments in a list named **sys.argv**. This list always contains at least one value—the name of the program that the user entered at the command line. The rest of the list contains the command-line arguments in the order in which the user passed those arguments to the program.

In our example, the program requires the user to pass two command-line arguments to the program: the name of the URL to obtain and the name of the file in which to save the URL's contents. Therefore, the length of list **sys.argv** should be 3 (the name of the program plus the two arguments). Lines 8–9 test this value and terminate the program if the user did not pass the correct number of arguments.

```
1   # Fig. 18.7: fig18_07.py
2   # Opens a Web page in a system-specific editor.
3
4   import os
5   import sys
6   import urllib
7
8   if len( sys.argv ) != 3:
9       sys.exit( "Incorrect number of arguments." )
10
11  # determine operating system and set editor command
12  if os.name == "nt" or os.name == "dos":
13      editor = "notepad.exe"
14  elif os.name == "posix":
15      editor = "vi"
16  else:
17      sys.exit( "Unsupported OS" )
18
19  # obtain Web page and store in file
20  urllib.urlretrieve( sys.argv[ 1 ], sys.argv[ 2 ] )
21
```

Fig. 18.7   **os.execvp** used to transfer control to another program. (Part 1 of 2.)

```
22    # editor expects to receive itself as an argument
23    os.execvp( editor, ( editor, sys.argv[ 2 ] ) )
24
25    print "This line never executes."
```

fig18_07.py http://www.deitel.com/test/test.txt test.txt

```
This is a test file to illustrate
downloading text from a file on a
web server using an HTTP connection
to the server.
~
~
~
```

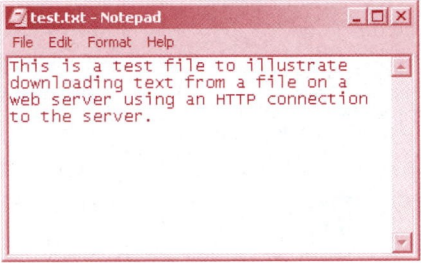

Fig. 18.7   **os.execvp** used to transfer control to another program. (Part 2 of 2.)

Lines 13 and 15 specify the editor command based on the operating-system type in variable **os.name**. If the operating system is Windows, the application uses the **Notepad** editor; if the operating system implements the POSIX standard, the application uses the **vi** editor. If the user is not using either of these systems, the program displays an error message and exits. [*Note*: On each platform, the **PATH** environment variable must include the path to the editor command. For example, the path to **notepad.exe** is **C:\WINDOWS** for Windows XP or **C:\WINNT** for Windows NT/2000. The path to **vi** on most UNIX systems is **/bin**.]

Line 20 calls function **urllib.urlretrieve** to obtain the Web page. The first argument passed to **urlretrieve** is the URL of the Web page (specified as a string). The second argument passed to **urlretrieve** is the filename to which the program should write the retrieved data.

Line 23 calls function **os.execvp** to replace the current process with the text editor application. This function is part of a family of functions that contain the prefix **exec**. Function **execvp** takes two arguments. The first argument is the name of the command to execute. The second argument is a tuple of arguments to pass to the command. This tuple follows the a special format—the first element of the tuple is the command itself, and subsequent elements correspond to command-line arguments for that command. In our example, we pass the name of the newly created file. Figure 18.8 lists the functions in the **exec** family.

Function name	Description
execl(*path, arg0, arg1, ...* **)**	Executes the program *path* with the given arguments.
execle(*path, arg0, arg1, ..., environment* **)**	Same as **execl**, but takes an additional argument—the *environment* in which the program executes. The environment is a dictionary with keys that are environment variables and with values that are environment variable values.
execlp(*path, arg0, arg1, ...* **)**	Same as **execl**, but searches for executable *path* in **os.environ["PATH"]**.
execv(*path, arguments* **)**	Same as **execl**, but arguments are contained in a single tuple or list.
excve(*path, arguments, environment* **)**	Same as **execle**, but arguments are contained in a single tuple or list.
execvp(*path, arguments* **)**	Same as **execlp**, but arguments are contained in a single tuple or list.
execvpe(*path, arguments, environment* **)**	Same as **execvp**, but takes an additional argument, *environment*, in which the program executes.

Fig. 18.8   **exec** family of functions.

18.4 Controlling Process Input and Output

A fundamental philosophy of UNIX systems is that programs should be small and should perform well-defined tasks. Users then can use multiple programs together to achieve a particular result. For example, the UNIX command **ls** lists the contents of a directory. The UNIX command **sort** sorts its input according to some ordering scheme (e.g., alphabetical order). By entering the following command-line, which uses these commands together, a user can produce a sorted list of a directory's contents.

        ls | sort

The above command uses the vertical-bar character (|) to "pipe" (transfer) the output from the **ls** command (**stdout**) to the input of the **sort** command (**stdin**). The **ls** command lists the directory's contents, and the **sort** command sorts those contents in alphabetical order to produce and ordered listing.

Python provides functions for accessing the contents of streams **stdout**, **stdin** and **stderr** (defined in Section 14.3), which enable programs to manipulate the input and output of other programs similarly to the above command line. These functions return one or more file objects that correspond to the input and output streams of a program. These file objects can be treated like any other file objects. To write information from one program to the input of another program, the first program prints or writes to the second program's input file object—the data is transferred to the input of the second program. To read the

output from the second program, the first program reads from the second program's output file object.

Figure 18.9 shows an example that produces a directory listing in reverse-sorted order by taking the output of one command and feeding that output to the input of another command. Our Python program then reads and displays the output from the second command. The sample outputs show the program running on a UNIX-compatible machine and a Windows machine, respectively.

The program calls the shell command to list the contents of the current directory, then passes that listing to another shell command to sort the entries in reverse-alphabetical order. Lines 8–15 determine the user's operating system and set the two commands appropriately.

Line 18 calls function **os.popen** to execute a command and obtain the **stdout** stream for the command (**dirOut**). The function takes two arguments—the shell command to execute and the "mode" to use when calling the function. A mode of **"r"** (i.e., read) means the function returns a file object that corresponds to the shell command's **stdout**; a mode of **"w"** (i.e., write) returns a file object for the command's **stdin**.

Line 21 calls function **os.popen2** to execute the sorting command and to obtain the **stdout** and **stdin** streams for the command. The function returns a tuple that contains two file objects. The first object—**sortIn**—corresponds to the command's **stdin** stream, and the second file object—**sortOut**—corresponds to the command's **stdout** stream.

Next, the program feeds the output from the first command to the input of the second command to sort the directory listing. Line 23 calls file method **read** to get the directory command's output. Line 28 prints this output. Line 30 then passes the output to the sorting command's **stdin** with file method **write**. This combination links the output from the first command to the input of the second command. The program then closes the two file objects (lines 32–33). Closing the file object for the sort command's **stdin** object is necessary, because this sends the end-of-file character to the sort command. The sort command waits to receive this character before it sorts the input.

After we close the sort command's **stdin** object, the sort command orders the directory listing in reverse, and we can read the command's output (line 38). The program finishes by closing the sort command's **stdout** object (line 40).

```
1   # Fig. 18.9: fig18_09.py
2   # Demonstrating popen and popen2.
3
4   import os
5
6   # determine operating system, then set directory-listing and
7   # reverse-sort commands
8   if os.name == "nt" or os.name == "dos":  # Windows system
9       fileList = "dir /B"
10      sortReverse = "sort /R"
11  elif os.name == "posix":  # UNIX-compatible system
12      fileList = "ls -1"
13      sortReverse = "sort -r"
```

Fig. 18.9 os.popen/os.popen2 used to connect two processes. (Part 1 of 3.)

```
14    else:
15        sys.exit( "OS not supported by this program." )
16
17    # obtain stdout of directory-listing command
18    dirOut = os.popen( fileList, "r" )
19
20    # obtain stdin, stdout of reverse-sort command
21    sortIn, sortOut = os.popen2( sortReverse )
22
23    filenames = dirOut.read()   # output from directory-listing command
24
25    # display output from directory-listing command
26    print "Before sending to sort"
27    print "(Output from '%s'):" % fileList
28    print filenames
29
30    sortIn.write( filenames )   # send to stdin of sort command
31
32    dirOut.close()   # close stdout of directory-listing command
33    sortIn.close()   # close stdin of sort command -- sends EOF
34
35    # display output from sort command
36    print "After sending to sort"
37    print "(Output from '%s'):" % sortReverse
38    print sortOut.read()   # output from sort command
39
40    sortOut.close()   # close stdout of sort command
```

```
Before sending to sort
(Output from 'ls -1'):
fig18_02.py
fig18_03.py
fig18_04.py
fig18_05.py
fig18_07.py
fig18_09.py
fig18_10.py
fig18_14.py
fig18_15.py

After sending to sort
(Output from 'sort -r'):
fig18_15.py
fig18_14.py
fig18_10.py
fig18_09.py
fig18_07.py
fig18_05.py
fig18_04.py
fig18_03.py
fig18_02.py
```

Fig. 18.9   os.popen/os.popen2 used to connect two processes. (Part 2 of 3.)

```
Before sending to sort
(Output from 'dir /B'):
fig18_02.py
fig18_03.py
fig18_04.py
fig18_05.py
fig18_07.py
fig18_09.py
fig18_10.py
fig18_14.py
fig18_15.py

After sending to sort
(Output from 'sort /R'):
fig18_15.py
fig18_14.py
fig18_10.py
fig18_09.py
fig18_07.py
fig18_05.py
fig18_04.py
fig18_03.py
fig18_02.py
```

Fig. 18.9 **os.popen/os.popen2** used to connect two processes. (Part 3 of 3.)

18.5 Interprocess Communication

The **os** module provides an interface to many *interprocess communication* (*IPC*) mechanisms. Processes use IPC mechanisms to pass information between processes. One IPC mechanism is the *pipe*, which is a file-like object that provides a one-way communication channel. Typically, pipes are used when a parent opens a pipe, then forks a child. The parent uses the pipe to write (send) information to the child, and the child uses the pipe to read information from the parent.

We create pipes in Python with function **os.pipe**. This function returns a tuple that contains two *file descriptors*. A file descriptor is a number with which the operating system represents an open file. The first file descriptor provides read access to the pipe; the second file descriptor provides write access to the pipe. The difference between file descriptors and Python file objects is that file objects encapsulate a file descriptor and provide methods for modifying the file's content. We can call functions **os.read** and **os.write** to read and write the files associated with file descriptors. Figure 18.10 uses pipes to communicate between a parent process and a child process.

Lines 8–9 call function **os.pipe** to create pipes through which the parent and child processes will communicate. In the example, the parent process sends information to the child, and the child process sends information to the parent. Line 8 creates a pipe through which the parent process can send information to the child process. Variable **fromParent** refers to the file descriptor that reads data from the pipe; variable **toChild** refers to the file descriptor that writes data to the pipe. Line 9 retrieves similar file descriptors for the child. Notice that the program creates the pipes before the program forks a child process (line 13). This enables both the parent and the child processes to access the file descriptors when those processes execute. The parent portion of the code (lines 19–33) first calls function **os.close** to close the two file descriptors that the parent will not use—**fromParent** and **toParent** (lines 20–21). In general, it is considered good practice for a process to close the end of the pipe that it does not require. The parent and the child each has its own copy of these variables; therefore, closing a file descriptor in one process does not close the file descriptor in the other process.

```
1   # Fig. 18.10: fig18_10.py
2   # Using os.pipe to communicate with a child process.
3
4   import os
5   import sys
6
7   # open parent and child read/write pipes
8   fromParent, toChild = os.pipe()
9   fromChild, toParent = os.pipe()
10
11  # parent about to fork child process
12  try:
13      pid = os.fork()   # create child process
14  except OSError:
15      sys.exit( "Unable to create child process." )
16
17  if pid != 0:   # am I parent process?
18
19      # close unnecessary pipe ends
20      os.close( toParent )
21      os.close( fromParent )
22
23      # write values from 1-10 to parent's write pipe and
24      # read 10 values from child's read pipe
25      for i in range( 1, 11 ):
26          os.write( toChild, str( i ) )
27          print "Parent: %d," % i,
28          print "Child: %s" % \
29              os.read( fromChild, 64 )
30
31      # close pipes
32      os.close( toChild )
33      os.close( fromChild )
34
35  elif pid == 0:   # am I child process?
36
37      # close unnecessary pipe ends
38      os.close( toChild )
39      os.close( fromChild )
40
41      # read value from parent pipe
42      currentNumber = os.read( fromParent, 64 )
43
```

Fig. 18.10 os.pipe used to communicate between a parent process and a child process. (Part 1 of 2.)

```
44      # if we receive number from parent,
45      # write number to child write pipe
46      while currentNumber:
47          newNumber = int( currentNumber ) * 20
48          os.write( toParent, str( newNumber ) )
49          currentNumber = os.read( fromParent, 64 )
50
51      # close pipes
52      os.close( toParent )
53      os.close( fromParent )
54      os._exit( 0 )  # terminate child process
```

```
Parent: 1, Child: 20
Parent: 2, Child: 40
Parent: 3, Child: 60
Parent: 4, Child: 80
Parent: 5, Child: 100
Parent: 6, Child: 120
Parent: 7, Child: 140
Parent: 8, Child: 160
Parent: 9, Child: 180
Parent: 10, Child: 200
```

Fig. 18.10 os.pipe used to communicate between a parent process and a child process. (Part 2 of 2.)

The diagrams in Figs. 18.11–18.13 demonstrate how a program creates two pipes through which parent and child processes communicate. Each process writes to its own pipe and reads from its counterpart's pipe. Figure 18.11 shows the initial stage: the parent process creates two pipes. At this stage, the parent process is the only process executing and can read and write to both pipes. Next, the parent process forks a new child process. The child process receives its own copies of all variables in the parent process, including the two pipes (Fig. 18.12). However, to communicate, the parent needs only to read from the child pipe and to write to the parent pipe. The child needs only to read from the parent pipe and to write to the child pipe. For this reason, each process closes the unneeded end of each pipe. The parent process closes the reading end of its pipe and the writing end of the child's pipe. Similarly, the child closes the reading end of its pipe and the writing end of the parent pipe. After these operations, the parent and child can communicate through the appropriate pipes (Fig. 18.13).

Lines 25–29 write the numbers 1–10 to the parent pipe. Function **os.write** takes as arguments a file descriptor and a string to be written to the file that corresponds to the file descriptor. The statement in line 26 inserts data into the pipe, and the data remains in the pipe until the child process reads that data.

Lines 28–29 read and print the data obtained from the child pipe. Function **os.read** takes as arguments a file descriptor and the size (in bytes) of the data to be read. This function blocks the calling process until data is available from the pipe. This means that function **os.read** does not return to the calling process until the pipe contains some data, thereby causing the parent process to block until the child process writes data to the pipe. After the child writes ten values to the parent pipe, the parent process closes the writing end of the parent's pipe and the reading end of the child's pipe.

The child process (lines 37–54) first closes its unneeded file descriptors—**toChild** and **fromChild** (lines 38–39). The child then reads a value from the parent pipe by calling function **os.read** (line 42). Lines 46–49 contain a **while** loop that multiplies the value read from the parent pipe by 20 and writes the product to the child pipe. The child then reads the next number from the parent. If the pipe is closed, function **os.read** returns the empty string. In this case, the **while** loop exits, and the child closes its remaining file descriptors.

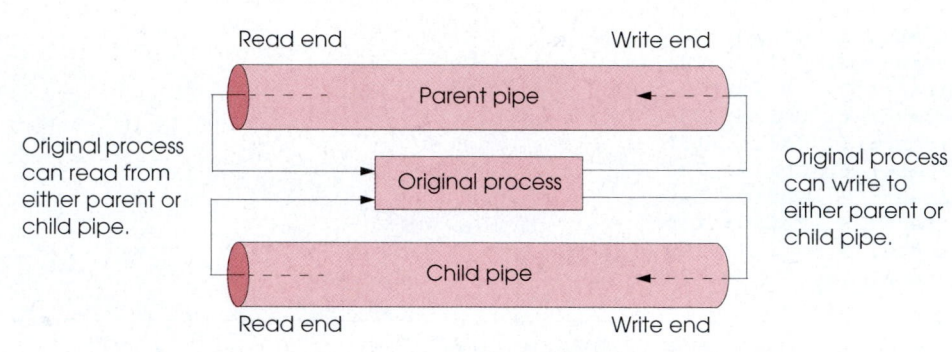

Fig. 18.11 Initial stage: Original process can read and write to both pipes.

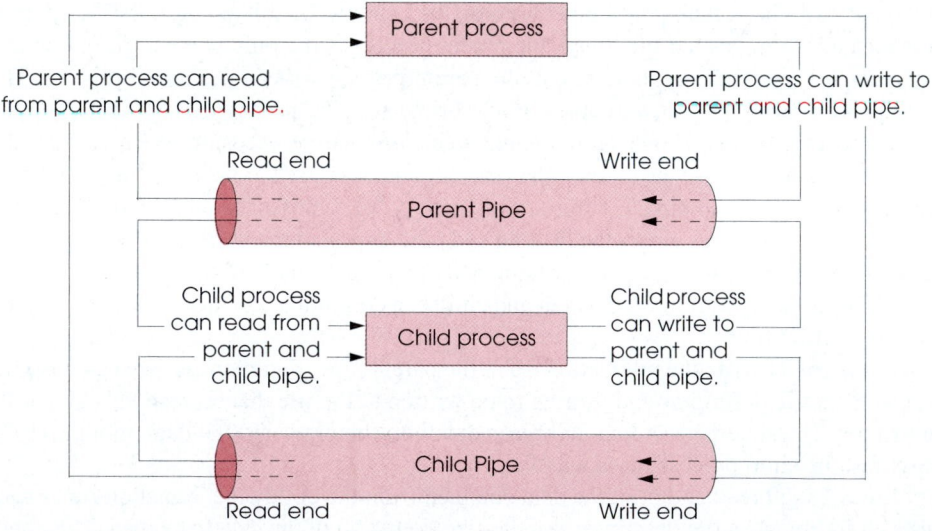

Fig. 18.12 Intermediate stage: Parent and child processes can read and write to both pipes.

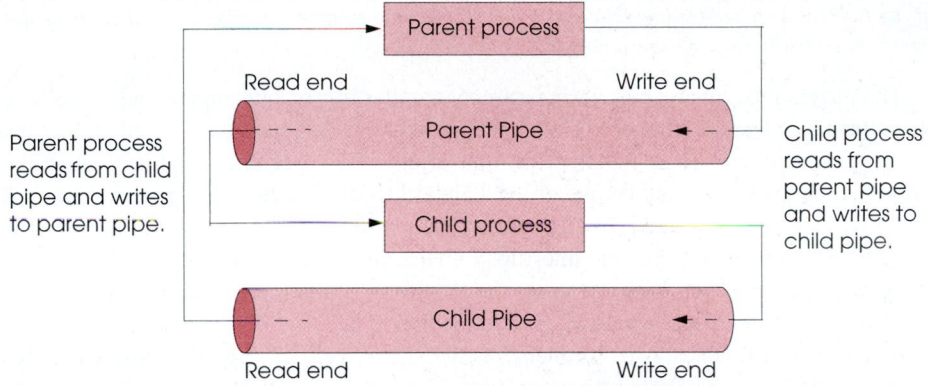

Fig. 18.13 Final stage: Parent and child processes close unneeded ends of the pipes.

Line 54 calls function **os._exit** to terminate the child process. Function **os._exit** is similar to **sys.exit**, but **os._exit** does not perform any cleanup (e.g., by flushing buffers). For this reason, **os._exit** is used specifically for exiting child processes. If, instead, the program used **sys.exit**, the operating system would reclaim the resources that the parent or other child processes may still need. The argument passed to **os._exit** must be the exit status of the process. An exit status of 0 indicates normal termination.

 Good Programming Practice 18.1

A process should close the end of the pipe that it does not need, since operating systems limit the number of file descriptors that can be open simultaneously.

18.6 Signal Handling

Processes also can communicate with *signals*, which are messages that operating systems deliver to programs asynchronously. For example, when the user presses *Ctrl-C* during the execution of a Windows or UNIX console program, the operating system sends an *interrupt signal* to the program. Usually, this signal causes the program to terminate. However, a program can specify actions to execute in response to any signal. In *signal processing*, a program receives a signal and performs an action based on that signal. Errors (e.g., writing to a closed pipe), events (e.g., when a timer goes to zero) and user input (e.g., *Ctrl-C*) can all generate signals. In addition, a program can generate signals internally.

Signal handlers execute in response to specific signals. Every Python program has a *default signal handler* for each signal. For example, when the Python interpreter receives a signal that indicates that the program wrote to a closed pipe or that the user typed a keyboard interrupt, Python raises an exception. When such exceptions occur, programs can use the default signal handlers or they can specify custom handlers.

Figure 18.14 shows an example of setting a custom handler for the interrupt signal. Pressing *Ctrl-C* on most platforms sends an interrupt signal. In this program, we override the interrupt signal handler so that the user must press *Ctrl-C* three times before the program terminates. Line 5 imports module **signal**, which provides signal-handling capabilities to Python programs.

Portability Tip 18.3

Each system defines a unique set of signals. Module **signal** *is a platform-specific module that contains only those signals that the system defines.*

The program begins by *registering* a signal handler for the interrupt signal using function **signal.signal** (line 15). This function takes two arguments: a signal and a function that corresponds to a handler for that signal. The second argument passed to **signal.signal** also may be one of the standard signal handlers: **signal.SIG_IGN** (ignore the signal) or **signal.SIG_DFL** (default handler for the signal). The value **signal.SIGINT** represents the interrupt signal, and **stop** is the name of the function we use as a signal handler. Line 15 causes the program to call function **stop** when the program receives an interrupt signal (e.g., when the user types *Ctrl-C*).

Function **stop** (lines 7–10) implements the signal handler. Signal handlers take two arguments. The first argument represents the signal that the program has received; the second argument contains the current stack frame. We discuss the first argument in more detail during the next example. (We discussed stack frames briefly in Section 12.7.) In this example, the signal handler decreases global variable **keepRunning** each time the signal handler executes.

If the user presses *Ctrl-C* after the signal handler has been registered, function **stop** executes. When the program receives a signal, the executing code is interrupted so the program can process the signal. Normally, this is not a problem, because after the signal is processed, the previously executing code can continue from where it terminated. In such a case, we say the code is *re-entrant*. Some code (e.g., some UNIX system calls or internal Python statements that manipulate memory) is not re-entrant and cannot be restarted after a signal has interrupted that code.

```
1   # Fig. 18.14: fig18_14.py
2   # Defining our own signal handler.
3
4   import time
5   import signal
6
7   def stop( signalNumber, frame ):
8      global keepRunning
9      keepRunning -= 1
10      print "Ctrl-C pressed; keepRunning is", keepRunning
11
12   keepRunning = 3
13
14   # set the handler for SIGINT to be function stop
15   signal.signal( signal.SIGINT, stop )
16
17   while keepRunning:
18      print "Executing..."
19      time.sleep( 1 )
20
21   print "Program terminating..."
```

Fig. 18.14 Custom signal handlers. (Part 1 of 2.)

```
Executing...
Executing...
Ctrl-C pressed; keepRunning is 2
Executing...
Executing...
Ctrl-C pressed; keepRunning is 1
Executing...
Executing...
Ctrl-C pressed; keepRunning is 0
Program terminating...
```

Fig. 18.14 Custom signal handlers. (Part 2 of 2.)

Line 12 initializes variable **keepRunning** to 3 and line 17 begins a **while** loop that executes as long as **keepRunning** is greater than zero. If the user presses *Ctrl-C* three times, the signal handler reduces the value of **keepRunning** to zero and the loop exits. At this point, the program prints a message and terminates (line 21).

18.7 Sending Signals

In the previous section, we demonstrated how a process can handle signals. It is also important to understand that an executing program can send signals to other processes. Function *os.kill* sends a signal to a particular process identified by its *pid*. In this section, we discuss an example (Fig. 18.15) in which a parent process sends a signal to its child process. The program handles the interrupt signal in the parent process, which then terminates the child process by sending a signal from the parent process to the child process.

```
 1   # Fig.  18.15:  fig18_15.py
 2   # Sending signals to child processes using kill
 3
 4   import os
 5   import signal
 6   import time
 7   import sys
 8
 9   # handles both SIGALRM and SIGINT signals
10   def parentInterruptHandler( signum, frame ):
11      global pid
12      global parentKeepRunning
13
14      # send kill signal to child process and exit
15      os.kill( pid, signal.SIGKILL )   # send kill signal
16      print "Interrupt received. Child process killed."
17
18      # allow parent process to terminate normally
19      parentKeepRunning = 0
20
21   # set parent's handler for SIGINT
22   signal.signal( signal.SIGINT, parentInterruptHandler )
```

Fig. 18.15 os.kill used to send signals to other processes. (Part 1 of 2.)

```
23
24   # keep parent running until child process is killed
25   parentKeepRunning = 1
26
27   # parent ready to fork child process
28   try:
29      pid = os.fork()   # create child process
30   except OSError:
31      sys.exit( "Unable to create child process." )
32
33   if pid != 0:   # am I parent process?
34
35      while parentKeepRunning:
36         print "Parent running. Press Ctrl-C to terminate child."
37         time.sleep( 1 )
38
39   elif pid == 0:   # am I child process?
40
41      # ignore interrupt in child process
42      signal.signal( signal.SIGINT, signal.SIG_IGN )
43
44      while 1:
45         print "Child still executing."
46         time.sleep( 1 )
47
48   print "Parent terminated child process."
49   print "Parent terminating normally."
```

```
Parent running. Press Ctrl-C to terminate child.
Child still executing.
Parent running. Press Ctrl-C to terminate child.
Child still executing.
Child still executing.
Parent running. Press Ctrl-C to terminate child.
Interrupt received. Child process killed.
Parent terminated child process.
Parent terminating normally.
```

Fig. 18.15 os.kill used to send signals to other processes. (Part 2 of 2.)

The program beings by defining a signal handler that enables the parent process to handle the interrupt signal (lines 10–19). Line 22 registers this signal handler in the parent process. Line 25 initializes variable **parentKeepRunning**, which the parent process uses to determine when the parent process should terminate.

Line 29 forks a new child process. Lines 42–46 execute only in this newly created child process. Line 42 registers the **signal.SIG_IGN** signal handler for the interrupt signal in the child process. This causes the child process to ignore the interrupt signal. Lines 44–46 are an infinite loop that keeps the child process running.

Lines 35–37 execute in the parent process. Line 36 prints instructions to the user. When the user presses *Ctrl-C*, the Python interpreter invokes the parent process's interrupt signal handler, **parentInterruptHandler** (lines 10–19). Line 15 invokes function *os.kill* to send the *kill signal* **signal.SIGKILL** to the child process. The first argument to function **os.kill** is the *pid* of the process to which the program should send the signal. The second argument specifies the type of signal to send. This program sends the kill signal, which terminates the child process. Line 19 then sets the **parentKeepRunning** flag to 0, which causes the loop on lines 35–37 to terminate and allows the parent process to terminate normally.

When a child process terminates in UNIX/Linux systems, the child process remains in the process table, so the parent can determine whether the child terminated normally. If many child processes are created and are not removed from the process table when they terminate, the process table accumulates dead processes, called *zombies*. Eliminating zombie processes is called *reaping* and is performed with functions **os.wait** or **os.waitpid**.

To avoid the accumulation of zombies, set a handler for the **signal.SIGCHLD** signal, which is sent to the parent when a child exits. This handler should call function **os.wait** or **os.waitpid** and perform additional operations as necessary. If additional tasks do not need to be performed when a child process terminates, register **signal.SIG_IGN** as the handler for the **SIGCHLD** signal. This handler causes the process to ignore the **SIGCHLD** signal and prevents the child from remaining in the process table.

SUMMARY

- Computers, perform operations concurrently. It is common for a desktop personal computer to compile a program, send a file to a printer and receive electronic mail messages over a network concurrently.

- Some programming languages do not enable programmers to specify concurrent activities. Rather, these programming languages provide control structures that allow programmers to organize successive actions; a program proceeds to the next action after the previous action is completed.

- The type of concurrency that computers perform today generally uses operating-system "primitives" available only to highly experienced "systems programmers."

- There are two primary ways to implement concurrency. One is to have each task, or process, operate in a separate memory space, each using its own section of memory in which to execute.

- Although processes may have separate memory spaces in which to execute, processes do not actually run "at the same time" unless they are executed on separate processors.

- On single-processor systems, the operating system uses time slicing to divide processor time among the many processes. The operating system allocates a short span of execution time—called a quantum—to a process. The process executes for the quantum of time, then the operating system allocates a quantum of time to another process.

- The operating system performs context switching to move the first process and its dependent data into memory, and to move the new processes and its dependent data into the processor.

- On multi-processor systems, each process can run on a separate processor to achieve true concurrency.

- Another way to implement concurrency is to enable multiple executions, also known as threads of execution, which operate in the same memory space. This is known as multithreading. Creating a thread is more efficient than creating a process, because the operating system does not create a separate memory space for each thread.

- Operating systems provide shells—programs that execute system commands on behalf of the user. UNIX users probably are familiar with shells such as the Bourne shell (**sh**) or the C shell (**csh**), which provide command-line interfaces for executing commands. Windows users probably are familiar with Windows Explorer, which is a graphical shell, and the MS-DOS prompt, which is a command-line interface. Macintosh OS users probably are familiar with the Finder, which is another graphical shell.

- Through module **os**, Python enables developers to access the shell to run other programs and control those programs' input and output.

- Some operating systems, (e.g., UNIX and Mac OS X) have built-in system commands that enable programmers to create and manage processes.

- The Portable Operating System Interface for UNIX (POSIX) standard defines these system commands for UNIX operating systems. Most UNIX operating systems implement the POSIX standard, and therefore provide the same set of functions for creating new processes programmatically. Python uses these underlying operating system commands to implement the process functions.

- Not all operating systems can create separate processes from within a running program. For this reason, process management is one of Python's least portable features.

- Creating new processes is useful in applications that can perform multiple tasks in parallel.

- One way to create a new process is to use function **os.fork**, which is available only on POSIX-compliant systems (e.g., most versions of UNIX and Linux).

- Module **os** on the Windows version of Python does not define function **os.fork**, because Windows does not support the creation of new processes by using **fork**. Instead, Windows applications programmers typically use multithreaded programming techniques to accomplish concurrency tasks.

- The parent process is the process that invokes **os.fork**. Any process that the parent process forks (creates) is a child process. Each process has a unique process id number, or pid, which identifies that process.

- When a process invokes function **fork**, the operating system creates a new child process that is essentially identical to the parent (original) process. The child process inherits copies of many values, such as global variables and environment variables, from the parent process.

- The only difference between a parent process and its child process is the return value of **fork**: The **child** process receives a return value of 0, and the parent process receives the child's *pid* as the return value.

- After the call to function **fork**, the two processes execute the same program concurrently, starting with the line of code that follows the invocation of **fork**. The parent and child processes execute concurrently and independently of one another (i.e., they execute "asynchronously").

- If the operating system is unable to create a new process, function **os.fork** raises an **OSError** exception

- If a program must perform different tasks in the parent and child processes, that program can use **if** statements to test the value that **fork** returns in each process. The processes then can perform the appropriate tasks based on the results of those **if** statements.

- Function **os.getpid** returns the *pid* of the currently executing process. A parent process can use the child's *pid* to manage the child process.

- Processes are asynchronous and concurrent. Asynchronous means that they operate independently of one another without synchronization. Concurrent means that they can proceed in parallel (i.e., they execute at the same time).

- We cannot predict the relative speeds of the child process and parent process. Once the child process is forked, the parent process sometimes will execute before the child process, and sometimes the child process will execute first.

- Function **os.wait** (available only on UNIX-compatible systems) waits for any one of the parent's child processes to complete before allowing the parent process to continue its execution. This function returns a two-element tuple that contains the *pid* of the finished child and the child's exit status—an integer that indicates the state in which the child process exited.

- An exit status of 0 indicates that the child process completed successfully; a positive integer indicates that the child process terminated with some error. Function **os.wait** raises an **OSError** exception if there are no children.

- To cause the parent process to wait for a specific child process to terminate, the parent can use function **os.waitpid**. This function (available only on UNIX-compatible systems) waits for a process to finish then returns a two-element tuple that contains the pid of that process and that process's exit status. If the pid does not exist or if the child terminated prior to the call to **waitpid**, function **waitpid** raises an **OSError** exception.

- Function **os.waitpid** takes as arguments a process id and an option. If the first argument is greater than 0, **waitpid** waits for the process with the specified pid. If the first argument is -1, **waitpid** waits for any child of the current process, which is a identical behavior to **os.wait**. The option argument passed to **os.waitpid** should be 0 for normal operation. Passing the constant **os.WNOHANG** as argument option specifies that the call to **waitpid** should return immediately if no status information is available for the process with the given pid.

- Python provides several ways to execute system commands and other programs from Python code. One way is to call function **os.system**, which executes a system command using a shell, then returns control to the original process (after the command completes).

- Another way to execute a program is through the **os.exec** family of functions. Unlike **os.system**, each **os.exec** function does not return control to the calling process after executing the specified command.

- When a program invokes an **os.exec** function, the program that the **os.exec** function executes "takes over" the Python process. In fact, the Python process terminates as soon as it calls the **os.exec** function. The invoked program then executes with the same *pid* under which the Python process executed previously.

- Function **os.execvp** replaces the Python process with the program executed via **os.execvp**. This is useful if one process wishes to terminate after handing control over to another process.

- On many systems—DOS and UNIX in particular—it is possible to pass information to programs from the command line as command-line arguments. Python stores command-line arguments in a list named **sys.argv**. This list always contains at least one value—the name of the program that the user entered at the command line. The rest of the list contains the command-line arguments in the order in which the user passed those arguments to the program.

- A fundamental philosophy of UNIX systems is that programs should be small and should perform well-defined tasks. Users then can use multiple programs together to achieve a particular result.

- Python provides functions for accessing the contents of streams **stdout**, **stdin** and **stderr**, which enable programs to manipulate the input and output of other programs. These functions return one or more file objects that correspond to the input and output streams of a program. These file objects can be treated like any other file objects.

- To write information from one program to the input of another program, the first program prints or writes to the second program's input file object—the data is transferred to the input of the second program. To read the output from the second program, the first program reads from the second program's output file object.

- Function **os.popen** takes two arguments—the shell command to execute and the "mode" to use when calling the function. A mode of **"r"** (i.e., read) means the function returns a file object that corresponds to the shell command's **stdout**; a mode of **"w"** (i.e., write) returns a file object for the command's **stdin**.

- Function **os.popen2** returns a tuple that contains two file objects. The first object corresponds to the command's **stdin** stream, and the second file object corresponds to the command's **stdout** stream.

- The **os** module provides an interface to many interprocess communication (IPC) mechanisms. Processes use IPC mechanisms to pass information between processes.

- One IPC mechanism is the pipe, which is a file-like object that provides a one-way communication channel. Typically, pipes are used when a parent opens a pipe, then forks a child. The parent uses the pipe to write (send) information to the child, and the child uses the pipe to read information from the parent.

- We create pipes in Python with function **os.pipe**. This function returns a tuple that contains two file descriptors. A file descriptor is a number with which the operating system represents an open file. The first file descriptor provides read access to the pipe; the second file descriptor provides write access to the pipe.

- Processes also can communicate with signals, which are messages that operating systems deliver to programs asynchronously. For example, when the user presses *Ctrl-C* during the execution of a Windows or UNIX console program, the operating system sends an interrupt signal to the program. Usually, this signal causes the program to terminate.

- A program can specify actions to execute in response to any signal. In signal processing, a program receives a signal and performs an action based on that signal. Errors (e.g., writing to a closed pipe), events (e.g., when a timer goes to zero) and user input (e.g., *Ctrl-C*) can all generate signals. In addition, a program can generate signals internally.

- Signal handlers execute in response to specific signals. Every Python program has a default signal handler for each signal. For example, when the Python interpreter receives a signal that indicates that the program wrote to a closed pipe or that the user typed a keyboard interrupt, Python raises an exception. When such exceptions occur, programs can use the default signal handlers or they can specify custom handlers.

- Each system defines a unique set of signals. Module **signal** is a platform-specific module that contains only those signals that the system defines.

- Function **signal.signal** takes two arguments: a signal and a function that corresponds to a handler for that signal. The second argument passed to **signal.signal** also may be one of the standard signal handlers: **signal.SIG_IGN** (ignore the signal) or **signal.SIG_DFL** (default handler for the signal).

- Function **os.kill** sends a signal to a particular process identified by its pid.

TERMINOLOGY

alarm function	**excve** function
alarm signal	**exec** function
AttributeError exception	**execl** function
blocking	**execle** function
child process	**execlp** function
clear command	**execv** function
clone	**execvp** function
cls command	**execvpe** function
concurrency	**_exit** function
console program	**exit** function

file descriptor
file object
interprocess communication (IPC)
interrupt signal
keyboard interrupt
kill function
kill signal
multithreading
normal termination
operating system
os module
os._exit function
os.close function
os.exec function
os.execvp function
os.fork function
os.kill function
os.name variable
os.pipe function
os.popen function
os.popen2 function
os.read function
os.system function
os.wait function
os.waitpid function
os.write function
OSError exception
parent process
pause function
pid (process id number)
pipe
Portable Operating System Interface for UNIX
    (POSIX)
"posix" operating system name
process
"r" file open mode
race condition
read file method

reaping zombies
re-entrant code
registering a signal handler
shell
SIG_IGN signal handler
SIGALRM signal
SIGCHLD signal
SIGINT signal
SIGKILL signal
signal
signal function
signal handler
signal handling
signal module
signal processing
signal.alarm function
signal.pause function
signal.SIG_IGN (ignore signal handler)
signal.SIGALRM signal
signal.SIGCHLD signal
signal.SIGINT signal
signal.SIGKILL signal
signal.signal function
specifying custom signal handlers
stderr
stdin
stdout
sys.argv argument list
sys.exit function
system call
threads of execution
time slicing
time.sleep function
"w" file mode
write file method
writing data to a pipe
writing to a closed pipe
zombie

SELF-REVIEW EXERCISES

18.1   Fill in the blanks in each of the following statements:

a) When two paths of execution run simultaneously but in separate memory spaces, they are known as _____. When they share a memory space, they are known as concurrent _____.

b) The **fork** function returns the _____ in the parent process and _____ in the child process.

c) There are two ways to execute other programs from within other programs. The first, and simplest, way is through function _____. The other way is through function _____.

d) To wait for a child process to complete, we can use the _____ or _____ func-
    tions.

e) The _____ function replaces the current process by running a shell command.

f) To create file descriptors that can be used to communicate between processes, we can use
    the _____ or _____ functions.

g) Messages sent by an OS to a process are known as _____.

h) To avoid collecting zombies, set a handler for the _____ signal.

i) The _____ message is sent when a child exits.

j) The _____ message is sent when *Ctrl-C* is pressed.

18.2   State whether each of the following is *true* or *false*. If *false*, explain why.

a) To execute separate programs concurrently, separate processes are required for each.

b) The function **os.fork** is available in Windows.

c) Function **os.wait** waits for the **SIGINT** signal.

d) If we want to wait for a specific process to complete, we can use the function **os.wait-pid**.

e) **os.system** and **os.exec** are available on both UNIX and Windows systems.

f) Python stores process information in **sys.argv**.

g) **os.pipe** is used to create files in Python.

h) Processes can communicate with signals.

i) **os.kill** sends a signal to a particular process.

ANSWERS TO SELF REVIEW EXERCISES

18.1   a) processes, thread. b) child's process id number, or *pid*, 0. c) **system**, **exec**. d) **wait**,
waitpid. e) **exec**. f) **popen**, **popen2**. g) signals. h) **SIGCHLD**. i) **SIGCHLD**. j) **SIGINT**.

18.2   a) True. b) False. **os.fork** is available only on UNIX machines. c) False. Function
os.wait waits for all the children of a particular parent process to finish. d) True. e) True. f) False.
Python stores command-line options in **sys.argv**. g) False. **os.pipe** creates pipes in Python.
h) True. i) True.

EXERCISES

18.3   [This question is for UNIX/Linux users.] Use functions **fork** and **exec** to emulate function
system. The parent should use the **wait** function to wait for the child process to finish before continuing. Run the command **"cat ex18_01.py"**.

18.4   Use function **exec** to create a menu that allows users to execute programs that they select.
Give the user a choice of three programs.

18.5   Create an output filter that performs word wrapping. If a line is longer than a certain number
of characters, split the line over multiple lines. The number of characters per line should be indicated
in the command line. The program should read keyboard input from the user, and format that input
as specified, placing the result in **file.txt**. Implement this using pipes and **fork** functions (child
gets input from user, parent performs the filtering).

18.6   [This question is for UNIX/Linux users.] Use function **kill** to end (terminate) a process.
First, end it using a **SIGINT** signal. Wait three seconds. If it does not respond to the **SIGINT** signal,
send the process to a **SIGKILL** signal.

18.7   Set a signal handler on **SIGINT** to query users if they want to quit after pressing *Ctrl-C*.

18.8   [This question is for UNIX/Linux users.] Use function **fork** to spawn a child and let the
child exit without leaving an entry in the process table.

Multithreading

Objectives

- To understand the concept of multithreading.
- To understand how multithreading can improve performance.
- To understand how to create, manage and destroy threads.
- To understand the thread life cycle.
- To study several examples of thread synchronization.

The spider's touch, how exquisitely fine!
Feels at each thread, and lives along the line.
Alexander Pope

Learn to labor and to wait.
Henry Wadsworth Longfellow

The most general definition of beauty…Multeity in Unity.
Samuel Taylor Coleridge

Outline

19.1 Introduction

In Chapter 18, Process Management, we discussed how to perform concurrent tasks using processes—code that executes in separate memory spaces. In this chapter, we discuss *multithreading* techniques for performing concurrent tasks in individual processes. *Threads* often are called "light-weight" processes, because operating systems generally require fewer resources to create and manage threads than to create and manage processes. Whereas operating systems allocate separate memory locations and data for forked processes, threads within a program execute in the same memory space and share many of the same resources. Multithreaded programs use computing resources more efficiently than do programs that fork multiple processes.

Python is different from many general-purpose programming languages in that it provides multithreading classes.[1] If the operating system on which a Python program is running supports multithreading, a programmer can use Python's ***threading*** module to create multithreaded applications. The programmer specifies that an application contains multiple threads of execution, and each thread designates a portion of a program that executes concurrently with other threads. Python's support for multithreaded programming gives the programmer access to powerful capabilities that may not be available directly in other languages.

Many tasks can benefit by multithreaded programming. When a Web browser downloads large files, such as audio clips or video clips, the user would prefer to start listening to the audio or watching the video immediately, rather than wait for the entire clip to download. While one thread downloads a clip, another thread can play the part of the clip that has been downloaded already; thus, allowing the activities to proceed concurrently. To

---

1. Many programming languages that do not provide multithreading capabilities directly, can still be used to implement multithreaded programs. Such programming languages use operating-system specific threading libraries. Programs implemented in this manner typically require modifications to execute on multiple platforms.

avoid choppy playback, the player thread should not begin until there is a sufficient amount of the data in the download clip. This strategy is known as *buffering*.

Performance Tip 19.1

A problem with single-threaded applications is that lengthy activities must complete before other activities can begin. In a multithreaded application, threads can share a processor (or set of processors), enabling multiple tasks to execute in parallel.

Although the human mind can perform tasks concurrently, people often find it difficult to jump between parallel "trains of thought." To perceive why multithreading can be difficult to program and understand, try the following experiment: Open three books to page one and try reading the books concurrently. Read a few words from the first book, then read a few words from the second book, then read a few words from the third book, then loop back and read the next few words from the first book, etc. After conducting this experiment, you will appreciate the challenges presented by multithreading. It is exceedingly difficult to switch between books, read each book briefly, remember your place in each book, move the book you are reading closer so you can see it and push books you are not reading aside. Moreover, it is nearly impossible to comprehend the content of the books amidst all this chaos!

19.2 Thread States: Life Cycle of a Thread

The Python interpreter controls all threads in a program. When the interpreter starts executing a program, the "main" thread begins execution. Each thread in a program can create and start other threads. When a program contains more than one running thread, these threads are *switched* in and out of the interpreter, after a specified interval (called a *quantum*). Python's *global interpreter lock (GIL)* ensures that the interpreter runs only one thread at any given time. Each time the GIL becomes available, a single thread obtains it. The interpreter then switches in this thread and executes the thread for its quantum. When the quantum expires, the interpreter switches out the thread, and frees the GIL. Certain operations cause a thread's quantum to be truncated (cut short). We discuss these operations momentarily.

At any time, a thread is said to be in one of several *thread states* (Fig. 19.1). This section discusses the various states, as well as the transitions between states. The section also discusses the objects and methods that cause threads to change state.

Multithreaded Python programs use the classes and functions of module **threading**. Programs can define threads by inheriting from class **threading.Thread** and overriding that class's functionality. When a program creates a new thread, the new thread begins its lifecycle in the *born* state. The thread remains in this state until the program invokes the thread's **start** method, which places the thread in the *ready* state (sometimes called the *runnable* state) and immediately returns control to the calling thread. The caller then executes concurrently with the launched thread and any other threads in the program.

Common Programming Error 19.1

*If a program calls method **start** for a thread that already has exited the born state, the method raises an **AssertionError** exception.*

When a class inherits from **Thread**, the derived class overrides the base class's **run** method. This method implements the tasks that the thread performs. A program that uses the thread does not call that thread's **run** method. Instead, a *ready* thread's **run** method begins executing when the thread obtains the GIL for the first time and becomes a *running*

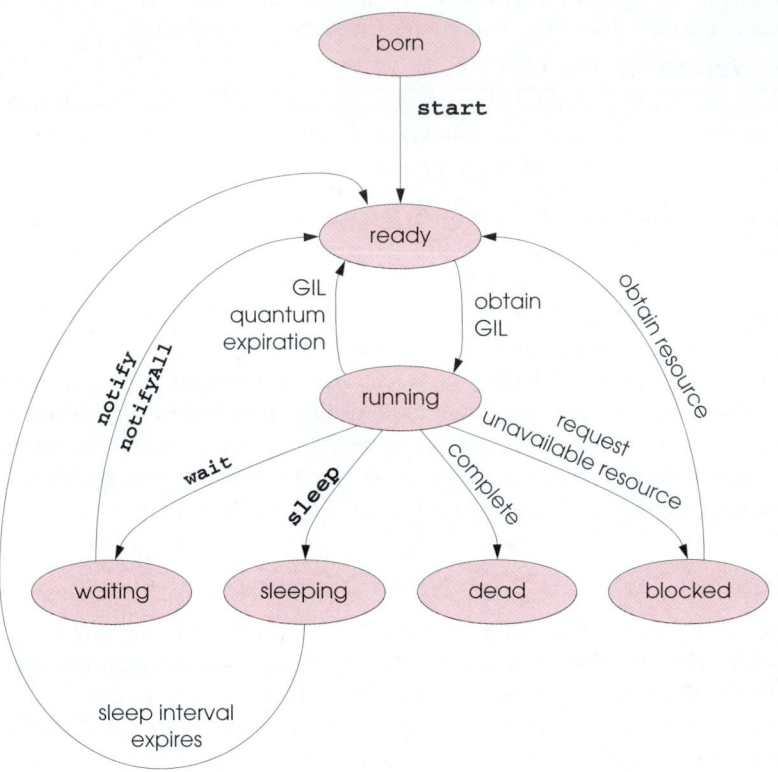

Fig. 19.1 State diagram showing the life cycle of a thread.

thread. The **run** method then executes until the method returns or raises an unhandled exception, or until the thread is switched out of the interpreter. When the interpreter switches out a *running* thread, the thread remembers its current point of execution. When the interpreter switches the thread back in, that thread continues executing from the point at which it was switched out of the interpreter. The only state in which a thread has obtained the GIL is the *running* state. If a thread exits the running state for any reason, the thread forfeits the GIL so another thread can execute.

A thread enters the *dead state* when its **run** method returns or terminates for any reason (e.g., an uncaught exception)—the interpreter eventually disposes of a *dead* thread. If a *running* thread calls another thread's ***join*** method, the *running* thread forfeits the GIL and waits for the ***join***ed thread to die before proceeding. A thread may not call its own **join** method. An optional argument that **join** accepts is a *timeout*, which is a floating-point number that indicates the number of seconds for which the caller will wait for the **join**ed thread to complete. Passing no argument to method **join** indicates that the caller will wait indefinitely for the target thread to die. Such waiting can be dangerous; it can lead to two particularly serious problems—*deadlock* and *indefinite postponement*. In deadlock, one or more threads wait forever for an event that cannot occur; in indefinite postponement, one or more threads is delayed for some unpredictably long time. We discuss deadlock in more detail in Section 19.4.

Most programs use external resources, such as network connections and files on disk, to perform their tasks. If such a resource is unavailable at the time a thread requests the resource, the thread will enter the *blocked* state until that resource becomes available to the thread. A common way for a thread to enter the *blocked* state occurs when the thread issues an *I/O (input/output) request*. When a thread performs an I/O request—such as reading a file from disk or sending a file to a printer—the thread that issues the request forfeits the GIL and is switched out of the interpreter, so that other threads may use the interpreter while the I/O is performed. An *I/O-bound program*—a program whose work consists mainly of I/O tasks—generally benefits most from multithreading, because the other threads in the program can use the interpreter while one thread waits for the I/O, thus using the processor more efficiently and reducing the program's total execution time. A thread *blocked* for I/O becomes *ready* when the I/O for which that thread is waiting completes. At that point the thread attempts to re-acquire the GIL.

When a *running* thread calls function **time.sleep**, that thread releases the GIL and enters the *sleeping state*. A *sleeping* thread returns to the *ready* state after the designated sleep time expires. A *sleeping* thread cannot use the interpreter even if the interpreter is available.

Often, threads in a program share data. If multiple threads modify that data, the data may become corrupted, and the program can produce unpredictable results. In such programs, it may be necessary to *synchronize* access to the shared data. This means that each thread that accesses shared data must first obtain a lock on a *synchronization object* associated with that data. Once the thread has finished with the data, the thread releases the synchronization object so that other threads may access the data. (We discuss the details of synchronization in Section 19.4–Section 19.8).

Sometimes, due to the logic requirements of a program, a *running* thread is unable to perform its task on shared data for which it has acquired a synchronization object. In this case, the thread can call the synchronization object's **wait** method to release the object, voluntarily. This causes the thread to release the GIL and enter a *waiting* state for that synchronization object. When another thread calls the synchronization object's **notify** method, one of that synchronization object's *waiting* threads becomes *ready*. That thread then resumes execution when it re-obtains the GIL. When a *running* thread calls **notifyAll** on the synchronization object, every thread in the *waiting* state for that object becomes *ready*. The interpreter then chooses one of the *ready* threads to execute.

Module **threading** provides several ways for a program to obtain information about its threads, including their current states. Function **threading.currentThread** returns a reference to the currently *running* **Thread**. Function **threading.enumerate** returns a list of all currently active objects of class **Thread** (i.e., a thread whose **run** method has started but not yet terminated). Function **threading.activeCount** returns the length of the list returned by **threading.enumerate**. **Thread** Method **isAlive** returns **1** if the thread's **start** method has been called and if the thread is not *dead* (i.e., its controlling **run** method has not terminated). Method **setName** sets the **Thread**'s name. Method **getName** returns the name of the **Thread**. Using the **print** statement on a **Thread** displays the thread's name and current state. Throughout this chapter, we use the various **Thread** methods and **threading** functions to obtain and display information about the threads our programs create.

19.3 threading.Thread Example

The program in Fig. 19.2 demonstrates how to create threads by defining a class that derives from **threading.Thread** and instantiating objects of that class. The application also demonstrates function **time.sleep**. Each of the three threads in this program displays its name after sleeping for a random amount of time between 1 and 5 seconds.

Class **PrintThread**, which inherits from **threading.Thread**, consists of attribute **sleepTime**, a constructor and a **run** method. Attribute **sleepTime** (line 15) stores a random integer value determined when a **PrintThread** object is constructed. When started, each **PrintThread** object sleeps for the amount of time specified by **sleepTime**, then outputs its name.

```python
1   # Fig. 19.2: fig19_02.py
2   # Multiple threads printing at different intervals.
3
4   import threading
5   import random
6   import time
7
8   class PrintThread( threading.Thread ):
9      """Subclass of threading.Thread"""
10
11     def __init__( self, threadName ):
12        """Initialize thread, set sleep time, print data"""
13
14        threading.Thread.__init__( self, name = threadName )
15        self.sleepTime = random.randrange( 1, 6 )
16        print "Name: %s; sleep: %d" % \
17           ( self.getName(), self.sleepTime )
18
19        # overridden Thread run method
20     def run( self ):
21        """Sleep for 1-5 seconds"""
22
23        print "%s going to sleep for %s second(s)" % \
24           ( self.getName(), self.sleepTime )
25        time.sleep( self.sleepTime )
26        print self.getName(), "done sleeping"
27
28  thread1 = PrintThread( "thread1" )
29  thread2 = PrintThread( "thread2" )
30  thread3 = PrintThread( "thread3" )
31
32  print "\nStarting threads"
33
34  thread1.start()    # invokes run method of thread1
35  thread2.start()    # invokes run method of thread2
36  thread3.start()    # invokes run method of thread3
37
38  print "Threads started\n"
```

Fig. 19.2 Multiple threads printing at random intervals. (Part 1 of 2.)

```
Name: thread1; sleep: 5
Name: thread2; sleep: 1
Name: thread3; sleep: 3

Starting threads
thread1 going to sleep for 5 second(s)
thread2 going to sleep for 1 second(s)
thread3 going to sleep for 3 second(s)
Threads started

thread2 done sleeping
thread3 done sleeping
thread1 done sleeping
```

Fig. 19.2   Multiple threads printing at random intervals. (Part 2 of 2.)

The **PrintThread** constructor (lines 11–17) first calls the base-class constructor, passing the object and the thread's name. A thread's name is specified with **Thread** keyword argument **name**. If no name is specified, the thread is assigned a unique name of the form **"Thread-***n***"**, where *n* is an integer. The constructor then initializes **sleepTime** to a random integer between 1 and 5, inclusive. Next, the program outputs the name of the thread and the value of **sleepTime**, to show the values for the particular **PrintThread** being constructed.

When a **PrintThread**'s **start** method (inherited from **Thread**) is invoked, the **PrintThread** object enters the *ready* state. When the interpreter switches in the **PrintThread** object, the thread enters the *running* state. If this is the first time the thread enters the running state, the thread's **run** method begins execution. Method **run** (lines 20–26) displays a message to indicate that the thread is going to sleep and invokes function **time.sleep** (line 25) to place the thread immediately into the *sleeping* state. The thread awakens after **sleepTime** seconds and is placed into the *ready* state again until it is switched into the interpreter. When a **PrintThread** object reenters the *running* state, the thread continues executing with the next statement after the **sleep** call (line 25) in which the thread outputs its name (indicating that the thread has finished sleeping). This completes the execution of the thread's **run** method, so the thread terminates and enters the *dead* state.

The main portion of the program (lines 28–38) creates three **PrintThread** objects and invokes the **Thread** class **start** method on each one to place all three **PrintThread** objects in a *ready* state. After this, the main program's thread terminates. However, the example continues running until the last **PrintThread** completes its **run** method.

19.4 Thread Synchronization

Often, multiple threads of execution manipulate shared data. If threads with access to shared data simply read that data, then there is no need to prevent the data from being accessed by more than one thread at a time because no thread will modify the data unexpectedly. However, when multiple threads share data and that data is modified by one or more of those threads, then indeterminate results may occur. If one thread is in the process of updating the data and another thread tries to update the data at the same time, the data will reflect the update that occurs second. If the data is an array or other data structure in which the threads could update separate parts of the data concurrently, it is possible that part of the data will reflect the information from one thread while another part of the data will reflect information from a different thread. When this happens, the program may have difficulty determining when the data has been updated properly. The sections of code that access shared data often are referred to as *critical sections*.

The problem can be solved by giving one thread at a time exclusive access to code that manipulates the shared data. During that time, other threads that attempt to manipulate the data should be kept waiting. When the thread with exclusive access to the data completes its manipulation of the data, one of the threads waiting to manipulate the data should be allowed to proceed. In this fashion, each thread that accesses the shared data excludes all other threads from doing so simultaneously. This is called *mutual exclusion* or *thread synchronization*.

Module **threading** provides many thread-synchronization mechanisms. The simplest synchronization mechanism is the *lock*. A lock object (created with class **threading.RLock**) defines two methods—*acquire* and *release*. When a thread calls the **acquire** method, the lock enters a *locked state*. Only one thread may acquire a lock at a time. If another thread attempts to invoke method **acquire** on the same lock object, the operating system places that thread in the *blocked* state until the lock becomes available. When the thread that owns the lock invokes method **release**, the lock enters the *unlocked state*. The blocked thread receives a notification and acquires the lock. If multiple threads are blocked, all of the threads are first unblocked. The operating system then selects one thread to acquire the lock, and blocks the remaining threads.

Locks can restrict access to critical sections. Multi-threaded programs are written such that threads must **acquire** a lock before entering a critical section and **release** the lock when exiting the critical section. Thus, if one thread is executing a critical section, other threads that attempt to enter a critical section will be blocked until the original thread has exited the critical section and released the lock.

 **Common Programming Error 19.2**

Be sure to enclose all critical sections between **acquire** *and* **release** *calls.*

Such a procedure provides only the most basic level of synchronization. Sometimes, we would like to create more sophisticated threads that access a critical section only when some event occurs (e.g., when a data value has changed). This is accomplished through *condition variables*. A thread uses a condition variable to monitor the state of an object or to be notified when an event occurs. When the object's state changes or the event occurs, the blocked threads are notified. We discuss condition variables throughout this chapter in the context of the classic producer/consumer problem. The solution involves a consumer thread that accesses a critical section only when notified by a producer thread, and vice versa.

Condition variables are created with class **threading.Condition**. As condition variables contain *underlying locks*, condition variables provide **acquire** and **release** methods. Other condition variable methods are **wait** and **notify**. After a thread successfully acquires an underlying lock, calling method **wait** causes the calling thread to release the lock and block until it is awakened by another thread's call to **notify** on the same condition variable. Method **notify** wakes up one thread waiting on the condition variable; method **notifyAll** wakes up all *waiting* threads.

Writing programs that use locks, condition variables or other synchronization mechanisms requires scrutiny to ensure that the program does not *deadlock*. A program or thread
deadlocks when it is blocked indefinitely (i.e., is waiting for a particular event to occur that
will never occur or for a particular resource that will never become available). For example,
consider the scenario where a thread enters a critical section that opens a file. If the file does
not exist and the thread does not catch the exception, the thread terminates before releasing
the lock. All other threads that attempt to access the file will deadlock, because they block
indefinitely after invoking the lock's **acquire** method.

Common Programming Error 19.3

Threads in the waiting *state for a condition variable must eventually be awakened explicitly
with a* **notify** *or the thread will wait forever. This may cause deadlock.*

Testing and Debugging Tip 19.1

Be sure that every call to **wait** *has a corresponding call to* **notify** *that eventually will end
the* waiting *or call* **notifyAll** *as a safeguard.*

Performance Tip 19.2

*Using synchronization to achieve correctness in multithreaded programs can make pro-
grams run more slowly, as a result of lock overhead and of the frequent moving of threads
between the different states.*

19.5 Producer/Consumer Relationship without Thread Synchronization

In a *producer/consumer relationship*, the *producer* portion of an application generates data
and the *consumer* portion of an application uses that data. In a multithreaded producer/con-
sumer relationship, a *producer thread* calls a *produce method* to generate data and place it
into a shared region of memory, called a *buffer*. A *consumer thread* calls a *consume method*
to read that data. If the producer waiting to put the next data into the buffer determines that
the consumer has not yet read the previous data from the buffer, the producer thread should
call **wait** on the condition variable; otherwise, the consumer never sees the previous data
and that data is lost to that application. When the consumer thread reads the message, it
should call **notify** on the condition variable to allow a waiting producer to proceed. If a
consumer thread finds the buffer empty or finds that the previous data has already been
read, the consumer should call **wait** on the condition variable; otherwise, the consumer
might read "garbage" from the buffer or the consumer might process a previous data item
more than once—each of these possibilities results in a logic error in the application. When
the producer places the next data into the buffer, the producer should call **notify** on the
condition variable to allow the consumer thread to proceed.

Let us consider how logic errors can arise if we do not synchronize access among multiple threads manipulating shared data. Consider a producer/consumer relationship in
which a producer thread writes a sequence of numbers (we use 1–4) into a *shared buffer*—
a memory location shared between multiple threads. The consumer thread reads this data
from the shared buffer then displays the data. We display in the program's output the values
that the producer writes (produces) and that the consumer reads (consumes). Figure 19.3–
Fig. 19.6 demonstrate a producer and a consumer accessing a single shared cell of memory
(**buffer**) without any synchronization. Both the consumer and the producer threads

access this single cell: The producer thread writes to the cell; the consumer thread reads from it. We would like each value the producer thread writes to the shared cell to be consumed exactly once by the consumer thread. However, the threads in this example are not synchronized. Therefore, data can be lost if the producer places new data into the slot before the consumer consumes the previous data. Also, data can be incorrectly repeated if the consumer consumes data again before the producer produces the next item. To show these possibilities, the consumer thread in the following example keeps a total of all the values it reads. The producer thread produces values from 1 to 4. If the consumer reads each value produced once and only once, the total would be 10. However, if you execute this program several times, you will see that the total is rarely, if ever, 10. Also, to emphasize our point, the producer and consumer threads in the example each sleep for random intervals of up to three seconds between performing their tasks. Thus, we do not know exactly when the producer thread will attempt to write a new value, nor do we know when the consumer thread will attempt to read a value. Figure 19.3 demonstrates a producer (defined in Fig. 19.4) and a consumer (defined in Fig. 19.5) that access a single shared cell of memory without any synchronization (defined in Fig. 19.6).

Figure 19.3 creates the shared **UnsynchronizedInteger** object **number** (line 9) and uses it as the argument to the constructors for the **ProduceInteger** object **producer** (line 10) and the **ConsumeInteger** object **consumer** (line 11). Next, the program invokes **Thread** method **start** on objects **producer** and **consumer** to place them in the *ready* state (lines 16–17). Lines 20–21 call **Thread** method **join** to ensure that the main program waits for both threads to terminate before continuing. Notice that line 23 executes only after both threads have terminated.

Class **ProduceInteger** (Fig. 19.4)—a subclass of **threading.Thread**—consists of attributes (**sharedObject**, **begin** and **end**), a constructor (lines 11–17) and a **run** method (lines 19–27). The constructor initializes attribute **sharedObject** (line 15) to refer to the **UnsynchronizedInteger** object passed as an argument.

Class **ProduceInteger**'s **run** method consists of a **for** structure that loops from **begin** to **end** (lines 22–24). Each iteration of the loop first invokes function **time.sleep** to put the **ProduceInteger** object into the *sleeping* state for a random time interval between 0 and 3 seconds. When the thread awakens, it invokes the shared object's **set** method (line 24) with the value of control variable **i** to set the shared object's data member. It is important to note that the shared object's **set** method is invoked from the **ProduceInteger** thread. The thread from which a method is called is the thread that executes the statements specified in the method definition. When the loop completes, the **ProduceInteger** thread displays a line in the command window indicating that it has finished producing data and that it is terminating; then, the thread terminates (i.e., the thread dies).

```
1   # Fig. 19.3: fig19_03.py
2   # Multiple threads modifying shared object.
3
4   from UnsynchronizedInteger import UnsynchronizedInteger
5   from ProduceInteger import ProduceInteger
6   from ConsumeInteger import ConsumeInteger
7
```

Fig. 19.3 Threads modifying unsynchronized shared object. (Part 1 of 3.)

```
 8    # initialize integer and threads
 9    number = UnsynchronizedInteger()
10    producer = ProduceInteger( "Producer", number, 1, 4 )
11    consumer = ConsumeInteger( "Consumer", number, 4 )
12
13    print "Starting threads...\n"
14
15    # start threads
16    producer.start()
17    consumer.start()
18
19    # wait for threads to terminate
20    producer.join()
21    consumer.join()
22
23    print "\nAll threads have terminated."
```

```
Starting threads...

Consumer reads -1
Consumer reads -1
Producer writes 1
Consumer reads 1
Producer writes 2
Consumer reads 2
Consumer read values totaling: 1.
Terminating Consumer.
Producer writes 3
Producer writes 4
Producer done producing.
Terminating Producer.

All threads have terminated.
```

```
Starting threads...

Producer writes 1
Producer writes 2
Producer writes 3
Consumer reads 3
Producer writes 4
Producer done producing.
Terminating Producer.
Consumer reads 4
Consumer reads 4
Consumer reads 4
Consumer read values totaling: 15.
Terminating Consumer.

All threads have terminated.
```

Fig. 19.3 Threads modifying unsynchronized shared object. (Part 2 of 3.)

```
Starting threads...

Producer writes 1
Consumer reads 1
Producer writes 2
Consumer reads 2
Producer writes 3
Consumer reads 3
Producer writes 4
Producer done producing.
Terminating Producer.
Consumer reads 4
Consumer read values totaling: 10.
Terminating Consumer.

All threads have terminated.
```

Fig. 19.3   Threads modifying unsynchronized shared object. (Part 3 of 3.)

```
1   # Fig. 19.4: ProduceInteger.py
2   # Integer-producing class.
3
4   import threading
5   import random
6   import time
7
8   class ProduceInteger( threading.Thread ):
9      """Thread to produce integers"""
10
11     def __init__( self, threadName, sharedObject, begin, end ):
12        """Initialize thread, set shared object"""
13
14        threading.Thread.__init__( self, name = threadName )
15        self.sharedObject = sharedObject
16        self.begin = begin
17        self.end = end
18
19     def run( self ):
20        """Produce integers in given range at random intervals"""
21
22        for i in range( self.begin, ( self.end + 1 ) ):
23           time.sleep( random.randrange( 4 ) )
24           self.sharedObject.set( i )
25
26        print "%s done producing." % self.getName()
27        print "Terminating %s." % self.getName()
```

Fig. 19.4   Integer-producer thread.

Class **ConsumeInteger** (Fig. 19.5)—a subclass of **threading.Thread**—consists of attributes (**sharedObject** and **amount**), a constructor (lines 11–16) and a **run** method (lines 18–30). The constructor initializes attribute **sharedObject** to refer to the **UnsynchronizedInteger** object passed as an argument (line 15).

```
1    # Fig. 19.5: ConsumeInteger.py
2    # Integer-consuming queue.
3
4    import threading
5    import random
6    import time
7
8    class ConsumeInteger( threading.Thread ):
9       """Thread to consume integers"""
10
11      def __init__( self, threadName, sharedObject, amount ):
12         """Initialize thread, set shared object"""
13
14         threading.Thread.__init__( self, name = threadName )
15         self.sharedObject = sharedObject
16         self.amount = amount
17
18      def run( self ):
19         """Consume given amount of values at random time intervals"""
20
21         sum = 0    # total sum of consumed values
22
23         # consume given amount of values
24         for i in range( self.amount ):
25            time.sleep( random.randrange( 4 ) )
26            sum += self.sharedObject.get()
27
28         print "%s read values totaling: %d." % \
29            ( self.getName(), sum )
30         print "Terminating %s." % self.getName()
```

Fig. 19.5   Integer-consumer thread.

Class **ConsumeInteger**'s **run** method consists of a **for** structure that loops **amount** times to read values from the **UnsynchronizedInteger** object to which **sharedObject** refers (lines 24–26). Each iteration of the loop invokes function **time.sleep** to put the **ConsumeInteger** object into a *sleeping* state for a random time interval between 0 and 3 seconds. Next, the thread calls the **get** method to get the value of the shared object's data member. Once again, it is important to note that the shared object's **set** method is invoked from the **ConsumeInteger** thread. The thread from which a method is called is the thread that executes the statements specified in the method definition. Then, the thread adds to variable **sum** the value returned by **get** (line 26). When the loop completes, the **ConsumeInteger** thread displays a line in the command window indicating that it has finished consuming data and that it is terminating; then, the thread terminates (i.e., the thread dies).

In Fig. 19.6, class **UnsynchronizedInteger** consists of attribute **buffer** (line 12), method **set** (lines 14–19) and method **get** (lines 21–28). Methods **set** and **get** do not synchronize access to attribute **buffer**. Ideally, we prefer every value produced by a **ProduceInteger** object to be consumed exactly once by a **ConsumeInteger** object. However, the example output of Fig. 19.3 shows that some of the values are lost (i.e., never seen by the consumer) and that some of the values are retrieved more than once by the consumer due to the lack of synchronization.

In fact, method **get** must perform some extra work to ensure that the output reflects the value of the data member accurately. Line 24 assigns the value of data member **buffer** to variable **tempNumber**. Lines 25–28 then use the value of **tempNumber** to print the message and return the value. If we did not use a temporary variable in this way, the following scenario could occur: The consumer calls method **get** and prints a message that displays the value of the data member. The interpreter might then switch out the consumer thread for the producer thread. The producer thread might then change the value of **buffer** by calling method **set**. Eventually, the interpreter switches the consumer back in and method **get** returns a value different from the value printed before the consumer was switched out.

Ideally, we would like every value produced by the **Producer** object to be consumed exactly once by the **Consumer** object. However, when we study the first output of Fig. 19.3, we see that the consumer retrieved the value (–1) twice before the producer ever placed a value in the shared buffer and that the values 3 and 4 were never consumed, because the consumer finished executing before the producer had an opportunity to produce those values. Therefore, those two values were lost. In the second output, we see that the values 1 and 2 were lost, because the values 1, 2 and 3 were produced before the consumer thread could read the value 1. Also, the value 4 was consumed three times. The last sample output demonstrates that it is possible, with some luck, to get a proper output in which each

```python
1   # Fig. 19.6: UnsynchronizedInteger.py
2   # Unsynchronized access to an integer.
3
4   import threading
5
6   class UnsynchronizedInteger:
7       """Class that provides unsynchronized access an integer"""
8
9       def __init__( self ):
10          """Initialize integer to -1"""
11
12          self.buffer = -1
13
14      def set( self, newNumber ):
15          """Set value of integer"""
16
17          print "%s writes %d" % \
18              ( threading.currentThread().getName(), newNumber )
19          self.buffer = newNumber
20
21      def get( self ):
22          """Get value of integer"""
23
24          tempNumber = self.buffer
25          print "%s reads %d" % \
26              ( threading.currentThread().getName(), tempNumber )
27
28          return tempNumber
```

Fig. 19.6 Unsynchronized integer value class.

value the producer produces is consumed once and only once by the consumer. This example clearly demonstrates that access to shared data by concurrent threads must be controlled carefully; otherwise, a program may produce incorrect results.

To solve the problems of lost data and data consumer more than once in the previous example, we will (in Fig. 19.7–Fig. 19.8) synchronize access of the concurrent producer and consumer threads to the code that manipulates the shared data by using condition variables and methods **acquire**, **release**, **wait** and **notify** mentioned previously. When threads that manipulate a shared object use the same condition to perform synchronization, each thread must first acquire the condition variable's lock before manipulating the shared object. Only one thread at a time can acquire the lock on a particular condition variable, so no other thread can acquire the lock for that condition variable at the same time.

19.6 Producer/Consumer Relationship with Thread Synchronization

The next program (Fig. 19.7 and Fig. 19.8) demonstrates a producer and a consumer that access a shared cell of memory with synchronization, so that the consumer consumes each value exactly once. The program also ensures that the consumer waits for the producer to execute first. Figure 19.7 from Fig. 19.3 only in that it passes an object of class **SynchronizedInteger** to the producer and consumer and that lines 15–17 print table headers and the initial state of the **SynchronizedInteger**. Classes **ProduceInteger** and **ConsumeInteger** are identical to the previous section, so they are not shown here.

Class **SynchronizedInteger** (Fig. 19.8) contains three attributes—**buffer**, **occupiedBufferCount** and **threadCondition**. Attribute **occupiedBufferCount** helps the **SynchronizedInteger** object determine whether it is the producer's turn or consumer's turn to manipulate the **buffer**. Attribute **threadCondition**—an object of class *Condition*—maintains the lock that prevents more than one thread from manipulating the **buffer** at the same time. The **Condition** object—sometimes called a *condition variable*—also contains methods that the threads use when they cannot perform their tasks and when they complete their tasks. We discuss these methods shortly.

Method **set** (lines 16–39) uses **occupiedBufferCount** and **threadCondition** to determine whether the thread that calls the method can write to the shared memory location. Method **get** (lines 41–66) uses **occupiedBufferCount** and **threadCondition** to determine whether the calling thread can read from the shared memory location. Method **displayState** (lines 68–72)) displays a message (the current operation) along with the current values of **buffer** and **occupiedBufferCount**.

```
1   # Fig. 19.7: fig19_07.py
2   # Multiple threads modifying shared object.
3
4   from SynchronizedInteger import SynchronizedInteger
5   from ProduceInteger import ProduceInteger
6   from ConsumeInteger import ConsumeInteger
7
8   # initialize number and threads
9   number = SynchronizedInteger()
10  producer = ProduceInteger( "Producer", number, 1, 4 )
```

Fig. 19.7   Threads modifying a synchronized shared object. (Part 1 of 4.)

```
11   consumer = ConsumeInteger( "Consumer", number, 4 )
12
13   print "Starting threads...\n"
14
15   print "%-35s %-9s%2s\n" % \
16       ( "Operation" , "Buffer", "Occupied Count" )
17   number.displayState( "Initial state" )
18
19   # start threads
20   producer.start()
21   consumer.start()
22
23   # wait for threads to terminate
24   producer.join()
25   consumer.join()
26
27   print "\nAll threads have terminated."
```

```
Starting threads...

Operation                            Buffer    Occupied Count

Initial state                        -1        0

Producer writes 1                    1         1

Consumer reads 1                     1         0

Consumer tries to read.
Buffer empty. Consumer waits.        1         0

Producer writes 2                    2         1

Consumer reads 2                     2         0

Producer writes 3                    3         1

Producer tries to write.
Buffer full. Producer waits.         3         1

Consumer reads 3                     3         0

Producer writes 4                    4         1

Producer done producing.
Terminating Producer.
Consumer reads 4                     4         0

Consumer read values totaling: 10.
Terminating Consumer.

All threads have terminated.
```

Fig. 19.7   Threads modifying a synchronized shared object. (Part 2 of 4.)

```
Starting threads...

Operation                            Buffer   Occupied Count

Initial state                        -1       0

Consumer tries to read.
Buffer empty. Consumer waits.        -1       0

Producer writes 1                    1        1

Consumer reads 1                     1        0

Producer writes 2                    2        1

Consumer reads 2                     2        0

Consumer tries to read.
Buffer empty. Consumer waits.        2        0

Producer writes 3                    3        1

Consumer reads 3                     3        0

Producer writes 4                    4        1

Producer done producing.
Terminating Producer.
Consumer reads 4                     4        0

Consumer read values totaling: 10.
Terminating Consumer.

All threads have terminated.
```

```
Starting threads...

Operation                            Buffer   Occupied Count

Initial state                        -1       0

Producer writes 1                    1        1

Consumer reads 1                     1        0

Producer writes 2                    2        1

Consumer reads 2                     2        0

Producer writes 3                    3        1
```

(continued)

Fig. 19.7　Threads modifying a synchronized shared object. (Part 3 of 4.)

```
Consumer reads 3                      3          0

Producer writes 4                     4          1

Producer done producing.
Terminating Producer.
Consumer reads 4                      4          0

Consumer read values totaling: 10.
Terminating Consumer.

All threads have terminated.
```

(continued from previous page)

Fig. 19.7   Threads modifying a synchronized shared object. (Part 4 of 4.)

```python
1   # Fig. 19.8: SynchronizedInteger.py
2   # Synchronized access to an integer with condition variable.
3
4   import threading
5
6   class SynchronizedInteger:
7      """Class that provides synchronized access an integer"""
8
9      def __init__( self ):
10        """Initialize integer, buffer count and condition variable"""
11
12        self.buffer = -1
13        self.occupiedBufferCount = 0    # number of occupied buffers
14        self.threadCondition = threading.Condition()
15
16     def set( self, newNumber ):
17        """Set value of integer--blocks until lock acquired"""
18
19        # block until lock released then acquire lock
20        self.threadCondition.acquire()
21
22        # while not producer's turn, release lock and block
23        while self.occupiedBufferCount == 1:
24           print "%s tries to write." % \
25              threading.currentThread().getName()
26           self.displayState( "Buffer full. " + \
27              threading.currentThread().getName() + " waits." )
28           self.threadCondition.wait()
29
30        # (lock has now been re-acquired)
31
32        self.buffer = newNumber           # set new buffer value
33        self.occupiedBufferCount += 1     # allow consumer to consume
34
35        self.displayState( "%s writes %d" % \
36           ( threading.currentThread().getName(), newNumber ) )
```

Fig. 19.8   Synchronized integer value class. (Part 1 of 2.)

```
37
38            self.threadCondition.notify()     # wake up a waiting thread
39            self.threadCondition.release()    # allow lock to be acquired
40
41    def get( self ):
42        """Get value of integer--blocks until lock acquired"""
43
44        # block until lock released then acquire lock
45        self.threadCondition.acquire()
46
47        # while producer's turn, release lock and block
48        while self.occupiedBufferCount == 0:
49            print "%s tries to read." % \
50                threading.currentThread().getName()
51            self.displayState( "Buffer empty. " + \
52                threading.currentThread().getName() + " waits." )
53            self.threadCondition.wait()
54
55        # (lock has now been re-acquired)
56
57        tempNumber = self.buffer
58        self.occupiedBufferCount -= 1 # allow producer to produce
59
60        self.displayState( "%s reads %d" % \
61            ( threading.currentThread().getName(), tempNumber ) )
62
63        self.threadCondition.notify()     # wake up a waiting thread
64        self.threadCondition.release()    # allow lock to be acquired
65
66        return tempNumber
67
68    def displayState( self, operation ):
69        """Display current state"""
70
71        print "%-35s %-9s%2s\n" % \
72            ( operation, self.buffer, self.occupiedBufferCount )
```

Fig. 19.8   Synchronized integer value class. (Part 2 of 2.)

Lines 12–13 initialize attributes **buffer** and **occupiedBufferCount** to **-1** and **0**, respectively, to indicate that the buffer is currently empty. Line 14 creates the thread condition variable by invoking the **threading.Condition** constructor. This creates a new lock for the condition variable. Variable **threadCondition** protects access to attribute **occupiedBufferCount** and **buffer**.

If **occupiedBufferCount** is **0**, no newly produced values exist and a producer can place a value into variable **buffer**. However, this also means that a consumer currently cannot read the value of **buffer**. If **occupiedBufferCount** is **1**, **buffer** contains a single newly produced value. This value must be read by a consumer before a producer can place another new value into **buffer**.

When the **ProduceInteger** thread invokes method **set** (lines 16–39), the thread acquires a lock on the condition variable (line 20). The **while** structure (lines 23–28) tests the **occupiedBufferCount** to determine if it is **1** (**buffer** is full). If so, the producer displays the current state and invokes the condition variable's **wait** method (line 28). This places the **ProduceInteger** thread object that called method **set** into the *waiting* state maintained by **threadCondition** and *releases the lock*. Now other threads can access the **SynchronizedInteger** object.

The **ProduceInteger** thread remains in the *waiting* state until it is notified that it may proceed—at which point it enters the *ready* state. When the **ProduceInteger** thread reenters the *running* state, the object implicitly reacquires the lock on **threadCondition**, and the **set** method continues executing in the **while** structure with the next statement after **wait**. There are no more statements, so the program reevaluates the **while** condition. If the condition is false (i.e., **occupiedBufferCount** is **0**), the **while** structure terminates. Line 32 then sets the current value of **buffer**. Line 33 increments **occupiedBufferCount** to indicate that the shared memory is now full (i.e., a consumer can read the value, and a producer cannot assign another value). Lines 35–36 call method **displayState** to show the newly produced value. Line 38 invokes **threadCondition**'s **notify** method. If there are any waiting threads in the *waiting* state maintained by **threadCondition**, one thread in the *waiting* state enters the *ready* state. That thread can now attempt its task again (after it is switched into the interpreter). Line 39 then releases the lock (so that the newly *ready* thread can obtain it) by calling **threadCondition**'s **release** method, then method **set** returns to its caller.

Common Programming Error 19.4

*Condition method **notify** does not release the underlying lock. Failure to call a Condition object's **release** method can result in deadlock.*

Methods **get** and **set** are implemented similarly. When the **ConsumeInteger** thread invokes method **get**, the method acquires a lock on **threadCondition**. The **while** structure (lines 48–53) determines whether variable **occupiedBufferCount** is **0** (i.e., there is nothing to consume). If so, the thread displays the current state and invokes **threadCondition**'s **wait** method. This places the **ConsumeInteger** thread that called method **get** into the *waiting* state maintained by **threadCondition** and releases the lock, so other threads may access it.

The **ConsumeInteger** thread remains in the *waiting* state until it is notified that it may proceed—at which point, it enters the *ready* state and waits to be switched into the interpreter. When the **ConsumeInteger** thread reenters the *running* state, the **set** method reacquires **threadCondition**'s lock, and method **set** continues executing in the **while** structure with the next statement after **wait**. There are no more statements, so the program tests the **while** condition again. If the **occupiedBufferCount** is **1**, the value of **buffer** is stored in variable **tempNumber** (line 57). Note that the value of **buffer** is retrieved only once and stored in variable **tempNumber** (while within the critical section). When the thread exits the critical section, it is possible that **buffer** could be modified by another thread. Line 66 (outside the critical section) uses the value of **tempNumber** rather than **buffer** to ensure that the caller receives the correct value that was stored in **tempNumber** before leaving the critical section. Line 58 decrements **occupiedBufferCount** to indicate that the shared memory is now empty. Lines 60–61 call method **displayState** to show the newly consumed value. Line 63 invokes **threadCondition**'s **notify** method. If there are any threads in the *waiting* state maintained by **threadCondition**, one of those threads enters the *ready* state, indicating that the thread can now attempt its task again (after it is switched into the interpreter). Line 54 releases **threadCondition**'s lock (so that the newly *ready* thread can obtain it), and line 56 returns the value of **tempNumber** to **get**'s caller.

Study the sample outputs in Fig. 19.7. In the first and second sample outputs, notice the lines indicating when the producer and consumer must wait to perform their respective tasks. In the third sample output, notice that the producer and consumer were able to perform their tasks without waiting. Also, observe in all three outputs that every integer produced is consumed once—no values are lost and no values are doubled.

19.7 Producer/Consumer Relationship: Module **Queue**

The program of Fig. 19.7–Fig. 19.8 uses thread synchronization to guarantee that two threads manipulate data in a shared buffer correctly. However, the application may not perform optimally. If the two threads operate at different speeds, one of the threads will spend more (or most) of its time waiting. For example, in Fig. 19.7 we shared a single buffer between the two threads. If the producer thread produces values faster than the consumer can consume those values, then the producer thread waits for the consumer, because there are no other locations in memory to place the next value. Similarly, if the consumer consumes faster than the producer can produce values, the consumer waits until the producer places the next value into the shared location in memory. Even when we have threads that operate at the same relative speeds, over a period of time, those threads may become "out of sync," causing one of the threads to wait for the other. We cannot make assumptions about the relative speeds of asynchronous concurrent threads. There are too many interactions that occur with the operating system, the network, the user and other components, which can cause the threads to operate at different speeds. When this happens, threads wait. When threads wait, programs become less productive, user-interactive programs become less responsive and network applications suffer longer delays because the processor is not used efficiently.

To minimize the waiting for threads that share resources and operate at the same relative speeds, we can use a *queue* that provides extra buffers into which the producer can place values and from which the consumer can retrieve those values. Queues represents a waiting line; insertions are made at the back (also referred to as the *tail*) of a queue, and removals are made from the front (also referred to as the *head*) of a queue. Queues are discussed in more detail in Chapter 22, Data Structures.

The Python standard library includes module ***Queue***, which defines class ***Queue***—a synchronized implementation of a queue. A queue may have either an infinite or a finite size. The size of an "infinite" queue is limited by memory resources. The **Queue** constructor accepts optional argument ***maxsize***. If **maxsize** is less than **1**, the queue size is infinite (i.e., the queue has no pre-defined size). Otherwise, **maxsize** defines the maximum number of items that may be placed into the queue.

A consumer consumes a value by calling **Queue** method ***get***, which removes and returns an item from the head of the queue. Method **get** accepts optional argument ***block***. If the queue is currently empty and **block** is **1** (default), method **get** blocks the calling thread until an item is available. If **block** is **0**, the queue raises an ***Empty*** exception, an exception defined in module **Queue**.

Similarly, a producer produces a value by calling **Queue** method ***put***, which inserts an item at the tail of the queue. Method **put** accepts up to two arguments. The first (required) argument is ***item***, which indicates the item to insert in the queue. The second (optional) argument is ***block***. If the queue is currently full and **block** is **1** (default), method **put** blocks the calling thread until a cell becomes available. If **block** is **0**, method **put** raises the *Full* exception.

The program of Fig. 19.9–Fig. 19.11 demonstrates a producer and a consumer accessing a synchronized queue. The queue size is infinite, therefore the queue has enough cells to handle any "extra" production. In the sample output of Fig. 19.9, notice that a consumer successfully retrieves a value only after a producer has inserted the value.

Class **ProduceToQueue** (Fig. 19.10) is similar to class **ProduceInteger** (Fig. 19.4) except that it has been modified to access a queue that is shared between the **ProduceToQueue** and **ConsumeFromQueue** (Fig. 19.11) threads. Class **ProduceToQueue**'s **run** method consists of a **for** structure (lines 20–23) that loops ten times and places the values in the range 11–20 into the queue. Each iteration of the loop first invokes function **time.sleep** to place the **ProduceToQueue** thread into the *sleeping* state for a random time interval between 0 and 3 seconds. When the thread awakens, it invokes the queue **sharedObject**'s **put** method (line 23) with the value of control variable **i** to insert the value into the queue. When the loop completes, the **ProduceToQueue** thread displays a line in the command window to indicate that it has finished producing data and that the thread is terminating; then, the thread terminates.

Class **ConsumeFromQueue** (Fig. 19.11) is similar to class **ConsumeInteger** (Fig. 19.5). Class **ConsumeFromQueue**'s **run** method consists of a **for** structure (lines 24–30) that loops ten times to read values from the **Queue** object to which **sharedObject** refers. Each iteration of the loop invokes function **time.sleep** to put the **ConsumeFromQueue** thread into the *sleeping* state for a random time interval between 0 and 3 seconds. Then, the thread calls **sharedObject**'s **get** method to get the next value in the queue. If the queue is currently empty, the thread will block until a value becomes available. When a value is obtained, the thread prints a message that displays the retrieved value (lines 29). Then, the thread adds the value of **current**—the value returned by **get**—to variable **sum** (line 30). When the loop completes, the **ConsumeFromQueue** thread displays a line in the command window indicating that it has finished consuming data and that the thread is terminating; then, the thread terminates.

In the sample output of Fig. 19.9, notice that when no values are available in the queue the **ConsumeFromQueue** thread automatically waits for the **ProduceToQueue** thread to produce a new value. Only then does the **ConsumeFromQueue** thread actually complete its read operation.

```
1   # Fig. 19.9: fig19_09.py
2   # Multiple threads producing/consuming values.
3
4   from Queue import Queue
5   from ProduceToQueue import ProduceToQueue
6   from ConsumeFromQueue import ConsumeFromQueue
7
8   # initialize number and threads
9   queue = Queue()
10  producer = ProduceToQueue( "Producer", queue )
11  consumer = ConsumeFromQueue( "Consumer", queue )
```

Fig. 19.9 Threads producing/consuming values from a queue. (Part 1 of 2.)

```
12
13   print "Starting threads...\n"
14
15   # start threads
16   producer.start()
17   consumer.start()
18
19   # wait for threads to terminate
20   producer.join()
21   consumer.join()
22
23   print "\nAll threads have terminated."
```

```
Starting threads...

Producer adding 11 to queue
Producer adding 12 to queue
Consumer attempting to read 11...
Consumer read 11
Consumer attempting to read 12...
Consumer read 12
Producer adding 13 to queue
Consumer attempting to read 13...
Consumer read 13
Producer adding 14 to queue
Consumer attempting to read 14...
Consumer read 14
Consumer attempting to read 15...
Producer adding 15 to queue
Consumer read 15
Consumer attempting to read 16...
Producer adding 16 to queue
Consumer read 16
Consumer attempting to read 17...
Producer adding 17 to queue
Consumer read 17
Producer adding 18 to queue
Producer adding 19 to queue
Consumer attempting to read 18...
Consumer read 18
Consumer attempting to read 19...
Consumer read 19
Producer adding 20 to queue
Producer finished producing values
Terminating Producer
Consumer attempting to read 20...
Consumer read 20
Consumer retrieved values totaling: 155
Terminating Consumer

All threads have terminated.
```

Fig. 19.9 Threads producing/consuming values from a queue. (Part 2 of 2.)

```
1   # Fig. 19.10: ProduceToQueue.py
2   # Integer-producing class.
3
4   import threading
5   import random
6   import time
7
8   class ProduceToQueue( threading.Thread ):
9      """Thread to produce integers"""
10
11     def __init__( self, threadName, queue ):
12        """Initialize thread, set shared queue"""
13
14        threading.Thread.__init__( self, name = threadName )
15        self.sharedObject = queue
16
17     def run( self ):
18        """Produce integers in range 11-20 at random intervals"""
19
20        for i in range( 11, 21 ):
21           time.sleep( random.randrange( 4 ) )
22           print "%s adding %s to queue" % ( self.getName(), i )
23           self.sharedObject.put( i )
24
25        print self.getName(), "finished producing values"
26        print "Terminating", self.getName()
```

Fig. 19.10 Integer-producer thread.

```
1   # Fig. 19.11: ConsumeFromQueue.py
2   # Integer-consuming queue.
3
4   import threading
5   import random
6   import time
7
8   class ConsumeFromQueue( threading.Thread ):
9      """Thread to consume integers"""
10
11     def __init__( self, threadName, queue ):
12        """Initialize thread, set shared queue"""
13
14        threading.Thread.__init__( self, name = threadName )
15        self.sharedObject = queue
16
17     def run( self ):
18        """Consume 10 values at random time intervals"""
19
20        sum = 0              # total sum of consumed values
21        current = 10         # last value retrieved
22
```

Fig. 19.11 Integer-consumer thread. (Part 1 of 2.)

```
23      # consume 10 values
24      for i in range( 10 ):
25          time.sleep( random.randrange( 4 ) )
26          print "%s attempting to read %s..." % \
27              ( self.getName(), current + 1 )
28          current = self.sharedObject.get()
29          print "%s read %s" % ( self.getName(), current )
30          sum += current
31
32      print "%s retrieved values totaling: %d" % \
33          ( self.getName(), sum )
34      print "Terminating", self.getName()
```

Fig. 19.11 Integer-consumer thread. (Part 2 of 2.)

19.8 Producer/Consumer Relationship: The Circular Buffer

The program of Fig. 19.9–Fig. 19.11 enables the producer to produce values faster than the consumer may consume them. In Fig. 19.12–Fig. 19.13, we demonstrate another data structure that can be used to minimize the waiting for threads that share resources and operate at the same relative speeds. A *circular buffer* that provides extra buffers into which the producer can place values and from which the consumer can retrieve those values. Let us assume the buffer is implemented as an array. The producer and consumer work from the beginning of the array. When either thread reaches the end of the array, it simply returns to the first element of the array to perform its next task. If the producer temporarily produces values faster than the consumer can consume them, the producer can write additional values into the extra buffers (if cells are available). This enables the producer to perform its task even though the consumer is not ready to receive the current value being produced. Similarly, if the consumer consumes faster than the producer produces new values, the consumer can read additional values from the buffer (if there are any). This enables the consumer to perform its task even though the producer is not ready to produce additional values.

Note that the circular buffer would be inappropriate if the producer and consumer operate at different speeds. If the consumer always executes faster than the producer, then a buffer at one location is enough. Additional locations would waste memory. If the producer always executes faster, a buffer with an infinite number of locations would be requires to absorb the extra production.

The key to using a circular buffer is to define it with enough extra cells to handle the anticipated "extra" production. If, over a period of time, we determine that the producer often produces as many as three more values than the consumer can consume, we can define a buffer of at least three cells to handle the extra production. We do not want the buffer to be too small, because that would cause threads to wait more. On the other hand, we do not want the buffer to be too large, because that would waste memory.

Performance Tip 19.3

Even when using a circular buffer, it is possible that a producer thread could fill the buffer, which would force the producer thread to wait until a consumer consumes a value to free an element in the buffer. Similarly, if the buffer is empty at any given time, the consumer thread must wait until the producer produces another value. The key to using a circular buffer is optimizing the buffer size to minimize the amount of thread-wait time.

The program of Fig. 19.12–Fig. 19.13 demonstrates a producer and a consumer accessing a synchronized circular buffer (in this case, a shared list of three cells). The consumer only consumes a value when the list contains one or more values; the producer only produces a value when the list contains one or more available cells. Figure 19.12 uses slightly modified versions of classes **ProduceInteger** (Fig. 19.4) and **ConsumeInteger** (Fig. 19.5) to produce and consume values in the range 11–20 (rather than 1–4). Notice in the sample output that, after the third value is placed in the third element of the buffer, the fourth value is inserted at the beginning of the list—thus providing the circular buffer effect.

```python
1   # Fig. 19.12: fig19_12.py
2   # Show multiple threads modifying shared object.
3
4   from CircularBuffer import CircularBuffer
5   from ProduceInteger import ProduceInteger
6   from ConsumeInteger import ConsumeInteger
7
8   # initialize number and threads
9   buffer = CircularBuffer()
10  producer = ProduceInteger( "Producer", buffer, 11, 20 )
11  consumer = ConsumeInteger( "Consumer", buffer, 10 )
12
13  print "Starting threads...\n"
14
15  buffer.displayState()
16
17  # start threads
18  producer.start()
19  consumer.start()
20
21  # wait for threads to terminate
22  producer.join()
23  consumer.join()
24
25  print "\nAll threads have terminated."
```

```
Starting threads...

(buffers occupied: 0)
buffers:     -1     -1     -1
             ----   ----   ----
              WR

Producer writes 11   (buffers occupied: 1)
buffers:     11     -1     -1
             ----   ----   ----
              R      W

Consumer reads 11   (buffers occupied: 0)
buffers:     11     -1     -1
             ----   ----   ----
                     WR
```

Fig. 19.12 Threads modifying a synchronized circular buffer. (Part 1 of 3.)

```
All buffers empty. Consumer waits.
Producer writes 12  (buffers occupied: 1)
buffers:    11      12      -1
            ----    ----    ----
                     R       W

Consumer reads 12  (buffers occupied: 0)
buffers:    11      12      -1
            ----    ----    ----
                            WR

All buffers empty. Consumer waits.
Producer writes 13  (buffers occupied: 1)
buffers:    11      12      13
            ----    ----    ----
             W               R

Consumer reads 13  (buffers occupied: 0)
buffers:    11      12      13
            ----    ----    ----
             WR

All buffers empty. Consumer waits.
Producer writes 14  (buffers occupied: 1)
buffers:    14      12      13
            ----    ----    ----
             R       W

Consumer reads 14  (buffers occupied: 0)
buffers:    14      12      13
            ----    ----    ----
                     WR

Producer writes 15  (buffers occupied: 1)
buffers:    14      15      13
            ----    ----    ----
                     R       W

Producer writes 16  (buffers occupied: 2)
buffers:    14      15      16
            ----    ----    ----
             W       R

Consumer reads 15  (buffers occupied: 1)
buffers:    14      15      16
            ----    ----    ----
             W               R

Producer writes 17  (buffers occupied: 2)
buffers:    17      15      16
            ----    ----    ----
                     W       R
```

Fig. 19.12 Threads modifying a synchronized circular buffer. (Part 2 of 3.)

```
Producer writes 18  (buffers occupied: 3)
buffers:    17      18      16
            ----    ----    ----
                            WR

All buffers full. Producer waits.
Consumer reads 16  (buffers occupied: 2)
buffers:    17      18      16
            ----    ----    ----
             R               W

Producer writes 19  (buffers occupied: 3)
buffers:    17      18      19
            ----    ----    ----
             WR

All buffers full. Producer waits.
Consumer reads 17  (buffers occupied: 2)
buffers:    17      18      19
            ----    ----    ----
             W       R

Producer writes 20  (buffers occupied: 3)
buffers:    20      18      19
            ----    ----    ----
                     WR

Producer done producing.
Terminating Producer.

Consumer reads 18  (buffers occupied: 2)
buffers:    20      18      19
            ----    ----    ----
                     W       R

Consumer reads 19  (buffers occupied: 1)
buffers:    20      18      19
            ----    ----    ----
             R       W

Consumer reads 20  (buffers occupied: 0)
buffers:    20      18      19
            ----    ----    ----
                     WR

Consumer read values totaling: 155.
Terminating Consume\r.

All threads have terminated.
```

Fig. 19.12 Threads modifying a synchronized circular buffer. (Part 3 of 3.)

Class **CircularBuffer** (Fig. 19.13) contains five attributes—**buffer** is a three-element list of integers that represents the circular buffer, **occupiedBufferCount** indicates how many occupied buffers exist, **readLocation** indicates the current position from which the next value can be read by a consumer, **writeLocation** indicates the next location in which a value can be placed by a producer and **threadCondition** is the condition variable that protects access to the buffer.

```
1   # Fig. 19.13: CircularBuffer.py
2   # Synchronized circular buffer of integer values
3
4   import threading
5
6   class CircularBuffer:
7
8      def __init__( self ):
9         """Set buffer, count, locations and condition variable"""
10
11         # each element in list is a buffer
12         self.buffer = [ -1, -1, -1 ]
13
14         self.occupiedBufferCount = 0     # count of occupied buffers
15         self.readLocation = 0            # current reading index
16         self.writeLocation = 0           # current writing index
17
18         self.threadCondition = threading.Condition()
19
20      def set( self, newNumber ):
21         """Set next buffer index value--blocks until lock acquired"""
22
23         # block until lock released then acquire lock
24         self.threadCondition.acquire()
25
26         # while all buffers are full, release lock and block
27         while self.occupiedBufferCount == len( self.buffer ):
28            print "All buffers full. %s waits." % \
29               threading.currentThread().getName()
30            self.threadCondition.wait()
31
32         # (there is an empty buffer, lock has been re-acquired)
33
34         # place value in writeLocation of buffer
35         # print string indicating produced value
36         self.buffer[ self.writeLocation ] = newNumber
37         print "%s writes %d " % \
38            ( threading.currentThread().getName(), newNumber ),
39
40         # produced value, so increment number of occupied buffers
41         self.occupiedBufferCount += 1
42
43         # update writeLocation for future write operation
44         # add current state to output
45         self.writeLocation = ( self.writeLocation + 1 ) % \
46            len( self.buffer )
47         self.displayState()
```

Fig. 19.13 Synchronized circular buffer of integers. (Part 1 of 3.)

```
48
49          self.threadCondition.notify()      # wake up a waiting thread
50          self.threadCondition.release()     # allow lock to be acquired
51
52      def get( self ):
53          """Get next buffer index value--blocks until lock acquired"""
54
55          # block until lock released then acquire lock
56          self.threadCondition.acquire()
57
58          # while all buffers are empty, release lock and block
59          while self.occupiedBufferCount == 0:
60              print "All buffers empty. %s waits." % \
61                  threading.currentThread().getName()
62              self.threadCondition.wait()
63
64          # (there is a full buffer, lock has been re-acquired)
65
66          # obtain value at current readLocation
67          # print string indicating consumed value
68          tempNumber = self.buffer[ self.readLocation ]
69          print "%s reads %d " % ( threading.currentThread().getName(),
70              tempNumber ),
71
72          # consumed value, so decrement number of occupied buffers
73          self.occupiedBufferCount -= 1
74
75          # update readLocation for future read operation
76          # add current state to output
77          self.readLocation = ( self.readLocation + 1 ) % \
78              len( self.buffer )
79          self.displayState()
80
81          self.threadCondition.notify()      # wake up a waiting thread
82          self.threadCondition.release()     # allow lock to be acquired
83
84          return tempNumber
85
86      def displayState( self ):
87          """Display current state"""
88
89          # display first line of state information
90          print "(buffers occupied: %d)" % self.occupiedBufferCount
91          print "buffers: ",
92
93          for item in self.buffer:
94              print " %d  " % item,
95
96          # display second line of state information
97          print "\n            ",
98
99          for item in self.buffer:
100             print "---- ",
```

Fig. 19.13 Synchronized circular buffer of integers. (Part 2 of 3.)

```
101
102            # display third line of state information
103            print "\n            ",
104
105            for i in range( len( self.buffer ) ):
106
107               if ( i == self.writeLocation ) and \
108                  ( self.writeLocation == self.readLocation ):
109                  print " WR  ",
110               elif ( i == self.writeLocation ):
111                  print " W   ",
112               elif ( i == self.readLocation ):
113                  print "  R  ",
114               else:
115                  print "     ",
116
117            print "\n"
```

Fig. 19.13 Synchronized circular buffer of integers. (Part 3 of 3.)

Method **set** (lines 20–50) performs the same tasks it did in Fig. 19.8 with a few modifications. The **while** structure in lines 27–30 determines whether the producer must wait (i.e., all buffers are full). If the producer thread must wait, lines 28–29 print a message indicating that the producer is waiting to perform its task, and line 30 invokes **Condition** method **wait**. When execution continues at line 36 after the **while** structure, the value written by the producer is placed in the circular buffer at location **writeLocation**. Next, lines 37–38 print a message that contains the produced value. Line 41 increments **occupiedBufferCount**, because the buffer now contains at least one value that the consumer can read. Then, lines 45–46 update **writeLocation** for the next call to the **set** method. Line 47 calls **CircularBuffer** method **displayState** (lines 86–117) to create output that indicates the number of occupied buffers, the contents of the buffers and the current **writeLocation** and **readLocation**. Next, condition variable method **notify** is invoked to indicate that a *waiting* thread (if there is one) should move to the *ready* state. Finally, condition variable method **release** is invoked to release the condition variable's underlying lock and allow another thread to acquire the lock and access the shared buffer.

Method **get** (line 52–84) also performs the same tasks in this example as those it performed in Fig. 19.8, with a few modifications. The **while** structure in lines 59–62 determines whether the consumer must wait (i.e., all buffers are empty). If so, lines 60–61 print a message to indicate that the consumer is waiting to perform its task, and line 62 invokes **Condition** method **wait**. When execution eventually continues at line 68 after the **while** structure, **tempNumber** is assigned the value at location **readLocation** in the circular buffer. Lines 69–70 print a message that contains the consumed value. Line 73 decrements **occupiedBufferCount**, because the buffer now contains at least one open position in which the producer thread can place a value. Then, lines 77–78 update **readLocation** for the next call to method **get**. Line 79 then calls method **displayState** to create output indicating the number of occupied buffers, the contents of the buffers and the current **writeLocation** and **readLocation**. Next, condition variable method **notify** is invoked to indicate that a *waiting* thread (if there is one) should move to the *ready* state.

Finally, condition variable method **release** is invoked to release the condition variable's underlying lock. Finally, line 84 returns the retrieved value to the calling thread.

19.9 Semaphores

A *semaphore* is a variable that controls access to a common resource or a critical section. A semaphore maintains a counter that specifies the number of threads that can use the resource or enter the critical section simultaneously. The counter is decremented each time a thread acquires the semaphore. When the counter is zero, the semaphore blocks other threads from accessing the semaphore until the semaphore has been released by another thread. Figure 19.14 uses a restaurant scenario to demonstrate using semaphores to control access to a critical section.

```python
1   # Figure 19.14: fig19_14.py
2   # Semaphore to control access to a critical section.
3
4   import threading
5   import random
6   import time
7
8   class SemaphoreThread( threading.Thread ):
9      """Class using semaphores"""
10
11     availableTables = [ "A", "B", "C", "D", "E" ]
12
13     def __init__( self, threadName, semaphore ):
14        """Initialize thread"""
15
16        threading.Thread.__init__( self, name = threadName )
17        self.sleepTime = random.randrange( 1, 6 )
18
19        # set the semaphore as a data attribute of the class
20        self.threadSemaphore = semaphore
21
22     def run( self ):
23        """Print message and release semaphore"""
24
25        # acquire the semaphore
26        self.threadSemaphore.acquire()
27
28        # remove a table from the list
29        table = SemaphoreThread.availableTables.pop()
30        print "%s entered; seated at table %s." % \
31           ( self.getName(), table ),
32        print SemaphoreThread.availableTables
33
34        time.sleep( self.sleepTime )   # enjoy a meal
35
36        # free a table
37        print "   %s exiting; freeing table %s." % \
38           ( self.getName(), table ),
```

Fig. 19.14 Semaphore to control access to a critical section. (Part 1 of 2.)

```
39              SemaphoreThread.availableTables.append( table )
40              print SemaphoreThread.availableTables
41
42              # release the semaphore after execution finishes
43              self.threadSemaphore.release()
44
45  threads = []  # list of threads
46
47  # semaphore allows five threads to enter critical section
48  threadSemaphore = threading.Semaphore(
49     len( SemaphoreThread.availableTables ) )
50
51  # create ten threads
52  for i in range( 1, 11 ):
53     threads.append( SemaphoreThread( "thread" + str( i ),
54        threadSemaphore ) )
55
56  # start each thread
57  for thread in threads:
58     thread.start()
```

```
thread1 entered; seated at table E. ['A', 'B', 'C', 'D']
thread2 entered; seated at table D. ['A', 'B', 'C']
thread3 entered; seated at table C. ['A', 'B']
thread4 entered; seated at table B. ['A']
thread5 entered; seated at table A. []
   thread2 exiting; freeing table D. ['D']
thread6 entered; seated at table D. []
   thread1 exiting; freeing table E. ['E']
thread7 entered; seated at table E. []
   thread3 exiting; freeing table C. ['C']
thread8 entered; seated at table C. []
   thread4 exiting; freeing table B. ['B']
thread9 entered; seated at table B. []
   thread5 exiting; freeing table A. ['A']
thread10 entered; seated at table A. []
   thread7 exiting; freeing table E. ['E']
   thread8 exiting; freeing table C. ['E', 'C']
   thread9 exiting; freeing table B. ['E', 'C', 'B']
   thread10 exiting; freeing table A. ['E', 'C', 'B', 'A']
   thread6 exiting; freeing table D. ['E', 'C', 'B', 'A', 'D']
```

Fig. 19.14 Semaphore to control access to a critical section. (Part 2 of 2.)

Lines 48–49 create a ***threading.Semaphore*** object that allows at most five threads to access the critical section in this example. An object of class **Semaphore** uses a counter to keep track of the number of threads that acquire and release the semaphore.

Lines 52–54 create a list of **SemaphoreThread** objects. Method **start** starts each thread in the list (lines 57–58).

Each object of class **SemaphoreThread** (lines 8–43) represents a single customer at a restaurant. Class attribute **availableTables** (line 11) keeps track of the available tables in the restaurant.

A **Semaphore** has a built-in counter to keep track of the number of calls to its **acquire** and **release** methods. The initial value of the internal counter can be passsed as an argument to the **Semaphore** constructor. The default value is 1. If the counter is greater than zero, **Semaphore** method **acquire** (line 26) obtains the semaphore for the thread and decrements the counter. If the counter is zero, the thread blocks until another thread releases the semaphore. A semaphore's counter can never be less than zero.

As a thread begins executing the critical section in class **SemaphoreThread**'s **run** method, list method **pop** (line 29) removes the last item from **availableTables** and assigns it to variable **table**. The program displays which thread entered the critical section and at which table the customer represented by that thread sat down. Then, the thread sleeps (occupies a table) for the random amount of time (line 34) that was calculated when the **SemaphoreThread** object was constructed. As a thread prepares to exit the critical section, line 39 appends the value of **table** to **availableTables** and displays the current list of available tables.

Semaphore method **release** (line 43) releases the semaphore when the thread finishes executing the critical section. The method call increments the **Semaphore**'s counter and notifies a waiting thread (if there is one) that it can become *ready* to execute.

Note, in Fig. 19.14, that if lines 26 and 43 are removed, more than five threads may attempt to remove an item from the shared list, resulting in an **IndexError** exception.

19.10 Events

Module **threading** defines class **Event**, which is useful for thread communication. An **Event** has an internal flag, which is either true or false. One or more threads may call the **Event** object's **wait** method to block until the event occurs. When the event occurs, the blocked thread or threads are awakened (in the order that they arrived) and resume execution. Figure 19.15 illustrates a situation in which a traffic light turns green every 3 seconds. We use an **Event** object to synchronize the threads, instead of a condition variable or other synchronization mechanism, because the threads do not share any data. Rather, the threads need only receive a notification when the light turns green.

Line 36 creates an **Event** object—**greenLight**—that simulates a traffic light. Lines 37–42 create a list of **VehicleThread**s. Class **VehicleThread** (lines 8–34) represents a vehicle at the intersection. Lines 44–45 start the vehicle threads. Each thread sleeps for a random amount of time, prints an arrival message, waits until the traffic light is green (i.e., **greenLight**'s internal flag is true) and prints a departing message.

The **while** structure (lines 47–57) loops until only the main thread remains active (i.e., all vehicle threads have terminated). Each iteration calls **Event** method **clear**, sleeps for three seconds, calls **Event** method **set** and sleeps for one second. **Event** methods **clear** and **set** change the value of an internal flag to false and true, respectively. Note that method **set** (line 56) awakens waiting vehicle threads in the order in which they arrived. At that point, each thread can print out that it is passing through the intersection.

```
1   # Fig. 19.15: fig19_15.py
2   # Event objects.
```

Fig. 19.15 Traffic-light example demonstrating an **Event** object. (Part 1 of 3.)

```
3
4    import threading
5    import random
6    import time
7
8    class VehicleThread( threading.Thread ):
9       """Class representing a motor vehicle at an intersection"""
10
11      def __init__( self, threadName, event ):
12         """Initializes thread"""
13
14         threading.Thread.__init__( self, name = threadName )
15
16         # ensures that each vehicle waits for a green light
17         self.threadEvent = event
18
19      def run( self ):
20         """Vehicle waits unless/until light is green"""
21
22         # stagger arrival times
23         time.sleep( random.randrange( 1, 10 ) )
24
25         # prints arrival time of car at intersection
26         print "%s arrived at %s" % \
27             ( self.getName(), time.ctime( time.time() ) )
28
29         # flag is false until light is green
30         self.threadEvent.wait()
31
32         # displays time that car departs intersection
33         print "%s passes through intersection at %s" % \
34             ( self.getName(), time.ctime( time.time() ) )
35
36   greenLight = threading.Event()
37   vehicleThreads = []
38
39   # creates and starts ten Vehicle threads
40   for i in range( 1, 11 ):
41      vehicleThreads.append( VehicleThread( "Vehicle" + str( i ),
42         greenLight ) )
43
44   for vehicle in vehicleThreads:
45      vehicle.start()
46
47   while threading.activeCount() > 1:
48
49      # sets the Event's flag to false -- block all incoming vehicles
50      greenLight.clear()
51      print "RED LIGHT! at", time.ctime( time.time() )
52      time.sleep( 3 )
53
54      # sets the Event's flag to true -- awaken all waiting vehicles
55      print "GREEN LIGHT! at", time.ctime( time.time() )
```

Fig. 19.15 Traffic-light example demonstrating an **Event** object. (Part 2 of 3.)

```
56      greenLight.set()
57      time.sleep( 1 )
```

```
RED LIGHT! at Fri Dec 21 18:10:44 2001
Vehicle7 arrived at Fri Dec 21 18:10:45 2001
Vehicle2 arrived at Fri Dec 21 18:10:46 2001
Vehicle8 arrived at Fri Dec 21 18:10:46 2001
GREEN LIGHT! at Fri Dec 21 18:10:47 2001
Vehicle7 passes through intersection at Fri Dec 21 18:10:47 2001
Vehicle2 passes through intersection at Fri Dec 21 18:10:47 2001
Vehicle8 passes through intersection at Fri Dec 21 18:10:47 2001
Vehicle1 arrived at Fri Dec 21 18:10:48 2001
Vehicle1 passes through intersection at Fri Dec 21 18:10:48 2001
Vehicle9 arrived at Fri Dec 21 18:10:48 2001
Vehicle9 passes through intersection at Fri Dec 21 18:10:48 2001
Vehicle10 arrived at Fri Dec 21 18:10:48 2001
Vehicle10 passes through intersection at Fri Dec 21 18:10:48 2001
RED LIGHT! at Fri Dec 21 18:10:48 2001
Vehicle4 arrived at Fri Dec 21 18:10:50 2001
Vehicle5 arrived at Fri Dec 21 18:10:50 2001
Vehicle6 arrived at Fri Dec 21 18:10:51 2001
GREEN LIGHT! at Fri Dec 21 18:10:51 2001
Vehicle4 passes through intersection at Fri Dec 21 18:10:51 2001
Vehicle5 passes through intersection at Fri Dec 21 18:10:51 2001
Vehicle6 passes through intersection at Fri Dec 21 18:10:51 2001
RED LIGHT! at Fri Dec 21 18:10:52 2001
Vehicle3 arrived at Fri Dec 21 18:10:53 2001
GREEN LIGHT! at Fri Dec 21 18:10:55 2001
Vehicle3 passes through intersection at Fri Dec 21 18:10:55 2001
```

Fig. 19.15 Traffic-light example demonstrating an **Event** object. (Part 3 of 3.)

In this chapter, we introduced multithreading and synchronization mechanisms. We used simple examples to demonstrate how programs access these classes to create threads and maintain data integrity. In the next chapter, we use these multithreading techniques to create a program that facilitates an Internet Tic-Tac-Toe game.

SUMMARY

- A thread is often called a "light-weight" process, because the operating system generally requires less resources to create and manage threads.

- While forked processes are allocated separate memory locations and data, threads execute in the same memory space and share the same resources.

- Python is different from many popular general-purpose programming languages in that it makes multithreading classes available to the application programmer.

- The programmer specifies that applications contain threads of execution, each thread designating a portion of a program that may execute concurrently with other threads.

- Programs create threads by creating objects of class **threading.Thread**.

- Usually, we create a subclass of class **Thread** that extends the basic capabilities of the class. The subclass is capable of performing additional tasks.

- The code that "does the real work" of a thread is placed in its **run** method, which is overridden in a subclass of **Thread**.

- A program launches a thread's execution by calling the thread's **start** method, which, in turn, calls the **run** method. After **start** launches the thread, **start** returns to its caller immediately. The caller then executes concurrently with the launched thread.

- If a thread has already been started, calling its **start** method again raises an **AssertionError** exception.

- Method **isAlive** returns 1 if **start** has been called for a given thread and the thread is not dead (i.e., its controlling **run** method has not completed execution).

- Method **setName** sets a **Thread**'s name.

- Method **getName** returns the name of the **Thread**.

- Using the **print** statement on a thread displays the thread's name and current state.

- Function **threading.currentThread** returns a reference to the currently executing **Thread**.

- Function **threading.enumerate** returns a list of all currently executing **Thread** objects, including the main thread.

- Function **threading.activeCount** returns the length of the list returned by **threading.enumerate**.

- Method **join** waits for the **Thread** to which the message is sent to die before allowing the calling **Thread** to proceed. A thread may not call its own **join** method—only those of other threads.

- An optional argument accepted by **join** is timeout, a floating-point number specifying the number of seconds that the caller waits. Passing no argument to method **join** indicates that the caller waits forever for the target **Thread** to die before the calling **Thread** proceeds.

- Waiting can be dangerous; it can lead to two particularly serious problems, called deadlock and indefinite postponement. In deadlock, one or more threads will wait forever for an event that cannot occur; in indefinite postponement, one or more threads will be delayed for some unpredictably long time.

- The Python interpreter controls all threads in a program. When the interpreter starts, the "main" thread begins. This thread invokes all other threads. When a program contains more than one running thread, these threads are switched in and out of the interpreter, after a specified interval (called a quantum).

- Python's global interpreter lock (GIL) ensures that the interpreter runs only one thread at any given time. Each time the GIL becomes available, a single thread obtains it. The interpreter then switches in this thread and executes the thread for its time interval. When the interval expires, the interpreter switches out the thread, and frees the GIL.

- A newly created thread is in the born state. The thread remains in this state until the program invokes the thread's **start** method, which causes the thread to enter the ready state (also known as the runnable state).

- A ready thread enters the running state (i.e., the thread begins executing) when the interpreter executes the thread (i.e., method **run** executes).

- A thread enters the dead state when its **run** method completes or terminates for any reason (e.g., an uncaught exception)—the interpreter eventually disposes of a dead thread.

- The only state in which a thread has obtained the GIL is the running state. In this state, the Python interpreter executes the thread's instructions. Any action which causes a thread to move to a state other than the running state causes that thread to forfeit the GIL.

- When a running thread requests an unavailable resource, that thread releases the GIL and enters the blocked state.

- One common way for a running thread to enter the blocked state occurs when a running thread calls **acquire** on an unavailable lock. A thread in the blocked state for a particular lock becomes ready on a call to **release** issued by another thread associated with that lock.

- Another common way for a thread to enter the blocked state occurs when the thread issues an input/output request. When a thread performs an I/O (input/output) request—such as reading a file from disk or sending a file to a printer—the thread that issues the request is promptly switched out of the interpreter (e.g., it releases the GIL), so that other threads may use the interpreter while the I/O is performed. While the thread is blocked for I/O by the operating system, another thread may acquire the GIL and perform some necessary computation, using the interpreter.

- I/O-bound processes generally benefit from multithreading, because such processes can use the interpreter while waiting for the I/O, thus reducing their total execution times.

- When a running thread calls function **time.sleep**, that thread releases the GIL and enters the sleeping state. A sleeping thread returns to the ready state after the designated sleep time expires. A sleeping thread cannot use the interpreter even if the interpreter is available.

- When a running thread calls **wait** on a particular synchronization mechanism, the thread releases the GIL and enters a waiting state for the particular mechanism on which **wait** was called. One thread in the waiting state for a particular mechanism becomes ready on a call to **notify** issued by another thread associated with that mechanism. Every thread in the waiting state for a given mechanism becomes ready on a call to **notifyAll** by another thread associated with that mechanism.

- A thread's name is specified with **Thread** keyword argument **name**. If no name is specified, the thread is assigned a unique name of the form **"Thread-n"**, where n is an integer.

- Multithreaded programs often contain code wherein two or more threads attempt to access or modify the value of a shared piece of data. The sections of code that access shared data often are referred to as critical sections.

- To prevent multiple threads from modifying data simultaneously, multithreaded programs typically restrict the number of threads that can execute critical sections concurrently. This restriction is accomplished through various synchronization mechanisms.

- Module **threading** provides many thread synchronization mechanisms. The most classes synchronization mechanism is the lock. A **lock** object (created with class **threading.RLock**) defines two methods—**acquire** and **release**.

- When a thread calls the **acquire** method, the lock enters a locked state. Only one thread may acquire a lock at a time. If another thread attempts to invoke method **acquire**, that thread will be blocked by the operating system until the lock becomes available.

- When the thread occupying the lock invokes method **release**, the lock enters the unlocked state. The blocked thread is notified (awakened), and it acquires the lock.

- If multiple threads are blocked, only one thread is notified of the lock's unlocked state.

- Locks can restrict access to critical sections.

- A thread uses a condition variable when the thread wants to monitor the state of some object or wants to be notified when some event occurs. When the object's state changes or the event occurs, blocked threads are notified.

- Condition variables are created with class **threading.Condition**.

- Condition variables contain an underlying lock and, therefore, provide **acquire** and **release** methods. Other condition variable methods are **wait** and **notify**.

- After a thread acquires a lock, invoking method **wait** releases the lock, and the thread is blocked until it is awakened by a call to **notify** on the same condition variable. Method **notify** wakes up one thread waiting on the condition variable; method **notifyAll** wakes up all waiting threads.

- Sometimes, threads need to wait for particular events to occur before proceeding with their executions. This is accomplished through an **Event** object (created with class **threading.Event**).
- A thread that calls **Event** method **wait** is blocked until the event occurs.
- Condition variable method **notify** does not release the underlying lock. Failure to call **release** can result in deadlock.
- Queues represents a waiting line; insertions are made at the back (also referred to as the tail) of a queue, and removals are made from the front (also referred to as the head) of a queue.
- Python includes module **Queue**, which contains class **Queue**—a synchronized implementation of a queue.
- A queue may either have an infinite or finite size. The size of an "infinite" queue is limited by memory resources. The **Queue** constructor accepts optional argument **maxsize**. If **maxsize** is less than 1, the queue size is infinite (i.e., the queue has no pre-defined size). Otherwise, **maxsize** defines the maximum number of items that may be placed into the queue.
- Method **get** removes and returns an item from the head of the queue.
- Method **get** accepts an optional argument **block**. If the queue is currently empty and **block** is 1 (default), method **get** blocks the calling thread until an item is available. If **block** is 0, the queue raises the **Empty** exception, an exception defined in module **Queue**.
- Method **put** inserts an item at the tail of the queue.
- Method **put** accepts from one to two arguments. The first (required) argument is **item**, which indicates the item to insert in the queue. The second (optional) argument is **block**. If the queue is currently full and **block** is 1 (default), method **put** blocks the calling thread until a cell becomes available. If **block** is 0, method **put** raises the **Full** exception.
- Similar to a queue, a circular buffer provides extra buffers into which the producer can place values and from which the consumer can retrieve those values. Let us assume the buffer is implemented as a finite size list. The producer and consumer work from the beginning of the list. When either thread reaches the end of the list, it simply returns to the first element of the list to perform its next task.
- Semaphores (created with class **threading.Semaphore**) are synchronization mechanisms that allow a set number of threads to access a critical section.
- The **Semaphore** uses a counter to keep track of the number of threads that acquire and release the semaphore. When the counter equals 0, all threads that invoke method **acquire** are blocked. Otherwise, if the counter is greater than 0, the threads acquire the semaphore and method **acquire** decrements the counter.
- Invoking method **release** releases the semaphore, increments the counter and notifies a blocked thread.
- The initial value of the internal counter can be passed as an argument to the **Semaphore** constructor (default is 1). The internal counter cannot equal a negative value, so specifying a negative value raises an **AssertionError** exception.
- An **Event** (created with class **threading.Event**) contains an internal flag that, initially, equals false (i.e., the event has not occurred).
- If a thread calls **Event** method **wait** when the internal flag equals false, the thread is blocked until a specified task occurs.
- After the event occurs, method **set** switches the flag to true and awakens all blocked threads.
- If a thread calls **Event** method **wait** when the internal flag equals true, the thread is not blocked, and it continues with its execution.
- **Event** method **isSet** returns true if the flag is true.

- Method **clear** sets the flag to false.
- A program or thread deadlocks when either one is blocked indefinitely (i.e., is waiting for a particular event to occur or for a particular resource).

TERMINOLOGY

acquire method of class **Condition**
acquire method of class **RLock**
acquire method of class **Semaphore**
back of a queue
block argument
blocked state
born state
buffering
circular buffer
clear method of class **Event**
Condition class of module **threading**
condition variable
consumer thread
critical section
currentThread function of module **threading**
dead state
deadlock
Empty exception
enumerate function of module **threading**
event
Event class of module **threading**
front of a queue
Full exception
get method of class **Queue**
getName method of class **Thread**
global interpreter lock (GIL)
head of a queue
I/O-bound process
indefinite postponement
isAlive method of class **Thread**
isSet method of class **Event**
item argument
join method of class **Thread**
lock
locked state
maxsize argument
multithreading

name keyword argument
notify method of class **Condition**
notifyAll method of class **Condition**
producer thread
producer/consumer relationship
put method of class **Queue**
quantum
queue
Queue class
Queue module
ready state
release method of class **Condition**
release method of class **RLock**
release method of class **Semaphore**
RLock class of module **threading**
run method of class **Thread**
runnable state
running state
Semaphore class of module **threading**
semaphore
set method of class **Event**
setName method of class **Thread**
sleeping state
start method of class **Thread**
switched
synchronization mechanism
tail of a queue
thread
Thread class of module **threading**
thread states
thread synchronization
threading module
timeout
underlying lock
unlocked state
wait method of class **Condition**
waiting state

SELF-REVIEW EXERCISES

19.1   Fill in the blanks in each of the following statements:
   a) Two reasons a thread that is alive could be not runnable are _____ and _____.
   b) A thread enters the *dead* state when _____.

    c) To wait for a designated number of seconds and then resume execution, a thread should call the _____ function.

    d) The _____ method moves a thread from the *waiting* state to the ready state.

    e) Four Python thread synchronization mechanisms are _____, _____, and _____.

    f) A program or thread _____ when the program or thread blocks forever on a needed resource.

    g) Insertions are made at the _____ of a queue, and removals are made from the _____ of a queue.

    h) The **Queue** constructor accepts optional argument _____, which specifies the size of the queue.

19.2 State whether each of the following is *true* or *false*. If *false*, explain why.

    a) While forked processes are allocated separate memory locations and data, threads execute in the same memory space and share the same resources.

    b) **Thread** method **wait** causes the calling **Thread** to wait for the corresponding **Thread** to die before it can proceed.

    c) When a program contains more than one *running* thread, these threads are switched in and out of the interpreter by the global interpreter lock (GIL) at specified intervals.

    d) Unlike a *blocked* thread, a *sleeping* thread may still use the interpreter.

    e) A *running* thread enters the *sleeping* state when the thread issues an input/output request.

    f) Semaphores provide **acquire** and **release** methods because they contain an underlying lock.

    g) A semaphore's counter can never be less than 0.

    h) Applications relying on I/O-bound processes generally benefit most from multithreading.

ANSWERS TO SELF-REVIEW EXERCISES

19.1 a) sleeping, blocked for input/output. b) its **run** method terminates. c) **time.sleep**. d) **notify**. e) locks, condition variables, semaphores, events. f) deadlocks. g) back/tail, front/head. h) **maxsize**.

19.2 a) True. b) False. **Thread** method **join** causes the calling **Thread** to wait for the corresponding **Thread** to die before it can proceed. c) True. d) False. A *sleeping* thread may not use the interpreter. e) False. A *running* thread enters the *blocked* state when the thread issues an input/output request. f) False. Condition variables contain an underlying lock. g) True. h) True.

EXERCISES

19.3 Describe one reason for entering each of the following states:

    a) *Sleeping* state.

    b) *Blocked* state.

    c) *Ready* state.

    d) *Dead* state.

    e) *Waiting* state.

19.4 Give an example of how deadlock can occur in a multithreaded Python program.

19.5 Choose the best threading-synchronization mechanism for each of the following situations:

    a) Halting thread execution until a particular event occurs.

    b) Allowing access to a critical section only when some event occurs.

    c) Restricting access to a critical section.

    d) Allowing a set number of threads to access a critical section simultaneously.

19.6   Write a multithreaded program that demonstrates **RLock**. Create two thread classes—**AddThread** and **MultiplyThread**. Class **AddThread** should increment a global variable by 1, sleep for two seconds and increment the variable again. Class **MultiplyThread** should double the global variable, sleep for two second and double the variable again. Protect these critical sections with a lock. After both threads terminate, print the final value of the shared variable. Also, try commenting out lines so that the lock is not used. Notice the different value the variable has.

19.7   Write a multithreaded simulation of a barbershop. Use a queue to share the available barbers. At the start of the program, insert barber names into the queue. Create a thread for each customer. As each customer arrives, the customer waits for an available barber, gets a haircut, returns the barber to the queue and exits the barber shop. Use random numbers and function **sleep** to stagger arrival times and to simulate haircut time.

19.8   (*Simulation: The Tortoise and the Hare*) In this problem, you will recreate one of the truly great moments in history, namely the classic race of the tortoise and the hare. You will use random-number generation and multithreading to develop a simulation of this memorable event.

Our contenders begin the race at "square 1" of 60 squares. Each square represents a possible position along the race course. The finish line is at square 60. The first contender to reach or pass square 60 is rewarded with a pail of fresh carrots and lettuce. The course weaves its way up the side of a slippery mountain, so occasionally the contenders lose ground.

There is a clock thread that ticks once per second. With each tick of the clock, your program should adjust the position of the animals according to the rules in Fig. 19.16. Place each of the animals in separate threads. Begin by calling the **start** method of the clock thread. At the start of the race, have the clock thread call the **start** methods for each of the animal threads. Use an **Event** object to synchronize the animals' activities.

Use variables to keep track of the positions of the animals (i.e., position numbers are 1–60). Start each animal at position 1 (i.e., the "starting gate"). If an animal slips left before square 1, move the animal back to square 1.

Generate the percentages in the preceding table by producing a random integer, i, in the range $0 \le i \le 9$. For the tortoise, perform a "fast plod" when $0 \le i \le 4$, a "slip" when $5 \le i \le 6$, a "slow plod" when $7 \le i \le 9$. Use a similar technique to move the hare.

Begin the race by printing

```
On your mark...
Get set...
Go!
```

Then, for each tick of the clock (i.e., each repetition of a loop), print a 60-position line showing the letter **T** in the position of the tortoise and the letter **H** in the position of the hare. Occasionally, the contenders will land on the same square. In this case, the tortoise bites the hare, and your program should print **OUCH!!!** beginning at that position. All print positions other than the **T**, the **H** or the **OUCH!!!** (in case of a tie) should be an asterisk.

After each line is printed, test for whether either animal has reached or passed square 60. If so, print the winner and terminate the simulation. If the tortoise wins, print **TORTOISE WINS!!! YAY!!!** If the hare wins, print **Hare wins. Yuch.** If both animals win on the same tick of the clock, you may want to favor the turtle (the "underdog") or you may want to print **It's a tie**. If neither animal wins, sleep for one second, then perform the loop again to simulate the next tick of the clock. When you are ready to run your program, assemble a group of fans to watch the race. You'll be amazed at how involved your audience gets!

Later in the book, we introduce a number of Python multimedia capabilities, such as graphics and sound. As you study those features, you might enjoy enhancing your tortoise-and-hare-contest simulation.

Animal	Move type	Percentage of the time	Actual move
Tortoise	Fast plod	50%	3 squares to the right
	Slip	20%	6 squares to the left
	Slow plod	30%	1 square to the right
Hare	Sleep	20%	No move at all
	Big hop	20%	9 squares to the right
	Big slip	10%	12 squares to the left
	Small hop	30%	1 square to the right
	Small slip	20%	2 squares to the left

Fig. 19.16 Tortoise and hare movement rules.

20

Networking

Objectives

- To understand the elements of Python networking—URLs, sockets and datagrams.
- To implement Python networking applications using sockets and datagrams.
- To understand the implementation client/server applications in Python.
- To understand how to create network-based collaborative applications.
- To construct a multithreaded server.

If the presence of electricity can be made visible in any part of a circuit, I see no reason why intelligence may not be transmitted instantaneously by electricity.
Samuel F. B. Morse

Mr. Watson, come here, I want you.
Alexander Graham Bell

Science may never come up with a better office-communication system than the coffee break.
Earl Wilson

It's currently a problem of access to gigabits through punybaud.
J. C. R. Licklider

20.1 Introduction

The Internet and World Wide Web have generated a great deal of excitement in the business and computing communities. The Internet ties the "information world" together; the Web makes the Internet easy to use while providing the flair of multimedia. Organizations regard both the Internet and the Web as crucial to their information-systems strategies. Python offers a number of built-in networking capabilities that facilitate Internet-based and Web-based applications development. Python not only can specify parallelism through multithreading, but also can enable programs to request information over the Web and collaborate with programs running on other computers internationally.

Chapter 6, Introduction to the Common Gateway Interface (CGI), began our presentation of Python's networking and distributed-computing capabilities. We discussed server-side Web technologies that enable users to generate dynamic Web content for Web clients to view. This chapter's networking discussion focuses on both sides of a *client/server relationship*. The *client* requests that the server perform some action; the *server* performs the action and responds to the client. A common implementation of this *request-response model* is between Web browsers and Web servers. When a user selects a Web site to view through a browser (the client application), the browser makes a request to the appropriate Web server (the server application). The server normally responds to the client by sending the appropriate Web pages.

This chapter focuses on Python's networking capabilities that can be used to build distributed applications. The chapter introduces Python's socket-based communications, which enable applications to view networking as if it were file I/O—a program can receive from a socket or send to a socket as simply as reading from a file or writing to a file. We show how to create and manipulate sockets. Python provides stream sockets and datagram sockets. With stream sockets, a process establishes a connection to another process. While the connection exists, data flows between the processes in continuous streams. Stream sockets provide connection-oriented services. The protocol used for transmission is the popular *Transmission Control Protocol (TCP)*, which we introduced in Chapter 6.

UDP enables connnectionless network communication with datagram sockets. This the not an efficient protocol for everyday users because, unlike TCP, the protocol uses the *User Datagram Protocol (UDP)*, which is a connectionless service and does not guarantee that packets arrive in a particular order. In fact, packets can be lost, can be duplicated and can even arrive out of sequence using the User Datagram Protocol. So, with UDP, significant additional programming is required on the user's part to deal with these problems (if the user chooses to do so). Stream sockets and the TCP protocol will be the most desirable for the vast majority of Python programmers.

20.2 Accessing URLs over HTTP

The Internet employs many protocols, some of which we introduce in Chapter 6. In this section, we review some of the Web's protocols and present an example that uses Python modules to display Web pages. One of the more important protocols is the *HyperText Transfer Protocol (HTTP)*, which is crucial to the transmission of data on the Web. HTTP uses *URLs (Uniform Resource Locators*, also called *Universal Resource Locators)* to locate content on the Internet. URLs represent files, directories or complex tasks, such as database lookups and Internet searches.

Figure 20.1 uses **Tkinter** and **Pmw** GUI components to display the contents of a file on a Web server in a Web browser. To accomplish this, we first define class **WebBrowser**, which acts as a Web browser. The user inputs the URL in the text field, the **Entry address**, at the top of the browser window, and the corresponding Web document (if one exists) displays in the **ScrolledText**.

```python
1   # Fig. 20.1: fig20_01.py
2   # Displays the contents of a file from a Web server in a browser.
3
4   from Tkinter import *
5   import Pmw
6   import urllib
7   import urlparse
8
9   class WebBrowser( Frame ):
10      """A simple Web browser"""
11
12      def __init__( self ):
13         """Create the Web browser GUI"""
14
15         Frame.__init__( self )
16         Pmw.initialise()
17         self.pack( expand = YES, fill = BOTH )
18         self.master.title( "Simple Web Browser" )
19         self.master.geometry( "400x300" )
20
21         self.address = Entry( self )
22         self.address.pack( fill = X, padx = 5, pady = 5 )
23         self.address.bind( "<Return>", self.getPage )
24
25         self.contents = Pmw.ScrolledText( self,
26            text_state = DISABLED )
27         self.contents.pack( expand = YES, fill = BOTH, padx = 5,
28            pady = 5 )
29
```

Fig. 20.1 URL connection used to read a file. (Part 1 of 2.)

```
30        def getPage( self, event ):
31            """Parse URL, add addressing scheme and retrieve file"""
32
33            # parse the URL
34            myURL = event.widget.get()
35            components = urlparse.urlparse( myURL )
36            self.contents.text_state = NORMAL
37
38            # if addressing scheme not specified, use http
39            if components[ 0 ] == "":
40                myURL = "http://" + myURL
41
42            # connect and retrieve the file
43            try:
44                tempFile = urllib.urlopen( myURL )
45                self.contents.settext( tempFile.read() ) # show results
46                tempFile.close()
47            except IOError:
48                self.contents.settext( "Error finding file" )
49
50            self.contents.text_state = DISABLED
51
52  def main():
53      WebBrowser().mainloop()
54
55  if __name__ == "__main__":
56      main()
```

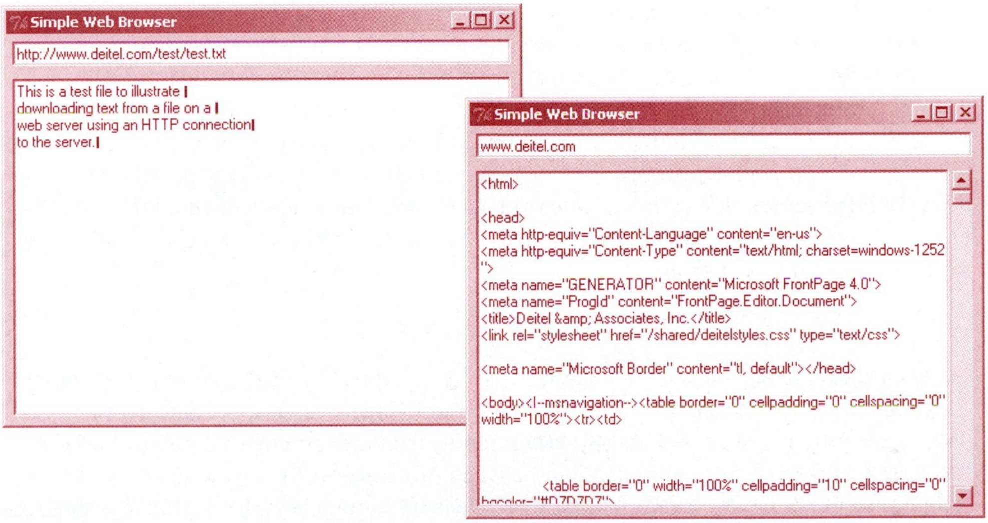

Fig. 20.1   URL connection used to read a file. (Part 2 of 2.)

Class **WebBrowser** contains **Entry** component **address**, into which the user enters the URL of the file to read. A **ScrolledText** component **contents** displays the contents of the file. When the user presses the *Enter* key in the **Entry** component, method **getPage** executes. Method **getPage** (lines 30–50) retrieves the specified file from the

Web server. Line 34 obtains the URL from component **address** by invoking its **get** method.

Module **urlparse** provides functions to parse URLs, as well as other functions that facilitate the manipulation of URLs. Function **urlparse.urlparse** takes a string as input and returns a six-element tuple. The first element of the tuple is the *addressing scheme*. This example uses **http** as the addressing scheme. Entering a URL beginning with **http** directs the Web server to retrieve and transfer the requested URL document. Line 39 checks for whether the user has entered a URL beginning with **"http://"**. If the user did not enter **"http://"**, the program assumes that the user has simply forgotten it and adds it to the URL (line 40).

Lines 43–48 attempt to connect to the Web server and retrieve the requested file using module **urllib**. Module **urllib** provides methods for accessing data referred to by a URL. Line 45 passes the URL to **urllib** function **urlopen** to retrieve the file. The function causes a *DNS* (*Domain Name System*) lookup to be performed. A DNS server translates a domain name, or URL, into an *IP address*, a unique identifier for a computer on a network. The module requests documents from the Web server. If successful, **urlopen** returns an object. This object behaves like a Python file object and can use file methods, such as **read**, **readline**, **readlines** and **close**. Line 45 reads the file and displays the results in component **contents**. Line 46 then closes the file. If **urlopen** fails, line 48 displays an error message to the user.

20.3 Establishing a Simple Server (Using Stream Sockets)

Typically, with TCP and stream sockets, a server "waits" for a connection request from a client. Often, the server-side application contains a control structure or block of code that executes continuously until the server receives a request for a connection. On receiving a request, the server establishes a connection with the client. The server then uses this connection to handle future requests from that client and to send data to the client.

The establishment of a simple server with TCP and stream sockets in Python requires module **socket**, which contains the function and class definitions that provide capabilities to build programs that communicate over a network. The establishment of this communication requires six steps. The first step is to create a **socket** object. A call to the **socket** constructor, such as

```
socket = socket.socket( family, type )
```

creates a socket using the specified address family and type. Typically, argument *family* is either **AF_INET** or **AF_UNIX**. The argument family specifies how to interpret any addresses used by the socket. The **AF_INET** family includes Internet addresses while the **AF_UNIX** family is for communication between processes on the same machine. In this chapter, we use only **AF_INET**. The typical values for argument *type* are **SOCK_STREAM** (for stream sockets) and **SOCK_DGRAM** (for datagram sockets). These constants are defined in module **socket**. For the purposes of our discussion, we assume that we have created a stream socket. Section 20.6 discusses the other type of socket—the datagram socket.

The second step in creating the server is to bind (assign) the **socket** to a specified address. This is performed via a call to a **socket** object's **bind** method, such as

```
socket.bind( address )
```

For a socket created by family **AF_INET**, *address* must be a two-element tuple in the form (*host*, *port*), in which *host* is a string representing the machine's hostname or IP address and *port* is a port number (i.e., integer). The preceding statement reserves a port in which the server waits for connections from clients. These clients connect to the server on this port. Method **bind** raises exception **socket.error** if the port is already in use, the hostname is incorrect or the port is reserved.

Software Engineering Observation 20.1

Port numbers can have values between 0 and 65535. Many operating systems reserve port numbers below 1024 for system services (such as e-mail and World Wide Web servers). Applications must be granted special privileges to use these reserved port numbers. Usually, a server-side application should not specify port numbers below 1024 as connection ports.

Common Programming Error 20.1

*Attempting to specify an already assigned port or and invalid port when creating a **socket** results in an exception.*

Once the socket is bound to an address, the socket must prepare to receive requests for connections (step 3). To achieve this, the **socket** method **listen**

```
socket.listen( backlog )
```

in which *backlog* specifies the maximum number of clients that can request connections to the server. The value of **backlog** should be at least 1. As connection requests are received, they are queued. If the queue is full, connection requests are refused.

In the fourth step, the server **socket** waits for a client to request a connection via **socket** method **accept**

```
connection, address = socket.accept()
```

The **socket** waits indefinitely (or *blocks*) when it calls method **accept**. When a client requests a connection, the method establishes the connection and returns to the server. Method **accept** returns a two-element tuple of the form (*connection*, *address*). The first element of the returned tuple (*connection*) is a new **socket** object, with which the server communicates with the client. The second element (*address*) corresponds to the client's Internet address.

The fifth step is the processing phase, in which the server and the client communicate (transmit data) using **socket** methods **send** and **recv**. The server sends information to the client by invoking **send** and passing the information in the form of a string. Method **send** returns the number of bytes sent. The server receives information from the client using **recv**. When calling **recv**, the server must specify an integer that corresponds to the maximum amount of data that can be received through one invocation of that method. Method **recv**, which blocks as it receives data, returns a string that represents the received data. If the amount of data sent is greater than **recv** allows, the data is truncated. The excess data is buffered on the receiving end. On a subsequent call to **recv**, the excess data is removed from the buffer (along with any additional data the client may have sent since the previous call to **recv**).

Common Programming Error 20.2

*A socket's **send** method accepts only a string argument. Trying to pass a value with a different type (e.g., an integer) results in an error.*

In step 6, the transmission completes, and the server closes the connection by invoking the **close** method on the **socket**.

Software Engineering Observation 20.2

Python's multithreading capabilities enable a programmer to create multithreaded servers that can manage many simultaneous client connections.

Software Engineering Observation 20.3

*A multithreaded server can be implemented to use the **socket** returned by each call to **accept** to create a thread that manages network I/O across that **socket**. Alternatively, a programmer can implement a multithreaded server to maintain a pool of threads to manage network I/O across newly created **socket**s.*

Performance Tip 20.1

*In high-performance systems with abundant memory, a multithreaded server can be implemented to create a pool of threads. These threads can be assigned quickly to handle network I/O across each newly created **socket**. Thus, when a connection is received, the server does not incur the overhead of thread creation.*

20.4 Establishing a Simple Client (Using Stream Sockets)

Establishing a simple client in Python requires four steps. The first step creates a **socket** to connect to the server:

```
socket = socket.socket( family, type )
```

Step two connects to the server using **socket** method **connect**. Method **connect** takes as input the address of the socket to which the client connects. For **AF_INET** client sockets, the call to **connect** has the form

```
socket.connect( ( host, port ) )
```

where *host* is a string that represents the server's hostname or IP address and *port* is the integer port number to which the server process is bound. If the connection attempt is successful, the client can communicate with the server through the **socket**. A connection attempt that fails raises the **socket.error** exception.

Common Programming Error 20.3

*A **socket.error** exception is raised when a server address indicated by a client cannot be resolved or when an error occurs while attempting to connect to a server.*

Step three is the processing phase in which the client and the server communicate via methods **send** and **recv**. In step four, when the transmission is complete, the client closes the connection by invoking method **close** of the **socket**.

20.5 Client/Server Interaction with Stream Socket Connections

The programs in Fig. 20.2 and Fig. 20.3 use stream sockets and techniques discussed in the previous two sections to construct a simple *client/server chat application*. The server waits for a client's request to make a connection. When a client application connects to the server, the server application sends a string to the client, which indicates that the connection was successful. The client then displays a message to notify that a connection has been established.

Both the client and the server applications enable the user to type a message and send it to the other application. When either the client or the server sends the string **"TERMI-NATE"**, the connection between the client and the server terminates. The server then waits for another client to request a connection. Figure 20.2 and Fig. 20.3 contains the definition of the server and the client, respectively. Figure 20.3 also contains sample output that demonstrates the execution between the client and the server.

```python
# Fig. 20.2: fig20_02.py
# Set up a server that will receive a connection
# from a client, send a string to the client,
# and close the connection.

import socket

HOST = "127.0.0.1"
PORT = 5000
counter = 0

# step 1: create socket
mySocket = socket.socket( socket.AF_INET, socket.SOCK_STREAM )

# step 2: bind the socket to address
try:
    mySocket.bind( ( HOST, PORT ) )
except socket.error:
    print "Call to bind failed"

while 1:

    # step 3: wait for connection request
    print "Waiting for connection"
    mySocket.listen( 1 )

    # step 4: establish connection for request
    connection, address = mySocket.accept()
    counter += 1
    print "Connection", counter, "received from:", address[ 0 ]

    # step 5: send and receive data via connection
    connection.send( "SERVER>>> Connection successful" )
    clientMessage = connection.recv( 1024 )

    while clientMessage != "CLIENT>>> TERMINATE":

        if not clientMessage:
            break

        print clientMessage
        serverMessage = raw_input( "SERVER>>> " )
        connection.send( "SERVER>>> " + serverMessage )
        clientMessage = connection.recv( 1024 )
```

Fig. 20.2 Server-side application that uses connection-oriented transmission to transmit data via sockets. (Part 1 of 2.)

```
45
46       # step 6: close connection
47       print "Connection terminated"
48       connection.close()
```

Fig. 20.2 Server-side application that uses connection-oriented transmission to transmit data via sockets. (Part 2 of 2.)

Lines 13–44 enable the server to wait for a connection request, establish a connection and transmit data through that connection. Line 13 creates **socket** object **mySocket** to wait for connection requests. Integer **counter** represents the total number of connections established (line 10).

Line 17 binds **mySocket** to port **5000**. If a **socket.error** occurs, the program prints an error message (line 19). Note that **HOST** is the string **"127.0.0.1"**. This IP address always refers to the local machine (also called **localhost**). [*Note*: We chose to demonstrate the client/server relationship by connecting between programs executing on a single computer, which is referred to as **localhost**. If this example had been client/server interaction over the Internet, this first argument typically would be a string that contains the Internet address of another computer.] Lines 21–44 contain a **while** loop, in which the server continually listens for each client request, then establishes a connection upon a request. Line 25 listens for a connection request from a client at port **5000**. Method **listen** takes as an argument the number of requests that can wait in a queue to connect to the server (**1** in this example). If the queue is full when a client requests a connection, the server refuses to establish the connection.

Method **listen** sets up a listener to wait for a client to request a connection. Once a request is received, **socket** method **accept** (line 28) creates a **socket** object that manages the connection. Recall that **accept** returns a two-element tuple. The first element is a new **socket** object that we call **connection**. The second element is the Internet address of the client computer that connected to this server (in the form (*host*, *port*) for **AF_INET** sockets). Once a new **socket** for the current connection exists, line 30 prints a message that displays the connection number and the client address.

Line 33 calls **socket** method **send** to send the string **"SERVER>>> Connection successful"** to the client. Line 34 calls **socket** method **recv** to receive a string from the client that contains up to 1024 bytes. The **while** loop in lines 36–44 loops until the server receives the message **"CLIENT>>> TERMINATE"**. Lines 38–39 determine whether the connection has been closed by the client. When a connection has been closed, **recv** returns an empty string. If this is the case, the **break** statement exits the loop. Otherwise, line 41 prints the message received from the client.

Function **raw_input** (line 42) reads a string from the user. The server sends this string to the client (line 43) and receives a message from the client (line 44). When the transmission is complete, line 48 closes the **socket**. The server awaits the next request from a client.

In our example, the server receives a request for a connection, establishes a connection and transmits data through it, closes the connection and waits for the next request. A more likely scenario would be a server that receives a request, sets up that connection to be managed by a separate thread of execution, then waits for additional requests. The separate threads that process existing connections can continue to execute while the server processes connection requests. In Exercise 20.6, we ask the reader to implement this multithreaded approach to the server application.

Figure 20.3 displays the client and its interaction with the server as a stream-socket connection is established. The sample output from this interaction is included.

Lines 12–33 connect the client to the server, enable the client to receive data from the server and enable the client to send data to the server. Line 12 creates a **socket** object—**mySocket**—to establish a connection. The client then requests a connection to the server by calling **socket** method **connect**. This method takes as an argument a two-element tuple (line 16). Setting variable **PORT** to the same value as that in Fig. 20.2 (**5000**) ensures that the client **socket** will request a connection on the port to which the server is bound. If the call to **connect** generates a **socket.error**, the **except** statement prints an error message.

```
1   # Fig. 20.3: fig20_03.py
2   # Set up a client that will read information sent
3   # from a server and display that information.
4
5   import socket
6
7   HOST = "127.0.0.1"
8   PORT = 5000
9
10  # step 1: create socket
11  print "Attempting connection"
12  mySocket = socket.socket( socket.AF_INET, socket.SOCK_STREAM )
13
14  # step 2: make connection request to server
15  try:
16      mySocket.connect( ( HOST, PORT ) )
17  except socket.error:
18      print "Call to connect failed"
19
20  print "Connected to Server"
21
22  # step 3: transmit data via connection
23  serverMessage = mySocket.recv( 1024 )
24
25  while serverMessage != "SERVER>>> TERMINATE":
26
27      if not serverMessage:
28          break
29
30      print serverMessage
31      clientMessage = raw_input( "CLIENT>>> " )
32      mySocket.send( "CLIENT>>> " + clientMessage )
33      serverMessage = mySocket.recv( 1024 )
34
35  # step 4: close connection
36  print "Connection terminated"
37  mySocket.close()
```

Fig. 20.3   Client-side application that uses connection-oriented transmission to transmit data via sockets. (Part 1 of 2.)

```
Waiting for connection
Connection 1 received from: 127.0.0.1
```

```
Attempting connection
Connected to Server
SERVER>>> Connection successful
CLIENT>>> Hi to person at server
```

```
Waiting for connection
Connection 1 received from: 127.0.0.1
CLIENT>>> Hi to person at server
SERVER>>> Hi back to you--client!
```

```
Attempting connection
Connected to Server
SERVER>>> Connection successful
CLIENT>>> Hi to person at server
SERVER>>> Hi back to you--client!
CLIENT>>> TERMINATE
```

```
Waiting for connection
Connection 1 received from: 127.0.0.1
CLIENT>>> Hi to person at server
SERVER>>> Hi back to you--client!
Connection terminated
Waiting for connection
```

Fig. 20.3   Client-side application that uses connection-oriented transmission to transmit data via sockets. (Part 2 of 2.)

If the connection is successful, line 16 prints a message indicating a successful connection. The **socket** method **recv** (line 23) receives a message from the server (i.e., **"SERVER>>> Connection successful"**). The **while** loop (lines 25–33) executes until the client receives the message **"SERVER>>> TERMINATE"**. As in the server program, line 27 examines each received message to determine whether the server has closed the connection. If so, the **break** statement exits the **while** loop (line 28).

Each iteration of the loop prints the message sent by the server (line 30) and calls function **raw_input** to read a string from the user (line 31). Line 32 sends this string to the server by invoking **socket** method **send**. The client then receives the next message from the server (line 33). When the transmission is complete, line 37 closes the **socket** object **mySocket**.

The programs in Fig. 20.2 and Fig. 20.3 provide basic client/server communication capabilities. More advanced capabilities require more complicated code. For example, the programs we present provide no ability for a server to handle more than one message from a client concurrently or messages larger than 1024 bytes. These issues begin to reveal the intricacies of writing professional networking applications.

20.6 Connectionless Client/Server Interaction with Datagrams

Up to this point, we have discussed connection-oriented, streams-based transmission. Now, we consider connectionless transmission using datagrams.

Connection-oriented transmission is similar to interaction over a telephone system, in which a user dials a number and is *connected* to the telephone of the party they wish to connect. The system maintains the connection for the duration of the phone call, regardless of whether the users are speaking.

By contrast, connectionless transmission via datagrams more closely resembles the way the postal service carries and delivers the mail. Connectionless transmission bundles and sends information in packets, called *datagrams*, which can be thought of as posted letters. If a large message will not fit in one envelope, that message is broken into separate message pieces and placed in separate, sequentially numbered envelopes. All the letters are mailed at once. The letters might arrive in order, out of order or not at all (although the last case is rare, it does happen). The person at the receiving end reassembles the message pieces into sequential order before attempting to interpret the message. If the message is small enough to fit in one envelope, the sequencing problem is eliminated, but it is still possible that the message will never arrive. One difference between datagrams and postal mail is that duplicates of datagrams can arrive on the receiving computer.

The programs of Fig. 20.4 and Fig. 20.5 use datagrams to send packets ("envelopes" that contain "messages") of information between a client application and a server application. In the client application, the user types a message and presses *Enter*. The client places the message in a datagram packet that is sent to the server. The server receives the packet and displays the packet's information, then *echoes*, or returns, the packet back to the client. When the client receives the packet, the client displays the packet's information.

The server code in Fig. 20.4 defines one **socket** object that sends and receives datagram (**SOCK_DGRAM**) packets. Note that the **socket** type is **SOCK_DGRAM**, which indicates that **mySocket** is a socket that uses datagrams for transmitting data. Line 14 binds the socket to a port (**5000**) in which a server can receive packets from clients, and clients sending packets to this server specify port **5000** in the packets they send.

```python
1   # Fig. 20.4: fig20_04.py
2   # Set up a server that will receive packets from a
3   # client and send packets to a client.
4
5   import socket
6
7   HOST = "127.0.0.1"
8   PORT = 5000
9
10  # step 1: create socket
11  mySocket = socket.socket( socket.AF_INET, socket.SOCK_DGRAM )
```

Fig. 20.4   Server-side application that uses connectionless-transmission to transmit data via datagrams. (Part 1 of 2.)

```
12
13    # step 2: bind socket
14    mySocket.bind( ( HOST, PORT ) )
15
16    while 1:
17
18        # step 3: receive packet
19        packet, address = mySocket.recvfrom( 1024 )
20
21        print "Packet received:"
22        print "From host:", address[ 0 ]
23        print "Host port:", address[ 1 ]
24        print "Length:", len( packet )
25        print "Containing:"
26        print "\t" + packet
27
28        # step 4: echo packet back to client
29        print "\nEcho data to client...",
30        mySocket.sendto( packet, address )
31        print "Packet sent\n"
32
33    mySocket.close()
```

```
Packet received:
From host: 127.0.0.1
Host port: 1645
Length: 20
Containing:
        first message packet

Echo data to client... Packet sent
```

Fig. 20.4   Server-side application that uses connectionless-transmission to transmit data via datagrams. (Part 2 of 2.)

The **while** loop in lines 16–31 receives packets from the client. First, line 19 waits for a packet to arrive. Method *recvfrom* blocks until a packet arrives. Once a packet arrives, **recvfrom** returns a string representing the data received and the address of the socket sending the data. The server then prints a message to the screen that contains the address of the client and the data the client sent.

Line 30 calls **socket** method **sendto** to echo the data back to the client. The method's first argument, **packet**, specifies the data to be sent. The second argument, **address**, is a tuple that indicates the client computer's Internet address to which the packet will be sent and the port on which the server waits to receive packets.

The client (Fig. 20.5) code is similar to the server code; however, the client sends packets only when the user enters a message to send, then presses the *Enter* key. The **while** loop in lines 13–29 uses method **sendto** (line 18) to send packets to the server, and uses method **recvfrom** (line 22) to wait for packets. Method **recvfrom** blocks until a packet arrives.

```
 1   # Fig. 20.5: fig20_05.py
 2   # Set up a client that will send packets to a
 3   # server and receive packets from a server.
 4
 5   import socket
 6
 7   HOST = "127.0.0.1"
 8   PORT = 5000
 9
10   # step 1: create socket
11   mySocket = socket.socket( socket.AF_INET, socket.SOCK_DGRAM )
12
13   while 1:
14
15       # step 2: send packet
16       packet = raw_input( "Packet>>>" )
17       print "\nSending packet containing:", packet
18       mySocket.sendto( packet, ( HOST, PORT ) )
19       print "Packet sent\n"
20
21       # step 3: receive packet back from server
22       packet, address = mySocket.recvfrom( 1024 )
23
24       print "Packet received:"
25       print "From host:", address[ 0 ]
26       print "Host port:", address[ 1 ]
27       print "Length:", len( packet )
28       print "Containing:"
29       print "\t" + packet + "\n"
30
31   mySocket.close()
```

```
Packet>>>first message packet

Sending packet containing: first message packet
Packet sent

Packet received:
From host: 127.0.0.1
Host port: 5000
Length: 20
Containing:
        first message packet

Packet>>>
```

Fig. 20.5   Client-side application that uses connectionless-transmission to transmit data via datagrams.

20.7 Client/Server Tic-Tac-Toe Using a Multithreaded Server

In this section, we present our capstone networking example—the popular game Tic-Tac-Toe, implemented with stream sockets with client/server techniques. The program consists

of a **TicTacToeServer** class (Fig. 20.6) that allows two **TicTacToeClient**s
(Fig. 20.7) to connect to the server and play the game. We display the output in Fig. 20.7.
When the server receives a client's request for connection, the server creates an object of
class **Player** (Fig. 20.6) to handle the request in a separate thread of execution. This enables the server to handle requests from both clients, which allows each to play the game
independently. The server assigns "X" to the first client that connects (player X makes the
first move), and then assigns "O" to the second client. Throughout the game, the server
maintains information regarding the status of the game board so that the server can validate
players' requested moves. Each **TicTacToeClient** maintains a GUI version of the Tic-
Tac-Toe board on which the game is displayed. The clients can place a mark only in an
empty square on the board.

```python
1   # Fig. 20.6: fig20_06.py
2   # Class TicTacToeServer maintains a game of Tic-Tac-Toe
3   # for two clients, each managed by a Player thread.
4
5   import socket
6   import threading
7
8   class Player( threading.Thread ):
9       """Thread to manage each Tic-Tac-Toe client individually"""
10
11      def __init__( self, connection, server, number ):
12          """Initialize thread and setup variables"""
13
14          threading.Thread.__init__( self )
15
16          # specify player's mark
17          if number == 0:
18              self.mark = "X"
19          else:
20              self.mark = "O"
21
22          self.connection = connection
23          self.server = server
24          self.number = number
25
26      def otherPlayerMoved( self, location ):
27          """Notify client of opponent's last move"""
28
29          self.connection.send( "Opponent moved." )
30          self.connection.send( str( location ) )
31
32      def run( self ):
33          """Play the game"""
34
35          # send client message indicating its mark (X or O)
36          self.server.display( "Player %s connected." % self.mark )
37          self.connection.send( self.mark )
38
```

Fig. 20.6 Server-side application of client/server Tic-Tac-Toe program. (Part 1 of 4.)

```
39              # wait for another player to arrive
40              if self.mark == "X":
41                  self.connection.send( "Waiting for another player..." )
42                  self.server.gameBeginEvent.wait()
43                  self.connection.send(
44                      "Other player connected. Your move." )
45              else:
46                  self.server.gameBeginEvent.wait()   # wait for server
47                  self.connection.send( "Waiting for first move..." )
48
49              # play game until over
50              while not self.server.gameOver():
51
52                  # get more location from client
53                  location = self.connection.recv( 1 )
54
55                  if not location:
56                      break
57
58                  # check for valid move
59                  if self.server.validMove( int( location ), self.number ):
60                      self.server.display( "loc: " + location )
61                      self.connection.send( "Valid move." )
62                  else:
63                      self.connection.send( "Invalid move, try again." )
64
65              # close connection to client
66              self.connection.close()
67              self.server.display( "Game over." )
68              self.server.display( "Connection closed." )
69
70  class TicTacToeServer:
71      """Server that maintains a game of Tic-Tac-Toe for two clients"""
72
73      def __init__( self ):
74          """Initialize variables and setup server"""
75
76          HOST = ""
77          PORT = 5000
78
79          self.board = []
80          self.currentPlayer = 0
81          self.turnCondition = threading.Condition()
82          self.gameBeginEvent = threading.Event()
83
84          for i in range( 9 ):
85              self.board.append( None )
86
87          # setup server socket
88          self.server = socket.socket( socket.AF_INET,
89              socket.SOCK_STREAM )
90          self.server.bind( ( HOST, PORT ) )
91          self.display( "Server awaiting connections..." )
```

Fig. 20.6 Server-side application of client/server Tic-Tac-Toe program. (Part 2 of 4.)

```
92
93      def execute( self ):
94          """Play the game--create and start both Player threads"""
95
96          self.players = []
97
98          # wait for and accept two client connections
99          for i in range( 2 ):
100             self.server.listen( 2 )
101             connection, address = self.server.accept()
102
103             # assign each client to a Player thread
104             self.players.append( Player( connection, self, i ) )
105             self.players[ -1 ].start()
106
107         self.server.close()    # no more connections to wait for
108
109         # players are suspended until player 0 connects
110         # resume players now
111         self.gameBeginEvent.set()
112
113     def display( self, message ):
114         """Display a message on the server"""
115
116         print message
117
118     def validMove( self, location, player ):
119         """Determine if a move is valid--if so, make move"""
120
121         # only one move can be made at a time
122         self.turnCondition.acquire()
123
124         # while not current player, must wait for turn
125         while player != self.currentPlayer:
126             self.turnCondition.wait()
127
128         # make move if location is not occupied
129         if not self.isOccupied( location ):
130
131             # set move on board
132             if self.currentPlayer == 0:
133                 self.board[ location ] = "X"
134             else:
135                 self.board[ location ] = "O"
136
137             # change current player
138             self.currentPlayer = ( self.currentPlayer + 1 ) % 2
139             self.players[ self.currentPlayer ].otherPlayerMoved(
140                 location )
141
142             # tell waiting player to continue
143             self.turnCondition.notify()
144             self.turnCondition.release()
```

Fig. 20.6   Server-side application of client/server Tic-Tac-Toe program. (Part 3 of 4.)

```
145
146                  # valid move
147                  return 1
148
149              # invalid move
150              else:
151                  self.turnCondition.notify()
152                  self.turnCondition.release()
153                  return 0
154
155          def isOccupied( self, location ):
156              """Determine if a space is occupied"""
157
158              return self.board[ location ]    # an empty space is None
159
160          def gameOver( self ):
161              """Determine if the game is over"""
162
163              # place code here testing for a game winner
164              # left as an exercise for the reader
165              return 0
166
167  def main():
168      TicTacToeServer().execute()
169
170  if __name__ == "__main__":
171      main()
```

```
Server awaiting connections...
Player X connected.
Player O connected.
loc: 0
loc: 4
loc: 3
loc: 1
loc: 7
loc: 5
loc: 2
loc: 8
loc: 6
```

Fig. 20.6   Server-side application of client/server Tic-Tac-Toe program. (Part 4 of 4.)

We now discuss the server-side application (Fig. 20.6). Line 168 instantiates a **Tic-TacToeServer** object and invokes its **execute** method. The **TicTacToeServer** constructor (lines 73–91) creates data member **currentPlayer** and condition variable **turnCondition**. The server uses these members to restrict access to method **valid-Move**—ensuring that only the current player can make a move. Line 82 creates **gameBeginEvent**—a **threading.Event** object used to synchronize the start of the game. Lines 84–85 then initialize the Tic-Tac-Toe board—a list of nine elements. Note that each location of the board is initialized to **None**, which indicates that the space is not yet occupied by either player. Locations are maintained as numbers from 0 to 8 (0 through 2 for the first row, 3 through 5 for the second row and 6 through 8 for the third row). Lines 88–90 prepare the **socket** on which the server listens for player connections and display a message that the server is ready.

Method **execute** (lines 93–111) loops twice, waiting each time for a connection from a client. When the server receives a connection, the server creates a **Player** object (lines 8–68) to manage the connection as a separate thread. The **Player** constructor (lines 11–24) takes as arguments the **socket** object representing the connection to the client, the **TicTacToeServer** object and a character indicating the player—X or O. Line 14 initializes the thread.

After the server creates each **Player** (line 104), the server invokes **Player**'s **start** method (line 105). The **Player**'s **run** method (lines 32–68) controls the information that is sent to and received from the client. First, the method passes to the client the character that the client will place on the board when a move is made, then the method sends a message that informs the client about the successful connection (lines 36–37). Lines 40–44 then cause player X to block until the game can begin (i.e., player O has joined). Similarly, lines 45–47 cause player O to block until the server begins the game. When both players have joined the game, the server closes its socket (line 107) and begins the game by calling **Event** method **set** (line 111).

At this point, each **Player**'s **run** method executes its **while** loop (lines 50–63). Each iteration of this **while** loop receives a string that represents the location where on the board the client wants to place a mark and invokes **TicTacToeServer** method **validMove** to determine whether the suggested move is legal. Lines 61 and 63 send a message to the client indicating whether the move was valid. The game continues until **TicTacToeServer** method **gameOver** (lines 160–165) indicates that the game has ended. Once the game terminates, lines 66–68 close the connection to the clients and display a message on the server. Note that the logic contained in method **gameOver**, which should determine if the game was won, lost or a draw, is left to the reader as an exercise.

Method **validMove** (lines 118–153 in class **TicTacToeServer**) uses condition variable methods **acquire** and **release** to permit only one player to move at a time. This prevents both players from simultaneously modifying the state information of the game. If the **Player** attempting to validate a move is not the current player (i.e., the one allowed to make a move), the **Player** is placed in a *wait* state until it is that player's turn to move. If another mark already occupies the position for the move, method **validMove** returns **0** (line 153). Otherwise, the server places a mark for the player in its local representation of the board and updates variable **currentPlayer**. The server then calls **Player** method **otherPlayerMoved** (lines 26–30) so the client can be notified, invokes the **notify** method so the waiting **Player** can validate a move and returns **1** to indicate that the move is valid (lines 143–147).

Next, we discuss the client-side application. When a **TicTacToeClient** (Fig. 20.7) begins execution, it creates a **Pmw ScrolledText** that displays messages from the server to the client and creates a representation of the board using nine **Tkinter Button**s. Class **TicTacToeClient** inherits from class **threading.Thread**. This inheritance enables a separate thread to be used for reading messages that are sent from the server to the client. The script's **run** method (lines 54–82) opens a connection to the server. After the client establishes a connection to the server, the method reads the mark character (X or O) from the server (line 65), initializes attribute **myTurn** to **0** (line 68) and loops continually to read messages from the server (lines 71–77). The messages are passed to the script's **processMessage** method for processing. When the game is over (i.e., the server closes the connection), lines 84–192 close the connection to each client and display a message to the user.

Method **processMessage** (lines 84–115) interprets messages from the server. If the message received is the string **"Valid move."**, the client displays the message **"Valid move, please wait."**, sets its mark in the square that the user clicked (indicated by attribute **currentSquare**) and colors the square white. If the client receives the message **"Invalid move, try again."**, the client displays the message and sets attribute **myTurn** to **1** so the user can click a different square. If the client receives the message **"Opponent moved."**, the client receives an integer from the server indicating where the opponent moved. The client then places the opponent's mark in that square of the board, colors the square gray, displays a message to the user and sets **myTurn** to **1**. If the client receives the message **"Other player connected. Your move."**, the client displays the message and sets **myTurn** to **1**. Note that this message is sent to player X only when player O initially connects (Fig. 20.6, lines 42–43). If the client receives any other message, the client displays that message.

When the player clicks a space on the board (a **Tkinter Button**), method **send-ClickedSquare** is invoked. Method **sendClickedSquare** (lines 117–124) first tests for whether it is the player's turn. If so, line 121 obtains the name of the button pressed by invoking **Widget** method **winfo_name** and stores the value in variable **name**. Lines 122–124 then update attribute **currentSquare**, send the move to the server and set attribute **myTurn** to **0**, so that the player cannot make another move until the client has received feedback from the server.

```
1   # Fig. 20.7: fig20_07.py
2   # Client for Tic-Tac-Toe program.
3
4   import socket
5   import threading
6   from Tkinter import *
7   import Pmw
8
9   class TicTacToeClient( Frame, threading.Thread ):
10      """Client that plays a game of Tic-Tac-Toe"""
11
12      def __init__( self ):
13         """Create GUI and play game"""
14
15         threading.Thread.__init__( self )
16
17         # initialize GUI
18         Frame.__init__( self )
19         Pmw.initialise()
20         self.pack( expand = YES, fill = BOTH )
21         self.master.title( "Tic-Tac-Toe Client" )
22         self.master.geometry( "250x325" )
23
```

Fig. 20.7   Client-side application of a client/server Tic-Tac-Toe program. (Part 1 of 5.)

```
24              self.id = Label( self, anchor = W )
25              self.id.grid( columnspan = 3, sticky = W+E+N+S )
26
27              self.board = []
28
29              # create and add all buttons to the board
30              for i in range( 9 ):
31                 newButton = Button( self, font = "Courier 20 bold",
32                    height = 1, width = 1, relief = GROOVE,
33                    name = str( i ) )
34                 newButton.bind( "<Button-1>", self.sendClickedSquare )
35                 self.board.append( newButton )
36
37              current = 0
38
39              # display buttons in 3x3 grid beginning with grid's row one
40              for i in range( 1, 4 ):
41
42                 for j in range( 3 ):
43                    self.board[ current ].grid( row = i, column = j,
44                       sticky = W+E+N+S )
45                    current += 1
46
47              # area for server messages
48              self.display = Pmw.ScrolledText( self, text_height = 10,
49                 text_width = 35, vscrollmode = "static" )
50              self.display.grid( row = 4, columnspan = 3 )
51
52              self.start()   # run thread
53
54           def run( self ):
55              """Control thread to allow continuous updated display"""
56
57              # setup connection to server
58              HOST = "127.0.0.1"
59              PORT = 5000
60              self.connection = socket.socket( socket.AF_INET,
61                 socket.SOCK_STREAM )
62              self.connection.connect( ( HOST, PORT ) )
63
64              # first get player's mark ( X or O )
65              self.myMark = self.connection.recv( 1 )
66              self.id.config( text = 'You are player "%s"' % self.myMark )
67
68              self.myTurn = 0
69
70              # receive messages sent to client
71              while 1:
72                 message = self.connection.recv( 34 )
73
74                 if not message:
75                    break
76
```

Fig. 20.7   Client-side application of a client/server Tic-Tac-Toe program. (Part 2 of 5.)

```
 77                 self.processMessage( message )
 78
 79         self.connection.close()
 80         self.display.insert( END, "Game over.\n" )
 81         self.display.insert( END, "Connection closed.\n" )
 82         self.display.yview( END )
 83
 84     def processMessage( self, message ):
 85         """Interpret server message to perform necessary actions"""
 86
 87         # valid move occurred
 88         if message == "Valid move.":
 89             self.display.insert( END, "Valid move, please wait.\n" )
 90             self.display.yview( END )
 91
 92             # set mark
 93             self.board[ self.currentSquare ].config(
 94                 text = self.myMark, bg = "white" )
 95
 96         # invalid move occurred
 97         elif message == "Invalid move, try again.":
 98             self.display.insert( END, message + "\n" )
 99             self.display.yview( END )
100             self.myTurn = 1
101
102         # opponent moved
103         elif message == "Opponent moved.":
104
105             # get move location
106             location = int( self.connection.recv( 1 ) )
107
108             # update board
109             if self.myMark == "X":
110                 self.board[ location ].config( text = "O",
111                     bg = "gray" )
112             else:
113                 self.board[ location ].config( text = "X",
114                     bg = "gray" )
115
116             self.display.insert( END, message + " Your turn.\n" )
117             self.display.yview( END )
118             self.myTurn = 1
119
120         # other player's turn
121         elif message == "Other player connected. Your move.":
122             self.display.insert( END, message + "\n" )
123             self.display.yview( END )
124             self.myTurn = 1
125
126         # simply display message
127         else:
128             self.display.insert( END, message + "\n" )
129             self.display.yview( END )
```

Fig. 20.7   Client-side application of a client/server Tic-Tac-Toe program. (Part 3 of 5.)

```
130
131      def sendClickedSquare( self, event ):
132          """Send attempted move to server"""
133
134          if self.myTurn:
135              name = event.widget.winfo_name()
136              self.currentSquare = int( name )
137
138              # send location to server
139              self.connection.send( name )
140              self.myTurn = 0
141
142  def main():
143      TicTacToeClient().mainloop()
144
145  if __name__ == "__main__":
146      main()
```

Fig. 20.7   Client-side application of a client/server Tic-Tac-Toe program. (Part 4 of 5.)

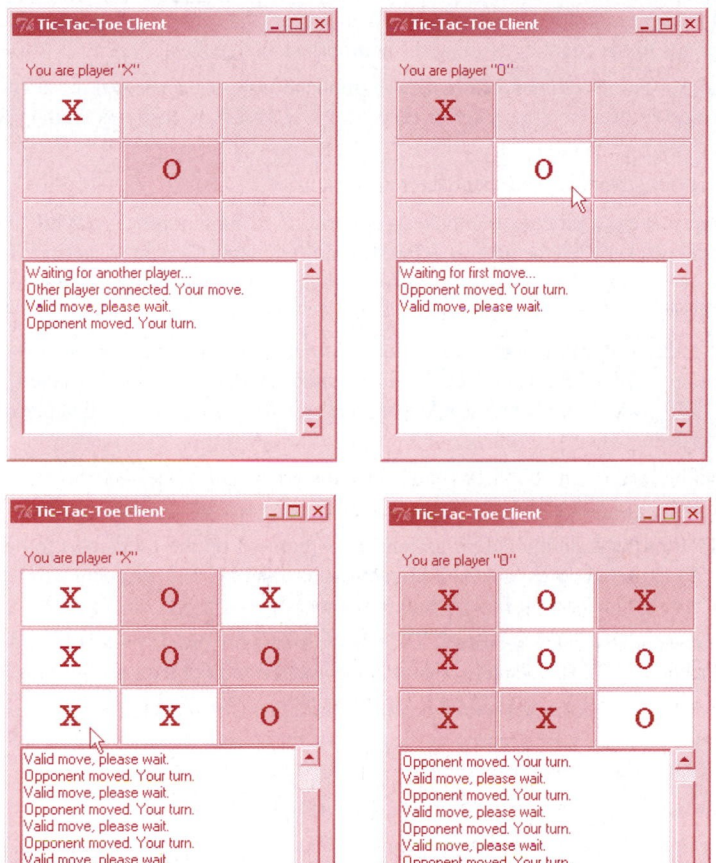

Fig. 20.7 Client-side application of a client/server Tic-Tac-Toe program. (Part 5 of 5.)

SUMMARY

- The Internet ties the "information world" together; the Web makes the Internet easy to use while providing the flair of multimedia.

- Organizations see both the Internet and the Web as crucial to their information-systems strategies.

- Python offers a number of built-in networking capabilities that facilitate Internet-based and Web-based applications development.

- Python not only can specify parallelism through multithreading, but also can enable programs to request information over the Web and collaborate with programs running on other computers internationally.

- The client requests that some action be performed; the server performs the action and responds to the clients. A common implementation of this request-response model is between Web browsers and Web servers.

- When users select Web sites that they wish to view through a browser (the client application), the browser makes a request to the appropriate Web server (the server application). The server normally responds to the client by sending the appropriate Web pages.

- Python's socket-based communications enable applications to view networking as file I/O—a program can receive data from a socket or send data to a socket as easily as reading from a file or writing to a file.

- Python provides stream sockets and datagram sockets.

- With stream sockets, a process establishes a connection to another process. While the connection exists, data flows between the processes in continuous streams. Stream sockets provide a connection-oriented services. The protocol used for transmission is the popular Transmission Control Protocol (TCP).

- Individual packets of information transmitted over networks uses datagram sockets. This the not an efficient protocol for everyday users because, unlike TCP, the protocol uses the User Datagram Protocol (UDP), which is a connectionless service and does not guarantee that packets arrive in a particular order.

- Packets can be lost, can be duplicated and can even arrive out of sequence using the User Datagram Protocol.

- With UDP, significant additional programming is required on the user's part to deal with these problems (if the user chooses to do so). Stream sockets and the TCP protocol will be the most desirable for the vast majority of Python programmers.

- The Internet employs many protocols. One of the more important protocols is the HyperText Transfer Protocol (HTTP), which is crucial to the transmission of data on the Web.

- HTTP uses URLs (Uniform Resource Locators, also called Universal Resource Locators) to locate content on the Internet. URLs represent files or directories and can represent complex tasks, such as database lookups and Internet searches.

- If you know a URL address, you can access data using **http**.

- Module **urlparse** provides functions to parse URLs, as well as other functions that facilitate the manipulation of URLs.

- Function **urlparse.urlparse** takes a string as input and returns a six-element tuple. The first element of the tuple is the addressing scheme. Entering a URL beginning with **http** directs the Web server to retrieve and transfer the requested URL document.

- Module **urllib** provides methods for accessing data referred to by a URL.

- Module **urllib** function **urlopen** to retrieve the file. The function causes a DNS (Domain Name System or Service) lookup to be performed. DNS translates a domain name, or URL, into an IP address, a unique identifier for a computer on a network. The module requests documents from the Web server. If successful, **urlopen** returns an object. This object behaves like a Python file object.

- Typically, with TCP and stream sockets, a server "waits" for a connection request from a client. Often, the server program contains a control structure or block of code that executes continuously until the server receives a request. On receiving a request, the server establishes a connection with the client. The server then uses this connection to handle future requests from that client and to transmit data to and from the client.

- The establishment of a server with TCP and stream sockets in Python requires module **socket**, which contains the function and class definitions that provide the capabilities to build programs that communicate over a network.

- A call to the **socket** constructor, such as **socket.socket**(*family*, *type*) creates a socket using the specified address family and type. Typically, argument *family* is either **AF_INET** or **AF_UNIX**.

The typical values for argument *type* are **SOCK_STREAM** (for stream sockets) and **SOCK_DGRAM** (for datagram sockets). These constants are defined in module **socket**.

- A call to a **socket** object's **bind** method, such as **socket**.bind(*address*) binds (assigns) the socket to a specified *address*. For a socket created by family **AF_INET**, *address* must be a two-element tuple in the form (*host*, *port*), in which *host* is a string representing the machine's hostname or IP address and *port* is a port number (i.e., integer). The preceding statement reserves a port in which the server waits for connections from clients. These clients ask to connect to the server on this port. Method **bind** raises the exception **socket.error** if the port is already in use, the hostname is incorrect or the port is reserved.

- Once the socket is bound to an address, the socket must prepare to receive connection requests. To achieve this, the socket object calls **socket** method **listen** as **socket**.listen(*backlog*) in which *backlog* specifies the maximum number of clients that can request connections to the server. The value of *backlog* should be at least 1. As connection requests are received, they are queued. If the queue is full, connection requests are refused.

- The server **socket** waits for a client to request a connection via **socket** method **accept**. The **socket** waits indefinitely (or blocks) when it calls method **accept**. When a client requests a connection, the method establishes the connection and returns to the server. Method **accept** returns a two-element tuple of the form (*connection*, *address*). The first element of the returned tuple (*connection*) is a new **socket** object that the server uses to communicate with the client. The second element (*address*) corresponds to the client's Internet address.

- The server and the client communicate (transmit data) using methods **socket** and **recv**.

- The server sends information to the client by invoking **socket** method **send** and passing the information in the form of a string. Method **send** returns the number of bytes sent.

- The server receives information from the client using **socket** method **recv**. When calling **recv**, the server must specify an integer that corresponds to the maximum amount of data that can be received through one invocation of that method. Method **recv**, which blocks as it receives data, returns a string representing the received data. If the amount of data sent is greater than **recv** allows, the data is truncated, and **recv** returns the maximum amount of data specified. The excess data is buffered on the receiving end. On a subsequent call to **recv**, the excess data is removed from the buffer (along with any additional data the client may have sent since the previous call to **recv**).

- The server closes the connection by invoking the **close** method on the **socket**.

- The IP address **127.0.0.1** always refers to the local machine (referred to as **localhost**).

- Connection-oriented transmission is similar to interaction over a telephone system, in which a user dials a number and is connected to the telephone of the party they wish to connect. The system maintains the connection for the duration of the phone call, regardless of whether the users are speaking.

- Connectionless transmission via datagrams resembles the way the postal service carries and delivers the mail. Connectionless transmission bundles and sends information in packets, called datagrams. If a large message will not fit in one envelope, that message is broken into separate message pieces and placed in separate, sequentially numbered envelopes. The letters might arrive in order, out of order or not at all.

- The **recvfrom** method blocks until a packet arrives.

- The **socket** method **sendto**'s first argument specifies the data to be sent. The second argument is a tuple that indicates the Internet address to which the packet will be sent and the port on which the server waits to receive packets.

TERMINOLOGY

accept method of **socket**	**listen** method of **socket**
address	**recv** method of **socket**
addressing scheme	**recvfrom** method of **socket**
AF_INET family	**send** method of **socket**
AF_UNIX family	**sendto** method of **socket**
backlog	server
bind method of **socket**	**SOCK_DGRAM** type
client	**SOCK_STREAM** type
client connection	socket
close method of **socket**	socket-based communications
connect method of **socket**	**socket.error** exception
connection	stream
connection-oriented transmission	stream-based transmission
connection port	stream socket
connectionless transmission	Transmission Control Protocol (TCP)
datagram	Uniform (or Universal) Resource Locator (URL)
datagram socket	**urllib** module
Domain Name System or Service (DNS)	**urlopen** method
HyperText Transfer Protocol (HTTP)	**urlparse** method
IP address	User Datagram Protocol (UDP)

SELF-REVIEW EXERCISES

20.1 Fill in the blanks in each of the following statements:

a) Module _____ provides methods for accessing data over the Internet.

b) Method **connect** accepts two arguments that represent the _____ and the _____ of the server.

c) Function _____ takes a string as input and returns a six-element tuple, which includes the addressing scheme.

d) Module _____ contains the function and class definitions that provide the capabilities to build socket-based programs that communicate with one another over a network.

e) Type _____ is used to create sockets for applications that use datagrams to transmit data.

f) Method _____ takes as an argument the maximum number of clients that can request connections to a server.

g) The two types of sockets we discussed in this chapter are _____ sockets and _____ sockets.

h) Method **recvfrom** _____ until a packet arrives.

i) The acronym UDP stands for _____.

j) _____ translates a domain name, or URL, into an IP address.

20.2 State whether each of the following is *true* or *false*. If *false*, explain why.

a) UDP is a connection-oriented protocol.

b) The IP address **127.0.0.1** refers to the local machine.

c) A server waits at a port for connection requests from clients.

d) Datagram packet transmission over a network is reliable—packets are guaranteed to arrive in sequence.

e) A socket's **send** method accepts only a string argument.

f) The server **socket** waits for a client to request a connection via **socket** method **listen**.

g) Port numbers can be between only **0** and **1024**.

h) A failed connection attempt raises the **socket.error** exception.

i) Method **recv**, which blocks as it receives data, returns the number of bytes received.

j) The Internet offers many protocols other than HTTP.

ANSWERS TO SELF-REVIEW EXERCISES

20.1   a) **urllib**. b) host, port. c) **urlparse.urlparse**. d) **socket**. e) **SOCK_DGRAM**.
f) **listen**. g) stream, datagram. h) blocks. i) User Datagram Protocol. j) Domain Name System or
Service (DNS).

20.2   a) False. UDP is a connectionless protocol and TCP is a connection-oriented protocol.
b) True. c) True. d) False. Packets could be lost and packets can arrive out of order. e) True. f) False.
The server **socket** waits for a client to request a connection via **socket** method **accept**. g) False.
Port numbers can be between 0 and 65535. h) True. i) False. Method **recv** returns a string representing the received data. j) True.

EXERCISES

20.3   Distinguish between connection-oriented network services and connectionless network services.

20.4   List under what circumstances a **socket.error** exception is raised.

20.5   Modify the client-server communication program of Fig. 20.2 and Fig. 20.3 to use **fork** to
handle client connections.

20.6   Create a multithreaded client/server program. Each client should send a message to the server. The server then echoes the message, in all uppercase letters, back to the client.

20.7   Write an application that uses a socket-based connection to enable a server to receive from a
client the name of a file; the server should return either the file's contents to the client, or a message
that the file does not exist.

20.8   *(Modifications to the Multithreaded Tic-Tac-Toe Program)* The programs of Fig. 20.6 and
Fig. 20.7 implemented a multithreaded, client/server version of the game Tic-Tac-Toe. Our goal in
developing this game was to demonstrate a multithreaded server that could process multiple connections from clients at the same time. The server in the example is really a mediator between the two
clients—it makes sure that each move is valid and that each client moves in the proper order. The
server does not determine who won or lost or if there was a draw. Modify the **TicTacToeServer**
class to test for a win, loss or draw on each move in the game. The server should send to each client
a message to each client that indicates the result of the game when the game is over.

21

Security

Objectives

- To understand the basic concepts of security.
- To understand public-key cryptography.
- To learn about popular security protocols, such as SSL.
- To understand digital signatures, digital certificates, certificate authorities and public-key infrastructure.
- To understand Python programming security issues.
- To learn to write restricted Python code.
- To become aware of various threats to secure systems.

Three may keep a secret, if two of them are dead.
Benjamin Franklin

Attack—Repeat—Attack.
William Frederick Halsey, Jr.

Private information is practically the source of every large modern fortune.
Oscar Wilde

There must be security for all—or not one is safe.
The Day the Earth Stood Still, screenplay by Edmund H. North

No government can be long secure without formidable opposition.
Benjamin Disraeli

Outline

21.1 Introduction

The explosion of e-business is forcing companies and consumers to focus on Internet and network security. Consumers are buying products, trading stocks and banking online.

They are submitting their credit card numbers, Social Security numbers and other confidential information to vendors through Web sites. Businesses are sending confidential information to clients and vendors, using the Internet. At the same time, an increasing number of security attacks are taking place on e-businesses, and companies and customers are vulnerable to these attacks. Data theft and cyber attacks can corrupt files and even shut down businesses. Preventing or protecting against such attacks is crucial to the success of e-business. In this chapter, we explore Internet security, including securing electronic transactions and networks. We discuss secure Python programming code. We also examine the fundamentals of secure business and how to secure e-commerce transactions using current technologies.

e-Fact 21.1

According to a study by International Data Corporation (IDC), organizations spent $6.2 billion on security consulting in 1999, and IDC expects the market to reach $14.8 billion by 2003.[1]

Modern computer security addresses the problems and concerns of protecting electronic communications and maintaining *network security*. There are four fundamental requirements for a successful, secure transaction: *privacy*, *integrity*, *authentication* and *nonrepudiation*. *The privacy issue is*: How do you ensure that the information you transmit over the Internet has not been captured or passed on to a third party without your knowledge? *The integrity issue is*: How do you ensure that the information you send or receive has not been compromised or altered? *The authentication issue is*: How do the sender and receiver of a message prove their identities to each other? *The nonrepudiation issue is*: How do you legally prove that a message was sent or received?

In addition to these requirements, network security addresses the issue of *availability*: How do we ensure that the network and the computer systems to which it connects will stay in continuous operation?

Python applications potentially can access files on the local computer on which the code is run. This chapter explains how a programmer can write secure, *restricted environment* Python code.

e-Fact 21.2

According to Forrester Research, it is predicted that organizations will spend 55% more on security in 2002 than they spent in 2000.[2]

We encourage you to visit the Web resources provided in Section 21.16 to learn more about the latest developments in e-business security. These resources include many informative and entertaining demos.

21.2 Ancient Ciphers to Modern Cryptosystems

The channels through which data passes are inherently unsecure; therefore, any private information passed through these channels must somehow be protected. To secure informa-

---

1. A. Harrison, "Xerox Unit Farms Out Security in $20M Deal," *Computerworld* 5 June 2000: 24.
2. "What the Experts are Saying About Security: Facts and Quotes," from an OKENA company Press kit.

tion, data can be encrypted. *Cryptography* transforms data using a *cipher*, or *cryptosystem*—a mathematical algorithm for encrypting messages. ("Algorithm" is a computer-science term for "procedure.") A *key*—a string of alpha-numeric characters that acts as a password—is input to the cipher. The cipher uses the key to make data incomprehensible to all but the sender and intended the receivers. Unencrypted data is called *plaintext*; encrypted data is called *ciphertext*. The algorithm is responsible for encrypting data, while the key acts as a variable—using different keys results in different ciphertext. Only the intended receivers should have the corresponding key to *decrypt* the ciphertext into plaintext.

Cryptographic ciphers have been used throughout history, as first recorded by the ancient Egyptians, to conceal and protect valuable information. In ancient cryptography, messages were encrypted by hand, usually with a method based on the alphabetic letters of the message. The two main types of ciphers were *substitution ciphers* and *transposition ciphers*. In a substitution cipher, every occurrence of a given letter is replaced by a different letter; for example, if every "a" is replaced by a "b," every "b" by a "c," etc., the word "security" would encrypt to "tfdvsjuz." The first prominent substitution cipher was credited to Julius Caesar and is referred to today as the *Caesar Cipher*. Using the Caesar Cipher, every instance of a letter is encrypted by replacing the letter in the alphabet three places to the right. For example, using the Caesar Cipher, the word "security" would encrypt to "vhfxulwb."

In a transposition cipher, the ordering of the letters is shifted; for example, if every other letter, starting with "s," in the word "security" creates the first word in the ciphertext, and the remaining letters create the second word in the ciphertext, the word "security" would encrypt to "scrt euiy." Complicated ciphers combine substitution and transposition ciphers. For example, using the substitution cipher first, followed by the transposition cipher, the word "security" would encrypt to "tdsu fvjz." The problem with many historical ciphers is that their security relied on the sender and receiver to remember the encryption algorithm and keep it secret. Such algorithms are called *restricted algorithms*. Restricted algorithms are not feasible to implement among a large group of people. Imagine if the security of U.S. government communications relied on every U.S. government employee to keep a secret; the encryption algorithm could easily be compromised.

Modern cryptosystems are digital. Their algorithms are based on the individual *bits* or *blocks* (a group of bits) of a message, rather than letters of the alphabet. A computer stores data as a *binary string*, which is a sequence of ones and zeros. Each digit in the sequence is called a bit. Encryption and decryption keys are binary strings with a given *key length*. For example, 128-bit encryption systems have a key length of 128 bits. Longer keys have stronger encryption; it takes more time and computing power to crack the message.

Until January 2000, the U.S. government placed restrictions on the strength of cryptosystems that could be exported from the United States by limiting the key length of the encryption algorithms. Today, the regulations on exporting products that employ cryptography are less stringent. Any cryptography product may be exported as long as the end user is not a foreign government or from a country with embargo restrictions on it.[3]

The Python module **rotor** is used to encrypt and decrypt messages. A **rotor** is a substitution cipher. Fig. 21.1 demonstrates encryption and decryption in Python. In the constructor (lines 11–41), we create a GUI with two buttons and one **Text** component. Lines 20–28 place two buttons—**Encrypt** and **Decrypt** buttons at the top of the output window.

---

3. "RSA Laboratories' Frequently Asked Questions About Today's Cryptography, Version 4.1," 2000 **<www.rsasecurity.com/rsalabs/faq>**.

Lines 30–35 add a **Text** component to the output window and set the default text to
"Text". Line 41 obtains a rotor by calling the function **newrotor** of the **rotor** module:

```
rotor.newrotor( "deitelkey", 12 )
```

Function **newrotor** takes two arguments, a key and a number of rotors, and returns a rotor
object. The first argument (the key) is used to randomly generate rotors. The second argument (number of rotors) is optional. By default, the number of rotors passed to the **newrotor** function is 6. To encrypt a character, the original character is permuted by the first
rotor. The result character of applying first rotor is then permuted by the second rotor and
so on, until all rotors are applied.

Function **encrypt** (lines 43–55) is called when the user clicks the **Encrypt** button.
Line 47 gets the text from the **Text** component. The ciphertext is obtained by passing the
plaintext to function **encrypt**

```
encryptedText = self.cipher.encrypt( text )
```

Line 55 places the encrypted text in the **Text** component.

Function **decrypt** (lines 57–69) is called when the user clicks the **Decrypt** button.
Line 61 gets the text from the **Text** component. The decrypted text is obtained by passing
the ciphertext to function **decrypt**

```
decryptedText = self.cipher.decrypt( text )
```

Line 69 places the encrypted text in the **Text** component.

```
1   # Fig. 21.01: fig21_01.py
2   # Demonstrating crypto system.
3
4   from Tkinter import *
5   import rotor
6   import string
7
8   class Crypto( Frame ):
9       """Demonstrate the cryptosystem"""
10
11      def __init__( self ):
12          """Create and grid several components into the frame"""
13
14          Frame.__init__( self )
15          self.grid( sticky = W+E+N+S )
16          self.master.title( "Python Encryption and Decryption" )
17          self.master.rowconfigure( 0, weight = 1 )
18          self.master.columnconfigure( 0, weight = 1 )
19
20          self.button1 = Button( self, text = "Encrypt",
21              width = 15, command = self.encrypt )
22
```

Fig. 21.1   Substitution cipher example using Python **rotor** module. (Part 1 of 3.)

```
23              # specify position of Button component button1
24              self.button1.grid( row = 0, column = 1, sticky = W+E+N+S )
25
26              self.button2 = Button( self, text = "Decrypt",
27                  width = 15, command = self.decrypt )
28              self.button2.grid( row = 0, column = 2, sticky = W+E+N+S )
29
30              self.text1 = Text( self, width = 30, height = 15 )
31
32              # text component spans three rows and all available space
33              self.text1.grid( row = 3, column = 1, columnspan = 2,
34                  sticky = W+E+N+S )
35              self.text1.insert( INSERT, "Text" )
36
37              # makes second row/column expand
38              self.rowconfigure( 1, weight = 1 )
39              self.columnconfigure( 1, weight = 1 )
40
41              self.cipher = rotor.newrotor( "deitelkey", 12 )
42
43          def encrypt( self ):
44              """Encrypt a text"""
45
46              # get text from Text component
47              text = self.text1.get( 1.0, END )
48              text = string.strip( text )
49
50              # encrypt text
51              encryptedText = self.cipher.encrypt( text )
52              self.text1.delete( 1.0, END )
53
54              # display encrypted text
55              self.text1.insert( END, encryptedText )
56
57          def decrypt( self ):
58              """Decrypt a text"""
59
60              # get text from Text component
61              text = self.text1.get( 1.0, END )
62              text = string.strip( text )
63
64              # decrypt text
65              decryptedText = self.cipher.decrypt( text )
66              self.text1.delete( 1.0, END )
67
68              # display decrypted text
69              self.text1.insert( END, decryptedText )
70
71      def main():
72          Crypto().mainloop()
73
74      if __name__ == "__main__":
75          main()
```

Fig. 21.1 Substitution cipher example using Python **rotor** module. (Part 2 of 3.)

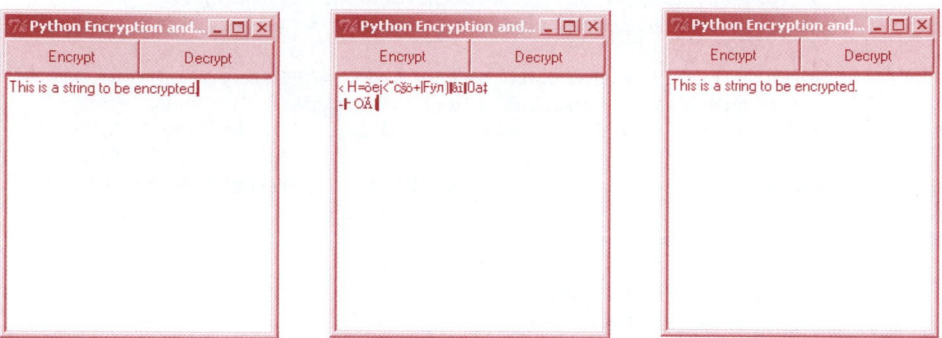

Fig. 21.1   Substitution cipher example using Python **rotor** module. (Part 3 of 3.)

21.3 Secret-Key Cryptography

In the past, organizations that wished to maintain secure computing environments used *symmetric cryptography*, also known as *secret-key cryptography*. Secret-key cryptography uses a single secret key to encrypt and decrypt a message (Fig. 21.2). In this case, the sender encrypts a message, using the secret key, then sends the encrypted message to the intended recipient. A fundamental problem with secret-key cryptography is that, before two people can communicate securely, they must find a secure way to exchange the secret key. One approach is to have the key delivered by a courier, such as a mail service or FedEx™. This approach can be feasible when two individuals communicate, but it is not efficient for securing communication in a large network, nor can it be considered completely secure. The privacy and the integrity of the message would be compromised if the key were intercepted as it is passed between the sender and the receiver over unsecure channels. Also, as both parties in the transaction use the same key to encrypt and decrypt a message, one cannot authenticate which party created the message. Finally, to keep communications private with each receiver, a sender needs a different secret key for each receiver. As a result, organizations would have huge numbers of secret keys to maintain.

An alternative approach to the key-exchange problem is to have a central authority, called a *key-distribution center* (*KDC*). The key-distribution center shares a (different) secret key with every user in the network. In this system, the key-distribution center generates a *session key* to be used for a transaction (Fig. 21.3). Next, the key-distribution center distributes the session key to the sender and receiver, encrypted with the secret key they each share with the key-distribution center. For example, say a merchant and a customer want to conduct a secure transaction. The merchant and the customer each have unique secret keys that they share with the key-distribution center. The key distribution center generates a session key for the merchant and customer to use in the transaction. The key-distribution center then sends the session key for the transaction to the merchant, encrypted with the secret key the merchant already shares with the center. The key-distribution center sends the same session key for the transaction to the customer, encrypted with the secret key the customer already shares with the key-distribution center. Once the merchant and the customer have the session key for the transaction, they can communicate with each other, encrypting their messages using the shared session key.

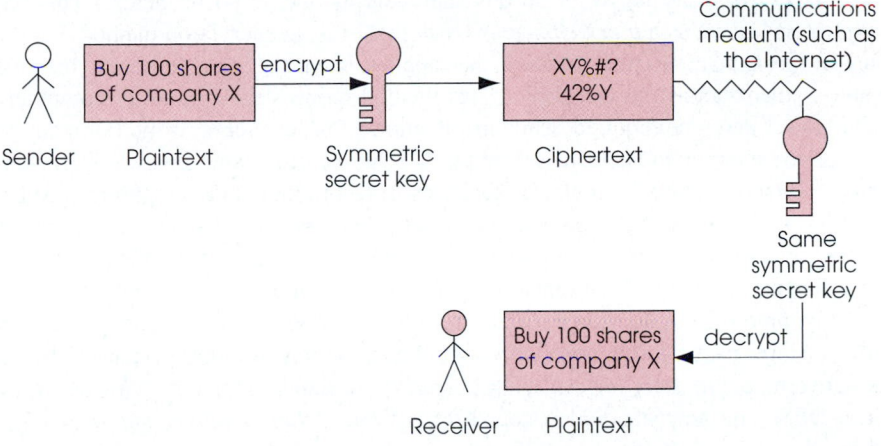

Fig. 21.2 Secret key used to encrypt and decrypt a message.

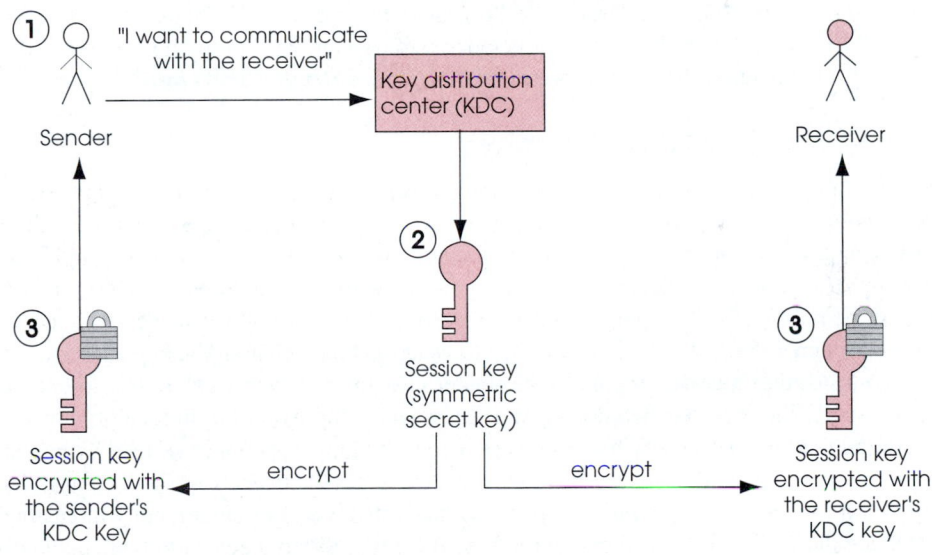

Fig. 21.3 Distributing a session key with a key-distribution center.

The use of a key-distribution center reduces the number of courier deliveries (again, by means such as mail or FedEx™) of secret keys to each user in the network. In addition, users can have a new secret key for each communication with other users in the network, which greatly increases the overall security of the network. However, if the security of the key-distribution center is compromised, then the security of the entire network is compromised.

One of the most commonly used symmetric-encryption algorithms is the *Data Encryption Standard (DES)*. Horst Feistel of IBM created the *Lucifer* algorithm, which was chosen as the DES by the United States government and the National Security Agency (NSA) in the

1970s.[4] DES has a key length of 56 bits and encrypts data in 64-bit blocks. This type of encryption is known as a *block cipher*. A block cipher is an encryption method that creates groups of bits from an original message, then applies an encryption algorithm to the block as a whole, rather than as individual bits. This method reduces the amount of computer processing power and time required, while maintaining a fair level of security. For many years, DES was the encryption standard set by the U.S. government and the *American National Standards Institute (ANSI)*. However, advances in technology and computing speed mean that DES is no longer considered secure. In the late 1990s, specialized *DES cracker machines* were built that recovered DES keys after just several hours.[5] As a result, the old standard of symmetric encryption has been replaced by *Triple DES*, or *3DES*, a variant of DES that is essentially three DES systems in a row, each with its own secret key. Though 3DES is more secure, the three passes through the DES algorithm result in slower performance. The United States government recently selected a new, more secure standard for symmetric encryption to replace DES. The new standard is called the *Advanced Encryption Standard (AES)*. The *National Institute of Standards and Technology* (NIST), which sets the cryptographic standards for the U.S. government, is evaluating *Rijndael* as the encryption method for AES. Rijndael is a block cipher developed by Dr. Joan Daemen and Dr. Vincent Rijmen of Belgium. Rijndael can be used with key sizes and block sizes of 128, 192 or 256 bits. Rijndael was chosen over four other finalists as the AES candidate because of its high security, performance, efficiency, flexibility and low memory requirement for computing systems.[6] For more information about AES, visit **csrc.nist.gov/encryption/aes**.

21.4 Public-Key Cryptography

In 1976, Whitfield Diffie and Martin Hellman, researchers at Stanford University, developed *public-key cryptography* to solve the problem of exchanging keys securely. Public-key cryptography is asymmetric. It uses two inversely related keys: A *public key* and a *private key*. The private key is kept secret by its owner, while the public key is freely distributed. If the public key encrypts a message, only the corresponding private key can decrypt it and vice versa (Fig. 21.4). Each party in a transaction has both a public key and a private key. To transmit a message securely, the sender uses the receiver's public key to encrypt the message. The receiver then decrypts the message, using his or her unique private key. Assuming that the private key has been kept secret, the message cannot be read by anyone other than the intended receiver. Thus, the system ensures the privacy of the message. The defining property of a secure *public-key algorithm* is that it is "computationally infeasible" to deduce the private key from the public key. Although the two keys are mathematically related, deriving one from the other would take enormous amounts of computing power and time, enough to discourage attempts to deduce the private key. An outside party cannot participate in communication without the correct keys. The security of the entire process is based on the secrecy of the private keys. Therefore, if a third party obtains the private key used in decryption, the security of the whole system is compromised. If a system's integrity is compromised, the user can simply change the key, instead of changing the entire encryption or decryption algorithm.

---

4. <www-math.cudenver.edu/~wcherowi/courses/m5410/m5410des.html>
5. M. Dworkin, "Advanced Encryption Standard (AES) Fact Sheet," 5 March 2001.
6. <www.esat.kuleuven.ac.be/~rijmen/rijndael>

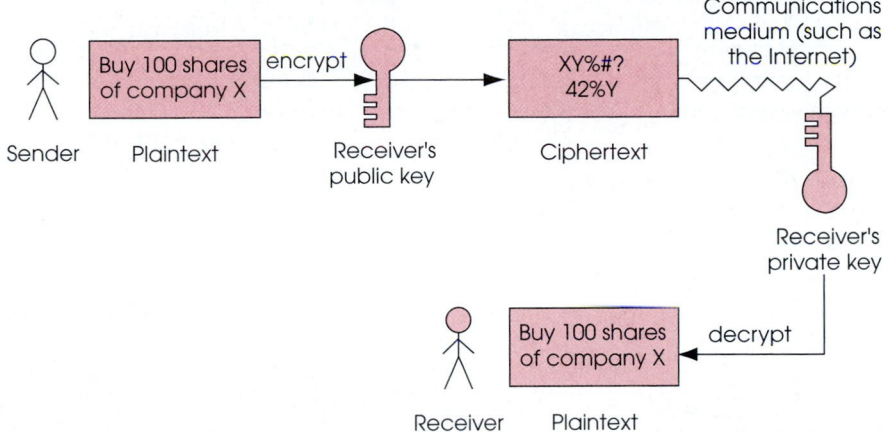

Fig. 21.4 Encrypting and decrypting a message using public-key cryptography.

Either the public key or the private key can encrypt or decrypt a message. For example, if a customer uses a merchant's public key to encrypt a message, only the merchant can decrypt the message, using the merchant's private key. Thus, the merchant's identity can be authenticated, because only the merchant knows the private key. However, the merchant has no way of validating the customer's identity, because the encryption key the customer used is publicly available.

If the decryption key is the sender's public key and the encryption key is the sender's private key, the sender of the message can be authenticated. For example, suppose a customer sends a merchant a message encrypted with the customer's private key. The merchant decrypts the message, using the customer's public key. The customer encrypted the message with his or her private key, so the merchant can be confident of the customer's identity. This process authenticates the sender, but does not ensure confidentiality; anyone could decrypt the message with the sender's public key. This system works as long as the merchant can be sure that the public key with which the merchant decrypted the message belongs to the customer and not to a third party posing as the customer.

These two methods of public-key encryption can actually be used together to authenticate both participants in a communication (Fig. 21.5). Suppose a merchant wants to send a message securely to a customer so that only the customer can read it, and suppose also that the merchant wants to provide proof to the customer that the merchant (not an unknown third party) actually sent the message. First, the merchant encrypts the message with the customer's public key. This step guarantees that only the customer can read the message. Then the merchant encrypts the result with the merchant's private key, which proves the identity of the merchant. The customer decrypts the message in reverse order. First, the customer uses the merchant's public key. Only the merchant could have encrypted the message with the inversely related private key, so this step authenticates the merchant. Then the customer uses the customer's private key to decrypt the next level of encryption. This step ensures that the content of the message was kept private in the transmission, because only the customer has the key to decrypt the message. Although this system provides extremely secure transactions, the setup cost and time required prevent widespread use.

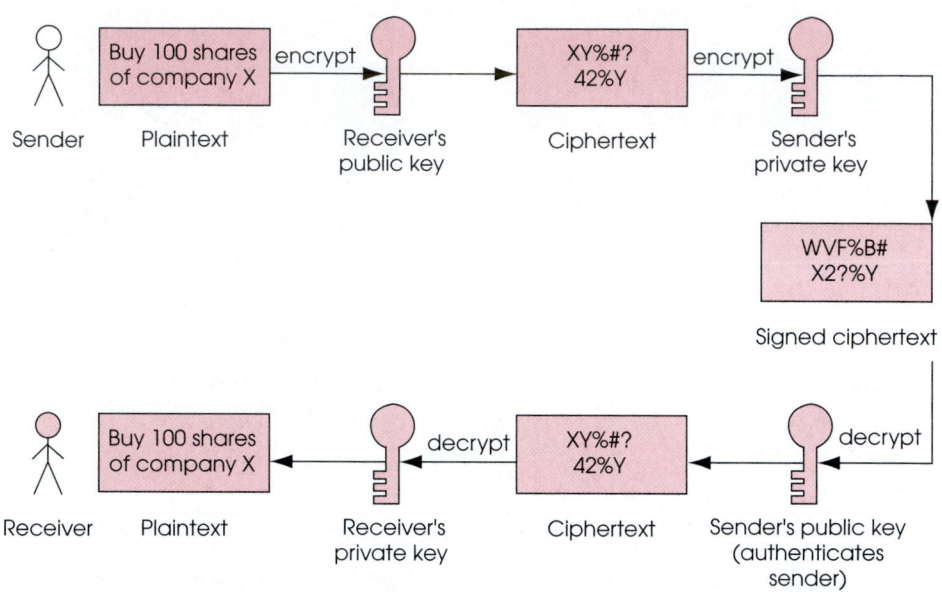

Fig. 21.5   Authentication with a public-key algorithm.

The most commonly used public-key algorithm is *RSA*, an encryption system developed in 1977 by MIT professors Ron Rivest, Adi Shamir and Leonard Adleman.[7] Today, most Fortune 1000 companies and leading e-commerce businesses use their encryption and authentication technologies. With the emergence of the Internet and the World Wide Web, Rivest, Shamir and Adleman's security work has become even more significant, and it plays a crucial role in e-commerce transactions. Their encryption products are built into hundreds of millions of copies of the most popular Internet applications, including Web browsers, commerce servers and e-mail systems. Most secure e-commerce transactions and communications on the Internet use RSA products. For more information about RSA, cryptography and security, visit **www.rsasecurity.com**.

Pretty Good Privacy (PGP) is a public-key encryption system used for the encryption of e-mail messages and files. PGP was designed in 1991, by Phillip Zimmermann.[8] PGP can also provide digital signatures (see Section 21.8, Digital Signatures) that confirm the author of an e-mail or public posting. PGP is based on a "web of trust"; each client in a network can vouch for another client's identity to prove ownership of a public key. This "web of trust" authenticates each client. If users know the identity of a public-key holder, through personal contact or another secure method, they validate the key by signing it with their own key. The web grows as more users validate the keys of others. To learn more about PGP and to download a free copy of the software, go to the MIT Distribution Center for PGP at **web.mit.edu/network/pgp.html**.

---

7. **<www.rsasecurity.com/rsalabs/rsa_algorithm>**
8. **<www.pgpi.org/doc/overview>**

21.5 Cryptanalysis

Even if keys are kept secret, it could be possible to compromise the security of a system. Trying to decrypt ciphertext without knowledge of the decryption key is known as *cryptanalysis*. Commercial encryption systems are constantly being researched by cryptologists to ensure that the systems are not vulnerable to a *cryptanalytic attack*. The most common form of cryptanalytic attacks is that in which the encryption algorithm is analyzed to find relations between bits of the encryption key and bits of the ciphertext. Often, these relations are only statistical in nature and incorporate an analyzer's outside knowledge about the plaintext. The goal of such an attack is to determine the key from the ciphertext.

Weak statistical trends between ciphertext and keys can be exploited to gain knowledge about the key if enough ciphertext is known. Proper key management and expiration dates on keys help prevent cryptanalytic attacks. When a key is used for long periods of time, more ciphertext is generated that can be beneficial to an attacker trying to derive a key. If a key is recovered secretly by an attacker, it can decrypt every message for the life of that key.

21.6 Key-Agreement Protocols

A drawback of public-key algorithms is that they are not efficient for sending large amounts of data. They require significant computer power, which slows down communication. Public-key algorithms should not be thought of as a replacement for secret-key algorithms. Instead, public-key algorithms allow two parties to agree on a key to be used for secret-key encryption over an unsecure medium. The process by which two parties can exchange keys over an unsecure medium is called a *key-agreement protocol*. A *protocol* sets the rules for communication: Exactly what encryption algorithm(s) is (are) going to be used?

The most common key-agreement protocol is a *digital envelope* (Fig. 21.6). With a digital envelope, the message is encrypted using a secret key (Step 1), and the secret key is encrypted with public-key encryption (Step 2). The sender attaches the encrypted secret key to the encrypted message and sends the receiver the entire package. The sender could also digitally sign the package before sending it to prove the sender's identity to the receiver (Section 21.8). To decrypt the package, the receiver first decrypts the secret key, using the receiver's private key. Then, the receiver uses the secret key to decrypt the actual message. Only the receiver can decrypt the encrypted secret key, so the sender can be sure that only the intended receiver is reading the message.

21.7 Key Management

Maintaining the secrecy of private keys is crucial to keeping cryptographic systems secure. Poor *key management* (e.g., the mishandling of private keys, resulting in key theft) results in more security compromises than attacks that attempt to guess the keys.[9]

A main component of key management is *key generation*—the process by which keys are created. A malicious third party could try to decrypt a message using every possible decryption key, a process known as *brute-force cracking*. Key-generation algorithms are sometimes unintentionally constructed to choose from only a small subset of possible keys. If the subset is too small, then the encrypted data is more susceptible to brute-force attacks.

---

9. `<www.rsasecurity.com/rsalabs/faq>`.

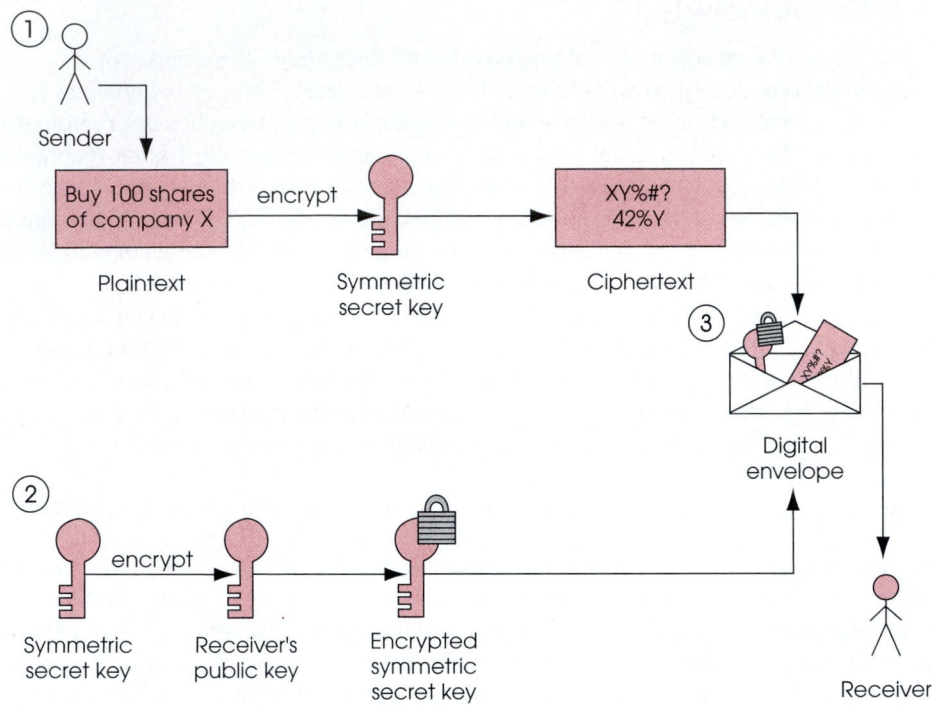

Fig. 21.6   Digital envelope creation.

Therefore, it is important to have a key-generation program that can generate a large number of keys as randomly as possible. Keys are made more secure by choosing a key length so large that it is computationally infeasible to try all combinations.

21.8 Digital Signatures

Digital signatures, the electronic equivalent of written signatures, were developed to be used in public-key cryptography to solve the problems of authentication and integrity. A digital signature authenticates the sender's identity, and, like a written signature, it is difficult to forge.

To create a digital signature, a sender first takes the original plaintext message and runs it through a *hash function*, which is a mathematical calculation that gives the message a *hash value*. A *one-way hashing function* generates a string of characters that is unique to the input file. The *Secure Hash Algorithm* (*SHA-1*) is the current standard for hashing functions. In using SHA-1, the phrase "Buy 100 shares of company X" could produce the hash value *D8 A9 B6 9F 72 65 0B D5 6D 0C 47 00 95 0D FD 31 96 0A FD B5*. *MD5* is another popular hash function, which was developed by Ronald Rivest to verify data integrity through a 128-bit hash value of the input file.[10] The interactive session (Fig. 21.7) demonstrates SHA-1.

---

10. **<userpages.umbc.edu/~mabzug1/cs/md5/md5.html>**.

```
Python 2.2b2 (#26, Nov 16 2001, 11:44:11) [MSC 32 bit (Intel)] on win32
Type "help", "copyright", "credits" or "license" for more information.
>>> import sha
>>> m1 = sha.new( "Buy 100 shares of company X" )
>>> print m1.hexdigest()
d8a9b69f72650bd56d0c4700950dfd31960afdb5
>>> m2 = sha.new()
>>> m2.update( "Buy 100 shares " )
>>> print m2.hexdigest()
4269dec883d1a763250d701c881defd34171809a
>>> m2.update( "of company X" )
>>> print m2.hexdigest()
d8a9b69f72650bd56d0c4700950dfd31960afdb5
>>>
```

Fig. 21.7   SHA-1 hash in Python.

Examples of SHA-1 and MD5 are available at **home.istar.ca/~neutron/ messagedigest**. At this site, users can input text or files into a program to generate the hash value, known as a *message digest*. *Collision* occurs when multiple messages have the same hash value. The likelihood of collision in SHA-1 and MD5 is computationally infeasible. It is also computationally infeasible to compute a message from its hash value or to find two messages with the same hash value.

Next, the sender uses the sender's private key to encrypt the message digest. This step creates a digital signature and authenticates the sender, because only the owner of that private key could encrypt the message. A message that includes the digital signature, hash function and original message (encrypted with the receiver's public key) is sent to the receiver. The receiver uses the sender's public key to decipher the original digital signature and reveal the message digest. The receiver then uses his or her own private key to decipher the original message. Finally, the receiver applies the hash function to the original message. If the hash value of the original message matches the message digest included in the signature, there is *message integrity*; the message has not been altered in transmission.

There is a fundamental difference between digital signatures and handwritten signatures. A handwritten signature is independent of the document being signed. Thus, if someone can forge a handwritten signature, they can use that signature to forge multiple documents. A digital signature is created using the contents of the document. Therefore, your digital signature is different for each document you sign.

Digital signatures do not provide proof that a message has been sent. Consider the following situation: A contractor sends a company a digitally signed contract, which the contractor later would like to revoke. The contractor could do so by releasing the private key and then claiming that the digitally signed contract came from an intruder who stole the contractor's private key. *Timestamping*, which binds a time and date to a digital document, can help solve the problem of nonrepudiation. For example, suppose the company and the contractor are negotiating a contract. The company requires the contractor to sign the contract digitally and then have the document digitally timestamped by a third party called a *timestamping agency*. The contractor sends the digitally-signed contract to the time-stamping agency. The privacy of the message is maintained, because the timestamping agency sees only the encrypted, digitally-signed message (as opposed to the original plaintext message).

The timestamping agency affixes the time and date of receipt to the encrypted, signed message and digitally signs the whole package with the timestamping agency's private key. The timestamp cannot be altered by anyone except the timestamping agency, because no one else possesses the timestamping agency's private key. Unless the contractor reports the private key to have been compromised before the document was timestamped, the contractor cannot legally prove that the document was signed by an unauthorized third party. The sender could also require the receiver to sign the message digitally and timestamp it as proof of receipt. To learn more about timestamping, visit **AuthentiDate.com**.

The U.S. government's digital-authentication standard is called the *Digital Signature Algorithm (DSA)*. The U.S. government recently passed a digital-signature legislation that makes digital signatures as binding legally as handwritten signatures. This legislation is expected to increase e-business dramatically. For the latest news about U.S. government legislation in information security, visit **www.itaa.org/infosec**. For more information about the bills, visit the following government sites:

```
thomas.loc.gov/cgi-bin/bdquery/z?d106:hr.01714:
thomas.loc.gov/cgi-bin/bdquery/z?d106:s.00761:
```

21.9 Public-Key Infrastructure, Certificates and Certificate Authorities

One problem with public-key cryptography is that anyone with a set of keys could potentially assume another party's identity. For example, say a customer wants to place an order with an online merchant. How does the customer know that the Web site indeed belongs to that merchant and not to a third party that posted a site and is *masquerading* as a merchant to steal credit-card information? *Public-Key Infrastructure* (*PKI*) provides a solution to these problems. PKI integrates public-key cryptography with *digital certificates* and *certificate authorities* to authenticate parties in a transaction.

e-Fact 21.3

The Aberdeen Group predicts that approximately 98% of all Global 2000 companies will implement PKI solutions by 2003.[11]

A digital certificate is a digital document used to identify a user and issued by a certificate authority (CA). A digital certificate includes the name of the subject (the company or individual being certified), the subject's public key, a serial number, an expiration date, the signature of the trusted certificate authority and any other relevant information (Fig. 21.8). A CA is a financial institution or other trusted third party, such as *VeriSign*. Once issued, the digital certificates are publicly available and are held by the certificate authority in *certificate repositories*.

The CA signs the certificate by encrypting either the subject's public key or a hash value of the public key, using the CA's own private key. The CA has to verify every subject's public key. Thus, users must trust the public key of a CA. Usually, each CA is part of a *certificate authority hierarchy*. This hierarchy is similar to a chain of trust in which each link relies on another link to provide authentication information. A certificate

---

11. T. Russell, "The Cryptographic Landscape for PKI Smart Cards," *Internet Security Advisor* March/April 2001: 22.

Fig. 21.8   VeriSign digital certificate. (Courtesy of VeriSign, Inc.)

authority hierarchy is a chain of certificate authorities, starting with the *root certificate authority*, which is the *Internet Policy Registration Authority (IPRA)*. The IPRA signs certificates, using the *root key*. The root key signs certificates only for *policy creation authorities*, which are organizations that set policies for obtaining digital certificates. In turn, policy creation authorities sign digital certificates for CAs. CAs then sign digital certificates for individuals and organizations. The CA takes responsibility for authentication, so it must check the information carefully before issuing a digital certificate. In one case, human error caused VeriSign to issue two digital certificates to an impostor posing as a Microsoft employee.[12] Such an error is significant: The inappropriately issued certificates can cause users to download malicious code unknowingly onto their machines. (See Authentication: *Microsoft Authenticode* feature.)

VeriSign, Inc., is a leading certificate authority. For more information about VeriSign, visit **www.verisign.com**. For a listing of other digital-certificate vendors, please see Section 21.16.

---

12. G. Hulme, "VeriSign Gave Microsoft Certificates to Imposter," *Information Week* 3 March 2001.

e-Fact 21.4

It can take a year and cost from $5 million to $10 million for a financial firm to build a digital certificate infrastructure, according to Identrus, a consortium of global financial companies that is providing a framework for trusted business-to-business e-commerce.[13]

Periodically changing key pairs is necessary in maintaining a secure system, for a private key could be compromised without a user's knowledge. The longer a key pair is used, the more vulnerable the keys are to attack and cryptanalysis. As a result, to force users to switch key pairs, digital certificates are created with an expiration date. If a private key is compromised before its expiration date, the digital certificate can be canceled, and the user can get a new key pair and digital certificate. Canceled and revoked certificates are placed on a *certificate revocation list (CRL)*. CRLs are stored with the certificate authority that issued the certificates. It is essential for users to report immediately if they suspect that their private keys have been compromised, because the issue of nonrepudiation makes certificate owners responsible for anything appearing with their digital signatures. In states with laws on digital signatures, certificates legally bind certificate owners to any transactions involving their certificates.

CRLs are similar to old paper lists of revoked credit-card numbers that were used at the points of sale in stores.[14] This makes for a great inconvenience when checking the validity of a certificate. An alternative to CRLs is the *Online Certificate Status Protocol (OCSP)*, which validates certificates in real time. OCSP technology is currently under development. For an overview of OCSP, read "X.509 Internet Public-Key Infrastructure Online Certificate Status Protocol—OCSP" located at `ftp.isi.edu/in-notes/rfc2560.txt`.

Many people still consider e-commerce unsecure. However, transactions using PKI and digital certificates can be more secure than exchanging private information over phone lines or through the mail and even paying by credit card in person. After all, when you go to a restaurant and the waiter takes your credit card to process your bill, how do you know that the waiter did not write down your credit card information? In contrast, the key algorithms used in most secure online transactions are nearly impossible to compromise. By some estimates, the key algorithms used in public-key cryptography are so secure that even millions of today's computers working in parallel could not break the codes in a century. However, as computing power increases, key algorithms considered strong today could be broken in the future.

Digital-certificate capabilities are built into many e-mail packages. For example, in Microsoft Outlook, you can go to the **Tools** menu and select **Options**. Then click on the **Security** tab. At the bottom of the dialog box, you will see the option to obtain a *digital ID*. Selecting the option will take you to a Microsoft Web site with links to several worldwide certificate authorities. Once you have a digital certificate, you can sign your e-mail messages digitally.

To obtain a digital certificate for your personal e-mail messages, visit `www.verisign.com` or `www.thawte.com`. VeriSign offers a free 60-day trial, or you can purchase the service for a yearly fee. Thawte Corporation offers free digital certificates for personal e-mail. Web-server certificates may also be purchased through VeriSign and Thawte; however, they are more expensive than e-mail certificates.

---

13. R. Yasin, "PKI Rollout to Get Cheaper, Quicker," *InternetWeek* 24 July 2000: 28.
14. C. Ellison and B. Schneier, "Ten Risks of PKI: What You're not Being Told about Public Key Infrastructure," *Computer Security Journal* 2000.

Authentication: Microsoft Authenticode

How do you know that the software you ordered online is safe and has not been altered? How can you be sure that you are not downloading a computer virus that could wipe out your computer? Do you trust the source of the software? With the emergence of e-commerce, software companies are offering their products online, so that customers can download software directly onto their computers. Security technology is used to ensure that the downloaded software is trustworthy and has not been altered. Microsoft Authenticode, combined with VeriSign digital certificates (or digital IDs), authenticates the publisher of the software and detects whether the software has been altered. Authenticode is a security feature built into Microsoft Internet Explorer.

To use Microsoft Authenticode technology, each software publisher must obtain a digital certificate specifically designed for the purpose of publishing software; such certificates may be obtained through certificate authorities, such as VeriSign (Section 21.9). To obtain a certificate, a software publisher must provide its public key and identification information and sign an agreement that it will not distribute harmful software. This requirement gives customers legal recourse if any downloaded software from certified publishers causes harm.

Microsoft Authenticode uses digital-signature technology to sign software (Section 21.8). The signed software and the publisher's digital certificate provide proof that the software is safe and has not been altered.

When a customer attempts to download a file, a dialog box appears on the screen, displaying the digital certificate and the name of the certificate authority. Links to the publisher and the certificate authority are provided so that customers can learn more about each party before they agree to download the software. If Microsoft Authenticode determines that the software has been compromised, the transaction is terminated.

To learn more about Microsoft Authenticode, visit the following sites:

```
msdn.microsoft.com/workshop/security/authcode/signfaq.asp
msdn.microsoft.com/workshop/security/authcode/authwp.asp
```

21.9.1 Smart Cards

One of the fastest growing applications of PKI is the *smart card*. A smart card generally looks like a credit card and can serve many different functions, from authentication to data storage. The most popular smart cards are *memory cards* and *microprocessor cards*. Memory cards are similar to floppy disks. Microprocessor cards are similar to small computers, with operating systems, security and storage. Smart cards also have different *interfaces*, via which they interact with reading devices. One type of interface is a *contact interface*, in which smart cards are inserted into a reading device and physical contact between the device and the card is necessary. The alternative to this method is a *contactless interface*, in which data is transferred to a reader via an embedded wireless device in the card, without the card and the device having to make physical contact.[15]

---

15. "What's So Smart About Smart Cards?" *Smart Card Forum*.

Smart cards store private keys, digital certificates and other information necessary for implementing PKI. They may also store credit card numbers, personal contact information and so on. Each smart card is used in combination with a *personal identification number* (*PIN*). This combination provides two levels of security by requiring the user both to possess a smart card and to know the corresponding PIN to access the information stored on the card. As an added measure of security, some microprocessor cards will delete or corrupt stored data if malicious attempts at tampering with the card occur. Smart-card PKI is portable, allowing users to access information from multiple devices with the same smart card.

21.10 Security Protocols

Everyone using the Web for e-business and e-commerce needs to be concerned about the security of their personal information. In this section, we discuss network security protocols, such as *Internet Protocol Security (IPSec),* and transport-layer security protocols, such as *Secure Sockets Layer (SSL)*. Network security protocols protect communications between networks; transport layer security protocols are used to establish secure connections for data to pass through.

21.10.1 Secure Sockets Layer (SSL)

Currently, most e-businesses use SSL for secure online transactions, although SSL is not designed specifically for securing transactions. Rather, SSL secures World Wide Web connections. SSL protocol, developed by Netscape Communications, is a nonproprietary protocol commonly used to secure communication between two computers on the Internet and the Web.[16] SSL is built into many Web browsers, including Netscape Communicator and Microsoft Internet Explorer, and numerous other software products. It operates between the Internet's TCP/IP communications protocol and the application software.[17]

In a standard correspondence over the Internet, a sender's message is passed to a *socket*, which receives and transmits information from a network. *Transmission Control Protocol/Internet Protocol* (*TCP/IP*) is the standard set of protocols used for connecting computers and networks to a network of networks, known as the Internet. Most Internet transmissions are sent as sets of individual message pieces, called *packets*. At the sending side, the packets of one message are numbered sequentially, and error-control information is attached to each packet. IP is primarily responsible for routing packets to avoid traffic jams, so each packet might travel a different route over the Internet. The destination of a packet is determined by the *IP address*—an assigned number used to identify a computer on a network, similar to the address of a house in a neighborhood. At the receiving end, the TCP makes sure that all of the packets have arrived, puts them in sequential order and determines whether the packets have been corrupted. If the packets have been accidentally altered or any data has been lost, TCP requests retransmission. However, TCP is not sophisticated enough to determine that packets have been altered maliciously during transmission; malicious packets can be disguised as valid ones. When all of the data successfully reaches TCP/IP, the message is passed to the socket at the receiver end. The socket translates the message back into a form that can be read by the receiver's application.[18] In a transaction using SSL, the sockets are secured by public-key cryptography.

16. S. Abbot, "The Debate for Secure E-Commerce," *Performance Computing* February 1999: 37–42.
17. T. Wilson, "E-Biz Bucks Lost Under the SSL Train," *Internet Week* 24 May 1999: 1, 3.

SSL implements public-key technology using the RSA algorithm and digital certificates to authenticate the server in a transaction and to protect private information as it passes from one party to another over the Internet. SSL transactions do not require client authentication; many servers require only a valid credit-card number to process purchases. To begin, a client sends a message to a server. The server responds and sends its digital certificate to the client for authentication. Using public-key cryptography to communicate securely, the client and server negotiate *session keys* to continue the transaction. Session keys are secret keys that are used for the duration of that transaction. Once the keys are established, the communication proceeds between the client and the server, the session keys and digital certificates. Encrypted data is passed through TCP/IP, just as regular packets travel over the Internet. However, before sending a message with TCP/IP, the SSL protocol breaks the information into blocks, compresses it and encrypts it. Conversely, after the data reaches the receiver through TCP/IP, the SSL protocol decrypts the packets, then decompresses and assembles the data. These extra processes provide an extra layer of security between TCP/IP and applications. SSL is primarily used to secure *point-to-point connections*—transmissions of data from one computer to another.[19] SSL allows for the authentication of the server, the client, both or neither; in most Internet SSL sessions, only the server is authenticated. The *Transport Layer Security* (*TLS*) protocol, designed by the Internet Engineering Task Force, is similar to SSL. For more information on TLS, visit **www.ietf.org/rfc/rfc2246.txt**.

Although SSL protects information as it is passed over the Internet, it does not protect private information, such as credit-card numbers, once the information is stored on the merchant's server. When a merchant receives credit-card information with an order, the information is often decrypted and stored on the merchant's server until the order is placed. If the server is not secure and the data is not encrypted, an unauthorized party can access the information. Hardware devices, such as *peripheral component interconnect (PCI) cards* designed for use in SSL transactions, can be installed on Web servers to process SSL transactions, thus reducing processing time and leaving the server free to perform other tasks.[20] Visit **www.sonicwall.com/products/trans.asp** for more information on these devices. For more information about the SSL protocol, check out the Netscape SSL tutorial at **developer.netscape.com/tech/security/ssl/protocol.html** and the Netscape Security Center site at **www.netscape.com/security/index.html**.

21.10.2 IPSec and Virtual Private Networks (VPN)

Networks allow organizations to link multiple computers together. *Local area networks* (*LANs*) connect computers that are physically close, generally in the same building. *Wide area networks* (*WANs*) are used to connect computers in multiple locations using private telephone lines or radio waves. Organizations are now taking advantage of the existing infrastructure of the Internet—the publicly available wires—to create *Virtual Private Networks* (*VPNs*), linking multiple networks, wireless users and other remote users. VPNs use the Internet infrastructure that is already in place; therefore, they are more economical than

18. H. Gilbert, "Introduction to TCP/IP," 2 February 1995 **<www.yale.edu/pclt/COMM/ TCPIP.HTM>**.
19. RSA Laboratories, "Security Protocols Overview," 1999 **<www.rsasecurity.com/standards/protocols>**.
20. M. Bull, "Ensuring End-to-End Security with SSL," *Network World* 15 May 2000: 63.

private networks such as WANs.[21] The encryption allows for VPNs to provide the same services as private networks over a public network.

A VPN is created by establishing a secure *tunnel* through which data passes between multiple networks over the Internet. IPSec is one of the technologies used to secure the tunnel through which the data passes, ensuring the privacy and integrity of the data, as well authenticating the users.[22] IPSec, developed by the *Internet Engineering Task Force* (*IETF*), uses public-key and symmetric-key cryptography to ensure authentication of the users, data integrity and confidentiality. The technology takes advantage of the standard that is already in place, in which information travels between two networks over the Internet via the IP. Information sent using IP, however, can easily be intercepted. Unauthorized users can access the network using a number of well-known techniques, such as *IP spoofing*—a method in which an attacker simulates the IP of an authorized user or host to get access to resources that would otherwise be off-limits. The SSL protocol enables secure, point-to-point connections between two applications; IPSec enables the secure connection of an entire network. The *Diffie-Hellman and RSA algorithms* are commonly used in the IPSec protocol for key exchange, and DES or 3DES are used for secret-key encryption (depending on system and encryption needs). An IP packet is encrypted, then sent inside a regular IP packet that creates the tunnel. The receiver discards the outer IP packet, then decrypts the inner IP packet.[23] VPN security relies on three concepts: authentication of the user, encryption of the data sent over the network and controlled access to corporate information.[24] To address these three security concepts, IPSec is composed of three pieces. The *Authentication Header* (*AH*) attaches additional information to each packet, which verifies the identity of the sender and proves that data was not modified in transit. The *Encapsulating Security Payload* (*ESP*) encrypts the data, using symmetric-key ciphers to protect the data from eavesdroppers, while the IP packet is being sent from one computer to another. The *Internet Key Exchange* (*IKE*) is the key-exchange protocol used in IPSec to determine security restrictions and to authenticate the encryption keys.

VPNs are becoming increasingly popular in businesses. However, VPN security is difficult to manage. To establish a VPN, all of the users on the network must have similar software or hardware. Although it is convenient for a business partner to connect to another company's network via VPN, access to specific applications and files should be limited to certain authorized users versus all users on a VPN.[25] Firewalls, intrusion-detection software and authorization tools can secure valuable data (Section 21.14).

For more information about IPSec, visit the *IPSec Developers Forum* at **www.ip-sec.com**. Also, check out the Web site for the *IPSec Working Group* of the IETF at **www.ietf.org/html.charters/ipsec-charter.html**.

21.11 Authentication

As we discuss throughout the chapter, authentication is one of the fundamental requirements for e-business and m-business (mobile business) security. In this section, we will dis-

21. <**www.cisco.com/warp/public/44/solutions/network/vpn.shtml**>.
22. S. Burnett and S. Paine, *RSA Security's Official Guide to Cryptography* (Berkeley: Osborne/ McGraw-Hill, 2001) 210.
23. D. Naik, *Internet Standards and Protocols* Microsoft Press 1998: 79–80.
24. M. Grayson, "End the PDA Security Dilemma," *Communication News* February 2001: 38–40.
25. T. Wilson, "VPNs Don't Fly Outside Firewalls," *Internet Week*, 28 May 2001.

cuss some of the technologies used to authenticate users in a network, such as *Kerberos*, *biometrics* and *single sign-on*. We conclude the section with a discussion of Microsoft Passport—a technology that combines several methods of authentication.

21.11.1 Kerberos

Firewalls do not protect users from internal security threats to their local area network. Internal attacks are common and can be extremely damaging. For example, disgruntled employees with network access can wreak havoc on an organization's network or steal valuable proprietary information. It is estimated that 70 percent to 90 percent of attacks on corporate networks are internal.[26] *Kerberos* is a freely available, open-source protocol developed at MIT. It employs secret-key cryptography to authenticate users in a network and to maintain the integrity and privacy of network communications.

Authentication in a Kerberos system is handled by a main Kerberos system and a secondary *Ticket-Granting Service* (*TGS*). This system is similar to the key-distribution centers described in Section 21.3. The main Kerberos system authenticates a client's identity to the TGS; the TGS authenticates a client's rights to access specific network services.

Each client in the network shares a secret key with the Kerberos system. This secret key may be used by multiple TGSs in the Kerberos system. The client starts by entering a login name and password into the Kerberos authentication server. The authentication server maintains a database of all clients in the network. The authentication server returns a *Ticket-Granting Ticket* (*TGT*) encrypted with the client's secret key that it shares with the authentication server. The secret key is known only by the authentication server and the client, so only the client can decrypt the TGT, thus authenticating the client's identity. Next, the client's system sends the decrypted TGT to the Ticket-Granting Service to request a *service ticket*. The service ticket authorizes the client's access to specific network services. Service tickets have a set expiration time. Tickets may be renewed by the TGS. This process helps ensure network security, since access to specific network services is granted on an as-needed basis; clients must be reauthorized to access the services when a service ticket expires.

21.11.2 Biometrics

Biometrics uses unique personal information, such as fingerprints, eyeball iris scans or face scans, to identify a user. This system eliminates the need for passwords, which are much easier to steal. Have you ever written down your passwords on a piece of paper and put the paper in your desk drawer or wallet? These days, people have passwords and PIN codes for everything—Web sites, networks, e-mail, ATM cards and even for their cars. Managing all of those codes can become a burden. Recently, the cost of biometrics devices has dropped significantly. Keyboard-mounted fingerprint-scanning, face-scanning and eye-scanning devices are being used in place of passwords to log into systems, check e-mail or access secure information over a network. Each user's iris scan, face scan or fingerprint is stored in a secure database. Each time a user logs in, his or her scan is compared with the database. If a match is made, the login is successful. Two companies that specialize in biometrics devices are IriScan (**www.iriscan.com**) and Keytronic (**www.keytronic.com**). For additional resources, see Section 21.16.

---

26. S. Gaudin, "The Enemy Within," *Network World* 8 May 2000: 122–126.

Currently, passwords are the predominant means of authentication; however, we are beginning to see a shift to smart cards and biometrics. Microsoft recently announced that it will include the *Biometric Application Programming Interface (BAPI)* in future versions of Windows, which will make it possible for companies to integrate biometrics into their systems.[27] *Two-factor authentication* uses two means to authenticate the user, such as biometrics or a smart card used in combination with a password. Although the smart-card system could be compromised, using two methods of authentication is more secure than just using passwords alone.

Keyware Inc., has already implemented a wireless biometrics system that stores user voiceprints on a central server. Keyware also created *layered biometric verification (LBV)*, which uses multiple physical measurements—face-, finger- and voice-prints—simultaneously. The LBV feature enables a wireless biometrics system to combine biometrics with other authentication methods, such as PIN and PKI.[28]

Identix Inc., also provides biometrics authentication technology for wireless transactions. The Identix fingerprint-scanning device is embedded in handheld devices. The Identix service offers *transaction management* and *content protection* services. Transaction management services prove that transactions took place, and content protection services control access to electronic documents, including limiting a user's ability to download or copy documents.[29]

Wireless biometrics is not widely used at this point. Fingerprint scanners must be accompanied by fingerprint readers installed in mobile devices. Wireless-device manufacturers are hesitant to build fingerprint readers, because the technology is expensive. Laptops have begun to accommodate biometric security, but cell phones are slower to advance, having limited memory and processing power.[30]

One of the major concerns with biometrics is the issue of privacy. Implementing fingerprint scanners means that organizations will be keeping databases with each employee's fingerprint. Do people want to provide their employers with such personal information? What if that data is compromised? To date, most organizations that have implemented biometrics systems have received little, if any, resistance from employees.

21.11.3 Single Sign-On

To access multiple applications on different servers, users must provide a separate password for authentication on each. Remembering multiple passwords is cumbersome. People tend to write their passwords down, creating security threats.

Single sign-on systems allow users to login once with a single password. Users can then access multiple applications. It is important to secure single sign-on passwords, because if the password becomes available to crackers, all applications can be accessed and attacked.

There are three types of single sign-on services: *workstation logon scripts, authentication server scripts* and *tokens.* Workstation logon scripts are the simplest form of single sign-on. Users login at their workstations, then choose applications from a menu. The workstation logon script sends the user's password to the application servers, and the user

---

27. D. Deckmyn, "Companies Push New Approaches to Authentication," *Computerworld* 15 May 2000: 6.
28. "Centralized Authentication," `<www.keyware.com>`.
29. J. Vijayan, "Biometrics Meet Wireless Internet," *Computerworld* 17 July 2000: 14.
30. C. Nobel, "Biometrics Targeted for Wireless Devices," *eWEEK* 31 July 2000: 22.

is authenticated for future access to those applications. Workstation logon scripts do not provide a sufficient amount of security, because user passwords are stored on the PC in plaintext. Anyone who can access the workstation can take the user's password. Authentication server scripts authenticate users with a central server. The central server controls connections between the user and the applications the user wishes to access. Authentication server scripts are more secure than workstation logon scripts because passwords are kept on the server, which is more secure than the individual PC.

The most advanced single sign-on systems use token-based authentication. Once a user is authenticated, a nonreusable token is issued to the user to access specific applications. The logon for creating the token is secured with encryption or with a single password, which is the only password the user needs to remember or change. The only problem with token authentication is that all applications must be built to accept tokens instead of traditional logon passwords.[31]

21.11.4 Microsoft® Passport

Microsoft Passport incorporates authentication, online purchasing, single sign-on and several other technologies that we have discussed into one product that can be used over several different sites on the Internet. Passport users sign in only once with the main Passport authentication server; after signing in, they are recognized as a unique user at each of the Passport-enabled sites they visit. This technology allows users to check e-mail, chat with friends and make purchases online without entering a password for each application.

Once a user logs in, the Passport provides authentication information to the participating sites, but the actual Passport password is safe with the secured database. Passport uses SSL to send the username, password and digital wallet data to the central server.[32] The authentication information that sites receive is in the form of a digital key. This key is unique to each user and is verifiable by the Passport database (similar to the PKI architecture). To provide a greater level of security, each key has an expiration date. The less time that a key is in circulation, the less time an attacker has to analyze the key or use a compromised key. Microsoft Passport also provides for protection from brute-force cracking. If an attacker enters a certain number of incorrect passwords at the login prompt, Passport temporarily suspends the account for several minutes. This action prevents brute-force programs from repeatedly trying passwords until finding the correct one.

Cookies on the user's computer store profile information after it has been encrypted. When a user logs out of the Passport, all of the personal information that was stored in the cookies is deleted.

Microsoft incorporates Passport technology into many of its upcoming products. Windows XP, the .NET framework and Hailstorm are based on Microsoft Passport. For more information on Microsoft Passport and to sign up for a free Passport account, visit **www.passport.com**.

21.12 Security Attacks

Recent cyberattacks on e-businesses have made the front pages of newspapers worldwide. *Denial-of-service attacks* (*DoS*), *viruses* and *worms* have cost companies billions of dol-

---

31. F. Trickey, "Secure Single Sign-On: Fantasy or Reality," *CSI* <www.gocsi.com>
32. <memberservices.passport.com/HELP/MSRV_HELP_howsecure.asp>.

lars. In this section, we will discuss the different types of attacks and the steps you can take to protect your information.

21.12.1 Denial-of-Service (DoS) Attacks

A denial-of-service attack occurs when a system is forced to behave improperly. In many DoS attacks, a network's resources are taken up by unauthorized traffic, restricting the access of legitimate users. Typically, the attack is performed by flooding servers with *data packets*. Denial-of-service attacks usually require the power of a network of computers working simultaneously, although some skillful attacks can be achieved with a single machine. Denial-of-service attacks can cause networked computers to crash or disconnect, disrupting service on a Web site or even shutting down critical systems such as telecommunications or flight-control centers

e-Fact 21.5

Approximately 4,000 sites experience denial of service every week.[33, 34]

Another type of denial-of-service attack targets the *routing tables* of a network. Routing tables are the road map of a network, providing directions for data to get from one computer to another. This type of attack is accomplished by modifying the routing tables, thus disabling network activity. For example, the routing tables can be changed to send all data to one address in the network.

In a *distributed denial-of-service attack*, the packet flooding comes not from a single source, but from many separate computers. Actually, such an attack is rarely the concerted work of many individuals. Instead, it is the work of a single individual who has installed viruses on various computers, gaining illegitimate use of the computers to carry out the attack. Distributed denial-of-service attacks can be difficult to stop; it is not clear which requests on a network are from legitimate users and which are part of the attack. In addition, it is particularly difficult to catch the culprit of such attacks, because the attacks are not carried out directly from the attacker's computer.

Who is responsible for viruses and denial-of-service attacks? Most often the responsible parties are referred to as *hackers* or *crackers*. Although the terms are often confused, generally hackers are skilled programmers while crackers use programs, often written by others, to break into systems. According to some, crackers break into systems just for the thrill of it, without causing any harm to the compromised systems (except, perhaps, humbling and humiliating their owners). Either way, crackers break the law by accessing or damaging private information and computers. Crackers have malicious intent and are usually interested in breaking into a system to shut down services or steal data. In February 2000, distributed denial-of-service attacks shut down a number of high-traffic Web sites, including Yahoo!, eBay, CNN Interactive and Amazon. In this case, a cracker used a network of computers to flood the Web sites with traffic that overwhelmed the sites' computers. Although denial-of-service attacks merely shut off access to a Web site and do not affect the victim's data, they can be extremely costly. For example, when eBay's Web site went down for a 24-hour period on August 6, 1999, its stock value declined dramatically.[35]

33. D. Moore, G. Voelker and S. Savage, "Inferring Internet Denial-of-Service Activity."
34. J. Schwartz, "Computer Vandals Clog Antivandalism Web Site," *The New York Times* 24 May 2001.

21.12.2 Viruses and Worms

Viruses are pieces of code—often sent as attachments or hidden in audio clips, video clips and games—that attach to or overwrite other programs to replicate themselves. Viruses can corrupt files or even wipe out a hard drive. Before the Internet was invented, viruses spread through files and programs (such as video games) were transferred to computers by removable disks. Today, viruses are spread over a network simply by sharing "infected" files embedded in e-mail attachments, documents or programs. A worm is similar to a virus, except that it can spread and infect files on its own over a network; worms do not need to be attached to another program to spread. Once a virus or worm is released, it can spread rapidly, often infecting millions of computers worldwide within minutes or hours.

There are many classes of computer viruses. A *transient virus* attaches itself to a specific computer program. The virus is activated when the program is run and deactivated when the program is terminated. A more powerful type of virus is a *resident virus*, which, once loaded into the memory of a computer, operates for the duration of the computer's use. Another type of virus is the *logic bomb*, which triggers when a given condition is met, such as a *time bomb* that is activated when the clock on the computer matches a certain time or date.

A *Trojan horse* is a malicious program that hides within a friendly program or simulates the identity of a legitimate program or feature, while actually causing damage to the computer or network in the background. The Trojan horse gets its name from the story of the Trojan War in Greek history. In this story, Greek warriors hid inside a wooden horse, which the Trojans took within the walls of the city of Troy. When night fell and the Trojans were asleep, the Greek warriors came out of the horse and opened the gates to the city, letting the Greek army enter the gates and destroy the city of Troy. Trojan-horse programs can be particularly difficult to detect, because they appear to be legitimate and useful applications. Also commonly associated with Trojan horses are *backdoor programs*, which are usually resident viruses that give the sender complete, undetected access to the victim's computer resources. These types of viruses are especially threatening to the victim, for they can be set up to log every keystroke (capturing all passwords, credit card numbers, etc.) No matter how secure the connection between a PC supplying private information and the server receiving the information, if a backdoor program is running on a computer, the data is intercepted before any encryption is implemented. In June 2000, news spread of a Trojan horse virus disguised as a video clip sent as an e-mail attachment. The Trojan horse virus was designed to give the attacker access to infected computers, potentially to launch a denial-of-service attack against Web sites.[36]

Two of the most famous viruses to date are *Melissa*, which struck in March 1999, and the *ILOVEYOU virus* that hit in May 2000. Both viruses cost organizations and individuals billions of dollars. The Melissa virus spread in Microsoft Word documents sent via e-mail. When the document was opened, the virus was triggered. Melissa accessed the Microsoft Outlook address book on that computer and automatically sent the infected Word attachment by e-mail to the first 50 people in the address book. Each time another person opened the attachment, the virus would send out another 50 messages. Once in a system, the virus infected any subsequently saved files.

---

35. "Securing B2B," *Global Technology Business* July 2000: 50–51.
36. H. Bray, "Trojan Horse Attacks Computers, Disguised as a Video Chip," *The Boston Globe* 10 June 2000: C1+.

The ILOVEYOU virus was sent as an attachment to an e-mail posing as a love letter. The message in the e-mail said "Kindly check the attached love letter coming from me." Once opened, the virus accessed the Microsoft Outlook address book and sent out messages to the addresses listed, helping to spread the virus rapidly worldwide. The virus corrupted all types of files, including system files. Networks at companies and government organizations worldwide were shut down for days trying to remedy the problem and contain the virus. This virus accentuated the importance of scanning file attachments for security threats before opening them. Either that, or it highlights the importance of using a more secure operating system and secure software.

e-Fact 21.6

Estimates for damage caused by the ILOVEYOU virus were as high as $10 billion to $15 billion, with the majority of the damage done in just a few hours.

Why do these viruses spread so quickly? One reason is that many people are too willing to open executable files from unknown sources. Have you ever opened an audio clip or video clip from a friend? Have you ever forwarded that clip to other friends? Do you know who created the clip and whether any viruses are embedded in it? Did you open the ILOVEYOU file to see what the love letter said?

Most antivirus software is reactive, going after viruses once they are discovered, rather than protecting against unknown viruses. New antivirus software, such as Finjan Software's SurfinGuard® (`www.finjan.com`), looks for executable files attached to e-mail and runs the executables in a secure area to test whether they attempt to access and harm files. For more information about antivirus software, see the `McAfee.com`: Antivirus Utilities feature.

McAfee.com: *Antivirus Utilities*

`McAfee.com` provides a variety of antivirus utilities (and other utilities) for users whose computers are not continuously connected to a network, for users whose computers are continuously connected to a network (such as the Internet) and for users connected to a network via wireless devices, such as personal digital assistants.

For computers that are not continuously connected to a network, McAfee provides its antivirus software *VirusScan®*. This software is configurable to scan files for viruses on demand or to scan continuously in the background as the user does his or her work.

For computers that are network and Internet accessible, McAfee provides its online `McAfee.com` Clinic. Users with a subscription to McAfee Clinic can use the online virus software from any computer they happen to be using. As with VirusScan software on stand-alone computers, users can scan their files on demand. A major benefit of the Clinic is its *ActiveShield* software. Once installed, ActiveShield can be configured to scan every file that is used on the computer or just the program files. It can also be configured to check automatically for virus definition updates and notify the user when such updates become available. The user simply clicks on the supplied hyperlink in an update notification to connect to the Clinic site and clicks on another hyperlink to download the update. Thus, users can keep their computers protected with the most up-to-date virus definitions at all times, an important factor in protection from viruses.

McAfee.com: *Antivirus Utilities (Cont.)*

McAfee.com *VirusScan Wireless* provides virus protection for Palm™ handhelds, Pocket PC and other handheld devices. VirusScan Wireless is installed on the user's PC. Each time the user syncs the handheld device, the software scans for viruses. If a virus is detected, the sync is terminated until the user deletes the virus. For more information about McAfee, visit **www.mcafee.com**. Also, check out Norton Internetsecurity products from Symantec, at **www.symantec.com**. Symantec is a leading security software vendor. Its product Norton™ Internet Security 2000 provides protection against crackers, viruses and threats to privacy for both small businesses and individuals.

21.12.3 Software Exploitation, Web Defacing and Cybercrime

Another problem plaguing e-businesses is *software exploitation* by crackers. In addition to constantly updating virus and firewall programs, every program on a networked machine should be checked for vulnerabilities. However, with millions of software products available and more vulnerabilities discovered daily, this becomes an enormous task. One common vulnerability exploitation method is a *buffer overflow*, in which a program is overwhelmed by an input of more data than it has allocated space for. Buffer overflow attacks can cause systems to crash or, more dangerously, allow arbitrary code to be run on a machine. *BugTraq* was created in 1993 to list vulnerabilities, how to exploit them and how to repair them. For more information about BugTraq, visit **www.securityfocus.com**.

Web defacing is another popular form of attack, wherein the crackers illegally enter an organization's Web site and change the contents. CNN Interactive has issued a special report titled "Insurgency on the Internet," with news stories about crackers and their online attacks. Included is a gallery of defaced sites. One notable case of Web defacing occurred in 1996, when Swedish crackers changed the Central Intelligence Agency Web site (**www.odci.gov/cia**) to read "Central Stupidity Agency." The vandals put obscenities, political messages, notes to system administrators and links to adult-content sites on the page. Many other popular and large Web sites have been defaced. Defacing Web sites has become overwhelmingly popular amongst crackers today, causing archives of affected sites (with records of more than 15,000 vandalized sites) to close because of the volume in which sites were being vandalized daily.[37]

Cybercrime can have significant financial implications on an organization.[38] Companies need to protect their data, intellectual property, customer information and so on. Implementing a *security policy* is key to protecting an organization's data and network. When developing a security plan, organizations must assess their vulnerabilities and the possible threats to security. What information do they need to protect? Who are the possible attackers and what is their intent—data theft or damaging the network? How will the organization respond to incidents?[39] For more information about security and security plans,

---

37. T. Bridis, "U.S. Archive of Hacker Attacks to Close Because It Is Too Busy," *The Wall Street Journal* 24 May 2001: B10.
38. R. Marshland, "Hidden Cost of Technology," *Financial Times* 2 June 2000: 5.
39. F. Avolio, "Best Practices in Network Security," *Network Computing* 20 March 2000: 60fl72.

visit **www.cerias.com** and **www.sans.org**. Visit **www.baselinesoft.com** to check out books and CD-ROMs on security policies. Baseline Software's book, *Information Policies Made Easy: Version 7* includes over 1000 security policies. This book is used by numerous Fortune 200 companies.

e-Fact 21.7

According to the GartnerGroup, 70% of computer crime is committed by disgruntled employees.[40]

The rise in cybercrimes has prompted the U.S. government to take action. Under the National Information Infrastructure Protection Act of 1996, denial-of-service attacks and distribution of viruses are federal crimes punishable by fines and jail time. For more information about the U.S. government's efforts against cybercrime or to read about recently prosecuted cases, visit the U.S. Department of Justice Web site, at **www.usdoj.gov/criminal/cybercrime/compcrime.html**. Also check out **www.cybercrime.gov**, a site maintained by the Criminal Division of the U.S. Department of Justice.

The *Computer Emergency Response Team (CERT®) Coordination Center* at Carnegie Mellon University's Software Engineering Institute responds to reports of viruses and denial-of-service attacks and provides information on network security, including how to determine whether a system has been compromised. It provides detailed incident reports of viruses and denial-of-service attacks, including descriptions of the incidents, their impact and solutions. The site also includes reports of vulnerabilities in popular operating systems and software packages. The *CERT Security Improvement Modules* are excellent tutorials on network security. These modules describe the issues and technologies used to solve network security problems. For more information, visit the CERT Web site, at **www.cert.org**.

To learn more about how you can protect yourself or your network from hacker attacks, visit AntiOnline™ at **www.antionline.com**. This site has security-related news and information, a tutorial titled "Fight-back! Against Hackers," information about hackers and an archive of hacked sites. You can find additional information about denial-of-service attacks and how to protect your site at **www.irchelp.org/irchelp/nuke**.

After obtaining a basic idea about security issues and solution, it is the time to learn how Python can protect your local machine or network.

21.13 Running Restricted Python Code

Python code is platform independent; once Python code is written, it can be run virtually anywhere. Many programmers access Python code remotely by downloading and running it via a Python interpreter installed on the local system. This method raises security issues; when the code executes on the local machine, the code could gain unauthorized access to local files or otherwise misuse the machine.

One way to prevent executing damaging code is to run code in a restricted environment. A restricted environment is a virtual machine that provides access to only those resources that the program may need. If the code is unable to access sensitive resources (such as a hard drive or network,) it will not be able to damage such resources.

---

40. "Industry Statistics," from an AbsoluteSoftware company Press kit.

21.13.1 Module `rexec`

Module *rexec* contains the *RExec* class for executing Python code in a restricted environment. An **RExec** object supports several methods such as *r_eval* that execute code in a restricted environment. Code that executes in this environment has limited access to standard modules and built-in Python functions—the programmer has complete control over the environment in which the untrusted code runs. A default restricted environment imports several modules, including **__builtins__** and **sys**. **RExec** can restrict access to some resources, such as a disk or network, but it cannot limit the amount of memory or CPU time that the code in the restricted environment uses. Restricted code can generate exceptions and, if the program does not catch and handle those exceptions, the program could terminate. Therefore, programmers should execute untrusted code from within **try/catch** clauses that catch all exceptions.

21.13.2 Module `Bastion`

Module *Bastion* restricts access to specific objects, rather than the entire environment. The **Bastion** object wraps an object and controls the access to this object. **Bastion** provides precise control over the methods of the object, achieved by supplying a filter function when creating a **Bastion** object. The filter function takes a method name as an argument and returns true if that method can be accessed. By default, methods of the object that begin with an underscore are not accessible.

When code tries to access a restricted method, an **AttributeError** exception is raised. This happens because the code does not recognize the method. In the restricted environment, this method is never defined and thus is not accessible. Note that **Bastion** must execute in a restricted environment, such as a **RExec** environment, to enhance a program's security.

21.13.3 Restricted Web Browser

Figure 21.9 demonstrates a modified version of the Web browser we presented in Chapter 20, Networking (Fig. 20.1). The modified browser checks on whether the requested page ends with the **.py** extension. If so, the browser runs the Python code in a restricted environment.

```
1   # Fig. 21.9: fig21_09.py
2   # Displays the contents of a file on a Web server.
3
4   from Tkinter import *
5   import tkMessageBox
6   import Pmw
7   import urllib
8   import urlparse
9   import Bastion
10  import rexec
11
12  class WebBrowser( Frame ):
13      """A simple Web browser"""
14
```

Fig. 21.9   Restricted Web browser. (Part 1 of 4.)

```
15       def __init__( self ):
16           """Create the Web browser GUI"""
17
18           Frame.__init__( self )
19           Pmw.initialise()
20           self.pack( expand = YES, fill = BOTH )
21           self.master.title( "Simple Web Browser" )
22           self.master.geometry( "400x300" )
23
24           self.address = Entry( self )
25           self.address.pack( fill = X, padx = 5, pady = 5 )
26           self.address.bind( "<Return>", self.getPage )
27
28           self.contents = Pmw.ScrolledText( self,
29              text_state = DISABLED )
30           self.contents.pack( expand = YES, fill = BOTH, padx = 5,
31              pady = 5 )
32
33           # create restricted environment
34           self.restricted = rexec.RExec()
35           self.module = self.restricted.add_module( "__main__" )
36           self.environment = self.module.__dict__
37
38           # add browser to environment
39           self.environment[ "browser" ] = Bastion.Bastion( self )
40
41       def setColor( self, color ):
42           """Set browser's background color"""
43
44           self.configure( background = color )
45
46       def _setColor( self, color ):
47           """Set browser's background"""
48
49           self.configure( background = color )
50
51       def setText( self, text ):
52           """Set the text of the ScrolledText component"""
53
54           self.contents.settext( text )
55
56       def runCode( self, statement ):
57           """Run a Python statement in restricted environment"""
58
59           try:
60              self.restricted.r_exec( statement ) # execute in rexec
61           except AttributeError, name:
62              tkMessageBox.showerror( "Error",
63                 "Restricted code tried to access forbidden " + \
64                 "attribute:" + str( name ) )
65
66       def getPage( self, event ):
67           """Parse the URL and addressing scheme and retrieve file"""
```

Fig. 21.9   Restricted Web browser. (Part 2 of 4.)

```
68
69          # parse the URL
70          myURL = event.widget.get()
71          components = urlparse.urlparse( myURL )
72          self.contents.text_state = NORMAL
73
74          # if addressing scheme not specified, use http
75          if components[ 0 ] == "":
76             myURL = "http://" + myURL
77
78          # connect and retrieve the file
79          try:
80             tempFile = urllib.urlopen( myURL ).read()
81          except IOError:
82             self.contents.settext( "Error finding file" )
83          else:
84             tempFile = tempFile.replace( "\r\n", "\n" )
85
86             if myURL[ -3: ] == ".py":
87                self.runCode( tempFile )
88             else:
89                self.contents.settext( tempFile ) # show results
90
91             self.contents.text_state = DISABLED
92
93   def main():
94      WebBrowser().mainloop()
95
96   if __name__ == "__main__":
97      main()
```

Fig. 21.9   Restricted Web browser. (Part 3 of 4.)

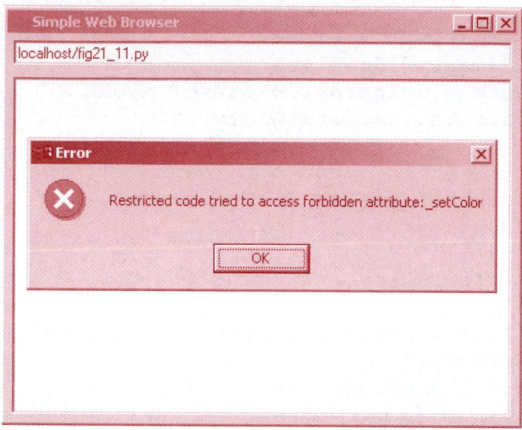

Fig. 21.9 Restricted Web browser. (Part 4 of 4.)

Line 34 creates an object of class **RExec**. Line 35 gets the environment's **__main__** module of that environment. The object defines an environment that contains a list of accessible modules and built-in functions (e.g., **raw_input** or **abs**). It has its own environment, including a list of accessible modules and built-in methods. Method **add_module** adds a new module to the list of the modules allowed in the restricted environment and returns a reference to that module. If the environment already permits access to the module, method **add_module** simply returns a reference to the specified module. Method **add_module** does not import the module into the restricted environment; the method only modifies the list of modules that the restricted code may import.

Line 34 gets the reference to the dictionary **__dict__** that contains the module-global bindings for the restricted environment. A **Bastion** module wraps a Web browser component and adds it to the module-global namespace of the restricted environment (line 39). The restricted code now may access and manipulate the Web-browser component. By wrapping the Web-browser component with class **Bastion**, we allow the program to control how the restricted code accesses the browser. By default, code many not access a **Bastion** object's data member or any methods that begin with the underscore (_) letter. The code may access methods that do not begin with the underscore character.

To demonstrate code execution, lines 41–49 add two methods to the **WebBrowser**. Both **setColor** (lines 41–44) and **_setColor** (lines 46–49) set the foreground color of the **WebBrowser**. By default, code may not access a **Bastion**-wrapped browser object's **_setColor** method.

A request for a Python program results in a call to method **runCode** (lines 56–64). The **try** statement (lines 59–64) executes the Python program in the restricted environment. If the program attempts to access **_setColor** method, the program catches the **AttributeError** exception and displays a warning in a message box. In a more realistic example, the **try** statement would include an empty **except** clause. This **except** clause would catch other exceptions raised by the code whether the errors are intentional or accidental. The program might write a message to an error file or display a message in a dialog box or on the console. The main goal is to prevent an error in downloaded code from terminating the program.

The screenshots in Fig. 21.9 demonstrate the result of running the code in Fig. 21.10 and Fig. 21.11. The first screenshot is the browser in its original state. The second screenshot is the result of running the code in Fig. 21.10. The browser has changed its background color to blue. The final screenshot demonstrates what happens when the code in Fig. 21.9 attempts to change color via restricted **_setColor**.

21.14 Network Security

The goal of network security is to allow authorized users access to information and services, while preventing unauthorized users from gaining access to, and possibly corrupting, the network. There is a trade-off between network security and network performance: Increased security often decreases the efficiency of the network.

In this section, we will discuss the various aspects of network security. We will discuss firewalls, which keep unauthorized users out of the network, and authorization servers, which allow users to access specific applications based on a set of predefined criteria. We will then look at intrusion-detection systems that actively monitor a network for intrusions and attacks.

21.14.1 Firewalls

A basic tool in network security is the *firewall*. The purpose of a firewall is to protect a LAN from intruders outside the network. For example, most companies have internal networks that allow employees to share files and access company information. Each LAN can be connected to the Internet through a *gateway*, which usually includes a firewall. For years, one of the biggest threats to security came from employees inside the firewall. Now that businesses rely heavily on access to the Internet, an increasing number of security threats are originating outside the firewall—from the hundreds of millions of people connected to the company network by the Internet.[41] A firewall acts as a safety barrier for data flowing into and out of the LAN. Firewalls can prohibit all data flow not expressly allowed or can allow all data flow that is not expressly prohibited. The choice between these two models is up to the network-security administrator and should be based on the need for security versus the need for functionality.

```
1   # Fig. 21.10: fig21_10.py
2   # Calls method setColor to set background color.
3
4   browser.setColor( "blue" )
```

Fig. 21.10 setColor used to set background color.

```
1   # Fig. 21.11: fig21_11.py
2   # Method _setColor raises attribute error in restricted enviroment.
3
4   browser._setColor( "red" )
```

Fig. 21.11 _setColor used to set background color.

41. R. Marshland, "Hidden Cost of Technology," *Financial Times* 2 June 2000: 5.

There are two main types of firewalls: *packet-filtering firewalls* and *application-level gateways*. A packet-filtering firewall examines all data sent from outside the LAN and rejects any data packets that have local network addresses. For example, if a cracker from outside the network obtains the address of a computer inside the network and tries to sneak a harmful data packet through the firewall, the packet-filtering firewall will reject the data packet: It has an internal address, but originated from outside the network. A problem with packet-filtering firewalls is that they consider only the source of data packets; they do not examine the actual data. As a result, malicious viruses can be installed on an authorized user's computer, giving the cracker access to the network without the authorized user's knowledge. The goal of an application-level gateway is to screen the actual data. If the message is deemed safe, then the message is sent through to the intended receiver.

Using a firewall is probably the most effective and easiest way to add security to a small network.[42] Often, small companies or home users who are connected to the Internet through permanent connections, such as DSL lines, do not employ strong security measures. As a result, their computers are prime targets for crackers to use in denial-of-service attacks or to steal information. It is important for all computers connected to the Internet to have some degree of security for their systems. Numerous firewall software products are available. Several products are listed in the Web resources in Section 21.16.

Air-gap technology is a network security solution that complements the firewall. It secures private data from external traffic accessing the internal network. The *air gap* separates the internal network from the external network, and the organization decides which information will be made available to external users. *Whale Communications* created the *e-Gap System*, which is composed of two computer servers and a *memory bank*. The memory bank does not run an operating system; therefore, crackers cannot take advantage of common operating system weaknesses to access network information.

Air-gap technology does not allow outside users to view the network's structure, preventing crackers from searching the layout for weak spots or specific data. The e-Gap *Web Shuttle* feature allows safe external access by restricting the system's *back office*, which is where an organization's most sensitive information and IT-based business processes are controlled. Users who want to access a network hide behind the air gap, where the authentication server is located. Authorized users gain access through a single sign-on capability, allowing them to use one login password to access authorized areas of the network.

The e-Gap *Secure File Shuttle* feature moves files into and out of the network. Each file is inspected behind the air gap. If the file is deemed safe, it is carried by the File Shuttle into the network.[43]

Air-gap technology is used by e-commerce organizations to allow their clients and partners to access information automatically, thus reducing the cost of inventory management. Military, aerospace and government industries, which store highly sensitive information, use air-gap technology.

21.14.2 Intrusion-Detection Systems

What happens if a cracker gets inside your firewall? How do you know that an intruder has penetrated the firewall? Also, how do you know that unauthorized employees are accessing

42. T. Spangler, "Home Is Where the Hack Is," *Inter@ctive Week* 10 April 2000: 28–34.
43. "Air Gap Technology," *Whale Communications* **<www.whale-com.com>**.

SANS Institute: Security Research and Education

The *System Administration, Networking and Security Institute (SANS)*, founded in 1989, is a security research and education organization with over 96,000 members (**www.sans.org**). SANS sells security training, certification programs and publications. The organization also offers several free, publicly available services such as security alerts and news.

Each year, SANS publishes the *Roadmap to Security Tools and Services Poster*—a resource that includes information about key-security technologies, lists of security vendors that specialize in each technology and URLs with additional security information. The poster also includes directions on how to order approximately 20 white papers. To order a copy of the poster and to request copies of the technical white papers, go to **www.sans.org/tools.htm**.

The SANS Information Security Reading Room is an excellent resource for security information. The site has hundreds of articles and case studies organized by security topic. Topics include authentication, attacking attackers, intrusion-detection, securing code, standards and many more. For more information, visit **www.sans.org/infosecFAQ/index.htm**.

SANS offers three free newsletters. *SANS NewsBites* is a free weekly e-mail newsletter that lists key security news articles with a short summary of each article and a link to the complete resource. Go to **www.sans.org/newlook/digests/newsbites.htm** to view the latest newsletter, to view past newsletters or to subscribe. *Security Alert Consensus (SAC)* is a weekly summary of new security alerts and countermeasures. Subscribers can opt to receive information on specific operating systems for their particular needs. The *SANS Windows Security Digest* lists Windows NT security updates, threats and bugs. To subscribe to any of the SANS e-mail newsletters, go to **www.sans.org/sansnews**.

The SANS *Global Incident Analysis Center (GIAC)* records current attacks and analyzes each attack. Network and systems administrators can use this information to help them defend their networks and systems against attacks. Reports are made readily available to the public at **www.sans.org/giac.htm** and **www.incidents.org**.

restricted applications? *Intrusion-detection systems* monitor networks and application *log files*—files containing information on files, including who accessed them and when—so if an intruder makes it into the network or an unauthorized application, the system detects the intrusion, halts the session and sets off an alarm to notify the system administrator.[44]

Host-based intrusion-detection systems monitor system and application log files. They can scan for Trojan horses, for example. *Network-based intrusion-detection* software monitors traffic on a network for any unusual patterns that might indicate DoS attacks or attempted entry into a network by an unauthorized user. Companies can then check their log files to determine whether indeed there was an intrusion and, if so, they can attempt to track the offender. Check out the intrusion-detection products from Cisco (**www.cisco.com/**

44. O. Azim and P. Kolwalkar, "Network Intrusion Monitoring," *Advisor.com/Security* March/April 2001: 16–19.

`warp/public/cc/pd/sqsw/sqidsz`),   Hewlett-Packard   (`www.hp.com/secu-rity/home.html`) and Symantec (`www.symantec.com`).

The *Operationally Critical Threat, Asset and Vulnerability Evaluation (OCTAVE[SM]) method*, under development at the Software Engineering Institute at Carnegie Mellon University, is a process for evaluating security threats to a system. There are three phases in OCTAVE: building threat profiles, identifying vulnerabilities, and developing security solutions and plans. In the first stage, the organization identifies its important information and assets, and then evaluates the levels of security required to protect them. In the second phase, the system is examined for weaknesses that could compromise the valuable data. The third phase is to develop a security strategy as advised by an analysis team of three to five security experts assigned by OCTAVE. This approach is one of the first of its kind, in which the owners of computer systems not only get to have professionals analyze their systems, but also participate in prioritizing the protection of crucial information.[45]

21.15 Steganography

Steganography is the practice of hiding information within other information. The term literally means "covered writing." Like cryptography, steganography has been used since ancient times. Steganography allows you to take a piece of information, such as a message or image, and hide it within another image, a message or even an audio clip. Steganography takes advantage of insignificant space in digital files, in images or on removable disks.[46] Consider a simple example: If you have a message that you want to send secretly, you can hide the information within another message, so that no one but the intended receiver can read it. For example, if you want to tell your stockbroker to buy a stock and your message must be transmitted over an unsecure channel, you could send the message "BURIED UNDER YARD." If you have agreed in advance that your message is hidden in the first letters of each word, the stock broker picks these letters off and sees "BUY."

An increasingly popular application of steganography is *digital watermarks* for intellectual property protection. An example of a conventional watermark is shown in Fig. 21.12. A digital watermark can be either visible or invisible. It is usually a company logo, copyright notification or other mark or message that indicates the owner of the document. The owner of a document could show the hidden watermark in a court of law, for example, to prove that the watermarked item was stolen.

Digital watermarking could have a substantial impact on e-commerce. Consider the music industry. Music publishers are concerned that MP3 technology is allowing people to distribute illegal copies of songs and albums. As a result, many publishers are hesitant to put content online; digital content is easy to copy. Also, CD-ROMs are digital, so people are able to upload their music and share it over the Web. Using digital watermarks, music publishers can make indistinguishable changes to a part of a song at a frequency that is not audible to humans, to show that the song was, in fact, copied. Microsoft Research is developing a watermarking system for digital audio, which would be included with default Windows media players. In this digital watermarking system, data such as licensing information is embedded into a song; the media player will not play files with invalid information.

---

45. "OCTAVE Information Security Risk Evaluation," 30 January 2001 <`www.cert.org/oc-tave/methodintro.html`>.
46. S. Katzenbeisser and F. Petitcolas, *Information Hiding: Techniques for Steganography and Digital Watermarking* (Norwood: Artech House, Inc., 2000) 1–2.

e-Fact 21.8

Record Companies are losing approximately $5 billion per year to piracy.[47]

Blue Spike's Giovanni™ digital watermarking software uses cryptographic keys to generate and embed steganographic digital watermarks into digital music and images (Fig. 21.13). The watermarks can be used as proof of ownership to help digital publishers protect their copyrighted material. The watermarks are undetectable by anyone who is not privy to the embedding scheme and therefore cannot be identified and removed. The watermarks are placed randomly.

Giovanni incorporates cryptography and steganography. It generates a secret key based on an encryption algorithm and the contents of the audio or image file. The key is then used to place (and eventually decode) the watermark in the file. The software identifies the perceptually insignificant areas of the image or audio file, enabling a digital watermark to be embedded inaudibly, invisibly and in such a way that, if the watermark is removed, the content is likely to be damaged.

Digital watermarking capabilities are built into some image-editing software applications, such as Adobe PhotoShop 5.5 (`www.adobe.com`). Companies that offer digital watermarking solutions include Digimarc (`www.digimark.com`) and Cognicity (`www.cognicity.com`).

Fig. 21.12 Conventional watermark example. (Courtesy of Blue Spike, Inc.)

47. D.McCullagh, "MS May Have File-Trading Answer," 1 May 2001 `<www.wired.com/news/print/0,1294,43389,00.html>`.

Fig. 21.13 Steganography example: Blue Spike's Giovanni digital watermarking process. (Courtesy of Blue Spike, Inc.)

21.16 Internet and World Wide Web Resources

Security Resource Sites

www.securitysearch.com
This is a comprehensive resource for computer security. The site has thousands of links to products, security companies, tools and more. It also offers a free weekly newsletter with information about vulnerabilities.

www.esecurityonline.com
This site is a great resource for information on online security. It has links to news, tools, events, training and other valuable security information and resources.

theory.lcs.mit.edu/~rivest/crypto-security.html
The *Ronald L. Rivest: Cryptography and Security* site has an extensive list of links to security resources, including newsgroups, government agencies, FAQs, tutorials and more.

www.w3.org/Security/Overview.html
The *W3C Security Resources* site has FAQs, information about W3C security and e-commerce initiatives and links to other security-related Web sites.

web.mit.edu/network/ietf/sa
The *Internet Engineering Task Force* (*IETF*), which is an organization concerned with the architecture of the Internet, has working groups dedicated to Internet security. Visit the *IETF Security Area* to learn about the working groups, join the mailing list or check out the latest drafts of the IETF's work.

dir.yahoo.com/Computers_and_Internet/Security_and_Encryption
The *Yahoo Security and Encryption* page is a great resource for links to Web sites security and encryption.

www.counterpane.com/hotlist.html
The Counterpane Internet Security, Inc., site includes links to downloads, source code, FAQs, tutorials, alert groups, news and more.

www.rsasecurity.com/rsalabs/faq
This site is an excellent set of FAQs about cryptography from RSA Laboratories, one of the leading makers of public-key cryptosystems.

www.nsi.org/compsec.html
Visit the National Security Institute's *Security Resource Net* for the latest security alerts, government standards and legislation, plus security FAQs links and other helpful resources.

www.itaa.org/infosec
The Information Technology Association of America (ITAA) *InfoSec* site has information about the latest U.S. government legislation related to information security.

staff.washington.edu/dittrich/misc/ddos
The *Distributed Denial of Service Attacks* site has links to news articles, tools, advisory organizations and even a section on security humor.

www.infoworld.com/cgi-bin/displayNew.pl?/security/links/
security_corner.htm
The Security Watch site on **Infoword.com** has loads of links to security resources.

www.antionline.com
AntiOnline has security-related news and information, a tutorial titled "Fight-back! Against Hackers," information about hackers and an archive of hacked sites.

www.microsoft.com/security/default.asp
The Microsoft security site has links to downloads, security bulletins and tutorials.

www.grc.com
This site offers a service to test the security of your computer's Internet connection.

www.sans.org/giac.html
Sans Institute presents information on system and security updates, along with new research and discoveries. The site offers current publications, projects and weekly digests.

www.packetstorm.securify.com
The Packet Storm page describes the 20 latest advisories, tools and exploits. This site also provides links to the top security news stories.

www.xforce.iss.net
This site allows one to search a virus by name, reported date, expected risk or affected platforms. Updated news reports can be found on this page.

www.ntbugtraq.com
This site provides a list and description of various Windows NT Security Exploits/Bugs encountered by Windows NT users. One can download updated service applications.

nsi.org/compsec.html
The Security Resource Net page states various warnings, threats, legislation and documents of viruses and security in an organized outline.

www.securitystats.com
This computer security site provides statistics on viruses, web defacements and security spending.

www.psionic.com/abacus/hostsentry
Python application that monitors logins to a system.

Magazines, Newsletters and News sites

www.networkcomputing.com/consensus
The *Security Alert Consensus* is a free weekly newsletter with information about security threats, holes, solutions and more.

www.atstake.com/security_news
Visit this site for daily security news.

www.infosecuritymag.com
Information Security Magazine has the latest Web security news and vendor information.

www.issl.org/cipher.html
Cipher is an electronic newsletter on security and privacy from the Institute of Electrical and Electronics Engineers (IEEE). You can view current and past issues online.

securityportal.com
The *Security Portal* has news and information about security, cryptography and the latest viruses.

www.scmagazine.com
SC Magazine has news, product reviews and a conference schedule for security events.

www.cnn.com/TECH/specials/hackers
Insurgency on the Internet from CNN Interactive has news on hacking, plus a gallery of hacked sites.

Government Sites for Computer Security

www.cit.nih.gov/security.html
This site has links to security organizations, security resources and tutorials on PKI, SSL and other protocols.

cs-www.ncsl.nist.gov
The *Computer Security Resource Clearing House* is a resource for network administrators and others concerned with security. This site has links to incident-reporting centers, information about security standards, events, publications and other resources.

www.cdt.org/crypto
Visit the Center for Democracy and Technology for U. S. legislation and policy news regarding cryptography.

www.epm.ornl.gov/~dunigan/security.html
This site has links to loads of security-related sites. The links are organized by subject and include resources on digital signatures, PKI, smart cards, viruses, commercial providers, intrusion detection and several other topics.

www.alw.nih.gov/Security
The *Computer Security Information* page is an excellent resource, providing links to news, newsgroups, organizations, software, FAQs and an extensive number of Web links.

www.fedcirc.gov
The Federal Computer Incident Response Capability deals with the security of government and civilian agencies. This site has information about incident statistics, advisories, tools, patches and more.

axion.physics.ubc.ca/pgp.html
This site has a list of freely available cryptosystems, along with a discussion of each system and links to FAQs and tutorials.

www.ifccfbi.gov
The Internet Fraud Complaint Center, founded by the Justice Department and the FBI, fields reports of Internet fraud.

www.disa.mil/infosec/iaweb/default.html
The Defense Information Systems Agency's *Information Assurance* page includes links to sites on vulnerability warnings, virus information and incident-reporting instructions, plus other helpful links.

www.nswc.navy.mil/ISSEC/
The objective of this site is to provide information on protecting your computer systems from security hazards. It contains a page on hoax versus real viruses.

www.cit.nih.gov/security.html
You can report security issues at this site. The site also lists official federal security policies, regulations and guidelines.

cs-www.ncsl.nist.gov/
The Computer Security Resource Center provides services for vendors and end users. The site includes information on security testing, management, technology, education and applications.

www.ssh.com
This site is the SSH Communications Security home page. It provides links for downloading SSH products.

Advanced Encryption Standard (AES)

csrc.nist.gov/encryption/aes
The official site for the AES includes press releases and a discussion forum.

www.esat.kuleuven.ac.be/~rijmen/rijndael/
Visit this site for information about the Rijndael algorithm.

home.ecn.ab.ca/~jsavard/crypto/co040801.htm
This AES site includes an explanation of the algorithm with helpful diagrams and examples.

Internet Security Vendors

www.rsasecurity.com
RSA is one of the leaders in electronic security. Visit its site for more information about its current products and tools, which are used by companies worldwide.

www.ca.com/protection
Computer Associates is a vendor of Internet security software. It has various software packages to help companies set up a firewall, scan files for viruses and protect against viruses.

www.checkpoint.com
Check Point™ Software Technologies Ltd. is a leading provider of Internet security products and services.

www.opsec.com
The Open Platform for Security (OPSEC) has over 200 partners that develop security products and solutions using OPSEC to allow for interoperability and increased security over a network.

www.baltimore.com
Baltimore Security is an e-commerce security solutions provider. Their UniCERT digital certificate product is used in PKI applications.

www.ncipher.com
nCipher is a vendor of hardware and software products, including an SSL accelerator that increases the speed of secure Web server transactions and a secure-key management system.

www.entrust.com
Entrust Technologies provides e-security products and services.

www.antivirus.com
ScanMail® is an e-mail virus detection program for Microsoft Exchange.

www.zixmail.com
Zixmail™ is a secure e-mail product that allows you to encrypt and digitally sign your messages, using different e-mail programs.

web.mit.edu/network/pgp.html
Visit this site to download *Pretty Good Privacy®* freeware. PGP allows you to send messages and files securely.

www.certicom.com
Certicom provides security solutions for the wireless Internet.

www.raytheon.com
Raytheon Corporation's *SilentRunner* monitors activity on a network to find internal threats, such as data theft or fraud.

SSL

developer.netscape.com/tech/security/ssl/protocol.html
This Netscape page has a brief description of SSL, plus links to an SSL tutorial and FAQs.

www.netscape.com/security/index.html
The Netscape Security Center is an extensive resource for Internet and Web security. You will find news, tutorials, products and services on this site.

psych.psy.uq.oz.au/~ftp/Crypto
This FAQs page has an extensive list of questions and answers about SSL technology.

www.visa.com/nt/ecomm/security/main.html
Visa International's security page includes information on SSL and SET. The page includes a demonstration of an online shopping transaction, which explains how SET works.

www.openssl.org
The *Open SSL Project* provides a free, open source toolkit for SSL.

Public-Key Cryptography

www.entrust.com
Entrust produces effective security software products, using Public Key Infrastructure.

www.cse.dnd.ca
The Communication Security Establishment has a short tutorial on Public-Key Infrastructure that defines PKI, public-key cryptography and digital signatures.

www.magnet.state.ma.us/itd/legal/pki.htm
The Commonwealth of Massachusetts Information Technology page has loads of links to sites related to PKI that contain information about standards, vendors, trade groups and government organizations.

www.ftech.net/~monark/crypto/index.htm
The Beginner's Guide to Cryptography is an online tutorial and includes links to other sites on privacy and cryptography.

www.faqs.org/faqs/cryptography-faq
The *Cryptography FAQ* has an extensive list of questions and answers.

www.pkiforum.org
The PKI Forum promotes the use of PKI.

www.counterpane.com/pki-risks.html
Visit the Counterpane Internet Security, Inc.'s site to read the article "Ten Risks of PKI: What You're Not Being Told About Public Key Infrastructure."

Digital Signatures

www.ietf.org/html.charters/xmldsig-charter.html
The *XML Digital Signatures* site was created by a group working to develop digital signatures using XML. You can view the group's goals and drafts of their work.

www.elock.com
E-Lock Technologies is a vendor of digital-signature products used in Public-Key Infrastructure. This site has an FAQs list covering cryptography, keys, certificates and signatures.

www.digsigtrust.com
The Digital Signature Trust Co. is a vendor of Digital Signature and Public-Key Infrastructure products. It has a tutorial titled "Digital Signatures and Public Key Infrastructure (PKI) 101."

Digital Certificates

www.verisign.com
VeriSign creates digital IDs for individuals, small businesses and large corporations. Check out its Web site for product information, news and downloads.

www.thawte.com
Thawte Digital Certificate Services offers SSL, developer and personal certificates.

www.silanis.com/index.htm
Silanis Technology is a vendor of digital-certificate software.

www.belsign.be
Belsign issues digital certificates in Europe. It is the European authority for digital certificates.

www.certco.com
Certco issues digital certificates to financial institutions.

www.openca.org
Set up your own CA, using open-source software from The OpenCA Project.

Digital Wallets

www.globeset.com
GlobeSet is a vendor of digital-wallet software. Its site has an animated tutorial demonstrating the use of an electronic wallet in an SET transaction.

www.trintech.com
Trintech digital wallets handle SSL and SET transactions.

wallet.yahoo.com
The *Yahoo! Wallet* is a digital wallet that can be used at thousands of Yahoo! Stores worldwide.

Firewalls

www.interhack.net/pubs/fwfaq
This site provides an extensive list of FAQs on firewalls.

www.spirit.com/cgi-bin/report.pl
Visit this site to compare firewall software from a variety of vendors.

`www.zeuros.co.uk/generic/resource/firewall`
Zeuros is a complete resource for information about firewalls. You will find FAQs, books, articles, training and magazines on this site.

`www.thegild.com/firewall`
The *Firewall Product Overview* site has an extensive list of firewall products, with links to each vendor's site.

`csrc.ncsl.nist.gov/nistpubs/800-10`
Check out this firewall tutorial from the U.S. Department of Commerce.

`www.watchguard.com`
WatchGuard® Technologies, Inc., provides firewalls and other security solutions for medium to large organizations.

Kerberos

`www.nrl.navy.mil/CCS/people/kenh/kerberos-faq.html`
This site is an extensive list of FAQs on Kerberos from the Naval Research Laboratory.

`web.mit.edu/kerberos/www`
Kerberos: The Network Authentication Protocol is a list of FAQs provided by MIT.

`www.contrib.andrew.cmu.edu/~shadow/kerberos.html`
The Kerberos Reference Page has links to several informational sites and technical sites.

`www.pdc.kth.se/kth-krb`
Visit this site to download various Kerberos white papers and documentation.

Biometrics

`www.iosoftware.com/products/integration/fiu500/index.htm`
This site describes a security device that scans a user's fingerprint to verify identity.

`www.identix.com/flash_index.html`
Identix specializes in fingerprinting systems for law enforcement, access control and network security. Using the company's fingerprint scanners, you can log on to your system, encrypt and decrypt files and lock applications.

`www.iriscan.com`
Iriscan's *PR Iris*™ can be used for e-commerce, network and information security. The scanner takes an image of the user's eye for authentication.

`www.keytronic.com`
Key Tronic manufactures keyboards with fingerprint recognition systems.

IPSec and VPNs

`www.checkpoint.com`
Check Point™ offers combined firewall and VPN solutions. Visit their resource library for links to numerous white papers, industry groups, mailing lists and other security and VPN resources.

`www.ietf.org/html.charters/ipsec-charter.html`
The IPSec Working Group of the Internet Engineering Task Force (IETF) is a resource for technical information related to the IPSec protocol.

`www.icsalabs.com/html/communities/ipsec/certification/`
`certified_products/index.shtml`
Visit this site for a list of certified IPSec products, plus links to an IPSec glossary and other related resources.

www.ip-sec.com

The IPSec Developers Forum allows vendors and users to test the interoperability of different IPSec products. The site includes technical documents related to the IPSec protocol.

www.vpnc.org

The Virtual Private Network Consortium, which has VPN standards, white papers, definitions and archives. VPNC also offers compatibility testing with current VPN standards.

Steganography and Digital Watermarking

www.bluespike.com/giovanni/giovmain.html

Blue Spike's *Giovanni* watermarks help publishers of digital content protect their copyrighted material and track their content that is distributed electronically.

www.outguess.org

Outguess is a freely available steganographic tool.

www.cl.cam.ac.uk/~fapp2/steganography/index.html

The Information Hiding Homepage has technical information, news and links related to digital watermarking and steganography.

www.demcom.com

DemCom's *Steganos Security Suite* software allows you to encrypt and hide files within audio, video, text or HTML files.

www.cognicity.com

Cognicity specializes in digital-watermarking solutions for the music and entertainment industries.

Python Security

www.python.org/doc/current/lib/module-Bastion.html

This site has detailed information on Python **Bastion** module.

www.python.org/doc/current/lib/module-rexec.html

This site has detailed information on Python **rexec** module.

www.python.org/doc/current/lib/module-md5.html

This site has detailed information on Python **md5** module.

www.post1.com/home/ngps/m2

Package M2Crypto lets Python access RSA, DSA, DH, HMAC, SSL, HTTPS, etc.

directory.google.com/Top/Computers/Programming/Languages/Python/ Modules/Cryptography/

This site lists a few sites relevant to Python and security, including the M2Crypto side and others such as pyRijndael which is a pure Python implementation of Rijndael and PyGPG which is a Python wrapper of "GNU Privacy Guard".

pygss.sourceforge.net

PyGSS is a Python wrapper to Kerberos' Generic Security Service API.

Newsgroups

news:comp.security.firewalls

news:comp.security.unix

news:comp.security.misc

news:comp.protocols.kerberos

SUMMARY

- The field of security places most emphasis on the following issues: privacy, integrity, authentication and nonrepudiation.

- Python applications potentially can access files on the local computer on which the code is run.

- To secure information, data can be encrypted. Cryptography transforms data using a cipher, or cryptosystem—a mathematical procedure for encrypting messages.

- A key—a string of alphanumeric characters that acts as a password—is input to the cipher. The algorithm uses the key to make data incomprehensible to all but the sender and intended receiver.

- In a substitution cipher, every occurrence of a given letter is replaced by a different letter. In a transposition cipher, the ordering of the letters is shifted.

- Modern cryptosystems are digital. Their algorithms are based on the individual bits or blocks—a group of bits, treated as a single unit—of a message.

- Secret-key cryptography uses the same secret key to encrypt and decrypt a message.

- One of the most commonly used symmetric encryption algorithms is DES. The new standard is called AES. Rijndael was chosen as the AES candidate.

- Public-key cryptography was designed to solve the problem of exchanging keys securely. Public-key cryptography is asymmetric. It uses two inversely related keys: a public key and a private key.

- The most common key agreement protocol is a digital envelope. With a digital envelope, the message is encrypted using a secret key, and the secret key is encrypted using public-key encryption.

- Digital signatures, the electronic equivalent of written signatures, were developed to be used in public-key cryptography to solve the problems of authentication and integrity. A digital signature authenticates the sender's identity, and like a written signature, they are difficult to forget.

- Timestamping, which binds a time and date to a digital document, can help solve the problem of nonrepudiation.

- Public-Key Infrastructure integrates public-key cryptography with digital certificates and certificate authorities to authenticate parties in a transaction.

- A digital certificate is a digital document used to identify a user public key that is issued by a certificate authority.

- Digital certificates are created with an expiration date, to force users to switch key pairs. The longer a key pair is used, the more vulnerable the keys are to attack and cryptanalysis.

- A smart card generally looks like a credit card and can serve many functions, from authentication to data storage.

- Trying to decrypt ciphertext without knowledge of the decryption key is known as cryptanalysis.

- SSL is primarily used to secure point-to-point connections—transmissions of data from one computer to another.

- Transmission Control Protocol/Internet Protocol (TCP/IP) is the standard set of protocols used for connecting computers and networks to the Internet.

- Virtual Private Networks (VPNs) use the Internet infrastructure that is already in place. VPNs provide the same services as private networks, but use a different technique for connecting devices.

- IPSec uses public-key and symmetric-key cryptography to ensure authentication of the users, data integrity and confidentiality. IPSec enables the secure connections of an entire VPN.

- Microsoft Passport incorporates authentication, online purchasing, single sign-on and several other technologies into one product that can be used over several different sites on the Internet.

- Microsoft Passport also provides for protection from brute-force cracking.

- A denial-of-service attack occurs when a network's resources are taken up by an unauthorized individual, leaving the network unavailable for legitimate users.

- Viruses are computer programs that attach to, or overwrite, other programs to replicate themselves. Viruses can corrupt files or even wipe out a hard drive.

- Most antivirus software is reactive—going after viruses once they are discovered—rather than protecting against unknown viruses. Wireless devices lack sufficient memory and power to run most antivirus scanners.

- Software exploitation by crackers can cause systems to crash or, more dangerously, allow arbitrary code to be run on a machine.

- Web defacing is a popular form of attack, wherein the crackers illegally enter an organization's Web site and change the contents.

- Cybercrime can have significant financial implications on an organization. Companies need to protect their data, intellectual property and customer information.

- Module **rexec** contains the **RExec** class used to execute Python code in a restricted environment.

- A default restricted environment imports several modules, including **__builtins__** and **sys.** **RExec** can only restrict access to some resources such as a disk or network, but it cannot limit the amount of memory or CPU time used by the code in the restricted environment.

- Module **Bastion** restricts access to specific objects, rather than the entire environment. The **Bastion** object wraps an object and controls the access to this object.

- Method **add_module** adds a new module to the list of the modules allowed in the restricted environment and returns a reference to that module.

- The goal of network security is to allow authorized users access to information and services, while preventing unauthorized users from gaining access to, and possibly corrupting, the network.

- A basic tool in network security is the firewall. The purpose of a firewall is to protect a local area network (LAN) from intruders outside the network.

- Air-gap technology secures a business' data from external traffic accessing the internal network.

- Kerberos authenticates users in a network and maintains the integrity and privacy of network communications.

- Intrusion-detection systems monitor networks and application log files unauthorized users or unauthorized access of applications.

- Biometrics uses unique personal information, such as fingerprints, eyeball iris scans or face scans, to identify a user. This system eliminates the need for passwords.

- Steganograpy is the practice of hiding information within other information.

- Digital watermarking could have a substantial impact on e-commerce. Using digital watermarks, music publishers can make indistinguishable changes to a part of a song at a frequency that is not audible to humans, to show that the song was, in fact, copied.

TERMINOLOGY

128-bit
3DES
ActiveShield
add_module method of **RExec** class
Advanced Encryption Standard (AES)
air-gap technology
American National Standards Institute (ANSI)

application-level gateway
authentication
authentication header (AH)
authentication server scripts
availability
back office
backdoor program

Bastion module
binary string
Biometric Application Programming
    Interface (BAPI)
biometrics
bit
block
block cipher
brute-force cracking
buffer overflow
BugTraq
Caesar cipher
Computer Emergency Response Team (CERT)
CERT coordination center
CERT Security Improvement Modules
certificate authority (CA)
certificate-authority hierarchy
certificate repository
certificate revocation list (CRL)
cipher
ciphertext
collision
contact interface
contactless interface
content protection
CPU
cracker
cryptanalysis
cryptanalytic attack
cryptography
cryptosystem
cybercrime
Data Encryption Standard (DES)
data packet
decryption
denial-of-service (DoS) attack
DES cracker machine
Diffie-Hellman and RSA algorithm
digital certificate
digital envelope
digital ID
digital signature
Digital Signature Algorithm (DSA)
digital watermarking
distributed denial-of-service attack
e-gap system
Encapsulating Security Payload (ESP)
encryption
firewall
gateway

hacker
hash function
hash value
identity permissions
ILOVEYOU Virus
integrity
interfaces
Internet Engineering Task Force (IETF)
Internet Key Exchange (IKE)
Internet Policy Registration Authority (IPRA)
Internet Protocol Security(IPSec)
host-based intrusion detection
IP address
IP spoofing
Kerberos
key
key-agreement protocol
key-distribution center
key generation
key length
key management
layered biometric verification (LBV)
local area network (LAN)
log files
logic bomb
Lucifer
masquerading
MD5 hashing algorithm
md5 module
Melissa Virus
memory card
message digest
message integrity
microprocessor card
Microsoft Authenticode
Microsoft Passport
National Institute of Standards and
    Technology (NIST)
network-based intrusion detector
network security
nonrepudiation
one-way hashing function
Online Certificate Status Protocol (OCSP)
Operationally Critical Threat, Asset and
    Vulnerability Evaluation (OCTAVE
packet
packet-filtering firewall
peripheral component interconnect (PCI) card
personal identification number (PIN)
plaintext

point-to-point connection	smart card
policy creation authority	socket
Pretty Good Privacy (PGP)	software exploit
privacy	steganography
private key	substitution cipher
protocol	symmetric encryption algorithm
public key	Ticket Granting Service (TGS)
Public-Key Infrastructure (PKI)	Ticket Granting Ticket (TGT)
public-key algorithms	time bomb
public-key cryptography	timestamping
resident virus	timestamping agency
restricted algorithms	token
rexec module	transaction management
rexec.RExec class	transient virus
restricted environment	Transmission Control Protocol/Internet
r_eval method	Protocol (TCP/IP)
Rijndael	Transport Layer Security (TSL)
root certificate authority	Triple DES
root key	Trojan horse virus
routing table	two-factor authentication
secret key	VeriSign
secure file shuttle	Virtual Private Network (VPN)
secure hash algorithm (SHA-1)	virus
Secure Sockets Layer (SSL)	Web defacing
security policy file	Web shuttle
service ticket	Wide area network (WAN)
session key	workstation logon scripts
single sign-on	worm

SELF-REVIEW EXERCISES

21.1 State whether the following are *true* or *false*. If the answer is *false*, explain why.

a) In a public-key algorithm, one key is used for both encryption and decryption.
b) Digital certificates are intended to be used indefinitely.
c) Secure Sockets Layer protects data stored on a merchant's server.
d) Digital signatures can provide undeniable proof of the author of a document.
e) In a network of 10 users communicating using public-key cryptography, only 10 keys are needed in total.
f) The security of modern cryptosystems lies in the secrecy of the algorithm.
g) Increasing the security of a network often decreases its functionality and efficiency.
h) Firewalls are the single most effective way to add security to a small computer network.
i) Kerberos is an authentication protocol that is used over TCP/IP networks.
j) SSL can connect a network of computers over the Internet.
k) Cracker attacks, such as denial of service and viruses, can cause e-business to lose billions of dollars.
l) Python applications potentially can access files on the local computer on which the code is run.
m) Running code in a restricted environment prevents executing damaging code.

21.2 Fill in the blanks in each of the following statements:

a) Cryptographic algorithms in which the message's sender and receiver both hold an identical key are called _____.

b) A _____ authenticates the sender of a document.

c) In a _____, a document is encrypted using a secret key and sent with that secret key, encrypted via a public-key algorithm.

d) A certificate that needs to be revoked before its expiration date is placed on a _____.

e) The recent wave of network attacks that have hit companies such as eBay and Yahoo are known as _____.

f) A digital fingerprint of a document can be created using a _____.

g) The four main issues addressed by cryptography are _____, _____, _____ and _____.

h) A customer can store purchase information and data on multiple credit cards in an electronic purchasing and storage device called a _____.

i) Trying to decrypt ciphertext without knowing the decryption key is known as _____.

j) A barrier between a small network and the outside world is called a _____.

k) A cracker who tries every possible solution to crack a code is using a method known as _____.

l) Module _____ can execute Python code in a restricted environment.

m) Module _____ can be used restrict access to specific objects, rather than the entire environment.

ANSWERS TO SELF-REVIEW EXERCISES

21.1   a) False. The encryption key is different from the decryption key. One is made public, and the other is kept private. b) False. Digital certificates are created with an expiration date to encourage users to change their public- and private-key pair periodically. c) False. Secure Sockets Layer is an Internet security protocol, which secures the transfer of information in electronic communication. It does not protect data stored on a merchant's server. d) False. A user who digitally signed a document could later intentionally give up his or her private key and then claim that the document was written by an imposter. Thus, timestamping a document is necessary, so that users cannot repudiate documents written before the pubic- and private-key pair is reported as invalidated. e) False. Each user needs a public key and a private key. Thus, in a network of 10 users, 20 keys are needed in total. f) False. The security of modern cryptosystems lies in the secrecy of the encryption and decryption keys. g) True. h) True. i) True. j) False, IPSec can connect a whole network of computers, while SSL can only connect two secure systems. k) True. l) True. m) True.

21.2   a) symmetric-key algorithms. b) digital signature. c) digital envelope. d) certificate revocation list. e) distributed denial-of-service attacks. f) hash function. g) privacy, authentication, integrity, nonrepudiation. h) electronic wallet. i) cryptanalysis. j) firewall. k) brute-force hacking. l) `rexec`. m) **Bastion**.

EXERCISES

21.3   What can online businesses do to prevent cracker attacks, such as denial-of-service attacks and virus attacks?

21.4   Define the following security terms:
a) Digital signature.
b) Hash function.
c) Symmetric-key encryption.
d) Digital certificate.
e) Denial-of-service attack.
f) Worm.

g) Message digest.
h) Collision.
i) Triple DES.
j) Session keys.

21.5 Define each of the following security terms, and give an example of how it is used:
a) Secret-key cryptography.
b) Public-key cryptography.
c) Digital signature.
d) Digital certificate.
e) Hash function.
f) SSL.
g) Kerberos.
h) Firewall.

21.6 Write the full name and describe each of the following acronyms:
a) PKI.
b) IPSec.
c) CRL.
d) AES.
e) SSL.

21.7 List the four problems addressed by cryptography, and give a real-world example of each.

21.8 Compare symmetric-key algorithms with public-key algorithms. What are the benefits and drawbacks of each type of algorithm? How are these differences manifested in the real-world uses of the two types of algorithms?

22

Data Structures

Objectives

- To form linked data structures using self-referential classes and recursion.
- To create and manipulate dynamic data structures such as linked lists, queues, stacks and binary trees.
- To understand various important applications of linked data structures.
- To understand how to create reusable data structures with composition.

Much that I bound, I could not free;
Much that I freed returned to me.
Lee Wilson Dodd

'Will you walk a little faster?' said a whiting to a snail,
'There's a porpoise close behind us, and he's treading on my tail.'
Lewis Carroll

There is always room at the top.
Daniel Webster

Push on — keep moving.
Thomas Morton

I think that I shall never see
A poem lovely as a tree.
Joyce Kilmer

22.1 Introduction

This chapter introduces the general topic of *data structures* that underlies some of Python's basic data types, such as lists, tuples and dictionaries. *Linked lists* are collections of data items "lined up in a row;" insertions and removals are made anywhere in a linked list. *Stacks* are important in compilers and operating systems; insertions and removals are made only at one end of a stack—its *top*. *Queues* represent waiting lines; insertions are made at the back (also referred to as the *tail*) of a queue and removals are made from the front (also referred to as the *head*) of a queue. *Binary trees* facilitate high-speed searching and sorting of data, efficient elimination of duplicate data items, representation of file system directories and compilation of expressions into machine language.

In this chapter, we discuss the major types of data structures and implement programs that create and manipulate these data structures. We use classes and composition to create and package the data structures for reusability and maintainability.

Although basic Python lists can serve as stacks and queues, studying this chapter and creating these structures "from scratch" will provide solid preparation for higher level computer science courses. The examples provided in this chapter are practical programs that you will be able to use in more advanced courses and in industry applications.

22.2 Self-Referential Classes

A *self-referential class* contains a member that refers to an object of the same class. Consider a class **Node** that has two data members—member **data** and reference member **nextNode**. Member **nextNode** refers to an object of class **Node**—an object of the same class as the one being defined, hence the term "self-referential class." Member **nextNode** is referred to as a *link*—i.e., **nextNode** can be used to "tie" an object of class **Node** to another object of the same type. Class **Node** also has two methods: A constructor that receives a value to initialize member **data** and an **__str__** method that represents the node's data as a string.

Objects of self-referential classes can be linked together to form useful data structures such as lists, queues, stacks and trees. Figure 22.1 illustrates two objects of a self-referential class linked together to form a list. Note that a slash—representing a reference to **None**—is placed in the link member of the second object, to indicate that the link does not refer to another object. The slash is only for illustration purposes; it does not correspond to the backslash character in Python. A **None** reference normally indicates the end of a data structure.

Common Programming Error 22.1
*Not setting the link in the last node of a list to **None** is a logic error.*

22.3 Linked Lists

A *linked list* is a linear collection of objects of self-referential classes, called *nodes,* connected by reference *links*—hence, the term "linked list." A linked list is accessed via a reference to the first node of the list. Subsequent nodes are accessed via the reference link stored in each node. By convention, the link in the last node of a list is set to **None**, to mark the end of the list. Data are stored in a linked list dynamically—each node is created as necessary. A node can contain data of any type, including objects of other classes. Stacks and queues also are linear data structures and, as we will see, are constrained versions of linked lists. Trees are nonlinear data structures.

Linked lists can be maintained in sorted order by inserting each new element at the proper point in the list. Existing list elements do not need to be moved.

Performance Tip 22.1
Insertion and deletion in a regular sorted list can be time consuming—all the elements following the inserted or deleted element must be shifted appropriately. However, insertion and deletion in a sorted linked list requires at most three changes to reference links.

Nodes of a linked list normally are not stored contiguously in memory. Logically, however, the nodes of a linked list appear to be contiguous. Figure 22.2 illustrates a linked list with several nodes.

Figure 22.3 contains the definition for classes **Node** and **List**. The program of Fig. 22.4 provides the user with five options for manipulating an object of class **List**:

    1. Insert a value at the beginning of the list (method **insertAtFront**).

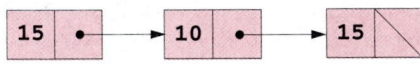

Fig. 22.1   Three linked objects of a self-referential class.

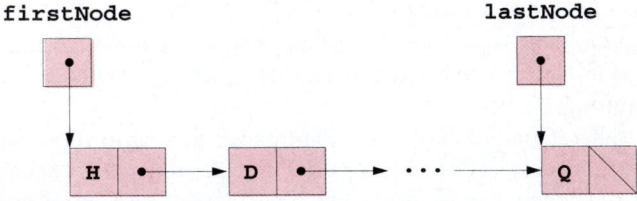

Fig. 22.2   Linked list graphical representation.

2. Insert a value at the end of the list (method **insertAtBack**).

3. Delete a value from the front of the list (method **removeFromFront**).

4. Delete a value from the end of the list (method **removeFromBack**).

5. Terminate the list processing.

A detailed discussion of **List** methods follows.

```
1   # Fig. 22.3: ListModule.py
2   # Classes List and Node definitions.
3
4   class Node:
5      """Single node in a data structure"""
6
7      def __init__( self, data ):
8         """Node constructor"""
9
10        self._data = data
11        self._nextNode = None
12
13     def __str__( self ):
14        """Node data representation"""
15
16        return str( self._data )
17
18  class List:
19     """Linked list"""
20
21     def __init__( self ):
22        """List constructor"""
23
24        self._firstNode = None
25        self._lastNode = None
26
27     def __str__( self ):
28        """List string representation"""
29
30        if self.isEmpty():
31           return "empty"
32
33        currentNode = self._firstNode
34        output = []
35
36        while currentNode is not None:
37           output.append( str( currentNode._data ) )
38           currentNode = currentNode._nextNode
39
40        return " ".join( output )
41
42     def insertAtFront( self, value ):
43        """Insert node at front of list"""
44
```

Fig. 22.3   Linked list representation—**ListModule.py**. (Part 1 of 3.)

```python
45            newNode = Node( value )
46
47            if self.isEmpty():  # List is empty
48                self._firstNode = self._lastNode = newNode
49            else:   # List is not empty
50                newNode._nextNode = self._firstNode
51                self._firstNode = newNode
52
53        def insertAtBack( self, value ):
54            """Insert node at back of list"""
55
56            newNode = Node( value )
57
58            if self.isEmpty():  # List is empty
59                self._firstNode = self._lastNode = newNode
60            else:  # List is not empty
61                self._lastNode._nextNode =  newNode
62                self._lastNode = newNode
63
64        def removeFromFront( self ):
65            """Delete node from front of list"""
66
67            if self.isEmpty():  # raise exception on empty list
68                raise IndexError, "remove from empty list"
69
70            tempNode = self._firstNode
71
72            if self._firstNode is self._lastNode:  # one node in list
73                self._firstNode = self._lastNode = None
74            else:
75                self._firstNode = self._firstNode._nextNode
76
77            return tempNode
78
79        def removeFromBack( self ):
80            """Delete node from back of list"""
81
82            if self.isEmpty():  # raise exception on empty list
83                raise IndexError, "remove from empty list"
84
85            tempNode = self._lastNode
86
87            if self._firstNode is self._lastNode:  # one node in list
88                self._firstNode = self._lastNode = None
89            else:
90                currentNode = self._firstNode
91
92                # locate second-to-last node
93                while currentNode._nextNode is not self._lastNode:
94                    currentNode = currentNode._nextNode
95
96                currentNode._nextNode = None
97                self._lastNode = currentNode
```

Fig. 22.3 Linked list representation—**ListModule.py**. (Part 2 of 3.)

```
98
99          return tempNode
100
101     def isEmpty( self ):
102         """Returns true if List is empty"""
103
104         return self._firstNode is None
```

Fig. 22.3 Linked list representation—**ListModule.py**. (Part 3 of 3.)

Figure 22.3 consists of two classes: **Node** and **List**. Encapsulated in each object of class **List** is a linked list of **Node**s. **Node** member **_nextNode** stores a reference to the next object of class **Node** in the linked list. Method **__str__** (lines 13–16) returns the string representation of the **Node**'s data.

The **List** class consists of members **_firstNode** (a reference to the first **Node** in a **List**) and **_lastNode** (a reference to the last **Node** in a **List**). The constructor initializes both links to **None** (lines 24–25). The primary methods of class **List** are **insertAtFront** (lines 42–51), **insertAtBack** (lines 53–62), **removeFromFront** (lines 64–77) and **removeFromBack** (lines 79–99).

Method **isEmpty** (lines 101–104) is called a *predicate method*—it does not alter the **List**. Rather, it determines if the **List** is empty (i.e., the reference to the first **Node** of the **List** is **None**). If the **List** is empty, **1** is returned; otherwise, **0** is returned. Method **__str__** (lines 27–40) displays the **List**'s contents.

Good Programming Practice 22.1

*Assign **None** to the link member of a new node.*

Software Engineering Observation 22.1

*Due to Python reference counting, when no references to an object of class **List** exist, the **List** and all **Node**s the **List** referenced are destroyed (assuming there are no other references to the **Node**s). However, in languages (such as C or C++) without reference counting or automatic garbage collection, it is necessary to remove all references to these objects and destroy them manually (in a destructor method, for example).*

```
1   # Fig. 22.4: fig22_04.py
2   # Driver to test class List.
3
4   from ListModule import List
5
6   # instructions for user
7   instructions = """Enter one of the following:
8       1 to insert at beginning of list
9       2 to insert at end of list
10      3 to delete from beginning of list
11      4 to delete from end of list
12      5 to end list processing\n"""
```

Fig. 22.4 Linked list representation—**fig22_04.py**. (Part 1 of 3.)

```
13
14   listObject = List()  # create empty List
15   print instructions  # print instructions
16
17   # obtain user choice until user chooses to quit (choice 5)
18   while 1:
19
20      choice = raw_input("\n? ")
21
22      # insert at front
23      if choice == "1":
24         listObject.insertAtFront( raw_input( "Enter value: " ) )
25         print "The list is: ", listObject
26
27      # insert at end
28      elif choice == "2":
29         listObject.insertAtBack( raw_input( "Enter value: " ) )
30         print "The list is: ", listObject
31
32      # delete from front
33      elif choice == "3":
34
35         try:
36            value = listObject.removeFromFront()
37         except IndexError, message:
38            print "Failed to remove:", message
39         else:
40            print value, "removed from list"
41            print "The list is: ", listObject
42
43      # delete from end
44      elif choice == "4":
45
46         try:
47            value = listObject.removeFromBack()
48         except IndexError, message:
49            print "Failed to remove:", message
50         else:
51             print value, "removed from list"
52            print "The list is: ", listObject
53
54      # exit
55      elif choice == "5":
56         break  # terminate while loop
57
58      # invalid choice
59      else:
60         print "Invalid choice:", choice
61         print instructions
62
63   print "End list test\n"
```

Fig. 22.4   Linked list representation—**fig22_04.py**. (Part 2 of 3.)

```
Enter one of the following:
    1 to insert at beginning of list
    2 to insert at end of list
    3 to delete from beginning of list
    4 to delete from end of list
    5 to end list processing


? 2
Enter value: 2
The list is:  2

? 2
Enter value: 3
The list is:  2 3

? 1
Enter value: 1
The list is:  1 2 3

? 3
1 removed from list
The list is:  2 3

? 4
3 removed from list
The list is:  2

? 3
2 removed from list
The list is:  empty

? 4
Failed to remove: remove from empty list

? 5
End list test
```

Fig. 22.4   Linked list representation—**fig22_04.py**. (Part 3 of 3.)

Over the next several pages, we discuss each of the methods of class **List** in detail. Method **insertAtFront** (lines 42–51 of Fig. 22.3) places a new node at the front of the list. The method consists of several steps (Fig. 22.5 illustrates the operation):

1. Create a new object of class **Node** and store the reference in variable **newNode** (line 45).

2. If the list is empty, then set both **_firstNode** and **_lastNode** to **newNode** (line 48).

3. If the list is not empty, the new node is "threaded" (not to be confused with the topic of multithreading) or "linked" into the list by assigning **newNode._nextNode** to the node referenced by **_firstNode** (so that the new

node now links to what used to be the first node in the list), then set **_firstNode** to reference **newNode** (lines 50–51).

In Fig. 22.5, part (a) shows the list and the new node during the **insertAtFront** operation and before the method threads the new node into the list. The dotted arrows in part (b) illustrate Step 3 of the **insertAtFront** operation, that enables the node containing **12** to become the new front of the list.

Method **insertAtBack** (lines 53–62 of Fig. 22.3) places a new node at the back of the list. The method consists of several steps (Fig. 22.6 illustrates the operation):

1. Create a new list node that contains **value** and assign the node to reference **newNode** (line 56).

2. If the list is empty, then set both **_firstNode** and **_lastNode** to **newNode** (line 59).

3. If the list is not empty, then thread the new node into the list by assigning **_lastNode._nextNode** to the node referenced by **newNode** (so that the node that used to be the last node now links to the new node), then set **_lastNode** to reference **newNode** (line 61–62).

In Fig. 22.6, part (a) shows the list and the new node during the operation and before the method inserts the new node. The dotted arrows in part (b) illustrate Step 3 of the **insertAtBack** operation that enables a new node to be added to the end of a list that is not empty.

Method **removeFromFront** (lines 64–77 of Fig. 22.3) removes the front node of the list and returns a reference to that node. The method raises an **IndexError** exception if an attempt is made to remove a node from an empty list. The method consists of several steps:

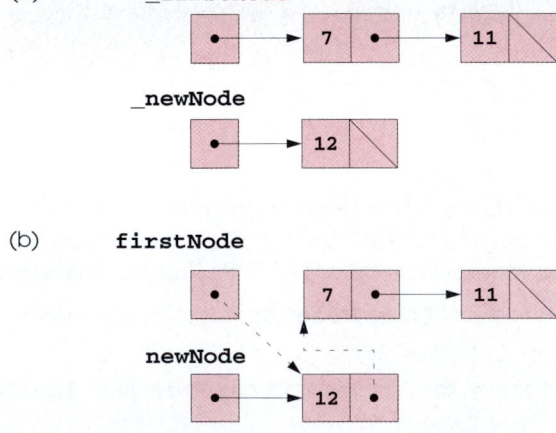

Fig. 22.5 Graphical representation of the **insertAtFront** operation.

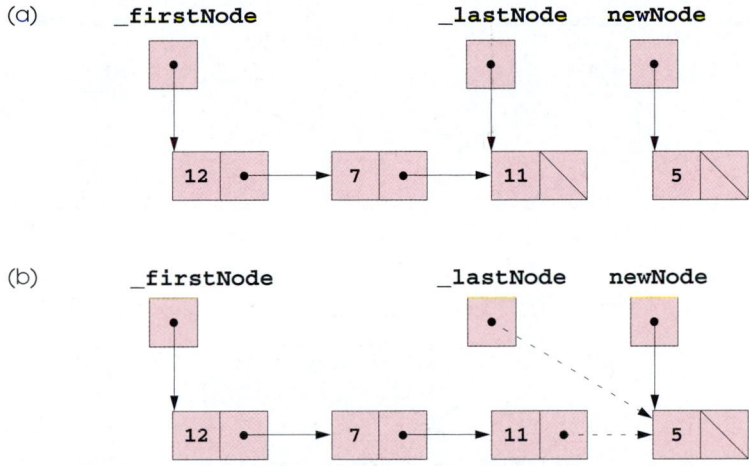

Fig. 22.6 Graphical representation of the **insertAtBack** operation.

1. If the list is empty, raise an **IndexError** exception (lines 67–68).

2. Assign a new reference called **tempNode** to the node referenced by **_firstNode** (line 70). The method eventually returns this reference.

3. If **_firstNode** refers to the same node as **_lastNode**—i.e., if the list has only one element prior to the removal attempt (line 72), then set **_firstNode** and **_lastNode** to **None** (line 73) to de-thread that node from the list (thereby leaving the list empty).

4. If the list has more than one node prior to the removal attempt, then leave **_lastNode** as is, and set **_firstNode** to the node referenced by **_firstNode._nextNode** (line 75)—i.e., modify **_firstNode** to refer to what was the second node prior to removal (and is the new first node now).

5. After all these reference manipulations have been completed, return the **tempNode** reference (line 77).

In Fig. 22.7 part (a) illustrates the list before the removal operation. Part (b) shows the actual reference manipulations.

Method **removeFromBack** (lines 79–99 of Fig. 22.3) removes the back node of the list and returns the value in that node. The method raises an **IndexError** exception if an attempt is made to remove a node from an empty list. The method consists of several steps:

1. If the list is empty, raise an **IndexError** exception (lines 82–83).

2. Assign a new reference called **tempNode** to the node referenced by **_lastNode** (line 85). The method eventually returns this reference.

3. If **_firstNode** refers to the same node as **_lastNode** (line 87), that is, if the list has only one element prior to the removal attempt, then set **_firstNode** and **_lastNode** to **None** (line 88) to de-thread that node from the list (thereby leaving the list empty).

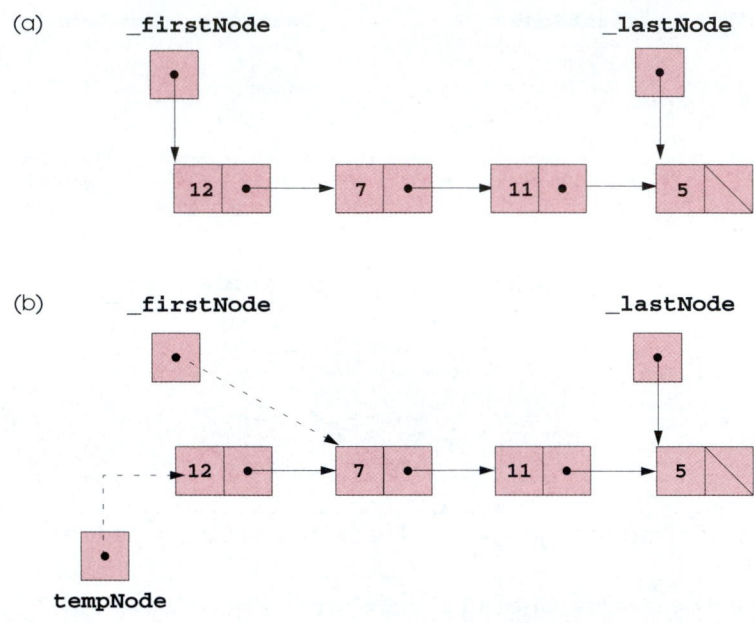

Fig. 22.7   Graphical representation of the **removeFromFront** operation.

4. If the list has more than one node prior to removal, then assign to **currentNode** the node to which **_firstNode** refers (line 90).

5. Now "walk the list" with **currentNode** until it refers to the node before the last node. This procedure is done with a **while** loop (lines 93–94) that assigns **currentNode** to the node referenced by **currentNode._nextNode** while **currentNode._nextNode** is not the node referenced by **_lastNode**.

6. Set the **_nextNode** of **currentNode** to **None** and assign **_lastNode** to **currentNode** (lines 96–97).

7. After all these reference manipulations have been completed, return the **tempN-ode** reference (line 99).

In Fig. 22.8, part (a) illustrates the list before the removal operation. Part (b) of the figure shows the actual reference manipulations. **List** method **__str__** (lines 27–40 of Fig. 22.3) first determines if the list is empty. If so, the method returns **"empty"**. Otherwise, it returns a string that contains each node's data. The method initializes **current-Node** as a reference to **firstNode** and initializes variable **output** as an empty list. While **currentNode** is not **None**, the string representation of **currentNode._data** is added to the list and **currentNode** is set to reference **currentNode._nextNode**. Once the final node's data has been added to the output list, method **__str__** returns the results of calling string method **join** on the output list. This creates a string that contains each node's data, separated by a space (**" "**) character. Note that if the link in the last node of the list is not **None**, the string-creation algorithm will erroneously continue past the end of the list. The string-creation algorithm is identical for linked lists, stacks and queues.

(a)

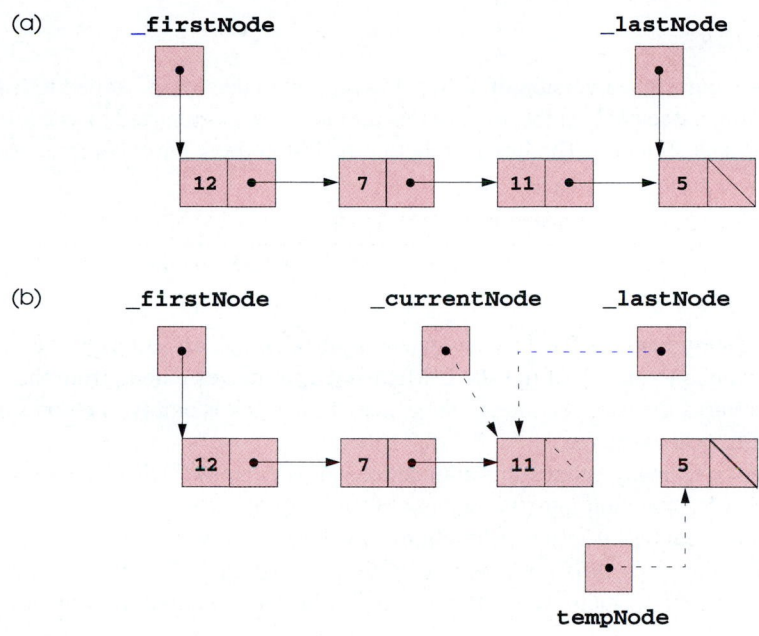

Fig. 22.8 Graphical representation of the **removeFromBack** operation.

The kind of linked list we have been discussing thus far is a *singly linked list*—the list begins with a reference to the first node, and each node contains a reference to the next node "in sequence." The list terminates with a node whose reference member is **None**. A singly linked list may be traversed in only one direction.

A *circular, singly linked list* begins with a reference to the first node, and each node contains a reference to the next node. The "last node" does not contain a reference to **None**; rather, the reference in the last node points back to the first node, thus closing the "circle."

A *doubly linked list* allows traversals both forward and backward. Such a list is often implemented with two "start references"—one that refers to the first element of the list, to allow front-to-back traversal of the list, and one that refers to the last element of the list, to allow back-to-front traversal of the list. Each node has both a forward reference to the next node in the list in the forward direction and a backward reference to the next node in the list in the backward direction. If the list contains an alphabetized telephone directory, for example, a search for someone whose name begins with a letter near the front of the alphabet might begin from the front of the list. A search for someone whose name begins with a letter near the end of the alphabet might begin from the back of the list.

In a *circular, doubly linked list*, the forward reference of the last node points to the first node, and the backward reference of the first node refers to the last node, thus closing the "circle."

22.4 Stacks

A *stack* is a constrained version of a linked list—new nodes can be added to a stack and removed from a stack only at the top. For this reason, a stack is referred to as a *last-in, first-out (LIFO)* data structure. The link member in the last node of the stack is set to **None** to indicate the bottom of the stack.

Common Programming Error 22.2

*Not setting the link at the bottom node of a stack to **None** is a logic error.*

The primary methods used to manipulate a stack are ***push*** and ***pop***. Method **push** adds a new node to the top of the stack. Method **pop** removes a node from the top of the stack and returns the popped value to the caller. If the stack is empty, method stack raises an **IndexError** exception.

Stacks have many interesting applications. For example, when a function call is made, the called function must know how to return to its caller, so the return address is pushed onto a stack. If a series of function calls occurs, the successive return values are pushed onto the stack in last-in, first-out order, so that each function can return to its caller. Stacks support recursive function calls in the same manner as conventional non-recursive calls.

Stacks contain the space created for local variables on each invocation of a function. When the function returns to its caller or raises an exception, the destructor (if any) for each local object is called. The space for that function's local variables is popped off the stack and those variables are no longer known to the program. Stacks are used by compilers in the process of evaluating expressions and generating machine-language code. The exercises at the end of this chapter explore applications of stacks.

We will take advantage of the close relationship between lists and stacks to implement a stack class primarily by reusing a list class. We implement the stack class with composition—the stack class has, as a data member, a reference to an object of class **List**. A stack also could be implemented with inheritance—by deriving a class **Stack** from class **List**. For this reason, we used the single-underscore naming notation for data in module **ListModule** (Fig. 22.3). The derived class can access the data of the list, if necessary, but clients of the class use the provided methods. One benefit of using composition to implement a stack is that the **Stack** class provides only the methods necessary for manipulating the stack (i.e., **push** and **pop**). The class does not expose the methods clients should not use to manipulate the stack but that would have been inherited from the base class (e.g., **removeFromBack**).

The program in Fig. 22.9 creates a **Stack** class with composition. Class **Stack** has private data member **_stackList**, an object of class **List** (defined in Fig. 22.3). We want the **Stack** to have methods **push** and **pop**. When we implement the **Stack**'s methods, we have each of these methods call the appropriate method of object **_stackList**—i.e., **push** calls **insertAtFront**, and **pop** calls **removeFromFront**. Of course, class **List** contains other methods (i.e., **insertAtBack** and **removeFromBack**) that the methods of class **Stack** do not call. The driver program (Fig. 22.10) uses class **Stack** to instantiate a stack object. Integers 0 through 3 are pushed onto the stack and popped off the stack.

```
1   # Fig. 22.9: StackModule.py
2   # Class Stack definition.
3
4   from ListModule import List
5
6   class Stack ( List ):
7      """Stack composed from linked list"""
8
9      def __init__( self ):
10        """Stack constructor"""
11
12        self._stackList = List()
13
14     def __str__( self ):
15        """Stack string representation"""
16
17        return str( self._stackList )
18
19     def push( self, element ):
20        """Push data onto stack"""
21
22        self._stackList.insertAtFront( element )
23
24     def pop( self ):
25        """Pop data from stack"""
26
27        return self._stackList.removeFromFront()
28
29     def isEmpty( self ):
30        """Return 1 if Stack is empty"""
31
32        return self._stackList.isEmpty()
```

Fig. 22.9 Stack implementation—**StackModule.py**.

```
1   # Fig. 22.10: fig22_010.py
2   # Driver to test class Stack.
3
4   from StackModule import Stack
5
6   stack = Stack()
7
8   print "Processing a Stack"
9
10  for i in range( 4 ):
11     stack.push( i )
12     print "The stack is:", stack
13
14  while not stack.isEmpty():
15     pop = stack.pop()
16     print pop, "popped from stack"
17     print "The stack is:", stack
```

Fig. 22.10 Stack implementation—**fig22_08.py**. (Part 1 of 2.)

```
Processing a Stack
The stack is: 0
The stack is: 1 0
The stack is: 2 1 0
The stack is: 3 2 1 0
3 popped from stack
The stack is: 2 1 0
2 popped from stack
The stack is: 1 0
1 popped from stack
The stack is: 0
0 popped from stack
The stack is: empty
```

Fig. 22.10 Stack implementation—`fig22_08.py`. (Part 2 of 2.)

22.5 Queues

A *queue* is similar to a supermarket checkout line—the first person in line is serviced first, and other customers enter the line at the end and wait to be serviced. Queue nodes are removed only from the *head* of the queue and are inserted only at the *tail* of the queue. For this reason, a queue is referred to as a *first-in, first-out (FIFO)* data structure. The insert and remove operations are known as **enqueue** and **dequeue** respectively.

Queues have many applications in computer systems. Most computers have only a single processor, so only one user at a time can be served. Entries for the other users are placed in a queue. Each entry gradually advances to the front of the queue as users receive service. The entry at the front of the queue is the next to receive service.

Queues also are used to support print spooling. A multiuser environment may have only a single printer. However, many users may be generating outputs to be printed. If the printer is busy, other outputs may still be generated. These outputs are "spooled" to disk (much as thread is wound onto a spool) where they wait in a queue until the printer becomes available.

Information packets also wait in queues in computer networks. Each time a packet arrives at a network node, it must be routed to the next node on the network along the path to the packet's final destination. The routing node routes one packet at a time, so additional packets are enqueued until the router can route them.

A file server in a computer network handles file access requests from many clients throughout the network. Servers have a limited capacity to service requests from clients. When that capacity is exceeded, client requests wait in queues.

Figure 22.11 creates class **Queue** primarily through composition. Class **Queue** has a private data member, **_queueList** of class **List** (defined in Fig. 22.3). We want the **Queue** to have methods **enqueue** and **dequeue**. We note that these methods essentially are the **insertAtBack** and **removeFromFront** methods, respectively, of class **List**. When we implement the **Queue**'s methods, we have each of the methods call the appropriate method of object **_queueList**—i.e., **enqueue** calls **insertAtBack** and **dequeue** calls **removeFromFront**. Of course, class **List** contains other methods (i.e., **insertAtFront** and **removeFromBack**) that the methods of class **Queue** do not call.

The driver program (Fig. 22.12) uses class **Queue** to instantiate a queue object. The program enqueues integer values 0 through 3 and then dequeues the values in first-in, first-out order.

```
1   # Fig. 22.11: QueueModule.py
2   # Class Queue definition.
3
4   from ListModule import List
5
6   class Queue:
7      """Queue composed from linked list"""
8
9      def __init__( self ):
10         """Queue constructor"""
11
12         self._queueList = List()
13
14      def __str__( self ):
15         """Queue string representation"""
16
17         return str( self._queueList )
18
19      def enqueue( self, element ):
20         """Enqueue element"""
21
22         self._queueList.insertAtBack( element )
23
24      def dequeue( self ):
25         """Dequeue element"""
26
27         return self._queueList.removeFromFront()
28
29      def isEmpty( self ):
30         """Return 1 if Queue is empty"""
31
32         return self._queueList.isEmpty()
```

Fig. 22.11 Queue implementation—**QueueModule.py**.

```
1   # Fig. 22.12: fig22_12.py
2   # Driver to test class QueueModule.
3
4   from QueueModule import Queue
5
6   queue = Queue()
7
8   print "processing a Queue"
9
10  for i in range( 4 ):
11     queue.enqueue( i )
12     print "The queue is:", queue
```

Fig. 22.12 Queue implementation—**fig22_09.py**. (Part 1 of 2.)

```
13
14   while not queue.isEmpty():
15       dequeue = queue.dequeue()
16       print dequeue, "dequeued"
17       print "The queue is:", queue
```

```
processing a Queue
The queue is: 0
The queue is: 0 1
The queue is: 0 1 2
The queue is: 0 1 2 3
0 dequeued
The queue is: 1 2 3
1 dequeued
The queue is: 2 3
2 dequeued
The queue is: 3
3 dequeued
The queue is: empty
```

Fig. 22.12 Queue implementation—**fig22_09.py**. (Part 2 of 2.)

22.6 Trees

Linked lists, stacks and queues are *linear data structures*. A tree is a nonlinear, two-dimensional data structure with special properties. Tree nodes contain two or more links. This section discusses *binary trees* (Fig. 22.13)—trees whose nodes all contain two links (one or both of which may be **None**). The *root node* is the first node in a tree. Each link in the root node refers to a *child*. The *left child* is the root node of the *left subtree*, and the *right child* is the root node of the *right subtree*. The children of a single node are called *siblings*. A node with no children is called a *leaf node*. Computer scientists normally draw trees from the root node down—exactly the opposite of trees in nature.

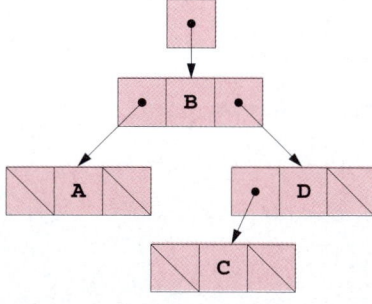

Fig. 22.13 Binary tree graphical representation.

In this section, we create a special binary tree called a *binary search tree (BST)*. A binary search tree (with no duplicate node values) has the characteristic that the values in any left subtree are less than the value in the subtree's parent node, and the values in any right subtree are greater than the value in the subtree's parent node. Figure 22.14 illustrates a binary search tree with 12 values. Note that the shape of the binary search tree that corresponds to a set of data can vary, depending on the order in which the values are inserted into the tree.

Common Programming Error 22.3

*Not setting the links in leaf nodes of a tree to **None** a logic error.*

Figure 22.15 defines class **Tree** as a binary search tree. The program in Fig. 22.16 creates an object of class **Tree** and traverses it (i.e., walks through all its nodes) three ways—using recursive *inorder*, *preorder* and *postorder traversals*.

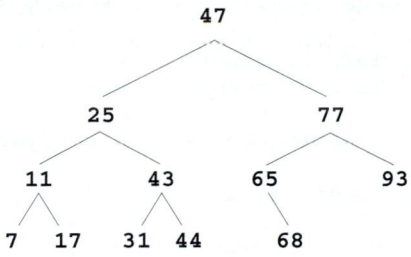

Fig. 22.14 Binary search tree graphical representation.

```
1   # Fig. 22.15: TreeModule.py
2   # Treenode and Tree definition.
3
4   class Treenode:
5      """Single Node in a Tree"""
6
7      def __init__( self, data ):
8         """Treenode constructor"""
9
10        self._left = None
11        self._data = data
12        self._right = None
13
14     def __str__( self ):
15        """Tree string representation"""
16
17        return str( self._data )
18
```

Fig. 22.15 Binary tree implementation—**TreeModule.py**. (Part 1 of 3.)

```
19   class Tree:
20       """Binary search tree"""
21
22       def __init__( self ):
23           """Tree Constructor"""
24
25           self._rootNode = None
26
27       def insertNode( self, value ):
28           """Insert node into tree"""
29
30           if self._rootNode is None:  # tree is empty
31               self._rootNode = Treenode( value )
32           else:  # tree is not empty
33               self.insertNodeHelper( self._rootNode, value )
34
35       def insertNodeHelper( self, node, value ):
36           """Recursive helper method"""
37
38           if value < node._data:  # insert to left
39
40               if node._left is None:
41                   node._left = Treenode( value )
42               else:
43                   self.insertNodeHelper ( node._left, value )
44
45           elif value > node._data:
46
47               if node._right is None:  # insert to right
48                   node._right = Treenode( value )
49               else:
50                   self.insertNodeHelper( node._right, value )
51
52           else:  # duplicate node
53               print value, "duplicate"
54
55       def preOrderTraversal( self ):
56           """Preorder traversal"""
57
58           self.preOrderHelper( self._rootNode )
59
60       def preOrderHelper( self, node ):
61           """Preorder traversal helper function"""
62
63           if node is not None:
64               print node,
65               self.preOrderHelper( node._left )
66               self.preOrderHelper( node._right )
67
68       def inOrderTraversal( self ):
69           """Inorder traversal"""
70
71           self.inOrderHelper( self._rootNode )
```

Fig. 22.15 Binary tree implementation—**TreeModule.py**. (Part 2 of 3.)

```
72
73        def inOrderHelper( self, node ):
74            """Inorder traversal helper function"""
75
76            if node is not None:
77                self.inOrderHelper( node._left )
78                print node,
79                self.inOrderHelper( node._right )
80
81        def postOrderTraversal( self ):
82            """Postorder traversal"""
83
84            self.postOrderHelper( self._rootNode )
85
86        def postOrderHelper( self, node ):
87            """Postorder traversal helper function"""
88
89            if node is not None:
90                self.postOrderHelper( node._left )
91                self.postOrderHelper( node._right )
92                print node,
```

Fig. 22.15 Binary tree implementation—**TreeModule.py**. (Part 3 of 3.)

The main program in Fig. 22.16 begins by instantiating a binary tree called **tree** (line 6). The program prompts for 10 integers, each of which is inserted in the binary tree through a call to **insertNode** (lines 10–11). Lines 23–24 then perform preorder, inorder and postorder traversals (these traversals are explained shortly) of **tree**.

```
1   # Fig. 22.16: fig22_16.py
2   # Driver to test Tree class.
3
4   from TreeModule import Tree
5
6   tree = Tree()
7   values = raw_input(
8       "Enter 10 integer values, separated by spaces:\n" )
9
10  for i in values.split():
11      tree.insertNode( int( i ) )
12
13  print "\nPreorder Traversal"
14  tree.preOrderTraversal()
15  print
16
17  print "Inorder Traversal"
18  tree.inOrderTraversal()
19  print
20
21  print "Postorder Traversal"
22  tree.postOrderTraversal()
23  print
```

Fig. 22.16 Binary tree implementation—**fig22_16.py**. (Part 1 of 2.)

```
Enter 10 integer values, separated by spaces:
50 25 75 12 33 67 88 6 13 68

Preorder Traversal
50 25 12 6 13 33 75 67 68 88
Inorder Traversal
6 12 13 25 33 50 67 68 75 88
Postorder Traversal
6 13 12 33 25 68 67 88 75 50
```

Fig. 22.16 Binary tree implementation—**fig22_16.py**. (Part 2 of 2.)

Now we discuss the class definitions (Fig. 22.15). Class **TreeNode** has as data the node's value (attribute **_data**), and it has references **_left** (to the node's left subtree) and **_right** (to the node's right subtree). The constructor (lines 7–12) sets member **_data** to the value supplied as a constructor argument and sets references **_left** and **_right** to **None** (thus initializing this node to be a leaf node).

Class **Tree** has data member **_rootNode**, a reference to the root node of the tree. The **Tree** constructor (lines 22–25) initializes **_rootNode** to **None** to indicate that the tree initially is empty. The class has methods **insertNode** (lines 22–25), which inserts a new node in the tree, and methods **preorderTraversal** (lines 55–58), **inorder-Traversal** (lines 68–71) and **postorderTraversal** (lines 81–84), each of which walks through the tree in the designated manner. Each of these methods calls its own separate recursive utility method to perform the appropriate operations on the internal representation of the tree.

A node can be inserted only as a leaf node in a binary search tree. Method **insert-Node** inserts a node in the tree. If the tree is empty, the method creates a new **TreeNode** and inserts it into the tree (line 31). Otherwise, the method calls utility method **insert-NodeHelper** (lines 35–53) to recursively insert the value into the tree.

If the tree is not empty, the program compares the value to be inserted with the value in the root node. If the insert value is smaller, the program recursively calls **insert-NodeHelper** to insert the value in the left subtree (line 43). If the insert value is larger, the program recursively calls **insertNodeHelper** to insert the value in the right subtree (line 50). If the value to be inserted is identical to the data value in the root node, the program prints the message **"duplicate"** and returns without inserting the duplicate value into the tree (lines 52–53).

Each of the methods **inOrderTraversal**, **preOrderTraversal** and **postOrderTraversal** traverse the tree and print the node values.

The steps for an **inOrderTraversal** are as follows:

1. Traverse the left subtree with an **inOrderTraversal**.

2. Process the value in the node (i.e., print the value in the node).

3. Traverse the right subtree with an **inOrderTraversal**.

The value in a node is not processed until the values in its left subtree are processed. The **inOrderTraversal** of the tree in Fig. 22.17 is

   6 13 17 27 33 42 48

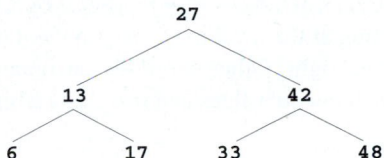

Fig. 22.17 A binary search tree.

Note that the **inOrderTraversal** of a binary search tree prints the values of the nodes in ascending order. The process of creating a binary search tree actually sorts the data—and thus this process is called the *binary-tree sort*.

The steps for a **preOrderTraversal** are as follows:

1. Process the value in the node.

2. Traverse the left subtree with a **preOrderTraversal**.

3. Traverse the right subtree with a **preOrderTraversal**.

The value in each node is processed as the node is visited. After the value in a given node is processed, the values in the left subtree are processed, and the values in the right subtree are processed. The **preOrderTraversal** of the tree in Fig. 22.17 is

    27 13 6 17 42 33 48

The steps for a **postOrderTraversal** are as follows:

1. Traverse the left subtree with a **postOrderTraversal**.

2. Traverse the right subtree with a **postOrderTraversal**.

3. Process the value in the node.

The value in each node is not printed until the values of its children are printed. The **postOrderTraversal** of the tree in Fig. 22.17 is

    6 17 13 33 48 42 27

The binary search tree facilitates *duplicate elimination*. As the tree is being created, an attempt to insert a duplicate value will be recognized because a duplicate will follow the same "go left" or "go right" decisions on each comparison as the original value did. Thus, the duplicate value eventually will be compared with a node containing the same value. The duplicate value may be discarded at this point.

Searching a binary tree for a value that matches a key value is fast. If the tree is *balanced*, then each level contains about twice as many elements as the previous level. So a binary search tree with n elements would have a maximum of $\log_2 n$ levels; thus, a maximum of $\log_2 n$ comparisons would have to be made either to find a match or to determine that no match exists. This means, for example, that when searching a (balanced) 1000-element binary search tree, no more than 10 comparisons need to be made, because $2^{10} > 1000$. When searching a (balanced) 1,000,000-element binary search tree, no more than 20 comparisons need to be made, because $2^{20} > 1,000,000$.

The exercises at the end of this chapter, present an algorithm for performing a level-order traversal of a binary tree. The *level-order traversal* of a binary tree visits the nodes of the tree row by row, starting at the level of the root node. On each level of the tree, the nodes are visited from left to right. Other exercises on binary trees include allowing a binary search tree to contain duplicate values and searching a binary search tree for a value.

SUMMARY

- A self-referential class contains a member that refers to an object of the same class.

- A link "ties" an object of class one class to another object of the same type.

- Objects of self-referential classes can be linked together to form useful data structures such as lists, queues, stacks and trees.

- A **None** reference normally indicates the end of a data structure.

- A linked list is a linear collection of objects of self-referential classes, called nodes, connected by reference links—hence, the term "linked list."

- A linked list is accessed via a reference to the first node of the list. Subsequent nodes are accessed via the reference link stored in each node.

- By convention, the link in the last node of a list is set to **None**, to mark the end of the list.

- Data are stored in a linked list dynamically—each node is created as necessary.

- A node can contain data of any type, including objects of other classes.

- Linked lists can be maintained in sorted order by inserting each new element at the proper point in the list. Existing list elements do not need to be moved.

- Nodes of a linked list are normally not stored contiguously in memory. Logically, however, the nodes of a linked list appear to be contiguous.

- A singly linked list begins with a reference to the first node, and each node contains a reference to the next node "in sequence." The list terminates with a node whose reference member is **None**. A singly linked list may be traversed in only one direction.

- A circular, singly linked list begins with a reference to the first node, and each node contains a reference to the next node. The "last node" does not contain a reference to **None**; rather, the reference in the last node points back to the first node, thus closing the "circle."

- A doubly linked list allows traversals both forward and backward. Such a list is often implemented with two "start references"—one that refers to the first element of the list, to allow front-to-back traversal of the list, and one that refers to the last element of the list, to allow back-to-front traversal of the list. Each node has both a forward reference to the next node in the list in the forward direction and a backward reference to the next node in the list in the backward direction.

- In a circular, doubly linked list, the forward reference of the last node points to the first node, and the backward reference of the first node refers to the last node, thus closing the "circle."

- A stack is a constrained version of a linked list—new nodes can be added to a stack and removed from a stack only at the top. For this reason, a stack is referred to as a last-in, first-out (LIFO) data structure. The link member in the last node of the stack is set to **None** to indicate the bottom of the stack.

- Stacks have many interesting applications. For example, when a function call is made, the called function must know how to return to its caller, so the return address is pushed onto a stack. If a series of function calls occurs, the successive return values are pushed onto the stack in last-in, first-out order, so that each function can return to its caller. Stacks support recursive function calls in the same manner as conventional nonrecursive calls.

- Stacks contain the space created for local variables on each invocation of a function. When the function returns to its caller or raises an exception, the destructor (if any) for each local object is called. The space for that function's local variables is popped off the stack and those variables are no longer known to the program.

- Stacks are used by compilers in the process of evaluating expressions and generating machine-language code.

- A queue is similar to a supermarket checkout line—the first person in line is serviced first, and other customers enter the line at the end and wait to be serviced. Queue nodes are removed only from the head of the queue and are inserted only at the tail of the queue. For this reason, a queue is referred to as a first-in, first-out (FIFO) data structure. The insert and remove operations are known as **enqueue** and **dequeue** respectively.

- Queues have many applications in computer systems. Most computers have only a single processor, so only one user at a time can be served. Entries for the other users are placed in a queue. Each entry gradually advances to the front of the queue as users receive service. The entry at the front of the queue is the next to receive service.

- Queues also are used to support print spooling. A multiuser environment may have only a single printer. However, many users may be generating outputs to be printed. If the printer is busy, other outputs may still be generated. These outputs are "spooled" to disk (much as thread is wound onto a spool) where they wait in a queue until the printer becomes available.

- Information packets wait in queues in computer networks. Each time a packet arrives at a network node, it must be routed to the next node on the network along the path to the packet's final destination. The routing node routes one packet at a time, so additional packets are enqueued until the router can route them.

- A file server in a computer network handles file access requests from many clients throughout the network. Servers have a limited capacity to service requests from clients. When that capacity is exceeded, client requests wait in queues.

- Linked lists, stacks and queues are linear data structures.

- A tree is a nonlinear, two-dimensional data structure with special properties.

- Tree nodes contain two or more links.

- Binary trees have nodes that contain two links (one or both of which may be **None**).

- The root node is the first node in a tree.

- Each link in the root node refers to a child.

- The left child is the root node of the left subtree, and the right child is the root node of the right subtree.

- The children of a single node are called siblings.

- A node with no children is called a leaf node.

- A binary search tree (with no duplicate node values) has the characteristic that the values in any left subtree are less than the value in the subtree's parent node, and the values in any right subtree are greater than the value in the subtree's parent node.

- A program can traverse a binary search tree using recursive inorder, preorder and postorder traversals.

- A node can be inserted only as a leaf node in a binary search tree.

- An inorder traversal of a binary tree traverses the left subtree inorder, processes the value in the root node and then traverse the right subtree inorder. The value in a node is not processed until the values in its left subtree are processed.

- A preorder traversal processes the value in the root node, traverses the left subtree preorder and then traverses the right subtree preorder. The value in a node is processed as the node is encountered.

- A postorder traversal traverses the left subtree postorder, traverses the right subtree postorder then processes the value in the root node. The value in each node is not processed until the values in both its subtrees are processed.

- The binary search tree facilitates duplicate elimination. As the tree is being created, an attempt to insert a duplicate value will be recognized because a duplicate will follow the same "go left" or "go right" decisions on each comparison as the original value did. Thus, the duplicate value will eventually be compared with a node containing the same value. The duplicate value may be discarded at this point.

- Searching a binary tree for a value that matches a key value is fast. If the tree is balanced, then each level contains about twice as many elements as the previous level. So a binary search tree with n elements would have a maximum of $\log_2 n$ levels; thus, a maximum of $\log_2 n$ comparisons would have to be made either to find a match or to determine that no match exists.

TERMINOLOGY

binary search tree
binary tree
binary tree sort
child
circular, doubly linked list
circular, singly linked list
data structure
dequeue queue method
doubly linked list
duplicate elimination
enqueue queue method
first-in, first-out (FIFO) data structure
head of a queue
inorder traversal
last-in, last-out (LIFO) data structure
leaf node
left child
left subtree
link
linked list

node
parent node
pop stack method
postorder traversal
predicate method
preorder traversal
push stack method
queue
right child
right subtree
self-referential class
sibling
singly linked list
stack
subtree
tail of a queue
top of a stack
tree
tree sort

SELF-REVIEW EXERCISES

22.1 Fill in the blanks in each of the following statements:
  a) A self-_____ class forms dynamic data structures that can grow and shrink at execution time.
  b) A _____ is a constrained version of a linked list in which nodes can be inserted and deleted only from the start of the list and node values are returned in last-in, first-out order.
  c) A function that does not alter a linked list, but looks at the list to determine if it is empty, is referred to as a _____ function.
  d) A queue is referred to as a _____ data structure because the first nodes inserted are the first nodes removed.

e) The reference to the next node in a linked list is referred to as a _____.

f) A _____ is a constrained version of a linked list in which nodes can be inserted only at the end of the list and deleted only from the start of the list.

g) A _____ is a nonlinear, two-dimensional data structure that contains nodes with two or more links.

h) The nodes of a _____ tree contain two link members.

i) The first node of a tree is the _____ node.

j) The three traversal algorithms we mentioned in the text for binary search trees are _____, _____ and _____.

22.2 State whether each of the following is *true* or *false*. If *false*, explain why.

a) A tree node that has no children is called a **None** node.

b) Each link a tree node refers to is a child or a subtree of that node.

c) A stack is referred to as a LIFO data structure because it is a linear data structure.

d) The level-order traversal of a binary tree visits the nodes of the tree, starting at a leaf and progressing toward the root node level.

e) A sibling of a leaf in a tree can be a parent.

f) A link can be used to tie an object of a class to another object of the same type.

g) Nodes of a linked list are stored contiguously in memory to allow quick access to the items in the list.

h) Each node of a circular, doubly linked list has a backward and a forward reference.

i) A queue can be described as a constrained version of a stack.

j) A binary search tree can contain duplicate values.

ANSWERS TO SELF-REVIEW EXERCISES

22.1   a) referential. b) stack. c) predicate functions. d) first-in, first-out (FIFO). e) link. f) queue. g) tree. h) binary. i) root. j) inorder, preorder, postorder.

22.2   a) False. A tree node that has no children is called a leaf. b) True. c) False. A stack is referred to as a LIFO data structure because nodes are removed from and added to the stack at its top. d) False. The level-order traversal of a binary tree visits the nodes of the tree row by row, starting at the root node level. e) True. f) True. g) False. The nodes of a linked list often are not stored contiguously in memory. h) True. i) False. A queue can be described as a constrained version of a linked list. j) True.

EXERCISES

22.3   Manually provide the inorder, preorder and postorder traversals of the binary search tree of Fig. 22.18.

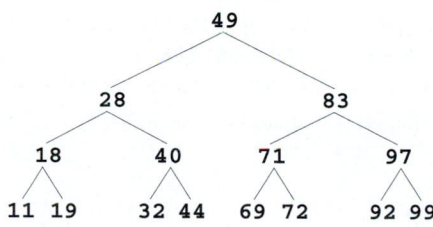

Fig. 22.18 15-node binary search tree.

22.4   (*Recursively Print a Queue Backwards*) Write a method `printQueueBackwards` that recursively outputs the items in a linked list object in reverse order. Write a test program that creates a list of integers and prints the list in reverse order.

22.5   Stacks are used by compilers to help in the process of evaluating expressions and generating machine language code. In this and the next exercise, we investigate how compilers evaluate arithmetic expressions consisting only of constants, operators and parentheses.

Humans generally write expressions like **3 + 4** and **7 / 9** in which the operator (**+** or **/** here) is written between its operands—this is called *infix notation*. Computers "prefer" *postfix notation* in which the operator is written to the right of its two operands. The preceding infix expressions would appear in postfix notation as **3 4 +** and **7 9 /**, respectively.

To evaluate a complex infix expression, a compiler would first convert the expression to postfix notation and then evaluate the postfix version of the expression. Each of these algorithms requires only a single left-to-right pass of the expression. Each algorithm uses a stack object in support of its operation, and in each algorithm the stack is used for a different purpose.

In this exercise, you will write a Python version of the infix-to-postfix conversion algorithm. In the next exercise, you will write a Python version of the postfix expression evaluation algorithm.

Write a program that converts an ordinary infix arithmetic expression (assume a valid expression is entered) with single-digit integers such as

```
(6 + 2) * 5 - 8 / 4
```

to a postfix expression. The postfix version of the preceding infix expression is

```
6 2 + 5 * 8 4 / -
```

The program should read the expression into a sequence **infix**, and use modified versions of the stack functions implemented in this chapter to help create the postfix expression in sequence **postfix**. The algorithm for creating a postfix expression is as follows:
1) Push a left parenthesis **'('** onto the stack.
2) Append a right parenthesis **')'** to the end of **infix**.
3) While the stack is not empty, read **infix** from left to right and do the following:
      If the current character in **infix** is a digit, copy it to the next element of **postfix**.
      If the current character in **infix** is a left parenthesis, push it onto the stack.
      If the current character in **infix** is an operator,
            Pop operators (if there are any) at the top of the stack while they have equal or
               higher precedence than the current operator, and insert the popped
               operators in **postfix**.
      Push the current character in **infix** onto the stack.
      If the current character in **infix** is a right parenthesis
            Pop operators from the top of the stack and insert them in **postfix** until a left
               parenthesis is at the top of the stack.
            Pop (and discard) the left parenthesis from the stack.

The following arithmetic operations are allowed in an expression:
        +   addition
        –   subtraction
        *   multiplication
        /   division
      **   exponentiation
        %   modulus

The stack should be maintained with stack nodes that each contain a data member and a reference to the next stack node.

Some of the functional capabilities you may want to provide are:

a) Function **convertToPostfix** that converts the infix expression to postfix notation.
b) Function **isOperator** that determines if **c** is an operator.
c) Function **precedence** that determines if the precedence of **operator1** is less than, equal to or greater than the precedence of **operator2**. The function returns -1, 0 and 1, respectively.
d) Function **push** that pushes a value onto the stack.
e) Function **pop** that pops a value off the stack.
f) Function **stackTop** that returns the top value of the stack without popping the stack.
g) Function **isEmpty** that determines if the stack is empty.
h) Function **printStack** that prints the stack.

22.6   Write a postfix evaluator, which evaluates a postfix expression (assume it is valid) such as

    6 2 + 5 * 8 4 / -

The program should read a postfix expression, such as the one created in Exercise 22.5. Using modified versions of the stack methods implemented in this chapter, the program should scan the expression and evaluate it. The algorithm is as follows:

1) Read the expression from right to left.
        If the current character is a digit:
                Push it on the stack.
        Otherwise, if the current character is an *operator*:
                Pop the two top elements of the stack into variables **x** and **y**.
                Calculate **y** *operator* **x**.
                Push the result of the calculation onto the stack.
2) At the end of the postfix expression, pop the top value of the stack. This is the result of the postfix expression.

[*Note*: In 1) above (based on the sample expression at the beginning of this exercise), if the operator is '**/**', the top of the stack is **2** and the next element in the stack is **8**, then pop **2** into **x**, pop **8** into **y**, evaluate **8 / 2** and push the result, **4**, back on the stack.]

The following arithmetic operations are allowed in an expression:

    +   addition
    –   subtraction
    *   multiplication
    /   division
    **   exponentiation
    %   modulus

The stack should be maintained with stack nodes that each contain a data member and a reference to the next stack node.

Some of the functional capabilities you may want to provide are:

a) Method **evaluatePostfixExpression**, which evaluates the postfix expression.
b) Method **calculate**, which evaluates the expression **op1 operator op2**. [*Note*: Method **eval** returns the result of an expression. For example, **eval('2**4')** returns 16.]
c) Method **push**, which pushes a value on the stack.
d) Method **pop**, which pops a value off the stack.
e) Method **isEmpty**, which determines if the stack is empty.
f) Method **printStack**, which prints the stack.

22.7   (*Binary tree search*) Write method **binaryTreeSearch**, which attempts to locate a specified value in a binary search tree object. The function should take a search key to be located as an argument. If the node containing the search key is found, the function should return a reference to that node; otherwise, the function should return **None**. In addition, modify the program of Fig. 22.16 to allow the binary tree object to contain duplicates.

22.8   (*Level-order binary tree traversal*) The program of Fig. 22.16 illustrated three recursive methods of traversing a binary tree—inorder, preorder and postorder traversals. This exercise presents the *level-order traversal* of a binary tree in which the node values are printed level by level, starting at the root node level. The nodes on each level are printed from left to right. The level-order traversal is not a recursive algorithm. It uses a queue object to control the output of the nodes. The algorithm is as follows:

    1) Insert the root node in the queue

    2) While there are nodes left in the queue,

            Get the next node in the queue

            Print the node's value

            If the reference to the left child of the node is not **None**

                    Insert the left child node in the queue

            If the reference to the right child of the node is not **None**

                    Insert the right child node in the queue.

Write method **levelOrder** to perform a level-order traversal of a binary tree object. Modify the program of Fig. 22.16 to use this function. [*Note*: You will also need to modify and incorporate the queue-processing functions of Fig. 22.11 in this program.]

Case Study: Online Bookstore

Objectives

- To build a three-tier, client/server, distributed Web application using Python and CGI.
- To understand the concept of an HTTP session.
- To use a **Session** class to keep track of an HTTP session between pages.
- To create XML from a script and use XSL transformations to convert the XML into a format the client can display.
- To deploy an application on an Apache Web server.
- To extend the application to handle wireless clients.

The world is a book, and those who do not travel, read only a page.
Saint Augustine

We must take the current when it serves, or lose our ventures.
William Shakespeare

If it's a good script I'll do it. And if it's a bad script, and they pay me enough, I'll do it.
George Burns

Outline

23.1 Introduction

In this chapter, we implement a bookstore Web application that integrates many technologies we cover in this book and serves as a capstone for our presentation of Python CGI. The technologies used in the application include CGI (Chapter 6), XML, XSL and XSLT (Chapters 15–16), MySQL and the Python DB-API (Chapter 17), XHTML (Appendix I and Appendix J) and Cascading Style Sheets (Appendix K). The case study also illustrates additional features, such as *Wireless Markup Language (WML)* and XHTML Basic. We discuss these new elements as we introduce them. We deploy this application on the Apache Web server so that after reading this chapter, the reader should be able to implement a substantial Web application on an Apache Web server.

23.2 HTTP Sessions and Session-Tracking Technologies

Web sites that provide custom Web pages and functionality tailored to clients can implement e-commerce applications. One example of such a Web-site application is the online shopping cart we build for this chapter's online bookstore case study. To enable this application to process orders correctly, the server must distinguish one client from another to ensure proper shipping and payment. *Session-tracking* technologies allow servers to distinguish between clients. In this section, we introduce and explain two session-tracking methods—*cookies* and *embedded state information*—and how they operate via Internet protocols.

Each request that a Web browser makes to a Web server creates a new connection. Once the Web server processes the client request, the connection terminates. If a Web server needs to maintain information about a client across several requests, the client must identify itself each time.

One method that a client can use to identify itself is *cookies*, small text files sent by the server (or Web site) as part of a response to a client request. During a client's first visit, a Web site can store a cookie on the client's computer to record user preferences or other information (e.g., the client's user name). The Web site then can retrieve the cookie during that client's subsequent visits. For example, many Web sites use cookies to store clients' zip codes. The Web site can retrieve the zip code from the cookie and provide weather reports and new updates tailored to the user's region.

Every HTTP-based interaction between a client and a server includes a *header* that contains information about the *request* (communication from the client to the server) or information about the *response* (communication from the server to the client). When a Python script receives a request, the header includes information, such as the request type (e.g., *get* or *post*) and cookies that the server previously stored on the client. When the server formulates its response, the header information includes any cookies the server wants to store on the client computer.

Depending on the *maximum age* of a cookie, the Web browser either maintains the cookie for the duration of the browsing session (i.e., until the user closes the Web browser) or stores the cookie on the client computer for future use. When the browser makes a request to a server, the client returns to that server any cookies the server stored on the client in previous interactions. The Web browser deletes cookies when they *expire* (i.e., when these cookies reach their maximum age).

Cookies often are the easiest way for Web applications to distinguish clients. However, not all client computers or Web browsers support cookies. For example, users who are concerned about the privacy and security implications of cookies can disable cookies in their Web browsers, thus becoming unable to interact with cookie-dependent sites. For these reasons, we have chosen not to use cookies to track sessions in our online bookstore.

Portability Tip 23.1

Some browsers (especially older browsers) do not support cookies. Designing a server that uses cookies might exclude some users from accessing your site.

Another method of session tracking involves embedding *state information* in each communication between client and server. State information may contain a username, password or specific information that might be helpful when a user returns to a Web site. The first time a client connects to a server, the Web application assigns the client a unique *session ID*. When the client makes additional requests, the client's session ID is compared with the session IDs stored in the server's memory.

The ID must be passed from page to page so the Web application can track the session ID of the current client, thereby distinguishing clients. This can be done in different ways. One method of passing the ID is to place it in a hidden form field in each Web page. The Web application can access the ID as a normal CGI parameter. Another method is to add the ID to the URL by adding the ID to a hyperlink that points to the next page. The next page then extracts the ID from the URL. For more information on passing CGI parameters, review Chapter 6.

Tracking session information via embedded session IDs has both advantages and disadvantages. One advantage is that Web browsers cannot disable session IDs. A disadvantage is that Web-page addresses that include session IDs are much longer than usual, because the session ID is embedded in every hyperlink. This can be a problem with older Web browsers that do not support long URLs. Another disadvantage is that embedding such information presents a potential security risk. Storing the session ID in the Web page or URL allows a person other than the user to view the ID and to gain access to the user's data. Nonetheless, we have chosen this method to track HTTP sessions in our online bookstore.

Good Programming Practice 23.1

Both cookies and embedded state information have advantages and disadvantages. Research and carefully consider each technique before selecting one for a site.

23.3 Tracking Sessions in the Bookstore

Before we begin building our Web application, we discuss class **Session**, which uses embedded state information to keep track of HTTP sessions (Fig. 23.1). When a user first enters the bookstore, a new **Session** object is created to establish the session-tracking. The new **Session** object contains a unique session ID as well as a dictionary of session data. This session data is pickled and stored on the server. For more information on pickling, please review Chapter 14, File Processing and Serialization. As the client navigates through the bookstore, the session ID is passed between scripts as part of the query string. Each subsequent script can extract the ID and obtain the session information. As we demonstrate shortly, this is done by creating a **Session** object with argument **1**.

When a **Session** instance is created and if **createNew** (the argument passed to the constructor) contains a value other than **0** (the default), a new session is created. In this case, execution begins with a call to method **generateID** (line 82). Method **generateID** (lines 146–153) uses module **sha** to generate a unique ID. Lines 150–151 create a string that consists of the time of the session, the client address and the client port. Lines 152–153 then create and return a unique ID, using this string. The Web application uses this ID to identify the client uniquely throughout the client's interactions with the application. For more information on **sha**, please review Chapter 21, Security.

```
1    # Fig. 23.1: Session.py
2    # Contains a Session class that keeps track of an http session
3    # by assigning a session ID and pickling session information.
4
5    import os
6    import sha
7    import cgi
8    import time
9    import urlparse
10   import urllib
11   import cPickle
12
13   def getClientType():
14       """Return client type and corresponding file extension"""
15
```

Fig. 23.1   Utility functions and **Session** class that track an HTTP session. (Part 1 of 4.)

```
16        # search environment variables for identifying strings
17        if os.environ[ "HTTP_USER_AGENT" ].find( "MSIE" ) > -1 or \
18           os.environ[ "HTTP_USER_AGENT" ].find( "Netscape" ) > -1:
19
20           # MSIE and Netscape represent XHTML clients (.html)
21           return ( "xhtml", "html" )
22
23        elif os.environ[ "HTTP_ACCEPT" ].find(
24           "text/vnd.wap.wml" ) > -1:
25
26           # text/vnd.wap.wml represents WML clients (.wml)
27           return ( "wml", "wml" )
28
29        else:
30
31           # otherwise, assume XHTML Basic client (.html)
32           return ( "xhtml_basic", "html" )
33
34  def getContentType():
35     """Return the contents of the client's contentType.txt file"""
36
37        # obtain contentType.txt located in client's subfolder
38        try:
39           file = open( getClientType()[ 0 ] + "/contentType.txt" )
40        except:
41           raise SessionError( "Missing file: contentType.txt" )
42
43        contentType = file.read()
44        file.close()
45        return contentType
46
47  def redirect( URL ):
48     """Redirect the client to a relative URL"""
49
50        # use urljoin to append full path to relative URL
51        print "Location: %s\n" % \
52           urlparse.urljoin( "http://" + os.environ[ "HTTP_HOST" ] +
53              os.environ[ "REQUEST_URI" ], URL )
54
55  class SessionError( Exception ):
56     """User-defined exception for Session class"""
57
58     def __init__( self, error ):
59        """Set error message"""
60
61           # use quote_plus to replace spaces with '+'
62           self.error = urllib.quote_plus( error )
63
64     def __str__( self ):
65        """Return error message"""
66
67           return self.error
68
```

Fig. 23.1   Utility functions and **Session** class that track an HTTP session. (Part 2 of 4.)

```
69   class IDError( Exception ):
70       """User-defined exception for Session class"""
71
72       pass
73
74   class Session:
75       """Session class keeps track of an HTTP session"""
76
77       def __init__( self, createNew = 0 ):
78           """Create a new session or load an existing session"""
79
80           # create new session
81           if createNew:
82               self.sessionID = self.generateID()
83               self.fileName = os.getcwd() + "/sessions/." + \
84                   self.sessionID
85
86               # newly generated ID already exists
87               if self.sessionExists():
88                   raise IDError
89
90               self.data = {}  # dictionary is empty
91
92               # store ID, empty cart, content type and agent type
93               self.data[ "ID" ] = self.sessionID
94               self.data[ "cart" ] = {}
95               self.data[ "content type" ] = getContentType()
96               self.data[ "agent" ], self.data[ "extension" ] = \
97                   getClientType()
98
99           # attempt to load previously created session
100          else:
101
102              # session ID is passed in query string
103              queryString = cgi.parse_qs( os.environ[ "QUERY_STRING" ] )
104
105              # no ID has been supplied in query string
106              if not queryString.has_key( "ID" ):
107                  raise SessionError( "No ID given" )
108
109              self.sessionID = queryString[ "ID" ][ 0 ]
110              self.fileName = os.getcwd() + "/sessions/." + \
111                  self.sessionID
112
113              # supplied ID is invalid
114              if not self.sessionExists():
115                  raise SessionError( "Nonexistent ID given" )
116
117              # load pickled session dictionary
118              self.loadSession()
119
```

Fig. 23.1 Utility functions and **Session** class that track an HTTP session. (Part 3 of 4.)

```
120    def sessionExists( self ):
121        """Determine if the specified session file exists"""
122
123        return os.path.exists( self.fileName )
124
125    def loadSession( self ):
126        """Unpickle dictionary of existing session"""
127
128        if self.sessionExists():
129            sessionFile = open( self.fileName )
130            data = cPickle.load( sessionFile )
131            sessionFile.close()
132            self.data = data
133
134    def saveSession( self ):
135        """Pickle session dictionary to session file"""
136
137        sessionFile = open( self.fileName, "w" )
138        cPickle.dump( self.data, sessionFile )
139        sessionFile.close()
140
141    def deleteSession( self ):
142        """Delete session file"""
143
144        os.remove( self.fileName )
145
146    def generateID( self ):
147        """Use sha to generate a unique ID"""
148
149        # generate ID using time, client address and port
150        randomString = str( time.time() ) + \
151            os.environ[ "REMOTE_ADDR" ] + os.environ[ "REMOTE_PORT" ]
152        ID = sha.new( randomString )
153        return ID.hexdigest()
```

Fig. 23.1 Utility functions and **Session** class that track an HTTP session. (Part 4 of 4.)

When the **Session** obtains its new ID from **generateID**, it stores the name of its session file, **fileName**, and determines whether the session already exists (line 87). If the session file already exists, **Session** raises the user-defined exception **IDError** (line 88). Note that the filename of a session is a period (**.**) followed by the session ID. All session files reside in a subdirectory, **sessions**, of the current working directory (i.e., **cgi-bin**). Each file contains a pickled session dictionary for a unique HTTP session. Each session dictionary contains information about the client such as the client type (e.g., XHTML) as well as the user's shopping cart, represented by a dictionary. As the user progresses through the bookstore application, each script uses the session ID to obtain the user's session file. Thus, the client's information is available to each script in the application.

Class **Session** stores session information in dictionary **data**. Line 90 initializes **data** by creating an empty session dictionary. Line 93 stores the session ID in this dictionary. Line 94 creates an empty dictionary that represents an empty shopping cart. Line 95 stores the results of function **getContentType** in the session dictionary. Function **get-ContentType** (lines 34–45) opens the **contentType.txt** file, which resides in a subdirectory named after the client type, and returns the contents of the file. File **contentType.txt** contains a browser-specific HTTP header that must be prepended to every page sent to the client. Figure 23.2 contains an example of such a file. Lines 96–97 obtain the client type from function **getClientType** and stores it in the session dictionary. Function **getClientType** (lines 13–32) searches the **HTTP_USER_AGENT** and **HTTP_ACCEPT** environment variables for certain values to determine the client type and returns a two-element tuple that consists of the client type and its corresponding file extension. Storing information about the client type ensures that every script in the bookstore will generate output that the client can render.

To save session data between pages, a program must invoke method **saveSession** (lines 134–139). This method creates a new session file that corresponds to the value of attribute **fileName**. Line 138 uses module **cPickle** to pickle the session dictionary (**self.data**) and **dump** it into the session file. Storing session information using **cPickle** allows us to store Python objects with the session easily.

Once the application has established a session ID for a client, the remaining scripts in the application create **Session** objects with **createNew** set to **0** (default). This causes the **Session** object to load the existing state information from the appropriate session file. In this case, execution begins at line 103. Session IDs are passed between scripts as part of the query string. Line 103 obtains the query string and parses it. If no ID is specified, the constructor raises a **SessionError** exception (line 107); otherwise, the session ID is extracted, and the filename is determined (lines 109–111). **SessionError** contains attribute **error**, which contains the error message specified. This is used to help the user understand the cause of the error (Section 23.13). Line 114 then checks whether the specified session ID already exists. If the session does not exist, the constructor raises a **SessionError** exception (line 115); otherwise, the constructor calls method **loadSession**. This method (lines 125–132) opens the session file (line 129). It then uses **cPickle** to **load** the session dictionary it contains (line 130). This dictionary is stored in the session dictionary (**self.data**).

When a Web application no longer needs to store a particular session, the application can remove that session by invoking method **deleteSession** (lines 141–144). This method deletes the session file by calling **os.remove**.

To redirect a client to another page, we use function **redirect**, which redirects a client to a relative URL (lines 47–53). Function **redirect** provides a convenient way for scripts in the application to perform redirection. Lines 52–54 use function **url-parse.urljoin** to combine the base URL with the URL specified. The base URL is obtained from the **HTTP_HOST** and **REQUEST_URI** environment variables. The redirection is then achieved through a **Location** header.

```
1   Content-type: text/html
2
```

Fig. 23.2 contentType.txt for XHTML clients.

23.4 Bookstore Architecture

This section overviews the architecture of the bookstore application. We present a diagram of the interactions between various Python scripts (Fig. 23.3). Also, we present a table of the files used in the case study (Fig. 23.4).

The shopping-cart case study contains a series of XHTML documents, XHTML Basic documents, WML documents, XSLT documents and Python scripts that interact to form an online bookstore that sells Deitel publications. This case study is implemented as a *distributed, three-tier, Web-based application*. The user's Web browser represents the *client tier*, or *top tier*. The browser displays either *static* documents or *dynamic* documents that allow the user to interact with the server. The application creates these documents based upon the user's client type. The *server tier*, or *middle tier*, consists of several scripts that act on behalf of the client. These scripts perform tasks such as creating a list of publications, creating documents that contain details about publications, adding items to the shopping cart, viewing the shopping cart and processing the final order. The *information tier* (also called the *data tier* or the *bottom tier*) maintains data for the application. The information tier uses the **Books** database introduced in Chapter 17, Python DB-API.

Figure 23.3 illustrates the interactions among the bookstore application's components. After the application creates a **Session** for the user, the application redirects the user to **allBooks.py**, which interacts with a database to create the list of books dynamically. The result is an XML document that contains the list of books. This XML document is then processed against a browser-specific XSLT style sheet (**allBooks.xsl**) to produce a page that contains links to **displayBook.py**. **displayBook.py** receives the ISBN number of the selected book and uses the ISBN to retrieve information on that book and to produce another XML document for the selected book. This XML is then processed against a different browser-specific XSLT style sheet (**displayBook.xsl**) to produce a document that contains the information for that book. From this document, the user can use GUI components (in this case, buttons) to place the current book in the shopping cart or view the shopping cart.

Adding a book to a shopping cart invokes **addToCart.py**. Viewing the cart's contents invokes **viewCart.py**, which returns a browser-specific document (again, created

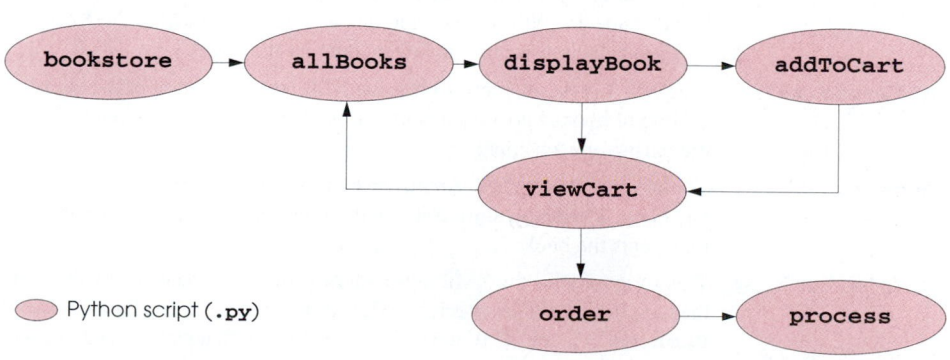

Fig. 23.3 Bookstore component interactions.

by processing XML with XSLT) that lists the contents in the cart, the subtotal dollar cost of each item and the total dollar cost of all the items in the cart. When the user adds an item to the shopping cart, **addToCart.py** processes the user's request, then forwards the request to **viewCart.py**, which creates the document that displays the contents of the current cart. At this point, the user either can continue shopping (**allBooks.py**) or can proceed to checkout (**order.py**). In the latter case, the user is presented with a form to input name, address and credit-card information. Then, the user submits the form to invoke **process.py**, which completes the transaction by sending a confirmation document to the user. Figure 23.4 overviews the scripts and other files used in this case study.

File	Description
Session.py	Contains the **Session** class. An instance of this class keeps track of an HTTP session by assigning each user a unique session ID and pickling a dictionary of data for each ID. It also contains three utility functions for redirecting the client, determining the user's client type and determining the client's content type (stored in **contentType.txt**).
contentType.txt	Contains the line that specifies the content type of the data. This file is created for each client type.
bookstore.py	This is the default home page for the bookstore. Here, a new **Session** is created for the user to track the HTTP session. The user is then forwarded to **allBooks.py**.
styles.css	This *Cascading Style Sheet (CSS)* file is linked to all XHTML and XHTML Basic documents rendered on the client. The CSS file allows us to apply uniform formatting across all the static and dynamic documents rendered.
allBooks.py	This script uses **Book** instances to create a document that contains the product list. It queries the **Books** database to obtain the list of titles in the database. The results are processed and placed into a list of **Book** instances. The list is stored as a session attribute for the client. The script creates an XML document that represents all the books, then applies a browser-specific XSL transformation (**allBooks.xsl**) to the XML to produce a document that can be rendered by the client.
allBooks.xsl	This XSLT style sheet transforms the XML representation of the entire catalog of books into a document that the client browser can render. This file exists for each client type.
Book.py	Contains the **Book** class. An instance of this class represents the data for one book. The **Book**'s **getXML** method returns an XML **Element** that represents the book.
displayBook.py	This script obtains the XML representation of a book selected by the user, then applies a browser-specific XSL transformation (**display-Book.xsl**) to the XML to produce a document that can be rendered by diverse clients.

Fig. 23.4   Components for bookstore case study. (Part 1 of 2.)

File	Description
displayBook.xsl	This XSLT style sheet transforms the XML representation of a book into a document that a browser can render. This file exists for each client type.
CartItem.py	Contains the **CartItem** class. An instance of this class maintains a **Book** and the current quantity for that book in the shopping cart. **CartItem**s are stored in a dictionary that represents the shopping cart contents.
addToCart.py	This script updates the shopping cart. If a **CartItem** representing the selected item is already in the cart, the script updates the quantity of that item. Otherwise, the script creates a new **CartItem** with a quantity of 1. After updating the cart, the user is forwarded to **viewCart.py** to view the current cart contents.
viewCart.py	This script extracts the **CartItem**s from the shopping cart, subtotals each item in the cart, totals all the items in the cart and creates an XML document that represents all items in the cart. The script then applies a browser-specific XSL transformation (**viewCart.xsl**) to the XML to produce a document that can be rendered by the client.
viewCart.xsl	This XSLT style sheet transforms the XML representation of all of the **CartItem**s in the cart into a document that the client browser can render. This file exists for each client type.
order.py	When viewing the cart, the user can click a **Check Out** button to execute this script. This script displays a browser-specific order form. In this example, the form has no functionality.
orderForm.html, orderForm.wml	These static documents contain order forms. They are displayed by **order.py**.
process.py	This final script simulates the processing of the user's credit-card information and loads a browser-specific document indicating that the order was processed and the total order value.
thankYou.html, thankYou.wml	These static documents, displayed by **process.py**, contain messages that the orders were processed and specify the total order value.
error.py	This script executes when an error occurs. It creates an XML document that represents the error. It then processes the XML against a browser-specific XSLT style sheet (**error.xsl**) to produce a document that can be rendered by the client. This document indicates to the user the error that occurred.
error.xsl	This XSLT style sheet transforms the XML representation of an error into a document that the client browser can render. This file exists for each client type.

Fig. 23.4   Components for bookstore case study. (Part 2 of 2.)

23.5 Configuring the Bookstore

All bookstore files are located in the Chapter 23 examples directory on the CD-ROM that accompanies this book. To set up the bookstore on Apache, copy the contents of subdirectory **htdocs** from the Chapter 23 examples directory to the root of Apache's HTML document directory. On a Windows platform, the root directory, **htdocs**, resides in the **C:\Program Files\Apache Group\Apache** directory; on Linux platforms, the directory may be called either **htdocs** or **html**. This directory should reside in one of two possible directories: **/var/www** or **/usr/local/httpd**. [*Note*: Most bookstore files depend on the names and relative locations of these directories. The reader may need to alter the code if the directory structure of the system does not match the directory structure specified in the code.]

Next, copy the contents of the **cgi-bin** subdirectory from the Chapter 23 examples directory into Apache's **cgi-bin** directory. On Windows, **cgi-bin** resides in **C:\Program Files\Apache Group\Apache**; on Linux, **cgi-bin** should reside in one of two possible directories: **/var/www** or **/usr/local/httpd**. Finally, start Apache. Figure 23.5 illustrates the directory structure for Apache on a Windows platform.

[*Note*: The bookstore case study requires the following software: 4Suite (Chapter 16), PyXML (Chapter 16), MySQL (Chapter 17) and the **Books** database (Chapter 17). Install this software before deploying the bookstore; installation instructions for the software can be found at **www.deitel.com**.]

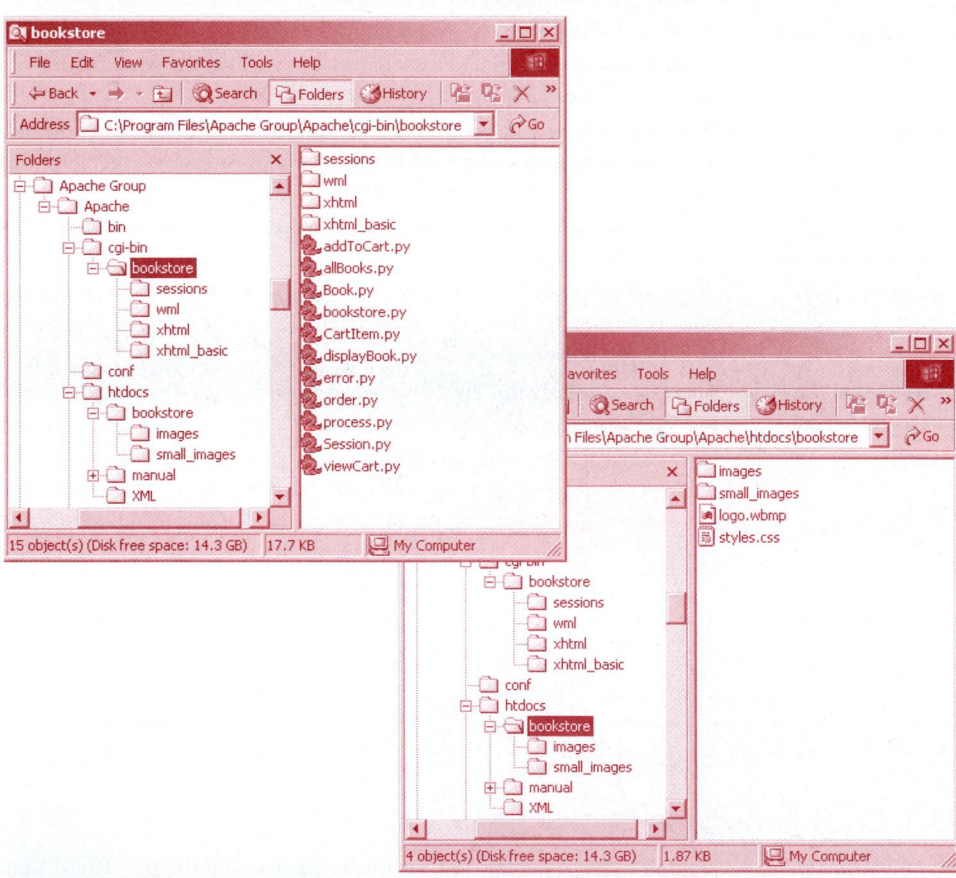

Fig. 23.5   Apache directory structure for online bookstore.

23.6 Entering the Bookstore

Figure 23.6 (**bookstore.py**) is the default home page for the bookstore. This file is also known as the *welcome file*, for it is the first file users see when they access the bookstore. Once the bookstore application is installed on Apache, enter the following URL in your Web browser to display the home page:

```
http://localhost/cgi-bin/bookstore/bookstore.py
```

Line 9 initializes **session** to **None**, indicating that we have not yet created a new **Session**. The **for** structure attempts to create a unique session for the client (lines 12–28). Line 16 creates a new **Session**. Recall that, if the session-generated ID already exists, an **IDError** is raised (Section 23.3). In this case, the program sleeps for **0.1** seconds (so that the string used for **sha** changes) and makes another attempt. If three failed attempts occur, line 36 redirects the client to **error.py**—a script that displays an error

```
1   #!c:\Python\python.exe
2   # Fig. 23.6: bookstore.py
3   # Create a new Session for client.
4
5   import sys
6   import time
7   import Session
8
9   session = None   # Session not yet created
10
11  # attempt to create Session three times
12  for i in range( 3 ):
13
14      # create new Session
15      try:
16          session = Session.Session( 1 )
17
18      # ID already exists
19      except Session.IDError:
20          time.sleep( 0.1 )   # wait 0.1 seconds -- try again
21
22      # missing content type
23      except Session.SessionError, message:
24          Session.redirect( "error.py?message=%s" % message )
25          sys.exit()
26
27      else:
28          break   # Session created successfully
29
30  # if successful, save Session and re-direct to allBooks.py
31  if session:
32      nextPage = "allBooks.py?ID=%s" % session.data[ "ID" ]
33      session.saveSession()
34      Session.redirect( nextPage )
35  else:
36      Session.redirect( "error.py?message=Unable+to+create+Session" )
```

Fig. 23.6 Bookstore home page (**bookstore.py**).

message to the client (Section 23.13). If a **SessionError** exception occurs (e.g., **contentType.txt** does not exist), line 24 redirects the client to **error.py**.

If no exceptions occur, the program exits the loop (line 28) and executes lines 32–34. Line 32 creates the redirection string to send the client to **allBooks.py**. The session ID is stored in the URL as part of the query string. This ensures **allBooks.py** can determine the client's identity. Lines 33–34 save the session and call **Session** function **redirect** to send the client to **allBooks.py**, which lists the available books.

23.7 Obtaining the Book List from the Database

The Python script **allBooks.py** creates a document that contains the list of available books. However, before we can obtain a list of books, we first must create a representation for a single book (Fig. 23.7). An instance of class **Book** represents the properties (information) for a particular book, including the book's ISBN, title, copyright, cover image file name, edition number, publisher ID number and price, although this example does not use some of this information. **Book** method **getXML** returns an XML **Element** that represents the book.

```
1   # Fig. 23.7: Book.py
2   # Represents one book.
3
4   class Book:
5       """A Book instance contains the data for one book"""
6
7       def __init__( self ):
8           """Initialize Book data"""
9
10          self.isbn = None
11          self.title = None
12          self.price = None
13          self.imageFile = None
14          self.copyright = None
15          self.publisherID = None
16          self.editionNumber = None
17
18      def getXML( self, document ):
19          """Return an XML representation of the product"""
20
21          # create dictionary of Book information
22          data = { "isbn" : self.isbn,
23                   "title" : self.title,
24                   "price" : self.price,
25                   "imageFile" : self.imageFile,
26                   "copyright" : self.copyright,
27                   "publisherID" : self.publisherID,
28                   "editionNumber" : self.editionNumber }
29
30          # create product node
31          product = document.createElement( "product" )
32
```

Fig. 23.7   **Book** that represents a single book's information and defines the XML format of that information. (Part 1 of 2.)

```
33              # add element for each Book attribute
34              for key in data.keys():
35
36                  # create element, append as child of product
37                  temp = document.createElement( key )
38                  temp.appendChild( document.createTextNode(
39                      str( data[ key ] ) ) )
40                  product.appendChild( temp )
41
42              return product
```

Fig. 23.7 **Book** that represents a single book's information and defines the XML
format of that information. (Part 2 of 2.)

Method **getXML** (lines 18–42) uses the DOM **Document** and **Element** interfaces
to create an XML representation of the book data as part of the **Document** that is passed
as an argument. The complete information for one book is placed in a **product** element
(created in line 31). The elements for the individual properties of a book are appended to
the **product** element as children.

The for structure (lines 34–40) uses Document method createElement to create an Element node for each book attribute (line 37). Lines 38–39 use Document method createText-
Node to specify the text in the Element node and uses Element method appendChild to
append the text to the Element node. Note that the data is first converted to a string using
str because method createTextNode only accepts string arguments. Line 40 adds the Element node to product by calling Element method appendChild. Line 42 returns Element
node product to the caller. Fig. 23.8 shows an example of a product element returned by
method getXML. For more information about XML, please refer to Chapters 15–16.

Recall that, after creating a client session, **bookstore.py** redirects the user to **all-
Books.py**, which retrieves the list of books from the **Books** database and dynamically generates an XML document that represents the books. Script **allBooks.py** then processes
this document against a browser-specific XSLT style sheet called **allBooks.xsl**. The
results are then rendered on the client. Figure 23.9 contains **allBooks.py**.

```
1   <product>
2     <isbn>0130895601</isbn>
3     <title>Advanced Java 2 Platform How to Program</title>
4     <price>69.95</price>
5     <imageFile>advjhtp1.jpg</imageFile>
6     <copyright>2002</copyright>
7     <publisherID>1</publisherID>
8     <editionNumber>1</editionNumber>
9   </product>
```

Fig. 23.8 **product** element.

```
1   #!c:\Python\python.exe
2   # Fig. 23.9: allBooks.py
```

Fig. 23.9 **allBooks.py** returns to the client a document containing the book list.
(Part 1 of 3.)

```
 3    # Retrieve all books from database and store in session.
 4    # Display book list to client by retrieving XML and converting
 5    # to required format using browser-specific XSLT stylesheet.
 6
 7    import sys
 8    import Book
 9    import urllib
10    import Session
11    import MySQLdb
12    from xml.xslt import Processor
13    from xml.dom.DOMImplementation import implementation
14
15    # load Session
16    try:
17       session = Session.Session()
18    except Session.SessionError, message:  # invalid/no session ID
19       Session.redirect( "error.py?message=%s" % message )
20       sys.exit()
21
22    # setup mySQL statement
23    query = """SELECT ISBN, Title, EditionNumber,
24       Copyright, PublisherID, ImageFile, Price
25       FROM Titles ORDER BY Title"""
26
27    # attempt database connection and retrieve list of Books
28    try:
29
30       # connect to the database, retrieve a cursor and execute query
31       connection = MySQLdb.connect( db = "Books" )
32       cursor = connection.cursor()
33       cursor.execute( query )
34
35       # acquire results and close database connection
36       results = cursor.fetchall()
37       cursor.close()
38       connection.close()
39
40    # error occurred, redirect to error page
41    except MySQLdb.OperationalError, message:
42
43       # replace spaces with '+' for URL compatibility
44       message = urllib.quote_plus( str( message ) )
45       Session.redirect( "error.py?message=%s" % message )
46       sys.exit()
47
48    allBooks = []
49
50    # get row data
51    for row in results:
52
53       # create new Book and set attributes
54       book = Book.Book()
```

Fig. 23.9   allBooks.py returns to the client a document containing the book list.
(Part 2 of 3.)

```
55      book.isbn = row[ 0 ]
56      book.title = row[ 1 ]
57      book.editionNumber = row[ 2 ]
58      book.copyright = row[ 3 ]
59      book.publisherID = row[ 4 ]
60      book.imageFile = row[ 5 ]
61      book.price = row[ 6 ]
62
63      allBooks.append( book )   # one more Book created
64
65   session.data[ "titles" ] = allBooks
66
67   # generate XML
68   document = implementation.createDocument( None, None, None )
69   catalog = document.createElement( "catalog" )
70   document.appendChild( catalog )
71
72   # add all products to catalog
73   for book in allBooks:
74      catalog.appendChild( book.getXML( document ) )
75
76   # process XML against XSLT stylesheet
77   processor = Processor.Processor()
78   style = open( session.data[ "agent" ] + "/allBooks.xsl" )
79   processor.appendStylesheetString( style.read() % \
80      session.data[ "ID" ] )
81   results = processor.runNode( document )
82   style.close()
83
84   # save Session data and display processed XML
85   pageData = session.data[ "content type" ] + results
86   session.saveSession()
87   print pageData
```

Fig. 23.9   allBooks.py returns to the client a document containing the book list.
(Part 3 of 3.)

Lines 16–20 load the session. If the session ID is not specified in the query string or if the specified ID is invalid, **error.py** displays an error message (line 19). Lines 23–25 prepare the MySQL statement that **allBooks.py** uses when querying the **Books** database. Lines 31–38 then connect to the database and retrieve the list of books. If an error occurs (**MySQLdb.OperationalError**), **error.py** displays an error message, and the program exits (lines 45–46). Note that the error that **MySQLdb.Operational-Error** returns first must be converted to a string with all spaces replaced by a **+**. This is because **MySQLdb.OperationalError** returns a tuple. The spaces must be replaced so that the message transfers correctly in the query string.

Lines 51–61 create a **Book** instance for each book in the database, and append it to list **allBooks**. Line 65 stores the list of **Book** instances in the session dictionary (**data**) with key **titles**.

We then create an XML **Document** that represents the entire catalog of books. The **xml.dom.DOMImplementation.implementation** method **createDocument** creates an empty DOM **Document** named **document** (line 68). **Document** method

createElement creates the empty **catalog** element (line 69). Line 70 appends the **catalog** element to **document**. Lines 73–74 retrieve the **product** element for each **Book** and use method **appendChild** to append the element to **catalog**.

A browser-specific XSLT style sheet processes the XML **Document** (lines 77–82). Line 77 creates an XSLT **Processor**. The script then retrieves the XSLT style sheet called **allBooks.xsl** (line 78). Note that **allBooks.xsl** resides in the directory that corresponds to the client type. This ensures that the XSLT style sheet transforms the XML **Document** into a format that is compatible with the client type. Lines 79–80 append the style sheet to a list of acceptable style sheets for use by the **Processor**. The program must insert the session ID in the style sheet, because the XML **Document** transformed by the style sheet does not contain the session ID. Inserting the session ID into the style sheet causes the session ID to appear in each hyperlink. This ensures that the session ID does not get lost. Line 81 runs the **Processor** on **document**, and line 82 closes the style sheet file. We then display the transformed XML to the client. Line 85 creates the string that contains the content-type specification and the processor results. Lines 86–87 save the session and display the page to the user, respectively.

Figure 23.10 contains the XSLT style sheet that transforms the XML catalog representation into XHTML and displays the resulting XHTML document.

```
1   <?xml version = "1.0"?>
2
3   <!-- Fig. 23.10: allBooks.xsl                              -->
4   <!-- XSLT style sheet that transforms XML generated by    -->
5   <!-- books.py into XHTML.                                  -->
6
7   <xsl:stylesheet version = "1.0"
8      xmlns:xsl = "http://www.w3.org/1999/XSL/Transform">
9
10     <xsl:output method = "xml" omit-xml-declaration = "no"
11        indent = "yes" doctype-system = "DTD/xhtml1-strict.dtd"
12        doctype-public = "-//W3C//DTD XHTML 1.0 Strict//EN"/>
13
14  <!-- template for catalog element -->
15  <xsl:template match = "catalog">
16
17     <html xmlns = "http://www.w3.org/1999/xhtml">
18
19        <head>
20           <title>Book List</title>
21           <link rel = "stylesheet" href = "/bookstore/styles.css"
22              type = "text/css" />
23        </head>
24
25        <body>
26
27           <p class = "bigFont">Available Books</p>
28           <p class = "bold">
29              Click a link to view book information</p>
```

Fig. 23.10 allBooks.xsl for an XHTML client type that transforms the XML representation of the catalog into XHTML. (Part 1 of 2.)

```
30
31              <!-- match product elements to product template -->
32              <xsl:apply-templates select = "/catalog/product">
33
34                  <!-- sort products by title -->
35                  <xsl:sort select = "title" />
36
37              </xsl:apply-templates>
38
39          </body>
40
41      </html>
42
43  </xsl:template>
44
45  <!-- template for building row of product information -->
46  <xsl:template match = "product">
47
48      <a href = "displayBook.py?ID=%s&amp;isbn={isbn}">
49          <strong><xsl:value-of select = "title" />, <xsl:value-of
50          select = "editionNumber" />e</strong>
51      </a><br />
52
53  </xsl:template>
54
55  </xsl:stylesheet>
```

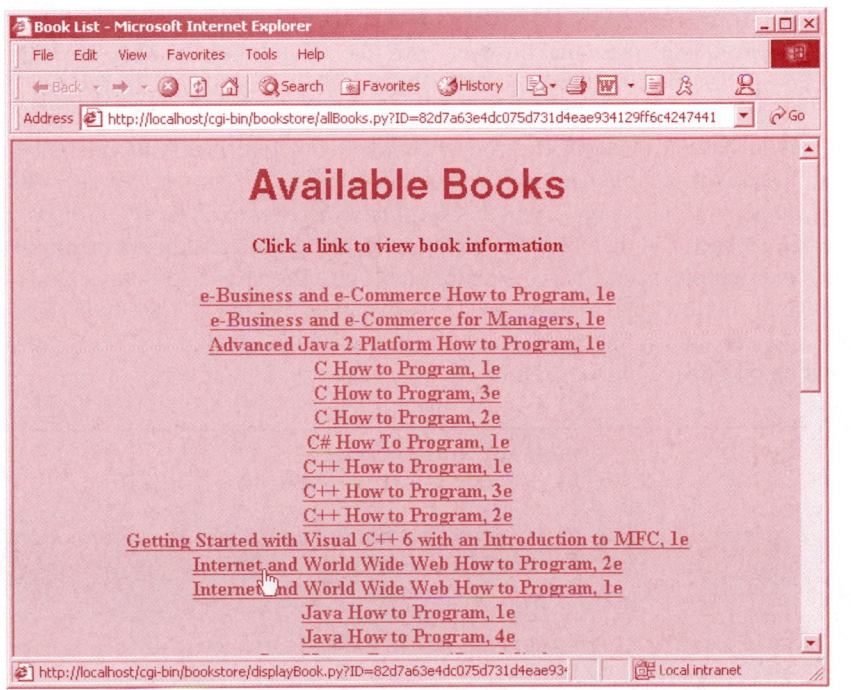

Fig. 23.10 `allBooks.xsl` for an XHTML client type that transforms the XML representation of the catalog into XHTML. (Part 2 of 2.)

An **xsl:template** defines a template for **catalog** elements (lines 15–43). Within this template, we insert matches of the **product** template (lines 32–37). These matches are sorted by their **title** elements (line 35). This ensures that the book list appears in alphabetical order by the title.

Lines 46–53 define an **xsl:template** for **product** elements. Line 48 specifies an **anchor** tag with attribute **href**. The value of the **href** attribute references **display-Book.py** with a query string. Recall that **allBooks.py** inserts the session ID into this query string, which enables the session-tracking mechanism. The **isbn** of the current **product** is inserted using **{isbn}**. The complete query string ensures that **display-Book** can identify the client and display the book. The anchor tag contains text and the values of the **title** and **editionNumber** elements of an XML document (lines 49–50).

The XSLT document (Fig. 23.10) specifies a linked style sheet, **styles.css** (lines 21–22). All XHTML documents sent to the client use **styles.css** to achieve uniform formatting. Figure 23.11 contains **styles.css**.

Portability Tip 23.2

Different browsers have different levels of support for CSS documents.

Lines 1–2 center the text in the **body** element and set the background color to steel blue. The hexadecimal number **#b0c4de** represents the background color. Line 3 defines class **.bold** to apply bold font weight to text. Lines 4–7 define class **.bigFont** with four CSS attributes. These attributes apply a bold, Helvetica font to elements that access the class. Also, **.bigFont** doubles the size of the font and sets the color to dark blue (**#00008b**). If the Helvetica font is not available, the browser uses the Arial font; if that font is not available, then the browser uses the default font, **sans-serif**. Class **.italic** applies italic font style to text (line 8). Class **.right** right-justifies the text (line 9). Lines 10–11 specify that all **table**, **th** (table head data) and **td** (table data) elements should have a three-pixel, grooved border with five pixels of internal padding between the text in a table cell and the border of that cell. Lines 12–14 specify that all **table** elements should have a blue background color (represented by the hexadecimal number **#6495ed**) and that all **table** elements should use pre-defined margins on both their left and right sides. The margins center a table on a Web page. Although the style sheet does not apply all the styles to every XHTML document, having a single style sheet allows programmers to modify the appearance of an application quickly and easily. For more information on CSS, refer to Appendix K.

```
1    body              { text-align: center;
2                        background-color: #boc4de }
3    .bold             { font-weight: bold }
4    .bigFont          { font-family: helvetica, arial, sans-serif;
5                        font-weight: bold;
6                        font-size: 2em;
7                        color: #00008b }
8    .italic           { font-style: italic }
9    .right            { text-align: right }
```

Fig. 23.11 **styles.css** applies common formatting across XHTML documents rendered on the client. (Part 1 of 2.)

```
10   table, th, td   { border: 3px groove;
11                     padding: 5px }
12   table           { background-color: #6495ed;
13                     margin-left: auto;
14                     margin-right: auto }
```

Fig. 23.11 styles.css applies common formatting across XHTML documents rendered on the client. (Part 2 of 2.)

23.8 Viewing a Book's Details

Selecting a book in **allBooks.py** forwards the user to **displayBook.py** (Fig. 23.12). This program extracts the ISBN from the query string and determines which book the user selected. The program then obtains the XML representation of the book and processes that representation against a browser-specific XSLT style sheet (**display-Book.xsl**). The results are sent to the user.

If the ISBN is not specified in the query string, the program redirects the user to **error.py** (line 17). Otherwise, **displayBook.py** loads the session (line 22). If successful, **displayBook.py** obtains the list of **Book**s from variable **session** (line 27). Line 28 sets the **session.data** key, **bookToAdd**, to value **None**, which indicates that the specified ISBN has not yet been found in the list of **Book**s stored in variable **titles**.

```
1   #!c:\Python\python.exe
2   # Fig. 23.12: displayBook.py
3   # Retrieve one book's XML representation, convert
4   # to required format using browser-specific XSLT
5   # stylesheet and display results.
6
7   import cgi
8   import sys
9   import Session
10  from xml.xslt import Processor
11  from xml.dom.DOMImplementation import implementation
12
13  form = cgi.FieldStorage()
14
15  # ISBN has not been specified
16  if not form.has_key( "isbn" ):
17     Session.redirect( "error.py?message=No+ISBN+given" )
18     sys.exit()
19
20  # load Session
21  try:
22     session = Session.Session()
23  except Session.SessionError, message:   # invalid/no session ID
24     Session.redirect( "error.py?message=%s" % message )
25     sys.exit()
26
```

Fig. 23.12 displayBook.py converts the XML representation of the selected book to a browser-specific format, using an XSLT style sheet. (Part 1 of 2.)

```
27   titles = session.data[ "titles" ]    # get titles
28   session.data[ "bookToAdd" ] = None   # book has not been found
29
30   # locate Book object for selected book
31   for book in titles:
32
33       if form[ "isbn" ].value == book.isbn:
34           session.data[ "bookToAdd" ] = book
35           break
36
37   # book has been found
38   if session.data[ "bookToAdd" ] is not None:
39
40       # get XML from selected book
41       document = implementation.createDocument( None, None, None )
42       document.appendChild( session.data[ "bookToAdd" ].getXML(
43           document ) )
44
45       # process XML against XSLT style sheet
46       processor = Processor.Processor()
47       style = open( session.data[ "agent" ] + "/displayBook.xsl" )
48       processor.appendStylesheetString( style.read() % \
49           ( session.data[ "ID" ], session.data[ "ID" ] ) )
50       results = processor.runNode( document )
51       style.close()
52
53       # save Session data and display processed XML
54       pageData = session.data[ "content type" ] + results
55       session.saveSession()
56       print pageData
57   else:
58
59       # invalid ISBN has been specified
60       Session.redirect( "error.py?message=Nonexistent+ISBN" )
```

Fig. 23.12 `displayBook.py` converts the XML representation of the selected book to a browser-specific format, using an XSLT style sheet. (Part 2 of 2.)

Lines 31–35 iterate over **titles**, searching for a **Book** with the corresponding ISBN. If a book exists with the specified ISBN, **session.data** key **bookToAdd** is set to the matching **Book** instance, and the loop terminates. If no book matches the specified ISBN, the loop terminates with **session.data** key **bookToAdd** still having the value **None**.

Line 38 determines whether a matching book exists. If a match exists (i.e., **session.data** key **bookToAdd** is not **None**), lines 40–56 execute. Line 41 creates a new XML **Document**. Lines 42–43 append the **product** element of the matching **Book** to the **Document**, using the **appendChild** method. Lines 46–51 process the XML **Document** against a browser-specific XSLT style sheet called **displayBook.xsl**. The style sheet resides in the subdirectory of the current directory named after the client type. Note that the program must insert the session ID into the style sheet before processing the XML **Document**. We then save the session and display the results to the client (lines 54–56). If the book does not exist, line 60 redirects the client to **error.py**.

Figure 23.13 contains the **displayBook.xsl** style sheet. The values of six elements in the XML document are placed in the resulting XHTML document.

```
1   <?xml version = "1.0"?>
2
3   <!-- Fig. 23.13: displayBook.xsl                          -->
4   <!-- XSLT style sheet that transforms XML generated by -->
5   <!-- displayBook.py into XHTML.                            -->
6
7   <xsl:stylesheet version = "1.0"
8       xmlns:xsl = "http://www.w3.org/1999/XSL/Transform">
9
10      <xsl:output method = "xml" omit-xml-declaration = "no"
11          indent = "yes" doctype-system = "DTD/xhtml1-strict.dtd"
12          doctype-public = "-//W3C//DTD XHTML 1.0 Strict//EN"/>
13
14  <!-- specify the root of the XML document  -->
15  <!-- that references this style sheet       -->
16  <xsl:template match = "product">
17
18      <html xmlns = "http://www.w3.org/1999/xhtml">
19
20          <head>
21
22              <!-- obtain book title from script to place in title -->
23              <title><xsl:value-of select = "title" /></title>
24
25              <link rel = "stylesheet" href = "/bookstore/styles.css"
26                  type = "text/css" />
27          </head>
28
29          <body>
30
31              <p class = "bigFont"><xsl:value-of select = "title" /></p>
32
33              <table>
34                  <tr>
35
36                      <!-- create table cell for product image -->
37                      <td rowspan = "5">  <!-- cell spans 5 rows -->
38                          <img src = "/bookstore/images/{imageFile}"
39                              alt = "{title}" />
40                      </td>
41
42                      <!-- create table cells for price in row 1 -->
43                      <td class = "bold">Price:</td>
44
45                      <td><xsl:value-of select = "price" /></td>
46                  </tr>
47
48                  <tr>
```

Fig. 23.13 XSLT style sheet that transforms a book's XML representation into an XHTML document. (Part 1 of 3.)

```
49
50                        <!-- create table cells for ISBN in row 2 -->
51                        <td class = "bold">ISBN #:</td>
52
53                        <td><xsl:value-of select = "isbn" /></td>
54                    </tr>
55
56                    <tr>
57
58                        <!-- create table cells for edition in row 3 -->
59                        <td class = "bold">Edition:</td>
60
61                        <td><xsl:value-of select = "editionNumber" /></td>
62                    </tr>
63
64                    <tr>
65
66                        <!-- create table cells for copyright in row 4 -->
67                        <td class = "bold">Copyright:</td>
68
69                        <td><xsl:value-of select = "copyright" /></td>
70                    </tr>
71
72                    <tr>
73
74                        <!-- create Add to Cart button in row 5 -->
75                        <td>
76                            <form method = "post"
77                                action = "addToCart.py?ID=%s">
78                                <p><input type = "submit"
79                                        value = "Add to Cart" /></p>
80                            </form>
81                        </td>
82
83                        <!-- create View Cart button in row 5 -->
84                        <td>
85                            <form method = "post"
86                                action = "viewCart.py?ID=%s">
87                                <p><input type = "submit"
88                                        value = "View Cart" /></p>
89                            </form>
90                        </td>
91                    </tr>
92                </table>
93
94          </body>
95
96      </html>
97
98  </xsl:template>
99
100 </xsl:stylesheet>
```

Fig. 23.13 XSLT style sheet that transforms a book's XML representation into an XHTML document. (Part 2 of 3.)

Fig. 23.13 XSLT style sheet that transforms a book's XML representation into an XHTML document. (Part 3 of 3.)

Lines 23 and 31 place the book's **title** in the document's **title** element and in a paragraph at the beginning of the document's **body** element, respectively. Line 38 specifies an **img** element that contains the value of the **imageFile** element of an XML document. This element specifies the name of the file that represents the book's cover image. Line 39 specifies the **alt** attribute of the **img** element, using the book's **title**. Lines 45, 53, 61 and 69 place the book's **price**, **isbn**, **editionNumber** and **copyright** in table cells, respectively. Lines 76–80 and lines 85-89 create **Add to Cart** (**addToCart.py**) and **View Cart** (**viewCart.py**) buttons, respectively. Both buttons use the *post* form method to pass the session ID to their target files. The session ID is inserted in lines 77 and 86 by **displayBook.py**.

23.9 Adding an Item to the Shopping Cart

When the user presses the **Add to Cart** button in the document produced by Fig. 23.13, the **addToCart.py** program updates the shopping cart. **CartItem** instances represent the items in the shopping cart. An instance of this class stores an item and the current quantity for that item in the shopping cart. For use with our online bookstore, a **CartItem** maintains a **Book** instance and the quantity of that **Book** in the cart. If a user selects an item that already exists in the shopping cart, the quantity of that item is updated in the **CartItem**. Otherwise, the script creates a new **CartItem** with a quantity of 1. After updating the cart, the user is forwarded to **viewCart.py** to view the cart's contents. Figure 23.14 and Fig. 23.15 show classes **CartItem** and **addToCart**.

```
1   # Fig. 23.14: CartItem.py
2   # Maintains an item and a quantity.
3
4   class CartItem:
5       """Class that maintains an item and its quantity"""
6
7       def __init__( self, itemToAdd, number ):
8           """Initialize a CartItem"""
9
10          self.item = itemToAdd
11          self.quantity = number
```

Fig. 23.14 CartItems contain an **item** and the **quantity** of an item in the shopping cart.

```
1   #!c:\Python\python.exe
2   # Fig. 23.15: addToCart.py
3   # Create new/update CartItem for selected Book object
4
5   import sys
6   import Session
7   import CartItem
8
9   # load Session
10  try:
11      session = Session.Session()
12  except Session.SessionError, message:   # invalid/no session ID
13      Session.redirect( "error.py?message=%s" % message )
14      sys.exit()
15
16  book = session.data[ "bookToAdd" ]
17  cart = session.data[ "cart" ]
18
19  # if book is already in cart, update quantity
20  if book.isbn in cart.keys():
21      cartItem = cart[ book.isbn ]
22      cartItem.quantity += 1
23
24  # otherwise, create and add a new CartItem to cart
25  else:
26      cart[ book.isbn ] = CartItem.CartItem( book, 1 )
27
28  # update cart attribute
29  session.data[ "cart" ] = cart
30
31  # save Session data and send user to viewCart.py
32  nextPage = "viewCart.py?ID=%s" % session.data[ "ID" ]
33  session.saveSession()
34  Session.redirect( nextPage )
```

Fig. 23.15 addToCart.py places an item in the shopping cart and invokes **viewCart.py** to display the cart contents.

The program first obtains the **Session** instance for the client (lines 10–14). If a session does not exist for this client, the client is forwarded to **error.py** (line 13). Otherwise, line 16 obtains the value of **session.data** key **bookToAdd**—the **Book** to add to the shopping cart. Line 17 obtains the value of **session.data** key **cart**—the dictionary that represents the shopping cart. The **if** statement in line 20 determines whether the shopping cart already contains the specified book. If so, line 21 obtains the **CartItem** that represents the book, and line 22 increments the quantity for that **CartItem**. Otherwise, line 26 creates a new **CartItem** with a quantity of **1** and puts the item into the shopping cart, keyed by the book's ISBN. Line 29 sets **session.data** key **cart** to the updated dictionary (**cart**). Then, lines 32-34 save the session and forward the user to **viewCart.py** to display the cart contents.

23.10 Viewing the Shopping Cart

Program **viewCart.py** (Fig. 23.16) extracts the **CartItem**s from the shopping cart, subtotals each item in the cart, totals all the items in the cart and creates a document that allows the client to view the cart in tabular format.

We first load the session (lines 13–17). If an error occurs, the program redirects the user to **error.py** (line 16). Line 19 obtains the session shopping-cart. Line 20 initializes variable **total** to **0**. We then create a new XML **Document** and append a **cart** element to **Document** (lines 23–25).

```
1   #!c:\Python\python.exe
2   # Fig. 23.16: viewCart.py
3   # Generate XML representing cart, convert
4   # to required format using browser-specific XSLT
5   # style sheet and display results.
6
7   import sys
8   import Session
9   from xml.xslt import Processor
10  from xml.dom.DOMImplementation import implementation
11
12  # load Session
13  try:
14      session = Session.Session()
15  except Session.SessionError, message:    # invalid/no session ID
16      Session.redirect( "error.py?message=%s" % message )
17      sys.exit()
18
19  cart = session.data[ "cart" ]
20  total = 0  # total for all ordered items
21
22  # generate XML representing cart object
23  document = implementation.createDocument( None, None, None )
24  cartNode = document.createElement( "cart" )
25  document.appendChild( cartNode )
```

Fig. 23.16 viewCart.py obtains the shopping cart and outputs a document with the cart contents in tabular format. (Part 1 of 2.)

```
26
27  # add XML representation for each cart item
28  for cartItem in cart.values():
29
30      # get book data, calculate subtotal and total
31      book = cartItem.item
32      quantity = cartItem.quantity
33      price = book.price
34      subtotal = quantity * price
35      total += subtotal
36
37      # create an orderProduct element
38      orderProduct = document.createElement( "orderProduct" )
39
40      # create a product element and append to orderProduct
41      productNode = book.getXML( document )
42      orderProduct.appendChild( productNode )
43
44      # create a quantity element and append to orderProduct
45      quantityNode = document.createElement( "quantity" )
46      quantityNode.appendChild( document.createTextNode( "%d" %
47          quantity ) )
48      orderProduct.appendChild( quantityNode )
49
50      # create a subtotal element and append to orderProduct
51      subtotalNode = document.createElement( "subtotal" )
52      subtotalNode.appendChild( document.createTextNode( "%.2f" %
53          subtotal ) )
54      orderProduct.appendChild( subtotalNode )
55
56      # append orderProduct to cartNode
57      cartNode.appendChild( orderProduct )
58
59  # set the total attribute of cart element
60  cartNode.setAttribute( "total", "%.2f" % total )
61
62  # make current total a session attribute
63  session.data[ "total" ] = total
64
65  # process generated XML against XSLT style sheet
66  processor = Processor.Processor()
67  style = open( session.data[ "agent" ] + "/viewCart.xsl" )
68  processor.appendStylesheetString( style.read() % \
69      ( session.data[ "ID" ], session.data[ "ID" ] ) )
70  results = processor.runNode( document )
71  style.close()
72
73  # save Session data and display processed XML
74  pageData = session.data[ "content type" ] + results
75  session.saveSession()
76  print pageData
```

Fig. 23.16 viewCart.py obtains the shopping cart and outputs a document with
the cart contents in tabular format. (Part 2 of 2.)

Lines 28–57 compute the total of the items in the cart. Lines 31–32 retrieve the **Book** instance and the **quantity** from the **CartItem**. Line 33 obtains the **price** of the **Book**. Line 34 calculates the subtotal for the **CartItem**. Line 35 updates the total cost of all cart items. Line 38 creates an XML **orderProduct** element for each item in the cart.

Each **orderProduct** element contains 3 child elements: **product**, **quantity** and **subtotal**. We first retrieve the **product** element that represents the current **Book** (line 41). Line 42 adds this **product** element to the **orderProduct** element by calling method **appendChild**. Lines 45–48 then create and append the **quantity** element. Note that the program must convert the quantity of the current **CartItem** to a string before creating the **quantity** element. Lines 51-54 create and append the **subtotal** child of **orderProduct**. The **subtotal** element contains the subtotal of the current **CartItem**, formatted to two decimal places. Line 57 appends the current **order-Product** to the **cart** element.

When a single **orderProduct** element has been created and appended to the **cart** element for each **CartItem**, the program then sets the **total** attribute of the **cart** element (line 60). Line 63 stores the current sales total (i.e., the sum of all **subtotals**) in the session dictionary, keyed by **total**. Lines 66–71 process the XML **Document** against a browser-specific XSLT style sheet (**viewCart.xsl**). The session ID must be inserted into the style sheet before processing. Lines 74–76 save the session and display the transformed XML to the client.

Figure 23.17 contains the **viewCart.xsl** style sheet file used in the XSLT transformation for an XHTML client.

```
1   <?xml version = "1.0"?>
2
3   <!-- Fig. 23.17: viewCart.xsl                        -->
4   <!-- XSLT style sheet that transforms XML generated by -->
5   <!-- viewCart.py into XHTML.                           -->
6
7   <xsl:stylesheet version = "1.0"
8      xmlns:xsl = "http://www.w3.org/1999/XSL/Transform">
9
10     <xsl:output method = "xml" omit-xml-declaration = "no"
11         indent = "yes" doctype-system = "DTD/xhtml1-strict.dtd"
12         doctype-public = "-//W3C//DTD XHTML 1.0 Strict//EN"/>
13
14  <xsl:template match = "cart">
15
16     <html xmlns = "http://www.w3.org/1999/xhtml">
17
18        <head>
19           <title>Your Online Shopping Cart</title>
20           <link rel = "stylesheet" href = "/bookstore/styles.css"
21              type = "text/css" />
22        </head>
23
24        <body>
```

Fig. 23.17 XSLT style sheet that transforms a cart's XML representation into an XHTML document. (Part 1 of 3.)

```
25
26                 <p class = "bigFont">Shopping Cart</p>
27
28             <xsl:choose>
29                 <xsl:when test = "@total = '0.00'">
30                     <p class = "bold">
31                         Your shopping cart is currently empty.</p>
32                 </xsl:when>
33
34                 <xsl:otherwise>   <!-- total != 0.00 -->
35                     <table class = "cart">
36                         <tr>
37                             <th>Product</th>
38                             <th>Quantity</th>
39                             <th>Price</th>
40                             <th>Total</th>
41                         </tr>
42
43                         <xsl:apply-templates select = "orderProduct">
44
45                             <!-- sort orderProducts by product/title -->
46                             <xsl:sort select = "product/title" />
47
48                         </xsl:apply-templates>
49
50                         <tr>
51                             <td colspan = "4" class = "bold right">
52                                 Total: <xsl:value-of select = "@total" />
53                             </td>
54                         </tr>
55                     </table>
56
57                 </xsl:otherwise>
58             </xsl:choose>
59
60             <p class = "bold green">
61                 <a href = "allBooks.py?ID=%s">Continue Shopping</a>
62             </p>
63
64             <form method = "post" action = "order.py?ID=%s">
65                 <p><input type = "submit" value = "Check Out" /></p>
66             </form>
67
68         </body>
69
70     </html>
71
72 </xsl:template>
73
74 <xsl:template match = "orderProduct">
75
76     <tr>
```

Fig. 23.17 XSLT style sheet that transforms a cart's XML representation into an XHTML document. (Part 2 of 3.)

```
77          <td><xsl:value-of select = "product/title" />,
78              <xsl:value-of select = "product/editionNumber" />e</td>
79          <td><xsl:value-of select = "quantity" /></td>
80          <td class = "right"><xsl:value-of select =
81              "product/price" /></td>
82          <td class = "bold right"><xsl:value-of select =
83              "subtotal" /></td>
84      </tr>
85
86  </xsl:template>
87
88  </xsl:stylesheet>
```

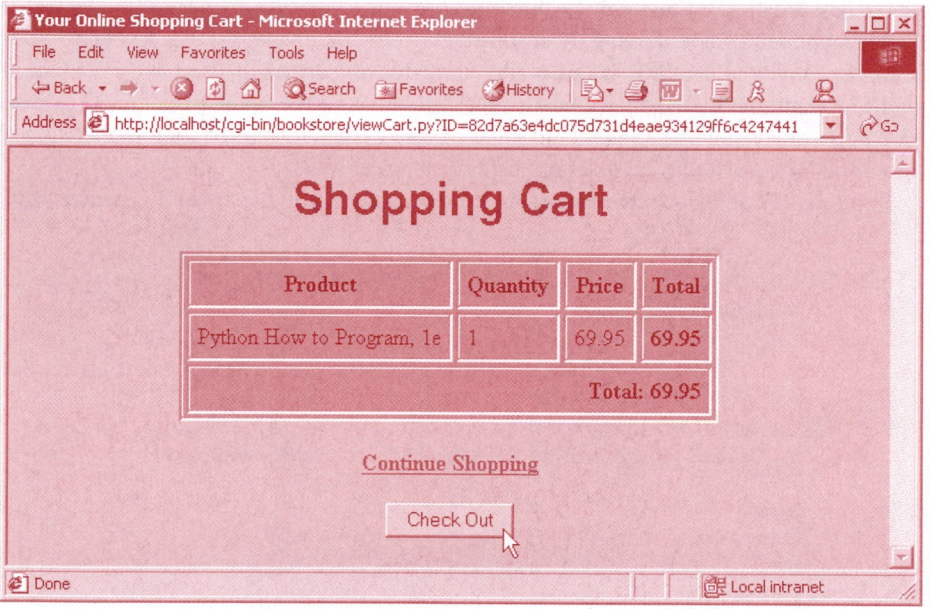

Fig. 23.17 XSLT style sheet that transforms a cart's XML representation into an XHTML document. (Part 3 of 3.)

The first **xsl:template** (lines 14–72) matches **cart** elements. Line 28 begins an **xsl:choose** element. If **cart** attribute (denoted by **@**) **total** equals **"0.00"**, the program displays a message to the client indicating the shopping cart is currently empty (lines 30–31); otherwise, the program creates a table for all the items in the cart (lines 34-57).

Lines 43–48 insert all matches into the **orderProduct** template, sorted by their **product/title** elements. The **orderProduct** template (lines 74–86) matches (i.e., describes how to transform) **orderProduct** elements. Lines 77–83 insert the **orderProduct**'s **product/title**, **product/editionNumber**, **quantity**, **product/price** and **subtotal** in table cells. Lines 50–54 then insert a table row displaying the total for all items. We then create two options for the user. The first is a hyperlink that references **allBooks.py** (line 61). The second is a **Check Out** button that redirects the user to **order.py** (lines 64-66).

23.11 Checking Out

When viewing the cart, the user can click a **Check Out** button to proceed to **order.py** (Fig. 23.18). This script retrieves a static page called **orderForm**, which varies with each client type. The correct file resides in a subdirectory named after the client type (e.g. **xhtml/orderForm.html** for an XHTML client). Form **orderForm** requests users to enter their names, addresses, phone number and credit-card information. The form helps complete the application. In this example, the form has no functionality. Normally, there would be some server-side validation of form elements (e.g. testing for a valid credit card). When the user submits the form, the client is forwarded to **process.py** to finalize the book order.

Lines 9–13 first load the session. If an error occurs, the program redirects the user to **error.py** (line 12). Lines 16–17 open the browser-specific order form. Note that the directory name does not necessarily correspond to the file extension (e.g., XHTML Basic clients use directory **xhtml_basic** and file extension **html**). Lines 18–19 create the string that contains the client's content type header (e.g., the header contained in **contentType.txt**) and the contents of page **orderForm**, formatted with the session ID. Lines 23–24 then save the session and display the order form.

Figure 23.19 shows **orderForm.html**, the order form displayed by **order.py** to XHTML clients.

```
1   #!c:\Python\python.exe
2   # Fig. 23.18: order.py
3   # Display order form to get information from customer
4
5   import sys
6   import Session
7
8   # load Session
9   try:
10      session = Session.Session()
11  except Session.SessionError, message:   # invalid/no session ID
12      Session.redirect( "error.py?message=%s" % message )
13      sys.exit()
14
15  # display content type and orderForm for specific client-type
16  content = open( "%s/orderForm.%s" % ( session.data[ "agent" ],
17      session.data[ "extension" ] ) )
18  pageData = session.data[ "content type" ] + content.read() % \
19      session.data[ "ID" ]
20  content.close()
21
22  # save Session data and display order form
23  session.saveSession()
24  print pageData
```

Fig. 23.18 order.py retrieves, formats and displays a static order-form page for the client.

```
1   <!-- Fig. 23.19: orderForm.html                        -->
2   <!-- Static XHTML to be displayed by order.py           -->
3
4   <!DOCTYPE html PUBLIC "-//W3C//DTD XHTML 1.0 Strict//EN"
5       "DTD/xhtml1-strict.dtd">
6
7   <html xmlns = "http://www.w3.org/1999/xhtml">
8
9       <head>
10          <title>Order</title>
11          <link rel = "stylesheet" href = "/bookstore/styles.css"
12              type = "text/css" />
13      </head>
14
15      <body>
16
17          <p class = "bigFont">Shopping Cart Check Out</p>
18
19          <!-- form to input user information and credit card.   -->
20          <!-- note: no need to input real data in this example. -->
21          <form method = "post" action = "process.py?ID=%s">
22              <p style = "font-weight: bold">
23                  Please input the following information</p>
24
25              <table>
26                  <tr>
27                      <td class = "right bold">First name:</td>
28
29                      <td>
30                          <input type = "text" name = "firstname"
31                              size = "25" />
32                      </td>
33                  </tr>
34                  <tr>
35                      <td class = "right bold">Last name:</td>
36
37                      <td>
38                          <input type = "text" name = "lastname"
39                              size = "25" />
40                      </td>
41                  </tr>
42                  <tr>
43                      <td class = "right bold">Street:</td>
44
45                      <td>
46                          <input type = "text" name = "street"
47                              size = "25" />
48                      </td>
49                  </tr>
50                  <tr>
51                      <td class = "right bold">City:</td>
52
```

Fig. 23.19 `orderForm.html` is the order form displayed by `order.py` for XHTML clients. (Part 1 of 3.)

```
53                      <td>
54                          <input type = "text" name = "city"
55                              size = "25" />
56                      </td>
57                  </tr>
58                  <tr>
59                      <td class = "right bold">State:</td>
60
61                      <td>
62                          <input type = "text" name = "state"
63                              size = "2" />
64                      </td>
65                  </tr>
66                  <tr>
67                      <td class = "right bold">Zip code:</td>
68
69                      <td>
70                          <input type = "text" name = "zipcode"
71                              size = "10" />
72                      </td>
73                  </tr>
74                  <tr>
75                      <td class = "right bold">Phone #:</td>
76
77                      <td>
78                          <input type = "text" name = "phone"
79                              size = "12" />
80                      </td>
81                  </tr>
82                  <tr>
83                      <td class = "right bold">Credit Card #:</td>
84
85                      <td>
86                          <input type = "text" name = "creditcard"
87                              size = "25" />
88                      </td>
89                  </tr>
90                  <tr>
91                      <td class = "right bold">Expiration (mm/yyyy):</td>
92
93                      <td>
94                          <input type = "text" name = "expires"
95                              size = "2" />
96
97                          <input type = "text" name = "expires2"
98                              size = "4" />
99                      </td>
100                 </tr>
101             </table>
102
103             <p><input type = "submit" value = "Submit" /></p>
104
```

Fig. 23.19 orderForm.html is the order form displayed by **order.py** for XHTML
clients. (Part 2 of 3.)

```
105              </form>
106
107          </body>
108
109      </html>
```

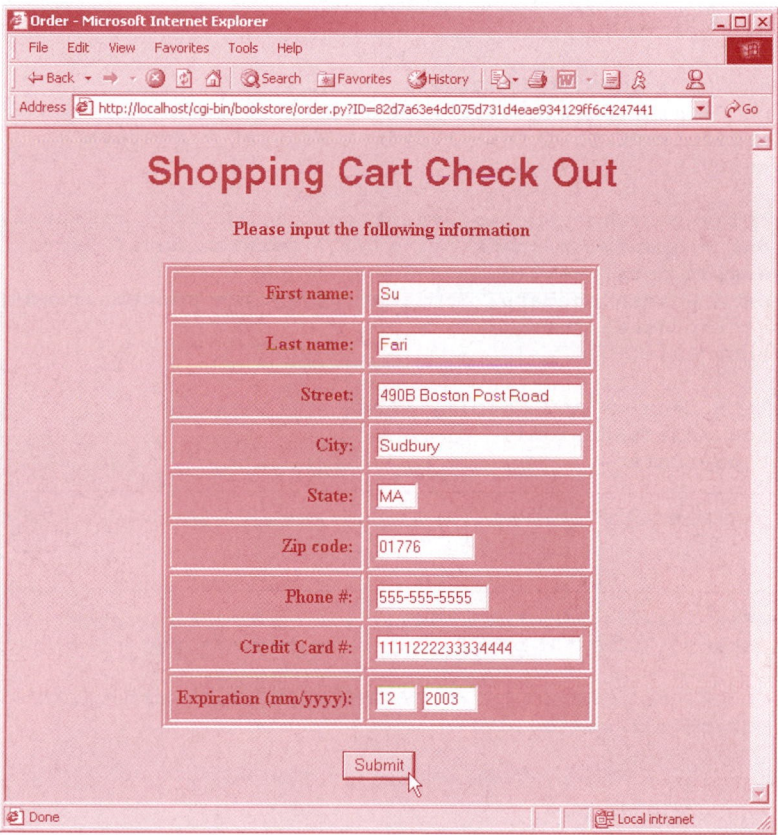

Fig. 23.19 `orderForm.html` is the order form displayed by `order.py` for XHTML clients. (Part 3 of 3.)

23.12 Processing the Order

Figure 23.20 (`process.py`) simulates the processing of the user's credit-card information and retrieves a browser-specific document called `thankYou`—a static page (lines 16–17). The correct file resides in a subdirectory named after the client type (e.g., `xhtml/thankYou.html` for an XHTML client). The program then inserts the final dollar total into the contents of `thankYou` (lines 18–19) and displays this page to the client. Our bookstore does not perform real credit-card processing, so the transaction is now complete. Line 23 invokes `Session` method `deleteSession` to discard the session file for the current client. In a real store, the session may not be invalidated until the purchase is confirmed by the credit-card company. Figure 23.21 shows file `thankYou` for an XHTML client.

```
 1   #!c:\Python\python.exe
 2   # Fig. 23.20: process.py
 3   # Display thank you page to customer and delete session
 4
 5   import sys
 6   import Session
 7
 8   # load session
 9   try:
10      session = Session.Session()
11   except Session.SessionError, message:    # invalid/no session ID
12      Session.redirect( "error.py?message=%s" % message )
13      sys.exit()
14
15   # display content type and thankYou for specific client-type
16   content = open( "%s/thankYou.%s" % ( session.data[ "agent" ],
17      session.data[ "extension" ] ) )
18   pageData = session.data[ "content type" ] + content.read() % \
19      session.data[ "total" ]
20   content.close()
21
22   # delete session and display thank you page
23   session.deleteSession()
24   print pageData
```

Fig. 23.20 process.py retrieves, formats and displays a static thank-you page.

```
 1   <!-- Fig. 23.21: thankYou.html                         -->
 2   <!-- Static XHTML to be displayed by process.py     -->
 3
 4   <!DOCTYPE html PUBLIC "-//W3C//DTD XHTML 1.0 Strict//EN"
 5      "DTD/xhtml1-strict.dtd">
 6
 7   <html xmlns = "http://www.w3.org/1999/xhtml">
 8
 9      <head>
10        <title>Thank You!</title>
11        <link rel = "stylesheet" href = "/bookstore/styles.css"
12           type = "text/css" />
13      </head>
14
15      <body>
16
17        <p class = "bigFont">Thank You</p>
18        <p>Your order has been processed.</p>
19        <p>Your credit card has been billed:
20           <span class = "bold">$%.2f</span>
21        </p>
22
23      </body>
```

Fig. 23.21 thankYou.html is the exit page displayed by **process.py** for XHTML clients. (Part 1 of 2.)

```
24
25    </html>
```

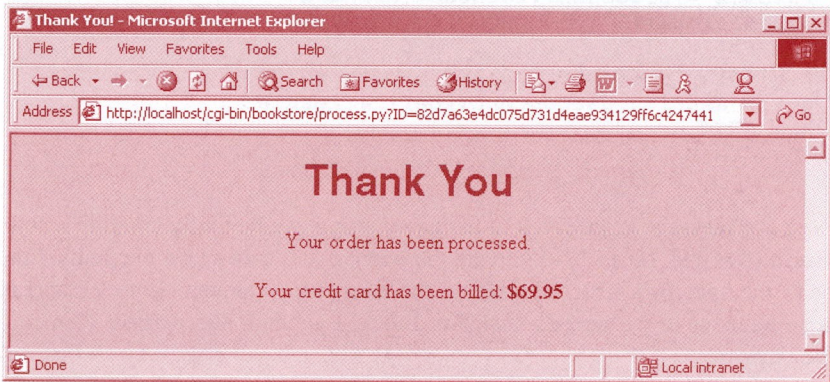

Fig. 23.21 thankYou.html is the exit page displayed by **process.py** for XHTML clients. (Part 2 of 2.)

23.13 Error Handling

When an error occurs in our online bookstore, the user is redirected to **error.py** (Fig. 23.22). This program displays an error message to the client.

```
1   #!c:\Python\python.exe
2   # Fig. 23.22: error.py
3   # Generate XML error message and display to user
4   # using a browser-specific XSLT style sheet.
5
6   import cgi
7   import Session
8   from xml.xslt import Processor
9   from xml.dom.DOMImplementation import implementation
10
11  form = cgi.FieldStorage()
12
13  if form.has_key( "message" ):
14
15      # create DOM for error message
16      document = implementation.createDocument( None, None, None )
17      error = document.createElement( "error" )
18      message = document.createElement( "message" )
19      message.appendChild( document.createTextNode(
20          form[ "message" ].value ) )
21      error.appendChild( message )
22      document.appendChild( error )
23
24      # process against XSLT style sheet
25      processor = Processor.Processor()
```

Fig. 23.22 error.py displays a dynamically created error page. (Part 1 of 2.)

```
26    style = open( Session.getClientType()[ 0 ] + "/error.xsl" )
27    processor.appendStylesheetStream( style )
28    results = processor.runNode( document )
29    style.close()
30
31    # display content type and processed XML
32    print Session.getContentType() + results
```

Fig. 23.22 `error.py` displays a dynamically created error page. (Part 2 of 2.)

If an error message is specified in the query string, we begin by creating a new XML **Document** (line 16). Lines 17–18 create the **error** and **message** elements. Lines 19–20 append the specified error message to the **message** element. Line 21 appends the **message** element to the **error** element. Line 22 appends the **error** element to the XML **Document**.

Lines 25–29 process the **Document** against a browser-specific XSLT style sheet (**error.xsl**). As **error.py** has no session, it must call **Session** functions **getClientType** and **getContentType** to determine the correct files to use. The results are displayed for the user (line 32).

Figure 23.23 contains the **error.xsl** style sheet file used in the XSLT transformation for an XHTML client. Lines 14–35 define an **xsl:template** that matches **error** elements. Line 28 inserts the value of the **message** element into a **paragraph** tag.

```
1    <?xml version = "1.0"?>
2
3    <!-- Fig. 23.23: error.xsl                              -->
4    <!-- XSLT style sheet that transforms XML generated by -->
5    <!-- error.py into XHTML.                               -->
6
7    <xsl:stylesheet version = "1.0"
8        xmlns:xsl = "http://www.w3.org/1999/XSL/Transform">
9
10       <xsl:output method = "xml" omit-xml-declaration = "no"
11           indent = "yes" doctype-system = "DTD/xhtml1-strict.dtd"
12           doctype-public = "-//W3C//DTD XHTML 1.0 Strict//EN"/>
13
14   <xsl:template match = "error">
15
16       <html xmlns = "http://www.w3.org/1999/xhtml">
17
18          <head>
19             <title>Error</title>
20             <link rel = "stylesheet" href = "/bookstore/styles.css"
21                 type = "text/css" />
22          </head>
23
24          <body>
25
```

Fig. 23.23 XSLT style sheet that transforms the XML representation of an error into an XHTML document. (Part 1 of 2.)

```
26              <p class = "bigFont">Error message:</p>
27              <p class = "bold">
28                  <xsl:value-of select = "message" />
29              </p>
30
31          </body>
32
33      </html>
34
35  </xsl:template>
36
37  </xsl:stylesheet>
```

Fig. 23.23 XSLT style sheet that transforms the XML representation of an error into an XHTML document. (Part 2 of 2.)

23.14 Handling Wireless Clients (XHTML Basic and WML)

In this section, we extend our bookstore case study to handle wireless clients. *Wireless clients*, such as *personal digital assistants (PDAs)* and *digital cell phones*, support different markup languages from *wireline clients* (e.g., Internet Explorer). In this section, we demonstrate the two most widely supported wireless markup languages—*XHTML Basic* and *WML*.

The *Wireless Application Protocol (WAP)*, which is a global standard for communications between wireless devices and the Internet supports both XHTML Basic and WML. WAP 2.0 is a revision of the Wireless Application Protocol. WAP 2.0 specifies XHTML Basic, a subset of XHTML, to replace WML as the markup language for Web content on wireless devices. However, because many devices do not support XHTML Basic, we provide support for both markup languages in our bookstore case study. For more information about WAP, visit the WAP Forum Web site at **www.wapforum.org**.

In the following subsections, we use a software application called a *microbrowser* to display the output. Microbrowsers are browsers designed with limited bandwidth and memory requirements. Various microbrowsers are available for different types of devices. For instance, Openwave's Mobile Browser is similar to Microsoft's Internet Explorer, except that the Mobile Browser runs on a wireless device, whereas Internet Explorer runs on a desktop computers.

This section demonstrates the extensibility of our bookstore case study. We show that new client types can be supported simply by creating new XSLT style sheets that support their markup language.

23.14.1 Introduction to XHTML Basic

XHTML Basic is the *World Wide Web Consortium's (W3C)* initiative to provide a common markup language for wireless devices and other small devices with limited memory. Like WML, XHTML Basic is derived from the *Extensible Markup Language (XML)*. As a smaller version of XHTML, XHTML Basic will not exceed the limited memory capacities of wireless devices. XHTML Basic excludes features of XHTML, such as nested tables, that are ill-suited for wireless clients. In addition, XHTML Basic takes advantage of XML's strict structural rules and its extensibility.

XHTML Basic documents are created with a text editor (e.g. Notepad, vi or emacs) and given either the **.html** or **.htm** file extension. In this section, we use the *Pixo Internet Microbrowser* to render XHTML Basic documents. Pixo is a company that develops software platforms and services for wireless-phone manufacturers. The Pixo Internet Microbrowser simulates a cell-phone interface that supports an Internet connection. In the following examples, the Pixo Internet Microbrowser renders XHTML Basic documents. The Pixo Internet Microbrowser 2.1 is available for free download at **www.pixo.com**. For installation instructions, visit the Deitel & Associates Web site at **www.deitel.com**.

Recall now that line 78 of **allBooks.py** opens the version of **allBooks.xsl** that resides in the directory that corresponds to the client type:

```
style = open( session.data[ "agent" ] + "/allBooks.xsl" )
```

For XHTML Basic clients, this file resides in the **xhtml_basic** subdirectory. Figure 23.24 shows the XHTML Basic version of **allBooks.xsl**. This document transforms the XML generated by **allBooks.py** (Fig. 23.9) into XHTML Basic that a wireless client can render. XHTML Basic is a subset of XHTML, so all XSLT documents for XHTML Basic clients resemble the XSLT documents for XHTML clients. Consequently, our explanation of these documents is rather brief.

Lines 10–13 output lines that are required in XHTML Basic documents to conform with proper XHTML Basic syntax. An **xsl:template** defines **catalog** elements (lines 16–44). Within this template, we insert any matches of the **product** template (lines 33–38). These matches are sorted by their **title** elements (line 36), to ensure the book list appears in alphabetical order by the title name.

Lines 47–54 define an **xsl:template** for **product** elements. Line 49 specifies an **anchor** tag with attribute **href**. The value of the **href** attribute references **displayBook.py** with a query string containing the session ID and the value of the **isbn** element of an XML document. Recall that line 71 of **allBooks.py** inserts the session ID into this query string. The **isbn** of the current **product** is inserted using **{isbn}**. The finalized query string ensures that **displayBook** can identify the client and display the book. The anchor tag contains text and the values of the **title** and **editionNumber** elements of an XML document (lines 50–51).

```
1   <?xml version = "1.0"?>
2
3   <!-- Fig. 23.24: allBooks.xsl                              -->
4   <!-- XSLT style sheet that transforms XML generated by     -->
```

Fig. 23.24 allBooks.xsl for XHTML Basic clients. (Courtesy of Pixo, Inc.) (Part 1 of 3.)

```
5   <!-- books.py into XHTML Basic.                    -->
6
7   <xsl:stylesheet version = "1.0"
8      xmlns:xsl = "http://www.w3.org/1999/XSL/Transform">
9
10     <xsl:output method = "xml" omit-xml-declaration = "no"
11         indent = "yes" doctype-system =
12         "http://www.w3.org/TR/xhtml-basic/xhtml-basic10.dtd"
13         doctype-public = "-//W3C//DTD XHTML Basic 1.0//EN"/>
14
15  <!-- template for catalog element -->
16  <xsl:template match = "catalog">
17
18     <html xmlns = "http://www.w3.org/1999/xhtml">
19
20        <head>
21           <title>Book List</title>
22           <link rel = "stylesheet" href = "/bookstore/styles.css"
23              type = "text/css" />
24        </head>
25
26        <body>
27
28           <p class = "bigFont">Available Books</p>
29           <p class = "bold">
30              Click a link to view book information</p>
31
32           <!-- match product elements to product template -->
33           <xsl:apply-templates select = "/catalog/product">
34
35              <!-- sort products by title -->
36              <xsl:sort select = "title" />
37
38           </xsl:apply-templates>
39
40        </body>
41
42     </html>
43
44  </xsl:template>
45
46  <!-- template for building row of Product information -->
47  <xsl:template match = "product">
48
49     <p><a href = "displayBook.py?ID=%s&amp;isbn={isbn}">
50        <strong><xsl:value-of select = "title" />, <xsl:value-of
51        select = "editionNumber" />e</strong>
52     </a></p>
53
54  </xsl:template>
55
56  </xsl:stylesheet>
```

Fig. 23.24 `allBooks.xsl` for XHTML Basic clients. (Courtesy of Pixo, Inc.) (Part 2 of 3.)

Fig. 23.24 allBooks.xsl for XHTML Basic clients. (Courtesy of Pixo, Inc.) (Part 3 of 3.)

Figure 23.25 shows **displayBook.xsl** for XHTML Basic clients. This document transforms the XML generated by **displayBook.py** (Fig. 23.12) into XHTML Basic the client can render.

```
1   <?xml version = "1.0"?>
2
3   <!-- Fig. 23.25: displayBook.xsl                          -->
4   <!-- XSLT style sheet that transforms XML generated by    -->
5   <!-- displayBook.py into XHTML Basic.                      -->
6
7   <xsl:stylesheet version = "1.0"
8      xmlns:xsl = "http://www.w3.org/1999/XSL/Transform">
9
10     <xsl:output method = "xml" omit-xml-declaration = "no"
11        indent = "yes" doctype-system =
12        "http://www.w3.org/TR/xhtml-basic/xhtml-basic10.dtd"
13        doctype-public = "-//W3C//DTD XHTML Basic 1.0//EN"/>
14
15   <!-- specify the root of the XML document -->
16   <!-- that references this style sheet      -->
17   <xsl:template match = "product">
```

Fig. 23.25 displayBook.xsl for XHTML Basic clients. (Courtesy of Pixo, Inc.) (Part 1 of 3.)

```
18
19      <html xmlns = "http://www.w3.org/1999/xhtml">
20
21         <head>
22
23            <!-- obtain book title from script to place in title -->
24            <title><xsl:value-of select = "title" /></title>
25
26            <link rel = "stylesheet" href = "/bookstore/styles.css"
27               type = "text/css" />
28         </head>
29
30         <body>
31            <p class = "bigFont">
32               <xsl:value-of select = "title" /></p>
33
34            <img src = "/bookstore/small_images/{imageFile}"
35               alt = "{title}" />
36
37            <!-- show price, ISBN, edition and copyright -->
38            <p class = "bold">Price:
39               <xsl:value-of select = "price" /></p>
40
41            <p class = "bold">ISBN:
42               <xsl:value-of select = "isbn" /></p>
43
44            <p class = "bold">Edition:
45               <xsl:value-of select = "editionNumber" /></p>
46
47            <p class = "bold">Copyright:
48               <xsl:value-of select = "copyright" /></p>
49
50            <!-- create Add to Cart button -->
51            <p>
52               <form method = "post" action = "addToCart.py?ID=%s">
53                  <p><input type = "submit"
54                     value = "Add to Cart" /></p>
55               </form>
56            </p>
57
58            <!-- create View Cart button -->
59            <p>
60               <form method = "post" action = "viewCart.py?ID=%s">
61                  <p><input type = "submit"
62                     value = "View Cart" /></p>
63               </form>
64            </p>
65
66         </body>
67
68      </html>
69
```

Fig. 23.25 `displayBook.xsl` for XHTML Basic clients. (Courtesy of Pixo, Inc.) (Part 2 of 3.)

```
70    </xsl:template>
71
72    </xsl:stylesheet>
```

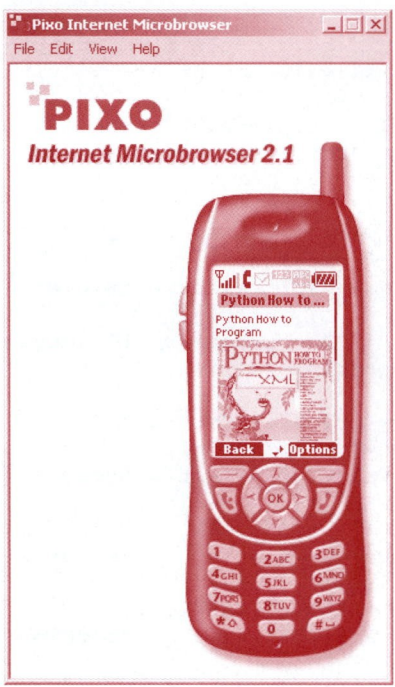

Fig. 23.25 displayBook.xsl for XHTML Basic clients. (Courtesy of Pixo, Inc.) (Part 3 of 3.)

Line 24 places the book's **title** in the document's **title** element, and line 32 places **title** in a paragraph at the beginning of the document's **body** element. Line 34 specifies an **img** element that contains the value of the **imageFile** element of an XML document. This element indicates the file name of the book's cover image. Notice that, for XHTML Basic clients, we use the images stored in subdirectory **small_images**. These images are the same as their larger counterparts, but have been reduced in size for display on wireless devices. Line 35 specifies the **alt** attribute of the **img** element, using the book's **title**. Lines 39, 42, 45 and 48 display the book's **price**, **isbn**, **edition-Number** and **copyright**, respectively. Lines 52–55 and lines 60-63 create **Add to Cart** (**addToCart.py**) and **View Cart** (**viewCart.py**) buttons, respectively. Both buttons use the **post** form method to pass the session IDs to their target files.

Figure 23.26 shows **viewCart.xsl** for XHTML Basic clients. This document transforms the XML generated by **viewCart.py** (Fig. 23.16) into XHTML Basic the client can render.

The first **xsl:template** (lines 15–65) matches **cart** elements. Line 21 specifies a **meta** tag with name **"PixoFriendly"** and content **"true"**. Although tables are not normally accepted by XHTML Basic clients, this line allows tables to be used with the Pixo Internet Microbrowser. Line 30 begins an **xsl:choose** element. If **cart** attribute

```
1    <?xml version = "1.0"?>
2
3    <!-- Fig. 23.26: viewCart.xsl                          -->
4    <!-- XSLT style sheet that transforms XML generated by  -->
5    <!-- viewCart.py into XHTML Basic.                       -->
6
7    <xsl:stylesheet version = "1.0"
8       xmlns:xsl = "http://www.w3.org/1999/XSL/Transform">
9
10      <xsl:output method = "xml" omit-xml-declaration = "no"
11         indent = "yes" doctype-system =
12         "http://www.w3.org/TR/xhtml-basic/xhtml-basic10.dtd"
13         doctype-public = "-//W3C//DTD XHTML Basic 1.0//EN"/>
14
15   <xsl:template match = "cart">
16
17      <html xmlns = "http://www.w3.org/1999/xhtml">
18
19         <head>
20            <title>Shopping Cart</title>
21            <meta name = "PixoFriendly" content = "true" />
22            <link rel = "stylesheet" href = "/bookstore/styles.css"
23               type = "text/css" />
24         </head>
25
26         <body>
27
28            <p class = "bigFont">Shopping Cart</p>
29
30            <xsl:choose>
31               <xsl:when test = "@total = '0.00'">
32                  <p class = "bold">
33                      Your shopping cart is currently empty.</p>
34               </xsl:when>
35
36               <xsl:otherwise>  <!-- total != 0.00 -->
37
38                     <table border = "true">
39                     <xsl:apply-templates select = "orderProduct">
40
41                        <!-- sort orderProducts by product/title -->
42                        <xsl:sort select = "product/title" />
43
44                     </xsl:apply-templates>
45                     </table>
46
47                     <p class = "bold right">Total: <xsl:value-of
48                        select = "@total" /></p>
49
50               </xsl:otherwise>
51            </xsl:choose>
52
```

Fig. 23.26 `viewCart.xsl` for XHTML Basic clients. (Courtesy of Pixo, Inc.) (Part 1 of 2.)

```
53              <p class = "bold green">
54                  <a href = "allBooks.py?ID=%s">Continue Shopping</a>
55              </p>
56
57              <form method = "post" action = "order.py?ID=%s">
58                  <p><input type = "submit" value = "Check Out" /></p>
59              </form>
60
61          </body>
62
63      </html>
64
65  </xsl:template>
66
67  <xsl:template match = "orderProduct">
68
69      <tr><td><ul>Product:<br />
70          <xsl:value-of select = "product/title" />,
71          <xsl:value-of select = "product/editionNumber" />e<br />
72        Quantity: <xsl:value-of select = "quantity" /><br />
73        Price: <xsl:value-of select = "product/price" /><br />
74        Subtotal: <xsl:value-of select = "subtotal" /><br />
75      </ul></td></tr>
76
77  </xsl:template>
78
79  </xsl:stylesheet>
```

Fig. 23.26 `viewCart.xsl` for XHTML Basic clients. (Courtesy of Pixo, Inc.) (Part 2 of 2.)

(denoted by **@**) **total** equals **"0.00"**, the program displays a message to the client indicating the shopping cart is currently empty (lines 32–33). Otherwise, if **total** does not equal **"0.00"**, the program creates a table for all items in the cart (lines 36–50).

Lines 39–44 insert all matches to the **orderProduct** template, sorted by their **product/title** element. The **orderProduct** template (lines 67–77) matches **orderProduct** elements. Lines 70–74 insert the **orderProduct**'s **product/title**, **product/editionNumber**, **quantity**, **product/price** and **subtotal** in a single table cell (for clarity on XHTML Basic clients, we use only one cell for each **orderProduct**). Lines 47–48 then display the total for all items. Lines 53–59 create two options for the user. The first is a hyperlink that points to **allBooks.py** (line 54). The second is a **Check Out** button that takes the user to **order.py** (lines 57–59).

Figure 23.27 shows **orderForm.html** for XHTML Basic clients. This document is the order form displayed by **order.py** (Fig. 23.18) to XHTML Basic clients.

Figure 23.28 shows **thankYou.html** for XHTML Basic clients. This document is displayed by **process.py** (Fig. 23.20) to XHTML Basic clients.

```
1   <!-- Fig. 23.27: orderForm.html                    -->
2   <!-- Static XHTML Basic to be displayed by order.py    -->
3
4   <!DOCTYPE html PUBLIC "-//W3C//DTD XHTML Basic 1.0//EN"
5       "http://www.w3.org/TR/xhtml-basic/xhtml-basic10.dtd">
6
7   <html xmlns = "http://www.w3.org/1999/xhtml">
8
9      <head>
10        <title>Order</title>
11        <meta name = "PixoFriendly" content = "true" />
12        <link rel = "stylesheet" href = "/bookstore/styles.css"
13            type = "text/css" />
14     </head>
15
16     <body>
17
18        <p class = "bigFont">Shopping Cart Check Out</p>
19
20        <!-- form to input user information and credit card   -->
21        <!-- note: no need to input real data in this example -->
22        <form method = "post" action = "process.py?ID=%s">
23           <p style = "font-weight: bold">
24              Input the following:</p>
25
26           <table border = "true">
27              <tr>
28                 <td class = "right bold">First name:<br />
29                    <input type = "text" name = "firstname"
30                       size = "25" />
31                 </td>
32              </tr>
```

Fig. 23.27 orderForm.html for XHTML Basic clients. (Courtesy of Pixo, Inc.) (Part 1 of 3.)

```
33                <tr>
34                    <td class = "right bold">Last name:<br />
35                        <input type = "text" name = "lastname"
36                            size = "25" />
37                    </td>
38                </tr>
39                <tr>
40                    <td class = "right bold">Street:<br />
41                        <input type = "text" name = "street"
42                            size = "25" />
43                    </td>
44                </tr>
45                <tr>
46                    <td class = "right bold">City:<br />
47                        <input type = "text" name = "city"
48                            size = "25" />
49                    </td>
50                </tr>
51                <tr>
52                    <td class = "right bold">State:
53                        <input type = "text" name = "state"
54                            size = "2" />
55                    </td>
56                </tr>
57                <tr>
58                    <td class = "right bold">Zip code:
59                        <input type = "text" name = "zipcode"
60                            size = "10" />
61                    </td>
62                </tr>
63                <tr>
64                    <td class = "right bold">Phone #:
65                        <input type = "text" name = "phone"
66                            size = "12" />
67                    </td>
68                </tr>
69                <tr>
70                    <td class = "right bold">Credit Card #:<br />
71                        <input type = "text" name = "creditcard"
72                            size = "25" />
73                    </td>
74                </tr>
75                <tr>
76                    <td class = "right bold">Expiration (mm/yyyy):
77                        <br />
78                        <input type = "text" name = "expires"
79                            size = "2" />
80                        <input type = "text" name = "expires2"
81                            size = "4" />
82                    </td>
83                </tr>
84            </table>
```

Fig. 23.27 `orderForm.html` for XHTML Basic clients. (Courtesy of Pixo, Inc.) (Part 2 of 3.)

```
85
86              <p><input type = "submit" value = "Submit" /></p>
87
88          </form>
89
90      </body>
91
92  </html>
```

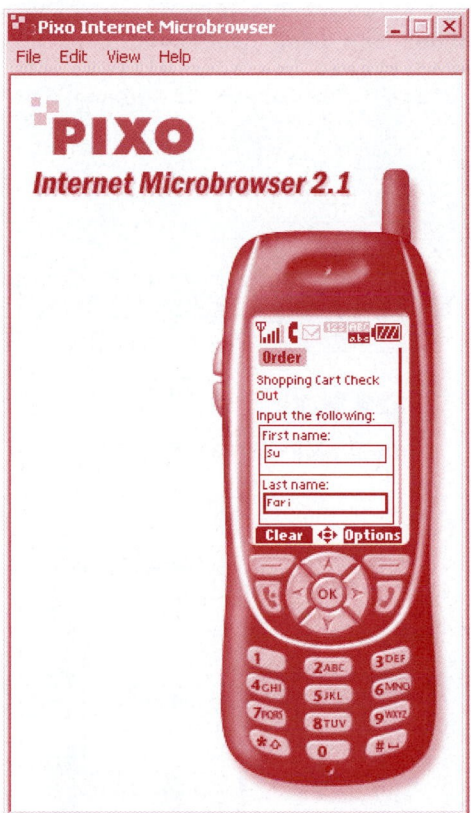

Fig. 23.27 orderForm.html for XHTML Basic clients. (Courtesy of Pixo, Inc.) (Part 3 of 3.)

```
1   <!-- Fig. 23.28: thankYou.html                        -->
2   <!-- Static XHTML Basic to be displayed by process.py  -->
3
4   <!DOCTYPE html PUBLIC "-//W3C//DTD XHTML Basic 1.0//EN"
5       "http://www.w3.org/TR/xhtml-basic/xhtml-basic10.dtd">
6
7   <html xmlns = "http://www.w3.org/1999/xhtml">
```

Fig. 23.28 thankYou.html for XHTML Basic clients. (Courtesy of Pixo, Inc.) (Part 1 of 2.)

```
 8
 9      <head>
10         <title>Thank You!</title>
11         <link rel = "stylesheet" href = "/bookstore/styles.css"
12            type = "text/css" />
13      </head>
14
15      <body>
16
17         <p class = "bigFont">Thank You</p>
18         <p>Your order has been processed.</p>
19         <p>Your credit card has been billed:
20            <span class = "bold">$%.2f</span>
21         </p>
22
23      </body>
24
25   </html>
```

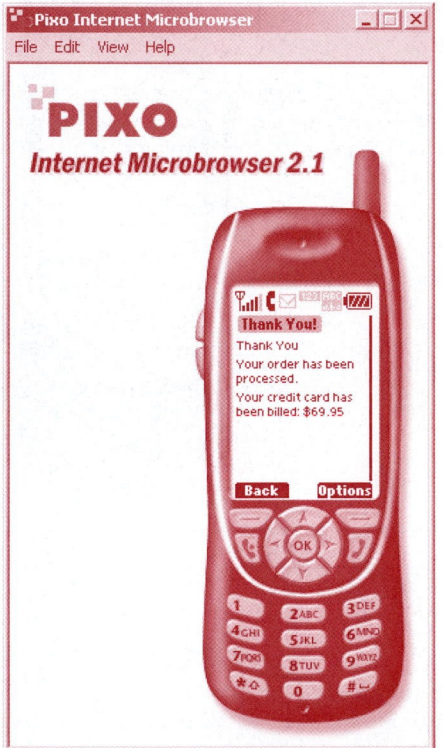

Fig. 23.28 thankYou.html for XHTML Basic clients. (Courtesy of Pixo, Inc.) (Part 2 of 2.)

Figure 23.29 shows **error.xsl** for XHTML Basic clients. This document transforms the XML generated by **error.py** (Fig. 23.22) into XHTML Basic the client can render. Lines 15–37 define an **xsl:template** that matches **error** elements. Line 30 inserts the value of the **message** element into a **paragraph** tag.

23.14.2 Introduction to WML

This section introduces wireless programming with the *Wireless Markup Language (WML)*. WML, like XHTML Basic, is a markup language that identifies the elements of a document so that a wireless device can render the document. WML is ideal for use with wireless devices because it is designed to accommodate their limited memory capacities and small display screens. We use WML in accordance with the WAP standard.

```
1   <?xml version = "1.0"?>
2
3   <!-- Fig. 23.29: error.xsl                              -->
4   <!-- XSLT style sheet that transforms XML generated by  -->
5   <!-- error.py into XHTML Basic.                          -->
6
7   <xsl:stylesheet version = "1.0"
8      xmlns:xsl = "http://www.w3.org/1999/XSL/Transform">
9
10     <xsl:output method = "xml" omit-xml-declaration = "no"
11         indent = "yes" doctype-system =
12         "http://www.w3.org/TR/xhtml-basic/xhtml-basic10.dtd"
13         doctype-public = "-//W3C//DTD XHTML Basic 1.0//EN"/>
14
15  <xsl:template match = "error">
16
17     <html xmlns = "http://www.w3.org/1999/xhtml">
18
19        <head>
20           <title>Error</title>
21           <link rel = "stylesheet" href = "/bookstore/styles.css"
22              type = "text/css" />
23        </head>
24
25        <body>
26
27           <p class = "bigFont">Error message:</p>
28
29           <p class = "bold">
30              <xsl:value-of select = "message" />
31           </p>
32
33        </body>
34
35     </html>
36
37  </xsl:template>
38
39  </xsl:stylesheet>
```

Fig. 23.29 error.xsl for XHTML Basic clients. (Courtesy of Pixo, Inc.) (Part 1 of 2.)

Fig. 23.29 error.xsl for XHTML Basic clients. (Courtesy of Pixo, Inc.) (Part 2 of 2.)

A WML document is called a *deck*; each deck contains one or more pages, called *cards*. Cards are renderable units of WML documents useful for WAP clients (a WAP client being any WAP-enabled device) that generally have limited screen sizes. Each card can contain both text content and navigational controls to facilitate user interaction. Though only one card can be viewed at a time, navigation between cards is rapid, because the entire deck is stored on the microbrowser.

WML documents are created with a text editor (e.g. Notepad, vi, emacs, etc.) and given the **.wml** file extension. In this section, we use the Openwave (**www.openwave.com**) simulator to render WML documents. The Openwave Simulator is part of the *Openwave Software Development Kit (SDK) WAP Edition*, which can be downloaded for free from

   developer.openwave.com/download/license_50.html

For installation instructions, visit **www.deitel.com**.

Figure 23.30 shows the version of **allBooks.xsl** for WML clients. This document, located in subdirectory **wml**, transforms the XML generated by **allBooks.py** (Fig. 23.9) into WML that a wireless client can render.

Lines 10–13 output lines that are required in WML documents to conform with proper WML syntax. An **xsl:template** defines **catalog** elements (lines 16–46). Line 18 defines the start of the **wml** element. This element is called a deck, because it contains one or more logical pages or information called cards, which are marked up with **card** elements (line 25).

```
1   <?xml version = "1.0"?>
2
3   <!-- Fig. 23.30: allBooks.xsl                          -->
4   <!-- XSLT style sheet that transforms XML generated by  -->
5   <!-- books.py into WML.                                 -->
6
7   <xsl:stylesheet version = "1.0"
8       xmlns:xsl = "http://www.w3.org/1999/XSL/Transform">
9
10      <xsl:output method = "xml" omit-xml-declaration = "no"
11          indent = "yes" doctype-system =
12          "http://www.wapforum.org/DTD/wml12.dtd"
13          doctype-public = "-//WAPFORUM//DTD WML 1.2//EN"/>
14
15  <!-- template for catalog element -->
16  <xsl:template match = "catalog">
17
18      <wml>
19
20          <head>
21              <meta forua = "true" http-equiv = "Cache-Control"
22                  content = "max-age=0" />
23          </head>
24
25          <card title = "Book List">
26
27              <p>
28
29                  <b>Available Books</b><br />
30                  Click a link to view book information<br />
31
32                  <!-- match product elements to product template -->
33                  <xsl:apply-templates select = "/catalog/product">
34
35                      <!-- sort products by title -->
36                      <xsl:sort select = "title" />
37
38                  </xsl:apply-templates>
39
40              </p>
41
42          </card>
43
44      </wml>
45
46  </xsl:template>
47
48  <!-- template for building row of Product information -->
49  <xsl:template match = "product">
50
```

Fig. 23.30 allBooks.xsl for WML clients. (Openwave, the Openwave logo, Openwave SDK, Openwave SDK Universal Edition, Openwave SDK WAP Edition are trademarks of Openwave Systems Inc. All rights reserved.) (Part 1 of 2.)

```
51        <a href = "displayBook.py?ID=%s&amp;isbn={isbn}">
52           <xsl:value-of select = "title" />, <xsl:value-of
53              select = "editionNumber" />e
54        </a><br />
55
56     </xsl:template>
57
58     </xsl:stylesheet>
```

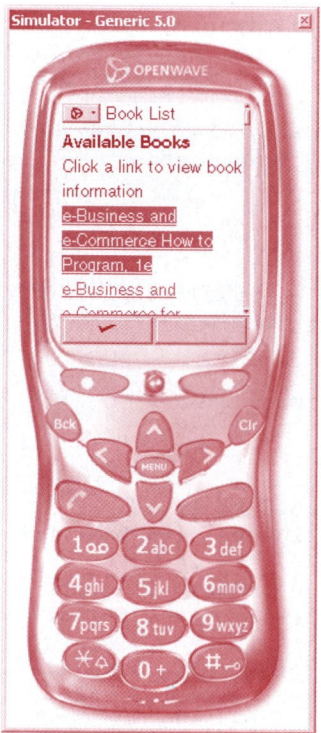

Fig. 23.30 `allBooks.xsl` for WML clients. (Openwave, the Openwave logo, Openwave SDK, Openwave SDK Universal Edition, Openwave SDK WAP Edition are trademarks of Openwave Systems Inc. All rights reserved.) (Part 2 of 2.)

Common Programming Error 23.1

WML element names are case sensitive and must be written in lowercase. Writing a WML element name that contains uppercase characters is a syntax error. This type of error prevents the page from being displayed by a microbrowser.

Lines 20–23 define the **head** element. Although the **head** element is not specifically required by WML, the **head** element in this example contains a **meta** tag that ensures a the client does not cache the current page. Due to their limited bandwidth, most WML clients *cache* (or store) downloaded pages in memory for future use. By storing previously visited pages, a Web client sometimes does not display the most current version of a Web page. However, the **meta** tag in lines 21–22 ensures that the client receives the most recent version of every page.

Line 25 defines the start of the **card** element. We define a **card** element with attribute *title*. The **title** attribute describes the **card**. This attribute's value often is displayed at the top of the screen by microbrowsers (see screen output). Line 27 defines the start of the **p** element. In WML documents, text paragraph tags (**<p>** and **</p>**) mark up text for display in a microbrowser. All text in a WML document must be placed between **<p>** tags, which are nested within **<card>** tags. Lines 33–38 insert any matches of the **product** template into the document. These matches are sorted by their **title** elements (line 36). This ensures the book list appears in alphabetical order by the title name.

Lines 49–56 define an **xsl:template** for **product** elements. Line 51 specifies an **anchor** tag with attribute **href**. The value of the **href** attribute references **display-Book.py** with a query string that contains the session ID and the value of the **isbn** element of an XML document. Recall that line 71 of **allBooks.py** inserts the session ID into this query string. The **isbn** of the current **product** is inserted with **{isbn}**. The finalized query string ensures that **displayBook** can identify the client and display the book. The anchor tag contains text and the values of the **title** and **editionNumber** elements of an XML document (lines 52–53).

Figure 23.31 shows **displayBook.xsl** for WML clients. This document transforms the XML generated by **displayBook.py** (Fig. 23.12) into WML the client can render.

Line 27 places the book's **title** in the **title** attribute of the document's **card** element, and line 31 places **title** in a paragraph at the beginning of the document's **p** element. Line 33 specifies an **img** element with **src** value **"/bookstore/logo.wbmp"** and **alt** value **"logo"**. This element specifies the name of the image to be displayed below the book's title.

Notice that, for WML clients, we use a single image called **logo.wbmp**, located in root folder **bookstore**. This image is a wireless bitmap image. Most microbrowsers support *bitmap* (*.bmp*) images, but some (such as the Openwave simulator) support only *wireless bitmap* (*.wbmp*) images. Bitmap images are images represented by groups of *bits* (i.e., binary digits with values 0 or 1) that correspond to *pixels*, or "picture elements." Pixels denote dots of color on the screen. Such images can be created in software such as Paint Shop™ Pro (**www.jasc.com**) or Photoshop® Elements (**www.adobe.com**).

Conversion programs, such as Pic2WBMP, translate bitmap images to wireless bitmap format. Pic2WBMP can be downloaded for free from **www.gingco.de/wap**. Another way of translating bitmap images to wireless bitmap format is to extend the capabilities of Photoshop Elements to support the **.wbmp** format. RCP Distributed Systems offers a plug-in that enables Photoshop Elements to support wireless bitmap images. The download, which includes installation instructions, is available for free at **www.rcp.co.uk/dis-tributed/Downloads**.

Lines 37, 38, 39 and 41 display the book's **price**, **isbn**, **editionNumber** and **copyright**, respectively. Lines 45–46 create **Add to Cart** (**addToCart.py**) and **View Cart** (**viewCart.py**) hyperlinks, respectively. Note that we create hyperlinks rather than buttons for simplicity on WML clients (WML forms are introduced in Fig. 23.33).

```
1   <?xml version = "1.0"?>
2
3   <!-- Fig. 23.31: displayBook.xsl                          -->
4   <!-- XSLT style sheet that transforms XML generated by    -->
5   <!-- displayBook.py into WML.                              -->
6
7   <xsl:stylesheet version = "1.0"
8      xmlns:xsl = "http://www.w3.org/1999/XSL/Transform">
9
10     <xsl:output method = "xml" omit-xml-declaration = "no"
11        indent = "yes" doctype-system =
12        "http://www.wapforum.org/DTD/wml12.dtd"
13        doctype-public = "-//WAPFORUM//DTD WML 1.2//EN"/>
14
15  <!-- specify the root of the XML document -->
16  <!-- that references this style sheet      -->
17  <xsl:template match = "product">
18
19     <wml>
20
21        <head>
22           <meta forua = "true" http-equiv = "Cache-Control"
23              content = "max-age=0" />
24        </head>
25
26        <!-- obtain book title from script to place in title -->
27        <card title = "{title}">
28
29           <p>
30
31              <xsl:value-of select = "title" /><br />
32
33              <img src = "/bookstore/logo.wbmp" alt = "logo" />
34              <br />
35
36              <!-- show price, ISBN, edition and copyright -->
37              Price: <xsl:value-of select = "price" /><br />
38              ISBN: <xsl:value-of select = "isbn" /><br />
39              Edition: <xsl:value-of select = "editionNumber" />
40              <br />
41              Copyright: <xsl:value-of select = "copyright" /><br />
42              <br />
43
44              <!-- add links to shopping cart -->
45              <a href = "addToCart.py?ID=%s">Add to Cart</a><br />
46              <a href = "viewCart.py?ID=%s">View Cart</a><br />
47
48           </p>
49
50        </card>
```

Fig. 23.31 displayBook.xsl for WML clients. (Openwave, the Openwave logo, Openwave SDK, Openwave SDK Universal Edition, Openwave SDK WAP Edition are trademarks of Openwave Systems Inc. All rights reserved.) (Part 1 of 2.)

```
51
52      </wml>
53
54  </xsl:template>
55
56  </xsl:stylesheet>
```

Fig. 23.31 `displayBook.xsl` for WML clients. (Openwave, the Openwave logo, Openwave SDK, Openwave SDK Universal Edition, Openwave SDK WAP Edition are trademarks of Openwave Systems Inc. All rights reserved.) (Part 2 of 2.)

Figure 23.32 shows **viewCart.xsl** for WML clients. This document transforms the XML generated by **viewCart.py** (Fig. 23.16) into WML the client can render.

```
1   <?xml version = "1.0"?>
2
3   <!-- Fig. 23.32: viewCart.xsl                              -->
4   <!-- XSLT style sheet that transforms XML generated by -->
5   <!-- viewCart.py into WML.                                 -->
```

Fig. 23.32 `viewCart.xsl` for WML clients. (Openwave, the Openwave logo, Openwave SDK, Openwave SDK Universal Edition, Openwave SDK WAP Edition are trademarks of Openwave Systems Inc. All rights reserved.) (Part 1 of 3.)

```
 6
 7   <xsl:stylesheet version = "1.0"
 8      xmlns:xsl = "http://www.w3.org/1999/XSL/Transform">
 9
10      <xsl:output method = "xml" omit-xml-declaration = "no"
11         indent = "yes" doctype-system =
12         "http://www.wapforum.org/DTD/wml12.dtd"
13         doctype-public = "-//WAPFORUM//DTD WML 1.2//EN"/>
14
15   <xsl:template match = "cart">
16
17      <wml>
18
19         <head>
20            <meta forua = "true" http-equiv = "Cache-Control"
21               content = "max-age=0" />
22         </head>
23
24         <card title = "Shopping Cart">
25
26            <p>
27
28               <b>Shopping Cart</b><br /><br />
29
30               <xsl:choose>
31                  <xsl:when test = "@total = '0.00'">
32                     Your shopping cart is currently empty.<br />
33                     <br />
34                  </xsl:when>
35
36                  <xsl:otherwise>   <!-- total != 0.00 -->
37
38                     <xsl:apply-templates select = "orderProduct">
39
40                        <!-- sort orderProducts by title -->
41                        <xsl:sort select = "product/title" />
42
43                     </xsl:apply-templates>
44
45                     <b>Total: <xsl:value-of
46                        select = "@total" /></b><br />
47
48                  </xsl:otherwise>
49               </xsl:choose>
50
51               <a href = "allBooks.py?ID=%s">Continue Shopping</a>
52               <br />
53               <a href = "order.py?ID=%s">Check Out</a>
54
55            </p>
```

Fig. 23.32 `viewCart.xsl` for WML clients. (Openwave, the Openwave logo, Openwave SDK, Openwave SDK Universal Edition, Openwave SDK WAP Edition are trademarks of Openwave Systems Inc. All rights reserved.) (Part 2 of 3.)

```
56
57          </card>
58
59      </wml>
60
61  </xsl:template>
62
63  <xsl:template match = "orderProduct">
64
65      Product:<br />
66      <xsl:value-of select = "product/title" />,
67      <xsl:value-of select = "product/editionNumber" />e<br />
68      Quantity: <xsl:value-of select = "quantity" /><br />
69      Price: <xsl:value-of select = "product/price" /><br />
70      Subtotal: <xsl:value-of select = "subtotal" /><br />
71      <br />
72
73  </xsl:template>
74
75  </xsl:stylesheet>
```

Fig. 23.32 viewCart.xsl for WML clients. (Openwave, the Openwave logo, Openwave SDK, Openwave SDK Universal Edition, Openwave SDK WAP Edition are trademarks of Openwave Systems Inc. All rights reserved.) (Part 3 of 3.)

The first **xsl:template** (lines 15–61) matches **cart** elements. Line 30 begins an **xsl:choose** element. If **cart** attribute (denoted by **@**) **total** equals **"0.00"**, the program displays a message to the client indicating the shopping cart is currently empty (lines 32–33). Otherwise, if **total** does not equal **"0.00"**, the program displays all the items in the cart (lines 36–48).

Lines 38–43 insert all matches to the **orderProduct** template, sorted by their **product/title** element. The **orderProduct** template (lines 63–73) matches **orderProduct** elements. Lines 66–70 display the **orderProduct**'s **product/title**, **product/editionNumber**, **quantity**, **product/price** and **subtotal** on separate lines. Lines 45–46 then display the total for all items. Lines 51–53 create two options for the user—hyperlinks that point to **allBooks.py** and to **order.py**, respectively.

Figure 23.33 shows **orderForm.wml** for WML clients. This document is the order form displayed by **order.py** (Fig. 23.18) to WML clients.

Lines 23–36 create *input* elements to obtain information from the user. The **input** element creates an area in the display called a *text field* where users can input information through the wireless devices's keypad. Lines 38–58 introduce the use of the *do* and *go* elements. The **do** element creates the *soft keys* of the wireless device. Soft keys are the physical buttons on a wireless device that enable a user to navigate between documents. The value of the **do** element's *label* attribute displays on the screen above the appropriate button. Pressing the soft key performs the action of the **go** element.

One attribute of the **do** element is *type*. The two most common values for the **type** attribute are **"accept"** and **"options"**. A **type** of **"accept"** corresponds to the left soft key, and a **type** attribute of **"options"** corresponds to the right soft key.

Lines 38–58 create a soft-key link, using the **do** and the **go** elements. The **type** attribute's value is **"accept"**, so the value of the **label** attribute, **"Submit"**, appears in the bottom left-hand corner of the display window to indicate the current function of the left soft key (after the user scrolls down to the bottom of the form). Pressing the soft key performs the action of the **go** element, which sends the user to **process.py**.

```
1   <!-- Fig. 23.33: orderForm.wml                        -->
2   <!-- Static WML to be displayed by order.py           -->
3
4   <!DOCTYPE wml PUBLIC "-//WAPFORUM//DTD WML 1.2//EN"
5       "http://www.wapforum.org/DTD/wml12.dtd">
6
7   <wml>
8
9       <head>
10         <meta forua = "true" http-equiv = "Cache-Control"
11             content = "max-age=0"/>
12      </head>
13
14      <card title = "Order">
```

Fig. 23.33 orderForm.wml for WML clients. (Openwave, the Openwave logo, Openwave SDK, Openwave SDK Universal Edition, Openwave SDK WAP Edition are trademarks of Openwave Systems Inc. All rights reserved.) (Part 1 of 3.)

```
15
16          <p>
17
18              <b>Shopping Cart Check Out</b><br /><br />
19
20              <!-- form to input user information and credit card     -->
21              <!-- note: no need to input real data in this example -->
22              Input the following:<br />
23              First name: <input type = "text" name = "firstname" />
24              <br />
25              Last name: <input type = "text" name = "lastname" />
26              <br />
27              Street: <input type = "text" name = "street" /><br />
28              City: <input type = "text" name = "city" /><br />
29              State: <input type = "text" name = "state" /><br />
30              Zip code: <input type = "text" name = "zipcode" /><br />
31              Phone #: <input type = "text" name = "phone" /><br />
32              Credit Card #: <input type = "text"
33                  name = "creditcard" /><br />
34              Expiration (mm): <input type = "text" name = "expires" />
35              Expiration (yyyy): <input type = "text"
36                  name = "expires2" /><br />
37
38              <do type = "accept" label = "Submit">
39
40                  <go method = "post" href = "process.py?ID=%s">
41                      <postfield name = "firstname"
42                          value = "$(firstname)" />
43                      <postfield name = "lastname"
44                          value = "$(lastname)" />
45                      <postfield name = "street" value = "$(street)" />
46                      <postfield name = "city" value = "$(city)" />
47                      <postfield name = "state" value = "$(state)" />
48                      <postfield name = "zipcode" value = "$(zipcode)" />
49                      <postfield name = "phone" value = "$(phone)" />
50                      <postfield name = "creditcard"
51                          value = "$(creditcard)" />
52                      <postfield name = "expires"
53                          value = "$(expires)" />
54                      <postfield name = "expires2"
55                          value = "$(expires2)" />
56                  </go>
57
58              </do>
59
60          </p>
61
62      </card>
63
64  </wml>
```

Fig. 23.33 `orderForm.wml` for WML clients. (Openwave, the Openwave logo, Openwave SDK,Openwave SDK Universal Edition, Openwave SDK WAP Edition are trademarks of Openwave Systems Inc. All rights reserved.) (Part 2 of 3.)

Fig. 23.33 `orderForm.wml` for WML clients. (Openwave, the Openwave logo, Openwave SDK, Openwave SDK Universal Edition, Openwave SDK WAP Edition are trademarks of Openwave Systems Inc. All rights reserved.) (Part 3 of 3.)

The **go** element is similar to the **a** element in that both link to resources. The value of the **go** element's ***href*** attribute defines a link's address. In Fig. 23.33, the **go** element links to **process.py**, using the **post** form method and specifying the session ID in the query string (line 40).

Lines 41–55 insert the data into the **go** element, using ***postfield*** elements. The **postfield** elements have two required attributes—***name*** and ***value***. As with XHTML **input** elements, **postfield** attribute **name** specifies the name that references the data, and attribute **value** specifies the actual data. In Fig. 23.33, the value of each **value** attribute is obtained from its corresponding **input** element. For example, the value of the **value** attribute is **"$(lastname)"** (line 44). This means that the value passed is to be retrieved from the **input** field with **name** attribute **lastname** (line 25). The data will be passed to the destination specified by the **href** attribute of the **go** element. When the client submits the form, the data values are obtained, and the **go** element redirects the user to **process.py**.

Figure 23.34 shows **thankYou.wml** for WML clients. This document is displayed by **process.py** (Fig. 23.20) to WML clients.

Figure 23.35 shows **error.xsl** for WML clients. This document transforms the XML generated by **error.py** (Fig. 23.22) into WML the client can render. Lines 15–37

```
1   <!-- Fig. 23.34: thankYou.wml                          -->
2   <!-- Static WML to be displayed by process.py           -->
3
4   <!DOCTYPE wml PUBLIC "-//WAPFORUM//DTD WML 1.2//EN"
5       "http://www.wapforum.org/DTD/wml12.dtd">
6
7   <wml>
8
9      <head>
10        <meta forua = "true" http-equiv = "Cache-Control"
11           content = "max-age=0" />
12     </head>
13
14     <card title = "Thank You!">
15
16        <p>
17
18           <b>Thank You</b><br /><br />
19           Your order has been processed.<br />
20           Your credit card has been billed: <b>%.2f</b>
21
22        </p>
23
24     </card>
25
26  </wml>
```

Fig. 23.34 thankYou.wml for WML clients. (Openwave, the Openwave logo, Openwave SDK, Openwave SDK Universal Edition, Openwave SDK WAP Edition are trademarks of Openwave Systems Inc. All rights reserved.)

define an **xsl:template** that matches **error** elements. Line 29 inserts the value of the **message** element into the **paragraph** tag (line 26).

23.15 Internet and World Wide Web Resources

Visit the following sites for additional information on topics discussed in this chapter.

www.wapforum.org
The WAP Forum is the consortium that makes WAP recommendations. The WAP Forum's goal is to establish wireless-device interoperability. This Web site holds a variety of information regarding WAP's history and its present status.

```
1   <?xml version = "1.0"?>
2
3   <!-- Fig. 23.35: error.xsl                           -->
4   <!-- XSLT style sheet that transforms XML generated by  -->
5   <!-- error.py into WML.                                -->
6
7   <xsl:stylesheet version = "1.0"
8       xmlns:xsl = "http://www.w3.org/1999/XSL/Transform">
9
10      <xsl:output method = "xml" omit-xml-declaration = "no"
11          indent = "yes" doctype-system =
12          "http://www.wapforum.org/DTD/wml12.dtd"
13          doctype-public = "-//WAPFORUM//DTD WML 1.2//EN"/>
14
15  <xsl:template match = "error">
16
17      <wml>
18
19          <head>
20              <meta forua = "true" http-equiv = "Cache-Control"
21                  content = "max-age=0" />
22          </head>
23
24          <card title = "Error">
25
26              <p>
27
28                  <b>Error message:</b><br />
29                  <xsl:value-of select = "message" />
30
31              </p>
32
33          </card>
34
35      </wml>
36
37  </xsl:template>
38
39  </xsl:stylesheet>
```

Fig. 23.35 error.xsl for WML clients. (Part 1 of 2.) (Openwave, the Openwave logo, Openwave SDK, Openwave SDK Universal Edition, Openwave SDK WAP Edition are trademarks of Openwave Systems Inc. All rights reserved.)

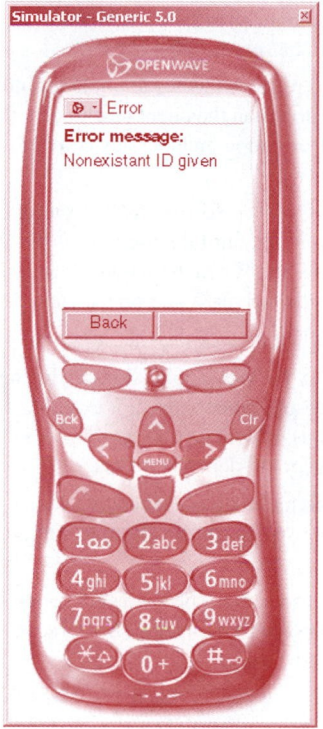

Fig. 23.35 error.xsl for WML clients. (Part 2 of 2.) (Openwave, the Openwave logo, Openwave SDK,Openwave SDK Universal Edition, Openwave SDK WAP Edition are trademarks of Openwave Systems Inc. All rights reserved.)

www.w3.org/TR/xhtml-basic
The *XHTML Basic Recommendation* contains all the nuances and fine points of XHTML Basic.

www.zvon.org/xxl/xhtmlBasicReference/Output/index.html
This site is an XHTML Basic reference that contains many examples.

www.softsteel.co.uk/tutorials/wmltut/
This site provides a short tutorial on WML.

www.webtools.com/story/html/TLS20000818S0001
This site provides a brief introduction and short tutorial on WML.

SUMMARY

- Session-tracking technologies allow servers to distinguish between clients.

- Each request that a Web browser makes to a Web server creates a new connection. Once the Web server processes the client request, the connection terminates. If a Web server needs to maintain information about a client across several requests, the client must identify itself each time.

- Cookies are small text files sent by the Web server as part of a response to a client request.

- A Web site can store a cookie on a client's computer to record user preferences or other information (e.g., the client's user name). The Web site can then retrieve the cookie during that client's subsequent visits.

- Every HTTP-based interaction between a client and a server includes a header that contains information about the request (communication from the client to the server) or information about the response (communication from the server to the client).

- When a Python script receives a request, the header includes information, such as the request type (e.g., *get* or *post*), and cookies stored on the client machine by the server. When the server formulates its response, the header information includes any cookies the server wants to store on the client computer.

- Depending on the maximum age of a cookie, the Web browser either maintains the cookie for the duration of the browsing session (i.e., until the user closes the Web browser) or stores the cookie on the client computer for future use. When the browser makes a request to a server, the client returns to that server any cookies the server stored on the client in previous interactions.

- Web browsers delete cookies when they expire (i.e., when they reach their maximum age).

- Cookies often are the easiest way for Web applications to distinguish clients. However, not all client computers or Web browsers support cookies. For example, users who are concerned about the privacy and security implications of cookies can disable cookies in their Web browsers, thus becoming unable to interact with cookie-dependent sites.

- Another method of session tracking involves embedding state information. State information may contain a username, password or specific information that might be helpful when a user returns to a Web site.

- The first time a client connects to a server, the Web application assigns the client a unique session ID. When the client makes additional requests, the client's session ID is compared with the session IDs stored in the server's memory.

- The ID must be passed from page to page so each Web page file will know the session ID of the current client, thereby distinguishing clients. This can be done in different ways.

- One method of passing the ID is to place it in a hidden form field in each page. The Web application can access the ID as a normal CGI parameter.

- Another method is to add the ID to the URL by adding the ID to a hyperlink that points to the next page. The next page then extracts the ID from the URL.

- Tracking session information via embedded session IDs has both advantages and disadvantages. One advantage is that Web browsers cannot disable session IDs. One disadvantage is that Web-page addresses are much longer than usual, because the session ID is embedded in every hyperlink. Another disadvantage is that embedding information presents a potential security risk. Storing the session ID in the Web page or URL allows a person other than the user to view the ID and to gain access to the user's data.

- The bookstore case study is implemented as a distributed, three-tier, Web-based application. The user's Web browser represents the client tier.

- The server tier, or middle tier, consists of several scripts on the server that act on behalf of the client.

- The information tier (also called the data tier or the bottom tier) maintains data for the application.

- Wireless clients, such as personal digital assistants (PDAs) and digital cell phones, support different markup languages from wireline clients (e.g., Internet Explorer).

- The Wireless Application Protocol (WAP), which is a global standard for communications between wireless devices and the Internet supports both XHTML Basic and WML.

- WAP 2.0 is a revision of the Wireless Application Protocol. WAP 2.0 specifies XHTML Basic, a subset of XHTML, to replace WML as the markup language for Web content on wireless devices.

- Microbrowsers are browsers designed with limited bandwidth and memory requirements.

- Various microbrowsers are available for different types of devices. For instance, Openwave's Mobile Browser is similar to Microsoft's Internet Explorer, except that the Mobile Browser runs on a wireless device, whereas Internet Explorer runs on a desktop computer.

- XHTML Basic is the World Wide Web Consortium's (W3C) initiative to provide a common markup language for wireless devices and other small devices with limited memory.

- Like WML, XHTML Basic is derived from the Extensible Markup Language (XML).

- As a smaller version of XHTML, XHTML Basic does not compromise the limited memory of a wireless device. XHTML Basic excludes features of XHTML, such as nested tables, that are ill-suited for wireless clients. In addition, XHTML Basic takes advantage of XML's strict structural rules and its extensibility.

- XHTML Basic documents are created with a text editor (e.g., Notepad, vi or emacs) and given either the **.html** or the **.htm** file extension.

- WML, like XHTML Basic, is a markup language that identifies the elements of a document so that a wireless device can render the document.

- WML is ideal for use with wireless devices because it is designed to accommodate their limited memory capacities and small display screens.

- A WML document is called a deck; each deck contains one or more pages, called cards.

- Cards are renderable units of WML documents useful for WAP clients (WAP-enabled devices) that generally use the devices with limited screen sizes.

- Each card can contain both text content and navigational controls to facilitate user interaction.

- Though only one card can be viewed at a time, navigation between cards is rapid, because the entire deck is stored by the microbrowser.

- WML documents are created with a text editor and given the **.wml** file extension.

- The **wml** element is called a deck because it contains one of more logical pages or information called cards, which are marked up with **card** elements.

- WML element names are case sensitive and must be written in lowercase. Writing a WML element name that contains uppercase characters is a syntax error. This type of error prevents the page from being displayed by a microbrowser.

- Due to their limited bandwidth, most WML clients cache (or store) downloaded pages in memory for future use.

- The **title** attribute of a **card** element often is displayed at the top of the screen by microbrowsers.

- In WML documents, text paragraph tags (**<p>** and **</p>**) mark up text for display in a microbrowser. All text in a WML document must be placed between **<p>** tags nested within **<card>** tags.

- Most microbrowsers support bitmap (**.bmp**) images, but some support only wireless bitmap (**.wbmp**) images.

- Bitmap images are images represented by groups of bits (i.e., binary digits with values 0 or 1) that correspond to pixels, or "picture elements." Pixels denote dots of color on the screen. Such images can be created in software such as Paint Shop™ Pro (**www.jasc.com**) or Photoshop Elements® (**www.adobe.com**).

- Conversion programs, such as Pic2WBMP, translate bitmap images to wireless bitmap format. Pic2WBMP can be downloaded from **www.gingco.de/wap**.

- Another way of translating bitmap images to wireless bitmap format is to extend the capabilities of Photoshop Elements to support the **.wbmp** format. RCP Distributed Systems offers a plug-in that enables Photoshop Elements to support such images. The download, which includes installation instructions, is available for free at **www.rcp.co.uk/distributed/Downloads**.

- The **input** element creates an area in the display called a text field where users can input information, using the wireless devices's keypad.

- The **do** element creates the soft keys of the wireless device. The value of the **do** element's **label** attribute displays on the screen above the appropriate button.

- Soft keys are the physical buttons on a wireless device that enable a user to navigate between documents.

- Pressing the soft key performs the action of the **go** element.

- One attribute of the **do** element is **type**. The two most common values for the **type** attribute are **"accept"** and **"options"**. A **type** attribute of **"accept"** corresponds to the left soft key, and a **type** attribute of **"options"** corresponds to the right soft key.

- The **go** element is similar to the **a** element in that both link to resources. The value of the **go** element's **href** attribute defines a link's address.

- The **postfield** elements have two required attributes—**name** and **value**.

- As with XHTML **input** elements, **postfield** attribute **name** specifies the name that references the data, and attribute **value** specifies the actual data.

TERMINOLOGY

.html, .htm	middle tier
.wml	**name** attribute of **postfield** element
.bmp (bitmap image)	Openwave Software Development Kit
bit	(SDK) WAP Edition
bottom tier	personal digital assistants (PDAs)
cache	pixel
card element	Pixo Internet Microbrowser
card	**postfield** element
client tier	request
cookie	response
data tier	server tier
deck	session ID
digital cell phone	session tracking
distributed, three-tier, Web-based application	soft key
do element	static document
dynamically created document	text field
expire	**title** attribute of **card** element
Extensible Markup Language (XML)	top tier
go element	**type** attribute of **do** element
head element	**value** attribute of **postfield** element
header	Wireless Application Protocol (WAP)
href attribute of **go** element	wireless bitmap (**.wbmp**) image
HyperText Transfer Protocol (HTTP)	wireless client
information tier	Wireless Markup Language (WML)
input element	wireline client
label attribute of **do** element	WML
maximum age	**wml** element
meta tag	World Wide Web Consortium's (W3C)
microbrowser	XHTML Basic

SELF-REVIEW EXERCISES

23.1 Fill in the blanks in each of the following statements:

a) _____ are small text files sent by the server as part of a response to a client.

b) Method _____ of class **Session** discards the session instance for the current client.

c) Class **Session** uses module _____ to pickle the session dictionary and dump it into the session file.

d) A three-tier, distributed Web application consists of _____, _____ and _____ tiers.

e) **Book** method _____ returns an XML **Element** representing the book.

f) Python script _____ obtains the XML representation of the book and processes it against a browser-specific XSLT style sheet.

g) Each **orderProduct** element contains 3 child elements: _____, _____ and _____.

h) _____ clients, such as personal digital assistants (PDAs) and digital cell phones, support different markup languages than do _____ clients (e.g., Internet Explorer).

23.2 State whether each of the following is *true* or *false*. If *false*, explain why.

a) Cookies are not accepted by all client types or browsers.

b) When embedding state information, a client is assigned a unique session ID by the server.

c) Each **CartItem** maintains a **Book** instance and the quantity of that **Book** in the cart.

d) WAP 2.0 specifies WML to replace XHTML Basic as the markup language for Web content on wireless devices.

e) Most wireless browsers support wireless bitmap images, but some support only bitmap images.

f) Web browsers that run on wireless devices are called "mobilebrowsers."

g) **postfield** elements have two required attributes—**name** and **value**.

h) The two most common values for the **type** attribute are **"left"** and **"right"**.

ANSWERS TO SELF-REVIEW EXERCISES

23.1 a) Cookies. b) **deleteSession**. c) **cPickle**. d) client/top, server/middle, information/data/bottom. e) **getXML**. f) **displayBook.py**. g) **product**, **quantity**, **subtotal**. h) Wireless, wireline.

23.2 a) True. b) True. c) True. d) False. WAP 2.0 specifies XHTML Basic to replace WML as the markup language for Web content on wireless devices. e) False. Most wireless browsers support bitmap images, but some support only wireless bitmap images. f) False. They are called "microbrowsers." g) True. h) False. The two most common values for the **type** attribute are **"accept"** and **"options"**.

EXERCISES

23.3 Explain the negative aspects of using cookies and embedding state information.

23.4 Modify the bookstore case study to enable the client to change the quantity of an item currently in the shopping cart. Modify **viewCart.xsl** to display the quantity in an **input form** element of type **text**. For each **text** element, provide the user with a **submit** button with the value **Update** that enables the user to submit the form to a script—**updateQuantity.py**—that updates the quantity of the items in the cart. The script should forward the request to **viewCart.py** so the user can see the updated cart contents.

23.5 Enhance the bookstore case study's **allBooks.py** to obtain author information from the **Books** database. Incorporate that author data into the **Book** class, and display the author information as part of the Web page users see when they select a book and view that book's information. The only files you need to modify are **allBooks.py**, **Book.py** and **displayBook.xsl**. Review Chapter 17 for more information on the **Books** database.

23.6   Add server-side form validation to the order form in the bookstore case study. Check that the credit-card expiration date is after today's date. If not, redirect the user to **error.py** with the message **"Expired credit card."** Also, make all fields in the form required fields. When the user does not supply data for all required fields, redirect the user back to **order.py**.

23.7   Create an **OrderInfo** table and an **OrderItems** table in the **Books** database to store orders placed by customers. The **OrderInfo** table should store an **OrderID**, an **OrderDate** and the **Email** address of the customer who placed the order. [*Note*: You will need to modify the form to include the customer's e-mail address.] The **OrderItems** table should store the **OrderID, ISBN, Price** and **Quantity** of each book in the order. Modify **process.py** so that it stores the order information in the **OrderInfo** and **OrderItems** tables.

23.8   Further modify **process.py** to display the client's order history. The script should obtain the necessary information (from the **OrderInfo** and **OrderItems** tables) for the e-mail address the user supplied. It should then generate XML representing this information and parse it against a browser-specific XSLT style sheet, displaying the results to the client. Note that because **process.py** is no longer displaying a static thank-you page (e.g., **thankYou.html**), the XSLT style sheet should also display the total for the current order.

24

Multimedia

Objectives

- To introduce multimedia-applications programming using Python.
- To learn to create three-dimensional objects using module **PyOpenGL**.
- To manipulate three-dimensional objects using Python and Alice.
- To learn to create multimedia applications using Python and **pygame**.

One picture is worth ten thousand words.
Chinese proverb

Treat nature in terms of the cylinder, the sphere, the cone, all in perspective.
Paul Cezanne

Nothing ever becomes real till it is experienced—even a proverb is no proverb to you till your life has illustrated it.
John Keats

A picture shows me at a glance what it takes dozens of pages of a book to expound.
Ivan Sergeyevich

Outline

24.1 Introduction

A decade ago, the typical desktop computer's power, although considered substantial at the time, made it impossible to think of integrating high-quality audio and video into applications. Since then, the rapid growth of the computing industry has brought multimedia to our desktops in the form of CD-ROMs, DVDs and streaming audio and video over the Web. In this chapter, we overview Python's multimedia capabilities using three technologies—**PyOpenGL**, **Alice** and **pygame**—to create interactive applications.

24.2 Introduction to **PyOpenGL**

Python module *PyOpenGL*,[1] which encapsulates the capabilities of the *OpenGL Application Programming Interface (API),* is a library for rendering *two-dimensional (2D)* and *three-dimensional (3D)* graphics. Programmers use the **PyOpenGL** module to incorporate colorful and interactive 2D and 3D graphics into Python programs. While this chapter does not teach OpenGL, the information about **PyOpenGL** should be valuable to programmers who do not have previous experience with OpenGL.

The *OpenGL Utility Toolkit (GLUT),* **wxPython**, **Tkinter** and **FxPy** are APIs that provide an OpenGL *context* (i.e., an electronic "canvas") in which to display **OpenGL**-rendered graphics. The examples in this chapter use **Tkinter** as OpenGL's context.

Module **PyOpenGL** includes the **Tkinter** component **Opengl**, which displays OpenGL graphics and allows the programmer to use **Tkinter** components and layout managers as well. In addition, the **Opengl** component already has an event bound to each mouse button. The **Opengl** component allows users to move objects by pressing and holding the left mouse button. To rotate an object, users hold the middle mouse button (if one is available). To resize objects, a user drags the mouse while holding the right mouse button.

Module **PyOpenGL** is available for download for both Windows and Linux/UNIX systems at **pyopengl.sourceforge.net**. This chapter's examples use **PyOpenGL**

---

1. This section assumes the reader is familiar with OpenGL (**www.opengl.org**).

version 2.0.0.44. Installation instructions are available for **PyOpenGL** on the Deitel & Associates, Inc., Web site, **www.deitel.com**.

24.3 PyOpenGL Examples

This section presents two **PyOpenGL** examples that create three-dimensional shapes. Figure 24.1 uses **PyOpenGL** coloring and transformations to create a rotating, colored box. Note that the program structure of the **PyOpenGL** examples in this chapter is similar to that of the GUI programs presented in Chapters 10 and 11 because the examples use **Tkinter**—Python's standard GUI tool—to create windows in which to display the **PyOpenGL** graphics.

Line 83 creates an object of class **ColorBox** (lines 8–80) and invokes its **mainloop** method to start the GUI. The **ColorBox** constructor (lines 11–28) creates and initializes the **Tkinter** window (lines 14–17). Lines 20–21 create and pack an **Opengl** component—*openGL*—which renders the OpenGL objects. Component **opengl**'s attribute **double** is set to 1 so that *double buffering* is used. Double buffering maintains two screen buffers—one for display purposes (the *on-screen buffer*) and the other for drawing purposes (the *off-screen buffer*). The application draws the next frame—the next image to be displayed—on the off-screen buffer. When the program finishes drawing the next frame, the program swaps the two buffers to display the new frame's contents. In contrast, when single buffering is used, the program draws directly to the screen. In this case, the display is not as smooth, because the program clears the drawing area before drawing each new frame. Depending on the speed of your computer system, this clearing operation may result in a brief flash of the background color before the next frame is displayed.

```
1    # Fig 24.1: fig24_01.py
2    # Colored, rotating box (with open top and bottom).
3
4    from Tkinter import *
5    from OpenGL.GL import *
6    from OpenGL.Tk import *
7
8    class ColorBox( Frame ):
9       """A colorful, rotating box"""
10
11      def __init__( self ):
12         """Initialize GUI and OpenGL"""
13
14         Frame.__init__( self )
15         self.master.title( "Color Box" )
16         self.master.geometry( "300x300" )
17         self.pack( expand = YES, fill = BOTH )
18
19         # create and pack Opengl -- use double buffering
20         self.openGL = Opengl( self, double = 1 )
21         self.openGL.pack( expand = YES, fill = BOTH )
22
23         self.openGL.redraw = self.redraw    # set redraw function
24         self.openGL.set_eyepoint( 20 )      # move away from object
```

Fig. 24.1 **PyOpenGL** used with **Tkinter** context. (Part 1 of 3.)

```
25
26         self.amountRotated = 0    # total degrees of rotation
27         self.increment = 2        # rotate amount in degrees
28         self.update()             # begin rotation
29
30     def redraw( self, openGL ):
31         """Draw box on black background"""
32
33         # clear background and disable lighting
34         glClearColor( 1.0, 1.0, 1.0, 0.0 )   # set clearing color
35         glClear( GL_COLOR_BUFFER_BIT )        # clear background
36         glDisable( GL_LIGHTING )
37
38         # constants
39         red = ( 1.0, 0.0, 0.0 )
40         green = ( 0.0, 1.0, 0.0 )
41         blue = ( 0.0, 0.0, 1.0 )
42         purple = ( 1.0, 0.0, 1.0 )
43
44         vertices = \
45            [ ( ( -3.0, 3.0, -3.0 ), red ),
46              ( ( -3.0, -3.0, -3.0 ), green ),
47              ( ( 3.0, 3.0, -3.0 ), blue ),
48              ( ( 3.0, -3.0, -3.0 ), purple ),
49              ( ( 3.0, 3.0, 3.0 ), red ),
50              ( ( 3.0, -3.0, 3.0 ), green ),
51              ( ( -3.0, 3.0, 3.0 ), blue ),
52              ( ( -3.0, -3.0, 3.0 ), purple ),
53              ( ( -3.0, 3.0, -3.0 ), red ),
54              ( ( -3.0, -3.0, -3.0 ), green ) ]
55
56         glBegin( GL_QUAD_STRIP )   # begin drawing
57
58         # change color and plot point for each vertex
59         for vertex in vertices:
60             location, color = vertex
61             apply( glColor3f, color )
62             apply( glVertex3f, location )
63
64         glEnd()  # stop drawing
65
66     def update( self ):
67         """Rotate box"""
68
69         if self.amountRotated >= 500:   # change rotation direction
70             self.increment = -2         # rotate left
71         elif self.amountRotated <= 0:   # change rotation direction
72             self.increment = 2          # rotate right
73
74         # rotate box around x, y, z axis ( 1.0, 1.0, 1.0 )
75         glRotate( self.increment, 1.0, 1.0, 1.0 )
76         self.amountRotated += self.increment
77
```

Fig. 24.1 **PyOpenGL** used with **Tkinter** context. (Part 2 of 3.)

```
78          self.openGL.tkRedraw()            # redraw geometry
79          self.openGL.after( 10, self.update )  # call update in 10ms
80
81  def main():
82      ColorBox().mainloop()
83
84  if __name__ == "__main__":
85      main()
```

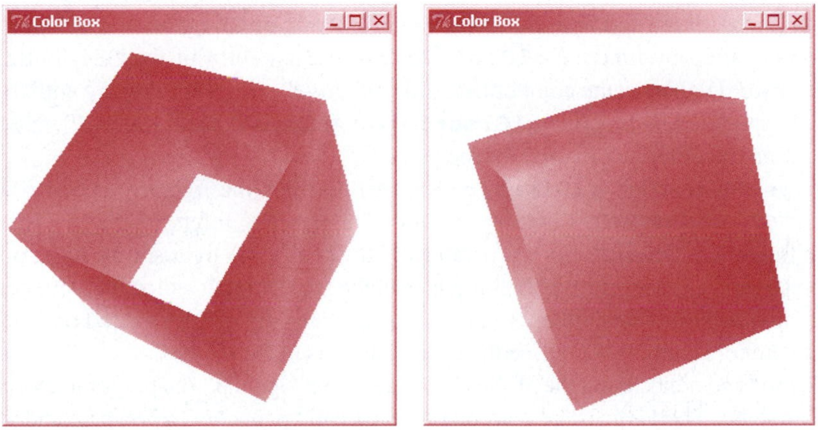

Fig. 24.1 **PyOpenGL** used with **Tkinter** context. (Part 3 of 3.)

Line 23 sets **opengl**'s *redraw* method, which the program calls to update the on-screen display each time the image changes. Line 24 calls **PyOpenGL** method **set_eyepoint** to move the *camera* away from the *scene* (i.e., the three-dimensional image) by a programmer-specified amount. The camera defines the viewer's perspective in relation to the scene. Passing larger values to **set_eyepoint** make the image smaller on the screen as the eye point moves further from the image. Negative argument values enable the user to view the image from behind.

Lines 26–27 initialize variables **amountRotated** and **increment**. These values control the number of degrees of rotation of the box. In this program, we increment the number of degrees by two each time we rotate the image. We store the total number of degrees of rotation in variable **amountRotated**. After the image rotates 500 total degrees, we can change the rotation direction. Finally, line 28 invokes method **update** (defined at lines 66–79) to rotate the image, redraw the image and specify that the program should call **update** again in **10** milliseconds.

Method **redraw** (lines 30–65) sets the background to the color white and draws the box. Line 34 calls **PyOpenGL** function **glClearColor** to specify the color that function **glClear** uses. Typically, colors are represented by either a three-element tuple containing values in the range 0.0–1.0 for the red, green and blue portions of a color, respectively; or a four-element tuple in which the first three elements represent the red, green and blue portions of the color and the last element represents the *alpha* (also called the *transparency*). The alpha value of a color determines how that color is combined with other colors when those colors are layered in an image. The alpha value represents whether the color is solid (alpha value 0.0) or transparent (alpha value 1.0). Alpha values between 0.0

and 1.0, indicate the amount of transparency. Function **glClearColor** requires a color with red, green, blue and alpha values as an argument. By combining different values, programmers can specify various colors—for example, solid white is (1.0, 1.0, 1.0, 0.0) and solid black is (0.0, 0.0, 0.0, 0.0).

Line 35 calls **PyOpenGL** function *glClear* to render a white background. The value passed to **glClear**—*GL_COLOR_BUFFER_BIT*—states that the function should clear the *color buffer*. The color buffer stores information about each of the window's *pixels* ("picture elements"), which represent dots of color on the screen. The color buffer stores each pixel's red, green and blue color components. **PyOpenGL** function **glClear** stores the color specified by function **glClearColor** in each entry of the color buffer. This replaces any old values in the color buffer. This effectively clears the display with the color previously specified by function **glClearColor**, setting the background to white. Lines 39–42 define the other colors used for the box.

PyOpenGL function *glDisable* (line 36) disables the *lighting* (specified by the argument *GL_LIGHTING*). Lighting in computer graphics refers to the placements of lights in the scene. **OpenGL** has ten parameters to specify the light source (e.g., position, direction, lighting color, etc.). If lighting is enabled, the object's color is calculated from the light-source parameters; otherwise, the color specified by **glClearColor** is used for the light source. Lines 39–42 define the other colors used for the box.

The program next creates the 3D box. To draw using OpenGL, the programmer specifies *vertices* (points). The vertices are placed between a call to function *glBegin* and a call to function *glEnd*. The argument passed to **glBegin** defines what type of shape is drawn.

Lines 44–54 create a list of the vertices that define the box's shape. Each tuple of the list contains a vertex location and a designated color. Lines 56–64 draw the box. Line 56 calls **PyOpenGL** function **glBegin** with argument *GL_QUAD_STRIP*, which instructs OpenGL to draw a group of connected quadrilaterals (i.e., four-sided figures). The program uses the first four vertices in the list (vertices 1–4) to draw the first quadrilateral. The second quadrilateral is defined by vertices 3–6 in the list, and so on. Note that the list defined in lines 44–54 has 10 vertices and the last pair of vertices is the same as the first pair, because **GL_QUAD_STRIP** needs the last two vertices to draw the quadrilateral (defined by vertices 7–10) that closes the box. The result is a series of connected polygons defined by the vertices specified before the call to function **glEnd** (line 64). Review the OpenGL documentation at **www.opengl.org/developers/documentation/man_pages/hardcopy/ GL/html/gl/begin.html** for other arguments available for **glBegin**.

The box is drawn by specifying the vertices as 3D points. Line 60 unpacks a tuple in the list to obtain the vertex location and color for each vertex. Line 61 uses function **apply** to call **PyOpenGL** function *glColor3f*, which changes the current drawing color. Function **glColor3f** takes three floating-point numbers that represent an RGB color as arguments. Each vertex has a unique color, and **PyOpenGL** blends the colors as they meet at the center of a side. Function *apply* (line 62) calls function **glVertex3f** to draw a point in three-dimensional space. Function *apply* takes a function as its first argument and a tuple of the values to be passed to the function as its second argument. The method calls the function, passing it the parameters. Function **glVertex3f** takes three floating-point arguments, which specify the location of a point.

This example also shows how to add animation to three-dimensional graphics. Method **update** (lines 66–79) rotates the box. Lines 70–73 alter the rotational direction that is represented by variable **increment**. A positive value for **increment** causes the box to rotate counterclockwise, while a negative value for **increment** rotates the box clockwise. After the box has rotated 500 degrees in one direction, the program switches the direction of the rotation (lines 70–73). Method *glRotate* (line 76) accepts four arguments. The first argument, in this case variable **increment**, sets the angle of rotation in degrees. The last three floating-point numbers describe the line around which the shape rotates. The line passes through the origin *(0.0, 0.0, 0.0)* and the specified point *(1.0, 0.0, 0.0)*. Line 77 increments variable **amountRotated**, which stores how many degrees the box has rotated. The call to method *tkRedraw* (line 79) updates the **Opengl** component with the rotated shape. Method *after* (line 80) takes two parameters—the value **10** and the method **update**. As a result, **mainloop**, the event loop of the program, schedules **update** to be called every **10** milliseconds.

Figure 24.2 demonstrates how to create three-dimensional shapes using several methods of module *OpenGL.GLUT* (the *GL Utilities Toolkit*). The example creates a GUI in which a programmer can preview object colors and shapes.

```
1   # Fig. 24.2: fig24_02.py
2   # Demonstrating various GLUT shapes.
3
4   from Tkinter import *
5   import Pmw
6   from OpenGL.GL import *
7   from OpenGL.Tk import *
8   from OpenGL.GLUT import *
9
10  class ChooseShape( Frame ):
11      """Allow user to preview different shapes and colors"""
12
13      def __init__( self ):
14          """Initialize GUI and OpenGL"""
15
16          Frame.__init__( self )
17          Pmw.initialise()
18          self.master.title( "Choose a shape and color" )
19          self.master.geometry( "300x300" )
20          self.pack( expand = YES, fill = BOTH )
21
22          # create and pack MenuBar
23          self.choices = Pmw.MenuBar( self )
24          self.choices.pack( fill = X )
25
26          # create and pack Opengl -- use double buffering
27          self.openGL = Opengl( self, double = 1 )
28          self.openGL.pack( expand = YES, fill = BOTH )
29
30          self.openGL.redraw = self.redraw        # set redraw function
31          self.openGL.set_eyepoint( 20 )          # move away from object
32          self.openGL.autospin_allowed = 1        # allow auto-spin
33
34          self.choices.addmenu( "Shape", None )   # Shape submenu
```

Fig. 24.2 **GLUT** used to create various shapes. (Part 1 of 3.)

```
35
36            # possible shapes and arguments
37            self.shapes = { "glutWireCube" : ( 3, ),
38                            "glutSolidCube": ( 3, ),
39                            "glutWireIcosahedron" : (),
40                            "glutSolidIcosahedron" : (),
41                            "glutWireCone" : ( 3, 3, 50, 50 ),
42                            "glutSolidCone" : ( 3, 3, 50, 50 ),
43                            "glutWireTorus" : ( 1, 3, 50, 50 ),
44                            "glutSolidTorus" : ( 1, 3, 50, 50 ),
45                            "glutWireTeapot" : ( 3, ),
46                            "glutSolidTeapot" : ( 3, ) }
47
48            self.selectedShape = StringVar()
49            self.selectedShape.set( "glutWireCube" )
50
51            sortedShapes = self.shapes.keys()
52            sortedShapes.sort()   # sort names before adding to menu
53
54            # add items to Shape menu
55            for shape in sortedShapes:
56                self.choices.addmenuitem( "Shape", "radiobutton",
57                    label = shape, variable = self.selectedShape,
58                    command = self.refresh )
59
60            self.choices.addmenu( "Color", None )   # Color submenu
61
62            # possible colors and their values
63            self.colors = { "Black" : ( 0.0, 0.0, 0.0 ),
64                            "Blue" : ( 0.0, 0.0, 1.0 ),
65                            "Red" : ( 1.0, 0.0, 0.0 ),
66                            "Green" : ( 0.0, 1.0, 0.0 ),
67                            "Magenta" : ( 1.0, 0.0, 1.0 ) }
68
69            self.selectedColor = StringVar()
70            self.selectedColor.set( "Black" )
71
72            # add items to Color menu
73            for color in self.colors.keys():
74                self.choices.addmenuitem( "Color", "radiobutton",
75                    label = color, variable = self.selectedColor,
76                    command = self.refresh )
77
78        def redraw( self, openGL ):
79            """Draw selected shape on white background"""
80
81            # clear background and disable lighting
82            glClearColor( 1.0, 1.0, 1.0, 0.0 ) # select clearing color
83            glClear( GL_COLOR_BUFFER_BIT )      # clear background
84            glDisable( GL_LIGHTING )
85
86            # obtain and set selected color
87            color = self.selectedColor.get()
```

Fig. 24.2   **GLUT** used to create various shapes. (Part 2 of 3.)

```
88              apply( glColor3f, self.colors[ color ] )
89
90              # obtain and draw selected shape
91              shape = self.selectedShape.get()
92              apply( eval( shape ), self.shapes[ shape ] )
93
94          def refresh( self ):
95              self.openGL.tkRedraw()
96
97      def main():
98          ChooseShape().mainloop()
99
100     if __name__ == "__main__":
101         main()
```

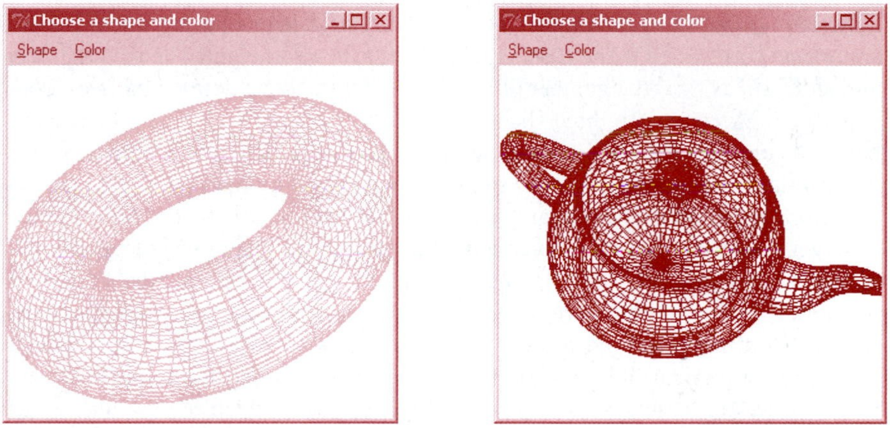

Fig. 24.2 GLUT used to create various shapes. (Part 3 of 3.)

Line 98 creates an object of class **ChooseShape** (lines 10–95) and invokes **mainloop** begin the application's event loop. Lines 16–20 initialize the GUI window. Lines 23–24 create and pack a **MenuBar** component. In lines 27–32, the **OpenGL** component is initialized. Line 32 sets **autospin_allowed** to **1**, which allows users to rotate a shape continuously by holding down the middle mouse button on a three-button mouse, dragging the mouse in the direction of the desired rotation and releasing the mouse button.

Our example provides users with a menu of shapes to preview, including cubes, icosa-hedrons (20-sided shapes), cones, tori (doughnut shapes) and teapots. Both wire-frame and solid shapes can be viewed. The screenshots of Fig. 24.2 show a wire-frame torus and a wire-frame teapot.

Dictionary **shapes** (lines 37–46) contains GLUT shapes as its keys. Each key corresponds to the name of a function that draws a 3D shape. The keys' values are possible arguments for those function. The program also allows the user to choose the color of the shape. Dictionary **colors** (lines 63–67) contains a list of color names as keys. Each color has its RGB tuple as its value. The GUI provides a **Pmw MenuBar** with radio-button menu items for each shape and color, default selection is a white-wire cube. Lines 73–76 add items to the **Color** menu. Selecting an item in the **Color** menu calls method **refresh** (lines 94–95).

Selecting an item from the menu updates the display. First, method **refresh** calls **tkRedraw** to update the window. Function **tkRedraw** calls the window's associated **redraw** function. Method **redraw** (lines 78–92) sets the background to white and disables lighting. Line 87 retrieves the selected color. Method **apply** (line 89) passes the color's RGB value to function **glColor3f**, which sets the drawing color. Similarly, line 91 gets the selected shape. Function *eval* changes the string representation of the shape function to a function call, and **apply** calls the indicated function on any arguments associated with the shape's dictionary key.

The **GLUT** library provides the functions that draw the three-dimensional shapes available in this example. Functions *glutWireCube* and *glutSolidCube* accept the length of the cube's side as an argument—3, in this case. Functions *glutWireIcosahedron* and *glutSolidIcosahedron*, which take no arguments, create a 20-sided shape with a radius of 1.0.

Functions *glutWireCone* and *glutSolidCone* take four arguments. The first two arguments correspond to the base's radius and the cone's height. The next argument is the number of *slices* (i.e., the number of subsections of the cone defined by lines from the tip to the base). A cone with three slices resembles a pyramid with sides. Increasing the number of slices gives the cone a more rounded appearance. The fourth argument sets the number of *stacks*—the number of cone subdivisions created by lines parallel to the base.

Functions *glutWireTorus* and *glutSolidTorus* also accept four arguments. The first two specify the inner and total radii of the doughnut shape. The inner radius is the radius of the inner space (e.g, the "doughnut hole") while the total radius is the distance from the torus's center to the outermost edge (e.g., the radius of the entire doughnut-shaped object). The third argument specifies the number of lines going around the entire torus shape. The last argument indicates the number of lines dividing the torus into sections. Functions *glutWireTeapot* and *glutSolidTeapot*, which draw a teapot, accept the relative size of the shape as an argument.

24.4 Introduction to Alice

Alice (**www.alice.org**) is a 3D *Interactive Graphics Programming Environment* that makes 3D modeling accessible even to novice Python programmers. Alice is designed for Microsoft Windows operating systems and provides an environment in which programmers can develop scripts to control the behavior of objects (i.e., animation). In addition to the objects included with Alice, users can import many common 3D-modeling formats.

A programmer can use Python to control the Alice environment. Alice provides a simple and intuitive interface that allows a developer to place objects in the Alice "world." The world is the virtual 3D scene. After the programmer designs the initial scene, a Python script animates the objects in the Alice world. Python programmers also can create animations by accessing the list of actions for each object that is available in the Alice environment. To view a completed world in Internet Explorer, download the browser plug-in at **www.alice.org/downloads/plugin**.

Alice uses a version of the Python interpreter to parse Python code. Although Python normally is case sensitive, the Alice interpreter does not treat Python as a case-sensitive language. Users of Python 2.2 and earlier versions also will expect integer division to always result in an integer. In Alice, division may result in a floating-point number; for example, the fraction 1/2 evaluates to 0.5, rather than 0 as it would in the standard Python interpreter.

24.5 Fox, Chicken and Seed Problem

We present the Fox, Chicken and Seed problem as a game to demonstrate programming with Alice (Fig. 24.3). The rules to this game are simple: Alice Liddell needs to transport a fox, a chicken and a seed across a river with a boat. The boat is small; it can accommodate only one additional passenger. However, the fox will eat the chicken if the two remain on the shore alone and the chicken cannot be left alone with the seed for the same reason.

Before running this example, the *Alice Authoring Tool* must be installed. [*Note*: Installation instructions can be found at **www.alice.org**.] To run the example, start the Alice Authoring Tool and open the **"FoxChickenAndSeed"** world, which is available on the CD-ROM that accompanies this text. Select the **Animations** tab and click the green **Start** button to begin the animation. For example, to move the fox into the boat, select the **fox** radio button, and click the **Get into the boat** button.

Figure 24.3 shows the game control panel and the Python code used to create the game. [*Note*: In this example, we use a flower pot, which is supplied as an object by Alice, to represent the seed.] We do not include the Alice code that renders the scene. This code can be found in **World_scene.py** on the CD-ROM that accompanies this text. [*Note*: We do not include a screenshot of the Alice world because the limited colors of this text would not give an accurate picture of the world.]

```
1   ### We omit the code generated by Alice. ###
2   # Fig. 24.3: fig24_03.py
3   # Fox, Chicken and Seed problem.
4
5   FollowTheBoat = Loop( camera.PointAt
6      ( AliceLiddell.dress.rthigh ) )
7
8   # run two animations together with given pause time
9   def AnimateWithPause( Animation1, Animation2, Object, time ):
10
11      return Loop( DoInOrder( DoTogether( Animation1, Animation2 ),
12         Object.Move( Forward, 0, Duration = time ) ) )
13
14   # create two fish following continuous animation pattern
15   LoopingFish = Loop( AnimateWithPause
16      ( Fish.Move( Forward, 50, Duration = 5 ),
17         Fish.Turn( Down, 1, Duration = 5 ), Fish, 15 ) )
18
19   LoopingFish2 = Loop( AnimateWithPause
20      ( Fish2.Move( Forward, 70, Duration = 8 ),
21         Fish2.Turn( Down, 1, Duration = 8 ), Fish2, 25 ) )
22
23   # lists that keep track of object position
24   thisBank = [ "Fox", "Chicken", "Flower" ]
25   theBoat = []
26   otherBank = []
```

Fig. 24.3 Fox, Chicken and Seed game. (Part 1 of 4.)

```
27
28   currentBank = thisBank
29   targetBank = otherBank
30   selected = None
31
32   # animal select callback
33   def animalSelect( value ):
34
35      global selected
36      selected = value
37
38   # put object into boat
39   def ObjectInBoat( Object ):
40
41      Object.RespondToCollisionWith( FishBoat.deck, Object.Stop )
42      Object.MoveTo( FishBoat.period )
43      Object.Move( Down, 2, Duration = 3 )
44
45   # get object out of boat
46   def ObjectOutOfBoat( Object ):
47
48      Object.RespondToCollisionWith( Ground, Object.Stop )
49      Object.Move( Left, 1 - int( ( len( Object._name ) - 1 ) / 3 ))
50      Object.Move( Back, 7 )
51      Object.Move( Down, 3, Duration = 3 )
52
53   # put the currently selected object into boat
54   def getIntoBoat():
55
56      if selected in currentBank and
57            ( len( theBoat ) == 0 ) and boatArrived():
58         currentBank.remove( selected )
59         theBoat.append( selected )
60         ObjectInBoat( eval( selected ) )
61
62   # remove currently selected object from boat
63   def getOutOfBoat():
64
65      if selected in theBoat and boatArrived():
66         theBoat.remove( selected )
67         currentBank.append( selected )
68         ObjectOutOfBoat( eval( selected ) )
69
70   # send boat to other shore
71   def toOtherShore():
72
73      if not boatArrived():        # boat is still in transit
74         return
75
76      global currentBank, thisBank, otherBank
77
```

Fig. 24.3   Fox, Chicken and Seed game. (Part 2 of 4.)

```
78        if len( theBoat ) == 1:   # someone is on boat
79            DoInOrder( eval( theBoat[ 0 ] ).Move( Forward, 16,
80            Duration = 3 ), eval( theBoat[ 0 ] ).Turn( Left, 1/2, 1,
81            AsSeenby = FishBoat ) )
82
83        # move boat then set alarm to check rules
84        DoInOrder( FishBoat.Move( Forward, 16, Duration = 3 ),
85            FishBoat.Turn( Left, 1/2 ) )
86        Alice.SetAlarm( 1, checkRules, ( currentBank ) )
87
88        if currentBank == thisBank:   # switch currentBank reference
89            currentBank = otherBank
90        else:
91            currentBank = thisBank
92
93  # boat has arrived
94  def boatArrived():
95
96        # check to see if the boat is at the shore
97        if AliceLiddell.DistanceTo( period ) < .01 or
98            AliceLiddell.DistanceTo( period2 ) < .01:
99            return 1
100       else:
101           return 0
102
103  # check to see if rules have been violated
104  def checkRules( currentBank ):
105
106       Animation1 = DoInOrder()
107       Animation2 = DoInOrder()
108
109       if "Chicken" in currentBank:
110
111           # chicken eats flower (i.e., seed)
112           if "Flower" in currentBank:
113               Animation1 = DoInOrder( camera.PointAt( Flower ),
114               Flower.destroy() )
115
116           # fox eats chicken
117           if "Fox" in currentBank:
118               Animation2 = DoInOrder( camera.PointAt( Chicken ),
119               Chicken.destroy() )
120
121           # player has lost
122           if ( "Flower" in currentBank ) or
123               ( "Fox" in currentBank ):
124               finishGame( Animation1, Animation2, GAMEOVER )
125
126       # player wins if nothing left on current bank
127       if len( currentBank ) == 0 and
128           not ( currentBank == targetBank ):
129           finishGame( Animation1, Animation2, CONGRATULATIONS )
130
```

Fig. 24.3   Fox, Chicken and Seed game. (Part 3 of 4.)

```
131  # game over, AnimationX defaults to an empty sequence
132  def finishGame( Animation1, Animation2, final ):
133
134     controlPanel.destroy()
135     FollowTheBoat.stop()
136     final.Show()
137     DoInOrder( Animation1, Animation2,
138     DoInOrder( camera.Place( len( final._name ) + 2,
139        InFrontOf, final ), camera.PointAt( final ) ) )
140
141  # create control panel and buttons
142  controlPanel = AControlPanel( Caption = "Game Control Panel" )
143  animalListBox = \
144     controlPanel.MakeOptionButtonSet( List = thisBank[ : ],
145     Command = animalSelect)
146  buttonToBoat = \
147     controlPanel.MakeButton( Caption = "Get into the boat" )
148  buttonFromBoat = \
149     controlPanel.MakeButton( Caption = "Get out of the boat" )
150  buttonMoveBoat = \
151     controlPanel.MakeButton( Caption = "Go to the other shore" )
152
153  # associate buttons with callbacks
154  buttonToBoat.SetCommand( getIntoBoat )
155  buttonFromBoat.SetCommand( getOutOfBoat )
156  buttonMoveBoat.SetCommand( toOtherShore )
157
158  # initial selection defaults to first element (fox)
159  animalListbox._children[ 0 ].SetValue( 1 )
160  selected = "Fox"
```

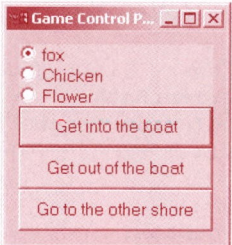

Fig. 24.3   Fox, Chicken and Seed game. (Part 4 of 4.)

The initial scene was created using the Alice environment and its predefined objects–
Alice Liddell, the fox, the hen, the flowerpot, the river and the boat. The Alice Liddell
figure is attached to the boat. The chicken, fox and seed initially are placed next to the boat
on the same side of the shore.

All other objects in the scene are inserted purely for visual interest and do not participate in the game. For instance, lines 15–22 create two jumping fish animations. The program animates each fish to move and turn. Method **Move** (line 16) takes three arguments—
the direction of the movement, the amount of the movement in meters and the amount of
time the movement should take in seconds. In the case of **LoopingFish**, the object
spends five seconds moving forward 50 meters. Method **Turn** (line 17) takes three argu-

ments as well—the direction of the turn, the amount of the turn in rotations and the duration of the turn. **LoopingFish** rotates once in the downward direction for five seconds.

We would like to run the animations of the fish jumping out of the water with a pause between the jumps, so we call function **AnimateWithPause** inside a call to **Loop** (lines 15–17). Function **Loop** calls the function it receives as an argument continuously. Function **AnimateWithPause** (lines 9–12) animates the movements of a fish so that each fish jumps once in the air and repeats this action a specified number of seconds later. The function takes two animations, the object and a time in seconds. This function is called for each fish. Lines 15–17 and lines 19–21 pass the two fish animations—movement and rotation—to **animateWithPause**. The function calls **DoTogether** (line 11), which takes two animations, to run the movement and rotation of a fish simultaneously. Line 12 forces the object to stop its forward motion by calling function **Move** with the amount of movement set to **0**. Function **DoInOrder** accepts a comma-separated list of animations and performs them sequentially. Function **DoInOrder** (lines 11–12) takes the calls to **DoTogether** and **Move** and performs their result in sequence.

Now that we have set up the scene and introduced animation, we create a control panel to allow the user to play the game. Function **AControlPanel** (line 142) creates the window **controlPanel** to which all the control buttons will be attached and sets the window's title to **"Game Control Panel"**. Lines 143–145 create a set of radio buttons, using the initial list of objects at the beginning shore. Each radio button is associated with an object at the bank—the fox, the hen or the flowerpot. The option **Command** associates the selection of a radio button with function **animalSelect** (lines 33–36).

We add three buttons to **controlPanel** that allow users to perform the actions necessary to play the game—placing an object in the boat, moving the boat across the shore and removing an object from the boat. Calls to function **MakeButton** creates the three buttons, **buttonToBoat**, **buttonFromBoat** and **buttonMoveBoat**. The label displayed on each button is the string assigned to **Caption**. Lines 154–156 call function **SetCommand** to associate each button with its event handler. Finally, lines 159–160 set the initial selection to **"fox"**.

A player follows the action in the game as Alice moves back and forth between shores. Lines 5–6 center the camera on Alice Liddell. The camera shows the action of the game as the boat travels between the two shores. Function **Loop** ensures that the camera continuously follows the Alice Liddell object.

The game status is preserved in Python lists and variables (lines 24–30). List **thisBank** refers to the shore at which the game begins. Initially, the three objects are in this list. List **otherBank** refers to the opposite shore, which initially is empty. Variable **currentBank** always refers to the shore at which the boat is docked, while **targetBank** refers to the side of the river to which the boat is headed. Variable **selected** (line 30) holds the currently selected object. When the user selects a radio button corresponding to an object (lines 143–145), callback **animalSelect** (lines 33–36) sets **selected** to the chosen animal object. Note that **selected** is a global variable, which enables the other functions to access its value.

A player places an object in the boat by selecting the object's radio button and clicking **Get into the boat** button (lines 146–147), which calls function **getIntoBoat** (lines 54–60). Callback **getIntoBoat** determines whether a selected object can be placed in the boat. If the object is on the current shore (i.e., the shore at which the boat has docked), and no other object is in the boat (lines 56–57), the function removes the selected object from the current bank's list and adds it to **theBoat**.

Line 60 calls function **ObjectInBoat** (lines 39–43) to move the object onto the boat. Function **RespondToCollisionWith** (line 41) sets the **FishBoat**'s response to a collision with the shore as **Object.Stop**. Function **MoveTo** moves the object to the boat, but the function sets the object above the boat. To set the object in the boat, function **Move** shifts the object down two meters where it intersects with the deck.

When the player wants to move an object from the boat to the shore, the player clicks the **Get out of the boat** button (lines 149–150). The callback **getOutOfBoat** (lines 63–68) determines whether the selected object is in the boat and whether the boat has arrived at the shore. If these conditions are met, the program removes the object from **the-Boat** and appends it to the current bank's list.

Line 68 calls function **ObjectOutOfBoat** (lines 46–51), which moves an object off the boat and onto the shore. The object is placed on the shore according to its length (lines 49–51); thus, each object is placed at a different position on the shore. Lines 50–51 move the object out of the boat and down onto the shore.

When the user selects the **Go to the other shore** button (lines 150–151), callback function **toOtherShore** (lines 71–91) sends the boat to the opposite shore. When the boat is in transit, this function returns **None** (lines 73–74). Line 76 makes the global variables that refer to the shores accessible within the function. If there is an object on the boat, the object is animated with the boat (lines 78–81). An object on the boat is not a part of the boat, so a separate animation is created to synchronize the object's position with the boat's movement. Function **DoInOrder** (lines 78–80) move the object forward 16 meters for three seconds and then turn the object half a rotation for 1 second. The fourth argument to function **Turn** sets **AsSeenby** to the **FishBoat**. This rotates the object to face the shore with the boat when the boat lands at a shore; if the object were not rotated with the boat, the object would appear to be in the back of the boat after its rotation. Lines 84–85 animate the boat's movement to follow the same path as the object's.

Function **boatArrived** (lines 94–101) determines the status of the boat. If the boat is moving across the river, this function returns **0**; otherwise, it returns **1**. This is accomplished with two **period** objects (two small dots) at both river banks. By checking the distance between a **period** object and Alice Liddell, we are able to determine whether she has arrived.

Line 86 sets an *alarm*. An alarm triggers an event after a specified amount of time. **Alice.SetAlarm** takes the time to wait as the first argument and a function to call when that time quantum expires. In this example, a second after the boat leaves the shore, the alarm calls function **checkRules** (lines 104–129).

Function **checkRules** (lines 104–129) determines if a rule has been violated, e.g. the fox and the chicken are alone on the same shore. If a rule has been violated, the animation changes accordingly and function **finishGame** (lines 132–139) is called with parameter **GAMEOVER**. If the player loses, method **PointAt** moves the camera so that its forward direction faces the object to be destroyed (i.e., the fox eats the hen or the hen eats the flower). Method **destroy** eliminates the "eaten" object from the scene. If the rules have not been violated, but the current shore is empty, **finishGame** receives **CONGRATULATIONS** as a parameter because all objects were transported to the opposite shore successfully.

Function **finishGame** (lines 132–139) destroys **controlPanel** and stops the boat animation. At the end of the game, we display the text **GAMEOVER** or **CONGRATULATIONS** away. Function **Place** (lines 138–139) accepts three arguments to place the camera relative to the text object—the distance from the text object, the relative placement of the camera and the text object. The function places the camera in front the text object. Then, method **PointAt** directs the camera at **final**, the text object.

24.6   Introduction to pygame

In Sections 24.7, 24.8 and 24.9, we present **pygame**, a set of Python modules written by Pete Shinners that are designed to create multimedia programs and games. The **pygame** modules use the *Simple DirectMedia Layer* (*SDL*), which is a cross-platform library that provides a uniform API to access multimedia hardware. Module **pygame** allows programmers to access this library through Python. For more information about **pygame**, including extensive documentation, visit **www.pygame.org**.

24.7 Python CD Player

In the first example, we demonstrate how to create a simple CD-ROM player, using **pygame**'s *cdrom* module (Fig. 24.4). Module **cdrom** contains class **CD** and methods to initialize a CD-ROM subsystem. Class **CD** represents the user's CD-ROM drive. Methods of class **CD** allow users to access an audio compact disc (CD) in a computer's CD-ROM drive. The program in Fig. 24.4 also uses **Tkinter** and **Pmw** to create the CD-player interface. **Tkinter** and **Pmw** are introduced in Chapters 10 and 11.

```
1   # Fig. 24.4: fig24_04.py
2   # Simple CD player using Tkinter and pygame.
3
4   import sys
5   import string
6   import pygame, pygame.cdrom
7   from Tkinter import *
8   from tkMessageBox import *
9   import Pmw
10
11  class CDPlayer( Frame ):
12      """A GUI CDPlayer class using Tkinter and pygame"""
13
14      def __init__( self ):
15          """Initialize pygame.cdrom and get CDROM if one exists"""
16
17          pygame.cdrom.init()
18
19          if pygame.cdrom.get_count() > 0:
20              self.CD = pygame.cdrom.CD( 0 )
21          else:
22              sys.exit( "There are no available CDROM drives." )
23
```

Fig. 24.4   Python CD player. (Part 1 of 5.)

```
24            self.createGUI()
25            self.updateTime()
26
27        def destroy( self ):
28            """Stop CD, uninitialize pygame.cdrom and destroy GUI"""
29
30            if self.CD.get_init():
31                self.CD.stop()
32
33            pygame.cdrom.quit()
34            Frame.destroy( self )
35
36        def createGUI( self ):
37            """Create CDPlayer widgets"""
38
39            Frame.__init__( self )
40            self.pack( expand = YES, fill = BOTH )
41            self.master.title( "CD Player" )
42
43            # display current track playing
44            self.trackLabel = IntVar()
45            self.trackLabel.set( 1 )
46            self.trackDisplay = Label( self, font = "Courier 14",
47                textvariable = self.trackLabel, bg = "black",
48                fg = "green" )
49            self.trackDisplay.grid( sticky = W+E+N+S )
50
51            # display current time of track playing
52            self.timeLabel = StringVar()
53            self.timeLabel.set( "00:00/00:00" )
54            self.timeDisplay = Label( self, font = "Courier 14",
55                textvariable = self.timeLabel, bg = "black",
56                fg = "green" )
57            self.timeDisplay.grid( row = 0, column = 1, columnspan = 3,
58                sticky = W+E+N+S )
59
60            # play/pause CD
61            self.playLabel = StringVar()
62            self.playLabel.set( "Play" )
63            self.play = Button( self, textvariable = self.playLabel,
64                command = self.playCD, width = 10 )
65            self.play.grid( row = 1, column = 0, columnspan = 2,
66                sticky = W+E+N+S )
67
68            # stop CD
69            self.stop = Button( self, text = "Stop", width = 10,
70                command = self.stopCD )
71            self.stop.grid( row = 1, column = 2, columnspan = 2,
72                sticky = W+E+N+S )
73
74            # skip to previous track
75            self.previous = Button( self, text = "|<<", width = 5,
76                command = self.previousTrack )
```

Fig. 24.4 Python CD player. (Part 2 of 5.)

```
77         self.previous.grid( row = 2, column = 0, sticky = W+E+N+S )
78
79         # skip to next track
80         self.next = Button( self, text = ">>|", width = 5,
81            command = self.nextTrack )
82         self.next.grid( row = 2, column = 1, sticky = W+E+N+S )
83
84         # eject CD
85         self.eject = Button( self, text = "Eject", width = 10,
86            command = self.ejectCD )
87         self.eject.grid( row = 2, column = 2, columnspan = 2,
88            sticky = W+E+N+S )
89
90      def playCD( self ):
91         """Play/Pause CD if disc is loaded"""
92
93         # if disc has been ejected, reinitialize drive
94         if not self.CD.get_init():
95            self.CD.init()
96            self.currentTrack = 1
97
98            # if no disc in drive, uninitialize and return
99            if self.CD.get_empty():
100               self.CD.quit()
101               return
102
103            # if disc is loaded, obtain disc information
104            else:
105               self.totalTracks = self.CD.get_numtracks()
106
107         # if CD is not playing, play CD
108         if not self.CD.get_busy() and not self.CD.get_paused():
109            self.CD.play( self.currentTrack - 1 )
110            self.playLabel.set( "| |" )
111
112         # if CD is playing, pause disc
113         elif not self.CD.get_paused():
114            self.CD.pause()
115            self.playLabel.set( "Play" )
116
117         # if CD is paused, resume play
118         else:
119            self.CD.resume()
120            self.playLabel.set( "| |" )
121
122      def stopCD( self ):
123         """Stop CD if disc is loaded"""
124
125         if self.CD.get_init():
126            self.CD.stop()
127            self.playLabel.set( "Play" )
128
```

Fig. 24.4 Python CD player. (Part 3 of 5.)

```python
129     def playTrack( self, track ):
130         """Play track if disc is loaded"""
131
132         if self.CD.get_init():
133             self.currentTrack = track
134             self.trackLabel.set( self.currentTrack )
135
136             # start beginning of track
137             if self.CD.get_busy():
138                 self.CD.play( self.currentTrack - 1 )
139             elif self.CD.get_paused():
140                 self.CD.play( self.currentTrack - 1 )
141                 self.playCD()    # re-pause CD
142
143     def nextTrack( self ):
144         """Play next track on CD if disc is loaded"""
145
146         if self.CD.get_init() and \
147             self.currentTrack < self.totalTracks:
148             self.playTrack( self.currentTrack + 1 )
149
150     def previousTrack( self ):
151         """Play previous track on CD if disc is loaded"""
152
153         if self.CD.get_init() and self.currentTrack > 1:
154             self.playTrack( self.currentTrack - 1 )
155
156     def ejectCD( self ):
157         """Eject CD from drive"""
158
159         response = askyesno( "Eject pushed", "Eject CD?" )
160
161         if response:
162             self.CD.init()    # CD must be initialized to eject
163             self.CD.eject()
164             self.CD.quit()
165             self.trackLabel.set( 1 )
166             self.timeLabel.set( "00:00/00:00" )
167             self.playLabel.set( "Play" )
168
169     def updateTime( self ):
170         """Update time display if disc is loaded"""
171
172         if self.CD.get_init():
173             seconds = int( self.CD.get_current()[ 1 ] )
174             endSeconds = int( self.CD.get_track_length(
175                 self.currentTrack - 1 ) )
176
177             # if reached end of current track, play next track
178             if seconds >= ( endSeconds - 1 ):
179                 self.nextTrack()
```

Fig. 24.4 Python CD player. (Part 4 of 5.)

```
180              else:
181                  minutes = seconds / 60
182                  endMinutes = endSeconds / 60
183                  seconds = seconds - ( minutes * 60 )
184                  endSeconds = endSeconds - ( endMinutes * 60 )
185
186                  # display time in format mm:ss/mm:ss
187                  trackTime = string.zfill( str( minutes ), 2 ) + \
188                      ":" + string.zfill( str( seconds ), 2 )
189                  endTime = string.zfill( str( endMinutes ), 2 ) +  \
190                      ":" + string.zfill( str( endSeconds ), 2 )
191
192                  if self.CD.get_paused():
193
194                      # alternate pause symbol and time in display
195                      if not self.timeLabel.get() == "      ||      ":
196                          self.timeLabel.set( "      ||      " )
197                      else:
198                          self.timeLabel.set( trackTime + "/" + endTime )
199
200                  else:
201                      self.timeLabel.set( trackTime + "/" + endTime )
202
203          # call updateTime method again after 1000ms ( 1 second )
204          self.after( 1000, self.updateTime )
205
206  def main():
207      CDPlayer().mainloop()
208
209  if __name__ == "__main__":
210      main()
```

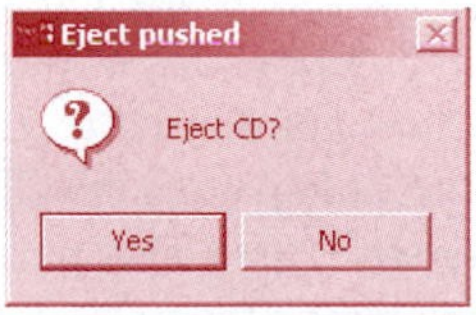

Fig. 24.4   Python CD player. (Part 5 of 5.)

Line 207 creates a **CDPlayer** object and invokes its **mainloop** method to start the application. The **CDPlayer** constructor (lines 14–25) initializes module **cdrom** (line 17). Initializing module **cdrom** gives a program access to methods for controlling and querying any CD-ROM drives on a machine. The **if/else** structure (lines 19–22) determines available CD-ROM drives on the machine by invoking **cdrom**'s **get_count** function. Method **get_count** returns the number of CD-ROM drives on the computer. If at least one drive is present, line 20 creates a **CD** object called **CD**. The value passed to the **CD** constructor is the identification (ID) number of the CD-ROM drive. If more than one CD-ROM drive is installed on a computer system, the program uses the primary CD-ROM drive. The constructor receives **0** as an argument, because the primary CD-ROM's drive identification number is always **0**. The program exits (line 22) if no CD-ROM exists.

After the program identifies that a CD-ROM drive exists, the program constructs a GUI with which users interact. Line 24 invokes method **createGUI** to create the CDplayer interface, which is composed of various GUI components. Method **createGUI** (lines 36–88) adds the components to the display (each component's action is discussed later in this section). Both the **Label** created to display the track number (**trackDisplay**) and the **Label** that displays the current track time (**timeDisplay**) have **textvariable**s—**trackLabel** and **timeLabel**—that update the CD-player display. Notice also that **Button play** has a **textvariable**—**playLabel**—which changes its display when the user pauses or plays a CD.

Once the GUI has been created, the constructor calls method **updateTime** (discussed momentarily). The program then enters the **mainloop**, in which the user can play, stop, pause, fast forward and backtrack through a CD by manipulating the CD player's GUI.

The other methods provide all the functionality of a basic CD player. The **Play** button has callback method **playCD** (lines 90–120), which plays or pauses the CD. Line 94 determines whether the CD-ROM is initialized by invoking **CD** method **get_init**. If the CD-ROM is not initialized, **playCD** initializes it and sets **currentTrack** to **1**. Variable **currentTrack** stores the number of the current audio track. Line 99 determines whether the CD-ROM drive is empty by invoking **CD** method **get_empty**. If the drive is empty, line 100 uninitializes the object with **CD** method **quit** and returns. Otherwise, line 105 obtains the total number of audio tracks on the disc from **CD** method **get_numtracks** and stores that value in object attribute **totalTracks**.

Method **playCD** tests for three cases—the CD is not playing, the CD is not paused and or the CD is paused. Line 108 determines whether the CD is not playing and not paused using methods **get_busy** and **get_paused**, respectively. If both these conditions are true, line 109 calls method **play**. The method call specifies which track to play. Because the track numbers for a CD object begin with **0** and **currentTrack** is initialized to **1**, the value passed to method **play** is **1** less than **currentTrack** (line 109). Line 110 sets the **Play** button's text to contain the symbols for the pause button, | | so the user can properly control the CD-ROM application.

Line 113 determines whether the CD is paused by invoking **get_paused**. If the CD is playing and not paused (e.g., the user has not pressed the pause button), **CD** method **pause** (line 114) pauses the CD. Line 114 sets the **Play** button's text to contain the word **Play**. Otherwise, the CD is paused, and the program calls **CD** method **resume** (line 119) to continue playing the track. As in line 110, the program sets the label on the button to the symbols for the **Paused** button.

The **Stop** button's associated callback is **stopCD** (lines 122–127). When a user presses the **Stop** button, line 125 determines whether the **CD** object is initialized. If it is, **CD** method **stop** is invoked to stop the CD, and the **Play** button is set to read **"Play"** once more. Calling **stop** on a **CD** that is not playing does nothing; however, line 125 determines whether the **CD** object is initialized because, if it is not, calling **stop** generates an error.

This application plays the audio tracks sequentially, but the user can press the |<< or the >>| button to move backward or forward, respectively, through the audio tracks on the CD. The >>| button is associated with callback **nextTrack**, which skips to the next track on the CD (lines 143–148). If **CD** is initialized and the current track is not the last one, method **playTrack** is invoked, with the next track number specified (**currentTrack + 1**). Similarly, the |<< button is associated with callback **previousTrack**, which skips to the previous track on a CD (lines 150–154). If **CD** is initialized and the current track is not the first one, method **playTrack** is invoked, with the previous track number specified (**currentTrack – 1**).

Method **playTrack** (lines 129–141) plays a CD track. If the CD is initialized, line 133 sets **currentTrack** to the indicated number. Line 134 sets **trackLabel** to the new track number. If the CD is playing another song, line 138 plays the indicated track instead. If the CD is paused, however, lines 140–141 switch to the specified song and then leave the disc paused.

Callback **ejectCD** (lines 156–167) is bound to the **Eject** button. When a user clicks the **Eject** button, line 159 displays a **tkMessageBox** window with a message that asks the user whether the CD should be ejected. This is a safeguard against accidentally ejecting the CD. If the user chooses to eject the CD, **CD** is initialized because, if the user never played the CD, it was never initialized and trying to eject an uninitialized **CD** object is an error. Once the **CD** object has been initialized, the disc is ejected with **CD** method **eject** and **CD** is uninitialized (lines 162–164). Lines 165–167 set the CD-player interface to its initial appearance.

The CD player updates its display using method **updateTime** (lines 169–204), originally called in line 25. Line 172 determines whether **CD** is initialized. If it is not, execution skips to line 204.

Often, audio CDs list the duration of each track. This program displays the time that a song has been playing to the user. If the **CD** is initialized, **CD** method **get_current** returns the number of seconds that the track has played and assigns that number to variable **seconds** (line 173). Method **get_current** returns a two-element tuple of the current track number and the number of seconds that the song has been playing. Lines 174–175 obtain the track length from **CD** method **get_track_length**, specifying the current track (**currentTrack – 1**). This value is assigned to variable **endSeconds**. Lines 178–179 ensure that the tracks play consecutively until the entire disk has been played. Lines 181–184 use **seconds** and **endSeconds** to determine the current time and end time in minutes and seconds.

Lines 187–188 create a string for the current track time (**trackTime**). The string is in the form *mm:ss,* in which *mm* is minutes and *ss* is seconds. Note that **string** function **zfill** pads the string with zeros so that it occupies the correct number of spaces. This ensures that both minutes and seconds are displayed with two digits.

Line 192 determines whether the CD is paused. If the CD is not paused, **timeDisplay** is updated to display the current time (line 201). Otherwise, **timeDisplay** is updated to either the current time or to the symbol that represents pause (lines 195–198). This causes the display to flash between the track time and the pause symbol when paused.

Method **updateTime** invokes component method **after**. Method **after** registers a callback that executes after a specified number of milliseconds. Line 204 ensures that method **updateTime** is called approximately every 1000 milliseconds (one second).

When the user is finished with the CD player, the program destroys the window, and invokes the **CDPlayer**'s **destroy** method to terminate the CD player (lines 27–34). Line 30 determines whether **CD** is initialized. If **CD** is initialized, **CD** method **stop** is invoked to stop the CD. If the program does not call method **stop**, the CD would continue to play after the user destroys the window. Lines 33–34 uninitialize the **pygame cdrom** module and destroy the frame by calling **Frame** method **destroy**.

Good Programming Practice 24.1

*For Tkinter programs, a **destroy** method acts as a destructor.*

24.8 Python Movie Player

This section demonstrates **pygame**'s *movie* module, by creating a simple movie player (Fig. 24.5). The **movie** module contains a method that creates a **Movie** object, which represents an open *moving pictures experts group (MPEG)* file. Class **Movie** provides methods to play, stop, pause and rewind movies.

```
1   # Fig. 24.5: fig24_05.py
2   # Playing an MPEG movie.
3
4   import os
5   import sys
6   import pygame, pygame.movie
7   import pygame.mouse, pygame.image
8   from pygame.locals import *
9
10  def createGUI( file ):
11
12      # load movie
13      movie = pygame.movie.Movie( file )
14      width, height = movie.get_size()
15
16      # initialize display window
17      screen = pygame.display.set_mode( ( width, height + 100 ) )
18      pygame.display.set_caption( "Movie Player" )
19      pygame.mouse.set_visible( 1 )
20
21      # play button
22      playImageFile = os.path.join( "data", "play.png" )
23      playImage = pygame.image.load( playImageFile ).convert()
24      playImageSize = playImage.get_rect()
25      playImageSize.center = width / 2, height + 50
26
27      # copy play button to screen
28      screen.blit( playImage, playImageSize )
29      pygame.display.flip()
30
31      # set output surface for movie's video
32      movie.set_display( screen )
33
34      return movie, playImageSize
35
36  def main():
37
38      # check command line arguments
39      if len( sys.argv ) != 2:
40          sys.exit( "Incorrect number of arguments." )
```

Fig. 24.5 Python movie player. (Part 1 of 2.)

```
41        else:
42            file = sys.argv[ 1 ]
43
44        # initialize pygame
45        pygame.init()
46
47        # initialize GUI
48        movie, playImageSize = createGUI( file )
49
50        # wait until player wants to close program
51        while 1:
52            event = pygame.event.wait()
53
54            # close window
55            if event.type == QUIT or \
56                ( event.type == KEYDOWN and event.key == K_ESCAPE ):
57                break
58
59            # click play button and play movie
60            pressed = pygame.mouse.get_pressed()[ 0 ]
61            position = pygame.mouse.get_pos()
62
63            # button pressed
64            if pressed:
65
66                if playImageSize.collidepoint( position ):
67                    movie.play()
68
69    if __name__ == "__main__":
70        main()
```

Fig. 24.5 Python movie player. (Part 2 of 2.)

When the movie application runs, function **main** (lines 36–67) executes. Lines 39–42 determines whether the appropriate number of command-line arguments were provided by the user. To run this example, the user needs to provide a command-line argument that specifies the location of the movie file, such as

```
python fig24_05.py "c:\bailey.mpg"
```

The movie file **bailey.mpg** is on the CD-ROM that accompanies the text. An error message displays if the user does not provide a file name.

Line 45 initializes **pygame**. Method **pygame.init** initializes every **pygame** module, including the ones used by this example, **pygame.movie**, **pygame.mouse** and **pygame.image**. This call to **init** is a shortcut—the program does not have to call each module's **init** method separately. Line 49 calls method **createGUI** (lines 10–34) to initialize the GUI for the application and to obtain the movie object and play button.

Method **createGUI** (lines 10–34) loads the MPEG movie and produces the display window. Line 13 calls method **pygame.movie.Movie** to create a **Movie** object. method **pygame.movie.Movie** takes one argument—the movie file name. The **Movie** object's method **get_size** (line 14) returns the movie's size as a tuple containing the width and height.

The program (lines 17–19) initializes the display window's size to accommodate for the movie and a play button. Line 17 sets the current display size using **pygame.display** method **set_mode**. The argument passed to **set_mode** is a two-element tuple that indicates a display mode in **width** and (**height + 100**) pixels. The value returned by **set_mode** is a **pygame Surface** object, which is a blank canvas where the program displays the movie. This **Surface** object is assigned to variable **screen**. Line 18 sets the window caption to **"Movie Player"**, by invoking **pygame.display** method **set_caption**.

The user starts the movie by pressing the play button. Method **createGUI** enables users to see the mouse pointer in the display and places the play button on the GUI. Line 19 calls **pygame.mouse** method **set_visible** with argument **1**, so that the mouse pointer appears over the window. The play-button image is located in the **"data"** subdirectory. Method **os.path.join** (line 22) takes two arguments, the subdirectory and the name of the image file **"play.png"**. This method locates the file by combining the subdirectory and the file name in a system-specific way. For example, in a Windows file directory, the path is **"data\play.png"**. The image returned is assigned to **playImageFile**.

Line 23 loads the play button image with **pygame.image** method **load** and method **convert** creates a copy of the **Surface** object with the button image's pixel format converted to the display's. Pixels with the same format are represented by the same number of bits. Setting the surface and the button to the same pixel format enables the program to *blit* (i.e., place one surface on another) more quickly. Method **load** places the converted button onto the **pygame Surface**.

We would like to specify exactly where to place the image on the display. The *Rect* class allows us to accomplish this task. Line 24 gets the play-button image size by invoking method *get_rect* of the **Surface** object **playImage**. The object returned by **get_rect** is a **Rect** object (i.e., a **pygame** rectangle), which is assigned to **playImageSize**. A **Rect** object represents a rectangle that covers the entire surface of the play button image. Line 25 sets the play-button position by modifying the **center** attribute of the play-button image.

Finally, the play button image is added to the display. Line 28 draws the play-button image onto the screen at position **playImageSize**. Position **(0, 0)** represents the upper-left corner of the screen. Line 29 calls method **flip** of module **pygame.display** to update the display. Method **flip** updates the entire display surface. In the next section, we discuss why this is not always necessary (or efficient).

Next, line 32 sets up the display so that the movie is rendered onto the **Surface** object **screen**. Method **set_display** of class **Movie** takes two arguments—the output **Surface** object for the movie and the position of the top-left corner of the movie. The second argument is optional. If the second argument is not supplied, the default value, **(0, 0)**, is used. Line 34 returns the **movie** object and the **playImageSize** rectangle, which is the play button.

After control returns to function **main**, the initial display on the Surface object **screen** is a round play button beneath an empty screen. The **while** loop waits for the users to start the movie or to close the application (lines 51–67). Line 52 invokes **pygame.event** method **wait**, which waits for and returns the next **Event** object waiting in the queue. If the event is a request to quit the program (**QUIT**) or is a **KEYDOWN** event with **key** attribute **K_ESCAPE**, the program exits the **while** loop (line 57) and the application terminates.

To play the movie, users click the right-mouse button. Line 60 determines whether the users click the right-mouse button. Method **pygame.mouse.get_pressed** returns a sequence of three values that indicate whether the mouse's left, middle or right button has been clicked. The status of the right mouse button is the first item in the sequence. If the right-mouse button has been pressed, this value evaluates to true.

The program needs to detect if the play button has been pressed. The **Rect** object **playImageSize** provides this functionality. First, line 61 obtains the mouse pointer's position by invoking method **pygame.mouse.get_pos**. If the right-mouse button has been pressed (line 66) method **collidepoint** of class **Rect** (line 67) determines whether the mouse click was inside or on the border of the button. This method takes one argument, which specifies the given point's position, and returns true if the point is inside the rectangle or on its border. Line 67 plays the movie by calling method **play** of class **Movie**.

24.9 Pygame Space Cruiser

Although other types of programs are developed with **pygame**, the most common applications are games. Figure 24.6 uses various **pygame** modules to create a simple "Space Cruiser" where the player has 60 seconds to navigate the space ship through an asteroid field. After 60 seconds, the ship's fuel is exhausted and the game is over. A clock in the upper-left corner of the screen shows the remaining time. Whenever the ship collides with an asteroid, 5 seconds are deducted from the remaining time. However, the ship also may pick up energy packs; each energy pack adds 5 extra seconds to the timer. The player controls the ship with the keyboard's arrow keys.

```
1   # Fig. 24.6: fig24_06.py
2   # Space Cruiser game using pygame.
3
4   import os
5   import sys
6   import random
```

Fig. 24.6   pygame Space Cruiser example. (Part 1 of 10.)

```
7   import pygame, pygame.image, pygame.font, pygame.mixer
8   from pygame.locals import *
9
10  class Sprite:
11      """An object to place on the screen"""
12
13      def __init__( self, image ):
14          """Initialize object image and calculate rectangle"""
15
16          self.image = image
17          self.rectangle = image.get_rect()
18
19      def place( self, screen ):
20          """Place object on the screen"""
21
22          return screen.blit( self.image, self.rectangle )
23
24      def remove( self, screen, background ):
25          """Place background over image to remove it"""
26
27          return screen.blit( background, self.rectangle,
28              self.rectangle )
29
30  class Player( Sprite ):
31      """Player Sprite with 4 different states"""
32
33      def __init__( self, images, crashImage,
34          centerX = 0, centerY = 0 ):
35          """Store images and set initial Player state"""
36
37          self.movingImages = images
38          self.crashImage = crashImage
39          self.centerX = centerX
40          self.centerY = centerY
41          self.playerPosition = 1     # start player facing down
42          self.speed = 0
43          self.loadImage()
44
45      def loadImage( self ):
46          """Load Player image and calculate rectangle"""
47
48          if self.playerPosition == -1:    # player has crashed
49              image = self.crashImage
50          else:
51              image = self.movingImages[ self.playerPosition ]
52
53          Sprite.__init__( self, image )
54          self.rectangle.centerx = self.centerX
55          self.rectangle.centery = self.centerY
56
57      def moveLeft( self ):
58          """Change Player image to face one position to left"""
59
```

Fig. 24.6 pygame Space Cruiser example. (Part 2 of 10.)

```
60         if self.playerPosition == -1:   # player crashed
61            self.speed = 1
62            self.playerPosition = 0      # move left of obstacle
63         elif self.playerPosition > 0:
64            self.playerPosition -= 1
65
66         self.loadImage()
67
68      def moveRight( self ):
69         """Change Player image to face one position to right"""
70
71         if self.playerPosition == -1:   # player crashed
72            self.speed = 1
73            self.playerPosition = 2      # move right of obstacle
74         elif self.playerPosition < ( len( self.movingImages ) - 1 ):
75            self.playerPosition += 1
76
77         self.loadImage()
78
79      def decreaseSpeed( self ):
80
81         if self.speed > 0:
82            self.speed -= 1
83
84      def increaseSpeed( self ):
85
86         if self.speed < 10:
87            self.speed += 1
88
89         # player crashed, start player facing down
90         if self.playerPosition == -1:
91            self.playerPosition = 1
92            self.loadImage()
93
94      def collision( self ):
95         """Change Player image to crashed player"""
96
97         self.speed = 0
98         self.playerPosition = -1
99         self.loadImage()
100
101      def collisionBox( self ):
102         """Return smaller bounding box for collision tests"""
103
104         return self.rectangle.inflate( -20, -20 )
105
106      def isMoving( self ):
107         """Player is not moving if speed is 0"""
108
109         if self.speed == 0:
110            return 0
111         else:
112            return 1
```

Fig. 24.6 pygame Space Cruiser example. (Part 3 of 10.)

```
113
114    def distanceMoved( self ):
115       """Player moves twice as fast when facing straight down"""
116
117       xIncrement, yIncrement = 0, 0
118
119       if self.isMoving():
120
121          if self.playerPosition == 1:
122             xIncrement = 0
123             yIncrement = 2 * self.speed
124          else:
125             xIncrement = ( self.playerPosition - 1 ) * self.speed
126             yIncrement = self.speed
127
128       return xIncrement, yIncrement
129
130 class Obstacle( Sprite ):
131    """Moveable Obstacle Sprite"""
132
133    def __init__( self, image, centerX = 0, centerY = 0 ):
134       """Load Obstacle image and initialize rectangle"""
135
136       Sprite.__init__( self, image )
137
138       # move Obstacle to specified location
139       self.positiveRectangle = self.rectangle
140       self.positiveRectangle.centerx = centerX
141       self.positiveRectangle.centery = centerY
142
143       # display Obstacle in moved position to buffer visible area
144       self.rectangle = self.positiveRectangle.move( -60, -60 )
145
146    def move( self, xIncrement, yIncrement ):
147       """Move Obstacle location up by specified increments"""
148
149       self.positiveRectangle.centerx -= xIncrement
150       self.positiveRectangle.centery -= yIncrement
151
152       # change position for next pass
153       if self.positiveRectangle.centery < 25:
154          self.positiveRectangle[ 0 ] += \
155             random.randrange( -640, 640 )
156
157       # keep rectangle values from overflowing
158       self.positiveRectangle[ 0 ] %= 760
159       self.positiveRectangle[ 1 ] %= 600
160
161       # display obstacle in moved position to buffer visible area
162       self.rectangle = self.positiveRectangle.move( -60, -60 )
163
164    def collisionBox( self ):
165       """Return smaller bounding box for collision tests"""
```

Fig. 24.6   pygame Space Cruiser example. (Part 4 of 10.)

```
166
167            return self.rectangle.inflate( -20, -20 )
168
169   class Objective( Sprite ):
170        """Moveable Objective Sprite"""
171
172        def __init__( self, image, centerX = 0, centerY = 0 ):
173            """Load Objective image and initialize rectangle"""
174
175            Sprite.__init__( self, image )
176
177            # move Objective to specified location
178            self.rectangle.centerx = centerX
179            self.rectangle.centery = centerY
180
181        def move( self, xIncrement, yIncrement ):
182            """Move Objective location up by specified increments"""
183
184            self.rectangle.centerx -= xIncrement
185            self.rectangle.centery -= yIncrement
186
187   # place a message on screen
188   def displayMessage( message, screen, background ):
189        font = pygame.font.Font( None, 48 )
190        text = font.render( message, 1, ( 250, 250, 250 ) )
191        textPosition = text.get_rect()
192        textPosition.centerx = background.get_rect().centerx
193        textPosition.centery = background.get_rect().centery
194        return screen.blit( text, textPosition )
195
196   # remove outdated time display and place updated time on screen
197   def updateClock( time, screen, background, oldPosition ):
198        remove = screen.blit( background, oldPosition, oldPosition )
199        font = pygame.font.Font( None, 48 )
200        text = font.render( str( time ), 1, ( 250, 250, 250 ),
201            ( 0, 0, 0 ) )
202        textPosition = text.get_rect()
203        post = screen.blit( text, textPosition )
204        return remove, post
205
206   def main():
207
208        # constants
209        WAIT_TIME = 20                    # time to wait between frames
210        COURSE_DEPTH = 50 * 480           # 50 screens long
211        NUMBER_ASTEROIDS = 20             # controls number of asteroids
212
213        # variables
214        distanceTraveled = 0              # vertical distance
215        nextTime = 0                      # time to generate next frame
216        courseOver = 0                    # the course has not been completed
217        allAsteroids = []                 # randomly generated obstacles
218        dirtyRectangles = []              # screen positions that have changed
```

Fig. 24.6 **pygame** Space Cruiser example. (Part 5 of 10.)

```
219   energyPack = None          # current energy pack on screen
220   timeLeft = 60              # time left to finish course
221   newClock = ( 0, 0, 0, 0 )  # location of clock
222
223   # find path to sounds
224   collisionFile = os.path.join( "data", "collision.wav" )
225   chimeFile = os.path.join( "data", "energy.wav" )
226   startFile = os.path.join( "data", "toneup.wav" )
227   applauseFile = os.path.join( "data", "applause.wav" )
228   gameOverFile = os.path.join( "data", "tonedown.wav" )
229
230   # find path to images
231   shipFiles = []
232   shipFiles.append( os.path.join( "data", "shipLeft.gif" ) )
233   shipFiles.append( os.path.join( "data", "shipDown.gif" ) )
234   shipFiles.append( os.path.join( "data", "shipRight.gif" ) )
235   shipCrashFile = os.path.join( "data", "shipCrashed.gif" )
236   asteroidFile = os.path.join( "data", "Asteroid.gif" )
237   energyPackFile = os.path.join( "data", "Energy.gif" )
238
239   # obtain user preference
240   fullScreen = int( raw_input(
241      "Fullscreen? ( 0 = no, 1 = yes ): " ) )
242
243   # initialize pygame
244   pygame.init()
245
246   if fullScreen:
247      screen = pygame.display.set_mode( ( 640, 480 ), FULLSCREEN )
248   else:
249      screen = pygame.display.set_mode( ( 640, 480 ) )
250
251   pygame.display.set_caption( "Space Cruiser!" )
252   pygame.mouse.set_visible( 0 )   # make mouse invisible
253
254   # create background and fill with black
255   background = pygame.Surface( screen.get_size() ).convert()
256
257   # blit background onto screen and update entire display
258   screen.blit( background, ( 0, 0 ) )
259   pygame.display.update()
260
261   collisionSound = pygame.mixer.Sound( collisionFile )
262   chimeSound = pygame.mixer.Sound( chimeFile )
263   startSound = pygame.mixer.Sound( startFile )
264   applauseSound = pygame.mixer.Sound( applauseFile )
265   gameOverSound = pygame.mixer.Sound( gameOverFile )
266
267   # load images, convert pixel format and make white transparent
268   loadedImages = []
269
270   for file in shipFiles:
271      surface = pygame.image.load( file ).convert()
```

Fig. 24.6 **pygame** Space Cruiser example. (Part 6 of 10.)

```
272            surface.set_colorkey( surface.get_at( ( 0, 0 ) ) )
273            loadedImages.append( surface )
274
275        # load crash image
276        shipCrashImage = pygame.image.load( shipCrashFile ).convert()
277        shipCrashImage.set_colorkey( shipCrashImage.get_at( ( 0, 0 ) ) )
278
279        # initialize theShip
280        centerX = screen.get_width() / 2
281        theShip = Player( loadedImages, shipCrashImage, centerX, 25 )
282
283        # load asteroid image
284        asteroidImage = pygame.image.load( asteroidFile ).convert()
285        asteroidImage.set_colorkey( asteroidImage.get_at( ( 0, 0 ) ) )
286
287        # place asteroid in randomly generated spot
288        for i in range( NUMBER_ASTEROIDS ):
289            allAsteroids.append( Obstacle( asteroidImage,
290                random.randrange( 0, 760 ), random.randrange( 0, 600 ) ) )
291
292        # load energyPack image
293        energyPackImage = pygame.image.load( energyPackFile ).convert()
294        energyPackImage.set_colorkey( surface.get_at( ( 0, 0 ) ) )
295
296        startSound.play()
297        pygame.time.set_timer( USEREVENT, 1000 )
298
299        while not courseOver:
300
301            # wait if moving too fast for selected frame rate
302            currentTime = pygame.time.get_ticks()
303
304            if currentTime < nextTime:
305                pygame.time.delay( nextTime - currentTime )
306
307            nextTime = currentTime + WAIT_TIME
308
309            # remove objects from screen
310            dirtyRectangles.append( theShip.remove( screen,
311                background ) )
312
313            for asteroid in allAsteroids:
314                dirtyRectangles.append( asteroid.remove( screen,
315                    background ) )
316
317            if energyPack is not None:
318                dirtyRectangles.append( energyPack.remove( screen,
319                    background ) )
320
321            # get next event from event queue
322            event = pygame.event.poll()
323
```

Fig. 24.6 **pygame** Space Cruiser example. (Part 7 of 10.)

```
324         # if player quits program or presses escape key
325         if event.type == QUIT or \
326            ( event.type == KEYDOWN and event.key == K_ESCAPE ):
327            sys.exit()
328
329         # if up arrow key was pressed, slow ship
330         elif event.type == KEYDOWN and event.key == K_UP:
331            theShip.decreaseSpeed()
332
333         # if down arrow key was pressed, speed up ship
334         elif event.type == KEYDOWN and event.key == K_DOWN:
335            theShip.increaseSpeed()
336
337         # if right arrow key was pressed, move ship right
338         elif event.type == KEYDOWN and event.key == K_RIGHT:
339            theShip.moveRight()
340
341         # if left arrow key was pressed, move ship left
342         elif event.type == KEYDOWN and event.key == K_LEFT:
343            theShip.moveLeft()
344
345         # one second has passed
346         elif event.type == USEREVENT:
347            timeLeft -= 1
348
349         # 1 in 100 odds of creating new energyPack
350         if energyPack is None and not random.randrange( 100 ):
351            energyPack = Objective( energyPackImage,
352               random.randrange( 0, 640 ), 480 )
353
354         # update obstacle and energyPack positions if ship moving
355         if theShip.isMoving():
356            xIncrement, yIncrement = theShip.distanceMoved()
357
358            for asteroid in allAsteroids:
359               asteroid.move( xIncrement, yIncrement )
360
361            if energyPack is not None:
362               energyPack.move( xIncrement, yIncrement )
363
364               if energyPack.rectangle.bottom < 0:
365                  energyPack = None
366
367            distanceTraveled += yIncrement
368
369         # check for collisions with smaller bounding boxes
370         # for better playability
371         asteroidBoxes = []
372
373         for asteroid in allAsteroids:
374            asteroidBoxes.append( asteroid.collisionBox() )
375
```

Fig. 24.6 **pygame** Space Cruiser example. (Part 8 of 10.)

```
376         # retrieve list of obstacles colliding with player
377         collision = theShip.collisionBox().collidelist(
378            asteroidBoxes )
379
380         # move asteroid one screen down
381         if collision != -1:
382            collisionSound.play()
383            allAsteroids[ collision ].move( 0, -540 )
384            theShip.collision()
385            timeLeft -= 5
386
387         # determine whether player has gotten energyPack
388         if energyPack is not None:
389
390            if theShip.collisionBox().colliderect(
391               energyPack.rectangle ):
392               chimeSound.play()
393               energyPack = None
394               timeLeft += 5
395
396         # place objects on screen
397         dirtyRectangles.append( theShip.place( screen ) )
398
399         for asteroid in allAsteroids:
400            dirtyRectangles.append( asteroid.place( screen ) )
401
402         if energyPack is not None:
403            dirtyRectangles.append( energyPack.place( screen ) )
404
405         # update time
406         oldClock, newClock = updateClock( timeLeft, screen,
407            background, newClock )
408         dirtyRectangles.append( oldClock )
409         dirtyRectangles.append( newClock )
410
411         # update changed areas of display
412         pygame.display.update( dirtyRectangles )
413         dirtyRectangles = []
414
415         # check for course end
416         if distanceTraveled > COURSE_DEPTH:
417            courseOver = 1
418
419         # check for game over
420         elif timeLeft <= 0:
421            break
422
423      if courseOver:
424         applauseSound.play()
425         message = "Asteroid Field Crossed!"
426      else:
427         gameOverSound.play()
428         message = "Game Over!"
```

Fig. 24.6   pygame Space Cruiser example. (Part 9 of 10.)

```
429
430        pygame.display.update( displayMessage( message, screen,
431          background ) )
432
433        # wait until player wants to close program
434        while 1:
435          event = pygame.event.poll()
436
437          if event.type == QUIT or \
438            ( event.type == KEYDOWN and event.key == K_ESCAPE ):
439            break
440
441 if __name__ == "__main__":
442    main()1
```

Fig. 24.6 **pygame** Space Cruiser example. (Part 10 of 10.)

When the program runs, function **main** (lines 206–439) executes. Lines 209–221 create constants and variables that the program uses. These are explained in the discussion. Lines 224–237 locate the sound and image files in the **"data"** subdirectory. The program prompts the player to select either fullscreen or windowed mode. The full-screen mode sets the game window to be the size of the computer screen whereas the windowed mode sets a smaller game display. The player's response is assigned to variable **fullScreen** as **0** (windowed mode) or **1** (full-screen mode).

Line 244 initializes **pygame**. This call to **init** bypasses the need to call each module's **init** method separately. Lines 246–249 set the current display mode with **pygame.display** method **set_mode**. The first argument passed to **set_mode** is a two-element tuple that indicates a display that measures 640 pixels wide and 480 pixels high. If the player selects fullscreen mode, the program passes **set_mode** the constant **FULLSCREEN**. If the player does not select fullscreen mode, the program does not pass an argument to the method. Method **set_mode** returns a **pygame Surface** object, which is a blank canvas onto which the program draws the game. This **Surface** object is assigned to variable **screen**. Line 251 sets the window caption to read **"Space Cruiser!"** by invoking **pygame.display** method **set_caption**. Line 252 calls **pygame.mouse** method **set_visible** with argument **0**, which ensures that the mouse cursor does not appear in the window.

Line 255 creates the game's black background. The program creates a **pygame Surface** that is the same size as the window. The window size is obtained from **screen** method **get_size**. We would like to add objects to the display as quickly as possible. Converting a surface to the same pixel format as the background accomplishes this. **Surface** method **convert** is invoked on the background to convert the surface's pixel format to the display format.

Line 258 blits the background onto the screen. The call to **screen**'s **blit** method in line 258 draws the background onto the screen at position **(0, 0)**—the upper-left corner of the screen. Although the background has been placed on **screen**, the display has not been updated. The **pygame.display** method **update** (line 259) redraws the display. If passed no arguments, **update** redisplays the entire display **Surface**. Method **update** performs in a manner similar to the OpenGL double buffer—**update** draws to a background buffer, then switches it with the current display.

Lines 261–265 load the required sound files. Each line creates a **Sound** object (defined in **pygame.mixer**) from a path created in lines 224–228. Lines 268–276 load the ship images. In this game, the ship has four possible states: *moving left*, *moving down*, *moving right* and *crashed*. The paths to the ship images that represent the first three states are appended to list **shipFiles** (lines 231–233). We explain more about this momentarily when class **Player** is discussed. The **for** loop at line 270–273 iterates over this list, and loads each image. Line 271 loads an image with **pygame.image** method **load**. Note that, just as the background's pixel format was converted, the pixel format of each loaded image must be converted. This increases the speed with which the application places these images on the display. The value returned by **load** is a **pygame Surface** object, which is assigned to variable **surface**.

Line 272 invokes **surface** method **get_at** to obtain the color at position **(0, 0)** of the image. The images used in the game, such as the spaceship and the asteroid, are rectangles in which any extra space has a solid white background color. To create transparency, set the color key to the color of the pixels that should not be drawn. Method **set_colorkey** is passed the color white. The effect is that the color white will not be drawn and, therefore, appear transparent for each surface. Each surface is appended to list **loadedImages**. Lines 276–277 similarly load the image representing the *crashed* state.

Line 280 invokes **screen** method **get_width** to obtain the width of the window. We want our ship to appear halfway across the screen, so we assign **centerX** half of this value. Line 281 creates a **Player** object and assigns it to variable **theShip**. The arguments passed to the **Player** constructor ensure that the ship appears halfway across the screen, 25 pixels from the top. We now discuss two classes, **Sprite** and **Player**, which represent the objects that we next insert on the display.

Class **Sprite** (lines 10–28) defines a *sprite*, which is any 2D image that we place on the screen. The **Sprite** constructor takes a **pygame Surface** object called **image** as input. Line 16 stores this **Surface** in class attribute **image**. Line 17 obtains the image's *bounding rectangle* with **Surface** method **get_rect** and stores the bounding rectangle in class attribute **rectangle**. A bounding rectangle defines the boundaries of the object. The object returned by **get_rect** is a **pygame** *rectstyle* object.

The **pygame** rectstyles are different ways of describing a rectangular object. The first form is a four-element sequence with the syntax [*xpos*, *ypos*, *width*, *height*], in which *xpos* and *ypos* are the coordinates of the upper-left corner of the rectangle, and *width* and *height* are the dimensions of the rectangle. The second form is a pair of sequences represented as [[*xpos*, *ypos*], [*width*, *height*]]. The third form is an object of class **pygame.Rect**. A **Rect** object represents a rectangle. The *rectstyle* returned by **get_rect** is a **Rect** object in which *xpos* and *ypos* are both **0**. Many **pygame** methods accept *rectstyles* as arguments rather than **Rect** objects (including the **Rect** constructor). For such methods, it is possible (and more convenient) simply to pass the method a four-element sequence.

Now, we display image objects on the screen. **Sprite** method **place** (lines 19–22) inserts a given object on the screen. Method **place** takes as an argument a **Surface** object called **screen**. Line 22 invokes the **screen**'s **blit** method to draw the object at position **rectangle**. Note that changes to **Rect** object **rectangle** draws the object in a different location. Method **place** then calls method **blit**, which returns a **Rect** object representing the area updated.

A programmer eliminates an object from the display by using **Sprite** method **remove** (lines 24–28) to draw the background over an object (lines 27–28). This method calls to **blit** with three arguments, two of which are **Rect** objects. The third argument specifies what section of **background** to draw at the position specified by the **Rect** object. If no third argument is specified, the entire background is displayed at the position specified by **rectangle**. Method **remove** returns a **Rect** representing the blitted area.

Next, the program implements the player's object—**theShip**. Class **Player** (lines 30–128) represents the player-controlled object, which appears to move across the screen. The game simulates ship movement by moving the asteroids up the screen. The player attempts to navigate the space ship safely through an asteroid field. Players manipulate their objects' movements until the game is over. **Player** inherits from class **Sprite**. Line 281 creates a **Player** object, which invokes **Player**'s constructor (lines 33–43). Lines 37–40 assign the image surfaces and starting position to class attributes **movingImages**, **crashImage**, **centerX** and **centerY**. Line 41 sets **playerPosition** to 1. Variable **playerPosition** is the index of the displayed image; the displayed image depends on the direction of the ship. Attribute **movingImages** is a list of length three in which the indices **0**, **1** and **2** represent *moving left*, *moving down* and *moving right*, respectively. Thus, line 42 starts the **Player** in state *moving down*. Attribute **playerPosition**, with a value **−1**, indicates the player *crashed*. As a result of the crash, line 42 sets attribute **speed** to **0**, and line 43 calls method **loadImage**.

As a player moves through the game by pressing keys on a keyboard, method **loadImage** (lines 45–55) updates the **Player** attributes. Lines 48–51 determine the correct image to use. If the player has not crashed, the program uses the image that represents the current player state (line 51). Line 53 invokes **Sprite**'s constructor to update the **image** and **rectangle** attributes. Lines 54–55 move the object to the correct position by changing **rectangle**'s **centerx** and **centery** attributes.

Player methods **moveLeft** and **moveRight** are called when the player presses the left and right arrow keys, respectively. The two methods are similar, so we discuss them together. First, an **if** statement determines whether the player has crashed (i.e., **playerPosition** is **−1**). If so, **speed** is reduced to 1, and the program positions the player to either the left (line 62) or the right (line 73) of the obstacle. If the player is not as far left or right as possible, the program moves the player left (line 64) or right (line 75) one position when a player presses the left or right arrow key, respectively. Finally, method **loadImage** updates the image and the position.

Method **decreaseSpeed** (lines 79–82) is called when the user presses the up arrow key to decrease attribute **speed** by **1**. Pressing the down arrow key invokes method **increaseSpeed**, which increases **speed** by **1** (lines 84–92). Lines 90–92 determine whether the player crashed. If so, **playerPosition** is set to **1** (*moving down*) and the image is updated (line 92).

Player method **collision** (lines 94–99) is called when the ship collides with an asteroid. Method **collision** sets **speed** to **0**, sets **playerPosition** to **−1** (*crashed*) and invokes method **loadImage**. Collisions are determined with the **Rect** returned by method **collisionBox** (lines 101–104), which calls **Rect** method **inflate** and returns the results. Note that we test for collisions with smaller bounding rectangles because the spaceship image does not completely fill its rectangle. Players would get frustrated if collisions occurred when bounding rectangles intersected, but images did not. Using smaller bounding rectangles for collision detection is sometimes referred to as *sub-rect-angle collision*. We achieve a smaller bounding rectangle by calling method **inflate**, which returns a new **Rect**. The method arguments, in this example, **-20** and **-20**, specify the amount by which the calling **Rect** is scaled. A negative parameter reduces the rectangle while a positive method argument enlarges the rectangle around its center by the specified amount.

Method **distanceMoved** (lines 114–128) determines the change in the player's position. Line 119 invokes method **isMoving** (lines 106–112) to test whether the player is moving. If the player is moving, the program must calculate **xIncrement** and **yIncrement**. Lines 121–126 use **playerPosition** and **speed** to determine the distance moved. When the player *moves down*, the player moves twice as fast in the vertical direction than when *moving left* or *moving right*.

Class **Obstacle** (lines 130–167) inherits from **Sprite**. An **Obstacle** represents an object that the player must avoid. In this game, the object is an asteroid. When an **Obstacle** is created, its constructor (lines 133–144) is invoked. Line 136 calls the **Sprite** constructor to initialize the **image** and **rectangle** attributes.

After instantiating a **Player** (line 281), the program creates the asteroids. Lines 284–285 load the asteroid image and makes the image's white pixels transparent. The **for** loop (lines 288–290) creates the number of asteroids specified by **NUMBER_ASTEROID**, reusing the asteroid image for each one. Each asteroid is an object of class **Obstacle**. The arguments passed to **Obstacle**'s constructor ensure that each asteroid is positioned randomly on the screen. Note that the values passed to **random.randrange** are larger than the screen size, to ensure that asteroids move onto the screen, rather than suddenly appearing. The direction the asteroids move depends on the current state of the ship. When an asteroid moves off the top of the screen, it is placed on the bottom of the screen again, creating a scrolling effect.

In this game, the asteroids move off the screen completely (i.e., into negative screen coordinates) before the program removes them and then places them back on the screen. To achieve this, the program buffers the visible area by tracking two locations for each **Obstacle**. Method **rectangle** represents the actual location of the asteroid. This is where we **place** the object. Object attribute **positiveRectangle** represents the coordinates of **rectangle** shifted into positive screen coordinates. Lines 139–141 create and initialize the position of **positiveRectangle**. Line 144 updates **rectangle** by invoking **Rect** method **move**. After this method call, **rectangle** is now a rectangle of the same dimensions as **positiveRectangle**, but shifted by **-60** pixels in both the *x* and *y* directions. This translation moves the ship away from the asteroid with which it collided.

Obstacle method **move** (lines 146–162) translates the object to a new location. Method **move** requires arguments **xIncrement** and **yIncrement**. Recall that class **Player** has method **distanceMoved**. This method returns the necessary values. Lines 149–150 move the position of **positiveRectangle** up the screen by the specified amounts. The **if** statement at line 153 determines whether the asteroid has reached the top of the screen. If so, lines 154–155 add a random integer to the *xpos* of **positiveRect-angle**. This ensures that the asteroid does not have the same *x*-coordinate as on its previous pass the next time the asteroid appears on the screen. This randomizes where the asteroid reappears on the screen. The program treats **Rect** object **positiveRect-**

angle as if it were a four-element sequence of the form [*xpos*, *ypos*, *width*, *height*]. Lines 158–159 ensure that the *xpos* and *ypos* of **positiveRectangle** are within range. Finally, now that **positiveRectangle** has been updated, **Rect** method **move** (line 162) obtains the new **rectangle** value.

As with class **Player**, **Obstacle** collisions are evaluated with the **Rect** returned by method **collisionBox**, which calls **Rect** method **inflate** and returns the results (lines 164–169).

The game also includes energy-pack images. When a player collects one, time is added to the clock. After creating the asteroids (lines 288–290), methods **load** and **convert** load and convert the energy-pack image (line 293), setting white to transparent (line 294). During gameplay, energy packs are created from class **Objective**. Class **Objective** (lines 169–184) has a constructor (lines 172–179) and method **move** (lines 181–185) similar to those of class **Obstacle**. Line 296 invokes **Sound** method **play** to play **start-Sound**. The player hears this sound when the game begins. Line 297 invokes **pygame.time** method **set_timer** to generate a **USEREVENT** every **1000** milliseconds (one second). **USEREVENT** is a **pygame** constant that represents a user-defined event. The effect of line 297 is that, a **USEREVENT** event is placed onto the event queue once per second. Module **pygame**'s *event system* is discussed in detail later in this section.

The **while** loop in lines 299–421 plays the game. Each iteration determines whether **courseOver** is **0**. If so, the player's spaceship has not completed crossing the asteroid field and gameplay continues. Lines 302–307 use **pygame** module **time** to ensure that the game does not execute too quickly. Line 302 invokes **pygame.time** method **get_ticks**, which returns the time in milliseconds since **pygame.time** was imported. This value is stored in variable **currentTime**. If **currentTime** is less than **next-Time**—the previous number of "ticks" plus the constant **WAIT_TIME**—we invoke **time** method **delay** (line 305) to pause execution for a given number of milliseconds. The value passed to **delay** is the number of milliseconds remaining until **nextTime**.

Next, the program updates the display. To update the positions of all objects on the screen, the program removes each object, changes its position and places (i.e., blits) it on the screen. Then **pygame.display.update** (as in line 259) updates the entire display. However, updating the entire display is inefficient and slow. A popular method used to speed up screen updates is called *dirty rectangle animation*. In dirty rectangle animation, a list of rectangles (representing areas of the display) that have been altered (i.e., have become "dirty") is recorded. After removing of an object from the screen, that object's current rectangle is appended to the list, then the object's position is updated. Finally, the program places the object back on the screen and appends its new rectangle to the list. Method **update** is called with the list of "dirty" rectangles. The effect is that **update** redraws only those parts of the display that have changed. This dramatically improves game performance. Note that the list of rectangles passed to **update** can be a list of any *rectstyle*.

This game implements dirty rectangle animation. Lines 310–319 remove the ship, each asteroid and the energy pack (if one is present) from the screen by invoking their **remove** methods. Each call to **remove** returns a **Rect** representing the area changed. Each **Rect** is appended to the list **dirtyRectangles**.

We now discuss **pygame** event handling. As with **Tkinter**, events can be generated from the keyboard or mouse. Module **pygame** also handles other events, including joystick events. One method of **pygame** event handling uses the event queue. As events are detected, they are placed in the queue. Each **Event** object in the queue has a **type** attribute. Keypress **Event**s have **type KEYDOWN**. Most user-defined events have type **USEREVENT**. A request to quit the game results in a **QUIT** event.

Line 322 invokes **pygame.event** method **poll**, which returns the next **Event** waiting in the queue. This object is assigned to variable **event**. If **event** is a request to quit the game (**QUIT**) or a **KEYDOWN** event with **key** attribute **K_ESCAPE**, the program exits (line 327). Lines 329–343 determine whether **event** was generated by any of the four arrow keys (**K_UP**, **K_DOWN**, **K_RIGHT** or **K_LEFT**). If so, the program invokes the corresponding **Player** method. Recall now that line 297 places one **USEREVENT** event on the event queue each second. Line 346 determines whether **event** is one of these. If so, **timeLeft**, the time remaining to cross the asteroid field, is reduced by **1** (line 347).

Lines 350–352 attempt to create a new energy pack. If an energy pack does not exist (**energyPack** is **None**) and **randrange** returns **0**, the program creates a new **energyPack** from class **Objective**. The arguments passed to **Objective**'s constructor ensure that the pack starts at a random position at the bottom of the screen. Note that the odds of creating a new pack if one does not exist are 1 in 100 because the method call passes **100** to **randrange**.

The program then updates the positions of the asteroids and energy packs (if any exist). If the ship is moving (i.e., **speed > 0**), the program retrieves the **xIncrement** and **yIncrement** from **Player** method **distanceMoved** (line 356). The program also updates the position of each asteroid (lines 358–359) and the position of the energy pack (lines 361–362). Line 364 determines whether the energy pack has moved off the top of the screen. If so, the program destroys the current energy pack (line 365). Line 367 increments **distanceTraveled**.

Next, the program tests for asteroid collisions. Lines 371–374 create a list, **asteroidBoxes**, of **Rect**s returned from each asteroid's **collisionBox** method. Lines 377–378 then passes this list to **Rect** method **collidelist**, which returns the index of the first *rectstyle* in a list that overlaps the base rectangle. The base rectangle is the **Rect** returned from the ship's **collisionBox** method. When an overlap is found, **collideList** stops checking the remaining list. If no overlap is found, **collideList** returns **–1**. If the ship collides with an asteroid (line 381), the program plays a collision sound (line 382) and moves the offending asteroid out of the way (line 383). Lines 384–385 invoke the ship's **collision** method and deduct **5** seconds from the time remaining.

Lines 388–394 determine whether the player obtained an energy pack. Lines 390–391 invoke **Rect** method **colliderect**. Method **colliderect** returns **true** if the calling **Rect** overlaps the argument *rectstyle*. If the player obtained an energy pack, the game plays **chimeSound**, removes the energy pack and adds **5** seconds to the clock (lines 392–394).

Next, the program displays the clock so that the user can view the time that remains to cross the asteroid field. Lines 397–403 **place** all the objects back on the screen and append their rectangles to **dirtyRectangles**. Lines 406–409 update the clock in the upper-left corner of the screen. Method **updateClock** (lines 197–204) removes the previous clock **Surface**, creates a new clock and places it onto the screen. A **pygame.font.Font** object (line 199) allows the program to render text into a **Surface**. The **Font** constructor takes two arguments. The first is the name of the font file to use. If **None** is specified, **Font** uses the **pygame** default font file (**bluebold.ttf**). The second argument is the size of the font. Line 199 creates a game clock with a **Font** of type *bluebold* and size **48**. Lines 200–201 invoke **font**'s **render** method to create a new **Surface** with specified text. Method **render** accepts up to four arguments. The first argument is the text to create. The second specifies whether to use *antialiasing* (edge smoothing). The third argument is the font's RGB color. The fourth is the RGB color of the background. If no fourth argument is specified, the text background will be transparent. Function **updateClock** returns both the old (**remove**) and new (**post**) rectangles.

Once the clock has been created and blitted onto the screen, lines 408–409 append the clock's previous rectangle and current rectangle to **dirtyRectangles**. Line 412 is the final step in the rectangle animation in which the program updates every altered area. Without this line, the player would not see any change in the display. Line 413 initializes **dirtyRectangles** for the next iteration.

If the player has crossed the asteroid field (line 416), the program sets **courseOver** to **1**. This ensures that the **while** loop exits after the current iteration. If the player has not completed crossing the asteroid field, the program determines whether the player has run out of time (line 420). If so, the program exits the **while** loop.

When the **while** loop terminates, execution continues at line 423 and determines whether the player won or lost the game. If the player won, the game plays **applauseSound** and sets **message** to **"Asteroid Field Crossed!"**. Otherwise, the program plays **gameOverSound** and sets **message** to **"Game Over!"**. Lines 430–431 invoke **pygame.display** method **update** to display **message** to the player. Method **displayMessage** returns the *rectstyle* passed to **update**. Method **displayMessage** (lines 188–194) places a message onto the screen and returns the area of the screen that has been modified. The **while** loop in lines 434–439 continues executing until the user to exit the program. Figure 24.7 shows a sample screen capture of the space-cruiser game.

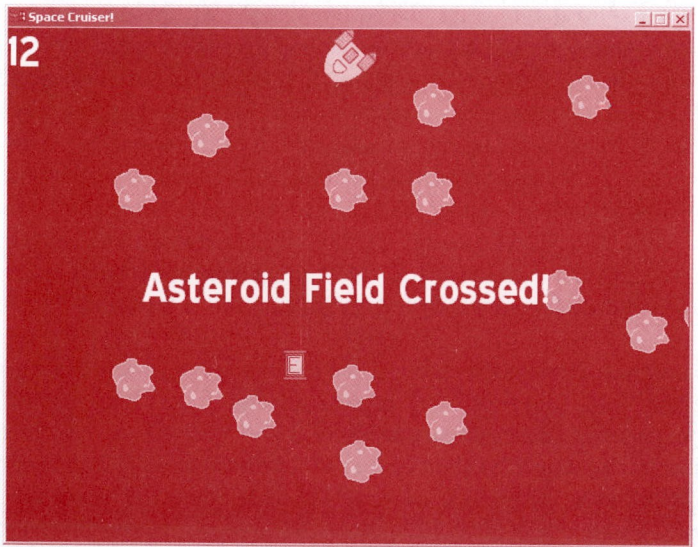

Fig. 24.7   Space-cruiser game.

24.10 Internet and World Wide Web Resources

pyopengl.sourceforge.net
The main Web site of the **PyOpenGL** module describes the module and provides links to documentation and to a download page.

www.wag.caltech.edu/home/rpm/python_course/Lecture_7.pdf
This series of lecture slides discusses the interaction between Python and **OpenGL**. The slides include a few introductory examples.

www.opengl.org
The **OpenGL** Web site includes a FAQ, downloads, documentation and forums.

www.alice.org
The Alice Web site provides links to downloads and documentation.

www.pygame.org
The **pygame** Web site offers module **pygame** for download. The site also offers links to documentation and sample code.

SUMMARY

- Python module **PyOpenGL**, which encapsulates the capabilities of the OpenGL Application Programming Interface (API), is a library for rendering two-dimensional (2D) and three-dimensional (3D) graphics.

- The OpenGL Utility Toolkit (GLUT), **wxPython**, **Tkinter** and **FxPy** are APIs that provide an OpenGL context (i.e., an electronic "canvas") in which to display OpenGL-rendered graphics.

- Module **PyOpenGL** includes the **Tkinter** component **Opengl**, which displays OpenGL graphics and allows the programmer to use **Tkinter** components and layout managers as well.

- The **Opengl** component has an event bound to each mouse button. The **Opengl** component allows users to move objects by pressing and holding the left mouse button. To rotate an object, users hold the middle mouse button (if one is available). To resize objects, users drag the mouse while holding the right mouse button.

- Setting the **Opengl** component's attribute **double** to **1** enables double buffering. Double buffering maintains two screen buffers—one for display purposes (the on-screen buffer) and the other for drawing purposes (the off-screen buffer). The application draws the next frame—the next image to be displayed—on the off-screen buffer. When the program finishes drawing the next frame, the program swaps the two buffers to display the new frame's contents. In contrast, when single buffering is used, the program draws directly to the screen. In this case, the display is not as smooth, because the program clears the drawing area before drawing each new frame. Depending on the speed of your computer system, this clearing operation may result in a brief flash of the background color before the next frame is displayed.

- A program calls **opengl**'s **redraw** method to update the on-screen display each time the image changes.

- **PyOpenGL** method **set_eyepoint** moves the camera away from the scene (i.e., the three-dimensional image) by a programmer-specified amount. The camera defines the viewer's perspective in relation to the scene. Passing larger values to **set_eyepoint** make the image smaller on the screen as the eye point moves further from the image. Negative argument values enable the user to view the image from behind.

- **PyOpenGL** function **glClearColor** specifies the color that function **glClear** uses. Function **glClearColor** requires a color with red, green, blue and alpha values as an argument.

- Typically, colors are represented by either a three-element tuple containing values in the range 0.0–1.0 for the red, green and blue portions of a color, respectively; or a four-element tuple in which the first three elements represent the red, green and blue portions of the color and the last element represents the alpha (also called the transparency).

- The alpha value of a color determines how that color is combined with other colors when those colors are layered in an image. The alpha value represents whether the color is solid (alpha value 0.0) or transparent (alpha value 1.0). Alpha values between 0.0 and 1.0, indicate the amount of transparency.

- The value **GL_COLOR_BUFFER_BIT** passed to **glClear** states that the function should clear the color buffer. The color buffer stores information about each of the window's pixels ("picture elements"), which represent dots of color on the screen. The color buffer stores each pixel's red, green and blue color components.

- **PyOpenGL** function **glClear** stores the color specified by function **glClearColor** in each entry of the color buffer. This replaces any old values in the color buffer. This effectively clears the display with the color previously specified by function **glClearColor**.

- **PyOpenGL** function **glDisable** disables the lighting (specified by the argument **GL_LIGHTING**). Lighting in computer graphics refers to the placements of lights in the scene. **OpenGL** has ten parameters to specify the light source (e.g., position, direction, lighting color, etc.). If lighting is enabled, the object's color is calculated from the light-source parameters; otherwise, the color specified by **glClearColor** is used for the light source.

- To draw using OpenGL, the programmer specifies vertices (points). The vertices are placed between a call to function **glBegin** and a call to function **glEnd**. The argument passed to **glBegin** defines what type of shape is drawn.

- Function **glBegin** called with argument **GL_QUAD_STRIP** instructs OpenGL to draw a group of connected quadrilaterals (i.e., four-sided figures). The function uses the first four vertices in the list (vertices 1–4) to draw the first quadrilateral. The second quadrilateral is defined by vertices 3–6 in the list, and so on. **GL_QUAD_STRIP** needs the last two vertices to be the same as the first two vertices to draw the quadrilateral. The result is a series of connected polygons defined by the vertices specified before the call to function **glEnd**.

- **PyOpenGL** function **glColor3f** changes the current drawing color. Function **glColor3f** takes three floating-point numbers that represent an RGB color as arguments.

- Function **glVertex3f** draws a point in three-dimensional space. Function **glVertex3f** takes three floating-point arguments, which specify the location of a point.

- Function **apply** takes a function as its first argument and a tuple of the values to be passed to the function as its second argument. The method calls the function, passing it the parameters.

- Method **glRotate** accepts four arguments. The first argument sets the angle of rotation in degrees. The last three floating-point numbers describe the line around which the shape rotates. The line passes through the origin *(0.0, 0.0, 0.0)* and the specified point *(1.0, 0.0, 0.0)*.

- Method **tkRedraw** updates the **Opengl** component.

- Setting **autospin_allowed** to **1** allows users to rotate a shape continuously by holding down the middle-mouse button on a three-button mouse, dragging the mouse in the direction of the desired rotation and releasing the mouse button.

- The **GLUT** library provides functions that draw three-dimensional shapes.

- Functions **glutWireCube** and **glutSolidCube** accept the length of the cube's side as an argument—**3**, in this case.

- Functions **glutWireIcosahedron** and **glutSolidIcosahedron**, which take no arguments, create a 20-sided shape with a radius of 1.0.

- Functions **glutWireCone** and **glutSolidCone** take four arguments. The first two arguments correspond to the base's radius and the cone's height. The next argument is the number of slices (i.e., the number of subsections of the cone defined by lines from the tip to the base). A cone with three slices resembles a pyramid with sides. Increasing the number of slices gives the cone a more rounded appearance. The fourth argument sets the number of stacks—the number of cone subdivisions created by lines parallel to the base.

- Functions **glutWireTorus** and **glutSolidTorus** accept four arguments. The first two specify the inner and total radii of the doughnut shape. The inner radius is the inner space (e.g, the "doughnut hole") while the total radius is the distance from the torus's center to the outermost edge (e.g., the radius of the entire doughnut-shaped object). The third argument specifies the number of lines going around the entire torus shape. The last argument indicates the number of lines dividing the torus into sections.

- Functions **glutWireTeapot** and **glutSolidTeapot**, which draw a teapot, accept the relative size of the shape as an argument.

- Alice is a 3D Interactive Graphics Programming Environment that makes 3D modeling accessible even to novice Python programmers.

- A programmer can use Python to control the Alice environment. Alice provides a simple and intuitive interface that allows a developer to place objects in the Alice "world." After the programmer designs the initial scene, a Python script animates the objects in the Alice world.

- Alice uses a version of the Python interpreter to parse Python code. Although Python normally is case sensitive, the Alice interpreter does not treat Python as a case-sensitive language.

- Alice function **Move** takes three arguments—the direction of the movement, the amount of the movement in meters and the amount of time the movement should take in seconds.

- Alice function **Turn** takes three arguments as well—the direction of the turn, the amount of the turn in rotations and the duration of the turn.

- Alice function **DoInOrder** accepts a comma-separated list of animations and performs them sequentially.

- Alice function **AControlPanel** creates a window to which all the control buttons are attached.

- Alice option **Command** associates the selection of a radio button with a callback.

- A call to Alice function **MakeButton** creates a button. The label displayed on each button is the string assigned to **Caption**.

- Alice function **RespondToCollisionWith** sets an object's response to a collision with another object as an action, such as **Object.Stop**.

- Alice function **MoveTo** moves an object to another specified object.

- An alarm triggers an event after a specified amount of time. **Alice.SetAlarm** takes the time to wait as the first argument and a function to call when that time quantum expires.

- **pygame** is a set of modules are written by Pete Shinners that allow programmers to create multimedia programs and games.

- The **pygame** modules use the Simple DirectMedia Layer (SDL), which is a cross-platform library that provides a uniform API to access multimedia hardware.

- **pygame**'s contains class **CD** and methods to initialize a CD-ROM subsystem.

- Class **CD** represents the user's CD-ROM drive. Methods of class **CD** allow users to access an audio compact disc (CD) in a computer's CD-ROM drive.

- Module **cdrom**'s **get_count** method returns the number of CD-ROM drives on the computer.
- The value passed to the **CD** constructor is the identification (ID) number of the CD-ROM drive. If more than one CD-ROM drive is installed on a computer system, the program uses the primary CD-ROM drive. The constructor receives **0** as an argument, because the primary CD-ROM's drive identification number is always **0**.
- Method **get_init** determines whether the CD-ROM is initialized.
- **CD** method **get_empty** determines whether the CD-ROM drive is empty.
- **CD** method **quit** uninitializes a **CD** object.
- Method **get_numtracks** gets the total number of audio tracks on the CD disc.
- Method **stop** stops the CD.
- A disc is ejected with **CD** method **eject**.
- **CD** method **get_current** returns the number of seconds that the track has played.
- **CD** method **get_track_length** returns the track length.
- **pygame**'s **movie** module contains a method that creates a **Movie** object, which represents an open moving pictures experts group (MPEG) file. Method **pygame.movie.Movie** takes one argument—the movie file name. Class **Movie** provides methods to play, stop, pause and rewind movies.
- Method **pygame.init** initializes every **pygame** module. This call is a shortcut—the program does not have to call each module's **init** method separately.
- The **Movie** object's method **get_size** returns the movie's size as a tuple containing the width and height.
- Method **pygame.display set_mode** takes as an argument a two-element tuple that indicates a display width and height in pixels. The value returned by **set_mode** is a **pygame Surface** object, which is a blank canvas where the program displays the movie.
- Passing **1** to **pygame.mouse** method **set_visible** enables the mouse pointer.
- Method **convert** creates a copy of a **Surface** object with the object's pixel format converted to the display's. Pixels with the same format are represented by the same number of bits. Setting the surface and the button to the same pixel format enables the program to blit (i.e., place one surface on another) more quickly.
- Method **load** places an item onto the **pygame Surface**.
- Method **get_rect** of the **Surface** object returns a **Rect** object (i.e., a **pygame** rectangle).
- Method **flip** of module **pygame.display** updates the entire display surface.
- Method **set_display** of class **Movie** takes two arguments—the output **Surface** object for the movie and the position of the top-left corner of the movie. The second argument is optional. If the second argument is not supplied, the default value, **(0, 0)**, is used.
- Method **pygame.event wait** waits for and returns the next **Event** object waiting in the queue.
- Method **pygame.mouse.get_pressed** returns a sequence of three values that indicate whether the mouse's left, middle or right button has been clicked. The status of the right mouse button is the first item in the sequence. If the right-mouse button has been pressed, this value evaluates to true.
- Method **collidepoint** of class **Rect** determines whether the mouse click was inside or on the border of the button. This method takes one argument, which specifies the given point's position, and returns true if the point is inside the rectangle or on its border.

- Although other types of programs are developed with **pygame**, the most common applications are games.

- Passing the constant **FULLSCREEN** to method **set_mode** set the window to the screen size.

- The window size is obtained from **Surface** object method **get_size**.

- **Surface** method **get_at** obtains the color at a specified position of the image.

- **Surface** method **get_width** returns the width of the window.

- A sprite is any 2D image that is placed on the screen.

- **Surface** method **get_rect** returns an image's bounding rectangle.

- The **pygame** rectstyles are different ways of describing a rectangular object. The first possible way is a four-element sequence of the form [*xpos, ypos, width, height*], in which *xpos* and *ypos* are the coordinates of the upper-left corner of the rectangle, and *width* and *height* are the dimensions of the rectangle. The second form is a pair of sequences represented as [[*xpos, ypos*], [*width, height*]]. The third is an object of class **pygame.Rect**, which represents a rectangle. The *rectstyle* returned by **get_rect** is a **Rect** object in which *xpos* and *ypos* are both **0**. Many **pygame** methods accept *rectstyles* as arguments rather than **Rect** objects (including the **Rect** constructor). For such methods, it is possible (and more convenient) simply to pass the method a four-element sequence.

- Method **pygame.display.update** updates the entire display. However, updating the entire display is inefficient and slow. A popular method used to speed up screen updates is called dirty rectangle animation. In dirty rectangle animation, a list of rectangles (representing areas of the display) that have been altered (i.e., have become "dirty") is recorded. After removing of an object from the screen, that object's current rectangle is appended to the list, then the object's position is updated. Finally, the program places the object back on the screen and appends its new rectangle to the list.

- One method of **pygame** event handling uses the event queue. As events are detected, they are placed in the queue. Each **Event** object in the queue has a **type** attribute. Keypress **Event**s have **type KEYDOWN**. Most user-defined events have type **USEREVENT**. A request to quit the game results in a **QUIT** event.

- **pygame.event** method **poll** returns the next **Event** waiting in the queue.

- A **pygame.font.Font** object allows the program to render text into a **Surface**. The **Font** constructor takes two arguments. The first is the name of the font file to use. If **None** is specified, **Font** uses the **pygame** default font file (**bluebold.ttf**). The second argument is the size of the font.

- A **Font** object's **render** method creates a new **Surface** with specified text. Method **render** accepts up to four arguments. The first argument is the text to create. The second specifies whether to use antialiasing (edge smoothing). The third argument is the font's RGB color. The fourth is the RGB color of the background. If no fourth argument is specified, the text background will be transparent.

TERMINOLOGY

after method
Alice Interactive Graphics Programming
   Environment
Alice SetAlarm function
angle of rotation
animation

antialiasing
blit method
bounding rectangle
cdrom module
centery attribute
collidelist method

two-dimensional game　　　　　　　**USEREVENT** event
type attribute　　　　　　　　　　windowed mode
user-defined event　　　　　　　　　**zfill** function

SELF-REVIEW EXERCISES

24.1　Fill in the blanks in each of the following statements:

a) Module _____ allows the programmer to write Python programs that create colorful, interactive 2D/3D graphics.

b) In an **Opengl** component, by default, the _____ button (in a three-button mouse) rotates objects.

c) **PyOpenGL** module _____ provides ways to create three-dimensional shapes.

d) **pygame** modules use the _____ library.

e) The _____ module decodes MPEG movies.

f) The three events handled by **pygame** are _____, _____ and _____.

g) Flag _____, an _____ constant, indicates fullscreen mode.

h) Method **load** returns _____ object.

i) Method _____ creates transparency.

j) The **pygame.display** method _____ redraws a display.

24.2　State whether each of the following is *true* or *false*. If *false*, explain why.

a) When double buffering is used, OpenGL maintains two screen buffers—one to display, and one to update.

b) Although Alice imposes several significant modifications on Python, Python remains case sensitive in Alice.

c) The **CD** module initializes the CD-ROM.

d) The **movie** module can decode all types of movies.

e) Calling **pygame.display.update** with no argument updates the entire display screen.

f) The **Opengl** component provides default bindings for a two-button mouse.

g) Method **glutWireCube** takes the vertices of its corners as arguments.

h) **CD** method **get_song_length** returns the length of a song on a CD.

i) A **destroy** method acts as a destructor for Tkinter programs.

j) Games are the most common applications developed with **pygame**.

ANSWERS TO SELF REVIEW EXERCISES

24.1 a) **PyOpenGL**. b) middle. c) **GLUT**. d) Simple DirectMedia Layer (SDL). e) **pygame.movie**. f) keyboard, mouse, joystick. g) **FULLSCREEN, SDL**. h) **pygame Surface**. i) **set_colorkey**. j) **update**.

24.2　a) True. b) False. In Alice, Python is case insensitive. c) False. **CD** is a **pygame** class, not a **pygame** module. To initialize the CD-ROM, use the **cdrom** module. d) False. The **movie** module can decode only MPEG movies. e) True. g) False. Method **glutWireCube** accepts the length of the cube's side as its only argument. h) False. **CD** method **get_track_length** returns the length of a song on a CD. i) True. j) True.

EXERCISES

24.3　Modify **fig24_01.py** so that it allows users to start rotation, stop rotation and change the rotation direction.

24.4   Modify **fig24_02.py** to make the shape spin.

24.5   Modify **fig24_05.py** by adding a track list to the output Window, so that the user can listen to a specific track.

24.6   Modify **fig24_06.py** to allow the user to play, stop, pause and rewind a movie.

24.7   Modify the solution from Exercise 24.6 so that the program displays times in the following format: "00:00/00:00." The first "00:00" represents the current time. The second "00:00" represents the total time.

24.8   Modify **fig24_07.py** to add stars to the program. Each time the space ship comes in contact with a star, the player collects 10 points. Display the points next to the time. [*Note*: The star image file is provided on the CD-ROM that accompanies this text.]

25

Python Server Pages (PSP)

Objectives

- To be able to create and deploy Python Server Pages (PSP).
- To use Python and PSP's implicit objects to create dynamic Web pages.
- To understand PSP actions.
- To embed Python scriptlets in XHTML.
- To specify global-PSP information using directives.
- To create an XML-based message forum.

A tomato does not communicate with a tomato, we believe. We could be wrong.
Gustav Eckstein

A donkey appears to me like a horse translated into Dutch.
Georg Christoph Lichtenberg

A fair request should be followed by the deed in silence.
Dante Alighieri

Talent is a question of quantity. Talent does not write one page: it writes three hundred.
Jules Renard

Every action must be due to one or other of seven causes: chance, nature, compulsion, habit, reasoning, anger, or appetite.
Aristotle

25.1 Introduction

This chapter introduces *Python Server Pages (PSP)*, which simplify the generation and delivery of dynamic Web content. PSP enables Web-application programmers to create dynamic content by reusing predefined components and by interacting with components through server-side scripting.

This chapter employs *Webware*, a suite of software that facilitates generating dynamic Web content in Python. Webware's WebKit package acts as a *Python servlet engine* that produces XHTML. WebKit is an application server that manages and executes Python *servlets*, which are Python objects that respond to client requests and execute in a Web server. Webware's PSP capabilities are built on WebKit, so Webware's WebKit package must be installed and configured. For installation and configuration instructions, please visit **www.deitel.com**. We developed the examples in this chapter using Webware 0.6 and Python 2.2b2. The Python servlets and PSPs introduced in this chapter are specific to Webware, which is a separate entity from the Python Software Foundation.

WebKit provides a set of core classes for creating Python servlets and PSPs, in addition to helper classes that provide functionality that Web developers often need. Classes for programming servlets are located in the **Webware/WebKit** directory; classes specific to PSP programming are located in the directory **Webware/PSP**. We discuss many of these classes throughout this chapter as we present PSP fundamentals. For more information on PSP, visit **Webware/PSP/Docs/UsersGuide.html**.

25.2 Python Servlets[1]

Before we discuss PSP, let us briefly look at Python servlets. When a client sends a PSP request to the Web server, the Web server calls the servlet *container*, which is a process that manages servlet requests. In Webware, **AppServer** acts as the servlet container. When called, the container translates the PSP into a new program, called a servlet, that handles the PSP request.

A servlet's life cycle begins when the servlet container loads the servlet into memory—normally, in response to the first request that the servlet receives. Before the servlet can handle a request, the servlet container invokes the servlet's **awake** method to initialize the servlet. After **awake** completes, the servlet can respond to the request. The servlet's **respond** method receives and processes the request, and sends a response to the client. When a request is done, the container invokes the servlet's **sleep** method to release servlet resources. By default, a servlet is constructed once, then processes many requests. During a servlet's life cycle, the container invokes methods **awake**, **respond** and **sleep** for each request that the servlet processes.

The servlet container uses classes and methods that WebKit provides. When a client sends a PSP request to the Web server, WebKit's **ServletFactory** (an abstract class that defines protocols used by applications to create servlets) creates a servlet instance to handle the request. A Web application uses the servlet factory to create servlets for *transactions*. In Webware, a transaction is an object that contains all of the objects involved in a single request-response cycle. Each time a client's Web browser fetches a page, a new transaction object is created and is destroyed after the transaction object finishes processing that page. Classes that are involved in a transaction include **Application**, **Request**, **Response**, **Session** and **Servlet**.

The **Application** class, together with various classes in the WebKit, manages (i.e., creates and destroys) servlets in a transaction. The **Request** class contains information about a client's request (e.g., the time and location from which the request was made.) Web developers typically use subclass **HTTPRequest**, which extends the functionality of class **Request** by adding capabilities such as session tracking, cookies and authentication. The **Response** class is capable of sending a response to the client. Similar to **HTTPRequest**, Web developers often use subclass **HTTPResponse**, which extends the functionality of class **Response** by adding capabilities for easy manipulation of response-header information, such as cookie support. The **Session** class creates a session object that is associated

---

1. The details of Python servlets are beyond the scope of this chapter. In fact, it is not necessary to understand Python servlets to understand the material presented in this chapter. Readers who are interested in a deeper treatment of Python servlets can visit:
   webware.sourceforge.net/Webware/WebKit/Docs/Source/
   ClassHier.html

with a specific user for a specified amount of time; PSPs use **Session** objects to track user information (e.g., pages that the user has visited) on the server.

The **Servlet** subclass *HTTPServlet* supports *get*, *post*, *put*, *delete*, *options* and *trace* requests. A *get* request is used to get data from a server; a *post* request is used to send data to a server. A *put* or *delete* request normally is used to store or delete a file on the server, respectively. An *options* request returns information to the client indicating the HTTP options supported by the server. A *trace* request normally is used for debugging. The **Page** class, a subclass of **HTTPServlet**, provides convenient methods for creating XHTML pages that respond to *get* and *post* requests. When developing servlets, Web developers often subclass **Page** to inherit its implementation and override its methods. Figure 25.1 shows methods that are available in the **Servlet** class.

25.3 Python Server Pages Overview

There are three key components to PSPs: *directives*, *actions* and *scriptlets*. Directives are messages to the PSP container that enable the programmer to specify page settings and to include content from other resources. Scriptlets, or *scripting elements*, enable programmers to insert Python code that interacts with components in a PSP (and possibly other Web-application components) to perform request processing. Actions encapsulate functionality in predefined tags that programmers can embed in a PSP. Actions often are based on information sent to the server as part of a particular client request. Also, actions can create Python objects for use in PSP scriptlets. These PSP component types are discussed in detail in subsequent sections.

Method	Description
name()	This method returns the class name.
awake(*transaction* **)**	This method is defined by a servlet programmer to initialize the servlet. The *transaction* argument is supplied by the servlet container that executes the servlet.
respond(*transaction* **)**	The servlet container calls this method to respond to a client request to the servlet.
sleep(*transaction* **)**	This "cleanup" method is called when a servlet is terminated by its servlet container. Resources that the servlet uses, such as open files or temporary database connections, should be deallocated here. Attributes of the servlet that are no longer required should be removed.
log(*message* **)**	This method prints servlet information, which is useful for debugging.
canBeThreaded()	This method returns **1** if the servlet can be multithreaded. Otherwise returns **0**. The default return value is **0**.

Fig. 25.1   Servlet class methods (**WebKit/Servlet.py**). (Part 1 of 2.)

Method	Description
`canBeReused()`	This method returns **1** if the servlet can be reused. Otherwise returns **0**. The default return value is **1**.
`serverSidePath( path )`	This method returns the path of the page on the server.

Fig. 25.1 **Servlet** class methods (**WebKit/Servlet.py**). (Part 2 of 2.)

In many ways, Python Server Pages look like standard HTML or XHTML documents. In fact, PSPs normally include XHTML or HTML markup. Such markup is known as *fixed-template data* or *fixed-template text*. The need for fixed-template data often helps a programmer decide whether to use either a servlet or a PSP. Programmers tend to use PSPs when most of the content sent to the client is fixed-template data and only a small portion of the content is generated dynamically with Python code. Programmers use servlets when only a small portion of the content sent to the client is fixed-template data. In fact, some servlets do not produce content. Rather, they perform tasks on behalf of clients, then invoke other servlets or PSPs to provide responses. Note that, in most cases, servlet and PSP technologies are interchangeable. As with servlets, PSPs normally execute as part of a Web server.

When a PSP-enabled server receives the first request for a PSP, the PSP container translates that request into a Python servlet that handles the current request and future requests to the PSP. If there are any errors during the compiling of the new servlet, these errors result in *generation-time errors*. The PSP may respond directly to the request or may invoke other Web-application components to assist in the processing of the request. Any errors that occur during request processing are known as *request-time errors*.

Overall, the request/response mechanism and life cycle of a PSP are the same as those of a servlet. PSPs can override methods **awake** and **sleep** from class **Servlet**, which the PSP container invokes when initializing a PSP and terminating a PSP, respectively. PSP programmers can define these methods through PSP page directives and actions.

25.4 First Python Server Page Example

We begin our introduction to Python Server Pages with a simple example (Fig. 25.2) that inserts the current date and time into a Web page. We import the **time** module with a **page** directive and use the module's **ctime** function in a PSP expression to insert the date and time.

```
1   <!DOCTYPE html PUBLIC "-//W3C//DTD XHTML 1.0 Strict//EN"
2      "http://www.w3.org/TR/xhtml1/DTD/xhtml1-strict.dtd">
3
4   <!-- Fig. 25.2: fig25_02.psp                    -->
5   <!-- Displays date and time every 60 seconds. -->
6
```

Fig. 25.2 PSP **page** directive and Python expression that insert the date and time into response Web page. (Part 1 of 3.)

```
7   <%-- import time module --%>
8   <%@ page imports = "time" %>
9
10  <html xmlns = "http://www.w3.org/1999/xhtml">
11
12     <head>
13        <meta http-equiv = "refresh" content = "60" />
14
15        <title>A Simple PSP Example</title>
16
17        <style type = "text/css">
18           .big { font-family: helvetica, arial, sans-serif;
19                  font-weight: bold;
20                  font-size: 2em; }
21        </style>
22     </head>
23
24     <body>
25        <p class = "big">Simple PSP Example</p>
26
27        <table style = "border: 6px outset;">
28           <tr>
29              <td style = "background-color: black;">
30                 <p class = "big" style = "color: cyan;">
31
32                    <!-- PSP expression to insert date/time -->
33                    <%= time.ctime() %>
34
35                 </p>
36              </td>
37           </tr>
38        </table>
39     </body>
40
41  </html>
```

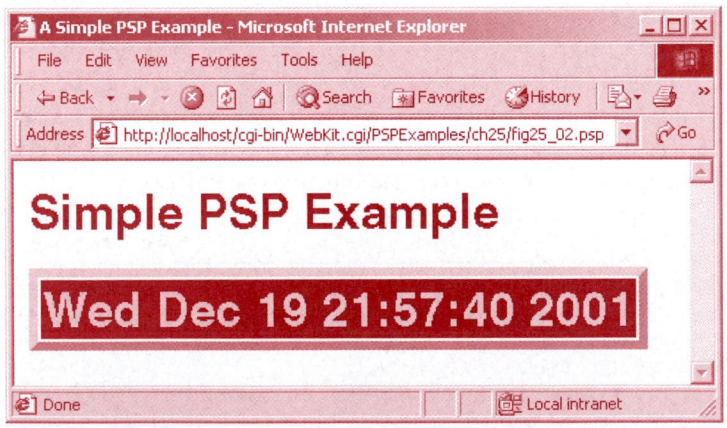

Fig. 25.2   PSP **page** directive and Python expression that insert the date and time into response Web page. (Part 2 of 3.)

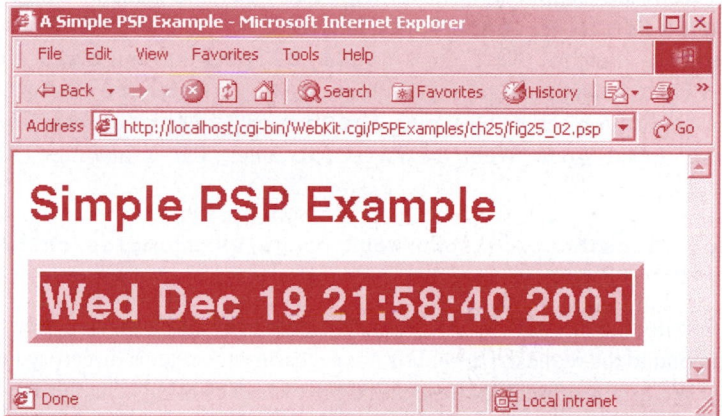

Fig. 25.2   PSP **page** directive and Python expression that insert the date and time into response Web page. (Part 3 of 3.)

Most of the code in Fig. 25.2 consists of XHTML markup. In cases like Fig. 25.2, PSPs are easier to implement than servlets. In a servlet that performs the same task as this PSP, each line of XHTML markup typically is a separate Python statement that outputs the string that represents the markup as part of the response to the client. Writing code to output markup often can lead to errors.

Software Engineering Observation 25.1

Python Server Pages are easier to implement than servlets when the responses to client requests consist primarily of markup that remains constant between requests.

The PSP of Fig. 25.2 generates an XHTML document that displays the current date and time. The key line in this PSP (line 33) is the expression

```
<%= time.ctime() %>
```

PSP expressions are delimited by **<%=** and **%>**. This particular expression calls function **ctime** of module **time**. When the client requests this PSP, the preceding expression inserts the string representation of the date and time in the response to the client. To use module **time**, the PSP first must import the module. Line 8 imports the **time** module by setting the **imports** attribute of the **page** directive. The **page** directive specifies settings for the current PSP.

The **imports** attribute instructs the PSP parser to import a Python module for use in the page. We discuss the **page** directive in detail in Section 25.8.1.

Software Engineering Observation 25.2

The PSP container converts the result of every PSP expression into a string that is output as part of the response to the client.

Note that we use the XHTML *meta* element on line 13 to set a *refresh interval* of 60 seconds for the document. This causes the browser to request **fig25_02.psp** every 60 seconds. For each request, the PSP container reevaluates the expression on line 33, thereby obtaining the server's current date and time.

We use Webware's application server (**AppServer**) and Apache Web server to test our PSPs. To test **fig25_02.psp**, create a new directory called **ch25** in the **Webware/PSP/Examples** directory. Next, copy **fig25_02.psp** into the **ch25** directory and start Apache. Open a command-prompt window, go to the **Webware/WebKit** directory and start the application server by typing **AppServer** (**./AppServer** for UNIX and Linux users). Open your Web browser, and enter the following URL to test **fig25_02.psp**:

```
http://localhost/cgi-bin/WebKit.cgi/PSPExamples/ch25/
    fig25_02.psp
```

When you first invoke the PSP, WebKit translates the PSP into a servlet, then invokes the servlet to respond to the request. [*Note*: It is not necessary to create a directory named **ch25** in Webware. We use this directory to separate the examples in this chapter from examples supplied by Webware.]

25.5 Implicit Objects

Implicit objects provide programmers with access to many servlet capabilities in the context of a Python Server Page. Figure 25.3 describes the PSP implicit objects, which act as local variables to PSP instances. All PSPs can access these objects.

Note that implicit objects extend the classes discussed in Section 25.2. Thus, PSPs can use the same methods that servlets use to interact with these objects. Most of the examples in this chapter use one or more of the implicit objects listed in Fig. 25.3.

25.6 Scripting

Python Server Pages often include dynamically generated content as part of each XHTML document sent to the client in response to a request. In some cases, the content is static and is output only if certain conditions are met during a request (such as entering values into a **form** that submits a request). PSP programmers can insert Python code and logic into PSPs through scripting.

Implicit Object	Description
trans	In Webware, a transaction is an object that contains all of the objects involved in a single request-response cycle. This **WebKit.Transaction** object represents the container in which the PSP executes.
res	This object represents the response to the client. The object is an instance of class **WebKit.HTTPResponse**.
req	This object represents the client request. The object is an instance of class **WebKit.HTTPRequest**.

Fig. 25.3   PSP implicit objects.

25.6.1 Scripting Components

PSP scripting components include scriptlets, comments and expressions. This section describes each of these scripting components. Many of these scripting components are demonstrated in Fig. 25.4 at the end of Section 25.6.2.

Scriptlets are blocks of code delimited by `<%` and `%>`. PSPs support three comment styles: PSP comments, XHTML comments and comments from the scripting language. *PSP comments* are delimited by `<%--` and `--%>`. Such comments can be placed throughout a PSP, but not inside scriptlets. *XHTML comments* are delimited with `<!--` and `-->`. These comments can be placed throughout a PSP, but not inside scriptlets. Scriptlets can use Python's single-line comments (delimited by `#`) and multiline docstrings (delimited by `"""` and `"""`).

Common Programming Error 25.1

Placing a PSP comment or XHTML comment inside a scriptlet is a generation-time syntax error that prevents the PSP from being translated properly.

PSP comments and Python comments are ignored and do not appear in the response to a client. When clients view the source code of a PSP response, they see only the XHTML comments in the source code. The different comment styles are useful for separating comments that the user should be able to see from comments that document logic processed on the server.

A PSP expression, delimited by `<%=` and `%>`, contains a Python expression that is evaluated when a client requests the PSP containing the expression. The container converts the result of a PSP expression to a string, then outputs the string as part of the response to the client.

25.6.2 Scripting Example

The PSP of Fig. 25.4 demonstrates basic scripting capabilities by responding to *get* requests. This PSP enables the user to input a first name, then outputs that name as part of the response. Using scripting, the PSP determines whether a **firstName** parameter was passed to the PSP as part of the request; if not, the PSP returns an XHTML document containing a **form** through which the user can input a first name. Otherwise, the PSP obtains the **firstName** value and uses it as part of an XHTML document that welcomes the user to Python Server Pages.

Similar to the program in Fig. 25.2, the majority of the code in Fig. 25.4 is XHTML markup (i.e., fixed-template data). Throughout the **body** element are several scriptlets (lines 21–25, 32–37 and 47–51) and a PSP expression (line 28). Note that all three comment styles appear in this PSP.

For every request, the fixed-template data at lines 1–6 and 9–19 are sent to the client as part of the response. Line 21 begins a scriptlet that contains an **if** evaluation statement (line 23). Line 23 uses method **hasField** of PSP implicit object **req** (an **HTTPRequest** object) to determine whether the PSP has a parameter named **firstName**. Notice the use of braces (`{ }`) in lines 23 and 34 to delimit the **if** suite code. Recall that Python code uses white space to identify suites and blocks of code. This indentation type reduces the readability in PSPs. To create readable XHTML code, Webware uses three special syntaxes to handle Python blocks. This example uses one of them—*braces*, as specified in line 8:

```
<%@ page indentType = "braces" %>
```

This line informs the compiler that the current PSP uses braces to signify suites and blocks of code in scriptlets. Braces are placed at the beginning and end of a suite or block. Within these braces, tabs and other whitespace at the beginning of each line are ignored. Section 25.8.1 discusses the **page** directive **indentType** in detail.

```
 1   <!DOCTYPE html PUBLIC "-//W3C//DTD XHTML 1.0 Strict//EN"
 2      "http://www.w3.org/TR/xhtml1/DTD/xhtml1-strict.dtd">
 3
 4   <!-- Fig. 25.4: fig25_04.psp                               -->
 5   <!-- PSP that processes a "get" request containing data. -->
 6
 7   <%-- specify indent type --%>
 8   <%@ page indentType = "braces" %>
 9
10   <html xmlns = "http://www.w3.org/1999/xhtml">
11
12      <!-- head section of document -->
13      <head>
14         <title>Processing "get" requests with data</title>
15      </head>
16
17      <!-- body section of document -->
18      <body>
19
20         <%-- generate a form --%>
21         <% # begin scriptlet
22
23            if req.hasField( "firstName" ): {
24
25         %> <%-- end scriptlet to insert fixed template data --%>
26
27            <h1>
28               Hello <%= req.field( "firstName" ) %>, <br />
29               Welcome to Python Server Pages!
30            </h1>
31
32         <% # continue scriptlet
33
34            } # end if
35            else: {
36
37         %> <%-- end scriptlet to insert fixed template data --%>
38
39               <form action = "fig25_04.psp" method = "get">
40                  <p>Type your first name and press Submit</p>
41
42                  <p><input type = "text" name = "firstName" />
43                     <input type = "submit" value = "Submit" />
44                  </p>
45               </form>
```

Fig. 25.4   Scripting a Python Server Page (**fig25_04.psp**). (Part 1 of 2.)

```
46
47        <% # continue scriptlet
48
49            } # end else
50
51        %> <%-- end scriptlet --%>
52    </body>
53
54  </html>   <!-- end XHTML document -->
```

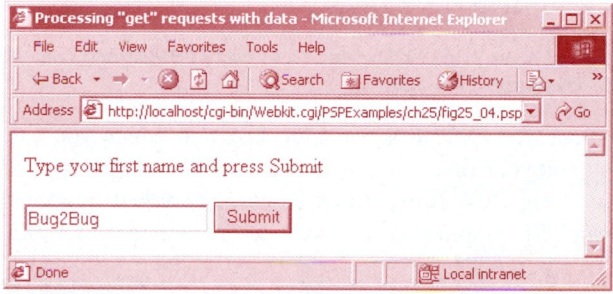

Fig. 25.4   Scripting a Python Server Page (**fig25_04.psp**). (Part 2 of 2.)

   Software Engineering Observation 25.3

*Once programmers specify braces as the indentation type in a **page** directive, they must use braces for all suites and blocks.*

    If the condition at line 23 evaluates to true, lines 21–25 terminate temporarily so that
the fixed-template data at lines 27–30 can be output. The PSP expression in line 28 outputs
the first name passed to the PSP as a request parameter. The scriptlet continues at lines 32–
37 with the closing curly brace of the **if** structure's body and the beginning of the **else**
part of the **if/else** structure. If the condition at line 23 is false, lines 27–30 are not output.
Instead, lines 39–45 output a **form** element that enables the client to submit a first name
in a *get* request to PSP **fig24_04.psp**. The user can type a first name in the **form** and
press the **Submit** button to request the PSP again and execute the **if** structure's body
(lines 27–30).

   Software Engineering Observation 25.4

Scriptlets, expressions and fixed-template data can be intermixed in a PSP to create dynamic responses appropriate to each PSP request.

Testing and Debugging Tip 25.1

*It is sometimes difficult to debug errors in a PSP, because the line numbers reported by a PSP container refer to the servlet that represents the translated PSP, not the original PSP line numbers. Finding the line number reported in the servlet can help debug the original PSP. The servlets are located in the **Webware/WebKit/Cache/PSP** directory.*

To test Fig. 25.4 in Webware, copy **fig25_04.psp** into the **Webware/PSP/Examples/ch25** directory. Make sure Webware's application server (**AppServer**) and Apache Web Server are running. Open your Web browser, and enter the following URL to test **fig25_04.psp**:

```
http://localhost/cgi-bin/WebKit.cgi/PSPExamples/ch25/
    fig25_04.psp
```

When you first execute the PSP, it displays the **form** in which you can enter your first name. After you submit your first name, your browser should appear as shown in the second screen capture of Fig. 25.4. It is possible to pass *get* request arguments as part of the URL. The following URL supplies the **firstName** parameter to **fig25_04.psp**:

```
http://localhost/cgi-bin/WebKit.cgi/PSPExamples/ch25/
    fig25_04.psp?firstName=Paul
```

25.7 Standard Actions

We continue our PSP discussion with the *PSP standard actions* (Fig. 25.5). These actions provide PSP programmers with access to several of the most common tasks performed in a PSP, such as including content from other resources and creating or overriding methods of a servlet class. PSP containers process actions at request time. Actions are delimited by **<psp:***action***>** and **</psp:***action***>** tags, where *action* is the standard action name (i.e., **include**, **insert** or **method**). PSP requires the closing **</psp:***action***>** tag only for the **method** action; the closing tag is optional for all other actions. We use action tags in the next several subsections.

Action	Description
<psp:include>	Includes another resource in a PSP dynamically. As the PSP executes, the referenced resource is included and processed.
<psp:insert>	Inserts another resource in a PSP. As the PSP executes, the referenced resource is included but the PSP contents are not parsed.
<psp:method>	Declares new methods of the **Servlet** class a PSP produces, or overrides the methods in the base class from which the PSP extends. Must have **</psp:method>** specified to indicate the end of method.

Fig. 25.5   PSP standard actions.

25.7.1 `<psp:include>` Action

Python Server Pages support two include mechanisms—the *`<psp:include>`* *action* and the *`include` directive*. Action `<psp:include>` enables PSPs to reuse content from existing PSPs, XHTML documents, etc. If the included resource changes between requests, subsequent requests to the PSP that contain the `<psp:include>` action will reflect those changes made to the included resource. On the other hand, the `include` directive copies the content into the PSP once, at PSP generation time. If the included resource changes, the new content will not be reflected in the PSP that used the `include` directive, unless the WebKit application server is restarted. Figure 25.6 describes the attribute of action `<psp:include>`.

Performance Tip 25.1

The `<psp:include>` action is more flexible than the `include` directive, but requires more overhead when page contents change frequently. Use the `<psp:include>` action only when dynamic content is necessary.

Common Programming Error 25.2

Specifying a page in a `<psp:include>` action that the application server cannot find is a request-time error.

The next example demonstrates action `<psp:include>` using XHTML and PSP documents that represent both static and dynamic content. `banner.html` (Fig. 25.7) and `toc.html` (Fig. 25.8) are static XHTML documents; `clock2.psp` (Fig. 25.9) is a PSP. Python Server Page `include.psp` (Fig. 25.10) combines these three documents to create a new XHTML document in which `banner.html` spans two columns across the top of the `table`, `toc.html` is the left column of the second row and `clock2.psp` (a simplified version of Fig. 25.2) is the right column of the second row. Figure 25.10 uses three `<psp:include>` actions (lines 38, 47 and 54) as the content in `td` elements of the `table`. Fig. 25.10 demonstrates that PSPs can include both static and dynamic content.

Attribute	Description
`path`	Specifies the URL path of the resource to include. The PSP parser supports both absolute paths and relative paths. A relative path does not start with `"/"` and is relative to the current page. An absolute path starts with `"/"`, which indicates to the PSP parser that the path is a absolute path rather than a path relative to the current page. The application server must be able to locate the page.

Fig. 25.6 `<psp:include>` action attribute.

```
1   <!-- Fig. 25.7: banner.html                    -->
2   <!-- Banner to include in another document. -->
3
```

Fig. 25.7 Banner (`banner.html`) to add to the top of the XHTML document created by Fig. 25.10. (Part 1 of 2.)

```
4    <div style = "width: 500px">
5       <p>
6          Java(TM), C, C++, Visual Basic(R),
7          Object Technology, and <br />Internet and
8          World Wide Web Programming Training <br />
9          On-Site Seminars Delivered Worldwide
10      </p>
11
12      <p>
13         <a href = "mailto:deitel@deitel.com">
14            deitel@deitel.com</a><br />
15
16         978.579.9911<br />
17         490B Boston Post Road, Suite 200,
18         Sudbury, MA 01776
19      </p>
20   </div>
```

Fig. 25.7   Banner (**banner.html**) to add to the top of the XHTML document created by Fig. 25.10. (Part 2 of 2.)

```
1    <!-- Fig. 25.8: toc.html                      -->
2    <!-- Contents to include in another document. -->
3
4    <p><a href = "http://www.deitel.com/books/index.html">
5       Publications/BookStore
6    </a></p>
7
8    <p><a href = "http://www.deitel.com/whatsnew.html">
9       What's New
10   </a></p>
11
12   <p><a href = "http://www.deitel.com/books/downloads.html">
13      Downloads/Resources
14   </a></p>
15
16   <p><a href = "http://www.deitel.com/faq/index.html">
17      FAQ (Frequently Asked Questions)
18   </a></p>
19
20   <p><a href = "http://www.deitel.com/intro.html">
21      Who we are
22   </a></p>
23
24   <p><a href = "http://www.deitel.com/index.html">
25      Home Page
26   </a></p>
27
28   <p>Send questions or comments about this site to
```

Fig. 25.8   Table of contents (**toc.html**) to include in a column on the left side of the XHTML document created by Fig. 25.10. (Part 1 of 2.)

```
29        <a href = "mailto:deitel@deitel.com">
30           deitel@deitel.com
31        </a><br />
32        Copyright 1995-2002 by Deitel &amp; Associates, Inc.
33        All Rights Reserved.
34     </p>
```

Fig. 25.8 Table of contents (`toc.html`) to include in a column on the left side of the XHTML document created by Fig. 25.10. (Part 2 of 2.)

```
1    <!-- Fig. 25.9: clock2.psp                        -->
2    <!-- Date and time to include in another document. -->
3
4    <%-- import time module --%>
5    <%@ page imports = "time"%>
6
7    <table>
8       <tr>
9          <td style = "background-color: black">
10            <p class = "big" style = "color: cyan; font-size: 3em;
11               font-weight: bold">
12
13               <%= time.ctime() %>
14            </p>
15         </td>
16      </tr>
17   </table>
```

Fig. 25.9 PSP `clock2.psp` to include as the main content in the XHTML document created by `include.psp`.

To test Fig. 25.10, Webware's application (**AppServer**) and Apache Web server must be running. Copy **banner.html**, **toc.html**, **clock2.psp**, **include.psp** and the **images** directory into the **PSP/Examples/ch25** directory. Open a Web browser and enter the following URL to test **include.psp**:

> **http://localhost/cgi-bin/WebKit.cgi/PSPExamples/ch25/**
> **include.psp**

Note that when we run a PSP, we provide the full filename (i.e., **include.psp**). However, WebKit has a feature that allows you to run a PSP, servlet or even static XHTML page without including the file extension in the URL. This feature enables a Web site administrator to change a page from a PSP to a servlet or an XHTML page without changing all the links to that page. For example, line 54

> **<psp:include path = "clock2.psp" >**

can be replaced by

> **<psp:include path = "clock2" >**

```
 1  <!DOCTYPE html PUBLIC "-//W3C//DTD XHTML 1.0 Strict//EN"
 2      "http://www.w3.org/TR/xhtml1/DTD/xhtml1-strict.dtd">
 3
 4  <!-- Fig. 25.10: include.psp                         -->
 5  <!-- PSP that includes both static and dynamic content. -->
 6
 7  <html xmlns = "http://www.w3.org/1999/xhtml">
 8
 9      <head>
10          <title>Using psp:include</title>
11
12          <style type = "text/css">
13              body {
14                  font-family: tahoma, helvetica, arial, sans-serif;
15              }
16
17              table, tr, td {
18                  font-size: .9em;
19                  border: 3px groove;
20                  padding: 5px;
21                  background-color: #dddddd;
22              }
23          </style>
24      </head>
25
26      <body>
27          <table>
28              <tr>
29                  <td style = "width: 160px; text-align: center">
30                      <img src = "images/logotiny.png"
31                          width = "140" height = "93"
32                          alt = "Deitel &amp; Associates, Inc. Logo" />
33                  </td>
34
35                  <td>
36
37                      <%-- include contents of banner.html here --%>
38                      <psp:include path = "banner.html" >
39
40                  </td>
41              </tr>
42
43              <tr>
44                  <td style = "width: 160px">
45
46                      <%-- include contents of toc.html here --%>
47                      <psp:include path = "toc.html" >
48
49                  </td>
50
51                  <td style = "vertical-align: top">
52
```

Fig. 25.10 PSP `include.psp` adds resources using `<psp:include>`.
(Part 1 of 2.)

```
53                          <%-- include clock2.psp in this PSP --%>
54                          <psp:include path = "clock2.psp" >
55
56                      </td>
57                  </tr>
58              </table>
59          </body>
60      </html>
```

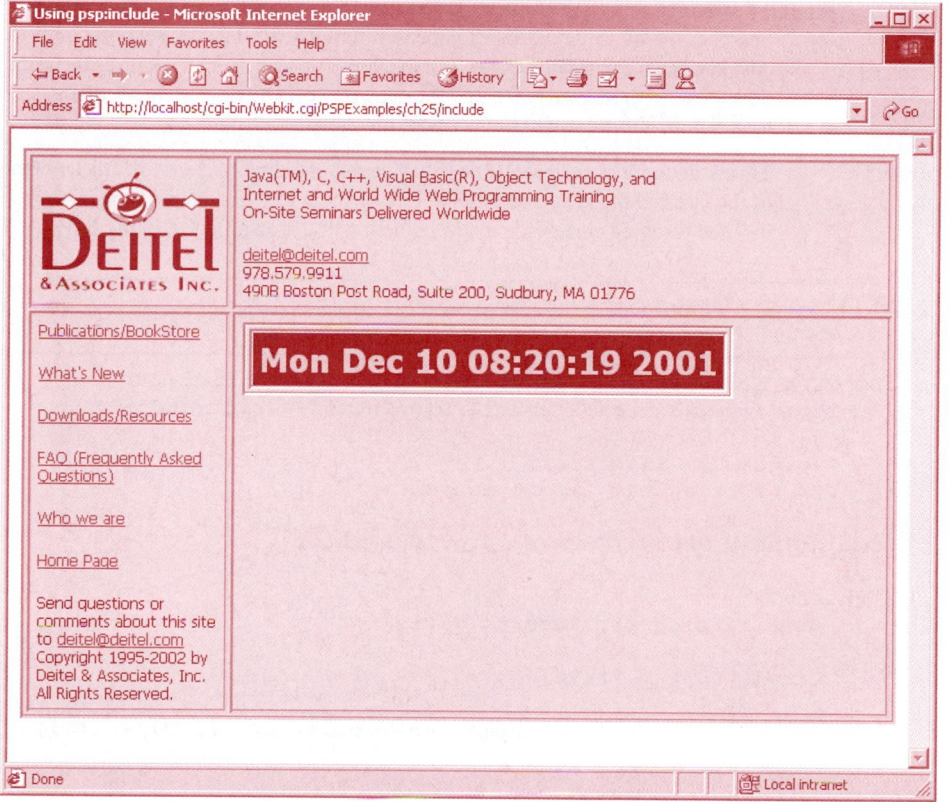

Fig. 25.10 PSP `include.psp` adds resources using `<psp:include>`.
(Part 2 of 2.)

25.7.2 `<psp:insert>` Action

Action `<psp:insert>` has the same functionality as action `<psp:include>`—`<psp:insert>` dynamically inserts a resource into a PSP. However, unlike `<psp:include>`, `<psp:insert>` instructs the PSP parser not to evaluate any scriptlets contained within the resource. Figure 25.11 describes the attributes of action `<psp:insert>`.

The next example (Fig. 25.12) demonstrates the difference between actions `<psp:include>` and `<psp:insert>`. Similar to Fig. 25.10, Fig. 25.12 uses three

<psp:insert> actions (lines 38, 47 and 54) as the content in **td** elements of the **table**. All the insert actions use relative paths to direct the page to the included files, which are located in the same directory as the PSP (Fig. 25.12). Line 38 sets the **static** attribute to **"true"**, which specifies that updates to **banner.html** will not be reflected in subsequent server responses.

Attribute	Description
file	Specifies the filename of the resource to insert. The PSP parser supports both absolute paths and relative paths. For example, **"test.psp"** retrieves the same document as **"/Webware/PSP/Examples/ch25/test.psp"** when issued from a PSP located in the **ch25** directory.
static	This is an optional attribute. If this attribute is set to **"true"** or **"1"**, the content of the inserted file is copied into the PSP once, at PSP generation time. If the inserted resource changes, the new content will not be reflected in the PSP.

Fig. 25.11 <psp:insert> action attributes.

```
1   <!DOCTYPE html PUBLIC "-//W3C//DTD XHTML 1.0 Strict//EN"
2       "http://www.w3.org/TR/xhtml11/DTD/xhtml1-strict.dtd">
3
4   <!-- Fig. 25.12: insert.psp           -->
5   <!-- Demonstrates the insert action. -->
6
7   <html xmlns = "http://www.w3.org/1999/xhtml">
8
9      <head>
10        <title>Using psp:insert</title>
11
12        <style type = "text/css">
13           body {
14              font-family: tahoma, helvetica, arial, sans-serif;
15           }
16
17           table, tr, td {
18              font-size: .9em;
19              border: 3px groove;
20              padding: 5px;
21              background-color: #dddddd;
22           }
23        </style>
24     </head>
25
26     <body>
27        <table>
28           <tr>
29              <td style = "width: 160px; text-align: center">
30                 <img src = "images/logotiny.png"
```

Fig. 25.12 PSP **insert.psp** includes resources with **<psp:insert>**. (Part 1 of 2.)

```
31                        width = "140" height = "93"
32                        alt = "Deitel &amp; Associates, Inc. Logo" />
33              </td>
34
35              <td>
36
37                  <%-- include banner.html in this PSP --%>
38                  <psp:insert file = "banner.html" static = "true" >
39
40              </td>
41          </tr>
42
43          <tr>
44              <td style = "width: 160px">
45
46                  <%-- include toc.html in this PSP --%>
47                  <psp:insert file = "toc.html" >
48
49              </td>
50
51              <td style = "vertical-align: top">
52
53                  <%-- include clock2.psp in this PSP --%>
54                  <psp:insert file = "clock2.psp" >
55
56              </td>
57          </tr>
58      </table>
59    </body>
60 </html>
```

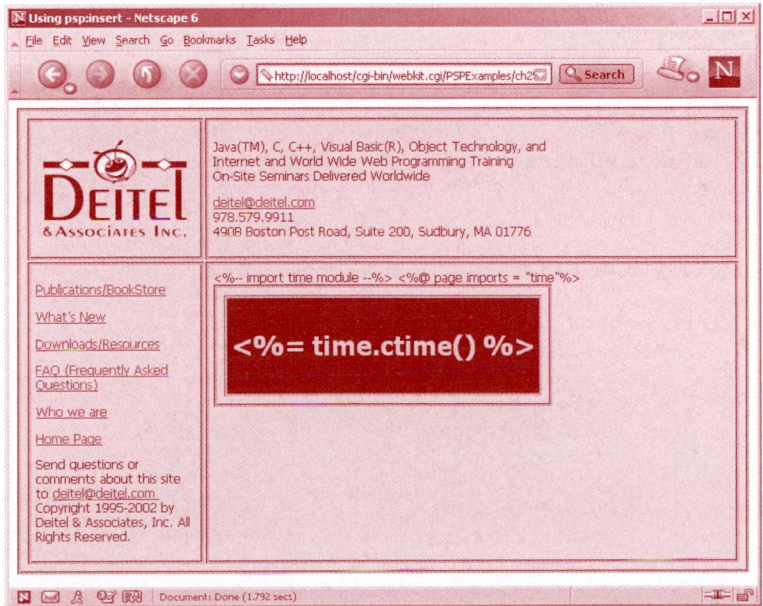

Fig. 25.12 PSP **insert.psp** includes resources with **<psp:insert>**. (Part 2 of 2.)

The output in Fig. 25.12 demonstrates that the **<psp:insert>** action inserts a document without interpreting any of the PSP scripting elements in the document. Action **<psp:insert>** inserts the contents of the document either dynamically at runtime or once at page-generation time based on the value of the status flag (**true** indicates page-generation time). In the bottom-right cell of this example document, notice that the original PSP code appears, instead of the result of parsing the script.

Performance Tip 25.2

*Documents containing **<psp:insert>** actions with the **static** attribute set to **"true"** are more efficient than those in which **static** is not set to **"true"**, because the insert action is not interpreted each time the document is requested. However, if the document is changed, the programmer must restart the WebKit application server (**AppServer**).*

25.7.3 **<psp:method>** Action

Action **<psp:method>** enables a PSP to override methods inherited from the servlet class and to declare new methods. Action **<psp:method>** has two attributes—**name** and **params**—that specify the method name and the method's parameter names, respectively. The code placed between **psp:method** elements is standard Python code. Neither raw XHTML nor scripts are allowed in **psp:method** elements.

The XHTML in **fig25_13.html** creates a form that prompts the user to input two numbers and select one of five operations—addition, subtraction, multiplication, true division or floor division. When a user clicks the **Submit** button, **fig25_14.psp** is invoked.

```
1   <!DOCTYPE html PUBLIC "-//W3C//DTD XHTML 1.0 Strict//EN"
2       "http://www.w3.org/TR/xhtml1/DTD/xhtml1-strict.dtd">
3
4   <!-- Fig. 25.13: fig25_13.html -->
5   <!-- Calculator form.           -->
6
7   <html xmlns = "http://www.w3.org/1999/xhtml">
8
9       <head>
10          <title>Calculator Input Data</title>
11      </head>
12
13      <body>
14          <h1>Python Calculator</h1>
15
16          <form method = "post" action = "fig25_14.psp">
17              <table width = "100%" border = "3">
18                  <tr>
19                      <th>operand 1</th>
20                      <th>Operator</th>
21                      <th>operand 2</th>
22                  </tr>
23                  <tr>
24                      <td><input type = "text" name = "operand1"/></td>
25                      <td><select name = "operator">
26                          <option value = "+">+
```

Fig. 25.13 Defining a form for **fig25_14.psp**. (Part 1 of 2.)

```
27                          <option value = "-">-
28                          <option value = "*">*
29                          <option value = "/">/
30                          <option value = "//">//
31                          </select>
32                       </td>
33                       <td><input type = "text" name = "operand2"/></td>
34                    </tr>
35                 </table><br />
36                 <input type = "submit" value = "Submit">
37              </form>
38
39        </body>
40     </html>
```

Fig. 25.13 Defining a form for `fig25_14.psp`. (Part 2 of 2.)

The PSP in Fig. 25.14 demonstrates the declaration of a method in PSP and the invocation of that method. Lines 8–10 are **page** directives that specify the page settings for the PSP. The indentation style is set to **"spaces"** in line 8. The number of spaces used for indentation is set to **3** (line 9). Line 10 contains a **page** directive that enables true division. [*Note*: We discuss true division in Chapter 2, Introduction to Python Programming.]

Lines 13–36 declare method **calculate**, which contains only Python code. Lines 13–14 contain the method start tag

```
<psp:method name = "calculate"
    params = "operand1, operator, operand2" >
```

Method **calculate** takes three parameters—**operand1**, **operator** and **operand2**. Lines 16–32 perform calculations on **operand1** and **operand2** using the **operator**. Line 34 returns the calculation result. The **</psp:method>** end tag terminates the method (line 36).

```
1   <!DOCTYPE html PUBLIC "-//W3C//DTD XHTML 1.0 Strict//EN"
2       "http://www.w3.org/TR/xhtml1/DTD/xhtml1-strict.dtd">
3
4   <!-- Fig. 25.14: fig25_14.psp                              -->
5   <!-- PSP that processes a "get" request containing data. -->
6
7   <%-- specify indent type --%>
8   <%@ page indentType = "spaces" %>
9   <%@ page indentSpaces = "3" %>
10  <%@ page imports = "__future__:division" %>
11
12  <%-- define a psp method --%>
13  <psp:method name = "calculate"
14      params = "operand1, operator, operand2" >
15
16  if operator == "+":         # addition operation
17      result = operand1 + operand2
```

Fig. 25.14 PSP `fig25_14.psp` defines a method with `<psp:method>`. (Part 1 of 3.)

```
18
19  elif operator == "-":      # subtraction operation
20     result = operand1 - operand2
21
22  elif operator == "*":      # multiplication operation
23     result = operand1 * operand2
24
25  elif operator == "/":      # division operation
26     result = operand1 / operand2
27
28  elif operator == "//":     # floor division
29     result = operand1 // operand2
30
31  else:                      # unrecognizable operator
32     result = None
33
34  return result
35
36  </psp:method> <%-- end psp method declaration --%>
37
38
39  <html xmlns = "http://www.w3.org/1999/xhtml">
40
41     <!-- head section of document -->
42     <head>
43        <title>Calculator Result</title>
44     </head>
45
46     <!-- body section of document -->
47     <body>
48        <h1>Python Calculator Result</h1>
49
50        <%-- get client input --%>
51        <%
52           try:
53              operand1 = float( req.field( "operand1" ) )
54              operator = req.field( "operator", "+" )
55              operand2 = float( req.field( "operand2" ) )
56              noError = 1 $%>
57        <% except Exception:
58              res.write( "You did not enter a number." )
59              noError = 0 $%>
60
61        <%-- display expression --%>
62        <% if noError: %>
63           <br />
64           <%= operand1 %> <%= operator %> <%= operand2 %> =
65           <%= self.calculate( operand1, operator, operand2 ) %>
66        <% end %>
67     </body>
68
69  </html>  <!-- end XHTML document -->
```

Fig. 25.14 PSP `fig25_14.psp` defines a method with `<psp:method>`.
(Part 2 of 3.)

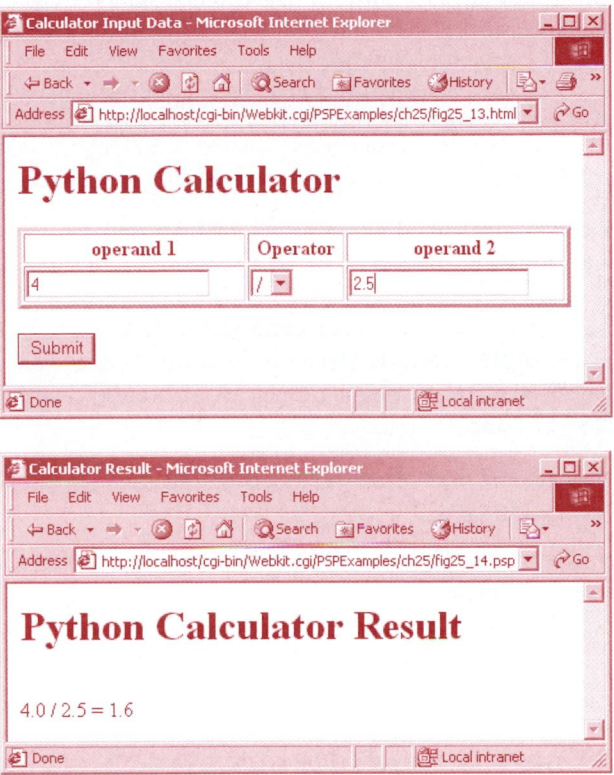

Fig. 25.14 PSP `fig25_14.psp` defines a method with `<psp:method>`.
(Part 3 of 3.)

The remainder of the file contains XHTML markup and scriptlets. The **body** element contains several scriptlets (lines 51–59 and lines 62, 64 and 67) and PSP expressions (lines 65–66). In Fig. 25.4, we discussed how PSP handles indentation when using braces. In this example, lines 51–56 and lines 57–59 introduce a second way PSP handles indentation, using the **$%>** tag to end a scriptlet. Lines 51–56 declare the first scriptlet, a **try** structure, which ends with a **$%>** tag. Within the scriptlet, the code is indented by three spaces (defined by lines 8–9). The **$%>** tag indicates to the PSP parser that the following template data belongs to the blocks of code started by the previous **<%** tag. The **$%>** enables Web developers to define blocks of code (e.g., loops) that can output template data. Opening a **<%** tag resets the indentation set by a previous **$%>** tag. For example, the scriptlet in lines 51–56 has the same indentation level as the scriptlet in lines 57–59.

The scriptlet in lines 51–56 retrieves the user-input operands and operator type. Line 54 gets the client-specified operator. The default operator is set to **"+"** by the call

```
operator = req.field( "operator", "+" )
```

The second argument method **req.field** method assigns a default value to **"operator"**. Method **calculate** uses this value if an **"operator"** is not declared. The scriptlet in lines 57–59 catches exceptions (e.g., if the client does not provide operands) and writes the error message.

Lines 62–66 introduce the third way PSP handles indentation—*automatic blocks*. The end script tag (`%>`) in line 62 declares the beginning of a block. Code in lines 62–65 is considered one block (the `if` structure); multiple blocks can be nested. The `<% end %>` tag terminates a block and decreases the indentation level by one for the remaining code (line 66).

Line 65 invokes method `calculate`

```
<%= self.calculate( operand1, operator, operand2 ) %>
```

Method `calculate` is available throughout the PSP file and can be accessed through `self.calculate`. Lines 65–66 use four PSP expressions to display the operation and the result.

To run this example in Webware, copy `fig25_13.html` and `fig25_14.psp` into the `PSP/Examples/ch25` directory. Make sure Webware's application server (`AppServer`) and Apache Web server are running. Open a Web browser, and enter the following URL to test `fig25_14.psp`:

```
http://localhost/cgi-bin/WebKit.cgi/PSPExamples/ch25/
    fig25_13.html
```

After completing the form, select the **Submit** button to invoke `fig25_14.psp`. Figure 25.14 displays the output.

25.8 Directives

Directives are instructions that enable programmers to specify page settings and content information to the PSP parser. Directives (delimited by `<%@` and `%>`) are processed at generation time. Thus, directives do not produce any immediate output, because they are processed before the PSP accepts any requests. Figure 25.15 summarizes the two directives; we discuss these directives in the following subsections.

25.8.1 page Directive

The ***page*** *directive* specifies global settings for the PSP in the PSP parser. There can be many ***page*** directives, provided that there is only one occurrence of each attribute. The exception to this rule is that the `imports` attribute, which imports Python modules used in the PSP, and the `method` attribute, which declares new methods or overrides methods from PSP's base class. Figure 25.16 summarizes the attributes of the ***page*** directive.

Common Programming Error 25.3

*Providing multiple **page** directives that contain the same attribute is a PSP generation-time error.*

Common Programming Error 25.4

*Providing a **page** directive with an attribute or value that is not recognized is a PSP generation-time error.*

We have discussed several attributes of the ***page*** directive in previous examples. Figure 25.14 uses the `<psp:method>` action to declare a new method, `calculate`, in the servlet class produced by the `fig25_14.psp`. In general, methods are declared in a servlet class from which the PSP inherits. The next example demonstrates how PSP inherits methods from the specified servlet class. Figure 25.17 specifies the servlet class from which **fig25_18.psp** inherits (Fig. 25.18).

Directive	Description
page	Defines page settings for the PSP parser to process.
include	Performs a generation-time insertion of another resource's content. As the PSP is translated into a servlet and compiled, the referenced file replaces the **include** directive and is translated as if it were originally part of the PSP.

Fig. 25.15 PSP directives.

Attribute	Description
extends	Specifies the servlet class from which the translated PSP inherits. By default, PSPs inherit from **Webware/WebKit/Page.py**. Webware allows PSPs to inherit from multiple classes. To specify multiple inheritance, use commas to separate the base classes.
imports	Specifies a comma-separated list of module names used in the current PSP. The **imports** attribute also supports importing objects from modules by placing the object name at the right-hand side of a colon and the module name at the left-hand side of a colon. For example, to import class **Ant** from module **bug**, the programmer can specify the **page** directive **<%@ page imports = "bug:Ant">**.
isThreadSafe	Specifies whether the page is thread safe. Possible values are **yes** and **no**. If **yes**, the page is considered to be thread safe, and it can process multiple requests at the same time. If **no** (the default), the page can process only one request at a time.
isInstanceSafe	Specifies whether it is safe to use this page multiple times. Possible values are **yes** and **no**. If **yes** (the default), the page is considered to be instance safe, and the PSP parser can invoke the servlet for multiple sequential client requests. If **no**, the PSP parser has to create a servlet for each client request, which can decrease performance.
method	Declares a new method that this PSP produces or overrides in the base class from which the PSP inherits.
indentType	Specifies the indentation style used in the servlet translated from the PSP. Possible values are **tabs**, **spaces** and **braces**. If **indentType** is set to **tabs**, the PSP parser treats tabs as indentation. If **indentType** is set to **spaces**, the PSP parser treats spaces as indentation. If **indentType** is set to **braces**, the PSP parser ignores indentation and uses braces to define the block structure. The default indentation style is **tab**.

Fig. 25.16 Attributes of the **page** directive. (Part 1 of 2.)

Attribute	Description
indentSpaces	When **indentType** is set to **spaces**, **indentSpaces** specifies the number of spaces used for indentation. If **indentSpaces** is not specified, the default value of **4** is used.

Fig. 25.16 Attributes of the **page** directive. (Part 2 of 2.)

```
1   # Fig. 25.17: fig25_17.py
2   # Subclass of the Page servlet.
3
4   from WebKit.Page import Page
5   from __future__ import division
6
7   class fig25_17( Page ):
8
9      def calculate( self, operand1, operator, operand2 ):
10         """Perform calculation"""
11
12         if operator == "+":        # addition operation
13            result = operand1 + operand2
14         elif operator == "-":      # subtraction operation
15            result = operand1 - operand2
16         elif operator == "*":      # multiplication operation
17            result = operand1 * operand2
18         elif operator == "/":      # division operation
19            result = operand1 / operand2
20         elif operator == "//":     # floor division
21            result = operand1 // operand2
22         else:                      # unrecognizable operator
23            result = None
24         return result
```

Fig. 25.17 Defining a servlet class inherited by **fig25_18.psp**.

Line 4 imports the **Page** servlet located in **WebKit/Page.py**. Line 6 indicates that the current servlet is a subclass of the **Page** servlet. Line 5 activates the new division behavior for this program, so we can use true division in line 19. Method **calculate** (lines 9–23) takes three arguments (the operands and operator type), performs the calculation and returns the result.

```
1   <!DOCTYPE html PUBLIC "-//W3C//DTD XHTML 1.0 Strict//EN"
2      "http://www.w3.org/TR/xhtml1/DTD/xhtml1-strict.dtd">
3
4   <!-- Fig. 25.18: fig25_18.psp            -->
5   <!-- PSP that extends a user-specified servlet. -->
6
7   <%-- specify indent type --%>
8   <%@ page indentType = "spaces" %>
```

Fig. 25.18 PSP **fig25_18.psp** extends **fig25_17** servlet. (Part 1 of 3.)

```
9   <%@ page indentSpaces = "3" %>
10  <%@ page imports =
11     "PSP.Examples.ch25.fig25_17:fig25_17" %>
12  <%@ page extends = "fig25_17" %>
13
14  <html xmlns = "http://www.w3.org/1999/xhtml">
15
16     <!-- head section of document -->
17     <head>
18        <title>Calculator Result</title>
19     </head>
20
21     <!-- body section of document -->
22     <body>
23        <h1>Python Calculator Result</h1>
24
25        <%-- get client input --%>
26        <%
27           try:
28              operand1 = float( req.field( "operand1" ) )
29              operator = req.field( "operator", "+" )
30              operand2 = float( req.field( "operand2" ) )
31              noError = 1 $%>
32        <% except ValueError:
33              res.write( "You did not enter a number." )
34              noError = 0 $%>
35
36        <%-- display expression --%>
37        <% if noError: %>
38           <br />
39           <%= operand1 %> <%= operator %> <%= operand2 %> =
40           <%= self.calculate( operand1, operator, operand2 ) %>
41        <% end %>
42     </body>
43
44  </html>  <!-- end XHTML document -->
```

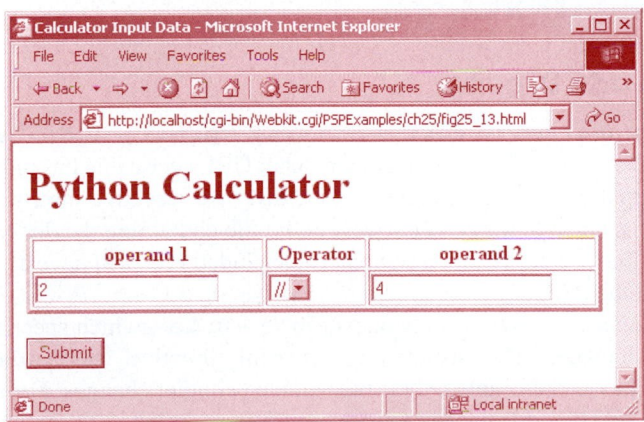

Fig. 25.18 PSP `fig25_18.psp` extends `fig25_17` servlet. (Part 2 of 3.)

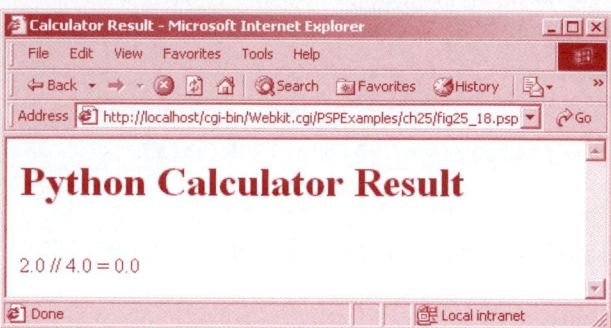

Fig. 25.18 PSP `fig25_18.psp` extends `fig25_17` servlet. (Part 3 of 3.)

Fig. 25.18 demonstrates how to use methods inherited from a servlet that is specified in the **extends** attribute of the **page** directive. Lines 8–12 define a list of page-directive attributes. Lines 8–9 indicate that the PSP parser should use the **space** indentation style and that the number of spaces for indentation is **3**. Lines 10–11 import the **fig25_17** servlet, which is defined in Fig. 25.17. Line 12 indicates to the PSP parser that the servlet produced by parsing the PSP file is derived from the **fig25_17** servlet.

The scriptlets in lines 26–41 are the same as those in Fig. 25.14. To run this example in Webware, copy **fig25_17.py** and **fig25_18.psp** into the **PSP/Examples/ch25** directory. Modify line 16 of **fig25_13.html** to

```
<form method = "post" action = "fig25_18.psp">
```

Make sure Webware's application server (**AppServer**) and Apache Web Server are running. Open your Web browser, and enter the following URL to test **fig25_18.psp**:

```
http://localhost/cgi-bin/WebKit.cgi/PSPExamples/ch25/
    fig25_13.html
```

After filling in the form, click the **Submit** button, so the PSP **fig25_18.psp** is invoked. Figure 25.18 displays the output.

25.8.2 `include` Directive

The **include** *directive* is different from the **<psp:include>** action. Action **<psp:include>** calls a PSP, servlet, or any other URL accessible through Webware and includes the output of the PSP or servlet. The **include** directive inserts the contents of another PSP file as though the contents were in the file containing the directive. The referenced resource must be a PSP, not a servlet. The included PSP will have access to all variables defined in the PSP.

The **include** directive has only one attribute—**file**—which specifies the URL of the page to include. The difference between directive **include** and action **<psp:include>** is noticeable only if the included content changes. For example, if the contents of an XHTML document changes after it is included with directive **include**, future requests of the PSP will show the original content of the XHTML document, not the new content. In contrast, action **<psp:include>** is processed each time the PSP is requested. Therefore, changes to included content would be shown in the subsequent requests to the PSP that uses action **<psp:include>**.

The PSP in Fig. 25.19 implements **include.psp** (Fig. 25.10) with **include** directives. To test **fig25_19.psp** in Webware, copy **fig25_19.psp** into the **PSP/Examples/ch25** directory. Make sure Webware's application server (**AppServer**) and Apache Web Server are running. Open a Web browser, and enter the following URL to test **fig25_19.psp**:

```
http://localhost/cgi-bin/WebKit.cgi/PSPExamples/ch25/
    fig25_19.psp
```

```
1   <!DOCTYPE html PUBLIC "-//W3C//DTD XHTML 1.0 Strict//EN"
2      "http://www.w3.org/TR/xhtml1/DTD/xhtml1-strict.dtd">
3
4   <!-- Fig. 25.19: fig25_19.psp             -->
5   <!-- Demonstrates the include directive. -->
6
7   <html xmlns = "http://www.w3.org/1999/xhtml">
8
9      <head>
10        <title>Using the include directive</title>
11
12        <style type = "text/css">
13           body {
14              font-family: tahoma, helvetica, arial, sans-serif;
15           }
16
17           table, tr, td {
18              font-size: .9em;
19              border: 3px groove;
20              padding: 5px;
21              background-color: #dddddd;
22           }
23        </style>
24     </head>
25
26     <body>
27        <table>
28           <tr>
29              <td style = "width: 160px; text-align: center">
30                 <img src = "images/logotiny.png"
31                    width = "140" height = "93"
32                    alt = "Deitel & Associates, Inc. Logo" />
33              </td>
34
35              <td>
36
37                 <%-- include banner.html in this PSP --%>
38                 <%@ include file = "banner.html" %>
39
```

Fig. 25.19 include directive used to include content at generation time.
(Part 1 of 2.)

```
40                    </td>
41                </tr>
42
43                <tr>
44                    <td style = "width: 160px">
45
46                        <%-- include toc.html in this PSP --%>
47                        <%@ include file = "toc.html" %>
48
49                    </td>
50
51                    <td style = "vertical-align: top">
52
53                        <%-- include clock2.psp in this PSP --%>
54                        <%@ include file = "clock2.psp" %>
55
56                    </td>
57                </tr>
58            </table>
59        </body>
60    </html>
```

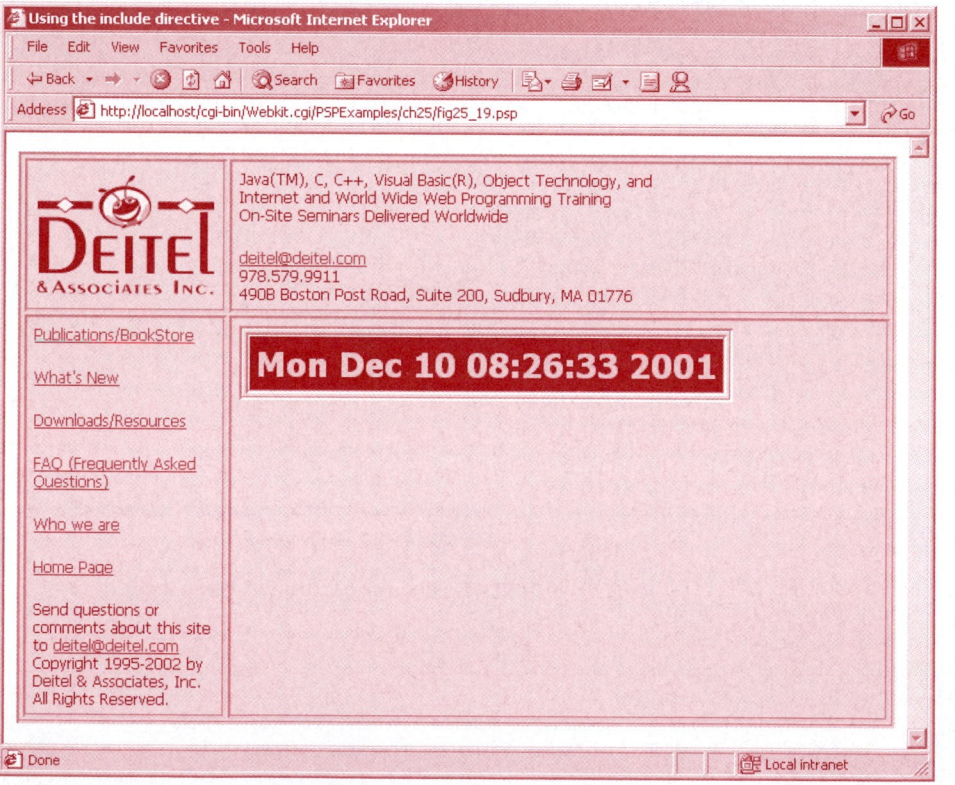

Fig. 25.19 `include` directive used to include content at generation time.
(Part 2 of 2.)

Software Engineering Observation 25.5

*Using the **include** directive to include a file is faster but less convenient than using the **<psp:include>** action. Setting the **include** directive makes it necessary for the programmer to restart the WebKit application server (**AppServer**) whenever the included file changes.*

25.9 Case Study: Message Forums with Python and XML[2]

In this section, we use XML[3] and several XML-related technologies to create one of the most popular types of Web sites: A *message forum*. Message forums are "virtual" bulletin boards where users discuss various topics. Common features of message forums include discussion groups, question-and-answer sections and general comments. Many Web sites host message forums. Some popular message forums are

```
groups.yahoo.com
web.eesite.com/forums
groups.google.com
```

This section recreates the message forum found in Chapter 16, Python XML Processing. In Chapter 16, we used CGI to implement the forum. In this section, we show how to implement the message forum using PSP.

Figure 25.20 summarizes the files that comprise the message forum. Figure 25.21 shows the directory structure for Apache running on Windows. Figure 25.22 illustrates some of the key interactions between the files. The main XHTML page generated by **default.psp** displays the list of available message forums, which are stored in the XML document **forums.xml**. Hyperlinks are provided to each XML message forum document and to script **addForum.psp**, which adds a forum to **forums.xml** and creates an XML message forum, using the markup in **template.xml** as a starting point.

Each XML document that contains a forum (e.g., **feedback.xml**) is transformed into an XHTML document by applying the XSLT document **formatting.xsl**. The XHTML generated is formatted by applying **site.css**. New messages are posted to a forum by **addPost.psp**.

File Name	Description
forums.xml	XML document listing all available forums and their filenames.
default.psp	Main page, providing navigational links to the forums.
template.xml	Template for a message forum XML document.
addForum.psp	Adds a new forum.

Fig. 25.20 Message-forum documents. (Part 1 of 2.)

---

2. The implementation of this message forum requires Internet Explorer 5 or higher, and msxml 3.0 or higher. In Section 25.9.3, we discuss how other client browsers, such as Netscape, may be used.
3. For more information on XML, refer to Chapter 15, Extensible Markup Language (XML) and Chapter 16, Python XML Processing.

File Name	Description
feedback.xml	Sample message forum.
formatting.xsl	XSLT document for transforming message forums into XHTML.
addPost.psp	Adds a message to a forum.
site.css	Style sheet for formatting XHTML documents.
forum.psp	Transforms XML documents to HTML for non-XSL browsers.

Fig. 25.20 Message-forum documents. (Part 2 of 2.)

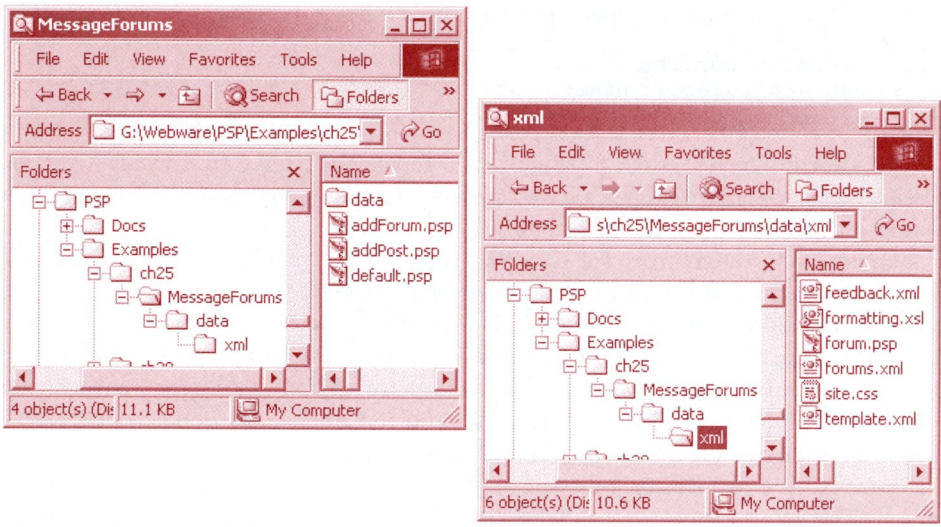

Fig. 25.21 Directory structure of message forum.

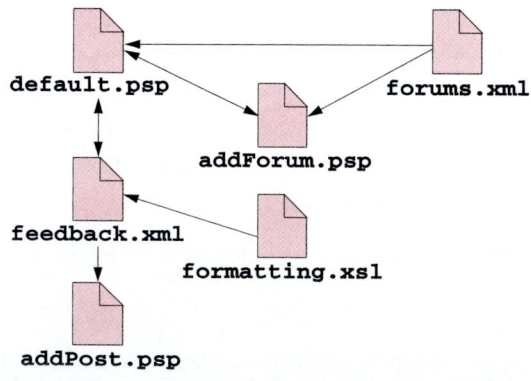

Fig. 25.22 Key interactions between message-forum documents.

25.9.1 Displaying the Forums

This section discusses how XML is used to mark up message forum data and the PSP—**default.psp**—that creates the message forum's main XHTML page. For this case study, we provide a sample forum named **feedback.xml** (Fig. 25.23) to show the structure of a forum document.

Notice the reference to the style sheet **formatting.xsl** (line 6). When applied by msxml, this XSLT document (which we discuss later in the chapter) transforms the XML into XHTML for display in Internet Explorer. Forum documents have root element **forum**, which contains attribute **file**. This attribute's value is the document's filename. Child elements include **name**, for specifying the title of the forum, and **message**, for marking up the message. Messages contain a user name, a title and the text, which are marked up by elements **user**, **title** and **text**, respectively. Messages also are given a **timestamp**.

The document **forums.xml** (Fig. 25.24) contains the filename and title for every message forum. As forums are created, this document is updated.

Root element **forums** (line 8) contains one or more **forum** child elements. Initially, one forum (i.e., **Feedback**) is present. Each **forum** element has attribute **filename** and child element **name**.

```
1   <?xml version = "1.0"?>
2
3   <!-- Fig. 25.23: feedback.xml          -->
4   <!-- XML document representing a forum. -->
5
6   <?xml:stylesheet type = "text/xsl" href = "formatting.xsl"?>
7
8   <forum file = "feedback.xml">
9      <name>Feedback</name>
10
11     <message timestamp = "Wed Jun 27 12:53:22 2001">
12        <user>Jessica</user>
13        <title>Nice forums!</title>
14        <text>These forums are great! Well done, all.</text>
15     </message>
16
17  </forum>
```

Fig. 25.23 XML document representing a forum containing one message.

```
1   <?xml version = "1.0"?>
2
3   <!-- Fig. 25.24: forums.xml            -->
4   <!-- XML document containing all forums. -->
5
6   <?xml:stylesheet type = "text/xsl" href = "formatting.xsl"?>
7
8   <forums>
9
```

Fig. 25.24 XML document containing data for all available forums. (Part 1 of 2.)

```
10      <forum filename = "feedback.xml">
11          <name>Feedback</name>
12      </forum>
13
14  </forums>
```

Fig. 25.24 XML document containing data for all available forums. (Part 2 of 2.)

Visitors to the message forum are greeted initially by the Web page that **default.psp** (Fig. 25.25) generates, which displays links to all forums and provides forum management options. Initially, only two links are active—one to view the **Feedback** forum (i.e., the sample forum) and one to create a forum. In the chapter exercises, we ask the reader to enhance the message forum by adding functionality for modifying and deleting forums.

This PSP uses package **4DOM** to parse **forums.xml**. Lines 15–19 print the XHTML header for the main page with a link to a Cascading Style Sheet (CSS) that formats the page. Lines 23–31 open **forums.xml**. Lines 35–36 instantiate a parser object, then load and parse **forums.xml**. Lines 39–70 output XHTML to the browser. The **for** loop (lines 53–60) retrieves all **Element** nodes that contain the tag name **forum**. Hyperlinks are created to each forum found in **forums.xml**. Lines 63–70 print the remaining XHTML, including a hyperlink to **addForum.psp**. Finally, line 72 releases the **Document** object from memory.

In this case study, we would like to take advantage of msxml's XML parsing and XSLT processing capabilities to reduce the amount of processing the server must perform. Method **req.environ** (line 44) returns a dictionary that contains the request's environment variables. Lines 44–45 determine whether the client is using Internet Explorer. If so, **prefix** is set to **"data/xml/"**. Otherwise, **prefix** is set to **"data/xml/forum.psp?file="**. Note that line 55 uses **prefix** to construct the hyperlinks to each forum. Clients who use Internet Explorer request the XML documents directly, while other clients request **forum.psp**. We discuss this in greater detail in Section 25.9.3.

```
1   <?xml version = "1.0"?>
2   <!DOCTYPE html PUBLIC "-//W3C//DTD XHTML 1.0 Strict//EN"
3       "http://www.w3.org/TR/xhtml1/DTD/xhtml1-strict.dtd">
4
5   <!-- Fig. 25.25: default.psp -->
6   <!-- Default message forums. -->
7
8   <%-- import time module --%>
9   <%@ page imports = "os" %>
10  <%@ page imports = "xml.dom.ext.reader:PyExpat" %>
11  <%@ page indentType = "braces" %>
12
13  <html xmlns = "http://www.w3.org/1999/xhtml">
14
15      <head>
16          <title>Bug2Bug Message Forums</title>
```

Fig. 25.25 Default page for XML message forums. (Part 1 of 3.)

```
17          <link rel = "stylesheet" href = "data/xml/site.css"
18             type = "text/css" />
19       </head>
20
21       <body>
22          <% # open forms.xml file
23             try: {
24                filePath = "PSP/Examples/ch25/MessageForums/"
25                XML = open( filePath + "data/xml/forums.xml" )
26                loadpage = 1
27             }
28             except IOError: {
29                res.write( "could not open file" )
30                loadpage = 0
31             }
32
33             # parse forums.xml and write XHTML markup
34             if loadpage: {
35                reader = PyExpat.Reader()
36                document = reader.fromStream( XML )
37                XML.close()
38
39                res.write( """<h1>Bug2Bug Message Forums</h1>
40                   <p style="font-weight:bold">Available Forums</p>
41                   <ul>""" )
42
43                # identify client browser type
44                if req.environ()['HTTP_USER_AGENT'].find( \
45                   "MSIE" ) != -1: {
46                   prefix = "data/xml/"
47                }
48                else: {
49                   prefix = "data/xml/forum.psp?file="
50                }
51
52                # get available forums from forums.xml
53                for forum in document.getElementsByTagName( \
54                   "forum" ): {
55                   link = prefix + forum.attributes.item( 0 ).value
56                   name = forum.getElementsByTagName( "name" )[ 0 ]
57                   nameText = name.childNodes[ 0 ].nodeValue
58                   res.write( '<li><a href = "%s">%s</a></li>' \
59                      % ( link, nameText ) )
60                }
61
62                # add XHTML markup
63                res.write( """</ul>
64                   <p style="font-weight:bold">Forum Management</p>
65                   <ul>
66                      <li><a href = "addForum.psp">
67                         Add a Forum</a></li>
68                      <li>Delete a Forum</li>
69                      <li>Modify a Forum</li>
```

Fig. 25.25 Default page for XML message forums. (Part 2 of 3.)

```
70                  </ul>""" )
71
72              reader.releaseNode( document )
73
74          } # end if
75
76      %> <!-- end script -->
77    </body>
78  </html>
```

Fig. 25.25 Default page for XML message forums. (Part 3 of 3.)

25.9.2 Adding Forums and Messages

In this section, we discuss the PSPs and documents that add forums and messages. The PSP that adds a new forum is shown in Fig. 25.26. This script uses modules in package **4DOM** to manipulate XML documents.

```
1   <?xml version = "1.0"?>
2   <!DOCTYPE html PUBLIC "-//W3C//DTD XHTML 1.0 Strict//EN"
3       "http://www.w3.org/TR/xhtml1/DTD/xhtml1-strict.dtd">
4
5   <!-- Fig. 25.26: addForum.psp          -->
6   <!-- Adds a forum to the list of forums. -->
7
8   <%-- import modules and specify indent type  --%>
9   <%@ page imports = "re" %>
10  <%@ page imports = "xml.dom.ext.reader:PyExpat" %>
11  <%@ page imports = "xml.dom.ext:PrettyPrint" %>
12  <%@ page indentType = "braces" %>
13
14  <html xmlns = "http://www.w3.org/1999/xhtml">
15
```

Fig. 25.26 PSP that adds a new forum to **forums.xml**. (Part 1 of 4.)

```
16      <head>
17         <title>Add a Forum</title>
18         <link rel = "stylesheet" href = "data/xml/site.css"
19            type = "text/css" />
20      </head>
21
22      <body>
23         <% # have form fields filled
24            if req.hasField( "name" ) and \
25               req.hasField( "filename" ): {
26               newFile = req.field( "filename" )
27
28               # filename must have suffix .xml
29               if not re.match( "\w+\.xml$", newFile ): {
30                  res.write( """<h1>Error: File name should
31                     end with ".xml".</h1>""" )
32               }
33               else: {
34
35                  # open xml files
36                  try: {
37                     filePath = "PSP/Examples/ch25/MessageForums" \
38                        + "/data/xml/"
39                     newForumFile = open( filePath + newFile, "w" )
40                     forumsFile = \
41                        open( filePath + "forums.xml", "r+" )
42                     templateFile = \
43                        open( filePath + "template.xml" )
44                     noError = 1
45                  }
46                  except IOError: {
47                     res.write(
48                        """<h1>Error: Cannot open files.</h1>""" )
49                     noError = 0
50                  }
51
52                  # update old files and create new file
53                  if noError: {
54
55                     # parse old forums document
56                     reader = PyExpat.Reader()
57                     document = reader.fromStream( forumsFile )
58
59                     # add new forum to DOM object
60                     forum = document.createElement( "forum" )
61                     forum.setAttribute( "filename", newFile )
62
63                     name = document.createElement( "name" )
64                     nameText = document.createTextNode(
65                        req.field( "name" ) )
66                     name.appendChild( nameText )
67                     forum.appendChild( name )
68
```

Fig. 25.26 PSP that adds a new forum to **forums.xml**. (Part 2 of 4.)

```
69              documentNode = document.documentElement
70              firstForum = documentNode.getElementsByTagName(
71                 "forum" )[ 0 ]
72              documentNode.insertBefore( forum, firstForum )
73
74              # write updated DOM object to forums document
75              forumsFile.seek( 0, 0 )
76              forumsFile.truncate()
77              PrettyPrint( document, forumsFile )
78              forumsFile.close()
79
80              # create document for new forum from
81              # template file
82              document = reader.fromStream( templateFile )
83              forum = document.documentElement
84              forum.setAttribute( "file", newFile )
85
86              name = document.createElement( "name" )
87              nameText = document.createTextNode(
88                 req.field( "name" ) )
89              name.appendChild( nameText )
90              forum.appendChild( name )
91
92              # write created DOM object to new forum file
93              PrettyPrint( document, newForumFile )
94              newForumFile.close()
95              templateFile.close()
96              reader.releaseNode( document )
97
98              # forward to default page
99              trans.application().forward(
100                trans, 'default.psp' )
101
102         } # end if
103
104       } # end else
105
106    } # end if
107
108    # create form
109    else: {
110       res.write( """
111          <form action = "addForum.psp" method="post">
112          Forum Name<br />
113             <input type = "text" name = "name"
114                size = "40" /><br />
115             Forum File Name<br />
116             <input type = "text" name = "filename"
117                size = "40" /><br />
118             <input type = "submit" name = "submit"
119                value = "Submit" />
120             <input type = "reset" value = "Reset" />
121          </form>
```

Fig. 25.26 PSP that adds a new forum to **forums.xml**. (Part 3 of 4.)

```
122
123                    <a href = "default.psp">
124                        Return to Main Page</a>""" )
125
126            } # end else
127
128         %> <!-- end script -->
129     </body>
130 </html>
```

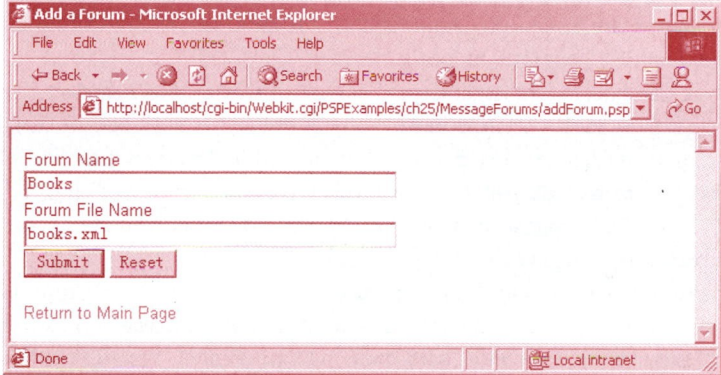

Fig. 25.26 PSP that adds a new forum to **forums.xml**. (Part 4 of 4.)

When the PSP is executed initially, it is not passed any parameters. Lines 24–25 call **req.hasField** to see if the required fields have been entered. Execution begins with the **else** block at line 109 because the form contains no values. Lines 110–124 output a form that prompts the user for a forum name and a filename for the XML document to be created. When the form is submitted, the script is re-requested and passed the user-entered form values. When this occurs, the condition (lines 24–25) is true, and lines 26–106 execute.

Line 29 examines the filename posted to the script to make sure it contains only alphanumeric characters and ends with **.xml**; if not, this PSP generates an error message. This prevents a malicious user from writing to a system file or otherwise gaining unrestricted access to the server. However, it is important to note that other solutions exist, such as generating filenames on the server. If the filename is permitted, line 39 attempts to create the file by calling function **open**.

Lines 40–41 open file **forums.xml** for reading and writing (**"r+"**). Lines 42–43 open the template XML document named **template.xml** (Fig. 25.27), which provides a forum's markup. The template contains an empty **forums** element, to which the forum name and filename are added programmatically. If an error occurs during an attempt to open any file, this PSP generates an error message.

Line 56 instantiates a DOM parser and assigns it to variable **reader**. Line 57 loads and parses **forums.xml**; the **Document** object created is assigned to variable **document**. Because we wish to create a **forum** element within **forums**, line 60 calls the **Document** object's **createElement** method with the name of the new element (**"forum"**). The **filename** attribute of the new **Element** node is set by calling **setAttribute** and passing the attribute's name and value.

The **forum** element contains only one piece of information—the forum name—added by lines 63–67. Line 63 creates another **Element** node named **name**. To add character data to the new **Element** node, a child **Text** node must be created. We call method **createTextNode** (lines 64–65) with the forum name from the form (i.e., **req.field("name")**). Line 66 appends the **Text** node to the **Element** node referenced by **name** by calling method **appendChild**. Line 67 adds the **Element** node referenced by **name** to the **Element** node referenced by **forum**.

Line 69 accesses the **documentElement** attribute of **document** to obtain the root element node (i.e., **forums**). Lines 70–71 obtain a **NodeList** of all **forum** elements by calling method **getElementsByTagName**, the first of which is assigned to variable **firstForum**. Line 72 inserts the new **Element** node referenced by **forum** before the first child node of **forums** by calling method **insertBefore**. With this technique, the most recently added forums appear first in the forum list.

To update **forums.xml**, line 75 **seek**s to the beginning and deletes any existing data (by truncating the file to size **0**). Line 77 then calls function **PrettyPrint** to write the updated XML to **forumsFile**.

Line 82 loads and parses file **template.xml** (Fig. 25.27) by calling method **fromStream** and assigns the **Document** object created to variable **document**. Line 83 uses **documentElement** to get the root element, and line 84 sets its **file** attribute's value to the specified filename. Lines 86–90 add the **name** node, and lines 93–94 output the updated XML to **newForumFile** and close the file. Lines 95–96 close **template.xml** and release the **Document** object from memory. The user is redirected to **default.psp** in lines 99–100 by calling method **forward** of the application object.

Figure 25.28 contains the PSP that allows users to add messages to a forum. When **formatting.xsl** (Fig. 25.29) is applied to a forum document, a link to **addPost.psp** is added to the page, which includes the current forum's filename. This filename is passed to **addPost.psp** (e.g., **addPost.psp?file=forum1.xml**).

```
1   <?xml version = "1.0"?>
2
3   <!-- Fig. 25.27: template.xml   -->
4   <!-- Empty forum file.          -->
5
6   <?xml:stylesheet type = "text/xsl" href = "formatting.xsl"?>
7   <forum>
8   </forum>
```

Fig. 25.27 XML template used to generate new forums.

Line 33 checks whether the user has entered a new *post*. The user has not yet submitted a new message; therefore, the form does not contain the value **"submit"**, and execution proceeds to line 106. If the form contains a single value (i.e., the filename), lines 107–127 output a form, which includes fields for the user name, message title, message text and the forum filename as a hidden value (lines 119–199). Note that, if no parameters are passed to the script, the script has been accessed in an inappropriate way, and the programs generates an error message (line 132).

When the form data are submitted, the posted information is processed. Line 34 obtains the specified filename. As in the previous figure, the filename is checked for an **.xml** extension, and the file is opened (lines 37–53). Lines 59–66 parse the forum file, create an **Element** node with tag name **message** and set the node's **timestamp** attribute by calling method **setAttribute**.

Lines 69–84 create **Element** nodes that represent the **user**, **title** and **text** and add text that corresponds to the values entered in the form. Note that, if a field has been left blank, **"(Field left blank)"** is entered for that field. Each new **Element** node is appended to the node referenced by **message** (line 84).

```
1   <?xml version = "1.0"?>
2   <!DOCTYPE html PUBLIC "-//W3C//DTD XHTML 1.0 Strict//EN"
3       "http://www.w3.org/TR/xhtml1/DTD/xhtml1-strict.dtd">
4
5   <!-- Fig. 25.28: addPost.psp    -->
6   <!-- Adds a message to a forum. -->
7
8   <%-- import modules and specify indent type --%>
9   <%@ page imports = "re, time" %>
10  <%@ page imports = "xml.dom.ext.reader:PyExpat" %>
11  <%@ page imports = "xml.dom.ext:PrettyPrint" %>
12  <%@ page indentType = "braces" %>
13
14  <html xmlns = "http://www.w3.org/1999/xhtml">
15
16      <head>
17          <title>Add a Posting</title>
18          <link rel = "stylesheet" href = "data/xml/site.css"
19              type = "text/css" />
20      </head>
21
```

Fig. 25.28 PSP that adds a message to a forum. (Part 1 of 4.)

```
22      <body>
23          <% # identify client browser type
24              if req.environ()['HTTP_USER_AGENT'].find( \
25                  "MSIE" ) != -1: {
26                  prefix = "data/xml/"
27              }
28              else: {
29                  prefix = "data/xml/forum.psp?file="
30              }
31
32              # submit form
33              if req.hasField( "submit" ): {
34                  filename = req.field( "file" )
35
36                  # filename must have suffix .xml
37                  if not re.match( "\w+\.xml$", filename ): {
38                      res.write( """<h1>Error:
39                          File name should end with ".xml".</h1>""" )
40                  }
41                  else: {
42
43                      # open forum xml file
44                      try: {
45                          forumFile = open( "PSP/Examples/ch25/" + \
46                              "MessageForums/data/xml/" + filename, "r+" )
47                          noError = 1
48                      }
49                      except IOError: {
50                          res.write( """<h1>Error:
51                              Cannot open files.</h1>""" )
52                          noError = 0
53                      }
54
55                      # add message to forum xml file
56                      if noError: {
57
58                          # parse old forum document
59                          reader = PyExpat.Reader()
60                          document = reader.fromStream( forumFile )
61                          documentNode = document.documentElement
62
63                          # create new message element
64                          message = document.createElement( "message" )
65                          message.setAttribute(
66                              "timestamp", time.ctime( time.time() ) ) )
67
68                          # add elements to message
69                          messageElements = [ "user", "title", "text" ]
70
71                          for item in messageElements: {
72
```

Fig. 25.28 PSP that adds a message to a forum. (Part 2 of 4.)

```
73                          if not req.field( item ): {
74                              text = "( Field left blank )"
75                          }
76                          else: {
77                              text = req.field( item )
78                          }
79
80                          element = document.createElement( item )
81                          elementText = document.createTextNode(
82                              text )
83                          element.appendChild( elementText )
84                          message.appendChild( element )
85                      }
86
87                      # append new message to forum
88                      documentNode.appendChild( message )
89                      forumFile.seek( 0, 0 )
90                      forumFile.truncate()
91                      PrettyPrint( document, forumFile )
92                      forumFile.close()
93                      reader.releaseNode( document )
94
95                      # forward to default page
96                      trans.application().forward(
97                          trans, 'default.psp' )
98
99                  } # end if
100
101              } # end else
102
103          } # end if
104
105          # create form
106          elif req.hasField( "file" ): {
107              res.write( """
108                  <form action = "addPost.psp" method="post">
109                  User<br />
110                      <input type = "text" name = "user"
111                          size = "40" /><br />
112                      Message Title<br />
113                      <input type = "text" name = "title"
114                          size = "40" /><br />
115                      Message Text<br />
116                      <textarea name = "text" cols = "40"
117                          rows = "5"></textarea><br />
118                      <input type = "hidden" name = "file"
119                          value = "%s" />
120                      <input type = "submit" name = "submit"
121                          value = "Submit" />
122                      <input type = "reset" value = "Reset" />
123                  </form>
124
```

Fig. 25.28 PSP that adds a message to a forum. (Part 3 of 4.)

```
125                    <a href = "%s">Return to Forum</a>""" % \
126                        ( req.field( "file" ), prefix + \
127                        req.field( "file" ) ) )
128
129            } # end elif
130
131            else: {
132                res.write( """<h1>Error occured</h1>""" )
133            }
134
135        %> <!-- end script -->
136    </body>
137 </html>
```

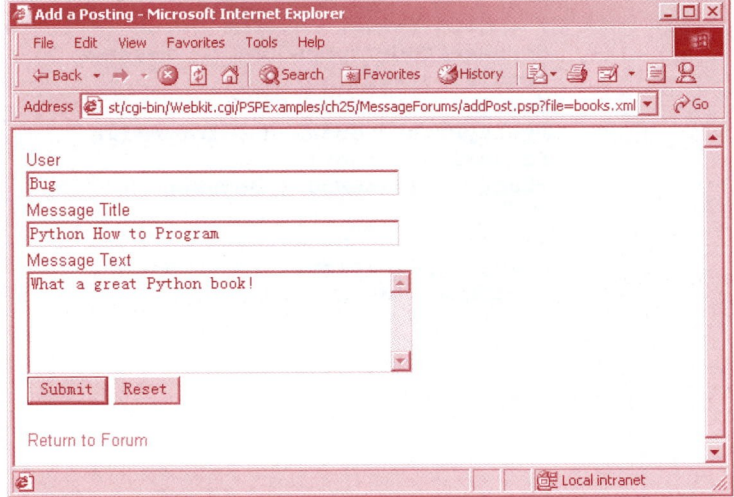

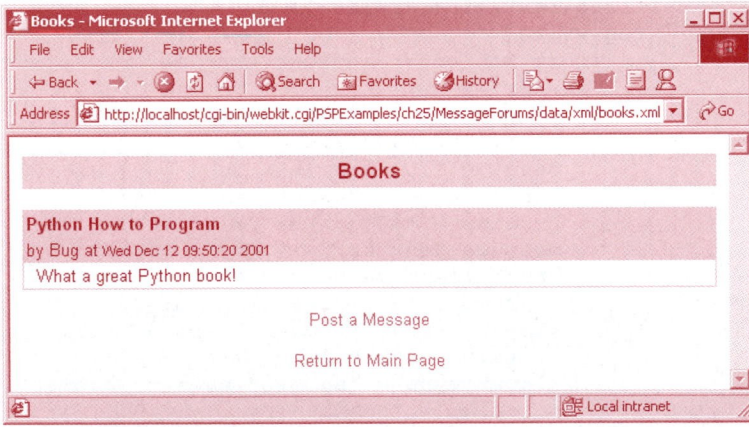

Fig. 25.28 PSP that adds a message to a forum. (Part 4 of 4.)

Line 88 appends the node referenced by **message** to the node referenced by **doc-umentNode**. Lines 89–91 then **seek** and **truncate** the XML file to eliminate the file's content and write the updated XML markup. Lines 92–93 close the file and free the **Document** object from memory. The user is redirected to the main forum page (**default.psp**) in lines 96–97.

25.9.3 Alterations for Browsers Without XML and XSLT Support

This case study uses an Extensible Stylesheet Language Transformations (XSLT) style sheet (**formatting.xsl** in Fig. 25.29) to transform XML data into XHTML that is rendered in Internet Explorer. Recall that each XML document sent to Internet Explorer contains a processing instruction that references this style sheet.

Support for XSLT currently is available only for Internet Explorer 5 and higher. This means that our message forum application could send XML content to some browsers (e.g., Netscape Communicator 6) that do not have built-in XML parsers and XSLT processors. To create a more client-independent application, we can parse the XML on the server and apply the XSLT transformation on the server.

```
1   <?xml version = "1.0"?>
2
3   <!-- Fig. 25.29: formatting.xsl   -->
4   <!-- Style sheet for forum files. -->
5
6   <xsl:stylesheet version = "1.0"
7       xmlns:xsl = "http://www.w3.org/1999/XSL/Transform">
8
9       <!-- match document root -->
10      <xsl:template match = "/">
11          <html xmlns = "http://www.w3.org/1999/xhtml">
12
13              <!-- apply for all elements -->
14              <xsl:apply-templates select = "*" />
15          </html>
16      </xsl:template>
17
18      <!-- match forum elements -->
19      <xsl:template match = "forum">
20          <head>
21              <title><xsl:value-of select = "name" /></title>
22              <link rel = "stylesheet" type = "text/css"
23                  href = "site.css" />
24          </head>
25
26          <body>
27              <table width = "100%" cellspacing = "0"
28                  cellpadding = "2">
29                  <tr>
30                      <td class = "forumTitle">
31                          <xsl:value-of select = "name" />
32                      </td>
33                  </tr>
34              </table>
```

Fig. 25.29 XSLT style sheet that transforms XML into XHTML. (Part 1 of 2.)

```
35
36                <!-- apply templates for message only -->
37                <br />
38                    <xsl:apply-templates select = "message" />
39                <br />
40
41                <div style = "text-align: center">
42                    <a>
43                        <!-- href attribute for an element -->
44                        <xsl:attribute name = "href">../../ad-
dPost.psp?file=<xsl:value-of select = "@file" />
45                        </xsl:attribute>
46                        Post a Message
47                    </a>
48                    <br /><br />
49                    <a href = "../../default.psp">Return to Main Page</a>
50                </div>
51
52        </body>
53    </xsl:template>
54
55    <!-- match message elements -->
56    <xsl:template match = "message">
57        <table width = "100%" cellspacing = "0"
58            cellpadding = "2">
59            <tr>
60                <td class = "msgTitle">
61                    <xsl:value-of select = "title" />
62                </td>
63            </tr>
64
65            <tr>
66                <td class = "msgInfo">
67                    by
68                    <xsl:value-of select = "user" />
69                    at
70                    <span class = "date">
71                        <xsl:value-of select = "@timestamp" />
72                    </span>
73                </td>
74            </tr>
75
76            <tr>
77                <td class = "msgText">
78                    <xsl:value-of select = "text" />
79                </td>
80            </tr>
81
82        </table>
83    </xsl:template>
84
85  </xsl:stylesheet>
```

Fig. 25.29 XSLT style sheet that transforms XML into XHTML. (Part 2 of 2.)

4XSLT, which is a package included in **4Suite**, contains an XSLT processor for transforming XML into HTML. We can create an instance of this processor for applying style sheets to XML documents.

Recall how the **prefix** variable in **default.psp** (Fig. 25.25) and **addPost.psp** (Fig. 25.28) was used to define where links or redirection statements sent clients. By allowing Internet Explorer's XML parser and XSLT processor to parse the XML and apply a style sheet to the XML, we reduce the load on the server. For browsers without XML and XSLT support, however, we direct clients to a PSP that parses the XML document and sends HTML to the client.

We therefore insert a browser test at line 44 of **default.psp** and at line 24 of **addPost.psp**:

```
if req.environ()['HTTP_USER_AGENT'].find( \
   "MSIE" ) != -1: {
   prefix = "data/xml/"
}
else: {
   prefix = "data/xml/forum.psp?file="
}
```

Variable **prefix** is set according to whether *MSIE* (Microsoft Internet Explorer) appears in the **HTTP_USER_AGENT** environment variable. For simplicity, we assume Internet Explorer 5 or higher (with msxml 3.0 or higher) is the only version of MSIE being used and do not test for older versions.

Once **prefix** has been set, we may use its value to customize the URLs generated by the scripts. One example occurs in line 55 of **default.psp**:

```
link = prefix + forum.attributes.item( 0 ).value
```

This line directs Internet Explorer users to the specified XML forum file located in **data/xml/**, but sends users of other browsers to **data/xml/forum.psp?file=**, a PSP that receives a single parameter (i.e., the filename).

Figure 25.30 shows **forum.psp**, which transforms XML documents to HTML on the server. The figure also includes the rendered HTML output displayed in Netscape Communicator.

```
1   <?xml version = "1.0"?>
2   <!DOCTYPE html PUBLIC "-//W3C//DTD XHTML 1.0 Strict//EN"
3      "http://www.w3.org/TR/xhtml1/DTD/xhtml1-strict.dtd">
4
5   <!-- Fig. 25.30: forum.psp                          -->
6   <!-- Display forums for non-Internet Explorer browsers. -->
7
8   <%-- import modules and specify indent type --%>
9   <%@ page imports = "re" %>
10  <%@ page imports = "xml.xslt:Processor" %>
11  <%@ page indentType = "braces" %>
12
```

Fig. 25.30 PSP that transforms XML into HTML for browsers without XSL support. (Part 1 of 3.)

```
13    <html xmlns = "http://www.w3.org/1999/xhtml">
14
15       <head>
16          <title>Add a Forum</title>
17       </head>
18
19       <body>
20          <% # get xml filename
21             if req.hasField( "file" ): {
22                fileName = req.field( "file" )
23
24                # filename must have suffix .xml
25                if not re.match( "\w+\.xml$", fileName ): {
26                   res.write( "<h1>Error:Invalid xml file</h1>" )
27                }
28                else: {
29
30                   # open forum xml file and style sheet
31                   try: {
32                      filePath = "PSP/Examples/ch25/MessageForums" \
33                         + "/data/xml/"
34                      style = open( filePath + "formatting.xsl" )
35                      XMLFile = open( filePath + fileName )
36                      noError = 1
37                   }
38                   except IOError: {
39                      noError = 0
40                   }
41
42                   # translate xml to html
43                   if noError: {
44                      processor = Processor.Processor()
45                      processor.appendStylesheetStream( style )
46                      results = processor.runStream( XMLFile )
47                      style.close()
48                      XMLFile.close()
49                      res.write( results )
50                   }
51
52                } # end else
53
54             } # end if
55
56             else: {
57                res.write( "Error: No file supplied" )
58             }
59
60          %> <!-- end script -->
61       </body>
62    </html>
```

Fig. 25.30 PSP that transforms XML into HTML for browsers without XSL support.
(Part 2 of 3.)

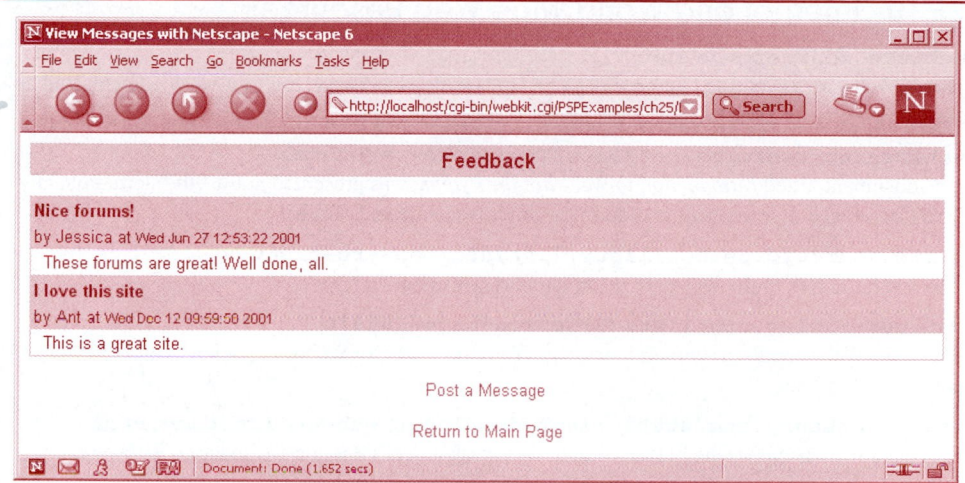

Fig. 25.30 PSP that transforms XML into HTML for browsers without XSL support.
(Part 3 of 3.)

If a filename is not passed to the script, an error message is generated (line 57). Otherwise, line 22 obtains the filename. Lines 25–26 determine whether the specified filename ends in **.xml**. If so, lines 34–35 open the XSLT style sheet (**formatting.xsl**) and the specified XML document, respectively.

The XML then is transformed into HTML for display. Line 44 instantiates a **4XSLT Processor** object, which transforms XML into HTML, by applying an XSLT style sheet. Line 45 specifies the appropriate XSLT style sheet by invoking **processor**'s **appendStyleSheetStream** method. This method appends a style sheet to the list of style sheets a **Processor** can use. Note that more than one style sheet can be appended (i.e., **appendStyleSheetStream** can be called multiple times) so that the same **Processor** object can be used to transform an XML document to many different formats. The argument passed to **appendStyleSheetStream** must be a Python file object. Other methods for appending style sheets to a **4XSLT Processor** are **appendStyleSheetString**, **appendStyleSheetNode** and **appendStyleSheetUri**, which accept as arguments a string containing an XSLT style sheet, a DOM tree containing a style sheet and a URI that references a style sheet, respectively. The specified URI may be a URL (in the form of a string) that represents the location of the style sheet on the Web.

Line 46 invokes the **Processor**'s **runStream** method to apply the style sheet to the XML document. As with **appendStyleSheetStream**, the object passed to **runStream** must be a Python file object. Other methods used for applying style sheets are **runString**, **runNode** and **runUri**, which accept as arguments a string containing XML, a DOM tree containing XML and a URI that references an XML document, respectively.

Lines 47–48 close the XSLT and XML files used by the script. The transformed XML is then sent to the client as HTML (line 49).

25.10 Internet and World Wide Web Resources

`webware.sourceforge.net`
This is Webware's Web site that provides links to download software and to view documents and archives.

`webware.sourceforge.net/Docs/IntroToWebware.html`
This document, titled *Introduction to Webware for Python*, was presented at the 9th International Python Conference. It introduces and discusses both Webware and WebKit.

`lists.sourceforge.net/lists/listinfo/webware-discuss`
This site has a link to the Webware discussion-archives page.

`www.geocrawler.com/lists/3/SourceForge/3854/0/`
This is the Webware discussion-archives page. You can search for Webware packages and PSP-related messages at this site.

`www.colorstudy.com/static/ianb/downloads/webware/Anatomy.html`
This document discusses the process that occurs when an HTTP request is made to Webware.

`pyxml.sourceforge.net`
This is the **PyXML** site. It has links for documentation and special interest groups.

`4suite.org`
This is the **4Suite** Web site. It offers links to downloads, documentation, resources and support.

`py-howto.sourgeforge.net/xml-howto/contents.html`
This site provides a tutorial for Python XML processing. Some topics discussed include **xml.sax** and **4DOM**.

SUMMARY

- Python Server Pages enable Web-application programmers to create dynamic content by using predefined components and by interacting with components through server-side scripting.

- Webware is a suite of software for writing dynamic Web contents in Python. The WebKit suite in Webware acts as a Python servlet engine and produces standard XHTML.

- Webware's Python Server Pages require WebKit to be installed and configured.

- Classes for programming servlets are located at **Webware/WebKit** directory; classes specific to Python Server Pages programming are located in directory **Webware/PSP**.

- In Webware, a transaction is an object that contains all Python servlets. Classes that participate in a transaction include: **Application**, **Request**, **Response**, **Session** and **Servlet**.

- A servlet's life cycle begins when the servlet container loads the servlet into memory—normally, in response to the first request that the servlet receives. Before the servlet can handle that request, the servlet container invokes the servlet's **awake** method.

- After **awake** completes execution, the servlet can respond to its first request. All requests are handled by a servlet's **respond** method, which receives the request, processes the request and sends a response to the client.

- When the servlet container terminates the servlet, the servlet's **sleep** method is called to release servlet resources.

- There are three key components to PSPs: directives, actions and scriptlets.

- Directives specify global information that is not associated with a particular PSP request.

- Actions encapsulate functionality in predefined tags that programmers can embed in a PSP.

- Scriptlets, or scripting elements, enable programmers to insert Python code that interacts with components in a PSP (and possibly other Web application components) to perform request processing.

- PSP normally include XHTML markup. Such markup is known as fixed-template data or fixed-template text.

- Programmers tend to use PSP when most of the content sent to the client is fixed-template data and only a small portion of the content is generated dynamically with Python code.

- Programmers use servlets when only a small portion of the content is fixed-template data.

- When a PSP-enabled server receives the first request for a PSP, the PSP container translates that PSP into a Python servlet that handles the current request and future requests to the PSP.

- The request/response mechanism and life cycle of a PSP are the same as those of a servlet.

- PSP can define methods **awake** and **sleep** that are invoked when the container initializes a PSP and when the container terminates a PSP, respectively.

- PSP expressions are delimited by **<%=** and **%>**. The results of such expressions are converted to **String**s by the PSP container and are output as part of the response.

- The XHTML **meta** element can set a refresh interval for a document that is loaded into a browser. This causes the browser to request the document at the specified interval.

- When you first invoke a PSP in WebKit, there is a delay as WebKit translates the PSP into a servlet and invokes the servlet to respond to your request.

- Implicit objects provide programmers with servlet capabilities in the context of a Python Server Page.

- PSP scripting components include scriptlets, comments and expressions.

- Scriptlets are blocks of code delimited by **<%** and **%>**.

- PSP comments and Python comments are ignored and do not appear in the response.

- A PSP expression, delimited by **<%=** and **%>**, contains a Python expression that is evaluated when a client requests the PSP containing the expression. The container converts the result of a PSP expression to a string, then outputs the string as part of the response to the client.

- PSP standard actions provide PSP programmers with access to several of the most common tasks performed in a PSP. PSP containers process actions at request time.

- Python Server Pages support two **include** mechanisms—the **<psp:include>** action and the **include** directive.

- Action **<psp:include>** enables dynamic content to be included in a Python Server Page. If the included resource changes between requests, the next request to the PSP containing the **<psp:include>** action includes the new content of the resource.

- The **include** directive is processed once, at PSP generation time, and causes the content to be copied into the PSP. If the included resource changes, the new content will not be reflected in the PSP that used the **include** directive unless the WebKit application server is restarted.

- The difference between an **insert** action and an **include** action is that the PSP contents in a resource included by the **insert** action are not parsed by the PSP parser.

- Action **<psp:method>** enables a PSP to override methods inherited from the servlet class that the PSP extends and declare new methods of the servlet class.

- PSP programmers need to use the **</psp:method>** tag to end the method definition. The code placed in between the **<psp:method>** and **</psp:method>** tags is standard Python code. No raw XHTML or scripts are allowed between the method start and close tags.

- The **page** directive defines information that is available globally in a PSP. Directives are delimited by **<%@** and **%>**.

- Attribute **extends** of the **page** directive enables programmers to specify the servlet class from which the translated PSP will be inherited.

- Attribute **imports** of the **page** directive enables programmers to specify Python modules and objects that are used in the context of a PSP.

- Attribute **method** of the **page** directive enables programmers to declare new methods of the servlet class this PSP is producing and override the methods in the base class that the PSP extends.

- Attributes **indentType** and **indentSpaces** of the **page** directive enable programmers to specify the indentation style.

- Directives are messages to the PSP container that enable the programmer to specify page settings, to include content from other resources.

- The page directive specifies global settings for a PSP in the PSP container. There can be many page directives, provided that there is only one occurrence of each attribute. The only exception to this rule are the **imports** attribute, which can be used repeatedly to import Python modules used in the PSP, and the **method** attribute, which can be used repeatedly to declare new methods or to override methods in the base class.

TERMINOLOGY

$%> tag
<!-- and **-->** XHTML comment delimiters
<%-- and **--%>** PSP comment delimiters
<% and **%>** scriptlet delimiters
<%= and **%>** JSP expression delimiters
<%@ and **%>** directive delimiters
4DOM package
4Suite package
4XSLT package
appendChild method of element **name**
appendStyleSheetNode method of class
   Processor
appendStyleSheetStream method of class
   Processor
appendStyleSheetString method of class
   Processor
appendStyleSheetUri method of class
   Processor
Application class
awake method of class **Servlet**
container
createElement method of class **Document**
createTextNode method of class **Document**
directive
DOM parser
dynamic content
environ method of implicit object **req**
expression
extends attribute of **page** directive
field method of implicit object **req**
file attribute of **<psp:insert>** action

file attribute of **include** directive
fixed-template data
fixed-template text
forward method
freeing the DOM from memory
fromStream method of class **Reader**
generation-time error
generation-time include
hasField method of implicit object **req**
HTTPRequest class
HTTPResponse class
HTTPServlet class
implicit object
imports attribute of **page** directive
include directive
indentSpaces attribute of **page** directive
indentType attribute of **page** directive
isInstanceSafe attribute of **page** directive
isThreadSafe attribute of **page** directive
meta element
method attribute of **page** directive
name attribute of **<psp:method>** action
page attribute of **<jsp:forward>** action
page attribute of **<jsp:include>** action
page directive
page directive attribute
page implicit object
param attribute of **<psp:method>**
path attribute of **<psp:include>** action
PSP action
PSP comment

PSP directive
PSP expression
PSP expression delimiters **<%=** and **%>**
PSP implicit object
<psp:include> action
<psp:insert> action
<psp:method> action
PSP scriptlet
Python Server Pages (PSP)
refresh interval
req implicit object
Request class
request-time error
res implicit object
Response class
runNode method of class **Processor**
runStream method of class **Processor**
runString method of class **Processor**
runUri method of class **Processor**
scripting element

scriptlet
seek method of file handle **forumsFile**
Servlet class
servlet factory
Session class
setAttribute method of element **forum**
sleep method of class **Servlet**
static attribute of **<psp:insert>** action
trans implicit object
transaction object
WebKit.HTTPRequest class
WebKit.HTTPResponse class
WebKit.Request class
WebKit.Response class
WebKit.Transaction class
Webware
XHTML document
xsl:apply-templates element
XSLT style sheet

SELF-REVIEW EXERCISES

25.1   Fill in the blanks in each of the following statements:
  a) There are three key components to PSP: _____, _____ and _____.
  b) A PSP can specify its indentation style with _____ attribute of the **page** directive.
  c) _____ are messages to the PSP parser that enable the programmer to specify page settings and to include content from other resources.
  d) The _____ directive is processed once, at PSP generation time, and causes content to be copied into the PSP.
  e) The optional attribute _____ of the **<psp:insert>** action indicates to the PSP parser that the content of the inserted file is copied into the PSP once, at PSP generation time.
  f) PSP scripting components include _____, _____ and _____.

25.2   State whether each of the following is *true* or *false*. If *false*, explain why.
  a) In a Web application, an object with page scope exists in every PSP.
  b) Directives specify global information that is not associated with a particular PSP request.
  c) Action **<psp:include>** is evaluated once at page generation time.
  d) Like XHTML comments, PSP comments and Python comments appear in the response to the client.
  e) Action **<psp:include>** behaves in the same way as directive **include**, except that action **<psp:include>** includes the referenced material only once.
  f) Each page has its own instances of the page-scope implicit objects.

ANSWERS TO SELF-REVIEW EXERCISES

25.1   a) directives, actions and scriptlets. b) **indentType**. c) Directives (page and request). d) **include**. e) **static**. f) scriptlets, comments and expressions.

25.2 a) False. Objects with page scope exist only as part of the page in which they are used. b) True. c) False. Action **<psp:include>** enables dynamic content to be included in a Python Server Page. d) False. PSP comments and Python comments are ignored and do not appear in the response. e) False. Directive **include** includes the referenced material only once. f) True.

EXERCISES

25.3   Modify Fig. 25.12 to use an absolute path to specify the path of the included file.

25.4   Reimplement Fig. 25.14, using **braces** for the indentation style.

25.5   Write a PSP that displays HTTP environment variables.

25.6   Write a PSP that determines whether an e-mail address is input correctly. Verify that the input begins with series of characters, followed by the **@** character, another series of characters, a period (**.**) and a final series of characters. Test your program, using both valid and invalid e-mail addresses.

25.7   Reimplement Fig. 17.27 (in Chapter 17) with PSP.

25.8   Reimplement Exercise 6.8 (in Chapter 6) with PSP.

Operator Precedence Chart

This appendix contains the operator precedence chart for Python (Fig. A.1). Operators are shown in decreasing order of precedence from top to bottom.

Operator	Type	Associativity
` `	string conversion	left to right
{ }	dictionary creation	left to right
[ ]	list creation	left to right
( )	tuple creation	left to right
( )	function call	left to right
[:]	slicing	left to right
[ ]	subscript access	left to right
.	member access	left to right
~	bitwise not	left to right
+ –	unary plus unary minus	right to left
**	exponentiation	left to right
* / %	multiplication division modulus (remainder)	left to right
+ –	addition subtraction	left to right

Fig. A.1 Python operator precedence chart. (Part 1 of 2.)

Operator	Type	Associativity
`<<` `>>`	left shift right shift	left to right
`&`	bitwise AND	left to right
`^`	bitwise XOR	left to right
`|`	bitwise OR	left to right

`<`
`<=`
`>`
`>=`
`<>, !=`
`==`
	less than
	less than or equal
	greater than
	greater than or equal
	not equal
	equal
		right to left

`is`, `is not`	identity	left to right
`in`, `not in`	membership tests	left to right
`not`	boolean NOT	left to right
`and`	boolean AND	left to right
`or`	boolean OR	left to right
`lambda`	lambda expressions (anonymous functions)	left to right

Fig. A.1   Python operator precedence chart. (Part 2 of 2.)

ASCII Character Set

	0	1	2	3	4	5	6	7	8	9
0	nul	soh	stx	etx	eot	enq	ack	bel	bs	ht
1	nl	vt	ff	cr	so	si	dle	dc1	dc2	dc3
2	dc4	nak	syn	etb	can	em	sub	esc	fs	gs
3	rs	us	sp	!	"	#	$	%	&	`
4	(	)	*	+	,	-	.	/	0	1
5	2	3	4	5	6	7	8	9	:	;
6	<	=	>	?	@	A	B	C	D	E
7	F	G	H	I	J	K	L	M	N	O
8	P	Q	R	S	T	U	V	W	X	Y
9	Z	[	\	]	^	_	'	a	b	c
10	d	e	f	g	h	i	j	k	l	m
11	n	o	p	q	r	s	t	u	v	w
12	x	y	z	{	|	}	~	del		

Fig. B.1   ASCII character set.

The digits at the left of the table are the left digits of the decimal equivalent (0-127) of the character code, and the digits at the top of the table are the right digits of the character code. For example, the character code for "F" is 70, and the character code for "&" is 38.

Most users of this book are interested in the ASCII character set used to represent English characters on many computers. The ASCII character set is a subset of the Unicode character set used by scripting languages to represent characters from most of the world's languages. For more information on the Unicode character set, see Appendix F.

Number Systems

Objectives

- To understand basic number system concepts such as base, positional value and symbol value.
- To understand how to work with numbers represented in the binary, octal and hexadecimal number systems
- To be able to abbreviate binary numbers as octal numbers or hexadecimal numbers.
- To be able to convert octal numbers and hexadecimal numbers to binary numbers.
- To be able to covert back and forth between decimal numbers and their binary, octal and hexadecimal equivalents.
- To understand binary arithmetic and how negative binary numbers are represented using two's complement notation.

Here are only numbers ratified.
William Shakespeare

Nature has some sort of arithmetic-geometrical coordinate system, because nature has all kinds of models. What we experience of nature is in models, and all of nature's models are so beautiful.
It struck me that nature's system must be a real beauty, because in chemistry we find that the associations are always in beautiful whole numbers—there are no fractions.
Richard Buckminster Fuller

Outline

C.1 Introduction

In this appendix, we introduce the key number systems that programmers use, especially when they are working on software projects that require close interaction with "machine-level" hardware. Projects like this include operating systems, computer networking software, compilers, database systems, and applications requiring high performance.

When we write an integer such as 227 or –63 in a program, the number is assumed to be in the *decimal (base 10) number system*. The *digits* in the decimal number system are 0, 1, 2, 3, 4, 5, 6, 7, 8, and 9. The lowest digit is 0 and the highest digit is 9—one less than the *base* of 10. Internally, computers use the *binary (base 2) number system*. The binary number system has only two digits, namely 0 and 1. Its lowest digit is 0 and its highest digit is 1—one less than the base of 2. Figure C.1 summarizes the digits used in the binary, octal, decimal and hexadecimal number systems.

As we will see, binary numbers tend to be much longer than their decimal equivalents. Programmers who work in assembly languages and in high-level languages that enable programmers to reach down to the "machine level," find it cumbersome to work with binary numbers. So two other number systems—the *octal number system (base 8)* and the *hexadecimal number system (base 16)*—are popular primarily because they make it convenient to abbreviate binary numbers.

In the octal number system, the digits range from 0 to 7. Because both the binary number system and the octal number system have fewer digits than the decimal number system, their digits are the same as the corresponding digits in decimal.

The hexadecimal number system poses a problem because it requires sixteen digits—a lowest digit of 0 and a highest digit with a value equivalent to decimal 15 (one less than the base of 16). By convention, we use the letters A through F to represent the hexadecimal digits corresponding to decimal values 10 through 15. Thus in hexadecimal we can have numbers like 876 consisting solely of decimal-like digits, numbers like 8A55F consisting of digits and letters, and numbers like FFE consisting solely of letters. Occasionally, a hexadecimal number spells a common word such as FACE or FEED—this can appear strange to programmers accustomed to working with numbers. Fig. C.2 summarizes each of the number systems.

Each of these number systems uses positional notation—each position in which a digit is written has a different positional value. For example, in the decimal number 937 (the 9, the 3, and the 7 are referred to as symbol values), we say that the 7 is written in the ones position, the 3 is written in the tens position, and the 9 is written in the hundreds position. Notice that each of these positions is a power of the base (base 10), and that these powers begin at 0 and increase by 1 as we move left in the number (Fig. C.3).

For longer decimal numbers, the next positions to the left would be the thousands position (10 to the 3rd power), the ten-thousands position (10 to the 4th power), the hundred-thousands position (10 to the 5th power), the millions position (10 to the 6th power), the ten-millions position (10 to the 7th power) and so on.

In the binary number 101, we say that the rightmost 1 is written in the ones position, the 0 is written in the twos position, and the leftmost 1 is written in the fours position. Notice that each of these positions is a power of the base (base 2), and that these powers begin at 0 and increase by 1 as we move left in the number (Fig. C.4).

For longer binary numbers, the next positions to the left would be the eights position (2 to the 3rd power), the sixteens position (2 to the 4th power), the thirty-twos position (2 to the 5th power), the sixty-fours position (2 to the 6th power), and so on.

In the octal number 425, we say that the 5 is written in the ones position, the 2 is written in the eights position, and the 4 is written in the sixty-fours position. Notice that each of these positions is a power of the base (base 8), and that these powers begin at 0 and increase by 1 as we move left in the number (Fig. C.5).

Binary digit	Octal digit	Decimal digit	Hexadecimal digit
0	0	0	0
1	1	1	1
	2	2	2
	3	3	3
	4	4	4
	5	5	5
	6	6	6
	7	7	7
		8	8
		9	9
			A (decimal value of 10)
			B (decimal value of 11)
			C (decimal value of 12)
			D (decimal value of 13)
			E (decimal value of 14)
			F (decimal value of 15)

Fig. C.1   Digits of the binary, octal, decimal and hexadecimal number systems.

Attribute	Binary	Octal	Decimal	Hexadecimal
Base	2	8	10	16
Lowest digit	0	0	0	0
Highest digit	1	7	9	F

Fig. C.2 Comparison of the binary, octal, decimal and hexadecimal number systems.

Positional values in the decimal number system

Decimal digit	9	3	7
Position name	Hundreds	Tens	Ones
Positional value	100	10	1
Positional value as a power of the base (10)	10^2	10^1	10^0

Fig. C.3 Positional values in the decimal number system.

For longer octal numbers, the next positions to the left would be the five-hundred-and-twelves position (8 to the 3rd power), the four-thousand-and-ninety-sixes position (8 to the 4th power), the thirty-two-thousand-seven-hundred-and-sixty eights position (8 to the 5th power), and so on.

In the hexadecimal number 3DA, we say that the A is written in the ones position, the D is written in the sixteens position, and the 3 is written in the two-hundred-and-fifty-sixes position. Notice that each of these positions is a power of the base (base 16), and that these powers begin at 0 and increase by 1 as we move left in the number (Fig. C.6).

For longer hexadecimal numbers, the next positions to the left would be the four-thousand-and-ninety-sixes position (16 to the 3rd power), the sixty-five-thousand-five-hundred-and-thirty-six position (16 to the 4th power), and so on.

Positional values in the binary number system

Binary digit	1	0	1
Position name	Fours	Twos	Ones
Positional value	4	2	1
Positional value as a power of the base (2)	2^2	2^1	2^0

Fig. C.4 Positional values in the binary number system.

Positional values in the octal number system			
Decimal digit	4	2	5
Position name	Sixty-fours	Eights	Ones
Positional value	64	8	1
Positional value as a power of the base (8)	8^2	8^1	8^0

Fig. C.5   Positional values in the octal number system.

Positional values in the hexadecimal number system			
Decimal digit	3	D	A
Position name	Two-hundred-and-fifty-sixes	Sixteens	Ones
Positional value	256	16	1
Positional value as a power of the base (16)	16^2	16^1	16^0

Fig. C.6   Positional values in the hexadecimal number system.

C.2 Abbreviating Binary Numbers as Octal Numbers and Hexadecimal Numbers

The main use for octal and hexadecimal numbers in computing is for abbreviating lengthy binary representations. Figure C.7 highlights the fact that lengthy binary numbers can be expressed concisely in number systems with higher bases than the binary number system.

Decimal number	Binary representation	Octal representation	Hexadecimal representation
0	0	0	0
1	1	1	1
2	10	2	2
3	11	3	3
4	100	4	4
5	101	5	5
6	110	6	6
7	111	7	7

Fig. C.7   Decimal, binary, octal and hexadecimal equivalents. (Part 1 of 2.)

Decimal number	Binary representation	Octal representation	Hexadecimal representation
8	1000	10	8
9	1001	11	9
10	1010	12	A
11	1011	13	B
12	1100	14	C
13	1101	15	D
14	1110	16	E
15	1111	17	F
16	10000	20	10

Fig. C.7   Decimal, binary, octal and hexadecimal equivalents. (Part 2 of 2.)

A particularly important relationship that both the octal number system and the hexadecimal number system have to the binary system is that the bases of octal and hexadecimal (8 and 16 respectively) are powers of the base of the binary number system (base 2). Consider the following 12-digit binary number and its octal and hexadecimal equivalents. See if you can determine how this relationship makes it convenient to abbreviate binary numbers in octal or hexadecimal. The answer follows the numbers.

Binary Number	Octal equivalent	Hexadecimal equivalent
100011010001	4321	8D1

To see how the binary number converts easily to octal, simply break the 12-digit binary number into groups of three consecutive bits each, and write those groups over the corresponding digits of the octal number as follows

100	011	010	001
4	3	2	1

Notice that the octal digit you have written under each group of thee bits corresponds precisely to the octal equivalent of that 3-digit binary number as shown in Fig. C.7.

The same kind of relationship may be observed in converting numbers from binary to hexadecimal. In particular, break the 12-digit binary number into groups of four consecutive bits each and write those groups over the corresponding digits of the hexadecimal number as follows

1000	1101	0001
8	D	1

Notice that the hexadecimal digit you wrote under each group of four bits corresponds precisely to the hexadecimal equivalent of that 4-digit binary number as shown in Fig. C.7.

C.3 Converting Octal Numbers and Hexadecimal Numbers to Binary Numbers

In the previous section, we saw how to convert binary numbers to their octal and hexadecimal equivalents by forming groups of binary digits and simply rewriting these groups as their equivalent octal digit values or hexadecimal digit values. This process may be used in reverse to produce the binary equivalent of a given octal or hexadecimal number.

For example, the octal number 653 is converted to binary simply by writing the 6 as its 3-digit binary equivalent 110, the 5 as its 3-digit binary equivalent 101, and the 3 as its 3-digit binary equivalent 011 to form the 9-digit binary number 110101011.

The hexadecimal number FAD5 is converted to binary simply by writing the F as its 4-digit binary equivalent 1111, the A as its 4-digit binary equivalent 1010, the D as its 4-digit binary equivalent 1101, and the 5 as its 4-digit binary equivalent 0101 to form the 16-digit 1111101011010101.

C.4 Converting from Binary, Octal or Hexadecimal to Decimal

Because we are accustomed to working in decimal, it is often convenient to convert a binary, octal, or hexadecimal number to decimal to get a sense of what the number is "really" worth. Our diagrams in Section C.1 express the positional values in decimal. To convert a number to decimal from another base, multiply the decimal equivalent of each digit by its positional value, and sum these products. For example, the binary number 110101 is converted to decimal 53 as shown in Fig. C.8.

To convert octal 7614 to decimal 3980, we use the same technique, this time using appropriate octal positional values as shown in Fig. C.9.

Converting a binary number to decimal

Positional values:	32	16	8	4	2	1
Symbol values:	1	1	0	1	0	1
Products:	1*32=32	1*16=16	0*8=0	1*4=4	0*2=0	1*1=1
Sum:	= 32 + 16 + 0 + 4 + 0 + 1 = 53					

Fig. C.8   Converting a binary number to decimal.

Converting an octal number to decimal

Positional values:	512	64	8	1
Symbol values:	7	6	1	4
Products	7*512=3584	6*64=384	1*8=8	4*1=4
Sum:	= 3584 + 384 + 8 + 4 = 3980			

Fig. C.9   Converting an octal number to decimal.

To convert hexadecimal AD3B to decimal 44347, we use the same technique, this time using appropriate hexadecimal positional values as shown in Fig. C.10.

C.5 Converting from Decimal to Binary, Octal or Hexadecimal

The conversions of the previous section follow naturally from the positional notation conventions. Converting from decimal to binary, octal or hexadecimal also follows these conventions.

Suppose we wish to convert decimal 57 to binary. We begin by writing the positional values of the columns right to left until we reach a column whose positional value is greater than the decimal number. We do not need that column, so we discard it. Thus, we first write:

Positional values: **64   32   16   8   4   2   1**

Then we discard the column with positional value 64 leaving:

Positional values: **32   16   8   4   2   1**

Next we work from the leftmost column to the right. We divide 32 into 57 and observe that there is one 32 in 57 with a remainder of 25, so we write 1 in the 32 column. We divide 16 into 25 and observe that there is one 16 in 25 with a remainder of 9 and write 1 in the 16 column. We divide 8 into 9 and observe that there is one 8 in 9 with a remainder of 1. The next two columns each produce quotients of zero when their positional values are divided into 1 so we write 0s in the 4 and 2 columns. Finally, 1 into 1 is 1 so we write 1 in the 1 column. This yields:

Positional values: **32   16   8   4   2   1**
Symbol values: **1   1   1   0   0   1**

and thus decimal 57 is equivalent to binary 111001.

To convert decimal 103 to octal, we begin by writing the positional values of the columns until we reach a column whose positional value is greater than the decimal number. We do not need that column, so we discard it. Thus, we first write:

Positional values: **512   64   8   1**

Then we discard the column with positional value 512, yielding:

Positional values: **64   8   1**

Converting a hexadecimal number to decimal			
Positional values:	4096	256	16	1
Symbol values:	A	D	3	B
Products	A*4096=40960	D*256=3328	3*16=48	B*1=11
Sum:	= 40960 + 3328 + 48 + 11 = 44347			

Fig. C.10 Converting a hexadecimal number to decimal.

Next we work from the leftmost column to the right. We divide 64 into 103 and observe that there is one 64 in 103 with a remainder of 39, so we write 1 in the 64 column. We divide 8 into 39 and observe that there are four 8s in 39 with a remainder of 7 and write 4 in the 8 column. Finally, we divide 1 into 7 and observe that there are seven 1s in 7 with no remainder so we write 7 in the 1 column. This yields:

```
Positional values:      64    8    1
Symbol values:           1    4    7
```

and thus decimal 103 is equivalent to octal 147.

To convert decimal 375 to hexadecimal, we begin by writing the positional values of the columns until we reach a column whose positional value is greater than the decimal number. We do not need that column, so we discard it. Thus, we first write

```
Positional values:  4096 256   16    1
```

Then we discard the column with positional value 4096, yielding:

```
Positional values:       256   16    1
```

Next we work from the leftmost column to the right. We divide 256 into 375 and observe that there is one 256 in 375 with a remainder of 119, so we write 1 in the 256 column. We divide 16 into 119 and observe that there are seven 16s in 119 with a remainder of 7 and write 7 in the 16 column. Finally, we divide 1 into 7 and observe that there are seven 1s in 7 with no remainder so we write 7 in the 1 column. This yields:

```
Positional values:      256   16    1
Symbol values:            1    7    7
```

and thus decimal 375 is equivalent to hexadecimal 177.

C.6 Negative Binary Numbers: Two's Complement Notation

The discussion in this appendix has been focussed on positive numbers. In this section, we explain how computers represent negative numbers using *two's complement notation*. First we explain how the two's complement of a binary number is formed, and then we show why it represents the negative value of the given binary number.

Consider a machine with 32-bit integers. Suppose

```
number = 13
```

The 32-bit representation of **number** is

```
00000000 00000000 00000000 00001101
```

To form the negative of **number** we first form its *one's complement* by applying Python's ~ operator:

```
onesComplement = ~number
```

Internally, **onesComplement** is now **number** with each of its bits reversed—ones become zeros and zeros become ones as follows:

```
number:
00000000 00000000 00000000 00001101

onesComplement:
11111111 11111111 11111111 11110010
```

To form the two's complement of **number** we simply add one to **number** one's complement. Thus

```
Two's complement of number:
11111111 11111111 11111111 11110011
```

Now if this is in fact equal to –13, we should be able to add it to binary 13 and obtain a result of 0. Let us try this:

```
 00000000 00000000 00000000 00001101
+11111111 11111111 11111111 11110011
-------------------------------------
 00000000 00000000 00000000 00000000
```

The carry bit coming out of the leftmost column is discarded and we indeed get zero as a result. If we add the one's complement of a number to the number, the result would be all 1s. The key to getting a result of all zeros is that the twos complement is 1 more than the one's complement. The addition of 1 causes each column to add to 0 with a carry of 1. The carry keeps moving leftward until it is discarded from the leftmost bit, and hence the resulting number is all zeros.

Computers actually perform a subtraction such as

```
x = a - number
```

by adding the two's complement of **number** to **a** as follows:

```
x = a + ( onesComplement + 1 )
```

Suppose **a** is 27 and **number** is 13 as before. If the two's complement of **number** is actually the negative of **number**, then adding the two's complement of value to **a** should produce the result 14. Let us try this:

```
a  (i.e., 27)              00000000 00000000 00000000 00011011
+( onesComplement + 1 )   +11111111 11111111 11111111 11110011
                          -------------------------------------
                           00000000 00000000 00000000 00001110
```

which is indeed equal to 14.

SUMMARY

- When we write an integer such as 19 or 227 or –63 in a Python program, the number is automatically assumed to be in the decimal (base 10) number system. The digits in the decimal number system are 0, 1, 2, 3, 4, 5, 6, 7, 8, and 9. The lowest digit is 0 and the highest digit is 9—one less than the base of 10.

- Internally, computers use the binary (base 2) number system. The binary number system has only two digits, namely 0 and 1. Its lowest digit is 0 and its highest digit is 1—one less than the base of 2.

- The octal number system (base 8) and the hexadecimal number system (base 16) are popular primarily because they make it convenient to abbreviate binary numbers.

- The digits of the octal number system range from 0 to 7.

- The hexadecimal number system poses a problem because it requires sixteen digits—a lowest digit of 0 and a highest digit with a value equivalent to decimal 15 (one less than the base of 16). By convention, we use the letters A through F to represent the hexadecimal digits corresponding to decimal values 10 through 15.

- Each number system uses positional notation—each position in which a digit is written has a different positional value.

- A particularly important relationship that both the octal number system and the hexadecimal number system have to the binary system is that the bases of octal and hexadecimal (8 and 16 respectively) are powers of the base of the binary number system (base 2).

- To convert an octal number to a binary number, simply replace each octal digit with its three-digit binary equivalent.

- To convert a hexadecimal number to a binary number, simply replace each hexadecimal digit with its four-digit binary equivalent.

- Because we are accustomed to working in decimal, it is convenient to convert a binary, octal or hexadecimal number to decimal to get a sense of the number's "real" worth.

- To convert a number to decimal from another base, multiply the decimal equivalent of each digit by its positional value, and sum these products.

- Computers represent negative numbers using two's complement notation.

- To form the negative of a value in binary, first form its one's complement by applying Pyton's ~ operator. This reverses the bits of the value. To form the two's complement of a value, simply add one to the value's one's complement.

TERMINOLOGY

base	digit
base 2 number system	hexadecimal number system
base 8 number system	negative value
base 10 number system	octal number system
base 16 number system	one's complement notation
binary number system	positional notation
bitwise complement operator (~)	positional value
conversions	symbol value
decimal number system	two's complement notation

SELF-REVIEW EXERCISES

C.1   The bases of the decimal, binary, octal, and hexadecimal number systems are _____, _____, _____, and _____ respectively.

C.2   In general, the decimal, octal, and hexadecimal representations of a given binary number contain (more/fewer) digits than the binary number contains.

C.3   (True/False) A popular reason for using the decimal number system is that it forms a convenient notation for abbreviating binary numbers simply by substituting one decimal digit per group of four binary bits.

C.4   The (octal / hexadecimal / decimal) representation of a large binary value is the most concise (of the given alternatives).

C.5   (True/False) The highest digit in any base is one more than the base.

C.6   (True/False) The lowest digit in any base is one less than the base.

C.7   The positional value of the rightmost digit of any number in either binary, octal, decimal, or hexadecimal is always _____.

C.8   The positional value of the digit to the left of the rightmost digit of any number in binary, octal, decimal, or hexadecimal is always equal to _____.

C.9   Fill in the missing values in this chart of positional values for the rightmost four positions in each of the indicated number systems:

decimal	1000	100	10	1
hexadecimal	...	256	...	...
binary	...	...	...	...
octal	512	...	8	...

C.10   Convert binary **110101011000** to octal and to hexadecimal.

C.11   Convert hexadecimal **FACE** to binary.

C.12   Convert octal **7316** to binary.

C.13   Convert hexadecimal **4FEC** to octal. [Hint: First convert **4FEC** to binary then convert that binary number to octal.]

C.14   Convert binary **1101110** to decimal.

C.15   Convert octal **317** to decimal.

C.16   Convert hexadecimal **EFD4** to decimal.

C.17   Convert decimal **177** to binary, to octal, and to hexadecimal.

C.18   Show the binary representation of decimal **417**. Then show the one's complement of **417**, and the two's complement of **417**.

C.19   What is the result when the one's complement of a number is added to itself?

ANSWERS TO SELF-REVIEW EXERCISES

C.1   10, 2, 8, 16.

C.2   Fewer.

C.3   False.

C.4   Hexadecimal.

C.5   False. The highest digit in any base is one less than the base.

C.6   False. The lowest digit in any base is zero.

C.7   1 (the base raised to the zero power).

C.8   The base of the number system.

C.9   Fill in the missing values in this chart of positional values for the rightmost four positions in each of the indicated number systems:

decimal	1000	100	10	1
hexadecimal	4096	256	16	1
binary	8	4	2	1
octal	512	64	8	1

C.10   Octal **6530**; Hexadecimal **D58**.

C.11   Binary 1111 1010 1100 1110.

C.12   Binary 111 011 001 110.

C.13   Binary 0 100 111 111 101 100; Octal 47754.

C.14   Decimal 2+4+8+32+64=110.

C.15   Decimal 7+1*8+3*64=7+8+192=207.

C.16   Decimal 4+13*16+15*256+14*4096=61396.

C.17   Decimal 177
to binary:

```
256 128 64 32 16 8 4 2 1
128 64 32 16 8 4 2 1
(1*128)+(0*64)+(1*32)+(1*16)+(0*8)+(0*4)+(0*2)+(1*1)
10110001
```

to octal:

```
512 64 8 1
64 8 1
(2*64)+(6*8)+(1*1)
261
```

to hexadecimal:

```
256 16 1
16 1
(11*16)+(1*1)
(B*16)+(1*1)
B1
```

C.18   Binary:

```
512 256 128 64 32 16 8 4 2 1
256 128 64 32 16 8 4 2 1
(1*256)+(1*128)+(0*64)+(1*32)+(0*16)+(0*8)+(0*4)+(0*2)+
(1*1)
110100001
```

```
One's complement: 001011110
Two's complement: 001011111
Check: Original binary number + its two's complement
```

```
110100001
001011111
---------
000000000
```

C.19   Zero.

EXERCISES

C.20   Some people argue that many of our calculations would be easier in the base 12 number system because 12 is divisible by so many more numbers than 10 (for base 10). What is the lowest digit in base 12? What might the highest symbol for the digit in base 12 be? What are the positional values of the rightmost four positions of any number in the base 12 number system?

C.21 How is the highest symbol value in the number systems we discussed related to the positional value of the first digit to the left of the rightmost digit of any number in these number systems?

C.22 Complete the following chart of positional values for the rightmost four positions in each of the indicated number systems:

```
decimal    1000    100    10     1
base 6     ...     ...    6      ...
base 13    ...     169    ...    ...
base 3     27      ...    ...    ...
```

C.23 Convert binary 100101111010 to octal and to hexadecimal.

C.24 Convert hexadecimal 3A7D to binary.

C.25 Convert hexadecimal 765F to octal. (Hint: First convert 765F to binary, then convert that binary number to octal.)

C.26 Convert binary 1011110 to decimal.

C.27 Convert octal 426 to decimal.

C.28 Convert hexadecimal FFFF to decimal.

C.29 Convert decimal 299 to binary, to octal, and to hexadecimal.

C.30 Show the binary representation of decimal 779. Then show the one's complement of 779, and the two's complement of 779.

C.31 What is the result when the two's complement of a number is added to itself?

C.32 Show the two's complement of integer value –1 on a machine with 32-bit integers.

Python Development Environments

Objectives

- To become aware of the various development environments for Python.
- To learn to use the Integrated Development Environment for Python (IDLE).
- To become familiar with the features of various Python integrated development environments.
- To become with familiar BlackAdder, PythonWorks™, Wing IDE™, Pythonwin and Komodo.

Outline

D.1 Introduction

Python developers can use text editors (e.g., **Notepad**, vi, etc.) or specialized software, called *integrated development environments (IDEs)* to write programming code. IDEs allow developers to create, run, test and debug Python programs conveniently. Python programs can be written and edited with a variety of IDEs; this appendix discusses six—*Integrated Development Environment for Python (IDLE)*, *BlackAdder*, *PythonWorks™*, *Wing IDE™*, *Pythonwin* and *Komodo*. This appendix provides a detailed description of IDLE, including its GUI interface, Python shell, file editor and debugger, and we overview the other five applications. Links for text editors and IDEs are available at **www.python.org/editors**. [*Note*: The information in this appendix was current at the time of this writing, but is subject to change. For the most current information about an IDE, visit the Web site of that IDE.]

Before reading this appendix, the student should be familiar with the topics in Chapter 1, Introduction to Computers, Internet and World Wide Web; Chapter 2, Introduction to Python Programming; and Chapter 3, Control Structures.

D.2 Integrated Development Environment: IDLE

Python's creator, Guido van Rossum, used Python and **Tkinter**, a *graphical user interface (GUI)* application, to create IDLE. Every Python distribution since Python 2.0 includes a version of IDLE—the most current Python release, Python 2.2, downloads with IDLE version 0.8. Both Python and **Tkinter** must be installed for a programmer to use IDLE. Documentation on IDLE's features can be found at **www.python.org/idle/doc**.

D.2.1 Installing and Launching IDLE

Programmers can install IDLE when they install the Python software package. Visit **www.python.org/download** to download Python; for detailed installation instructions, visit **www.deitel.com**. During the Windows installation process, a developer selects the components to install (Fig. D.1). To install IDLE on Windows, the option labeled **Tcl/Tk** must be selected; by default, all options are selected in the dialog.

To launch IDLE, select **Programs** from the **Start** menu. Select the folder that contains the Python installation (e.g., **Python 2.2**) and select the **IDLE (Python GUI)** choice. IDLE components include a text editor (to create, save and modify Python programs), an *interactive interpreter* (to translate and execute Python statements), a *debugger* (to identify errors in Python programs) and a Python shell (to use the Python interpreter's capabilities inside IDLE). Figure D.2 illustrates the initial IDLE window, the **Python Shell**, which allows programmers to execute Python commands. The IDLE Python shell provides a direct interface to the Python interpreter.

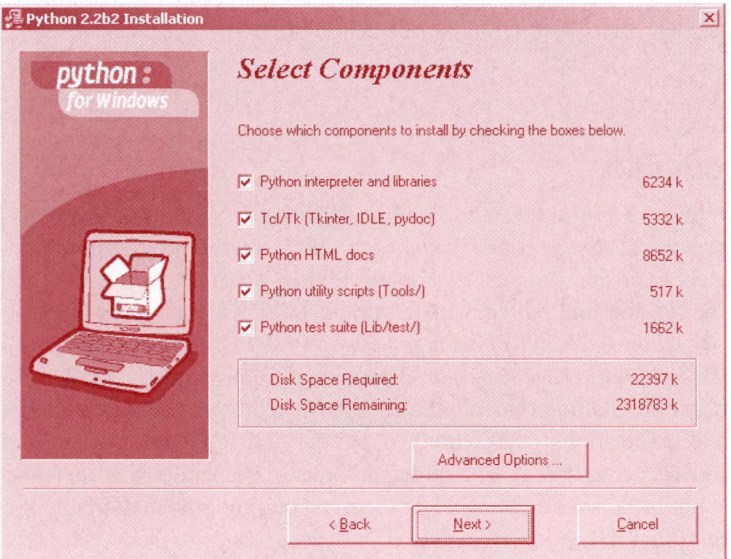

Fig. D.1   Installing Python with Tcl/Tk support.

```
Python 2.2b2 (#26, Nov 16 2001, 11:44:11) [MSC 32 bit (Intel)] on win32
Type "copyright", "credits" or "license" for more information.
IDLE 0.8 -- press F1 for help
>>> |
```

Fig. D.2   IDLE's Python shell.

D.2.2 Features

IDLE offers a rich set of features that allow a programmer to concentrate on applying programming code rather than with formatting and other issues. This section discusses such features as indentation, color coding, command history and word completion.

Indentation is crucial in Python, because Python uses indentation to delimit (distinguish) sections of code (i.e., *suites*). As a result, IDLE offers an automatic indentation feature, which places the cursor at a specified number of spaces, on the subsequent line. IDLE invokes automatic indentation after a programmer types a keyword that corresponds either to a control structure (e.g., **if**, **while**, **for**) or to a function definition (e.g., **def**) and presses the **Enter** key. By default, IDLE indents code by four spaces (or "one level"), the standard amount for Python code. However, a programmer can modify this setting by selecting **New indent width** (from the **Edit** menu). To unindent the cursor at the end of a suite, press the **Backspace** key. This command unindents the suite by one level. IDLE automatically unindents the cursor by one level after a **break**, **continue**, **raise**, **pass** or **return** keyword. Although IDLE supports automatic indentation, programmers should review their code, because IDLE does not detect all instances of indentation.

Another feature of IDLE is a highlighting scheme called *syntax coloring*, which applies various colors to programming code. By default, keywords appear in orange, comments in red, strings in green, definitions and interpreter's output in blue, and the console output appears in brown. IDLE applies syntax-color highlighting as a programmer types code and applies highlighting to all source files opened in IDLE. Syntax coloring is useful because it improves readability and minimizes errors. For instance, if a newly created variable name appears in orange, the syntax-coloring scheme indicates that the variable name is in fact a pre-defined keyword name; thus, the programmer should assign a different name to the variable.

The *command history* is an IDLE feature that tracks every command executed at the command line during a session. A programmer can retrieve these commands using the *Alt+P* shortcut at the command prompt. When the programmer presses this keyboard shortcut, IDLE iterates through the command history, displaying each command, starting with the most recent command. The user can move forward in this history by entering the command *Alt+N*. In addition, the user can place the cursor at a line and press **Enter** to copy that single statement or that block of statements to the current command line.

Word completion is another IDLE feature. The user enters one or more letters of the intended word and then either selects **Expand word** in the **Edit** menu or presses *Alt+ /* to display possible word endings. The program begins with user-specified words, then progresses through Python keywords that meet the criteria. For instance, assuming that a function **isOdd** has been defined, if the user enters **i** at the command prompt and continues to press *Alt+ /*, the program suggests **isOdd**, **is**, **in**, **import** and **if**.

IDLE also displays tips about method and function calls as the user types the calls. [*Note*: IDLE does not display tips about list, tuple or dictionary methods.] The tips about built-in methods or functions describe the arguments and, sometimes, offer brief descriptions about the arguments (Fig. D.3). IDLE also displays the docstrings supplied for user-defined methods and functions.

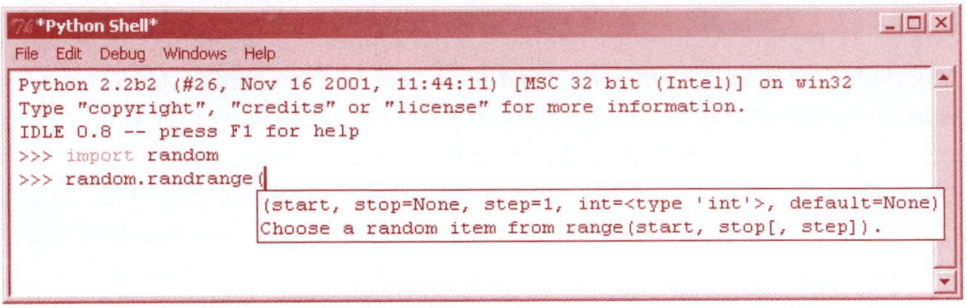

Fig. D.3   Built-in method tip.

D.2.3 Text Editor

The text editor and the shell share many similar capabilities, including word completion and the method/function-call tips. The following section describes how to create a Python file using IDLE and some of the text editor's features.

To create a new file, select **New window** from the **File** menu. Programmers can type their code in the resulting window, which contains an empty, untitled screen (Fig. D.4). Type the following sample program into the text editor.

```
# prompt user for input
integer = raw_input( "Enter an integer:\n" )
integer = int( integer )

if integer < 0:
    print "%d is less than zero" % integer
else:
    print "%d is not less than zero" % integer

print "Sum is", sum
```

The **Edit** menu offers many options that simplify the creation and modification of files. Figure D.5 lists some of these options, which are available in the Python shell and in the text editor.

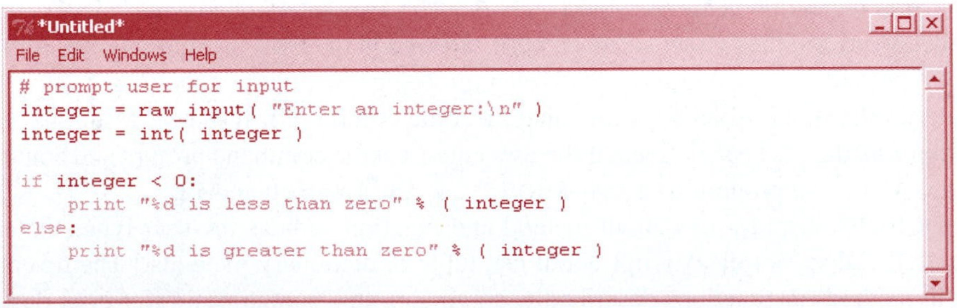

Fig. D.4   New, untitled file.

Menu item	Function
`Undo`	Reverse last change.
`Redo`	Redo last change.
`Cut`	Remove selected text and place it on clipboard.
`Copy`	Copy selected text onto clipboard.
`Paste`	Place text from clipboard at cursor position.
`Indent region`	Move selection right one level.
`Dedent region`	Move selection left one level.
`Comment out region`	Turn selected region into comments.
`Uncomment region`	Remove comment symbols from the start of each line in the selected region.
`Set indent width`	Set the width of each tab indent from 1 to 16. [*Note*: A width of 8 is equivalent to 4 spaces.]
`Toggle tabs`	Turn tabs on or off.
`Expand word`	Perform word completion.
`Find`	Find word or pattern in window.
`Find in files`	Find word or pattern in specified files.
`Replace`	Replace word or pattern.
`Go to line`	Place cursor at the beginning of the specified line.
`Import module`	Import or reload module in current window.
`Run script`	Execute the current file.

Fig. D.5   **Edit** menu items.

After creating the program, click **Save** (in the **File** menu) to save the file. When a programmer saves new files, the **Save As** dialog appears (Fig. D.6). In this dialog, a programmer can assign a name to the file and navigate to the directory where the file will reside. [*Note*: Although we save this example as `test.py` in the **C:\PythonTestFiles** directory, readers may select different filenames and directory locations.] After saving the file, the filename appears in the blue title bar located at the top of the screen. When a file has unsaved changes, asterisks appear at the beginning and the end of the filename in the title bar.

To execute `test.py` (or any other program) using IDLE, select **Run script** from the **Edit** menu. Figure D.7 shows the execution of the program in Fig. D.4.

Common Programming Error D.1

*If you execute a **Tkinter** program using IDLE, do not include a **mainloop** in the program. IDLE is a **Tkinter** application, which invokes **mainloop**. Another call to **mainloop** conflicts with IDLE's event loop and results in a runtime error.*

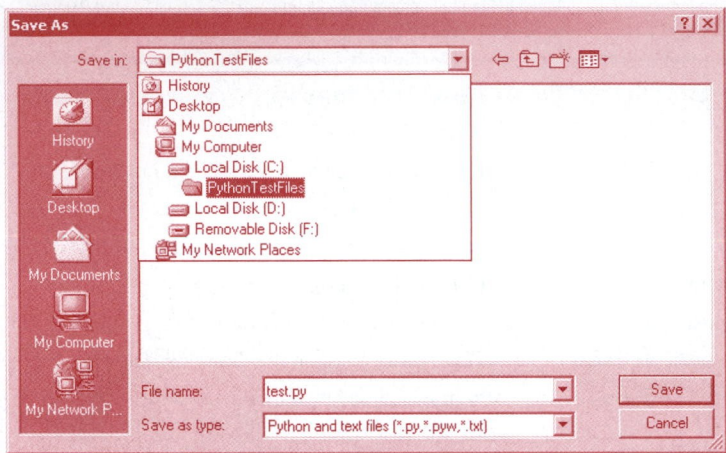

Fig. D.6 Saving a newly created file.

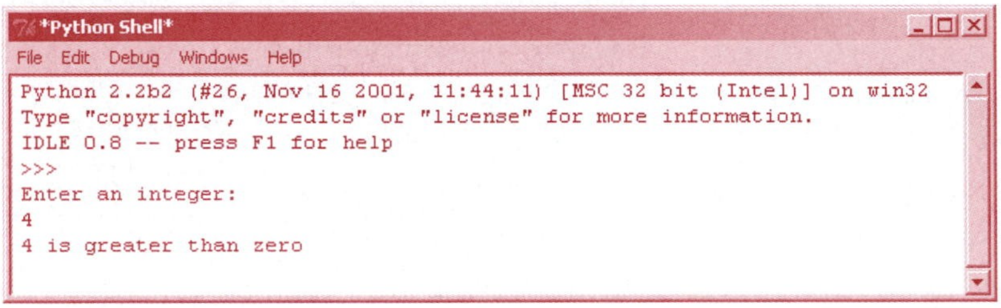

Fig. D.7 IDLE used to execute a Python program.

D.2.4 Debugger

Two types of errors occur during software development: *syntax errors* and *logic errors*. Syntax errors occur when program statements violate the grammatical rules of a programming language, such as failure to insert a colon (**:**) after an **if** statement. When the Python interpreter detects syntax errors, the interpreter terminates the program. By contrast, logic errors do not prevent programs from executing, but rather prevent programs from operating as expected.

Syntax errors are easier to fix than logic errors. Upon detecting a syntax error, IDLE gives the description and line number in the **Python Shell** window. This information gives the programmer a "clue" as to how to eliminate the error, so the interpreter can execute the program. For instance, if we remove the colon (**:**) that follows the **if** statement in **test.py** and execute the program, the **Python Shell** indicates that **test.py** contains a syntax error on line 5 (Fig. D.8). On the other hand, logic errors are more subtle and usually do not inform the user exactly where in the program the errors occurred.

Debugging is the process of finding and correcting logic errors in applications. Logic errors are more subtle than syntax errors because a program that contains a logic error executes successfully, but does not execute as expected. Logic errors often are difficult to debug, because the programmer cannot see the code as it executes. One strategy that novice programmers often use to debug programs is to display program data directly, using `print` statements. For example, the programmer might print the value referenced by a variable to determine whether the variable references the correct value. This approach is cumbersome, because programmers must insert a line of code wherever they suspect there might be a problem. Furthermore, once the program has been debugged, the programmer then must remove the extraneous statements, which often can be difficult to distinguish from the original program code.

A *debugger* is software that allows a programmer to analyze program data and trace the flow of program execution while the application executes. A debugger provides capabilities that allow the programmer to suspend program execution, examine and modify variables, call methods without changing the program code and more.

IDLE provides a debugger tool that helps a programmer detect logic errors. For more information on the debugger, visit `www.python.org/idle/doc/idlemain.html`.

Python module **pdb** also provides debugging capabilities. This module is used in the shell window. To obtain information on module **pdb**, visit

> `www.python.org/doc/current/lib/module-pdb.html`.

D.3 Other Integrated Development Environments

Although IDLE is a popular IDE and is packaged with the Python program, it is not the only development tool. This section introduces other Python IDEs and overviews examples of their capabilities. Each IDE provides similar basic elements, such as text editors, GUI designers and debuggers, and this text highlights those and additional features unique to each application.

D.3.1 BlackAdder

BlackAdder supports both Windows and Linux environments—i.e, a programmer can create a Python application that will run on either platform. The organization that maintains BlackAdder, **TheKompany.com**, offers a personal version of the software, which provides limited support, and a professional version of the software, which includes a license to create and distribute software that contains BlackAdder elements. The professional version is intended for commercial software developers.

```
*Python Shell*                                              _ □ ×
File  Edit  Debug  Windows  Help
Python 2.2b2 (#26, Nov 16 2001, 11:44:11) [MSC 32 bit (Intel)] on win32
Type "copyright", "credits" or "license" for more information.
IDLE 0.8 -- press F1 for help
>>>
  File "C:\PythonTestFiles\test.py", line 5
    if integer < 0
                  ^
SyntaxError: invalid syntax
```

Fig. D.8   Syntax error in a Python program.

In addition to a text editor, GUI designer and debugger, BlackAdder components include a project management elements and a Python interpreter. The text editor offers features such as automatic indentation, customizable color coding and *code folding*, which allows the user to hide the bodies of function, methods and classes. The debugger allows a developer to set one or more breakpoints and to view local and global variables as a program executes. A breakpoint is a "marker" that a programmer sets at a specific line of code that causes the debugger to suspend execution when the program reaches that line of code. Breakpoints help the programmer to verify that a programmer is executing correctly. BlackAdder also allows a programmer to organize Python programs into projects in which all programs in a project can be executed with a single mouse click. The interpreter can execute code while an application is running.

For more information on BlackAdder, visit **www.thekompany.com/products/blackadder**. A trial version with limited functionality is free for download at the site.

D.3.2 PythonWorks™

PythonWorks is distributed by SecretLabs, a company that designs tools for the development and deployment of Python projects. PythonWorks IDE is considered a *Rapid Application Development (RAD)* tool, which is software that allows programmers to create, debug and release programs quickly.

PythonWorks includes an HTML/XML editor, fully indexed documentation, a source-code management system for group projects, customizable code-editing features and a GUI layout editor. The IDE also allows users to package a project as source, as an executable and/or as a **.pyc** file for deployment. Similar to the other IDEs, PythonWorks includes a debugger. PythonWorks provides support for various Python versions as well as JPython. Purchasing a copy of PythonWorks entitles buyers to versions for Solaris, Linux (Red Hat and Suse); users also receive free updates. PythonWorks soon will be available for Windows.

Ordering information can be found at **www.pythonware.com/products/works/index.htm**. The site also provides a link to free evaluation copies for Windows and Linux users. A trial version of PythonWorks is available free for download at **www.pythonware.com/products/works/testdrive.htm**.

D.3.3 Wing IDE™

Wing IDE, developed and supported by Archaeopteryx Software, Inc., is available for Windows and Linux environments. The IDE provides a source-code analyzer and browser, project-management capabilities as well as a text editor and debugger.

Wing IDE is designed to offer support for group projects. A project manager component of the software helps to organize and access project files. In addition, Wing IDE supports integrating code written by group members using different development environments. Wing IDE is fully customizable to enable users to write and debug code more efficiently. This integrated development environment is written primarily in Python and includes Python source code. The buyer may customize the source code for internal use, but cannot distribute the modified code for profit.

A text editor offers syntax coloring, automatic indentation, automatic completion, code folding and customizable key bindings. A source-code analyzer presents a graphical view of class hierarchy, methods, functions and docstrings. The debugger is fully graphical and offers breakpoints, single stepping, variable inspection and an interactive command shell.

A fully functional demo of Wing IDE is available for download at **archaeopteryx.com/wingide.** Archaeopteryx also offers a version for purchase.

D.3.4 Pythonwin

The Pythonwin integrated development environment is included with ActiveState's ActivePython, a binary build of Python that includes module **expat** for XML processing and a suite of Windows tools. Whereas ActivePython is available for Linux, Solaris and Windows, Pythonwin runs only on the Windows platform.

Pythonwin's interactive shell and text editor offer standard features, such as color coding, source-code folding, word completion, and automatic indentation. The customizable interface includes the Tools menu, color coding, indentation spacing and keyboard bindings. In addition, Pythonwin offers visual tips in the form of scrollable lists to complete function and method calls. The debugger offers postmortem diagnostics, standard stepping, breakpoints and variable watching.

The ActivePython Web site provides a version free for download (**aspn.activestate.com/ActivePython**). The ActivePython download includes Pythonwin documentation.

D.3.5 Komodo

ActiveState offers a second IDE for Python, called Komodo. Komodo can be used to develop programs on both Windows and Linux, Furthermore, Komodo is an integrated development environment for Perl, PHP, Tcl, HTML, XML and XSLT.

Komodo's IDE offers a text editor, a project manager and a graphical debugger. The editor offers standard features, such as tips, syntax-coloring, code-folding and automatic word completion. Komodo issues warnings about syntax errors and incorrect indentations as the user enters code. The debugger includes breakpoint control, code stepping and variable watching. The debugger also can be run on remote files (i.e., files not on your local machine). Komodo also provides a sample project for first-time users to enable them to learn the Komodo interface quickly. In addition, the IDE contains a toolkit for creating and debugging regular expressions.

Unlike Linux users, Windows users need a license. The noncommercial license for students, home users and nonprofit organizations is free. The commercial license requires an annual fee, and provides access to free software upgrades and programming resources. A 21-day trial version of the commercial license is available at **www.activestate.com/Products/Komodo/pricing_and_licensing.plex**.

D.4 Internet and World Wide Web Resources

www.gnu.org/software/emacs
The GNU Emacs Web site provides background information on the Emacs text editor. From this site, users can register for mailing lists, join newsgroups and download the product.

www.math.fu-berlin.de/~guckes/vi
This Web site discusses the Vi text editor. It provides background information on Vi, lists the various versions of the text editor and contains links to other Web sites that provide documentation on Vi.

www.vim.org
The *VIM (Vi Improved) Home Page* introduces VIM, allows visitors to download the product and provides news information about the text editor.

Career Opportunities

Objectives

- To explore the various online career services.
- To examine the advantages and disadvantages of posting and finding jobs online.
- To review the major online career services Web sites available to job seekers.
- To explore the various online services available to employers seeking to build their workforces.

What is the city but the people?
William Shakespeare

A great city is that which has the greatest men and women,
If it be a few ragged huts it is still the greatest city in the
whole world.
Walt Whitman

To understand the true quality of people, you must look into
their minds, and examine their pursuits and aversions.
Marcus Aurelius

The soul is made for action, and cannot rest till it be
employed. Idleness is its rust. Unless it will up and think and
taste and see, all is in vain.
Thomas Traherne

Outline

E.1 Introduction

There are approximately 40,000 career-advancement services on the Internet today.[1] These services include large, comprehensive job sites, such as **Monster.com** (see the upcoming **Monster.com** feature), as well as interest-specific job sites such as **JustJava-Jobs.com**. Companies can reduce the amount of time spent searching for qualified employees by building recruiting features on their Web sites or establishing accounts with career sites. This results in a larger pool of qualified applicants, as online services can automatically select and reject resumes based on user-designated criteria. Online interviews, testing services and other resources also expedite the recruiting process.

Applying for a position online is a relatively new method of exploring career opportunities. Online recruiting services streamline the process and allow job seekers to concentrate their energies in careers that are of interest to them. Job seekers can explore opportunities according to geographic location, position, salary or benefits packages.

Job seekers can learn how to write resumes and cover letters, post them online and search through job listings to find the jobs that best suit their needs. *Entry-level positions*, or positions commonly sought by individuals who are entering a specific field or the job market for the first time; contracting positions; executive-level positions and middle-management-level positions are all available on the Web.

Job seekers will find a number of time-saving features when searching for jobs online. These include storing and distributing resumes digitally, e-mail notification of possible positions, salary and relocation calculators, job coaches, self-assessment tools and information on continuing education.

In this chapter, we explore online career services from the employer and employee's perspective. We suggest sites on which applications can be submitted, jobs can be searched and applicants can be reviewed. We also review services that build recruiting pages directly into e-businesses.

E.2 Resources for the Job Seeker

Finding a job online can greatly reduce the amount of time spent applying for a position. Instead of searching through newspapers and mailing resumes, job seekers can request a specific positions in specific industries through search engines. Some sites allow job seekers to setup intelligent agents to find jobs that meet their requirements. Intelligent agents are programs that search and arrange large amounts of data and report answers based on that data. When the agent finds a potential match, it sends it to the job seeker's inbox. Resumes can be stored digitally, customized quickly to meet job requirements and e-mailed instantaneously. A potential candidate also can learn more about a company by visiting its Web site. Most employment sites are free to job seekers. These sites typically generate their revenues by charging employers for posting job opportunities and by selling advertising space on their Web pages (see the **Monster.com** feature).

Career services, such as **FlipDog.com**, search a list of employer job sites to find positions. By searching links to employer Web sites, **FlipDog.com** is able to identify positions from companies of all sizes. This feature enables job seekers to find jobs that employers may not have posted outside the corporation's Web site.

Monster.com

Super Bowl ads and effective marketing have made **Monster.com** one of the most recognizable online brands (see Fig. E.1). In fact, in the 24 hours following Super Bowl XXXIV, 5 million job searches occurred on **Monster.com**.[2] The site allows people looking for jobs to post their resumes, search job listings, read advice and information about the job-search process and take proactive steps to improve their careers. These services are free to job seekers. Employers can post job listings, search resume databases and become featured employers.

Posting a resume at **Monster.com** is simple and free. **Monster.com** has a resume builder that allows users to post a resume to its site in 15–30 minutes. Each user can store up to 5 resumes and cover letters on the **Monster.com** server. Some companies offer their employment applications directly through the **Monster.com** site. **Monster.com** has job postings in every state and all major categories. Users can limit access to their personal identification information. As one of the leading recruiting sites on the Web, **Monster.com** is a good place to begin a job search or to find out more about the search process.

Monster.com *(Cont.)*

Fig. E.1   Monster.com home page. (Courtesy of **Monster.com**.)

Job seekers can visit **FlipDog.com** and choose, by state, the area in which they are looking for positions. Applicants also can conduct worldwide searches. After a user selects a region, **FlipDog.com** requests the user to choose a job category containing several specific positions. The user's choice causes a list of local employers to appear. The user can specify an employer or request that **FlipDog.com** search the employment databases for jobs offered by all employers (see Fig. E.2).

Other services, such as employment networks, also help job seekers in their search. Sites such as **Vault.com** (see the **Vault.com** feature) and **WetFeet.com** allow job seekers to post questions in designated chat rooms or on electronic bulletin boards about employers and positions.

E.3 Online Opportunities for Employers

Recruiting on the Internet provides several benefits over traditional recruiting. For example, Web recruiting reaches a much larger audience than posting an advertisement in a local newspaper. Given the breadth of the services provided by most online career services Web sites, the cost of posting online can be considerably less than posting positions through traditional means. Even newspapers, which depend greatly on career opportunity advertising, are starting online career sites.[3]

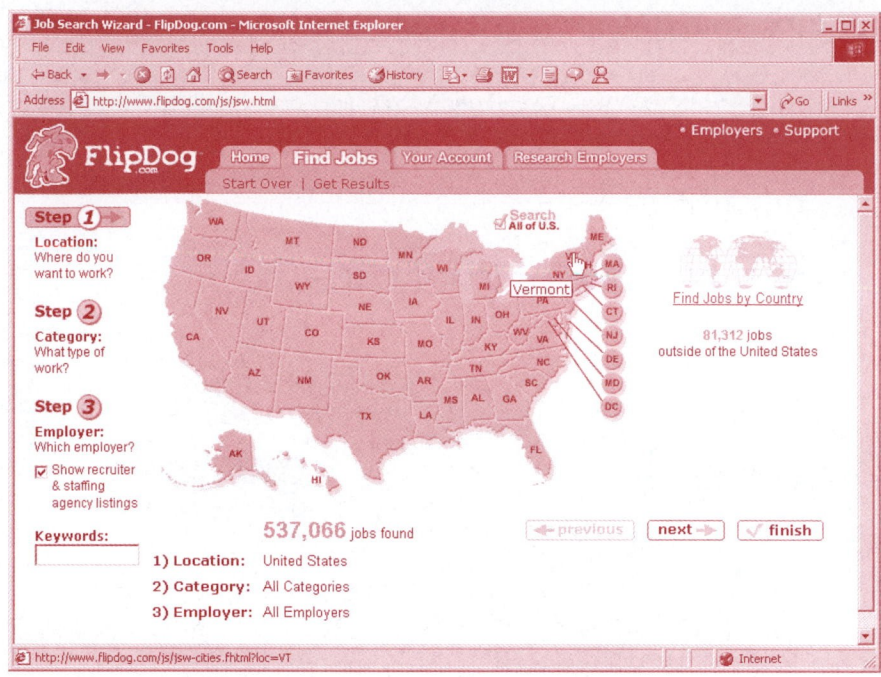

Fig. E.2   **FlipDog.com** job search. (Courtesy of **Flipdog.com**.)

Vault.com: Finding the Right Job on the Web[4]

Vault.com allows potential employees to seek out additional, third-party information for over 3000 companies. By visiting the *Insider Research* page, Web users have access to a profile on the company of their choice, as long as it exists in **Vault.com**'s database. In addition to **Vault.com**'s profile, there is a link to additional commentary by company employees. Most often anonymous, these messages can provide prospective employees with potentially valuable decision-making information. However, users must consider the integrity of the source. For example, a disgruntled employee may leave a posting that is not an accurate representation of the corporate culture of his or her company.

The **Vault.com** *Electronic Watercooler*™ is a message board that allows visitors to post stories, questions and concerns and to advise employees and job seekers. In addition, the site provides e-newsletters and feature stories designed to help job seekers in their search. Individuals seeking information on business, law and graduate schools can also find information on **Vault.com**.

Job-posting and career-advancement services for the job seeker are featured on **Vault.com**. These services include *VaultMatch*, a career service that e-mails job postings as requested, and *Salary Wizard*™, which helps job seekers determine the salary they are worth. Online guides with advice for fulfilling career ambitions are also available.

> ## Vault.com: Finding the Right Job on the Web[4] (Cont.)
>
> Employers can also use the site. *HR Vault*, a feature of **Vault.com**, provides employers with a free job-posting site. It offers career-management advice, employer-to-employee relationship management and recruiting resources.

e-Fact E.1

According to Forrester Research, 33 percent of today's average company's hiring budget goes toward online career services, while the remaining 66 percent is used for traditional recruiting mechanisms. Online use is expected to increase to 42 percent by 2004, while traditional mechanisms may be reduced to 10 percent.[5]

Generally, jobs posted online are viewed by a larger number of job seekers than jobs posted through traditional means. However, it is important not to overlook the benefits of combining online efforts with human-to-human interaction. There are many job seekers who are not yet comfortable with the process of finding a job online. Often, online recruiting is used as a means of freeing up a recruiter's time for the interviewing process and final selection.

e-Fact E.2

Cisco Systems cites a 39 percent reduction in cost-per-hire expenses, and a 60 percent reduction in the time spent hiring.[6]

E.3.1 Posting Jobs Online

When searching for job candidates online, there are many things employers need to consider. The Internet is a valuable tool for recruiting, but one that takes careful planning to acquire the best results. It provides a good supplementary tool, but should not be considered the complete solution for filling positions. Web sites, such as WebHire (**www.webhire.com**), enhance a company's online employment search (see the WebHire feature).

There are a variety of sites that allow employers to post jobs online. Some of these sites require a fee, which generally runs between $100–200. Postings typically remain on the Web site for 30–60 days. Employers should be careful to post to sites that are most likely to be visited by eligible candidates. As we discovered in the previous section, there are a variety of online career services focused on specific industries, and many of the larger, more comprehensive sites have categorized their databases by job category.

When designing a posting, the recruiter should consider the vast number of postings already on the Web. Defining what makes the job position unique, including information such as benefits and salary, might convince a qualified candidate to further investigate the position (see Fig. E.3).[7]

HotJobs.com career postings are cross-listed on a variety of other sites, thus increasing the number of potential employees who see the job listings. Like **Monster.com** and **jobfind.com**, **HotJobs.com** requires a fee per listing. Employers also have the option of becoming **HotJobs.com** members. Employers can gain access to HotJob's *Private Label Job Board*s (private corporate employment sites), online recruiting technology and online career fairs.

WebHire™[8]

Designed specifically for recruiters and employers, WebHire is a multifaceted service that provides employers with *end-to-end recruiting solutions*. The service offers job-posting services as well as candidate searches. The most comprehensive of the services, *WebHire™ Enterprise*, locates and ranks candidates found through resume-scanning mechanisms. Clients will also receive a report indicating the best resources for their search. Other services available through the *WebHire™ Employment Services Network* include preemployment screening, tools for assessing employees' skill levels and information on compensation packages. An employment law advisor helps organizations design interview questions.

WebHire™ Agent is an intelligent agent that searches for qualified applicants based on job specifications. When WebHire Agent identifies a potential candidate, an e-mail is sent to the candidate to generate interest. WebHire Agent then ranks applicants according to the skills information it gains from the Web search; the information is stored so that new applicants are distinguished from those who have already received an e-mail from the site.

Yahoo!® Resumes, a feature of WebHire, allows recruiters to find potential employees by typing in keywords on the Yahoo! Resumes search engine. Employers can purchase a year's membership to the recruiting solution for a flat fee; there are no per-use charges.

Job Seeker's Criteria

Position (responsibilities)

Salary

Location

Benefits (health, dental, stock options)

Advancement

Time Commitment

Training Opportunities

Tuition Reimbursement

Corporate Culture

Fig. E.3   List of a job seeker's criteria.

Boston Herald *Job Find* (**www.jobfind.com**) also charges employers to post on its site. The initial fee entitles the employer to post up to three listings. Employers have no limitations on the length of their postings.

Other Web sites providing employers with employee recruitment services include **CareerPath.com**, America's Job Bank (**www.ajb.dni.us/employer**), CareerWeb (**www.cweb.com**), **Jobs.com** and **Career.com**.

E.3.2 Problems with Recruiting on the Web

The large number of applicants presents a challenge to both job seekers and employers. On many recruitment sites, matching resumes to positions is conducted by *resume-filtering software*. The software scans a pool of resumes for keywords that match the job description. While this software increases the number of resumes that receive attention, it is not a foolproof system. For example, the resume-filtering software might overlook someone with similar skills to those listed in the job description, or someone whose abilities would enable them to learn the skills required for the position. Digital transmissions can also create problems because certain software platforms are not always acceptable by the recruiting software. This sometimes results in an unformatted transmission, or a failed transmission.

A lack of confidentiality is another disadvantage of online career services. In many cases, a job candidate will want to search for job opportunities anonymously. This reduces the possibility of offending the candidate's current employer. Posting a resume on the Web increases the likelihood that the candidate's employer might come across it when recruiting new employees. The traditional method of mailing resumes and cover letters to potential employers does not impose the same risk.

According to recent studies, the number of individuals researching employment positions through traditional means, such as referrals, newspapers and temporary agencies, far outweighs the number of job seekers researching positions through the Internet.[9] Optimists feel, however, that this disparity is largely due to the early stages of e-business development. Given time, online career services will become more refined in their posting and searching capabilities, decreasing the amount of time it takes for a job seeker to find jobs and employers to fill positions.

E.3.3 Diversity in the Workplace

Every workplace inevitably develops its own culture. Responsibilities, schedules, deadlines and projects all contribute to a working environment. Perhaps the most defining elements of a *corporate culture* are the employees. For example, if all employees were to have the same skills, same backgrounds and the same ideas, the workplace would lack diversity. It also might lack creativity and enthusiasm. One way to increase the dynamics of an organization is to employ people of different backgrounds and cultures.

The Internet hosts demographic-specific sites for employers seeking to increase diversity in the workplace. By recruiting people from different backgrounds, new ideas and perspectives are brought forth, helping businesses meet the needs of a larger, more diverse target audience.[10]

Blackvoices.com and **hirediversity.com** are demographic-specific Web sites. BlackVoices™, which functions primarily as a portal (a site offering news, sports and weather information, as well as Web searches), features job searching capabilities and the ability for prospective employees to post resumes. HireDiversity is divided into several categories, including opportunities for African Americans, Hispanics and women. Other online recruiting services place banner advertisements on ethnic Web sites for companies seeking diverse workforces.

The Diversity Directory (**www.mindexchange.com**) offers international career-searching capabilities. Users selecting the **Diversity** site can find job opportunities, information and additional resources to help them in their career search. The site can be searched according to demographics (African American, Hispanic, alternative lifestyle, etc.) or by subject (employer, position, etc.) via hundreds of links. Featured sites include **BilingualJobs.com**, *Latin World* and *American Society for Female Entrepreneurs*.

Many sites have sections dedicated to job seekers with disabilities. In addition to providing job-searching capabilities, these sites include additional resources, such as equal opportunity documents and message boards. The *National Business and Disability Council* (*NBDC*) provides employers with integration and accessibility information for employing people with disabilities, and the site also lists opportunities for job seekers.

E.4 Recruiting Services

There are many services on the Internet that help employers match individuals to positions. The time saved by conducting preliminary searches on the Internet can be dedicated to interviewing qualified candidates and making the best matches possible.

Advantage Hiring, Inc. (**www.advantagehiring.com**) provides employers with a resume-screening service. When a prospective employee submits a resume for a particular position, Advantage Hiring, Inc. presents *Net-Interview*™, a small questionnaire to supplement the information presented on the resume. The site also offers *SiteBuilder*, a service that helps employers build an employee recruitment site. An online demonstration can be found at **www.advantagehiring.com**. The demonstration walks the user through the Net-Interview software, as well as a number of other services offered by Advantage Hiring (see Fig. E.4).

Recruitsoft.com is an application service provider (ASP) that offers companies recruiting software on a *pay-per-hire* basis (Recruitsoft receives a commission on hires made via its service). *Recruiter WebTop*™ is the company's online recruiting software. It includes features such as Web-site hosting, an employee-referral program, skill-based resume screening, applicant-tracking capabilities and job-board posting capabilities. A demonstration of Recruiter WebTop's *Corporate Recruiting Solutions* can be found at **www.recruitsoft.com/process**. Other online recruiting services include **Hire.com**, and **Futurestep.com**™.

The Internet also provides employers with a cost-effective means of testing their prospective employees in such categories as decision making, problem solving and personality. Services such *eTest* help to reduce the cost of in-house testing and to make the interview process more effective. Test results, given in paragraph form, present employers with the interested individual's strengths and weaknesses. Based on these results, the report suggests interview methods, such as asking *open-ended questions*, which are questions that require more than a "yes" or "no" response. Sample reports and a free-trial test can be found at **www.etest.net**.

Employers and job seekers can also find career placement exercises at **www.advisorteam.net/User/ktsintro.asp**. Some of these services require a fee. The tests ask several questions regarding the individual's interests and working style. Results help candidates determine the best career for their skills and interests.

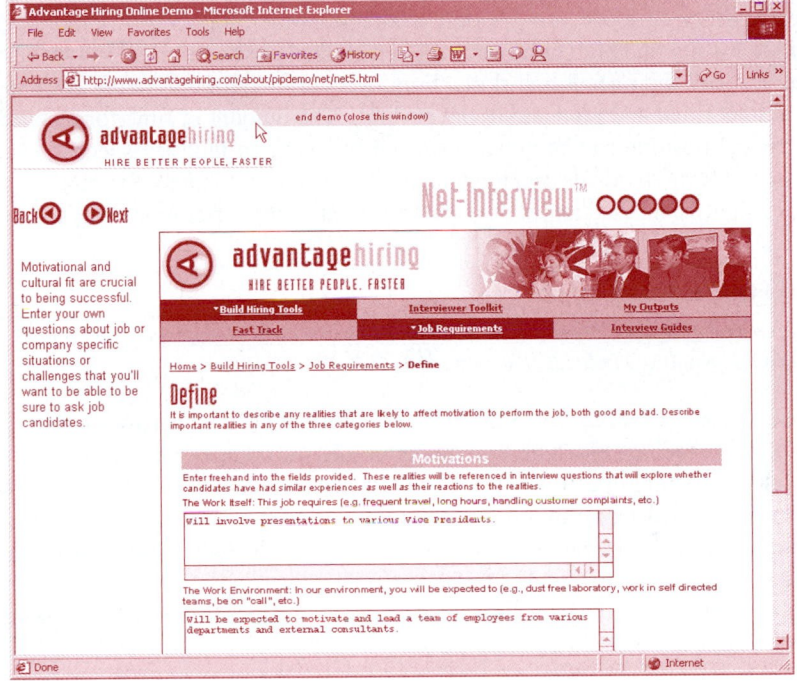

Fig. E.4   Advantage Hiring, Inc.'s Net-Interview™ service. (Courtesy of Advantage Hiring, Inc.)

E.5 Career Sites

Online career sites can be comprehensive or industry specific. In this section, we explore a variety of sites on the Web that accommodate the needs of both the job seeker and the employer. We review sites offering technical positions, free-lancing opportunities and contracting positions.

E.5.1 Comprehensive Career Sites

As mentioned previously, there are many sites on the Web that provide job seekers with career opportunities in multiple fields. **Monster.com** is the largest of these sites, attracting the greatest number of unique visitors per month. Other popular online recruiting sites include **JobsOnline.com**, **HotJobs.com**, **www.jobtrak.com** (a **Monster.com** site) and **Headhunter.net**.

Searching for a job online can be a conducted in a few steps. For example, during an initial visit to **JobsOnline.com**, a user is required to fill out a registration form. The form requests basic information, such as name, address and area of interest. After registering, members can search through job postings according to such criteria as job category, location and the number of days the job has been posted. Contact information is provided for additional communication.

E.5.2 Technical Positions

Technical positions are becoming widely available as the Internet grows more pervasive. Limited job loyalty and high turnover rates in technical positions allow job seekers to find jobs that best suit their needs and skills. Employers are required to rehire continuously to keep positions filled and productivity levels high. The amount of time for an employer to fill a technical position can be greatly reduced by using an industry-specific site. Career sites designed for individuals seeking technical positions are among the most popular on-line career sites. In this section, we review several sites that offer recruiting and hiring opportunities for technical positions.

e-Fact E.3

It costs a company 25 percent more to hire a new technical employee than it does to pay an already employed individual's salary.[11]

Dice.com (**www.dice.com**) is a recruiting Web site that focuses on technical fields. Company fees are based on the number of jobs the company posts and the frequency with which the postings are updated. Job seekers can post their resumes and search the job database for free. **JustTechJobs.com** directs job seekers toward 39 specific computer technologies for their job search. Language-specific sites include **JustJavaJobs.com**, **JustCJobs.com** and **JustPerlJobs.com**. Hardware, software and communications technology sites are also available. Other technology recruiting sites include **Hire-Ability.com**, and **HotDispatch.com**.

E.5.3 Wireless Positions

The wireless industry is developing rapidly. According to **WirelessResumes.com**, the number of wireless professionals is 328,000. This number is expected to increase 40 percent each year for the next five years. To accommodate this growth, and the parallel demand for professionals, **WirelessResumes.com** has created an online career site specifically for the purpose of filling wireless jobs (see the **WirelessResumes.com** feature).

WirelessResumes.com: *Filling Wireless Positions*

WirelessResumes.com is an online career site focused specifically on matching wireless professionals with careers in the industry. This narrow focus enables businesses to locate new employees quickly—reducing the time and expense attached to traditional recruiting methods. Similarly, candidates can limit their searches to precisely the job category of interest. Wireless carriers, device manufacturers, WAP and Bluetooth developers, e-commerce companies and application service providers (ASPs) are among those represented on the site.

   In addition to searching for jobs and posting a resume, **WirelessResumes.com** provides job seekers with resume writing tips, interviewing techniques, relocation tools and assistance in obtaining a Visa or the completion of other necessary paperwork. Employers can use the site to search candidates and post job opportunities.

The Caradyne Group (`www.pcsjobs.com`*)*, an executive search firm, connects job seekers to employers in the wireless technology field. Interested job seekers must first fill out a "Profile Questionnaire." This information is then entered into The Caradyne Group's database and is automatically matched to an open position in the job seeker's field of expertise. If there are no open positions, a qualified consultant from The Caradyne Group will contact the job seeker for further a interview and discussion.

E.5.4 Contracting Online

The Internet also serves as a forum for job seekers to find employment on a project-by-project basis. *Online contracting services* allow businesses to post positions for which they wish to hire outside resources, and individuals can identify projects that best suit their interests, schedules and skills.

 e-Fact E.4

Approximately six percent of America's workforce falls into the category of independent contractor.[12]

`Guru.com` (`www.guru.com`) is a recruiting site for contract employees. Independent contractors, private consultants and trainers use `guru.com` to find short-term and long-term contract assignments. Tips, articles and advice are available for contractors who wish to learn more about their industry. Other sections of the site teach users how to manage their businesses, buy the best equipment and deal with legal issues. `Guru.com` includes an online store where contractors can buy products associated with small-business management, such as printing services and office supplies. Companies wishing to hire contractors must register with `guru.com`, but individuals seeking contract assignments do not.

`Monster.com`'s Talent Market™ offers online auction-style career services to free agents. Interested users design a profile, listing their qualifications. After establishing a profile, free agents "Go Live" to start the bidding on their services. The bidding lasts for five days during which users can view the incoming bids. At the close of five days, the user can choose the job of his or her choice. The service is free for users, and bidding employers pay a commission on completed transactions.

`eLance.com` is another site where individuals can find contracting work. Interested applicants can search eLance's database by category, including business, finance and marketing (Fig. E.5). These projects, or *requests for proposals* (RFPs), are posted by companies worldwide. When users find projects for which they feel qualified, they submit bids on the projects. Bids must contain a user's required payment, a statement detailing the user's skills and a feedback rating drawn from other projects on which the user has worked. If a user's bid is accepted, the user is given the project, and the work is conducted over eLance's file-sharing system, enabling both the contractor and the employer to contact one another quickly and easily. For an online demonstration, visit `www.elance.com` and click on the **take a tour...** link.

Other Web sites that provide contractors with projects and information include eWork® Exchange (`www.ework.com`), `MBAFreeAgent.com`, `Aquent.com` and `WorkingSolo.com`.

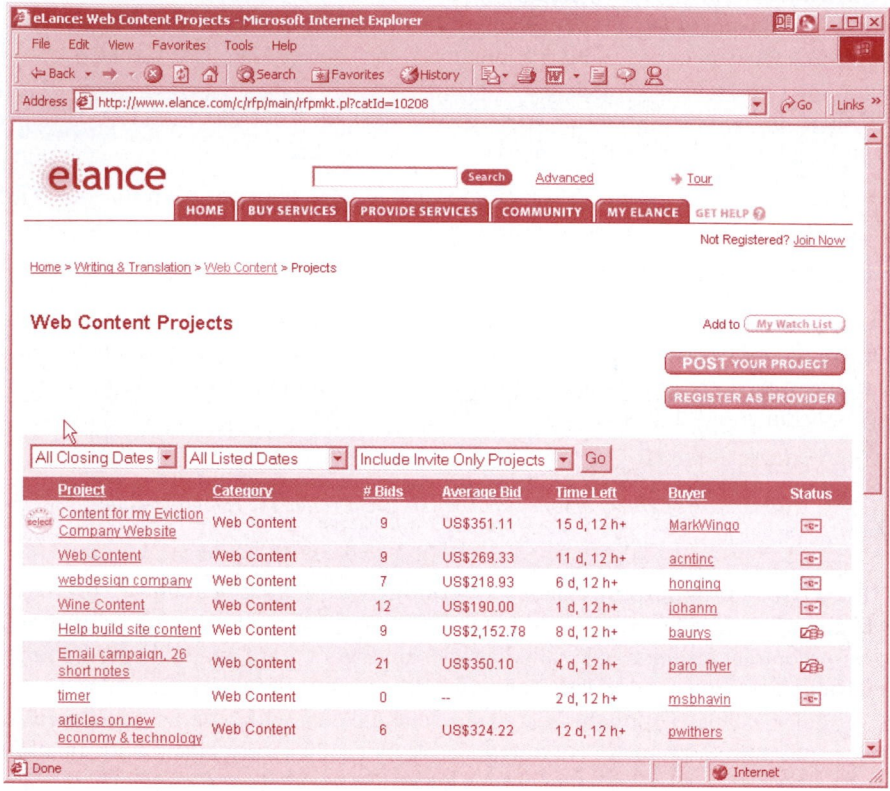

Fig. E.5   **eLance.com** request for proposal (RFP) example. (Courtesy of eLance, Inc.)

E.5.5 Executive Positions

In this section, we discuss the advantages and disadvantages of finding an executive position online. Executive career advancement sites usually include many of the features found on comprehensive job-search sites. Searching for an executive position online differs from finding an entry-level position online. The Internet allows individuals to continually survey the job market. However, candidates for executive-level positions must exercise a higher level of caution when determining who is able to view their resume. Applying for an executive position online is an extensive process. As a result of the high level of scrutiny passed on a candidate during the hiring process, the initial criteria presented by an executive level candidate often are more specific than the criteria presented by the first-time job seeker. Executive positions often are difficult to fill, due to the high demands and large amount of experience required for the jobs.

SixFigureJobs (**www.sixfigurejobs.com**) is a recruitment site designed for experienced executives. Resume posting and job searching is free to job seekers. Other sites that help executives find positions include **www.execunet.com**, **Monster.com**'s ChiefMonster™ (**www.chiefmonster.com**) and **www.nationjob.com**.

E.5.6 Students and Young Professionals

The Internet provides students and young professionals with tools to get them started in the job market. Individuals still in school and seeking internships, individuals who are just graduating and individuals who have been in the workforce for a few years make up the target market. Additional tools specifically designed for this *demographic* (a population defined by a specific characteristic) are available. For example, journals kept by previous interns provide prospective interns with information regarding what to look for in an internship, what to expect and what to avoid. Many sites will provide information to lead young professionals in the right direction, such as matching positions to their college or university major.

Experience.com is a career services Web site geared toward the younger population. Members can search for positions according to specific criteria, such as geographic location, job category, keywords, commitment (i.e. full time, part time, internship), amount of vacation and amount of travel time. After applicants register, they can send their resumes directly to the companies posted on the site. In addition to the resume, candidates provide a personal statement, a list of applicable skills and their language proficiency. Registered members also receive access to the site's *Job Agent*. Up to three Job Agents can be used by each member. The agents search for available positions, based on the criteria posted by the member. If a match is made, the site contacts the candidate via e-mail.[13,14]

Internships.wetfeet.com helps students find internships. In addition to posting a resume and searching for an internship, students can use the relocation calculator to compare the cost of living in different regions. Tips on building resumes and writing essays are provided. The *City Intern* program provides travel, housing and entertainment guides to interns interviewing or accepting a position in an unfamiliar city, making them feel more at home in a new location.

In addition to its internship locators, undergraduate, graduate, law school, medical school and business school services, the Princeton Review's Web site (**www.review.com**) offers career services to graduating students. While searching for a job, students and young professionals can also read through the site's news reports or even increase their vocabulary by visiting the "word for the day." Other career sites geared toward the younger population include **campuscareercenter.com**, **brassring-campus.com** and **collegegrad.com**.

E.5.7 Other Online Career Services

In addition to Web sites that help users find and post jobs online, there are a number of Web sites that offer features that will enhance searches, prepare users to search online, help applicants design resumes or help users calculate the cost of relocating.

Salary.com helps job seekers gauge their expected income, based on position, level of responsibility and years of experience. The search requires job category, ZIP code and specific job title. Based on this information, the site will return an estimated salary for an individual living in the specified area and employed in the position described. Estimates are returned based on the average level of income for the position.

In addition to helping applicants find employment, **www.careerpower.com** provides individuals with tests that will help them realize their strengths, weaknesses, values, skills and personality traits. Based on the results, which can be up to 10–12 pages per test, users can best decide what job categories they are qualified for and what career choice will be best suited to their personal ambitions. The service is available for a fee.

InterviewSmart™ is another service offered through CareerPower that prepares job seekers of all levels for the interviewing process. The service can be downloaded for a minimal fee or can be used on the Web for free. Both versions are available at **www.career-power.com/CareerPerfect/interviewing.htm#is.start.anchor**.

Additional services will help applicants find positions that meet their unique needs, or design their resumes to attract the attention of specific employers. **Dog-friendly.com**, organized by geographic location, helps job seekers find opportunities that allow them to bring their pets to work, and **cooljobs.com** is a searchable database of unique job opportunities.

E.6 Internet and World Wide Web Resources

Information Technology (IT) Career Sites

www.dice.com
This is a recruiting Web site that focuses on the computer industry.

www.guru.com
This is a recruiting site for contract employees. Independent contractors, private consultants and trainers can use **guru.com** to find short-term and long-term work.

www.hallkinion.com
This is a Web recruiting service for individuals seeking IT positions.

www.techrepublic.com
This site provides employers and job seekers with recruiting capabilities and information regarding developing technology.

www.justcomputerjobs.com
This site serves as a portal with access to language-specific sites, including Java, Perl, C and C++.

www.hotdispatch.com
This forum provides software developers with the opportunity to share projects, discuss code and ask questions.

www.techjobs.bizhosting.com/jobs.htm
This site directs job seekers to links of numerous technological careers listed by location, internet, type of field, etc.

Career Sites

www.careerbuilder.com
A network of career sites, including IT Careers, *USA Today* and MSN, CareerBuilder attracts 3 million unique job seekers per month. The site provides resume-builder and job-searching agents.

www.recruitek.com
This free site caters to jobs seekers, employers and contractors.

www.monster.com
This site, the largest of the online career sites, allows people looking for jobs to post their resumes, search job listings and read advice and information about the job-search process. It also provides a variety of recruitment services for employers.

www.jobsonline.com
Similar to **Monster.com**, this site provides opportunities for job seekers and employers.

www.hotjobs.com
This online recruiting site offers cross-listing possibilities on additional sites.

www.jobfind.com
This job site is an example of locally targeted job-search resources. **JobFind.com** targets the Boston area.

www.flipdog.com
This site allows online job candidates to search for career opportunities. It employs intelligent agents to scour the Web and return jobs matching the candidate's request.

www.cooljobs.com
This site highlights unique job opportunities.

www.inetsupermall.com
This site aids job searchers in creating professional resumes and connecting with employers.

www.wirelessnetworksonline.com
This site helps connect job searchers to careers for which they are qualified.

www.careerweb.com
This site highlights featured employers and jobs and allows job seekers and employers to post and view resumes, respectively.

www.jobsleuth.com
On this site job seekers can fill out a form that indicates their desired field of employment. Job Sleuth™ searches the Internet and returns potential matches to the user's inbox. The service is free.

www.ajb.org
America's Job Bank is an online recruiting service provided through the Department of Labor and the state employment service. Searching for and posting positions on the site are free.

Executive Positions

www.sixfigurejobs.com
This is a recruitment site designed for experienced executives.

www.leadersonline.com
This career services Web site offers confidential job searches for mid-level professionals. Potential job matches are e-mailed to job candidates.

www.ecruitinginc.com
This site is designed to search for employees for executive positions.

Diversity

www.latpro.com
This site is designed for Spanish-speaking and Portuguese-speaking job seekers. In addition to providing resume-posting services, the site enables job seekers to receive matching positions via e-mail. Advice and information services are available.

www.blackvoices.com
This portal site hosts a career center designed to match African American job seekers with job opportunities.

www.hirediversity.com

In addition to services for searching for and posting positions, resume-building and updating services are also available on this site. The site targets a variety of demographics including African Americans, Asian Americans, people with disabilities, women and Latin Americans.

People with Disabilities

www.halftheplanet.com

This site represents people with disabilities. The site is large and includes many different resources and information services. A special section is dedicated to job seekers and employers.

www.wemedia.com

This site is designed to meet the needs of people with disabilities. It includes a section for job seekers and employers.

www.disabilities.com

This site provides users with a host of links to information resources on career opportunities.

www.mindexchange.com

The diversity section of this site provides users with several links to additional resources regarding people with disabilities and employment.

www.usdoj.gov/crt/ada/adahom1.htm

This is the Americans with Disabilities Act home page.

www.abanet.org/publicserv/mental.html

This is the Web site for The Commission on Mental and Physical Disability Law.

janweb.icdi.wvu.edu

The Job Accommodation Web site offers consulting services to employers regarding integration of people with disabilities into the workplace.

General Resources

www.vault.com

This site provides potential employees with "insider information" on over 3000 companies. In addition, job seekers can search through available positions and post and answer questions on the message board.

www.wetfeet.com

Similar to **vault.com**, this site allows visitors to ask questions and receive "insider information" on companies that are hiring.

Special Interest

www.eharvest.com/careers/

This Web site provides job seekers interested in agricultural positions with online career services.

www.opportunitynocs.org

This career services site is for both employers and job seekers interested in non-profit opportunities.

www.experience.com

This Web site is designed specifically for young professionals and students seeking full-time, part-time and internship positions.

www.internships.wetfeet.com

Students seeking internships can search job listings on this site. It also features City Intern, to help interns become acquainted with a new location.

www.brassringcampus.com
This site provides college grads and young professionals with less than five years of experience with job opportunities. Additional features help users buy cars or find apartments.

Online Contracting

www.ework.com
This online recruiting site matches outside contractors with companies needing project specialists. Other services provided through eWork include links to online training sites, benefits packages and payment services and online meeting and management resources.

www.elance.com
Similar to **eWork.com**, eLance matches outside contractors with projects.

www.MBAFreeAgent.com
This site is designed to match MBAs with contracting opportunities.

www.aquent.com
This site provides access to technical contracting positions.

www.WorkingSolo.com
This site helps contractors begin their own projects.

Recruiting Services

www.advantagehiring.com
This site helps employers screen resumes.

www.etest.net
This site provides employers with testing services to assess the strengths and weaknesses of prospective employees. This information can be used for better hiring strategies.

www.hire.com
Hire.com's eRecruiter is an application service provider that helps organizations streamline their Web-recruiting process.

www.futurestep.com
Executives can register confidentially at **Futurestep.com** to be considered for senior executive positions. The site connects registered individuals to positions. It also offers career management services.

www.webhire.com
This site provides employers with end-to-end recruiting solutions.

Wireless Career Resources

www.wirelessresumes.com/
This site connects employers and job seekers with resumes that focus on jobs revolving around wireless technology.

www.msua.org/job.htm
This site contains links to numerous wireless job-seeking Web sites.

www.wiwc.org
This site's focus is wireless communication job searching for women.

www.firstsearch.com
At this site a job seeker is able to discover part-time, full-time and salary-based opportunities in the wireless industry.

www.pcsjobs.com
This is the site for The Caradyne Group, which is an executive search firm that focuses on finding job seekers wireless job positions.

www.cnijoblink.com
CNI Career Networks offers confidential, no-charge job placement in the wireless and telecommunications industries.

SUMMARY

- The Internet can improve an employer's ability to recruit employees and help users find career opportunities worldwide.

- Job seekers can learn how to write a resume and cover letter, post them online and search through job listings to find the jobs that best suit their needs.

- Employers can post jobs that can be searched by an enormous pool of applicants.

- Job seekers can store and distribute resumes digitally, receive e-mail notification of possible positions, use salary and relocation calculators, consult job coaches and use self-assessment tools when searching for a job on the Web.

- There are approximately 40,000 career-advancement services on the Internet today.

- Finding a job online can greatly reduce the amount of time spent applying for a position. Potential candidates can also learn more about a company by visiting its Web site.

- Most sites are free to job seekers. These sites typically generate their revenues by charging employers who post their job opportunities, and by selling advertising space on their Web pages.

- Sites such as **Vault.com** and **WetFeet.com** allow job seekers to post questions about employers and positions in chat rooms and on bulletin boards.

- On many recruitment sites, the match of a resume to a position is conducted with resume-filtering software.

- A lack of confidentiality is a disadvantage of online career services.

- According to recent studies, the number of individuals researching employment positions through means other than the Internet, such as referrals, newspapers and temporary agencies, far outweighs the number of Internet job seekers.

- Career sites designed for individuals seeking technical positions are among the most popular online career sites.

- Online contracting services allow businesses to post positions for which they wish to hire outside resources, and allow individuals to identify projects that best suit their interests, schedules and skills.

- The Internet provides students and young professionals with some of the necessary tools to get them started in the job market. The target market is made up of individuals still in school and seeking internships, individuals who are just graduating and individuals who have been in the workforce for a few years.

- There are a number of Web sites that offer features that enhance job searches, prepare users to search online, help design applicants' resumes or help users calculate the cost of relocating.

- Web recruiting reaches a much larger audience than posting an advertisement in the local newspaper.

- There are a variety of sites that allow employers to post jobs online. Some of these sites require a fee, which generally runs between $100–$200. Postings remain on the Web site for approximately 30–60 days.

- Employers should try to post to sites that are most likely to be visited by eligible candidates.

- When designing a job posting, defining what makes a job position unique and including information such as benefits and salary might convince a qualified candidate to further investigate the position.

- The Internet hosts demographic-specific sites for employers seeking to increase diversity in the workplace.

- The Internet has provided employers with a cost-effective means of testing their prospective employees in such categories as decision making, problem solving and personality.

TERMINOLOGY

corporate culture
demographic
end-to-end recruiting solutions
entry-level position
online contracting service
open-ended question
pay-per-hire
request for proposal (RFP)
resume-filtering software

SELF-REVIEW EXERCISES

E.1   State whether each of the following is *true* or *false*, if *false*, explain why.
  a) Online contracting services allow businesses to post job listings for specific projects that can be viewed by job seekers over the Web.
  b) Employment networks are Web sites designed to provide information on a selected company to better inform job seekers of the corporate environment.
  c) The large number of applications received over the Internet is considered an advantage by most online recruiters.
  d) There is a greater number of individuals searching for work on the Web than through all other mediums combined.
  e) Sixteen percent of America's workforce is categorized as independent contractors.

E.2   Fill in the blanks in each of the following statements.
  a) There are approximately _____ online career services Web sites on the Internet today.
  b) The Internet hosts demographic-specific sites for employers seeking to increase _____ in the workplace.
  c) In the 24 hours following the Super Bowl, _____ job searches occurred on **Monster.com**.
  d) Many recruitment sites use _____ to filter through received resumes.
  e) Employers should try to post to sites that are most likely to be visited by _____ candidates.

ANSWERS TO SELF-REVIEW EXERCISES

E.1   a) True. b) True. c) False. The large number of applicants reduces the amount of time a recruiter can spend interviewing and making decisions. Despite screening processes, many highly qualified applicants can be overlooked. d) False. The number of individuals researching employment positions through other means, such as referrals, newspapers and temporary agencies, far outweighs the number of Internet job seekers. e) False. Six percent of America's workforce is categorized as independent consultants.

E.2   a) 40,000. b) diversity. c) 5 million. d) resume-filtering software. e) eligible.

EXERCISES

E.3   State whether each of the following is *true* or *false*, if *false*, explain why.
  a) RFP is the acronym for request for proposal.
  b) The Internet has provided employers with a cost-effective means of testing their prospective employees in such categories as decision making, problem solving and personality.
  c) Online job recruiting can completely replace other means of hiring employees.
  d) Posting a job online is less expensive than placing ads in more traditional media.
  e) A lack of confidentiality is a disadvantage of online career services.

E.4   Fill in the blanks in each of the following:
  a) Finding a job online can greatly _____ the amount of time spent applying for a position.
  b) _____ is an example of a Web site in which contractors can bid on projects.
  c) When designing a job posting, defining what makes the position unique and including information such as _____ and _____ might convince a qualified candidate to further investigate the position.
  d) The Internet hosts _____ for employers seeking to increase diversity in the workplace.
  e) The Internet provides employers with a cost-effective means of testing their prospective employees in such categories as _____, _____ and _____.

E.5   Define the following
  a) Corporate culture.
  b) Pay-per-hire.
  c) Request for proposal (RFP).
  d) Resume-filtering software.

E.6   (*Class discussion*). In this chapter, we discuss the short-comings and advantages of recruiting on the Internet. Using the text, additional reading material and personal accounts answer the following questions. Be prepared to discuss your answers.
  a) Do you think finding a job is easier on the Web? Why or why not?
  b) What disadvantages can you identify?
  c) What are some of the advantages?
  d) Which online recruiting services do you think will be most successful? Why?

E.7   Many of the career services Web sites we have discussed in this chapter offer resume-building capabilities. Begin building your resume, choosing an objective that is of interest to you. Think of your primary concerns. Are you searching for a paid internship or a volunteer opportunity? Do you have a specific location in mind? Do you have an opportunity for future employment? Are stock options important to you? Find several entry-level jobs that meet your requirements. Write a short summary of your results. Include any obstacles and opportunities.

E.8   In this chapter, we have discussed online contracting opportunities. Visit eLance (**www.elance.com**) and search the requests for proposals for contracting opportunities that interest you or visit **guru.com** and create a profile.

E.9   In this chapter, we have discussed many career services Web sites. Choose three sites. Explore the opportunities and resources offered by the sites. Visit any demonstrations, conduct a job search, build your resume and calculate your salary or relocation expenses. Answer the following questions.
  a) Which site provides the best service? Why?
  b) What did you like? Dislike?
  c) Write a brief summary of your findings, including descriptions of any features that you would add.

WORKS CITED

The notation <**www.domain-name.com**> indicates that the citation is for information found at the Web site.

1. J. Gaskin, "Web Job Sites Face Tough Tasks," *Inter@ctive Week*, 14 August 2000: 50.

2. J. Gaskin, 50.

3. M. Berger, "Jobs Supermarket," *Upside*, November 2000: 224.

4. <**www.vault.com**>.

5. M. Berger, 224.

6. Cisco Advertisement, *The Wall Street Journal,* 19 October 2000: B13.

7. M. Feffer, "Posting Jobs on the Internet," 18 August 2000 <**www.webhire.com/hr/ spotlight.asp**>.

8. <**www.webhire.com**>.

9. J. Gaskin, 51.

10. C. Wilde, "Recruiters Discover Diverse Value in Web Sites," *Information Week*, 7 February 2000: 144.

11. A.K. Smith, "Charting Your Own Course," *U.S. News and World Report*, 6 November 2000: 58.

12. D. Lewis, "Hired! By the Highest Bidder," *The Boston Globe*, 9 July 2000: G1.

13. <**www.experience.com**>.

14. M. French, "Experience Inc., E-Recruiting for Jobs for College Students," *Mass High Tech*, 7 February–13 February 2000: 29.

Unicode®

Objectives

- To become familiar with Unicode.
- To understand the mission of the Unicode Consortium.
- To understand the design basis of Unicode.
- To understand the three Unicode encoding forms: UTF-8, UTF-16 and UTF-32.
- To introduce characters and glyphs.
- To understand the advantages and disadvantages of using Unicode.
- To provide a brief tour of the Unicode Consortium's Web site.

Outline

F.1 Introduction

The use of inconsistent character *encodings* (i.e., numeric values associated with characters) when developing global software products causes serious problems, because computers use numbers to process information. For instance, the character "a" is converted to a numeric value, so that a computer can manipulate that piece of data. Many countries and corporations have developed their own encoding systems that are incompatible with the encoding systems of other countries and corporations. For example, the Microsoft Windows operating system assigns the value 0xC0 to the character "A" with a grave accent, while the Apple Macintosh operating system assigns the same value to an upside-down question mark. The misrepresentation and possible corruption of data can result when the data is not processed as intended.

In the absence of a widely implemented universal character encoding standard, global software developers had to *localize* their products extensively before distribution. Localization includes the language translation and cultural adaptation of content. The process of localization usually involves significant modifications to the source code (such as the conversion of numeric values and the underlying assumptions made by programmers), which results in increased costs and delays the release of the software. For example, some English-speaking programmers might design global software products, assuming that a single character can be represented by one byte. However, when those products are localized for Asian markets, the programmers' assumptions are no longer valid. Thus, the majority, if not the entirety, of the code needs to be rewritten. Localization is necessary with each release of a version of software. By the time a software product is localized for a particular market, a newer version, which needs to be localized as well, may be ready for distribution. As a result, it is cumbersome and costly to produce and distribute global software products in a market where there is no universal character-encoding standard.

In response to this situation, the *Unicode Standard*, an encoding standard that facilitates the production and distribution of software, was created. The Unicode Standard outlines a specification to produce consistent encoding of the world's characters and *symbols*. Software products that handle text encoded in the Unicode Standard need to be localized, but the localization process in Unicode is simpler and more efficient, because the numeric values need not be converted, and the assumptions made by programmers about the character encoding are universal. The Unicode Standard is maintained by a nonprofit organization called the *Unicode Consortium*, whose members include Apple, IBM, Microsoft, Oracle, Sun Microsystems, Sybase and many other companies.

When the Consortium envisioned and developed the Unicode Standard, it wanted an encoding system that was *universal*, *efficient*, *uniform* and *unambiguous*. A universal encoding system encompasses all commonly used characters. An efficient encoding system allows text files to be parsed easily. A uniform encoding system assigns fixed values to all characters. An unambiguous encoding system represents a given character in a consistent manner. These four terms are referred to as the Unicode Standard *design basis*.

F.2 Unicode Transformation Format (UTF)

Although Unicode incorporates the limited ASCII *character set* (i.e., a collection of characters), its character set is more comprehensive. In ASCII, each character is represented by a byte containing 0s and 1s. One byte is capable of storing the binary numbers from 0 to 255. Each character is assigned a number between 0 and 255. Thus, ASCII-based systems can support only 256 characters, which is a tiny fraction of the world's characters. Unicode extends the ASCII character set by encoding the vast majority of the world's characters. The Unicode Standard encodes all those characters in a uniform numerical space from 0 to 10FFFF hexadecimal. An implementation expresses these numbers in one of several transformation formats, choosing the one that best fits the particular application at hand.

Three such formats are in use—*UTF-8*, *UTF-16* and *UTF-32*—depending on the size of the units, in *bits,* being used. UTF-8, a variable-width encoding form, requires one to four bytes to express each Unicode character. UTF-8 data consists of 8-bit bytes (sequences of one, two, three or four bytes, depending on the character being encoded) and are well suited for ASCII-based systems when there is a predominance of one-byte characters. (As stated previously, ASCII represents characters as one byte.) Currently, UTF-8 is widely implemented in UNIX systems and in databases.

The variable-width UTF-16 encoding form expresses Unicode characters in units of 16 bits (i.e., as two adjacent bytes, or a short integer in many machines). Most characters of Unicode are expressed in a single 16-bit unit. However, characters with values above FFFF hexadecimal are expressed with an ordered pair of 16-bit units called *surrogates*. Surrogates are 16-bit integers in the range D800 through DFFF, which are used solely for the purpose of "escaping" into higher numbered characters. Approximately one million characters can be expressed in this manner. Although a surrogate pair requires 32 bits to represent characters, it is space-efficient to use these 16-bit units. Surrogates are rare characters in current implementations. Many string-handling implementations are written in terms of UTF-16. [*Note*: Details and sample code for UTF-16 handling are available on the Unicode Consortium Web site, **www.unicode.org**.]

Implementations that require significant use of rare characters or entire scripts encoded above FFFF hexadecimal should use UTF-32—a 32-bit, fixed-width encoding form that occasionally requires twice as much memory as do UTF-16 encoded characters. The major advantage of the fixed-width UTF-32 encoding form is that it uniformly expresses all characters, so it is easy to handle in arrays.

There are few guidelines that state when to use a particular encoding form. The best encoding form to use depends on computer systems and business protocols, not on the data themselves. Typically, the UTF-8 encoding form should be used where computer systems and business protocols require data to be handled in 8-bit units. This requirement occurs particularly in legacy systems that are being upgraded, because it often simplifies changes to existing programs. Likewise, UTF-16 is the encoding form of choice on Microsoft Windows applications. UTF-32 is likely to become more widely used in the future as more characters are encoded with values above FFFF hexadecimal. UTF-32 requires less sophisticated handling than UTF-16 in the presence of surrogate pairs.

Figure F.1 demonstrates the ways in which the three encoding forms handle character encoding.

F.3 Characters and Glyphs

The Unicode Standard consists of *characters*, which are written components (i.e., alphabetic letters, numerals, punctuation marks, accent marks, etc.) that can be represented by numeric values. An example of a character is U+0041 LATIN CAPITAL LETTER A. In the first character representation, U+*yyyy* is a *code value*, in which U+ refers to Unicode code values, as opposed to other hexadecimal values. The *yyyy* represents a four-digit hexadecimal number of an encoded character. Code values are bit combinations that represent encoded characters. Characters are represented by using *glyphs*, which are various shapes, fonts and sizes. There are no code values for glyphs in the Unicode Standard. Examples of glyphs are shown in Fig. F.2.

The Unicode Standard encompasses the alphabets, ideographs, syllabaries, punctuation marks, mathematical operators, *diacritics*, etc., that compose the written languages and scripts of the world. A diacritic is a special mark added to a character to distinguish it from another letter or to indicate an accent (e.g., in Spanish, the tilde "~" above the character "n"). Currently, Unicode provides code values for 94,140 character representations, with more than 880,000 code values reserved for future expansion.

Character	UTF-8	UTF-16	UTF-32
LATIN CAPITAL LETTER A	0x41	0x0041	0x00000041
GREEK CAPITAL LETTER ALPHA	0xCD 0x91	0x0391	0x00000391
CJK UNIFIED IDEOGRAPH-4E95	0xE4 0xBA 0x95	0x4E95	0x00004E95
OLD ITALIC LETTER A	0xF0 0x80 0x83 0x80	0xDC00 0xDF00	0x00010300

Fig. F.1   Correlation between the three encoding forms.

Fig. F.2   Various glyphs of the character **A**.

F.4 Advantages and Disadvantages of Unicode

The Unicode Standard has several significant advantages that promote its use. One benefit is the impact it has on the performance of the international economy. Unicode standardizes the characters for the world's writing systems to a uniform model that promotes the transfer and sharing of data. Programs developed using a standard schema maintain their accuracy, because each character has a single definition (e.g., *a* is always U+0061, % is always U+0025). Corporations can manage the high demands of international markets by processing different writing systems at the same time. Also, all characters can be managed in an identical manner, avoiding any confusion caused by different character code architectures. Managing data in a consistent manner eliminates data corruption, because data can be sorted, searched and manipulated using a consistent process.

Another advantage of the Unicode Standard is *portability* (i.e., the ability to execute software on disparate computers or with disparate operating systems). Most operating systems, databases, programming languages and Web browsers currently support, or are planning to support, Unicode.

Another advantage of the Unicode Standard is that it encompasses more characters than any other character set. Also, the Consortium has plans to increase it coverage by encompassing more characters.

A disadvantage of the Unicode Standard is the amount of memory required by UTF-16 and UTF-32. ASCII character sets are 8 bits in length, so they require less storage than the default 16-bit Unicode character set. However, the *double-byte character set* (*DBCS*) and the *multi-byte character set* (*MBCS*) that encode Asian characters (ideographs) require two to four bytes, respectively. In such instances, the UTF-16 or the UTF-32 encoding forms may be used with little hindrance on memory and performance.

Another disadvantage is that UTF-8 and UTF-16 are variable-width encoding forms, so characters occupy different amounts of memory.

F.5 Unicode Consortium's Web Site

If you would like to learn more about the Unicode Standard, visit **www.unicode.org**. This site provides a wealth of information about the Unicode Standard. Currently, the home page is organized into various sections: *New to Unicode, General Information, The Consortium, The Unicode Standard, Work in Progress* and *For Members*.

The *New to Unicode* section consists of two subsections: **What is Unicode?** and **How to Use this Site**. The first subsection provides a technical introduction to Unicode by describing design principles, character interpretations and assignments, text processing and Unicode conformance. This subsection is recommended reading for anyone new to Unicode. Also, this subsection provides a list of related links that provide the reader with additional information about Unicode. The **How to Use this Site** subsection contains information for navigating the site and hyperlinks to additional resources.

The *General Information* section contains six subsections: **Where is my Character?**, **Display Problems?**, **Useful Resources**, **Enabled Products**, **Mail Lists** and **Conferences**. The main areas covered in this section include a link to the Unicode code charts (a complete listing of code values) assembled by the Unicode Consortium and a detailed outline on how to locate an encoded character in the code chart. The section contains advice on how to configure different operating systems and Web browsers so that the

Unicode characters can be viewed properly. Moreover, from this section, the user can navigate to other sites that provide information on various topics such as fonts, linguistics and other standards, including *Armenian Standards Page* and the *Chinese GB 18030 Encoding Standard.*

The *Consortium* section consists of five subsections, including **Who we are**, **Our Members**, **How to Join**, **Press Info** and **Contact Us**. This section provides a list of the current Unicode Consortium members, as well as information on how to become a member. Privileges for each member type—*full, associate, specialist* and *individual*—and the fees assessed to each member are listed.

The *Unicode Standard* section consists of nine subsections: **Start Here**, **Latest Version**, **Technical Reports**, **Code Charts**, **Unicode Data**, **Updates & Errata**, **Unicode Policies**, **Glossary** and **Technical FAQ**. This section describes the updates applied to the latest version of the Unicode Standard and categorizes all defined encodings. The user can learn how the latest version of the standard has been modified to encompass more features and capabilities. For instance, one enhancement of Version 3.1 is that it contains additional encoded characters. If users are unfamiliar with vocabulary terms used by the Unicode Consortium, then they can navigate to the **Glossary** subsection.

The *Work in Progress* section consists of three subsections: **Calendar of Meetings**, **Proposed Characters** and **Submitting Proposals**. This section presents a catalog of the recent characters added to the Unicode Standard scheme and the characters being considered for inclusion. If users determine that a character has been overlooked, then they can submit a proposal for that character's inclusion. The **Submitting Proposals** subsection contains strict guidelines that must be adhered to when submitting written proposals.

The *For Members* section consists of two subsections: **Member Resources** and **Working Documents**. These subsections are password protected; only consortium members can access these links.

F.6 Using Unicode

Figure F.3 prints the text "Welcome to Unicode!" in 10 different languages: English, French, German, Japanese, Kannada (India), Portuguese, Russian, Simplified Chinese, Spanish, and Telugu (India). [*Note*: The Unicode Consortium's Web site contains a link to code charts that list the 16-bit Unicode code values.]

```
1   # Fig. F.3: figF_03.py
2   # Unicode encoding for 10 different languages
3
4   welcomes = [ u"Unicode Encoding" ]
5
6   welcomes.append( u"In English:\u0020\u0057\u0065\u006C\u0063" +
7      u"\u006F\u006D\u0065\u0020\u0074\u006F\u0020Unicode\u0021" )
8
9   welcomes.append( u"In French:\u0020\u0042\u0069\u0065\u006E" +
10     u"\u0076\u0065\u006E\u0075\u0065\u0020\u0061\u0075" +
11     u"\u0020Unicode\u0021" )
12
```

Fig. F.3   **Welcome to Unicode** in ten languages. (Part 1 of 2.)

```
13   welcomes.append( u"In German:\u0020\u0057\u0069\u006C\u006B" +
14      u"\u006F\u006D\u006D\u0065\u006E\u0020\u007A\u0075\u0020" +
15      u"Unicode\u0021" )
16
17   welcomes.append( u"In Japanese:\u0020Unicode\u3078\u3087" +
18      u"\u3045\u3053\u305D\u0021" )
19
20   welcomes.append( u"In Kannada:\u0020\u0CB8\u0CC1\u0CB8\u0CCD" +
21      u"\u0CB5\u0C97\u0CA4\u0020Unicode\u0021" )
22
23   welcomes.append( u"In Portuguese:\u0020\u0053\u00E9\u006A" +
24      u"\u0061\u0020\u0042\u0065\u006D\u0076\u0069\u006E\u0064" +
25      u"\u006F\u0020Unicode\u0021" )
26
27   welcomes.append( u"In Russian:\u0020\u0414\u043E\u0431\u0440" +
28      u"\u043E\u0020\u043F\u043E\u0436\u0430\u043B\u043E\u0432" +
29      u"\u0430\u0442\u044A\u0020\u0432\u0020Unicode\u0021" )
30
31   welcomes.append( u"In Simplified Chinese:\u0020\u6B22\u8FCE" +
32      u"\u4F7F\u7528\u0020Unicode\u0021" )
33
34   welcomes.append( u"In Spanish:\u0020\u0042\u0069\u0065\u006E" +
35      u"\u0076\u0065\u006E\u0069\u0064\u006F\u0020\u0061\u0020" +
36      u"Unicode\u0021" )
37
38   welcomes.append( u"In Telugu:\u0020\u0C38\u0C41\u0C38\u0C3E" +
39      u"\u0C35\u0C17\u0C24\u0C02\u0020Unicode\u0021" )
40
41   for welcome in welcomes:
42      print welcome.encode( "utf-8" )
43      print
```

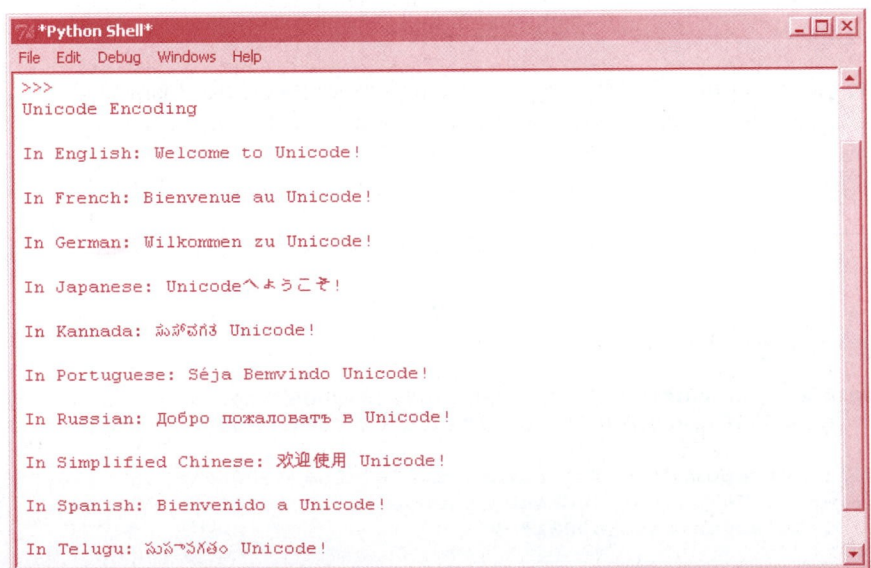

Fig. F.3   **Welcome to Unicode** in ten languages. (Part 2 of 2.)

The **figF_03.py** document creates **welcomes**—a list of Unicode strings. Inserting the letter **u** before a string of characters identifies that string as Unicode. Lines 6–7 contain the English "Welcome to Unicode!" message. The **Code Charts** page on the Unicode Consortium Web site contains the code values for the **Basic Latin** *block* (or category), which includes the English alphabet. When using Unicode in Python, the escape sequence is **\u***yyyy*, where *yyyy* represents the hexadecimal Unicode encoding. For example, the letter "W" (in "Welcome") is denoted by **\u0057**. The sequence **\u0020** represents a space. The Unicode for "Welcome" and "to" are on lines 6–7. The word "Unicode" is on line 7. "Unicode" is not encoded because it is a registered trademark and has no equivalent translation in most languages. Line 7 also contains the **\u0021** notation for the exclamation mark (**!**).

The remaining code (lines 9–39) contains the Unicode encoding for the other nine languages. The code values used for the French, German, Portuguese and Spanish text are located in the **Basic Latin** block, the code values used for the Simplified Chinese text are located in the **CJK Unified Ideographs** block, the code values used for the Russian text are located in the **Cyrillic** block, the code values for the Japanese text are located in the **Hiragana** block, and the code values used for the Kannada and Telugu texts are located in their respective blocks.

Method **encode** (line 42) encodes the Unicode string **welcomes** by implementing the UTF-8 encoding. A UTF-8 **encoding** indicates that the document conforms to the form of Unicode that uses sequences of one to four bytes.

F.7 Character Ranges

The Unicode Standard assigns code values, which range from **0000** (**Basic Latin**) to **E007F** (***Tags***), to the written characters of the world. Currently, there are code values for 94,140 characters. To simplify the search for a character and its associated code value, the Unicode Standard generally groups code values by *script* and function (i.e., Latin characters are grouped in a block, mathematical operators are grouped in another block, etc.). As a rule, a script is a single writing system that is used for multiple languages (e.g., the Latin script is used for English, French, Spanish, etc.). The **Code Charts** page on the Unicode Consortium Web site lists all the defined blocks and their respective code values. Figure F.4 lists some blocks (scripts) from the Web site and their range of code values.

Script	Range of Code Values
Arabic	U+0600–U+06FF
Basic Latin	U+0000–U+007F
Bengali (India)	U+0980–U+09FF
Cherokee (Native America)	U+13A0–U+13FF
CJK Unified Ideographs (East Asia)	U+4E00–U+9FAF
Cyrillic (Russia and Eastern Europe)	U+0400–U+04FF
Ethiopic	U+1200–U+137F
Greek	U+0370–U+03FF

Fig. F.4   Unicode character ranges. (Part 1 of 2.)

Script	Range of Code Values
Hangul Jamo (Korea)	U+1100–U+11FF
Hebrew	U+0590–U+05FF
Hiragana (Japan)	U+3040–U+309F
Khmer (Cambodia)	U+1780–U+17FF
Lao (Laos)	U+0E80–U+0EFF
Mongolian	U+1800–U+18AF
Myanmar	U+1000–U+109F
Ogham (Ireland)	U+1680–U+169F
Runic (Germany and Scandinavia)	U+16A0–U+16FF
Sinhala (Sri Lanka)	U+0D80–U+0DFF
Telugu (India)	U+0C00–U+0C7F
Thai	U+0E00–U+0E7F

Fig. F.4   Unicode character ranges. (Part 2 of 2.)

SUMMARY

- Before the advent of Unicode, software developers were plagued by the use of inconsistent character encoding (i.e., numeric values for characters). Most countries and organizations had their own encoding systems, which often were incompatible with each other. A good example of this phenomenon is the individual encoding systems on the Windows and Macintosh platforms.

- Computers process data by converting characters to numeric values. For instance, the character "a" is converted to a numeric value, so that a computer can manipulate that piece of data.

- Without Unicode, localization of global software requires significant modifications to the source code, which results in increased costs and in delays in releasing the product.

- Localization is necessary with each release of a version. By the time a software product is localized for a particular market, a newer version, which needs to be localized as well, is ready for distribution. As a result, it is cumbersome and costly to produce and distribute global software products in a market where there is no universal character-encoding standard.

- The Unicode Consortium developed the Unicode Standard in response to the serious problems created by multiple character encodings and the use of those encodings.

- The Unicode Standard facilitates the production and distribution of localized software. It outlines a specification for the consistent encoding of the world's characters and symbols.

- Software products that handle text encoded in the Unicode Standard need to be localized, but the localization process is simpler and more efficient, because the numeric values need not be converted.

- The Unicode Standard is designed to be universal, efficient, uniform and unambiguous.

- A universal encoding system encompasses all commonly used characters, an efficient encoding system parses text files easily, a uniform encoding system assigns fixed values to all characters and an unambiguous encoding system represents the same character for any given value.

- Unicode extends the limited ASCII character set to include all the major characters of the world.

- Unicode makes use of three Unicode Transformation Formats (UTFs)— UTF-8, UTF-16 and UTF—32, each of which may be appropriate for use in different contexts.

- UTF-8 data consists of 8-bit bytes (sequences of one, two, three or four bytes, depending on the character being encoded) and is well suited for ASCII-based systems when there is a predominance of one-byte characters. (ASCII represents characters as one byte.)

- UTF-8 is a variable-width encoding form that is more compact for text involving mostly Latin characters and ASCII punctuation.

- UTF-16 is the default encoding form of the Unicode Standard. It is a variable-width encoding form that uses 16-bit code units instead of bytes. Most characters are represented by a single unit, but some characters require surrogate pairs.

- Surrogate pairs are 16-bit integers in the range D800 through DFFF and are used solely for the purpose of "escaping" into higher numbered characters.

- Without surrogate pairs, the UTF-16 encoding form can only encompass 65,000 characters, but with the surrogate pairs, this range is expanded to include over one million characters.

- UTF-32 is a 32-bit encoding form. The major advantage of this fixed-width encoding form is that it uniformly expresses all characters, so that they are easy to handle in arrays and so forth.

- The Unicode Standard consists of characters. A character is any written component that can be represented by a numeric value.

- Characters are represented using glyphs—various shapes, fonts and sizes—for displaying characters.

- Code values are bit combinations that represent encoded characters. The Unicode notation for a code value is U+yyyy, in which U+ refers to the Unicode code values, as opposed to other hexadecimal values. The yyyy represents a four-digit hexadecimal number.

- Currently, the Unicode Standard provides code values for 94,140 character representations.

- An advantage of the Unicode Standard is its impact on the overall performance of the international economy. Applications that conform to an encoding standard can be processed easily by computers anywhere.

- Another advantage of the Unicode Standard is its portability. Applications written in Unicode can be easily transferred to different operating systems, databases, Web browsers, etc. Most companies currently support, or are planning to support, Unicode.

- Another advantage of the Unicode Standard is that it encompasses more characters than any other character set. Also, the Consortium has plans to increase coverage by encompassing more characters.

- To obtain more information about the Unicode Standard and the Unicode Consortium, visit **www.unicode.org**. This site contains a link to the code charts, which contain the 16-bit code values for the currently encoded characters.

- When writing Python programs, use the Unicode escape sequence \u*yyyy*;, where *yyyy* represents the hexadecimal code value.

TERMINOLOGY

\u*yyyy*; notation	glyph
ASCII	hexadecimal notation
block	localization
character	multi-byte character set (MBCS)
character set	portability
code value	script
diacritic	surrogate
double-byte character set (DBCS)	symbol
efficient (Unicode design basis)	unambiguous (Unicode design basis)
encode	Unicode Consortium

Unicode design basis   universal (Unicode design basis)
Unicode Standard   UTF-8
Unicode Transformation Format (UTF)   UTF-16
uniform (Unicode design basis)   UTF-32

SELF-REVIEW EXERCISES

F.1   Fill in the blanks in each of the following statements:
a) Global software developers have to _____ their products to a specific market before distribution.
b) The Unicode Standard is an _____ standard that facilitates the uniform production and distribution of software products.
c) The four terms that describe the design basis of the Unicode Standard are _____, _____, _____ and _____.
d) A _____ is the smallest written component that can be represented with a numeric value.
e) Software that can execute on different operating systems is said to be _____.

F.2   State whether each of the following is *true* or *false*. If *false*, explain why.
a) The Unicode Standard encompasses all the world's characters.
b) A Unicode code value is represented as U+*yyyy*, where *yyyy* represents a number in binary notation.
c) A diacritic is a character with a special mark that emphasizes an accent.
d) Unicode is portable.
e) When designing Python documents, the entity reference is denoted by **#U+***yyyy*.

ANSWERS TO SELF-REVIEW EXERCISES

F.1   a) localize. b) encoding. c) universal, efficient, uniform, unambiguous. d) character. e) portable.

F.2   a) False. It encompasses the majority of the world's characters. b) False. A code value is represented as U+*yyyy*, where the *yyyy* represents a hexadecimal number. c) False. A diacritic is a special mark added to a character to distinguish it from another letter or to indicate an accent. d) True. e) False. The entity reference is denoted by **\u***yyyy*.

EXERCISES

F.3   Navigate to the Unicode Consortium Web site (**www.unicode.org**), and write the hexadecimal code values for the given characters. In which block are they located?
a) Latin letter 'Z.'
b) Latin letter 'n' with the 'tilde' (~).
c) Greek letter 'delta.'
d) Mathematical operator 'less than or equal to.'
e) Punctuation symbol 'open quote' (").

F.4   Describe the design basis of the Unicode Standard.

F.5   Define the following terms:
a) Code value.
b) Surrogates.
c) Unicode Standard.
d) UTF-8.
e) UTF-16.
f) UTF-32.

F.6   Describe a scenario where it is optimal to store your data in UTF-16 format.

F.7   Using the Unicode Standard code values, create a Python dictionary with the letters of the English alphabet as keys and their Unicode equivalents as values. Create a program that displays each letter with its Unicode representation. The output should include both uppercase and lowercase letters.

F.8   Write a Python program that prints the Unicode code values for a word entered by the user. Use the dictionary created in Exercise F.7.

Introduction to HyperText Markup Language 4: Part 1

Objectives

- To understand the key components of an HTML document.
- To be able to use basic HTML elements to create World Wide Web pages.
- To be able to add images to your Web pages.
- To understand how to create and use hyperlinks to traverse Web pages.
- To be able to create lists of information.

To read between the lines was easier than to follow the text.
Henry James

Mere colour, unspoiled by meaning, and annulled with definite form, can speak to the soul in a thousand different ways.
Oscar Wilde

High thoughts must have high language.
Aristophanes

I've gradually risen from lower-class background to lower-class foreground.
Marvin Cohen

Outline

G.1 Introduction

In this appendix we introduce the basics of creating Web pages in HTML. We write many simple Web pages. In Appendix H, Introduction to HyperText Markup Language 4: Part 2, we introduce more sophisticated HTML techniques, such as *tables*, which are particularly useful for structuring information from databases. In this appendix, we do not present any Python programming.

In this appendix, we introduce basic HTML *elements* and *attributes*. A key issue when using HTML is the separation of the *presentation of a document* (i.e., how the document is rendered on the screen by a browser) from the *structure of that document*. In this appendix and in Appendix H, we discuss this issue in depth.

G.2 Markup Languages

HTML is a *markup language*. It is used to format text and information. This "marking up" of information is different from the intent of traditional programming languages, which is to perform actions in a designated order.

In HTML, text is marked up with *elements*, delineated by *tags* that are keywords contained in pairs of angle brackets. For example, the HTML *element* itself, which indicates that we are writing a Web page to be rendered by a browser, begins with the start tag **`<html>`** and terminates with the end tag **`</html>`**. These elements format your page in a specified way. Over the course of the next two appendices, we introduce many of the commonly used tags and how to use them.

Good Programming Practice G.1

HTML tags are not case sensitive. However, keeping all the letters in one case improves program readability. Although the choice of case is up to you, we recommend that you write all of your code in lowercase. Writing in lowercase ensures greater compatibility with future markup languages that are designed to be written with only lowercase tags and elements.

Common Programming Error G.1

Forgetting to include end tags for elements that require them is a syntax error and can grossly affect the formatting and look of your page. Unlike conventional programming languages, a syntax error in HTML does not usually cause page display in browsers to fail completely.

G.3 Editing HTML

In this appendix we show how to write HTML in its *source-code form*. We create *HTML documents* using a text editor and store them in files with either the **.html** or **.htm** file name extension. A wide variety of text editors exist. We recommend that you initially use a text editor called Notepad, which is built into Windows. Notepad can be found inside the **Accessories** panel of your **Program** list, inside the **Start** menu. You can also download a free HTML source-code editor called HTML-Kit at **www.chami.com/html-kit**. Unix users can use popular text editors like *vi* or *emacs*.

Good Programming Practice G.2

*Assign names to your files that describe their functionality. This practice can help you identify documents faster. It also helps people who want to link to your page, by giving them an easier-to-remember name for the file. For example, if you are writing an HTML document that will display your products, you might want to call it **products.html**.*

As mentioned previously, errors in conventional programming languages like C, C++ and Visual Basic often prevent the program from running. Errors in HTML markup are usually not fatal. The browser will make its best effort at rendering the page, but will probably not display the page as you intended.

The file name of your *home page* (the first of your HTML pages that a user sees when browsing your Web site) should be **index.html**, because when a browser does not request a specific file in a directory, the normal default Web server response is to return **index.html** (this may be different for your server) if it exists in that directory. For example, if you direct your browser to **www.deitel.com**, the server actually sends the file **www.deitel.com/index.html** to your browser.

G.4 Common Elements

Throughout these HTML appendices, we will present both HTML source code and a sample screen capture of the rendering of that HTML in Internet Explorer. Figure G.1 shows an HTML file that displays one line of text.

Lines 1 and 2

```
<!DOCTYPE HTML PUBLIC "-//W3C//DTD HTML 4.01//EN"
          "http://www.w3.org/TR/html4/strict.dtd">
```

are required in every HTML document and are used to specify the *document type*. The document type specifies which version of HTML is used in the document and can be used with a validation tool, such as the W3C's **validator.w3.org**, to ensure an HTML document conforms to the HTML recommendation. In these examples we create HTML version 4.01 documents. All of the examples in these appendices have been validated through the Web site **validator.w3.org**.

The HTML document begins with the opening **<html>** tag (line 3) and ends with the closing **</html>** tag (line 17).

```
1    <!DOCTYPE HTML PUBLIC "-//W3C//DTD HTML 4.01//EN"
2                "http://www.w3.org/TR/html4/strict.dtd">
3    <html>
4
5    <!-- Fig. G.1: main.html -->
6    <!-- Our first Web page. -->
7
8    <head>
9       <title>Python How to Program - Welcome</title>
10   </head>
11
12   <body>
13
14      <p>Welcome to Our Web Site!</p>
15
16   </body>
17   </html>
```

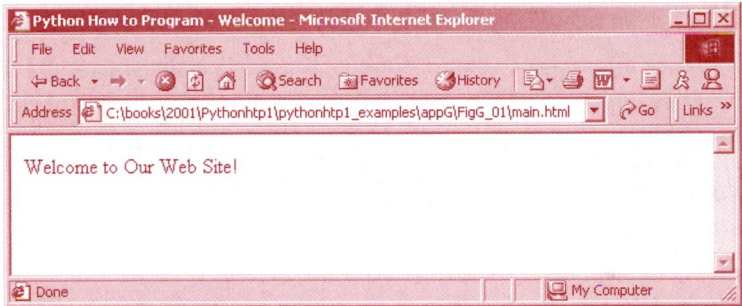

Fig. G.1   Basic HTML file.

Good Programming Practice G.3

Always include the **<html>...</html>** *tags in the beginning and end of your HTML document.*

Good Programming Practice G.4

Place comments throughout your code. Comments in HTML are placed inside the **<!--...**
--> *tags. Comments help other programmers understand the code, assist in debugging and list other useful information that you do not want the browser to render. Comments also help you understand your own code, especially if you have not looked at it for a while.*

We see our first *comments* (i.e., text that documents or describes the HTML markup) on lines 5 and 6

```
<!-- Fig. G.1: main.html -->
<!-- Our first Web page. -->
```

Comments in HTML always begin with **<!--** and end with **-->**. The browser ignores any text and/or tags inside a comment. We place comments at the top of each HTML document giving the figure number, the file name and a brief description of the purpose of the example. In subsequent examples, we also include comments in the markup, especially when we introduce new features.

Every HTML document contains a *head* element, which generally contains information about the document, and a **body** element, which contains the page content. Information in the **head** element is not generally rendered in the display window, but may be made available to the user through other means. Lines 8–10

```
<head>
   <title>Python How to Program - Welcome</title>
</head>
```

show the **head** element section of our Web page. Including a *title* element is required for every HTML document. To include a title in your Web page, enclose your chosen title between the pair of tags *<title>...</title>* in the **head** element.

 ### Good Programming Practice G.5

Use a consistent title-naming convention for all pages on your site. For example, if your site is called "Al's Web Site," then the title of your links page might best be "Al's Web Site - Links." This practice presents a clearer picture to those browsing your site.

The **title** element names your Web page. The title usually appears on the colored bar at the top of the browser window, and also will appear as the text identifying your page if a user adds your page to their list of **Favorites** or **Bookmarks**. The title is also used by search engines for cataloging purposes, so picking a meaningful title can help search engines direct a more focused group of people to your site.

Line 12

```
<body>
```

opens the *body* element. The body of an HTML document is the area where you place the content of your document. This includes text, images, links and forms. We discuss many elements that can be inserted in the **body** element later in this appendix. Remember to include the end **</body>** tag before the closing **</html>** tag.

Various elements enable you to place text in your HTML document. We see the *paragraph element* on line 14

```
<p>Welcome to Our Web Site!</p>
```

All text placed between the **<p>...</p>** tags forms one paragraph. Most Web browsers render paragraphs as set apart from all other material on the page by a line of vertical space both before and after the paragraph. The HTML in line 12 causes Internet Explorer to render the enclosed text as shown in Fig. G.1.

Our code example ends on lines 16 and 17 with

```
</body>
</html>
```

These two tags close the body and HTML sections of the document, respectively. As discussed earlier, the last tag in any HTML document should be **</html>**, which tells the browser that all HTML coding is complete. The closing **</body>** tag is placed before the **</html>** tag because the body section of the document is entirely enclosed by the HTML section. Therefore, the body section must be closed before the HTML section.

G.5 Headers

The six *headers* are used to delineate new sections and subsections of a page. Figure G.2 shows how these elements (**h1** through **h6**) are used. Note that the actual size of the text of each header element is selected by the browser and can vary significantly between browsers.

 Good Programming Practice G.6

Adding comments to the right of short HTML lines is a clean-looking way to comment code.

```
1   <!DOCTYPE HTML PUBLIC "-//W3C//DTD HTML 4.01//EN"
2           "http://www.w3.org/TR/html4/strict.dtd">
3   <html>
4
5   <!-- Fig. G.2: header.html -->
6   <!-- HTML headers.          -->
7
8   <head>
9      <title>Python How to Program - Headers</title>
10  </head>
11
12  <body>
13
14     <h1>Level 1 Header</h1>      <!-- Level 1 header -->
15     <h2>Level 2 header</h2>      <!-- Level 2 header -->
16     <h3>Level 3 header</h3>      <!-- Level 3 header -->
17     <h4>Level 4 header</h4>      <!-- Level 4 header -->
18     <h5>Level 5 header</h5>      <!-- Level 5 header -->
19     <h6>Level 6 header</h6>      <!-- Level 6 header -->
20
21  </body>
22  </html>
```

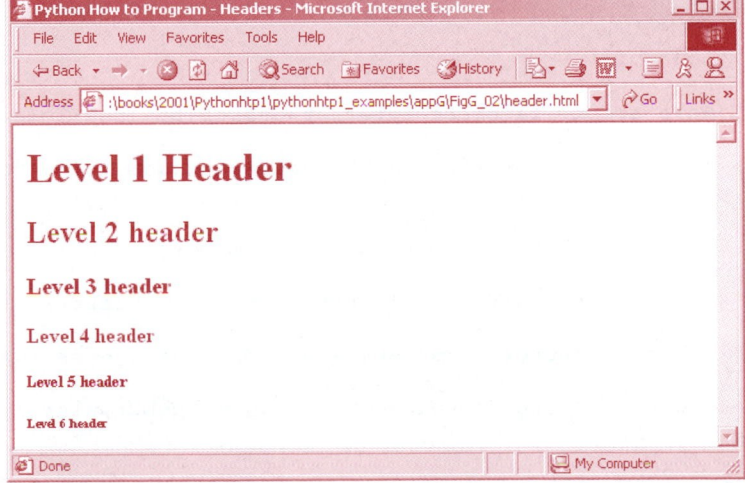

Fig. G.2   Header elements **h1** through **h6**.

Line 14

```
<h1>Level 1 Header</h1>
```

introduces the **h1** *header element*, with its start tag **<h1>** and its end tag **</h1>**. Any text to be displayed is placed between the two tags. All six header elements, **h1** through **h6**, follow the same pattern.

Good Programming Practice G.7

Putting a header at the top of every Web page helps those viewing your pages understand what the purpose of each page is.

G.6 Linking

The most important capability of HTML is its ability to create hyperlinks to other documents, making possible a worldwide network of linked documents and information. In HTML, both text and images can act as *anchors* to *link* to other pages on the Web. We introduce anchors and links in Fig. G.3.

The first link can be found on line 19

```
<p><a href = "http://www.yahoo.com">Yahoo</a></p>
```

```
1   <!DOCTYPE HTML PUBLIC "-//W3C//DTD HTML 4.01//EN"
2            "http://www.w3.org/TR/html4/strict.dtd">
3   <html>
4
5   <!-- Fig. G.3: links.html        -->
6   <!-- Introduction to hyperlinks. -->
7
8   <head>
9      <title>Python How to Program - Links</title>
10  </head>
11
12  <body>
13
14     <h1>Here are my favorite Internet Search Engines</h1>
15
16     <p><strong>Click on the Search Engine address to go to that
17        page.</strong></p>
18
19     <p><a href = "http://www.yahoo.com">Yahoo</a></p>
20
21     <p><a href = "http://www.altavista.com">AltaVista</a></p>
22
23     <p><a href = "http://www.askjeeves.com">Ask Jeeves</a></p>
24
25     <p><a href = "http://www.webcrawler.com">WebCrawler</a></p>
26
27  </body>
28  </html>
```

Fig. G.3   Linking to other Web pages. (Part 1 of 2.)

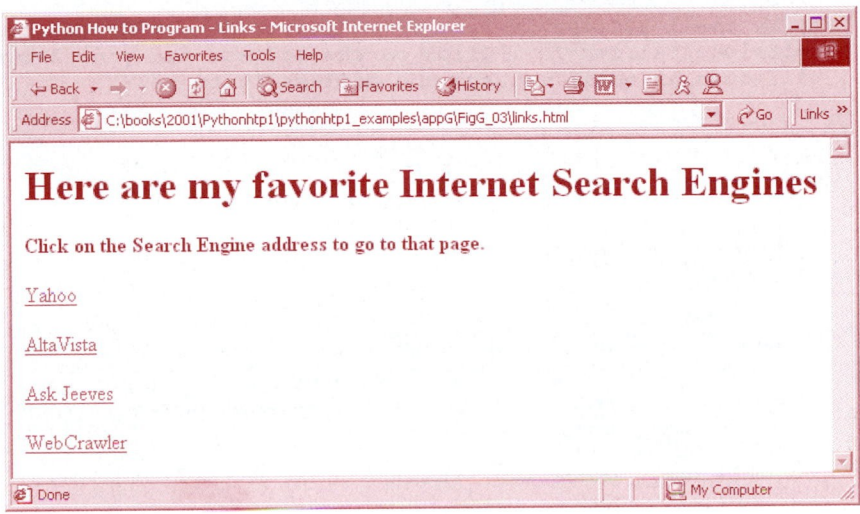

Fig. G.3   Linking to other Web pages. (Part 2 of 2.)

Links are inserted with the **a** *(anchor) element*. The anchor element is unlike the elements we have seen thus far in that it requires certain *attributes* (i.e., markup that provides information about the element) to specify the hyperlink. Attributes are placed inside an element's start tag and consist of a name and a value. The most important attribute for the **a** element is the location to which you would like the anchoring object to be linked. This location can be any resource on the Web, including pages, files and email addresses. To specify the address to link to, add the **href** *attribute* to the anchor element as follows: **<a href = "***address***">**. In this case, the address we are linking to is **http://www.yahoo.com**. The hyperlink (line 19) makes the text **Yahoo** a link to the address specified in **href**.

Anchors can use **mailto** URLs to provide links to email addresses. When someone selects this type of anchored link, most browsers launch the default email program to initiate an email message to the linked address. This type of anchor is demonstrated in Fig. G.4.

```
1   <!DOCTYPE HTML PUBLIC "-//W3C//DTD HTML 4.01//EN"
2              "http://www.w3.org/TR/html4/strict.dtd">
3   <html>
4
5   <!-- Fig. G.4: contact.html   -->
6   <!-- Adding email hyperlinks. -->
7
8   <head>
9      <title>Python How to Program - Contact Page</title>
10  </head>
11
```

Fig. G.4   Linking to an email address. (Part 1 of 2.)

```
12    <body>
13
14       <p>My email address is <a href = "mailto:deitel@deitel.com">
15       deitel@deitel.com</a>. Click on the address and your browser
16       will open an email message and address it to me.</p>
17
18    </body>
19    </html>
```

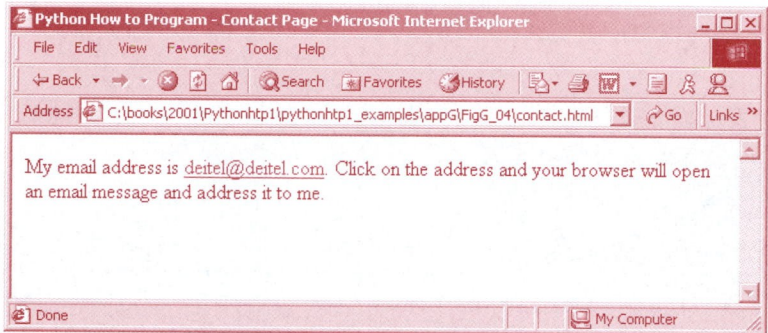

Fig. G.4   Linking to an email address. (Part 2 of 2.)

We see an email link on lines 14 and 15

```
<p>My email address is <a href = "mailto:deitel@deitel.com">
deitel@deitel.com</a>. Click on the address and your browser
```

The form of an email anchor is **<a href = "mailto:***emailaddress***">...</a>**. It is important that this whole attribute, including the **mailto:**, be placed in quotation marks.

G.7 Images

We have thus far dealt exclusively with text. We now show how to incorporate images into Web pages (Fig. G.5).

```
1    <!DOCTYPE HTML PUBLIC "-//W3C//DTD HTML 4.01//EN"
2              "http://www.w3.org/TR/html4/strict.dtd">
3    <html>
4
5    <!-- Fig. G.5: picture.html    -->
6    <!-- Adding images with HTML. -->
7
8    <head>
9       <title>Python How to Program - Welcome</title>
10   </head>
11
```

Fig. G.5   Placing images in HTML files. (Part 1 of 2.)

```
12   <body>
13
14      <p><img src = "pythonhtp.jpg" height = "238" width = "181"
15         alt = "Demonstration of the alt attribute"></p>
16
17   </body>
18   </html>
```

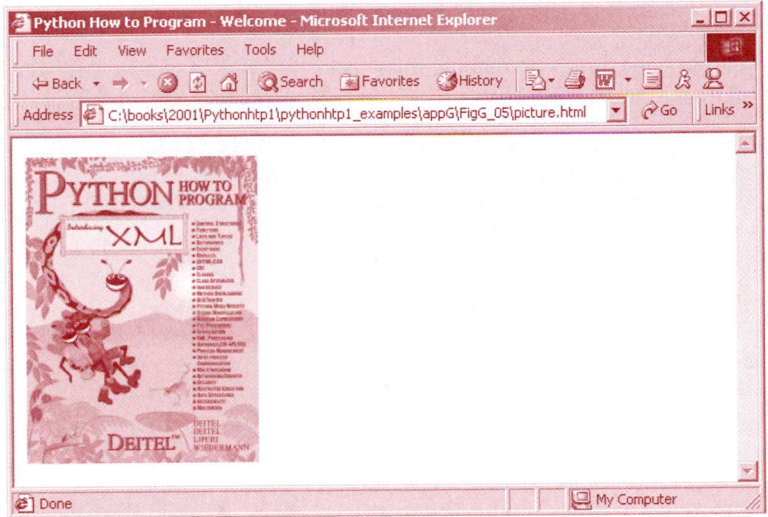

Fig. G.5   Placing images in HTML files. (Part 2 of 2.)

The image in this code example is inserted in lines 14 and 15:

```
<p><img src = "pythonhtp.jpg" height = "238" width = "181"
   alt = "Demonstration of the alt attribute"></p>
```

You specify the location of the image file in the ***img*** element. This is done by adding the ***src* = "***location***"** attribute. You can also specify the ***height*** and ***width*** of an image, measured in pixels. The term pixel stands for "picture element." Each pixel represents one dot of color on the screen. This image is 181 pixels wide and 238 pixels high.

Good Programming Practice G.8

Always include the ***height*** *and the* ***width*** *of an image inside the* ***img*** *tag. When the browser loads the HTML file, it will know immediately how much screen space to give the image and will therefore lay out the page properly, even before it downloads the image.*

Common Programming Error G.2

Entering new dimensions for an image that changes its inherent width-to-height ratio distorts the appearance of the image. For example, if your image is 200 pixels wide and 100 pixels high, you should always make sure that any new dimensions have a 2:1 width-to-height ratio.

The ***alt*** attribute is required for every **img** element. In Fig. G.5, the value of this attribute is

```
alt = "Demonstration of the alt attribute"
```

Attribute **alt** is provided for browsers that have images turned off or cannot view images (e.g., text-based browsers). The value of the **alt** attribute will appear on-screen in place of the image, giving the user an idea of what was in the image. The **alt** attribute is especially important for making Web pages *accessible* to users with disabilities, as discussed in Appendix L, Accessibility.

 Good Programming Practice G.9

*Include a description of the purpose of every image, using the **alt** attribute in the **img** tag.*

Now that we have discussed placing images on your Web page, we will show you how to transform images into anchors to provide links to other sites on the Internet (Fig. G.6).

```
1   <!DOCTYPE HTML PUBLIC "-//W3C//DTD HTML 4.01//EN"
2              "http://www.w3.org/TR/html14/strict.dtd">
3   <html>
4
5   <!-- Fig. G.6: nav.html          -->
6   <!-- Using images as link anchors. -->
7
8   <head>
9      <title>Python - Navigation Bar</title>
10  </head>
11
12  <body>
13
14     <p>
15        <a href = "links.html">
16        <img src = "buttons/links.jpg" width = "65" height = "50"
17           alt = "Links Page"></a><br>
18
19        <a href = "list.html">
20        <img src = "buttons/list.jpg" width = "65" height = "50"
21           alt = "List Example Page"></a><br>
22
23        <a href = "contact.html">
24        <img src = "buttons/contact.jpg" width = "65" height = "50"
25           alt = "Contact Page"></a><br>
26
27        <a href = "header.html">
28        <img src = "buttons/header.jpg" width = "65" height = "50"
29           alt = "Header Page"></a><br>
30
31        <a href = "table.html">
32        <img src = "buttons/table.jpg" width = "65" height = "50"
33           alt = "Table Page"></a><br>
34
35        <a href = "form.html">
36        <img src = "buttons/form.jpg" width = "65" height = "50"
37           alt = "Feedback Form"></a><br>
38     </p>
39
```

Fig. G.6   Using images as link anchors. (Part 1 of 2.)

```
40    </body>
41    </html>
```

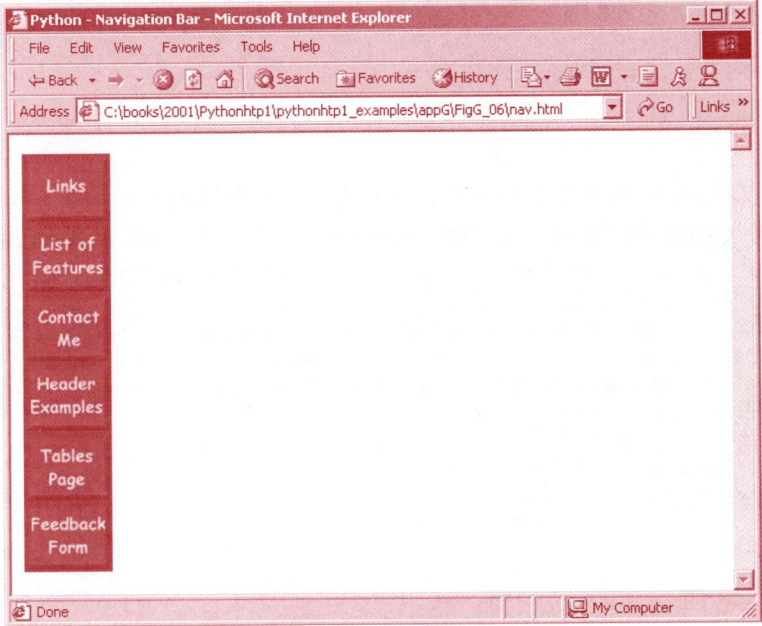

Fig. G.6   Using images as link anchors. (Part 2 of 2.)

We see an image hyperlink in lines 15–17

```
<a href = "links.html">
<img src = "buttons/links.jpg" width = "65" height = "50"
    alt = "Links Page"></a><br>
```

Here we use the **a** element and the **img** element. The anchor works the same way as when it surrounds text; the image becomes an active hyperlink to a location somewhere on the Internet, indicated by the **href** attribute inside the **<a>** tag. Remember to close the anchor element when you want the hyperlink to end.

If you direct your attention to the **src** attribute of the **img** element,

```
src = "buttons/links.jpg"
```

you will see that it is not in the same form as that of the image in the previous example. This is because the image we are using here, **links.jpg**, resides in a subdirectory called **buttons**, which is in the main directory for our site. We have done this so that we can keep all our button graphics in the same place, making them easier to find and edit.

You can always refer to files in different directories simply by putting the directory name in the correct format in the **src** attribute. If, for example, there was a directory inside the **buttons** directory called **images**, and we wanted to put a graphic from that directory onto our page, we would just have to make the source attribute reflect the location of the image: **src = "buttons/images/filename"**.

You can even insert an image from a different Web site into your site (after obtaining permission from the site's owner, of course). Just make the **src** attribute reflect the location and name of the image file.

On line 17

```
alt = "Links Page"></a><br>
```

we introduce the **br** *element*, which causes a *line break* to be rendered in most browsers.

G.8 Special Characters and More Line Breaks

In HTML, the old QWERTY typewriter setup no longer suffices for all our textual needs. HTML 4.01 has a provision for inserting special characters and symbols (Fig. G.7).

```
1   <!DOCTYPE HTML PUBLIC "-//W3C//DTD HTML 4.01//EN"
2           "http://www.w3.org/TR/html4/strict.dtd">
3   <html>
4
5   <!-- Fig. G.7: contact.html        -->
6   <!-- Inserting special characters. -->
7
8   <head>
9      <title>Python How to Program</title>
10  </head>
11
12  <body>
13
14     <!-- special characters are entered using the form &code; -->
15     <p>My email address is <a href = "mailto:deitel@deitel.com">
16     deitel@deitel.com</a>. Click on the address and your browser
17     will automatically open an email message and address it to my
18     address.</p>
19
20     <hr> <!-- inserts a horizontal rule -->
21
22     <p>All information on this site is <strong>&copy;</strong>
23     Deitel <strong>&amp;</strong> Associates, 2002.</p>
24
25     <!-- text can be struck out with a set of <del>...</del>    -->
26     <!-- tags, it can be set in subscript with <sub>...</sub>, -->
27     <!-- and it can be set into superscript with <sup...</sup> -->
28     <p><del>You may copy up to 3.14 x 10<sup>2</sup> characters
29     worth of information from this site.</del> Just make sure
30     you <sub>do not copy more information</sub> than is allowable.
31     </p>
32
33     <p>No permission is needed if you only need to use <strong>
34     &lt; &frac14;</strong> of the information presented here.</p>
35
36  </body>
37  </html>
```

Fig. G.7   Inserting special characters into HTML. (Part 1 of 2.)

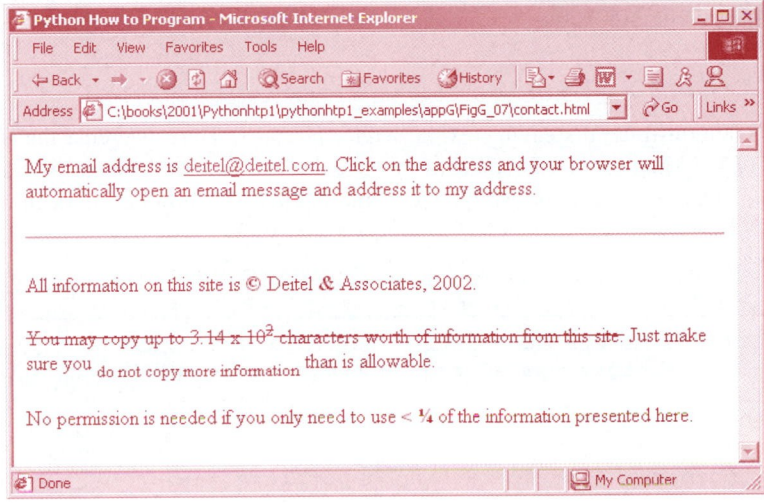

Fig. G.7   Inserting special characters into HTML. (Part 2 of 2.)

There are some *special characters* inserted into the text of lines 22 and 23:

```
<p>All information on this site is <strong>&copy;</strong>
Deitel <strong>&amp;</strong> Associates, 2002.</p>
```

All special characters are inserted in their code form. The format of the code is always **&*code*;**. An example of this is **&**, which inserts an ampersand. Codes are often abbreviated forms of the character (like **amp** for ampersand and **copy** for copyright) and can also be in the form of *hex codes*. (For example, the hex code for an ampersand is 38, so another method of inserting an ampersand is to use **&**.) Please refer to the chart in Appendix M for a listing of special characters and their respective codes.

In lines 28–31, we introduce three new styles.

```
<p><del>You may copy up to 3.14 x 10<sup>2</sup> characters
worth of information from this site.</del> Just make sure
you <sub>do not copy more information</sub> than is allow-
able.
</p>
```

You can indicate text that has been deleted from a document by including it in a ***del*** element. This could be used as an easy way to communicate revisions of an online document. Many browsers render the **del** element as strike-through text. To turn text into *superscript* (i.e., raised vertically to the top of the line and made smaller) or to turn text into *subscript* (the opposite of superscript, lowers text on a line and makes it smaller), use the ***sup*** or ***sub*** element, respectively.

Line 20

```
<hr> <!-- inserts a horizontal rule -->
```

inserts a horizontal rule, indicated by the **<hr>** tag. A horizontal rule is rendered by most browsers as a straight line going across the screen horizontally. The **hr** element also inserts a line break directly below it.

G.9 Unordered Lists

Figure G.8 demonstrates displaying text in an *unordered list*. Here, we reuse the HTML file from Fig. G.3, adding an unordered list to enhance the structure of the page. The *unordered list element* **ul** creates a list in which every line begins with a bullet mark in most Web browsers.

```
1   <!DOCTYPE HTML PUBLIC "-//W3C//DTD HTML 4.01//EN"
2              "http://www.w3.org/TR/html4/strict.dtd">
3   <html>
4
5   <!-- Fig. G.8: links.html              -->
6   <!-- Unordered list containing hyperlinks. -->
7
8   <head>
9      <title>Python How to Program - Links</title>
10  </head>
11
12  <body>
13
14     <h1>Here are my favorite Internet Search Engines</h1>
15
16
17     <p><strong>Click on the Search Engine address to go to that
18        page.</strong></p>
19
20     <ul>
21        <li>
22           <a href = "http://www.yahoo.com">Yahoo</a>
23        </li>
24
25        <li>
26           <a href = "http://www.altavista.com">AltaVista</a>
27        </li>
28
29        <li>
30           <a href = "http://www.askjeeves.com">Ask Jeeves</a>
31        </li>
32
33        <li>
34           <a href = "http://www.webcrawler.com">WebCrawler</a>
35        </li>
36     </ul>
37
38  </body>
39  </html>
```

Fig. G.8   Unordered lists in HTML. (Part 1 of 2.)

Fig. G.8   Unordered lists in HTML. (Part 2 of 2.)

The first list item appears in lines 21–23

```
<li>
    <a href = "http://www.yahoo.com">Yahoo</a>
</li>
```

Each entry in an unordered list is a *li* (*list item*) element. Most Web browsers render these elements with a line break and a bullet mark at the beginning of the line.

G.10 Nested and Ordered Lists

Figure G.9 demonstrates *nested lists* (i.e., one list inside another list). This feature is useful for displaying information in outline form.

```
1   <!DOCTYPE HTML PUBLIC "-//W3C//DTD HTML 4.01//EN"
2              "http://www.w3.org/TR/html4/strict.dtd">
3   <html>
4
5   <!-- Fig. G.9: list.html              -->
6   <!-- Advanced Lists: nested and ordered. -->
7
8   <head>
9      <title>Python How to Program - Lists</title>
10  </head>
11
12  <body>
13
14     <h1>The Best Features of the Internet</h1>
15
16     <ul>
17        <li>You can meet new people from countries around
18           the world.</li>
```

Fig. G.9   Nested and ordered lists in HTML. (Part 1 of 3.)

```html
19       <li>You have access to new media as it becomes public:
20
21           <!-- this starts a nested list, which -->
22           <!-- uses a modified bullet. The list -->
23           <!-- ends when you close the <ul> tag -->
24           <ul>
25               <li>New games</li>
26               <li>New applications
27
28                   <!-- another nested list -->
29                   <ul>
30                       <li>For business</li>
31                       <li>For pleasure</li>
32                   </ul> <!-- this ends the double nested list -->
33               </li>
34
35               <li>Around the clock news</li>
36               <li>Search engines</li>
37               <li>Shopping</li>
38               <li>Programming
39
40                   <ul>
41                       <li>Python</li>
42                       <li>Java</li>
43                       <li>HTML</li>
44                       <li>Scripts</li>
45                       <li>New languages</li>
46                   </ul>
47
48               </li>
49
50           </ul> <!-- this ends the first level nested list -->
51       </li>
52
53       <li>Links</li>
54       <li>Keeping in touch with old friends</li>
55       <li>It is the technology of the future!</li>
56
57   </ul>    <!-- this ends the primary unordered list -->
58
59   <h1>My 3 Favorite <em>CEOs</em></h1>
60
61   <!-- ordered lists are constructed in the same way as   -->
62   <!-- unordered lists, except their starting tag is <ol> -->
63   <ol>
64       <li>Ant Chovey</li>
65       <li>Anna Lee Tic</li>
66       <li>Albert Antstein</li>
67   </ol>
68
69 </body>
70 </html>
```

Fig. G.9   Nested and ordered lists in HTML. (Part 2 of 3.)

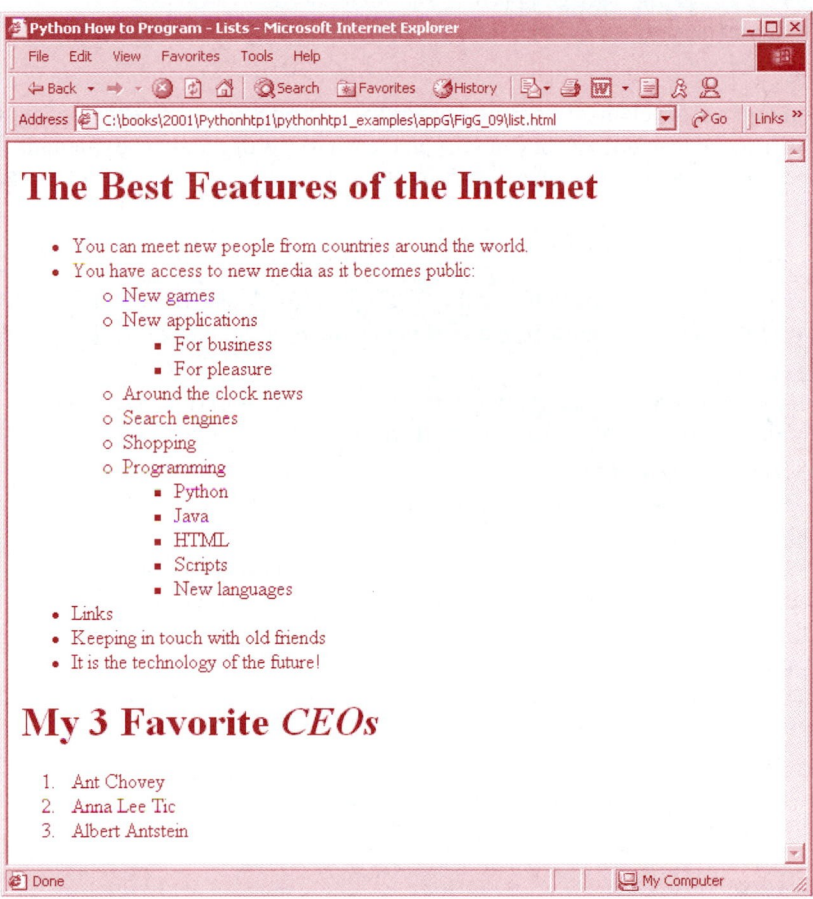

Fig. G.9   Nested and ordered lists in HTML. (Part 3 of 3.)

Our first nested list begins on line 24, and its first element is on 25.

```
<ul>
    <li>New games</li>
```

A nested list is created in the same way as the list in Fig. G.8, except that the nested list is itself contained in a list element. Most Web browsers render nested lists by indenting the list one level and changing the bullet type for the list elements.

Good Programming Practice G.10

Indenting each level of a nested list in your code makes the code easier to edit and debug.

In Fig. G.9, lines 16–57 show a list with three levels of nesting. When nesting lists, be sure to insert the closing **</ul>** tags in the appropriate places. Lines 63–67

```
<ol>
   <li>Lawrence J. Ellison</li>
   <li>Steve Jobs</li>
   <li>Michael Dell</li>
</ol>
```

define an *ordered list* element with the tags *<ol>...</ol>*. Most browsers render ordered lists with a sequence number for each list element instead of a bullet. By default, ordered lists use decimal sequence numbers (1, 2, 3, …).

G.11 Internet and World Wide Web Resources

There are many resources available on the World Wide Web that go into more depth on the topics we cover. Visit the following sites for additional information on this appendix's topics.

www.w3.org
The *World Wide Web Consortium* (W3C), is the group that makes HTML recommendations. This Web site holds a variety of information about HTML—both its history and its present status.

www.w3.org/TR/html401
The *HTML 4.01 Specification* contains all the nuances and fine points in HTML 4.01.

www.w3schools.com/html
The HTMl School. This site contains a complete guide to HTML, starting with an introduction to the WWW and ending with advanced HTML features. This site also has a good reference for the features of HTML.

www2.utep.edu/~kross/tutorial
This University of Texas at El Paso site contains another guide for simple HTML programming. The site is helpful for beginners, because it focuses on teaching and gives specific examples.

www.w3scripts.com/html
This site, an offshoot of *W3Schools*, is a repository for code examples exhibiting all of the features of HTML, from beginner to advanced.

SUMMARY

- HTML is not a procedural programming language like C, Fortran, Cobol or Pascal. It is a markup language that identifies the elements of a page so a browser can render that page on the screen.

- HTML is used to format text and information. This "marking up" of information is different from the intent of traditional programming languages, which is to perform actions in a designated order.

- In HTML, text is marked up with elements, delineated by tags that are keywords contained in pairs of angle brackets.

- HTML documents are created via text editors.

- All HTML documents stored in files require either the **.htm** or the **.html** file name extension.

- Making errors while coding in conventional programming languages like C, C++ and Java often produces a fatal error, preventing the program from running. Errors in HTML code are usually not fatal. The browser will make its best effort at rendering the page, but will probably not display the page as you intended. In our Common Programming Errors and Testing and Debugging Tips, we highlight common HTML errors and how to detect and correct them.

- For most Web servers, the filename of your home page should be **index.html**. When a browser requests a directory, the default Web server response is to return **index.html**, if it exists in that directory.

- The document type specifies which version of HTML is used in the document and can be used with a validation tool, such as the W3C's **validator.w3.org**, to ensure an HTML document conforms to the HTML specification.
- **<html>** tells the browser that everything contained between the opening **<html>** tag and the closing **</html>** tag is HTML.
- Comments in HTML always begin with **<!--** and end with **-->** and can span across several source lines. The browser ignores any text and/or tags placed inside a comment.
- Every HTML file is separated into a header section and a body.
- Including a title is mandatory for every HTML document. Use the **<title>**...**</title>** tags to do so. They are placed inside the header.
- **<body>** opens the **body** element. The body of an HTML document is the area where you place all content you would like browsers to display.
- All text between the **<p>**...**</p>** tags forms one paragraph. Most browsers render paragraphs as set apart from all other material on the page by a line of vertical space both before and after the paragraph.
- Headers are a simple form of text formatting that typically increase text size based on the header's "level" (**h1** through **h6**). They are often used to delineate new sections and subsections of a page.
- The purpose of HTML is to mark up text; the question of how it is presented is left to the browser itself.
- People who have difficulty seeing can use special browsers that read the text on the screen aloud. These browsers (which are text based and do not show images, colors or graphics) might read **strong** and **em** with different inflections to convey the impact of the styled text to the user.
- You should close tags in the reverse order from that in which they were started to ensure proper nesting.
- The most important capability of HTML is creating hyperlinks to documents on any server to form a worldwide network of linked documents and information.
- Links are inserted with the **a** (anchor) element. To specify the address you would like to link to, add the **href** attribute to the anchor element, with the address as the value of **href**.
- Anchors can link to email addresses. When someone clicks this type of anchored link, their default email program initiates an email message to the linked address.
- The term pixel stands for "picture element". Each pixel represents one dot of color on the screen.
- You specify the location of the image file with the **src = "***location***"** attribute in the **<img>** tag. You can specify the **height** and **width** of an image, measured in pixels.
- **alt** is provided for browsers that cannot view pictures or that have images turned off (text-based browsers, for example). The value of the **alt** attribute will appear on screen in place of the image, giving the user an idea of what was in the image.
- You can refer to files in different directories by including the directory name in the correct format in the **src** attribute. You can insert an image from a different Web site onto your site (after obtaining permission from the site's owner). Just make the **src** attribute reflects the location and name of the image file.
- The **br** element forces a line break. If the **br** element is placed inside a text area, the text begins a new line at the place of the **
** tag.
- HTML 4.01 has a provision for inserting special characters and symbols. All special characters are inserted in the format of the code, always **&***code***;**. An example of this is **&**, which inserts an ampersand. Codes are often abbreviated forms of the character (like **amp** for ampersand and **copy**

for copyright) and can also be in the form of hex codes. (For example, the hex code for an ampersand is 38, so another method of inserting an ampersand is to use `&#38;`.)

- The **del** element marks text as deleted, which is rendered with a strike through by most browsers. To turn text into superscript or subscript, use the **sup** or **sub** element, respectively.

- Most visual Web browsers place a bullet mark at the beginning of each element in an unordered list. All entries in an unordered list must be enclosed within `<ul>`…`</ul>` tags, which open and close the unordered list element.

- Each entry in an unordered list is contained in an **li** element. You then insert and format any text.

- Nested lists display information in outline form. A nested list is a list that is contained in an **li** element. Most visual Web browsers indent nested lists one level and change the bullet type to reflect the nesting.

- An ordered list (`<ol>`…`</ol>`) is rendered by most browsers with a sequence number instead of a bullet at the beginning of each list element. By default, ordered lists use decimal sequence numbers (1,2,3, …).

TERMINOLOGY

`&amp;`
`.htm`
`.html`
`<!--…-->` (comment)
`<body>`…`</body>`
`<hr>` element (horizontal rule)
a element (anchor; `<a>`…`</a>`)
`alt`
anchor
attributes of an HTML tag
`clear = "all"` in `<br>`
closing tag
color
comments
content of an HTML element
del element
em element (`<em>`…`</em>`)
emphasis
h1 element (`<h1>`…`</h1>`)
h2 element (`<h2>`…`</h2>`)
h3 element (`<h3>`…`</h3>`)
h4 element (`<h4>`…`</h4>`)
h5 element (`<h5>`…`</h5>`)
h6 element (`<h6>`…`</h6>`)
head element (`<head>`…`</head>`)
height
horizontal rule
href attribute of `<a>` element
HTML (HyperText Markup Language)
HTML document
html element (`<html>`…`</html>`)
HTML file
HTML tags

HTML-kit
hyperlink
hypertext
image
img element
`index.html`
line-break element (`<br>`)
link
link attribute of **body** element…
`mailto:`
markup language
opening tag
p element (paragraph; `<p>`…`</p>`)
presentation of a Web page
RGB colors
`size =` in `<font>`
source-code form
special characters
src attribute in **img** element
strong element (`<strong>`…`</strong>`)
structure of a Web page
sub (subscript)
sup (superscript)
tags in HTML
text in **body**
text-based browser
title element (`<title>`…`</title>`)
unordered list (`<ul>`…`</ul>`)
Web site
width attribute
width by percentage
width by pixel
World Wide Web

SELF-REVIEW EXERCISES

G.1 State whether the following statements are *true* or *false*. If *false*, explain why.
    a) The document type for an HTML document is optional.
    b) The use of the **em** and **strong** elements is deprecated.
    c) The name of your site's home page should always be **homepage.html**.
    d) It is a good programming practice to insert comments into your HTML document that explain what you are doing.
    e) A hyperlink is inserted around text with the **link** element.

G.2 Fill in the blanks in each of the following statements:
    a) The _____ element is used to insert a horizontal rule.
    b) Superscript is formatted with the _____ element and subscript is formatted with the _____ element.
    c) The _____ element is located within the **<head>...</head>** tags.
    d) The least important header is the _____ element and the most important text header is _____.
    e) The _____ element is used to create an unordered list.

G.3 Identify each of the following as either an element or attribute:
    a) **html**
    b) **width**
    c) **href**
    d) **br**
    e) **h3**
    f) **a**
    g) **src**

ANSWERS TO SELF-REVIEW EXERCISES

G.1 a) False. The document type is required for HTMl documents. b) False. The use of the **i** and **b** elements is deprecated. Elements **em** and **strong** may be used instead. c) False. The name of your home page should always be **index.html**. d) True. e) False. A hyperlink is inserted around text with the **a** (anchor) element.

G.2 a) **hr**. b) **sup**, **sub**. c) **title**. d) **h6**, **h1**. e) **ul**.

G.3 a) Tag. b) Attribute. c) Attribute. d) Tag. e) Tag. f) Tag. g) Attribute.

EXERCISES

G.4 Use HTML to mark up the first paragraph of this appendix. Use **h1** for the section header, **p** for text, **strong** for the first word of every sentence, and **em** for all capital letters.

G.5 Why is this code valid? (*Hint*: you can find the W3C specification for the **p** element at **www.w3.org/TR/html4**)

```
<p>Here's some text...
<hr>
<p>And some more text...</p>
```

G.6 Why is this code invalid? [*Hint*: you can find the W3C specification for the **br** element at the same URL given in Exercise G.5.]

```
<p>Here's some text...<br></br>
And some more text...</p>
```

G.7   We have an image named **deitel.gif** that is 200 pixels wide and 150 pixels high. Use the **width** and **height** attributes of the **img** tag to a) increase image size by 100%; b) increase image size by 50%; c) change the width-to-height ratio to 2:1, keeping the width attained in a).

G.8   Create a link to each of the following: a) **index.html**, located in the **files** directory; b) **index.html**, located in the **text** subdirectory of the **files** directory; c) **index.html**, located in the **other** directory in your *parent directory* [*Hint*: **..** signifies parent directory.]; d) A link to the President of the United States' email address (**president@whitehouse.gov**); e) An **FTP** link to the file named **README** in the **pub** directory of **ftp.cdrom.com**. [*Hint*: remember to use **ftp://**.]

Introduction to HyperText Markup Language 4: Part 2

Objectives

- To be able to create tables with rows and columns of data.
- To be able to control the display and formatting of tables.
- To be able to create and use forms.
- To be able to create and use image maps to aid hyperlinking.
- To be able to make Web pages accessible to search engines.
- To be able to use the **frameset** element to create more interesting Web pages.

Yea, from the table of my memory
I'll wipe away all trivial fond records.
William Shakespeare

Outline	
H.1	**Introduction**
H.2	**Basic HTML Tables**
H.3	**Intermediate HTML Tables and Formatting**
H.4	**Basic HTML Forms**
H.5	**More Complex HTML Forms**
H.6	**Internal Linking**
H.7	**Creating and Using Image Maps**
H.8	**`meta` Elements**
H.9	**`frameset` Element**
H.10	**Nested `framesets`**
H.11	**Internet and World Wide Web Resources**

Summary • Terminology • Self-Review Exercises • Answers to Self-Review Exercises • Exercises

H.1 Introduction

In Appendix G, Introduction to HyperText Markup Language 4: Part 1, we discussed some basic HTML features. We built several complete Web pages featuring text, hyperlinks, images and such formatting tools as horizontal rules and line breaks.

In this appendix, we discuss more substantial HTML elements and features. We will see how to present information in *tables*. We discuss how to use forms to collect information from people browsing a site. We explain how to use *internal linking* and *image maps* to make pages more navigable. We also discuss how to use *frames* to make navigating Web sites easier. By the end of this appendix, you will be familiar with most commonly used HTML tags and features. You will then be able to create more complex Web sites. In this appendix, we do not present any Python programming.

H.2 Basic HTML Tables

HTML 4.0 *tables* are used to mark up tabular data, such as data stored in a database. The table in Fig. H.1 organizes data into rows and columns.

```
1   <!DOCTYPE HTML PUBLIC "-//W3C//DTD HTML 4.01//EN"
2           "http://www.w3.org/TR/html4/strict.dtd">
3   <html>
4
5   <!-- Fig. H.1: table.html -->
6   <!-- Basic table design.  -->
7
8   <head>
9      <title>Python How to Program - Tables</title>
10  </head>
```

Fig. H.1   HTML table. (Part 1 of 2.)

```
11
12   <body>
13
14      <h1>Table Example Page</h1>
15
16      <!-- the <table> tag opens a new table and lets you -->
17      <!-- put in design options and instructions        -->
18      <table border = "1" width = "40%">
19
20         <!-- use the <caption> tag to summarize the table's -->
21         <!-- contents (this helps the visually impaired)    -->
22         <caption>Here is a small sample table.</caption>
23
24         <!-- The <thead> is the first (non-scrolling)  -->
25         <!-- horizontal section. <th> inserts a header -->
26         <!--  cell and displays bold text              -->
27         <thead>
28            <tr><th>This is the head.</th></tr>
29         </thead>
30
31         <!-- All of your important content goes in the <tbody>. -->
32         <!-- Use this tag to format the entire section          -->
33         <!-- <td> inserts a data cell, with regular text        -->
34         <tbody>
35            <tr><td>This is the body.</td></tr>
36         </tbody>
37
38      </table>
39
40   </body>
41   </html>
```

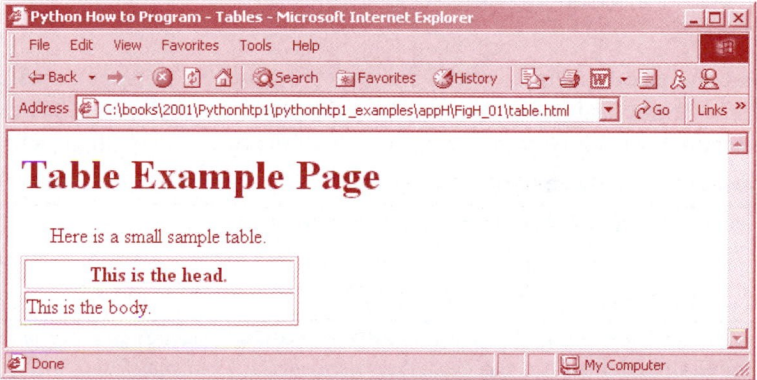

Fig. H.1   HTML table. (Part 2 of 2.)

All tags and text that apply to the table go inside the **<table>** element, which begins on line 18:

```
<table border = "1" width = "40%">
```

The **_border_** *attribute* lets you set the width of the table's border in pixels. If you want the border to be invisible, you can specify **border = "0"**. In the table shown in Fig. H.1, the value of the border attribute is set to **1**. The **_width_** attribute sets the width of the table as either a number of pixels or a percentage of the screen width.

Line 22

```
<caption>Here is a small sample table.</caption>
```

inserts a **_caption_** element into the table. The text inside the **caption** element is inserted directly above the table in most visual browsers. The caption text is also used to help *text-based browsers* interpret the table data.

Tables can be split into distinct horizontal and vertical sections. The first of these sections, the head area, appears in lines 27–29

```
<thead>
    <tr><th>This is the head.</th></tr>
</thead>
```

Put all header information (for example, the titles of the table and column headers) inside the **_thead_** element. The **_tr_**, or *table row element*, is used to create rows of table cells. All of the cells in a row belong in the **<tr>** element for that row.

The smallest unit of the table is the *data cell*. There are two types of data cells, one type—the **th** element—is located in the table header. The other type—the **td** element—is located in the table body. The code example in Fig. H.1 inserts a header cell, using the **th** element. Header cells, which are placed in the **<thead>** element, are suitable for column headings.

The second grouping section, the **_tbody_** element, appears in lines 34–36

```
<tbody>
    <tr><td>This is the body.</td></tr>
</tbody>
```

Like **thead**, the **_tbody_** element is used for formatting and grouping purposes. Although there is only one row and one cell (line 35) in the above example, most tables will use **tbody** to group the majority of their content in multiple rows and multiple cells.

Look-and-Feel Observation H.1

Use tables in your HTML pages to mark up tabular data.

Common Programming Error H.1

*Forgetting to close any of the elements inside the **table** element is an error and can distort the table format. Be sure to check that every element is opened and closed in its proper place to make sure that the table is structured as intended.*

H.3 Intermediate HTML Tables and Formatting

In the previous section and code example, we explored the structure of a basic table. In Fig. H.2, we extend our table example with more structural elements and attributes

```
1   <!DOCTYPE HTML PUBLIC "-//W3C//DTD HTML 4.01//EN"
2           "http://www.w3.org/TR/html4/strict.dtd">
3   <html>
4
5   <!-- Fig. H.2: table.html        -->
6   <!-- Intermediate table design. -->
7
8   <head>
9       <title>Python How to Program - Tables</title>
10  </head>
11
12  <body>
13
14      <h1>Table Example Page</h1>
15
16      <table border = "1">
17          <caption>Here is a more complex sample table.</caption>
18
19          <!-- <colgroup> and <col> are used to format      -->
20          <!-- entire columns at once. SPAN determines how -->
21          <!-- many columns the <col> tag effects.         -->
22          <colgroup>
23              <col align = "right">
24              <col span = "4">
25          </colgroup>
26
27          <thead>
28
29              <!-- rowspans and colspans combine the indicated -->
30              <!-- number of cells vertically or horizontally  -->
31              <tr>
32                  <th rowspan = "2">
33                      <img src = "snake.gif" width = "205"
34                          height = "167" alt = "Picture of a snake">
35                  </th>
36                  <th colspan = "4" valign = "top">
37                      <h1>Python comparison</h1><br>
38                      <p>Approximate as of 12/2/2001</p>
39                  </th>
40              </tr>
41
42              <tr valign = "bottom">
43                  <th>Average Length (Feet)</th>
44                  <th>Indigenous region</th>
45                  <th>Aboreal?</th>
46                  <th>Habitat</th>
47              </tr>
48
49          </thead>
50
```

Fig. H.2   Complex HTML table. (Part 1 of 2.)

```
51          <tbody>
52
53             <tr>
54                <th>Indian Python</th>
55                <td>20</td>
56                <td>Southeast Asia</td>
57                <td rowspan = "2">Indian Python</td>
58                <td>Jungles, rocky hill slopes and rivers</td>
59             </tr>
60
61             <tr>
62                <th>Royal Python</th>
63                <td>4</td>
64                <td>Equatorial West Africa</td>
65                <td>Savvana and sparsely wooded plains</td>
66             </tr>
67          </tbody>
68
69       </table>
70
71    </body>
72    </html>
```

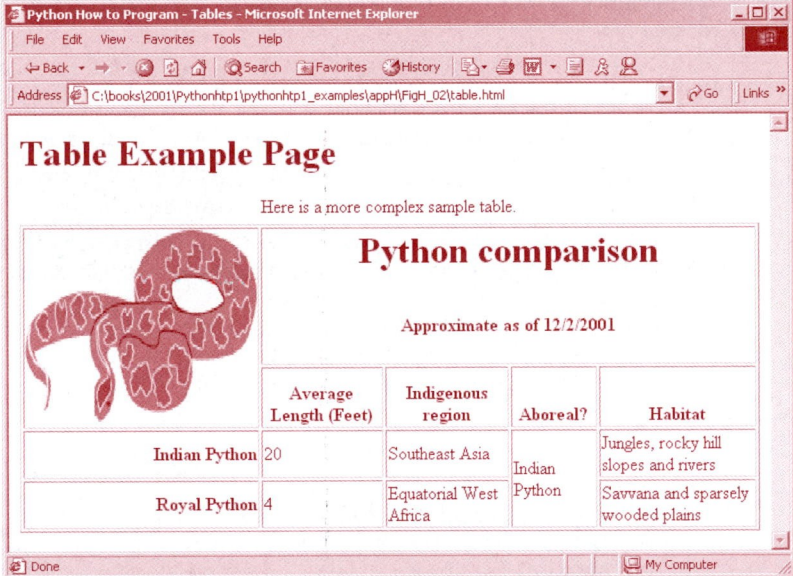

Fig. H.2   Complex HTML table. (Part 2 of 2.)

The table begins on line 16. The **colgroup** *element*, used for grouping columns, is shown on lines 22–25

```
<colgroup>
   <col align = "right">
```

```
    <col span = "4">
</colgroup>
```

The **colgroup** element can be used to group and format columns. Each **col** element in the **<colgroup>**...**</colgroup>** tags can format any number of columns (specified with the **span** attribute). Any formatting to be applied to a column or group of columns can be specified in both the **colgroup** and **col** tags. In this case, we align the text inside the leftmost column to the right. Another useful attribute to use here is **width**, which specifies the width of the column.

Most visual Web browsers automatically format data cells to fit the data they contain. However, it is possible to make some data cells larger than others. This effect is accomplished with the *rowspan* and *colspan* attributes, which can be placed inside any data cell element. The value of the attribute specifies the number of rows or columns to be occupied by the cell, respectively. For example, **rowspan = "2"** tells the browser that this data cell will span the area of two vertically adjacent cells. These cells will be joined vertically (and will thus span over two rows). An example of **colspan** appears in line 36,

```
<th colspan = "4" valign = "top">
```

where the header cell is widened to span four cells.

We also see here an example of vertical alignment formatting. The *valign* attribute accepts the following values: **"top"**, **"middle"**, **"bottom"** and **"baseline"**. All cells in a row whose **valign** attribute is set to **"baseline"** will have the first text line occur on a common baseline. The default vertical alignment in all data and header cells is **valign = "middle"**.

The remaining code in Fig. H.2 demonstrates other uses of the **table** attributes and elements outlined above.

 Common Programming Error H.2

*When using **colspan** and **rowspan** in table data cells, consider that the modified cells will cover the areas of other cells. Compensate for this in your code by reducing the number of cells in that row or column. If you do not, the formatting of your table will be distorted, and you could inadvertently create more columns and/or rows than you originally intended.*

H.4 Basic HTML Forms

HTML provides several mechanisms to collect information from people viewing your site; one is the *form* (Fig. H.3).

```
1   <!DOCTYPE HTML PUBLIC "-//W3C//DTD HTML 4.01//EN"
2              "http://www.w3.org/TR/html4/strict.dtd">
3   <html>
4
5   <!-- Fig. H.3: form.html     -->
6   <!-- Form design example 1. -->
7
8   <head>
9      <title>Python How to Program - Forms</title>
10  </head>
```

Fig. H.3   Simple form with hidden fields and a text box. (Part 1 of 2.)

```
11
12   <body>
13
14      <h1>Feedback Form</h1>
15
16      <p>Please fill out this form to help us improve our site.</p>
17
18      <!-- This tag starts the form, gives the method of sending -->
19      <!-- information and the location of form scripts.         -->
20      <!-- Hidden inputs give the server non-visual information   -->
21      <form method = "post" action = "/cgi-bin/formmail">
22
23      <p>
24         <input type = "hidden" name = "recipient"
25            value = "deitel@deitel.com">
26
27         <input type = "hidden" name = "subject"
28            value = "Feedback Form">
29
30         <input type = "hidden" name = "redirect"
31            value = "main.html">
32      </p>
33
34      <!-- <input type = "text"> inserts a text box -->
35      <p><label>Name:
36         <input name = "name" type = "text" size = "25">
37      </label></p>
38
39      <p>
40         <!-- input types "submit" and "reset" insert buttons -->
41         <!-- for submitting or clearing the form's contents   -->
42         <input type = "submit" value = "Submit Your Entries">
43         <input type = "reset" value = "Clear Your Entries">
44      </p>
45
46      </form>
47
48   </body>
49   </html>
```

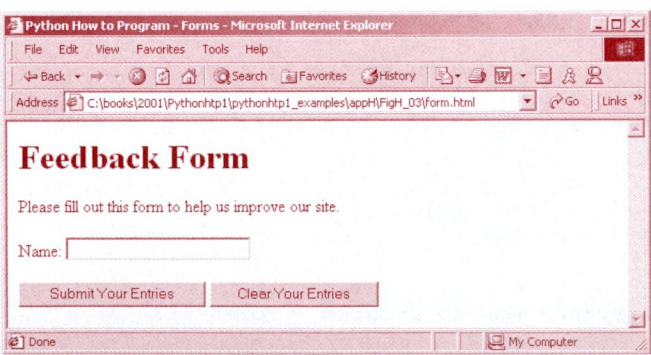

Fig. H.3   Simple form with hidden fields and a text box. (Part 2 of 2.)

The form begins on line 21

```
<form method = "post" action = "/cgi-bin/formmail">
```

with the **form** element. The **method** attribute indicates the way the information gathered in the form will be sent to the *Web server* for processing. Use **method = "post"** in a form that causes changes to server data, for example when updating a database. The form data will be sent to the server as an *environment variable,* which scripts are able to access. The other possible value, **method = "get"**, should be used when your form does not cause any changes in server-side data, for example when making a database request. The form data from **method = "get"** is appended to the end of the URL (for example, **/cgi-bin/formmail?name=bob&order=5**). Also be aware that **method = "get"** is limited to standard characters and cannot submit any special characters.

A *Web server* is a machine that runs a software package like Microsoft's PWS (Personal Web Server), Microsoft's IIS (Internet Information Server) or Apache. Web servers handle browser requests. When a browser requests a page or file somewhere on a server, the server processes the request and returns an answer to the browser. In this example, the data from the form goes to a CGI (Common Gateway Interface) script, which is a means of interfacing an HTML page with a script (i.e., a program) written in Perl, C, Tcl or other languages. The script then handles the data fed to it by the server and typically returns some information for the user. The **action** attribute in the **form** tag is the URL for this script; in this case, it is a simple script that emails form data to an address. Most Internet Service Providers (ISPs) will have a script like this on their site, so you can ask your system administrator how to set up your HTML to use the script correctly.

For this particular script, there are several pieces of information (not seen by the user) needed in the form. Lines 24–31

```
<input type = "hidden" name = "recipient"
   value = "deitel@deitel.com">

<input type = "hidden" name = "subject"
   value = "Feedback Form">

<input type = "hidden" name = "redirect"
   value = "main.html">
```

specify this information using *hidden input elements*. The **input** element is common in forms and always requires the **type** attribute. Two other attributes are **name**, which provides a unique identifier for the **input** element, and **value**, which indicates the value that the **input** element sends to the server upon submission.

As shown above, hidden inputs always have the attribute **type = "hidden"**. The three hidden inputs shown are typical for this kind of CGI script: An email address to which the data will be sent, the subject line of the email and a URL to which the user is redirected after submitting the form.

Good Programming Practice H.1

Place hidden **input** *elements in the beginning of a form, right after the opening* **<form>** *tag. This makes these elements easier to find and identify.*

The usage of an **input** element is defined by the value of its **type** attribute. We introduce another of these options in lines 35–37:

```
<p><label>Name:
   <input name = "name" type = "text" size = "25">
</label></p>
```

The input **type = "text"** inserts a one-line text box into the form (line 36). A good use of the textual input element is for names or other one-line pieces of information. The **label** element on lines 35–37 provide a description for the **input** element on line 36.

We also use the **size** attribute of the **input** element to specify the width of the text input, measured in characters. You can also set a maximum number of characters that the text input will accept using the **maxlength** attribute.

Good Programming Practice H.2

*When using **input** elements in forms, be sure to leave enough space with the **maxlength** attribute for users to input the pertinent information.*

Common Programming Error H.3

*Forgetting to include a **label** element for each form element is a design error. Without these labels, users will have no way of knowing what the function of individual form elements is.*

There are two types of **input** elements in lines 42–43

```
<input type = "submit" value = "Submit Your Entries">
<input type = "reset" value = "Clear Your Entries">
```

that should be inserted into every form. The **type = "submit" input** element allows the user to submit the data entered in the form to the server for processing. Most visual Web browsers place a button in the form that submits the data when clicked. The **value** attribute changes the text displayed on the button (the default value is **"submit"**). The input element **type = "reset"** allows a user to reset all form elements to the default values. This can help the user correct mistakes or simply start over. As with the **submit** input, the **value** attribute of the **reset input** element affects the text of the button on the screen, but does not affect its functionality.

Common Programming Error H.4

*Be sure to close your form code with the **</form>** tag. Neglecting to do so is an error and can affect the functionality of other forms on the same page.*

H.5 More Complex HTML Forms

We introduce additional form input options in Fig. H.4.

```
1   <!DOCTYPE HTML PUBLIC "-//W3C//DTD HTML 4.01//EN"
2             "http://www.w3.org/TR/html4/strict.dtd">
3   <html>
4
5   <!-- Fig. H.4: form.html     -->
6   <!-- Form design example 2. -->
7
8   <head>
9      <title>Python How to Program - Forms</title>
10  </head>
```

Fig. H.4   Form including textareas, password boxes and checkboxes. (Part 1 of 3.)

```
11
12   <body>
13
14      <h1>Feedback Form</h1>
15
16      <p>Please fill out this form to help us improve our site.</p>
17
18      <form method = "post" action = "/cgi-bin/formmail">
19
20         <p>
21            <input type = "hidden" name = "recipient"
22               value = "deitel@deitel.com">
23
24            <input type = "hidden" name = "subject"
25               value = "Feedback Form">
26
27            <input type = "hidden" name = "redirect"
28               value = "main.html">
29         </p>
30
31         <p><label>Name:
32            <input name = "name" type = "text" size = "25">
33         </label></p>
34
35         <!-- <textarea> creates a textbox of the size given -->
36         <p><label>Comments:
37            <textarea name = "comments" rows = "4" cols = "36">
38            </textarea>
39         </label></p>
40
41         <!-- <input type = "password"> inserts textbox whose -->
42         <!-- readout will be in *** not regular characters   -->
43         <p><label>Email Address:
44            <input name = "email" type = "password" size = "25">
45         </label></p>
46
47         <p>
48            <strong>Things you liked:</strong><br>
49
50            <label>Site design
51            <input name = "thingsliked" type = "checkbox"
52               value = "Design"></label>
53
54            <label>Links
55            <input name = "thingsliked" type = "checkbox"
56               value = "Links"></label>
57
58            <label>Ease of use
59            <input name = "thingsliked" type = "checkbox"
60               value = "Ease"></label>
61
62            <label>Images
```

Fig. H.4   Form including textareas, password boxes and checkboxes. (Part 2 of 3.)

```
63              <input name = "thingsliked" type = "checkbox"
64                 value = "Images"></label>
65
66              <label>Source code
67              <input name = "thingsliked" type = "checkbox"
68                 value = "Code"></label>
69           </p>
70
71           <p>
72              <input type = "submit" value = "Submit Your Entries">
73              <input type = "reset" value = "Clear Your Entries">
74           </p>
75
76        </form>
77
78     </body>
79     </html>
```

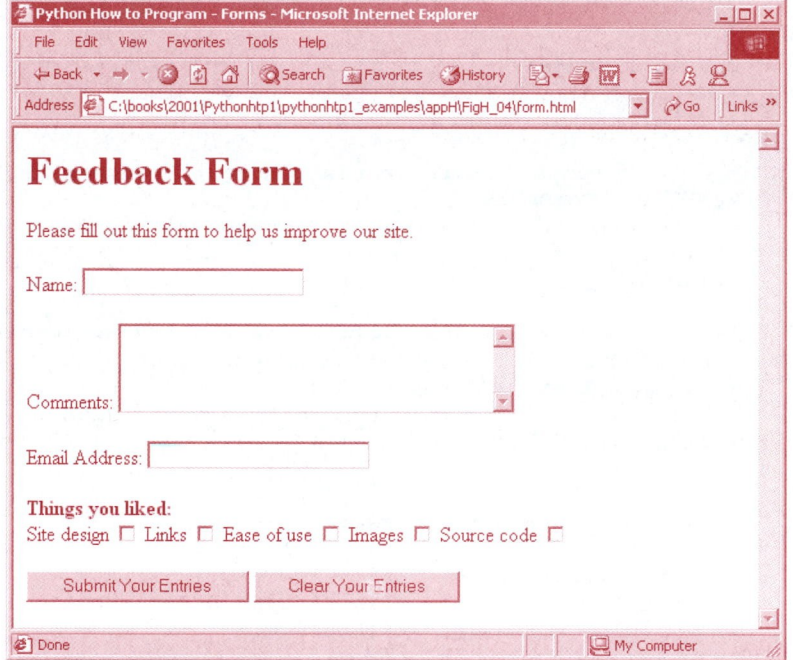

Fig. H.4   Form including textareas, password boxes and checkboxes. (Part 3 of 3.)

Lines 37–38

```
<textarea name = "comments" rows = "4" cols = "36">
</textarea>
```

introduce the **textarea** element. The **textarea** element inserts a text box into the form. You specify the size of the box with the **rows** *attribute*, which sets the number of rows that will appear in the **textarea**. With the **cols** *attribute*, you specify how wide the **textarea** should be. This **textarea** is four rows of characters tall and 36 characters wide. Any default text that you want to place inside the **textarea** should be contained in the **textarea** element.

The input *type = "password"* (line 44)

```
<input name = "email" type = "password" size = "25">
```

inserts a text box with the indicated size. The password input field provides a way for users to enter information that the user would not want others to be able to read on the screen. In visual browsers, the data the user types into a password input field is shown as asterisks. However, the actual value the user enters is sent to the server. Nonvisual browsers may render this type of input field differently.

Lines 50–68 introduce another type of form element, the checkbox. Every **input** element with **type = "checkbox"** creates a new checkbox item in the form. Checkboxes can be used individually or in groups. Each checkbox in a group should have the same **name** (in this case, **name = "thingsliked"**). This notifies the script handling the form that all of the checkboxes are related to one another.

Common Programming Error H.5

*When your form has several checkboxes with the same **name**, you must make sure that they have different **value**s, or else the script will have no way of distinguishing between them.*

Additional form elements are introduced in Fig. H.5. In this form example, we introduce two new types of input options. The first of these is the *radio button*, introduced in lines 80–97. Inserted into forms with the **input** attribute *type = "radio"*, radio buttons are similar in function and usage to checkboxes. Radio buttons are different in that only one element in the group may be selected at any time. All of the **name** attributes of a group of radio inputs must be the same and all of the **value** attributes different. Insert the attribute *checked* to indicate which radio button you would like selected initially. The **checked** attribute can also be applied to checkboxes.

Common Programming Error H.6

*When you are using a group of radio inputs in a form, forgetting to set the **name** values to the same name will let the user select all the radio buttons at the same time—an undesired result.*

```
1   <!DOCTYPE HTML PUBLIC "-//W3C//DTD HTML 4.01//EN"
2              "http://www.w3.org/TR/html4/strict.dtd">
3   <html>
4
5   <!-- Fig. H.5: form.html    -->
6   <!-- Form design example 3. -->
7
8   <head>
9      <title>Python How to Program - Forms</title>
10  </head>
11
12  <body>
13
14     <h1>Feedback Form</h1>
15
```

Fig. H.5   Form including radio buttons and pulldown lists. (Part 1 of 4.)

```
16      <p>Please fill out this form to help us improve our site.</p>
17
18      <form method = "post" action = "/cgi-bin/formmail">
19
20         <p>
21            <input type = "hidden" name = "recipient"
22               value = "deitel@deitel.com">
23
24            <input type = "hidden" name = "subject"
25               value = "Feedback Form">
26
27            <input type = "hidden" name = "redirect"
28               value = "main.html">
29         </p>
30
31         <p><label>Name:
32            <input name = "name" type = "text" size = "25">
33         </label></p>
34
35         <p><label>Comments:
36            <textarea name = "comments" rows = "4" cols = "36">
37               </textarea>
38         </label></p>
39
40         <p><label>Email Address:
41            <input name = "email" type = "password" size = "25">
42         </label></p>
43
44         <p>
45            <strong>Things you liked:</strong><br>
46
47            <label>Site design
48               <input name = "things" type = "checkbox"
49                  value = "Design">
50            </label>
51
52            <label>Links
53               <input name = "things" type = "checkbox"
54                  value = "Links">
55            </label>
56
57            <label>Ease of use
58               <input name = "things" type = "checkbox"
59                  value = "Ease">
60            </label>
61
62            <label>Images
63               <input name = "things" type = "checkbox"
64                  value = "Images">
65            </label>
66
67            <label>Source code
```

Fig. H.5   Form including radio buttons and pulldown lists. (Part 2 of 4.)

```
68              <input name = "things" type = "checkbox"
69                 value = "Code">
70          </label>
71      </p>
72
73      <!-- <input type = "radio"> creates one radio button -->
74      <!-- radio buttons and checkboxes differ in that      -->
75      <!-- only one radio button in group can be selected   -->
76      <p>
77          <strong>How did you get to our site?:</strong><br>
78
79          <label>Search engine
80              <input name = "how get to site" type = "radio"
81                 value = "search engine" checked></label>
82
83          <label>Links from another site
84              <input name = "how get to site" type = "radio"
85                 value = "link"></label>
86
87          <label>Deitel.com Web site
88              <input name = "how get to site" type = "radio"
89                 value = "deitel.com"></label>
90
91          <label>Reference in a book
92              <input name = "how get to site" type = "radio"
93                 value = "book"></label>
94
95          <label>Other
96              <input name = "how get to site" type = "radio"
97                 value = "other"></label>
98
99      </p>
100
101     <!-- <select> tags present drop down menus    -->
102     <!-- with choices indicated by <option> tags  -->
103     <p>
104         <label>Rate our site:
105
106         <select name = "rating">
107             <option selected>Amazing:-)</option>
108             <option>10</option>
109             <option>9</option>
110             <option>8</option>
111             <option>7</option>
112             <option>6</option>
113             <option>5</option>
114             <option>4</option>
115             <option>3</option>
116             <option>2</option>
117             <option>1</option>
118             <option>The Pits:-(</option>
119         </select>
120
```

Fig. H.5   Form including radio buttons and pulldown lists. (Part 3 of 4.)

```
121            </label>
122        </p>
123
124        <p>
125            <input type = "submit" value = "Submit Your Entries">
126            <input type = "reset" value = "Clear Your Entries">
127        </p>
128
129    </form>
130
131 </body>
132 </html>
```

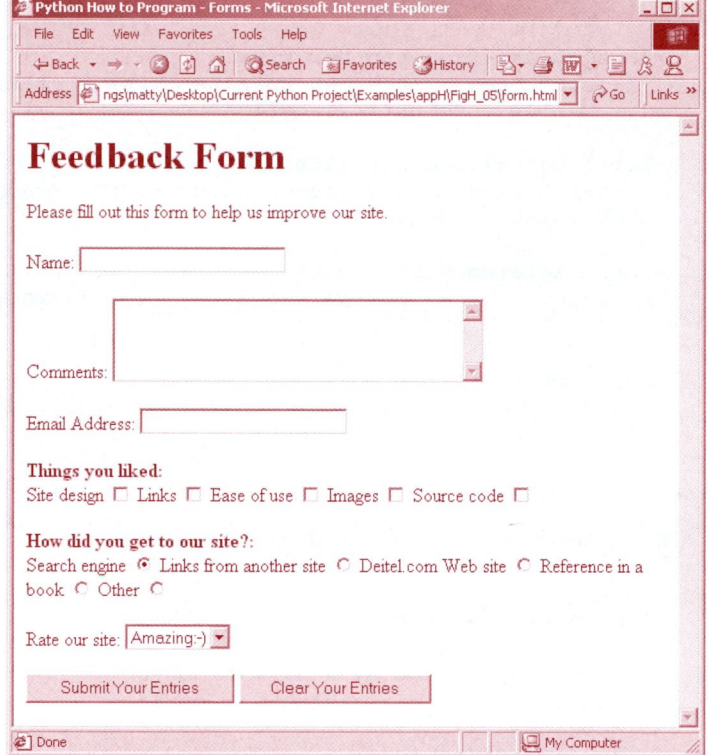

Fig. H.5 Form including radio buttons and pulldown lists. (Part 4 of 4.)

The last type of form input that we introduce here is the ***select*** element (lines 106–119). This will place a selectable list of items inside your form.

```
<select name = "rating">
    <option selected>Amazing:-)</option>
    <option>10</option>
    <option>9</option>
    <option>8</option>
    <option>7</option>
    <option>6</option>
```

```
        <option>5</option>
        <option>4</option>
        <option>3</option>
        <option>2</option>
        <option>1</option>
        <option>The Pits:-(</option>
    </select>
```

This type of form input is created via a **select** element. Inside the opening **<select>** tag, be sure to include the **name** attribute.

To add an item to the list, add to the **select** element an **option** element containing the text to be displayed. The **selected** attribute, like the **checked** attribute for radio buttons and checkboxes, applies a default selection to your list.

The preceding code will generate a pull-down list of options in most visual browsers, as shown in Fig. H.5. You can change the number of list options visible at one time, using the **size** attribute of the **select** element. Use this attribute if you prefer an expanded version of the list to the one-line expandable list.

H.6 Internal Linking

In Appendix G, Introduction to HyperText Markup Language 4: Part 1, we discussed how to link one Web page to another with text and image anchors. Figure I.6 introduces *internal linking*, which lets you create named anchors for hyperlinks to particular parts of an HTML document.

```
1   <!DOCTYPE HTML PUBLIC "-//W3C//DTD HTML 4.01//EN"
2            "http://www.w3.org/TR/html4/strict.dtd">
3   <html>
4
5   <!-- Fig. H.6: links.html -->
6   <!-- Internal linking.     -->
7
8   <head>
9      <title>Python How to Program - List</title>
10  </head>
11
12  <body>
13
14     <!-- <a name = ".."></a> makes internal hyperlinks -->
15     <p>
16        <a name = "features"></a>
17     </p>
18
19     <h1>The Best Features of the Internet</h1>
20
21     <!-- internal link's address is "xx.html#linkname" -->
22     <p>
23        <a href = "#ceos">Go to <em>Favorite CEOs</em></a>
24     </p>
25
```

Fig. H.6   Using internal hyperlinks to make your pages more navigable. (Part 1 of 3.)

```
26    <ul>
27        <li>You can meet people from countries around the world.
28        </li>
29
30        <li>You have access to new media as it becomes public:
31
32            <ul>
33                <li>New games</li>
34                <li>New applications
35
36                    <ul>
37                        <li>For Business</li>
38                        <li>For Pleasure</li>
39                    </ul>
40
41                </li>
42
43                <li>Around the Clock news</li>
44                <li>Search Engines</li>
45                <li>Shopping</li>
46                <li>Programming
47
48                    <ul>
49                        <li>HTML</li>
50                        <li>Java</li>
51                        <li>Dynamic HTML</li>
52                        <li>Scripts</li>
53                        <li>New languages</li>
54                    </ul>
55
56                </li>
57            </ul>
58
59        </li>
60
61        <li>Links</li>
62        <li>Keeping In touch with old friends</li>
63        <li>It is the technology of the future!</li>
64    </ul>
65
66    <p><a name = "ceos"></a></p>
67
68    <h1>My 3 Favorite <em>CEOs</em></h1>
69
70    <p>
71        <a href = "#features">Go to <em>Favorite Features</em></a>
72    </p>
73
74    <ol>
75        <li>Ant Chovy</li>
76        <li>Ant Lee Tic</li>
77        <li>Albert Antstein</li>
78    </ol>
```

Fig. H.6   Using internal hyperlinks to make your pages more navigable. (Part 2 of 3.)

```
79
80    </body>
81    </html>
```

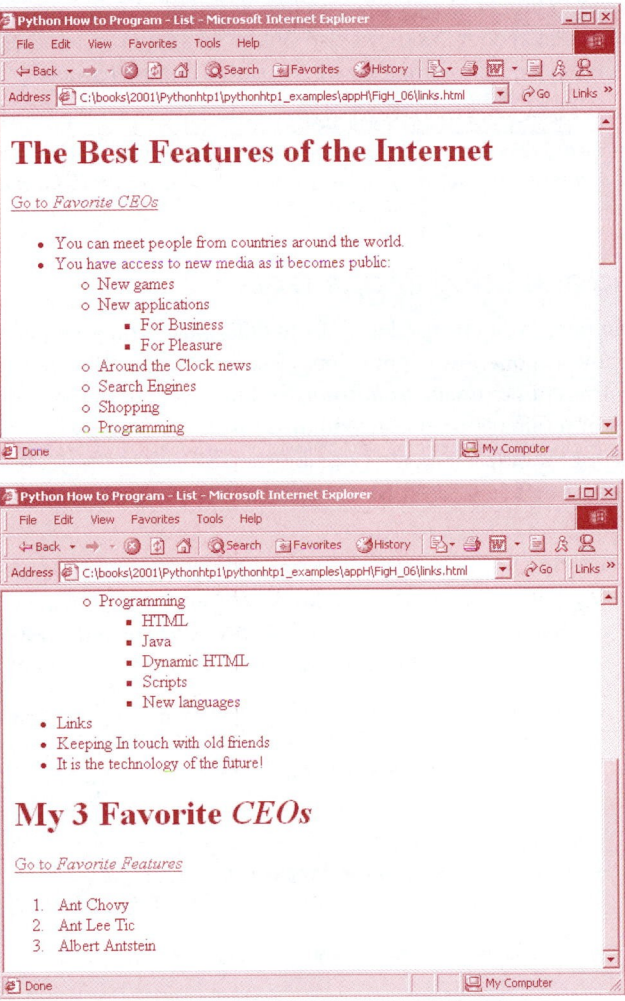

Fig. H.6   Using internal hyperlinks to make your pages more navigable. (Part 3 of 3.)

Lines 15–17

```
<p>
   <a name = "features"></a>
</p>
```

show a named anchor for an internal hyperlink. A named anchor is created via an **a** element with a **name** attribute. Line 15 creates an anchor named **features**. Because the name of the page is **list.html**, the URL of this anchor in the Web page is **list.html#fea-**
tures. Line 71

```
<a href = "#features">Go to <em>Favorite Features</em></a>
```

shows a hyperlink with the anchor **features** as its target. Selecting this hyperlink in a visual browser would scroll the browser window to the **features** anchor (line 16). Examples of this occur in Fig. H.6, which shows two different screen captures from the same page, each at a different anchor. You can also link to an anchor in another page, using the URL of that location (using the format **href = "*page.html#name*"**).

Look-and-Feel Observation H.2

Internal hyperlinks are most useful in large HTML files with lots of information. You can link to various points on the page to save the user from having to scroll down and find a specific location.

H.7 Creating and Using Image Maps

We have seen that images can be used as links to other places on your site or elsewhere on the Internet. We now discuss how to create *image maps* (Fig. H.7), which allow you to designate certain sections of the image as *hotspots* and then use these hotspots as links.

All elements of an image map are contained inside the **<map>**...**</map>** tags. The required attribute for the *map* element is **name** (line 18):

```
<map name = "picture">
```

As we will see, this attribute is needed for referencing purposes. A hotspot on the image is designated with the *area* element. Every *area* element has the following attributes: **href** sets the target for the link on that spot, *shape* and *coords* set the characteristics of the area and **alt** functions just as it does in the **img** element.

```
 1    <!DOCTYPE HTML PUBLIC "-//W3C//DTD HTML 4.01//EN"
 2             "http://www.w3.org/TR/html4/strict.dtd">
 3    <html>
 4
 5    <!-- Fig. H.7: picture.html        -->
 6    <!-- Creating and using imape maps. -->
 7
 8    <head>
 9      <title>Python How to Program - Image Map</title>
10    </head>
11
12    <body>
13
14      <p>
15
16      <!-- <map> opens and names image map formatting -->
17      <!-- area and to be referenced later           -->
18      <map name = "picture">
19
20         <!-- "shape = rect" indicates rectangular -->
21         <!-- area, with coordinates of the        -->
22         <!-- upper-left and lower-right corners    -->
```

Fig. H.7   Picture with links anchored to an image map. (Part 1 of 2.)

```
23          <area href = "form.html" shape = "rect"
24             coords = "3, 122, 73, 143"
25             alt = "Go to the feedback form">
26
27          <area href = "contact.html" shape = "rect"
28             coords = "109, 123, 199, 142"
29             alt = "Go to the contact page">
30
31          <area href = "main.html" shape = "rect"
32             coords = "1, 2, 72, 17"
33             alt = "Go to the homepage">
34
35          <area href = "links.html" shape = "rect"
36             coords = "155, 0, 199, 18"
37             alt = "Go to the links page">
38
39          <!-- "shape = polygon" indicates area of -->
40          <!-- cusotmizable shape, with the        -->
41          <!-- coordinates of every vertex listed   -->
42          <area href = "mailto:deitel@deitel.com" shape = "poly"
43          coords = "28, 22, 24, 68, 46, 114, 84, 111, 99, 56, 86, 13"
44             alt = "Email the Deitels">
45
46          <!-- "shape = circle" indicates circular -->
47          <!-- area with center and radius listed   -->
48          <area href = "mailto:deitel@deitel.com" shape = "circle"
49             coords = "146, 66, 42" alt = "Email the Deitels">
50       </map>
51
52       <!-- <img src=... usemap = "#name"> says that    -->
53       <!-- indicated image map will be used with image -->
54       <img src = "deitel.gif" width = "200" height = "144"
55          alt = "Harvey and Paul Deitel" usemap = "#picture">
56       </p>
57
58    </body>
59    </html>
```

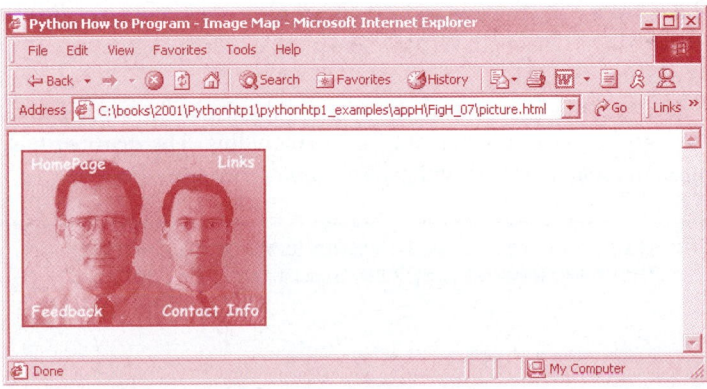

Fig. H.7   Picture with links anchored to an image map. (Part 2 of 2.)

The markup on lines 23–25

```
<area href = "form.html" shape = "rect"
   coords = "3, 122, 73, 143" alt = "Go to the feedback form">
```

causes a *rectangular hotspot* to be drawn around the *coordinates* given in the **coords** element. A coordinate pair consists of two numbers, which are the locations of the point on the *x* and *y* axes. The *x* axis extends horizontally from the upper-left corner, the *y* axis vertically. Every point on an image has a unique *x–y* coordinate. In the case of a rectangular hotspot, the required coordinates are those of the upper-left and lower-right corners of the rectangle. In this case, the upper-left corner of the rectangle is located at 3 on the *x* axis and 122 on the *y* axis, annotated as (*3, 122*). The lower-right corner of the rectangle is at (*73, 143*).

Another map area is in lines 42–44

```
<area href = "mailto:deitel@deitel.com" shape = "poly"
   coords = "28, 22, 24, 68, 46, 114, 84, 111, 99, 56, 86, 13
   alt = "Email the Deitels">
```

In this case, we use the value **poly** for the **shape** attribute. This creates a hotspot in the shape of a polygon, using the coordinates in the **coords** attribute. These coordinates represent each vertex, or corner, of the polygon. The browser will automatically connect these points with lines to form the area of the hotspot.

shape = "circle" is the last shape attribute that is commonly used in image maps. It creates a *circular hotspot*, and requires both the coordinates of the center of the circle and the radius of the circle, in pixels.

To use the image map with an **img** element, you must insert the **usemap = "#***name***"** attribute into the **img** element, where *name* is the value of the **name** attribute in the **map** element. Lines 54–55

```
<img src = "deitel.gif" width = "200" height= "144" alt =
"Harvey and Paul Deitel" usemap = "#picture">
```

show how the image map **name = "picture"** is applied to the **img** element.

H.8 meta Elements

People use search engines to find interesting Web sites. Search engines usually catalog sites by following links from page to page and saving identification and classification information for each page visited. The main HTML element that search engines use to catalog pages is the **meta** element (Fig. H.8).

A **meta** element contains two attributes that should always be used. The first of these, **name**, identifies the type of **meta** element you are including. The **content** attribute provides information the search engine will catalog about your site.

```
1    <!DOCTYPE HTML PUBLIC "-//W3C//DTD HTML 4.01//EN"
2              "http://www.w3.org/TR/html4/strict.dtd">
3    <html>
4
5    <!-- Fig. H.8: main.html          -->
6    <!-- <meta> and <!doctype> tags. -->
```

Fig. H.8   Using **meta** to provide keywords and a description. (Part 1 of 2.)

```
 7
 8    <head>
 9       <!-- <meta> tags give search engines information -->
10       <!-- they need to catalog your site            -->
11       <meta name = "keywords" content = "Webpage, design, HTML,
12          tutorial, personal, help, index, form, contact, feedback,
13          list, links, frame, deitel">
14
15       <meta name = "description" content = "This Web site will help
16          you learn the basics of HTML and Webpage design through the
17          use of interactive examples and instruction.">
18
19       <title>Python How to Program - Welcome</title>
20    </head>
21
22    <body>
23
24       <h1>Welcome to Our Web Site!</h1>
25
26       <p>
27          We have designed this site to teach about the wonders of
28          <em>HTML</em>. We have been using <em>HTML</em> since
29          version <strong>2.0</strong>, and we enjoy the features
30          that have been added recently. It seems only a short
31          time ago that we read our first <em>HTML</em> book.
32          Soon you will know about many of the great new
33          features of HTML 4.01.
34       </p>
35
36       <p>Have Fun With the Site!</p>
37
38    </body>
39    </html>
```

Fig. H.8   Using **meta** to provide keywords and a description. (Part 2 of 2.)

Lines 11–13 demonstrate the **meta** element.

```
<meta name = "keywords" content = "Webpage, design, HTML,
   tutorial, personal, help, index, form, contact, feedback,
   list, links, frame, deitel">
```

The **content** of a **meta** element with *name = "keywords"* provides search engines with a list of words that describe key aspects of your site. These words are used to match with searches—if someone searches for some of the terms in your **keywords meta** element, they have a better chance of being notified about your site in the search-engine output. Thus, including **meta** elements and their **content** information will draw more viewers to your site.

The *description* attribute value (lines 15–17)

```
<meta name = "description" content = "This Web site will help
   you learn the basics of HTML and Webpage design through the
   use of interactive examples and instruction.">
```

is quite similar to the **keywords** value. Instead of giving a list of words describing your page, the **content**s of the keywords **meta** element should be a readable 3-to-4-line description of your site, written in sentence form. This description is also used by search engines to catalog and display your site.

Software Engineering Observation H.1

meta elements are not visible to users of the site and must be placed inside the header section of your HTML document.

H.9 frameset Element

All of the Web pages we have designed so far have the ability to link to other pages but can display only one page at a time. Figure I.9 introduces *frames*, which can help you display more than one HTML file at a time. Frames, when used properly, can make your site more readable and usable for your users.

```
1   <!DOCTYPE HTML PUBLIC "-//W3C//DTD HTML 4.01 Frameset//EN"
2               "http://www.w3.org/TR/html4/frameset.dtd">
3   <html>
4
5   <!-- Fig. H.9: index.html -->
6   <!-- HTML Frames I.        -->
7
8   <head>
9      <meta name = "keywords" content = "Webpage, design, HTML,
10         tutorial, personal, help, index, form, contact, feedback,
11         list, links, frame, deitel">
12
13     <meta name = "description" content = "This Web site will help
14         you learn the basics of HTML and Webpage design through the
15         use of interactive examples and instruction.">
16
17     <title>Python How to Program - Main</title>
18  </head>
19
20  <!-- the <frameset> tag gives dimensions of your frame -->
21  <frameset cols = "110,*">
22
23     <!-- the individual frame elements specify -->
24     <!-- which pages appear in given frames     -->
25     <frame name = "nav" src = "nav.html">
26     <frame name = "main" src = "main.html">
27
28     <noframes>
29        <p>
30           This page uses frames, but your browser
31              does not support them.
32        </p>
33
```

Fig. H.9   Web site using two frames—navigation and content. (Part 1 of 2.)

```
34            <p>
35                Please, <a href = "nav.html">follow this link to
36                browse our site without frames</a>.
37            </p>
38        </noframes>
39
40    </frameset>
41    </html>
```

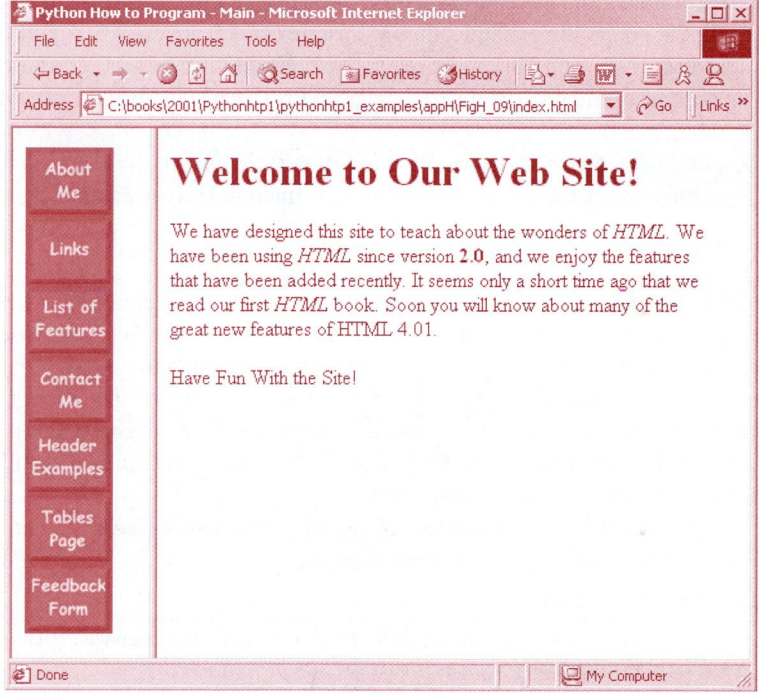

Fig. H.9   Web site using two frames—navigation and content. (Part 2 of 2.)

On lines 1 and 2,

```
<!DOCTYPE HTML PUBLIC "-//W3C//DTD HTML 4.01 Frameset//EN"
            "http://www.w3.org/TR/html4/frameset.dtd">
```

we encounter a new document type. The document type specified here indicates that this HTML document uses frames. You should use this document type whenever you use frames in your HTML document.

The framed page begins with the opening **frameset** tag, on line 21

```
<frameset cols = "110,*">
```

This tag tells the browser that the page contains frames. The **cols** attribute of the opening **frameset** tag gives the layout of the frameset. The value of **cols** (or **rows**, if you will be writing a frameset with a horizontal layout) gives the width of each frame, either in pixels or as a percentage of the screen. In this case, the attribute **cols = "110,*"** tells the browser that there are two frames. The first one extends 110 pixels from the left edge of the screen, and the second frame fills the remainder of the screen (as indicated by the asterisk).

Now that we have defined the page layout, we have to specify what files will make up the frameset. We do this with the ***frame*** element in lines 25 and 26:

```
<frame name = "nav" src = "nav.html">
<frame name = "main" src = "main.html">
```

In each **frame** element, the **src** attribute gives the URL of the page that will be displayed in the frame. In the preceding example, the first frame (which covers 110 pixels on the left side of the **frameset**) will display the page **nav.html** and has the attribute **name = "nav"**. The second frame will display the page **main.html** and has the attribute **name = "main"**.

The purpose of a **name** attribute in the **frame** element is to identify the frame, enabling hyperlinks in a **frameset** to load in their intended target **frame**. For example,

```
<a href = "links.html" target = "main">
```

would load **links.html** in the frame whose **name** attribute is **"main"**.

A target in an anchor element can also be set to a number of preset values: **target="_blank"** loads the page in a new blank browser window, **target="_self"** loads the page into the same window as the anchor element, **target="_parent"** loads it in the parent **frameset** (i.e., the **frameset** which contains the current frame) and **target="_top"** loads the page into the full browser window (the page loads over the **frameset**).

In lines 28–38 of the code example in Fig. H.9, the **noframes** element displays HTML in those browsers that do not support frames.

Portability Tip H.1

*Not everyone uses a browser that supports frames. Use the **noframes** element inside the **frameset** to direct users to a nonframed version of your site.*

Look-and-Feel Observation H.3

Frames are capable of enhancing your page, but are often misused. Never use frames to accomplish what you could with other, simpler HTML formatting.

H.10 Nested **framesets**

You can use the **frameset** element to create more complex layouts in a framed Web site by nesting **frameset** areas as in Fig. H.10.

The first level of **frameset** tags is on lines 21 and 22

```
<frameset cols = "110,*">
    <frame name = "nav"src = "nav.html">
```

The **frameset** and **frame** elements here are constructed in the same manner as in Fig. H.9. We have one frame that extends over the first 110 pixels, starting at the left edge.

The second (nested) level of the **frameset** element covers only the remaining **frame** area that was not included in the primary **frameset**. Thus, any frames included in the second **frameset** will not include the leftmost 110 pixels of the screen. Lines 26–29 show the second level of **frameset** tags.

```
<frameset rows = "175,*">
    <frame name = "picture" src = "picture.html">
    <frame name = "main" src = "main.html">
</frameset>
```

In this **frameset** area, the first frame extends 175 pixels from the top of the screen, as indicated by the **rows = "175,*"**. Be sure to include the correct number of **frame** elements inside the second **frameset** area. Also, be sure to include a **noframes** element and to close both of the **frameset** areas at the end of the Web page.

```
1   <!DOCTYPE HTML PUBLIC "-//W3C//DTD HTML 4.01 Frameset//EN"
2           "http://www.w3.org/TR/html4/frameset.dtd">
3   <html>
4
5   <!-- Fig. H.10: index.html   -->
6   <!-- HTML frames II.          -->
7
8   <head>
9
10     <meta name = "keywords" content = "Webpage, design, HTML,
11         tutorial, personal, help, index, form, contact, feedback,
12         list, links, frame, deitel">
13
14     <meta name = "description" content = "This Web site will help
15         you learn the basics of HTML and Webpage design through
16         the use of interactive examples and instruction.">
17
18     <title>Python How to Program - Main</title>
19   </head>
20
21   <frameset cols = "110,*">
22     <frame name = "nav" src = "nav.html">
23
24     <!-- nested framesets are used to change formatting -->
25     <!-- and spacing of frameset as whole                -->
26     <frameset rows = "175,*">
27         <frame name = "picture" src = "picture.html">
28         <frame name = "main" src = "main.html">
29     </frameset>
30
31     <noframes>
32         <p>
33             This page uses frames, but your browser does
34                 not support them.
35         </p>
36
37         <p>
38             Please, <a href = "nav.html">follow this link
39                 to browse our site without frames</a>.
```

Fig. H.10 Framed Web site with a nested frameset. (Part 1 of 2.)

```
40          </p>
41      </noframes>
42
43  </frameset>
44  </html>
```

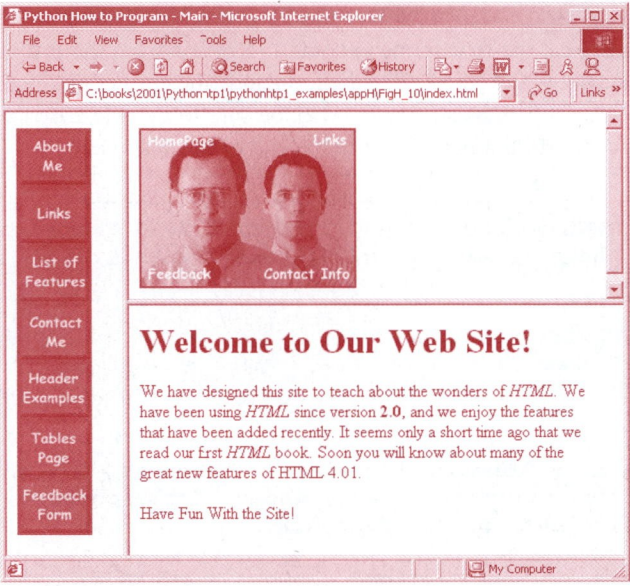

Fig. H.10 Framed Web site with a nested frameset. (Part 2 of 2.)

Testing and Debugging Tip H.1

When using nested **frameset** *elements, indent every level of* **frame** *tag. This makes the page clearer and easier to debug.*

Look-and-Feel Observation H.4

Nested **frameset***s can help you create visually pleasing, easy-to-navigate Web sites.*

H.11 Internet and World Wide Web Resources

There are many Web sites that cover the more advanced and difficult features of HTML. Several of these sites are featured here.

www.geocities.com/SiliconValley/Orchard/5212
Adam's Advanced HTML Page is geared to those looking to master the more advanced techniques of HTML. It includes instructions for creating tables, frames and marquees and other advanced topics.

www.w3scripts.com/html
This site, an offshoot of *W3Schools*, is a repository for code examples exhibiting all of the features of HTML, from beginner to advanced.

www.blooberry.com/indexdot/html
Index Dot HTML, The Advance HTML Reference... The name speaks for itself. This site has a great directory and tree-based index of all HTML elements, plus more.

`www.neiljohan.com/html/advancedhtml.htm`
The *Advanced HTML Guide* gives insights into improving your site using HTML in ways you might not have thought possible.

SUMMARY

- HTML tables organize data into rows and columns. All tags and text that apply to a table go inside the **`<table>`**…**`</table>`** tags. The **border** attribute lets you set the width of the table's border in pixels. The **width** attribute sets the width of the table—you specify either a number of pixels or a percentage of the screen width.

- The text inside the **`<caption>`**…**`</caption>`** tags is inserted directly above the table in the browser window. The caption text is also used to help text-based browsers interpret the table data.

- Tables can be split into distinct horizontal and vertical sections. Put all header information (such as table titles and column headers) inside the **`<thead>`**…**`</thead>`** tags. The **tr** (table row) element is used for formatting the cells of individual rows. All of the cells in a row belong within the **`<tr>`**…**`</tr>`** tags of that row.

- The smallest area of the table that we are able to format is the data cell. There are two types of data cells: ones located in the header (**`<th>`**…**`</th>`**) and ones located in the table body (**`<td>`**…**`</td>`**). Header cells, usually placed in the **`<thead>`** area, are suitable for titles and column headings.

- Like **thead**, the **tbody** is used for formatting and grouping purposes. Most tables use **tbody** to house the majority of their content.

- **td** table data cells are left aligned by default. **th** cells are centered by default.

- Just as you can use the **thead** and **tbody** elements to format groups of table rows, you can use the **colgroup** element to group and format columns. **colgroup** is used by setting in its opening tag the number of columns it affects and the formatting it imposes on that group of columns.

- Each **col** element contained inside the **`<colgroup>`**…**`</colgroup>`** tags can in turn format a specified number of columns.

- It is possible to make some table data cells larger than others by using the **rowspan** and **colspan** attributes. The attribute value extends the data cell to span the specified number of cells.

- The **valign** (vertical alignment) attribute of a table data cell accepts the following values: **`"top"`**, **`"middle"`**, **`"bottom"`** and **`"baseline"`**.

- All cells in a table row whose **valign** attribute is set to **`"baseline"`** will have the first text line on a common baseline.

- The default vertical alignment in all data and header cells is **`valign="middle"`**.

- HTML provides several mechanisms—including the **form**—to collect information from people viewing your site.

- Use **`method = "post"`** in a form that causes changes to server data, for example when updating a database. The form data will be sent to the server as an environment variable, which scripts are able to access. The other possible value, **`method = "get"`**, should be used when your form does not cause any changes in server-side data, for example when making a database request. The form data from **`method = "get"`** is appended to the end of the URL. Because of this, the amount of data submitted using this **method** is limited to 4K. Also be aware that **`method = "get"`** is limited to standard characters and cannot submit any special characters.

- A Web server is a machine that runs a software package like Apache or IIS; servers are designed to handle browser requests. When a user uses a browser to request a page or file somewhere on the server, the server processes this request and returns an answer to the browser.

- The **action** attribute in the **form** tag is the path to a script that processes the form data.

- The input element is common in forms and always requires the **type** attribute. Two other attributes are **name**, which provides a unique identification for the **input**, and **value**, which indicates the value that the **input** element sends to the server upon submission.

- The input **type="text"** inserts a one-line text bar into the form. The value of this **input** element and the information that the server sends to you from this **input** is the text that the user types into the bar. The **size** attribute determines the width of the text input, measured in characters. You can also set a maximum number of characters that the text input will accept by inserting the **maxlength="***length***"** attribute.

- You must make sure to include a **label** element for each form element to indicate the function of the element.

- The **type="submit" input** element places a button in the form that submits data to the server when clicked. The **value** attribute of the **submit** input changes the text displayed on the button.

- The **type="reset"** input element places a button on the form that, when clicked, will clear all entries the user has entered into the form.

- The **textarea** element inserts a box into the form. You specify the size of the box (which is scrollable) inside the opening **<textarea>** tag with the **rows** attribute and the **cols** attribute.

- Data entered in a **type="password"** input appears on the screen as asterisks. The password is used for submitting sensitive information that the user would not want others to be able to read. It is just the browser that displays asterisks—the real form data is still submitted to the server.

- Every **input** element with **type="checkbox"** creates a new checkbox in the form. Checkboxes can be used individually or in groups. Each checkbox in a group should have the same **name** (in this case, **name="things"**).

- Inserted into forms by means of the **input** attribute **type="radio"**, radio buttons are different from checkboxes in that only one in the group may be selected at any time. All of the **name** attributes of a group of radio inputs must be the same and all of the **value** attributes different.

- Insert the attribute **checked** to indicate which radio button you would like selected initially.

- The **select** element places a selectable list of items inside your form. To add an item to the list, insert an **option** element in the **<select>...</select>** area and type what you want the list item to display on the same line. You can change the number of list options visible at one time by including the **size="***size***"** attribute inside the **<select>** tag. Use this attribute if you prefer an expanded version of the list to the one-line expandable list.

- A location on a page is marked by including a **name** attribute in an **a** element. Clicking this hyperlink in a browser would scroll the browser window to that point on the page.

- An image map allows you to designate certain sections of the image as hotspots and then use these hotspots as anchors for linking.

- All elements of an image map are contained inside the **<map>...</map>** tags. The required attribute for the **map** element is **name**.

- A hotspot on the image is designated with the ***area*** element. Every **<area>** tag has the following attributes: **href** sets the target for the link on that spot, ***shape*** and ***coords*** set the characteristics of the area and **alt** function just as it does in **<img>** tags.

- **shape="rect"** creates a rectangular hotspot around the *coordinates* of a **coords** element.

- A coordinate pair consists of two numbers, which are the locations of the point on the *x* and *y* axes. The *x* axis extends horizontally from the upper-left corner, the *y* axis vertically. Every point on an image has a unique *x*–*y* coordinate, annotated as *(x, y)*.

- In the case of a rectangular hotspot, the required coordinates are those of the upper-left and lower-right corners of the rectangle.
- The **shape="poly"** creates a hotspot of no preset shape—you specify the shape of the hotspot in the **coords** attribute by listing the coordinates of every vertex, or corner of the hotspot.
- **shape="circle"** creates a circular hotspot; it requires both the coordinates of the center of the circle and the length of the radius, in pixels.
- To use an image map with a graphic on your page, you must insert the **usemap="#*name*"** attribute into the **img** element, where "name" is the value of the **name** attribute in the **map** element.
- The main element that interacts with search engines is the **meta** element.
- **meta** tags contain two attributes that should always be used. The first of these, **name**, is an identification of the type of **meta** tag you are including. The **content** attribute gives the information the search engine will be cataloging.
- The **content** of a **meta** tag with **name="keywords"** provides the search engines with a list of words that describe the key aspects of your site. By including **meta** tags and their content information, you can give precise information about your site to search engines. This will help you draw a more focused audience to your site.
- The **description** value of the **name** attribute in the **meta** tag should be a 3-to-4-line description of your site, written in sentence form. This description is used by the search engine to catalog and display your site.
- **meta** elements are not visible to users of the site and should be placed inside the header section of your HTML document.
- The **frameset** tag tells the browser that the page contains frames.
- **cols** or **rows** gives the width of each frame in pixels or as a percentage of the screen.
- In each **frame** element, the **src** attribute gives the URL of the page that will be displayed in the specified frame.
- The purpose of a **name** attribute in the **frame** element is to give an identity to that specific frame, in order to enable hyperlinks in a **frameset** to load their intended **frame**. The **target** attribute in an anchor element is set to the **name** of the **frame** in which the new page should load.
- A target in an anchor element can be set to a number of preset values: **target="_blank"** loads the page in a new blank browser window, **target="self"** loads the page into the same window as the anchor element, **target="_parent"** loads the page into the parent **frameset** and **target="_top"** loads the page into the full browser window.
- Not everyone viewing a page has a browser that can handle frames. You therefore need to include a **noframes** element inside of the **frameset**. You should include regular HTML tags and elements within the **<noframes>...</noframes>** tags. Use this area to direct the user to a non-framed version of the site.
- By nesting **frameset** elements, you can create more complex layouts.

TERMINOLOGY

<!doctype...>	cell of a table
<meta> tag	CGI script
<option>	**checked**
ACTION attribute in **form** element	circular hotspot
area	**col** element
border property of **table** element	**colgroup** element
caption element	**cols** attribute of **table** element

colspan attribute of **td** element
column of a table
coords attribute inside **area** element
data cell
environment variable
form
frame element (**<frame>**...**</frame>**)
frameset element
header cell
hotspot
image map
indenting lists
input element (**<input>**...**</input>**)
input type="button"
input type="checkbox"
input type="password"
input type="radio"
input type="reset"
input type="submit"
input type="text"
input type="textarea"
internal linking
list
map element
maxlength="#"
method="get"
method="post"
name attribute in **input** element
name="recipient" in **input** element
name="redirect" in **input** element
name="subject" in **input** element
nested lists

noframes
noresize attribute in **frame**
ol (ordered list) element (**<ol>**...**</ol>**)
rectangular hotspot
row of a table
rowspan attribute of **td** element
scrolling attribute in **frame**
select element (**<select>**...**</select>**)
shape attribute inside **area** element
size attribute in **select**
src attribute of **frame** element
table
table element (**<table>**...**</table>**)
target="_blank"
target="_parent"
target="_top"
tbody
td (table data) element (**<td>**...**</td>**)
text-based browser
th (header cell) element (**<th>**...**</th>**)
thead element (**<thead>**...**</thead>**)
tr (table row) element (**<tr>**...**</tr>**)
type=1 attribute of **<ol>**
type=a attribute of **<ol>**
type=A attribute of **<ol>**
type=i attribute of **<ol>**
type=I attribute of **<ol>**
ul (unordered list) element (**<ul>**...**</ul>**)
usemap="name" attribute in **img**
value attribute of **input** element
Web server

SELF-REVIEW EXERCISES

H.1   State whether the following statements are *true* or *false*. If *false*, explain why.
   a)   The width of all data cells in a table must be the same.
   b)   The **thead** element is mandatory in a **table**.
   c)   You are limited to a maximum of 100 internal links per page.
   d)   All browsers can render **frameset**s.

H.2   Fill in the blanks in each of the following statements.
   a)   The _____ attribute in an **input** element inserts a button that, when clicked, will clear the contents of the form.
   b)   The spacing of a **frameset** is set by including the _____ attribute or the _____ attribute inside of the **<frameset>** tag.
   c)   The _____ element inserts a new item in a list.
   d)   The _____ element tells the browser what version of HTML is included on the page. Two types of this element are _____ and _____.
   e)   The common shapes used in image maps are _____, _____ and _____.

H.3   Write HTML tags to accomplish the following tasks:

    a) Insert a framed Web page with the first frame extending 300 pixels across the page from the left side.

    b) Insert an ordered list that will have numbering by lowercase Roman numerals.

    c) Insert a scrollable list (in a form) that will always display four entries of the list.

    d) Insert an image map onto a page, using **deitel.gif** as an image and **map** with **name="hello"** as the image map, and have "**hello**" be the **alt** text.

ANSWERS TO SELF-REVIEW EXERCISES

H.1   a) False. You can specify the width of any column either in pixels or as a percentage of the total width of the table. b) False. The **thead** element is used only for formatting purposes and is optional (but it is recommended that you include it). c) False. You can have an unlimited number of hyperlink locations on any page. d) False. Text-based browsers are unable to render a **frameset** and must therefore rely on the information that you include inside the **<noframes>...</noframes>** tag.

H.2   a) **type = "reset"**. b) **cols**, **rows**. c) **li**. d) **<!doctype...>**, **transitional**, **frameset**. e) **poly**, **circle**, **rect**.

H.3   a) **<frameset cols = "300,*">...</frameset>** b) **<ol type = "i">...</ol>** c) **<select size = "4">...</select>** d) **<img src = "deitel.gif" alt = "hello" usemap = "#hello">**

EXERCISES

H.4   Categorize each of the following as an element or an attribute:

    a) **width**
    b) **td**
    c) **th**
    d) **frame**
    e) **name**
    f) **select**
    g) **type**

H.5   What will the **frameset** produced by the following code look like? Assume that the pages being imported are blank with white backgrounds and that the dimensions of the screen are 800 by 600. Sketch the layout, approximating the dimensions.

```
<frameset rows = "20%,*">
<frame src = "hello.html" name = "hello">
   <frameset cols = "150,*">
   <frame src = "nav.html" name = "nav">
   <frame src = "deitel.html" name = "deitel">
   </frameset>
</frameset>
```

H.6   Assume that you have a document with many subsections. Write the HTML markup to create a frame with a table of contents on the left side of the window, and have each entry in the table of contents use internal linking to scroll down the document frame to the appropriate subsection.

Introduction to XHTML: Part 1

Objectives

- To understand important components of XHTML documents.
- To use XHTML to create World Wide Web pages.
- To add images to Web pages.
- To understand how to create and use hyperlinks to navigate Web pages.
- To mark up lists of information.

To read between the lines was easier than to follow the text.
Henry James

High thoughts must have high language.
Aristophanes

Outline

I.1 Introduction

In this appendix, we begin unlocking the power of Web-based application development with *XHTML*[1]—the *Extensible Hypertext Markup Language*. In later appendices, we introduce more sophisticated XHTML techniques, such as *tables*, which are particularly useful for structuring information from *databases* (i.e., software that stores structured sets of data), and *Cascading Style Sheets (CSS)*, which make Web pages more visually appealing.

Unlike procedural programming languages such as C, Fortran, Cobol and Pascal, XHTML is a *markup language* that specifies the format of text that is displayed in a Web browser such as Microsoft's Internet Explorer or Netscape's Communicator.

One key issue when using XHTML[2] is the separation of the *presentation of a document* (i.e., the document's appearance when rendered by a browser) from the *structure of the document's information*. Over the next several appendices, we discuss this issue in depth.

I.2 Editing XHTML

In this appendix, we write XHTML in its *source-code form*. We create *XHTML documents* by typing them in with a text editor (e.g., *Notepad, Wordpad, vi,* or *emacs*), saving the documents with either the **.html** or the **.htm** file-name extension.

---

1. XHTML has replaced the HyperText Markup Language (HTML) as the primary means of describing Web content. XHTML provides more robust, richer and more extensible features than HTML. For more on XHTML/HTML, visit **www.w3.org/markup**.

2. As this book was being submitted to the publisher, XHTML 1.1 became a World Wide Web Consortium (W3C) Recommendation. The XHTML examples presented in this book are based upon the XHTML 1.0 Recommendation, because Internet Explorer 5.5 does not support the full set of XHTML 1.1 features. In the future, Internet Explorer and other browsers will support XHTML 1.1. When this occurs, we will update our Web site (**www.deitel.com**) with XHTML 1.1 examples and information.

Good Programming Practice I.1

Assign documents file names that describe their functionality. This practice can help you identify documents faster. It also helps people who want to link to a page, by giving them an easy-to-remember name. For example, if you are writing an XHTML document that contains product information, you might want to call it **products.html***.*

Machines running specialized software called *Web servers* store XHTML documents. Clients (e.g., Web browsers) request specific *resources* from the Web server. For example, typing **www.deitel.com/books/downloads.htm** into a Web browser's address field requests **downloads.htm** from the Web server running at **www.deitel.com**. This document resides in a directory named **books**. For now, we simply place the XHTML documents on our machine and open them using Internet Explorer.

I.3 First XHTML Example[3]

In this appendix and the next, we present XHTML markup and provide screen captures that show how Internet Explorer 5.5 renders (i.e., displays) the XHTML. Every XHTML document we show has line numbers for the reader's convenience. These line numbers are not part of the XHTML documents.

Our first example (Fig. I.1) is an XHTML document named **main.html** that displays the message "Welcome to XHTML!" in the browser.

The key line in the program is line 14, which tells the browser to display "Welcome to XHTML!" Now let us consider each line of the program.

Lines 1 is the optional *XML declaration* that identifies the **version** of XML used in the document. Line 2–3 is required for XHTML documents to conform with proper XHTML syntax.

Lines 5–6 are *XHTML comments*. Comments do not cause the browser to perform any action when the user loads the XHTML document into the Web browser to view the document. XHTML comments always start with **<!--** and end with **-->**. Each of our XHTML examples include comments that specify the figure number and file name and provide a brief description of the example's purpose. Subsequent examples include comments in the markup, especially to highlight new features.

```
1   <?xml version = "1.0"?>
2   <!DOCTYPE html PUBLIC "-//W3C//DTD XHTML 1.0 Strict//EN"
3      "http://www.w3.org/TR/xhtml1/DTD/xhtml1-strict.dtd">
4
5   <!-- Fig. I.1: main.html -->
6   <!-- Our first Web page. -->
7
8   <html xmlns = "http://www.w3.org/1999/xhtml">
9      <head>
10        <title>Python How to Program - Welcome</title>
11     </head>
```

Fig. I.1   First XHTML example. (Part 1 of 2.)

___

3. All of the examples presented in this book are available at **www.deitel.com** and on the CD-ROM that accompanies this book.

```
12
13     <body>
14        <p>Welcome to XHTML!</p>
15     </body>
16  </html>
```

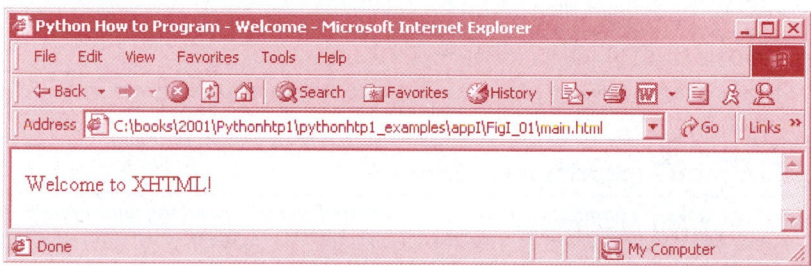

Fig. I.1   First XHTML example. (Part 2 of 2.)

XHTML markup contains text that represents the content of a document and *elements* that specify a document's structure. Some important elements of an XHTML document include the **html** element, the **head** element and the **body** element. The **html** element encloses the *head section* (represented by the **head** *element*) and the *body section* (represented by the **body** *element*). The head section contains information about the XHTML document, such as the *title* of the document. The head section also can contain special document formatting instructions called *style sheets* and client-side programs called *scripts* for creating dynamic Web pages. (We introduce style sheets in Appendix K.) The body section contains the page's content that the browser displays when the user visits the Web page.

XHTML documents delimit an element with *start* and *end* tags. A start tag consists of the element name in angle brackets (e.g., **<html>**). An end tag consists of the element name preceded by a **/** in angle brackets (e.g., **</html>**). In this example, lines 8 and 16 define the start and end of the **html** element. Note that the end tag on line 16 has the same name as the start tag, but is preceded by a **/** inside the angle brackets. Many start tags define *attributes* that provide additional information about an element. Browsers can use this additional information to determine how to process the element. Each attribute has a *name* and a *value*, which is in quotation marks, separated by an equal sign (**=**). Line 8 specifies a required attribute (**xmlns**) and value (**http://www.w3.org/1999/xhtml**) for the **html** element in an XHTML document. Simply copy and paste the **html** element start tag on line 8 into your XHTML documents.

 Common Programming Error I.1

Not enclosing attribute values in either single or double quotes is a syntax error.

 Common Programming Error I.2

Using uppercase letters in an XHTML element or attribute name is a syntax error.

An XHTML document divides the **html** element into two sections—head, and body. Lines 9–11 define the Web page's head section with a **head** element. Line 10 specifies a

title element. This is called a *nested element*, because it is enclosed in the **head** element's start and end tags. The **head** element also is a nested element, because it is enclosed in the **html** element's start and end tags. The **title** element describes the Web page. Titles usually appear in the *title bar* at the top of the browser window and also as the text identifying a page when users add the page to their list of **Favorites** or **Bookmarks**, which enable users to return to their favorite sites. Search engines (i.e., sites that allow users to search the Web) also use the **title** for cataloging purposes.

Good Programming Practice I.2

Indenting nested elements emphasizes a document's structure and promotes readability.

Common Programming Error I.3

XHTML does not permit tags to overlap—a nested element's end tag must appear in the document before the enclosing element's end tag. For example, the nested XHTML tags **<head><title>hello</head></title>** *cause a syntax error, because the enclosing* **head** *element's ending* **</head>** *tag appears before the nested* **title** *element's ending* **</title>** *tag.*

Good Programming Practice I.3

Use a consistent **title** *naming convention for all pages on a site. For example, if a site is named "Bailey's Web Site," then the* **title** *of the main page might be "Bailey's Web Site—Links." This practice can help users better understand the Web site's structure.*

Line 13 opens the document's ***body*** element. The body section of an XHTML document specifies the document's content, which may include text and tags.

Some tags, such as the *paragraph tags* (**<p>** and **</p>**) in line 14, mark up text for display in a browser. All text placed between the **<p>** and **</p>** tags forms one paragraph. Typically, the browser renders a paragraph with a blank linepreceding and following the paragraph.

This document ends with two closing tags (lines 15–16). These tags close the **body** and **html** elements, respectively. The ending **</html>** tag in an XHTML document informs the browser that the XHTML markup is complete.

To view this example in Internet Explorer, perform the following steps:

1. Copy the Appendix I examples onto your machine from the CD that accompanies this book (or download the examples from **www.deitel.com**).

2. Launch Internet Explorer and select **Open...** from the **File** Menu. This displays the **Open** dialog.

3. Click the **Open** dialog's **Browse...** button to display the **Microsoft Internet Explorer** file dialog.

4. Navigate to the directory containing the Appendix I examples and select the file **main.html**, then click **Open**.

5. Click **OK** to have Internet Explorer render the document. Other examples are opened in a similar manner.

At this point your browser window should appear similar to the sample screen capture shown in Fig. I.1. (Note that we resized the browser window to save space in the book.)

I.4 W3C XHTML Validation Service

Programming Web-based applications can be complex, and XHTML documents must be written correctly to ensure that browsers process them properly. To promote correctly written documents, the *World Wide Web Consortium (W3C)* provides a *validation service* (**validator.w3.org**) for checking a document's syntax. Documents can be validated from either a URL that specifies the location of the file or by uploading a file to the site **validator.w3.org/file-upload.html**. Uploading a file copies the file from the user's computer to another computer on the Internet. Figure I.2 shows **main.html** (Fig. I.1) being uploaded for validation. Although the W3C's Web page indicates that the service name is **HTML Validation Service**,[4] the service validates the syntax of XHTML documents. All the XHTML examples in this book are validated successfully using **validator.w3.org**.

By clicking **Browse...**, users can select files on their own computers for upload. After selecting a file, clicking the **Validate this document** button uploads and validates the file. Figure I.3 shows the results of validating **main.html**. This document does not contain any syntax errors. If a document does contain syntax errors, the validation service displays error

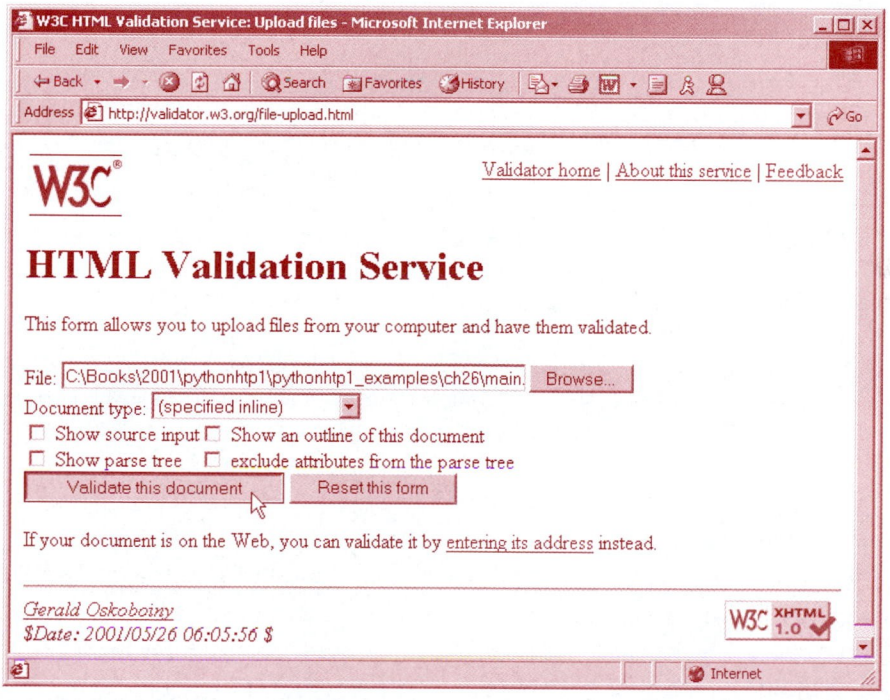

Fig. I.2   Validating an XHTML document. (Courtesy of World Wide Web Consortium (W3C).)

---

4. HTML (HyperText Markup Language) is the predecessor of XHTML designed for marking up Web content. HTML is a deprecated technology.

messages describing the errors. Figure I.4 shows the results of validating the **main.html** document, which contains a syntax error—the closing **</p>** tag is omitted. In Exercise I.13, we ask readers to create an invalid XHTML document (i.e., one that contains syntax errors) and to check the document's syntax, using the validation service. This enables readers to see the types of error messages generated by the validator.

Testing and Debugging Tip I.1

Use a validation service, such as the W3C HTML Validation Service, to confirm that an XHT-ML document is correct syntactically.

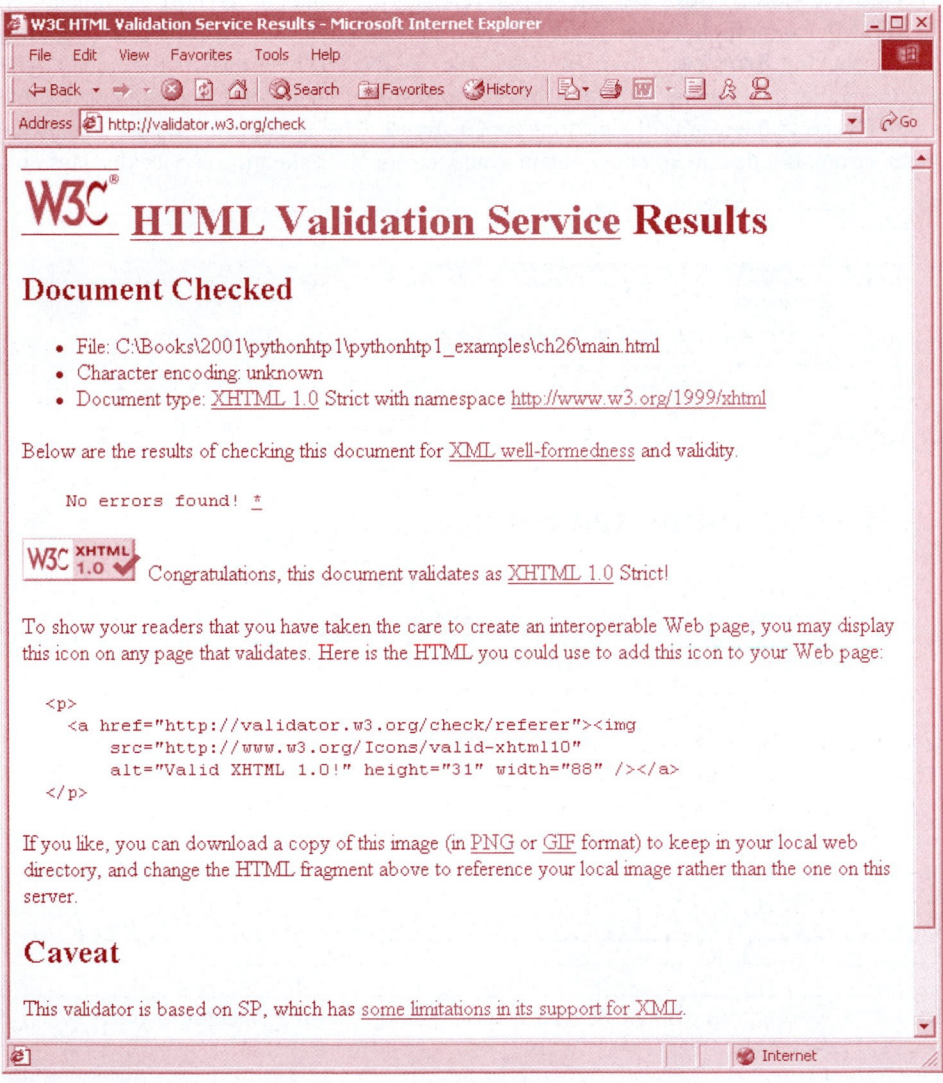

Fig. I.3   XHTML validation results of **main.html**, containing no syntax errors. (Courtesy of World Wide Web Consortium (W3C).)

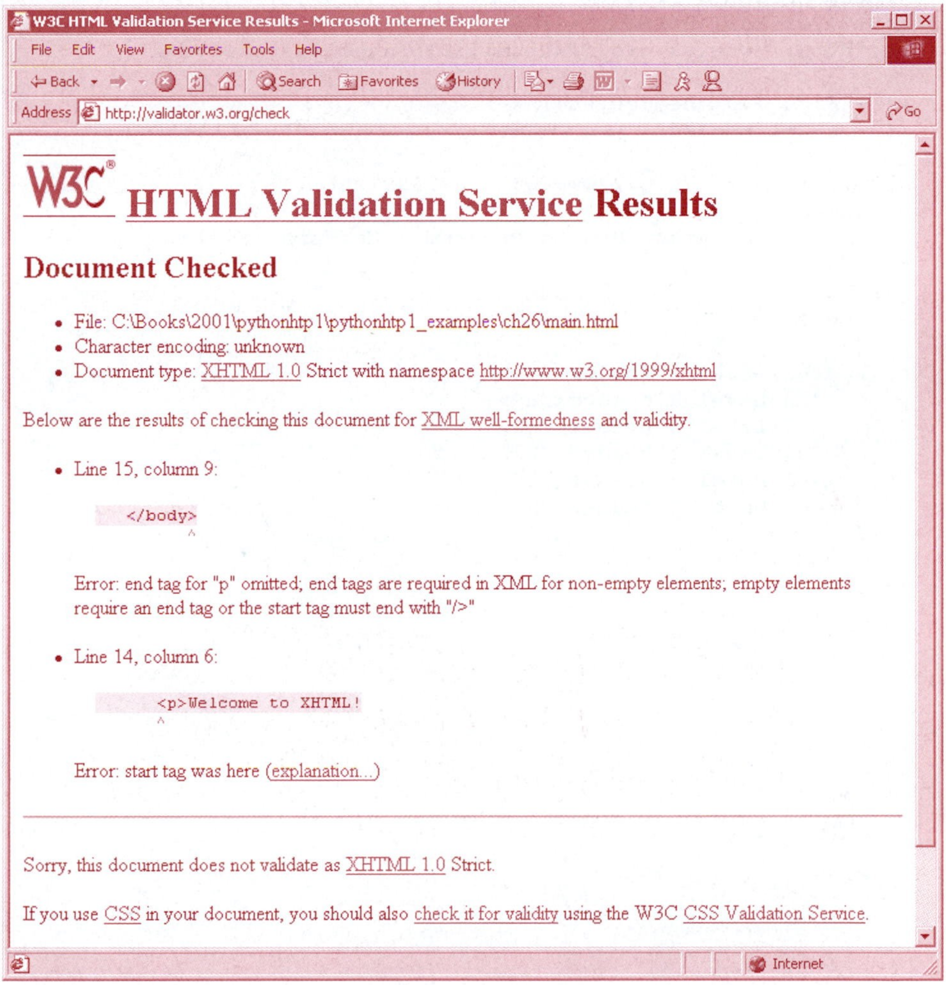

![W3C HTML Validation Service Results screenshot]

W3C HTML Validation Service Results – Microsoft Internet Explorer

File   Edit   View   Favorites   Tools   Help

Back   →   ·   Search   Favorites   History   ·   ·   ·

Address   http://validator.w3.org/check   Go

W3C® HTML Validation Service Results

Document Checked

- File: C:\Books\2001\pythonhtp1\pythonhtp1_examples\ch26\main.html
- Character encoding: unknown
- Document type: XHTML 1.0 Strict with namespace http://www.w3.org/1999/xhtml

Below are the results of checking this document for XML well-formedness and validity.

- Line 15, column 9:

```
        </body>
            ^
```

  Error: end tag for "p" omitted; end tags are required in XML for non-empty elements; empty elements require an end tag or the start tag must end with "/>"

- Line 14, column 6:

```
        <p>Welcome to XHTML!
       ^
```

  Error: start tag was here (explanation...)

___

Sorry, this document does not validate as XHTML 1.0 Strict.

If you use CSS in your document, you should also check it for validity using the W3C CSS Validation Service.

Internet

Fig. I.4   XHTML validation results of **main.html** containing a syntax error. (Courtesy of World Wide Web Consortium (W3C).)

I.5 Headers

Some text in an XHTML document may be more important than others. For example, the text in this section is considered more important than a footnote. XHTML provides six *headers*, called *header elements*, for specifying the relative importance of information. Figure I.5 demonstrates these elements (**h1** through **h6**).

Portability Tip I.1

The text size used to display each header element can vary significantly between browsers. In Appendix K, we discuss how to control the text size and other text properties.

```
1   <?xml version = "1.0"?>
2   <!DOCTYPE html PUBLIC "-//W3C//DTD XHTML 1.0 Strict//EN"
3       "http://www.w3.org/TR/xhtml1/DTD/xhtml1-strict.dtd">
4
5   <!-- Fig. I.5: header.html -->
6   <!-- XHTML headers.          -->
7
8   <html xmlns = "http://www.w3.org/1999/xhtml">
9      <head>
10        <title>Python How to Program - Headers</title>
11     </head>
12
13     <body>
14
15        <h1>Level 1 Header</h1>
16        <h2>Level 2 header</h2>
17        <h3>Level 3 header</h3>
18        <h4>Level 4 header</h4>
19        <h5>Level 5 header</h5>
20        <h6>Level 6 header</h6>
21
22     </body>
23  </html>
```

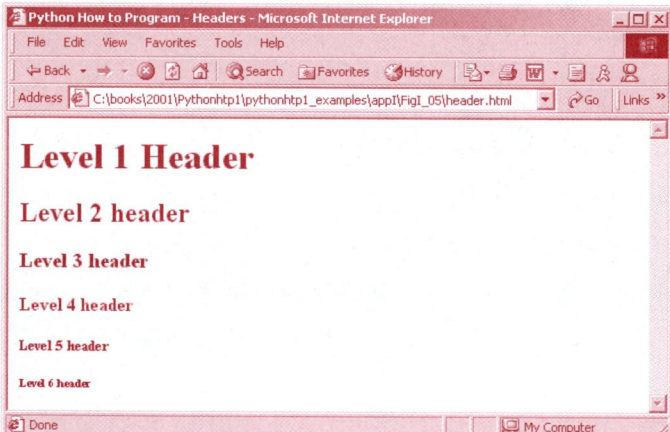

Fig. I.5   Header elements **h1** through **h6**.

Header element **h1** (line 15) is considered the most significant header and is rendered in a larger font than the other five headers (lines 16–20). Each successive header element (i.e., **h2**, **h3**, etc.) is rendered in a smaller font.

Look-and-Feel Observation I.1

Placing a header at the top of every XHTML page helps viewers understand the purpose of each page.

Look-and-Feel Observation I.2

Use larger headers to emphasize more important sections of a Web page.

I.6 Linking

One of the most important XHTML features is the *hyperlink,* which references (or *links* to) other resources such as XHTML documents and images. In XHTML, both text and images can act as hyperlinks. Web browsers typically underline text hyperlinks and color their text blue by default, so that users can distinguish hyperlinks from plain text. In Fig. I.6, we create text hyperlinks to four different Web sites.

Line 17 introduces the **<strong>** tag. Browsers typically display text marked up with **<strong>** in a bold font.

Links are created using the **a** (*anchor*) *element.* Line 20 defines a hyperlink that links the text **Deitel** to the URL assigned to attribute **href**, which specifies the location of a linked resource, such as a Web page, a file or an e-mail address. This particular anchor element links to a Web page located at **http://www.deitel.com**. When a URL does not indicate a specific document on the Web site, the Web server returns a default Web page. This pages often is called **index.html**; however, most Web servers can be configured to to use any file as the default Web page for the site. (Open **http://www.deitel.com** in one browser window and **http://www.deitel.com/index.html** in a second browser window to confirm that they are identical.) If the Web server cannot locate a requested document, the server returns an error indication to the Web browser, and the browser displays an error message to the user.

```
1   <?xml version = "1.0"?>
2   <!DOCTYPE html PUBLIC "-//W3C//DTD XHTML 1.0 Strict//EN"
3       "http://www.w3.org/TR/xhtml1/DTD/xhtml1-strict.dtd">
4
5   <!-- Fig. I.6: links.html        -->
6   <!-- Introduction to hyperlinks. -->
7
8   <html xmlns = "http://www.w3.org/1999/xhtml">
9      <head>
10        <title>Python How to Program - Links</title>
11     </head>
12
13     <body>
14
15        <h1>Here are my favorite sites</h1>
16
17        <p><strong>Click a name to go to that page.</strong></p>
18
19        <!-- create four text hyperlinks -->
20        <p><a href = "http://www.deitel.com">Deitel</a></p>
21
22        <p><a href = "http://www.prenhall.com">Prentice Hall</a></p>
23
24        <p><a href = "http://www.yahoo.com">Yahoo!</a></p>
25
26        <p><a href = "http://www.usatoday.com">USA Today</a></p>
27
28     </body>
29  </html>
```

Fig. I.6   Linking to other Web pages. (Part 1 of 2.)

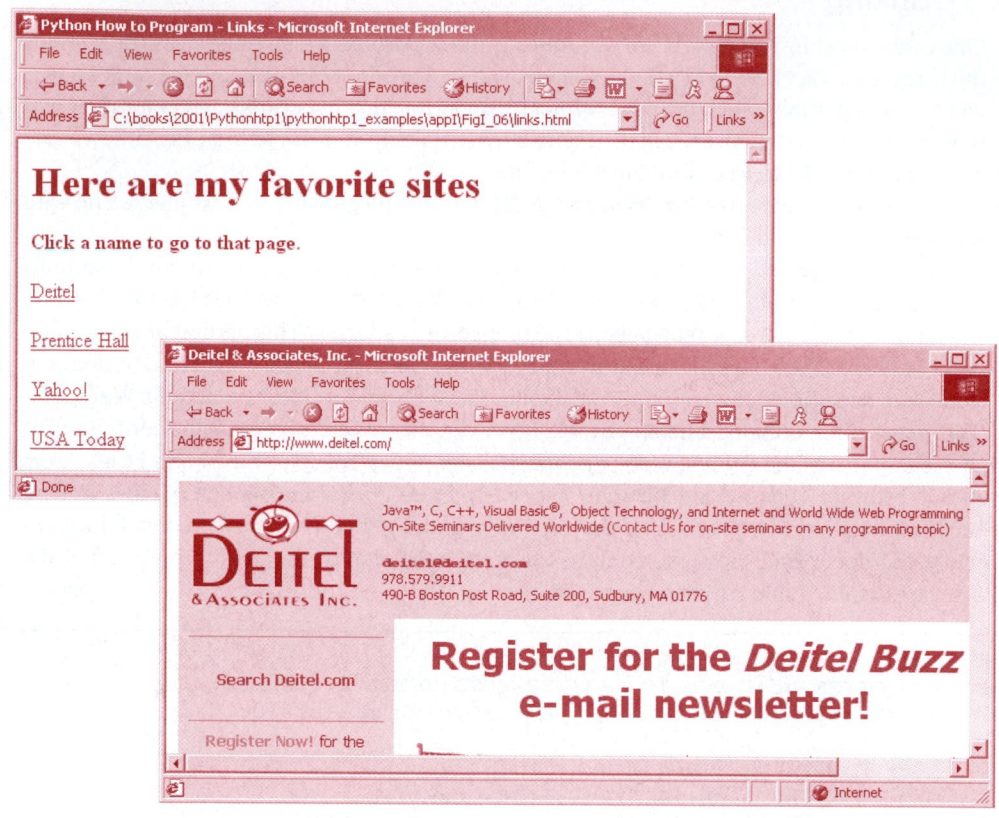

Fig. I.6   Linking to other Web pages. (Part 2 of 2.)

Anchors can link to e-mail addresses using a **mailto:** URL. When someone clicks this type of anchored link, most browsers launch the default e-mail program (e.g., Outlook Express) to enable the user to write an e-mail message to the linked address. Figure I.7 demonstrates this type of anchor.

```
1   <?xml version = "1.0"?>
2   <!DOCTYPE html PUBLIC "-//W3C//DTD XHTML 1.0 Strict//EN"
3      "http://www.w3.org/TR/xhtml1/DTD/xhtml1-strict.dtd">
4
5   <!-- Fig. I.7: contact.html    -->
6   <!-- Adding email hyperlinks. -->
7
8   <html xmlns = "http://www.w3.org/1999/xhtml">
9      <head>
10        <title>Python How to Program - Contact Page
11        </title>
12     </head>
13
```

Fig. I.7   Linking to an e-mail address. (Part 1 of 2.)

```
14      <body>
15
16          <p>My email address is
17              <a href = "mailto:deitel@deitel.com">
18                  deitel@deitel.com
19              </a>
20              . Click the address and your browser will
21              open an e-mail message and address it to me.
22          </p>
23      </body>
24  </html>
```

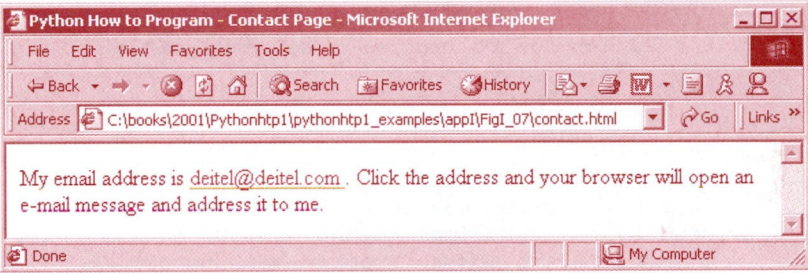

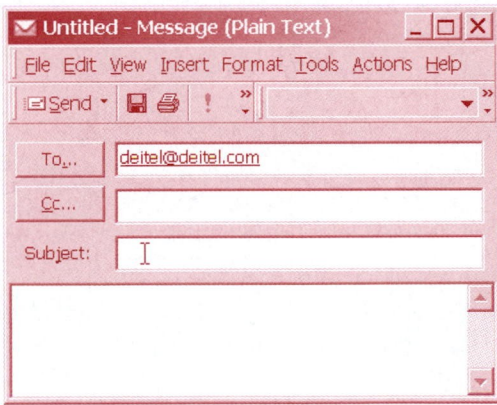

Fig. I.7   Linking to an e-mail address. (Part 2 of 2.)

Lines 17–19 contain an e-mail link. The form of an e-mail anchor is **<a href = "mailto:***emailaddress***">...</a>**. In this case, we link to the e-mail address **deitel@deitel.com**.

I.7 Images

The examples discussed so far demonstrated how to mark up documents that contain only text. However, most Web pages contain both text and images. In fact, images are an equal and essential part of Web-page design. The two most popular image formats used by Web developers are *Graphics Interchange Format (GIF)* and *Joint Photographic Experts Group (JPEG)* images. Users can create images using specialized software such as Adobe Photo-

Shop Elements and Jasc Paint Shop Pro.[5] Images may also be acquired from various Web sites, such as **gallery.yahoo.com**. Figure I.8 demonstrates how to incorporate images into Web pages.

```
1   <?xml version = "1.0"?>
2   <!DOCTYPE html PUBLIC "-//W3C//DTD XHTML 1.0 Strict//EN"
3       "http://www.w3.org/TR/xhtml1/DTD/xhtml1-strict.dtd">
4
5   <!-- Fig. I.8: picture.html     -->
6   <!-- Adding images with XHTML. -->
7
8   <html xmlns = "http://www.w3.org/1999/xhtml">
9      <head>
10        <title>Python How to Program - Welcome</title>
11     </head>
12
13     <body>
14
15        <p><img src = "pythonhtp.jpg" height = "238" width = "183"
16            alt = "Python How to Program book cover" />
17           <img src = "jhtp.jpg" height = "238" width = "183"
18            alt = "Java How to Program book cover" />
19        </p>
20     </body>
21  </html>
```

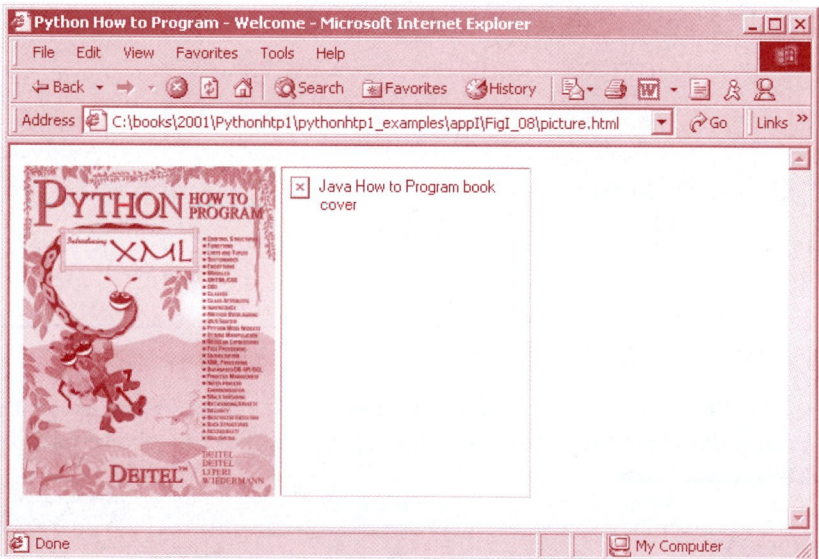

Fig. I.8   Placing images in XHTML files.

---

5. The CD-ROM that accompanies this book contains a 90-day evaluation version of Paint Shop Pro.™

Lines 15–16 use an *img* element to insert an image in the document. The image file's location is specified with the **img** element's *src* attribute. In this case, the image is located in the same directory as this XHTML document, so only the image's file name is required. Optional attributes *width* and *height* specify the image's width and height, respectively. The document author can scale an image by increasing or decreasing the values of the image **width** and **height** attributes. If these attributes are omitted, the browser uses the image's actual width and height. Images are measured in *pixels* ("picture elements"), which represent dots of color on the screen. The image in Fig. I.8 is **183** pixels wide and **238** pixels high.

Good Programming Practice I.4

Always include the **width** *and the* **height** *of an image in the* **<img>** *tag. When the browser loads the XHTML file, it knows immediately from these attributes how much screen space to provide for the image and lays out the page properly, even before it downloads the image.*

Performance Tip I.1

Including the **width** *and* **height** *attributes in an* **<img>** *tag can result in the browser loading and rendering pages faster.*

Common Programming Error I.4

Entering new dimensions for an image that change its inherent width-to-height ratio distorts the appearance of the image. For example, if your image is 200 pixels wide and 100 pixels high, you should ensure that any new dimensions have a 2:1 width-to-height ratio.

Every **img** element in an XHTML document has an *alt* attribute. If a browser cannot render an image, the browser displays the **alt** attribute's value. A browser may not be able to render an image for several reasons. It may not support images—as is the case with a *text-based browser* (i.e., a browser that can display only text)—or the client may have disabled image viewing to reduce download time. Figure I.8 shows Internet Explorer 5.5 rendering the **alt** attribute's value when a document references a nonexistent image file (**jhtp.jpg**).

Some XHTML elements (called *empty elements*) contain only attributes and do not mark up text (i.e., text is not placed between the start and end tags). Empty elements (e.g., **img**) must be terminated, either by using the *forward slash character* (*/*) inside the closing right angle bracket (**>**) of the start tag or by explicitly including the end tag. When using the forward slash character, we add a space before the forward slash to improve readability (as shown at the ends of lines 16 and 18). Rather than using the forward slash character, lines 17–18 could be written with a closing **</img>** tag as follows:

```
<img src = "jhtp.jpg" height = "238" width = "183"
    alt = "Java How to Program book cover"></img></p>
```

By using images as hyperlinks, Web developers can create graphical Web pages that link to other resources. In Fig. I.9, we create six different image hyperlinks.

Lines 17–20 create an *image hyperlink* by nesting an **img** element nested in an anchor (**a**) element. The value of the **img** element's **src** attribute value specifies that this image (**links.jpg**) resides in a directory named **buttons**. The **buttons** directory and the XHTML document are in the same directory. Images from other Web documents also can be referenced (after obtaining permission from the document's owner) by setting the **src** attribute to the name and location of the image.

On line 20, we introduce the *br element*, which most browsers render as a *line break*. Any markup or text following a **br** element is rendered on the next line. Like the **img** ele-

ment, **br** is an example of an empty element terminated with a forward slash. We add a
space before the forward slash to enhance readability.

```
1   <?xml version = "1.0"?>
2   <!DOCTYPE html PUBLIC "-//W3C//DTD XHTML 1.0 Strict//EN"
3       "http://www.w3.org/TR/xhtml1/DTD/xhtml1-strict.dtd">
4
5   <!-- Fig. I.9: nav.html              -->
6   <!-- Using images as link anchors. -->
7
8   <html xmlns = "http://www.w3.org/1999/xhtml">
9       <head>
10          <title>Python How to Program - Navigation Bar
11          </title>
12      </head>
13
14      <body>
15
16          <p>
17              <a href = "links.html">
18                  <img src = "buttons/links.jpg" width = "65"
19                      height = "50" alt = "Links Page" />
20              </a><br />
21
22              <a href = "list.html">
23                  <img src = "buttons/list.jpg" width = "65"
24                      height = "50" alt = "List Example Page" />
25              </a><br />
26
27              <a href = "contact.html">
28                  <img src = "buttons/contact.jpg" width = "65"
29                      height = "50" alt = "Contact Page" />
30              </a><br />
31
32              <a href = "header.html">
33                  <img src = "buttons/header.jpg" width = "65"
34                      height = "50" alt = "Header Page" />
35              </a><br />
36
37              <a href = "table.html">
38                  <img src = "buttons/table.jpg" width = "65"
39                      height = "50" alt = "Table Page" />
40              </a><br />
41
42              <a href = "form.html">
43                  <img src = "buttons/form.jpg" width = "65"
44                      height = "50" alt = "Feedback Form" />
45              </a><br />
46          </p>
47
48      </body>
49  </html>
```

Fig. I.9   Images used as link anchors. (Part 1 of 2.)

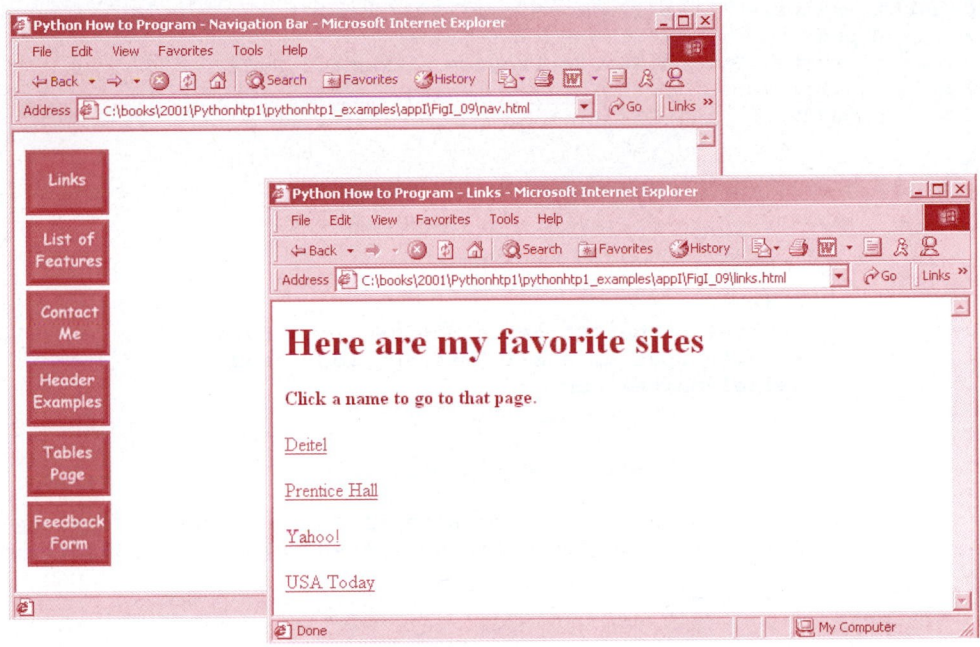

Fig. I.9   Images used as link anchors. (Part 2 of 2.)

I.8 Special Characters and More Line Breaks

In the marking up of text, certain characters or symbols (e.g., **<**) may be difficult to embed directly into an XHTML document. Some keyboards may not provide these symbols, or the presence of these symbols may cause syntax errors. For example, the markup

```
<p>if x < 10 then increment x by 1</p>
```

results in a syntax error because it uses the less-than character (**<**), which is reserved for start tags and end tags such as **<p>** and **</p>**. XHTML provides *special characters* or *entity references* (in the form **&*code*;**) for representing these characters. We could correct the previous line by writing

```
<p>if x &lt; 10 then increment x by 1</p>
```

which uses the special character **<** for the less-than symbol. Figure I.10 demonstrates how to use special characters in an XHTML document.

```
1   <?xml version = "1.0"?>
2   <!DOCTYPE html PUBLIC "-//W3C//DTD XHTML 1.0 Strict//EN"
3       "http://www.w3.org/TR/xhtml1/DTD/xhtml1-strict.dtd">
4
5   <!-- Fig. I.10: contact2.html        -->
6   <!-- Inserting special characters. -->
7
```

Fig. I.10   Inserting special characters into XHTML. (Part 1 of 2.)

```
 8   <html xmlns = "http://www.w3.org/1999/xhtml">
 9      <head>
10         <title>Python How to Program - Contact Page
11         </title>
12      </head>
13
14      <body>
15
16         <!-- special characters are entered -->
17         <!-- using the form &code;              -->
18         <p>
19            Click
20            <a href = "mailto:deitel@deitel.com">here
21            </a> to open an e-mail message addressed to
22            deitel@deitel.com.
23         </p>
24
25         <hr /> <!-- inserts a horizontal rule -->
26
27         <p>All information on this site is <strong>&copy;</strong>
28            Deitel <strong>&amp;</strong> Associates, Inc. 2002.</p>
29
30         <!-- to strike through text use <del> tags    -->
31         <!-- to subscript text use <sub> tags         -->
32         <!-- to superscript text use <sup> tags       -->
33         <!-- these tags are nested inside other tags -->
34         <p><del>You may download 3.14 x 10<sup>2</sup>
35            characters worth of information from this site.</del>
36            Only <sub>one</sub> download per hour is permitted.</p>
37
38         <p>Note: <strong>&lt; &frac14;</strong> of the information
39            presented here is updated daily.</p>
40
41      </body>
42   </html>
```

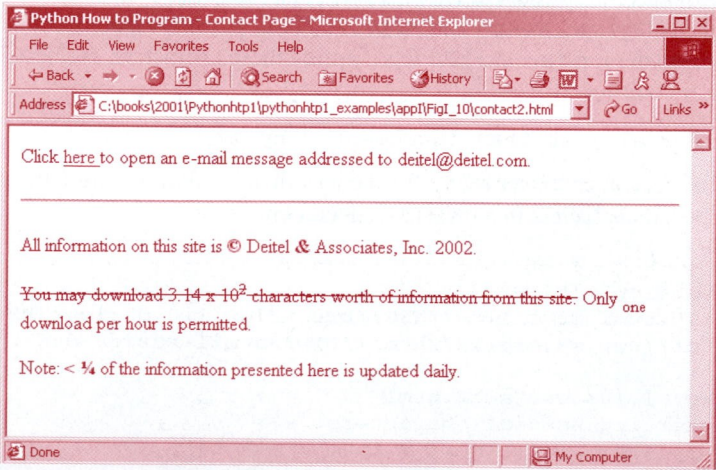

Fig. I.10   Inserting special characters into XHTML. (Part 2 of 2.)

Lines 27–28 contain other special characters, which are expressed as either word abbreviations (e.g., **amp** for ampersand and **copy** for copyright) or *hexadecimal (hex)* values (e.g., **&** is the hexadecimal representation of **&**). Hexadecimal numbers are base-16 numbers—digits in a hexadecimal number have values from 0 to 15 (a total of 16 different values). The letters A–F represent the hexadecimal digits corresponding to decimal values 10–15. Thus in hexadecimal notation we can have numbers like 876 consisting solely of decimal-like digits, numbers like DA19F consisting of digits and letters, and numbers like DCB consisting solely of letters. We discuss hexadecimal numbers in detail in Appendix C, Number Systems.

In lines 34–36, we introduce three new elements. Most browsers render the *del* element as strike-through text. With this format users can easily indicate document revisions. To *superscript* text (i.e., raise text on a line with a decreased font size) or *subscript* text (i.e., lower text on a line with a decreased font size), use the *sup* and *sub* elements, respectively. We also use special characters **<** for a less-than sign and *¼* for the fraction 1/4 (line 38).

In addition to special characters, this document introduces a *horizontal rule*, indicated by the **<hr />** tag in line 24. Most browsers render a horizontal rule as a horizontal line. The **<hr />** tag also inserts a line break above and below the horizontal line.

I.9 Unordered Lists

Up to this point, we have presented basic XHTML elements and attributes for linking to resources, creating headers, using special characters and incorporating images. In this section, we discuss how to organize information on a Web page, using lists. In Appendix J, Introduction to XHTML: Part 2, we introduce another feature for organizing information, called a table. Figure I.11 displays text in an *unordered list* (i.e., a list that does not order its items by letter or number). The *unordered list element* **ul** creates a list in which each item begins with a bullet symbol (called a *disc*).

Each entry in an unordered list (element **ul** in line 20) is an *li* (*list item*) element (lines 23, 25, 27 and 29). Most Web browsers render these elements with a line break and a bullet symbol indented from the beginning of the new line.

```
1   <?xml version = "1.0"?>
2   <!DOCTYPE html PUBLIC "-//W3C//DTD XHTML 1.0 Strict//EN"
3      "http://www.w3.org/TR/xhtml1/DTD/xhtml1-strict.dtd">
4
5   <!-- Fig. I.11: links2.html              -->
6   <!-- Unordered list containing hyperlinks. -->
7
8   <html xmlns = "http://www.w3.org/1999/xhtml">
9      <head>
10         <title>Python How to Program - Links</title>
11      </head>
12
13      <body>
14
15         <h1>Here are my favorite sites</h1>
```

Fig. I.11   Unordered lists in XHTML. (Part 1 of 2.)

```
16
17            <p><strong>Click on a name to go to that page.</strong></p>
18
19            <!-- create an unordered list -->
20            <ul>
21
22                <!-- add four list items -->
23                <li><a href = "http://www.deitel.com">Deitel</a></li>
24
25                <li><a href = "http://www.w3.org">W3C</a></li>
26
27                <li><a href = "http://www.yahoo.com">Yahoo!</a></li>
28
29                <li><a href = "http://www.cnn.com">CNN</a></li>
30            </ul>
31        </body>
32    </html>
```

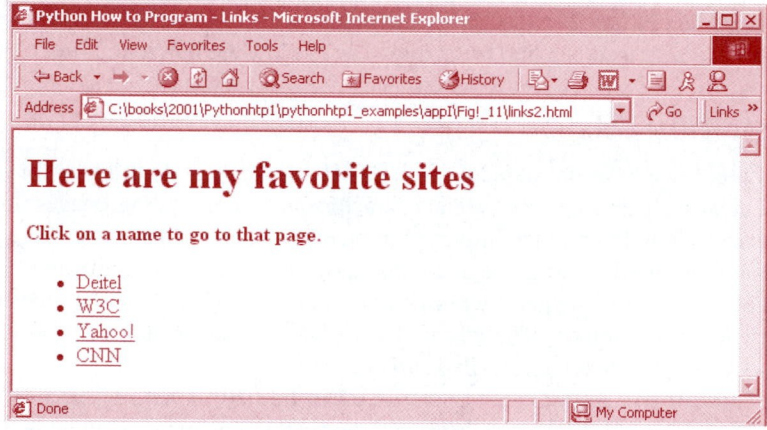

Fig. I.11   Unordered lists in XHTML. (Part 2 of 2.)

I.10 Nested and Ordered Lists

Lists may be nested to represent hierarchical relationships, as in an outline format.
Figure I.12 demonstrates nested lists and *ordered lists* (i.e., list that order their items by letter or number).

```
1    <?xml version = "1.0"?>
2    <!DOCTYPE html PUBLIC "-//W3C//DTD XHTML 1.0 Transitional//EN"
3        "http://www.w3.org/TR/xhtml1/DTD/xhtml1-transitional.dtd">
4
5    <!-- Fig. I.12: list.html              -->
6    <!-- Advanced Lists: nested and ordered. -->
7
8    <html xmlns = "http://www.w3.org/1999/xhtml">
```

Fig. I.12   Nested and ordered lists in XHTML. (Part 1 of 3.)

```
 9      <head>
10         <title>Python How to Program - Lists</title>
11      </head>
12
13      <body>
14
15         <h1>The Best Features of the Internet</h1>
16
17         <!-- create an unordered list -->
18         <ul>
19            <li>You can meet new people from countries around
20               the world.</li>
21            <li>
22               You have access to new media as it becomes public:
23
24               <!-- this starts a nested list, which uses a -->
25               <!-- modified bullet. The list ends when you -->
26               <!-- close the <ul> tag.                     -->
27               <ul>
28                  <li>New games</li>
29                  <li>
30                     New applications
31
32                     <!-- ordered nested list -->
33                     <ol type = "I">
34                        <li>For business</li>
35                        <li>For pleasure</li>
36                     </ol>
37                  </li>
38
39                  <li>Around the clock news</li>
40                  <li>Search engines</li>
41                  <li>Shopping</li>
42                  <li>
43                     Programming
44
45                     <!-- another nested ordered list -->
46                     <ol type = "a">
47                        <li>XML</li>
48                        <li>Java</li>
49                        <li>XHTML</li>
50                        <li>Python</li>
51                        <li>New languages</li>
52                     </ol>
53
54                  </li>
55
56               </ul> <!-- ends the nested list of line 27 -->
57            </li>
58
59            <li>Links</li>
60            <li>Keeping in touch with old friends</li>
61            <li>It is the technology of the future!</li>
```

Fig. I.12   Nested and ordered lists in XHTML. (Part 2 of 3.)

```
62
63      </ul>    <!-- ends the unordered list of line 18 -->
64
65      <h1>My 3 Favorite <em>CEOs</em></h1>
66
67      <!-- ol elements without a type attribute          -->
68      <!-- have a numeric sequence type (i.e., 1, 2, ...) -->
69      <ol>
70         <li>Ant Chovy</li>
71         <li>Anna Lee Tic</li>
72         <li>Albert Antstein</li>
73      </ol>
74
75   </body>
76 </html>
```

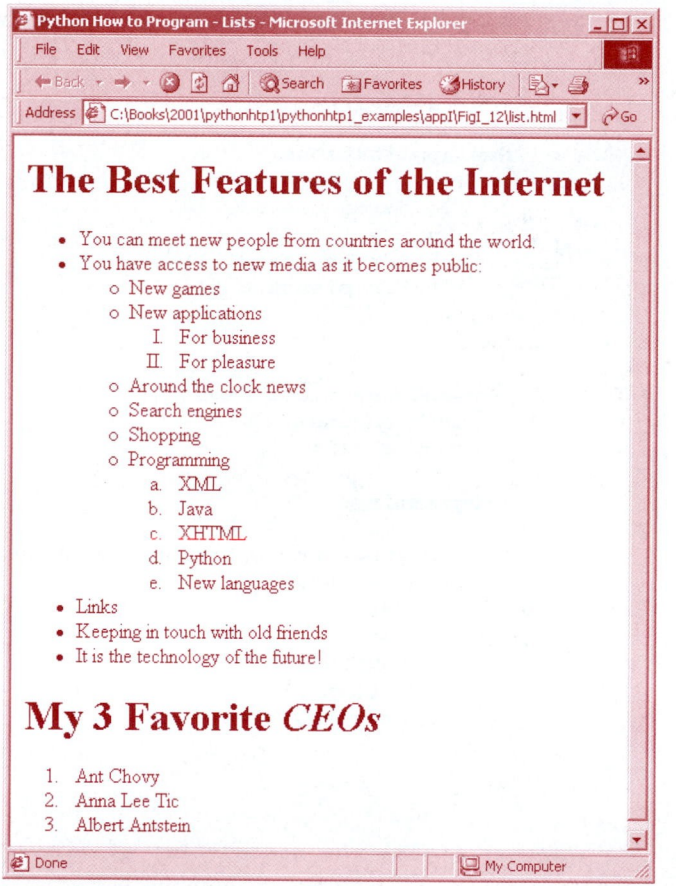

Fig. I.12   Nested and ordered lists in XHTML. (Part 3 of 3.)

   The first ordered list begins on line 33. Attribute **type** specifies the *sequence type* (i.e., the set of numbers or letters used in the ordered list). In this case, setting **type** to **"I"** specifies upper-case Roman numerals. Line 46 begins the second ordered list and sets attribute

type to **"a"**, specifying lowercase letters for the list items. The last ordered list (lines 64–68) does not use attribute **type**. By default, the list's items are enumerated from 1 to 3.

A Web browser indents each nested list to indicate a hierarchal relationship. By default, the items in the outermost unordered list (line 18) are preceded by discs. List items nested inside the unordered list of line 18 are preceded by *circles*. Although not demonstrated in this example, subsequent nested list items are preceded by *squares*. Unordered list items may be explicitly set to discs, circles or squares by setting the **ul** element's **type** attribute to **"disc"**, **"circle"** or **"square"**, respectively.

XHTML is based on HTML (HyperText Markup Language)—a legacy technology of the World Wide Web Consortium (W3C). In HTML, it was common to specify the document's content, structure and formatting. Formatting might specify where the browser places an element in a Web page or the fonts and colors used to display an element. The so called *strict* form of XHTML allows only a document's content and structure to appear in a valid XHTML document, and not that document's formatting. Our first several examples used only the strict form of XHTML. In fact, the purpose of lines 2–3 in each of the examples before Fig. I.12 was to indicate to the browser that each document conformed to the strict XHTML definition. This enables the browser to confirm that the document is valid. There are other XHTML document types as well. This particular example uses the XHTML *transitional* document type. This document type exists to enable XHTML document creators to use legacy HTML technologies in an XHTML document. In this example, the **type** attribute of the **ol** element (lines 33 and 46) is a legacy HTML technology. Changing lines 2–3 as shown in this example enables us to demonstrate ordered lists with different numbering formats. Normally, such formatting is specified with style sheets (Appendix K, Cascading Style Sheets).

Testing and Debugging Tip 25.2

Most current browsers still attempt to render XHTML documents, even if they are invalid.

I.11 Internet and World Wide Web Resources

www.w3.org/TR/xhtml1
The *XHTML 1.0 Recommendation* contains XHTML 1.0 general information, compatibility issues, document type definition information, definitions, terminology and much more.

www.xhtml.org
XHTML.org provides XHTML development news and links to other XHTML resources, which include books and articles.

www.w3schools.com/xhtml/default.asp
The *XHTML School* provides XHTML quizzes and references. This page also contains links to XHTML syntax, validation and document type definitions.

validator.w3.org
This is the W3C XHTML validation service site.

hotwired.lycos.com/webmonkey/00/50/index2a.html
This site provides an article about XHTML. Key sections of the article overview XHTML and discuss tags, attributes and anchors.

wdvl.com/Authoring/Languages/XML/XHTML
The Web Developers Virtual Library provides an introduction to XHTML. This site also contains articles, examples and links to other technologies.

www.w3.org/TR/1999/xhtml-modularization-19990406/DTD/doc
The XHTML 1.0 DTD documentation site provides links to DTD documentation for the strict, transitional and frameset document type definitions.

SUMMARY

- XHTML (Extensible Hypertext Markup Language) is a markup language for creating Web pages.

- A key issue when using XHTML is the separation of the presentation of a document (i.e., the document's appearance when rendered by a browser) from the structure of the information in the document.

- In XHTML, text is marked up with elements, delimited by tags that are names contained in pairs of angle brackets. Some elements may contain additional markup called attributes, which provide additional information about the element.

- A machine that runs specialized piece of software called a Web server stores XHTML documents and sends them to client machines that request them.

- XHTML documents that are syntactically correct are guaranteed to render properly. XHTML documents that contain syntax errors might not display properly.

- Validation services (e.g., **validator.w3.org**) ensure that an XHTML document is syntactically correct.

- Every XHTML document contains a start **<html>** tag and an end **</html>** tag.

- Comments in XHTML always begin with **<!--** and end with **-->**. The browser ignores all text inside a comment.

- Every XHTML document contains a **head** element, which generally contains information, such as a title, and a **body** element, which contains the page content. Information in the **head** element generally is not rendered in the display window but may be made available to the user through other means.

- The **title** element names a Web page. The title usually appears in the colored bar (called the title bar) at the top of the browser window and also appears as the text identifying a page when users add your page to their list of **Favorites** or **Bookmarks**.

- The body of an XHTML document is the area in which the document's content is placed. The content may include text and tags.

- All text placed between the **<p>** and **</p>** tags forms one paragraph.

- XHTML provides six headers (**h1** through **h6**) for specifying the relative importance of information. Header element **h1** is considered the most significant header and is rendered in a larger font than the other five headers. Each successive header element (i.e., **h2**, **h3**, etc.) is rendered in a smaller font.

- Web browsers typically underline text hyperlinks and color them blue by default.

- The **<strong>** tag renders text in a bold font.

- Users can insert links with the **a** (anchor) element. The most important attribute for the **a** element is **href**, which specifies the resource (e.g., page or e-mail address) being linked.

- Anchors can link to an e-mail address, using a **mailto:** URL. When someone clicks this type of anchored link, most browsers launch the default e-mail program (e.g., Outlook Express) to initiate e-mail messages to the linked addresses.

- The **img** element's **src** attribute specifies an image's location. Optional attributes **width** and **height** specify the image width and height, respectively. Images are measured in pixels ("picture elements"), which represent dots of color on the screen. Every **img** element in a valid XHTML document must have an **alt** attribute, which contains text that is displayed if the client cannot render the image.

• The **alt** attribute makes Web pages more accessible to users with disabilities, especially those with vision impairments.

• Some XHTML elements are empty elements and contain only attributes and do not mark up text. Empty elements (e.g., **img**) must be terminated, either by using the forward slash character (**/**) or by explicitly writing an end tag.

• The **br** element causes most browsers to render a line break. Any markup or text following a **br** element is rendered on the next line.

• XHTML provides special characters or entity references (in the form **&***code***;**) for representing characters that cannot be marked up.

• Most browsers render a horizontal rule, indicated by the **<hr />** tag, as a horizontal line. The **hr** element also inserts a line break above and below the horizontal line.

• The unordered list element **ul** creates a list in which each item in the list begins with a bullet symbol (called a disc). Each entry in an unordered list is an **li** (list item) element. Most Web browsers render these elements with a line break and a bullet symbol at the beginning of the line.

• Lists may be nested to represent hierarchical data relationships.

• Attribute **type** specifies the sequence type (i.e., the set of numbers or letters used in the ordered list).

TERMINOLOGY

<!--...--> (XHTML comment)
a element
alt attribute
& (& special character)
anchor
angle brackets (**< >**)
attribute
body element
br (line break) element
comments in XHTML
© (© special character)
disc
element
e-mail anchor
empty tag
Extensible Hypertext Markup
    Language (XHTML)
head element
header
header elements (**h1** through **h6**)
height attribute
hexadecimal code
<hr /> tag (horizontal rule)
href attribute
.htm (XHTML file-name extension)
<html> tag
.html (XHTML file-name extension)
hyperlink

image hyperlink
img element
level of nesting
<li> (list item) tag
linked document
mailto: URL
markup language
nested list
ol (ordered list) element
p (paragraph) element
special character
src attribute (**img**)
<strong> tag
sub element
subscript
superscript
syntax
tag
text editor
title element
type attribute
unordered-list element (**ul**)
valid document
Web page
width attribute
World Wide Web (WWW)
XHTML (Extensible Hypertext
    Markup Language)

XHTML comment	XML declaration
XHTML markup	**xmlns** attribute
XHTML tag	

SELF-REVIEW EXERCISES

I.1 State whether the following are *true* or *false*. If *false*, explain why.
  a) Attribute **type**, when used with an **ol** element, specifies a sequence type.
  b) An ordered list cannot be nested inside an unordered list.
  c) XHTML is an acronym for XML HTML.
  d) Element **br** represents a line break.
  e) Hyperlinks are marked up with **<link>** tags.

I.2 Fill in the blanks in each of the following statements:
  a) The _____ element inserts a horizontal rule.
  b) A superscript is marked up using element _____, and a subscript is marked up using element _____.
  c) The least important header element is _____, and the most important header element is _____.
  d) Element _____ marks up an unordered list.
  e) Element _____ marks up a paragraph.

ANSWERS TO SELF-REVIEW EXERCISES

I.1 a) True. b) False. An ordered list can be nested inside an unordered list. c) False. XHTML is an acronym for Extensible HyperText Markup Language. d) True. e) False. A hyperlink is marked up with **<a>** tags.

I.2 a) **hr**. b) **sup**, **sub**. c) **h6**, **h1**. d) **ul**. e) **p**.

EXERCISES

I.3 Use XHTML to create a document that contains the correct elements to mark up the following text:

> *Python How to Program*
> *Welcome to the world of Python programming. We have provided extensive coverage on Python.*

Use **h1** for the title (the first line of text), **p** for text (the second and third lines of text) and **sub** for each word that begins with a capital letter. Insert a horizontal rule between the **h1** element and the **p** element. Open your new document in a Web browser to view the marked up document.

I.4 Why is the following markup invalid?

```
<p>Here is some text...
<hr />
<p>And some more text...</p>
```

I.5 Why is the following markup invalid?

```
<p>Here is some text...<br>
And some more text...</p>
```

I.6 An image named **deitel.gif** is 200 pixels wide and 150 pixels high. Use the **width** and **height** attributes of the **<img>** tag to (a) increase the size of the image by 100%; (b) increase the size of the image by 50%; and (c) change the width-to-height ratio to 2:1, keeping the **width** attained in part (a). Write separate XHTML statements for parts (a), (b) and (c).

I.7   Create a link to each of the following: (a) **index.html**, located in the **files** directory; (b) **index.html**, located in the **text** subdirectory of the **files** directory; (c) **index.html**, located in the **other** directory in your *parent directory* (*Hint*: **..** signifies parent directory.); and (d) A link to the President of the United States' e-mail address (**president@whitehouse.gov**).

I.8   Create an XHTML document that marks up your resume.

I.9   Create an XHTML document containing three ordered lists: ice cream, soft serve and frozen yogurt. Each ordered list should contain a nested, unordered list of your favorite flavors. Provide a minimum of three flavors in each unordered list.

I.10   Create an XHTML document that uses an image as an e-mail link. Use attribute **alt** to provide a description of the image and link.

I.11   Create an XHTML document that contains an unordered list of your favorite Web sites. Your page should contain the header "My Favorite Web Sites."

I.12   Create an XHTML document that contains links to all the examples presented in this appendix. (*Hint*: Place all the appendix examples in one directory.)

I.13   Modify the XHTML document (**picture.html**) in Fig. I.8 by removing all end tags. Validate this document via the W3C validation service. What happens? Next remove the **alt** attributes from the **<img>** tags and revalidate your document. What happens?

I.14   Identify each of the following as either an element or an attribute:
   a) **html**.
   b) **width**.
   c) **href**.
   d) **br**.
   e) **h3**.
   f) **a**.
   g) **src**.

I.15   State which of the following statements are *true* and which are *false*. If *false*, explain why.
   a) A valid XHTML document can contain uppercase letters in element names.
   b) Tags need not be closed in a valid XHTML document.
   c) XHTML documents can have the file extension **.htm**.
   d) Valid XHTML documents can contain tags that overlap.
   e) **&less;** is the special character for the less-than (**<**) character.
   f) In a valid XHTML document, **<li>** can be nested inside either **<ol>** or **<ul>** tags.

I.16   Fill in the blanks for each of the following statements:
   a) XHTML comments begin with **<!--** and end with _____.
   b) In XHTML, attribute values must be enclosed in _____.
   c) _____ is the special character for an ampersand.
   d) Element _____ can be used to bold text.

Introduction to XHTML: Part 2

Objectives

- To create tables with rows and columns of data.
- To control table formatting.
- To create and use forms.
- To create and use image maps to aid in Web-page navigation.
- To make Web pages accessible to search engines using **`<meta>`** tags.
- To set the **`frameset`** element to display multiple Web pages in a single browser window.

Yea, from the table of my memory
I'll wipe away all trivial fond records.
William Shakespeare

J.1 Introduction

In the previous appendix, we introduced XHTML. We built several complete Web pages featuring text, hyperlinks, images, horizontal rules and line breaks. In this appendix, we discuss more substantial XHTML features, including presentation of information in *tables* and *incorporation of forms* for collecting information from a Web-page visitor. We also introduce *internal linking* and *image maps* for enhancing Web-page navigation and *frames* for displaying multiple documents in the browser.

By the end of this appendix, you will be familiar with the most commonly used XHTML features and will be able to create more complex Web documents. In Appendix K, Cascading Style Sheets (CSS), we discuss how to make Web pages more visually appealing by manipulating fonts, colors and text.

J.2 Basic XHTML Tables

This section presents XHTML *tables*—a frequently used feature that organizes data into rows and columns. Our first example (Fig. J.1) uses a table with six rows and two columns to display price information for fruit.

Tables are defined with the **table** element. Lines 16–18 specify the start tag for a table element that has several attributes. The **border** attribute specifies the width of the table's border, in pixels. To create a table without a border, set **border** to **"0"**. This example assigns (**"40%"**) to attribute **width** to set the table's width to 40 percent of the browser's width. A developer can also set attribute **width** to a specified number of pixels.

Testing and Debugging Tip J.1

Resize the browser window to see how the width of the window affects the width of the table.

As its name implies, attribute **summary** (line 17) describes the table's contents. Speech devices use this attribute to make the table more accessible to users with visual

```
 1   <?xml version = "1.0"?>
 2   <!DOCTYPE html PUBLIC "-//W3C//DTD XHTML 1.0 Strict//EN"
 3      "http://www.w3.org/TR/xhtml1/DTD/xhtml1-strict.dtd">
 4
 5   <!-- Fig. J.1: table1.html    -->
 6   <!-- Creating a basic table. -->
 7
 8   <html xmlns = "http://www.w3.org/1999/xhtml">
 9      <head>
10         <title>A simple XHTML table</title>
11      </head>
12
13      <body>
14
15         <!-- the <table> tag opens a table -->
16         <table border = "1" width = "40%"
17            summary = "This table provides information about
18               the price of fruit">
19
20            <!-- the <caption> tag summarizes the table's     -->
21            <!-- contents (this helps the visually impaired) -->
22            <caption><strong>Price of Fruit</strong></caption>
23
24            <!-- the <thead> is the first section of a table -->
25            <!-- it formats the table header area            -->
26            <thead>
27               <tr>                <!-- <tr> inserts a table row -->
28                  <th>Fruit</th> <!-- insert a heading cell -->
29                  <th>Price</th>
30               </tr>
31            </thead>
32
33            <!-- all table content is enclosed  -->
34            <!-- within the <tbody>              -->
35            <tbody>
36               <tr>
37                  <td>Apple</td> <!-- insert a data cell -->
38                  <td>$0.25</td>
39               </tr>
40
41               <tr>
42                  <td>Orange</td>
43                  <td>$0.50</td>
44               </tr>
45
46               <tr>
47                  <td>Banana</td>
48                  <td>$1.00</td>
49               </tr>
50
51               <tr>
52                  <td>Pineapple</td>
53                  <td>$2.00</td>
```

Fig. J.1   XHTML table. (Part 1 of 2.)

```
54                          </tr>
55                      </tbody>
56
57                      <!-- the <tfoot> is the last section of a table -->
58                      <!-- it formats the table footer                 -->
59                      <tfoot>
60                          <tr>
61                              <th>Total</th>
62                              <th>$3.75</th>
63                          </tr>
64                      </tfoot>
65
66              </table>
67
68          </body>
69      </html>
```

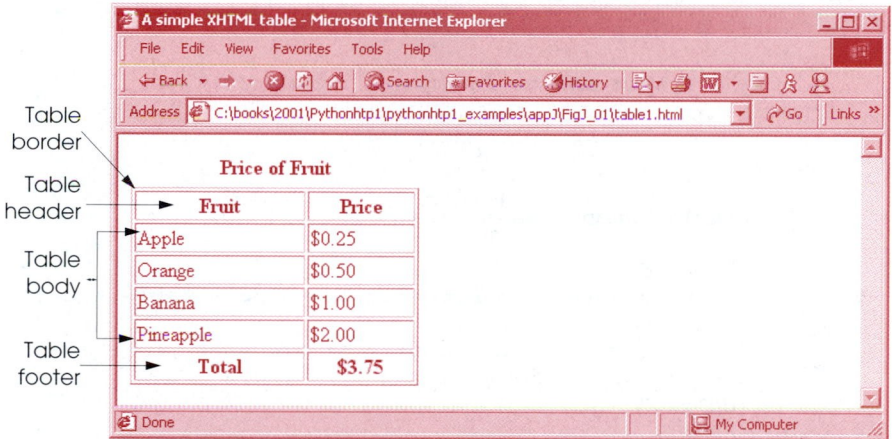

Fig. J.1   XHTML table. (Part 2 of 2.)

impairments. The **caption** element (line 22) describes the table's content and helps text-based browsers interpret the data in the table. Text inside the **<caption>** tag is rendered above the table by most browsers. Attribute **summary** and element **caption** are two of many XHTML features that make Web pages more accessible to users with disabilities.

A table has three distinct sections—*head*, *body* and *foot*. The head section (or *header cell*) is defined with a **thead** element (lines 26–31), which contains header information such as column names. Each **tr** element (lines 27–30) defines an individual *table row*. The columns in the head section are defined with **th** elements. Most browsers center and display text formatted by **th** (table header column) elements in bold. Table header elements are nested inside table row elements.

The body section, or *table body*, contains the table's primary data. The table body (lines 35–55) is defined in a **tbody** element. *Data cells* contain individual pieces of data and are defined with **td** (*table data*) elements.

The foot section (lines 59–64) is defined with a **tfoot** (table foot) element and represents a footer. Common text placed in the footer includes calculation results and footnotes. Like other sections, the foot section can contain table rows, and each row can contain columns.

J.3 Intermediate XHTML Tables and Formatting

In the previous section, we explored the structure of a basic table. In Fig. J.2, we enhance our discussion of tables by introducing elements and attributes that allow the author of the document to build more complex tables.

```
1    <?xml version = "1.0"?>
2    <!DOCTYPE html PUBLIC "-//W3C//DTD XHTML 1.0 Strict//EN"
3       "http://www.w3.org/TR/xhtml1/DTD/xhtml1-strict.dtd">
4
5    <!-- Fig. J.2: table2.html      -->
6    <!-- Intermediate table design. -->
7
8    <html xmlns = "http://www.w3.org/1999/xhtml">
9       <head>
10         <title>Python How to Program - Tables</title>
11      </head>
12
13      <body>
14
15         <h1>Table Example Page</h1>
16
17         <table border = "1">
18            <caption>Here is a more complex sample table.</caption>
19
20            <!-- <colgroup> and <col> tags are used to -->
21            <!-- format entire columns                 -->
22            <colgroup>
23
24               <!-- span attribute determines how many columns -->
25               <!-- the <col> tag affects                      -->
26               <col align = "right" span = "1" />
27            </colgroup>
28
29            <thead>
30
31               <!-- rowspans and colspans merge the specified   -->
32               <!-- number of cells vertically or horizontally  -->
33               <tr>
34
35                  <!-- merge two rows -->
36                  <th rowspan = "2">
37                     <img src = "snake.gif" width = "220"
38                        height = "100" alt = "python picture" />
39                  </th>
40
41                  <!-- merge four columns -->
42                  <th colspan = "4" valign = "top">
43                     <h1>Python comparison</h1><br />
```

Fig. J.2   Complex XHMTL table. (Part 1 of 2.)

```
44                      <p>Approximate as of 12/2001</p>
45                  </th>
46              </tr>
47
48              <tr valign = "bottom">
49                  <th>Average Length (Feet)</th>
50                  <th>Indigenous region</th>
51                  <th>Arboreal?</th>
52              </tr>
53
54          </thead>
55
56          <tbody>
57
58              <tr>
59                  <th>Indian Python</th>
60                  <td>20</td>
61                  <td>southeast Asia</td>
62                  <td rowspan = "2">Indian Python</td>
63              </tr>
64
65              <tr>
66                  <th>Royal Python</th>
67                  <td>4</td>
68                  <td>equatorial West Africa</td>
69              </tr>
70
71          </tbody>
72
73      </table>
74
75  </body>
76 </html>
```

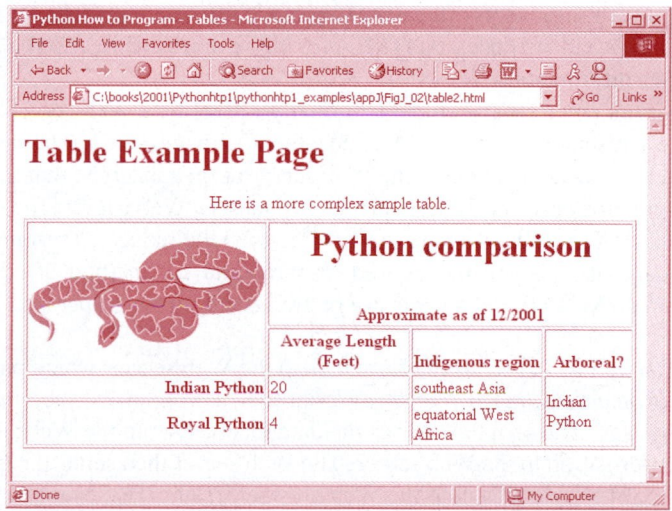

Fig. J.2   Complex XHMTL table. (Part 2 of 2.)

The table begins on line 17. Element **colgroup** (lines 22–27) groups and formats columns. The **col** element (line 26) specifies two attributes in this example. The **align** attribute determines the alignment of text in the column. The **span** attribute determines how many columns the **col** element formats. In this case, we set **align**'s value to **"right"** and **span**'s value to **"1"** to right-align text in the first column (the column containing the picture of the camel in the sample screen capture).

Table cells are sized to fit the data they contain. Document authors can create large data cells by using attributes **rowspan** and **colspan**. The values assigned to these attributes specify the number of rows or columns, respectively, occupied by a cell. The **th** element in lines 36–39 uses the attribute **rowspan = "2"** to allow the cell containing the picture of the camel to use two vertically adjacent cells. Thus, the cell *spans* two rows. The **th** element in lines 42–45 uses the attribute **colspan = "4"** to widen the header cell (containing **Python comparison** and **Approximate as of 12/2001**) to span four cells.

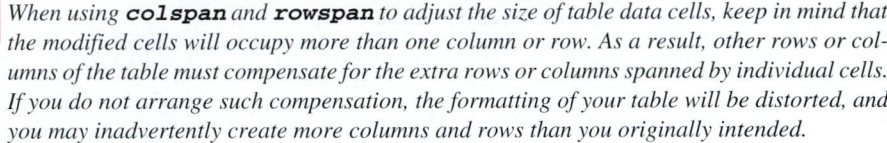

Common Programming Error J.1

*When using **colspan** and **rowspan** to adjust the size of table data cells, keep in mind that the modified cells will occupy more than one column or row. As a result, other rows or columns of the table must compensate for the extra rows or columns spanned by individual cells. If you do not arrange such compensation, the formatting of your table will be distorted, and you may inadvertently create more columns and rows than you originally intended.*

Line 42 introduces attribute **valign**, which aligns data vertically and may be assigned one of four values: **"top"** aligns data with the top of the cell, **"middle"** vertically centers data (the default for all data and header cells), **"bottom"** aligns data with the bottom of the cell and **"baseline"** ignores the fonts used for the row data and sets the bottom of all text in the row on a common *baseline* (i.e., the horizontal line to which each character in a word is aligned).

J.4 Basic XHTML Forms

When browsing Web sites, users often need to provide information such as e-mail addresses, search keywords and zip codes. XHTML provides a mechanism, called a *form*, for collecting such user information.

Data that users enter on a Web page normally is sent to a Web server that provides access to a site's resources (e.g., XHTML documents, images, etc.). These resources are either located on the same machine as the Web server or on a machine that the Web server can access through the network. When a browser requests a Web page or file that is located on a server, the server processes the request and returns the requested resource. A request contains the name and path of the desired resource and the method of communication (called a *protocol*). XHTML documents use or are served by the HyperText Transfer Protocol (HTTP).

The program in Fig. J.3 sends the form data to the Web server, which passes the form data to a *CGI* (*Common Gateway Interface*) script (i.e., a program) written in Python, C or some other language. The script processes the data received from the Web server and typically returns information to the Web server. The Web server then sends the information in the form of an XHTML document to the Web browser. [*Note*: This example demonstrates client-side functionality only. If the form is submitted (by clicking **Submit Your Entries**), an error occurs.]

```
1    <?xml version = "1.0"?>
2    <!DOCTYPE html PUBLIC "-//W3C//DTD XHTML 1.0 Strict//EN"
3        "http://www.w3.org/TR/xhtml1/DTD/xhtml1-strict.dtd">
4
5    <!-- Fig. J.3: form.html    -->
6    <!-- Form Design Example 1. -->
7
8    <html xmlns = "http://www.w3.org/1999/xhtml">
9       <head>
10         <title>Python How to Program - Forms</title>
11      </head>
12
13      <body>
14
15         <h1>Feedback Form</h1>
16
17         <p>Please fill out this form to help
18            us improve our site.</p>
19
20         <!-- this tag starts the form, gives the   -->
21         <!-- method of sending information and the -->
22         <!-- location of form scripts              -->
23         <form method = "post" action = "/cgi-bin/formmail">
24
25            <p>
26               <!-- hidden inputs contain nonvisual  -->
27               <!-- information                      -->
28               <input type = "hidden" name = "recipient"
29                  value = "deitel@deitel.com" />
30               <input type = "hidden" name = "subject"
31                  value = "Feedback Form" />
32               <input type = "hidden" name = "redirect"
33                  value = "main.html" />
34            </p>
35
36            <!-- <input type = "text"> inserts a text box -->
37            <p><label>Name:
38                  <input name = "name" type = "text" size = "25"
39                     maxlength = "30" />
40               </label></p>
41
42            <p>
43
44               <!-- input types "submit" and "reset" insert  -->
45               <!-- buttons for submitting and clearing the   -->
46               <!-- form's contents                          -->
47               <input type = "submit" value =
48                  "Submit Your Entries" />
49               <input type = "reset" value =
50                  "Clear Your Entries" />
51            </p>
52
53         </form>
```

Fig. J.3   Simple form with hidden fields and a text box. (Part 1 of 2.)

```
54
55    </html>
```

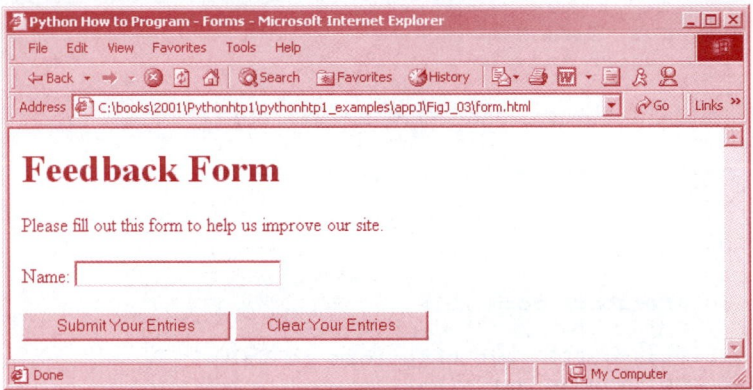

Fig. J.3   Simple form with hidden fields and a text box. (Part 2 of 2.)

Forms can contain visual and nonvisual components. Visual components include clickable buttons and other graphical user interface components with which users interact. Nonvisual components, called *hidden inputs*, store data that the document author specifies, such as e-mail addresses and XHTML document file names that act as links. The form begins on line 23 with the **form** element. Attribute **method** specifies how the form's data is sent to the Web server.

method = "post" appends form data to the browser's request, which contains the protocol (i.e., HTTP) and the requested resource's URL. Scripts located on the Web server's computer (or on a computer accessible through the network) can access the form data sent as part of the request. For example, a script may take the form information and update an electronic mailing list. The other possible value, **method = "get"**, appends the form data directly to the end of the URL. For example, the URL **/cgi-bin/formmail** might have the form information **name = Nicole** appended to it as in Fig. J.4.

The **action** attribute in the **<form>** tag specifies the URL of a script on the Web server; in this case, it specifies a script that e-mails form data to an address. Most *Internet Service Providers* (*ISPs*) have a script like this on their site; ask the Web site's system administrator how to set up an XHTML document to use the script correctly.

Lines 28–33 define three **input** elements that specify data to provide to the script that processes the form (also called the *form handler*). These three **input** elements have **type** attribute **"hidden"**, which allows the document author to send form data that is not entered by a user to a script.

The three hidden inputs are an e-mail address to which the data will be sent, the e-mail's subject line and a URL where the browser will be redirected after submitting the form. Two other **input** attributes are **name**, which identifies the **input** element, and **value**, which provides the value that will be sent (or posted) to the Web server.

Good Programming Practice J.1

*Place hidden **input** elements at the beginning of a form, immediately after the opening* **<form>** *tag, so document authors can locate hidden **input** elements quickly.*

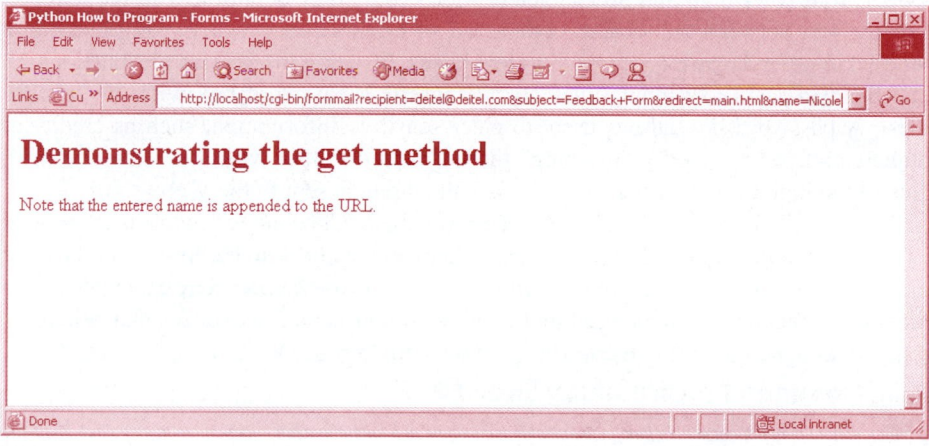

Fig. J.4   Method **get** appending entry to a URL.

We introduce another **type** of **input** in lines 38–39. The **"text"** input inserts a *text box* into the form. Users can type data in text boxes. The **label** element (lines 37–40) provides users with information about the **input** element's purpose.

Common Programming Error J.2

*Failure to include a **label** element for each form element is a design error. Without these labels, users cannot determine the purpose of individual form elements.*

The **input** element's **size** attribute specifies the number of characters visible in the text box. Optional attribute **maxlength** limits the number of characters input into the text box. In this case, the user is not permitted to type more than **30** characters into the text box.

There are two types of **input** elements in lines 47–50. The **"submit"** input element is a button. When the user presses a **"submit"** button, the browser sends the data in the form to the Web server for processing. The **value** attribute sets the text displayed on the button (the default value is **Submit**). The **"reset"** input element allows a user to reset all **form** elements to their default values. The **value** attribute of the **"reset"** **input** element sets the text displayed on the button (the default value is **Reset**).

J.5 More Complex XHTML Forms

In the previous section, we introduced basic forms. In this section, we introduce elements and attributes for creating more complex forms. Figure J.5 contains a form that solicits user feedback about a Web site.

The **textarea** element (lines 37–39) inserts a multiline text box, called a *text area*, into the form. The number of rows is specified with the **rows** *attribute*, and the number of columns (i.e., characters) is specified with the **cols** *attribute*. In this example, the **text-**

area is four rows high and 36 characters wide. To display default text in the text area, place the text between the **<textarea>** and **</textarea>** tags. Default text can be specified in other **input** types, such as text boxes, by using the **value** attribute.

The ***"password"*** input (lines 46–47), inserts a password box with the specified **size**. A password box allows users to enter sensitive information, such as credit-card numbers and passwords, by "masking" the information input with asterisks. The actual value of the input, not the asterisks that mask the input, is sent to the Web server.

Lines 54–71 introduce the *checkbox* **form** element. Checkboxes enable users to select from a set of options. When a user selects a checkbox, a check mark appears in the check box. Otherwise, the checkbox remains empty. Each ***"checkbox"*** **input** creates a new checkbox. Checkboxes can be used individually or in groups. Checkboxes that belong to a group are assigned the same **name** (in this case, **"thingsliked"**).

Common Programming Error J.3

*When your **form** has several checkboxes with the same **name**, you must make sure that they have different **values**, or the scripts running on the Web server will not be able to distinguish between them.*

```
1   <?xml version = "1.0"?>
2   <!DOCTYPE html PUBLIC "-//W3C//DTD XHTML 1.0 Strict//EN"
3      "http://www.w3.org/TR/xhtml1/DTD/xhtml1-strict.dtd">
4
5   <!-- Fig. J.5: form2.html   -->
6   <!-- Form Design Example 2. -->
7
8   <html xmlns = "http://www.w3.org/1999/xhtml">
9      <head>
10        <title>Python How to Program - Forms</title>
11     </head>
12
13     <body>
14
15        <h1>Feedback Form</h1>
16
17        <p>Please fill out this form to help
18           us improve our site.</p>
19
20        <form method = "post" action = "/cgi-bin/formmail">
21
22           <p>
23              <input type = "hidden" name = "recipient"
24                 value = "deitel@deitel.com" />
25              <input type = "hidden" name = "subject"
26                 value = "Feedback Form" />
27              <input type = "hidden" name = "redirect"
28                 value = "main.html" />
29           </p>
30
```

Fig. J.5   Form with text areas, password boxes and checkboxes. (Part 1 of 3.)

```
31                <p><label>Name:
32                    <input name = "name" type = "text" size = "25" />
33                </label></p>
34
35                <!-- <textarea> creates a multiline textbox -->
36                <p><label>Comments:<br />
37                    <textarea name = "comments" rows = "4" cols = "36">
38    Enter your comments here.
39                    </textarea>
40                </label></p>
41
42                <!-- <input type = "password"> inserts a    -->
43                <!-- textbox whose display is masked with    -->
44                <!-- asterisk characters                      -->
45                <p><label>E-mail Address:
46                    <input name = "email" type = "password"
47                        size = "25" />
48                </label></p>
49
50                <p>
51                    <strong>Things you liked:</strong><br />
52
53                    <label>Site design
54                    <input name = "thingsliked" type = "checkbox"
55                        value = "Design" /></label>
56
57                    <label>Links
58                    <input name = "thingsliked" type = "checkbox"
59                        value = "Links" /></label>
60
61                    <label>Ease of use
62                    <input name = "thingsliked" type = "checkbox"
63                        value = "Ease" /></label>
64
65                    <label>Images
66                    <input name = "thingsliked" type = "checkbox"
67                        value = "Images" /></label>
68
69                    <label>Source code
70                    <input name = "thingsliked" type = "checkbox"
71                        value = "Code" /></label>
72                </p>
73
74                <p>
75                    <input type = "submit" value =
76                        "Submit Your Entries" />
77                    <input type = "reset" value =
78                        "Clear Your Entries" />
79                </p>
80
81        </form>
82    </html>
```

Fig. J.5   Form with text areas, password boxes and checkboxes. (Part 2 of 3.)

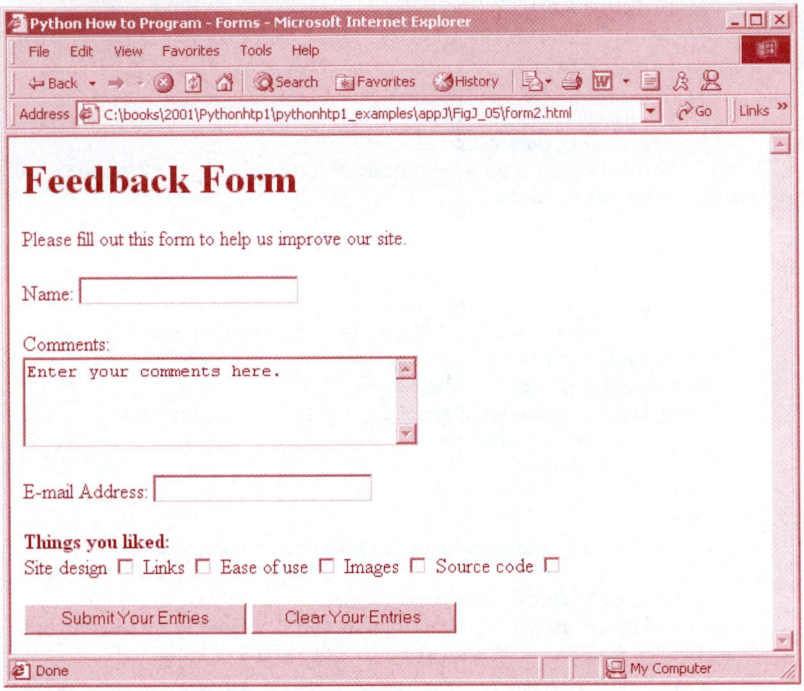

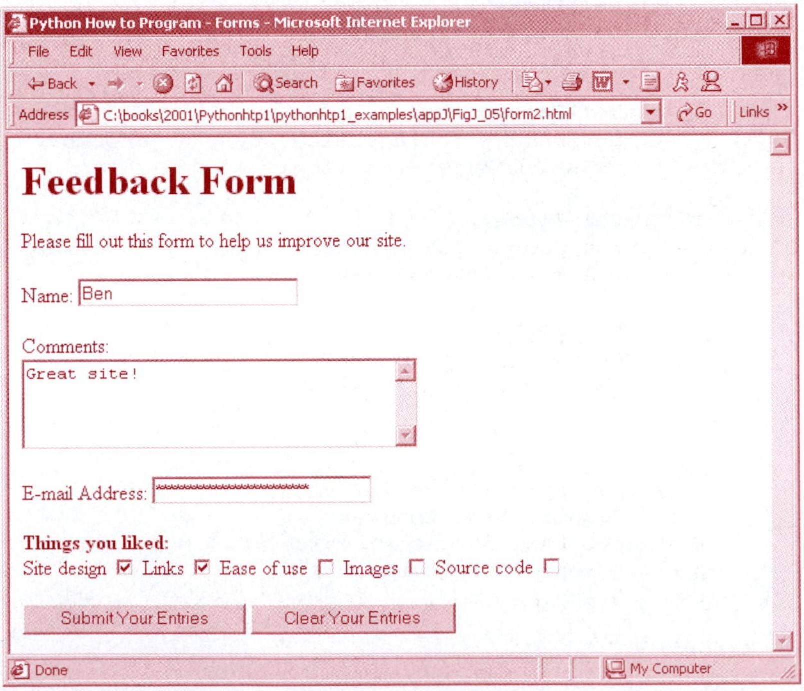

Fig. J.5   Form with text areas, password boxes and checkboxes. (Part 3 of 3.)

We continue our discussion of forms by presenting a third example that introduces several more form elements from which users can make selections (Fig. J.6). In this example, we introduce two new **input** types. The first type is the *radio button* (lines 76–94), specified with type **"radio"**. Radio buttons are similar to checkboxes, except that only one radio button in a group of radio buttons may be selected at any time. All radio buttons in a group have the same **name** attributes and are distinguished by their different **value** attributes. The attribute–value pair ***checked = "checked"*** (line 77) indicates which radio button, if any, is selected initially. The **checked** attribute also applies to checkboxes.

Common Programming Error J.4

*When using a group of radio buttons in a form, forgetting to set the **name** attributes of the radio buttons to the same name lets the user select all the radio buttons at the same time, which is a logic error.*

The ***select*** element (lines 104–117) provides a drop-down list of items from which the user can make a selection. The **name** attribute identifies the drop-down list. The ***option*** element (lines 105–116) adds items to the drop-down list. The **option** element's ***selected*** attribute specifies which item initially is displayed as the selected item in the **select** element.

```
1   <?xml version = "1.0"?>
2   <!DOCTYPE html PUBLIC "-//W3C//DTD XHTML 1.0 Strict//EN"
3       "http://www.w3.org/TR/xhtml1/DTD/xhtml1-strict.dtd">
4
5   <!-- Fig. J.6: form3.html    -->
6   <!-- Form Design Example 3. -->
7
8   <html xmlns = "http://www.w3.org/1999/xhtml">
9      <head>
10         <title>Python How to Program - Forms</title>
11      </head>
12
13      <body>
14
15         <h1>Feedback Form</h1>
16
17         <p>Please fill out this form to help
18            us improve our site.</p>
19
20         <form method = "post" action = "/cgi-bin/formmail">
21
22            <p>
23               <input type = "hidden" name = "recipient"
24                  value = "deitel@deitel.com" />
25               <input type = "hidden" name = "subject"
26                  value = "Feedback Form" />
```

Fig. J.6   Form including radio buttons and drop-down lists. (Part 1 of 4.)

```
27              <input type = "hidden" name = "redirect"
28                 value = "main.html" />
29          </p>
30
31          <p><label>Name:
32              <input name = "name" type = "text" size = "25" />
33          </label></p>
34
35          <p><label>Comments:<br />
36              <textarea name = "comments" rows = "4"
37                 cols = "36"></textarea>
38          </label></p>
39
40          <p><label>E-mail Address:
41              <input name = "email" type = "password"
42                 size = "25" /></label></p>
43
44          <p>
45              <strong>Things you liked:</strong><br />
46
47              <label>Site design
48                 <input name = "thingsliked" type = "checkbox"
49                    value = "Design" /></label>
50
51              <label>Links
52                 <input name = "thingsliked" type = "checkbox"
53                    value = "Links" /></label>
54
55              <label>Ease of use
56                 <input name = "thingsliked" type = "checkbox"
57                    value = "Ease" /></label>
58
59              <label>Images
60                 <input name = "thingsliked" type = "checkbox"
61                    value = "Images" /></label>
62
63              <label>Source code
64                 <input name = "thingsliked" type = "checkbox"
65                    value = "Code" /></label>
66          </p>
67
68          <!-- <input type = "radio" /> creates a radio     -->
69          <!-- button. The difference between radio buttons -->
70          <!-- and checkboxes is that only one radio button -->
71          <!-- in a group can be selected.                  -->
72          <p>
73              <strong>How did you get to our site?:</strong><br />
74
75              <label>Search engine
76                 <input name = "howtosite" type = "radio"
77                    value = "search engine" checked = "checked" />
78              </label>
79
```

Fig. J.6   Form including radio buttons and drop-down lists. (Part 2 of 4.)

```
80                    <label>Links from another site
81                        <input name = "howtosite" type = "radio"
82                            value = "link" /></label>
83
84                    <label>Deitel.com Web site
85                        <input name = "howtosite" type = "radio"
86                            value = "deitel.com" /></label>
87
88                    <label>Reference in a book
89                        <input name = "howtosite" type = "radio"
90                            value = "book" /></label>
91
92                    <label>Other
93                        <input name = "howtosite" type = "radio"
94                            value = "other" /></label>
95
96              </p>
97
98              <p>
99                  <label>Rate our site:
100
101                      <!-- the <select> tag presents a drop-down -->
102                      <!-- list with choices indicated by the     -->
103                      <!-- <option> tags                           -->
104                  <select name = "rating">
105                      <option selected = "selected">Amazing</option>
106                      <option>10</option>
107                      <option>9</option>
108                      <option>8</option>
109                      <option>7</option>
110                      <option>6</option>
111                      <option>5</option>
112                      <option>4</option>
113                      <option>3</option>
114                      <option>2</option>
115                      <option>1</option>
116                      <option>Awful</option>
117                  </select>
118
119              </label>
120          </p>
121
122          <p>
123              <input type = "submit" value =
124                  "Submit Your Entries" />
125              <input type = "reset" value = "Clear Your Entries" />
126          </p>
127
128      </form>
129
130   </body>
131 </html>
```

Fig. J.6   Form including radio buttons and drop-down lists. (Part 3 of 4.)

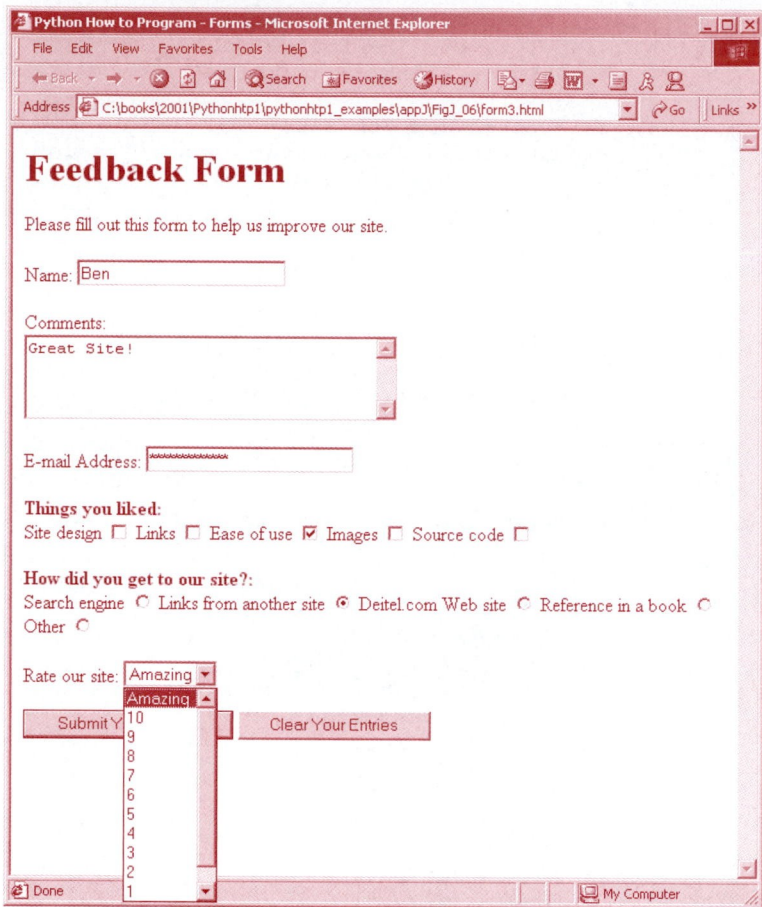

Fig. J.6   Form including radio buttons and drop-down lists. (Part 4 of 4.)

J.6 Internal Linking

In Appendix I, Introduction to XHTML: Part 1, we discussed how to hyperlink one Web page to another. Figure J.7 introduces *internal linking*—a mechanism that enables the user to jump between locations in the same document. Internal linking is useful for long documents that contain many sections. Clicking an internal link enables users to find a section without scrolling through the entire document.

```
1   <?xml version = "1.0"?>
2   <!DOCTYPE html PUBLIC "-//W3C//DTD XHTML 1.0 Strict//EN"
3       "http://www.w3.org/TR/xhtml1/DTD/xhtml1-strict.dtd">
4
5   <!-- Fig. J.7: links.html -->
6   <!-- Internal Linking.    -->
```

Fig. J.7   Internal hyperlinks for making Web pages more navigable. (Part 1 of 3.)

```
 7
 8   <html xmlns = "http://www.w3.org/1999/xhtml">
 9      <head>
10         <title>Python How to Program - List</title>
11      </head>
12
13      <body>
14
15         <!-- <a name = ".."></a> creates an internal hyperlink -->
16         <p><a name = "features"></a></p>
17         <h1>The Best Features of the Internet</h1>
18
19         <!-- an internal link's address is "#linkname"        -->
20         <p><a href = "#ceos">Go to <em>Favorite CEOs</em></a></p>
21
22         <ul>
23            <li>You can meet people from countries
24               around the world.</li>
25
26            <li>You have access to new media as it becomes public:
27               <ul>
28                  <li>New games</li>
29                  <li>New applications
30                     <ul>
31                        <li>For Business</li>
32                        <li>For Pleasure</li>
33                     </ul>
34                  </li>
35
36                  <li>Around the clock news</li>
37                  <li>Search Engines</li>
38                  <li>Shopping</li>
39                  <li>Programming
40                     <ul>
41                        <li>XHTML</li>
42                        <li>Java</li>
43                        <li>Python</li>
44                        <li>Scripts</li>
45                        <li>New languages</li>
46                     </ul>
47                  </li>
48               </ul>
49            </li>
50
51            <li>Links</li>
52            <li>Keeping in touch with old friends</li>
53            <li>It is the technology of the future!</li>
54         </ul>
55
56         <!-- named anchor -->
57         <p><a name = "ceos"></a></p>
58         <h1>My 3 Favorite <em>CEOs</em></h1>
59
```

Fig. J.7   Internal hyperlinks for making Web pages more navigable. (Part 2 of 3.)

```
60        <p>
61
62            <!-- internal hyperlink to features -->
63            <a href = "#features">Go to <em>Favorite Features</em>
64            </a></p>
65
66        <ol>
67            <li>Ant Chovy</li>
68            <li>Anna Lee Tic</li>
69            <li>Albert Antstein</li>
70        </ol>
71
72    </body>
73 </html>
```

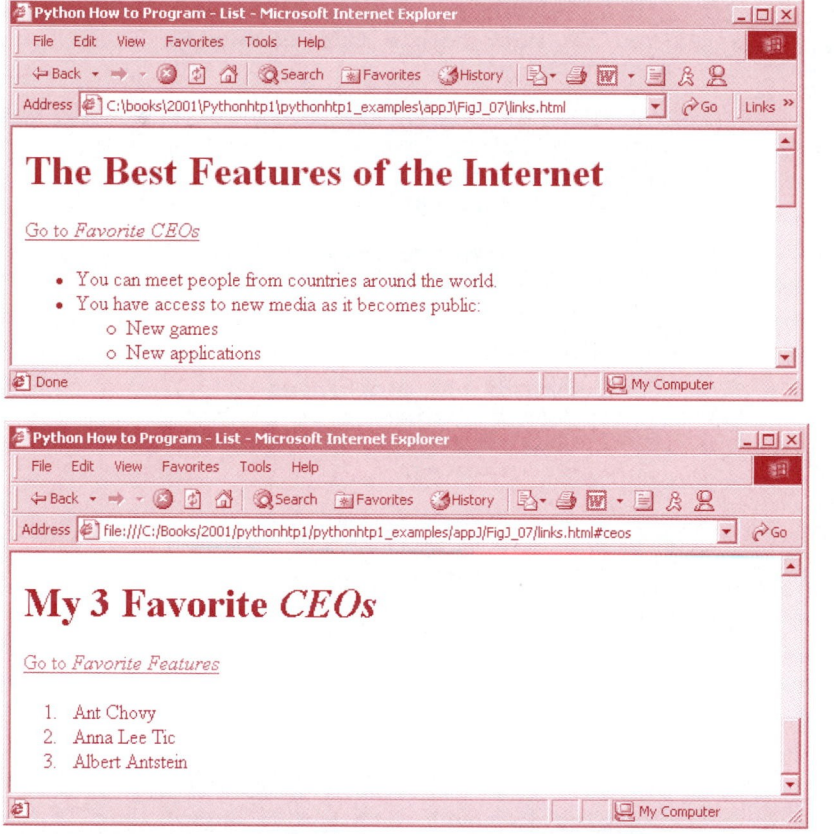

Fig. J.7   Internal hyperlinks for making Web pages more navigable. (Part 3 of 3.)

Line 16 contains a *named anchor* (called **features**) for an internal hyperlink. To link to this type of anchor inside the same Web page, the **href** attribute of another anchor element should include the named anchor preceded by a pound sign (as in **#features**). Lines 63–64 contain a hyperlink with the anchor **features** as its target. Selecting this hyperlink in a Web browser scrolls the browser window to the **features** anchor at line 16.

Look-and-Feel Observation J.1

Internal hyperlinks are useful in XHTML documents that contain large amounts of informa-
tion. Internal links to various sections on the page makes it easier for users to navigate the
page; the users do not have to scroll to find a specific section.

Although not demonstrated in this example, a hyperlink can specify an internal link in another document by specifying the document name followed by a pound sign and the named anchor, as in

        href = "*page.html#name*"

For example, to link to a named anchor called **booklist** in **books.html**, **href** is assigned **"books.html#booklist"**.

J.7 Creating and Using Image Maps

In Appendix I, Introduction to XHTML: Part 1, we demonstrated how images can be used as hyperlinks to link to other resources on the Internet. In this section, we introduce another technique for image linking called *image maps*, which designate certain areas of an image (called *hotspots*) as links. Figure J.8 introduces image maps and hotspots.

```
 1   <?xml version = "1.0" ?>
 2   <!DOCTYPE html PUBLIC "-//W3C//DTD XHTML 1.0 Strict//EN"
 3      "http://www.w3.org/TR/xhtml1/DTD/xhtml1-strict.dtd">
 4
 5   <!-- Fig. J.8: picture.html          -->
 6   <!-- Creating and Using Image Maps. -->
 7
 8   <html xmlns = "http://www.w3.org/1999/xhtml">
 9      <head>
10         <title>
11            Python How to Program - Image Map
12         </title>
13      </head>
14
15      <body>
16
17         <p>
18
19         <!-- the <map> tag defines an image map -->
20         <map id = "picture">
21
22            <!-- shape = "rect" indicates a rectangular  -->
23            <!-- area, with coordinates for the upper-left -->
24            <!-- and lower-right corners                 -->
25            <area href = "form.html" shape = "rect"
26               coords = "2,123,54,143"
27               alt = "Go to the feedback form" />
28            <area href = "contact.html" shape = "rect"
29               coords = "126,122,198,143"
30               alt = "Go to the contact page" />
```

Fig. J.8   Image with links anchored to an image map. (Part 1 of 2.)

```
31              <area href = "main.html" shape = "rect"
32                  coords = "3,7,61,25" alt = "Go to the homepage" />
33              <area href = "links.html" shape = "rect"
34                  coords = "168,5,197,25"
35                  alt = "Go to the links page" />
36
37              <!-- value "poly" creates a hotspot in the shape -->
38              <!-- of a polygon, defined by coords              -->
39              <area shape = "poly" alt = "E-mail the Deitels"
40                  coords = "162,25,154,39,158,54,169,51,183,39,161,26"
41                  href = "mailto:deitel@deitel.com" />
42
43              <!-- shape = "circle" indicates a circular -->
44              <!-- area with the given center and radius -->
45              <area href = "mailto:deitel@deitel.com"
46                  shape = "circle" coords = "100,36,33"
47                  alt = "E-mail the Deitels" />
48          </map>
49
50          <!-- <img src =... usemap = "#id"> indicates that the -->
51          <!-- specified image map is used with this image       -->
52          <img src = "deitel.gif" width = "200" height = "144"
53              alt = "Deitel logo" usemap = "#picture" />
54          </p>
55      </body>
56  </html>
```

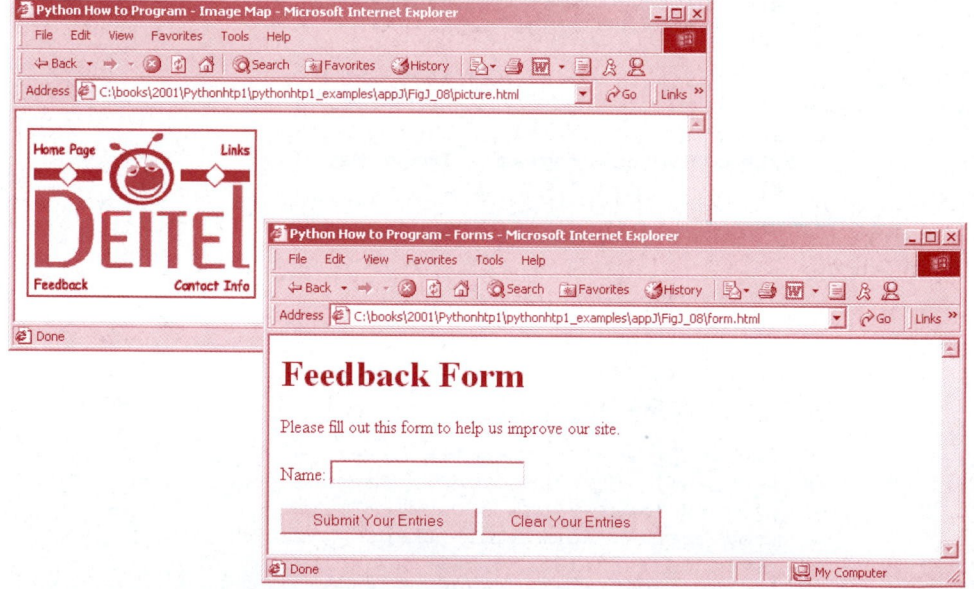

Fig. J.8   Image with links anchored to an image map. (Part 2 of 2.)

Lines 20–48 define image maps using a **map** element. Attribute **id** (line 20) identifies the image map. If **id** is omitted, the map cannot be referenced by an image. We discuss how to reference an image map momentarily. Hotspots are defined with **area** elements (as shown in lines 25–27). Attribute **href** (line 25) specifies the link's target (i.e., the resource to which to link). Attributes **shape** (line 25) and **coords** (line 26) specify the hotspot's shape and coordinates, respectively. Attribute **alt** (line 27) provides alternative text for the link.

Common Programming Error J.5

*Not specifying an **id** attribute for a **map** element prevents an **img** element from using the map's **area** elements to define hotspots.*

The markup on lines 25–27 creates a *rectangular hotspot* (**shape = "rect"**) for the *coordinates* specified in the **coords** attribute. A coordinate pair consists of two numbers that represent the location of a point on the *x*-axis and the *y*-axis, respectively. The *x*-axis extends horizontally and the *y*-axis extends vertically from the upper left corner of the image. Every point on an image has a unique *x–y*-coordinate. For rectangular hotspots, the required coordinates are those of the upper-left and lower right corners of the rectangle. In this case, the upper left corner of the rectangle is located at coordinate 2 on the *x*-axis and coordinate 123 on the *y*-axis, annotated as *(2,123)*. The lower right corner of the rectangle is at *(54,143)*. Coordinates are measured in pixels.

Common Programming Error J.6

Overlapping coordinates of an image map cause the browser to render the first hotspot it encounters for the area.

The map **area** (lines 39–41) assigns the **shape** attribute **"poly"** to create a hotspot in the shape of a polygon, using the coordinates in attribute **coords**. These coordinates represent each *vertex*, or corner, of the polygon. The browser connects these points with lines to form the hotspot's area.

The map **area** (lines 45–47) assigns the **shape** attribute **"circle"** to create a *circular hotspot*. In this case, the **coords** attribute specifies the coordinates of the circle's center and the circle's radius, in pixels.

To use an image map with an **img** element, the **img** element's **usemap** attribute is assigned the **id** of a **map**. Lines 52–53 reference the image map named **"picture"**. The image map resides within the same document, so we use internal linking.

J.8 meta Elements

People use search engines to find useful Web sites. Search engines usually catalog sites by following links from page to page and saving identification and classification information for each page. One way that search engines catalog pages is by reading the content in each page's **meta** elements, which specify information about a document (Fig. J.9).

Two important attributes of the **meta** element are **name**, which identifies the type of **meta** element, and **content**, which provides the information that search engines use to catalog pages. Figure J.9 introduces the **meta** element.

Lines 14–16 demonstrate a **"keywords"** **meta** element. The **content** attribute of such a **meta** element provides search engines with a list of words that describe a page. These words are compared with words in search requests. Thus, including **meta** elements and their **content** information exposes Web sites to a wider audience.

```
1   <?xml version = "1.0"?>
2   <!DOCTYPE html PUBLIC "-//W3C//DTD XHTML 1.0 Strict//EN"
3      "http://www.w3.org/TR/xhtml1/DTD/xhtml1-strict.dtd">
4
5   <!-- Fig. J.9: main.html -->
6   <!-- <meta> tag.          -->
7
8   <html xmlns = "http://www.w3.org/1999/xhtml">
9      <head>
10        <title>Python How to Program - Welcome</title>
11
12        <!-- <meta> tags provide search engines with -->
13        <!-- information used to catalog a site      -->
14        <meta name = "keywords" content = "Web page, design,
15           XHTML, tutorial, personal, help, index, form,
16           contact, feedback, list, links, frame, deitel" />
17
18        <meta name = "description" content = "This Web site will
19           help you learn the basics of XHTML and Web page design
20           through the use of interactive examples and
21           instruction." />
22
23     </head>
24
25     <body>
26
27        <h1>Welcome to Our Web Site!</h1>
28
29        <p>We have designed this site to teach about the wonders
30        of <strong><em>XHTML</em></strong>. <em>XHTML</em> is
31        better equipped than <em>HTML</em> to represent complex
32        data on the Internet. <em>XHTML</em> takes advantage of
33        XML's strict syntax to ensure well-formedness. Soon you
34        will know about many of the great new features of
35        <em>XHTML.</em></p>
36
37        <p>Have Fun With the Site!</p>
38
39     </body>
40   </html>
```

Fig. J.9   **meta** used to provide keywords and a description.

Lines 18–21 demonstrate a **"description" meta** element. The **content** attribute of such a **meta** element provides a three- to four-line description of a site, written in sentence form. Search engines also use this description to catalog your site and sometimes display this information as part of the search results.

Software Engineering Observation 25.6

*meta elements are not visible to users and must be placed inside the **head** section of your XHTML document. If **meta** elements are not placed in this section, they will not be read by search engines.*

J.9 `frameset` Element

All the Web pages we have presented in this book thus far have the ability to link to other pages, but can display only one page at a time. Figure J.10 uses *frames*, which allow the browser to display more than one XHTML document simultaneously, to display the documents in Fig. J.10 and Fig. J.11.

Most of our prior examples conformed to the strict XHTML document type. This particular example uses the *frameset* document type—a special XHTML document type specifically for framesets. This new document type is specified in lines 2–3 and is required for documents that define framesets.

```
1   <?xml version = "1.0"?>
2   <!DOCTYPE html PUBLIC "-//W3C//DTD XHTML 1.0 Frameset//EN"
3       "http://www.w3.org/TR/xhtml1/DTD/xhtml1-frameset.dtd">
4
5   <!-- Fig. J.10: index.html -->
6   <!-- XHTML Frames I.        -->
7
8   <html xmlns = "http://www.w3.org/1999/xhtml">
9       <head>
10          <title>Python How to Program - Welcome</title>
11          <meta name = "keywords" content = "Webpage, design,
12              XHTML, tutorial, personal, help, index, form,
13              contact, feedback, list, links, frame, deitel" />
14
15          <meta name = "description" content = "This Web site will
16              help you learn the basics of XHTML and Web page design
17              through the use of interactive examples
18              and instruction." />
19
20      </head>
21
22      <!-- the <frameset> tag sets the frame dimensions      -->
23      <frameset cols = "110,*">
24
25          <!-- frame elements specify which pages -->
26          <!-- are loaded into a given frame       -->
27          <frame name = "leftframe" src = "nav.html" />
28          <frame name = "main" src = "main.html" />
29
30          <noframes>
31              <p>This page uses frames, but your browser does not
32              support them.</p>
33
34              <p>Please, <a href = "fig27_11.html">follow this link
35              to browse our site without frames</a>.</p>
36          </noframes>
37
38      </frameset>
39  </html>
```

Fig. J.10 Web document containing two frames—navigation and content. (Part 1 of 2.)

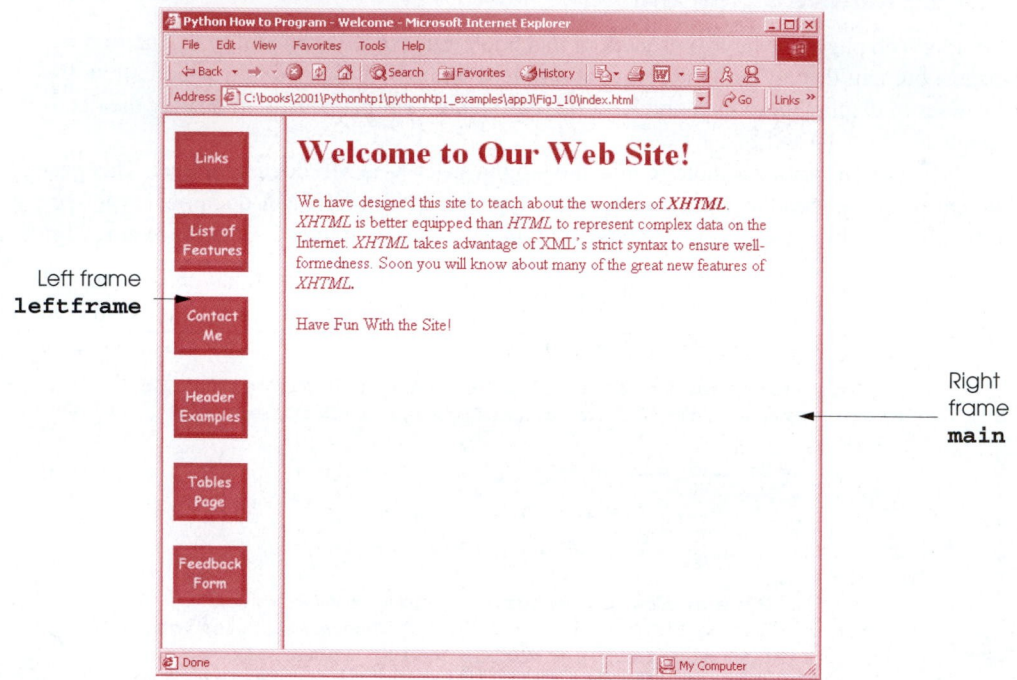

Left frame
leftframe

Right
frame
main

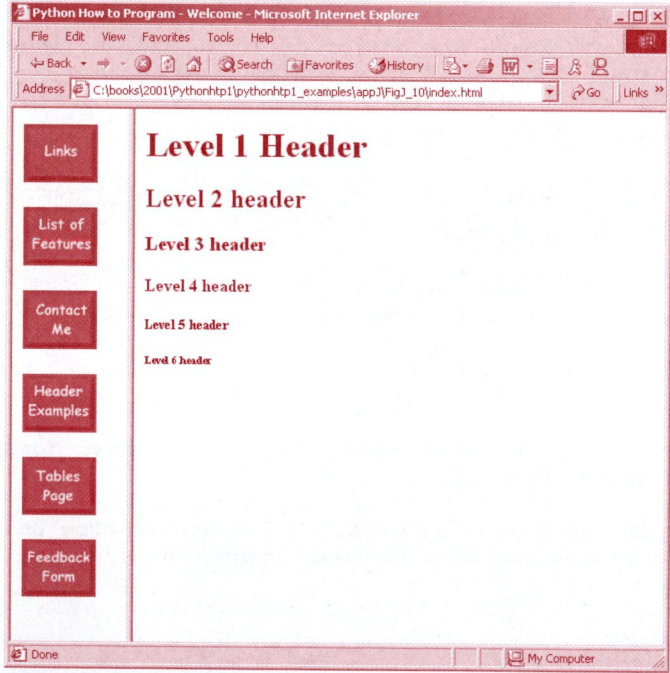

Fig. J.10   Web document containing two frames—navigation and content.
             (Part 2 of 2.)

A document that defines a frameset normally consists of an **html** element that contains a **head** element and a *frameset* element. The **<frameset>** tag (line 23) informs the browser that a page contains frames. Attribute *cols* specifies the frameset's column layout. The value of **cols** gives the width of each frame, either in pixels or as a percentage of the browser width. In this case, the attribute **cols = "110,*"** informs the browser that there are two vertical frames. The first frame extends **110** pixels from the left edge of the browser window, and the second frame fills the remainder of the browser width (as indicated by the asterisk). Similarly, **frameset** attribute *rows* specifies the number of rows and the size of each row in a frameset.

The documents that will be loaded into the **frameset** are specified with *frame* elements (lines 27–28 in this example). Attribute **src** specifies the URL of the page to display in the frame. Each frame has **name** and **src** attributes. The first frame (which covers **110** pixels on the left side of the **frameset**) is named **leftframe** and displays the page **nav.html** (Fig. J.11). The second frame is named **main** and displays the page **main.html**.

Attribute **name** identifies a frame, enabling hyperlinks in a **frameset** to specify the *target frame* in which a linked document should display when the user clicks the link. For example,

```
<a href = "links.html" target = "main">
```

loads **links.html** in the frame whose **name** is **"main"**.

Not all browsers support frames. XHTML provides the *noframes* element (lines 30–36) to enable designers of XHTML documents to specify alternative content for browsers that do not support frames.

 Portability Tip J.1

*Some browsers do not support frames. Use the **noframes** element inside a **frameset** to direct users to a nonframed version of your site.*

Fig. J.11 is the Web page displayed in the left frame of Fig. J.10. This XHTML document provides the navigation buttons that, when clicked, determine which document is displayed in the right frame.

```
1   <?xml version = "1.0"?>
2   <!DOCTYPE html PUBLIC "-//W3C//DTD XHTML 1.0 Transitional//EN"
3       "http://www.w3.org/TR/xhtml1/DTD/xhtml1-transitional.dtd">
4
5   <!-- Fig. J.11: nav.html          -->
6   <!-- Using images as link anchors. -->
7
8   <html xmlns = "http://www.w3.org/1999/xhtml">
9
10      <head>
11          <title>Python How to Program - Navigation Bar
12          </title>
13      </head>
```

Fig. J.11   XHTML document displayed in the left frame of the Web document in
Fig. J.10. (Part 1 of 2.)

```
14
15     <body>
16
17        <p>
18           <a href = "links.html" target = "main">
19              <img src = "buttons/links.jpg" width = "65"
20                 height = "50" alt = "Links Page" />
21           </a><br />
22
23           <a href = "list.html" target = "main">
24              <img src = "buttons/list.jpg" width = "65"
25                 height = "50" alt = "List Example Page" />
26           </a><br />
27
28           <a href = "contact.html" target = "main">
29              <img src = "buttons/contact.jpg" width = "65"
30                 height = "50" alt = "Contact Page" />
31           </a><br />
32
33           <a href = "header.html" target = "main">
34              <img src = "buttons/header.jpg" width = "65"
35                 height = "50" alt = "Header Page" />
36           </a><br />
37
38           <a href = "table1.html" target = "main">
39              <img src = "buttons/table.jpg" width = "65"
40                 height = "50" alt = "Table Page" />
41           </a><br />
42
43           <a href = "form.html" target = "main">
44              <img src = "buttons/form.jpg" width = "65"
45                 height = "50" alt = "Feedback Form" />
46           </a><br />
47        </p>
48
49     </body>
50  </html>
```

Fig. J.11   XHTML document displayed in the left frame of the Web document in Fig. J.10. (Part 2 of 2.)

Line 27 (Fig. J.10) displays the XHTML page in Fig. J.11. Anchor attribute **target** (line 18 in Fig. J.11) specifies that the linked documents are loaded in frame **main** (line 28 in Fig. J.10). A **target** can be set to a number of preset values: **"_blank"** loads the page into a new browser window, **"_self"** loads the page into the frame in which the anchor element appears and **"_top"** loads the page into the full browser window (i.e., it removes the **frameset**).

J.10 Nested **frameset**s

You can use the **frameset** element to create more complex layouts in a Web page by nesting **frameset**s, as demonstrated in Fig. J.12. The nested **frameset** in this example displays the XHTML documents in Fig. J.8, Fig. J.9 and Fig. J.11.

The outer **frameset** element (lines 23–41) defines two columns. The left frame extends over the first 110 pixels from the left edge of the browser, and the right frame occupies the rest of the window's width. The **frame** element on line 24 specifies that the document **nav.html** (Fig. J.11) displays in the left column.

Lines 28–31 define a nested **frameset** element for the second column of the outer **frameset**. This **frameset** defines two rows. The first row extends 175 pixels from the top of the browser window, as indicated by **rows = "175,*"**. The second row occupies the remainder of the browser window's height. The **frame** element on line 29 specifies that the first row of the nested **frameset** displays **picture.html** (Fig. J.8). The **frame** element on line 30 specifies that the second row of the nested **frameset** displays **main.html** (Fig. J.10).

```
1   <?xml version = "1.0"?>
2   <!DOCTYPE html PUBLIC "-//W3C//DTD XHTML 1.0 Frameset//EN"
3       "http://www.w3.org/TR/xhtml11/DTD/xhtml11-frameset.dtd">
4
5   <!-- Fig. J.12: index2.html   -->
6   <!-- XHTML Frames II.         -->
7
8   <html xmlns = "http://www.w3.org/1999/xhtml">
9      <head>
10        <title>Python How to Program - Main</title>
11
12        <meta name = "keywords" content = "Webpage, design,
13           XHTML, tutorial, personal, help, index, form,
14           contact, feedback, list, links, frame, deitel" />
15
16        <meta name = "description" content = "This Web site will
17           help you learn the basics of XHTML and Web page design
18           through the use of interactive examples
19           and instruction." />
20
21     </head>
22
23     <frameset cols = "110,*">
24        <frame name = "leftframe" src = "nav.html" />
25
26        <!-- nested framesets are used to change the -->
27        <!-- formatting and layout of the frameset   -->
28        <frameset rows = "175,*">
29           <frame name = "picture" src = "picture.html" />
30           <frame name = "main" src = "main.html" />
31        </frameset>
32
33        <noframes>
34           <p>This page uses frames, but your browser does not
35           support them.</p>
36
37           <p>Please, <a href = "fig27_10.html">follow this link
38           to browse our site without frames</a>.</p>
39        </noframes>
```

Fig. J.12 Nested **frameset** used in a Web site. (Part 1 of 2.)

```
40
41        </frameset>
42   </html>
```

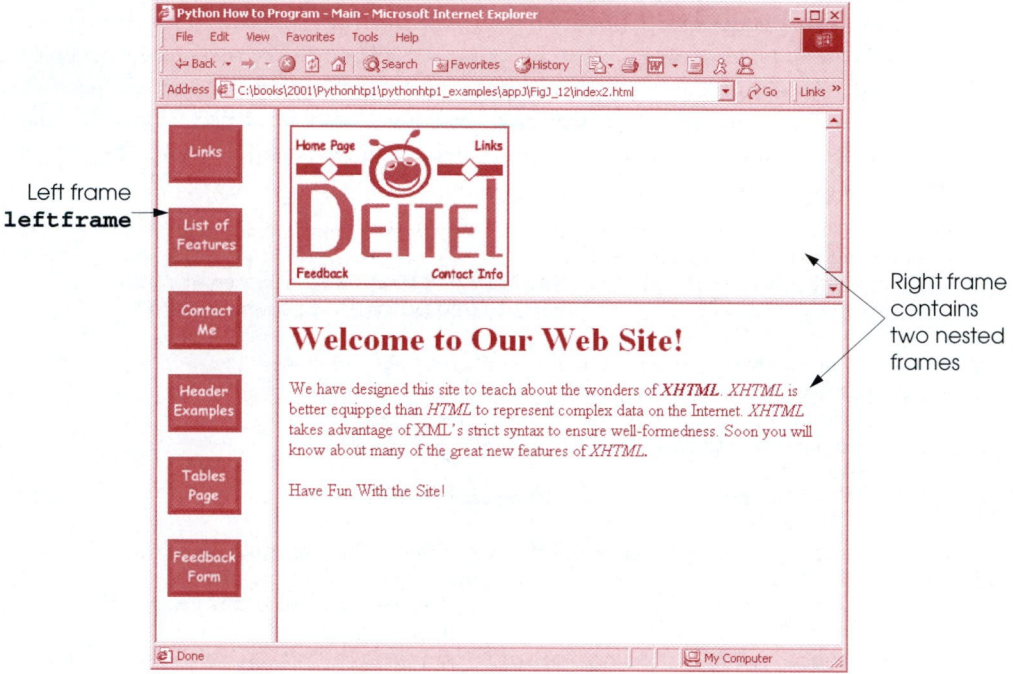

Left frame
leftframe

Right frame
contains
two nested
frames

Fig. J.12   Nested **frameset** used in a Web site. (Part 2 of 2.)

Testing and Debugging Tip 25.3

*When using nested **frameset** elements, indent every level of **<frame>** tag. This practice makes the page clearer and easier to debug.*

In this appendix, we have presented XHTML for marking up information in tables, creating forms for gathering user input, linking to sections within the same document, using **<meta>** tags and creating frames. In Appendix K, Cascading Style Sheets, we build upon the XHTML introduced in this appendix by discussing how to make Web pages more visually appealing with Cascading Style Sheets.

J.11 Internet and World Wide Web Resources

courses.e-survey.net.au/xhtml/index.html
The *Web Page Design - XHTML* site provides descriptions of and examples for various XHTML features, such as links, tables, frames and forms. Users can e-mail questions or comments to the Web Page Design support staff.

www.vbxml.com/xhtml/articles/xhtml_tables
The *VBXML.com* Web site contains a tutorial on creating XHTML tables.

www.webreference.com/xml/reference/xhtml.html
This Web page contains a list of the frequently used XHTML tags, such as header tags, table tags, frame tags and form tags. It also provides a description of each tag.

www.xhtml.org
This site offers links to recommendations, mailing lists, a newsgroup and other Internet resources related to XHTML topics.

SUMMARY

- XHTML tables mark up tabular data and are one of the most frequently used features in XHTML.

- The **table** element defines an XHTML table. Attribute **border** specifies the width of the table's border, in pixels. For tables without borders, this attribute is set to **"0"**.

- Attribute **summary** describes the table's contents. Speech devices use this attribute to make the table more accessible to users with visual impairments.

- Element **caption** describe's the table's content. The text inside the **<caption>** tag is rendered above the table in most browsers.

- A table can be split into three distinct sections: head (**thead**), body (**tbody**) and foot (**tfoot**). The head section contains information such as table titles and column headers. The table body contains the primary table data. The table foot contains information such as footnotes.

- Element **tr**, or table row, defines individual table rows. Element **th** defines a header cell. Text in **th** elements usually is centered and displayed in bold by most browsers. This element can be present in any section of the table.

- Data within a row are defined with **td**, or table data, elements.

- Element **colgroup** groups and formats columns. Each **col** element can format any number of columns (specified with the **span** attribute).

- The document author has the ability to merge data cells with the **rowspan** and **colspan** attributes. The values assigned to these attributes specify the number of rows or columns, respectively, occupied by the cell. These attributes can be placed inside any data-cell tag.

- XHTML provides forms for collecting information from users. Forms contain visual components such as buttons that users click. Forms may also contain nonvisual components, called hidden inputs, which store data, such as e-mail addresses and file names of XHTML documents used for linking.

- A form begins with the **form** element. Attribute **method** specifies how the form's data is sent to the Web server.

- The **"text"** input inserts a text box into a form. Text boxes allow the user to input data.

- The **input** element's **size** attribute specifies the number of characters visible in the **input** element. Optional attribute **maxlength** limits the number of characters input into a text box.

- The **"submit"** input submits the data entered in the form to the Web server for processing. Most Web browsers create a button that submits the form data when clicked. The **"reset"** input allows a user to reset all **form** elements to their default values.

- The **textarea** element inserts a multiline text box, called a text area, into a form. The number of rows in the text area is specified with the **rows** attribute, and the number of columns (i.e., characters) is specified with the **cols** attribute.

- The **"password"** input inserts a password box into a form. A password box allows users to enter sensitive information, such as credit-card numbers and passwords, by "masking" the information input with another character. Asterisks are the masking character used for password boxes. The actual value input, not the asterisks that mask the input, is sent to the Web server.

- The checkbox input allows the user to make a selection. When the checkbox is selected, a check mark appears in the checkbox. Otherwise, the checkbox is empty. Checkboxes can be used individually or in groups. Checkboxes that are part of the same group have the same **name**.

- A radio button is similar in function to a checkbox, except that only one radio button in a group can be selected at any time. All radio buttons in a group have the same **name** attribute value and different attribute **value**s.

- The **select** input provides a drop-down list of items. The **name** attribute identifies the drop-down list. The **option** element adds items to the drop-down list. The **selected** attribute, like the **checked** attribute for radio buttons and checkboxes, specifies which item in the list is displayed initially.

- Image maps designate certain sections of an image as links. These links are more properly called hotspots.

- Image maps are defined with **map** elements. Attribute **id** identifies the image map. Hotspots are defined with the **area** element. Attribute **href** specifies the link's target. Attributes **shape** and **coords** specify the hotspot's shape and coordinates, respectively, and **alt** provides alternative text.

- One way that search engines catalog pages is by reading the **meta** elements's contents. Two important attributes of the **meta** element are **name**, which identifies the type of **meta** element, and **content**, which provides information that search engines use to catalog a page.

- Frames allow the browser to display more than one XHTML document simultaneously. The **frameset** element informs the browser that the page contains frames. Not all browsers support frames. XHTML provides the **noframes** element to specify alternative content for browsers that do not support frames.

- You can use the **frameset** element to create more complex layouts in a Web page by nesting **frameset**s.

TERMINOLOGY

action attribute	**input** element
area element	internal hyperlink
border attribute	internal linking
browser request	**map** element
<caption> tag	**maxlength** attribute
checkbox	**meta** element
checked attribute	**method** attribute
col element	**name** attribute
colgroup element	navigational frame
cols attribute	nested **frameset** element
colspan attribute	nested tag
coords element	**noframes** element
form	password box
form element	**"radio"** (attribute value)
frame element	**rows** attribute (**textarea**)
frameset element	**rowspan** attribute (**tr**)
header cell	**selected** attribute
hidden input element	**size** attribute (**input**)
hotspot	**table** element
href attribute	**target = "_blank"**
image map	**target = "_self"**
img element	**target = "_top"**

tbody element
td element
text area
textarea element
tfoot (table foot) element
<thead>...</thead>
tr (table row) element

type attribute
usemap attribute
valign attribute (**th**)
value attribute
Web server
XHTML form
x–y-coordinate

SELF-REVIEW EXERCISES

J.1   State whether the following statements are *true* or *false*. If *false*, explain why.
   a) The width of all data cells in a table must be the same.
   b) **frameset**s can be nested.
   c) You are limited to a maximum of 100 internal links per page.
   d) All browsers can render **frameset**s.

J.2   Fill in the blanks in each of the following statements:
   a) Assigning attribute **type** _____ in an **input** element inserts a button that, when
       clicked, clears the contents of the form.
   b) The layout of a **frameset** is set by including the _____ attribute or the
       _____ attribute inside the **<frameset>** tag.
   c) The _____ element marks up a table row.
   d) _____ are used as masking characters in a password box.
   e) The common shapes used in image maps are _____, _____ and _____.

J.3   Write XHTML markup to accomplish each of the following tasks:
   a) Insert a framed Web page, with the first frame extending 300 pixels across the page from
       the left side.
   b) Insert a table with a border of **8**.
   c) Indicate alternative content to a **frameset**.
   d) Insert an image map into a page, using **deitel.gif** as the image and **map** with **name**
       = "hello" as the image map, and set the **alt** text to "**hello**".

ANSWERS TO SELF-REVIEW EXERCISES

J.1   a) False. You can specify the width of any column, either in pixels or as a percentage of the
table width. b) True. c) False. You can have an unlimited number of internal links. d) False. Some
browsers are unable to render a **frameset** and must therefore rely on the information that you include inside the **<noframes>...</noframes>** tags.

J.2   a) **"reset"**. b) **cols**, **rows**. c) **tr**. d) Asterisks. e) **poly** (polygons), **circle**s, **rect**
(rectangles).

J.3   a) **<frameset cols = "300,*">...</frameset>**
       b) **<table border = "8">...</table>**
       c) **<noframes>...</noframes>**
       d) **<img src = "deitel.gif" alt = "hello" usemap = "#hello" />**

EXERCISES

J.4   Categorize each of the following as an element or an attribute:
   a) **width**.
   b) **td**.
   c) **th**.

d) `frame`.

e) `name`.

f) `select`.

g) `type`.

J.5   What will the **frameset** produced by the given code look like? Assume that the pages referenced are blank with white backgrounds and that the dimensions of the screen are 800 by 600. Sketch the layout, approximating the dimensions.

```
<frameset rows = "20%,*">
    <frame src = "hello.html" name = "hello" />
        <frameset cols = "150,*">
            <frame src = "nav.html" name = "nav" />
            <frame src = "deitel.html" name = "deitel" />
        </frameset>
</frameset>
```

J.6   Write the XHTML markup to create a frame with a table of contents on the left side of the window, and have each entry in the table of contents use internal linking to scroll down the document's frame to the appropriate subsection.

J.7   Create XHTML markup that produces the table shown in Fig. J.13. Use **<em>** and **<strong>** tags as necessary. The image (**snake.gif**) is included in the Appendix J examples directory on the CD-ROM that accompanies this book.

J.8   Write an XHTML document that produces the table shown in Fig. J.14.

J.9   A local university has asked you to create an XHTML document that allows potential students to provide feedback about their campus visits. Your XHTML document should contain a form with text boxes for names, addresses and e-mail addresses. Provide checkboxes that allow prospective students to indicate what they liked most about the campus. There should be checkboxes for students, location, campus, atmosphere, dorm rooms and sports. Also, provide radio buttons that ask prospective students how they became interested in the university. Options should include friends, television, Internet and other. In addition, provide a text area for additional comments, a submit button and a reset button.

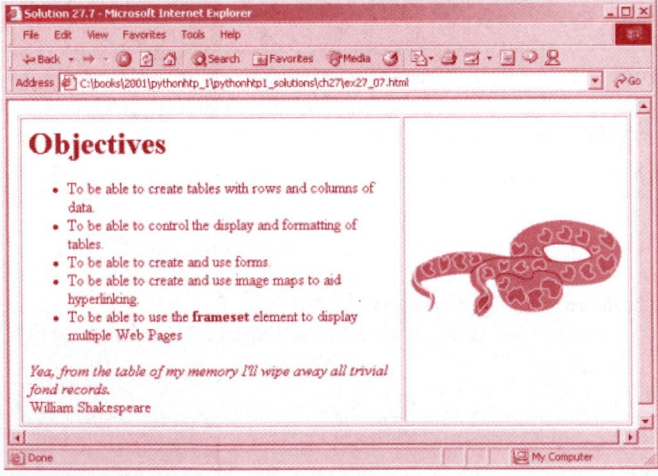

Fig. J.13   XHTML table for Exercise J.7.

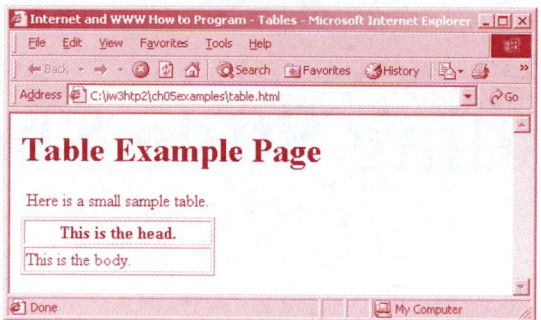

Fig. J.14   XHTML table for Exercise J.8.

J.10   Create an XHTML document that displays a tic-tac-toe table with player X winning. Use `<h2>` to mark up both Xs and Os. Center the letters in each cell horizontally. Use an `<h1>` tag to title the game. This title should span all three columns. Set the table border to `1`.

Cascading Style Sheets™ (CSS)

Objectives

- To take control of the appearance of a Web site by creating style sheets.
- To use a style sheet to give all the pages of a Web site the same look and feel.
- To use the `class` attribute to apply styles.
- To specify the precise font, size, color and other properties of displayed text.
- To specify element backgrounds and colors.
- To understand the box model and how to control the margins, borders and padding.
- To use style sheets to separate presentation from content.

Fashions fade, style is eternal.
Yves Saint Laurent

A style does not go out of style as long as it adapts itself to its period. When there is an incompatibility between the style and a certain state of mind, it is never the style that triumphs.
Coco Chanel

How liberating to work in the margins, outside a central perception.
Don DeLillo

I've gradually risen from lower-class background to lower-class foreground.
Marvin Cohen

Outline

K.1 Introduction

In Appendix I and Appendix J, we introduced the Extensible Hyper Text Markup Language (XHTML) for marking up information. In this appendix, we shift our focus from marking up information to formatting and presenting information, using a W3C technology called *Cascading Style Sheets (CSS)* that allows document authors to specify the presentation of elements on a Web page (spacing, margins, etc.) separately from the structure of the document (section headers, body text, links, etc.). This *separation of structure from presentation* simplifies maintaining and modifying a website's document layout.

K.2 Inline Styles

A Web developer can declare document styles in many ways. In this section, we present *inline styles* that declare an individual element's format, using *attribute* `style`. Figure K.1 applies inline styles to `p` elements to alter their font sizes and colors.

```
1   <?xml version = "1.0"?>
2   <!DOCTYPE html PUBLIC "-//W3C//DTD XHTML 1.0 Strict//EN"
3      "http://www.w3.org/TR/xhtml1/DTD/xhtml1-strict.dtd">
4
5   <!-- Fig. K.1: inline.html -->
6   <!-- Using inline styles.  -->
7
8   <html xmlns = "http://www.w3.org/1999/xhtml">
9      <head>
10        <title>Inline Styles</title>
11     </head>
```

Fig. K.1   Inline styles. (Part 1 of 2.)

```
12
13      <body>
14
15         <p>This text does not have any style applied to it.</p>
16
17         <!-- The style attribute allows you to declare -->
18         <!-- inline styles. Separate multiple styles    -->
19         <!-- with a semicolon.                          -->
20         <p style = "font-size: 20pt">This text has the
21         <em>font-size</em> style applied to it, making it 20pt.
22         </p>
23
24         <p style = "font-size: 20pt; color: #0000ff">
25         This text has the <em>font-size</em> and
26         <em>color</em> styles applied to it, making it
27         20pt. and blue.</p>
28
29      </body>
30   </html>
```

Fig. K.1   Inline styles. (Part 2 of 2.)

The first inline style declaration appears in line 20. Attribute **style** specifies the style for an element. Each *CSS property* (the **font-size** property in this case) is followed by a colon and a value. On line 20, we declare the **p** element to have 20-point text size. Line 21 uses element **em** to "emphasize" text, which most browsers do by making the font italic.

Line 24 specifies the two properties, **font-size** and **color**, separated by a semi-colon. In this line, we set the text's **color** to blue, using the hexadecimal code **#0000ff**. Color names may be used in place of hexadecimal codes, as we demonstrate in the next example. [*Note*: Inline styles override any other styles applied via the techniques we discuss later in this appendix.]

K.3 Embedded Style Sheets

In this section, we present a second technique for using style sheets, called *embedded style sheets*. Embedded style sheets enable a Web-page author to embed an entire CSS document within an XHTML document's **head** section. Figure K.2 creates an embedded style sheet containing four styles.

```
1   <?xml version = "1.0"?>
2   <!DOCTYPE html PUBLIC "-//W3C//DTD XHTML 1.0 Strict//EN"
3       "http://www.w3.org/TR/xhtml1/DTD/xhtml1-strict.dtd">
4
5   <!-- Fig. K.2: declared.html                        -->
6   <!-- Declaring a style sheet in the header section. -->
7
8   <html xmlns = "http://www.w3.org/1999/xhtml">
9       <head>
10          <title>Style Sheets</title>
11
12          <!-- this begins the style sheet section -->
13          <style type = "text/css">
14
15              em          { background-color: #8000ff;
16                            color: white }
17
18              h1          { font-family: arial, sans-serif }
19
20              p           { font-size: 14pt }
21
22              .special { color: blue }
23
24          </style>
25      </head>
26
27      <body>
28
29          <!-- this class attribute applies the .blue style -->
30          <h1 class = "special">Deitel & Associates, Inc.</h1>
31
32          <p>Deitel & Associates, Inc. is an internationally
33          recognized corporate training and publishing organization
34          specializing in programming languages, Internet/World
35          Wide Web technology and object technology education.
36          Deitel & Associates, Inc. is a member of the World Wide
37          Web Consortium. The company provides courses on Java,
38          C++, Visual Basic, C, Internet and World Wide Web
39          programming, and Object Technology.</p>
40
41          <h1>Clients</h1>
42          <p class = "special"> The company's clients include many
43          <em>Fortune 1000 companies</em>, government agencies,
44          branches of the military and business organizations.
45          Through its publishing partnership with Prentice Hall,
46          Deitel & Associates, Inc. publishes leading-edge
47          programming textbooks, professional books, interactive
48          CD-ROM-based multimedia Cyber Classrooms, satellite
49          courses and World Wide Web courses.</p>
```

Fig. K.2   **head** element used to declare styles in a document. (Part 1 of 2.)

```
50
51        </body>
52    </html>
```

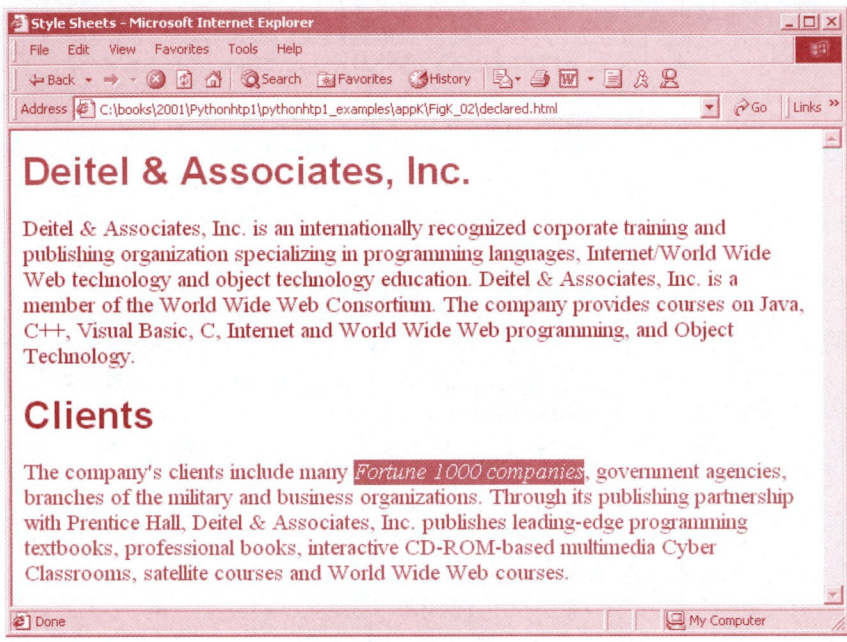

Fig. K.2   **head** element used to declare styles in a document. (Part 2 of 2.)

The **style** element (lines 13–24) defines the embedded style sheet. Styles placed in the **head** apply to matching elements in the entire document, not just to a single element. The **type** attribute specifies the *Multipurpose Internet Mail Extension* (*MIME) type* that describes a file's content. CSS documents use the MIME type **text/css**. Other MIME types include **image/gif** (for GIF images) and **text/javascript** (for the JavaScript scripting language).

The body of the style sheet (lines 15–22) declares the *CSS rules* for the style sheet. We declare rules for **em** (lines 15–16), **h1** (line 18) and **p** (line 20) elements. When the browser renders this document, it applies the properties defined in these rules to each element to which the rule applies. For example, the rule on lines 15–16 will be applied to all **em** elements. The body of each rule is enclosed in curly braces (**{** and **}**). We declare a *style class* named **special** in line 22. Class declarations are preceded with a period and are applied to elements of that class only. We discuss how to apply a style class in a moment.

CSS rules that embedded style sheets use the same syntax as inline styles; the property name is followed by a colon (**:**) and the value of that property. Multiple properties are separated by *semicolons* (**;**). In this example, the **color** property specifies the color of text in an element line, and property **background-color** specifies the background color of the element.

The **font-family** property (line 18) specifies the name of the font to use. In this case, we use the **arial** font. The second value, **sans-serif**, is a *generic font family*.

Not all users have the same fonts installed on their computers, so Web-page authors often specify a comma-separated list of fonts to use for a particular style. The browser attempts to use the fonts in the order of the list. Many Web-page authors end a font list with a generic font family name, in case the other fonts are not installed on the user's computer. In this example, if the **arial** font is not found on the system, the browser instead displays a generic **sans-serif** font such as **helvetica** or **verdana**. Other generic font families include **serif** (e.g., **times new roman**, **Georgia**), **cursive** (e.g., **script**), **fantasy** (e.g., **critter**) and **monospace** (e.g., **courier**, **fixedsys**).

The *font-size* *property* (line 20) specifies a 14-point font. Other possible measurements, in addition to *pt* (point), are introduced later in the appendix. Relative values— *xx-small*, *x-small*, *small*, *smaller*, *medium*, *large*, *larger*, *x-large* and *xx-large* also can be used. Generally, relative values for **font-size** are preferred over point sizes because an author does not know the specific measurements of the display for each client. For example, a user may wish to view a Web page on a handheld device with a small screen. Specifying an 18-point font size in a style sheet prevents such a user from seeing more than one or two characters at a time. However, if a relative font size is specified, such as **large** or **larger**, the actual size is determined by the browser that displays the font.

Line 30 uses attribute *class* in an **h1** element to apply a *style class*—in this case, class **special** (declared as **.special** in the style sheet). When the browser renders the **h1** element, notice that the text appears on screen with both the properties of an **h1** element (**arial** or **sans-serif** font defined at line 18) and the properties of the **.special** style class applied (the color **blue** defined on line 22).

The **p** element and the **.special** class style are applied to the text in lines 42–49. All styles applied to an element (the *parent*, or *ancestor*, *element*) also apply to that element's nested elements (*descendant elements*). The **em** element *inherits* the style from the **p** element (namely, the 14-point font size in line 20), but retains its italic style. However, this property overrides the **color** property of the **special** class, because the **em** element has its own **color** property. We discuss the rules for resolving these conflicts in the next section.

K.4 Conflicting Styles

Cascading Style Sheets are "cascading" because styles may be defined by a user, an author or a *user agent* (e.g., a Web browser). Styles defined by authors take precedence over styles defined by the user, and styles defined by the user take precedence over styles defined by the user agent. Styles defined for parent and ancestor elements are also inherited by child and descendant elements. In this section, we discuss the rules for resolving conflicts between styles defined for elements and styles inherited from parent and ancestor elements.

Figure K.2 presented an example of *inheritance* in which a child **em** element inherited the **font-size** property from its parent **p** element. However, in Fig. K.2, the child **em** element had a **color** property that conflicted with (i.e., had a value different from) the **color** property of its parent **p** element. Properties defined for child and descendant elements have a greater *specificity* than properties defined for parent and ancestor elements. According to the W3C CSS Recommendation, conflicts are resolved in favor of properties with a higher specificity. In other words, the styles defined for the child (or descendant) are more specific than the styles for that child's parent (or ancestor) element; therefore, the child's styles take precedence. Figure K.3 illustrates examples of inheritance and specificity.

```
 1   <?xml version = "1.0"?>
 2   <!DOCTYPE html PUBLIC "-//W3C//DTD XHTML 1.0 Strict//EN"
 3       "http://www.w3.org/TR/xhtml1/DTD/xhtml1-strict.dtd">
 4
 5   <!-- Fig K.3: advanced.html        -->
 6   <!-- More advanced style sheets. -->
 7
 8   <html xmlns = "http://www.w3.org/1999/xhtml">
 9       <head>
10           <title>More Styles</title>
11
12           <style type = "text/css">
13
14               a.nodec   { text-decoration: none }
15
16               a:hover   { text-decoration: underline;
17                           color: red;
18                           background-color: #ccffcc }
19
20               li em     { color: red;
21                           font-weight: bold }
22
23               ul        { margin-left: 75px }
24
25               ul ul     { text-decoration: underline;
26                           margin-left: 15px }
27
28           </style>
29       </head>
30
31       <body>
32
33           <h1>Shopping list for <em>Monday</em>:</h1>
34
35           <ul>
36               <li>Milk</li>
37               <li>Bread
38                   <ul>
39                       <li>White bread</li>
40                       <li>Rye bread</li>
41                       <li>Whole wheat bread</li>
42                   </ul>
43               </li>
44               <li>Rice</li>
45               <li>Potatoes</li>
46               <li>Pizza <em>with mushrooms</em></li>
47           </ul>
48
49           <p><a class = "nodec" href = "http://www.food.com">
50           Go to the Grocery store</a></p>
51
52       </body>
53   </html>
```

Fig. K.3   Inheritance in style sheets. (Part 1 of 2.)

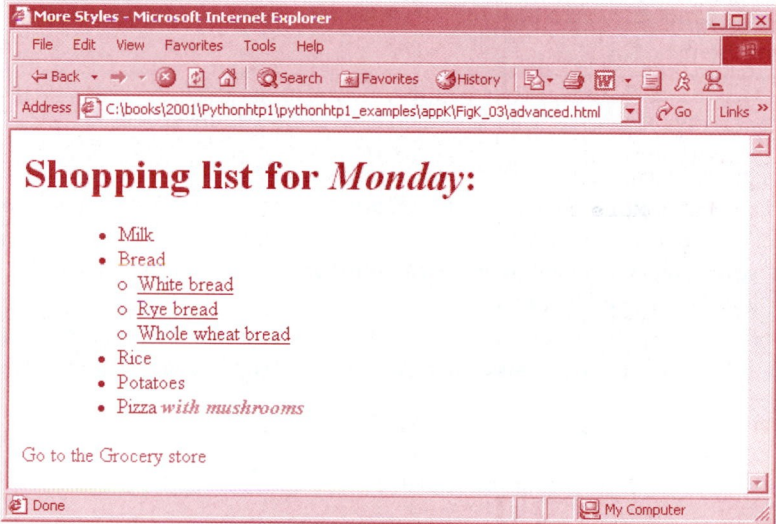

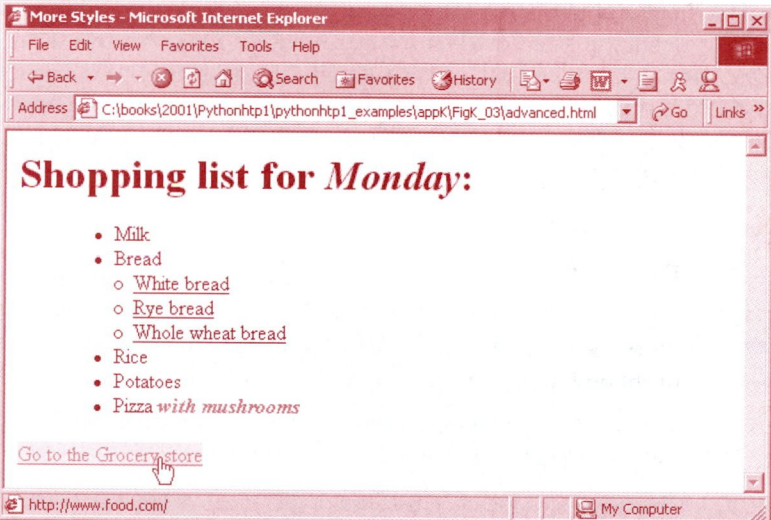

Fig. K.3   Inheritance in style sheets. (Part 2 of 2.)

Line 14 applies property **text-decoration** to all **a** elements whose **class** attribute is set to **nodec**. The **text-decoration** property applies *decorations* to text within an element. By default, browsers underline the text marked up with an **a** element. Here, we set the **text-decoration** property to **none** to indicate that the browser should not underline hyperlinks. Other possible values for **text-decoration** include *blink*, *overline*, *line-through* and *underline*. The **.nodec** appended to **a** is an extension of class styles; this style applies only to **a** elements that specify **nodec** as their class.

Lines 16–18 specify a style for **hover**, which is a *pseudoclass*. Pseudoclasses give the author access to content not specifically declared in the document. The **hover** pseudoclass is activated dynamically when the user moves the mouse cursor over an element.

Portability Tip K.1

To ensure that your style sheets work in various Web browsers, test your style sheets on all client Web browsers that will render documents using your styles.

Lines 20–21 declare a style for all **em** elements that are descendants of **li** elements. In the screen output of Fig. K.3, notice that **Monday** (which line 33 contains in an **em** element) does not appear in bold red, because the **em** element is not in an **li** element. However, the **em** element containing **with mushrooms** (line 46) is in an **li** element; therefore, it is formatted in bold red.

The syntax for applying rules to multiple elements is similar. For example, to apply the rule in lines 20–21 to all **li** and **em** elements, you would separate the elements by commas, as follows:

```
li, em   { color: red;
           font-weight: bold }
```

Lines 25–26 specify that all nested lists (**ul** elements that are descendants of **ul** elements) be underlined and have a left-hand margin of 15 pixels. A pixel is a *relative-length measurement*—it varies in size, based on screen resolution. Other relative lengths are **em** (the so-called "*M*-height" of the font, which is usually set to the height of an uppercase *M*), **ex** (the so-called "*x*-height" of the font, which is usually set to the height of a lowercase *x*) and percentages (e.g., **margin-left: 10%**). To set an element to display text at 150% of its default text size, the author could use the syntax

```
font-size: 1.5em
```

Other units of measurement available in CSS are *absolute-length measurements*—i.e., units that do not vary in size based on the system. These units are **in** (inches), **cm** (centimeters), **mm** (millimeters), **pt** (points; 1 **pt**=1/72 **in**) and **pc** (picas—1 **pc** = 12 **pt**).

Good Programming Practice K.1

Whenever possible, use relative-length measurements. If you use absolute-length measurements, your document might not be readable on some client browsers (e.g., wireless phones).

In Fig. K.3, the entire list is indented because of the 75-pixel left-hand margin for top-level **ul** elements. However, the nested list is indented only 15 pixels more (not another 75 pixels), because the child **ul** element's **margin-left** property overrides the parent **ul** element's **margin-left** property.

K.5 Linking External Style Sheets

Style sheets are a convenient way to create a document with a uniform theme. With *external style sheets* (i.e., separate documents that contain only CSS rules), Web-page authors can provide a uniform look and feel to an entire Web site. Different pages on a site can all use the same style sheet. Then, when changes to the style are required, the Web-page author needs to modify only a single CSS file to make style changes across the entire Web site.

Figure K.4 presents an external style sheet and Fig. K.5 contains an XHTML document that references the style sheet.

```
1   /* Fig. K.4: styles.css   */
2   /* External stylesheet.   */
3
4   a         { text-decoration: none }
5
6   a:hover { text-decoration: underline;
7             color: red;
8             background-color: #ccffcc }
9
10  li em    { color: red;
11            font-weight: bold;
12            background-color: #ffffff }
13
14  ul        { margin-left: 2cm }
15
16  ul ul    { text-decoration: underline;
17            margin-left: .5cm }
```

Fig. K.4   External style sheet (**styles.css**).

```
1   <?xml version = "1.0"?>
2   <!DOCTYPE html PUBLIC "-//W3C//DTD XHTML 1.0 Strict//EN"
3       "http://www.w3.org/TR/xhtml1/DTD/xhtml1-strict.dtd">
4
5   <!-- Fig. K.5: external.html        -->
6   <!-- Linking external style sheets. -->
7
8   <html xmlns = "http://www.w3.org/1999/xhtml">
9      <head>
10         <title>Linking External Style Sheets</title>
11         <link rel = "stylesheet" type = "text/css"
12            href = "styles.css" />
13      </head>
14
15      <body>
16
17         <h1>Shopping list for <em>Monday</em>:</h1>
18         <ul>
19            <li>Milk</li>
20            <li>Bread
21               <ul>
22                  <li>White bread</li>
23                  <li>Rye bread</li>
24                  <li>Whole wheat bread</li>
25               </ul>
26            </li>
27            <li>Rice</li>
28            <li>Potatoes</li>
```

Fig. K.5   Linking an external style sheet. (Part 1 of 2.)

```
29              <li>Pizza <em>with mushrooms</em></li>
30          </ul>
31
32          <p>
33          <a href = "http://www.food.com">Go to the Grocery store</a>
34          </p>
35
36      </body>
37  </html>
```

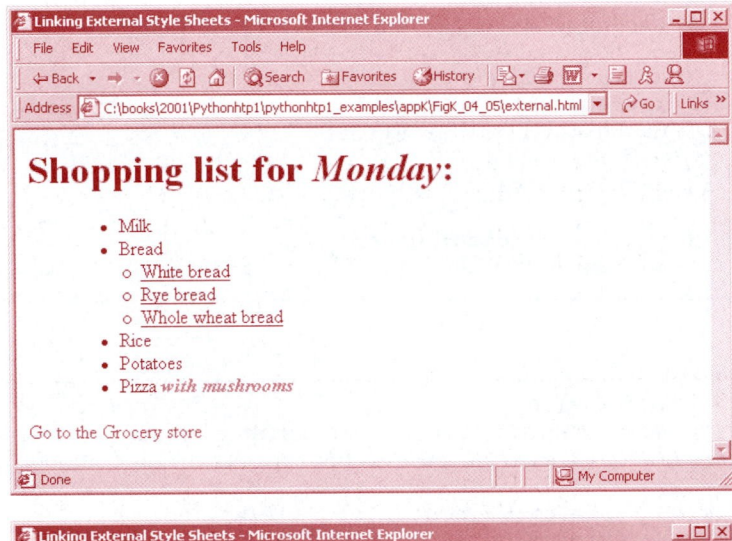

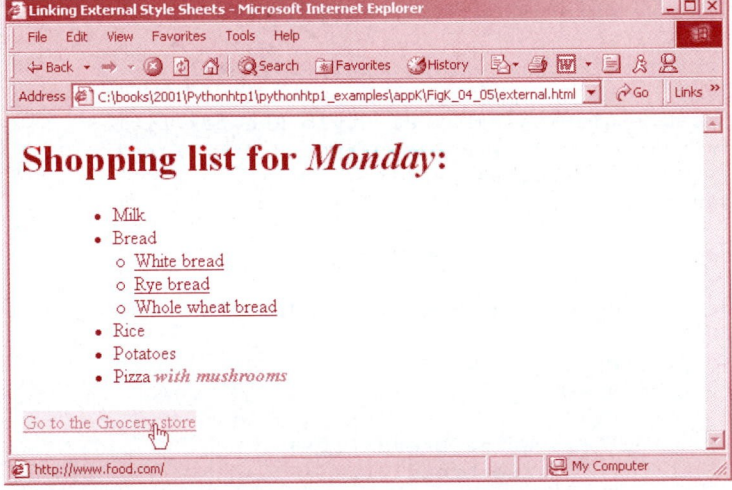

Fig. K.5   Linking an external style sheet. (Part 2 of 2.)

Lines 11–12 (Fig. K.5) show a **link** *element*, which uses the **rel** *attribute* to specify a *relationship* between the current document and another document. In this case, we declare the linked document to be a **stylesheet** for this document. The **type** attribute specifies the MIME type as **text/css**. The **href** attribute provides the URL for the document containing the style sheet .

Software Engineering Observation K.1

Style sheets are reusable. Creating them once and reusing them reduces programming effort.

Software Engineering Observation K.2

*The **link** element can be placed only in the **head** element. The user can specify **next** and **previous**, which allows the user to link a whole series of documents. This feature allows browsers to print a large collection of related documents at once. (In Internet Explorer, select **Print all linked documents** in the **Print...** submenu of the **File** menu.)*

K.6 W3C CSS Validation Service

The W3C provides a validation service (**jigsaw.w3.org/css-validator**) that validates external CSS documents to ensure that they conform to the W3C CSS Recommendation. Like XHTML validation, CSS validation ensures that style sheets have correct syntax. The validator provides three options—either entering the CSS document's URL, pasting the CSS document's contents into a text area or uploading a CSS document from disk. Figure K.6 illustrates uploading a CSS document from a disk.

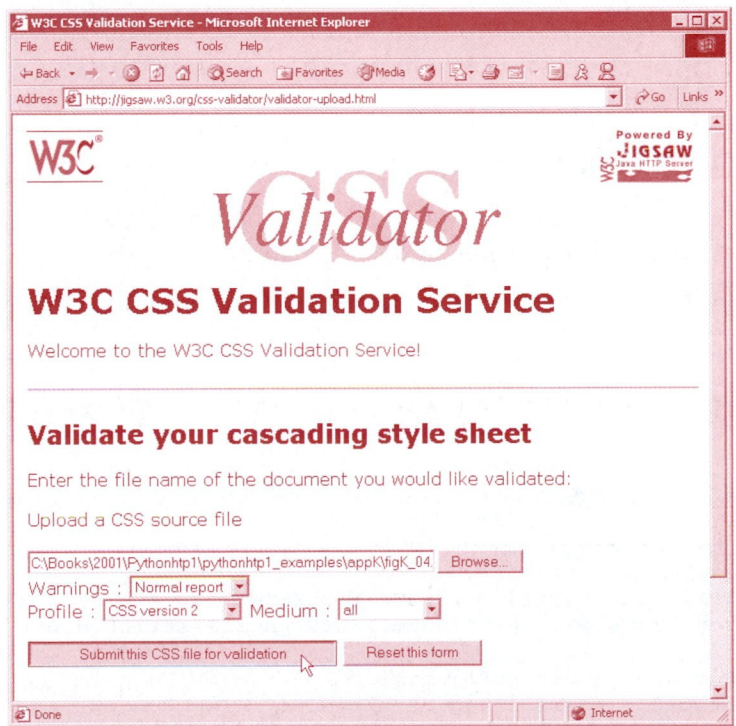

Fig. K.6   CSS document validation. (Courtesy of World Wide Web Consortium (W3C).)

Figure K.7 shows the results of validating **figK_04.css** via the file upload feature available at

jigsaw.w3.org/css-validator/validator-upload.html

To validate the document, click the **Browse** button to locate the file on your computer. After locating the file, click **Submit this CSS file for validation** to upload the file for validation. [*Note*: Like many W3C technologies, CSS is being developed in stages (or *versions*). The current version under development is Version 3.]

K.7 Positioning Elements

Prior to CSS, controlling the positioning of elements in an XHTML document was difficult—the browser determined positioning. CSS introduces the *position* property and a capability called *absolute positioning*, which provides authors greater control over how document elements are displayed. Figure K.8 demonstrates absolute positioning.

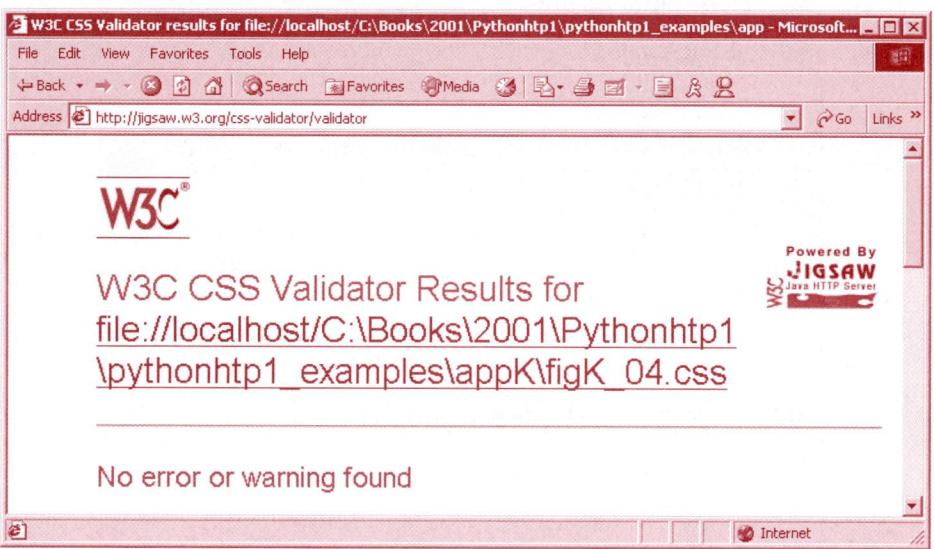

Fig. K.7   CSS validation results. (Courtesy of World Wide Web Consortium (W3C).)

```
1   <?xml version = "1.0"?>
2   <!DOCTYPE html PUBLIC "-//W3C//DTD XHTML 1.0 Strict//EN"
3       "http://www.w3.org/TR/xhtml1/DTD/xhtml1-strict.dtd">
4
5   <!-- Fig K.8: positioning.html              -->
6   <!-- Absolute positioning of elements. -->
7
8   <html xmlns = "http://www.w3.org/1999/xhtml">
```

Fig. K.8   Positioning elements with CSS. (Part 1 of 2.)

```
9      <head>
10        <title>Absolute Positioning</title>
11     </head>
12
13     <body>
14
15        <p><img src = "i.gif" style = "position: absolute;
16           top: 0px; left: 0px; z-index: 1"
17           alt = "First positioned image" /></p>
18        <p style = "position: absolute; top: 50px; left: 50px;
19           z-index: 3; font-size: 20pt;">Positioned Text</p>
20        <p><img src = "circle.gif" style = "position: absolute;
21           top: 25px; left: 100px; z-index: 2" alt =
22           "Second positioned image" /></p>
23
24     </body>
25  </html>
```

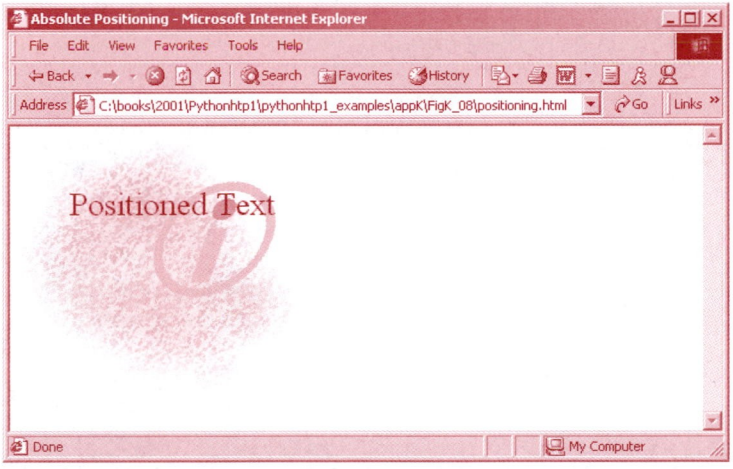

Fig. K.8   Positioning elements with CSS. (Part 2 of 2.)

Lines 15–17 position the first **img** element (**i.gif**) on the page. Specifying an element's **position** as *absolute* removes the element from the normal flow of elements on the page, instead positioning the element according to the distance from the **top**, **left**, **right** or **bottom** margins of its *containing block* (i.e., an element such as **body** or **p**). Here, we position the element to be **0** pixels away from both the **top** and **left** margins of the **body** element.

The *z-index* attribute allows you to layer overlapping elements properly. Elements that have higher **z-index** values are displayed in front of elements with lower **z-index** values. In this example, **i.gif** has the lowest **z-index** (**1**), so it displays in the background. The **img** element at lines 20–22 (**circle.gif**) has a **z-index** of **2**, so it displays in front of **i.gif**. The **p** element at lines 18–19 (**Positioned Text**) has a **z-index** of **3**, so it displays in front of the other two. If you do not specify a **z-index** or if elements have the same **z-index** value, the elements are placed from background to foreground in the order they are encountered in the document.

Absolute positioning is not the only way to specify page layout. Figure K.9 demonstrates *relative positioning* in which elements are positioned relative to other elements.

Setting the **position** property to **relative**, as in class **super** (lines 21–22), lays out the element on the page and offsets the element by the specified **top**, **bottom**, **left** or **right** values. Unlike absolute positioning, relative positioning keeps elements in the general flow of elements on the page, so positioning is relative to other elements in the flow.

```
1   <?xml version = "1.0"?>
2   <!DOCTYPE html PUBLIC "-//W3C//DTD XHTML 1.0 Strict//EN"
3      "http://www.w3.org/TR/xhtml1/DTD/xhtml1-strict.dtd">
4
5   <!-- Fig. K.9: positioning2.html          -->
6   <!-- Relative positioning of elements. -->
7
8   <html xmlns = "http://www.w3.org/1999/xhtml">
9      <head>
10        <title>Relative Positioning</title>
11
12        <style type = "text/css">
13
14           p            { font-size: 1.3em;
15                          font-family: verdana, arial, sans-serif }
16
17           span         { color: red;
18                          font-size: .6em;
19                          height: 1em }
20
21           .super       { position: relative;
22                          top: -1ex }
23
24           .sub         { position: relative;
25                          bottom: -1ex }
26
27           .shiftleft   { position: relative;
28                          left: -1ex }
29
30           .shiftright  { position: relative;
31                          right: -1ex }
32
33        </style>
34     </head>
35
36     <body>
37
38        <p>The text at the end of this sentence
39        <span class = "super">is in superscript</span>.</p>
40
41        <p>The text at the end of this sentence
42        <span class = "sub">is in subscript</span>.</p>
43
44        <p>The text at the end of this sentence
45        <span class = "shiftleft">is shifted left</span>.</p>
```

Fig. K.9   Relative positioning of elements. (Part 1 of 2.)

```
46
47              <p>The text at the end of this sentence
48              <span class = "shiftright">is shifted right</span>.</p>
49
50       </body>
51   </html>
```

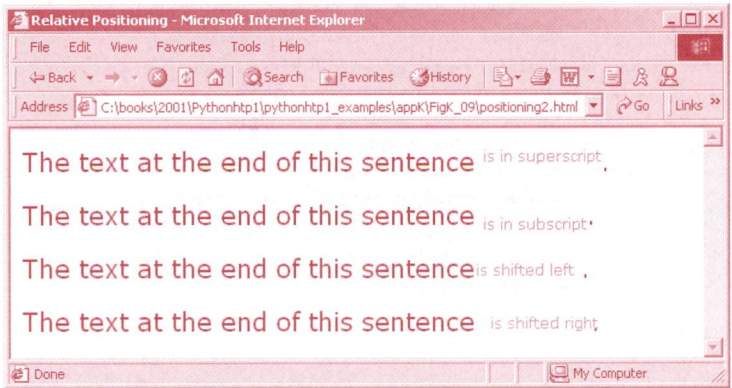

Fig. K.9   Relative positioning of elements. (Part 2 of 2.)

We introduce the ***span*** element in line 39. Element **span** is a *grouping element*—it does not apply any inherent formatting to its contents. Its primary purpose is to apply CSS rules or ***id*** *attributes* to a block of text. Element **span** is an *inline-level element*—it is displayed inline with other text and with no line breaks. Lines 17–19 define the CSS rule for **span**. A similar element is the ***div*** element, which also applies no inherent styles but is displayed on its own line, with margins above and below (a *block-level element*).

Common Programming Error K.1

Because relative positioning keeps elements in the flow of text in your documents, be careful to avoid unintentionally overlapping text.

K.8 Backgrounds

CSS also provides control over the element backgrounds. In previous examples, we introduced the **background-color** property. CSS also can add background images to documents. Figure K.10 adds a corporate logo to the bottom-right corner of the document. This logo stays fixed in the corner, even when the user scrolls up or down the screen.

```
1   <?xml version = "1.0"?>
2   <!DOCTYPE html PUBLIC "-//W3C//DTD XHTML 1.0 Strict//EN"
3       "http://www.w3.org/TR/xhtml1/DTD/xhtml1-strict.dtd">
4
5   <!-- Fig. K.10: background.html                    -->
6   <!-- Adding background images and indentation. -->
7
```

Fig. K.10   Adding a background image with CSS. (Part 1 of 2.)

```
 8   <html xmlns = "http://www.w3 .org/1999/xhtml">
 9      <head>
10         <title>Background Images</title>
11
12         <style type = "text/css">
13
14            body   { background-image: url(logo.gif);
15                     background-position: bottom right;
16                     background-repeat: no-repeat;
17                     background-attachment: fixed; }
18
19            p      { font-size: 18pt;
20                     color: #aa5588;
21                     text-indent: 1em;
22                     font-family: arial, sans-serif; }
23
24            .dark { font-weight: bold; }
25
26         </style>
27      </head>
28
29      <body>
30
31         <p>
32         This example uses the background-image,
33         background-position and background-attachment
34         styles to place the <span class = "dark">Deitel
35         & Associates, Inc.</span> logo in the bottom,
36         right corner of the page. Notice how the logo
37         stays in the proper position when you resize the
38         browser window.
39         </p>
40
41      </body>
42   </html>
```

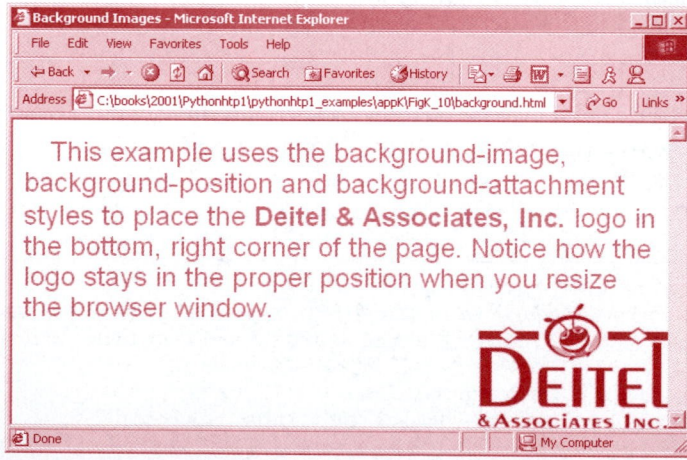

Fig. K.10   Adding a background image with CSS. (Part 2 of 2.)

The ***background-image*** *property* (line 14) specifies the image URL for the image `logo.gif` in the format `url(`*fileLocation*`)`. The Web-page author can set the **back-ground-color** in case the image is not found. The image is overlaid on top of the background color if the image is available.

The ***background-position*** *property* (line 15) places the image on the page. The keywords ***top***, ***bottom***, ***center***, ***left*** and ***right*** are used individually or in combination for vertical and horizontal positioning. Images can be positioned using lengths by that specify the horizontal length followed by the vertical length. For example, to position the image as vertically centered (positioned at 50% of the distance across the screen) and 30 pixels from the top, use

```
background-position: 50% 30px;
```

The ***background-repeat*** *property* (line 16) controls the *tiling* of the background image. Tiling places multiple copies of the image next to each other to fill the background. Here, we set the tiling to ***no-repeat*** to display only one copy of the background image. The **background-repeat** property can be set to ***repeat*** (the default) to tile the image vertically and horizontally, ***repeat-x*** to tile the image only horizontally or ***repeat-y*** to tile the image only vertically.

The final property setting, ***background-attachment: fixed*** (line 17), fixes the image in the position specified by **background-position**. Scrolling the browser window does not move the image from its position. The default value, ***scroll***, moves the image as the user scrolls through the document.

Line 21 indents the first line of text in the element by the specified amount, in this case **1em**. An author might use this property to create a Web page that reads more like a novel, in which the first line of every paragraph is indented.

Line 24 uses the ***font-weight*** *property* to specify the "boldness" of text. Possible values are ***bold***, ***normal*** (the default), ***bolder*** (bolder than **bold** text) and ***lighter*** (lighter than **normal** text). Boldness also can be specified with multiples of 100, from 100 to 900 (e.g., **100**, **200**, …, **900**). Text specified as **normal** is equivalent to **400**, and **bold** text is equivalent to **700**. However, many systems do not have fonts that scale this finely, so using the values from **100** to **900** might not display the desired effect.

Another CSS property that formats text is the ***font-style*** *property*, which allows the developer to set text to ***none***, ***italic*** or ***oblique*** (**oblique** defaults to **italic** if the system does not support oblique text).

K.9 Element Dimensions

In addition to positioning elements, CSS rules can specify the actual dimensions of each page element. Figure K.11 demonstrates how to set the dimensions of elements.

```
1   <?xml version = "1.0"?>
2   <!DOCTYPE html PUBLIC "-//W3C//DTD XHTML 1.0 Strict//EN"
3      "http://www.w3.org/TR/xhtml1/DTD/xhtml1-strict.dtd">
4
5   <!-- Fig. K.11: width.html                          -->
6   <!-- Setting box dimensions and aligning text. -->
```

Fig. K.11   Setting box dimensions and aligning text. (Part 1 of 2.)

```
7
8   <html xmlns = "http://www.w3.org/1999/xhtml">
9      <head>
10        <title>Box Dimensions</title>
11
12        <style type = "text/css">
13
14           div { background-color: #ffccff;
15                 margin-bottom: .5em }
16        </style>
17
18     </head>
19
20     <body>
21
22        <div style = "width: 20%">Here is some
23        text that goes in a box which is
24        set to stretch across twenty percent
25        of the width of the screen.</div>
26
27        <div style = "width: 80%; text-align: center">
28        Here is some CENTERED text that goes in a box
29        which is set to stretch across eighty percent of
30        the width of the screen.</div>
31
32        <div style = "width: 20%; height: 30%; overflow: scroll">
33        This box is only twenty percent of
34        the width and thirty percent of the height.
35        What do we do if it overflows? Set the
36        overflow property to scroll!</div>
37
38     </body>
39  </html>
```

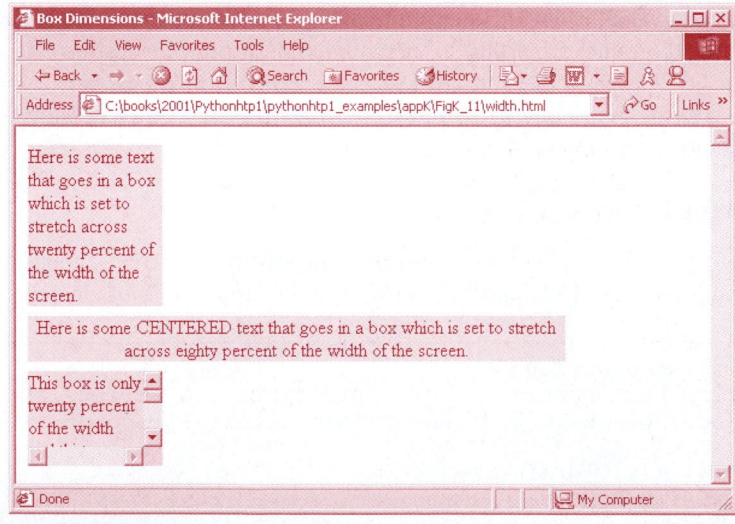

Fig. K.11   Setting box dimensions and aligning text. (Part 2 of 2.)

The inline style in line 22 illustrates how to set the **width** of an element on screen; here, we indicate that the **div** element should occupy 20% of the screen width. Most elements are left-aligned by default; however, this alignment can be altered to position the element elsewhere. The height of an element can be set similarly, using the **height** property. The **height** and **width** values also can be assigned relative and absolute lengths. For example

```
width: 10em
```

sets the element's width to be equal to 10 times the font size. Line 27 sets text in the element to be **center** aligned; some other values for the **text-align** property are **left** and **right**.

One problem with setting both dimensions of an element is that the content inside the element can exceed the set boundaries, in which case the element is simply made large enough for all the content to fit. However, in line 32, we set the **overflow** property to **scroll**, a setting that adds scrollbars if the text overflows the boundaries.

K.10 Text Flow and the Box Model

A browser normally places text and elements on screen in the order in which they appear in the XHTML document. However, as we have seen with absolute positioning, it is possible to remove elements from the normal flow of text. *Floating* allows you to move an element to one side of the screen; other content in the document then flows around the floated element. In addition, each block-level element has a box drawn around it, known as the *box model*. The properties of this box can be adjusted to control the amount of padding inside the element and the margins outside the element (Fig. K.12).

In addition to text, whole elements can be *floated* to the left or right of content. This means that any nearby text wraps around the floated element. For example, in lines 30–32, we float a **div** element to the **right** side of the screen. As you can see from the sample screen capture, the text from lines 34–41 flows cleanly to the left and underneath the **div** element.

The second property on line 30, **margin**, specifies the distance between the edge of the element and any other element on the page. When the browser renders elements in the box model, the content of each element is surrounded by *padding*, a *border* and a *margin* (Fig. K.13).

Margins for individual sides of an element can be specified by using **margin-top**, **margin-right**, **margin-left** and **margin-bottom**.

Lines 43–47 specify a **div** element that floats at the right side of the content. Property **padding** for the **div** element is set to **.5em**. *Padding* is the distance between the content inside an element and the element's border. Like the **margin**, the **padding** can be set for each side of the box, with **padding-top**, **padding-right**, **padding-left** and **padding-bottom**.

A portion of lines 56–57 shows that you can interrupt the flow of text around a **float**ed element by setting the **clear** property to the same direction as that in which the element is **float**ed—**right** or **left**. Setting the **clear** property to **all** interrupts the flow on both sides of the document.

Note that the text in the result window is justified. This is done by setting the **text-align** property to **justify** (line 19). The **text-align** property determines how text is aligned within an element.

```
 1   <?xml version = "1.0"?>
 2   <!DOCTYPE html PUBLIC "-//W3C//DTD XHTML 1.0 Strict//EN"
 3       "http://www.w3.org/TR/xhtml1/DTD/xhtml1-strict.dtd">
 4
 5   <!-- Fig. K.12: floating.html            -->
 6   <!-- Floating elements and element boxes. -->
 7
 8   <html xmlns = "http://www.w3.org/1999/xhtml">
 9      <head>
10         <title>Flowing Text Around Floating Elements</title>
11
12         <style type = "text/css">
13
14            div { background-color: #ccffcc;
15                  margin-bottom: .5em;
16                  font-size: 1.5em;
17                  width: 50% }
18
19            p   { text-align: justify; }
20
21         </style>
22
23      </head>
24
25      <body>
26
27         <div style = "text-align: center">
28            Deitel & Associates, Inc.</div>
29
30         <div style = "float: right; margin: .5em;
31            text-align: right">
32            Corporate Training and Publishing</div>
33
34         <p>Deitel & Associates, Inc. is an internationally
35         recognized corporate training and publishing organization
36         specializing in programming languages, Internet/World
37         Wide Web technology and object technology education.
38         Deitel & Associates, Inc. is a member of the World Wide
39         Web Consortium. The company provides courses on Java,
40         C++, Visual Basic, C, Internet and World Wide Web
41         programming, and Object Technology.</p>
42
43         <div style = "float: right; padding: .5em;
44            text-align: right">
45            Leading-edge Programming Textbooks, e-learning products
46            and interactive Multimedia-intensive teaching tutorials
47         </div>
48
49         <p>The company's clients include many Fortune 1000
50         companies, government agencies, branches of the military
51         and business organizations. Through its publishing
52         partnership with Prentice Hall, Deitel & Associates,
53         Inc. publishes leading-edge programming textbooks,
```

Fig. K.12 Floating elements, aligning text and setting box dimensions. (Part 1 of 2.)

```
54        professional books, interactive CD-ROM-based multimedia
55        Cyber Classrooms, satellite courses and World Wide Web
56        courses.<span style = "clear: right"> Here is some
57        unflowing text. Here is some unflowing text.</span></p>
58
59     </body>
60  </html>
```

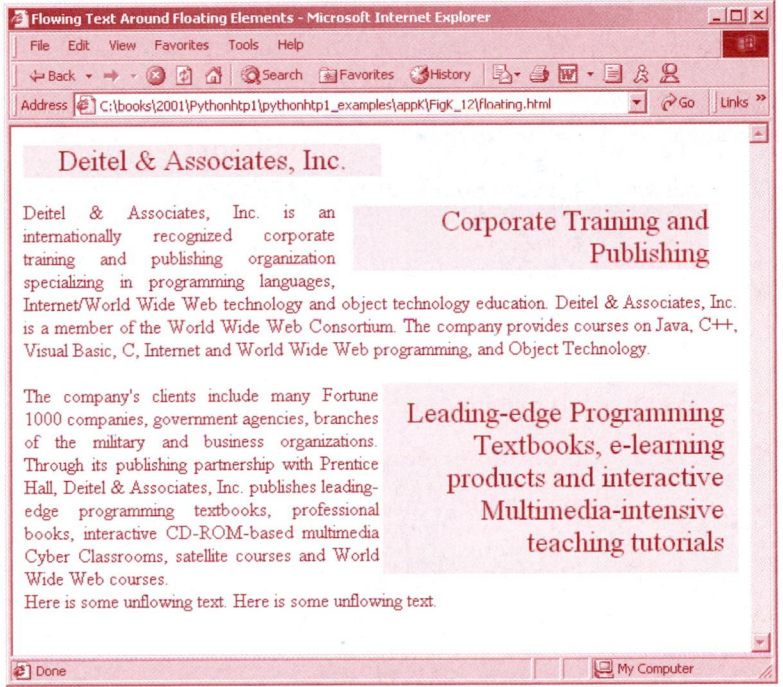

Fig. K.12   Floating elements, aligning text and setting box dimensions. (Part 2 of 2.)

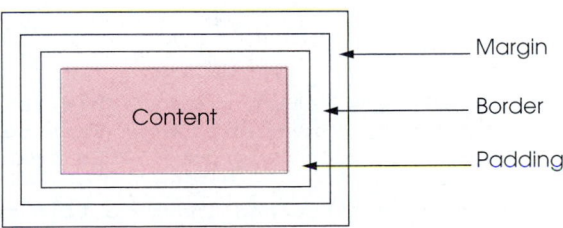

Fig. K.13   Box model for block-level elements.

Another property of every block-level element on screen is the border, which lies between the padding space and the margin space and has numerous properties for adjusting its appearance as shown in Fig. K.14.

```
1   <?xml version = "1.0"?>
2   <!DOCTYPE html PUBLIC "-//W3C//DTD XHTML 1.0 Strict//EN"
3      "http://www.w3.org/TR/xhtml1/DTD/xhtml1-strict.dtd">
4
5   <!-- Fig. K.14: borders.html        -->
6   <!-- Setting borders of an element. -->
7
8   <html xmlns = "http://www.w3.org/1999/xhtml">
9      <head>
10         <title>Borders</title>
11
12         <style type = "text/css">
13
14            body    { background-color: #ccffcc }
15
16            div     { text-align: center;
17                      margin-bottom: 1em;
18                      padding: .5em }
19
20            .thick  { border-width: thick }
21
22            .medium { border-width: medium }
23
24            .thin   { border-width: thin }
25
26            .groove { border-style: groove }
27
28            .inset  { border-style: inset }
29
30            .outset { border-style: outset }
31
32            .red    { border-color: red }
33
34            .blue   { border-color: blue }
35
36         </style>
37      </head>
38
39      <body>
40
41         <div class = "thick groove">This text has a border</div>
42         <div class = "medium groove">This text has a border</div>
43         <div class = "thin groove">This text has a border</div>
44
45         <p class = "thin red inset">A thin red line...</p>
46         <p class = "medium blue outset">
47            And a thicker blue line</p>
48
49      </body>
50   </html>
```

Fig. K.14 Applying borders to elements. (Part 1 of 2.)

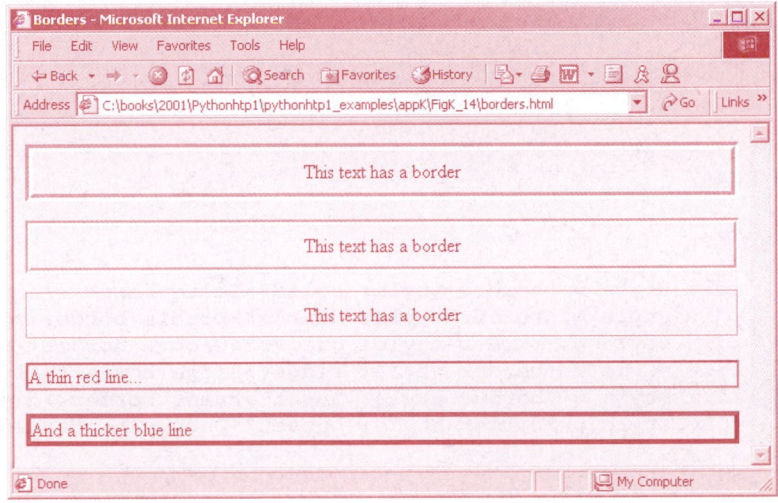

Fig. K.14 Applying borders to elements. (Part 2 of 2.)

In this example, we set three properties—**border-width**, **border-color** and **border-style**. The **border-width** property may be set to any of the CSS lengths or to a predefined value—*thin*, *medium* or *thick*. The **border-color** property sets the color. (This property has different meanings for different borders.)

As with **padding** and **margin**s, each of the border properties may be set for individual sides of the box (e.g., **border-top-style** or **border-left-color**). A developer can assign more than one class to an XHTML element by using the **class** attribute as shown in line 41.

The **border-style**s are *none*, *hidden*, *dotted*, *dashed*, *solid*, *double*, *groove*, *ridge*, *inset* and *outset*. Borders **groove** and **ridge** have opposite effects, as do *inset* and *outset*. Figure K.15 illustrates these border styles.

```
1   <?xml version = "1.0"?>
2   <!DOCTYPE html PUBLIC "-//W3C//DTD XHTML 1.0 Strict//EN"
3      "http://www.w3.org/TR/xhtml11/DTD/xhtml11-strict.dtd">
4
5   <!-- Fig. K.15: borders2.html   -->
6   <!-- Various border-styles.     -->
7
8   <html xmlns = "http://www.w3.org/1999/xhtml">
9      <head>
10        <title>Borders</title>
11
12        <style type = "text/css">
13
14           body    { background-color: #ccffcc }
15
```

Fig. K.15 Various **border-style**s. (Part 1 of 2.)

```
16              div       { text-align: center;
17                          margin-bottom: .3em;
18                          width: 50%;
19                          position: relative;
20                          left: 25%;
21                          padding: .3em }
22          </style>
23      </head>
24
25      <body>
26
27          <div style = "border-style: solid">Solid border</div>
28          <div style = "border-style: double">Double border</div>
29          <div style = "border-style: groove">Groove border</div>
30          <div style = "border-style: ridge">Ridge border</div>
31          <div style = "border-style: inset">Inset border</div>
32          <div style = "border-style: outset">Outset border</div>
33
34      </body>
35  </html>
```

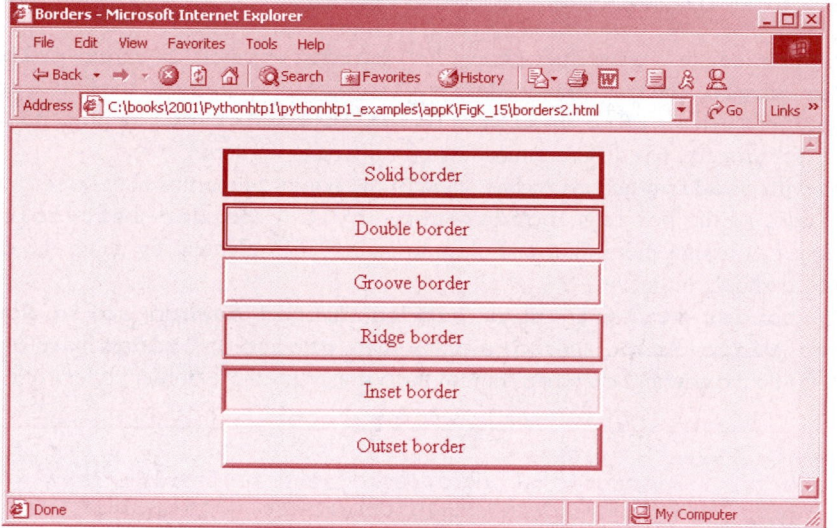

Fig. K.15   Various **border-style**s. (Part 2 of 2.)

K.11 User Style Sheets

Users can define their own *user style sheets* to format pages based on their preferences. For example, people with visual impairments may want to increase the page's text size. A Web-page author needs to be careful because they may inadvertently override user preferences with defined styles. This section discusses possible conflicts between *author styles* and *user styles*.

Figure K.16 contains an author style. The **font-size** is set to **9pt** for all **<p>** tags that have class **note** applied to them.

User style sheets are external style sheets. Figure K.17 shows a user style sheet that sets the **body**'s **font-size** to **20pt**, **color** to **yellow** and **background-color** to **#000080**.

User style sheets are not **link**ed to a document; rather, they are set in the browser's options. To add a user style sheet in Internet Explorer 5.5, select **Internet Options...**, located in the **Tools** menu. In the **Internet Options** dialog (Fig. K.18), select **Accessibility...**, Check the **Format documents using my style sheet** check box and type the location of the user style sheet. Internet Explorer 5.5 applies the user style sheet to any document it loads.

```
1   <?xml version = "1.0"?>
2   <!DOCTYPE html PUBLIC "-//W3C//DTD XHTML 1.0 Strict//EN"
3       "http://www.w3.org/TR/xhtml1/DTD/xhtml1-strict.dtd">
4
5   <!-- Fig. K.16: user_absolute.html -->
6   <!-- User styles.               -->
7
8   <html xmlns = "http://www.w3.org/1999/xhtml">
9      <head>
10        <title>User Styles</title>
11
12        <style type = "text/css">
13
14           .note { font-size: 9pt }
15
16        </style>
17     </head>
18
19     <body>
20
21        <p>Thanks for visiting my Web site. I hope you enjoy it.
22        </p><p class = "note">Please Note: This site will be
23        moving soon. Please check periodically for updates.</p>
24
25     </body>
26  </html>
```

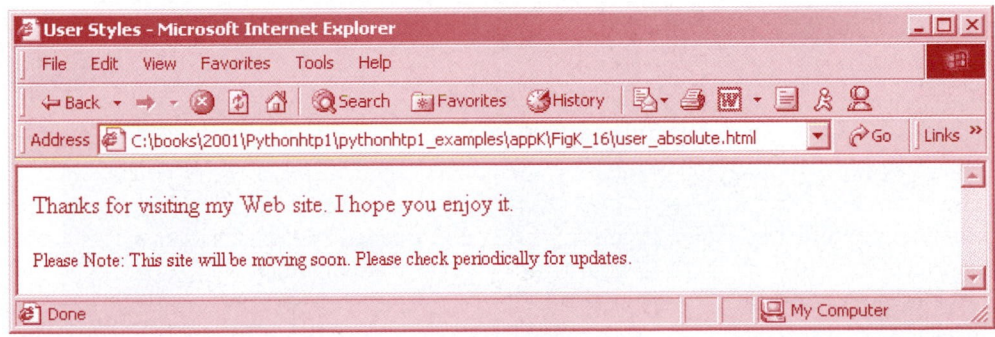

Fig. K.16 **pt** measurement used to modify text size.

```
1   /* Fig. K.17: userstyles.css */
2   /* User stylesheet.          */
3
4   body       { font-size: 20pt;
5                color: yellow;
6                background-color: #000080 }
```

Fig. K.17   User style sheet.

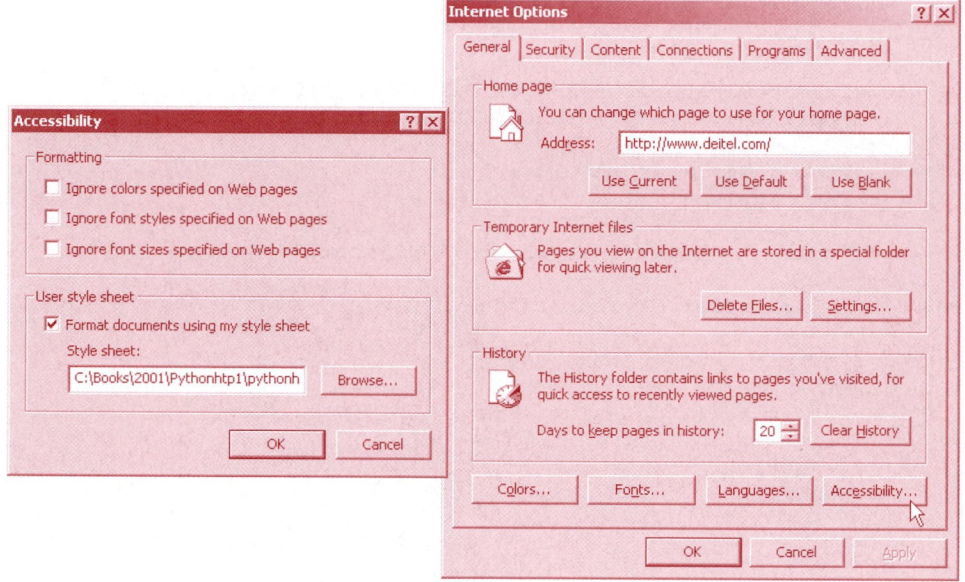

Fig. K.18   User style sheet added in Internet Explorer 5.5.

The Web page from Fig. K.16 is displayed in Fig. K.19, with the application of the user style sheet from Fig. K.17.

Fig. K.19   Web page with user styles applied.

In this example, if users define their own **font-size** in user style sheets, the author styles have higher precedence and override the user styles. The **9pt** font specified in the author style sheet overrides the **20pt** font specified in the user style sheet. This small font may make pages difficult to read, especially for individuals with visual impairments. A developer can avoid this problem by using relative measurements (such as **em** or **ex**) instead of absolute measurements such as **pt**. Figure K.20 changes the **font-size** property to use a relative measurement (line 14), which does not override the user style set in Fig. K.17. Instead, the font size displayed is relative to that specified in the user style sheet. In this case, text enclosed in the **<p>** tag displays as **20pt** and **<p>** tags that have class **note** applied to them are displayed in **15pt** (**.75** times **20pt**).

```
1   <?xml version = "1.0"?>
2   <!DOCTYPE html PUBLIC "-//W3C//DTD XHTML 1.0 Strict//EN"
3       "http://www.w3.org/TR/xhtml1/DTD/xhtml1-strict.dtd">
4
5   <!-- Fig. K.20: user_relative.html -->
6   <!-- User styles.                 -->
7
8   <html xmlns = "http://www.w3.org/1999/xhtml">
9       <head>
10          <title>User Styles</title>
11
12          <style type = "text/css">
13
14              .note { font-size: .75em }
15
16          </style>
17      </head>
18
19      <body>
20
21          <p>Thanks for visiting my Web site. I hope you enjoy it.
22          </p><p class = "note">Please Note: This site will be
23          moving soon. Please check periodically for updates.</p>
24
25      </body>
26  </html>
```

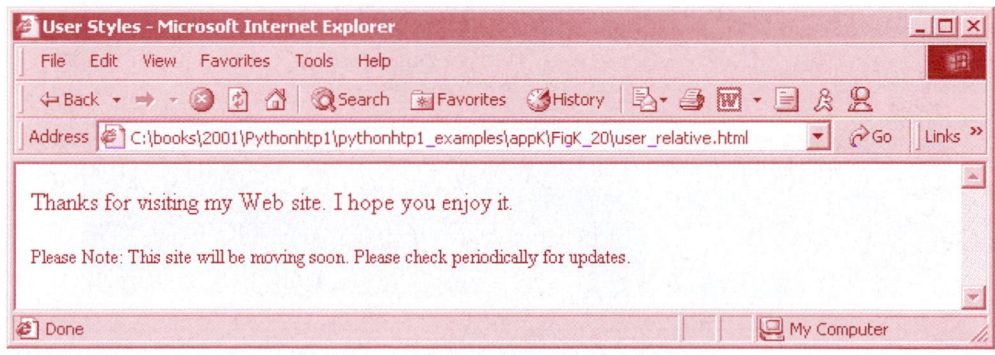

Fig. K.20   **em** measurement used to modify text size.

Fig. K.21 displays the Web page from Fig. K.20 with the application of the user style sheet from Fig. K.16. Notice that the second line of text displayed is larger than the same line of text in Fig. K.19.

K.12 Internet and World Wide Web Resources

www.w3.org/TR/REC-CSS2
The W3C *Cascading Style Sheets, Level 2* specification contains a list of all the CSS properties. The specification also provides helpful examples detailing the use of many of the properties.

www.webreview.com/style
This site has several charts of CSS properties, including a list detailing which browsers support what attributes and to what extent.

tech.irt.org/articles/css.htm
This site contains articles dealing with CSS.

www.web-weaving.net
This site contains many CSS articles.

SUMMARY

- The inline style allows a developer to declare a style for an individual element by using the **style** attribute in that element's opening XHTML tag.
- Each CSS property is followed by a colon and the value of the attribute.
- The **color** property sets text color. Color names and hexadecimal codes may be used as the value.
- Styles that are placed in the **<style>** tag apply to the entire document.
- **style** element attribute **type** specifies the MIME type (the specific encoding format) of the style sheet. Style sheets use **text/css**.
- Each rule body begins and ends with a curly brace (**{** and **}**).
- Style class declarations are preceded by a period and are applied to elements of that specific class.
- The CSS rules in a style sheet use the same format as inline styles: The property is followed by a colon (**:**) and the value of that property. Multiple properties are separated by semicolons (**;**).
- The **background-color** attribute specifies the background color of the element.

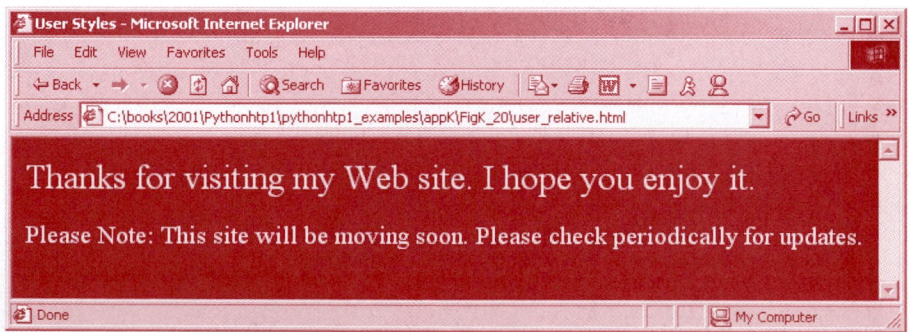

Fig. K.21   Relative measurements in author styles.

- The **font-family** attribute names a specific font that should be displayed. Generic font families allow authors to specify a type of font instead of a specific font, in case a browser does not support a specific font. The **font-size** property specifies the size used to render the font.

- The **class** attribute applies a style class to an element.

- Pseudoclasses provide the author access to content not specifically declared in the document. The **hover** pseudoclass is activated when the user moves the mouse cursor over an element.

- The **text-decoration** property applies decorations to text within an element, such as **underline**, **overline**, **line-through** and **blink**.

- To apply rules to multiple elements, separate the elements with commas in the style sheet.

- A pixel is a relative-length measurement: It varies in size based on screen resolution. Other relative lengths are **em**, **ex** and percentages.

- The other units of measurement available in CSS are absolute-length measurements—i.e., units that do not vary in size. These units can be **in** (inches), **cm** (centimeters), **mm** (millimeters), **pt** (points; 1 **pt**=1/72 **in**) and **pc** (picas; 1 **pc** = 12 **pt**).

- External linking can create a uniform look for a Web site; separate pages can all use the same styles. Modifying a single file makes changes to styles across an entire Web site.

- **link**'s **rel** attribute specifies a relationship between two documents.

- The CSS **position** property allows absolute positioning, which provides greater control over where elements reside. Specifying an element's **position** as **absolute** removes it from the normal flow of elements on the page and positions it according to distance from the **top**, **left**, **right** or **bottom** margins of its parent element.

- The **z-index** property allows a developer to layer overlapping elements. Elements that have higher **z-index** values are displayed in front of elements with lower **z-index** values.

- Unlike absolute positioning, relative positioning keeps elements in a general flow on the page and offsets them by the specified **top**, **left**, **right** or **bottom** values.

- Property **background-image** specifies the URL of the image, in the format **url(***fileLocation***)**. The property **background-position** places the image on the page using the values **top**, **bottom**, **center**, **left** and **right** individually or in combination for vertical and horizontal positioning. You can also position by using lengths.

- The **background-repeat** property controls the tiling of the background image. Setting the tiling to **no-repeat** displays one copy of the background image on screen. The **background-repeat** property can be set to **repeat** (the default) to tile the image vertically and horizontally, to **repeat-x** to tile the image only horizontally or to **repeat-y** to tile the image only vertically.

- The property setting **background-attachment: fixed** fixes the image in the position specified by **background-position**. Scrolling the browser window does not move the image from its set position. The default value, **scroll**, moves the image as the user scrolls the window.

- The **text-indent** property indents the first line of text in the element by the specified amount.

- The **font-weight** property specifies the "boldness" of text. Values besides **bold** and **normal** (the default) are **bolder** (bolder than **bold** text) and **lighter** (lighter than **normal** text). The value also may be justified with multiples of 100, from 100 to 900 (i.e., **100**, **200**, …, **900**). Text specified as **normal** is equivalent to **400**, and **bold** text is equivalent to **700**.

- The **font-style** property allows the developer to set text to **none**, **italic** or **oblique**. (**oblique** will default to **italic** if the system does not have a separate font file for oblique text, which is normally the case.)

- **span** is a generic grouping element; it does not apply any inherent formatting to its contents. Its main use is to apply styles or **id** attributes to a block of text. Element **span** is displayed inline (an inline element) with other text and with no line breaks. A similar element is the **div** element, which also applies no inherent styles, but is displayed on a separate line, with margins above and below (a block-level element).

- The dimensions of elements on a page can be set with CSS by using the **height** and **width** properties.

- Text within an element can be **center**ed using **text-align**; other values for the **text-align** property are **left** and **right**.

- One problem with setting both dimensions of an element is that the content inside the element might sometimes exceed the set boundaries, in which case the element must be made large enough for all the content to fit. However, a developer can set the **overflow** property to **scroll**; this setting adds scroll bars if the text overflows the boundaries set for it.

- Browsers normally place text and elements on screen in the order in which they appear in the XHTML file. Elements can be removed from the normal flow of text. Floating allows you to move an element to one side of the screen; other content in the document will then flow around the floated element.

- Each block-level element has a box drawn around it, known as the box model. The properties of this box are easily adjusted.

- The **margin** property determines the distance between the element's edge and any outside text.

- CSS uses a box model to render elements on screen. The content of each element is surrounded by padding, a border and margins.

- Margins for individual sides of an element can be specified by using **margin-top**, **margin-right**, **margin-left** and **margin-bottom**.

- The padding is the distance between the content inside an element and the edge of the element. Padding can be set for each side of the box by using **padding-top**, **padding-right**, **padding-left** and **padding-bottom**.

- A developer can interrupt the flow of text around a **float**ed element by setting the **clear** property to the same direction in which the element is **float**ed—**right** or **left**. Setting the **clear** property to **all** interrupts the flow on both sides of the document.

- A property of every block-level element on screen is its border. The border lies between the padding space and the margin space and has numerous properties with which to adjust its appearance.

- The **border-width** property may be set to any of the CSS lengths or to the predefined values **thin**, **medium** and **thick**.

- The **border-style**s available are **none**, **hidden**, **dotted**, **dashed**, **solid**, **double**, **groove**, **ridge**, **inset** and **outset**.

- The **border-color** property sets the color used for the border.

- The class attribute allows more than one class to be assigned to an XHTML element.

TERMINOLOGY

absolute positioning	**background-repeat**
absolute-length measurement	**blink**
arial font	block-level element
background	border
background-attachment	**border-color**
background-color	**border-style**
background-image	**border-width**
background-position	box model

Cascading Style Sheets (CSS)
class attribute
clear property value
cm (centimeter)
colon (**:**)
color
CSS rule
cursive generic font family
dashed border-style
dotted border-style
double border-style
em (size of font)
embedded style sheet
ex (*x*-height of font)
floated element
font-style property
generic font family
groove border style
hidden border style
href attribute
in (inch)
inline style
inline-level element
inset border-style
large relative font size
larger relative font size
left
line-through text decoration
link element
linking to an external style sheet
margin
margin-bottom property
margin-left property
margin-right property
margin-top property
medium relative border width
medium relative font size
mm (millimeter)
monospace
none border-style

outset border-style
overflow property
overline text decoration
padding
parent element
pc (pica)
pseudoclass
pt (point)
rel attribute (**link**)
relative positioning
relative-length measurement
repeat
ridge border-style
right
sans-serif generic font family
scroll
separation of structure from content
serif generic font family
small relative font size
smaller relative font size
solid border-style
span element
style
style attribute
style class
style in header section of the document
text flow
text/css MIME type
text-align
text-decoration property
text-indent
thick border width
thin border width
user-style sheet
x-large relative font size
x-small relative font size
xx-large relative font size
xx-small relative font size
z-index

SELF-REVIEW EXERCISES

K.1   Fill in the blanks in each of the following statements:

    a) Using the _____ element allows authors to use external style sheets in their pages.

    b) To apply a CSS rule to more than one element at a time, separate the element names with a _____.

    c) Pixels are a(n) _____ -length measurement unit.

    d) The **hover** _____ is activated when the user moves the mouse cursor over the specified element.

e) Setting the **overflow** property to _____ provides a mechanism for containing inner content without compromising specified box dimensions.

f) Whereas _____ is a generic inline element that applies no inherent formatting; _____ is a generic block-level element that applies no inherent formatting.

g) Setting the **background-repeat** property to _____ tiles the specified **background-image** only vertically.

h) If you **float** an element, you can stop the flowing text by using property _____.

i) The _____ property allows you to indent the first line of text in an element.

j) Three components of the box model are the _____, _____ and _____.

K.2   Assume that the size of the base font on a system is 12 points. State whether each of the following is *true* or *false*. If *false*, explain why.

a) 36-point font equals to 3 **em**s.

b) 8-point font equals to 1.5 **em**s.

c) 24-point font equals to 3 picas.

d) 12-point font equals to 1/6 inches.

e) 1-inch font equals to 12 picas.

ANSWERS TO SELF-REVIEW EXERCISES

K.1   a) **link**. b) comma. c) relative. d) pseudoclass. e) **scroll**. f) **span, div**. g) **y-repeat**. h) **clear**. i) **text-indent**. j) padding, border, margin.

K.2   a) True. b) False. 8-point font equals to 0.75 **em**s. c) False. 24-point font equals to 3 picas. d) True. e) False. 1-inch font equals to 6 picas.

EXERCISES

K.3   Write a CSS rule that makes all text 1.5 times larger than the base font of the system and colors the text red.

K.4   Write a CSS rule that removes the underline from all links inside list items (**li**) and shifts them left by 3 **em**s.

K.5   Write a CSS rule that places a background image halfway down the page, tiling it horizontally. The image should remain in place when the user scrolls up or down.

K.6   Write a CSS rule that gives all **h1** and **h2** elements a padding of 0.5 **em**s, a **groove**d border style and a margin of 0.5 **em**s.

K.7   Write a CSS rule that changes the color of all elements containing attribute **class = "greenMove"** to green and shifts them down 25 pixels and right 15 pixels.

K.8   Write an XHTML document that shows the results of a color survey. The document should contain a form, with radio buttons, that allows each user to vote for a favorite color. One of the colors should be selected as a default. The document should also contain a table showing various colors and the corresponding percentage of votes for each color. (Each row should be displayed in the color to which it is referring.) Use attributes to format width, border and cell spacing for the table.

Accessibility

Objectives

- To introduce the World Wide Web Consortium's Web Content Accessibility Guidelines 1.0 (WCAG 1.0).
- To understand how to use the **alt** attribute of the **<img>** tag to describe images to people with visual impairments, mobile-Web-device users, search engines, etc.
- To understand how to make XHTML tables more accessible to page readers.
- To understand how to verify that XHTML tags are used properly and to ensure that Web pages are viewable on any type of display or reader.
- To understand how VoiceXML™ and CallXML™ are changing the way people with disabilities access information on the Web.
- To introduce the various accessibility aids offered in Windows 2000.

'Tis the good reader that makes the good book...
Ralph Waldo Emerson

Outline

L.1 Introduction

Enabling a Web site to meet the needs of individuals with disabilities is a concern for all businesses. People with disabilities are a significant portion of the population, and legal ramifications exist for Web sites that discriminate by not providing adequate and universal access to their resources. In this chapter, we explore the *Web Accessibility Initiative*, its guidelines, various laws regarding businesses and their availability to people with disabilities and how some companies have developed systems, products and services to meet the needs of this demographic.

L.2 Web Accessibility

In 1999, the National Federation for the Blind (NFB) filed a lawsuit against *America On Line (AOL)* for not supplying access to its services for people with visual disabilities. The *Americans with Disabilities Act (ADA)* and many other efforts address Web accessibility laws (Fig. L.1).

Act	Purpose
Americans with Disabilities Act	The ADA prohibits discrimination on the basis of disability in employment, state and local government, public accommodations, commercial facilities, transportation and telecommunications.
Telecommunications Act of 1996	The Telecommunications Act of 1996 contains two amendments to Section 255 and Section 251(a)(2) of the Communications Act of 1934. These amendments require that communication devices, such as cell phones, telephones and pagers, be accessible to individuals with disabilities.
Individuals with Disabilities Education Act of 1997	Education materials in schools must be made accessible to children with disabilities.
Rehabilitation Act	Section 504 of the Rehabilitation Act states that college sponsored activities receiving federal funding cannot discriminate against individuals with disabilities. Section 508 mandates that all government institutions receiving federal funding design their Web sites such that they are accessible to individuals with disabilities. Businesses that service the government also must abide by this act.

Fig. L.1   Acts designed to protect access to the Internet for people with disabilities.

WeMedia.com™ (Fig. L.2) is a Web site dedicated to providing news, information, products and services for the millions of people with disabilities, their families, friends and caregivers. There are 54 million Americans with disabilities, representing an estimated $1 trillion in purchasing power.

The Internet enables individuals with disabilities to work in a vast array of new fields. Technologies such as voice activation, visual enhancers and auditory aid, afford more employment opportunities. People with visual impairments may use computer monitors with enlarged text, while people with physical impairments may use head pointers with on-screen keyboards.

Federal regulations will be applied to the Internet to accommodate the needs of people with hearing, vision and speech impairments. In the following sections, we explore a variety of products and services that provide Internet access for people with disabilities.

L.3 Web Accessibility Initiative

On April 7, 1997, the World Wide Web Consortium (W3C) launched the *Web Accessibility Initiative* (WAI™). Although accessibility can refer to buildings or objects that can be used by people with disabilities, the W3C *accessibility* refers to the usability of an application or Web site by people with disabilities. Currently, many Web sites are considered either partially or totally inaccessible to people with visual, learning or mobility impairments. In many cases, total accessibility is difficult to achieve because people have varying types of disabilities, language barriers and computer hardware and software inconsistencies. However, Web sites can attain high levels of accessibility. As more people with disabilities use the Internet, it is essential that Web-site designers increase the accessibility of their sites. The WAI's mission is to encourage high levels of accessibility, as discussed on its Web site at **www.w3.org/WAI**.

This appendix explains some of the techniques for developing accessible Web sites. The WAI published the *Web Content Accessibility Guidelines (WCAG) 1.0* to help businesses determine whether, and to what level, their Web sites are accessible. The WCAG 1.0 (**www.w3.org/TR/WCAG10**) provides checkpoints to indicate specific accessibility requirements. Each checkpoint has an associated priority, indicating its importance. *Priority-one checkpoints* are goals that must be met to ensure accessibility; we focus on these points in this chapter. *Priority-two checkpoints*, though not essential, are highly recommended. If priority-two checkpoints are not satisfied, people with certain disabilities will experience difficulty accessing Web sites. *Priority-three checkpoints* specify requirements that only minimally improve accessibility.

To determine whether a Web site is WCAG complaint, the *Center for Applied Special Technology (CAST)* has developed *Bobby 3.2* (**www.cast.org/bobby**), a software program that scans a Web page and identifies non-accessibility issues. Bobby categorizes the issues by WAI checkpoints.

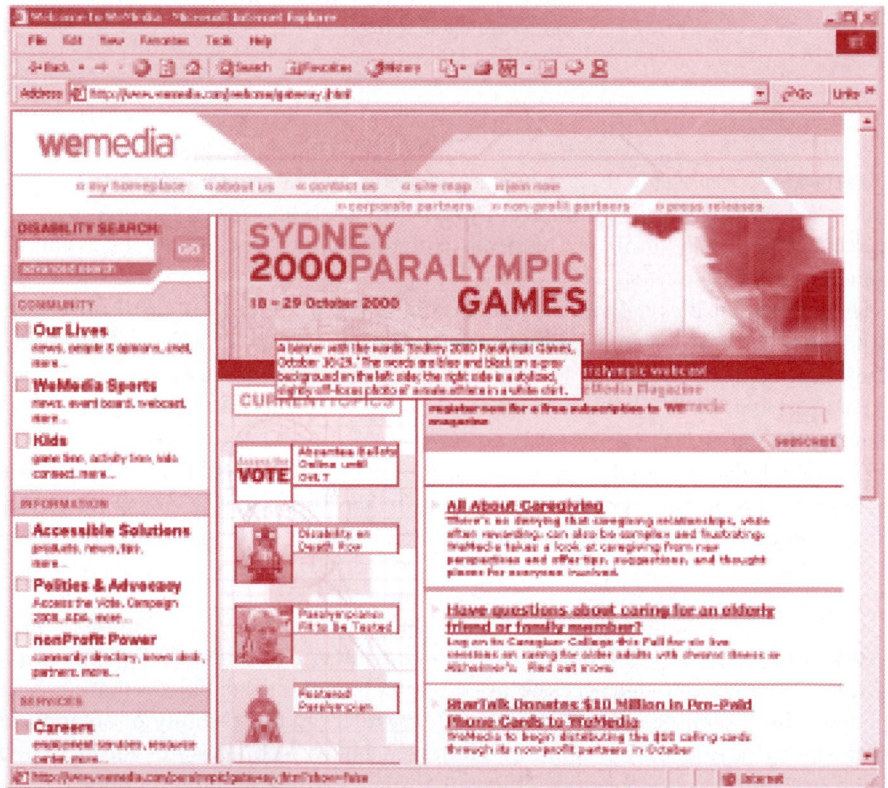

Fig. L.2   Wemedia.com home page. (Courtesy of We Media Inc.)

At the time of this writing, the WAI is working on the *WCAG 2.0* draft, which will supersede WCAG 1.0. In the revision, a single checkpoint in the WCAG 2.0 Working Draft may encompass several checkpoints from WCAG 1.0. The WCAG 2.0 supports a wider range of markup languages (i.e., XML, WML etc.) and content types than its predecessor. To obtain more information about the WCAG 2.0 Working Draft, visit **www.w3.org/ TR/WCAG20**.

For people interested in a summary of Web site accessibility issues, the WAI offers a supplemental checklist of *quick tips*, which presents ten important points for accessible Web site design. More information on the WAI Quick Tips resides at **www.w3.org/ WAI/References/Quicktips**.

L.4 Providing Alternatives for Images

One important WAI requirement is to ensure that every image on a Web page is accompanied by a textual description that clearly defines the purpose of the image. To accomplish this task, use the **alt** attribute of the **<applet>**, **<area>**, **<img>** and **<input>** tags to include a text equivalent of each item. A text equivalent for images, defined using the **object** element, is the text between the start and end **<object>** tags.

Web developers who do not use the **alt** attribute to provide text equivalents increase the difficulty people with visual impairments experience in navigating the Web. Specialized *user agent*s, such as *screen readers* (programs that allow users to hear text and text descriptions displayed on their screens) and *braille displays* (devices that receive data from screen-reading software and output the data as braille), allow people with visual impairments to access text-based information displayed on the screen. A user agent visually interprets Web-page source code and translates it into formatted text and images. Web browsers, such as Microsoft Internet Explorer and Netscape Communicator, and the screen readers mentioned throughout this chapter are examples of user agents.

Web pages that do not provide text equivalents for video and audio clips are difficult for people with visual and hearing impairments to access. Screen readers cannot read images, movies and other nonXHTML objects from these Web pages. Providing multimedia-based information in a variety of ways (e.g., using the **alt** attribute or providing inline descriptions of images) helps maximize the content's accessibility.

Web designers should provide useful text equivalents in the **alt** attribute for use in nonvisual user agents. For example, if the **alt** attribute describes a sales growth chart, the attribute should provide a brief summary of the data; it should not describe the data in the chart. Instead, a complete description of the chart's data should be included in the **longdesc** attribute, which is intended to augment the **alt** attribute's description. The **longdesc** attribute contains the URL that links to a Web page describing the image or multimedia content. Currently, most Web browsers do not support the **longdesc** attribute. An alternative for the **longdesc** attribute is *D-link*, which provides descriptive text about graphs and charts. More information on D-links can be obtained at the *CORDA Technologies* Web site (**www.corda.com**).

Using a screen reader for Web-site navigation can be time consuming and frustrating, as screen readers cannot interpret pictures and other graphical content. A link at the top of each Web page that provides direct access to the page's content allows users to bypass a long list of navigation links or other inaccessible elements. This jump can save time and eliminate frustration for individuals with visual impairments.

L.5 Maximizing Readability by Focusing on Structure

Many Web sites use tags for aesthetic purposes rather than for the appropriate purpose. For example, the `<h1>` heading tag often is used erroneously to make text large and bold rather than as a major section head for content. The desired visual effect may be achieved, but it creates a problem for screen readers. When the screen-reader software encounters the `<h1>` tag, it verbally may inform the user that a new section has been reached when it is not the case, which can confuse users. Use the **h1** only in accordance with its XHTML specifications (e.g., as headings to introduce important sections of a document). Instead of using **h1** to make text large and bold, use CSS (discussed in Appendix K, Cascading Style Sheets) or XSL (discussed in Chapter 15, Extensible Markup Language) to format and style the text. For further examples, refer to the WCAG 1.0 Web site at **www.w3.org/TR/ WCAG10**. [*Note:* The `<strong>` tag also may be used to make text bold; however, screen readers emphasize bold text, which affects the inflection of what is spoken.]

Another accessibility issue is *readability*. When creating a Web page intended for the general public, it is important to consider the reading level (i.e., the comprehension and level of understanding) at which it is written. Web site designers can make their sites easier to read by using shorter words. Designers should also limit slang terms and other nontraditional language that may be problematic for users from other countries.

WCAG 1.0 suggests using a paragraph's first sentence to convey its subject. Stating the point of the paragraph in its first sentence makes it easier to find crucial information and allows readers to bypass unwanted material.

The *Gunning Fog Index*, a formula that produces a readability grade when applied to a text sample, evaluates a Web site's readability. More information about the Gunning Fog Index can be obtained at **www.trainingpost.org/3-2-inst.htm**.

L.6 Accessibility in XHTML Tables

Complex Web pages often contain tables for formatting content and presenting data. Many screen readers are incapable of translating tables correctly unless the tables are designed properly. For example, the *CAST eReader*, a screen reader developed by the Center for Applied Special Technology (**www.cast.org**), starts at the top-left-hand cell and reads columns from left to right, top to bottom. This procedure is known as reading a table in a *linearized* manner. The CAST eReader reads the table in Fig. L.3 as follows:

```
Price of Fruit Fruit Price Apple $0.25 Orange $0.50 Banana
$1.00 Pineapple $2.00
```

This reading does not present the content of the table adequately. WCAG 1.0 recommends using CSS instead of tables, unless the tables' content linearizes in an understandable manner.

If the table in Fig. L.3 were large, the screen reader's linearized reading would be even more confusing to users. Modifying the `<td>` tag with the **headers** attribute and modifying *header cells* (cells specified by the `<th>` tag) with the **id** attribute can help a table be read as intended. Figure L.4 demonstrates how these modifications change the way a table is interpreted.

```
 1   <?xml version = "1.0"?>
 2   <!DOCTYPE html PUBLIC "-//W3C//DTD XHTML 1.0 Strict//EN"
 3      "http://www.w3.org/TR/xhtml1/DTD/xhtml1-strict.dtd">
 4
 5   <!-- Fig. L.3: withoutheaders.html -->
 6   <!-- Table without headers.          -->
 7
 8   <html>
 9      <head>
10         <title>XHTML Table Without Headers</title>
11
12         <style type = "text/css">
13            body { background-color: #ccffaa;
14                   text-align: center }
15         </style>
16      </head>
17
18      <body>
19
20         <p>Price of Fruit</p>
21
22         <table border = "1" width = "50%">
23
24            <tr>
25               <td>Fruit</td>
26               <td>Price</td>
27            </tr>
28
29            <tr>
30               <td>Apple</td>
31               <td>$0.25</td>
32            </tr>
33
34            <tr>
35               <td>Orange</td>
36               <td>$0.50</td>
37            </tr>
38
39            <tr>
40               <td>Banana</td>
41               <td>$1.00</td>
42            </tr>
43
44            <tr>
45               <td>Pineapple</td>
46               <td>$2.00</td>
47            </tr>
48
49         </table>
50
51      </body>
52   </html>
```

Fig. L.3   XHTML table without accessibility modifications. (Part 1 of 2.)

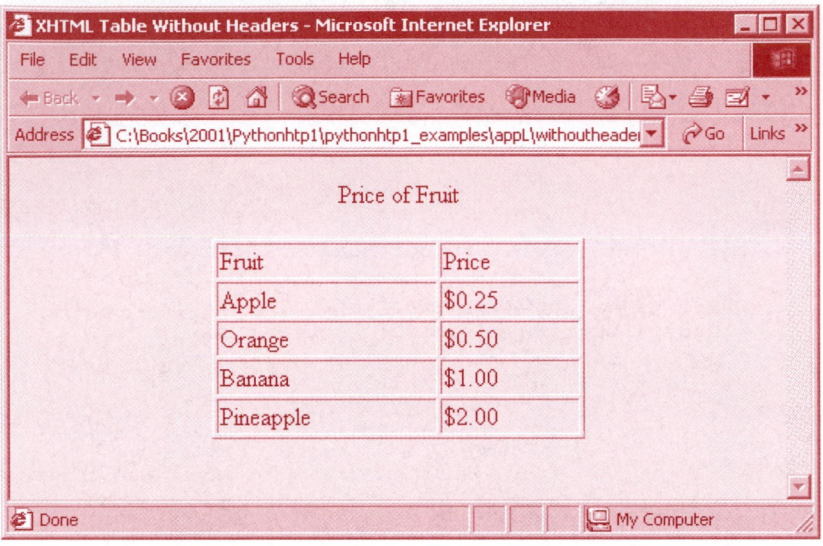

Fig. L.3   XHTML table without accessibility modifications. (Part 2 of 2.)

This table does not appear to be different from a standard XHTML table. However, the table is read in a more intelligent manner by a screen reader. A screen reader vocalizes the data from the table in Fig. L.4 as follows:

```
Caption: Price of Fruit
Summary: This table uses th and the id and headers attributes
to make the table readable by screen readers.
Fruit: Apple, Price: $0.25
Fruit: Orange, Price: $0.50
Fruit: Banana, Price: $1.00
Fruit: Pineapple, Price: $2.00
```

Every cell in the table is preceded by its corresponding header when read by the screen reader. This format helps the listener understand the table. The ***headers*** *attribute* is intended specifically for tables that hold large amounts of data. Most small tables linearize well as long as the **<th>** tag is used properly. The **summary** attribute and the **caption** element are also suggested. For more examples demonstrating how to make tables accessible, visit **www.w3.org/TR/WCAG**.

```
1   <?xml version = "1.0"?>
2   <!DOCTYPE html PUBLIC "-//W3C//DTD XHTML 1.0 Strict//EN"
3      "http://www.w3.org/TR/xhtml1/DTD/xhtml1-strict.dtd">
4
5   <!-- Fig. L.4: withheaders.html -->
6   <!-- Table with headers.         -->
7
```

Fig. L.4   **headers** attribute used to optimize table for screen reading. (Part 1 of 3.)

```
 8    <html>
 9       <head>
10          <title>XHTML Table With Headers</title>
11
12          <style type = "text/css">
13              body { background-color: #ccffaa;
14                     text-align: center }
15          </style>
16       </head>
17
18       <body>
19
20       <!-- this table uses the id and headers attributes to   -->
21       <!-- ensure readability by text-based browsers. It also -->
22       <!-- uses a summary attribute, used screen readers to    -->
23       <!-- describe the table                                 -->
24
25          <table width = "50%" border = "1"
26              summary = "This table uses th elements and id and
27              headers attributes to make the table readable
28              by screen readers">
29
30              <caption><strong>Price of Fruit</strong></caption>
31
32              <tr>
33                  <th id = "fruit">Fruit</th>
34                  <th id = "price">Price</th>
35              </tr>
36
37              <tr>
38                  <td headers = "fruit">Apple</td>
39                  <td headers = "price">$0.25</td>
40              </tr>
41
42              <tr>
43                  <td headers = "fruit">Orange</td>
44                  <td headers = "price">$0.50</td>
45              </tr>
46
47              <tr>
48                  <td headers = "fruit">Banana</td>
49                  <td headers = "price">$1.00</td>
50              </tr>
51
52              <tr>
53                  <td headers = "fruit">Pineapple</td>
54                  <td headers = "price">$2.00</td>
55              </tr>
56
57          </table>
58
59       </body>
60    </html>
```

Fig. L.4   **headers** attribute used to optimize table for screen reading. (Part 2 of 3.)

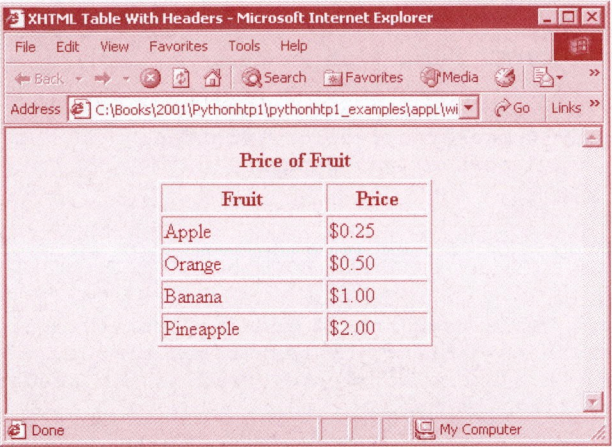

Fig. L.4   **headers** attribute used to optimize table for screen reading. (Part 3 of 3.)

L.7 Accessibility in XHTML Frames

Web designers often use frames to display more than one XHTML file in a single browser window. Frames are a convenient way to ensure that certain content always displays on the screen. Unfortunately, frames often lack proper descriptions, which prevents users with text-based browsers or users listening with speech synthesizers from navigating the Web site.

A site with frames must have meaningful descriptions in the **<title>** tag for each frame. Examples of good titles include "*Navigation Frame*" and "*Main Content Frame.*" Users with text-based browsers, such as Lynx, must choose which frame they want to open; descriptive titles make this choice simpler. However, assigning titles to frames does not solve all the navigation problems associated with frames. The **<noframes>** tag allows Web designers to offer alternative content for browsers that do not support frames. To make a Web page truly accessible, **<noframes>** tags are required.

Good Programming Practice L.1

Always provide titles for frames to ensure that user agents which do not support frames have alternatives.

Good Programming Practice L.2

*Include a title for each frame's contents with the **frame** element, and, if possible, provide links to the individual pages within the frameset so that users still can navigate through the Web pages. To provide access to browsers that do not support frames, use the **<noframes>** tag. It also provides better access to browsers that have limited support.*

WCAG 1.0 suggests using CSS as an alternative to frames, because CSS provides similar functionality and are highly customizable. Unfortunately, the ability to display multiple XHTML documents in a single browser window requires the complete support of HTML 4, which is not widespread. The second generation of Cascading Style Sheets (CSS2) displays a single document as if it were several documents. However, CSS2 is not yet fully supported by many Web browsers.

L.8 Accessibility in XML

XML allows developers to create new markup languages, which may not necessarily incorporate accessibility features. To prevent the proliferation of inaccessible languages, the WAI is developing guidelines—the *XML Guidelines* (*XML GL*)—for creating accessible XML documents. The XML GL recommends including a text description, similar to XHTML's `<alt>` tag, for each nontext object on a page. To facilitate accessibility further, element types should allow grouping and classification and should identify important content. Without an accessible user interface, other efforts to implement accessibility are less effective, so it is essential to create XSLT or CSS style sheets that can produce multiple outputs, including document outlines.

Many XML languages, including Synchronized Multimedia Integration Language (SMIL) and Scalable Vector Graphics (SVG), implement WAI guidelines. The WAI XML Accessibility Guidelines can be found at `www.w3.org/WAI/PF/xmlgl.htm`.

L.9 Using Voice Synthesis and Recognition with VoiceXML™

A joint effort by AT&T®, IBM®, Lucent™ and Motorola® has created an XML vocabulary that marks up information for *speech synthesizers*, which enable computers to speak to users. This technology, called *VoiceXML*, has tremendous implications for people with visual impairments and for the illiterate. VoiceXML-enabled applications read Web pages to the user and understand words spoken into a microphone through *speech recognition* technology. An example of a speech recognition tool is IBM's *ViaVoice* (`www-4.ibm.com/software/speech`).

A VoiceXML interpreter and VoiceXML browser process VoiceXML, a platform-independent XML-based technology. Web browsers may incorporate these interpreters in the future. When a VoiceXML document is loaded, a *voice server* initiates a "conversation" between the user and the computer.

IBM *WebSphere Voice Server SDK 1.5* is a VoiceXML interpreter that tests VoiceXML documents on a desktop computer. To download the VoiceServer SDK, visit `www.alphaworks.ibm.com/tech/voiceserversdk`. [*Note*: To run the VoiceXML program in Fig. L.5, download *Java 2 Platform Standard Edition* (Java SDK) 1.3 from `www.java.sun.com/j2se/1.3`. To obtain installation instructions for the VoiceServer SDK and the Java SDK, visit the Deitel & Associates, Inc. Web site at `www.deitel.com`.]

Figure L.5 and Fig. L.6 show examples of VoiceXML that would be appropriate for a Web site. The document's text is spoken to the user, and the text embedded in the VoiceXML tags allows for interactivity between the user and the browser. The output included in Fig. L.6 demonstrates a conversation that might take place between a user and a computer after the loading of this document.

```
1   <?xml version = "1.0"?>
2   <vxml version = "1.0">
3
4   <!-- Fig. L.5: main.vxml -->
5   <!-- Voice page.          -->
```

Fig. L.5   VoiceXML used to design a home page. (Part 1 of 3.)

```
6
7   <link next = "#home">
8      <grammar>home</grammar>
9   </link>
10
11  <link next = "#end">
12     <grammar>exit</grammar>
13  </link>
14
15  <var name = "currentOption" expr = "'home'"/>
16
17  <form>
18     <block>
19        <emp>Welcome</emp> to the voice page of Deitel and
20        Associates. To exit any time say exit.
21        To go to the home page any time say home.
22     </block>
23     <subdialog src = "#home"/>
24  </form>
25
26  <menu id = "home">
27     <prompt count = "1" timeout = "10s">
28        You have just entered the Deitel home page.
29        Please make a selection by speaking one of the
30        following options:
31        <break msecs = "1000" />
32        <enumerate/>
33     </prompt>
34
35     <prompt count = "2">
36        Please say one of the following.
37        <break msecs = "1000" />
38        <enumerate/>
39     </prompt>
40
41     <choice next = "#about">About us</choice>
42     <choice next = "#directions">Driving directions</choice>
43     <choice next = "publications.vxml">Publications</choice>
44  </menu>
45
46  <form id = "about">
47     <block>
48     About Deitel and Associates, Inc.
49     Deitel and Associates, Inc. is an internationally
50     recognized corporate training and publishing organization,
51     specializing in programming languages, Internet and World
52     Wide Web technology and object technology education.
53     Deitel and Associates, Inc. is a member of the World Wide
54     Web Consortium. The company provides courses on Java, C++,
55     Visual Basic, C, Internet and World Wide Web programming
56     and Object Technology.
57        <assign name = "currentOption" expr = "'about'"/>
58        <goto next = "#repeat"/>
```

Fig. L.5   VoiceXML used to design a home page. (Part 2 of 3.)

```
59      </block>
60   </form>
61
62   <form id = "directions">
63      <block>
64         Directions to Deitel and Associates, Inc.
65         We are located on Route 20 in Sudbury,
66         Massachusetts, equidistant from route
67      <sayas class = "digits">128</sayas> and route
68      <sayas class = "digits">495</sayas>.
69      <assign name = "currentOption" expr = "'directions'"/>
70      <goto next = "#repeat"/>
71      </block>
72   </form>
73
74   <form id = "repeat">
75      <field name = "confirm" type = "boolean">
76         <prompt>
77            To repeat say yes. To go back to home, say no.
78         </prompt>
79
80         <filled>
81            <if cond = "confirm == true">
82               <goto expr = "'#' + currentOption"/>
83            <else/>
84               <goto next = "#home"/>
85            </if>
86         </filled>
87
88      </field>
89   </form>
90
91   <form id = "end">
92      <block>
93         Thank you for visiting Deitel and Associates voice page.
94         Have a nice day.
95         <exit/>
96      </block>
97   </form>
98
99   </vxml>
```

Fig. L.5   VoiceXML used to design a home page. (Part 3 of 3.)

A VoiceXML document contains a series of dialogs and subdialogs, which result in spoken interaction between the user and the computer. The **<form>** and **<menu>** tags implement the dialogs. A **form** element presents information and gathers data from the user. A **menu** element provides users with options based on users' selections and transfers control to other dialogs.

Lines 7–9 use element **link** to create an active link to the home page. Attribute **next** specifies the URI navigated to when the link is selected. Element **grammar** marks up the text that the user must speak to select the link. In the **link** element, we navigate to the element with **id home** when users speak the word **home**. Lines 11–13 use element **link** to create a link to **id end** when users speak the word **exit**.

Lines 17–24 create a form dialog, using element **form**, which collects information from the user. Lines 18–22 present introductory text. Element **block**, which can exist only within a **form** element, groups elements that perform an action or an event. Element **emp** states that a section of text should be spoken with emphasis. If the level of emphasis is not specified, then the default level—*moderate*—is used. Our example uses the default level. [*Note*: To specify an emphasis level, use the **level** attribute. This attribute accepts the following values: *strong*, *moderate*, *none* and *reduced*.]

The **menu** element on line 26 enables users to select the page to which they would like to link. The **choice** element, which is always part of either a **menu** or a **form**, presents the options. The **next** attribute indicates the page to be loaded when a user makes a selection. The user selects a **choice** element by speaking the text marked up between the tags into a microphone. In this example, the first and second **choice** elements on lines 41–42 transfer control to a *local dialog* (i.e., a location within the same document) when they are selected. The third **choice** element transfers the user to the document **publications.vxml**. Lines 27–33 use element ***prompt*** to instruct the user to make a selection. Attribute ***count*** maintains the number of times a prompt is spoken (i.e., each time a prompt is read, **count** increments by one). The **count** attribute transfers control to another prompt once a certain limit has been reached. Attribute **timeout** specifies how long the program should wait after outputting the prompt for users to respond. In the event that the user does not respond before the timeout period expires, lines 35–39 provide a second, shorter prompt to remind the user to make a selection.

When the user chooses the **publications** option, the **publications.vxml** (Fig. L.6) loads into the browser. Lines 106–111 define **link** elements that provide links to **main.vxml**. Lines 112–114 provide links to the **menu** element (lines 118–138), which asks users to select one of the publications: Java, C or C++. The **form** elements on lines 140–214 describe each of the books on these topics. Once the browser speaks the description, control transfers to the **form** element with an **id** attribute that has a value equal to **repeat** (lines 216–231).

```
1   <?xml version = "1.0"?>
2   <vxml version = "1.0">
3
4   <!-- Fig. L.6: publications.vxml              -->
5   <!-- Voice page for various publications. -->
6
7   <link next = "main.vxml#home">
8      <grammar>home</grammar>
9   </link>
10  <link next = "main.vxml#end">
11     <grammar>exit</grammar>
12  </link>
13  <link next = "#publication">
14     <grammar>menu</grammar>
15  </link>
16
```

Fig. L.6   Publication page of Deitel's VoiceXML page. (Part 1 of 4.)

```
17    <var name = "currentOption" expr = "'home'"/>
18
19    <menu id = "publication">
20
21        <prompt count = "1" timeout = "12s">
22            Following are some of our publications. For more
23            information visit our web page at www.deitel.com.
24            To repeat the following menu, say menu at any time.
25            Please select by saying one of the following books:
26            <break msecs = "1000" />
27            <enumerate/>
28        </prompt>
29
30        <prompt count = "2">
31          Please select from the following books.
32            <break msecs = "1000" />
33            <enumerate/>
34        </prompt>
35
36        <choice next = "#java">Java.</choice>
37        <choice next = "#c">C.</choice>
38        <choice next = "#cplus">C plus plus.</choice>
39    </menu>
40
41    <form id = "java">
42        <block>
43            Java How to program, third edition.
44            The complete, authoritative introduction to Java.
45            Java is revolutionizing software development with
46            multimedia-intensive, platform-independent,
47            object-oriented code for conventional, Internet,
48            Intranet and Extranet-based applets and applications.
49            This Third Edition of the world's most widely used
50            university-level Java textbook carefully explains
51            Java's extraordinary capabilities.
52          <assign name = "currentOption" expr = "'java'"/>
53          <goto next = "#repeat"/>
54        </block>
55    </form>
56
57    <form id = "c">
58        <block>
59            C How to Program, third edition.
60            This is the long-awaited, thorough revision to the
61            world's best-selling introductory C book! The book's
62            powerful "teach by example" approach is based on
63            more than 10,000 lines of live code, thoroughly
64            explained and illustrated with screen captures showing
65            detailed output.World-renowned corporate trainers and
66            best-selling authors Harvey and Paul Deitel offer the
67            most comprehensive, practical introduction to C ever
68            published with hundreds of hands-on exercises, more
69            than 250 complete programs written and documented for
```

Fig. L.6   Publication page of Deitel's VoiceXML page. (Part 2 of 4.)

```
70        easy learning, and exceptional insight into good
71        programming practices, maximizing performance, avoiding
72        errors, debugging, and testing. New features include
73        thorough introductions to C++, Java, and object-oriented
74        programming that build directly on the C skills taught
75        in this book; coverage of graphical user interface
76        development and C library functions; and many new,
77        substantial hands-on projects.For anyone who wants to
78        learn C, improve their existing C skills, and understand
79        how C serves as the foundation for C++, Java, and
80        object-oriented development.
81     <assign name = "currentOption" expr = "'c'"/>
82     <goto next = "#repeat"/>
83   </block>
84 </form>
85
86 <form id = "cplus">
87   <block>
88        The C++ how to program, second edition.
89        With nearly 250,000 sold, Harvey and Paul Deitel's C++
90        How to Program is the world's best-selling introduction
91        to C++ programming. Now, this classic has been thoroughly
92        updated! The new, full-color Third Edition has been
93        completely revised to reflect the ANSI C++ standard, add
94        powerful new coverage of object analysis and design with
95        UML, and give beginning C++ developers even better live
96        code examples and real-world projects. The Deitels' C++
97        How to Program is the most comprehensive, practical
98        introduction to C++ ever published with hundreds of
99        hands-on exercises, roughly 250 complete programs written
100       and documented for easy learning, and exceptional insight
101       into good programming practices, maximizing performance,
102       avoiding errors, debugging, and testing. This new Third
103       Edition covers every key concept and technique ANSI C++
104       developers need to master: control structures, functions,
105       arrays, pointers and strings, classes and data
106       abstraction, operator overloading, inheritance, virtual
107       functions, polymorphism, I/O, templates, exception
108       handling, file processing, data structures, and more. It
109       also includes a detailed introduction to Standard
110       Template Library containers, container adapters,
111       algorithms, and iterators.
112    <assign name = "currentOption" expr = "'cplus'"/>
113    <goto next = "#repeat"/>
114  </block>
115 </form>
116
117 <form id = "repeat">
118   <field name = "confirm" type = "boolean">
119
120     <prompt>
121         To repeat say yes. Say no, to go back to home.
122     </prompt>
```

Fig. L.6   Publication page of Deitel's VoiceXML page. (Part 3 of 4.)

```
123
124        <filled>
125            <if cond = "confirm == true">
126                <goto expr = "'#' + currentOption"/>
127            <else/>
128                <goto next = "#publication"/>
129            </if>
130        </filled>
131    </field>
132 </form>
133 </vxml>
```

Computer:
Welcome to the voice page of Deitel and Associates. To exit any time
say exit. To go to the home page any time say home.

User:
Home

Computer:
You have just entered the Deitel home page. Please make a selection by
speaking one of the following options: About us, Driving directions,
Publications.

User:
Driving directions

Computer:
Directions to Deitel and Associates, Inc.
We are located on Route 20 in Sudbury,
Massachusetts, equidistant from route 128
and route 495.
To repeat say yes. To go back to home, say no.

Fig. L.6   Publication page of Deitel's VoiceXML page. (Part 4 of 4.)

Figure L.6 provides a brief description of each VoiceXML tag used in the previous example (Fig. L.6).

VoiceXML Tag	Description
`<assign>`	Assigns a value to a variable.
`<block>`	Presents information to users without any interaction between the user and the computer (i.e., the computer does not expect any input from the user).
`<break>`	Instructs the computer to pause its speech output for a specified period of time.
`<choice>`	Specifies an option in a **menu** element.
`<enumerate>`	Lists all the available options to the user.
`<exit>`	Exits the program.

Fig. L.7   VoiceXML tags. (Part 1 of 2.)

VoiceXML Tag	Description
`<filled>`	Contains elements to be executed when the computer receives user input for a **form** element.
`<form>`	Gathers information from the user for a set of variables.
`<goto>`	Transfers control from one dialog to another.
`<grammar>`	Specifies grammar for the expected input from the user.
`<if>`, `<else>`, `<elseif>`	Control statements used for making logic decisions.
`<link>`	A transfer of control similar to the `goto` statement, but a `link` can be executed at any time during the program's execution.
`<menu>`	Provides user options and transfers control to other dialogs, based on the selected option.
`<prompt>`	Specifies text to be read to the user when a selection is needed.
`<subdialog>`	Calls another dialog. After executing the subdialog, the calling dialog resumes control.
`<var>`	Declares a variable.
`<vxml>`	The top-level tag specifying that the document should be processed by a VoiceXML interpreter.

Fig. L.7   VoiceXML tags. (Part 2 of 2.)

L.10 CallXML™

Another advancement in voice technology for people with visual impairments is *CallXML*, a technology created and supported by *Voxeo* (**www.voxeo.com**). CallXML creates phone-to-Web applications that control incoming and outgoing telephone calls. Some examples of CallXML applications include voice mail, interactive voice response systems and Internet call waiting. CallXML, like VoiceXML, can assist individuals with visual impairments by reading Web pages—in other words, accessing Web-based content through the telephone, a device that most people won, without the need for a personal computer. Such an application typically utilizes a *text-to-speech (TTS)* engine to read information contained within CallXML elements to the caller (a TTS engine converts text to an automated voice). Web applications then can tailor their responds to the caller's input. [*Note*: A touch-tone phone is required to access CallXML functions.]

Typically, other CallXML applications might play prerecorded audio clips or text as output, requesting a response as input. An audio clip might contain a greeting that introduces callers to the application or to a menu of options that requires callers to make touch-tone entries. Certain applications, such as voice mail, may require verbal and touch-tone input. Once the input is received, the application responds by invoking CallXML elements such as **text**, which either contains the information a TTS engine reads to users or which will stream audio content over the phone. If the application does not receive input within a designated time frame, the application can even prompt the user to enter valid input.

When a user accesses a CallXML application, the incoming telephone call is referred to as a *session*, although a call that makes a subsequent outbound call can have multiple session (e.g., a conferencing application). An individual CallXML application can support numerous sessions or calls, enabling the same script to receive multiple telephone calls simultaneously. Each session is independent of the others and is assigned a unique *sessionID* for identification. A session terminates either when the user hangs up the telephone or when the CallXML application invokes the **hangup** element. Our first CallXML example shows the classic **Hello World** example (Fig. L.8).

Line 1 contains the optional *XML declaration*. Value ***version*** indicates the XML version to which the document conforms. Currently, this is **version = 1.0**. Value ***encoding*** indicates the type of *Unicode* encoding to use. This example uses UTF-8, which requires eight bits to transfer and receive data. More information on Unicode may be found in Appendix G, Unicode®.

The **<callxml>** tag on line 6 declares the contents of a CallXML document. Line 7 contains the **Hello World text**. All text spoken by a text-to-speech (TTS) engine needs to reside within **<text>** tags.

To deploy a CallXML application (or even a VoiceXML application), register with the *Voxeo* Community (**community.voxeo.com**), a Web resource for creating, debugging and deploying phone applications. For the most part, Voxeo is a free Web resource. However, the company charges fees when CallXML applications are deployed commercially. The

```
1   <?xml version = "1.0" encoding = "UTF-8"?>
2
3   <!-- Fig. L.8: hello.xml          -->
4   <!-- Classic Hello World example. -->
5
6   <callxml>
7      <text>Hello World.</text>
8   </callxml>
```

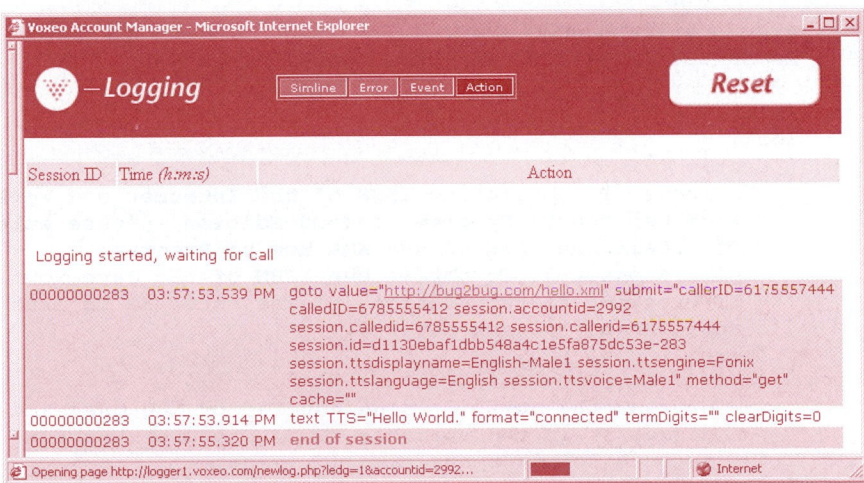

Fig. L.8   CallXML **Hello World** example. (Courtesy of Voxeo, © Voxeo Corporation 2000-2001.)

Voxeo Community can assign a unique telephone number to a CallXML application so that external users may access and interact with the application. [*Note*: Voxeo assigns telephone numbers to applications that reside on the Internet. If you have access to a Web server (IIS, PWS, Apache, etc.), use it to post your CallXML application. Otherwise, open an Internet account, using one of the many Internet-service companies (e.g., **www.geocities.com**, **www.angelfire.com**). These companies allow you to post documents on the Internet using their Web servers.]

Figure L.8 demonstrates the *logging* feature of the **Voxeo Account Manager**, which is accessible to registered members. The logging feature records and displays the "conversation" between the user and the application. The first row of the logging feature displays the URL of the CallXML application and the *global variables* associated with each session. The application (program) creates and assigns values to global variables, which the entire application can access and modify, at the start of each session. The subsequent row(s) display(s) the "conversation." This example shows a one-way conversation (because the application does not accept any input from the user) in which the TTS says **Hello World**. The last row shows the **end of session** message, which states that the phone call has terminated. The logging feature assists developers in debugging their applications. By observing the "conversation," a developer can determine at which point the application terminates. If the application terminates abruptly ("crashes"), the logging feature states the type and location of the error, so that a developer knows the particular section of the application on which to focus.

The next example (Fig. L.9) shows a CallXML application that reads the ISBN values of three Deitel textbooks—*Internet and World Wide Web How to Program: Second Edition*, *XML How to Program* and *Java How to Program: Fourth Edition*—based on the user's touch-tone input. [*Note*: The following code has been formatted for presentation purposes.]

```
1   <?xml version = "1.0" encoding = "UTF-8"?>
2
3   <!-- Fig. L.9: isbn.xml                    -->
4   <!-- Reads the ISBN value of three Deitel books -->
5
6   <callxml>
7      <block>
8         <text>
9            Welcome. To obtain the ISBN of the Internet and World
10           Wide Web How to Program: Second Edition, please enter 1.
11           To obtain the ISBN of the XML How to Program,
12           please enter 2. To obtain the ISBN of the Java How
13           to Program: Fourth Edition, please enter 3. To exit the
14           application, please enter 4.
15        </text>
16
17        <!-- obtains the numeric value entered by the user and -->
18        <!-- stores it in the variable ISBN. The user has 60   -->
19        <!-- seconds to enter one numeric value               -->
```

Fig. L.9   CallXML example that reads three ISBN values. (Courtesy of Voxeo, © Voxeo Corporation 2000-2001.) (Part 1 of 3.)

```
20          <getDigits var = "ISBN"
21             maxDigits = "1"
22             termDigits = "1234"
23             maxTime = "60s" />
24
25          <!-- requests that the user enter a valid numeric -->
26          <!-- value after the elapsed time of 60 seconds   -->
27          <onMaxSilence>
28             <text>
29                Please enter either 1, 2, 3 or 4.
30             </text>
31
32             <getDigits var = "ISBN"
33                termDigits = "1234"
34                maxDigits = "1"
35                maxTime = "60s" />
36
37          </onMaxSilence>
38
39          <onTermDigit value = "1">
40             <text>
41                The ISBN for the Internet book is 0130308978.
42                Thank you for calling our CallXML application.
43                Good-bye.
44             </text>
45          </onTermDigit>
46
47          <onTermDigit value = "2">
48             <text>
49                The ISBN for the XML book is 0130284173.
50                Thank you for calling our CallXML application.
51                Good-bye.
52             </text>
53          </onTermDigit>
54
55          <onTermDigit value = "3">
56             <text>
57                The ISBN for the Java book is 0130341517.
58                Thank you for calling our CallXML application.
59                Good-bye.
60             </text>
61          </onTermDigit>
62
63          <onTermDigit value = "4">
64             <text>
65                Thank you for calling our CallXML application.
66                Good-bye.
67             </text>
68          </onTermDigit>
69       </block>
70
```

Fig. L.9   CallXML example that reads three ISBN values. (Courtesy of Voxeo, ©
Voxeo Corporation 2000-2001.) (Part 2 of 3.)

```
71        <!-- event handler that terminates the call -->
72        <onHangup />
73   </callxml>
```

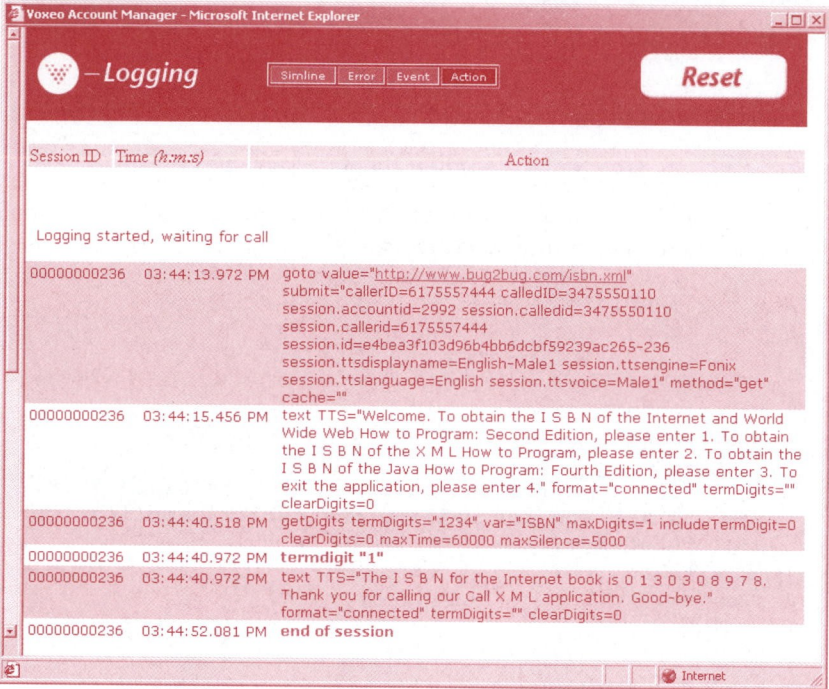

Fig. L.9   CallXML example that reads three ISBN values. (Courtesy of Voxeo, ©
Voxeo Corporation 2000-2001.) (Part 3 of 3.)

The **<block>** tag (line 7) encapsulates other CallXML tags. Usually, CallXML tags
that perform a similar task should be enclosed within **<block>...</block>**. The **block**
element in this example encapsulates the **<text>**, **<getDigits>**, **<onMaxSilence>**
and **<onTermDigit>** tags. A **block** element can contain nested **block** elements.

Lines 20–23 show some attributes of the **<getDigits>** tag. The **getDigits** element obtains the user's touch-tone response and stores it in the variable declared by the
var attribute (i.e., **ISBN**). The **maxDigits** attribute (line 21) indicates the maximum
number of digits that the application can accept. This application accepts only one character. If no number is stated, then the application uses the default value—*nolimit*.

The **termDigits** attribute (line 22) contains the list of characters that terminate user
input. When a character from this list is received as input, the CallXML application is notified that the last acceptable input has been received and that any character entered after this
point is invalid. These characters do not terminate the call; they simply notify the application to proceed to the next step because the necessary input has been received. In our
example, the values for **termDigits** are one, two, three or four. The default value for
termDigits is the null value (**""**).

The **maxTime** attribute (line 23) indicates the maximum amount of time to wait for a
user response (i.e., 60 seconds). If no input is received within the given time frame, then

the CallXML application may terminate—a drastic measure. The default value for this attribute is 30 seconds.

The *onMaxSilence* element (lines 27–37) is an *event handler* that is invoked when the **maxTime** (or **maxSilence**) expires. An event handler notifies the application of the appropriate action to perform. In this case, the application asks the user to enter a value because the **maxTime** has expired. After receiving input, **getDigits** (line 32) stores the value in the **ISBN** variable.

The *onTermDigit* element (lines 39–68) is an event handler that notifies the application of the appropriate action to perform when users select one of the **termDigits** characters. At least one **<onTermDigit>** tag must be associated with the **getDigits** element, even if the default value (**""**) is used. We provide four actions that the application can perform depending on the user-entered value. For example, if the user enters **1**, the application reads the ISBN value of the *Internet and World Wide Web How to Program: Second Edition* textbook.

Line 72 contains the **<onHangup/>** event handler, which terminates the telephone call when the user hangs up the telephone. Our **<onHangup>** event handler is an empty tag (i.e., there is no action to perform when this tag is invoked).

The logging feature in Fig. L.9 displays the "conversation" between the application and the user. The first row displays the URL of the application and the global variables of the session. The subsequent rows display the "conversation"—the application asks the caller which ISBN value to read, the caller enters **1** (*Internet and World Wide Web How to Program: Second Edition*) and the application reads the corresponding ISBN. The **end of session** message states that the application has terminated.

Brief descriptions of several logic and action CallXML elements are provided in Fig. L.10. *Logic elements* assign values to, and clear values from, the session variables, and *action elements* perform specified tasks, such as answering and terminating a telephone call during the current session. A complete list of CallXML elements is available at:

```
www.oasis-open.org/cover/callxmlv2.html
```

Elements	Description
assign	Assigns a **value** to a variable, **var**.
clear	Clears the contents of the **var** attribute.
clearDigits	Clears all digits that the user has entered.
goto	Navigates to another section of the current CallXML application or to a different CallXML application. The **value** attribute specifies the application URL. The **submit** attribute lists the variables that are passed to the invoked application. The **method** attribute states whether to use the HTTP *get* or *post* request types when sending and retrieving information. A *get* request retrieves data from a Web server without modifying the contents, while the *post* request sends modified data.

Fig. L.10   CallXML elements. (Part 1 of 2.)

Elements	Description
run	Starts a new CallXML session for each call. The **value** attribute specifies which CallXML application to retrieve. The **submit** attribute lists the variables that are passed to the invoked application. The **method** attribute states whether to use the HTTP *get* or *post* request type. The **var** attribute stores the identification number of the session.
sendEvent	Allows multiple sessions to exchange messages. The **value** attribute stores the message, and the **session** attribute specifies the identification number of the session that receives the message.
answer	Answers an incoming telephone call.
call	Calls the URL specified by the **value** attribute. The **callerID** attribute contains the phone number that is displayed on a CallerID device. The **maxTime** attribute specifies the length of time to wait for the call to be answered before disconnecting.
conference	Connects multiple sessions so that people can participate in a conference call. The **targetSessions** attribute specifies the identification numbers of the sessions, and the **termDigits** attribute indicates the touch-tone keys that terminate the call.
wait	Waits for user input. The **value** attribute specifies how long to wait. The **termDigits** attribute indicates the touch-tone keys that terminate the **wait** element.
play	Plays an audio file or a value that is stored as a number, date or amount of money and is indicated by the **format** attribute. The **value** attribute contains the information (location of the audio file, number, date or amount of money) that corresponds to the **format** attribute. The **clearDigits** attribute specifies whether or not to delete the previously entered input. The **termDigits** attribute indicates the touch-tone keys that terminate the audio file, etc.
recordAudio	Records an audio file and stores it at the URL specified by **value**. The **format** attribute indicates the file extension of the audio clip. Other attributes include **termDigits**, **clearDigits**, **maxTime** and **maxSilence**.

Fig. L.10   CallXML elements. (Part 2 of 2.)

L.11 JAWS® for Windows

JAWS (Job Access with Sound) is one of the leading screen readers on the market today. Henter-Joyce, a division of Freedom Scientific™, created this application to help people with visual impairments use technology.

Visit **www.hj.com/JAWS/JAWS37DemoOp.htm** to download a demonstration version of JAWS. Select the **JAWS 3.7 FREE Demo** link. The demo expires after 40 minutes. The computer must be rebooted before another 40-minute session can be started.

The JAWS demo is fully functional and includes an extensive, highly customized help system. Users can select the voice to use and the rate at which text is spoken. Users also can create keyboard shortcuts. Although the demo is in English, the full version of JAWS 3.7 allows the user to choose one of several supported languages.

JAWS also includes special key commands for popular programs such as Microsoft Internet Explorer and Microsoft Word. For example, when browsing in Internet Explorer, JAWS' capabilities extend beyond reading the content on the screen. If JAWS is enabled, pressing *Insert + F7* in Internet Explorer opens a **Links List** dialog, which displays all the links available on a Web page. For more information about JAWS and the other products offered by Henter-Joyce, visit **www.hj.com**.

L.12 Other Accessibility Tools

Many additional accessibility products are available to assist people with disabilities. This section describes a variety of accessibility products, including hardware items and advanced technologies.

A *braille keyboard*, in addition to having each key labeled with the letter it represents, has the equivalent braille symbol printed on the key. Braille keyboards are combined most often with a speech synthesizer or a braille display, so users can interact with the computer to verify that their typing is correct.

Speech synthesis is another research-intensive area that benefits people with disabilities. Speech synthesizers aid those who are unable to communicate verbally. However, the growing popularity of the Web has prompted a great deal of work in the field of speech synthesis and speech recognition. These technologies are allowing individuals with disabilities to use computers more than ever before. The development of speech synthesizers is also enabling the improvement of other technologies, such as VoiceXML and *AuralCSS* (**www.w3.org/TR/REC-CSS2/aural.html**). These tools allow people with visual impairment and the illiterate to access Web sites.

Despite the existence of adaptive software and hardware for people with visual impairments, the accessibility of computers and the Internet is still hampered by the high costs, rapid obsolescence and unnecessary complexity of current technology. Moreover, almost all software currently available requires installation by a person who can see. *Ocularis* is a project launched in the open-source community to help address these problems. Open-source software for people with visual impairments already exists, and although it is often superior to its proprietary, closed-source counterparts, it has not yet reached its full potential. Ocularis ensures that the blind can use the Linux operating system fully, by providing an *Audio User Interface (AUI)*. Products that integrate with Ocularis include a word processor, calculator, basic finance application, Internet browser and e-mail client. A screen reader will also be included with programs that have command-line interfaces. The official Ocularis Web site is located at **ocularis.sourceforge.net**.

Emacspeak is a screen interface that allows greater Internet access to individuals with visual disabilities by translating text to voice data. The open source product also implements auditory icons that play various sounds. Emacspeak can be customized with Linux operating systems and provides support for the IBM *ViaVoice* speech engine. More information, including purchasing details, about the ViaVoice speech engine can be found at **www-4.ibm.com/software/speech**. The Emacspeak Web site is located at **www.cs.cornell.edu/home/raman/emacspeak/emacspeak.html**.

In March 2001, We Media introduced the "WeMedia Browser," which allows people with poor vision and cognitive disabilities (e.g., dyslexia) to use the Internet more conveniently. The *WeMedia Browser i*mproves upon the traditional browser by providing over-sized buttons and keystroke commands for navigation. The user can control the speed and volume at which the browser "reads" Web page text. The WeMedia Browser is available for free download at **www.wemedia.com**.

IBM Home Page Reader (HPR) is another browser that "reads" text selected by the user. The HPR uses the IBM ViaVoice technology to synthesize a voice. A trial version of HPR is available at **www-3.ibm.com/able/hpr.html**.

People with visual impairments are not the only beneficiaries of the effort being made to improve markup languages. People with hearing impairments also have a number of tools to help them interpret auditory information delivered over the Web, such as *Synchronized Multimedia Integration Language* (SMIL™), discussed in Chapter 15, Extensible Markup Language. This markup language adds extra *tracks*—layers of content found within a single audio or video file—to multimedia content. The additional tracks can contain closed captioning.

Technologies also are being designed to help people with severe disabilities, such as *quadriplegia*, a form of paralysis that affects the body from the neck down. One such technology, *EagleEyes*, developed by researchers at Boston College (**www.bc.edu/eagleeyes**), is a system that translates eye movements into mouse movements. Users move the mouse cursors by moving their eyes or heads and thereby can control computers.

The company CitXCorp is developing technology that translates Web information through the telephone. Information on a specific topic can be accessed by dialing the designated number. The new software is expected to be made available to users for $10 per month. For more information on regulations governing the design of Web sites to accommodate people with disabilities, visit **www.access-board.gov**.

In alliance with Microsoft, GW Micro, Henter-Joyce and Adobe Systems, Inc. are also working on software to aid people with disabilities. JetForm Corp also is accommodating the needs of people with disabilities by developing server-based XML software. The new software allows users to download a format that best meets their needs.

There are many services on the Web that assist e-business owners in designing their Web sites to be accessible to individuals with disabilities. For additional information, the U.S. Department of Justice (**www.usdoj.gov**) provides extensive resources detailing legal issues and current technologies related to people with disabilities.

These examples are just a few of the accessibility projects and technologies that currently exist. For more information on Web and general computer accessibility, see the resources provided in Section L.14, Internet and World Wide Web Resources.

L.13 Accessibility in Microsoft® Windows® 2000

Beginning with Microsoft *Windows 95*, Microsoft has included accessibility features in its operating systems and many of its applications, including *Office 97*, *Office 2000* and *Netmeeting*. In Microsoft *Windows 2000*, the accessibility features have been significantly enhanced. All the accessibility options provided by Windows 2000 are available through the **Accessibility Wizard**, which guides users through all the Windows 2000 accessibility features and configures their computers according to the chosen specifications. This section guides users through the configuration of their Windows 2000 accessibility options using the **Accessibility Wizard**.

To access the **Accessibility Wizard**, users must have Microsoft Windows 2000. Select the **Start** button and select **Programs** followed by **Accessories**, **Accessibility** and **Accessibility Wizard**. When the wizard starts, the **Welcome** screen is displayed. Select **Next** to display a dialog (Fig. L.11) that asks the user to select a font size. Click **Next**.

Figure L.12 shows the next dialog displayed. This dialog allows the user to activate the font size settings chosen in the previous window, change the screen resolution, enable the *Microsoft Magnifier* (a program that displays an enlarged section of the screen in a separate window) and disable personalized menus (a feature which hides rarely used programs from the start menu, which can be a hindrance to users with disabilities). Make selections and select **Next**.

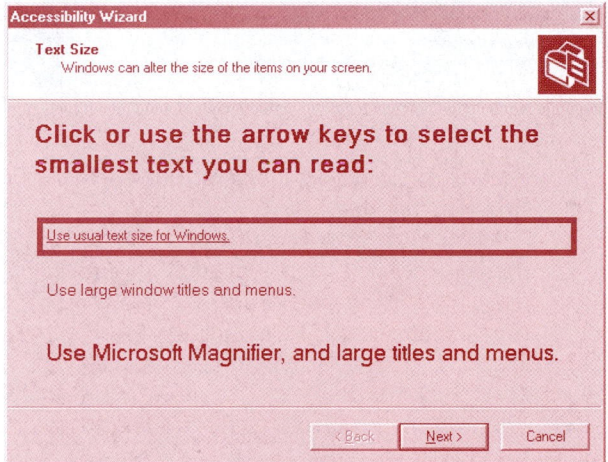

Fig. L.11   Text Size dialog.

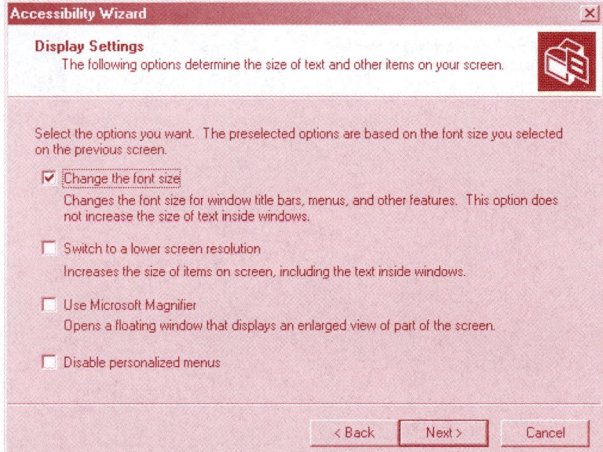

Fig. L.12   Display Settings dialog.

The next dialog (Fig. L.13) inquires about the user's disabilities. By checking the appropriate boxes, the **Accessibility Wizard** customizes Windows to accommodate the users needs. We selected everything for demonstration purposes. Select **Next** to continue.

L.13.1 Tools for People with Visual Impairments

When we checked all the options in Fig. L.13, the wizard configured Windows for people with visual impairments. As shown in Fig. L.14, the dialog box allows users to resize the scroll bars and window borders to increase their visibility. Select **Next** to proceed to the next dialog.

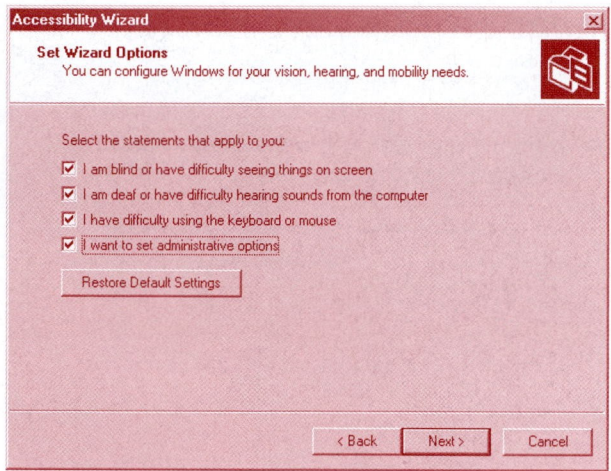

Fig. L.13   Accessibility Wizard initialization options.

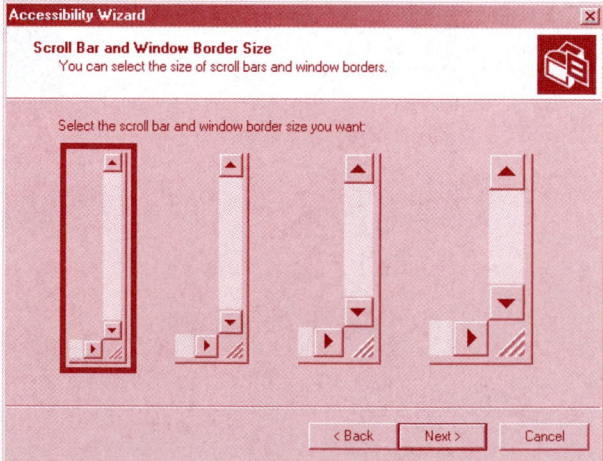

Fig. L.14   Scroll Bar and Window Border Size dialog.

The dialog in Fig. L.15 allows users to resize icons. Users with poor vision, as well as users who have trouble reading, benefit from large icons.

Selecting **Next** displays the **Display Color Settings** dialog (Fig. L.16). These settings allow users to change Windows' color schemes and resize various screen elements. Select **Next** to view the dialog (Fig. L.17) for customizing the mouse cursor.

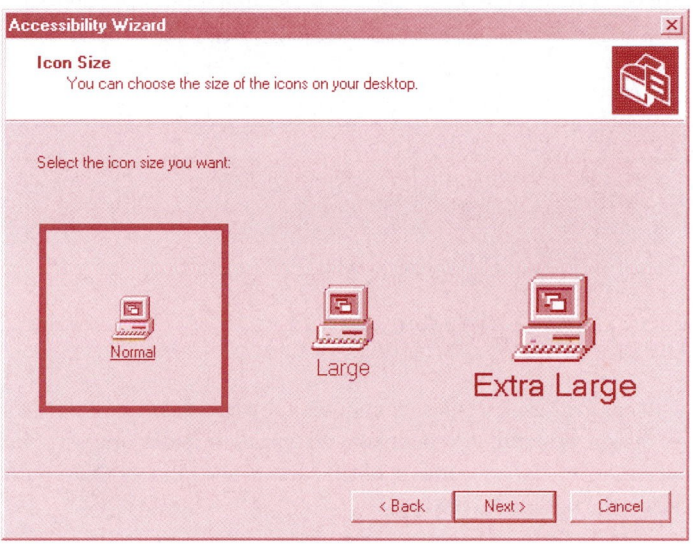

Fig. L.15   Setting up window element sizes.

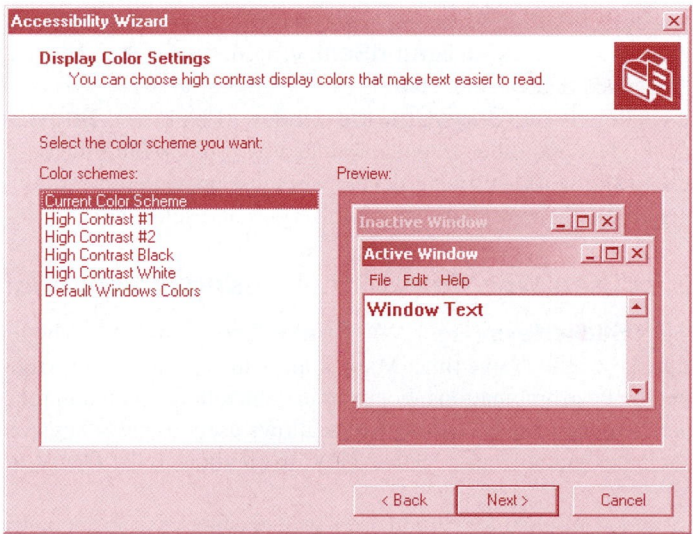

Fig. L.16   **Display Color Settings** options.

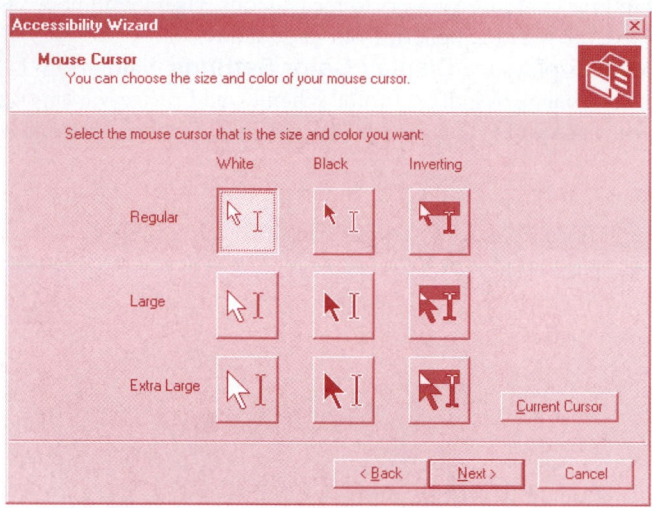

Fig. L.17   Accessibility Wizard mouse cursor adjustment tool.

Anyone who has ever used a laptop computer knows how difficult it is to see the mouse cursor. This is also a problem for people with visual impairments. To help solve this problem, the wizard offers larger cursors, black cursors and cursors that invert the colors of objects underneath them. Select **Next**.

L.13.2 Tools for People with Hearing Impairments

This section, which focuses on accessibility for people with hearing impairments, begins with the **SoundSentry** window (Fig. L.18). **SoundSentry** creates visual signals when system events occur. For example, people with hearing impairments are unable to hear the beeps that normally warn users, so **SoundSentry** flashes the screen when a beep occurs. To continue to the next dialog, select **Next**.

The next window is the **ShowSounds** window (Fig. L.19). **ShowSounds** adds captions to spoken text and other sounds produced by today's multimedia-rich software. For **ShowSounds** to work, software developers must provide the captions and spoken text specifically within their software. Make selections and select **Next**.

L.13.3 Tools for Users Who Have Difficulty Using the Keyboard

The next dialog is **StickyKeys** (Fig. L.20). **StickyKeys** helps users who have difficulty pressing multiple keys at the same time. Many important computer commands are invoked by pressing specific key combinations. For example, the reboot command requires pressing *Ctrl+Alt+Delete* simultaneously. **StickyKeys** allows users to press key combinations in sequence rather than simultaneously. Select **Next** to continue to the **BounceKeys** dialog (Fig. L.21).

Another common problem for certain users with disabilities is accidentally pressing the same key more than once. This problem typically results from pressing a key for a long period of time. **BounceKeys** force the computer to ignore repeated keystrokes. Select **Next**.

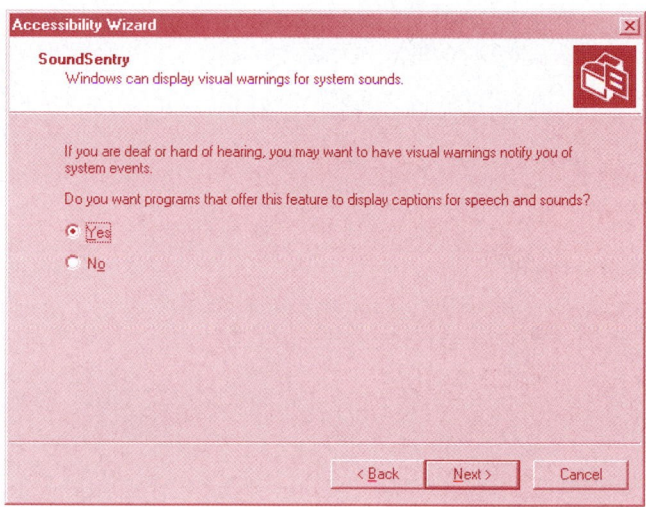

Fig. L.18   SoundSentry dialog.

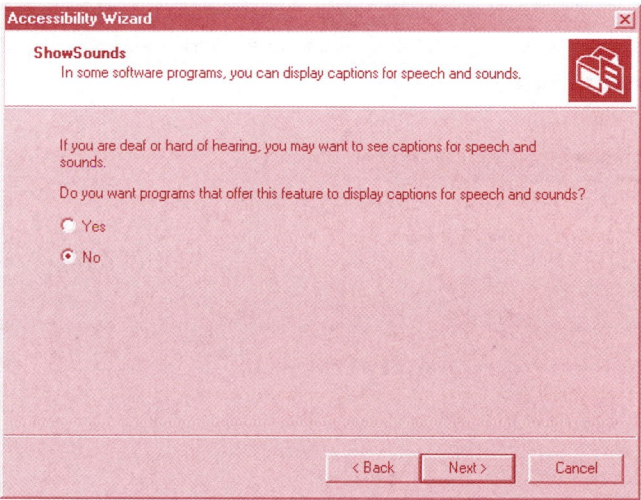

Fig. L.19   ShowSounds dialog.

ToggleKeys (Fig. L.22) alerts users that they have pressed one of the lock keys (i.e., *Caps Lock*, *Num Lock* and *Scroll Lock*) by sounding an audible beep. Make selections and select **Next**.

The **Extra Keyboard Help** dialog (Fig. L.23) activates a tool that displays such information as keyboard shortcuts and tool tips, when they are available. Like **Show-Sounds**, this tool requires that software developers provide the content to be displayed. Selecting **Next** loads the **MouseKeys** (Fig. L.24) customization window.

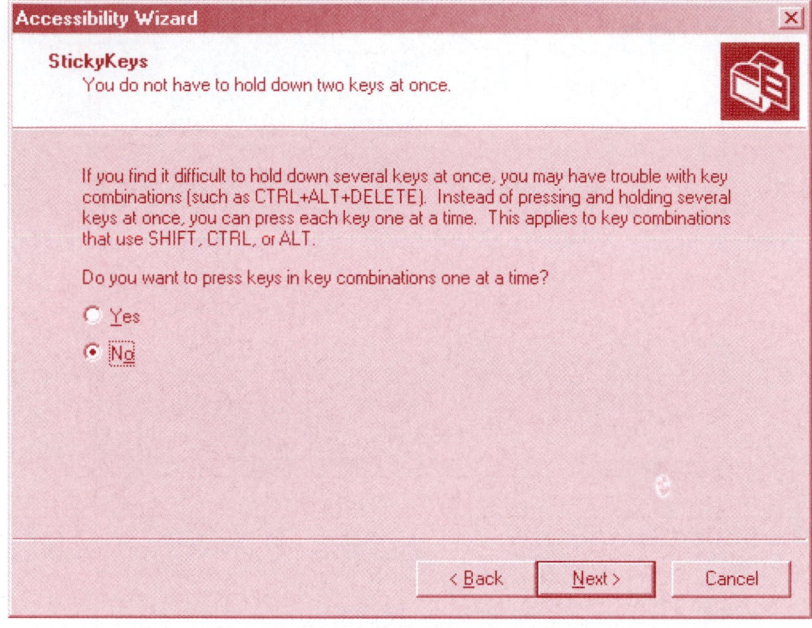

Fig. L.20   StickyKeys window.

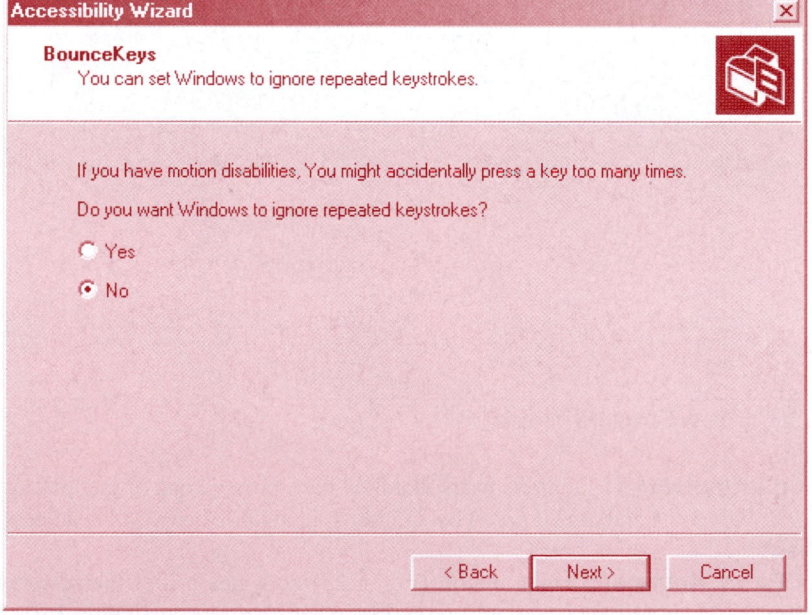

Fig. L.21   BounceKeys dialog.

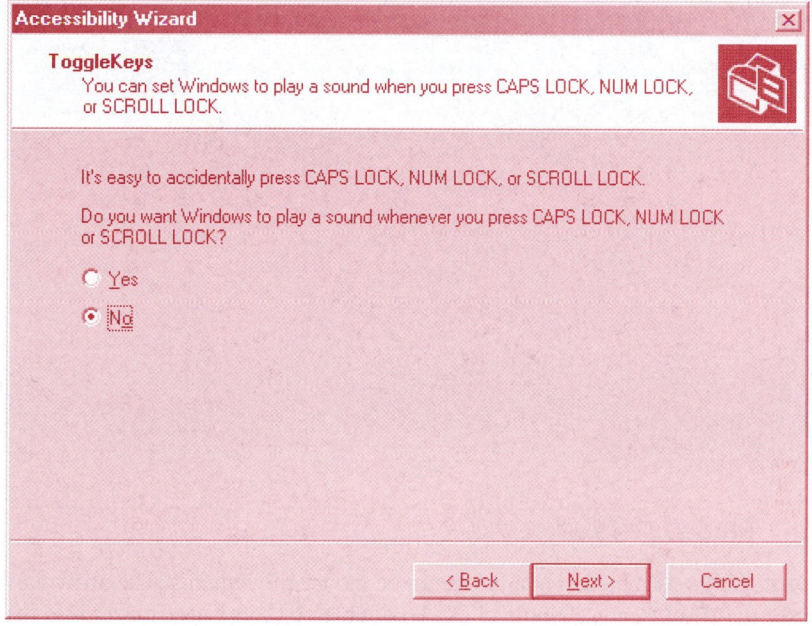

Fig. L.22   ToggleKeys window.

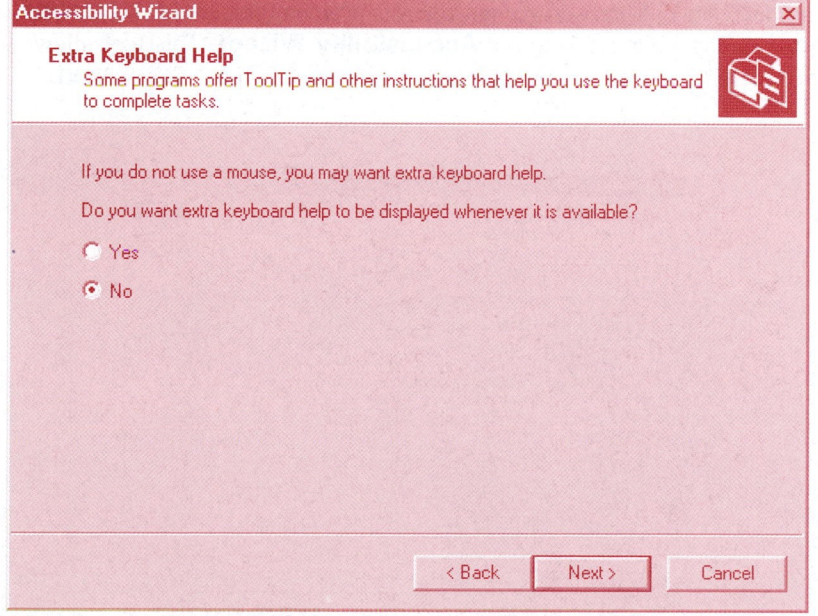

Fig. L.23   Extra Keyboard Help dialog.

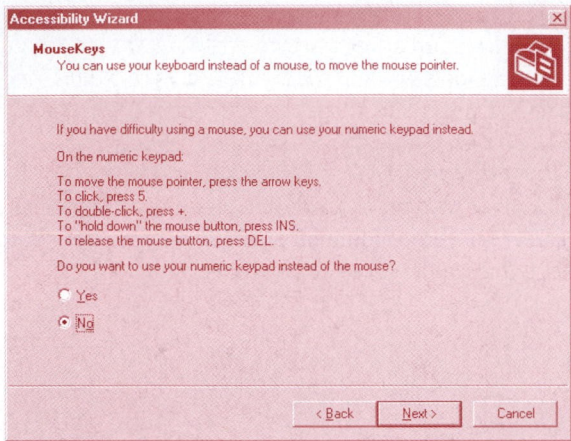

Fig. L.24   MouseKeys window.

MouseKeys uses the keyboard to emulate mouse movements. The arrow keys direct the mouse; the *5* key sends a single click. To double click, the user must press the + key; to simulate holding down the mouse button, the user must press the *Ins* (*Insert*) key; and to release the mouse button, the user must press the *Del* (*Delete*) key. To continue to the next screen in the **Accessibility Wizard**, select **Next**.

Today's computer tools are made almost exclusively for right-handed users, including most computer mice. Microsoft recognized this problem and added the *Mouse Button Settings* window (Fig. L.25) to the **Accessibility Wizard**. This tool allows users to create virtual left-handed mice by swapping the button functions. Select **Next**.

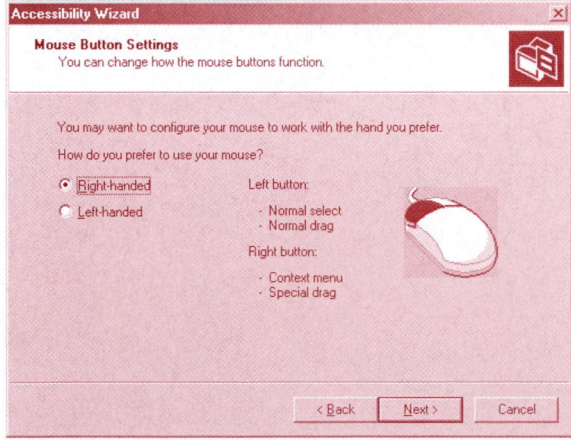

Fig. L.25   Mouse Button Settings window.

Mouse speed is adjusted by using the **MouseSpeed** (Fig. L.26) dialog of the **Accessibility Wizard**. Dragging the scroll bar changes the speed. Selecting the **Next** button sets the speed and displays the wizard's **Set Automatic Timeouts** window (Fig. L.27).

Although accessibility tools are important to users with disabilities, they can be a hindrance to users who do not need them. In situations where varying accessibility needs exist, it is important that users be able to turn the accessibility tools on and off as necessary. The ***Set Automatic Timeouts*** window specifies a *timeout* period for the tools. A timeout either enables or disables a certain action after the computer has idled for a specified amount of time. A screen saver is a common example of a program with a timeout period. Here, a timeout is set to toggle the accessibility tools.

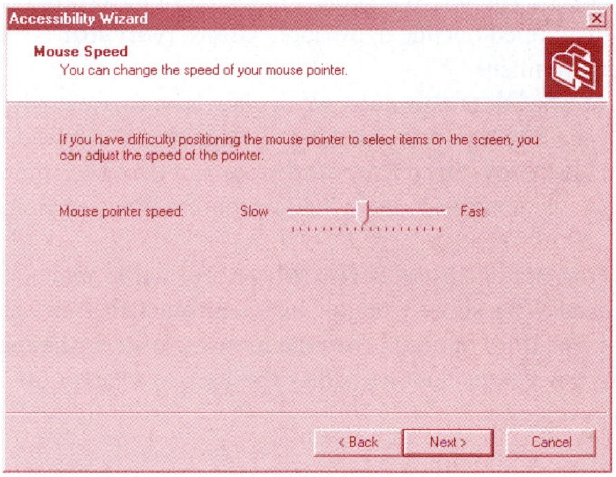

Fig. L.26   Mouse Speed dialog.

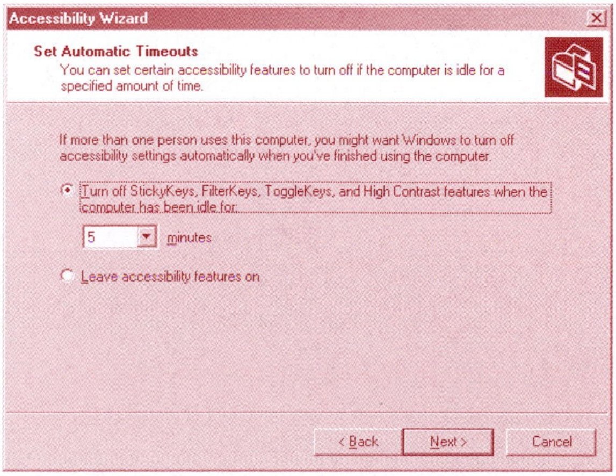

Fig. L.27   Set Automatic Timeouts dialog.

After selecting **Next**, the **Save Settings to File** dialog appears (Fig. L.28). This dialog determines whether the accessibility settings should be used as the *default settings*, which are loaded when the computer is rebooted, or after a timeout. Set the accessibility settings as the default if the majority of users need them. Users can save the accessibility settings as well, by creating an **.acw** file, which, when clicked, activates the saved accessibility settings on any Windows 2000 computer.

L.13.4 Microsoft Narrator

Microsoft **Narrator** is a text-to-speech program for people with visual impairments. It reads text, describes the current desktop environment and alerts users when certain Windows events occur. **Narrator** aids in configuring Microsoft Windows. It is a screen reader that works with Internet Explorer, *Wordpad*, *Notepad* and most programs in the **Control Panel**. Although it is limited outside these applications, **Narrator** is excellent at navigating the Windows environment.

To get an idea of what **Narrator** does, we explain how to use it with various Windows applications. Select the **Start** button and select **Programs**, followed by **Accessories**, **Accessibility** and **Narrator**. Once **Narrator** is open, it describes the current foreground window. It then reads the text inside the window aloud to the user. Selecting **OK** displays the dialog in Fig. L.29.

Checking the first option instructs **Narrator** to describe menus and new windows when they are opened. The second option instructs **Narrator** to speak the characters entered by the user. The third option moves the mouse cursor to the region being read by **Narrator**. Clicking the **Voice** button enables the user to change the pitch, volume and speed of the narrator voice.

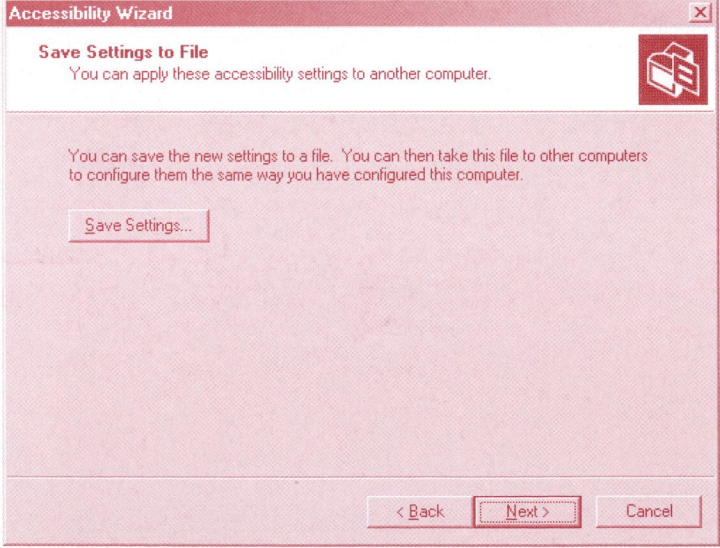

Fig. L.28   *Saving new accessibility settings.*

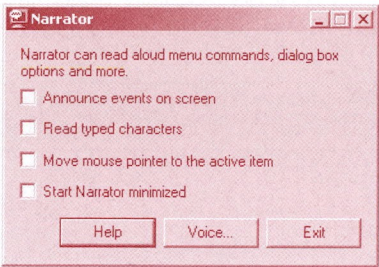

Fig. L.29 Narrator window.

With **Narrator** running, open **Notepad** and select the **File** menu. **Narrator** announces the opening of the program and begins to describe the items in the **File** menu. When scrolling down the list, **Narrator** reads the current item to which the mouse is pointing. Type some text, and press *Ctrl-Shift-Enter* to hear **Narrator** read it (Fig. L.30). If the **Read typed characters** option is checked, **Narrator** reads each character as it is typed. The direction arrows on the keyboard can be used to make **Narrator** read. The up and down arrows cause **Narrator** to speak the lines adjacent to the current mouse position, and the left and right arrows cause **Narrator** to speak the characters adjacent to the current mouse position.

L.13.5 Microsoft On-Screen Keyboard

Some computer users lack the ability to use a keyboard but can use a pointing device such as a mouse. For these users, the *On-Screen Keyboard* is helpful. To access the On-Screen Keyboard, select the **Start** button and select **Programs** followed by **Accessories**, **Accessibility** and **On-Screen Keyboard**. Figure L.31 shows the layout of the Microsoft On-Screen Keyboard.

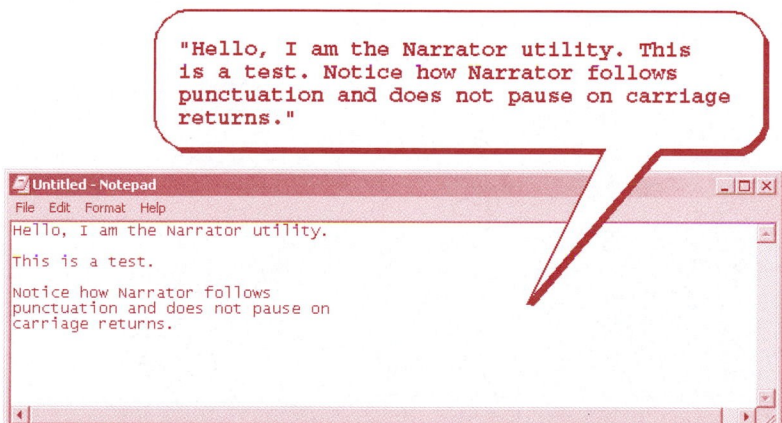

Fig. L.30 Narrator reading **Notepad** text.

Fig. L.31 Microsoft **On-Screen Keyboard**.

Users who have difficulty using the On-Screen Keyboard should purchase more sophisticated products, such as *Clicker 4*™ by *Inclusive Technology*. Clicker 4 aids people who cannot use a keyboard effectively. Its main feature is its ability to be customized. Keys can have letters, numbers, entire words or even pictures on them. For more information regarding Clicker 4, visit **www.inclusive.co.uk/catalog/clicker.htm**.

L.13.6 Accessibility Features in Microsoft Internet Explorer 5.5

Internet Explorer 5.5 offers a variety of options to improve usability. To access IE5.5's accessibility features, launch the program, select the **Tools** menu and select **Internet Options...**. From the **Internet Options** menu, press the button labeled **Accessibility...** to open the accessibility options (Fig. L.32).

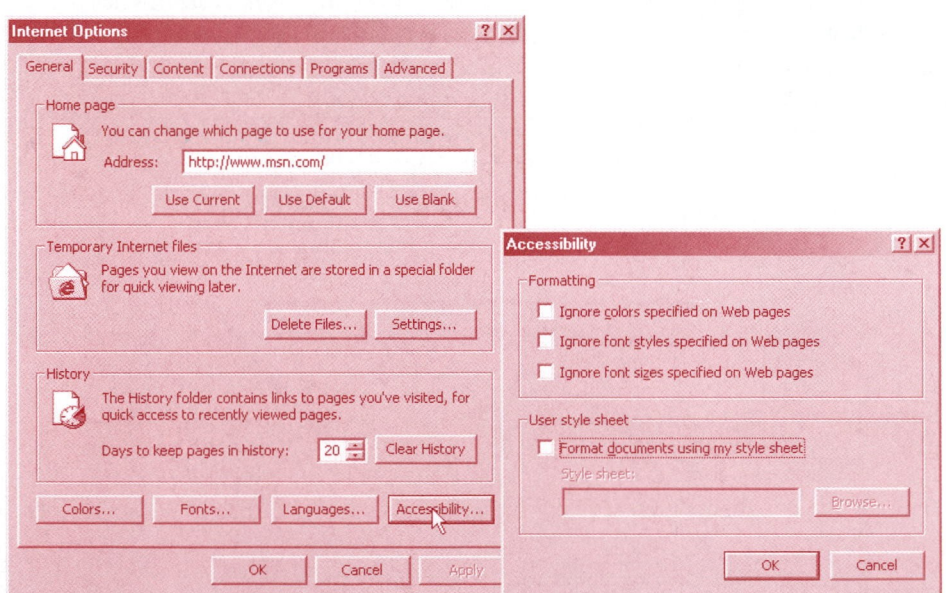

Fig. L.32 Microsoft Internet Explorer 5.5's accessibility options.

The accessibility options in IE5.5 augment users' Web browsing. Users can ignore Web colors, Web fonts and font size tags. This eliminates problems that arise from poor Web page design and allows users to customize their Web browsers. Users can even specify a *style sheet,* which formats every Web site visited according to users' personal preferences.

These are not the only accessibility options offered in IE5.5. In the **Internet Options** dialog click the **Advanced** tab. This opens the dialog shown in Fig. L.33. The first option that can be set is labeled **Always expand ALT text for images**. By default, IE5.5 hides some of the `<alt>` text if it exceeds the size of the image it describes. This option forces all the text to be shown. The second option reads: **Move system caret with focus/ selection changes**. This option is intended to make screen reading more effective. Some screen readers use the *system caret* (the blinking vertical bar associated with editing text) to decide what is read. If this option is not activated, screen readers might not read Web pages correctly.

Web designers often forget to take accessibility into account when creating Web sites, and they use fonts that are too small. Many user agents have addressed this problem by allowing the user to adjust the text size. Select the **View** menu and then **Text Size** to change the font size when using IE5.5. By default, the text size is set to **Medium**.

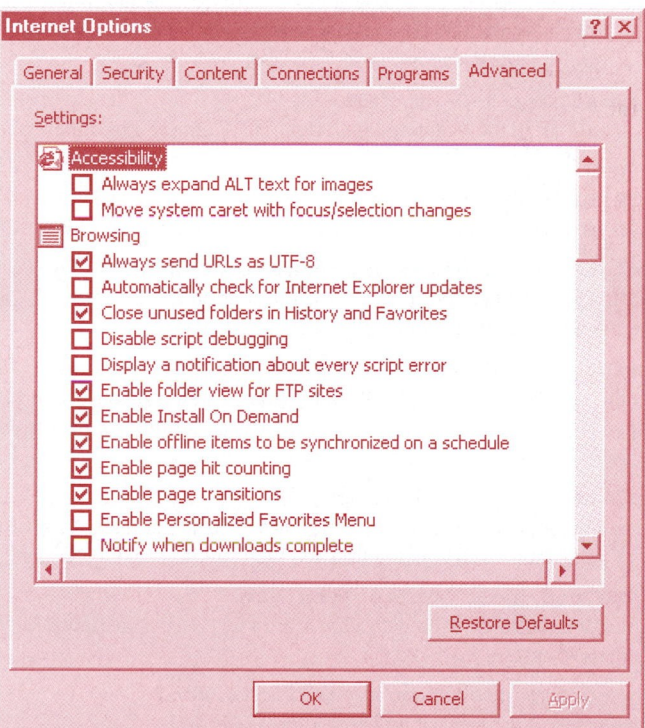

Fig. L.33   Advanced accessibility settings in Microsoft Internet Explorer 5.5.

L.14 Internet and World Wide Web Resources

There are many accessibility resources on the Internet and World Wide Web, and this section lists a variety of these resources.

www.synapseadaptive.com/joel/natlink.htm
Python module **natlink** allows the user to access and control Dragon NaturallySpeaking, software that provides a speech recognition system for Windows 95/98/NT.

sourceforge.net/projects/ocularis
This Web site contains information about the development status, environment and intended audience of project Ocularis. The site also provides links to mailing lists related to the project.

www.w3.org/WAI
The World Wide Web Consortium's *Web Accessibility Initiative (WAI)* site promotes the design of universally accessible Web sites. This site contains the current guidelines and forthcoming standards for Web accessibility.

www.w3.org/WAI/bcase/benefits
This W3C site provides a business case on the benefits of the designing accessible Web sites.

deafness.about.com/health/deafness/msubmenu6.htm
This is the home page of **deafness.about.com**. It is a resource to find information pertaining to deafness.

www.cast.org
CAST (Center for Applied Special Technology) offers software, including a valuable accessibility checker, that help individuals with disabilities use a computer. The accessibility checker is a Web-based program that validates the accessibility of Web sites.

www.trainingpost.org/3-2-inst.htm
This site presents a tutorial on the Gunning Fog Index. The Gunning Fog Index grades text based on its readability.

www.w3.org/TR/REC-CSS2/aural.html
This page discusses Aural Style Sheets, outlining the purpose and uses of this new technology.

laurence.canlearn.ca/English/learn/newaccessguide/indie
INDIE stands for "Integrated Network of Disability Information and Education." This site is home to a search engine that helps users find information on disabilities.

java.sun.com/products/java-media/speech/forDevelopers/JSML
This site outlines the specifications for JSML, Sun Microsystem's Java Speech Markup Language. This language, like VoiceXML, could drastically improve accessibility for people with visual impairments.

www.slcc.edu/webguide/lynxit.html
Lynxit is a development tool that allows users to view any Web site as a text-only browser would. The site's form allows you to enter a URL and returns the Web site in text-only format.

www.trill-home.com/lynx/public_lynx.html
This site allows users to browse the Web with a Lynx browser. Users can view how Web pages appear to users without the most current technologies.

www.wgbh.org/wgbh/pages/ncam/accesslinks.html
This site provides links to other accessibility pages across the Web.

ocfo.ed.gov/coninfo/clibrary/software.htm
This page is the U.S. Department of Education's Web site for software accessibility requirements. It helps developers produce accessible products.

www-3.ibm.com/able/access.html
The homepage of IBM's accessibility site provides information on IBM products and their accessibility and discusses hardware, software and Web accessibility.

www.w3.org/TR/voice-tts-reqs
This page explains the speech-synthesis markup requirements for voice markup languages.

www.voicexmlcentral.com
This site contains information about VoiceXML, such as the specification and the document type definition (DTD).

deafness.about.com/health/deafness/msubvib.htm
This site provides information on vibrotactile devices, which allow individuals with hearing impairments to experience audio in the form of vibrations.

web.ukonline.co.uk/ddmc/software.html
This site provides links to software for people with disabilities.

www.hj.com
Henter-Joyce is a division of Freedom Scientific, which provides software for people with visual impairments. It is the home of JAWS.

www.abledata.com/text2/icg_hear.htm
This page contains a consumer guide that discusses technologies for people with hearing impairments.

www.washington.edu/doit
The University of Washington's DO-IT (Disabilities, Opportunities, Internetworking and Technology) site provides information and Web development resources for creating universally accessible Web sites.

www.webable.com
WebABLE contains links to many disability-related Internet resources and is geared towards those developing technologies for people with disabilities.

www.webaim.org
The *WebAIM* site provides a number of tutorials, articles, simulations and other useful resources that demonstrate how to design accessible Web sites. The site provides a screen reader simulation.

www.speech.cs.cmu.edu/comp.speech/SpeechLinks.html
The *Speech Technology Hyperlinks* page has over 500 links to sites related to computer-based speech and speech-recognition tools.

www.islandnet.com/~tslemko
The *Micro Consulting Limited* site contains shareware speech-synthesis software.

www.chantinc.com/technology
This page is the *Chant* Web site, which discusses speech technology and how it works. Chant also provides speech-synthesis and speech-recognition software.

whatis.techtarget.com/definition
This site provides definitions and information about several topics, including CallXML. Its thorough definition of CallXML differentiates CallXML from VoiceXML, another technology developed by Voxeo. The site contains links to other published articles discussing CallXML.

www.oasis-open.org/cover/callxmlv2.html
This site provides a comprehensive list of the CallXML tags, complete with descriptions of each tag. Short examples on how to apply the tags in various applications are provided.

SUMMARY

- Enabling a Web site to meet the needs of individuals with disabilities is an issue relevant to all business owners.

- Legal ramifications exist for Web sites that discriminate against people with disabilities (i.e., by not providing them with adequate access to the site's resources).

- Technologies such as voice activation, visual enhancers and auditory aids enable individuals with disabilities to work in more positions.

- On April 7, 1997, the World Wide Web Consortium (W3C) launched the Web Accessibility Initiative (WAI). The WAI is an attempt to make the Web more accessible; its mission is described at **www.w3.org/WAI**.

- Accessibility refers to the level of usability of an application or Web site for people with disabilities. Total accessibility is difficult to achieve because there are many different disabilities, language barriers and hardware and software inconsistencies.

- The majority of Web sites are considered either partially or totally inaccessible to people with visual, learning or mobility impairments.

- The WAI publishes the Web Content Accessibility Guidelines 1.0, which assigns priorities to a three-tier structure of checkpoints. The WAI currently is working on a draft of the Web Content Accessibility Guidelines 2.0.

- One important WAI requirement is to ensure that every image, movie and sound on a Web site is accompanied by a description that clearly defines the object's purpose; this is called an **<alt>** tag.

- Specialized user agents, such as screen readers (programs that allow users to hear what is being displayed on their screen) and braille displays (devices that receive data from screen-reading software and output the data as braille), allow people with visual impairments to access text-based information that is normally displayed on the screen.

- Using a screen reader to navigate a Web site can be time consuming and frustrating, because screen readers are unable to interpret pictures and other graphical content that do not have alternative text.

- Including links at the top of each Web page provides easy access to page's main content.

- Web pages with large amounts of multimedia content are difficult for user agents to interpret unless they are designed properly. Images, movies and most nonXHTML objects cannot be read by screen readers.

- Web designers should avoid misuse of the **alt** attribute; it is intended to provide a short description of an XHTML object that may not load properly on all user agents.

- The value of the **longdesc** attribute is a text-based URL, linked to a Web page, that describes the image associated with the attribute.

- When creating a Web page intended for the general public, it is important to consider the reading level at which it is written. Web site designers can make their sites more readable through the use of shorter words, as some users may have difficulty reading long words. In addition, users from other countries may have difficulty understanding slang and other nontraditional language.

- Web designers often use frames to display more than one XHTML file at a time and are a convenient way to ensure that certain content is always on screen. Unfortunately, frames often lack proper descriptions, which prevents users with text-based browsers, or users who lack sight, from navigating the Web site.

- The **<noframes>** tag allows the designer to offer alternative content to users whose browsers do not support frames.

- VoiceXML has tremendous implications for people with visual impairments and for the illiterate. VoiceXML, a speech recognition and synthesis technology, reads Web pages to users and understands words spoken into a microphone.

- A VoiceXML document is made up of a series of dialogs and subdialogs, which result in spoken interaction between the user and the computer. VoiceXML is a voice-recognition technology.

- CallXML, a language created and supported by Voxeo, creates phone-to-Web applications.

- When a user accesses a CallXML application, the incoming telephone call is referred to as a session. A CallXML application can support multiple sessions that enable the application to receive multiple telephone calls at any given time.

- A session terminates either when the user hangs up the telephone or when the CallXML application invokes the **hangup** element.

- The contents of a CallXML application are inserted within the **<callxml>** tag.

- CallXML tags that perform similar tasks should be enclosed within the **<block>** and **</block>** tags.

- To deploy a CallXML application, register with the Voxeo Community, which assigns a telephone number to the application so that other users may access it.

- Voxeo's logging feature enables developers to debug their telephone application by observing the "conversation" between the user and the application.

- Braille keyboards are similar to standard keyboards, except that in addition to having each key labeled with the letter it represents, braille keyboards have the equivalent braille symbol printed on the key. Most often, braille keyboards are combined with a speech synthesizer or a braille display, so users can interact with the computer to verify that their typing is correct.

- People with visual impairments are not the only beneficiaries of the effort to improve markup languages. Individuals with hearing impairments also have a great number of tools to help them interpret auditory information delivered over the Web.

- Speech synthesis is another research area that helps people with disabilities.

- Open-source software for people with visual impairments already exists and is often superior to most of its proprietary, closed-source counterparts.

- People with hearing impairments benefit from Synchronized Multimedia Integration Language (SMIL). This markup language adds extra tracks—layers of content found within a single audio or video file. The additional tracks can contain data such as closed captioning.

- EagleEyes, developed by researchers at Boston College (**www.bc.edu/eagleeyes**), translates eye movements into mouse movements. Users move the mouse cursor by moving their eyes or heads and are thereby are able to control computers.

- All of the accessibility options provided by Windows 2000 are available through the **Accessibility Wizard**. The **Accessibility Wizard** takes a user, step-by-step, through all of the Windows accessibility features and configures his or her computer according to the chosen specifications.

- Microsoft Magnifier enlarges the section of your screen surrounding the mouse cursor.

- To solve problems seeing the mouse cursor, Microsoft offers the ability to use larger cursors, black cursors and cursors that invert objects underneath them.

- **SoundSentry** is a tool that creates visual signals when system events occur.

- **ShowSounds** adds captions to spoken text and other sounds produced by today's multimedia-rich software.

- **StickyKeys** is a program that helps users who have difficulty pressing multiple keys at the same time.

- **BounceKeys** forces the computer to ignore repeated keystrokes, solving the problem of accidentally pressing the same key more than once.
- **ToggleKeys** causes an audible beep to alert users that they have pressed one of the lock keys (i.e., *Caps Lock*, *Num Lock*, or *Scroll Lock*).
- **MouseKeys** is a tool that uses the keyboard to emulate mouse movements.
- The **Mouse Button Settings** tool allows you to create a virtual left-handed mouse by swapping the button functions.
- A timeout either enables or disables a certain action after the computer has idled for a specified amount of time. A common example of a timeout is a screen saver.
- You can create an `.acw` file that, when clicked, will automatically activate the saved accessibility settings on any Windows 2000 computer.
- Microsoft **Narrator** is a text-to-speech program for people with visual impairments. It reads text, describes the current desktop environment and alerts the user when certain Windows events occur.

TERMINOLOGY

accessibility
Accessibility Wizard
Accessibility Wizard: Display Color Settings
Accessibility Wizard: Icon Size
Accessibility Wizard: Mouse Cursor
Accessibility Wizard: Scroll Bar and Window Border Size
action element
`alt` attribute
Americans with Disabilities Act (ADA)
`<assign>` tag in VoiceXML
AuralCSS
`<b>` tag (bold)
`<block>` tag in VoiceXML
BounceKeys
braille display
braille keyboard
`<break>` tag in VoiceXML
CallXML
`<callxml>` tag in CallXML
`caption`
Cascading Style Sheets (CSS)
`<choice>` tag in VoiceXML
`count` attribute in VoiceXML
CSS2
D-link
default setting
EagleEyes
`encoding`
`<enumerate>` tag in VoiceXML
event handler
`<exit>` tag in VoiceXML

`field` variable
`<filled>` tag in VoiceXML
`<form>` tag in VoiceXML
frames
get request type
`<getDigits>` tag in CallXML
global variable
`<goto>` tag in VoiceXML
`<grammar>` tag in VoiceXML
Gunning Fog Index
`<h1>` tag
header cells
`headers` attribute
IBM ViaVoice
`id` attribute
`<img>` tag
JAWS (Job Access With Sound)
`level` attribute in VoiceXML
linearize
`<link>` tag in VoiceXML
local dialog
logging feature
logic element
`longdesc` attribute
Lynx
markup language
`maxDigits` attribute in CallXML
`maxTime` attribute in CallXML
`<menu>` tag in VoiceXML
Microsoft Magnifier
Microsoft Narrator
Mouse Button Settings window
MouseKeys

Narrator
`<next>` tag in VoiceXML
`<noframes>` tag
nolimit (default value)
Ocularis
`<onHangup>` tag in CallXML
`<onMaxSilence>` tag in CallXML
On-Screen Keyboard
`<onTermDigits>` tag in CallXML
post request type
priority-1 checkpoint
priority-2 checkpoint
priority-3 checkpoint
`<prompt>` tag in VoiceXML
quick tip
readability
Read typed characters
screen reader
session
sessionID
Set Automatic Timeout window
ShowSounds
SoundSentry
speech recognition
speech synthesizer
StickyKeys
`<strong>` tag
style sheet
system caret

`<subdialog>` tag in VoiceXML
summary attribute
Synchronized Multimedia Integration
      Language (SMIL)
tables
`<td>` tag
termDigits attribute in CallXML
`<text>` tag in CallXML
text-to-speech (TTS)
`<th>` tag
timeout
`<title>` tag
ToggleKeys
track
Unicode
user agent
`<var>` tag in VoiceXML
var attribute in CallXML
`version`
ViaVoice
voice server
Voice Server SDK
VoiceXML
Voxeo Community
`<vxml>` tag in VoiceXML
Web Accessibility Initiative (WAI)
Web Content Accessibility Guidelines 1.0
XML declaration
XML Guidelines (XML GL)

SELF-REVIEW EXERCISES

L.1   Expand the following acronyms:
   a) W3C.
   b) WAI.
   c) JAWS.
   d) SMIL.
   e) CSS.

L.2   Fill in the blanks in each of the following statements:
   a) The highest priority of the Web Accessibility Initiative ensures that each _____, _____ and _____ is accompanied by a description that clearly defines its purpose.
   b) Technologies such as _____, _____ and _____ enable individuals with disabilities to work in a large number of positions.
   c) Although they can be used as a great layout tool, _____ are difficult for screen readers to interpret and convey clearly to a user.
   d) To make a frame accessible to individuals with disabilities, it is important to include _____ tags on a Web page.
   e) _____ and _____ often assist blind people using computers.

f) CallXML creates _____ applications that allow businesses to receive and send telephone calls.

g) A _____ tag must be associated with the **`<getDigits>`** tag.

ANSWERS TO SELF-REVIEW EXERCISES

L.1   a) World Wide Web Consortium. b) Web Accessibility Initiative. c) Job Access with Sound. d) Synchronized Multimedia Integration Language. e) Cascading Style Sheets.

L.2   a) image, movie, sound. b) voice activation, visual enhancers, auditory aids. c) tables. d) **`<noframes>`**. e) Braille displays, braille keyboards. f) phone-to-Web. g) **`<onTermDigit>`**.

EXERCISES

L.3   State whether each of the following is *true* or *false*. If *false*, explain why.
- a) Screen readers have no problem reading and translating images.
- b) When writing pages for the general public, it is important to consider the reading difficulty level of the text.
- c) The **`<alt>`** tag helps screen readers describe images in a Web page.
- d) Left-handed people have been helped by the improvements made in speech-recognition technology more than any other group of people.
- e) VoiceXML lets users interact with Web content using speech recognition and speech synthesis technologies.
- f) Elements such as **`onMaxSilence`** and **`onTermDigit`** are event handlers because they perform a specified task when invoked.
- g) The debugging feature of the **Voxeo Account Manager** assists developers in debugging their CallXML application.

L.4   Insert XHTML markup into each segment to make the segment accessible to someone with disabilities. The contents of images and frames should be apparent from the context and filenames.

- a) `<img src = "dogs.jpg" width = "300" height = "250" />`
- b)
```
<table width    "75%">
    <tr><th>Language</th><th>Version</th></tr>
    <tr><td>XHTML</td><td>1.0</td></tr>
    <tr><td>Perl</td><td>5.6.0</td></tr>
    <tr><td>Java</td><td>1.3</td></tr>
</table>
```

L.5   Define the following terms:
- a) Action element.
- b) Gunning Fog Index.
- c) Screen reader.
- c) Session.
- d) Web Accessibility Initiative (WAI).

L.6   Describe the three-tier structure of checkpoints (priority-1, priority-2 and priority-3) set forth by the WAI.

L.7   Why do misused **`<h1>`** heading tags create problems for screen readers?

L.8   Use CallXML to create a voice mail system that plays a voice mail greeting and records the message. Have friends and classmates call your application and leave a message.

HTML/XHTML
Special Characters

The table of Fig. M.1 shows many commonly used HTML/XHTML special characters—called *character entity references* by the World Wide Web Consortium. For a complete list of character entity references, see the site

`www.w3.org/TR/REC-html40/sgml/entities.html`

Character	HTML/XHTML encoding	Character	HTML/XHTML encoding
non-breaking space	` `	ê	`&#234;`
§	`&#167;`	ì	`&#236;`
©	`&#169;`	í	`&#237;`
®	`&#174;`	î	`&#238;`
π	`&#188;`	ñ	`&#241;`
∫	`&#189;`	ò	`&#242;`
Ω	`&#190;`	ó	`&#243;`
à	`&#224;`	ô	`&#244;`
á	`&#225;`	õ	`&#245;`
â	`&#226;`	÷	`&#247;`
ã	`&#227;`	ù	`&#249;`
å	`&#229;`	ú	`&#250;`
ç	`&#231;`	û	`&#251;`
è	`&#232;`	•	`&#8226;`
é	`&#233;`	™	`&#8482;`

Fig. M.1   XHTML special characters.

HTML/XHTML Colors

Colors may be specified by using a standard name (such as **aqua**) or a hexadecimal RGB value (such as **#00FFFF** for **aqua**). Of the six hexadecimal digits in an RGB value, the first two represent the amount of red in the color, the middle two represent the amount of green in the color, and the last two represent the amount of blue in the color. For example, **black** is the absence of color and is defined by **#000000**, whereas **white** is the maximum amount of red, green and blue and is defined by **#FFFFFF**. Pure **red** is **#FF0000**, pure green (which is called **lime**) is **#00FF00** and pure **blue** is **#0000FF**. Note that **green** in the standard is defined as **#008000**. Figure N.1 contains the HTML/XHTML standard color set. Figure N.2 contains the HTML/XHTML extended color set.

Color name	Value	Color name	Value
aqua	#00FFFF	navy	#000080
black	#000000	olive	#808000
blue	#0000FF	purple	#800080
fuchsia	#FF00FF	red	#FF0000
gray	#808080	silver	#C0C0C0
green	#008000	teal	#008080
lime	#00FF00	yellow	#FFFF00
maroon	#800000	white	#FFFFFF

Fig. N.1 HTML/XHTML standard colors and hexadecimal RGB values.

Color name	Value	Color name	Value
aliceblue	#F0F8FF	deeppink	#FF1493
antiquewhite	#FAEBD7	deepskyblue	#00BFFF
aquamarine	#7FFFD4	dimgray	#696969
azure	#F0FFFF	dodgerblue	#1E90FF
beige	#F5F5DC	firebrick	#B22222
bisque	#FFE4C4	floralwhite	#FFFAF0
blanchedalmond	#FFEBCD	forestgreen	#228B22
blueviolet	#8A2BE2	gainsboro	#DCDCDC
brown	#A52A2A	ghostwhite	#F8F8FF
burlywood	#DEB887	gold	#FFD700
cadetblue	#5F9EA0	goldenrod	#DAA520
chartreuse	#7FFF00	greenyellow	#ADFF2F
chocolate	#D2691E	honeydew	#F0FFF0
coral	#FF7F50	hotpink	#FF69B4
cornflowerblue	#6495ED	indianred	#CD5C5C
cornsilk	#FFF8DC	indigo	#4B0082
crimson	#DC1436	ivory	#FFFFF0
cyan	#00FFFF	khaki	#F0E68C
darkblue	#00008B	lavender	#E6E6FA
darkcyan	#008B8B	lavenderblush	#FFF0F5
darkgoldenrod	#B8860B	lawngreen	#7CFC00
darkgray	#A9A9A9	lemonchiffon	#FFFACD
darkgreen	#006400	lightblue	#ADD8E6
darkkhaki	#BDB76B	lightcoral	#F08080
darkmagenta	#8B008B	lightcyan	#E0FFFF
darkolivegreen	#556B2F	lightgoldenrodyellow	#FAFAD2
darkorange	#FF8C00	lightgreen	#90EE90
darkorchid	#9932CC	lightgrey	#D3D3D3
darkred	#8B0000	lightpink	#FFB6C1
darksalmon	#E9967A	lightsalmon	#FFA07A
darkseagreen	#8FBC8F	lightseagreen	#20B2AA
darkslateblue	#483D8B	lightskyblue	#87CEFA
darkslategray	#2F4F4F	lightslategray	#778899
darkturquoise	#00CED1	lightsteelblue	#B0C4DE
darkviolet	#9400D3	lightyellow	#FFFFE0

Fig. N.2   XHTML extended colors and hexadecimal RGB values. (Part 1 of 2.)

Color name	Value	Color name	Value
limegreen	#32CD32	mediumblue	#0000CD
mediumpurple	#9370DB	mediumorchid	#BA55D3
mediumseagreen	#3CB371	plum	#DDA0DD
mediumslateblue	#7B68EE	powderblue	#B0E0E6
mediumspringgreen	#00FA9A	rosybrown	#BC8F8F
mediumturquoise	#48D1CC	royalblue	#4169E1
mediumvioletred	#C71585	saddlebrown	#8B4513
midnightblue	#191970	salmon	#FA8072
mintcream	#F5FFFA	sandybrown	#F4A460
mistyrose	#FFE4E1	seagreen	#2E8B57
moccasin	#FFE4B5	seashell	#FFF5EE
navajowhite	#FFDEAD	sienna	#A0522D
oldlace	#FDF5E6	skyblue	#87CEEB
olivedrab	#6B8E23	slateblue	#6A5ACD
orange	#FFA500	slategray	#708090
orangered	#FF4500	snow	#FFFAFA
orchid	#DA70D6	springgreen	#00FF7F
palegoldenrod	#EEE8AA	steelblue	#4682B4
palegreen	#98FB98	tan	#D2B48C
paleturquoise	#AFEEEE	thistle	#D8BFD8
palevioletred	#DB7093	tomato	#FF6347
papayawhip	#FFEFD5	turquoise	#40E0D0
peachpuff	#FFDAB9	violet	#EE82EE
peru	#CD853F	wheat	#F5DEB3
pink	#FFC0CB	whitesmoke	#F5F5F5
mediumaquamarine	#66CDAA	yellowgreen	#9ACD32

Fig. N.2   XHTML extended colors and hexadecimal RGB values. (Part 2 of 2.)

Additional Python 2.2 Features

Objectives

- To introduce the concept of iterators.
- To create classes that support iterators by defining methods __iter__ and next.
- To introduce generators and keyword yield.
- To create generators that compute the Fibonacci sequence.
- To introduce the concept of functional programming.
- To introduce nested scopes.

Outline

O.1 Introduction

In Chapter 9, Object-Oriented Programming: Inheritance, we discussed the major changes to Python for version 2.2, intended to address the differences between built-in types and classes (programmer-defined types). With the type-class unification, programmers now can inherit from built-in types, to extend their functionality. Python 2.2 adds other object-oriented features, including static methods and properties.

   In this appendix, we present an overview of additional new features in Python 2.2 that allow programmers to express algorithms more clearly and simply. We first introduce *iterators*—special objects for progressing through a sequences of values. *Generators*—functions that return iterators—are resumable functions that are especially well suited for computing the values of a recursive sequence. *Nested scopes* address how identifier lookup takes place in nested functions. We discuss iterators and generators in the context of a series of examples that examine how programs can compute sequences of values in an efficient and elegant manner. Nested scoping behavior is most useful for programs that employ a functional-style of programming. This text focuses mostly on the object-oriented aspects of Python, so we provide only an introductory example to motivate the inclusion of nested scopes. We then provide further resources for the reader to explore.

O.2 Iterators

In Chapter 12, Exceptions, we mentioned that Python **for** loops use exceptions to determine when the end of a sequence has been reached. This makes it possible to write classes whose objects may be used with **for** loops. In earlier versions of Python, the class author provided method **__getitem__**, which enabled clients to perform list- or dictionary-like subscript access for objects of the class. As an example, Fig. O.1 defines class **MyRange**, a class that simulates a sequence returned from a call to built-in function **range**. A client creates an object of class **MyRange** by passing to the constructor values for parameters **start**, **stop** and **step**, which the method simply passes to function **range** (line 10). The class stores the return value from **range** in attribute **__sequence**.

```
1   # Fig. O.1: NewRange.py
2   # __getitem__ used in a for loop.
3
4   class MyRange:
5       """Simple class to simulate a range of integer values"""
```

Fig. O.1   **__getitem__** method to emulate iteration. (Part 1 of 2.)

```
6
7       def __init__( self, start, stop, step ):
8          """Class MyRange constructor; takes start, stop and step"""
9
10         self.__sequence = range( start, stop, step )
11
12      def __getitem__( self, subscript ):
13         """Overridden sequence element access"""
14
15         return self.__sequence[ subscript ]
```

```
Python 2.2b2 (#26, Nov 16 2001, 11:44:11) [MSC 32 bit (Intel)] on win32
Type "help", "copyright", "credits" or "license" for more information.
>>>
>>> from NewRange import MyRange
>>> myRange = MyRange( 0, 10, 1 )
>>>
>>> print myRange[ 0 ]
0
>>> print myRange[ 8 ]
8
>>>
>>> for value in myRange:
...     print value,
...
0 1 2 3 4 5 6 7 8 9
```

Fig. O.1   __getitem__ method to emulate iteration. (Part 2 of 2.)

Method __getitem__ provides subscript access (using operator **[]**) for objects of the class. The method takes one argument—**subscript**—and returns the element stored in __sequence[subscript]. If the specified subscript lies outside the bounds of the sequence, Python raises an **IndexError** exception.

The interactive session that follows the class definition creates an object of class **MyRange** with the values 0–9 and demonstrates random attribute access (lines 4–10). When the interpreter encounters the statements in lines 12–13 of the interactive session, the interpreter translates the code into successive subscript operations on object **myRange**. The interactive session in Fig. O.2 simulates how Python executes the **for** loop from the previous session. The interpreter starts at index 0 (variable **currentIndex**). The session then enters a **for** loop that attempts to access the value stored in object **myRange** at index **currentIndex**, which implicitly calls the object's __getitem__ method. If the index lies outside the bounds for that object, method __getitem__ raises an **IndexError** exception; otherwise, the interpreter assigns the returned value to control variable **value**. If the attribute access in line 11 of the interactive session does not raise an **IndexError** exception, the interpreter prints variable **value** and increments the control variable. Then, program control returns to the top of the **while** loop, where the interpreter attempts to access the second value in sequence **myRange**. The interpreter continues to increment the control variable and access the sequence's corresponding element until method __getitem__ raises an **IndexError** exception. At this point, the **except** clause in lines 12-13 of the interactive session breaks out of the **while** loop.

```
Python 2.2b2 (#26, Nov 16 2001, 11:44:11) [MSC 32 bit (Intel)] on win32
Type "help", "copyright", "credits" or "license" for more information.
>>>
>>> from NewRange import MyRange
>>> myRange = MyRange( 0, 10, 1 )
>>>
>>> currentIndex = 0
>>>
>>> while 1:
...     try:
...         value = myRange[ currentIndex ]
...     except IndexError:
...         break
...     else:
...         print value,
...         currentIndex += 1
...
0 1 2 3 4 5 6 7 8 9
```

Fig. O.2 ___getitem___ and **for** loops.

Although method **___getitem___** provides a way for clients to use an object with **for**/**in** syntax, method **___getitem___** was intended for random attribute access (e.g., index access for lists or key lookup for dictionaries), rather than iteration.[1] The designers of the language felt it would be cleaner to separate the random attribute access operation from the object iteration operation.[2] To address this issue, Python 2.2 introduces the concept of *iterators*—special objects that define operations for progressing through sequences. Iterators are useful for many kinds of sequences, including list-like objects (such as built-in types **list** and **tuple**), programmer-defined container objects (e.g., trees) or unbounded sequences—sequences whose length is unknown or cannot be determined in advance (e.g., input and output streams).

Figure O.3 contains a new implementation of class **MyRange**—called **Range-Iterator**—that supports iterators. Before we discuss the class definition, consider the main program (lines 29–71) that uses iterators to progress through the sequences defined by objects of class **RangeIterator**. Line 32 creates object **range1** that contains the values 0–9. Lines 36–37 use the object in a **for** loop, to iterate over the object's elements. The **for**-loop syntax for an object of class **RangeIterator** is identical to that of an object of the class as defined in Fig. O.1, even though the new class definition does not define method **___getitem___**.

```
1   # Fig. O.3: NewRangeIterator.py
2   # Iterator class that defines a sequence.
3
```

Fig. O.3   Iterator class that defines a sequence. (Part 1 of 3.)

1. A. Kuchling, "What's New in Python 2.2," <www.amk.ca/python/2.2>.
2. G. van Rossum and K. Yee, "Iterators," 30 April 2001 <python.sourceforge.net/peps/pep-0234.html>.

```python
4   class RangeIterator:
5       """Simple class to simulate a range"""
6
7       def __init__( self, start, stop, step ):
8           """RangeIterator constructor; takes start, stop and step"""
9
10          self.__sequence = range( start, stop, step )
11          self.__nextValue = 0   # subscript of next value to produce
12
13      def __iter__( self ):
14          """Returns iterator for object of class RangeIterator"""
15
16          return self
17
18      def next( self ):
19          """Iterator method to produce next value in sequence"""
20
21          try:
22              value = self.__sequence[ self.__nextValue ]
23          except IndexError:
24              raise StopIteration
25          else:
26              self.__nextValue += 1
27              return value
28
29  def main():
30
31      # create object of class RangeIterator, use for loop to iterate
32      range1 = RangeIterator( 0, 10, 1 )
33
34      print "Iterate over the values in range1 using a for loop:"
35
36      for value in range1:
37          print value,
38
39      print
40
41      # create object of class RangeIterator, call next to iterate
42      range2 = RangeIterator( 0, 10, 1 )
43      range2Iterator = iter( range2 )   # retrieve iterator for range2
44
45      print "\nCall method next for range2Iterator:"
46
47      while 1:
48
49          try:
50              value = range2Iterator.next()
51          except StopIteration:
52              break
53          else:
54              print value,
55
56      print
```

Fig. O.3 Iterator class that defines a sequence. (Part 2 of 3.)

```
57
58       # create one object of class RangeIterator two iterators
59       # for that object
60       range3 = RangeIterator( 0, 10, 1 )
61       range3Iterator1 = iter( range3 )
62       range3Iterator2 = iter( range3 )
63
64       print "\nCall next for two iterators of the same object:"
65
66       for i in range( 10 ):
67          print "Loop iteration %d: range3Iterator1.next() = %d" % \
68             ( i, range3Iterator1.next() )
69          print "Loop iteration %d: range3Iterator2.next() = %d" % \
70             ( i, range3Iterator2.next() )
71          print
72
73   if __name__ == "__main__":
74       main()
```

```
Iterate over the values in range1 using a for loop:
0 1 2 3 4 5 6 7 8 9

Call method next for range2Iterator:
0 1 2 3 4 5 6 7 8 9

Call next for two iterators of the same object:
Loop iteration 0: range3Iterator1.next() = 0
Loop iteration 0: range3Iterator2.next() = 1

Loop iteration 1: range3Iterator1.next() = 2
Loop iteration 1: range3Iterator2.next() = 3

Loop iteration 2: range3Iterator1.next() = 4
Loop iteration 2: range3Iterator2.next() = 5

Loop iteration 3: range3Iterator1.next() = 6
Loop iteration 3: range3Iterator2.next() = 7

Loop iteration 4: range3Iterator1.next() = 8
Loop iteration 4: range3Iterator2.next() = 9

Traceback (most recent call last):
  File "newrange3.py", line 74, in ?
    main()
  File "newrange3.py", line 67, in main
    print "Loop iteration %d: range3Iterator1.next() = %d" % \
  File "newrange3.py", line 24, in next
    raise StopIteration
StopIteration
```

Fig. O.3   Iterator class that defines a sequence. (Part 3 of 3.)

Just as earlier versions of Python "rewrite" **for** loops to call an object's __getitem__ method, Python 2.2 rewrites **for** loops to progress through an object's iterator. Lines 42–54 simulate how a Python **for** loop works on an object that supports iterators. Line 42 creates **range2**—an object of class **RangeIterator**. All objects that support (i.e., provide) iterators define two methods—**__iter__** and **next**. A client obtains an iterator for an object by passing the object's name to built-in function **iter** (line 43). This function implicitly invokes the object's **__iter__** method, which allows Python to create an iterator for that object. The **while** loop in lines 47–54 corresponds to the **for** loop in lines 36–37. A program progresses through the values in an object's sequence by calling method **next** for an iterator of that object (line 50). This method either returns the next element in the object's sequence—in which case line 54 prints the value— or raises the **StopIteration** exception, to indicate that the sequence contains no more values—in which case line 52 breaks out of the **while** loop.

Software Engineering Observation O.1

*If a program uses a **for** loop to iterate over an object that does not support iteration through methods **__iter__** and **next**, Python uses the object's **__getitem__** method instead. If that object also does not define a **__getitem__** method, Python raises a **TypeError** exception when the program attempts to iterate over the object.*

A client may obtain more than one iterator for a particular sequence (lines 61–62). In this case, each call to the iterator's **next** method retrieves the next value in the sequence. Sometimes, this can lead to subtle logic errors. The **for** suite in lines 67–71 executes 10 times, each time calling **next** on two iterators for the same object. Even though **range3Iterator1** and **range3Iterator2** are two different iterator objects, their **next** methods retrieve values from the same sequence (i.e., **range3**). Therefore, the program exhausts **range3**'s values after only 5 executions of the **for** suite, causing the program to terminate on a **StopIteration** exception. It is possible for a class to provide a unique iterator object for each call to function **iter**. For example, calling **iter** on an object that is a built-in list returns a unique iterator for that list's sequence. For programmer-defined classes, returning a unique iterator for an object sometimes requires complex state information. In these cases, the programmer-defined class may provide a generator (discussed in Section O.3) to produce the values in an object's sequence.

Common Programming Error O.1

*Iterating past the end of a sequence raises a **StopIteration** exception. Enclose in a **try** statement any code that calls an iterator's **next** method explicitly and which may therefore iterate past the end of a sequence.*

We now discuss the class definition in lines 4–27. The constructor defines attribute **__sequence**, which contains an object's sequence values, and attribute **__nextValue**, a control variable that an object of the class uses to mark the next value to produce in the sequence. Any class whose objects support iterators must define method **__iter__**, either explicitly or through inheritance. This method takes only the object reference argument (**self**) and should return an iterator object for the class. An iterator object is an object that defines method **next**, which clients can call to retrieve the next value in the sequence, and which raises **StopIteration** when the sequence values have been exhausted. Line 16 simply returns the object reference argument, because class **Range-Iterator** defines an appropriate **next** method.

Method **next** (lines 18–27) retrieves the next value from an object of class **RangeIterator**. The method attempts to retrieve the value that corresponds to the current location in an object's sequence (i.e., the index indicated by attribute **__nextValue**). If the current subscript location is out of bounds for the sequence, Python raises an **Index-Error** exception. We catch this exception in lines 23–24 and raise a **StopIteration** exception to indicate that the sequence values have been exhausted; otherwise, lines 26–27 increment the control variable and return the retrieved value.

A class that supports iteration is not required to define **next**. If a class does not define **next**, the class's **__iter__** method should return an object that provides this message. For example, in Fig. O.3, we could have omitted the definition for method **next** and implemented method **__iter__** as follows:

```
def __iter__( self ):
    return iter( self.__sequence )
```

In this case, the **__iter__** method returns the result of passing a list to function **iter**. Lists are not iterators themselves, because they do not define method next; however when a program passes a list to function **iter**, Python creates an iterator (that defines method **next**) for that list.

Common Programming Error O.2

*It is a logic error if a class's **__iter__** method does not return an object that defines method **next**.*

Software Engineering Observation O.2

*Calling **iter** on a a built-in type such as a list, tuple or dictionary object returns a unique iterator for that object. Calling **next** on one iterator of an object built-in type does not affect any other iterators on that object.*

One benefit of iterators is that a client can retrieve a sequence's values one at a time. This technique is much more memory efficient for cases where the sequence contains many values. For example, dictionaries now support iterators that make processing dictionary contents much more efficient than in earlier versions of Python. Dictionary methods **iterkeys**, **itervalues** and **iteritems** return iterator objects for looping over the keys, values and items of a dictionary, respectively. Method **iterkeys** is more memory-efficient than method **keys**, because method **iterkeys** does not produce the entire list of keys at once. Rather, **iterkeys** returns an iterator that may be used by a **for** loop to retrieve the dictionary's keys, as needed. If the **for** suite terminates after only a few executions, the iterator technique of obtaining values provides significant performance improvement over obtaining the entire sequence in advance (e.g., through method **keys**). Python 2.2 also defines how a dictionary may be used in a **for** loop. The statement

```
for key in dictionaryObject:
    process key
```

implicitly calls the dictionary's **iterkeys** method to obtain an iterator.

In addition, dictionaries may be used with the syntax

```
if key in dictionaryObject:
    process key
```

which is equivalent to

```
if dictionary.has_key( key ):
    process key
```

Files also support iterators and the **for**/**in** syntax. The statement

```
for line in fileObject:
    print line
```

creates an iterator object for the file and calls the iterator's **next** method to retrieve each line in the file. A file's iterator provides a more efficient means for processing the contents of a file.

Another case in which an iterator is useful occurs when a program needs to process a sequence whose length cannot be determined. For example, a program may use an iterator to process input from a file stream (e.g., **stdin**) continually. In this case, the program simply calls **next** on the file stream to retrieve the next piece of input. Figure O.4 defines a class (**ComputerGuessingGame**) whose objects produce sequences of indeterminate length. The program simulates a random guessing game where the user supplies a number and the **ComputerGuessingGame** randomly guesses numbers until one of the guesses matches the user-supplied value.

 Common Programming Error O.3

*Calling function **len** on an iterator object raises a **TypeError** exception, because an iterator's length cannot always be determined at runtime.*

ComputerGuessingGame's constructor takes an argument that corresponds to the number that the computer is should try to guess (**value**) and arguments that correspond to the lower- and upper-bounds (**lowerBound** and **upperBound**, respectively) on the range of values from which the game produces guesses. Lines 16–24 ensure that the number to guess lies within the lower- and upper-bounds. If the constructor failed to do this, the user could pass to the constructor a value that lies outside the range from which the **ComputerGuessingGame** chooses guess, causing the program to execute indefinitely.

```
1   # Fig. O.4: GuessingGame.py
2   # Class and program to simulate computer guessing game.
3
4   import random
5
6   class ComputerGuessingGame:
7       """Class to guess a number randomly"""
8
9       def __init__( self, value, lowerBound = 0, upperBound = 10 ):
10          """ComputerGuesser constructor; takes secret number, lower
11          and upper bounds"""
12
13          self.realValue = value
14
15          # keep value within upper and lower bound
16          if value < lowerBound:
17              self.lower = value
```

Fig. O.4   Guessing game. (Part 1 of 3.)

```
18            else:
19                self.lower = lowerBound
20
21            if value > upperBound:
22                self.upper = value + 1
23            else:
24                self.upper = upperBound
25
26        def __iter__( self ):
27            """Return iterator for object of class ComputerGuesser"""
28
29            return self
30
31        def next( self ):
32            """Guesses a new value. If correct, raises StopIteration;
33            otherwise returns guess"""
34
35            guess = random.randrange( self.lower, self.upper )
36
37            if guess == self.realValue:
38                raise StopIteration
39            else:
40                return guess
41
42    def main():
43
44        # retrieve an integer from the user
45        while 1:
46
47            try:
48                secretNumber = int(
49                    raw_input( "Enter number for computer to guess: " ) )
50            except ValueError:
51                print "Please enter an integer."
52            else:
53                break
54
55        print
56
57        computerGuesser = ComputerGuessingGame( secretNumber )
58        numberOfWrongGuesses = 0
59
60        # print the incorrect guesses
61        for wrongGuess in computerGuesser:
62            numberOfWrongGuesses += 1
63            print "Computer guessed: %d" % wrongGuess
64
65        print "\nGot secret number after %d wrong guesses." % \
66            numberOfWrongGuesses
67
68    if __name__ == "__main__":
69        main()
```

Fig. O.4   Guessing game. (Part 2 of 3.)

```
Enter number for computer to guess: 6

Computer guessed: 1
Computer guessed: 7
Computer guessed: 1
Computer guessed: 1
Computer guessed: 3
Computer guessed: 9
Computer guessed: 9
Computer guessed: 1
Computer guessed: 8

Got secret number after 9 wrong guesses.
```

```
Enter number for computer to guess: 100

Computer guessed: 31
Computer guessed: 41
Computer guessed: 61
Computer guessed: 77
Computer guessed: 92
Computer guessed: 80
Computer guessed: 11
Computer guessed: 46
Computer guessed: 43
Computer guessed: 31
Computer guessed: 21
Computer guessed: 6
Computer guessed: 7

Got secret number after 13 wrong guesses.
```

Fig. O.4   Guessing game. (Part 3 of 3.)

Method **next** (lines 31–40) produces a series of random guesses. Each time the client calls **next** on an iterator for an object of class **ComputerGuessingGame**, the method produces a new, random value (line 35). If the random value matches the value the object is trying to guess, the method raises a **StopIteration** exception, to indicate the end of the sequence of guesses. Otherwise, the method returns the randomly-guessed, incorrect value.

The main program retrieves an integer from the user and creates **computer-Guesser**—an object of class **ComputerGuessingGame**. The **for** loop in lines 61–63 implicitly creates an iterator for object **computerGuesser**. Before each execution of the **for** suite, Python calls the object's **next** method. If the method produces an incorrect guess, Python assigns that value to control variable **wrongGuess** and executes the statements in the **for** suite. When method **next** guesses the correct value, the method raises a **StopIteration** exception, the **for** loop terminates and program execution resumes in lines 65.

The example in Fig. O.4 demonstrates how an iterator's **next** method generates values for a sequence of indeterminate length. An iterator can produce values in a variety of ways. The example in Fig. O.3 defined a class that maintains information about its current state (i.e., the next value in the sequence). Programmers often can keep track of a iterator's state with relative ease. Sometimes, however, maintaining an iterator's state requires complex program logic and large amounts of data storage. In the next section, we discuss generators—resumable functions that are a useful tool for creating iterators whose state may be difficult to maintain.

O.3 Generators

In the previous section, we discussed iterators—special objects that provide operations for getting the next value from a sequence. We also discussed how iterators can be more efficient for processing a sequence of values, especially when we may choose to stop processing the values before we have reached the end of the sequence. This concept of producing and processing values "as-needed" can be exceptionally useful for iterating over a sequence of recursively-generated values.

Consider function **fibonacci** in Fig. O.5, which computes the nth number in the Fibonacci sequence for a given n. This definition is similar to the one we presented in Chapter 4, Functions. Now suppose we want to find the smallest Fibonacci number that is greater than 1000. To compute this value, lines 20–22 contain a **while** loop that calls function **fibonacci** on a control variable, as long as the function returns a value less than 1000.

```
1   # Fig. O.5: figO_05.py
2   # Inefficient, recursive fibonacci calls.
3
4   def fibonacci( n ):
5
6      if n < 0:
7         raise ValueError, \
8            "Cannot computer fibonacci on negative number"
9
10     elif n == 0 or n == 1:
11        return n
12
13     else:
14        return fibonacci( n - 1 ) + fibonacci( n - 2 )
15
16  n = 0
17  value = 0
18
19  # compute smallest fibonacci( n ) > 1000
20  while value < 1000:
21     value = fibonacci( n )
22     n += 1
23
24  print "The smallest fibonacci number greater than 1000 is:", value
```

Fig. O.5 **fibonacci** function. (Part 1 of 2.)

```
The smallest fibonacci number greater than 1000 is: 1597
```

Fig. O.5   `fibonacci` function. (Part 2 of 2.)

Although the program produces the correct answer, the computation of the answer is inefficient, because the program makes several redundant calls to function **fibonacci**. Each time the function executes for a number *n*, the function must re-compute all the fibonacci values in the range 0-(*n*-1). Additionally, the recursive function calls themselves make redundant function calls. For example, to compute **fibonacci(3)** recursively, a program must compute the value of **fibonacci(1)** three times. For a value of *n*, the amount of recursive calls generated by **fibonacci(n)** grows quickly enough and may soon consume more than the available amount of memory. This example demonstrates that the overhead of recursive function calls sometimes outweighs the benefits of the ease with which programs can express recursive algorithms.

It would be more efficient to write **fibonacci** so that a program could obtain the sequence's values on an as-needed basis, rather than by performing redundant computations as in the previous example. Python 2.2 introduces the *generator*—a special kind of function that can suspend computation, "remember" its local variables and later resume where the previous computation left off. Figure O.6, defines **fibonacci** as a generator.

```python
1   # Fig. O.6: figO_06.py
2   # fibonacci generator.
3
4   from __future__ import generators
5
6   def fibonacci():
7
8       nextItem = 0   # next value in the sequence
9       beyondItem = 1   # value *after* the next value in the sequence
10
11      while 1:
12          yield nextItem   # return fibonacci( n )
13
14          # function resumes here when program calls next on
15          # fibonacci's iterator
16
17          # compute the next fibonacci( n ) and fibonacci( n + 1 )
18          nextItem, beyondItem = beyondItem, nextItem + beyondItem
19
20  fibIterator = fibonacci()   # create iterator for Fibonacci sequence
21  result = 0
22
23  # find smallest Fibonacci number greater than 1000
24  while result < 1000:
25      result = fibIterator.next()
26
27  print "The smallest fibonacci number greater than 1000 is:", result
```

Fig. O.6   `fibonacci` generator. (Part 1 of 2.)

```
The smallest fibonacci number greater than 1000 is: 1597
```

Fig. O.6   fibonacci generator. (Part 2 of 2.)

Generators use keyword **yield** to suspend execution and return to the caller an intermediate value. Introducing a new keyword to Python can cause problems for existing programs that used the keyword as a variable name. These programs now would contain a syntax error, because Python does not allow the programmer to assign values to keywords. In Chapter 2, Introduction to Python Programming, we discussed that Python uses a **from __future__ import** statement (line 4) to "phase in" language changes that may cause errors in programs that were written for an earlier version of Python. If a Python 2.2 program defines generators, the program must import the generator functionality explicitly; in future versions, the **import** statement will not be necessary.

Common Programming Error O.4

*If a program uses **yield** as an identifier, Python 2.2 prints a **SyntaxWarning** message, but does not raise an exception that may cause a program to terminate. In a program that imports generators or that executes under a post-2.2 version of Python, using **yield** as an identifier raises a **SyntaxError** exception.*

Generators can be called just like functions. In Fig. O.6, line 20 calls generator **fibonacci** and assigns the return value to variable **fibonacciIterator**. As the name of the variable indicates, the value returned by calling a generator is an iterator.[1] Essentially, a generator defines how to produce the values of a sequence. A program calls a generator to obtain an iterator for that sequence. When the program calls the returned iterator's **next** method, the generator computes and produces the next value in the sequence. Lines 24–25 contain a **while** loop that assigns the next value in the Fibonacci sequence to variable **value**, until the iterator's **next** method returns a value greater than 1000.

Lines 6–18 define the **fibonacci** generator. Local variables **nextItem** and **beyondItem** initially refer to the first and second items in the sequence, respectively. As the generator executes, **nextItem** is always the next value in the Fibonacci sequence and **beyondItem** is always the value that comes after the next value.

Lines 11–18 contain an infinite **while** loop that computes the Fibonacci sequence. When a function definition contains keyword **yield** (line 12)—and if generators have been activated—Python identifies that function as a generator. Generators behave differently than functions. In a generator, program execution continues normally until Python encounters keyword **yield**. At this point, the function returns the value of the expression that follows **yield** (in this case, the value of local variable **nextItem**). Unlike traditional functions, however, Python "remembers" two important pieces of information about the state of execution when a generator yields: the values of all the generator's local variables and the point from which the generator yielded. This means that when the program calls method **next** again, the generator's execution resumes with the first statement that follows the **yield** statement.

The flow of control in a program that uses generators can be difficult to follow. Let us examine the order of execution in Fig. O.6 step-by-step. First, Python encounters the

---

1. Calling a generator actually returns a special kind of iterator called a generator-iterator.

import statement in line 4. This tells Python that the program intends to define a generator. Python then encounters the definition for **fibonacci**. This definition contains keyword **yield**, so Python designates **fibonacci** as a generator. Next, line 20 calls **fibonacci**. Calling a generator returns an iterator, and the program assigns this iterator to variable **fibIterator**. Line 21 assigns the value 0 to variable **result**. The program uses **result** to determine when the desired return value has been obtained. Next the **while** loop (lines 24–25) begins executing.

On the first execution of the **while** loop, Python determines that the value of **result** (0) is less than 1000, so program control enters the **while** suite. Line 25 invokes **fibIterator**'s **next** method for the first time. At this point, program control jumps to the first statement in **fibonacci** (line 8). This statement and the subsequent statement assign the values 0 and 1 to local variables **nextItem** and **beyondItem**, respectively. These values represent the first and second values in the Fibonacci sequence. Next, the **while** loop in lines 11–18 begins execution. The first statement in the **while** suite yields the value of variable **nextItem** (in this case, 0). This means that program control returns to the caller (line 25 in the main program) and assigns the value 0 to variable **result**. The program then re-tests the **while**-loop condition in line 24. The condition is true (i.e., 0 is less than 1000), so program control again enters the **while** suite at line 25 and invokes **fibIterator.next**. This time, program control resumes in **fibonacci** at line 18, because a generator "remembers" where it yielded previously. A generator also remembers the values of its local variables. This means that before line 18 executes, **nextItem** is 0 and **beyondItem** is 1. After line 18 executes, **nextItem** is 1 (i.e., it is the old value of **beyondItem**) and **beyondItem** is 1 (i.e., the result of adding 0 and 1). These values represent the second and third values in the Fibonacci sequence, respectively. Line 18 is the last line of the **while** suite, so program execution continues at the top of the **while** loop. Line 12 yields the new value of **nextItem** (i.e., 1) to line 25 of the main program. The main program then continues to test control variable **result** and to execute the statement in the **while** suite until the generator returns a value that is greater than 1000. At this point, the **while** loop terminates and the program prints the value of variable **result**.

The fact that generators return iterators when called enables programmers to use generators with **for** loops. Figure O.7 redefines the fibonacci generator to take one argument, **n**. The generator produces all the Fibonacci sequence values up through and including the nth value. The main program does not explicitly create an iterator for the Fibonacci sequence. Instead, Python implicitly creates an iterator the first time the program calls **fibonacci** in line 33. Then, Python repeatedly calls the iterator's **next** method to retrieve values for control variable **result**. Notice that **fibonacci** never raises a **StopIteration** exception to signal the end of the sequence. When a generator returns, either through a **return** statement or when program execution reaches the end of the function's block, a **StopIteration** exception is raised implicitly. This signals to the **for** loop in lines 33–35 that the end of the sequence has been reached. Program control then exits the **for** suite and the program terminates, because it contains no more statements.

As these simple examples illustrate, generators provide a simple and efficient way for programmers to compute a sequence of values. Generators are well-suited for computing more complicated recursive algorithms, as well. For example, in Chapter 22, we presented a binary tree data structure that used recursive helper methods to traverse the tree and print the values of each node. With generators, we can write traversal methods that are easy to define in the traditional, recursive manner but which have the added benefit that a program can compute node values on an as-needed basis.

```python
1   # Fig O.7: figO_07.py
2   # fibonacci generator for nth Fibonacci sequence element.
3
4   from __future__ import generators
5
6   def fibonacci( n ):
7
8      nextItem = 0   # next value in the sequence
9      beyondItem = 1   # value *after* the next value in the sequence
10     currentN = 0   # n for which the generator is producing a value
11
12     while currentN <= n:
13        yield nextItem   # return fibonacci( n )
14
15        # compute the next fibonacci( n ) and fibonacci( n + 1 )
16        nextItem, beyondItem = beyondItem, nextItem + beyondItem
17        currentN += 1
18
19  while 1:
20
21     # retrieve number from user
22     try:
23        fibNumber = int( raw_input( "Enter a number: " ) )
24     except ValueError:
25        print "Please enter an integer."
26     else:
27        break
28
29  print
30  counter = 0
31
32  # print fibonacii( n ) for all n <= fibNumber
33  for result in fibonacci( fibNumber ):
34     print "fibonacci( %d ) = %d" % ( counter, result )
35     counter += 1
```

```
Enter a number: 20

fibonacci( 0 ) = 0
fibonacci( 1 ) = 1
fibonacci( 2 ) = 1
fibonacci( 3 ) = 2
fibonacci( 4 ) = 3
fibonacci( 5 ) = 5
fibonacci( 6 ) = 8
fibonacci( 7 ) = 13
fibonacci( 8 ) = 21
fibonacci( 9 ) = 34
```
continued at top of next page

Fig. O.7   **fibonacci** generator for *n*th Fibonacci sequence element. (Part 1 of 2.)

continued from previous page

```
fibonacci( 10 ) = 55
fibonacci( 11 ) = 89
fibonacci( 12 ) = 144
fibonacci( 13 ) = 233
fibonacci( 14 ) = 377
fibonacci( 15 ) = 610
fibonacci( 16 ) = 987
fibonacci( 17 ) = 1597
fibonacci( 18 ) = 2584
fibonacci( 19 ) = 4181
fibonacci( 20 ) = 6765
```

Fig. O.7 **fibonacci** generator for *n*th Fibonacci sequence element. (Part 2 of 2.)

O.4 Nested Scopes

Python allows programmers to define nested functions—functions within functions. The reason programmers define nested functions often is because the inner function performs some of the internal operations of the outer function that users of the outer function express-ly do not need to perform. For example, in Chapter 22, Data Structures, we defined a **Tree** class and provided operations for pre-, in- and post-order traversal. Each traversal method called another "helper" method that performed the recursive tree traversal operation and printed the value of each node. The helper methods were defined at the same level as the traversal methods, which means that the helper methods were bound to their class's scope. A better way to design the class might have been to define nested helper functions within the traversal methods. This design makes the **Tree** interface cleaner, because a client sees only those methods that the client needs to traverse the **Tree**. In this section, we introduce the technique of defining nested functions and discuss how nested scoping enables an inner function to access variables that appear in the function's outer scope.

The program in Fig. O.8 defines two functions—**outer** and **inner**. The definition of function **outer** (lines 4–14) first defines function **inner** (lines 6–9), which simply prints messages to indicate that the function is executing and calls built-in function **dir** to print a list of the objects in the function's scope. Because the definition of function **inner** appears in the code block that corresponds to function **outer**, Python binds the name **inner** to function **outer**'s local scope. The identifier **inner** behaves like any other local identifier, which means that the value to which it is bound (i.e., the **inner** function definition) cannot be seen by any enclosing scopes and the identifier goes out of scope once the **outer** function block terminates.

The main program (lines 16–21) first calls function **dir** to print a list of the objects in the global scope. Notice from the output that identifier **outer** appears in the list, but not identifier **inner**. This underscores the fact that **inner** can be accessed only in the local scope of function **outer**.

One problem with nested scopes in older versions of Python is that variable lookup from the inner scope did not behave as many programmers expected. This raised consider-able issues for programmers who used Python with a *functional programming* style. In functional programming, the programmer places emphasis on writing expressions that the interpreter evaluates, reduces to a simpler expression, re-evaluates to reduce to a simpler expression, and so on. A functional programmer often creates expressions through a series of nested function calls. Each nested function call is evaluated, and the resulting value is passed to an outer function call.

Figure O.9 uses a typical functional-style programming technique. Function **centerLength** is a function that takes one argument **length**—the length of a string of whitespace in which another string is to be centered. Function **centerLength** contains a nested function **centerString** that takes a string object and calls the object's **center** method, passing the value of the **length** argument from the outer scope. Then, line 9 in function **centerLength** returns function **centerString** to the caller.

Lines 5–8 of the interactive session in Fig. O.9 demonstrate that the return value of calling function **centerLength** is another function. When we call the returned function (**centerString10**), and pass the string **"python"**, the function returns the string, centered in a string of length 10.

```
1   # Fig. O.8: figO_08.py
2   # Nested functions.
3
4   def outer():
5
6       def inner():
7           print "\nFunction inner executing"
8           print "The objects in inner's scope are:", dir()
9           print "Function inner finishing"
10
11      print "Function outer executing"
12      print "The objects in outer's scope are:", dir()
13      inner()
14      print "\nFunction outer finishing"
15
16  print "The objects in the global scope are:"
17  print dir()
18
19  print "\nCalling function outer\n"
20  outer()
21  print "\nFunction outer finished"
```

```
The objects in the global scope are:
['__builtins__', '__doc__', '__name__', 'outer']

Calling function outer

Function outer executing
The objects in outer's scope are: ['inner']

Function inner executing
The objects in inner's scope are: []
Function inner finishing

Function outer finishing

Function outer finished
```

Fig. O.8   Nested functions.

```
1   # Fig O.9: CenterLength.py
2   # Functional definition of string justification.
3
4   def centerLength( length ):
5
6      def centerString( stringValue ):
7         return stringValue.center( length )
8
9      return centerString
10
```

```
Python 2.2b2 (#26, Nov 16 2001, 11:44:11) [MSC 32 bit (Intel)] on win32
Type "help", "copyright", "credits" or "license" for more information.
>>>
>>> import CenterLength
>>> centerString10 = CenterLength.centerLength( 10 )
>>>
>>> type( centerString10 )
<type 'function'>
>>>
>>> centerString10( "python" )
'  python  '
```

Fig. O.9   Functional-style programming.

Notice that the definition of function **centerString** relies on the value of **length** from the outer scope. This is an example of nested scopes. In previous versions of Python, inner functions did not have access to the variables in their containing scopes. The interactive session in Fig. O.10 attempts to import our function definition in Python 2.1.1, which does not support nested scopes by default. Notice that Python issues a **SyntaxWarning** when we import the module that contains our function definition, because Python 2.1.1 does not know how to resolve the name **"length"** in function **centerString**. When we attempt to invoke the function returned from function **centerLength**, Python raises a **NameError**, because variable **length** is not defined in the local scope of the function, nor is it defined in the global (module) or __**builtin**__ scopes.

Python 2.2's nested-scope behavior also makes it easier for programmers to write *lambda expressions*. A **lambda** expression—when evaluated—produces a function, much in the same way that function **centerLength**—when called—returns a function. Many programmers use **lambda** expressions to define callbacks for GUI applications. In this text, we have chosen to focus on object-oriented programming in Python, rather than on functional or procedural programming. The Web resources in the next session provide additional information about functional programming in Python.

O.5 Internet and World Wide Web Resources

python.sourceforge.net/peps
This page hosts the Python Enhancement Proposals (PEPs), each of which describes a suggestion language addition or modification. These include iterators (PEP 234), generators (PEP 255) and nested scopes (PEP 227).

```
Python 2.1.1 (#20, Jul 20 2001, 01:19:29) [MSC 32 bit (Intel)] on win32
Type "copyright", "credits" or "license" for more information.
>>>
>>> import CenterLength
CenterLength.py:4: SyntaxWarning: local name 'length' in 'centerLength'
shadows
use of 'length' as global in nested scope 'centerString'
  def centerLength( length ):
>>>
>>> centerString10 = CenterLength.centerLength( 10 )
>>> centerString10( "python" )
Traceback (most recent call last):
  File "<stdin>", line 1, in ?
  File "CenterLength.py", line 7, in centerString
    return stringValue.center( length )
NameError: global name 'length' is not defined
```

Fig. O.10 Nested-scopes and older versions of Python.

www.amk.ca/python/2.2
This page provides an overview of the language changes for version 2.2 and includes many small examples.

sourceforge.net/projects/python
The SourceForge™ project page for Python is located here. Visitors can view the current status of the language and browse the latest version of the source code.

comp.lang.python
This newsgroup hosts active discussions on the Python language. Topics often include language suggestions, design questions, programming suggestions and help for beginners.

www-106.ibm.com/developerworks/linux/library/l-prog.html
This is the first of three articles that addresses functional programming in Python.

Bibliography

Altom, T. and M. Chapman. *Programming with Python*. Rocklin, CA: Prima Publishing, 1999.

Beazley, D.M. *Python Essential Reference*. Indianapolis, IN: New Riders, 2000.

Blaha, M. R., W. J. Premerlani and J. E. Rumbaugh. "Relational Database Design Using an Object-Oriented Methodology." *Communications of the ACM*, Vol. 31, No. 4, April 1988, 414–427.

Brown, M.C. *Python: Annotated Archives*. Berkeley, CA: Osborne/McGraw Hill, 2000.

Chun, W.J. *Core Python Programming*. Upper Saddle River, NJ: Prentice Hall, 2001.

Codd, E. F. "A Relational Model of Data for Large Shared Data Banks." *Communications of the ACM*, June 1970.

Codd, E. F. "Fatal Flaws in SQL." *Datamation*, Vol. 34, No. 16, August 15, 1988, 45–48.

Codd, E. F. "Further Normalization of the Data Base Relational Model." *Courant Computer Science Symposia*, Vol. 6, *Data Base Systems*. Upper Saddle River, N.J.: Prentice Hall, 1972.

Date, C. J. *An Introduction to Database Systems, Seventh Edition*. Reading, MA: Addison-Wesley, 2000.

Deitel, H. M. *Operating Systems, Second Edition*. Reading, MA: Addison-Wesley, 1990.

Deitel, H. M. and P.J. Deitel, *Java How To Program, Fourth Edition*. Upper Saddle River, NJ: Prentice Hall, 2001

Deitel, H. M., P. J. Deitel, T. R. Nieto, T. M. Lin and P. Sadhu. *XML How To Program*. Upper Saddle River, NJ: Prentice Hall, 2001

Dejong, J. "Raising the Bar." *Software Development Times*, March 2001, 29–30.

Friedl, Jeffrey E. F. *Mastering Regular Expressions*. Sebastopol, CA: O'Reilly and Associates, 1997.

Gauld, A. *Learn to Program Using Python*. Reading, MA: Addison-Wesley, 2001.

Grayson, J.E. *Python and Tkinter Programming*. Greenwich, CT: Manning, 2000.

Harms, D. and K. McDonald. *The Quick Python Book*. Greenwich, CT: Manning, 2000.

Houlette, F. *SQL: A Beginner's Guide*. Berkeley, CA: Osborne/McGraw Hill, 2001.

Hulme, G, V. "XML Specification May Ease PKI Integration." *Information Week*, December 2000, 38.

Hutchinson, J. "Can't Fit Another Byte." *Network Computing*, March 2001, 14.

Lessa, A. *Python: Developer's Handbook*. Indianapolis, IN: SAMS, 2001.

Levitt, J. "Plug-And-Play Redefined." *Information Week*, April 2001, 63–68.

Lutz, M. *Programming Python*. Sebastopol, CA: O'Reilly and Associates, 2001.

Lutz, M. and D. Ascher. *Learning Python*. Sebastopol, CA: O'Reilly and Associates, 1999.

Moran, B. "Questions, Answers, and Tips." *SQL Server Magazine*, April 2001, 19–20.

MySQL Manual. MySQL Web site <**www.mysql.com/doc/**>.

Nichols, B., D. Buttlar, and J. Proulx Farrell. *Pthreads Programming*. Sebastopol, CA: O'Reilly and Associates, 1996.

Relational Technology, *INGRES Overview*. Alameda, CA: Relational Technology, 1988.

Rizzo, T. "Moving to Square One." *Internet World*, March 2001, 4–5.

Rollman, R. "XML Q & A." *SQL Server Magazine*, April 2001, 57–58.

Rubinstein, D. "Play It Again, XML." *Software Development Times*, March 2001, 12.

Scott, G. "Putting on the Breaks." *EntMag*, December 2000, 54.

Stonebraker, M. "Operating System Support for Database Management." *Communications of the ACM*, Vol. 24, No. 7, July 1981, 412–418.

Whitney, R. "XML for Analysis." *SQL Server Magazine*, April 2001, 63–66.

Winston, A. "A Distributed Database Primer." *UNIX World*, April 1988, 54–63.

Woo, M., J. Neider, T. Davis and D. Shreiner. *OpenGL Programming Guide, Third Edition*. Boston, MA: Addison-Wesley, 1999.

Yarger, R.J., G. Reese and T. King. *MySQL and mSQL*. Sebastopol, CA: O'Reilly and Associates, 1999.

Index

Prentice Hall License Agreement and Limited Warranty

READ THE FOLLOWING TERMS AND CONDITIONS CAREFULLY BEFORE OPENING THIS SOFT-WARE PACKAGE. THIS LEGAL DOCUMENT IS AN AGREEMENT BETWEEN YOU AND PRENTICE-HALL, INC. (THE "COMPANY"). BY OPENING THIS SEALED SOFTWARE PACKAGE, YOU ARE AGREEING TO BE BOUND BY THESE TERMS AND CONDITIONS. IF YOU DO NOT AGREE WITH THESE TERMS AND CONDITIONS, DO NOT OPEN THE SOFTWARE PACKAGE. PROMPTLY RETURN THE UNOPENED SOFTWARE PACKAGE AND ALL ACCOMPANYING ITEMS TO THE PLACE YOU OBTAINED THEM FOR A FULL REFUND OF ANY SUMS YOU HAVE PAID.

1.   GRANT OF LICENSE: In consideration of your purchase of this book, and your agreement to abide by the terms and conditions of this Agreement, the Company grants to you a nonexclusive right to use and display the copy of the enclosed software program (hereinafter the "SOFTWARE") on a single computer (i.e., with a single CPU) at a single location so long as you comply with the terms of this Agreement. The Company reserves all rights not expressly granted to you under this Agreement.

2.   OWNERSHIP OF SOFTWARE: You own only the magnetic or physical media (the enclosed media) on which the SOFTWARE is recorded or fixed, but the Company and the software developers retain all the rights, title, and ownership to the SOFTWARE recorded on the original media copy(ies) and all subsequent copies of the SOFTWARE, regardless of the form or media on which the original or other copies may exist. This license is not a sale of the original SOFTWARE or any copy to you.

3.   COPY RESTRICTIONS: This SOFTWARE and the accompanying printed materials and user manual (the "Documentation") are the subject of copyright. The individual programs on the media are copyrighted by the authors of each program. Some of the programs on the media include separate licensing agreements. If you intend to use one of these programs, you must read and follow its accompanying license agreement. You may not copy the Documentation or the SOFTWARE, except that you may make a single copy of the SOFTWARE for backup or archival purposes only. You may be held legally responsible for any copying or copyright infringement which is caused or encouraged by your failure to abide by the terms of this restriction.

4.   USE RESTRICTIONS: You may not network the SOFTWARE or otherwise use it on more than one computer or computer terminal at the same time. You may physically transfer the SOFTWARE from one computer to another provided that the SOFTWARE is used on only one computer at a time. You may not distribute copies of the SOFTWARE or Documentation to others. You may not reverse engineer, disassemble, decompile, modify, adapt, translate, or create derivative works based on the SOFTWARE or the Documentation without the prior written consent of the Company.

5.   TRANSFER RESTRICTIONS: The enclosed SOFTWARE is licensed only to you and may not be transferred to any one else without the prior written consent of the Company. Any unauthorized transfer of the

SOFTWARE shall result in the immediate termination of this Agreement.

6.   TERMINATION: This license is effective until terminated. This license will terminate automatically without notice from the Company and become null and void if you fail to comply with any provisions or limitations of this license. Upon termination, you shall destroy the Documentation and all copies of the SOFTWARE. All provisions of this Agreement as to warranties, limitation of liability, remedies or damages, and our ownership rights shall survive termination.

7.   MISCELLANEOUS: This Agreement shall be construed in accordance with the laws of the United States of America and the State of New York and shall benefit the Company, its affiliates, and assignees.

8.   LIMITED WARRANTY AND DISCLAIMER OF WARRANTY: The Company warrants that the SOFTWARE, when properly used in accordance with the Documentation, will operate in substantial conformity with the description of the SOFTWARE set forth in the Documentation. The Company does not warrant that the SOFTWARE will meet your requirements or that the operation of the SOFTWARE will be uninterrupted or error-free. The Company warrants that the media on which the SOFTWARE is delivered shall be free from defects in materials and workmanship under normal use for a period of thirty (30) days from the date of your purchase. Your only remedy and the Company's only obligation under these limited warranties is, at the Company's option, return of the warranted item for a refund of any amounts paid by you or replacement of the item. Any replacement of SOFTWARE or media under the warranties shall not extend the original warranty period. The limited warranty set forth above shall not apply to any SOFTWARE which the Company determines in good faith has been subject to misuse, neglect, improper installation, repair, alteration, or damage by you. EXCEPT FOR THE EXPRESSED WARRANTIES SET FORTH ABOVE, THE COMPANY DISCLAIMS ALL WARRANTIES, EXPRESS OR IMPLIED, INCLUDING WITHOUT LIMITATION, THE IMPLIED WARRANTIES OF MERCHANTABILITY AND FITNESS FOR A PARTICULAR PURPOSE. EXCEPT FOR THE EXPRESS WARRANTY SET FORTH ABOVE, THE COMPANY DOES NOT WARRANT, GUARANTEE, OR MAKE ANY REPRESENTATION REGARDING THE USE OR THE RESULTS OF THE USE OF THE SOFTWARE IN TERMS OF ITS CORRECTNESS, ACCURACY, RELIABILITY, CURRENTNESS, OR OTHERWISE.

IN NO EVENT, SHALL THE COMPANY OR ITS EMPLOYEES, AGENTS, SUPPLIERS, OR CONTRACTORS BE LIABLE FOR ANY INCIDENTAL, INDIRECT, SPECIAL, OR CONSEQUENTIAL DAMAGES ARISING OUT OF OR IN CONNECTION WITH THE LICENSE GRANTED UNDER THIS AGREEMENT, OR FOR LOSS OF USE, LOSS OF DATA, LOSS OF INCOME OR PROFIT, OR OTHER LOSSES, SUSTAINED AS A RESULT OF INJURY TO ANY PERSON, OR LOSS OF OR DAMAGE TO PROPERTY, OR CLAIMS OF THIRD PARTIES, EVEN IF THE COMPANY OR AN AUTHORIZED REPRESENTATIVE OF THE COMPANY HAS BEEN ADVISED OF THE POSSIBILITY OF SUCH DAMAGES. IN NO EVENT SHALL LIABILITY OF THE COMPANY FOR DAMAGES WITH RESPECT TO THE SOFTWARE EXCEED THE AMOUNTS ACTUALLY PAID BY YOU, IF ANY, FOR THE SOFTWARE.

SOME JURISDICTIONS DO NOT ALLOW THE LIMITATION OF IMPLIED WARRANTIES OR LIABILITY FOR INCIDENTAL, INDIRECT, SPECIAL, OR CONSEQUENTIAL DAMAGES, SO THE ABOVE LIMITATIONS MAY NOT ALWAYS APPLY. THE WARRANTIES IN THIS AGREEMENT GIVE YOU SPECIFIC LEGAL RIGHTS AND YOU MAY ALSO HAVE OTHER RIGHTS WHICH VARY IN ACCORDANCE WITH LOCAL LAW.

ACKNOWLEDGMENT

YOU ACKNOWLEDGE THAT YOU HAVE READ THIS AGREEMENT, UNDERSTAND IT, AND AGREE TO BE BOUND BY ITS TERMS AND CONDITIONS. YOU ALSO AGREE THAT THIS AGREEMENT IS THE COMPLETE AND EXCLUSIVE STATEMENT OF THE AGREEMENT BETWEEN YOU AND THE COMPANY AND SUPERSEDES ALL PROPOSALS OR PRIOR AGREEMENTS, ORAL, OR WRITTEN, AND ANY OTHER COMMUNICATIONS BETWEEN YOU AND THE COMPANY OR ANY REPRESENTATIVE OF THE COMPANY RELATING TO THE SUBJECT MATTER OF THIS AGREEMENT.

Should you have any questions concerning this Agreement or if you wish to contact the Company for any reason, please contact in writing at the address below.

Robin Short
Prentice Hall PTR
One Lake Street
Upper Saddle River, New Jersey 07458

IBM International License Agreement for Non-Warranted Programs

PART 1 - GENERAL TERMS

PLEASE READ THIS AGREEMENT CAREFULLY BEFORE USING THE PROGRAM. IBM WILL LICENSE THE PROGRAM TO YOU ONLY IF YOU FIRST ACCEPT THE TERMS OF THIS AGREEMENT. BY USING THE PROGRAM YOU AGREE TO THESE TERMS. IF YOU DO NOT AGREE TO THE TERMS OF THIS AGREEMENT, PROMPTLY RETURN THE UNUSED PROGRAM TO THE PARTY (EITHER IBM OR ITS RESELLER) FROM WHOM YOU ACQUIRED IT TO RECEIVE A REFUND OF THE AMOUNT YOU PAID.

The Program is owned by International Business Machines Corporation or one of its subsidiaries (IBM) or an IBM supplier, and is copyrighted and licensed, not sold.

The term "Program" means the original program and all whole or partial copies of it. A Program consists of machine-readable instructions, its components, data, audio-visual content (such as images, text, recordings, or pictures), and related licensed materials. This Agreement includes Part 1 - General Terms and Part 2 - Country-unique Terms and is the complete agreement regarding the use of this Program, and replaces any prior oral or written communications between you and IBM. The terms of Part 2 may replace or modify those of Part 1.

1. License

Use of the Program

IBM grants you a nonexclusive license to use the Program. You may 1) use the Program to the extent of authorizations you have acquired and 2) make and install copies to support the level of use authorized, providing you reproduce the copyright notice and any other legends of ownership on each copy, or partial copy, of the Program. If you acquire this Program as a program upgrade, your authorization to use the Program from which you upgraded is terminated. You will ensure that anyone who uses the Program does so only in compliance with the terms of this Agreement. You may not 1) use, copy, modify, or distribute the Program except as provided in this Agreement; 2) reverse assemble, reverse compile, or otherwise translate the Program except as specifically permitted by law without the possibility of contractual waiver; or 3) sublicense, rent, or lease the Program.

Transfer of Rights and Obligations

You may transfer all your license rights and obligations under a Proof of Entitlement for the Program to another party by transferring the Proof of Entitlement and a copy of this Agreement and all documentation. The transfer of your license rights and obligations terminates your authorization to use the Program under the Proof of Entitlement.

2. Proof of Entitlement

The Proof of Entitlement for this Program is evidence of your authorization to use this Program and of your eligibility for future upgrade program prices (if announced) and potential special or promotional opportunities.

3. Charges and Taxes

IBM defines use for the Program for charging purposes and specifies it in the Proof of Entitlement. Charges are based on extent of use authorized. If you wish to increase the extent of use, notify IBM or its reseller and pay any applicable charges. IBM does not give refunds or credits for charges already due or paid. If any authority imposes a duty, tax, levy or fee, excluding those based on IBM's net income, upon the Program supplied by IBM under this Agreement, then you agree to pay that amount as IBM specifies or supply exemption documentation.

4. No Warranty

SUBJECT TO ANY STATUTORY WARRANTIES WHICH CAN NOT BE EXCLUDED, IBM MAKES NO WARRANTIES OR CONDITIONS EITHER EXPRESS OR IMPLIED, INCLUDING WITHOUT LIMITATION, THE WARRANTY OF NON-INFRINGEMENT AND THE IMPLIED WARRANTIES OF MERCHANTABILITY AND FITNESS FOR A PARTICULAR PURPOSE, REGARDING THE PROGRAM OR TECHNICAL SUPPORT, IF ANY. IBM MAKES NO WARRANTY REGARDING THE CAPABILITY OF THE PROGRAM TO CORRECTLY PROCESS, PROVIDE AND/OR RECEIVE DATE DATA WITHIN AND BETWEEN THE 20TH AND 21ST CENTURIES.

The exclusion also applies to any of IBM's subcontractors, suppliers, or program developers (collectively called "Suppliers"). Manufacturers, suppliers, or publishers of non-IBM Programs may provide their own warranties

5. Limitation of Liability

NEITHER IBM NOR ITS SUPPLIERS WILL BE LIABLE FOR ANY DIRECT OR INDIRECT DAMAGES, INCLUDING WITHOUT LIMITATION, LOST PROFITS, LOST SAVINGS, OR ANY INCIDENTAL, SPECIAL, OR OTHER ECONOMIC CONSEQUENTIAL DAMAGES, EVEN IF IBM IS INFORMED OF THEIR POSSIBILITY. SOME JURISDICTIONS DO NOT ALLOW THE EXCLUSION OR LIMITATION OF INCIDENTAL OR CONSEQUENTIAL DAMAGES, SO THE ABOVE EXCLUSION OR LIMITATION MAY NOT APPLY TO YOU.

6. General

Nothing in this Agreement affects any statutory rights of consumers that cannot be waived or limited by contract. IBM may terminate your license if you fail to comply with the terms of this Agreement. If IBM does so, you must immediately destroy the Program and all copies you made of it. You agree to comply with applicable export laws and regulations. Neither you nor IBM will bring a legal action under this Agreement more than two years after the cause of action arose unless otherwise provided by local law without the possibility of contractual waiver or limitation.

Neither you nor IBM is responsible for failure to fulfill any obligations due to causes beyond its control. IBM does not provide program services or technical support, unless IBM specifies otherwise.

The laws of the country in which you acquire the Program govern this Agreement, except 1) in Australia, the laws of the State or Territory in which the transaction is performed govern this Agreement; 2) in Albania, Armenia, Belarus, Bosnia/Herzegovina, Bulgaria, Croatia, Czech Republic, Georgia, Hungary, Kazakhstan, Kirghizia, Former Yugoslav Republic of Macedonia (FYROM), Moldova, Poland, Romania, Russia, Slovak Republic, Slovenia, Ukraine, and Federal Republic of Yugoslavia, the laws of Austria govern this Agreement; 3) in the United Kingdom, all disputes relating to this Agreement will be governed by English Law and will be submitted to the exclusive jurisdiction of the English courts; 4) in Canada, the laws in the Province of Ontario govern this Agreement; and 5) in the United States and Puerto Rico, and People's Republic of China, the laws of the State of New York govern this Agreement.

PART 2 - COUNTRY-UNIQUE TERMS

AUSTRALIA:

No Warranty (Section 4):
The following paragraph is added to this Section:

Although IBM specifies that there are no warranties, you may have certain rights under the Trade Practices Act 1974 or other legislation and are only limited to the extent permitted by the applicable legislation. Limitation of Liability (Section 5): The following paragraph is added to this Section: Where IBM is in breach of a condition or warranty implied by the Trade Practices Act 1974, IBM's liability is limited to the repair or replacement of the goods, or the supply of equivalent goods. Where that condition or warranty relates to right to sell, quiet possession or clear title, or the goods are of a kind ordinarily acquired for personal, domestic or household use or consumption, then none of the limitations in this paragraph apply.

GERMANY:

No Warranty (Section 4):

The following paragraphs are added to this Section:

The minimum warranty period for Programs is six months. In case a Program is delivered without Specifications, we will only warrant that the Program information correctly describes the Program and that the Program can be used according to the Program information. You have to check the usability according to the Program information within the "money-back guaranty" period. Limitation of Liability (Section 5): The following paragraph is added to this Section: The limitations and exclusions specified in the Agreement will not apply to damages caused by IBM with fraud or gross negligence, and for express warranty.

INDIA:

General (Section 6):

The following replaces the fourth paragraph of this Section:

If no suit or other legal action is brought, within two years after the cause of action arose, in respect of any claim that either party may have against the other, the rights of the concerned party in respect of such claim will be forfeited and the other party will stand released from its obligations in respect of such claim.

IRELAND:

No Warranty (Section 4):

The following paragraph is added to this Section:

Except as expressly provided in these terms and conditions, all statutory conditions, including all warranties implied, but without prejudice to the generality of the foregoing, all warranties implied by the Sale of Goods Act 1893 or the Sale of Goods and Supply of Services Act 1980 are hereby excluded.

ITALY:

Limitation of Liability (Section 5):

This Section is replaced by the following:

Unless otherwise provided by mandatory law, IBM is not liable for any damages which might arise.

NEW ZEALAND:

No Warranty (Section 4):

The following paragraph is added to this Section:

Although IBM specifies that there are no warranties, you may have certain rights under the Consumer Guarantees Act 1993 or other legislation which cannot be excluded or limited. The Consumer Guarantees Act 1993 will not apply in respect of any goods or services which IBM provides, if you require the goods and services for the purposes of a business as defined in that Act.

Limitation of Liability (Section 5):

The following paragraph is added to this Section:

Where Programs are not acquired for the purposes of a business as defined in the Consumer Guarantees Act 1993, the limitations in this Section are subject to the limitations in that Act.

PEOPLE'S REPUBLIC OF CHINA:

Charges (Section 3):

The following paragraph is added to the Section:

All banking charges incurred in the People's Republic of China will be borne by you and those incurred outside the People's Republic of China will be borne by IBM.

UNITED KINGDOM:

Limitation of Liability (Section 5):

The following paragraph is added to this Section at the end of the first paragraph:

The limitation of liability will not apply to any breach of IBM's obligations implied by Section 12 of the Sales of Goods Act 1979 or Section 2 of the Supply of Goods and Services Act 1982. Z125-5589-01 (10/97) LICENSE INFORMATION The Programs listed below are licensed under the following terms and conditions in addition to those of the International License Agreement for Non-Warranted Programs.

Program Name: IBM WebSphere Voice Server SDK v2.0

Program Number: CY12TNA

Guarantee: 1

Authorization for Use on Home/Portable Computer: 1

EXPLANATIONS OF TERMS:

Guarantee:

The Program has a money-back guarantee. If for any reason you are unsatisfied with the Program, you may return it to the party (either IBM or its resellers) from whom you acquired it, to receive a refund of the amount you paid. "1" means that this Program has a 30 day money-back guarantee. "2" means that this Program has a 2 month money-back guarantee. Authorization for Use on Home/Portable Computer: "1" means that the Program may be stored on the primary machine and another machine, provided that the Program is not in active use on both machines at the same time. "2" means that you may not copy and use this Program on another computer without paying additional license fees.

Specified Operating Environment

The Program Specifications and Specified Operating Environment information may be found in documentation accompanying the Program such as the Installation/Users Guide.

Program-unique Terms

THIRD PARTY CODE: The Program contains, and future updates and fixpacks to the Program may contain, certain third party components which are provided to you under terms and conditions which are different from this Agreement, or which require IBM to provide you with certain notices and/or information. For each such third party component, either IBM will identify such third party component in the Program's "README" file (or in an updated file accompanying the fixpack or update), or in a file or files referenced in such "README" files (and shall include any associated license agreement, notices and other related information therein), or the third party component will contain or be accompanied by its own license agreement (for example, provided when installing or starting such component, or accompanying such component in a file entitled "README, "COPYING", "LICENSE" or a substantially similar title, or included among the Program's paper documentation, if any). Your use of each third party component which contains or is accompanied by its own license agreement, or for which IBM has identified a license agreement in one of the above "README" files (or in a file or files referenced therein), will be subject to the terms and conditions of such other license agreement, and not this Agreement. By using or not uninstalling such third party components after the initial installation of such third party components (thereby giving you access to the applicable license agreements, notices and information), you acknowledge and agree to all such license agreements, notices and information, including those provided only in the English language. You agree to review any updated "README" file which accompany updates and fixpacks to the Program.

U.S. Government Users Restricted Rights

U.S. Government Users Restricted Rights - Use, duplication, or disclosure restricted by the GSA ADP Schedule Contract with the IBM Corporation.

D/N: L-LWRT-53YN2X

P/N: L-LWRT-53YN2X

The DEITEL & DEITEL Suite of Products...

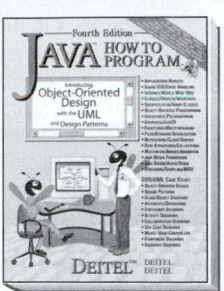

C# How to Program

`BOOK / CD-ROM`

©2002, 1400 pp., paper
(0-13-062221-4)

An exciting new addition to the *How to Program* series, *C# How to Program* provides a comprehensive introduction to Microsoft's new object-oriented language. C# builds on the skills already mastered by countless C++ and Java programmers, enabling them to create powerful Web applications and components—ranging from XML-based Web services on Microsoft's .NET platform to middle-tier business objects and system-level applications. *C# How to Program* begins with a strong foundation in the introductory and intermediate programming principles students will need in industry. It then explores such essential topics as object-oriented programming and exception handling. Graphical user interfaces are extensively covered, giving readers the tools to build compelling and fully interactive programs. Internet technologies such as XML, ADO .NET and Web services are also covered as well as topics including regular expressions, multithreading, networking, databases, files and data structures.

Visual Basic .NET How to Program
Second Edition

`BOOK / CD-ROM`

©2002, 1400 pp., paper
(0-13-029363-6)

Teach Visual Basic .NET programming from the ground up! This introduction of Microsoft's .NET Framework marks the beginning of major revisions to all of Microsoft's programming languages. This book provides a comprehensive introduction to the next version of Visual Basic—Visual Basic .NET—featuring extensive updates and increased functionality. *Visual Basic .NET How to Program, Second Edition* covers introductory programming techniques as well as more advanced topics, featuring enhanced treatment of developing Web-based applications. Other topics discussed include an extensive treatment of XML and wireless applications, databases, SQL and ADO .NET, Web forms, Web services and ASP .NET.

Also coming soon in the Deitels' *.NET Series*:
• *Visual C++ .NET How to Program*

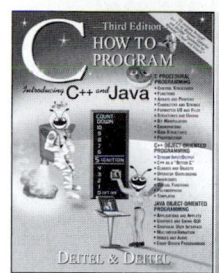

C How to Program
Third Edition

`BOOK / CD-ROM`

©2001, 1253 pp., paper
(0-13-089572-5)

Highly practical in approach, the Third Edition of the world's best-selling C text introduces the fundamentals of structured programming and software engineering and gets up to speed quickly. This comprehensive book not only covers the full C language, but also reviews library functions and introduces object-based and object-oriented programming in C++ and Java. The Third Edition includes a new 346-page introduction to Java 2 and the basics of GUIs, and the 298-page introduction to C++ has been updated to be consistent with the most current ANSI/ISO C++ standards. Plus, icons throughout the book point out valuable programming tips such as Common Programming Errors, Portability Tips and Testing and Debugging Tips.

C++ How to Program
Third Edition

`BOOK / CD-ROM`

©2001, 1168 pp., paper
(0-13-089571-7)

The world's best-selling C++ text teaches programming by emphasizing object-oriented programming, software reuse and component-oriented software construction. This comprehensive book uses the Deitels' signature LIVE-CODE™ Approach, presenting every concept in the context of a complete, working C++ program followed by a screen capture showing the program's output. It also includes a rich collection of exercises and valuable insights in its set of Common Programming Errors, Software Engineering Observations, Portability Tips and Testing and Debugging Tips. The Third Edition features an extensive treatment of the Standard Template Library and includes a new case study that focuses on object-oriented design with the UML, illustrating the entire process of object-oriented design from conception to implementation. In addition, it adheres to the latest ANSI/ISO C++ standards. The accompanying CD-ROM contains Microsoft® Visual C++™ 6.0 Introductory Edition software, source code for all examples in the text and hyperlinks to C++ demos and Internet resources.

Getting Started with Microsoft® Visual C++™ 6 with an Introduction to MFC

`BOOK / CD-ROM`

©2000, 163 pp., paper (0-13-016147-0)

XML How to Program

BOOK / CD-ROM

©2001, 934 pp., paper (0-13-028417-3)

This book is a comprehensive guide to programming in XML. It teaches how to use XML to create customized tags and includes chapters that address standard custom-markup languages for science and technology, multimedia, commerce and many other fields. Concise introductions to Java, JavaServer Pages, VBScript, Active Server Pages and Perl/CGI provide readers with the essentials of these programming languages and server-side development technologies to enable them to work effectively with XML. The book also covers cutting-edge topics such as XSL, DOM™ and SAX, plus a real-world e-commerce case study and a complete chapter on Web accessibility that addresses Voice XML. It includes tips such as Common Programming Errors, Software Engineering Observations, Portability Tips and Debugging Hints. Other topics covered include XHTML, CSS, DTD, schema, parsers, XPath, XLink, namespaces, XBase, XInclude, XPointer, XSLT, XSL Formatting Objects, JavaServer Pages, XForms, topic maps, X3D, MathML, OpenMath, CML, BML, CDF, RDF, SVG, Cocoon, WML, XBRL, and BizTalk™ and SOAP™ Web resources.

Perl How to Program

BOOK / CD-ROM

©2001, 1057 pp., paper (0-13-028418-1)

This comprehensive guide to Perl programming emphasizes the use of the Common Gateway Interface (CGI) with Perl to create powerful, dynamic multi-tier Web-based client/server applications. The book begins with a clear and careful introduction to programming concepts at a level suitable for beginners, and proceeds through advanced topics such as references and complex data structures. Key Perl topics such as regular expressions and string manipulation are covered in detail. The authors address important and topical issues such as object-oriented programming, the Perl database interface (DBI), graphics and security. Also included is a treatment of XML, a bonus chapter introducing the Python programming language, supplemental material on career resources and a complete chapter on Web accessibility. The text includes tips such as Common Programming Errors, Software Engineering Observations, Portability Tips and Debugging Hints.

e-Business & e-Commerce How to Program

BOOK / CD-ROM

©2001, 1254 pp., paper (0-13-028419-X)

This innovative book explores programming technologies for developing Web-based e-business and e-commerce solutions, and covers e-business and e-commerce models and business issues. Readers learn a full range of options, from "build-your-own" to turnkey solutions. The book examines scores of the top e-businesses (examples include Amazon, eBay, Priceline, Travelocity, etc.), explaining the technical details of building successful e-business and e-commerce sites and their underlying business premises. Learn how to implement the dominant e-commerce models—shopping carts, auctions, name-your-own-price, comparison shopping and bots/ intelligent agents—by using markup languages (HTML, Dynamic HTML and XML), scripting languages (JavaScript, VBScript and Perl), server-side technologies (Active Server Pages and Perl/CGI) and database (SQL and ADO), security and online payment technologies. Updates are regularly posted to **www.deitel.com** and the book includes a CD-ROM with software tools, source code and live links.

www.InformIT.com/deitel

Deitel & Associates, Inc. is partnering with Prentice Hall's parent company, Pearson PLC, and its information technology Web site, InformIT (`www.informit.com`) to launch the Deitel InformIT site at `www.InformIT.com/deitel`. The Deitel InformIT kiosk will be up and running in Q1 2002 with information on the continuum of Deitel products, including:

 • **Free informational articles**

 • **Deitel e-Matter**

• **Books and new e-Books**

• **Instructor-led training**

• **Web-based training**

• *Complete Training Courses/Cyber Classrooms*

Deitel will contribute to a weekly column in the popular InformIT newsletter, currently subscribed to by more than 800,000 IT professionals worldwide (for opt-in registration, see `www.informit.com`). This column will provide information on topics including:

- Deitel publications and products including the complete Deitel Catalog for product ordering information and updates
- Resources and articles on leading-edge technologies and IT issues
- WBT and e-learning updates
- Instructor-led training information
- Programming tips and methods
- Progress reports on forthcoming publications
- Deitel research and development activities

Web-Based Tutorials

Deitel is committed to continuous research and development in e-learning and is enhancing its series of self-paced CD-ROM and Web-based tutorials using content from the Deitel *How to Program Series* textbooks. The tutorials are appropriate for distance education and on-campus courses. Our instructional designers are currently developing features that include:

- Interactive Macromedia® Flash™ animations demonstrating key programming concepts.
- Interactive Questions (with answers) relating to specific lines of code.
- Dynamic Glossary linking designated keywords or phrases to small windows containing definitions.
- More abundant audio, including some examples with animated, interactive code walk-throughs highlighting each section of code as it is mentioned.

A Sneak Peek at the Interactive Animation in the *Java Multimedia Cyber Classroom 4/e*

1. When the animation starts a ball is dropped into a bucket signifying that the flow through the flowchart has begun. The ball continues through the flowchart stopping three times along the way.

2. First, the loop-continuation condition is checked; next, a line is drawn in a simulated output window...

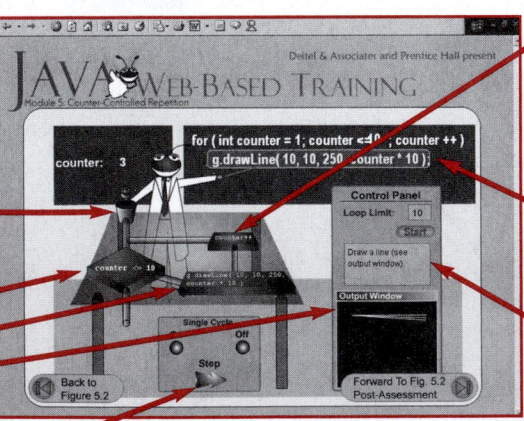

3. ...then the value of the conditional variable is incremented.

4. At each step, the appropriate code is highlighted...

5. ...and a short description of that step is given on the control panel.

If the user misses something in the animation, it can be repeated as needed. The animation may also be switched to "single-cycle" mode, allowing the student to step through the code manually one action at a time.

Future Publications

Here are some new titles we are considering for 2002/2003 release:

Computer Science Series: *Theory and Principles of Operating Systems: a Simulation Approach, Data Structures in C++, Data Structures in Java, Theory and Principles of Database Systems.*

Database Series: *Oracle How to Program, SQL Server How to Program, MySQL How to Program.*

Internet and Web Programming Series: *Open Source Software Development: Apache, Linux, MySQL and PHP How to Program, Perl 6 How to Program 2/e.*

Programming Series: *Flash™ How to Program, Multimedia How to Program.*

.NET Programming Series: *Advanced C# .NET How to Program, Advanced Visual Basic .NET How to Program, Visual C++ .NET™ How to Program, Advanced Visual C++ .NET How to Program, ASP .NET How to Program.*

Object Technology Series: *OOAD with the UML, Design Patterns, Java and XML.*

Advanced Java Series: *JDBC How to Program, Enterprise JavaBeans How to Program, Java Media Framework (JMF) How to Program, Java Security and Java Cryptography (JCE) How to Program, Java Servlets How to Program, Java2D and Java3D How to Program, JavaServer Pages (JSP) How to Program, JINI How to Program, Java 2 Micro Edition (J2ME) How to Program.*

Deitel Newsletter

Deitel and Associates, Inc. is launching a free, opt-in newsletter that will include:

- Updates and commentary on industry trends and developments
- Resources and links to articles from our published books and upcoming publications.
- Information on the Deitel publishing plans, including future publications and product-release schedules

To sign up for the Deitel Newsletter, visit `www.deitel.com`.

E-Books

We are committed to providing our content in traditional print formats and in emerging electronic formats, such as e-books, to fulfill our customers' needs. We are currently exploring several solutions. Visit `www.deitel.com` for periodic updates.

E-Learning

(Cyber Classrooms, Web-Based Training and Course Management Systems)

Deitel is committed to continuous research and development in e-Learning. On the page to the left, we provide a sneak peek at our plans for Web-based training, including a five-way Macromedia® Flash™ animation of a `for` loop in Java. We are pleased to announce that we have incorporated this example into the *Java 2 Multimedia Cyber Classroom, 4/e* (which is included in *The Complete Java 2 Training Course, 4/e*). Our instructional designers and Flash animation team are developing additional simulations that demonstrate key programming concepts. We are enhancing the *Multimedia Cyber Classroom* products to include more audio, pre- and post-assessment questions and Web-based labs with solutions for the benefit of professors and students alike. In addition, our *Multimedia Cyber Classroom* products, available in both CD and Web-based formats, are being ported to Pearson's CourseCompass course-management system—a powerful e-platform for teaching and learning.

Turn the page to find out more about Deitel & Associates!

License Agreement and Limited Warranty

Using the CD-ROM

Microsoft Windows users may access the contents of this CD through the interface provided in the file **AUTORUN.EXE**. If a startup screen does not pop up automatically when you insert the CD into your computer, double click on the icon for **AUTORUN.EXE** to launch the program or launch the file **INDEX.HTM** in your browser. Linux users should launch **INDEX.HTM** in a browser to get started.

Contents of the CD-ROM

- Alice 99 Interactive 3D Graphics Programming System
- Python 2.2 (Windows/ Linux)
- Apache Web Server 1.3.22 from the Apache Software Foundation
- Webware 0.6 for Python (Windows/ Linux)
- Pixo™ Internet Microbrowser 2.1
- IBM® WebSphere® Voice Server SDK 2.0 for Windows® 2000, for Evaluation.
- Live links to websites mentioned in the book *Python How to Program*
- Live code examples from the book *Python How to Program*

Software and Hardware System Requirements

- Intel Pentium 166 MHz or faster (IBM® WebSphere® Voice Server SDK 2.0 for Windows® 2000 requires a 366 MHz or higher processor.)
- Windows 9x, Windows NT or later. Some software packages supplied on this CD may require a specific version of Windows. (IBM® WebSphere® Voice Server SDK 2.0 for Windows® 2000, for Evaluation; requires Windows NT 4.0 or Windows 2000; and Pixo Internet Microbrowser 2.1 requires Windows 98, NT 4.0 2000, or above)
- Red Hat Linux 6.2 or later
- 64 MHz RAM (128 MHz for NT 4.0/2000 systems) (The IBM WebSphere Voice Server SDK requires a minimum of 128 MB RAM)
- CD-ROM drive
- Internet connection and web browser